Approaching Literature in the 21st Century

Fiction • Poetry • Drama

Approaching Literature in the 21st Century

Fiction • Poetry • Drama

Peter Schakel
Hope College

Jack Ridl
Hope College

Bedford/St. Martin's   Boston ◆ New York

To Karen and Julie

For Bedford/St. Martin's

Developmental Editor: Genevieve Hamilton Day
Production Editor: Arthur Johnson
Production Supervisor: Chris Gross
Marketing Manager: Jenna Bookin Barry
Editorial Assistant: Jeffrey Voccola
Production Assistants: Kristen Merrill, Amy Derjue
Copyeditor: Lisa Wehrle
Text Design: Glenna Collett
Cover Design: Kim Cevoli
Cover Art: Sherman Alexie photo, *Cowboys & Indians*/Murrae Haynes; Judith Ortiz Cofer
    photo by Sortino; *Nathaniel Hawthorne,* painting by George P. A. Healy (New Hamp-
    shire Historical Society); Ernest Hemingway portrait © Bettmann/Corbis; Gish Jen
    photo courtesy of the author; photo of Jhumpa Lahiri at Barnes & Noble book signing
    © Marc Brasz/Corbis; American novelist John Updike photo © Michael Brennan/
    Corbis.
Composition: Stratford Publishing Services, Inc.
Printing and Binding: Quebecor World Kingsport

President: Joan E. Feinberg
Editorial Director: Denise B. Wydra
Editor in Chief: Karen S. Henry
Director of Marketing: Karen Melton Soeltz
Director of Editing, Design, and Production: Marcia Cohen
Managing Editor: Elizabeth M. Schaaf

Library of Congress Control Number: 2004102681

9   8   7   6   5   4
f   e   d   c   b   a

For information, write: Bedford/St. Martin's, 75 Arlington Street, Boston, MA 02116
(617-399-4000)

ISBN: 0–312–40756–4
EAN: 978–0–312–40756–8

Acknowledgments

Chinua Achebe, "Dead Men's Path" from *Girls at War and Other Stories.* Copyright © 1972, 1973 by
Chinua Achebe. Reprinted by permission of Harold Ober Associates, Inc., and Doubleday, a division of Random House, Inc.

*Acknowledgments and copyrights are continued at the back of the book on pages 1521-29, which constitute an
extension of the copyright page. It is a violation of the law to reproduce these selections by any means whatsoever
without the written permission of the copyright holder.*

Preface

Approaching Literature in the 21st Century offers a fresh, accessible entry to literature for all students, whatever their previous exposure to fiction, poetry, and drama. It contributes to a richer, more dynamic and valuable reading experience for students while in class, and demonstrates why and how reading is an important part of their lives in school and beyond.

In selecting works, we have sought to make this anthology widely representative. One of the great messages of literature has always been its affirmation of a democracy of voices. Our table of contents concurs with this. It includes voices that have been heard, voices that need to be heard, and voices that deserve to be heard by a wider audience. The most frequently taught texts from the traditional canon are here, mingled, juxtaposed, and connected in provocative ways with diverse authors and works from the twentieth and twenty-first centuries.

Approaching Literature in the 21st Century leads students to consider the human value of reading any effective literary work. By focusing on the reading process, it expands the notion of what a work is "about": It is about a lot of things, not a single topic or theme that readers must figure out through what to many beginning students seems a mysterious and esoteric method. In this textbook, students' experiences and cultural backgrounds are affirmed, and they are welcomed as readers to the study of literature. They are empowered by being shown that reading literature involves an exploration of all that can be discovered in a work — and that such exploration starts from wherever they are, whatever their background. Focusing on readers restores the tradition of the humanities as being profoundly "useful" and recognizes that works exist in a dynamic relationship with readers, one that inevitably influences readers' lives.

The emphasis on "active reading" throughout the text leads directly into student writing. Writing is introduced sequentially, starting with observations that students write in the margins of books as they read and progressing by natural, gradual steps to notes, journal writing, short critical papers, and longer research papers. The sequencing is not presented as hierarchical, as if one form of writing is more valuable than another, but it is there for a practical reason: to show that each form is both valuable in itself and helpful to mastering the next. Students develop skills and confidence in writing about literature as they are given detailed, practical advice about how to proceed in literature papers generally and how to approach the specific challenges posed by different genres.

The general principles outlined above have guided us in all of our work developing this book. Now we turn to a more detailed look at how these principles influenced and shaped specific elements of our text.

Fresher and More Diverse Selections Than in Traditional Anthologies

The most striking aspect of *Approaching Literature in the 21st Century* is found in its table of contents. Predominately multicultural and multinational, the stories, poems, and plays not only speak more directly to today's diverse student body but also prepare more homogeneous classrooms for a multicultural and global future. As Lucille Clifton has said, "In the polyglot we call America, literature *has* to include all voices. Nothing else makes sense." This anthology connects multicultural texts with the central, most frequently taught texts from the traditional canon. Students are introduced to important works, which in turn are refreshed by the imaginative ways the two strains are juxtaposed and interrelated. A principal criterion for selecting all of the texts was that they be teachable, effective, and interesting for students to read and write about. The casebooks on Langston Hughes, Judith Ortiz Cofer, and Sherman Alexie in Part 5, "Approaching Writers in Depth," offer just one example. These casebooks introduce students to an in-depth look at three diverse authors and feature multiple selections for each author, including biographical information, critical essays, interviews, and photographs.

Student-Friendly Approach

Approaching Literature in the 21st Century recognizes that students enter Introduction to Literature or Literature for Composition courses with varied levels of preparation for reading literature. It bridges those levels by offering solid explanations that do not presuppose prior knowledge of or experience with literature, but that are sufficiently fresh in their reader-oriented approach to stretch and enhance the understanding of students with prior literary knowledge and experience.

The elements of each genre are explained in nontechnical language that beginning literature students will grasp easily. Boxed checklists near the end of each chapter are designed for ready review of the material. Each chapter on the literary elements opens with a short work of fiction, poetry, or drama that is discussed in depth to model close reading techniques and to provide clear illustrations of the element being treated. Instructional text is written in a relaxed style that students will find engaging and appealing, and the imaginative interior design makes the book inviting to use.

With any work of literature, I engage the words in terms of their beauty and truth. It is difficult while I am reading to keep so many elements in my mind's eye: historical context, form, diction, theme, and all of the infinite theoretical approaches that are possible for a single work of literature. Evaluating the worth of writing is similar to assessing a precious diamond — as a whole or from far away we see its shimmering, universal beauty, but its true worth is bestowed according to the tiny details, angles, and cuts that can be seen only through a magnified lens.   Dan Carter

I watched the PBS television show *Reading Rainbow* as I was growing up. I can still hear the theme song in my head, and it always makes me smile. The best part is that I totally agree with the writers of the song. I really can go places when I read a book. Characters become real to me. I can read for personal growth, too. Literature is essential for cultivating my mind.   Annie Otto

I'm writing in my head constantly. Sometimes the words appear in print or in cursive on the chalkboard of my mind, but the act of writing is what matters. Writing is not something I can stop. I'm constantly writing in my head, with a pen and paper, by computer, or scribbling in the dirt with my fingers.   Kristina Martinez

Focus on Active Reading

Approaching Literature in the 21st Century aims to help students become active readers, able to enjoy and appreciate literature. Every aspect of the book focuses on this goal. The opening chapter presents a clear, step-by-step explanation of the reading process that challenges students to be active readers. It begins with a personal essay by Sherman Alexie and ends with a story by Julia Alvarez on the way reading "saved their lives." Throughout its pages, this textbook stresses that reading powerful literature offers readers the chance to participate fully with a work, to respond to it intellectually, emotionally, and imaginatively. Students are given ways to use and apply technical material as soon as it is presented and are invited to reflect and analyze by the "Approaching the Reading" prompts that follow stories, poems, and plays in the chapters. The emphasis is not on what techniques and elements *are* but on what readers *do* with them, how readers *engage* with them, revealing how techniques and elements are the ways works are brought to life.

Practical, Detailed Explanations of the Writing Process

Five chapters on writing present clear, step-by-step guidance, beginning with how to find possibilities to write about and how to shape these into successful topics, then continuing through the organization and development of ideas into convincing, well-supported arguments. Four sample student papers, introduced by the students themselves, along with sample exam answers and journal entries, provide accessible models for students to emulate.

- **Overview of Writing**   A full chapter discusses responding to literature through various kinds of writing and alternative, nontraditional responses. Coverage is thorough, clear, and firmly grounded in details and examples.
- **Genre-Specific Writing**   Each genre section concludes with a chapter on the writing challenges that are specific to that genre. These chapters discuss basic strategies and offer practical tips for writing successfully about the genre and are designed to help students apply what they've learned in the preceding chapters to longer, more polished essays.
- **Student Writers at Work**   The writing chapter in each genre section includes a model student essay prefaced by the student writer's own step-by-step explanation of how she or he carried out the assignment.
- **Writing Assignments**   End-of-chapter writing assignments offer not only standard writing suggestions such as journal writing and critical analyses, but also alternative ideas for responding to literature through music, art, or performance. Many assignments emphasize connections to other selections in the book, encouraging comparison and dialogue between more recent multicultural writing and that from the established canon.

Clear, Sensible Guidance on Literary Research in the Twenty-First Century

Approaching Literature in the 21st Century's section on literary research guides students step by step through the literary research process, from finding material to reading it, evaluating it, incorporating it effectively, citing it accurately in papers, and avoiding plagiarism. It is particularly attentive to twenty-first-century research challenges and includes clear, specific coverage of the benefits and pitfalls involved in using electronic resources.

- **Critical Essays**   An innovation in this anthology is its chapter providing basic, practical instruction on how to approach and read academic and critical essays. An annotated critical essay on Alice Walker's "Everyday Use" models the kinds of questions students should be asking of a critical work.
- **Documentation Guide**   The research section offers thorough, detailed, easy-to-use information about parenthetical citations and bibliography form.
- **Sample Student Research Paper**   Students are guided through the steps of the research process, culminating in an annotated sample paper that provides a clear, helpful model for handling various aspects they may encounter and that is introduced by a first-person account of how the writer moved from conception to completion.
- **Multigenre Casebooks**   A unique feature is the inclusion of casebooks featuring works by Langston Hughes, Judith Ortiz Cofer, and Sherman Alexie in multiple genres. These chapters introduce students to the life and work of three diverse authors and include accessible introductions, photographs, biographical information, reviews, interviews, and critical essays, along with a generous selection of primary texts. These casebooks offer a natural starting point for research projects.

Fully Integrated with Electronic Resources

Approaching Literature in the 21st Century is fully integrated with its companion Web site and with the *LiterActive* CD-ROM, using a variety of new media to expand the world of literature for students. Marginal icons throughout the book direct students to relevant, informative, and stimulating resources.

The Companion Web Site, *bedfordstmartins.com/approachinglit*

- **LitLinks**   These annotated links to carefully chosen Web sites supplement the book's biographical and contextual coverage, providing biographical, critical, and cultural information for every fiction writer and playwright and for many of the book's celebrated poets.

- **LitQuiz Online Quizzes**   Students can use the online quizzes — provided for each story and play — for self-study with immediate feedback, and instructors can use them for assessment, with results collated automatically and available online.
- **The VirtuaLit Interactive Literature Tutorials**   For fiction, poetry, and drama, students are guided step by step as they explore the literary elements, critical perspectives, and cultural contexts of eleven featured works, helping them to become engaged readers. (See the back cover of this book for more on the companion Web site.)

LiterActive CD-ROM

An innovative new CD-ROM, *LiterActive*, is packed with hundreds of images, contextual documents, audio and video clips, activities for exploring literature, and help with research and documentation.

- **VirtuaLit Interactive Tutorials** (same resource as on the companion Web site)
- A **Multimedia & Document Library** provides hundred of images, audio clips, and contextual documents supporting forty-three authors, enriching students' experience and comprehension of literature.

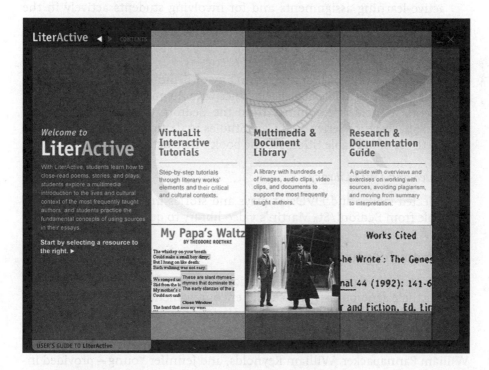

- A **Research and Documentation Guide** gives students concrete advice for working with sources — how to find, evaluate, summarize, interpret, and document them. The inclusion of scorable exercises as well as advice for avoiding plagiarism help students evaluate and improve their research and documentation practices.

Innovative Instructor's Resources

The Instructor's Manual

Resources for Teaching APPROACHING LITERATURE IN THE 21ST CENTURY, written by Peter Schakel and Jack Ridl, is a comprehensive, practical guide to the selections in the book and to teaching Introduction to Literature and Literature for Composition courses.

- **Entry Points**   In-depth comments on each selection provide entry points into content, themes, and style, and suggest ways of handling the work in the classroom.
- **Provocative Pairings**   Each selection is paired with at least one similar or contrasting work to which it is related in subject matter, theme, technique, or form.
- **Teaching Tips**   Practical ideas and activities are suggested for designing active-learning assignments and for involving students actively in the classroom.

Literary Reprints

Additional works of literature from any of Bedford/St. Martin's literary reprint series are available at a special price with *Approaching Literature in the 21st Century,* including volumes from the Bedford Cultural Editions, the Bedford Shakespeare Series, and Case Studies in Critical Controversy. (For a complete list of available titles, see the book's instructor's manual.)

Video and DVD Library

Selected videos and DVDs of plays and stories included in the text are available from Bedford/St. Martin's video library to qualified adopters.

Acknowledgments

We want to express our appreciation to many colleagues at Hope College for their generous assistance and encouragement as we worked on *Approaching Literature in the 21st Century.* Various members of the Department of English — including John Cox, Heather Sellers DeZwaan, Natalie Dykstra, Curtis Gruenler, Stephen Hemenway, Rhoda Janzen, Marla Lunderberg, William Pannapacker, William Reynolds, and Jennifer Young — provided information and offered advice in areas of their expertise. Charles Huttar read almost every page of the typescript, critiqued them attentively, gave us much wise counsel, and made countless corrections and suggestions. David Klooster read Parts 1 and 2 and made valuable suggestions that improved the book as a whole. Jesse Montaño, in addition to his talents as a photographer, assisted with translations from Spanish, as did Miguel De La Torre from the Department of Religion. Ion Agheana, from the Department of Modern and Classical Languages, contributed significantly to particular translations and to the section "Reading Poems in Translation." Jane Currie, a reference librarian at the Van Wylen Library, read parts of the chapter on literary research and provided helpful guidance. And Myra Kohsel, office manager for the English department, assisted us willingly in her usual capable, cheerful, and efficient way.

We are grateful also to our students at Hope College, from whom we learn as they learn, and especially to Alicia Abood, Dan Carter, Kortney DeVito, Kristina Martinez, Annie Otto, and Caleb Sheng for allowing us to include their writing in the book.

We appreciate also the help given by colleagues elsewhere, especially Kamala Balasubramanian, Grossmont College; Sue Beebe, Southwest Texas State University; Daniel Cano, Santa Monica College; Emily Dial-Driver, Rogers State University; Tamara Kuzmenkov, Tacoma Community College; Laurie F. Leach, Hawaii Pacific University; Refugio Romo, Northwest Vista College; Tracy L. Schaelen, Southwestern College; William E. Sheidley, Colorado State University–Pueblo; James G. Van Belle, Edmonds Community College; and Sallie Wolf, Arapahoe Community College.

Finally, we are deeply grateful to those at Bedford/St. Martin's who made this book possible and worked hard on it. We especially want to thank Charles Christensen and Joan Feinberg for their support of the project and their vision for what the book should be; Steve Scipione for his help over several years in developing the project and his excellent advice on many facets of the book; Denise Wydra and Karen Henry for their editorial insights; Arthur Johnson for his creative and meticulous guidance of the book through the production process; Lisa Wehrle for her brilliant copyediting; Elisabeth Gehrlein for her careful, alert work on permissions; Jeff Voccola and Harriet Wald for their development of the companion Web site. Most of all, we thank Genevieve Hamilton for her superb editing of the book. Genevieve contributed more to this book, through her intelligence, creativity, attentiveness to detail, good sense, and hard work, than we can possibly describe. We are deeply indebted to her.

Brief Contents

Contents

PART 3   Approaching POETRY   453

9   Reading Poetry   455

10   Words and Images   460

15   Writing about Poetry   582

A Collection of Poems   596

PART **4**   **Approaching DRAMA**   **787**

16   **Reading Drama**   **789**

24   Sherman Alexie: Listening for Stories   1319

PART 6   Approaching LITERARY RESEARCH   1361

25   Reading Critical Essays   1363

26 Writing a Literary Research Paper   1376

Using This Book

- Terms that are **boldface** in the text are defined in the Glossary of Literary Terms at the end of the book.
- The dates provided for stories indicate their earliest publication; dates for poems give the first publication in a book; dates for plays are for their initial performance. For some poems, when publication was delayed, the probable date of composition is given as well, in *italics*.
- A row of asterisks (* * *) indicates a space break (in a story) or a stanza break (in a poem) that falls at the bottom or top of a page and otherwise might be undetectable.
- For untitled poems, the first line is often used as a convenient form of reference, though it should not be thought of as a title and thus does not follow the capitalization rules for titles.

Approaching Literature in the 21st Century

Fiction • Poetry • Drama

Approaching LITERATURE

Overleaf: The novelist, essayist, poet, and children's book author Julia Alvarez was photographed in her home in Vermont, where she has lived and worked since 1988. Alvarez teaches creative writing and is currently the writer-in-residence at Middlebury College. Alvarez and her husband divide their time between their home in Vermont and a cooperative coffee farm — a sustainable farm–literacy center called Alta Gracia — in the Dominican Republic, where Alvarez was raised. When asked why she writes in so many different genres, she says, "I blame my life. Something happens which sends me in a new direction . . . and the telling requires a different form, rhythm, voice." (See p. 1416 for a short biography.)

Reprinted by permission of Cameron Davidson.

I read because it takes me out of myself, it enlarges me. Reading is a transformative activity.

Kathleen Norris

Reading Literature

Why read? Why write? Why take the time and effort a story, poem, or play requires when we have movies, television, and DVD? The answer this book assumes is that we need to, we all need to. Writing and reading fill a human need to express, communicate, and experience connection and communion in ways that are of deep personal value. To be ourselves in the fullest sense, we need to enter the worlds and experiences of other selves, and reading is one of the best ways to do this. Although writing and reading may seem at first like individual acts, they are by their nature shared and communal: We write so that others will read, and we read what others have written. Writing and reading are sources of ideas, challenges, and meaning as well as invitations to understanding, empathy, sympathy, judgment, and compassion. They enable us to connect with others, to enter the thoughts, feelings, and experiences of those both similar to and different from ourselves. Writing and reading fill a deep need, assisting us in our endless growth toward being fully human and fully humane.

For some people, reading forms a central part of their lives. It is so vital to them that a day without some time for reading seems empty or incomplete—much as a pianist wants to spend time at the piano every day and a jogger is frustrated if she or he can't get in a daily run. And just as a musician or runner can become devoted to music and running, so can anyone get hooked on reading. The following essay was written by Sherman Alexie, who grew up on the Spokane Indian Reservation in Wellpinit, Washington, where—surprisingly, he says—he found that first reading and then writing became essential to his very being. As you read it, pay attention to the way Alexie began reading—not at all a passive taking in, but an active engagement with the work before him. Notice also what goes on as you read the essay, how it requires you also to actively involve yourself in the process.

Sherman Alexie   b. 1966

Superman and Me   [1997]

I learned to read with a *Superman* comic book. Simple enough, I suppose. I cannot recall which particular *Superman* comic book I read, nor can I remember which villain he fought in that issue. I cannot remember the plot, nor the means by which I obtained the comic book. What I can remember is this: I was three years old, a Spokane Indian boy living with his family on the Spokane Indian Reservation in eastern Washington state. We were poor by most standards, but one of my parents usually managed to find some minimum-wage job or another, which made us middle class by reservation standards. I had a brother and three sisters. We lived on a combination of irregular paychecks, hope, fear, and government-surplus food.

My father, who is one of the few Indians who went to Catholic school on purpose, was an avid reader of westerns, spy thrillers, murder mysteries, gangster epics, basketball-player biographies, and anything else he could find. He bought his books by the pound at Dutch's Pawn Shop, Goodwill, Salvation Army, and Value Village. When he had extra money, he bought new novels at supermarkets, convenience stores, and hospital gift shops. Our house was filled with books. They were stacked in crazy piles in the bathroom, bedrooms, and living room. In a fit of unemployment-inspired creative energy, my father built a set of bookshelves and soon filled them with a random assortment of books about the Kennedy assassination, Watergate, the Vietnam War, and the entire twenty-three-book series of the Apache westerns. My father loved books, and since I loved my father with an aching devotion, I decided to love books as well.

I can remember picking up my father's books before I could read. The words themselves were mostly foreign, but I still remember the exact moment when I first understood, with a sudden clarity, the purpose of a paragraph. I didn't have the vocabulary to say "paragraph," but I realized that a paragraph was a fence that held words. The words inside a paragraph worked together for a common purpose. They had some specific reason for being inside the same fence. This knowledge delighted me. I began to think of everything in terms of paragraphs. Our reservation was a small paragraph within the United States. My family's house was a paragraph, distinct from the other paragraphs of the LeBrets to the north, the Fords to our south, and the Tribal School to the west. Inside our house, each family member existed as a separate paragraph, but still had genetics and common experiences to link us. Now, using this logic, I can see my changed family as an essay of seven paragraphs: mother, father, older brother, the deceased sister, my younger twin sisters, and our adopted little brother.

At the same time I was seeing the world in paragraphs, I also picked up that *Superman* comic book. Each panel, complete with picture, dialogue, and narrative, was a three-dimensional paragraph. In one panel, Superman breaks through a door. His suit is red, blue, and yellow. The brown door shatters into many pieces. I look at the narrative above the picture. I cannot read the words, but I assume it tells me that Superman is breaking down the door. Aloud, I pretend to read the words and say "Superman is breaking down the door." Words, dialogue, also float out of Superman's mouth. Because he is breaking down the door, I assume he says, "I am breaking down the door." Once again, I pretend to read the words and say aloud, "I am breaking down the door." In this way, I learned to read.

This might be an interesting story all by itself. A little Indian boy teaches himself to read at an early age and advances quickly. He reads *Grapes of Wrath* in kindergarten when other children are struggling through Dick and Jane. If he'd been anything but an Indian boy living on the reservation, he might have been called a prodigy. But he is an Indian boy living on the reservation, and is simply an oddity. He grows into a man who often speaks of his childhood in the third-person, as if it will somehow dull the pain and make him sound more modest about his talents.

A smart Indian is a dangerous person, widely feared and ridiculed by Indians and non-Indians alike. I fought with my classmates on a daily basis. They wanted me to stay quiet when the non-Indian teacher asked for answers, for volunteers, for help. We were Indian children who were expected to be stupid. Most lived up to those expectations inside the classroom, but subverted them on the outside. They struggled with basic reading in school, but could remember how to sing a few dozen powwow songs. They were monosyllabic in front of their non-Indian teachers, but could tell complicated stories and jokes at the dinner table. They submissively ducked their heads when confronted by a non-Indian adult, but would slug it out with the Indian bully who was ten years older. As Indian children, we were expected to fail in the non-Indian world. Those who failed were ceremonially accepted by other Indians and appropriately pitied by non-Indians.

I refused to fail. I was smart. I was arrogant. I was lucky. I read books late into the night, until I could barely keep my eyes open. I read books at recess, then during lunch, and in the few minutes left after I had finished my classroom assignments. I read books in the car when my family traveled to powwows or basketball games. In shopping malls, I ran to the bookstores and read bits and pieces of as many books as I could. I read the books my father brought home from the pawnshops and secondhand stores. I read the books I borrowed from the library. I read the backs of cereal boxes. I read the newspaper. I read the bulletins posted on the walls of the school, the clinic, the tribal offices, the post office. I read junk mail. I read auto-repair manuals. I read magazines. I read anything that had words and paragraphs. I read with equal parts joy and desperation. I loved those books, but I also knew that love had only one purpose. I was trying to save my life.

Despite all the books I read, I am still surprised I became a writer. I was going to be a pediatrician. These days, I write novels, short stories, and poems. I visit schools and teach creative writing to Indian kids. In all my years in the reservation school system, I was never taught how to write poetry, short stories, or novels. I was certainly never taught that Indians wrote poetry, short stories, and novels. Writing was something beyond Indians. I cannot recall a single time that a guest teacher visited the reservation. There must have been visiting teachers. Who were they? Where are they now? Do they exist? I visit the schools as often as possible. The Indian kids crowd the classroom. Many are writing their own poems, short stories, and novels. They have read my books. They have read many other books. They look at me with bright eyes and arrogant wonder. They are trying to save their lives. Then there are the sullen and already defeated Indian kids who sit in the back rows and ignore me with theatrical precision. The pages of their notebooks are empty. They carry neither pencil nor pen. They stare out the window. They refuse and resist. "Books," I say to them. "Books," I say. I throw my weight against their locked doors. The door holds. I am smart. I am arrogant. I am lucky. I am trying to save our lives.

APPROACHING THE READING

1. This chapter opens by giving some reasons people need to read. Which of those reasons do you think apply to Alexie? Why does he need to read?

2. List some things in Alexie's life that made love of reading difficult to sustain, that worked against his learning and growth. Think briefly about your own life. Do you love to read, the way Alexie did? If not, are there factors that work against reading, that make it difficult to do or love?

3. Think about what is involved in the process of reading. How do ideas, feelings, and descriptions get from Alexie's heart and mind to your heart and mind? In what sense are you essential for the communication process to be complete?

Alexie says he read to save his life. He doesn't mean surviving physically, of course. Rather, he realized that his mind and heart and imagination required regular nourishment, which he found could come from books. Without this nourishment, parts of himself, parts essential to his very identity that make him who he really is, would weaken and perhaps eventually starve. You may be just like him, someone who loves to read and reads to live. Or you may not be at that point yet, or may have lost your love of reading, or may never have enjoyed literature. In that case, we hope this course and this book will lead you to the real value of making reading and writing a vital part of your life, and perhaps even change your life. We hope that you will give reading a new chance, will put into reading the attentiveness and receptivity it requires and deserves. If it doesn't *save* your life, at least it certainly will *enrich* it.

"Superman and Me" is a personal essay. An *essay* is a brief discussion, usually in prose, of a limited topic or idea; a *personal* essay deals with a particular part of the author's life and experience. An essay is not a story. It is *expository writing* (an explanation and discussion of ideas), not *imaginative writing* (at least partially "made up"). Most of this textbook concerns creative writing—fiction (made-up stories), poetry, and drama, and all of the examples included in the book are considered works of literature.

In his essay, Alexie says that he is a writer of "novels, short stories, and poems"; he also has written screenplays for two award-winning films, *Smoke Signals* and *The Business of Fancydancing*. Alexie's works are considered works of literature, their lasting value based on their artistic quality and the way they portray and reflect on issues important to human experience. Alexie's writing explores personal identity, ethnicity, alienation, and love. The works selected for inclusion in this book examine those issues as well. They ask readers to notice and reflect on *borders* that divide and connect people, on the *diversity of voices* we hear when we are willing to listen, and on the way many people are treated as *outsiders*. Reading such works can be personally rewarding, deepen your understanding of others, and expand the borders of your own world.

THE NATURE OF READING

If reading is so important, it only makes sense to look more closely at it. What *is* reading? What goes on when you read? How does a person "read well"? One view appears in the movie *Driving Miss Daisy*. Reading is easy, Daisy Werthan tells Hoke, her chauffeur. "If you know your letters, then you can read." She draws a *B* and an *R* in the dust and then sends him off to find a tombstone marked *BAUER*.

Reading used to be thought of that way—as just taking in the letters and combinations of letters on the page. The meaning was "there" in the marks on paper, waiting to be extracted. And because each reader was looking at the same marks, it was assumed that the meaning would be the same for everyone.

That is not, however, either an adequate or an accurate view of this human activity called reading. We are not mechanical decoders like a radio set receiving signals and emitting sounds. Nevertheless, this idea is still common and sometimes misleads students in a literature class. What actually happens when we read?

Most reading specialists agree that reading is interactive. It is a sense-*making* activity. It involves an encounter between an author, a text, and a reader in a cultural context. The writer puts ideas, details, and emotions into words (a *text*). The reader takes in the writer's words, processes them mentally, relates them to knowledge and information she or he already possesses, and constructs out of them pictures, feelings, and meanings. The writer depends on the reader to complete the communication process, to lift the inert marks off the page and fill them with life and meaning.

Understanding writing and reading as a three-way transaction between author, text, and reader makes it clear that what is written does not convey the same thing to every reader. Your engagement with a writer's words is an individual act; it depends on your mind and your personality. Each reader gains an understanding of the words in relation to her or his knowledge and experience, to the specific context and cultural situation, and even to the stage of life in which she or he is reading.

Take, for example, a writer who provides a detailed description of an Indian reservation in the mountains of eastern Washington. The pictures you form in your mind are a key part of the meaning of such a text. The mental pictures are not there on the page; what the writer started is not completed until you interact with the text, form mental images related to the written words, and respond to them with your senses and emotions.

If you have seen reservations in Washington or elsewhere, those experiences will help form sharp, precise mental pictures as you read the text and bring its meaning to life. Your mental pictures will be richer and more precise than ones formed by someone who has never been on a reservation or knows about them only from watching Western movies.

But your response as a reader is not confined to just the precision of the mental pictures (or, for more complex material, the ideas) formed. If you have been to Washington, for example, you also recall emotions associated with traveling in the mountains and being with certain companions. Those emotions also influence the understanding you construct; they become part of the meaning of what is being read, of what makes the reading itself meaningful.

ACTIVE READING

As we read, we constantly relate what we see on the page to our own knowledge and experiences. We grasp ideas, imagine details, and feel emotions as we process words to things stored in our memories; we bring our prior knowledge, attitudes, and assumptions to bear as we take in what the author wrote. Reading as a sense-making activity is inevitably personal and individual. That doesn't mean, of course, that a text means anything a reader says it means. "It is going to snow" cannot mean "An elephant is doing math," no matter what a particular reader asserts. There is a text; there are words and sentences on the page that we must look at, take in, and respond to. But we fill the words with meaning—personal meaning. Thus, readers in Michigan may read "It is going to snow" differently from the ways readers in Hawaii read the same sentence, just as an elephant trainer in India may read "An elephant is doing math" differently from the way a literature professor in Michigan reads the same sentence.

The stories, poems, and plays in this book are not objects, not just writing on the page, but potential works that need to be *completed in the reader's mind*. There can be a text (the words of the writer, written or spoken) without a reader (we "read" a spoken text just as we do a written one), but there can't be a living literary work (a story, poem, or play) without a reader (or listener) to complete what the writer began. Texts are similar to musical scores: The notes on paper are only potential music until a musician brings them to life by performing them. So too the reader "performs" a story, poem, or play by bringing it to life in his or her mind through the method of active reading.

Meaning, then, is the result of an interaction between a piece of writing and an individual reader. Since no two people have the same personality and the same experiences, the story, poem, or play they actualize out of the same text, though perhaps similar, will not be identical. The rooms filled with books that you see in your mind's eye as you read "Superman and Me" may be similar to those someone else imagines, but they won't be the same, and we shouldn't gloss over the difference by saying that it is only what they have in common that really matters. Thus, also, although you as a reader can reread the same text, you cannot experience the work in the same way a second time. Your second reading is different because you know from the beginning what is ahead, so you see things differently: It is a new story (or poem or play). If a good bit of time passes between the readings, you also are a different person, bringing new knowledge, experiences, and maturity to the process. The text does not change, but as you the reader change and the context changes, the experience of the story, poem, or play changes.

Reading is an *active* process. Your whole being — intellect, imagination, emotions, values — can be and should be involved. As we read, we select from our memories definitions and pictures that make sense of the words and phrases we encounter; we anticipate what may be ahead; we revise our earlier anticipations in light of what we find later; we make judgments about what is said and done, and sometimes need to revise those judgments and come to a different conclusion. Reading is not a spectator sport — we do not observe passively from the sidelines. To be a good reader, you need to participate, to be actively involved at every moment, with every word.

All reading is not the same. Active reading of a chemistry book takes different skills from those used in actively reading a novel; reading an Internet site actively is different from actively reading a newspaper. Reading literature actively requires you to pay attention to the way things are written as well as to what is said, and to the techniques a writer uses to develop a work. Such attentiveness doesn't happen automatically — we all, at some point, have to learn how to pay attention and to judge what is worth attending to. Active reading of literary texts entails imagining characters, forming mental images, visualizing locations and series of actions, and listening for sounds and rhythms. This book is designed to help you do these things. Its chapters introduce features and techniques that will enrich your reading experience and develop your skills at "literary observation." It describes specific strategies for reading fiction, poetry, and drama, and it introduces strategies for writing about each of them.

Active reading also involves asking questions, wondering "why? why? why?" It includes talking with other readers, talking back to the author or text, underlining words and phrases, jotting notes in the margins, and perhaps writing an outline or drawing a map inside the back cover. (More is said about these active reading strategies in Chapter 2.)

An active reader pays attention not just to what is in the text but also to what is left out ("gaps" in the text). Some gaps we close, consciously or not, by guessing what might fill them (who is the murderer in a detective story?); some gaps we ignore as unimportant. When we do fill them, we often need to revise our idea later (the clues initially point toward a murderous gardener, but he has an alibi, so maybe the butler is the guilty party?). What is left out often is very much a part of the total meaning of a text. For example, if a male writer completely ignores a female perspective, it may say a lot about the writer and make a big difference in how we interpret what he says. Paying attention not just to what is there but also to what is not there requires alert, active involvement in a *process*. Reading this way is demanding, but the rewards are well worth the effort.

By now it should be clear that Hoke in *Driving Miss Daisy* isn't really reading. He identifies the first and last letters of a word, but he lacks the skills and the background for interacting dynamically with that word. *Bauer* means nothing to him; he hadn't known the Bauers, and their name provokes no cluster of memories and emotions as it does for Miss Daisy, clusters of associations that are crucial to the construction of meaning that constitutes real reading. Active reading is a complicated skill, but an exciting one. We hope this book encourages you to want to get better and better at it and helps you find greater and greater pleasure and enrichment from your reading.

Here is a story about the importance reading and writing came to have in the life of a young woman whose family emigrated from the Dominican Republic to New York City. The point is similar to that in "Superman and Me," but notice the difference in form. As an essay, "Superman and Me" explains and discusses personal experiences and their effect on the author. "Daughter of Invention" brings a personal experience to life, telling it as a story, through characters and a sequence of events. As you read, practice the kinds of active reading skills we've just discussed — paying close attention to everything in the text, imagining, visualizing, listening, asking questions, noticing what's left out, filling gaps, underlining words and phrases you might want to look at again, and jotting notes in the margins.

Julia Alvarez b. 1950

Daughter of Invention   [1988]

She wanted to invent something, my mother. There was a period after we arrived in this country, until five or so years later, when my mother was inventing. They were never pressing, global needs she was addressing with her pencil and pad. She would have said that was for men to do, rockets and engines that ran on gasoline and turned the wheels of the world. She was just fussing with little house things, don't mind her.

She always invented at night, after settling her house down. On his side of the bed my father would be conked out for an hour already, his Spanish newspaper draped over his chest, his glasses, propped up on his bedside table, looking out eerily at the darkened room like a disembodied guard. But in her lighted corner, like some devoted scholar burning the midnight oil, my mother was inventing, sheets pulled to her lap, pillows propped up behind her, her reading glasses riding the bridge of her nose like a schoolmarm's. On her lap lay one of those innumerable pads of paper my father always brought home from his office, compliments of some pharmaceutical company, advertising tranquilizers or antibiotics or skin cream; in her other hand, my mother held a pencil that looked like a pen with a little cylinder of lead inside. She would work on a sketch of something familiar, but drawn at such close range so she could attach a special nozzle or handier handle, the thing looked peculiar. Once, I mistook the spiral of a corkscrew for a nautilus shell, but it could just as well have been a galaxy forming.

It was the only time all day we'd catch her sitting down, for she herself was living proof of the *perpetuum mobile* machine so many inventors had sought over the ages. My sisters and I would seek her out now when she seemed to have a moment to talk to us: We were having trouble at school or we wanted her to persuade my father to give us permission to go into the city or to a shopping mall or a movie—in broad daylight! My mother would wave us out of her room. "The problem with you girls . . ." I can tell you right now what the problem always boiled down to: We wanted to become Americans and my father—and my mother, at first—would have none of it.

"You girls are going to drive me crazy!" She always threatened if we kept nagging. "When I end up in Bellevue, you'll be safely sorry!"

She spoke in English when she argued with us, even though, in a matter of months, her daughters were the fluent ones. Her English was much better than my father's, but it was still a mishmash of mixed-up idioms and sayings that showed she was "green behind the ears," as she called it.

If my sisters and I tried to get her to talk in Spanish, she'd snap, "When in Rome, do unto the Romans . . ."

I had become the spokesman for my sisters, and I would stand my ground in that bedroom. "We're not going to that school anymore, Mami!"

"You have to." Her eyes would widen with worry. "In this country, it is against the law not to go to school. You want us to get thrown out?"

"You want us to get killed? Those kids were throwing stones today!"

"Sticks and stones don't break bones . . ." she chanted. I could tell, though, by the look on her face, it was as if one of those stones the kids had aimed at us had hit her. But she always pretended we were at fault. "What did you do to provoke them? It takes two to tangle, you know."

"Thanks, thanks a lot, Mom!" I'd storm out of that room and into mine. I never called her *Mom* except when I wanted her to feel how much she had failed us in this country. She was a good enough Mami, fussing and scolding and giving advice, but a terrible girlfriend parent, a real failure of a Mom.

Back she'd go to her pencil and pad, scribbling and tsking and tearing off paper, finally giving up, and taking up her *New York Times*. Some nights, though, she'd get a good idea, and she'd rush into my room, a flushed look on her face, her tablet of paper in her hand, a cursory knock on the door she'd just thrown open: "Do I have something to show you, Cukita!"

This was my time to myself, after I'd finished my homework, while my sisters were still downstairs watching TV in the basement. Hunched over my small desk, the overhead light turned off, my lamp shining poignantly on my paper, the rest of the room in warm, soft, uncreated darkness, I wrote my secret poems in my new language.

"You're going to ruin your eyes!" My mother would storm into my room, turning on the overly bright overhead light, scaring off whatever shy passion I had just begun coaxing out of a labyrinth of feelings with the blue thread of my writing.

"Oh Mami!" I'd cry out, my eyes blinking up at her. "I'm writing."

"Ay, Cukita." That was her communal pet name for whoever was in her favor. "Cukita, when I make a million, I'll buy you your very own type-writer." (I'd been nagging my mother for one just like the one father had bought her to do his order forms at home.) "Gravy on the turkey" was what she called it when someone was buttering her up. She'd butter and pour. "I'll hire you your very own typist."

Down she'd plop on my bed and hold out her pad to me. "Take a guess, Cukita?" I'd study her rough sketch a moment: soap sprayed from the nozzle head of a shower when you turned the knob a certain way? Coffee with creamer already mixed in? Time-released water capsules for your plants when you were away? A key chain with a timer that would go off when your parking meter was about to expire? (The ticking would help you find your keys easily if you mislaid them.) The famous one, famous only in hindsight, was the stick person dragging a square by a rope—a suitcase with wheels? "Oh, of course," we'd humor her. "What every household needs: a shower like a car wash, keys ticking like a bomb, luggage on a leash!" By now, as you can see, it'd become something of a family joke, our Thomas Edison Mami, our Benjamin Franklin Mom.

Her face would fall. "Come on now! Use your head." One more wrong guess, and she'd tell me, pressing with her pencil point the different high-lights of this incredible new wonder. "Remember that time we took the car to Bear Mountain, and we re-ah-lized that we had forgotten to pack an opener with our pick-a-nick?" (We kept correcting her, but she insisted this is how it should be said.) "When we were ready to eat we didn't have any way to open the refreshments cans?" (This before fliptop lids, which she claimed had crossed her mind.) "You know what this is now?" A shake of my head. "Is a car bumper, but see this part is a removable can opener. So simple and yet so necessary, no?"

"Yeah, Mami. You should patent it." I'd shrug. She'd tear off the scratch paper and fold it, carefully, corner to corner, as if she were going to save it. But then, she'd toss it in the wastebasket on her way out of the room and give a little laugh like a disclaimer. "It's half of one or two dozen of another . . ."

I suppose none of her daughters was very encouraging. We resented her spending time on those dumb inventions. Here, we were trying to fit in America among Americans; we needed help figuring out who we were, why these Irish kids whose grandparents were micks two generations ago, why they were calling us spics. Why had we come to the country in the first place? Important, crucial, final things, you see, and here was our own mother, who didn't have a second to help us puzzle any of this out, inventing gadgets to make life easier for American moms. Why, it seemed as if she were arming our own enemy against us!

One time, she did have a moment of triumph. Every night, she liked to read *The New York Times* in bed before turning off her light, to see what the Americans were up to. One night, she let out a yelp to wake up my father beside her, bolt upright, reaching for his glasses which, in his haste, he knocked across the room. *"Que pasa? Que pasa?"* What is wrong? There was terror in his voice, fear she'd seen in his eyes in the Dominican Republic before we left. We were being watched there; he was being followed; he and mother had often exchanged those looks. They could not talk, of course, though they must have whispered to each other in fear at night in the dark bed. Now in America, he was safe, a success even; his Centro Medico in Brooklyn was thronged with the sick and the homesick. But in dreams, he went back to those awful days and long nights, and my mother's screams confirmed his secret fear: we had not gotten away after all; they had come for us at last.

"Ay, Papi, I'm sorry. Go back to sleep, Cukito. It's nothing, nothing really." My mother held up the *Times* for him to squint at the small print, back page headline, one hand tapping all over the top of the bedside table for his glasses, the other rubbing his eyes to wakefulness.

"Remember, remember how I showed you that suitcase with little wheels so we would not have to carry those heavy bags when we traveled? Someone stole my idea and made a million!" She shook the paper in his face. She shook the paper in all our faces that night. "See! See! This man was no *bobo*! He didn't put all his pokers on a back burner. I kept telling you, one of these days my ship would pass me by in the night!" She wagged her finger at my sisters and my father and me, laughing all the while, one of those eerie laughs crazy people in movies laugh. We had congregated in her room to hear the good news she'd been yelling down the stairs, and now we eyed her and each other. I suppose we were all thinking the same thing: Wouldn't it be weird and sad if Mami did end up in Bellevue as she'd always threatened she might?

"Ya, ya! Enough!" She waved us out of her room at last. "There is no use trying to drink spilt milk, that's for sure."

It was the suitcase rollers that stopped my mother's hand; she had weather vaned a minor brainstorm. She would have to start taking herself seriously. That blocked the free play of her ingenuity. Besides, she had also begun working at my father's office, and at night, she was too tired and busy filling in columns with how much money they had made that day to be fooling with gadgets!

She did take up her pencil and pad one last time to help me out. In ninth grade, I was chosen by my English teacher, Sister Mary Joseph, to deliver the teacher's day address at the school assembly. Back in the Dominican Republic, I was a terrible student. No one could ever get me to sit down to a book. But in New York, I needed to settle somewhere, and the natives were unfriendly, the country inhospitable, so I took root in the language. By high school, the nuns were reading my stories and compositions out loud to my classmates as examples of imagination at work.

This time my imagination jammed. At first I didn't want and then I couldn't seem to write that speech. I suppose I should have thought of it as a "great honor," as my father called it. But I was mortified. I still had a pronounced lilt to my accent, and I did not like to speak in public, subjecting myself to my classmates' ridicule. Recently, they had begun to warm toward my sisters and me, and it took no great figuring to see that to deliver a eulogy for a convent full of crazy, old overweight nuns was no way to endear myself to the members of my class.

But I didn't know how to get out of it. Week after week, I'd sit down, hoping to polish off some quick, noncommittal little speech. I couldn't get anything down.

The weekend before our Monday morning assembly I went into a panic. My mother would just have to call in and say I was in the hospital, in a coma. I was in the Dominican Republic. Yeah, that was it! Recently, my father had been talking about going back home to live.

My mother tried to calm me down. "Just remember how Mister Lincoln couldn't think of anything to say at the Gettysburg, but then, Bang! 'Four score and once upon a time ago,'" she began reciting. Her version of history was half invention and half truths and whatever else she needed to prove a point. "Something is going to come if you just relax. You'll see, like the Americans say, 'Necessity is the daughter of invention.' I'll help you."

All weekend, she kept coming into my room with help. "Please, Mami, just leave me alone, please," I pleaded with her. But I'd get rid of the goose only to have to contend with the gander. My father kept poking his head in the door just to see if I had "fulfilled my obligations," a phrase he'd used when we were a little younger, and he'd check to see whether we had gone to the bathroom before a car trip. Several times that weekend around the supper table, he'd recite his valedictorian speech from when he graduated from high school. He'd give me pointers on delivery, on the great orators and their tricks. (Humbleness and praise and falling silent with great emotion were his favorites.)

My mother sat across the table, the only one who seemed to be listening to him. My sisters and I were forgetting a lot of our Spanish, and my father's formal, florid diction was even harder to understand. But my mother smiled softly to herself, and turned the Lazy Susan at the center of the table around and around as if it were the prime mover, the first gear of attention.

That Sunday evening, I was reading some poetry to get myself inspired: Whitman in an old book with an engraved cover my father had picked up in a thrift shop next to his office a few weeks back. "I celebrate myself and sing myself . . ." "He most honors my style who learns under it to destroy the teacher." The poet's words shocked and thrilled me. I had gotten used to the nuns, a literature of appropriate sentiments, poems with a message, expurgated texts. But here was a flesh and blood man, belching and laughing and sweating in poems. "Who touches this book touches a man."

That night, at last, I started to write, recklessly, three, five pages, looking up once only to see my father passing by the hall on tiptoe. When I was done, I read over my words, and my eyes filled. I finally sounded like myself in English!

As soon as I had finished that first draft, I called my mother to my room. She listened attentively, as she had to my father's speech, and in the end, her eyes were glistening too. Her face was soft and warm and proud. "That is a beautiful, beautiful speech, Cukita. I want for your father to hear it before he goes to sleep. Then I will type it for you, all right?"

Down the hall we went, the two of us, faces flushed with accomplishment. Into the master bedroom where my father was propped up on his pillows, still awake, reading the Dominican papers, already days old. He had become interested in his country's fate again. The dictatorship had been toppled. The interim government was going to hold the first free elections in thirty years. There was still some question in his mind whether or not we might want to move back. History was in the making, freedom and hope were in the air again! But my mother had gotten used to the life here. She did not want to go back to the old country where she was only a wife and a mother (and a failed one at that, since she had never had the required son). She did not come straight out and disagree with my father's plans. Instead, she fussed with him about reading the papers in bed, soiling those sheets with those poorly printed, foreign tabloids. "*The Times* is not that bad!" she'd claim if my father tried to humor her by saying they shared the same dirty habit.

The minute my father saw my mother and me, filing in, he put his paper down, and his face brightened as if at long last his wife had delivered a son, and that was the news we were bringing him. His teeth were already grinning from the glass of water next to his bedside lamp, so he lisped when he said, "Eh-speech, eh-speech!"

"It is so beautiful, Papi," my mother previewed him, turning the sound off on his TV. She sat down at the foot of the bed. I stood before both of them, blocking their view of the soldiers in helicopters landing amid silenced gun reports and explosions. A few weeks ago it had been the shores of the Dominican Republic. Now it was the jungles of Southeast Asia they were saving. My mother gave me the nod to begin reading.

I didn't need much encouragement. I put my nose to the fire, as my mother would have said, and read from start to finish without looking up. When I was done, I was a little embarrassed at my pride in my own words. I pretended to quibble with a phrase or two I was sure I'd be talked out of changing. I looked questioningly to my mother. Her face was radiant. She turned to share her pride with my father.

But the expression on his face shocked us both. His toothless mouth had collapsed into a dark zero. His eyes glared at me, then shifted to my mother, accusingly. In barely audible Spanish, as if secret microphones or informers were all about, he whispered, "You will permit her to read *that*?"

My mother's eyebrows shot up, her mouth fell open. In the old country, any whisper of a challenge to authority could bring the secret police in their black V.W.'s. But this was America. People could say what they thought. "What is wrong with her speech?" my mother questioned him.

"What ees wrrrong with her eh-speech?" My father wagged his head at her. His anger was always more frightening in his broken English. As if he had mutilated the language in his fury—and now there was nothing to stand between us and his raw, dumb anger. "What is wrong? I will tell you what is wrong. It shows no gratitude. It is boastful. 'I celebrate myself'? 'The best student learns to destroy the teacher'?" He mocked my plagiarized words. "That is insubordinate. It is improper. It is disrespecting of her teachers—" In his anger he had forgotten his fear of lurking spies: Each wrong he voiced was a decibel higher than the last outrage. Finally, he was yelling at me, "As your father, I forbid you to say that eh-speech!"

My mother leapt to her feet, a sign always that she was about to make a speech or deliver an ultimatum. She was a small woman, and she spoke all her pronouncements standing up, either for more protection or as a carry-over from her girlhood in convent schools where one asked for, and literally took, the floor in order to speak. She stood by my side, shoulder to shoulder; we looked down at my father. "That is no tone of voice, Eduardo—" she began.

By now, my father was truly furious. I suppose it was bad enough I was rebelling, but here was my mother joining forces with me. Soon he would be surrounded by a house full of independent American women. He too leapt from his bed, throwing off his covers. The Spanish newspapers flew across the room. He snatched my speech out of my hands, held it before my panicked eyes, a vengeful, mad look in his own, and then once, twice, three, four, countless times, he tore my prize into shreds.

"Are you crazy?" My mother lunged at him. "Have you gone mad? That is her speech for tomorrow you have torn up!"

"Have *you* gone mad?" He shook her away. "You were going to let her read that . . . that insult to her teachers?"

"Insult to her teachers!" My mother's face had crumpled up like a piece of paper. On it was written a love note to my father. Ever since they had come to this country, their life together was a constant war. "This is America, Papi, America!" she reminded him now. "You are not in a savage country any more!"

I was on my knees, weeping wildly, collecting all the little pieces of my speech, hoping that I could put it back together before the assembly tomorrow morning. But not even a sibyl could have made sense of all those scattered pieces of paper. All hope was lost. "He broke it, he broke it," I moaned as I picked up a handful of pieces.

Probably, if I had thought a moment about it, I would not have done what I did next. I would have realized my father had lost brothers and comrades to the dictator Trujillo. For the rest of his life, he would be haunted by blood in the streets and late night disappearances. Even after he had been in the states for years, he jumped if a black Volkswagen passed him on the street. He feared anyone in uniform: the meter maid giving out parking tickets, a museum guard approaching to tell him not to touch his favorite Goya at the Metropolitan.

I took a handful of the scraps I had gathered, stood up, and hurled them in his face. "Chapita!" I said in a low, ugly whisper. "You're just another Chapita!"

It took my father only a moment to register the hated nickname of our dictator, and he was after me. Down the halls we raced, but I was quicker than he and made it to my room just in time to lock the door as my father threw his weight against it. He called down curses on my head, ordered me on his authority as my father to open that door this very instant! He throttled that doorknob, but all to no avail. My mother's love of gadgets saved my hide that night. She had hired a locksmith to install good locks on all the bedroom doors after our house had been broken into while we were away the previous summer. In case burglars broke in again, and we were in the house, they'd have a second round of locks to contend with before they got to us.

"Eduardo," she tried to calm him down. "Don't you ruin my new locks."

He finally did calm down, his anger spent. I heard their footsteps retreating down the hall. I heard their door close, the clicking of their lock. Then, muffled voices, my mother's peaking in anger, in persuasion, my father's deep murmurs of explanation and of self-defense. At last, the house fell silent, before I heard, far off, the gun blasts and explosions, the serious, self-important voices of newscasters reporting their TV war.

A little while later, there was a quiet knock at my door, followed by a tentative attempt at the doorknob. "Cukita?" my mother whispered. "Open up, Cukita."

"Go away," I wailed, but we both knew I was glad she was there, and I needed only a moment's protest to save face before opening that door.

What we ended up doing that night was putting together a speech at the last moment. Two brief pages of stale compliments and the polite commonplaces on teachers, wrought by necessity without much invention by mother for daughter late into the night in the basement on the pad of paper and with the same pencil she had once used for her own inventions, for I was too upset to compose the speech myself. After it was drafted, she typed it up while I stood by, correcting her misnomers and mis-sayings.

She was so very proud of herself when I came home the next day with the success story of the assembly. The nuns had been flattered, the audience had stood up and given "our devoted teachers a standing ovation," what my mother had suggested they do at the end of my speech.

She clapped her hands together as I recreated the moment for her. "I stole that from your father's speech, remember? Remember how he put that in at the end?" She quoted him in Spanish, then translated for me into English.

That night, I watched him from the upstairs hall window where I'd retreated the minute I heard his car pull up in front of our house. Slowly, my father came up the driveway, a grim expression on his face as he grappled with a large, heavy cardboard box. At the front door, he set the package down carefully and patted all his pockets for his house keys—precisely why my mother had invented her ticking key chain. I heard the snapping open of the locks downstairs. Heard as he struggled to maneuver the box through the narrow doorway. Then, he called my name several times. But I would not answer him.

"My daughter, your father, he love you very much," he explained from the bottom of the stairs. "He just want to protect you." Finally, my mother came up and pleaded with me to go down and reconcile with him. "Your father did not mean to harm. You must pardon him. Always it is better to let bygones be forgotten, no?"

I guess she was right. Downstairs, I found him setting up a brand new electric typewriter on the kitchen table. It was even better than the one I'd been begging to get like my mother's. My father had outdone himself with all the extra features: a plastic carrying case with my initials, in decals, below the handle, a brace to lift the paper upright while I typed, an erase cartridge, an automatic margin tab, a plastic hood like a toaster cover to keep the dust away. Not even my mother, I think, could have invented such a machine!

But her inventing days were over just as mine were starting up with my schoolwide success. That's why I've always thought of that speech my mother wrote for me as her last invention rather than the suitcase rollers everyone else in the family remembers. It was as if she had passed on to me her pencil and pad and said, "Okay, Cukita, here's the buck. You give it a shot."

APPROACHING THE READING

1. "Daughter of Invention" divides into two parts. The first third provides background: about the family relocating to New York, about the mother's inventions, about the difficulties the sisters face in adjusting to a new country and a different culture. The rest of the story, beginning at "She did take up her pencil and pad one last time to help me out," deals with the speech

the speaker must deliver at the school assembly. *Invention* in the first part refers primarily to what the mother dreams up; in the second part, it refers mostly to the speech they are making up, or inventing. In both parts, could *invention* have a wider application? Are the characters engaged in other forms of invention as they adjust to a new place and culture?

2. Reflect on things you engaged with as you read the text actively. What questions did you raise? At what points did you feel concern, anticipating possible difficulty for the characters? (Think about how you would experience those points differently on a second reading.) What gaps did you notice, and how did you fill them? What parts did you enjoy most? Why? Which parts were you able to imagine most vividly, perhaps drawing on past experiences? Which ones left your visualizings less sharp and distinct?

3. Make a list of tensions and conflicts among the family members: the mother and father, the daughters and the parents, the sisters and their mother, the speaker and her mother, the speaker and her father. Reflect on those tensions and conflicts. Which ones would exist regardless of whether the family had moved to the United States? Which ones are created or heightened by their relocation?

4. Why does writing become so important to the speaker? Was she writing to save her life? In what ways is reading also important, and how does it relate to her writing? If you have not read anything by Walt Whitman before, read some of the parts of his long poem *Song of Myself* (included in this book on p. 748)—that's an element of active reading, too. What is it in Whitman that Alvarez finds so inspiring? Why would Whitman be so influential in her particular life situation?

5. The speaker, like Sherman Alexie, reads (and writes) to save her life. Reflect on similarities between what reading and writing mean to both of them. Consider also ways in which their situations are different, making the ways that reading and writing save them different as well.

6. List some gaps in the story. Be ready to discuss why you think things were left out and whether the gaps are unimportant or become a part of the total meaning of the story.

7. Reflect on the last two paragraphs. Why does her father give the speaker the gift that he does? What is he saying through it? What do the final paragraphs suggest about the continuing importance of writing in his daughter's life?

eading makes me want to write, and writing makes me want to read. And both reading and writing make it a joy to be a part of the great human adventure we call life.

Katherine Patterson

CHAPTER **2**

Responding to Literature

Responding to literature is like participating in a great, ongoing conversation—perhaps like posting messages in the most gigantic chatroom the world has ever known because it has postings from the distant past as well as the present and all times in between. Some portions of this conversation are personal and some are public, and they cover an endlessly wide range of subjects. Included are conversations between authors and existing literary works, held directly or indirectly (see **allusion**, p. 205); conversations between a work and its readers; conversations between readers and other readers; conversations held orally, in writing, or through other media and art forms. This chapter offers specific suggestions for ways an active reader—the kind described in Chapter 1—can take part in some of these conversations.

Throughout this chapter, we draw illustrations from a very short story by Alice Walker. Read it and reflect on it before you move on.

Alice Walker   b. 1944

The Flowers   [1973]

It seemed to Myop as she skipped lightly from hen house to pigpen to smokehouse that the days had never been as beautiful as these. The air held a keenness that made her nose twitch. The harvesting of the corn and cotton, peanuts and squash, made each day a golden surprise that caused excited little tremors to run up her jaws.

Myop carried a short, knobby stick. She struck out at random at chickens she liked, and worked out the beat of a song on the fence around the pigpen. She felt light and good in the warm sun. She was ten, and nothing existed for her but her song, the stick clutched in her dark brown hand, and the tat-de-ta-ta-ta of accompaniment.

Turning her back on the rusty boards of her family's sharecropper cabin, Myop walked along the fence till it ran into the stream made by the spring. Around the spring, where the family got drinking water, silver ferns and wildflowers grew. Along the shallow banks pigs rooted. Myop watched the tiny white bubbles disrupt the thin black scale of soil and the water that silently rose and slid away down the stream.

She had explored the woods behind the house many times. Often, in late autumn, her mother took her to gather nuts among the fallen leaves. Today she made her own path, bouncing this way and that way, vaguely keeping an eye out for snakes. She found, in addition to various common but pretty ferns and leaves, an armful of strange blue flowers with velvety ridges and a sweetsuds bush full of the brown, fragrant buds.

By twelve o'clock, her arms laden with sprigs of her findings, she was a mile or more from home. She had often been as far before, but the strangeness of the land made it not as pleasant as her usual haunts. It seemed gloomy in the little cove in which she found herself. The air was damp, the silence close and deep.

Myop began to circle back to the house, back to the peacefulness of the morning. It was then she stepped smack into his eyes. Her heel became lodged in the broken ridge between brow and nose, and she reached down quickly, unafraid, to free herself. It was only when she saw his naked grin that she gave a little yelp of surprise.

He had been a tall man. From feet to neck covered a long space. His head lay beside him. When she pushed back the leaves and layers of earth and debris Myop saw that he'd had large white teeth, all of them cracked or broken, long fingers, and very big bones. All his clothes had rotted away except some threads of blue denim from his overalls. The buckles of the overalls had turned green.

Myop gazed around the spot with interest. Very near where she'd stepped into the head was a wild pink rose. As she picked it to add to her bundle she noticed a raised mound, a ring, around the rose's root. It was the rotted remains of a noose, a bit of shredding plowline, now blending benignly into the soil. Around an overhanging limb of a great spreading oak clung another piece. Frayed, rotted, bleached, and frazzled — barely there — but spinning restlessly in the breeze. Myop laid down her flowers.

And the summer was over.

WRITING IN THE MARGINS

Chapter 1 describes reading as an interactive process: The text speaks to the reader, and the reader responds to the text. Reading should never be a one-way "lecture," the reader merely taking in the work passively. You, as an active reader, can talk back to the work, agreeing with it, interrogating it, connecting with it, challenging it. One way of doing that is to read with a pencil in hand, jotting down your side of the conversation.

If you own the book you are reading, you can jot notes in and around the text itself. If you don't own the book you're reading, have paper available, maybe as a bookmark, and use it for keeping notes.

- Underline sentences or phrases that you really like or that strike you as especially important. But don't underline or highlight *everything* — then nothing stands out.
- Circle words you find particularly noteworthy.
- Put a star, a question mark, or an exclamation point, especially during a first reading, next to passages you might want to return to later to figure out a difficulty or to ponder in light of later events.
- Write comments in the margins as you move through a work: "What does this mean?" "Big point!" "Stupid idea!" "Tone shifts."
- Enter into dialogue with the work — raising questions, disagreeing with what is said, noting things that remind you of other works by the same writer or by a different writer or that connect you to something important, jotting down possibilities for papers.
- Write out definitions of words you had to look up.

This form of "engaged reading," writing in a book, is an ancient and honored tradition. Reading the marginal notes (or *marginalia*) that people of all ages wrote in their books can be interesting and informative. Billy Collins made it the subject of a poem (included in this book on p. 624).

Personally annotating a book is a way to make the book "yours." It now contains your ideas and inquiries as well as the author's. Try it in this book. You might find it interesting to revisit this book years from now, to reread stories, poems, and plays you liked especially, and to look again at the notes you wrote about them. You may wonder who that person was who wrote those notes; you might reacquaint yourself with who you were then; or you might discover how much you have added to your experience with literature since then.

To illustrate what we mean (not to prescribe how it should be done), here is some writing in the margins of "The Flowers" done by one of our students, Kortney DeVito (pictured at left). She later uses these notes to write a journal entry on the story (see p. 26), which she could use as the starting point for a paper.

Alice Walker

The Flowers

interesting name

It seemed to (Myop) as she skipped lightly from hen house to pigpen to smokehouse that the days had never been as beautiful as these. The air held a keenness that made her nose twitch. <u>The harvesting of the corn and cotton, peanuts and squash, made each day a golden surprise that caused excited little tremors to run up her jaws.</u>

Great imagery!

Myop carried a short, knobby stick. She struck out at random at chickens she liked, and worked out the beat of a song on the fence around the pigpen. She felt light and good in the warm sun. She was ten, and nothing existed for her but her song, the stick clutched in her dark brown hand, and the <u>tat-de-ta-ta-ta of accompaniment.</u>

I can nearly hear her sing.

Turning her back on the rusty boards of her family's share-cropper cabin, Myop walked along the fence till it ran into the stream made by the spring. Around the spring, where the family got drinking water, silver ferns and wildflowers grew. Along the shallow banks pigs rooted <u>Myop watched the tiny white bubbles disrupt the thin black scale of soil and the water that silently rose and slid away down the stream.</u>

I adore this description.

Does Myop see the stream the same way as the narrator?

She had explored the woods behind the house many times. Often, in late autumn, her mother took her to gather nuts among the fallen leaves. Today she made (her own path,) bouncing this way and that way, vaguely keeping an eye out for snakes. She found, in addition to various common but pretty ferns and leaves, an armful of strange blue flowers with velvety ridges and a sweet-suds bush full of the brown, fragrant buds.

growing older, independent

By twelve o'clock, her arms laden with sprigs of her find-ings, she was a mile or more from home. She had often been as far before, but the strangeness of the land made it not as pleas-ant as her usual haunts. <u>It seemed gloomy in the little cove in which she found herself. The air was damp, the silence close and deep.</u>

Uh-oh, fore-shadowing — sounds creepy.

Myop began to circle back to the house, back to the peaceful-ness of the morning. It was then she stepped smack into his eyes. <u>Her heel became lodged in the broken ridge between brow and nose,</u> and she reached down quickly, unafraid, to free herself. It

Yuck!

was only when she saw his naked grin that she gave a little yelp of surprise.

Past tense!   He had been a tall man. From feet to neck covered a long space. His head lay beside him. When she pushed back the leaves and layers of earth and debris Myop saw that he'd had large white teeth, all of them cracked or broken, long fingers, and very big bones. All

He had been there for a while.   his clothes had rotted away except some threads of blue denim from his overalls. The buckles of the overalls had turned green.

Most 10-year-olds would have run away!   Myop gazed around the spot with interest. Very near where she'd stepped into the head was a wild pink rose. As she picked it to add to her bundle she noticed a raised mound, a ring, around the rose's root. It was the rotted remains of a noose, a bit of

Gross!!!   shredding plowline, now blending benignly into the soil. Around an overhanging limb of a great spreading oak clung another piece. Frayed, rotted, bleached, and frazzled — barely there — but spinning restlessly in the breeze. Myop laid down her flowers.

And the summer was over.

For the dead man or her childhood and innocence?

JOURNAL WRITING

Journal writing enables you to go beyond the brief notes you jot in the margins of a book to longer responses in which you develop your reactions, insights, and ideas in greater detail. A journal is a good place to store information, quotations, related ideas, personal anecdotes, tangential insights — anything that might be connected to what you are studying or that can be extended from or associated with it.

Think of a journal as something you write primarily for yourself — something halfway between a diary and a class notebook. It's not intimate or confessional as diaries often are, nor is it as objective, remote, and impersonal as the notebook. A journal can contain personal reactions to literature and give practice in applying skills of analysis and interpretation. Not wholly private, it is not wholly public either. You can keep track of characters' names; notes on specific elements; lines you want to remember; unusual uses of form, diction, or sounds; things you were drawn to or put off by. You could regard your journal as an extension of the notes you take in class, reorganizing the notes, perhaps, and clarifying and expanding them (which can be a great help for reviewing later). A journal also provides a place where you can express ideas or emotions stimulated by what you read or by conversations with other people.

A journal can be kept in a notebook; some people divide it into two columns or use the left- and right-hand pages differently — one side for notes or information, the other side for reactions, reflections, and observations. Or it can be kept in a computer file or series of files — that's helpful for cutting and pasting notes from your journal into a paper later and for doing searches of related items. If you put entries in separate files, develop a good labeling system so you can find entries easily. If you put multiple entries in the same file, be sure to include searchable identifying tags introducing entries.

If a journal is assigned for your course or if keeping a journal simply appeals to you, buy a notebook or computer diskette and begin entering responses to literary works, to chapters of this book, or to discussions and assignments connected with this course. The suggestions for writing at the ends of chapters may stimulate some ideas; your teacher will bring up some; you will think of others yourself. Try to be specific and precise (include brief quotations and page numbers), and date each entry. Keeping journals can help you trace your own development and growth in taste, judgment, and attitudes. As mentioned before, it can be surprising, interesting, and helpful one day to look back at them.

In some courses, journals are assigned as part of the writing. A benefit (or intention) of this is to illustrate the value of keeping a journal so that students may decide to continue them after the course is over. Instructors who include journals in their courses do so because journals allow for immediate, reactive, personal, and flexible responses to reading. Often the writing itself emerges from a deeply intimate connection of the self with a literary work. We tap into the part of ourselves that seeks to respond, record, and retain things that feel meaningful to us. Many storywriters and poets keep notebooks or journals of impressions, reactions, names, and lists of words and phrases, not just from what they read but from what they experience daily.

Writing a journal as a class assignment changes its nature to some degree, especially if the journal is handed in and read by the teacher. A personal journal is usually private; an assigned journal is not. Assigned journals differ also in that some of the writing in them may be directed; that is, the teacher could ask you to focus on a specific topic in a given entry ("Identify and record examples of nature imagery in 'The Flowers' and discuss its effect in the story"). Teachers do not necessarily want specific answers or interpretations. Rather, they are looking for clear evidence that you have read the works carefully; that you have made a thoughtful effort to engage with the material and to respond sensibly and sensitively to its emotional, aesthetic, and intellectual dimensions; and that your comments are clear and specific. They are looking for evidence of your mind at work as you read. Here is a page from Kortney's journal on "The Flowers." Notice the places where she carries over ideas from her marginal notations and elaborates on or changes them.

Alice Walker, "The Flowers"

Why the need for a story such as this? Why combine such a beautiful beginning with such a hauntingly grotesque ending? It conveys that throughout life there is death — not just of others but of ourselves. Not one person can stay in one season of his/her life forever. Each season of our lives teaches something special, but at the same time each season becomes obsolete and passes away.

Myop was going through the season known as childhood at the beginning of the story. She thought there was nothing but beauty in the world; each day was a "golden surprise." When she encountered the head of the decaying man, she began to realize the harsh reality that life can possess. It was almost as if she was Eve eating from the Tree of Knowledge in the Garden of Eden — she began to see the horrible truths life is capable of delivering — not just death, but the evil of death by lynching. At the end of the story Myop "laid down her flowers." A question is: where and for whom? Some may say it was to the man whose life was cut short. I believe Myop laid the flowers down for her childhood — the innocence she once possessed was now dead to her.

DISCUSSING LITERATURE

Talking to someone is another way of responding to literature. We do that with most things that interest us. After a good concert or game or movie, we want to talk about it with somebody — to compare notes, share enthusiasms, relive favorite moments, ask questions about things we found puzzling or confusing. The same is true about literature. Most people who enjoy reading like to talk about books. Sometimes they form reading groups: Members get together to spend an evening discussing works they've read. Literature classes often try to replicate that situation by having classes small enough to be conducted mainly by discussion or by breaking large lecture classes into discussion groups.

To participate effectively in a discussion requires preparation. That's true for discussing other things as well. It's more fun to talk about baseball or movies with someone who watches closely, knows some background, and thinks before speaking. For a discussion group or class to work, it is essential that all members do the reading before the group or class meets. For a literature class, that means having the work in your mind, fresh and at the forefront — not as a vague memory of which the class will remind you. This requires reading works more than once before class.

Being prepared for discussion also requires thinking about the reading. The kind of active reading described in Chapter 1 and the marginal annotations illustrated in the first part of this chapter are good preparation. Writing down questions you might raise in class or points you might make also is good preparation, especially for those who are reserved and don't find it easy to join in. Even if you feel hesitant, are usually quiet, or lack confidence, try to add to the conversation by reading from your notations. It's the conjoining of a democracy of ideas and perspectives — each of them equal, all of them needed to form a whole — that makes a discussion interesting and valuable. Each member should feel welcome to take part.

Participating in a discussion does not require thoroughly thought-out statements or authoritative positions, but it does require honesty, alertness, a questioning attitude, and a willingness to stick one's neck out at least a little way. You can play a valuable role by sharing your enthusiasm for something, asking someone to elaborate on what she or he said, adding evidence for an idea someone else proposed, agreeing with someone, disagreeing, and so forth. Attentive, respectful listening, showing obvious interest in what is being said, or nodding your head in agreement are all valuable to a group. On the other hand, talking too often or too long or too assertively dampens others' enthusiasm and sense of community. Quality, not quantity, is important — along with genuineness, thoughtfulness, and timeliness.

Some students are confused about how to take notes during a discussion class. It seems easier to take notes on a lecture — things usually proceed in an orderly way, the professor does all the talking, and what she or he says is surely accurate and worth writing down. In a discussion, it's hard to tell whose ideas are "right" and therefore what to write down. It is important, however, that you take notes to have a record of the vital topics and ideas discussed. Here's a suggestion: Organize your notes for the discussion by writing down the *questions* taken up in class. Remembering the questions raised is often as important as the answers given. Then, jot down interesting ideas, with the names of the people who offered them. Having the names attached helps you remember the point and helps you evaluate it later.

In some classes, discussion is carried out partially or entirely by means of Web-based discussion boards. For people who express themselves better through a keyboard than through speaking, online discussions offer real advantages: You may hear insights from them that they never would offer in class. Online discussions also enable everyone to participate, something the size of a class might make impossible in the classroom. The principles of online participation are the same as in class: Ask questions, answer questions other people have posted, write comments expressing what you would have said about the works and authors in class. But there's a difference: Tone is difficult to control online, so you may hurt or offend others without intending to; and since you don't see the other person's face, you may not be as careful about what you say online.

Here are some guidelines for participating in online discussions.

1. Read what others have said on a topic before posting comments. The host usually retains the right to change the subject.
2. The rules of grammar, punctuation, and spelling still apply to Web posts. If your writing is sloppy, what you say won't be taken as seriously, even if it deserves to be.
3. Think before you post. Don't flame people. Be polite and reasonable. Never write anything obscene or libelous.
4. Remember that anything published on the Web with your name can follow you for the rest of your life, especially if the discussion board has open access to anyone surfing the Net. Once the Send button is pressed, your comment is public knowledge, now and possibly forever.

Getting the most from a discussion and growing as a reader requires follow-up as well as advance preparation. After class, reread the works discussed in class as well as your class notes. Usually you will find much more in them than you did before class, and the approaches and methods used in class will be imprinted much more deeply in your memory.

THINKING CRITICALLY

One important purpose for having discussions in a literature class is to foster the ability to think critically about literary works and about ideas proposed in response to them. Critical thinking, adapting a statement by Michael Scriven and Richard Paul on the *Critical Thinking Consortium* Web site (criticalthinking.org/university/univclass/defining.html), is an active, disciplined use of reason to question, analyze, evaluate, and apply information received through reading, listening, observing, and reflecting. Critical thinking has two components: a set of skills for examining information, and the habit of and commitment to using those skills to guide your actions. Critical thinking contrasts greatly with passively acquiring and remembering information, or merely possessing a set of skills — it is always active, practical, and applied. The development of critical thinking skills and of the disposition to use them is a never-completed, lifelong endeavor.

A central aim of this book is to foster a critical thinking attitude in students to help them improve their critical thinking skills. That emphasis begins in Chapter 1 with the discussion of active reading and the engaging, imagining, questioning, and challenging it involves. It continues in this chapter with its emphasis on reading with pencil in hand, participating in discussions, analyzing questions and topics, and developing argumentative theses and papers. The focus on critical thinking extends to the later chapters on the elements of fiction, poetry, and drama through their discussions of analyzing, interrogating, and evaluating literary texts. The "Approaching the Reading" topics in each chapter, which require active engagement with the works, and the suggested writing topics at the end of each chapter further encourage the development of critical thinking. The aim of the book is that you come to understand, appreciate, and enjoy reading and literature more and that you improve in your ability to think clearly, incisively, and sensibly, not just about literature, but in all areas of your life.

WRITING ESSAY EXAMINATION ANSWERS

Teachers often include essay questions on examinations to see how well students can think through a problem. The question and the answer become a sort of conversation between you and your teacher. Think of it as an opportunity for talking to your teacher one-on-one, of having your teacher's undivided attention for what you want to get across. The object is not just to find out *what* you know but also what you can *do with* what you know — synthesize it, apply it, see it in relation to other things, and respond to its challenges. Here are a few tips for writing essay answers.

Read the Question Carefully

Read the question several times and make sure you understand what it asks you to do. It is crucial to understand what the question is focusing on. Look for two things: a *subject* (the work, or character, or kind of images, or whatever it asks you to write about), and an *approach* (what it asks you to *do with* that subject, such as explain, compare, contrast, compare and contrast, or discuss).

> Explain [APPROACH] what the final sentence [SUBJECT] of "The Flowers" indicates about the long-term effect of this experience on Myop [SUBJECT].

> Compare and contrast [APPROACH] Myop's experience in "The Flowers" with that of the speaker as a young boy in Countee Cullen's "Incident" [SUBJECT].

If you need clarification of the subject or approach, ask your teacher for it rather than risk going at the essay incorrectly. If it's an open-book exam (one in which you are allowed to use your book in class), double-check about whether and how you may use notes or the marginalia you've jotted in your book.

Organize Your Thoughts

After reading the question, you probably will want to plunge right in since time is limited and you feel under pressure. But most students use their time more effectively if they pause briefly to plan and organize before beginning to write. Reflect on how the approach relates to the material (why was that approach selected for exploring this subject?), and think about what details you need to support what you want to say about the subject. Your answer should be more than just a list of comparisons and contrasts; the list should add up to something, make a point. Jot that point down as your "thesis" and make sure that you state it clearly in your answer — at the beginning, the end, or both. Sketch an outline of points that will clarify what you mean and will support and illustrate its validity.

Start Writing

The most efficient way to get moving is to state your central point in the first sentence of the answer. As you do, repeat words from the question to indicate that you are answering it directly, meeting it head-on. Keep your outline in mind but don't stick to it slavishly. An exciting part of writing is that in the process of thinking and searching, you make discoveries and get insights and ideas you didn't expect when you began. These often take off in new directions and may even be opposite to what you originally intended to say. When you're writing a paper, you can revise it to incorporate such discoveries in a unified way. But there's no time to revise essay exam answers. So, do you ignore the new insight and stick to the outline, or include it? We think it's better to include it, but you should explain that you're changing directions ("That's the way it looked to me at first, but as I examine the work more closely I see something different in it"). Don't leave the teacher thinking you don't realize that what you are saying now doesn't fit with the way you started.

Divide Your Answer into Paragraphs

Start a new paragraph when you move to a new subpoint. This makes the answer clearer and easier for your teacher to read and follow. And whatever you do, don't write so fast that your handwriting becomes illegible — the best ideas in the world are useless if your teacher can't read them.

Proofread Your Answer

Try to leave yourself a couple of minutes to read through your answer. Be sure you have offered support (explanations, details, quotations) for each subpoint. Check spelling and grammar.

The best way to learn how to write better essay answers is to look at examples of ineffective and effective ones. The second of these answers (the effective one) is by Annie Otto. In the first one, we rewrote Annie's answer to make it less effective.

LESS EFFECTIVE EXAMPLE   (30 minutes) Explain the difference in effect if Alice Walker's story had been titled "The Corpse" instead of "The Flowers."

Titles have a large influence on a reader. When one reads a title, one expects to read about things that relate to it. When I first saw "The Flowers" I thought of feelings and ideas. I imagined sunshine, fields, joy, beauty. As I started reading Alice Walker's short story, I got everything I expected.

The opening is too broad — not closely related to the topic.

If Alice Walker's story had been titled "The Corpse," I would not have been so surprised when Myop ran into the corpse, but as it was, I was shocked. When Myop first started picking the flowers, I expected her to skip back to her family's cabin to put them in a jar for display. I had no idea that they would be used for mourning a man's death.

Doesn't respond directly to the topic.

Myop is ten years old. She feels the sun shining warm rays down to her and she has her very own song to sing. She feels as though she needs to go for a walk and pick wild flowers. Walker includes specific pictures of sunshine, fields, joy, beauty, and a peaceful scene. Then Myop steps into the rotten corpse of a man who was hanged long ago. Whatever my expectations were for Myop, they were not for her to push the debris around to uncover the face of the corpse. Nor did I think that she would "gaze around the spot with interest." Why? Why would a little girl be interested in that?

Not outlined as clearly as it should be.

The cove that Myop found the corpse in gave me a cold feeling, an uncomfortable feeling. When Myop picked that wild pink rose that grew in the center of the rotted noose and added it to her bundle of flowers to lay down by the remains, she paid her respects to the man that used to be. That day she lost her childish innocence.

Includes specific details, but they're not connected to "effect."

The title of a piece of literature prepares readers for specific images. When the story twists so rapidly on us, it is quite unexpected. "The Flowers" ended entirely opposite of what I anticipated.

Never actually addresses the assigned topic.

MORE EFFECTIVE EXAMPLE   (30 minutes) Explain the difference in effect if Alice Walker's story had been titled "The Corpse" instead of "The Flowers."

The main difference in effect when "The Corpse" is substituted for "The Flowers" in Walker's story is that it wipes out the surprising twist built into the plot construction, and lessens the sense of horror the reader experiences.

Clear statement of central point in the opening sentence; repeats words from the topic.

Focuses well on "effect."

The title "The Flowers" puts an initial expectation into the reader's mind. Walker tells us of a little girl, Myop, skipping around her yard and enjoying the warm sun's rays. She goes for a walk to pick wild flowers. There is so much life in the story and the descriptions pull the reader into the scene. Walker includes specific pictures of sunshine, fields, joy, beauty, and harmony as seen through the eyes of a child.

Clear, logical outline throughout.

As I continued to read, I noticed words like "haunts" and "gloomy." I wondered why the author had added some darkness to the story. Myop wanted to turn back to the "peacefulness of the morning," which to me, meant that there was a whisper of unrest.

Good example of "effect."

Then there came a scream of surprise, shock and horror. That scream was not from the ten-year-old, Myop. It was from me, the twenty-year-old reader. Myop had stepped into the rotten corpse of a man who was hanged long ago. The shock effect was huge, in-

Good use of specific supporting details.

tensified by the contrast between the beauty of nature (the flowers) and the ugliness of a decayed body. I suppose that I tend to react extremely when I get startled as I did when reading this story. I expected that Myop would react similarly and run home screaming, not that she would "gaze around the spot with interest." Why? Why would a little girl be interested in that?

The realization of a person's death is a difficult thing for a child to handle, and death by lynching is an action full of hate. When Myop picked that wild pink rose that grew in the center of the rotted noose and added it to her bundle of flowers to lay down by the remains, she paid her respects to the man that used to be. That day she lost her childish innocence.

Clear contrast to actual title; wraps up discussion nicely.

If the story had been titled "The Corpse," I would have expected a corpse to appear and would not have been so surprised at what Myop found. As it was, I was shocked, and that shock intensified the horror I felt not only at Myop's finding a corpse, but also at the horrible way the man had met his end.

WRITING SHORT PAPERS

Think of writing papers on literature as an opportunity rather than as an obligation. Like essay exam answers, papers give you a chance to communicate directly with your teacher, to have your teacher's undivided attention for what you want to get across. They also give you the opportunity to think through a topic carefully, develop an idea or position about it, and express it for others to hear. Because papers on stories, poems, and plays handle topics and supporting material differently, specific suggestions for writing papers on each genre, and sample papers for each genre, are given at the end of Parts 2, 3, and 4. Here we offer suggestions that apply to literature papers of all kinds.

The most successful short papers focus on a specific problem and explore it in some depth: They develop an *idea,* or an *angle,* about the problem, an insightful approach to it; they show evidence of careful, perceptive reading and clear critical thinking; they avoid summary but use details and brief quotations as support and expansion of their idea or interpretation; they avoid broad generalizations; they grow out of asking probing questions.

Five Steps in the Writing Process

Most writers approach papers in a series of steps. We suggest five central steps:

1. Finding a topic
2. Narrowing and focusing that topic
3. Turning the topic into an argumentative thesis
4. Developing and supporting the thesis in the body of the paper
5. Revising and proofreading the paper

It's important to realize that writing is an individual act: Everyone does it differently. You as a writer may not follow these steps in this order or may not need to do all of them every time, though you'll need to achieve the result they are aimed at. Also, the steps overlap, so that you may be working on more than one at the same time. (In Chapter 8, you can find an example of a student paper going through these five steps — see p. 209.)

FINDING A TOPIC   Before choosing a topic for your paper, be sure you are clear about what is expected of you. Double-check the assignment and clear up any uncertainties about the expected length, form, subject matter, approach, format, and deadline.

Your teacher may give you a topic or a list of topics to choose from. You may feel that this limits your options, but it can also save you from the sometimes difficult and time-consuming task of coming up with a workable and interesting subject yourself. If you are given a topic, read the assignment carefully several times to make sure you understand the terms being used and what idea the topic is getting at. And keep in mind that although you are being given a topic, you still need to find a thesis that develops a central idea about the topic (see p. 35).

If you can choose your own topic, you have more freedom but also more work to do. Your marginal jottings and journal entries often are good places to start. Look through them for works that engaged you — ones that intrigued you, or puzzled you, or opened up new perceptions, insights, or ideas. Topics that struggle with a problem, suggest ambiguous resolutions, or explore a conflict often work well.

If you are given or choose an unfamiliar work to write about, use marginal writing and a journal entry to help you get into it. Look for an unusual technique or approach in the work, the most important or most intriguing issue in it, or a question or difficulty you struggled with while you read. If you write about something that you struggled with or that intrigued you, you are likely to interest your readers in it as well. Look for connections, patterns, focuses, questions, or problems. Begin asking *why:* Why is the speaker's tone this way? Why did the character make that decision? Why does the work end this way? Why was that word used to describe this character? Consider alternatives: Ask how the work's effect would change if it had used a different speaker or different metaphors, been arranged in a different order, or been written in third person instead of first.

NARROWING THE TOPIC   The process we just described generates ideas, which could lead you to an interesting subject area to work with. But it's important to remember that a key aspect of planning a paper involves narrowing and focusing that broad subject area to a clearly defined topic that you can explore in detail within the assigned length. Too large a topic for the length of the paper will prove ineffective; it will skim rather than cover. Too limited a topic can leave you without enough to say to fill the needed pages.

The topic also needs to focus on a disputable issue. Literary papers are *argumentative* papers in the sense of developing and presenting a reasoned argument in support of a position about which someone could disagree. Your tasks are to state your central idea in the first paragraph and then to present a series of paragraphs that explain the idea further and support it with reasons, explanations, and illustrations. If you don't focus on a disputable issue, you may end up with an *illustrative* paper instead of an argumentative one. Illustrative papers start with statements of fact (or summaries) in the first paragraph. Readers may learn from them, but there's nothing to disagree with (except whether the statements reflect the story accurately). The rest of an illustrative paper continues with statements of fact that expand and illustrate further the statements made in the first paragraph. But they do not argue for a central idea or try to convince readers of the writer's point of view.

In narrowing your topic to an argumentative issue, it's helpful to focus on questions. Phrase your topic as a question; the paper then provides your answer. Think of controversies in the text, things about which different readers will have different views. But be sure the controversy isn't too broad to handle in the space allotted. You may need to concentrate on one aspect of the issue or make just one point instead of covering everything about it. Limiting the topic in this way enables you to go into depth and achieve some fresh insights about a small slice of the topic. Attempting to touch on everything at a surface level makes both the paper and you come across as shallow or superficial. Or perhaps the complete point you want to make in a paper involves two or three steps or aspects, which together would take too long to develop. You might summarize all of the steps in the introduction or second paragraph and then say that, because of space limitations, you are dealing thoroughly with only one of the steps.

FRAMING AN ARGUMENTATIVE THESIS   Once you've narrowed the topic, you need to sharpen what you want to say about that topic. Readers can read a poem or story for themselves. They can follow the outline and pick out images. But what they can't know in any other way are *your* explanations, interpretations, observations, perceptions, and connections. That's what you need to get across, in as clear, inviting, and accessible a way as possible. The central point you want to make should be stated in a thesis, a proposition put forward for consideration and placed, usually, at or near the end of the first paragraph.

It's important to notice the difference between a topic and a thesis. A *topic* just names a subject area: "Point of view in 'The Flowers.'" It merely states a fact. A *thesis* adds a *comment* about the subject and turns it into something disputable: "The third-person, limited omniscient point of view is crucial to the effectiveness of the ending of 'The Flowers.'" A thesis states an idea that readers could disagree with or reject. Your job is to convince them that your point is worth accepting.

As you think about your topic and what to say about it, you might start by framing a working thesis, a statement of the main argument you think you will make in the paper. The working thesis often changes or develops as you write — that's natural. But beginning with a tentative argument, even one you know is not your final version, helps to organize the rest of the paper.

When you finish the first draft of your paper, reexamine the working thesis. Ask yourself if the arguments developed in the paper match the central point expressed in the thesis. If they don't, revise the thesis (if you're satisfied with the arguments) or revise the paragraphs (if you want to stay with the original thesis).

DEVELOPING AND SUPPORTING THE THESIS AS AN EFFECTIVE ARGUMENT Developing an argumentative paper begins with analysis of the thesis to determine what parts of it need to be explained and supported. A thesis such as "The third-person, limited omniscient point of view is crucial to the effectiveness of the ending of 'The Flowers'" implies a series of steps that will develop the argument. You will need to demonstrate that "The Flowers" is presented from a third-person, limited omniscient point of view; you will need to argue that this point of view is appropriate and crucial to the effectiveness of the story; and you will need to show that point of view is particularly important in setting up the story's conclusion. Here you have a potential outline for the body of the paper, a three-part or three-paragraph development. Analyzing the thesis carefully often yields an outline for the paper as well as an understanding of its central argument.

Having determined those steps, you need to develop and support each point in two ways: (1) by your explanations, and (2) by details and quotations from the story. The two need to go together. Details and quotations by themselves do not prove anything. Your explanations are needed to indicate what is important about them and to tie them in to the whole fabric you are weaving in the paper. Likewise, explanations without details and quotations are not specific enough and do not anchor themselves to the work. The key to a successful paper lies in its development and support of its ideas: explaining ideas so readers understand them readily and supporting ideas with details and quotations so readers have confidence that the points are well grounded and worth considering.

The way you start the paragraphs in the body of an argumentative paper is very important. Just as the thesis of your paper must state an idea, not just a fact, so should the first sentence of each paragraph. The opening sentence of a paragraph in an argumentative paper is a mini-thesis: It states the idea developed in that paragraph. If a paragraph starts with a statement of fact rather than with a statement of idea, the rest of the paragraph likely consists of summary and more factual statements, neither of which explores an idea or develops an argument. Many writers begin paragraphs with a short topic sentence stating the idea succinctly, followed by a sentence explaining the idea more fully, before they go on to support and illustrate it.

It is often helpful to have an outline—a plan, an advance sketch of the argumentative steps the paper will take the reader through. Some students write out a detailed, formal outline, one with roman numerals, letters, and arabic numerals as headings. Others jot down a list of subtopics. Still others have a plan clear in their heads and don't write it down. People work in different ways, so find what works best for you. For some, thinking ahead before beginning to write is essential for the essay to have a focus and direction from the start. Others begin by brainstorming or freewriting. For them, it's the writing that gets them thinking. If you have found an outlining system useful in other courses, you might also use it here.

REVISING AND PROOFREADING   Once you finish a draft of the paper, the next steps are to revise and then proofread it. Notice that these are separate steps. Revising doesn't mean correcting spelling and grammar errors: That's proofreading, the final step. Revising comes first. The word *revision* derives from the Latin words for *look* and *again:* Revising means examining closely what you've written, thinking through it again, and trying to find ways to improve its content, organization, and expression.

Look again at the order of the paragraphs: Are they in the most effective order? Do they build from one to the next? Would it be more effective to rearrange them? Pay attention to transitions between paragraphs: Are the connections clear and easy to follow? Examine the way ideas are explained and developed: Have you said enough to make your points convincing? Have you supplied enough details and examples to show that your points are well grounded in the work? Listen to the sentences: Is there variety in their length and structure? Do they read easily, with graceful, appealing rhythms? (Reading the paper aloud is a helpful way to test its style.)

It's hard to get a fresh look right after you finish writing. You are usually still too close to it to come up with different ways of explaining, arranging, or expressing. Revision often works best if you can lay your paper aside for a day or two or even more before thinking about changes. It also may help to have someone else read the paper, to check if ideas and organization are clear and adequately supported. You may have done this in a composition class; it often helps in a literature class, too. But choose this person wisely. Some friends worry about offending you. Give your reader clear direction about the kind of feedback you need.

For most people, revision is crucial to effective writing: Making your paper the best possible usually requires several drafts. You may be able to write one draft and get a C or even a B, but the writing simply won't be as good as it would be if you revised, and you won't learn as much about writing. Granted, you may not always have time to revise an essay several times, but you should always do at least one revision, and try to allow time for more. An old cliché says that good writing requires perspiration, not inspiration. That's trite, yes, but most of the time it's true.

Your paper also needs a title. Make sure you create a *title* (indicating the subject of or an idea about the paper — for instance, "Point of View in Alice Walker's 'The Flowers'"), not a heading (as, for example, "Point of View"). Don't use the title of the work as the label for your paper: "The Flowers" is Walker's title; it can't be yours. Your own title, when given on the title page or at the top of the paper, should not be put in quotation marks (see the sample paper on p. 213).

After revising your paper, edit (or proofread) it to check for errors in spelling and grammar, for inconsistencies, and for any awkward expressions. If you do your paper on a computer, use its programs to check spelling and grammar. There's no excuse for simple typos when spending a few minutes on spell-checking would catch them.

A computer check, of course, doesn't free you from the need to read closely as well. The computer can tell you that it doesn't recognize *thier* and ask if you intended to write *their;* but it won't notice if you wrote *their* when you should have used *there*. Again, distance (coming back after a couple of days) can be helpful because you may have become so familiar with your essay that it is hard to see what should be different. Some writers proofread by starting at the end and reading backwards as a way of looking at the words instead of getting caught up in the meaning. Again, having another person read your essay is sometimes useful — if she or he is a good speller and an attentive reader.

Even if you revise and proofread initially on a computer screen, we recommend at least one revision (and the final proofreading and editing) be done from a printed copy. It is helpful to see the sentences and paragraphs the way they will look on paper in the finished product.

Getting Started

Those are the central steps in the writing process. Before going on to five guidelines for effective papers, we should pause to touch on that sticky difficulty, getting started. It's not uncommon for someone to spend as much time trying to get going as doing the actual writing. The key to getting started is to *start*. Don't wait to be "in the right mood." Start writing, and more often than not you will find yourself getting caught up in your subject. Also, don't start by spending hours trying to come up with a wonderful introduction. The first paragraph you write is likely to be discarded anyhow.

To get going, you might read the work again so its words fill your mind. Do some more underlining and annotating as you read. Then, make yourself put words on paper or on your computer screen. Try starting with a bald, direct statement of your central point: "This paper will explain the point of view in 'The Flowers' and show how the powerful final sentence depends for its effect on the point of view." Such a sentence makes it clear to you what you need to do. When you get to the end of the paper, sharpen the thesis, in style and in the point it makes, and then develop an introduction that leads into it. That's right—do the introduction last. You will know better what will lead a reader into your paper after you've written the paper. In some cases, the last paragraph you write, the one you planned as the conclusion, becomes a good introduction.

If ideas don't start coming at first, try *freewriting*—writing anything that comes to mind about the topic for five minutes, in any order, without stopping, editing, or changing anything. Or try *clustering*: Write down your main point and circle it. Then write points related to the topic in a ring around the main point, circle them, and use lines to connect them to the first circle. For each circle in the ring, write any ideas, examples, facts, and details you think of and use lines to connect them to the points with which they are associated. On page 39 you can see some clustering that Annie Otto did to pull together her thinking about "The Flowers." For some writers, clustering is useful in grasping relationships among the various parts of a topic and clarifying what materials are available or needed for developing subtopics.

Many people find that it works best to write a first draft rapidly, getting their ideas down without worrying about neatness, grammar, or spelling. Others need to work more slowly, getting each sentence and each paragraph right before moving on to the next one. There is no single "right" process; discover the one that suits you best.

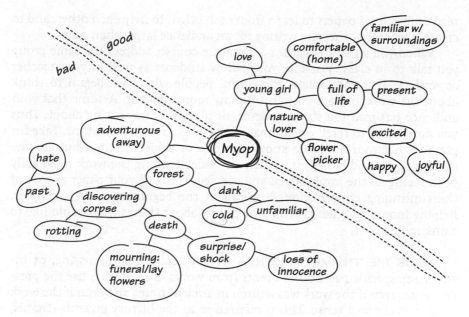

Annie Otto's clustering for "The Flowers"

Five Guidelines for Making Literary Papers Effective

In addition to the five central steps in the writing process, here are five suggested guidelines for making papers effective:

1. Adapting to your audience
2. Using the literary present
3. Handling quotations
4. Considering outside sources
5. Formatting the paper properly

Don't begin thinking about these guidelines only *after* the five steps in the writing process. They ought to be in your mind as you are conceptualizing the paper and developing its arguments.

ADAPTING TO YOUR AUDIENCE   All writers need to be aware of the audience they are addressing. Readers differ in age, reading ability, levels of understanding, background, interest in the subject, and so on. An effective writer takes those differences into account in planning and developing what she or he writes. A paper for a literature course should include a larger audience than your teacher. In practice, only your teacher may read it, but ideally other people would read it too. And that is how your teacher will read your paper, as if she or he is part of this larger audience. In some classes, students read each other's papers to learn from each other, to help each other, and to create a sense that they are writing for an audience larger than one.

When you write a paper for a literature course, address the same group you talk to in class. Visualize your fellow students as well as your teacher as readers. These are smart, thoughtful people who have begun to think about the work and are curious to know more about it. Assume that your audience has read the stories, poems, or plays you are writing about. Thus you don't need to retell or summarize the work. That's important. Take for granted that your audience knows the plot or subject matter, but assume that readers could benefit from help in understanding the work more fully or in seeing all the implications you can see. Think of your paper as part of the continuing conversation described at the beginning of this chapter, helping interested readers by talking clearly about things they would like to think more about.

USING THE "LITERARY PRESENT"   When describing, discussing, or introducing specific passages or events from works of literature, use the present tense, even if the work was written in ancient times and even if the work itself uses the past tense. This is referred to as the *literary present* — that is, action within a literary work continues to happen even if the telling about it looks back at it from a later point. Thus, if you are writing about Myop's character in Alice Walker's "The Flowers" (p. 20), the story says "She *was* ten, and nothing *existed* for her but her song," but you should say, "Myop *is* a ten-year-old whose happy songs *demonstrate* the innocent, carefree life she *leads* before encountering the skeleton." It may seem confusing at times or occasionally to defy logic, but always use present tense when writing about characters and events from literary works. Use past tense, however, to relate historical fact, as, for example, "Alice Walker first *published* 'The Flowers' in 1973."

Also, always use present tense when introducing quotes. Instead of writing, "The narrator in 'The Flowers' *noted* that 'Myop carried a short, knobby stick' as she *walked* through the barnyard," write, "The narrator in 'The Flowers' *points* out that 'Myop carried a short, knobby stick' as she *walks* through the barnyard." In some cases changing the tense of the verbs in a quotation to match those in the rest of your sentence (using square brackets to indicate the alternation) will make it read more smoothly: "The narrator in 'The Flowers' *points* out that 'Myop [*carries*] a short, knobby stick' as she *walks* through the barnyard." Better still, in a case like this one, you might decide to quote only the nouns, not the verb — if it's the nouns that you want to emphasize here: "The narrator in 'The Flowers' *tells* us that Myop *carries* 'a short, knobby stick' as she *walks* through the barnyard."

HANDLING QUOTATIONS   A literary paper almost always includes at least some quotations from the work or works being discussed. Quotations connect your explanations and interpretations directly to the work(s) and show that they are firmly based. How often you should quote requires good judgment based on specific situations. If you find your paragraphs using an alternating pattern — quotation, explanatory sentence, quotation, explanatory sentence — you're probably overdoing quotations. Keep most quotations brief. Pick out the most telling phrases and weave them into your sentence structures rather than quoting long, stand-alone blocks of text. Remember, a reader goes to your paper to learn your approach, your explanations, and your ideas. The work can be read elsewhere, but your ideas can't be.

To ensure the smooth incorporation of quotes into your writing, introduce them by indicating who you are quoting or where the quote comes from. Don't just insert a quotation after the end of your sentence:

> The crucial detail for Myop's growing up is discovering that the man whose skeleton she finds had been lynched. "It was the rotted remains of a noose."

Instead, lead into the quotation and incorporate it into your sentence:

> The crucial detail for Myop's growing up was discovering that the man whose skeleton she finds had been lynched. The narrator tells us that the ring Myop finds around a rose's root "was the rotted remains of a noose."

As a rule, avoid beginning a sentence with a quotation: Begin sentences with your own words. Doing so helps ensure that the reader understands how the quotation supports your argument.

Also, avoid referring to a quotation as one in your writing. Phrases such as "the following quotation shows" are awkward and not an informative introduction to the quoted material.

Beyond indicating who you are quoting or where a quotation comes from, also make sure that (1) the quote fits into your sentence grammatically — not "Esperanza's key realization occurs when *she* 'knew *I* had to have a house. A real house,'" but "Esperanza's key insight occurs when she realizes she 'had to have a house. A real house'" — and (2) the reader can easily understand all references within the quotation (pronouns, especially) — not "The narrator says '*she* struck out at random at chickens she liked,'" but "The narrator says *Myop* 'struck out at random at chickens she liked.'"

Avoid ending paragraphs with quotations: Literally, you should have the last word. When a paragraph ends in a quotation, it may suggest to the reader that you are relying too heavily on your cited source to make your case *for* you. Quotations should not *make* your primary points in an essay; instead, they should *support* or *illustrate* claims that you have already made in your own words. At the very least, close the paragraph by reiterating what is said in the quotation. Even if you are relying heavily on sources, have the final say in a paragraph yourself.

You need to make clear where any quoted lines or phrases can be found. For papers on literature, MLA (Modern Language Association) style is generally used for citations. (For a summary of MLA guidelines, see pp. 1393–1405.) If you're writing on one poem, story, or play from this book, it should be acceptable to put line or page numbers in parentheses at the end of the quotation. (See the sample papers on pp. 213, 592, 924, and 1408.) Note that the parenthesis goes outside the quotation marks (it is not a part of the quotation), and a period or comma, if needed, goes after the parenthesis (so it doesn't float unattached between sentences), except for block quotations. If you are discussing a work that's not in this book, include a footnote or bibliographic entry to inform the reader where the work can be found.

Passages from a story or play usually are cited by page numbers (except William Shakespeare's plays, which typically are cited by act, scene, and line numbers). But passages in poetry usually are referred to by line numbers, with page numbers given to indicate the location of the whole poem. If you include several works in the paper, you may need a shortened title as well as a line or page number in the parenthetical references to make the source clear. (For a more complete discussion of proper citation style, see Chapter 26.)

USING OUTSIDE SOURCES   Should you do library or Internet research on the work or author? That depends on what your teacher wants for a particular assignment. For some subjects, teachers may encourage you to see what you come up with on your own and may therefore ask you to refrain from reading interpretations by others. In other situations, teachers may have different objectives in mind and require such reading. When the assignment doesn't specify whether you may or should read critics, it's best to ask about it. If the answer is yes, go to Part 6 for help on doing literary research and writing research papers.

Some students think it's a good idea to read studies of a literary work before reading the work itself, to help them know what to look for. However, doing this robs you of discovering your own reactions uninfluenced by others. So, before reading any critical studies of a literary work, read the work itself at least twice and form your own ideas about it first, and your own questions — questions that continue to puzzle you and about which you feel a need for some hints from others. If you read about a work before reading the work itself, your understanding is shaped by someone else's perceptions rather than by your own experience.

A key issue in all academic work involves giving proper credit for anything taken from another source. If you do consult any books other than your course textbook and dictionaries, you must enclose within quotation marks words quoted directly from the source. You must also supply the location in which you found the passage. Even if you do not quote directly from an outside source, you must acknowledge in notes or a bibliography any sources you have consulted. (MLA style guidelines for citing sources can be found on pp. 1393–1405.) In fact, you should acknowledge *any* external assistance, like discussing the assigned poem with your former high school teacher or another student who is especially knowledgeable about the topic. Failure to do so, and thus presenting the ideas or work of others — intentionally or unintentionally — as if they were your own, is *plagiarism,* a very serious academic offense. (See pp. 1392–93.)

FORMATTING THE PAPER   Papers should be typed (word processed), double-spaced, with one-inch margins all around, in 12-point font. The guideline we use in classes is that papers of five pages or longer should have a title page (follow the format of the sample papers on pp. 213, 592, 924, and 1408), and that papers shorter than five pages should have the student's name, course number, instructor's name, and date in the upper right corner of the first page without a title page (save a tree, or a twig, at least). Check with your teacher about this: Some teachers prefer title pages for all papers. Check also whether your teacher prefers to have pages stapled or held by a paper clip.

Ten Guidelines for Formatting and Punctuating Quotations

1. In some cases it is most effective to introduce a quotation formally, with your sentence coming to a full stop, followed by a colon.

> The most powerful statement in "Superman and Me" comes when the speaker explains why he read everything he could get his hands on: "I was trying to save my life."

2. Often, however, you can use a less formal construction, blending the quotation smoothly and effectively into your sentence.

> Sherman Alexie described his father as "an avid reader of westerns" and of many other types of popular writing.

Commas are needed with the quotation marks only if the same words would require commas even if they were not a quotation.

3. Place quotation marks outside commas and periods ("." or ",") but inside semicolons and colons ("; or ":). U.S. punctuation conventions never put the period or comma outside quotation marks.

4. Always use double quotation marks ("), except for a quotation within a quotation, which is indicated by single marks ('). However, if an entire quotation consists of dialogue by one speaker and is so introduced, it is not necessary to use the extra single quotation marks.

5. Treat longer passages (more than three lines of poetry or more than four lines of a prose passage) as block quotations, set off from the rest of the text by starting a new line and indenting the passage ten spaces — sometimes more for poetry — from the left margin. (See the sample papers on pp. 213

and 592.) Treating a passage as a block quotation is the same as putting quotation marks around it. Use quotation marks around an indented passage only if it has quotation marks around it in the source. If, however, the entire quotation consists of dialogue by one speaker and is so introduced, quotation marks are not necessary.

6. The end punctuation of a quotation may be (often should be) dropped and replaced by punctuation appropriate to your sentence; thus, a period ending a quotation may be replaced with a comma if your sentence goes on (thus you should never have a .", or ,". in a paper) or it can be omitted if a parenthetical citation follows: " (source). If the quotation ends with a question mark, an additional period or comma should not be supplied.

7. In all other respects, quotations must be precisely accurate, including original spelling, capitalization, and punctuation. The initial letter of a line of poetry must be capitalized if it is capitalized in the original, even if the quotation is not indented. Always double-check quotations to be sure you have everything down correctly. If you need to insert a word into a quotation (if, for example, the part you are quoting needs a verb) or if you need to change a pronoun to a noun for clarity, place the inserted word not in parentheses but in square brackets: [ ].

8. In some cases, quotations are more effective if words or punctuation are omitted, to shorten them or to make them fit your sentence construction. Ellipsis marks (. . .) are used whenever you omit something from a quotation.

9. Ellipsis marks generally are not used at the beginning or end of a quotation since it is clear that almost always something comes before and after the words you quote.

10. You need not (even should not) start a new paragraph after a quotation. With rare exception, follow each quotation with an explanation of the point being illustrated, tying it into the rest of the paper.

Guidelines for Punctuating Titles

1. Titles of books or long poems (the names of any long work published by itself, with its name on the title page) and the names of TV shows, movies, or plays are underlined or italicized (either is acceptable; underlining is a mark editors use to tell typesetters "this should be italicized"). Titles of books, TV shows, movies, or plays are not placed within quotation marks.

2. Titles of short works (poems, short stories, essays), ones that name a part of a book rather than the whole, are placed within quotation marks:

"The Flowers" is found in Alice Walker's book *In Love & Trouble: Stories of Black Women.*

Quotation marks are also used around chapter titles in a book or titles of individual episodes of a TV series:

The final episode of *Baywatch* in 2001 was entitled "Rescue Me."

The authoritative guidebook to matters of style and punctuation is *The Chicago Manual of Style,* 15th edition (Chicago: University of Chicago Press, 2003). Or you can consult the *MLA Handbook for Writers of Research Papers,* 6th edition (New York: Modern Language Association of America, 2003), or a college writing handbook such as Andrea A. Lunsford, *The St. Martin's Handbook,* 5th edition (Boston: Bedford/St. Martin's, 2003).

WRITING PAPERS IN OTHER FORMATS

Papers can be developed in ways other than the standard explanation, analysis, or compare and contrast formats. Sometimes developing a paper as a letter — writing to a friend, to the author, to the narrator in the work, as an answer to a question from a former English teacher, or as a reply to a hostile critic — can stimulate ideas. The letter form supplies a context and an audience you can write to. If you're looking for a way to present both sides of an issue strongly or want to be more imaginative, try developing a paper as a dialogue or a debate in which you imagine the characters participating, expressing their voices as well as developing the ideas and positions you want to convey.

Alternative forms require the same preliminary steps as a conventional paper. You should review the ideas discussed in the preceding section on "Writing Short Papers": selecting and narrowing a topic, identifying a central point and framing a thesis, outlining the subpoints you will cover, and perhaps using freewriting or clustering to generate ideas. For a mock letter, the outline will be much like that for a conventional essay; for a dialogue or debate, an outline will likely become a plan for what the characters are like, what their opinions are, and what they will talk about. Realize, too, that adapting to your audience is just as important when using an alternative form.

If you have not worked before with an unconventional format, keep in mind that doing this type of paper can take just as much, or even more, time and effort as a traditional form. But this time and work may yield outstanding results if using such a format enables you to get into the material at a more thoughtful level or to present your ideas more clearly or in a more attractive and inviting manner. Before using such a format, however, check with your teacher to make sure it is acceptable. Sometimes practice in using a conventional approach is part of what a teacher wants students to gain in a particular assignment.

RESPONDING THROUGH OTHER ART FORMS

Not all communication relies on words. Some people are better at conversing nonverbally. One way of responding to literature as an art form is through another art form: through dance, a visual art, dramatics, film, or music.

There is a long tradition of original artistic responses. Choreographing a dance, creating music or artwork, making a film, or designing a set are ways of responding to a literary work. Many poets, from all ages, have written responses or replies to other poems, as, for example, the way Sir Walter Ralegh responded to Christopher Marlowe's "The Passionate Shepherd to His Love" (1599; see p. 687) by writing "The Nymph's Reply to the Shepherd" (1600; see p. 707). Many artists have created paintings or sculptures to depict characters or scenes from literature: from classical myths and legends, Dante's *Divine Comedy,* and John Milton's *Paradise Lost,* to mention only a few famous examples. The poet and artist William Blake did watercolor paintings and engravings of scenes from the works of many authors, including Virgil, Dante, Chaucer, and Milton; see, for example, the National Gallery of Victoria Web site's page on Blake, at ngv.vic.gov.au/blake/sections.html. For an example of how many artists do such illustrations, in a variety of styles, go to the *Paradise Lost Illustrated* Web site at pitt.edu/~ulin/Paradise/.

Countless poets have written poems in response to paintings or sculpture. Two are included in this book: W. H. Auden's "Musée des Beaux Arts" (1940), written as a response to a painting by Pieter Breughel the Elder, *Landscape with the Fall of Icarus* (see p. 600); and Cathy Song's "Girl Powdering Her Neck" (1983), responding to a painting by Kitagawa Utamaro (see p. 480). Composers have often responded to literature through music. You may have heard the music Felix Mendelssohn wrote in response to Shakespeare's *A Midsummer Night's Dream* (heard it perhaps without realizing it in the 1999 film version of the play directed by Michael Hoffman), or seen the musical *Cats* by Andrew Lloyd Webber, which was inspired by T. S. Eliot's *Old Possum's Book of Practical Cats* (1939). If you have talent in another art, you might try responding to a story, poem, or play through your art — if that is acceptable to your teacher. Be sure to ask first.

An alternative to creating original art as a nonverbal response to literature is connecting existing works into what seem to you meaningful pairs or groups. You might be reminded of some music that seems a perfect complement to the first several paragraphs of "The Flowers," for example, or of a photograph or painting that evokes the mood of a poem you come across later in this book. Or you might gather a variety of pictures into a collage that provides a visual representation of the content and complexity of a story, poem, or play. As you do, you may find that a nonverbal response can be expressive in ways and to degrees that a written response is unable to be.

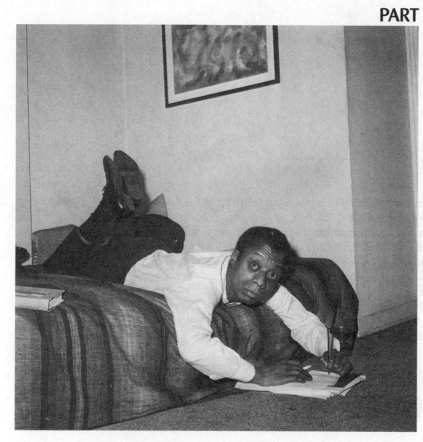

Approaching FICTION

Overleaf: The author James Baldwin in a relaxed portrait of a writer at work, photographed in his New York apartment in 1963. Not yet forty years old when this photograph was taken, Baldwin was already established as a major literary presence with the publication of his semiautographical first novel, Go Tell It on the Mountain *(1953), the essay collection* Notes of a Native Son *(1955), and his second novel,* Giovanni's Room *(1956), among other works. Baldwin's work explored what it means to be an African American in the twentieth century, and he was a lifelong and fierce defender of racial justice and equality. The responsibility of the writer, Baldwin told an interviewer, "is to excavate the experience of the people who produced him." (See p. 1418 for a short biography.)*

Literary works do not endure as objects but as presences. When you read anything worth remembering, you liberate a human voice; you release into the world again a companion spirit.

Louise Glück

Reading Fiction

What are your own stories? What books and movies do you love? What television shows do you follow? The stories that you own, that you love, may incline toward realism, or science fiction, or romance—each of us is different, with individual tastes. But almost all of us are drawn toward stories of some sort. What is it about stories that draws you into their world, that makes you not want to put the book down or miss the time the show is on, or want to rent the DVD a third and fourth time? We know that what we are reading or watching is not factual: These are made-up characters doing imaginary things. Yet we become deeply invested in their lives: We begin to think about the characters as if they are real, and we care about what happens to them. Why do we begin to sympathize deeply with a grieving mother or delight in the achievements of a college sophomore, neither of whom actually exists? The answer to these questions must start with the impressive power of imagination—with the way our imaginations respond to the imaginative creations of excellent writers. In the chapters to come, we look closely at such imaginative creations and at the way we use our own imaginations to enter, enjoy, and appreciate them.

WHAT IS FICTION?

Before we start that closer look, we need to clarify what it is we're talking about. *Story,* considered broadly, is any account of a related series of events in sequential order, usually chronological order (the order in which they happened). Stories did not start out as something to be read: long before people read stories or watched them being acted out in plays, they listened to stories being told or sung. From the time ancient peoples gathered around fires in the evening for warmth and safety, they told stories to each other. And although we no longer need campfires for warmth and protection, the storytelling tradition of "stories around the campfire" continue wherever people gather for companionship. Generation after generation of children around the world have said to parents, "Tell me a story."

Story, in this broad sense, includes events that are true or made up — an account of the invading of Normandy in World War II, the planning for the prom during your junior year in high school, or the landing of three-headed cyborgs in an Iowa cornfield. The account can be narrated (told by a story-teller) or dramatized (acted out in drama). It can be told in prose or verse. Chapters 4 to 7 deal only with narrated stories, only with stories in prose, and only with stories that are fictional.

Fiction refers to narrated stories that are drawn from the imagination or are an imaginative reworking of actual experiences. Incidents and details in a work of fiction can originate in fact, history, or everyday life, but the characters and events as a whole are primarily invented, or altered, in the author's imagination. Imaginative fiction (like movies) varies widely in types, from fast-paced adventures that focus on action to stories that examine characters and ideas in depth; they can be told at great length (**novels** or **epics**) or more briefly (**novellas** or **short stories**).

The works of fiction included in this book are **short stories**, relatively brief fictional narratives in prose that often focus on the essential aspects of a character (instead of showing character development over time, the way a novel can) and on a single event or episode — often a life-changing circumstance. It is characterized by careful, deliberate craftsmanship (in handling of plot, characterization, and point of view). The short stories included in this book explore the complexities of life and people; they lead us to interact imaginatively with significant human issues; they offer us an opportunity to expand our understanding of ourselves, others, and the multiple cultures we find ourselves living with and within. They are widely respected by other writers, scholars, and general readers for the way they handle the techniques of fiction (ones discussed in Chapters 4 to 7) and for their insights into people, their values, their experiences, and their cultures.

WHY READ FICTION?

What is the value of reading such stories? Most important, perhaps, is the way they can take us outside of ourselves and through our imaginations enable us to enter other lives, other selves, other places and cultures, other feelings and experiences. All of us live limited lives. We want to see more, expand our range of experiences, meet people whose lives are different from our own. That's why many people like to travel, and why many students want to go away to college. A story enables us, without leaving our chairs, to escape our boundaries and broaden our understanding and vision. Think again of Sherman Alexie (see p. 4) and what reading stories did to "save his life."

Author and literary critic C. S. Lewis explained the appeal of story this way: "We seek an enlargement of our being. We want to be more than ourselves. . . . We want to see with other eyes, to imagine with other imaginations, to feel with other hearts, as well as with our own" (*An Experiment in Criticism* [Cambridge University Press, 1961], p. 137). Fiction can do that. A story can mirror our own world, take us to a world that is not part of our daily experience, or create a world entirely new to us. To read fiction is to enter a place where you both disappear and find yourself — a place where, when you put the book down and look up, you feel even more yourself than you did before reading.

You have likely heard someone say, "Fiction? I don't read fiction. I want to read what's true." Fiction is not fact. It may contain facts, but it is still fiction. A literary scholar and a historian who were on a panel together were asked the difference between the two disciplines. The historian spoke about how important it was to get the facts correct in his work. The literary scholar then replied, "Yes. You deal with facts. I deal with truth." What was the literary scholar implying? Not that the historian wasn't searching for the truth within the facts, but that fiction is the embodiment of truth, at times factual truth, but always — if it is a fine work of fiction — the kind of truth that exists within, around, or beyond fact. This is a different kind of truth, the kind of truth that needs story to contain it, the truth of what it is like to live the facts, the kind of truth that exists and comes to life through what the writer "makes up." It is the truth of Captain Ahab's obsession with a white whale, Jane Eyre's dreams, Sherman Alexie's Superman. We need this truth. We need our stories.

ACTIVE READING: **Fiction**

The more you read, and the more widely you read, the more confident you will become in your ability to follow a story and understand the characters in it. The purpose of Chapters 4 to 7 is to help you become a more skilled reader of fiction — more alert to the richness of a work of fiction, to the fascinating variety of good things it has to offer. Most of the things covered in those chapters, however, should not concern you the first time you read a short story or novel. Here are some suggestions for the first time you go through a story with an active imagination.

- *Give the work a fair chance.* Writers generally try to catch a reader's interest immediately, but some short stories and novels start slowly. Don't quit reading after a few paragraphs or pages. Give yourself enough time to get involved in the action and characters.

- *Keep going.* Even if some things aren't completely clear, later events probably will clarify them.

- *Watch for what's happening.* As in movies, some stories are filled with action and excitement. Others, often ones that deal with inner struggles, move more deliberately and with less external action.

- *Watch for who it is happening to.* Pay attention to the characters — their appearances, personalities, values, attitudes, struggles, weaknesses, strengths, and so forth.

- *Watch for "why" — why does what happens happen?* What happens that leads to the situations and actions? What causes the action? What motivates the characters?

REREADING: Fiction

Experiencing a story fully requires reading it more than once. The first time through, you primarily concentrate on what's going on. The second and third times through, you begin paying attention to other things — to easily overlooked details and nuances concerning plot and character, and to the way the piece is written, the subtlety of techniques the author used.

You probably already do this with movies and music you love. Good movies, ones you really like, you watch twice, or many times, and you listen to favorite CDs over and over. We enjoy experiencing again the things we liked at first, of course; but our follow-up experience is different, richer, because we notice what we didn't notice before. It's the same for reading. Once you get into it, you'll enjoy rereading books or stories for the same reasons you like watching films or listening to music again. Here are some suggestions for rereading.

- *Slow down.* Let yourself absorb the flavor and style; roll the sentences and rhythms around on your tongue; reread paragraphs that aren't fully clear or that you find especially well written and enjoyable; go back to earlier parts to check on details that tie in with later ones.

- *Pay attention to the title.* Often it's significant and revealing, though its significance may not be evident during the first reading. In such cases, as you reread, it's worth reflecting on possible ways the title links to the actions and characters.

- *Look up things that aren't familiar.* Check unfamiliar words in a dictionary. The context often clarifies new words, but in other cases it doesn't, and you can miss something. Do some research on people from history, other literature, or historical events who are mentioned in the story. Look at a map when real places are used.

- *Pay attention to the first sentence and the first paragraph, especially for short stories.* Authors often embed within them a lot of important indicators about tone, style, setting, and subject. For the same reasons, pay close attention to the last paragraph and last sentence.

- *Pay attention to things that do not seem needed.* What appears insignificant may actually be a subtlety. Reflecting on its part in the whole can open up a deeper understanding of the characters or events.

*P*lot grows out of character . . . Characters should not,
conversely, serve as pawns for some plot.

Anne Lamott

CHAPTER **4** # Plot and Characters

Probably the first thing you notice as you read a story is what happened, to whom. Plot and characters: These are the foundation stones of fiction. As such, they're worth a closer look. We connect with those probably because they're so basic to life: We care about people (family, friends, the famous and influential) and about what goes on in their lives. In literature, we meet not with actual people and events but imaginative constructs; and as readers of literature, beyond our fascination with what happens to whom, we should be interested in the way they are constructed and brought to life. This chapter focuses on the skills and techniques we should be alert to in the development of plots and characters in fiction.

PLOT

The first thing to consider in reading fiction is plot. **Plot**, in a literary sense, is the way events are selected and arranged in narrative work to present them most effectively to the reader. Comparing *plot* with *story* can help clarify that. *Story,* as we used the word in Chapter 3, "Reading Fiction," is a straightforward account of everything that happens, in the order it happens. Story provides the materials (the events, the characters, the outcome) from which a plot is constructed. As a story is converted to a plot, some things are left out (ones that aren't essential for the effect and emphasis desired), things are sometimes rearranged (the story may start in the middle or at the end instead of at the beginning), and causal connections between key events are brought out. The interest in plot is not just in what happens but in why it happens and in the implications or results of what happens: What does it all "mean"? What does it "say" to us? Another way to put it is that plot provides the **structure** of a story, that is, the arrangement of material in it, the ordering of its parts, the design used to draw out and convey its significance.

Pay attention to plot in the following short story about an unexpected encounter between a young man and a young woman on a street in Los Angeles. In addition to what's going on in it, consider what details the author includes, how they are arranged, and how they relate to each other and work together to convey a unified effect.

Dagoberto Gilb b. 1950

Love in L.A.   [1993]

Jake slouched in a clot of near motionless traffic, in the peculiar gray of concrete, smog, and early morning beneath the overpass of the Hollywood Freeway on Alvarado Street. He didn't really mind because he knew how much worse it could be trying to make a left onto the onramp. He certainly didn't do that every day of his life, and he'd assure anyone who'd ask that he never would either. A steady occupation had its advantages and he couldn't deny thinking about that too. He needed an FM radio in something better than this '58 Buick he drove. It would have crushed velvet interior with electric controls for the L.A. summer, a nice warm heater and defroster for the winter drives at the beach, a cruise control for those longer trips, mellow speakers front and rear of course, windows that hum closed, snuffing out that nasty exterior noise of freeways. The fact was that he'd probably have to change his whole style. Exotic colognes, plush, dark nightclubs, maitais and daquiris, necklaced ladies in satin gowns, misty and sexy like in a tequila ad. Jake could imagine lots of possibilities when he let himself, but none that ended up with him pressed onto a stalled freeway.

Jake was thinking about this freedom of his so much that when he glimpsed its green light he just went ahead and stared bye bye to the steadily employed. When he turned his head the same direction his windshield faced, it was maybe one second too late. He pounced the brake pedal and steered the front wheels away from the tiny brakelights but the smack was unavoidable. Just one second sooner and it would only have been close. One second more and he'd be crawling up the Toyota's trunk. As it was, it seemed like only a harmless smack, much less solid than the one against his back bumper.

Jake considered driving past the Toyota but was afraid the traffic ahead would make it too difficult. As he pulled up against the curb a few carlengths ahead, it occurred to him that the traffic might have helped him get away too. He slammed the car door twice to make sure it was closed fully and to give himself another second more, then toured front and rear of his Buick for damage on or near the bumpers. Not an impressionable scratch even in the chrome. He perked up. Though the car's beauty was secondary to its ability to start and move, the body and paint were clean except for a few minor dings. This stood out as one of his few clearcut accomplishments over the years.

Before he spoke to the driver of the Toyota, whose looks he could see might present him with an added complication, he signaled to the driver of the car that hit him, still in his car and stopped behind the Toyota, and waved his hands and shook his head to let the man know there was no problem as far as he was concerned. The driver waved back and started his engine.

"It didn't even scratch my paint," Jake told her in that way of his. "So how you doin? Any damage to the car? I'm kinda hoping so, just so it takes a little more time and we can talk some. Or else you can give me your phone number now and I won't have to lay my regular b.s. on you to get it later."

He took her smile as a good sign and relaxed. He inhaled her scent like it was clean air and straighted out his less than new but not unhip clothes.

"You've got Florida plates. You look like you must be Cuban."

"My parents are from Venezuela."

"My name's Jake." He held out his hand.

"Mariana."

They shook hands like she'd never done it before in her life.

"I really am sorry about hitting you like that." He sounded genuine. He fondled the wide dimple near the cracked taillight. "It's amazing how easy it is to put a dent in these new cars. They're so soft they might replace waterbeds soon." Jake was confused about how to proceed with this. So much seemed so unlikely, but there was always possibility. "So maybe we should go out to breakfast somewhere and talk it over."

"I don't eat breakfast."

"Some coffee then."

"Thanks, but I really can't."

"You're not married, are you? Not that that would matter that much to me. I'm an openminded kinda guy."

She was smiling. "I have to get to work."

"That sounds boring."

"I better get your driver's license," she said.

Jake nodded, disappointed. "One little problem," he said. "I didn't bring it. I just forgot it this morning. I'm a musician," he exaggerated greatly, "and, well, I dunno, I left my wallet in the pants I was wearing last night. If you have some paper and a pen I'll give you my address and all that."

He followed her to the glove compartment side of her car.

"What if we don't report it to the insurance companies? I'll just get it fixed for you."

"I don't think my dad would let me do that."

"Your dad? It's not your car?"

"He bought it for me. And I live at home."

"Right." She was slipping away from him. He went back around to the back of her new Toyota and looked over the damage again. There was the trunk lid, the bumper, a rear panel, a taillight.

"You do have insurance?" she asked, suspicious, as she came around the back of the car.

"Oh yeah," he lied.

"I guess you better write the name of that down too."

He made up a last name and address and wrote down the name of an insurance company an old girlfriend once belonged to. He considered giving a real phone number but went against that idea and made one up.

"I act too," he lied to enhance the effect more. "Been in a couple of movies."

She smiled like a fan.

"So how about your phone number?" He was rebounding maturely.

She gave it to him.

"Mariana, you are beautiful," he said in his most sincere voice.

"Call me," she said timidly.

Jake beamed. "We'll see you, Mariana," he said holding out his hand. Her hand felt so warm and soft he felt like he'd been kissed.

Back in his car he took a moment or two to feel both proud and sad about his performance. Then he watched the rear view mirror as Mariana pulled up behind him. She was writing down the license plate numbers on his Buick, ones that he'd taken off a junk because the ones that belonged to his had expired so long ago. He turned the ignition key and revved the big engine and clicked into drive. His sense of freedom swelled as he drove into the now moving street traffic, though he couldn't stop the thought about that FM stereo radio and crushed velvet interior and the new car smell that would even make it better.

APPROACHING THE READING

1. Try sketching out the story, what happens in the order it happens. Then think about what is left out, and what added or emphasized, in plotting the story. Is what Jake was thinking about important to the basic story? If not, why is it included as part of the plot? Are the exact words Jake and Mariana use necessary to the story? Why are they included in the plot?

2. Reflect on the organization of the plot: Why does it start where it does? Why does it linger on certain sections and go into great detail? Why does it stop where it does and not follow through to the outcomes of what happened here?

3. What significance or implications seem to grow out of the decisions about what to include, what not to include, and how to organize? What's the "point" of it all?

Aristotle, in one of the earliest works on imaginative writing, said a plot must have a beginning, a middle, and an end. Those terms have been used as the basis for the way readers talk about plot ever since. *Beginning, middle, and end,* and other terminology such as *suspense* and *conflict,* grew out of analyses of drama, which focus on action and suspense. These terms were transferred successfully to the novel, also centered on action, and to the early short story. However, they are less applicable to some modern fiction, especially short stories, which focus often on inner struggles without much physical action or external conflict. In the following pages, we use the traditional terms but also note their limitations.

Beginning

A plot usually starts at a point that relates directly and significantly to the series of events being recorded: "Love in L.A." starts with Jake in his car caught in a traffic jam. Earlier events in his day are not included: what time he got up, whether he had breakfast, where he is going. These details may be important in Jake's larger life, but because they are not relevant to his encounter with Mariana, they do not concern readers. For fiction writers, decisions about what to leave out are as important as what to include.

Equally important is the arrangement of the events that follow the opening. "Love in L.A." is told in *chronological order,* the order in which the events occur. But that's not always the case for works of fiction. Sometimes the first events in the related sequence, though necessary to the story, are not the best place to start. The most interesting or exciting or important events occur later. Readers become more quickly and deeply involved when the plot starts at an engaging point well into the story and fills in the background events later as needed. In fact, for thousands of years this has been a common way for storytellers to proceed—the Latin phrase **in medias res** (meaning "into the middle of things") is used to describe it. The background events are usually filled in through a **flashback** (in which events prior to the beginning of a story or play are presented as an inserted narrative or a scene, perhaps with a character remembering earlier times) or through **exposition** (a nondramatized explanation, often a speech by a character or the narrator, explaining things that occurred before the initial action of a story or play). "Love in L.A." could have begun in the middle, with Jake's car bumping Mariana's, and then gone back to explain what Jake was daydreaming about instead of paying attention to his driving; and if Gilb had wanted to emphasize the accident instead of Jake's character, that probably would have been a better way to start.

Middle

Of course a story must have a middle—something has to come between the beginning and the end. But what goes into a middle? Can't a writer just lay out what happens the way it happens? Of course, but often that is not the best way to hold a reader's interest. Remember, plot involves the arrangement of the action whereby the story builds on the beginning and leads to the ending — that requires particular techniques for increasing intensity and holding the reader's interest.

At the heart of that pattern of action usually is some kind of **conflict**, some struggle or confrontation between opposing characters or a character and opposing forces. Usually, at least one side of the struggle involves the main character. The range of possible opposing forces is large, but ordinarily they fall into three broad categories.

PHYSICAL CONFLICT   One basic kind of conflict occurs as a physical struggle or confrontation between a character or group of characters and another character or group of characters: the showdown between a sheriff's posse and a gang of outlaws in an old Western, for example, or a fistfight between two rivals at a high school prom. Physical conflict can also involve humans struggling against nature: a group of sailors, perhaps led by a courageous captain, attempting to survive a fierce storm. "Love in L.A." has no physical conflict, but it's easy to imagine how the events could have turned into a road rage story with physical conflict at its center.

SOCIAL CONFLICT   A further type of conflict involves differences regarding personal or societal relationships or values. This is a common motif in modern fiction. Examples could include a teenager challenging her or his parents, the differing gender outlooks a man and a woman might bring to the same situation, or an activist confronting a social injustice. Part of the conflict in "Love in L.A." is the way Jake's lifestyle runs counter to social norms: Society expects drivers to have insurance and accept responsibility for any damage they cause to other people's property; it requires people to carry their driver's licenses and have accurate license plates on their cars. The story gives you as reader the options of identifying with Jake and enjoying the way he flaunts social expectations, or dismissing him as irresponsible, or perhaps feeling caught between accepting Jake's laid-back charm and rejecting what he does as illegal and immoral.

INTERNAL OR PSYCHOLOGICAL CONFLICT   Another variety of conflict deals with struggles within a character, as she or he wrestles with competing moral claims or a difficult decision. This has always been a central issue for literature. Numerous stories in this book show characters engaged in such inner struggles: Jig in "Hills Like White Elephants" (p. 120), the title characters in "Young Goodman Brown" (p. 252) and "Eveline" (p. 280), Farogh in "Departures" (p. 371), and Sammy in "A & P" (p. 386). Inner conflicts often appear at crucial moments in a person's life: facing the moment of death like the grandmother does in "A Good Man Is Hard to Find" (p. 341); an identity crisis when a crucial event forces a person to a new or deeper sense of self-knowledge or self-awareness, often a moment of maturation like Myop's in "The Flowers" (p. 20); a belief crisis when something causes a person to reexamine the foundation of what she or he puts faith or trust in, as in "Young Goodman Brown" (p. 252); a values crisis when something forces a person to decide how to make a moral or ethical decision, such as Mokopi's in "The Collector of Treasures" (p. 421), or sometimes to decide whether to adhere to standards she or he has held to — or should have ad-hered to — in the past. Equally important is a lack of inner conflict: One of the most revealing things about Jake in "Love in L.A." is his lack of internal struggle, despite doing some things that would trouble most readers' con-sciences at least somewhat.

Identifying a conflict is a helpful way to "get into" a story, when you want to look at the story's complexity more closely and discuss why the con-flict is one worth thinking about.

To hold readers' interest, the middle of a plot often creates some degree of **suspense**, some uncertainty and concern about how things will turn out, who did what, what the effects on the characters or events will be, or when disaster will fall or rescue will occur. The word *suspense* might be too strong for "Love in L.A." (as it is for much modern fiction), but we are curious, at least, to find out if Jake can get away with all that he's trying to.

The beginning and middle of a story often contain **foreshadowings**, anticipations of things that will happen later. For example, when the mother in "Daughter of Invention" (p. 10) says " 'When I make a million, I'll buy you your very own typewriter.' (I'd been nagging my mother for one just like the one father had bought her to do his order forms at home)," it foreshadows the ending where her father gives her "a brand new electric typewriter . . . even better than the one I'd been begging to get like my mother's" (pp. 12, 18). *Repetitions* are also often included to draw our at-tention to especially important aspects of the story. The repeated references to the mother's inventions, from the title on, set up the key invention later, when mother and daughter together invent a speech to replace the one the father tore up.

The middle of a plot holds its readers' attention by building, becoming more complex and more intense (sometimes referred to as **rising action** or **complication**), until it reaches a crisis of some sort, the **climax**, the thing the suspense builds toward. This terminology grew out of action-based plots, where the most intense moment is the peak of the physical conflict. The cli-max of a sci-fi action movie might come when, just before the gelatin-coated cyborg sends an earth-freezing probe into the center of the planet, the kung-fu master heroine shoots a laser into the monster's ultra-sensitive fifth eye and saves the world. In a story focusing on inner conflict, by contrast, the climax might be a moment of inner realization — the point at which the main character realizes that gambling is destroying his family and decides to go into rehab, which turns his life around.

Epiphany describes a moment when a character experiences a sudden moment of illumination or revelation, especially as the result of perceiving a commonplace object in a new way or through a new context. Esperanza in

"The House on Mango Street" might be said to experience an epiphany when the nun points to her third-floor apartment and says "You live *there?*" (p. 92). Suddenly she realizes how other people regard her house, what the house says about her and her family, how much she needs to have "a real house" to improve her sense of self-worth and identity.

Picking out a climax is not the same as understanding a work of fiction, nor is it a definite feature all readers identify in the same way. There can be differences of opinion about what a story's climax is or even about whether a given story has one. If "Love in L.A." has a climax, it might well come in the next-to-last paragraph when Jake seems not only to have avoided responsibility for the accident but also to have won Mariana's interest in him: "Her hand felt so warm and soft he felt like he'd been kissed" (p. 57).

A literary work can't (and shouldn't) include everything that happens during the series of events it is relating — reading or hearing everything would get pretty boring. But what things are omitted? Whatever is not significant to the action typically is left out. For example, if characters are ordinary people, they need to eat or get some sleep, but except where these activities are crucial to the overall story, they are omitted. Since lots of unimportant things are left out, you usually can assume that anything that *is* included is significant. You can be confident that almost everything in the work is there for a reason — every detail, maybe even every word. Excellent authors are very careful and deliberate in selecting what to include, presenting only those things that contribute something to the overall effect of the story.

Because an author can't include everything, stories inevitably leave *gaps*, that is, places where things are omitted or not filled in. As active readers, we need to use our imaginations to fill any significant gaps, supplying information or explanations the story doesn't spell out. Some gaps are insignificant and appear only to avoid cluttering the story with irrelevant detail. For example, we aren't told the circumstances under which the family in "Daughter of Invention" (p. 10) left the Dominican Republic. Even though we may wonder about why or how they went, that's not important to what the story is about. Other gaps, deliberate or unintentional, are important.

Authors often create gaps intentionally (sometimes withholding information in early parts of a story that will be supplied later) as a way of getting readers actively involved. Mystery and detective stories always create gaps (who did it? why?) as part of the structure. Part of the enjoyment of reading stories is reaching with our imaginations for what is omitted, seeking to supply missing details or connecting links, anticipating what may be ahead, and revising our earlier anticipations in light of what we find out later. In a milder way, as we read about the mother's ideas in "Daughter of Invention," we begin anticipating that this emphasis on inventions is leading to something. We begin wondering what, maybe trying to guess: Does she manage to come up with a crazily sane possibility that makes the family rich? In the end, we find that we were right. There was a last important invention, but inventing a speech was nothing that we could have predicted.

In some cases gaps are unintentional. But they are significant nonetheless. That women or servants fill invisible roles in a story might suggest a male-centered or an economically privileged outlook. Such an outlook *is* part of the whole meaning of the story, even if it never occurs to the author that it is. What the author does *not* think about is part of her or his idea framework, as much as what she or he consciously does think about.

Gaps also can indicate what is "meaningfully *not* important" — what the story recognizes as potentially meaningful, but is *not* interested in. If a story about the difficulties a pair of lovers encounters in their relationship ends before their marriage takes place, the gap indicates that their married life is not significant to the story; its interest is in their solving the difficulties they encounter in getting together. Gaps, on the other hand, can be used to signal what is *very* important, often putting even more emphasis on a detail or bit of information by having the reader supply it, even suggesting perhaps that the very process of working to fill the gap is crucial to the effect. "The Red Convertible" (p. 67), for example, says a lot about the Vietnam War by saying very little about it.

Ending

A story must end, of course — it can't go on forever. But it also can't just stop. The difference between just stopping and an effective ending is that the latter gives a sense of wholeness and leaves you satisfied, or satisfyingly unsatisfied, as a reader or listener. One of the big differences between fiction and real life is that life carries on after reaching a "big event," while the series of events in a fictional plot reaches a terminal point, the conflicts around which it was shaped are resolved (or shown to be unresolvable), and the story ends.

The French term **dénouement** is often used in discussing the ending of a story. It literally means "unknotting," the untying of the threads that are tangled and knotted, the solution of the mysteries, the explanation of the secrets and misunderstandings. An ending, in addition to unknotting tangles, often ties up the loose ends, leaving us with a sense of finality or a momentary stay against ordinary chaos. That doesn't mean that everything turns out happily — some stories have unresolved, unhappy endings. But it does mean that the questions and problems we have been involved with, if not solved or even resolved, at least are adequately accounted for. We know all that we need to know to comprehend and reflect on the story as a whole. The last paragraph of "Love in L.A." has a feeling of finality — the lives of Jake and Mariana do not end, but nothing that follows is relevant to the story of their encounter under the Alvarado Street overpass (though an active reader will imagine Mariana's pained and disappointed reaction, and her father's furious reaction, when they find out that all the information Jake gave her was false — and that may form an important part of how we feel about Jake's actions). Jake and Mariana have a personal encounter that could have touched Jake and made a difference in his life, but the last sentence shows that it didn't. The end takes us back to the beginning and the daydreams he prefers over reality.

ABDCE

Fiction writer Alice Adams suggests an ABDCE acronym for thinking about typical plot structure of a story:

- **Action:** Stories often begin in the middle, plunging us into action to get us immediately involved and interested.
- **Background:** Stories then fill in the background, the pertinent earlier events that make sense of the action we are plunged into, usually through a flashback or some exposition.
- **Development:** The story builds up as details are supplied and the conflicts become more intense. This is sometimes referred to as the rising action, or the complication, as problems become more difficult and relationships more intricate.
- **Climax:** Stories often build to a climax, or a crisis, a turning point of greatest importance or excitement (the term *reversal* is often applied). The climax is typically a point at which a key character does something, or learns something, or discovers something really important. Reversal suggests change: The climax often involves a life-changing realization, perhaps an opportunity for inner growth or maturation, or the beginning of a development into a wiser or better person.
- **Ending:** If the story reaches a peak in its climax, the ending involves a falling action, as things slow down, suspense is alleviated, pieces fall into place. There is a falling movement, as the reader or listener is brought back down to solid footing. The reversal allows the story to terminate, and the ending provides an indication of whether change or growth has occurred and will be lasting.

CHARACTERS

When you read a story, you may first be interested in the events of the plot. Important as the events are, however, they cannot be separated from the people involved in the events who carry out the actions. **Characters**, the created persons who appear or are referred to in narratives and dramas (and at times in poems), are in many cases the aspect that is of greatest appeal and interest in the work. Literature offers us the opportunity to learn about, and even imaginatively to enter the lives of, people we would otherwise never get close to, at least not close enough for us to understand their lives and situations to such a significant extent and to sympathize, even empathize, with them.

When we meet such people in literature, we want to know what they are like, what makes them tick, how they deal with the situations and relationships they encounter. **Characterization** refers to the methods and techniques an author uses to represent people and to enable us to know and relate to them. As we read a work of fiction, we understand characters more fully and accurately if we pay attention to the means by which we attain our knowledge, to the kind of techniques through which they are brought to life in the story.

Techniques of Characterization

Here are some of the most important means of characterization to pay attention to. They can appear individually or in a variety of combinations.

TELLING   In the most direct way of characterization, we are simply told what the characters are like, all at once as they are first introduced or bit by bit as they reappear in the story. That is the case for some aspects of Connie's character in "Where Are You Going, Where Have You Been?," especially aspects that would be difficult, or would take a lot of space, to demonstrate: "Everything about her had two sides to it, one for home and one for anywhere that was not home" (p. 76). Even the narrator's choice of words can be a way of telling something about a character: The use of *slouched* and *lied*, for example, gives us direct insight into Jake's character in "Love in L.A."

SHOWING   What a character is like can come out through the character's actions, which may be presented without interpretive comment, leaving the reader to conclude what a character is like from what she or he does. What Jake does in response to hitting Mariana's car shows the kind of person he is; words the narrator selects may suggest some reservations about Jake as a person, but the narrator does not explicitly evaluate his behavior. In many cases, showing is combined with telling, often with differing weights of emphasis. Only telling what a character is like is often less effective than showing what the character is like through her or his actions, or through a combination of telling and showing.

SAYING   What a character is like can be brought out by having other characters say things about her or him. It's important, however, to keep in mind that how we take what the characters say depends, of course, on how those characters relate to the main characters: What is said may need to be taken with a grain of salt because of a bias for or against the character. A great deal can also be revealed about a character by what she or he says — **dialogue** (conversation between characters) is an important characterization technique. Thus we gain valuable insights into Jake as a person when he says "You're not married, are you? Not that that would matter that much to me. I'm an openminded kinda guy" and "I left my wallet in the pants I was wearing last night" and "[I've] been in a couple of movies" (pp. 56, 57).

ENTERING A CHARACTER'S MIND   What a character is like can be revealed through her or his thoughts and feelings. The author takes us into a character's mind using techniques such as a partially or wholly omniscient narrator (the way the narrator shows us what goes on in Jake's mind through his daydreams, his thoughts, and things he observes), stream of consciousness, or interior monologue (see pp. 55–57).

NAMING   In some cases, the names an author gives to characters reveal aspects of what they are like. Henry Fielding, one of the first English novelists, names one of his characters Squire Allworthy to reveal how admirable he is in every respect. In other cases, Fielding uses an **allusion** (see p. 205) to the Bible in naming a character: Parson Abraham Adams, for example, is a man of great faith (like the biblical Abraham), but is also a person as innocent and trusting as the Adam of Genesis 2–3. In many cases, however, names are simply names, and yet they invariably somehow sound right (think of David Copperfield or Huckleberry Finn).

After you know what the characters are like, you will want to know why they do the things they do, why they make the kinds of decisions and choices they do. This important aspect of characterization is **motivation**, the reasons, explanations, or justifications behind a character's behavior. Motivation in fiction usually grows out of a sense of what a character deeply wants or desires, and how that leads the character to react in a specific situation.

A great deal is revealed about characters also by the *way* they handle situations — especially difficult, problematic, or tragic situations or relationships. For characters to be plausible, they must be consistent in the way they deal with circumstances. If they respond to a situation one way at one time and differently at another, there should be clear reasons for the difference (their inconsistency must be understandable and believable).

Types of Characterization

Our understanding and appreciation of characters in a story are enhanced when we are alert to the varying degrees of a character's complexity and importance. Here are some of the ways those varying degrees are indicated.

ROUND/FLAT   The novelist E. M. Forster used the terms *flat* and *round* to illustrate differences in complexity. **Round characters** are complex and sometimes even challenging to understand. We are offered many sides and facets of their lives and personalities, leading us sometimes to need to reconcile what seem to be incompatible ideas or behaviors. Round characters often are **dynamic**, shown as changing and growing because of what happens to them. They also can be **static**, not shown as changing, though they may be described in such rich detail that we have a clear sense of how they would, or will, change, even though we don't see it happening. We are shown enough about Connie in "Where Are You Going, Where Have You Been?" (p. 75) for her character to be rounded out; the story shows her changing, at least in the sense of having to confront a totally new area of experience.

Flat characters are generally developed less fully than round, or dynamic, characters. Usually they are static and are represented through only one or two main features or aspects. Unlike round characters, they often can be summed up in a sentence or two. If these one or two traits are developed in considerable detail, the characters may be very interesting and enjoyable to read about. But we can't come to know them as thoroughly and in as much depth as characters who are depicted with more complexity or developed more fully and shown to be changing and growing throughout the story. Jake and Mariana in "Love in L.A." are flat characters — a thoroughgoing cad and a rather gullible innocent. That's all they need to be and all that could be expected in such a short short story.

MAJOR/MINOR   Most major characters in a story or play are round characters, while minor characters are usually flat. Minor characters are at times **stock characters**, stereotypes easily recognized by readers or audiences from their frequent uses, such as the absent-minded professor, the evil stepmother, the nerdy computer geek, or the smart but quiet detective or police sergeant. Use of flat characters is not necessarily "bad writing." Some excellent fiction writers create central characters who are flat but are described in such rich detail that they come to life fully and in an enjoyable way. There isn't time in most short stories to develop more than one character in a rounded way, perhaps not even one. Even in a novel or play, the reader might find it too much to handle if every character were rounded out fully.

PROTAGONIST/ANTAGONIST   The terms *protagonist* and *antagonist* are often used to define relationships between characters. The **protagonist** is the central character in a work (the older term **hero** seems less useful because the central character doesn't have to be "heroic"). The **antagonist** is the character, force, or collected forces opposed to the protagonist that give rise to the central conflict of the work — the rival, opponent, or enemy of the protagonist (the older term *villain* works less well because the antagonist isn't always evil and isn't always a person). In the stories included in this chapter, Connie is the protagonist of "Where Are You Going, Where Have You Been?"; Arnold Friend is the antagonist. Henry is the protagonist of "The Red Convertible"; white society and the world outside the reservation are the antagonists.

WWW
Further explore plot and characters, including interactive exercises, with VirtuaLit Fiction at bedfordstmartins.com/approachinglit.

☑️ **CHECKLIST on Plot and Characters**

❏ Notice the structuring of plot:
 • the handling of beginning, middle, and ending
 • its use of action, background, development, climax, and conclusion
 • its use of gaps, flashbacks, suspense, foreshadowing, and repetition

❏ Look for conflicts—physical, social, internal—and use them as a way to get into the story and to explore its complexity.

❏ Be attentive to the methods of characterization: by noticing what we are told and shown, listening to what a character says and what other characters say about her or him, entering a character's mind, and considering the way she or he is named.

❏ Consider how fully characters are developed: whether they are round or flat, whether they change or stay pretty much the same.

FURTHER READING

Below are two stories for further reading, both about young persons encountering situations new to them that change their lives. The first is a story about two brothers and a car that comes to epitomize their love for each other. It was written by Louise Erdrich, who grew up near the Turtle Mountain Reservation and is a member of the Turtle Mountain Band of Chippewa. Many of the place names in the story can be found on maps of North and South Dakota. As you read and then think back on the story, pay attention to its handling of plot—which details the author includes, how these details are arranged, and how they relate to each other and work together to convey a unified effect. Note the story's handling of characters—what they are like and how you come to know them.

Louise Erdrich   b. 1954

The Red Convertible   [1984]

Lyman Lamartine

I was the first one to drive a convertible on my reservation. And of course it was red, a red Olds. I owned that car along with my brother Henry Junior. We owned it together until his boots filled with water on a windy night and he bought out my share. Now Henry owns the whole car, and his younger brother Lyman (that's myself), Lyman walks everywhere he goes.

How did I earn enough money to buy my share in the first place? My one talent was I could always make money. I had a touch for it, unusual in a Chippewa. From the first I was different that way, and everyone recognized it. I was the only kid they let in the American Legion Hall to shine shoes, for example, and one Christmas I sold spiritual bouquets for the mission door to door. The nuns let me keep a percentage. Once I started, it seemed the more money I made the easier the money came. Everyone encouraged it. When I was fifteen I got a job washing dishes at the Joliet Café, and that was where my first big break happened.

It wasn't long before I was promoted to busing tables, and then the short-order cook quit and I was hired to take her place. No sooner than you know it I was managing the Joliet. The rest is history. I went on managing. I soon became part owner, and of course there was no stopping me then. It wasn't long before the whole thing was mine.

After I'd owned the Joliet for one year, it blew over in the worst tornado ever seen around here. The whole operation was smashed to bits. A total loss. The fryalator was up in a tree, the grill torn in half like it was paper. I was only sixteen. I had it all in my mother's name, and I lost it quick, but before I lost it I had every one of my relatives, and their relatives, to dinner, and I also bought that red Olds I mentioned, along with Henry.

The first time we saw it! I'll tell you when we first saw it. We had gotten a ride up to Winnipeg, and both of us had money. Don't ask me why, because we never mentioned a car or anything, we just had all our money. Mine was cash, a big bankroll from the Joliet's insurance. Henry had two checks — a week's extra pay for being laid off, and his regular check from the Jewel Bearing Plant.

We were walking down Portage anyway, seeing the sights, when we saw it. There it was, parked, large as life. Really as *if* it was alive. I thought of the word *repose*, because the car wasn't simply stopped, parked, or whatever. That car reposed, calm and gleaming, a FOR SALE sign in its left front window. Then, before we had thought it over at all, the car belonged to us and our pockets were empty. We had just enough money for gas back home.

We went places in that car, me and Henry. We took off driving all one whole summer. We started off toward the Little Knife River and Mandaree in Fort Berthold and then we found ourselves down in Wakpala somehow, and then suddenly we were over in Montana on the Rocky Boy, and yet the summer was not even half over. Some people hang on to details when they travel, but we didn't let them bother us and just lived our everyday lives here to there.

I do remember this one place with willows. I remember I laid under those trees and it was comfortable. So comfortable. The branches bent down all around me like a tent or a stable. And quiet, it was quiet, even though there was a powwow close enough so I could see it going on. The air was not too still, not too windy either. When the dust rises up and hangs in the air around the dancers like that, I feel good. Henry was asleep with his arms thrown wide. Later on, he woke up and we started driving again. We were somewhere in Montana, or maybe on the Blood Reserve — it could have been anywhere. Anyway it was where we met the girl.

All her hair was in buns around her ears, that's the first thing I noticed about her. She was posed alongside the road with her arm out, so we stopped. That girl was short, so short her lumber shirt looked comical on her, like a nightgown. She had jeans on and fancy moccasins and she carried a little suitcase.

"Hop on in," says Henry. So she climbs in between us.

"We'll take you home," I says. "Where do you live?"

"Chicken," she says.

"Where the hell's that?" I ask her.

"Alaska."

"Okay," says Henry, and we drive.

We got up there and never wanted to leave. The sun doesn't truly set there in summer, and the night is more a soft dusk. You might doze off, sometimes, but before you know it you're up again, like an animal in nature. You never feel like you have to sleep hard or put away the world. And things would grow up there. One day just dirt or moss, the next day flowers and long grass. The girl's name was Susy. Her family really took to us. They fed us and put us up. We had our own tent to live in by their house, and the kids would be in and out of there all day and night. They couldn't get over me and Henry being brothers, we looked so different. We told them we knew we had the same mother, anyway.

One night Susy came in to visit us. We sat around in the tent talking of this and that. The season was changing. It was getting darker by that time, and the cold was even getting just a little mean. I told her it was time for us to go. She stood up on a chair.

"You never seen my hair," Susy said.

That was true. She was standing on a chair, but still, when she unclipped her buns the hair reached all the way to the ground. Our eyes opened. You couldn't tell how much hair she had when it was rolled up so neatly. Then my brother Henry did something funny. He went up to the chair and said, "Jump on my shoulders." So she did that, and her hair reached down past his waist, and he started twirling, this way and that, so her hair was flung out from side to side.

"I always wondered what it was like to have long pretty hair," Henry says. Well we laughed. It was a funny sight, the way he did it. The next morning we got up and took leave of those people.

On to greener pastures, as they say. It was down through Spokane and across Idaho then Montana and very soon we were racing the weather right along under the Canadian border through Columbus, Des Lacs, and then we were in Bottineau County and soon home. We'd made most of the trip, that summer, without putting up the car hood at all. We got home just in time, it turned out, for the army to remember Henry had signed up to join it.

I don't wonder that the army was so glad to get my brother that they turned him into a Marine. He was built like a brick outhouse anyway. We liked to tease him that they really wanted him for his Indian nose. He had a nose big and sharp as a hatchet, like the nose on Red Tomahawk, the Indian who killed Sitting Bull, whose profile is on signs all along the North Dakota highways. Henry went off to training camp, came home once during Christmas, then the next thing you know we got an overseas letter from him. It was 1970, and he said he was stationed up in the northern hill country. Whereabouts I did not know. He wasn't such a hot letter writer, and only got off two before the enemy caught him. I could never keep it straight, which direction those good Vietnam soldiers were from.

I wrote him back several times, even though I didn't know if those letters would get through. I kept him informed all about the car. Most of the time I had it up on blocks in the yard or half taken apart, because that long trip did a hard job on it under the hood.

I always had good luck with numbers, and never worried about the draft myself. I never even had to think about what my number was. But Henry was never lucky in the same way as me. It was at least three years before Henry came home. By then I guess the whole war was solved in the government's mind, but for him it would keep on going. In those years I'd put his car into almost perfect shape. I always thought of it as his car while he was gone, even though when he left he said, "Now it's yours," and threw me his key.

"Thanks for the extra key," I'd said. "I'll put it up in your drawer just in case I need it." He laughed.

When he came home, though, Henry was very different, and I'll say this: the change was no good. You could hardly expect him to change for the better, I know. But he was quiet, so quiet, and never comfortable sitting still anywhere but always up and moving around. I thought back to times we'd sat still for whole afternoons, never moving a muscle, just shifting our weight along the ground, talking to whoever sat with us, watching things. He'd always had a joke, then, too, and now you couldn't get him to laugh, or when he did it was more the sound of a man choking, a sound that stopped up the throats of other people around him. They got to leaving him alone most of the time, and I didn't blame them. It was a fact: Henry was jumpy and mean.

I'd bought a color TV set for my mom and the rest of us while Henry was away. Money still came very easy. I was sorry I'd ever bought it though, because of Henry. I was also sorry I'd bought color, because with black-and-white the pictures seem older and farther away. But what are you going to do? He sat in front of it, watching it, and that was the only time he was completely still. But it was the kind of stillness that you see in a rabbit when it freezes and before it will bolt. He was not easy. He sat in his chair gripping the armrests with all his might, as if the chair itself was moving at a high speed and if he let go at all he would rocket forward and maybe crash right through the set.

Once I was in the room watching TV with Henry and I heard his teeth click at something. I looked over, and he'd bitten through his lip. Blood was going down his chin. I tell you right then I wanted to smash that tube to pieces. I went over to it but Henry must have known what I was up to. He rushed from his chair and shoved me out of the way, against the wall. I told myself he didn't know what he was doing.

My mom came in, turned the set off real quiet, and told us she had made something for supper. So we went and sat down. There was still blood going down Henry's chin, but he didn't notice it and no one said anything, even though every time he took a bite of his bread his blood fell onto it until he was eating his own blood mixed in with the food.

While Henry was not around we talked about what was going to happen to him. There were no Indian doctors on the reservation, and my mom couldn't come around to trusting the old man, Moses Pillager, because he courted her long ago and was jealous of her husbands. He might take revenge through her son. We were afraid that if we brought Henry to a regular hospital they would keep him.

"They don't fix them in those places," Mom said; "they just give them drugs."

"We wouldn't get him there in the first place," I agreed, "so let's just forget about it."

Then I thought about the car.

Henry had not even looked at the car since he'd gotten home, though like I said, it was in tip-top condition and ready to drive. I thought the car might bring the old Henry back somehow. So I bided my time and waited for my chance to interest him in the vehicle.

One night Henry was off somewhere. I took myself a hammer. I went out to that car and I did a number on its underside. Whacked it up. Bent the tail pipe double. Ripped the muffler loose. By the time I was done with the car it looked worse than any typical Indian car that has been driven all its life on reservation roads, which they always say are like government promises — full of holes. It just about hurt me, I'll tell you that! I threw dirt in the carburetor and I ripped all the electric tape off the seats. I made it look just as beat up as I could. Then I sat back and waited for Henry to find it.

Still, it took him over a month. That was all right, because it was just getting warm enough, not melting, but warm enough to work outside.

"Lyman," he says, walking in one day, "that red car looks like shit."

"Well it's old," I says. "You got to expect that."

"No way!" says Henry. "That car's a classic! But you went and ran the piss right out of it, Lyman, and you know it don't deserve that. I kept that car in A-one shape. You don't remember. You're too young. But when I left, that car was running like a watch. Now I don't even know if I can get it to start again, let alone get it anywhere near its old condition."

"Well you try," I said, like I was getting mad, "but I say it's a piece of junk."

Then I walked out before he could realize I knew he'd strung together more than six words at once.

After that I thought he'd freeze himself to death working on that car. He was out there all day, and at night he rigged up a little lamp, ran a cord out the window, and had himself some light to see by while he worked. He was better than he had been before, but that's still not saying much. It was easier for him to do the things the rest of us did. He ate more slowly and didn't jump up and down during the meal to get this or that or look out the window. I put my hand in the back of the TV set, I admit, and fiddled around with it good, so that it was almost impossible now to get a clear picture. He didn't look at it very often anyway. He was always out with that car or going off to get parts for it. By the time it was really melting outside, he had it fixed.

I had been feeling down in the dumps about Henry around this time. We had always been together before. Henry and Lyman. But he was such a loner now that I didn't know how to take it. So I jumped at the chance one day when Henry seemed friendly. It's not that he smiled or anything. He just said, "Let's take that old shitbox for a spin." Just the way he said it made me think he could be coming around.

We went out to the car. It was spring. The sun was shining very bright. My only sister, Bonita, who was just eleven years old, came out and made us stand together for a picture. Henry leaned his elbow on the red car's windshield, and he took his other arm and put it over my shoulder, very carefully, as though it was heavy for him to lift and he didn't want to bring the weight down all at once.

"Smile," Bonita said, and he did.

That picture. I never look at it anymore. A few months ago, I don't know why, I got his picture out and tacked it on the wall. I felt good about Henry at the time, close to him. I felt good having his picture on the wall, until one night when I was looking at television. I was a little drunk and stoned. I looked up at the wall and Henry was staring at me. I don't know what it was, but his smile had changed, or maybe it was gone. All I know is I couldn't stay in the same room with that picture. I was shaking. I got up, closed the door, and went into the kitchen. A little later my friend Ray came over and we both went back into that room. We put the picture in a brown bag, folded the bag over and over tightly, then put it way back in a closet.

I still see that picture now, as if it tugs at me, whenever I pass that closet door. The picture is very clear in my mind. It was so sunny that day Henry had to squint against the glare. Or maybe the camera Bonita held flashed like a mirror, blinding him, before she snapped the picture. My face is right out in the sun, big and round. But he might have drawn back, because the shadows on his face are deep as holes. There are two shadows curved like little hooks around the ends of his smile, as if to frame it and try to keep it there — that one, first smile that looked like it might have hurt his face. He has his field jacket on and the worn-in clothes he'd come back in and kept wearing ever since. After Bonita took the picture, she went into the house and we got into the car. There was a full cooler in the trunk. We started off, east, toward Pembina and the Red River because Henry said he wanted to see the high water.

The trip over there was beautiful. When everything starts changing, drying up, clearing off, you feel like your whole life is starting. Henry felt it, too. The top was down and the car hummed like a top. He'd really put it back in shape, even the tape on the seats was very carefully put down and glued back in layers. It's not that he smiled again or even joked, but his face looked to me as if it was clear, more peaceful. It looked as though he wasn't thinking of anything in particular except the bare fields and windbreaks and houses we were passing.

The river was high and full of winter trash when we got there. The sun was still out, but it was colder by the river. There were still little clumps of dirty snow here and there on the banks. The water hadn't gone over the banks yet, but it would, you could tell. It was just at its limit, hard swollen, glossy like an old gray scar. We made ourselves a fire, and we sat down and watched the current go. As I watched it I felt something squeezing inside me and tightening and trying to let go all at the same time. I knew I was not just feeling it myself; I knew I was feeling what Henry was going through at that moment. Except that I couldn't stand it, the closing and opening. I jumped to my feet. I took Henry by the shoulders and I started shaking him. "Wake up," I says, "wake up, wake up, wake up!" I didn't know what had come over me. I sat down beside him again.

His face was totally white and hard. Then it broke, like stones break all of a sudden when water boils up inside them.

"I know it," he says. "I know it. I can't help it. It's no use."

We start talking. He said he knew what I'd done with the car. It was obvious it had been whacked out of shape and not just neglected. He said he wanted to give the car to me for good now, it was no use. He said he'd fixed it just to give it back and I should take it.

"No way," I says. "I don't want it."

"That's okay," he says, "you take it."

"I don't want it, though," I says back to him, and then to emphasize, just to emphasize, you understand, I touch his shoulder. He slaps my hand off.

"Take that car," he says.

"No," I say. "Make me," I say, and then he grabs my jacket and rips the arm loose. That jacket is a class act, suede with tags and zippers. I push Henry backwards, off the log. He jumps up and bowls me over. We go down in a clinch and come up swinging hard, for all we're worth, with our fists. He socks my jaw so hard I feel like it swings loose. Then I'm at his rib cage and land a good one under his chin so his head snaps back. He's dazzled. He looks at me and I look at him and then his eyes are full of tears and blood and at first I think he's crying. But no, he's laughing. "Ha! Ha!" he says. "Ha! Ha! Take good care of it."

"Okay," I says. "Okay, no problem. Ha! Ha!"

I can't help it, and I start laughing, too. My face feels fat and strange, and after a while I get a beer from the cooler in the trunk, and when I hand it to Henry he takes his shirt and wipes my germs off. "Hoof-and-mouth disease," he says. For some reason this cracks me up, and so we're really laughing for a while, and then we drink all the rest of the beers one by one and throw them in the river and see how far, how fast, the current takes them before they fill up and sink.

"You want to go on back?" I ask after a while. "Maybe we could snag a couple nice Kashpaw girls."

He says nothing. But I can tell his mood is turning again.

"They're all crazy, the girls up here, every damn one of them."

"You're crazy too," I say, to jolly him up. "Crazy Lamartine boys!"

He looks as though he will take this wrong at first. His face twists, then clears, and he jumps up on his feet. "That's right!" he says. "Crazier 'n hell. Crazy Indians!"

I think it's the old Henry again. He throws off his jacket and starts springing his legs up from the knees like a fancy dancer. He's down doing something between a grass dance and a bunny hop, no kind of dance I ever saw before, but neither has anyone else on all this green growing earth. He's wild. He wants to pitch whoopee! He's up and at me and all over. All this time I'm laughing so hard, so hard my belly is getting tied up in a knot.

"Got to cool me off!" he shouts all of a sudden. Then he runs over to the river and jumps in.

There's boards and other things in the current. It's so high. No sound comes from the river after the splash he makes, so I run right over. I look around. It's getting dark. I see he's halfway across the water already, and I know he didn't swim there but the current took him. It's far. I hear his voice, though, very clearly across it.

"My boots are filling," he says.

He says this in a normal voice, like he just noticed and he doesn't know what to think of it. Then he's gone. A branch comes by. Another branch. And I go in.

By the time I get out of the river, off the snag I pulled myself onto, the sun is down. I walk back to the car, turn on the high beams, and drive it up the bank. I put it in first gear and then I take my foot off the clutch. I get out, close the door, and watch it plow softly into the water. The headlights reach in as they go down, searching, still lighted even after the water swirls over the back end. I wait. The wires short out. It is all finally dark. And then there is only the water, the sound of it going and running and going and running and running.

APPROACHING THE READING

1. Outline the plot of the story. Then comment on the way it starts, the way it builds in the middle (what kinds of conflicts appear, how the material is arranged), and the way it ends. What effects are achieved through the way plot is organized and developed?

2. Think about what is left out and what is added or emphasized in plotting the story. What gaps are left in the story? How do they force you to become actively involved as a reader? What does the inclusion of the episodes about their travels — the place under the willows where they rested, and their taking Susy home to Alaska — contribute to the story? What would be lost if those details were not there?

Research this author in depth with cultural documents and multimedia resources on *LiterActive*.

3. Describe what the main characters are like and how we come to know them (telling? showing? saying? entering their minds? by their names?). Are they dynamic characters or static ones? To what extent does what we know about Henry depend on what we know about Lyman, and what difference does that make?

4. Why does Henry walk into the river? Does he intend to drown, or is it accidental? In what ways does he change in the story, and what things cause him to change? Why does Lyman roll the car into the river?

Here is another story about cars and young people, but in a very different style and tone (more like a psychological thriller). It was written by Joyce Carol Oates, whose work has extensively explored the nature of violence in America. It too is a carefully constructed story with interesting characters. Be alert to what is included, the way it is arranged, what the characters are like, and the ways in which they are developed.

Joyce Carol Oates   b. 1938

Where Are You Going, Where Have You Been?   [1966]

For Bob Dylan

Her name was Connie. She was fifteen and she had a quick, nervous giggling habit of craning her neck to glance into mirrors or checking other people's faces to make sure her own was all right. Her mother, who noticed everything and knew everything and who hadn't much reason any longer to look at her own face, always scolded Connie about it. "Stop gawking at yourself. Who are you? You think you're so pretty?" she would say. Connie would raise her eyebrows at these familiar old complaints and look right through her mother, into a shadowy vision of herself as she was right at that moment: she knew she was pretty and that was everything. Her mother had been pretty once too, if you could believe those old snapshots in the album, but now her looks were gone and that was why she was always after Connie.

"Why don't you keep your room clean like your sister? How've you got your hair fixed—what the hell stinks? Hair spray? You don't see your sister using that junk."

Her sister June was twenty-four and still lived at home. She was a secretary in the high school Connie attended, and if that wasn't bad enough—with her in the same building—she was so plain and chunky and steady that Connie had to hear her praised all the time by her mother and her mother's sisters. June did this, June did that, she saved money and helped clean the house and cooked and Connie couldn't do a thing, her mind was all filled with trashy daydreams. Their father was away at work most of the time and when he came home he wanted supper and he read the newspaper at supper and after supper he went to bed. He didn't bother talking much to them, but around his bent head Connie's mother kept picking at her until Connie wished her mother was dead and she herself was dead and it was all over. "She makes me want to throw up sometimes," she complained to her friends. She had a high, breathless, amused voice that made everything she said sound a little forced, whether it was sincere or not.

There was one good thing: June went places with girl friends of hers, girls who were just as plain and steady as she, and so when Connie wanted to do that her mother had no objections. The father of Connie's best girl friend drove the girls the three miles to town and left them at a shopping plaza so they could walk through the stores or go to a movie, and when he came to pick them up again at eleven he never bothered to ask what they had done.

They must have been familiar sights, walking around the shopping plaza in their shorts and flat ballerina slippers that always scuffed the sidewalk, with charm bracelets jingling on their thin wrists; they would lean together to whisper and laugh secretly if someone passed who amused or interested them. Connie had long dark blond hair that drew anyone's eye to it, and she wore part of it pulled up on her head and puffed out and the rest of it she let fall down her back. She wore a pullover jersey blouse that looked one way when she was at home and another way when she was away from home. Everything about her had two sides to it, one for home and one for anywhere that was not home: her walk, which could be childlike and bobbing, or languid enough to make anyone think she was hearing music in her head; her mouth, which was pale and smirking most of the time, but bright and pink on these evenings out; her laugh, which was cynical and drawling at home—"Ha, ha, very funny"—but high-pitched and nervous anywhere else, like the jingling of the charms on her bracelet.

Sometimes they did go shopping or to a movie, but sometimes they went across the highway, ducking fast across the busy road, to a drive-in restaurant where older kids hung out. The restaurant was shaped like a big bottle, though squatter than a real bottle, and on its cap was a revolving figure of a grinning boy holding a hamburger aloft. One night in midsummer they ran across, breathless with daring, and right away someone leaned out a car window and invited them over, but it was just a boy from high school they didn't like. It made them feel good to be able to ignore him. They went up through the maze of parked and cruising cars to the bright-lit, fly-infested restaurant, their faces pleased and expectant as if they were entering a sacred building that loomed up out of the night to give them what haven and blessing they yearned for. They sat at the counter and crossed their legs at the ankles, their thin shoulders rigid with excitement, and listened to the music that made everything so good: the music was always in the background, like music at a church service; it was something to depend upon.

A boy named Eddie came in to talk with them. He sat backwards on his stool, turning himself jerkily around in semicircles and then stopping and turning back again, and after a while he asked Connie if she would like something to eat. She said she would and so she tapped her friend's arm on her way out — her friend pulled her face up into a brave, droll look — and Connie said she would meet her at eleven, across the way. "I just hate to leave her like that," Connie said earnestly, but the boy said that she wouldn't be alone for long. So they went out to his car, and on the way Connie couldn't help but let her eyes wander over the windshields and faces all around her, her face gleaming with a joy that had nothing to do with Eddie or even this place; it might have been the music. She drew her shoulders up and sucked in her breath with the pure pleasure of being alive, and just at that moment she happened to glance at a face just a few feet from hers. It was a boy with shaggy black hair, in a convertible jalopy painted gold. He stared at her and then his lips widened into a grin. Connie slit her eyes at him and turned away, but she couldn't help glancing back and there he was, still watching her. He wagged a finger and laughed and said, "Gonna get you, baby," and Connie turned away again without Eddie noticing anything.

She spent three hours with him, at the restaurant where they ate hamburgers and drank Cokes in wax cups that were always sweating, and then down an alley a mile or so away, and when he left her off at five to eleven only the movie house was still open at the plaza. Her girl friend was there, talking with a boy. When Connie came up, the two girls smiled at each other and Connie said, "How was the movie?" and the girl said, "*You* should know." They rode off with the girl's father, sleepy and pleased, and Connie couldn't help but look back at the darkened shopping plaza with its big empty parking lot and its signs that were faded and ghostly now, and over at the drive-in restaurant where cars were still circling tirelessly. She couldn't hear the music at this distance.

Next morning June asked her how the movie was and Connie said, "So-so."

She and that girl and occasionally another girl went out several times a week, and the rest of the time Connie spent around the house — it was summer vacation — getting in her mother's way and thinking, dreaming about the boys she met. But all the boys fell back and dissolved into a single face that was not even a face but an idea, a feeling, mixed up with the urgent insistent pounding of the music and the humid night of July. Connie's mother kept dragging her back to the daylight by finding things for her to do or saying suddenly, "What's this about the Pettinger girl?"

And Connie would say nervously, "Oh, her. That dope." She always drew thick clear lines between herself and such girls, and her mother was simple and kind enough to believe it. Her mother was so simple, Connie thought, that it was maybe cruel to fool her so much. Her mother went scuffling around the house in old bedroom slippers and complained over the telephone to one sister about the other, then the other called up and the two of them complained about the third one. If June's name was mentioned her mother's tone was approving, and if Connie's name was mentioned it was disapproving. This did not really mean she disliked Connie, and actually Connie thought that her mother preferred her to June just because she was prettier, but the two of them kept up a pretense of exasperation, a sense that they were tugging and struggling over something of little value to either of them. Sometimes, over coffee, they were almost friends, but something would come up — some vexation that was like a fly buzzing suddenly around their heads — and their faces went hard with contempt.

One Sunday Connie got up at eleven — none of them bothered with church — and washed her hair so that it could dry all day long in the sun. Her parents and sister were going to a barbecue at an aunt's house and Connie said no, she wasn't interested, rolling her eyes to let her mother know just what she thought of it. "Stay home alone then," her mother said sharply. Connie sat out back in a lawn chair and watched them drive away, her father quiet and bald, hunched around so that he could back the car out, her mother with a look that was still angry and not at all softened through the windshield, and in the back seat poor old June, all dressed up as if she didn't know what a barbecue was, with all the running yelling kids and the flies. Connie sat with her eyes closed in the sun, dreaming and dazed with the warmth about her as if this were a kind of love, the caresses of love, and her mind slipped over onto thoughts of the boy she had been with the night before and how nice he had been, how sweet it always was, not the way someone like June would suppose but sweet, gentle, the way it was in movies and promised in songs; and when she opened her eyes she hardly knew where she was, the back yard ran off into weeds and a fence-like line of trees and behind it the sky was perfectly blue and still. The asbestos "ranch house" that was now three years old startled her — it looked small. She shook her head as if to get awake.

It was too hot. She went inside the house and turned on the radio to drown out the quiet. She sat on the edge of her bed, barefoot, and listened for an hour and a half to a program called XYZ Sunday Jamboree, record after record of hard, fast, shrieking songs she sang along with, interspersed by exclamations from "Bobby King": "An' look here, you girls at Napoleon's — Son and Charley want you to pay real close attention to this song coming up!"

And Connie paid close attention herself, bathed in a glow of slow-pulsed joy that seemed to rise mysteriously out of the music itself and lay languidly about the airless little room, breathed in and breathed out with each gentle rise and fall of her chest.

After a while she heard a car coming up the drive. She sat up at once, startled, because it couldn't be her father so soon. The gravel kept crunching all the way in from the road — the driveway was long — and Connie ran to the window. It was a car she didn't know. It was an open jalopy, painted a bright gold that caught the sunlight opaquely. Her heart began to pound and her fingers snatched at her hair, checking it, and she whispered, "Christ, Christ," wondering how bad she looked. The car came to a stop at the side door and the horn sounded four short taps, as if this were a signal Connie knew.

She went into the kitchen and approached the door slowly, then hung out the screen door, her bare toes curling down off the step. There were two boys in the car and now she recognized the driver: he had shaggy, shabby black hair that looked crazy as a wig and he was grinning at her.

"I ain't late, am I?" he said.

"Who the hell do you think you are?" Connie said.

"Toldja I'd be out, didn't I?"

"I don't even know who you are."

She spoke sullenly, careful to show no interest or pleasure, and he spoke in a fast, bright monotone. Connie looked past him to the other boy, taking her time. He had fair brown hair, with a lock that fell onto his forehead. His sideburns gave him a fierce, embarrassed look, but so far he hadn't even bothered to glance at her. Both boys wore sunglasses. The driver's glasses were metallic and mirrored everything in miniature.

"You wanta come for a ride?" he said.

Connie smirked and let her hair fall loose over one shoulder.

"Don'tcha like my car? New paint job," he said. "Hey."

"What?"

"You're cute."

She pretended to fidget, chasing flies away from the door.

"Don'tcha believe me, or what?" he said.

"Look, I don't even know who you are," Connie said in disgust.

"Hey, Ellie's got a radio, see. Mine broke down." He lifted his friend's arm and showed her the little transistor radio the boy was holding, and now Connie began to hear the music. It was the same program that was playing inside the house.

"Bobby King?" she said.

"I listen to him all the time. I think he's great."

"He's kind of great," Connie said reluctantly.

"Listen, that guy's *great*. He knows where the action is."

Connie blushed a little, because the glasses made it impossible for her to see just what this boy was looking at. She couldn't decide if she liked him or if he was just a jerk, and so she dawdled in the doorway and wouldn't come down or go back inside. She said, "What's all that stuff painted on your car?"

"Can'tcha read it?" He opened the door very carefully, as if he were afraid it might fall off. He slid out just as carefully, planting his feet firmly on the ground, the tiny metallic world in his glasses slowing down like gelatine hardening, and in the midst of it Connie's bright green blouse. "This here is my name, to begin with," he said. ARNOLD FRIEND was written in tarlike black letters on the side, with a drawing of a round, grinning face that reminded Connie of a pumpkin, except it wore sunglasses. "I wanta introduce myself, I'm Arnold Friend and that's my real name and I'm gonna be your friend, honey, and inside the car's Ellie Oscar, he's kinda shy." Ellie brought his transistor radio up to his shoulder and balanced it there. "Now, these numbers are a secret code, honey," Arnold Friend explained. He read off the numbers 33, 19, 17 and raised his eyebrows at her to see what she thought of that, but she didn't think much of it. The left rear fender had been smashed and around it was written, on the gleaming gold background: DONE BY CRAZY WOMAN DRIVER. Connie had to laugh at that. Arnold Friend was pleased at her laughter and looked up at her. "Around the other side's a lot more — you wanta come and seem them?"

"No."

"Why not?"

"Why should I?"

"Don'tcha wanta see what's on the car? Don'tcha wanta go for a ride?"

"I don't know."

"Why not?"

"I got things to do."

"Like what?"

"Things."

He laughed as if she had said something funny. He slapped his thighs. He was standing in a strange way, leaning back against the car as if he were balancing himself. He wasn't tall, only an inch or so taller than she would be if she came down to him. Connie liked the way he was dressed, which was the way all of them dressed: tight faded jeans stuffed into black, scuffed boots, a belt that pulled his waist in and showed how lean he was, and a white pullover shirt that was a little soiled and showed the hard small muscles of his arms and shoulders. He looked as if he probably did hard work, lifting and carrying things. Even his neck looked muscular. And his face was a familiar face, somehow: the jaw and chin and cheeks slightly darkened because he hadn't shaved for a day or two, and the nose long and hawklike, sniffing as if she were a treat he was going to gobble up and it was all a joke.

"Connie, you ain't telling the truth. This is your day set aside for a ride with me and you know it," he said, still laughing. The way he straightened and recovered from his fit of laughing showed that it had been all fake.

"How do you know what my name is?" she said suspiciously.

"It's Connie."

"Maybe and maybe not."

"I know my Connie," he said, wagging his finger. Now she remembered him even better, back at the restaurant, and her cheeks warmed at the thought of how she had sucked in her breath just at the moment she passed him — how she must have looked to him. And he had remembered her. "Ellie and I come out here especially for you," he said. "Ellie can sit in back. How about it?"

"Where?"

"Where what?"

"Where're we going?"

He looked at her. He took off the sunglasses and she saw how pale the skin around his eyes was, like holes that were not in shadow but instead in light. His eyes were like chips of broken glass that catch the light in an amiable way. He smiled. It was as if the idea of going for a ride somewhere, to someplace, was a new idea to him.

"Just for a ride, Connie sweetheart."

"I never said my name was Connie," she said.

"But I know what it is. I know your name and all about you, lots of things," Arnold Friend said. He had not moved yet but stood still leaning back against the side of his jalopy. "I took a special interest in you, such a pretty girl, and found out all about you — like I know your parents and sister are gone somewheres and I know where and how long they're going to be gone, and I know who you were with last night, and your best girl friend's name is Betty. Right?"

He spoke in a simple lilting voice, exactly as if he were reciting the words to a song. His smile assured her that everything was fine. In the car Ellie turned up the volume on his radio and did not bother to look around at them.

"Ellie can sit in the back seat," Arnold Friend said. He indicated his friend with a casual jerk of his chin, as if Ellie did not count and she should not bother with him.

"How'd you find out all that stuff?" Connie said.

"Listen: Betty Schultz and Tony Fitch and Jimmy Pettinger and Nancy Pettinger," he said in a chant. "Raymond Stanley and Bob Hutter —"

"Do you know all those kids?"

"I know everybody."

"Look, you're kidding. You're not from around here."

"Sure."

"But — how come we never saw you before?"

"Sure you saw me before," he said. He looked down at his boots, as if he were a little offended. "You just don't remember."

"I guess I'd remember you," Connie said.

"Yeah?" He looked up at this, beaming. He was pleased. He began to mark time with the music from Ellie's radio, tapping his fists lightly together. Connie looked away from his smile to the car, which was painted so bright it almost hurt her eyes to look at it. She looked at that name, ARNOLD FRIEND. And up at the front fender was an expression that was famil-iar — MAN THE FLYING SAUCERS. It was an expression kids had used the year be-fore but didn't use this year. She looked at it for a while as if the words meant something to her that she did not yet know.

"What're you thinking about? Huh?" Arnold Friend demanded. "Not worried about your hair blowing around in the car, are you?"

"No."

"Think I maybe can't drive good?"

"How do I know?"

"You're a hard girl to handle. How come?" he said. "Don't you know I'm your friend? Didn't you see me put my sign in the air when you walked by?"

"What sign?"

"My sign." And he drew an X in the air, leaning out toward her. They were maybe ten feet apart. After his hand fell back to his side the X was still in the air, almost visible. Connie let the screen door close and stood per-fectly still inside it, listening to the music from her radio and the boy's blend together. She stared at Arnold Friend. He stood there so stiffly relaxed, pre-tending to be relaxed, with one hand idly on the door handle as if he were keeping himself up that way and had no intention of ever moving again. She recognized most things about him, the tight jeans that showed his thighs and buttocks and the greasy leather boots and the tight shirt, and even that slippery friendly smile of his, that sleepy dreamy smile that all the boys used to get across ideas they didn't want to put into words. She recognized all this and also the singsong way he talked, slightly mocking, kidding, but serious and a little melancholy, and she recognized the way he tapped one fist against the other in homage to the perpetual music behind him. But all these things did not come together.

She said suddenly, "Hey, how old are you?"

His smile faded. She could see then that he wasn't a kid, he was much older — thirty, maybe more. At this knowledge her heart began to pound faster.

"That's a crazy thing to ask. Can'tcha see I'm your own age?"

"Like hell you are."

"Or maybe a coupla years older. I'm eighteen."

"Eighteen?" she said doubtfully.

He grinned to reassure her and lines appeared at the corners of his mouth. His teeth were big and white. He grinned so broadly his eyes became slits and she saw how thick the lashes were, thick and black as if painted with a black tarlike material. Then, abruptly, he seemed to become embar-rassed and looked over his shoulder at Ellie. "*Him*, he's crazy," he said. "Ain't he a riot? He's a nut, a real character." Ellie was still listening to the music. His sunglasses told nothing about what he was thinking. He wore a bright orange shirt unbuttoned halfway to show his chest, which was a pale, bluish chest and not muscular like Arnold Friend's. His shirt collar was turned up all around and the very tips of the collar pointed out past his chin as if they were protecting him. He was pressing the transistor radio up against his ear and sat there in a kind of daze, right in the sun.

"He's kinda strange," Connie said.

"Hey, she says you're kinda strange! Kinda strange!" Arnold Friend cried. He pounded on the car to get Ellie's attention. Ellie turned for the first time and Connie saw with shock that he wasn't a kid either—he had a fair, hairless face, cheeks reddened slightly as if the veins grew too close to the surface of his skin, the face of a forty-year-old baby. Connie felt a wave of dizziness rise in her at this sight and she stared at him as if waiting for something to change the shock of the moment, make it all right again. Ellie's lips kept shaping words, mumbling along with the words blasting in his ear.

"Maybe you two better go away," Connie said faintly.

"What? How come?" Arnold Friend cried. "We come out here to take you for a ride. It's Sunday." He had the voice of the man on the radio now. It was the same voice, Connie thought. "Don'tcha know it's Sunday all day? And honey, no matter who you were with last night, today you're with Arnold Friend and don't you forget it! Maybe you better step out here," he said, and this last was in a different voice. It was a little flatter, as if the heat was finally getting to him.

"No. I got things to do."

"Hey."

"You two better leave."

"We ain't leaving until you come with us."

"Like hell I am—"

"Connie, don't fool around with me. I mean—I mean, don't fool *around*," he said, shaking his head. He laughed incredulously. He placed his sunglasses on top of his head, carefully, as if he were indeed wearing a wig, and brought the stems down behind his ears. Connie stared at him, another wave of dizziness and fear rising in her so that for a moment he wasn't even in focus but was just a blur standing there against his gold car, and she had the idea that he had driven up the driveway all right but had come from nowhere before that and belonged nowhere and that everything about him and even about the music that was so familiar to her was only half real.

"If my father comes and sees you—"

"He ain't coming. He's at a barbecue."

"How do you know that?"

"Aunt Tillie's. Right now they're—uh—they're drinking. Sitting around," he said vaguely, squinting as if he were staring all the way to town and over to Aunt Tillie's back yard. Then the vision seemed to get clear and he nodded energetically. "Yeah. Sitting around. There's your sister in a blue dress, huh? And high heels, the poor sad bitch—nothing like you, sweetheart! And your mother's helping some fat woman with the corn, they're cleaning the corn—husking the corn—"

"What fat woman?" Connie cried.

"How do I know what fat woman, I don't know every goddamn fat woman in the world!" Arnold Friend laughed.

"Oh, that's Mrs. Hornsby. . . . Who invited her?" Connie said. She felt a little lightheaded. Her breath was coming quickly.

"She's too fat. I don't like them fat. I like them the way you are, honey," he said, smiling sleepily at her. They stared at each other for a while through the screen door. He said softly, "Now, what you're going to do is this: you're going to come out that door. You're going to sit up front with me and Ellie's going to sit in the back, the hell with Ellie, right? This isn't Ellie's date. You're my date. I'm your lover, honey."

"What? You're crazy—"

"Yes, I'm your lover. You don't know what that is but you will," he said. "I know that too. I know all about you. But look: it's real nice and you couldn't ask for nobody better than me, or more polite. I always keep my word. I'll tell you how it is, I'm always nice at first, the first time. I'll hold you so tight you won't think you have to try to get away or pretend anything because you'll know you can't. And I'll come inside you where it's all secret and you'll give in to me and you'll love me—"

"Shut up! You're crazy!" Connie said. She backed away from the door. She put her hands up against her ears as if she'd heard something terrible, something not meant for her. "People don't talk like that, you're crazy," she muttered. Her heart was almost too big now for her chest and its pumping made sweat break out all over her. She looked out to see Arnold Friend pause and then take a step toward the porch, lurching. He almost fell. But, like a clever drunken man, he managed to catch his balance. He wobbled in his high boots and grabbed hold of one of the porch posts.

"Honey?" he said. "You still listening?"

"Get the hell out of here!"

"Be nice, honey. Listen."

"I'm going to call the police—"

He wobbled again and out of the side of his mouth came a fast spat curse, an aside not meant for her to hear. But even this "Christ!" sounded forced. Then he began to smile again. She watched this smile come, awkward as if he were smiling from inside a mask. His whole face was a mask, she thought wildly, tanned down to his throat but then running out as if he had plastered makeup on his face but had forgotten about his throat.

"Honey—? Listen, here's how it is. I always tell the truth and I promise you this: I ain't coming in that house after you."

"You better not! I'm going to call the police if you—if you don't—"

"Honey," he said, talking right through her voice, "honey, I'm not coming in there but you are coming out here. You know why?"

She was panting. The kitchen looked like a place she had never seen before, some room she had run inside but that wasn't good enough, wasn't going to help her. The kitchen window had never had a curtain, after three years, and there were dishes in the sink for her to do — probably — and if you ran your hand across the table you'd probably feel something sticky there.

"You listening, honey? Hey?"

"— going to call the police —"

"Soon as you touch the phone I don't need to keep my promise and can come inside. You won't want that."

She rushed forward and tried to lock the door. Her fingers were shaking. "But why lock it," Arnold Friend said gently, talking right into her face. "It's just a screen door. It's just nothing." One of his boots was at a strange angle, as if his foot wasn't in it. It pointed out to the left, bent at the ankle. "I mean, anybody can break through a screen door and glass and wood and iron or anything else if he needs to, anybody at all, and specially Arnold Friend. If the place got lit up with a fire, honey, you'd come runnin' out into my arms, right into my arms an' safe at home — like you knew I was your lover and'd stopped fooling around." Part of those words were spoken with a slight rhythmic lilt, and Connie somehow recognized them — the echo of a song from last year, about a girl rushing into her boy friend's arms and coming home again —

Connie stood barefoot on the linoleum floor, staring at him. "What do you want?" she whispered.

"I want you," he said.

"What?"

"Seen you that night and thought, that's the one, yes sir. I never needed to look anymore."

"But my father's coming back. He's coming to get me. I had to wash my hair first —" She spoke in a dry, rapid voice, hardly raising it for him to hear.

"No, your daddy is not coming and yes, you had to wash your hair and you washed it for me. It's nice and shining and all for me. I thank you sweetheart," he said with a mock bow, but again he almost lost his balance. He had to bend and adjust his boots. Evidently his feet did not go all the way down; the boots must have been stuffed with something so that he would seem taller. Connie stared out at him and behind him at Ellie in the car, who seemed to be looking off toward Connie's right, into nothing. This Ellie said, pulling the words out of the air one after another as if he were just discovering them, "You want me to pull out the phone?"

"Shut your mouth and keep it shut," Arnold Friend said, his face red from bending over or maybe from embarrassment because Connie had seen his boots. "This ain't none of your business."

"What — what are you doing? What do you want?" Connie said. "If I call the police they'll get you, they'll arrest you —"

"Promise was not to come in unless you touch that phone, and I'll keep that promise," he said. He resumed his erect position and tried to force his shoulders back. He sounded like a hero in a movie, declaring something important. But he spoke too loudly and it was as if he were speaking to someone behind Connie. "I ain't made plans for coming in that house where I don't belong but just for you to come out to me, the way you should. Don't you know who I am?"

"You're crazy," she whispered. She backed away from the door but did not want to go into another part of the house, as if this would give him permission to come through the door. "What do you . . . you're crazy, you. . . ."

"Huh? What're you saying, honey?"

Her eyes darted everywhere in the kitchen. She could not remember what it was, this room.

"This is how it is, honey: you come out and we'll drive away, have a nice ride. But if you don't come out we're gonna wait till your people come home and then they're all going to get it."

"You want that telephone pulled out?" Ellie said. He held the radio away from his ear and grimaced, as if without the radio the air was too much for him.

"I toldja shut up, Ellie," Arnold Friend said, "you're deaf, get a hearing aid, right? Fix yourself up. This little girl's no trouble and's gonna be nice to me, so Ellie keep to yourself, this ain't your date — right? Don't hem in on me, don't hog, don't crush, don't bird dog, don't trail me," he said in a rapid, meaningless voice, as if he were running through all the expressions he'd learned but was no longer sure which of them was in style, then rushing on to new ones, making them up with his eyes closed. "Don't crawl under my fence, don't squeeze in my chipmunk hole, don't sniff my glue, suck my popsicle, keep your own greasy fingers on yourself!" He shaded his eyes and peered in at Connie, who was backed against the kitchen table. "Don't mind him, honey, he's just a creep. He's a dope. Right? I'm the boy for you and like I said, you come out here nice like a lady and give me your hand, and nobody else gets hurt, I mean, your nice old bald-headed daddy and your mummy and your sister in her high heels. Because listen: why bring them in this?"

"Leave me alone," Connie whispered.

"Hey, you know that old woman down the road, the one with the chickens and stuff — you know her?"

"She's dead!"

"Dead? What? You know her?" Arnold Friend said.

"She's dead —"

"Don't you like her?"

"She's dead — she's — she isn't here any more —"

"But don't you like her, I mean, you got something against her? Some grudge or something?" Then his voice dipped as if he were conscious of a rudeness. He touched the sunglasses perched up on top of his head as if to make sure they were still there. "Now, you be a good girl."

"What are you going to do?"

"Just two things, or maybe three," Arnold Friend said. "But I promise it won't last long and you'll like me the way you get to like people you're close to. You will. It's all over for you here, so come on out. You don't want your people in any trouble, do you?"

She turned and bumped against a chair or something, hurting her leg, but she ran into the back room and picked up the telephone. Something roared in her ear, a tiny roaring, and she was so sick with fear that she could do nothing but listen to it—the telephone was clammy and very heavy and her fingers groped down to the dial but were too weak to touch it. She began to scream into the phone, into the roaring. She cried out, she cried for her mother, she felt her breath start jerking back and forth in her lungs as if it were something Arnold Friend was stabbing her with again and again with no tenderness. A noisy sorrowful wailing rose all about her and she was locked inside it the way she was locked inside this house.

After a while she could hear again. She was sitting on the floor with her wet back against the wall.

Arnold Friend was saying from the door, "That's a good girl. Put the phone back."

She kicked the phone away from her.

"No, honey. Pick it up. Put it back right."

She picked it up and put it back. The dial tone stopped.

"That's a good girl. Now, you come outside."

She was hollow with what had been fear but what was now just an emptiness. All that screaming had blasted it out of her. She sat, one leg cramped under her, and deep inside her brain was something like a pinpoint of light that kept going and would not let her relax. She thought, I'm not going to see my mother again. She thought, I'm not going to sleep in my bed again. Her bright green blouse was all wet.

Arnold Friend said, in a gentle-loud voice that was like a stage voice, "The place where you came from ain't there any more, and where you had in mind to go is cancelled out. This place you are now—inside your daddy's house—is nothing but a cardboard box I can knock down any time. You know that and always did know it. You hear me?"

She thought, I have got to think. I have got to know what to do.

"We'll go out to a nice field, out in the country here where it smells so nice and it's sunny," Arnold Friend said. "I'll have my arms tight around you so you won't need to try to get away and I'll show you what love is like, what it does. The hell with this house! It looks solid all right," he said. He ran a fingernail down the screen and the noise did not make Connie shiver, as it would have the day before. "Now, put your hand on your heart, honey. Feel that? That feels solid too but we know better. Be nice to me, be sweet like you can because what else is there for a girl like you but to be sweet and pretty and give in?—and get away before her people come back?"

She felt her pounding heart. Her hand seemed to enclose it. She thought for the first time in her life that it was nothing that was hers, that belonged to her, but just a pounding, living thing inside this body that wasn't really hers either.

"You don't want them to get hurt," Arnold Friend went on. "Now, get up, honey. Get up all by yourself."

She stood.

"Now, turn this way. That's right. Come over here to me.—Ellie, put that away, didn't I tell you? You dope. You miserable creepy dope," Arnold Friend said. His words were not angry but only part of an incantation. The incantation was kindly. "Now, come out through the kitchen to me, honey, and let's see a smile, try it, you're a brave, sweet little girl and now they're eating corn and hot dogs cooked to bursting over an outdoor fire, and they don't know one thing about you and never did and honey, you're better than them because not a one of them would have done this for you."

Connie felt the linoleum under her feet; it was cool. She brushed her hair back out of her eyes. Arnold Friend let go of the post tentatively and opened his arms for her, his elbows pointing in toward each other and his wrists limp, to show that this was an embarrassed embrace and a little mocking, he didn't want to make her self-conscious.

She put out her hand against the screen. She watched herself push the door slowly open as if she were back safe somewhere in the other doorway, watching this body and this head of long hair moving out into the sunlight where Arnold Friend waited.

"My sweet little blue-eyed girl," he said in a half-sung sigh that had nothing to do with her brown eyes but was taken up just the same by the vast sunlit reaches of the land behind him and on all sides of him—so much land that Connie had never seen before and did not recognize except to know that she was going to it.

APPROACHING THE READING

1. Look closely at the way the story begins—at the first sentence and the first paragraph, for example—and think about what effect they have on you.

2. Pick out the steps in the story's development—outline the plot development. Why do you think the story includes the paragraphs about June, about trips to the mall, about evenings with Eddie and other friends? The plot changes direction with the seemingly harmless phrase "One Sunday Connie got up at eleven" (p. 78). Notice the way the encounter with Arnold Friend is organized to make it build in intensity and suspense.

3. Oates says the story grew out of reading about an actual serial rapist and murderer in Arizona. The story ends with Connie going out the door to join Arnold Friend. What do you assume would have happened next, if the story hadn't ended there? Why do you think the author chose not to continue the story further? In what ways might stopping there indicate what is of greatest interest or importance for the story, and what is not of central interest or importance?

4. Describe the main characters and comment on the techniques and approaches through which we come to know them. Are they round or flat? Are they static or dynamic? Consider characters' names and how they contribute to the story.

5. The story is dedicated to singer and composer Bob Dylan. References to music appear frequently in the story. Consider what these references say and what they contribute to effect and theme. If you aren't familiar with Bob Dylan's music, listen to some and do some research on him. Is his music the kind that "made everything so good" for Connie? Does the Dylan reference relate to the story, or is it simply an honorific dedication?

6. Suggest two or three different ways the title could relate to the story.

RESPONDING THROUGH WRITING

Journal Entries

1. Experiment with the basic principles of plot construction by writing a plot analysis of a TV show or a movie: its beginning, its handling of gaps, its use of flashbacks, its rising action or development (look for conflict, suspense, foreshadowing, and repetitions), and its ending. Apply the ABDCE steps to it (see p. 63). Write a journal entry summarizing the result and discussing whether, how, and why basic aspects of plot are the same everywhere.

2. Choose a crucial event from your past. In a journal entry, outline it as a plot. Consider what you need to include and what you can leave out, what order would be most effective for presenting it, and so on. Add a few sentences pointing out the techniques you bring in and discussing what you learn about plot construction.

> **www**
> Research the authors in this chapter with LitLinks, or take a quiz on the stories with LitQuiz, at bedfordstmartins.com/approachinglit.

3. Write an analysis of characterization techniques in a TV show or a movie: Look for how telling, showing, what a character says and what other characters say about her or him, conveying a character's thoughts, and the way she or he is named are used to reveal character. Consider which characters are round and which are flat. Write a journal entry summarizing the result and discussing whether, how, and why basic aspects of characterization are similar across different genres.

Literary Analysis Papers

4. Write a paper on the importance and handling of gaps in the plotting of Louise Erdrich's "The Red Convertible" (p. 67).

5. Write a paper examining relation of plot construction to title in Toni Morrison's "Recitatif" (p. 300) or Bharati Mukherjee's "Orbiting" (p. 315).

6. Write a paper discussing characterization techniques in Gish Jen's "Who's Irish?" (p. 272), Katherine Anne Porter's "The Jilting of Granny Weatherall" (p. 364), or Salman Rushdie's "The Prophet's Hair" (p. 442).

Making Connections

7. Write a paper comparing and contrasting Arnold Friend in Joyce Carol Oates's "Where Are You Going, Where Have You Been?" (p. 75) and the Misfit in Flannery O'Connor's "A Good Man Is Hard to Find" (p. 341).

8. Write a paper discussing how Tim O'Brien's "The Things They Carried" (p. 327) could be used to fill gaps left in Louise Erdrich's "The Red Convertible" (p. 67).

Cultural Criticism Papers

9. In the United States and many other societies, cars carry a lot of cultural importance. Write a paper on the place of cars in Dagoberto Gilb's "Love in L.A." (p. 55), Louise Erdrich's "The Red Convertible" (p. 67), Joyce Carol Oates's "Where Are You Going, Where Have You Been?" (p. 75), and your own experience. Consider what types of cars carry various meanings for different cultures. How do cars embody distinctions, and at times conflicts, between cultures? Consider ironies you find in this "car culture."

10. Henry's experiences on leaving the reservation to enter basic training and then on going to Vietnam for active service are not covered in Louise Erdrich's "The Red Convertible" (p. 67) because of the point of view. But they remain very much a part of the story. Do some reading about what Native Americans often encounter when they leave the reservation and about what military action in Vietnam was like. Then write a paper describing what Henry's experiences probably were like and why he had changed the way he did when he returned.

RESPONDING THROUGH THE ARTS

1. Respond to the references to Bob Dylan and to music in Joyce Carol Oates's "Where Are You Going, Where Have You Been?" (p. 75) by preparing a sound track to accompany the story.

2. Draw or paint a series of portraits of several characters from Sandra Cisneros's "The House on Mango Street" (p. 91), Joyce Carol Oates's "Where Are You Going, Where Have You Been?" (p. 75), or another story of your choice.

Point of View and Theme

This book is about *reading* literature, specifically reading in the interactive manner described in Chapters 1 and 2. But reading literature differs from most other reading: It is often more like listening to someone, more like hearing a voice, than what we usually think of as reading. You've probably heard the phrase "seeing with the mind's eye"; you can also hear with the mind's ear. Responding fully to literature requires training the ear so you can enjoy and benefit from hearing many voices from a variety of places and cultures. This chapter focuses on *voice* in stories, particularly as it is affected by the perspective from which the story is told, and on the way stories give voice to a central idea or *theme*.

Using your "mind's ear," listen to the following story as if it were being spoken directly to you. It is the first in a series of forty-six connected stories, or a *collective story,* told by a young girl, Esperanza Cordero, growing up in a Latino section of Chicago and seeking both to escape that world and to find herself.

Sandra Cisneros b. 1954

The House on Mango Street   [1983]

We didn't always live on Mango Street. Before that we lived on Loomis on the third floor, and before that we lived on Keeler. Before Keeler it was Paulina, and before that I can't remember. But what I remember most is moving a lot. Each time it seemed there'd be one more of us. By the time we got to Mango Street we were six—Mama, Papa, Carlos, Kiki, my sister Nenny and me.

The house on Mango Street is ours, and we don't have to pay rent to anybody, or share the yard with the people downstairs, or be careful not to make too much noise, and there isn't a landlord banging on the ceiling with a broom. But even so, it's not the house we'd thought we'd get.

We had to leave the flat on Loomis quick. The water pipes broke and the landlord wouldn't fix them because the house was too old. We had to leave fast. We were using the washroom next door and carrying water over in empty milk gallons. That's why Mama and Papa looked for a house, and that's why we moved into the house on Mango Street, far away, on the other side of town.

They always told us that one day we would move into a house, a real house that would be ours for always so we wouldn't have to move each year. And our house would have running water and pipes that worked. And inside it would have real stairs, not hallway stairs, but stairs inside like the houses on TV. And we'd have a basement and at least three washrooms so when we took a bath we wouldn't have to tell everybody. Our house would be white with trees around it, a great big yard and grass growing without a fence. This was the house Papa talked about when he held a lottery ticket and this was the house Mama dreamed up in the stories she told us before we went to bed.

But the house on Mango Street is not the way they told it at all. It's small and red with tight steps in front and windows so small you'd think they were holding their breath. Bricks are crumbling in places, and the front door is so swollen you have to push hard to get in. There is no front yard, only four little elms the city planted by the curb. Out back is a small garage for the car we don't own yet and a small yard that looks smaller between the two buildings on either side. There are stairs in our house, but they're ordinary hallway stairs, and the house has only one washroom. Everybody has to share a bedroom—Mama and Papa, Carlos and Kiki, me and Nenny.

Once when we were living on Loomis, a nun from my school passed by and saw me playing out front. The laundromat downstairs had been boarded up because it had been robbed two days before and the owner had painted on the wood YES WE'RE OPEN so as not to lose business.

Where do you live? she asked.

There, I said pointing up to the third floor.

You live *there*?

There. I had to look to where she pointed—the third floor, the paint peeling, wooden bars Papa had nailed on the windows so we wouldn't fall out. You live *there*? The way she said it made me feel like nothing. *There.* I lived *there.* I nodded.

I knew then I had to have a house. A real house. One I could point to. But this isn't it. The house on Mango Street isn't it. For the time being, Mama says. Temporary, says Papa. But I know how those things go.

APPROACHING THE READING

1. Describe the voice you hear in "The House on Mango Street." How old do you imagine the speaker is? What makes you think that? What else can you tell about her from the way she sounds as you listen to her?

2. What is the effect of having the voice and perspective be that of Esperanza? How do you think the story would differ if told by Esperanza's mother? Her father? One of her brothers?

> Research this author in depth with cultural documents and multimedia resources on *LiterActive*.

3. Considering the story as a whole, what central point comes through as you listen to what Esperanza says?

NARRATOR

As you read a work of fiction, one of the first things to listen for is who is telling, or narrating, the story. "The House on Mango Street" is told by a character in the story, or a **first-person narrator**. The *I* in any story, however, should *not* be assumed to be the author: The **narrator** in a story always is a *narrative construct,* an imagined speaker created by the writer.

True, many details about Esperanza's life parallels the author's: Cisneros was born in Chicago; was part of a large family (six brothers, no sisters); moved often during her childhood between Chicago and Mexico, where her father was born; and shared Esperanza's sense of dislocation and a lack of permanence. However, Cisneros was not writing an autobiographical essay, the way Sherman Alexie did in "Superman and Me" (p. 4). She clearly drew upon her own experiences as she wrote, but she used her imagination to alter the facts of her own life and to invent new ones. She constructed a character as the narrator, one who takes part in, as well as relates, the story. The story's power depends on hearing it from a child's perspective. We, as readers older than Esperanza is, can see implications in her story that she is not aware of yet, about poverty, class distinctions, housing patterns, and the power of landlords.

A first-person narrator who seems to speak directly for the author is often referred to as a **persona**: the "character" projected by the author, the *I* of a narrative poem or novel, or the speaker whose voice is heard in a lyric poem. Even if a first-person narrator seems to speak directly for the author or is given the author's name, the speaker created by the words of the story is not identical to the real-life author who writes the words.

POINT OF VIEW

The way a story is narrated is part of its **point of view**, the approach used in presenting the events of the story. Point of view usually includes a *person* and a *perspective*. Consideration of point of view starts with listening to who is telling the story: Is it being told in first person or third person (or, rarely, in second person)? Is the narrator given a name, or is the narrator an unnamed, unidentified voice relating what happens from above or outside the events? You cannot always identify a specific person as the narrator, but you usually can discern the narrator's relation to the action. Does the narrator participate in the action as a major or minor character, or does she or he observe the action, looking on from the outside?

Listening for the complexity of point of view continues with paying attention to the *perspective* from which the story is told. The narrator inevitably relates the story from a certain vantage point. To get the most from a story, it is important to determine what that vantage point is. Think of it in terms of camera angle in cinema: The camera can pull back and let you see everything, showing the scene from the outside ("objectively"), or it can seem to enter the mind of a particular character and show you only what that character sees and the way she or he sees it ("subjectively"). The film can show us one side of the events by focusing on one character or group of characters, or it can show two or more sides of the events by focusing alternately between characters or groups. Thus, a cops-and-robbers film shown from the perspective of the robbers looks very different from one presented from the perspective of the cops. And some films take advantage of that by moving back and forth between the two. Point of view matters — a lot.

The same is true in fiction. You can be told everything from both outside and inside the characters and events so that you know all that happens and the reasons why. Or you can hear everything from the outside but nothing from the inside, so you have to deduce the why (the characters' motivations) for yourself. You can hear about only what one character experiences and know only as much as she or he knows. Or you can be told things from different perspectives as the story progresses, sometimes switching back and forth. (This happens more often in longer works such as novels; with some exceptions, short stories don't have enough room for a lot of switching.) Each perspective has its own rewards and makes its own demands on the reader. Thus, for example, when a story is presented from the perspective of one character, as an active reader you should consider what that story would sound like from the perspective of other characters. Doing so gives you a deeper understanding of the character through whose eyes you are seeing the events as well as, in many cases, of the events themselves.

In fiction, the perspective of time also needs your consideration. Unlike film, which usually shows events as they are occurring, narrative necessarily relates events after they happened (a narrative in present tense would need to use the techniques of a play-by-play announcer at a sports event—but even here the announcer is describing not what *is* happening but what just did happen). As you read actively, therefore, you need to ask if the narrator is looking back to past events. If so, are they recent events or from the distant past? Can you tell how long ago? Does it matter how much time has passed? Does the narrator tell things differently now from the way she or he saw them earlier?

In describing and discussing point of view, you always need to include both a person and a perspective. It's not enough to say a story uses a third-person point of view. You need to add the *perspective* from which the third-person narrative is being presented, in as much precise detail as possible. "The House on Mango Street," for example, uses a first-person limited point of view, told from the perspective of the young girl Esperanza. Here are several possible combinations of point of view and perspective a story can employ.

First-Person Omniscient

Stories using an *I* or *we* are told from a first-person point of view. In rare instances, a first-person narrator is almost omniscient, or all knowing. A story narrated by a god, for example, might be first-person omniscient (though the author of such a story might find it more interesting to depict a god who is limited in knowledge or power). Or a story could have a first-person narrator who talks to all the people involved and learns everything about the events in the story—both what happened and why—and thus is able to describe them from an all-knowing perspective. As readers, then, we listen for a reliable account of what happened and what the people involved are like.

First-Person Limited

Ordinarily, however, a first-person point of view is limited to what the narrator observes, or is told, and is able to understand, like Esperanza in "The House on Mango Street." She knows what the family's dream house would be like, and she knows their present house falls far short of their dreams; but she doesn't understand, until the day the nun sees her playing out front, what the house they live in says about their social situation, and she doesn't realize the kind of economic realities her family is up against. In many cases, a first-person narrator is very knowledgeable about what has happened and why, often because the events happen either to the narrator or in the narrator's presence. But for just that reason, because the narrator is closely involved, the narrator's knowledge and understanding may be limited. The narrator knows what happened to her- or himself or to some other characters, but may not know all that is happening to others related to the events. The narrator may not understand now, or did not understand then, why things happened as they did. She or he may not understand things about her- or himself. Often the narrator is looking back at things that happened much earlier, which she or he did not understand fully at the time but comes to grasp more fully later.

Two specific variations on first-person limited perspectives should be noted. First is the use of a **naïve narrator**, a narrator too young or too inexperienced to understand fully the implications of what she or he is talking about. In such cases, active reading is even more important than usual, as the reader — who understands more than the narrator — must fill in implications the narrator cannot grasp. Such is the case in "The House on Mango Street": Much of the power of the story comes from our ability to understand the reasons behind Esperanza's pains and disappointments, even though she is not fully aware of them.

The other variation involves the use of a narrator who is not completely trustworthy. If the narrator tells her or his story accurately and honestly (as far as we can tell), the story has a **reliable narrator**: We can believe or rely on what she or he says. But in some cases, we may suspect that a narrator is not telling the whole truth or is distorting some things, perhaps deliberately to make them look better or unintentionally because they are too painful to face. The narrator may not have the mental capacity to provide a coherent account of events, or she or he may have prejudices (against a race or class, or against a particular individual in the story) that the reader perceives even though the narrator is unaware of them. The narrator may want to make her- or himself look better; the narrator in Gish Jen's "Who's Irish?" does just that (see pp. 272–80). In all these cases, the narrator is **unreliable**: We can't trust everything she or he says. Here active reading is even more essential because you must try to determine what you can take straightforwardly and where you need to raise questions and make allowances for or corrections in what you are being told.

Third-Person Omniscient

With an all-knowing, or **omniscient**, point of view, the narrator seems very much like the author, knowing everything that happens and why it happens (though not necessarily telling everything she or he knows), able to see into the minds and hearts of all the characters. But this can be a risky technique, because the characters can seem mere puppets. For an example of where it is handled well, look at Zora Neale Hurston's "Sweat" (p. 263): Things are shown sometimes from the perspective of Delia Jones, sometimes from that of the men sitting in front of the village store, and sometimes from that of Sykes, the husband who abuses Delia. At some points, we are able to look into Delia's consciousness ("A great terror took hold of her" — p. 263), and at times into that of her husband ("Inside, Sykes heard nothing until he knocked a pot lid off the stove while trying to reach the match safe in the dark" — p. 271).

Third-Person Objective

A third-person objective point of view differs in a crucial way from that of third-person omniscient. The narrator does not look into the mind of any of the characters or explain why any of the characters do what they do. The narrator describes events only from the outside, leaving it to the reader to draw conclusions from the details and dialogue provided. The invisible narrator in Ernest Hemingway's "Hills Like White Elephants" (p. 120), for example, simply describes where two characters are and what they do, and relates what they say to each other, never looking into their thoughts or commenting on or explaining what is going on between them.

Third-Person Limited

Third-person limited uses a narrator who is omniscient in some areas or to some extent, but is not completely all knowing. Such a narrator is described as having **limited omniscience**. Typically, the narrator knows everything about one character, including her or his thoughts and motivations (omniscient), and tells the story from that character's perspective while not being able to see into the minds or feelings of other characters (limited). "The Man to Send Rain Clouds" by Leslie Marmon Silko (p. 377), for example, is told from Leon's perspective: We follow where he goes, see what he sees, and at times enter his mind ("[The priest's] voice was distant, and Leon thought that his blue eyes looked tired" — p. 380); but we do not enter the priest's mind — we are aware of his inner struggle and misgivings only through what Leon sees (the priest's weariness, his hesitation) and what Leon hears him say. Or the narrator may know everything about some events in the story but not about other, related events. This is true in William Faulkner's "A Rose for Emily" (p. 108), where the townspeople know what goes on outside Miss Emily's house but not (until after she dies) what goes on inside.

A widely used variant on the third-person limited point of view is a **center of consciousness** perspective. In it, the narrator relates the story in the third person but does so through what is thought, felt, seen, and experienced by one of the characters. We are shown only what that character is conscious of; we are not given external, objective views, the way a perspective limited in other ways can. The character may be the central character or a minor character, an observer or a participant, but only that character's perceptions, thoughts, and feelings are shown. However, an author usually mixes some third-person limited external narration with center of consciousness, moving back and forth between them, as for example in "Where Are You Going, Where Have You Been?" (p. 75). The first two sentences of the opening paragraph are external, objective statements of fact, and such statements are interspersed throughout the story. In the third sentence, we enter Connie's consciousness and hear what she thinks about her mother and how and why her mother treats her as she does. Much of the rest of the story comes through Connie's consciousness.

> Her name was Connie. She was fifteen and she had a quick, nervous gig-gling habit of craning her neck to glance into mirrors or checking other people's faces to make sure her own was all right. Her mother, who noticed everything and knew everything and who hadn't much reason any longer to look at her own face, always scolded Connie about it. (p. 75)

Stream of Consciousness

A story, or parts of a story, can be told by conveying the continuous flow of what passes through the mind (consciousness) of a character. This in-cludes sense perceptions, thoughts, memories, and feelings — the total sense of awareness and the mental and emotional response to it. This approach is referred to as **stream of consciousness**. It should not be confused with the approach described just above: A *center of consciousness* story can use a *stream of consciousness* approach, but it doesn't need to. Usually, to capture the fact that much mental activity is nonverbal, stream of consciousness adopts a special style of writing. Often it does not use ordinary punctua-tion or complete sentences (after all, we don't always think in complete sentences), is associative rather than logical, and seems disjointed and hap-hazard. It is an unstructured, even at times chaotic, flow of random sense perceptions, mental pictures, sounds, thoughts, and details — an attempt to represent prerational mental activity before the mind orders it into a coher-ent form or shape.

Realizing that an author has selected these seemingly random thoughts and perceptions, an active reader must make connections between them and find a meaning the character is usually unaware of. Here, for example, is a stream of consciousness passage from James Joyce's novel *Ulysses* (1922), as the main character Leopold Bloom strolls through Dublin, with his mind absorbing impressions and connecting them to random thoughts and mem-ories: "Pineapple rock, lemon platt, butter scotch. A sugar-sticky girl shovel-ing scoopfuls of creams for a christian brother. Some school great. Bad for their tummies. Lozenge and comfit manufacturer to His Majesty the King. God. Save. Our. Sitting on his throne, sucking red jujubes white."

A technique often used in presenting stream of consciousness is **inte-rior monologue**. A *monologue* in drama is an extended, uninterrupted speech by a single speaker; an *interior monologue* is such a speech occurring within a character's mind. It is the representation of unspoken mental ac-tivity — thoughts, impressions, and memories — as if directly overheard by the reader without being selected and organized by a narrator. It can be the associative, disjointed, nonlogical, nongrammatical flow of stream of con-sciousness. Or it can be a more logical, grammatical flow of thoughts and memories moving through a person's mind, as if being spoken to an exter-nal listener (the way we rehearse in our minds what we plan to say to some-one later, but digress along the way, following things we are reminded of before getting back to the topic at hand).

In Tillie Olsen's "I Stand Here Ironing," for example, the narrator, while doing her ironing, runs through her mind what she would like to say, but probably never will, to the school counselor or social worker who asks her to come in to talk about her daughter, who the counselor feels is in need of help: "You think because I am her mother I have a key, or that in some way you could use me as a key? She has lived for nineteen years. There is all that life that has happened outside of me, beyond me" (p. 353). This whole story is an interior monologue. A story or novel, however, can be presented partly through interior monologue or stream of consciousness and partly through another point of view.

THEME

Along with listening for what happens to whom and who tells the story from what perspective, active readers listen for what the story as a whole says, what it is about in the sense of "what it all adds up to." Many people refer to what it all adds up to as the **theme**: the central idea or concept con-veyed by a literary work. The *all* in "what it all adds up to" is important — theme must take everything into account, all the different techniques used in telling the story (everything discussed in Chapters 4 to 7), and all the things that happen to all the characters. In a statement on theme, the *all* should be expressed in two parts: a *subject* and a *predicate* (something about the subject). The subject of "The House on Mango Street" could be said to be a poor immigrant family's search for adequate housing; a statement of the theme might be that a poor immigrant family's search for adequate housing reveals that the effect of inadequate housing goes beyond discomfort and in-convenience to undermining the occupants' sense of respect and self-worth.

Theme can never encompass the work as a whole; it is always less than the work and is never an adequate substitute for the work. Because theme is an artificial abstraction from the work, it has the risk of diminishing reading from a holistic experience, which involves the emotions and imagination as well as the intellect, to an intellectual one only. A good reader does not read simply for theme. Articulating a theme is one of the many ways of respond-ing to a work, but it is not the only or necessarily the most important one.

Theme is always at least somewhat subjective. Works rarely have a single, "right" theme that all readers find and express in the same way. Each of us may find different themes in a rich work of literature, and we may express them in different ways, but that does not mean that every interpretation is equally valid. If someone says the theme of "The House on Mango Street" is the importance of mothers in holding families together through difficult circumstances, there would be good reason to object that such an interpretation is not grounded in the story, that it is more an effort to extract a lesson from the story than to draw together what it all adds up to.

WWW Further explore point of view and theme, including interactive exercises, with VirtuaLit Fiction at bedfordstmartins.com/approachinglit.

Statements of theme must grow out of details in the story, not out of ideas, experiences, or values we bring to the story. Stating a theme should not be thought of as finding a moral or lesson in the work; there may be a lesson, but often a literary work is more interested in depicting human behavior than in judging it or drawing lessons from it. We do not need to agree with characters' beliefs or approve of their actions to enjoy and appreciate the work in which they appear.

☑ CHECKLIST on Point of View and Theme

❑ Notice who is telling the story (the narrator) and the point-of-view (the perspective, or vantage, from which the story is told):

- *First-person omniscient:* an all-knowing *I* or *we*
- *First-person limited:* a partially knowing *I* or *we* (possibly naïve or unreliable)
- *Third-person omniscient:* an all-knowing, often anonymous, reporter
- *Third-person objective:* a reporter of words and actions, not thoughts or motives
- *Third-person limited:* a partially knowing observer or participant (often using a center of consciousness — seeing a story through the consciousness of a particular character)
- *Stream of consciousness:* the seemingly unstructured perceptions, images, and reflections flowing through a mind (sometimes using interior monologue — direct presentation of a character's thoughts and memories, without intervention by a narrator)

❑ Think about a story's theme, the central idea or concept conveyed in the story — what it all adds up to. Be sure the theme you come up with is firmly grounded in the story and that you have specific details to support the theme's presence and importance.

FURTHER READING

The following story takes us back to the 1960s, when African Americans began turning back to Africa in their search for roots and identity, when Afro hairdos, African-influenced clothing, and adoption of African (or Muslim) names to connect with one's heritage were new and startling (especially in the old world of the rural South). As you read it, pay attention to the voice you hear and to the handling of point of view and perspective. Think about the extent to which the way the story "works," the way it achieves its effects, depends on the voice and personality of the narrator.

Alice Walker b. 1944

Everyday Use   [1973]

for your grandmama

I will wait for her in the yard that Maggie and I made so clean and wavy yesterday afternoon. A yard like this is more comfortable than most people know. It is not just a yard. It is like an extended living room. When the hard clay is swept clean as a floor and the fine sand around the edges lined with tiny, irregular grooves, anyone can come and sit and look up into the elm tree and wait for the breezes that never come inside the house.

Maggie will be nervous until after her sister goes: she will stand hopelessly in corners, homely and ashamed of the burn scars down her arms and legs, eyeing her sister with a mixture of envy and awe. She thinks her sister has held life always in the palm of one hand, that "no" is a word the world never learned to say to her.

You've no doubt seen those TV shows where the child who has "made it" is confronted, as a surprise, by her own mother and father, tottering in weakly from backstage. (A pleasant surprise, of course: What would they do if parent and child came on the show only to curse out and insult each other?) On TV mother and child embrace and smile into each other's faces. Sometimes the mother and father weep, the child wraps them in her arms and leans across the table to tell how she would not have made it without their help. I have seen these programs.

Sometimes I dream a dream in which Dee and I are suddenly brought together on a TV program of this sort. Out of a dark and soft-seated limousine I am ushered into a bright room filled with many people. There I meet a smiling, gray, sporty man like Johnny Carson who shakes my hand and tells me what a fine girl I have. Then we are on the stage and Dee is embracing me with tears in her eyes. She pins on my dress a large orchid, even though she has told me once that she thinks orchids are tacky flowers.

In real life I am a large, big-boned woman with rough, man-working hands. In the winter I wear flannel nightgowns to bed and overalls during the day. I can kill and clean a hog as mercilessly as a man. My fat keeps me hot in zero weather. I can work outside all day, breaking ice to get water for washing; I can eat pork liver cooked over the open fire minutes after it comes steaming from the hog. One winter I knocked a bull calf straight in the brain between the eyes with a sledge hammer and had the meat hung up to chill before nightfall. But of course all this does not show on television. I am the way my daughter would want me to be: a hundred pounds lighter, my skin like an uncooked barley pancake. My hair glistens in the hot bright lights. Johnny Carson has much to do to keep up with my quick and witty tongue.

But that is a mistake. I know even before I wake up. Who ever knew a Johnson with a quick tongue? Who can even imagine me looking a strange white man in the eye? It seems to me I have talked to them always with one foot raised in flight, with my head turned in whichever way is farthest from them. Dee, though. She would always look anyone in the eye. Hesitation was no part of her nature.

"How do I look, Mama?" Maggie says, showing just enough of her thin body enveloped in pink skirt and red blouse for me to know she's there, almost hidden by the door.

"Come out into the yard," I say.

Have you ever seen a lame animal, perhaps a dog run over by some careless person rich enough to own a car, sidle up to someone who is ignorant enough to be kind to him? That is the way my Maggie walks. She has been like this, chin on chest, eyes on ground, feet in shuffle, ever since the fire that burned the other house to the ground.

Dee is lighter than Maggie, with nicer hair and a fuller figure. She's a woman now, though sometimes I forget. How long ago was it that the other house burned? Ten, twelve years? Sometimes I can still hear the flames and feel Maggie's arms sticking to me, her hair smoking and her dress falling off her in little black papery flakes. Her eyes seemed stretched open, blazed open by the flames reflected in them. And Dee. I see her standing off under the sweet gum tree she used to dig gum out of; a look of concentration on her face as she watched the last dingy gray board of the house fall in toward the red-hot brick chimney. Why don't you do a dance around the ashes? I'd wanted to ask her. She had hated the house that much.

I used to think she hated Maggie, too. But that was before we raised the money, the church and me, to send her to Augusta to school. She used to read to us without pity; forcing words, lies, other folks' habits, whole lives upon us two, sitting trapped and ignorant underneath her voice. She washed us in a river of make-believe, burned us with a lot of knowledge we didn't necessarily need to know. Pressed us to her with the serious way she read, to shove us away at just the moment, like dimwits, we seemed about to understand.

Dee wanted nice things. A yellow organdy dress to wear to her graduation from high school; black pumps to match a green suit she'd made from an old suit somebody gave me. She was determined to stare down any disaster in her efforts. Her eyelids would not flicker for minutes at a time. Often I fought off the temptation to shake her. At sixteen she had a style of her own: and knew what style was.

I never had an education myself. After second grade the school was closed down. Don't ask my why: in 1927 colored asked fewer questions than they do now. Sometimes Maggie reads to me. She stumbles along good-naturedly but can't see well. She knows she is not bright. Like good looks and money, quickness passed her by. She will marry John Thomas (who has mossy teeth in an earnest face) and then I'll be free to sit here and I guess just sing church songs to myself. Although I never was a good singer. Never could carry a tune. I was always better at a man's job. I used to love to milk till I was hooked in the side in '49. Cows are soothing and slow and don't bother you, unless you try to milk them the wrong way.

I have deliberately turned my back on the house. It is three rooms, just like the one that burned, except the roof is tin; they don't make shingle roofs any more. There are no real windows, just some holes cut in the sides, like the portholes in a ship, but not round and not square, with rawhide holding the shutters up on the outside. This house is in a pasture, too, like the other one. No doubt when Dee sees it she will want to tear it down. She wrote me once that no matter where we "choose" to live, she will manage to come see us. But she will never bring her friends. Maggie and I thought about this and Maggie asked me, "Mama, when did Dee ever *have* any friends?"

She had a few. Furtive boys in pink shirts hanging about on washday after school. Nervous girls who never laughed. Impressed with her they worshiped the well-turned phrase, the cute shape, the scalding humor that erupted like bubbles in lye. She read to them.

When she was courting Jimmy T she didn't have much time to pay to us, but turned all her faultfinding power on him. He *flew* to marry a cheap city girl from a family of ignorant flashy people. She hardly had time to recompose herself.

When she comes I will meet—but there they are!

Maggie attempts to make a dash for the house, in her shuffling way, but I stay her with my hand. "Come back here," I say. And she stops and tries to dig a well in the sand with her toe.

It is hard to see them clearly through the strong sun. But even the first glimpse of leg out of the car tells me it is Dee. Her feet were always neat-looking, as if God himself had shaped them with a certain style. From the other side of the car comes a short, stocky man. Hair is all over his head a foot long and hanging from his chin like a kinky mule tail. I hear Maggie suck in her breath. "Uhnnnh," is what it sounds like. Like when you see the wriggling end of a snake just in front of your foot on the road. "Uhnnnh."

Dee next. A dress down to the ground, in this hot weather. A dress so loud it hurts my eyes. There are yellows and oranges enough to throw back the light of the sun. I feel my whole face warming from the heat waves it throws out. Earrings gold, too, and hanging down to her shoulders. Bracelets dangling and making noises when she moves her arm up to shake the folds of the dress out of her armpits. The dress is loose and flows, and as she walks closer, I like it. I hear Maggie go "Uhnnnh" again. It is her sister's hair. It stands straight up like the wool on a sheep. It is black as night and around the edges are two long pigtails that rope about like small lizards disappearing behind her ears.

"Wa-su-zo-Tean-o!" she says, coming on in that gliding way the dress makes her move. The short stocky fellow with the hair to his navel is all grinning and he follows up with "Asalamalakim, my mother and sister!" He moves to hug Maggie but she falls back, right up against the back of my chair. I feel her trembling there and when I look up I see the perspiration falling off her chin.

"Don't get up," says Dee. Since I am stout it takes something of a push. You can see me trying to move a second or two before I make it. She turns, showing white heels through her sandals, and goes back to the car. Out she peeks next with a Polaroid. She stoops down quickly and lines up picture after picture of me sitting there in front of the house with Maggie cowering behind me. She never takes a shot without making sure the house is included. When a cow comes nibbling around the edge of the yard she snaps it and me and Maggie *and* the house. Then she puts the Polaroid in the back seat of the car, and comes up and kisses me on the forehead.

Meanwhile Asalamalakim is going through motions with Maggie's hand. Maggie's hand is as limp as a fish, and probably as cold, despite the sweat, and she keeps trying to pull it back. It looks like Asalamalakim wants to shake hands but wants to do it fancy. Or maybe he don't know how people shake hands. Anyhow, he soon gives up on Maggie.

"Well," I say. "Dee."

"No, Mama," she says. "Not 'Dee,' Wangero Leewanika Kemanjo!"

"What happened to 'Dee'?" I wanted to know.

"She's dead," Wangero said. "I couldn't bear it any longer, being named after the people who oppress me."

"You know as well as me you was named after your aunt Dicie," I said. Dicie is my sister. She named Dee. We called her "Big Dee" after Dee was born.

"But who was *she* named after?" asked Wangero.

"I guess after Grandma Dee," I said.

"And who was she named after?" asked Wangero.

"Her mother," I said, and saw Wangero was getting tired. "That's about as far back as I can trace it," I said. Though, in fact, I probably could have carried it back beyond the Civil War through the branches.

"Well," said Asalamalakim, "there you are."

"Uhnnnh," I heard Maggie say.

"There I was not," I said, "before 'Dicie' cropped up in our family, so why should I try to trace it that far back?"

He just stood there grinning, looking down on me like somebody inspecting a Model A car. Every once in a while he and Wangero sent eye signals over my head.

"How do you pronounce this name?" I asked.

"You don't have to call me by it if you don't want to," said Wangero.

"Why shouldn't I?" I asked. "If that's what you want us to call you, we'll call you."

"I know it might sound awkward at first," said Wangero.

"I'll get used to it," I said. "Ream it out again."

Well, soon we got the name out of the way. Asalamalakim had a name twice as long and three times as hard. After I tripped over it two or three times he told me to just call him Hakim-a-barber. I wanted to ask him was he a barber, but I didn't really think he was, so I didn't ask.

"You must belong to those beef-cattle peoples down the road," I said. They said "Asalamalakim" when they met you, too, but they didn't shake hands. Always too busy: feeding the cattle, fixing the fences, putting up salt-lick shelters, throwing down hay. When the white folks poisoned some of the herd the men stayed up all night with rifles in their hands. I walked a mile and a half just to see the sight.

Hakim-a-barber said, "I accept some of their doctrines, but farming and raising cattle is not my style." (They didn't tell me, and I didn't ask, whether Wangero (Dee) had really gone and married him.)

We sat down to eat and right away he said he didn't eat collards and pork was unclean. Wangero, though, went on through the chitlins and corn bread, the greens and everything else. She talked a blue streak over the sweet potatoes. Everything delighted her. Even the fact that we still used the benches her daddy made for the table when we couldn't afford to buy chairs.

"Oh, Mama!" she cried. Then turned to Hakim-a-barber. "I never knew how lovely these benches are. You can feel the rump prints," she said, running her hands underneath her and along the bench. Then she gave a sigh and her hand closed over Grandma Dee's butter dish. "That's it!" she said. "I knew there was something I wanted to ask you if I could have." She jumped up from the table and went over in the corner where the churn stood, the milk in it clabber by now. She looked at the churn and looked at it.

"This churn top is what I need," she said. "Didn't Uncle Buddy whittle it out of a tree you all used to have?"

"Yes," I said.

"Uh huh," she said happily. "And I want the dasher, too."

"Uncle Buddy whittle that, too?" asked the barber.

Dee (Wangero) looked up at me.

"Aunt Dee's first husband whittled the dash," said Maggie so low you almost couldn't hear her. "His name was Henry, but they called him Stash."

"Maggie's brain is like an elephant's," Wangero said, laughing. "I can use the churn top as a centerpiece for the alcove table," she said, sliding a plate over the churn, "and I'll think of something artistic to do with the dasher."

When she finished wrapping the dasher the handle stuck out. I took it for a moment in my hands. You didn't even have to look close to see where hands pushing the dasher up and down to make butter had left a kind of sink in the wood. In fact, there were a lot of small sinks; you could see where thumbs and fingers had sunk into the wood. It was beautiful light yellow wood, from a tree that grew in the yard where Big Dee and Stash had lived.

After dinner Dee (Wangero) went to the trunk at the foot of my bed and started rifling through it. Maggie hung back in the kitchen over the dishpan. Out came Wangero with two quilts. They had been pieced by Grandma Dee and then Big Dee and me had hung them on the quilt frames on the front porch and quilted them. One was in the Lone Star pattern. The other was Walk Around the Mountain. In both of them were scraps of dresses Grandma Dee had worn fifty and more years ago. Bits and pieces of Grandpa Jarrell's Paisley shirts. And one teeny faded blue piece, about the size of a penny matchbox, that was from Great Grandpa Ezra's uniform that he wore in the Civil War.

"Mama," Wangero said sweet as a bird. "Can I have these old quilts?"

I heard something fall in the kitchen, and a minute later the kitchen door slammed.

"Why don't you take one or two of the others?" I asked. "These old things was just done by me and Big Dee from some tops your grandma pieced before she died."

"No," said Wangero. "I don't want those. They are stitched around the borders by machine."

"That'll make them last better," I said.

"That's not the point," said Wangero. "These are all pieces of dresses Grandma used to wear. She did all this stitching by hand. Imagine!" She held the quilts securely in her arms, stroking them.

"Some of the pieces, like those lavender ones, come from old clothes her mother handed down to her," I said, moving up to touch the quilts. Dee (Wangero) moved back just enough so that I couldn't reach the quilts. They already belonged to her.

"Imagine!" she breathed again, clutching them closely to her bosom.

"The truth is," I said, "I promised to give them quilts to Maggie, for when she marries John Thomas."

She gasped like a bee had stung her.

"Maggie can't appreciate these quilts!" she said. "She'd probably be backward enough to put them to everyday use."

"I reckon she would," I said. "God knows I been saving 'em for long enough with nobody using 'em. I hope she will!" I didn't want to bring up how I had offered Dee (Wangero) a quilt when she went away to college. Then she had told me they were old-fashioned, out of style.

"But they're *priceless!*" she was saying now, furiously; for she has a temper. "Maggie would put them on the bed and in five years they'd be in rags. Less than that!"

"She can always make some more," I said. "Maggie knows how to quilt."

Dee (Wangero) looked at me with hatred. "You just will not understand. The point is these quilts, *these* quilts!"

"Well," I said, stumped. "What would *you* do with them?"

"Hang them," she said. As if that was the only thing you *could* do with quilts.

Maggie by now was standing in the door. I could almost hear the sound her feet made as they scraped over each other.

"She can have them, Mama," she said, like somebody used to never winning anything, or having anything reserved for her. "I can 'member Grandma Dee without the quilts."

I looked at her hard. She had filled her bottom lip with checkerberry snuff and it gave her face a kind of dopey, hangdog look. It was Grandma Dee and Big Dee who taught her how to quilt herself. She stood there with her scarred hands hidden in the folds of her skirt. She looked at her sister with something like fear but she wasn't mad at her. This was Maggie's portion. This was the way she knew God to work.

When I looked at her like that something hit me in the top of my head and ran down to the soles of my feet. Just like when I'm in church and the spirit of God touches me and I get happy and shout. I did something I never had done before: hugged Maggie to me, then dragged her on into the room, snatched the quilts out of Miss Wangero's hands and dumped them into Maggie's lap. Maggie just sat there on my bed with her mouth open.

"Take one or two of the others," I said to Dee.

But she turned without a word and went out to Hakim-a-barber.

"You just don't understand," she said, as Maggie and I came out to the car.

"What don't I understand?" I wanted to know.

"Your heritage," she said. And then she turned to Maggie, kissed her, and said, "You ought to try to make something of yourself, too, Maggie. It's really a new day for us. But from the way you and Mama still live you'd never know it."

She put on some sunglasses that hid everything above the tip of her nose and her chin.

Maggie smiled; maybe at the sunglasses. But a real smile, not scared. After we watched the car dust settle I asked Maggie to bring me a dip of snuff. And then the two of us sat there just enjoying, until it was time to go in the house and go to bed.

APPROACHING THE READING

1. Describe the voice you hear in "Everyday Use." What can you tell about the narrator from the way she sounds as you listen to her? What kind of personality comes through what she says and the way she says it?

2. Identify the point of view and perspective used in the story. What is the particular effect of having the narrator address the reader as *you?* In what ways does the effect of story depend on its voice and perspective?

3. Explain the theme of the story, as you see it. What central point comes through, considering the story as a whole? Point to particular parts of the story that support what you say.

4. Look carefully at the final paragraph of the story. Does it fit well with what you said about voice and theme? Is it an effective and satisfying ending? If so, how and why? If you find it unsatisfying, explain why.

Like "Everyday Use," the following story is set in the South, but in a white community and earlier in the twentieth century. It tells of a reclusive elderly woman who seems a mystery to the other residents of her small town, especially the younger people with their new attitudes and changing ways of doing things that marginalize her all the more. It is a story that depends heavily on the point of view and perspective from which it is told. Notice them as you read or think back over it.

William Faulkner   1897–1962

A Rose for Emily   [1931]

I

When Miss Emily Grierson died, our whole town went to her funeral: the men through a sort of respectful affection for a fallen monument, the women mostly out of curiosity to see the inside of her house, which no one save an old manservant—a combined gardener and cook—had seen in at least ten years.

It was a big, squarish frame house that had once been white, decorated with cupolas and spires and scrolled balconies in the heavily lightsome style of the seventies, set on what had once been our most select street. But garages and cotton gins had encroached and obliterated even the august names of that neighborhood; only Miss Emily's house was left, lifting its stubborn and coquettish decay above the cotton wagons and the gasoline pumps—an eyesore among eyesores. And now Miss Emily had gone to join the representatives of those august names where they lay in the cedar-bemused cemetery among the ranked and anonymous graves of Union and Confederate soldiers who fell at the battle of Jefferson.

Alive, Miss Emily had been a tradition, a duty, and a care; a sort of hereditary obligation upon the town, dating from that day in 1894 when Colonel Sartoris, the mayor — he who fathered the edict that no Negro woman should appear on the streets without an apron — remitted her taxes, the dispensation dating from the death of her father on into perpetuity. Not that Miss Emily would have accepted charity. Colonel Sartoris invented an involved tale to the effect that Miss Emily's father had loaned money to the town, which the town, as a matter of business, preferred this way of repaying. Only a man of Colonel Sartoris' generation and thought could have invented it, and only a woman could have believed it.

When the next generation, with its more modern ideas, became mayors and aldermen, this arrangement created some little dissatisfaction. On the first of the year they mailed her a tax notice. February came, and there was no reply. They wrote her a formal letter, asking her to call at the sheriff's office at her convenience. A week later the mayor wrote her himself, offering to call or to send his car for her, and received in reply a note on paper of an archaic shape, in a thin, flowing calligraphy in faded ink, to the effect that she no longer went out at all. The tax notice was also enclosed, without comment.

They called a special meeting of the Board of Aldermen. A deputation waited upon her, knocked at the door through which no visitor had passed since she ceased giving china-painting lessons eight or ten years earlier. They were admitted by the old Negro into a dim hall from which a stairway mounted into still more shadow. It smelled of dust and disuse — a close, dank smell. The Negro led them into the parlor. It was furnished in heavy, leather-covered furniture. When the Negro opened the blinds of one window, they could see that the leather was cracked; and when they sat down, a faint dust rose sluggishly about their thighs, spinning with slow motes in the single sun-ray. On a tarnished gilt easel before the fireplace stood a crayon portrait of Miss Emily's father.

They rose when she entered — a small, fat woman in black, with a thin gold chain descending to her waist and vanishing into her belt, leaning on an ebony cane with a tarnished gold head. Her skeleton was small and spare; perhaps that was why what would have been merely plumpness in another was obesity in her. She looked bloated, like a body long submerged in motionless water, and of that pallid hue. Her eyes, lost in the fatty ridges of her face, looked like two small pieces of coal pressed into a lump of dough as they moved from one face to another while the visitors stated their errand.

She did not ask them to sit. She just stood in the door and listened quietly until the spokesman came to a stumbling halt. Then they could hear the invisible watch ticking at the end of the gold chain.

Her voice was dry and cold. "I have no taxes in Jefferson. Colonel Sartoris explained it to me. Perhaps one of you can gain access to the city records and satisfy yourselves."

"But we have. We are the city authorities, Miss Emily. Didn't you get a notice from the sheriff, signed by him?"

"I received a paper, yes," Miss Emily said. "Perhaps he considers himself the sheriff . . . I have no taxes in Jefferson."

"But there is nothing on the books to show that, you see. We must go by the—"

"See Colonel Sartoris. I have no taxes in Jefferson."

"But, Miss Emily—"

"See Colonel Sartoris." (Colonel Sartoris had been dead almost ten years.) "I have no taxes in Jefferson. Tobe!" The Negro appeared. "Show these gentlemen out."

II

So she vanquished them, horse and foot, just as she had vanquished their fathers thirty years before about the smell. That was two years after her father's death and a short time after her sweetheart—the one we believed would marry her—had deserted her. After her father's death she went out very little; after her sweetheart went away, people hardly saw her at all. A few of the ladies had the temerity to call, but were not received, and the only sign of life about the place was the Negro man—a young man then—going in and out with a market basket.

"Just as if a man—any man—could keep a kitchen properly," the ladies said; so they were not surprised when the smell developed. It was another link between the gross, teeming world and the high and mighty Griersons.

A neighbor, a woman, complained to the mayor, Judge Stevens, eighty years old.

"But what will you have me do about it, madam?" he said.

"Why, send her word to stop it," the woman said. "Isn't there a law?"

"I'm sure that won't be necessary," Judge Stevens said. "It's probably just a snake or a rat that nigger of hers killed in the yard. I'll speak to him about it."

The next day he received two more complaints, one from a man who came in diffident deprecation. "We really must do something about it, Judge. I'd be the last one in the world to bother Miss Emily, but we've got to do something." That night the Board of Aldermen met—three graybeards and one younger man, a member of the rising generation.

"It's simple enough," he said. "Send her word to have her place cleaned up. Give her a certain time to do it in, and if she don't . . ."

"Dammit, sir," Judge Stevens said, "will you accuse a lady to her face of smelling bad?"

So the next night, after midnight, four men crossed Miss Emily's lawn and slunk about the house like burglars, sniffing along the base of the brick-

work and at the cellar openings while one of them performed a regular sowing motion with his hand out of a sack slung from his shoulder. They broke
open the cellar door and sprinkled lime there, and in all the outbuildings. As
they recrossed the lawn, a window that had been dark was lighted and Miss
Emily sat in it, the light behind her, and her upright torso motionless as that
of an idol. They crept quietly across the lawn and into the shadow of the locusts that lined the street. After a week or two the smell went away.

That was when people had begun to feel really sorry for her. People
in our town, remembering how old lady Wyatt, her great-aunt, had gone
completely crazy at last, believed that the Griersons held themselves a little
too high for what they really were. None of the young men were quite
good enough for Miss Emily and such. We had long thought of them as a
tableau, Miss Emily a slender figure in white in the background, her father
a spraddled silhouette in the foreground, his back to her and clutching a
horsewhip, the two of them framed by the back-flung front door. So when
she got to be thirty and was still single, we were not pleased exactly, but vin-
dicated; even with insanity in the family she wouldn't have turned down all
of her chances if they had really materialized.

When her father died, it got about that the house was all that was left to
her; and in a way, people were glad. At last they could pity Miss Emily. Being
left alone, and a pauper, she had become humanized. Now she too would
know the old thrill and the old despair of a penny more or less.

The day after his death all the ladies prepared to call at the house and
offer condolence and aid, as is our custom. Miss Emily met them at the
door, dressed as usual and with no trace of grief on her face. She told them
that her father was not dead. She did that for three days, with the ministers
calling on her, and the doctors, trying to persuade her to let them dispose of
the body. Just as they were about to resort to law and force, she broke down,
and they buried her father quickly.

We did not say she was crazy then. We believed she had to do that. We
remembered all the young men her father had driven away, and we knew
that with nothing left, she would have to cling to that which had robbed
her, as people will.

III

She was sick for a long time. When we saw her again, her hair was cut
short, making her look like a girl, with a vague resemblance to those angels
in colored church windows — sort of tragic and serene.

The town had just let the contracts for paving the sidewalks, and in the
summer after her father's death they began the work. The construction
company came with niggers and mules and machinery, and a foreman
named Homer Barron, a Yankee — a big, dark, ready man, with a big voice
and eyes lighter than his face. The little boys would follow in groups to hear
him cuss the niggers, and the niggers singing in time to the rise and fall of

picks. Pretty soon he knew everybody in town. Whenever you heard a lot of laughing anywhere about the square, Homer Barron would be in the center of the group. Presently we began to see him and Miss Emily on Sunday afternoons driving in the yellow-wheeled buggy and the matched team of bays from the livery stable.

At first we were glad that Miss Emily would have an interest, because the ladies all said, "Of course a Grierson would not think seriously of a Northerner, a day laborer." But there were still others, older people, who said that even grief could not cause a real lady to forget *noblesse oblige*—without calling it *noblesse oblige*. They just said, "Poor Emily. Her kinsfolk should come to her." She had some kin in Alabama; but years ago her father had fallen out with them over the estate of old lady Wyatt, the crazy woman, and there was no communication between the two families. They had not even been represented at the funeral.

And as soon as the old people said, "Poor Emily," the whispering began. "Do you suppose it's really so?" they said to one another. "Of course it is. What else could . . ." This behind their hands; rustling of craned silk and satin behind jalousies closed upon the sun of Sunday afternoon as the thin, swift clop-clop-clop of the matched team passed: "Poor Emily."

She carried her head high enough—even when we believed that she was fallen. It was as if she demanded more than ever the recognition of her dignity as the last Grierson; as if it had wanted that touch of earthiness to reaffirm her imperviousness. Like when she bought the rat poison, the arsenic. That was over a year after they had begun to say "Poor Emily," and while the two female cousins were visiting her.

"I want some poison," she said to the druggist. She was over thirty then, still a slight woman, though thinner than usual, with cold, haughty black eyes in a face the flesh of which was strained across the temples and about the eye-sockets as you imagine a lighthouse-keeper's face ought to look. "I want some poison," she said.

"Yes, Miss Emily. What kind? For rats and such? I'd recom—"

"I want the best you have. I don't care what kind."

The druggist named several. "They'll kill anything up to an elephant. But what you want is—"

"Arsenic," Miss Emily said. "Is that a good one?"

"Is . . . arsenic? Yes, ma'am. But what you want—"

"I want arsenic."

The druggist looked down at her. She looked back at him, erect, her face like a strained flag. "Why, of course," the druggist said. "If that's what you want. But the law requires you to tell what you are going to use it for."

Miss Emily just stared at him, her head tilted back in order to look him eye for eye, until he looked away and went and got the arsenic and wrapped it up. The Negro delivery boy brought her the package; the druggist didn't come back. When she opened the package at home there was written on the box, under the skull and bones: "For rats."

IV

So the next day we all said, "She will kill herself"; and we said it would be the best thing. When she had first begun to be seen with Homer Barron, we had said, "She will marry him." Then we said, "She will persuade him yet," because Homer himself had remarked—he liked men, and it was known that he drank with the younger men in the Elks' Club—that he was not a marrying man. Later we said, "Poor Emily" behind the jalousies as they passed on Sunday afternoon in the glittering buggy, Miss Emily with her head high and Homer Barron with his hat cocked and a cigar in his teeth, reins and whip in a yellow glove.

Then some of the ladies began to say that it was a disgrace to the town and a bad example to the young people. The men did not want to interfere, but at last the ladies forced the Baptist minister—Miss Emily's people were Episcopal—to call upon her. He would never divulge what happened during that interview, but he refused to go back again. The next Sunday they again drove about the streets, and the following day the minister's wife wrote to Miss Emily's relations in Alabama.

So she had blood-kin under her roof again and we sat back to watch developments. At first nothing happened. Then we were sure that they were to be married. We learned that Miss Emily had been to the jeweler's and ordered a man's toilet set in silver, with the letters H. B. on each piece. Two days later we learned that she had bought a complete outfit of men's clothing, including a nightshirt, and we said, "They are married." We were really glad. We were glad because the two female cousins were even more Grierson than Miss Emily had ever been.

So we were not surprised when Homer Barron—the streets had been finished some time since—was gone. We were a little disappointed that there was not a public blowing-off, but we believed that he had gone on to prepare for Miss Emily's coming, or to give her a chance to get rid of the cousins. (By that time it was a cabal, and we were all Miss Emily's allies to help circumvent the cousins.) Sure enough, after another week they departed. And, as we had expected all along, within three days Homer Barron was back in town. A neighbor saw the Negro man admit him at the kitchen door at dusk one evening.

And that was the last we saw of Homer Barron. And of Miss Emily for some time. The Negro man went in and out with the market basket, but the front door remained closed. Now and then we would see her at a window for a moment, as the men did that night when they sprinkled the lime, but for almost six months she did not appear on the streets. Then we knew that this was to be expected too; as if that quality of her father which had thwarted her woman's life so many times had been too virulent and too furious to die.

When we next saw Miss Emily, she had grown fat and her hair was turning gray. During the next few years it grew grayer and grayer until it attained an even pepper-and-salt iron-gray, when it ceased turning. Up to the day of her death at seventy-four it was still that vigorous iron-gray, like the hair of an active man.

From that time on her front door remained closed, save for a period of six or seven years, when she was about forty, during which she gave lessons in china-painting. She fitted up a studio in one of the downstairs rooms, where the daughters and granddaughters of Colonel Sartoris' contemporaries were sent to her with the same regularity and in the same spirit that they were sent to church on Sundays with a twenty-five-cent piece for the collection plate. Meanwhile her taxes had been remitted.

Then the newer generation became the backbone and the spirit of the town, and the painting pupils grew up and fell away and did not send their children to her with boxes of color and tedious brushes and pictures cut from the ladies' magazines. The front door closed upon the last one and remained closed for good. When the town got free postal delivery, Miss Emily alone refused to let them fasten the metal numbers above her door and attach a mailbox to it. She would not listen to them.

Daily, monthly, yearly we watched the Negro grow grayer and more stooped, going in and out with the market basket. Each December we sent her a tax notice, which would be returned by the post office a week later, unclaimed. Now and then we would see her in one of the downstairs windows — she had evidently shut up the top floor of the house — like the carven torso of an idol in a niche, looking or not looking at us, we could never tell which. Thus she passed from generation to generation — dear, inescapable, impervious, tranquil, and perverse.

And so she died. Fell ill in the house filled with dust and shadows, with only a doddering Negro man to wait on her. We did not even know she was sick; we had long since given up trying to get any information from the Negro. He talked to no one, probably not even to her, for his voice had grown harsh and rusty, as if from disuse.

She died in one of the downstairs rooms, in a heavy walnut bed with a curtain, her gray head propped on a pillow yellow and moldy with age and lack of sunlight.

V

The Negro met the first of the ladies at the front door and let them in, with their hushed, sibilant voices and their quick, curious glances, and then he disappeared. He walked right through the house and out the back and was not seen again.

The two female cousins came at once. They held the funeral on the second day, with the town coming to look at Miss Emily beneath a mass of bought flowers, with the crayon face of her father musing profoundly above the bier and the ladies sibilant and macabre; and the very old men — some in their brushed Confederate uniforms — on the porch and the lawn, talking of Miss Emily as if she had been a contemporary of theirs, believing that they had danced with her and courted her perhaps, confusing time with its mathematical progression, as the old do, to whom all the past is not a diminishing road but, instead, a huge meadow which no winter ever quite touches, divided from them now by the narrow bottle-neck of the most recent decade of years.

Already we knew that there was one room in that region above stairs which no one had seen in forty years, and which would have to be forced. They waited until Miss Emily was decently in the ground before they opened it.

The violence of breaking down the door seemed to fill this room with pervading dust. A thin, acrid pall as of the tomb seemed to lie everywhere upon this room decked and furnished as for a bridal: upon the valance curtains of faded rose color, upon the rose-shaded lights, upon the dressing table, upon the delicate array of crystal and the man's toilet things backed with tarnished silver, silver so tarnished that the monogram was obscured. Among them lay a collar and tie, as if they had just been removed, which, lifted, left upon the surface a pale crescent in the dust. Upon a chair hung the suit, carefully folded; beneath it the two mute shoes and the discarded socks.

The man himself lay in the bed.

For a long while we just stood there, looking down at the profound and fleshless grin. The body had apparently once lain in the attitude of an embrace, but now the long sleep that outlasts love, that conquers even the grimace of love, had cuckolded him. What was left of him, rotted beneath what was left of the nightshirt, had become inextricable from the bed in which he lay; and upon him and upon the pillow beside him lay that even coating of the patient and biding dust.

Then we noticed that in the second pillow was the indentation of a head. One of us lifted something from it, and leaning forward, that faint and invisible dust dry and acrid in the nostrils, we saw a long strand of iron-gray hair.

APPROACHING THE READING

1. Telling a story from a first-person plural point of view is unusual. Who is the narrator? From what perspective is the story told? Consider how the effect would be different if in each case *our* was changed to *my* and *we* changed to *I*.

2. Do you think the story could have been told effectively from a third-person omniscient point of view? Describe ways it would be different. How would its effect be different?

Research this author in depth with cultural documents and multimedia resources on *LiterActive*.

3. Summarize Miss Emily's character. To what extent is what you know about her shaped and affected by the story's point of view? Would you know her

better if the story had used a third-person omniscient point of view? Would that have made the story more effective?

4. What do you think is the central theme of the story? What does it all add up to? In what ways does the title fit or relate to its theme?

RESPONDING THROUGH WRITING

Journal Entries

1. As a way of getting hold of point of view in fiction, pay attention to point of view in several TV shows or movies. Notice the perspective from which each is presented: Does it stick to one character or group of characters, or does it switch back and forth between two (or more) characters or groups of characters? Watch the use of the camera as an "eye": From what perspective does it let you see what's happening—only from "outside" and at a distance? Does it ever show you just what a character is seeing? Write a journal entry summarizing what you observe and discussing how what you observed might apply to or clarify point of view in fiction.

www Research the authors in this chapter with LitLinks, or take a quiz on the stories with LitQuiz, at bedfordstmartins.com/approachinglit.

2. In your journal, rewrite part of a story from a different perspective, as, for example, Sandra Cisneros's "The House on Mango Street" (p. 91) or John Updike's "A & P" (p. 386) from the perspective of the narrator's mother.

3. In your journal, rewrite part of a story using a different point of view— Sandra Cisneros's "The House on Mango Street" (p. 91) or John Updike's "A & P" (p. 386) as a third-person narrative instead of first-person, for example.

Literary Analysis Papers

4. Write a paper on how Alice Walker's "Everyday Use" (p. 101) combines saying and showing as techniques of characterization through the handling of its first-person narration.

5. Discussions of point of view usually center on the question of how appropriate and effective the point of view is in terms of the best way to present the action and characters and to develop the story's theme. Write a paper discussing the appropriateness and effectiveness, to presentation and theme, of the point of view in one of the following stories:

   - first-person unreliable in Gish Jen's "Who's Irish?" (p. 272) or Toni Morrison's "Recitatif" (p. 300)
   - first-person reliable in John Updike's "A & P" (p. 386)
   - third-person omniscient in Zora Neale Hurston's "Sweat" (p. 263)
   - third-person limited in Leslie Marmon Silko's "The Man to Send Rain Clouds" (p. 377)

- third-person limited and center of consciousness in Richard Wright's "The Man Who Was Almost a Man" (p. 395)
- third-person limited and stream of consciousness in Katherine Anne Porter's "The Jilting of Granny Weatherall" (p. 364)
- interior monologue in Tillie Olsen's "I Stand Here Ironing" (p. 353)

6. Write a paper discussing the title "Everyday Use" as it applies to Dee (Wangero) and to her mother and sister. Consider what Dee means by saying "You just don't understand" (p. 107). What does Dee not understand?

Making Connections

7. Write a paper exploring the mingling of love and death in Joyce Carol Oates's "Where Are You Going, Where Have You Been?" (p. 75) and William Faulkner's "A Rose for Emily" (p. 108).

8. Write a paper that compares and contrasts the handling of parent-child conflict in two of the following stories: Alice Walker's "Everyday Use" (p. 101), Lan Samantha Chang's "The Eve of the Spirit Festival" (p. 228), or Richard Wright's "The Man Who Was Almost a Man" (p. 395).

Cultural Criticism Papers

9. Stories about "outsiders" look different depending on the point of view from which they are told. Does a character feel, or is she or he made to feel, like an outsider? Does one character look at another as an outsider? Discuss both perspectives in a story dealing with an outsider—either Esperanza, Henry, or Arnold from the stories in this chapter, or characters in Lan Samantha Chang's "The Eve of the Spirit Festival" (p. 228), Ralph Ellison's "Battle Royal" (p. 237), or Chinua Achebe's "Dead Men's Path" (p. 405).

10. Write a paper discussing the cultural meaning of houses—of owning one's own place, of the type of house one owns and its location—focusing on Sandra Cisneros's "The House on Mango Street" (p. 91) and Alice Walker's "Everyday Use" (p. 101) as starting points. In what ways does the house one lives in affect one's self and life, have power, and lead to acceptance or conflict or rejection?

RESPONDING THROUGH THE ARTS

1. As a way of responding to a story through use of another art, make a collage of materials cut from magazines or newspapers and add appropriate captions. Think about using bits from both visual and written materials, juxtaposing images and language from hard and soft news, advertising, comics and cartoons, headlines, TV listings, and anywhere else you can find relevant material. For example, you could illustrate a story that works with contrasting perspectives, though it's told from one point of view—as, for

example, Gish Jen's "Who's Irish?" (p. 272) or Toni Morrison's "Recitatif" (p. 300).

2. Do some exploring into the importance of quilts as cultural artifacts. In what ways are they important beyond providing warmth? What do they reveal about the people who make them and the society that values them? Write a paper applying what you find to Alice Walker's "Everyday Use" (p. 101), showing how a deeper knowledge of quilts adds more meaning to the story.

The place of birth itself becomes a metaphor for the things we must all leave behind; the assimilation of a new culture is the coming into maturity by accepting the terms necessary for survival.

Judith Ortiz Cofer

Setting and Symbol

Of the memories we look back on, those involving places often carry particularly important emotional weight. We may have special memories of grandmother's house or a good friend's apartment; a street corner or a park down the street; a gymnasium or playground across town; or a theme park in Florida—or even nightmarish memories of an abandoned house in the country, a cemetery, or a back alley. Reflect for a moment on some significant places in your own life. Place (or setting) is very important in stories as well, as the area and context in which the characters live and where the events occur. Place may just be the key locale of a story, or it may convey a symbolic meaning, taking on an expanding significance beyond that of just the location of the action. This chapter explores setting and symbol to help you realize more fully what these two contribute to a story and how they sometimes interrelate.

SETTING

The **setting** of a story, poem, or play is its overall context—where, when, and in what circumstances the action occurs. In the following story, setting plays an important role. Two characters, a young woman named Jig and her male companion, are waiting for a train. As you read about them, listen for a major conflict in their relationship and what their discussion of it reveals about their characters. Focus also on where they are (the country, the part of the country, the specific building and its surroundings) and on how the place is described. Look for connections between where they are and what they are talking about.

Ernest Hemingway   1899–1961

Hills Like White Elephants   [1927]

The hills across the valley of the Ebro were long and white. On this side there was no shade and no trees and the station was between two lines of rails in the sun. Close against the side of the station there was the warm shadow of the building and a curtain, made of strings of bamboo beads, hung across the open door into the bar, to keep out flies. The American and the girl with him sat at a table in the shade, outside the building. It was very hot and the express from Barcelona would come in forty minutes. It stopped at this junction for two minutes and went on to Madrid.

"What should we drink?" the girl asked. She had taken off her hat and put it on the table.

"It's pretty hot," the man said.

"Let's drink beer."

"Dos cervezas,"° the man said into the curtain.

"Big ones?" a woman asked from the doorway.

"Yes. Two big ones."

The woman brought two glasses of beer and two felt pads. She put the felt pads and the beer glasses on the table and looked at the man and the girl. The girl was looking off at the line of hills. They were white in the sun and the country was brown and dry.

"They look like white elephants," she said.

"I've never seen one," the man drank his beer.

"No, you wouldn't have."

"I might have," the man said. "Just because you say I wouldn't have doesn't prove anything."

The girl looked at the bead curtain. "They've painted something on it," she said. "What does it say?"

"Anis del Toro. It's a drink."

"Could we try it?"

The man called "Listen" through the curtain. The woman came out from the bar.

"Four reales."

"We want two Anis del Toro."

"With water?"

"Do you want it with water?"

"I don't know," the girl said. "Is it good with water?"

"It's all right."

"You want them with water?" asked the woman.

"Yes, with water."

"It tastes like licorice," the girl said and put the glass down.

Dos cervezas: Two beers (Spanish).

"That's the way with everything."

"Yes," said the girl. "Everything tastes of licorice. Especially all the things you've waited so long for, like absinthe."

"Oh, cut it out."

"You started it," the girl said. "I was being amused. I was having a fine time."

"Well, let's try and have a fine time."

"All right. I was trying. I said the mountains looked like white elephants. Wasn't that bright?"

"That was bright."

"I wanted to try this new drink. That's all we do, isn't it — look at things and try new drinks?"

"I guess so."

The girl looked across at the hills.

"They're lovely hills," she said. "They don't really look like white elephants. I just meant the coloring of their skin through the trees."

"Should we have another drink?"

"All right."

The warm wind blew the bead curtain against the table.

"The beer's nice and cool," the man said.

"It's lovely," the girl said.

"It's really an awfully simple operation, Jig," the man said. "It's not really an operation at all."

The girl looked at the ground the table legs rested on.

"I know you wouldn't mind it, Jig. It's really not anything. It's just to let the air in."

The girl did not say anything.

"I'll go with you and I'll stay with you all the time. They just let the air in and then it's all perfectly natural."

"Then what will we do afterward?"

"We'll be fine afterward. Just like we were before."

"What makes you think so?"

"That's the only thing that bothers us. It's the only thing that's made us unhappy."

The girl looked at the bead curtain, put her hand out and took hold of two of the strings of beads.

"And you think then we'll be all right and be happy."

"I know we will. You don't have to be afraid. I've known lots of people that have done it."

"So have I," said the girl. "And afterward they were all so happy."

"Well," the man said, "if you don't want to you don't have to. I wouldn't have you do it if you didn't want to. But I know it's perfectly simple."

"And you really want to?"

"I think it's the best thing to do. But I don't want you to do it if you don't really want to."

"And if I do it you'll be happy and things will be like they were and you'll love me?"

"I love you now. You know I love you."

"I know. But if I do it, then it will be nice again if I say things are like white elephants, and you'll like it?"

"I'll love it. I love it now but I just can't think about it. You know how I get when I worry."

"If I do it you won't ever worry?"

"I won't worry about that because it's perfectly simple."

"Then I'll do it. Because I don't care about me."

"What do you mean?"

"I don't care about me."

"Well, I care about you."

"Oh, yes. But I don't care about me. And I'll do it and then everything will be fine."

"I don't want you to do it if you feel that way."

The girl stood up and walked to the end of the station. Across, on the other side, were fields of grain and trees along the banks of the Ebro. Far away, beyond the river, were mountains. The shadow of a cloud moved across the field of grain and she saw the river through the trees.

"And we could have all this," she said. "And we could have everything and every day we make it more impossible."

"What did you say?"

"I said we could have everything."

"We can have everything."

"No, we can't."

"We can have the whole world."

"No, we can't."

"We can go everywhere."

"No, we can't. It isn't ours any more."

"It's ours."

"No, it isn't. And once they take it away, you never get it back."

"But they haven't taken it away."

"We'll wait and see."

"Come on back in the shade," he said. "You mustn't feel that way."

"I don't feel any way," the girl said. "I just know things."

"I don't want you to do anything that you don't want to do—"

"Nor that isn't good for me," she said. "I know. Could we have another beer?"

"All right. But you've got to realize—"

"I realize," the girl said. "Can't we maybe stop talking?"

They sat down at the table and the girl looked across at the hills on the dry side of the valley and the man looked at her and at the table.

"You've got to realize," he said, "that I don't want you to do it if you don't want to. I'm perfectly willing to go through with it if it means anything to you."

"Doesn't it mean anything to you? We could get along."

"Of course it does. But I don't want anybody but you. I don't want any one else. And I know it's perfectly simple."

"Yes, you know it's perfectly simple."

"It's all right for you to say that, but I do know it."

"Would you do something for me now?"

"I'd do anything for you."

"Would you please please please please please please please stop talking?"

He did not say anything but looked at the bags against the wall of the station. There were labels on them from all the hotels where they had spent nights.

"But I don't want you to," he said, "I don't care anything about it."

"I'll scream," the girl said.

The woman came out through the curtains with two glasses of beer and put them down on the damp felt pads. "The train comes in five minutes," she said.

"What did she say?" asked the girl.

"That the train is coming in five minutes."

The girl smiled brightly at the woman, to thank her.

"I'd better take the bags over to the other side of the station," the man said. She smiled at him.

"All right. Then come back and we'll finish the beer."

He picked up the two heavy bags and carried them around the station to the other tracks. He looked up the tracks but could not see the train. Coming back, he walked through the barroom, where people waiting for the train were drinking. He drank an Anis at the bar and looked at the people. They were all waiting reasonably for the train. He went out through the bead curtain. She was sitting at the table and smiled at him.

"Do you feel better?" he asked.

"I feel fine," she said. "There's nothing wrong with me. I feel fine."

APPROACHING THE READING

1. Think first about what you saw as you read the story. References to Barcelona, Madrid, and the Ebro broadly identify the place where the scene happens as Spain. You might look at a map to identify where these places are and find a book with pictures of that area so you can visualize the scene more precisely. How does it affect you to have the story occur in Europe? How might the effect differ if it had occurred in the United States?

2. Think about the immediate location—a train junction out in the middle of nowhere. What is the effect of the rural train junction? How would it be different if the American and Jig were in a big train station in Madrid? Sitting in a coffee shop in Paris, or New York, or a small town in the United States?

3. White elephants are mentioned in the title and several times in the story. Jig says she is referring to elephants that are white. Could there be more to the words than that? Look them up in a dictionary. Might the words have a symbolic significance?

4. Consider possible connections between white elephants and the conflict, or conflicts, between the main characters. What do you think is the operation the man is urging on Jig? What details from the story support your answer? Is the operation their only conflict?

5. "We'll be fine afterward. Just like we were before," the American says to Jig (p. 121). This line opens an enormous gap — their future — for you to fill in. Where do you think they would go if the story continued? What would happen? How does ending where it does indicate what is important in the story? How do you respond to Jig's concluding lines?

Setting as Place

Basic to a story's context is place, or locale — the physical environment. We need to know the locale in a broad sense: Where does the action take place? What country? What city or regions of that country? We also need to know it in a specific, narrower sense: What kind of place — building, countryside, school, or street? What specific building, rural area, school, or street? Physical setting — whether street or house or farm or prison camp — can be presented through vibrant, specific details, or it can be sketched broadly with a few, quick strokes. The setting of "Hills Like White Elephants" is indicated in the first paragraph: the broad setting — eastern Spain, about a third of the way from Barcelona to Madrid — and the specific setting — a hot day at a rural train station, a junction where two lines meet in the middle of nowhere.

The description of a setting often evokes its significance, what it conveys and suggests. Reflect, for example, on the significance of the principal setting in "The Red Convertible" (p. 67) being a reservation. Ask yourself how the story would be different if Lyman and Henry lived in Chicago. Think about the locale of "Hills Like White Elephants," how by creating a sense of isolation, the story focuses us on the two people and their problem. There are other people in the bar, but we see no one else except the waitress — the other people are just there, like the chairs and tables. The location includes only a railway junction: No town or city is indicated, which increases the sense of isolation. There is no community to support or affect them in what they face or decide (especially in what Jig faces and must decide) — just two individuals, making an individual decision as if it affects no one but themselves (at least that's how the man views it). Using a train station as locale also creates a sense of transience — no roots, no home, no ties. And placing the story at a junction suggests that the characters are facing a decision about the direction in which they should go.

Setting as Time

Setting also includes the time in which the events occur, time in all its dimensions: the century, the year, the season, the day, the hour, maybe even the exact second. In some cases, a specific time is not indicated: The events are universal and could as well have occurred a minute or a millennium ago. Often, however, a specific or approximate time is either assumed (the time seems the same as when the story was written or published) or indicated — perhaps by giving a date in the story, by mentioning historical events that were going on at the time of the story, or by describing the way people talk, act, or dress. In those cases, the specific time may be significant, and knowing something about that time period may help you understand what is going on or the significance of what occurs. That may require asking questions and then doing some investigating — in an encyclopedia, or on the Internet, or through more specialized books, depending on the time period involved and the way the story uses its setting.

The action in "Hills Like White Elephants" is probably contemporaneous with when it was written, in the mid-1920s. To decide if that time setting is significant to the story, ask what was going on at that time, what was significant or noteworthy. You might check a time line of world or European historical events. You'll notice that the story takes place less than ten years after the end of World War I (1914–1918). To gain the full impact of the story's setting in time, you might need to do some reading about the war and its aftermath (an encyclopedia entry on the war probably would suffice). The war caused immense loss of life, physical suffering, and psychological and emotional damage from trench warfare and use of nerve gas. It is estimated that 8.5 million military personnel died (a high percentage of a whole generation's young men), along with 10 million civilians. Although the corresponding numbers in World War II were much greater, at the time the number of deaths and amount of devastation were unprecedented. It was called the Great War with good reason.

You would also need to learn something about the social changes that took place during and after the war. An encyclopedia or Internet articles probably would cover the years after as well as during the war. The war shattered the optimistic outlook held by much of the population in Western Europe and the United States. After the war ended, many people reacted by deciding to enjoy life fully in the present, since the war showed that life can end so quickly, and by rejecting older values (including prevailing sexual mores) and traditional roles (especially for women). The war led to changes in gender roles: With young men away in the military, young women had to work in factories instead of in homes, schools, or offices. Having seen large cities and other countries, young people found it difficult to return to the sheltered, conservative communities in which they grew up. Many of them wanted to travel and to live in more cosmopolitan locations. A large number of writers, artists, and socialites — Ernest Hemingway among them — moved from the United States to Europe, which they considered more sophisticated. The American man in "Hills Like White Elephants" seems to be one of them, and to reflect the sense of restlessness and desire to see new places and have new experiences. "That's all we do, isn't it," Jig says, "look at things and try new drinks?" (p. 121).

Setting as Cultural Context

Setting also involves the social circumstances of the time and place. Here too, active reading may require some extra reading or research. Beyond the historical events at the time, try to find what attitudes people held about what was going on. What social and political problems were people facing? How were people below the poverty line treated, and what were the attitudes of the economically secure? What kinds of social change were occurring? Such social and cultural contexts are closely related to the kind of historical events we discussed above — actually, all aspects of setting are interrelated and inseparable. So, for example, to understand "The Red Convertible" fully it helps to know something about the Vietnam War and attitudes toward it. Notice also how it involves transplanting a young Native American from his familiar, traditional culture to a strikingly different military culture and then to a strange foreign culture.

Like "The Red Convertible," "Hills Like White Elephants" involves cultural transplantation: an American writer, Ernest Hemingway, living in Paris, writing in English (thus mainly for an American audience), about an American traveling in Spain (a conservative, predominantly Catholic country) with a companion (to whom he does not seem to be married) from an unspecified country. The fact that he is called "the American" suggests that Jig is not American; she apparently is not from Spain since she cannot converse with the waitress (we are supposed to assume the man is talking to the waitress in Spanish, even though his words and hers are written in English). Such details economically and efficiently convey a mixture of cultures and values, as well as a cosmopolitan outlook.

The Effects of Setting

Setting, thus, provides a "world" for the story to take place in, a location and a background for the events. But as you pay even closer attention to setting, you'll see that it usually does more. Again, you need to ask questions, especially about further implications of when and where the events happen. Ask yourself what setting reveals about characters. What is suggested by where a person lives (the kind of house and furniture) or the place in which we encounter her or him (a bar, a gym, a library, a woods)? Does setting help clarify what she or he is like? Think, for example, about Connie in "Where Are You Going, Where Have You Been?" (p. 75). The amount of time she spends at the shopping mall and the drive-in restaurant reveals aspects of her character.

Ask yourself also how the setting affects the way you feel about the characters and events. Setting can be important in evoking **atmosphere** — that is, the mood or emotional aura that surround and permeate a literary work. A major part of the effect in "A Rose for Emily" (p. 108) is created by the eerie atmosphere of the house in which Miss Emily secludes herself for much of her life. And watch for possible connections between details in the setting and other aspects of the story, such as characters, conflicts, or actions. If handled well, setting adds to or reinforces meanings, ideas, or impressions in a work. Think, for example, about the effect of the setting in "Hills Like White Elephants." The isolated train station reflects the isolation of the two characters; and the barren aridity Jig sees on one side of the station and the fertile growth on the other echo the social conflict between her and the American as well as the internal conflict within her.

SYMBOLS

Works of literature not only help us see things in fresh and meaningful ways, they also can lead us to see deeply *into* and *beyond* things through the use of symbols. A **symbol** is something that represents both itself and something else. In literature, a symbol is usually an object, although it is sometimes a character or an action. Every day you encounter symbols. You send a rose to someone you love. A rose is an object in itself, something that can be touched and smelled. But of course you hope that the recipient will recognize it as more than itself, will know it suggests the depth of your love, concern, and support, and therefore will respond to its *symbolic* implications. A symbol's characteristics usually relate closely to the abstractions it represents: A rose is a symbol of love because it is beautiful, because it is the reproductive organ of a plant, and because its red color — the color of blood or a blush — has long been connected to passion. In contrast, a *sign* is an object that conveys an abstract meaning but does so through an arbitrary relationship: By common agreement, a red octagonal sign means "stop," but a white triangular sign could just as well mean "stop."

Recognizing Symbols

Even though almost anything can take on symbolic significance, not every object, character, or act in a literary work should be labeled a symbol. Symbols draw their power from standing out, and they don't stand out if we call everything a symbol. A prudent way to proceed is to assume that objects, characters, and actions are just themselves and are not meant to be taken as symbols *unless* a further sense of meaning forces itself on us. If you miss something others regard as a symbol, don't worry. Symbols add to a work's meaning, but a work usually doesn't depend on your recognizing them. It's better to miss a symbolic meaning than to impose one and reduce a work to a string of abstractions.

How, then, do you recognize a symbol? The key signal is *prominence:* Objects that are mentioned repeatedly, described in detail, or appear in noticeable or strategic positions (at the beginning or end, in the title, at a crucial moment, in the climactic lines) may point toward a meaning beyond themselves. The red convertible in Louise Erdrich's story (p. 67) certainly meets all these criteria. Signals, however, are not always structural. Another signal can be a sense of *weightiness* or *significance:* Sometimes you may notice that an image, character, or action differs from others, that it is beginning to embody an idea related to an area of major concern in the work. In such a case, it might be a symbol.

Be careful, however, not to undermine the use of concrete details by dismissing their crucial part in the work because you see them as symbols. Their literal role always comes first. A symbol is first an image, and its representation of an actual thing plays a key role in a work even if it also becomes a symbol. The quilts in "Everyday Use" (p. 101) come to symbolize the Johnson family's culture and heritage, but first and foremost they are actual quilts. At the end of the story, the narrator gives Maggie coverings she can put on a bed, not some abstract "heritage" (though the bed coverings carry that sense of heritage with them). To separate the symbolic meaning from the literal diminishes the richness of both. The warmth of the Johnsons' heritage comes alive in the warmth provided by the quilts. Be careful also not to turn an abstraction into a symbol. A rose can be a symbol of love, but love (an abstraction) can never be a symbol of something else. And be sure that the symbolic meaning seems plausible: Its connection to the image, character, or action must seem likely and convincing within the context of the story. To claim that the red convertible is a symbol of Lyman's Marxist leanings (since red was associated with communism during the Cold War) seems totally far-fetched and implausible.

Symbols appear in several overlapping varieties. Think of some things you keep—a toy, a hat, a photo, a souvenir—that for you carry personal meanings although for others suggest nothing more than what they are. These *private symbols* are objects that hold a special meaning for you because of certain experiences or people. Since it is difficult, if not impossible, to convey their meaning to another person, private symbols ordinarily are not used in literary works. Several types of symbols, however, are important for literature.

Literary Symbols

A *literary symbol* is an object, character, or action that is both part of the literal story in a literary work—it can be seen, touched, smelled, heard, tasted, encountered, or experienced by people in the story, poem, or play— and suggests abstract meanings beyond itself. The red convertible is a real object in Erdrich's story: Lyman and Henry buy a real car, fix it up, and drive around in it. But beyond being an object the brothers own, the car also represents their friendship and the bond they share. It suggests carefreeness, spontaneity, and freedom (think of the difference if the car was a tan mini-van); perhaps it even reflects Henry's life and soul. When Lyman rolls the car into the river, the red convertible becomes part of a symbolic act. He isn't just getting rid of the car; he is giving it to Henry, evidence of his love for and close connection with his brother.

The distant hills in "Hills Like White Elephants" are actual objects in the story, visible to the characters, and are prominent: included in the title and discussed several times in the story. They seem to convey a sense of longing for that which is distant and unattainable, "all the things you've waited so long for," as Jig puts it (p. 121). Note that *meanings* in the first sentence of the previous paragraph is plural. Symbols usually convey a cluster of possible meanings; they are rich, suggestive, and evocative. Knowledgeable readers do not reduce them to a single, definite meaning: The verb *suggests* may be safer to use than the verb *symbolizes* because it conveys better a sense of a symbol's openness, inclusivity, and plurality.

Conventional and Traditional Symbols

Symbols often derive their meanings from the context of the literary work itself. Red convertibles have a certain cultural status in society — they're sexy. But they do not carry the particular symbolic meanings that are relied on in Erdrich's story. The car in "The Red Convertible" develops its meanings from its specific associations with Lyman and Henry and their situation. It is a "story-specific" symbol, one that receives its significance from the work and may not have the same significance outside of that work. If you see a red convertible on the street, it may remind you of this story and its symbolic significance in the story, but it won't suggest the same significance for someone who hasn't read the story.

In contrast are conventional and traditional symbols. These do have significance outside literary works and can carry that significance into a work. *Conventional symbols* are objects like a national flag, a dove, a star of David; they are objects that can be seen and touched, but they also ripple with associations and meanings particular groups have consciously agreed to assign to them. *Traditional symbols* are objects that over years or even centuries have had certain meanings become attached to them in a culture, or in many cultures. The rose, to use that example again, an object that is beautiful and fragile, has by tradition, in many cultures, become a symbol of love; but the cultures did not deliberately decide to attach that significance to the rose.

Conventional and traditional symbols bring into a literary work the clusters of meaning they already possess outside the work. For us to respond to them according to usual expectations depends on our having, or our learning about, the shared background and experiences they depend on. No white elephants appear in the setting of Hemingway's story: They are the imaginative half of a simile. The title itself should make us begin asking in what ways hills are like white elephants. We should start with the physical, with the hills as images: In the story, Jig is looking at the line of hills, white in the sun, and says "They look like white elephants" (p. 120). She surely is talking about physical appearance: The hills are rounded and lumpy (not with sharp peaks and points), so they look sort of, a little bit, like the bodies of elephants. Jig says later, "They don't really look like white elephants. I just meant the coloring of their skin through the trees" (p. 121), but by then most readers probably have a visual image of their shape as well.

If that was the only time the phrase was used in the story, it would simply be a part of the description of the setting. But it is repeated three times, as well as being the title phrase. Dwelling on it this way suggests there is more to it than an imaginative description of setting. And if Jig had said only that the hills are like elephants, the phrase probably wouldn't get beyond the physical. But she says they are like white elephants. That takes us further, probably requiring us to explore what white elephants are. The *Oxford English Dictionary* gives the following definitions for *white elephant* (all current when Hemingway was writing):

> a. A rare albino variety of elephant which is highly venerated in some Asian countries. b. *fig.* A burdensome or costly possession (from the story that the kings of Siam were accustomed to make a present of one of these animals to courtiers who had rendered themselves obnoxious, in order to ruin the recipient by the cost of its maintenance). Also, an object, scheme, etc., considered to be without use or value.

White elephants have taken on traditional symbolic significance in Eastern cultures and, to some extent, Western societies. Some of that traditional symbolic significance is carried into "Hills Like White Elephants" through the repeated references to, and resulting prominence of, white elephants in the story. The story implies that Jig, unlike the man, has seen white elephants:

> "They look like white elephants," she said.
> "I've never seen one," the man drank his beer.
> "No, you wouldn't have." (p. 120)

If she has, she probably knows that they are both rare and venerated and (figuratively) a burdensome or useless possession. Their conversation goes from "all the things you've waited so long for" to "white elephants" to the operation: the "simple operation" that is "not really an operation at all." It's left to the reader to decide what the operation is. It might well be an abortion (see if that fits the way they talk about it). In that case, her use of *white elephant* suggests a contrast — whether she intends the application or not — between pregnancy and new life as, on the one hand, a highly valued treasure and, on the other, a burden or an object without value. In addition, the story implies that, if Jig stays pregnant, the man may soon think of her as a burdensome and unwanted possession.

Archetypal Symbols

A special type of traditional symbol is an *archetypal symbol*. **Archetypes** are original models or patterns from which later things are made: the first automobile that was constructed is the archetype of all later models. *Literary archetypes* are symbols, character types, and plot lines that trace back to original models or patterns, especially in early myths, folktales, fairy tales, and religious writings. They are used again and again in literature until they come to carry a wide, nearly universal significance and thus move most readers at a very deep emotional level.

Here is a list of some archetypal symbols — a small sampling of all those that could be listed — to illustrate what you can look for:

- A *meal* or *feast* as a symbol of harmony and union
- A *garden* or *park* as a type of paradise
- The *country* as a place of natural beauty, freedom, or innocence, in contrast to a *city* as a place of artificiality and corruption, or of order and community
- A *forest* as natural beauty, or as a scary place where one can be lost
- A *spring* or *fountain* as a symbol of purity and fertility
- The *sea* as a source of life, or as a symbol of danger, leading to death
- A *desert* or *wilderness* as a symbol of barrenness, emptiness
- A *river* as boundary between worlds, thus as death; sometimes as fertility and source of life
- Cycles of nature — the *phases of the day* (dawn, noon, sunset, and night) and the *seasons* (spring, summer, autumn, and winter) — suggesting the cycles of human life (birth and youth, adulthood, old age, and death)

Character types can also take on symbolic significance. Among archetypal characters used through the centuries are the hero, the villain, the witch, the wanderer, the benevolent ruler, the tyrant, the trickster, the siren, the angel, the keeper of wisdom. And narrative motifs can carry archetypal significance. Examples used throughout literature and now rich with symbolic implications include creation stories, salvation stories, and tales of temptation.

Among the most frequently used symbolic motifs, especially in longer stories and poems, is the archetype of the *journey,* which throughout the centuries has suggested growth or achievement or maturing, especially through experience and education. Because, in that sense, all of us are on a journey, stories, poems, and plays involving journeys are often especially meaningful and include some of the world's best-known literary works. The car as a symbol in "The Red Convertible" suggests that Lyman and Henry are on such a journey of growth and experience, with Henry's experiences in Vietnam, though implied rather described, forming a crucial part of his journey. The railway brings a similar significance into "Hills Like White Elephants," as the wanderings across Europe undertaken by Jig and the American (their luggage is covered with labels "from all the hotels where they had spent nights") echo the directionless journey or wandering that is shaping their lives.

ALLEGORY

Closely related to symbol is **allegory**: a form or manner, usually narrative, in which objects, persons, and actions are themselves in a story on the literal level, but also are equated in a sustained and obvious way with meanings that lie outside the story. In the case of allegory, those meanings often seem or are of more importance to the work than the literal story. The qualification *sustained* points to the allegory's key difference from symbolism: In a work using allegory, many (or all) details carry a related abstract meaning, not just prominent or repeated details. A classic example of allegory is John Bunyan's *Pilgrim's Progress* (1678), an allegorical dream vision in which a character named Christian undertakes a journey through the wilderness of this world, passing through such places as the Slough (swamp) of Despair and a carnival called Vanity Fair on his way to the Celestial City (heaven). Each character, place, and action in the narrative has an equivalent meaning in the Christian journey of faith and salvation. George Orwell's *Animal Farm* (1944) is an example of a satiric political allegory, with the farmer, various animals, and their actions representing aspects of a workers' revolution, the establishment of a communist state, and its corruption as the new leaders take on the same tyrannical attitudes the original owners had.

Be careful not to impose an allegorical way of reading (looking for representational meaning everywhere) on works that are not allegorical. This happens especially when readers are taught to search for "deeper meanings" in literary works and to ask, for almost every character, object, and event, "What does it stand for?" That may appear to be active reading, but it's not. Active readers wisely refrain from trying to find meanings hidden below the surface. Rather, they seek to engage actively with what is right there on the surface. It is vitally important to get to know characters, actions, and objects as themselves, to understand them as thoroughly as possible — which in some cases includes their representational significance but in most cases does not.

Symbols are powerful, among the most evocative experiences for a reader. If read undiscerningly, they can turn a literary work into a hunt for

www
Further explore setting and symbol, including interactive exercises, with VirtuaLit Fiction at bedfordstmartins.com/approachinglit.

"hidden meaning." But when read with thoughtful common sense, they add a rich, suggestive aura and depth to a work, and help us realize that meanings are not hidden but embodied and revealed, suggested, or evoked.

☑ **CHECKLIST on Setting and Symbol**

☐ Be attentive to setting in a literary work:
- setting in terms of place, in its broad sense and in its sense of narrower, individual places
- setting in time
- setting as historical, social, and cultural context

☐ Be aware of different effects setting can have in a work—revealing character, conveying atmosphere, reinforcing meaning, serving as a symbol or occasionally almost as a character.

☐ Be able to explain the difference between an image or action or character that is only itself and one used as a symbol (an image or action or character that also embodies an idea).

☐ Know the formal devices commonly used for indicating that an image, action, or character may be a symbol: repetition, description, prominent placement (title, beginning, ending, climactic scene), or a sense of weightiness or significance beyond the literal function in the work. Be able to use those signals to perceive when a work is using symbols.

☐ Be alert to different kinds of symbols (private, literary, conventional, traditional, and archetypal) and the various ways they affect works.

☐ Be able to recognize allegory (a sustained equating of objects, persons, or actions in a story with a pattern of abstract meaning outside the story, which is often more important than the literal story), and be able to differentiate that from symbol.

☐ Be comfortable with allowing details to be details.

FURTHER READING

Setting and symbol figure significantly in the following story, about how a young girl, a recent arrival to New Jersey with her family from Puerto Rico, attempts to find her way in a very different culture. Escaping the real world through romantic stories, she suddenly finds herself caught in a romantic story that is frightening because of its reality. References to Scheherazade, the storyteller in *Thousand and One Nights* (or *Arabian Nights*), a series of anonymous stories in Arabic, form an important thread in the story. Scheherezade, to keep her husband, King Shahryar, from killing her, gets him to wait until she finishes telling him a tale each night for 1,001 nights. A number of the tales have become well known, including those about Ali Baba, Sinbad the Sailor, and Aladdin.

Judith Ortiz Cofer b. 1952

Not for Sale   [1992]

El Árabe was what the Puerto Rican women called him. He sold them beautiful things from his exotic homeland in the afternoons, at that hour when the day's work is done and there is a little time before the evening duties. He did not carry anything men would buy. His merchandise, mostly linens, was impractical but exquisite. The bed covers were gorgeously woven into oriental tales that he narrated to his customers in his halting Spanish. My mother bought the Scheherazade. It was expensive, but she desired it for my bed, since it was the year when I was being denied everything by my father: no dating like other sixteen-year-olds (I was a decent Puerto Rican señorita, not a wild American teenager); no driver's license (the streets of Paterson, New Jersey, were too dangerous for an inexperienced driver — he would take me where I needed to go); no end-of-the-school-year weekend trip with my junior class to Seaside Heights (even though three teachers would be chaperoning us). *No, no, no,* with a short Spanish "o." Final: no lingering vowels in my father's pronouncements.

  She knew that I could be brought out of my surliness, my seething anger at my father's constant vigilance, by a visit from the storytelling salesman. On the days when I heard the heavy footfall on the staircase announcing his coming, I would emerge from my room, where I kept company only with my English-language books no one else in the house could read. Since I was not allowed to linger at the drugstore with my high school classmates nor to go out socially — unless my father could be persuaded to let me after interrogations and arguments I had come to dread — I had turned to reading in seclusion. Books kept me from going mad. They allowed me to imagine my circumstances as romantic: some days I was an Indian princess living in a *zenana,* a house of women, keeping myself pure, being trained for a brilliant future. Other days I was a prisoner: Papillon, preparing myself for my great flight to freedom. When El Árabe came to our door, bearing his immense stack of bed linens on his shoulder, I ran to let him in. Mother brought him a glass of cold water as he settled into a rocking chair. I sat on the linoleum floor Indian-style while he spread his merchandise in front of us. Sometimes he brought jewelry too. He carried the rings and bracelets in a little red velvet bag he pulled out of his coat pocket. The day he showed us the Scheherazade bedspread, he emptied the glittering contents of the velvet bag on my lap, then he took my hand and fitted a gold ring with an immense green stone on my finger. It was ornate and covered my finger up to the knuckle, scratching the tender skin in between fingers. Feeling nervous, I laughed and tried to take it off. But he shook his head no. He said that he wanted me to keep the ring on while he told me some of the stories woven on the bedspread. It was a magic ring, he said, that would help me understand. My mother gave me a little frown from the doorway behind El Árabe, meaning *Be polite but give it back soon.* El Árabe settled back to tell his stories. Every so often he would unfold another corner of the bedspread to illustrate a scene.

On a gold background with green threads running through it, glossy like the patina on the dome at city hall, the weavers had put the seated figure of the storytelling woman among the characters she had created. She seemed to be invisible to them. In each panel she sat slightly behind the action in the posture of wisdom, which the salesman demonstrated: mouth parted and arms extended toward her audience, like a Buddha or a sacred dancer. While Sinbad wields his sword at a pirate, Scheherazade sits calmly in between them. She can be found on the street corner, where Aladdin trades his new lamps for old. But he does not see her.

El Árabe spoke deliberately, but his Spanish was still difficult to understand. It was as if his tongue had trouble with certain of our sound combinations. But he was patient. When he saw that one of us had lost the thread of the story, he would begin again, sometimes at the beginning.

This usually drove my mother out of the room, but I understood that these tales were one continuous story to him. If broken, the pattern would be ruined. They had to be told all the way through. I looked at him closely as he spoke. He appeared to be about my father's age, but it was hard to tell, because a thick beard covered most of his face. His eyes revealed his fatigue. He was stooped from carrying his bundles from building to building, I assumed. No one seemed to know where he lived or whether he had a family. But on the day of the Scheherazade stories he told me about his son. The subject seemed to arise naturally out of the last tale. The king who beheaded his brides was captivated by the storytelling woman and spared her life. I felt uneasy with this ending, though I had read it before, not trusting the gluttonous King Shahryar to keep his word. And what would happen to Scheherazade when she ran out of stories? It was always the same with these fairy tales: the plot was fascinating, but the ending was unsatisfactory to me. "Happily ever after" was a loose knot tied on a valuable package.

El Árabe took the first payment on the bedspread from my mother who had, I knew, gotten the dollar bills out of her underwear drawer where she kept her "secret" little stash of money in the foot of a nylon stocking. She probably thought that neither my father nor I would have any reason to look there. But in that year of my seclusion, nothing was safe from my curiosity: if I could not go out and explore the world, I would learn what I could from within the four walls. Sometimes I was Anne Frank, and what little there was to discover from my keepers belonged by rights to me.

She counted out ten dollars slowly into his hand. He opened his little notebook with frayed pages. He wrote with a pencil: the full amount at the top, her name, the date, and "10.00" with a flourish. She winced a little as she followed his numbers. It would take her a long time to pay it off. She asked me if I really wanted it — three times. But she knew what it meant to me.

My mother left with the bedspread, explaining that she wanted to see how it would look on my bed. El Árabe seemed reluctant to leave. He lit a slender, aromatic cigarette he took out of a gold case with a little diamond in the middle. Then he repeated the story of Scheherazade's winning over of her husband. Though I was by now weary of the repetition, I listened politely. It was then that he said that he had a son, a handsome young man who wanted very much to come to America to take over the business. There was much money to be made. I nodded, not really understanding why he was telling me all this.

But I fell under the spell of his words as he described a heroic vision of a handsome man who rode thoroughbreds over a golden desert. Without my being aware of it, the afternoon passed quickly. It caught me entirely by surprise when I heard the key turning in the front door lock. I was really chagrined at being found out of my room by my father.

He walked in on us before I had time to rise from my childish position on the floor at El Árabe's feet.

He came in, smelling strongly of sweat and coffee from the factory where he was the watchman. I never understood why sacks of unprocessed coffee beans had to be watched, but that's all I knew about his job. He walked in, looking annoyed and suspicious. He did not like any interruption of his routines: he wanted to find my mother and me in our places when he came home. If she had a friend drop by, Mother had to make sure the visit ended before he arrived. I had stopped inviting my friends over after a while, since his silent hostility made them uncomfortable. Long ago, when I was a little girl, he had spent hours every evening playing with me and reading to me in Spanish. Now, since those activities no longer appealed to me, since I wanted to spend time with other people, he showed no interest in me, except to say no to my requests for permission to go out.

Mother tried to mediate between us by reminding me often of my father's early affection. She explained that teenage girls in Puerto Rico did not go out without chaperons as I wanted to do. They stayed home and helped their mothers and obeyed their fathers. Didn't he give me everything I needed?

I had felt furious at her absurd statements. They did not apply to me, or to the present reality of my life in Paterson, New Jersey. I would work myself into a shouting frenzy. I would scream out my protests that we were not living in some backward country where women were slaves.

"Look," I would point out of the window of our fifth-story apartment in a building at the core of the city. "Do you see palm trees, any sand or blue water? All I see is concrete. We are in the United States. I am an American citizen. I speak English better than Spanish and I am as old as you were when you got married!" The arguments would end with her in tears and the heavy blanket of angry silence falling over both of us. It was no use talking to him either. He had her to comfort him for the unfairness of twelve-hour days in a factory and for being too tired to do anything else but read *La Prensa* in the evenings. I felt like an exile in the foreign country of my parents' house.

My father walked into the living room and immediately focused his eyes on the immense ring on my finger. Without greeting the salesman, without acknowledging my mother who had just returned to the room, he kept pointing at my hand. El Árabe stood up and bowed his head to my father in a strange formal way. Then he said something very odd—something like *I greet you as a kinsman, the ring is a gift to your daughter from my son.* What followed was utter confusion. My father kept asking what? what? what? I struggled to my feet trying to remove the ring from my finger, but it seemed to be stuck. My mother waved me into the kitchen where we worked soap around the swollen finger. In silence we listened to the shouting match in the living room. Both men seemed to be talking at once.

From what I could make out, El Árabe was proposing to my father that I be sold to him—for a fair price—to be his son's bride. This was necessary, since his son could not immigrate quickly unless he married an American citizen. The old salesman was willing to bargain with my father over what I was worth in this transaction. I heard figures, a listing of merchandise, a certain number of cattle and horses his son could sell in their country for cash if that was what my father preferred.

My father seemed to be choking. He could not break through the expert haggler's multilingual stream of offers and descriptions of family wealth. My mother pulled the ring off my finger, scraping away some of the skin along with it. I tried not to cry out, but something broke in me when I heard my father's anguished scream of *Not for sale! Not for sale!* persisting until the salesman fell silent. My mother rushed the ring out to the living room while I tried to regain my self-control. But my father's hoarse voice repeating the one phrase echoed in my ears; even after there was the sound of a door being shut and the dull, heavy footsteps of a burdened man descending the stairs, I heard the pained protest.

Then my father came into the kitchen, where I was standing at the sink, washing the blood off my fingers. The ring had cut me deeply. He stood in silence and, unmoving in the doorway, looked at me as if he had not seen me in a long time or just then for the first time. Then he asked me in a soft voice if I was all right. I nodded, hiding my hand behind my back.

In the months that followed, my mother paid on her account at the door. El Árabe did not come into our apartment again. My father learned the word "yes" in English and practiced saying it occasionally, though "no" remained NO in both languages and easier to say for a nonnative speaker.

On my bed Scheherazade kept telling her stories, which I came to understand would never end—as I had once feared—since it was in my voice that she spoke to me, placing my dreams among hers, weaving them in.

APPROACHING THE READING

1. Find out something about Paterson, New Jersey—locate it on a map, look up information about it in an almanac, or research it through the Internet. Why is it appropriate as the locale of the story? What differences would it make if the story were set in New York City or New Orleans or a small town in the Southwest?

2. In this story, setting as cultural context is very important. Both the family and the salesman have been displaced from a familiar, homogenous culture to a new, diverse one. Inevitably they hold onto some familiar customs. How does setting as place contribute to a clash of cultural differences?

3. The Scheherazade bedspread seems to have the kind of prominence (frequent repetition, detailed description, noticeable positioning in the first and last paragraphs) and weightiness that would justify regarding it as a symbol. What meanings does the bedspread suggest? As you think about the bedspread's significance, ask yourself: Why does the mother buy the bedspread? Why does the speaker want it so much? What does it seem to mean to her? How does it contribute to her characterization and reveal aspects of her character?

The following is a rich, moving, beautifully written story about a young African American musician who struggles against his physical location, drugs, and lack of understanding by his family as he tries to find himself as a musician and as a man, and about the brother who fails to provide him the kind of help he needs. Both setting and symbol seem important in it. As you read, you'll be able to identify with the associations of its general settings—a high school, an apartment building in a crowded city, a family gathering, a night club—though connecting with its specific setting in the Harlem section of New York City might take some effort. Pay attention especially to the effects of setting on characters, on what happens, and on the theme.

James Baldwin   1924–1987

Sonny's Blues   [1957]

I read about it in the paper, in the subway, on my way to work. I read it, and I couldn't believe it, and I read it again. Then perhaps I just stared at it, at the newsprint spelling out his name, spelling out the story. I stared at it in the swinging lights of the subway car, and in the faces and bodies of the people, and in my own face, trapped in the darkness which roared outside.

It was not to be believed and I kept telling myself that, as I walked from the subway station to the high school. And at the same time I couldn't doubt

it. I was scared, scared for Sonny. He became real to me again. A great block
of ice got settled in my belly and kept melting there slowly all day long, while
I taught my classes algebra. It was a special kind of ice. It kept melting, sending trickles of ice water all up and down my veins, but it never got less.
Sometimes it hardened and seemed to expand until I felt my guts were going
to come spilling out or that I was going to choke or scream. This would always be at a moment when I was remembering some specific thing Sonny
had once said or done.

When he was about as old as the boys in my classes his face had been
bright and open, there was a lot of copper in it; and he'd had wonderfully
direct brown eyes, and great gentleness and privacy. I wondered what he
looked like now. He had been picked up, the evening before, in a raid on an
apartment downtown, for peddling and using heroin.

I couldn't believe it: but what I mean by that is that I couldn't find any
room for it anywhere inside me. I had kept it outside me for a long time. I
hadn't wanted to know. I had had suspicions, but I didn't name them, I kept
putting them away. I told myself that Sonny was wild, but he wasn't crazy.
And he'd always been a good boy, he hadn't ever turned hard or evil or disrespectful, the way kids can, so quick, so quick, especially in Harlem. I didn't
want to believe that I'd ever see my brother going down, coming to nothing,
all that light in his face gone out, in the condition I'd already seen so many
others. Yet it had happened and here I was, talking about algebra to a lot of
boys who might, every one of them for all I knew, be popping off needles
every time they went to the head. Maybe it did more for them than algebra
could.

I was sure that the first time Sonny had ever had horse, he couldn't have
been much older than these boys were now. These boys, now, were living as
we'd been living then, they were growing up with a rush and their heads
bumped abruptly against the low ceiling of their actual possibilities. They
were filled with rage. All they really knew were two darknesses, the darkness
of their lives, which was now closing in on them, and the darkness of the
movies, which had blinded them to that other darkness, and in which they
now, vindictively, dreamed, at once more together than they were at any
other time, and more alone.

When the last bell rang, the last class ended, I let out my breath. It
seemed I'd been holding it for all that time. My clothes were wet — I may
have looked as though I'd been sitting in a steam bath, all dressed up, all afternoon. I sat alone in the classroom a long time. I listened to the boys outside, downstairs, shouting and cursing and laughing. Their laughter struck
me for perhaps the first time. It was not the joyous laughter which — God
knows why — one associates with children. It was mocking and insular, its
intent to denigrate. It was disenchanted, and in this, also, lay the authority
of their curses. Perhaps I was listening to them because I was thinking about
my brother and in them I heard my brother. And myself.

One boy was whistling a tune, at once very complicated and very simple,
it seemed to be pouring out of him as though he were a bird, and it sounded

very cool and moving through all that harsh, bright air, only just holding its own through all those other sounds.

I stood up and walked over to the window and looked down into the courtyard. It was the beginning of the spring and the sap was rising in the boys. A teacher passed through them every now and again, quickly, as though he or she couldn't wait to get out of that courtyard, to get those boys out of their sight and off their minds. I started collecting my stuff. I thought I'd better get home and talk to Isabel.

The courtyard was almost deserted by the time I got downstairs. I saw this boy standing in the shadow of a doorway, looking just like Sonny. I almost called his name. Then I saw that it wasn't Sonny, but somebody we used to know, a boy from around our block. He'd been Sonny's friend. He'd never been mine, having been too young for me, and, anyway, I'd never liked him. And now, even though he was a grown-up man, he still hung around that block, still spent hours on the street corners, was always high and raggy. I used to run into him from time to time and he'd often work around to asking me for a quarter or fifty cents. He always had some real good excuse, too, and I always gave it to him, I don't know why.

But now, abruptly, I hated him. I couldn't stand the way he looked at me, partly like a dog, partly like a cunning child. I wanted to ask him what the hell he was doing in the school courtyard.

He sort of shuffled over to me, and he said, "I see you got the papers. So you already know about it."

"You mean about Sonny? Yes, I already know about it. How come they didn't get you?"

He grinned. It made him repulsive and it also brought to mind what he'd looked like as a kid. "I wasn't there. I stay away from them people."

"Good for you." I offered him a cigarette and I watched him through the smoke. "You come all the way down here just to tell me about Sonny?"

"That's right." He was sort of shaking his head and his eyes looked strange, as though they were about to cross. The bright sun deadened his damp dark brown skin and it made his eyes look yellow and showed up the dirt in his kinked hair. He smelled funky. I moved a little away from him and I said, "Well, thanks. But I already know about it and I got to get home."

"I'll walk you a little ways," he said. We started walking. There were a couple of kids still loitering in the courtyard and one of them said goodnight to me and looked strangely at the boy beside me.

"What're you going to do?" he asked me. "I mean, about Sonny?"

"Look. I haven't seen Sonny for over a year, I'm not sure I'm going to do anything. Anyway, what the hell *can* I do?"

"That's right," he said quickly, "ain't nothing you can do. Can't much help old Sonny no more, I guess."

It was what I was thinking and so it seemed to me he had no right to say it.

"I'm surprised at Sonny, though," he went on—he had a funny way of talking, he looked straight ahead as though he were talking to himself— "I thought Sonny was a smart boy, I thought he was too smart to get hung."

"I guess he thought so too," I said sharply, "and that's how he got hung. And how about you? You're pretty goddamn smart, I bet."

Then he looked directly at me, just for a minute. "I ain't smart," he said. "If I was smart, I'd have reached for a pistol a long time ago."

"Look. Don't tell *me* your sad story, if it was up to me, I'd give you one." Then I felt guilty—guilty, probably, for never having supposed that the poor bastard *had* a story of his own, much less a sad one, and I asked, quickly, "What's going to happen to him now?"

He didn't answer this. He was off by himself some place. "Funny thing," he said, and from his tone we might have been discussing the quickest way to get to Brooklyn, "when I saw the papers this morning, the first thing I asked myself was if I had anything to do with it. I felt sort of responsible."

I began to listen more carefully. The subway station was on the corner, just before us, and I stopped. He stopped, too. We were in front of a bar and he ducked lightly, peering in, but whoever he was looking for didn't seem to be there. The juke box was blasting away with something black and bouncy and I half watched the barmaid as she danced her way from the juke box to her place behind the bar. And I watched her face as she laughingly responded to something someone said to her, still keeping time to the music. When she smiled one saw the little girl, one sensed the doomed, still-struggling woman beneath the battered face of the semi-whore.

"I never *give* Sonny nothing," the boy said finally, "but a long time ago I come to school high and Sonny asked me how it felt." He paused, I couldn't bear to watch him, I watched the barmaid, and I listened to the music which seemed to be causing the pavement to shake. "I told him it felt great." The music stopped, the barmaid paused and watched the juke box until the music began again. "It did."

All this was carrying me some place I didn't want to go. I certainly didn't want to know how it felt. It filled everything, the people, the houses, the music, the dark, quicksilver barmaid, with menace; and this menace was their reality.

"What's going to happen to him now?" I asked again.

"They'll send him away some place and they'll try to cure him." He shook his head. "Maybe he'll even think he's kicked the habit. Then they'll let him loose"—he gestured, throwing his cigarette into the gutter. "That's all."

"What do you mean, that's *all?*"

But I knew what he meant.

"I *mean,* that's *all.*" He turned his head and looked at me, pulling down the corners of his mouth. "Don't you know what I mean?" he asked, softly.

"How the hell *would* I know what you mean?" I almost whispered it, I don't know why.

"That's right," he said to the air, "how would *he* know what I mean?" He turned toward me again, patient and calm, and yet I somehow felt him shaking, shaking as though he were going to fall apart. I felt that ice in my guts again, the dread I'd felt all afternoon; and again I watched the barmaid, moving about the bar, washing glasses, and singing. "Listen. They'll let him out and then it'll just start all over again. That's what I mean."

"You mean — they'll let him out. And then he'll just start working his way back in again. You mean he'll never kick the habit. Is that what you mean?"

"That's right," he said, cheerfully. "*You* see what I mean."

"Tell me," I said at last, "why does he want to die? He must want to die, he's killing himself, why does he want to die?"

He looked at me in surprise. He licked his lips. "He don't want to die. He wants to live. Don't nobody want to die, ever."

Then I wanted to ask him — too many things. He could not have answered, or if he had, I could not have borne the answers. I started walking. "Well, I guess it's none of my business."

"It's going to be rough on old Sonny," he said. We reached the subway station. "This is your station?" he asked. I nodded. I took one step down. "Damn!" he said, suddenly. I looked up at him. He grinned again. "Damn it if I didn't leave all my money home. You ain't got a dollar on you, have you? Just for a couple of days, is all."

All at once something inside gave and threatened to come pouring out of me. I didn't hate him any more. I felt that in another moment I'd start crying like a child.

"Sure," I said. "Don't sweat." I looked in my wallet and didn't have a dollar, I only had a five. "Here," I said. "That hold you?"

He didn't look at it — he didn't want to look at it. A terrible closed look came over his face, as though he were keeping the number on the bill a secret from him and me. "Thanks," he said, and now he was dying to see me go. "Don't worry about Sonny. Maybe I'll write him or something."

"Sure," I said. "You do that. So long."

"Be seeing you," he said. I went on down the steps.

And I didn't write Sonny or send him anything for a long time. When I finally did, it was just after my little girl died, he wrote me back a letter which made me feel like a bastard.

Here's what he said:

Dear brother,
    You don't know how much I needed to hear from you. I wanted to write you many a time but I dug how much I must have hurt you and so I didn't write. But now I feel like a man who's been trying to climb up out of some deep, real deep and funky hole and just saw the sun up there, outside. I got to get outside.

I can't tell you much about how I got here. I mean I don't know how to tell you. I guess I was afraid of something or I was trying to escape from something and you know I have never been very strong in the head (smile). I'm glad Mama and Daddy are dead and can't see what's happened to their son and I swear if I'd known what I was doing I would never have hurt you so, you and a lot of other fine people who were nice to me and who believed in me.

I don't want you to think it had anything to do with me being a musician. It's more than that. Or maybe less than that. I can't get anything straight in my head down here and I try not to think about what's going to happen to me when I get outside again. Sometime I think I'm going to flip and *never* get outside and sometime I think I'll come straight back. I tell you one thing, though, I'd rather blow my brains out than go through this again. But that's what they all say, so they tell me. If I tell you when I'm coming to New York and if you could meet me, I sure would appreciate it. Give my love to Isabel and the kids and I was sure sorry to hear about little Gracie. I wish I could be like Mama and say the Lord's will be done, but I don't know it seems to me that trouble is the one thing that never does get stopped and I don't know what good it does to blame it on the Lord. But maybe it does some good if you believe it.

Your brother,
Sonny

Then I kept in constant touch with him and I sent him whatever I could and I went to meet him when he came back to New York. When I saw him many things I thought I had forgotten came flooding back to me. This was because I had begun, finally, to wonder about Sonny, about the life that Sonny lived inside. This life, whatever it was, had made him older and thinner and it had deepened the distant stillness in which he had always moved. He looked very unlike my baby brother. Yet, when he smiled, when we shook hands, the baby brother I'd never known looked out from the depths of his private life, like an animal waiting to be coaxed into the light.

"How you been keeping?" he asked me.

"All right. And you?"

"Just fine." He was smiling all over his face. "It's good to see you again."

"It's good to see you."

The seven years' difference in our ages lay between us like a chasm: I wondered if these years would ever operate between us as a bridge. I was remembering, and it made it hard to catch my breath, that I had been there when he was born; and I had heard the first words he had ever spoken. When he started to walk, he walked from our mother straight to me. I caught him just before he fell when he took the first steps he ever took in this world.

"How's Isabel?"

"Just fine. She's dying to see you."

"And the boys?"

"They're fine, too. They're anxious to see their uncle."

"Oh, come on. You know they don't remember me."

"Are you kidding? Of course they remember you."

He grinned again. We got into a taxi. We had a lot to say to each other, far too much to know how to begin.

As the taxi began to move, I asked, "You still want to go to India?"

He laughed. "You still remember that. Hell, no. This place is Indian enough for me."

"It used to belong to them," I said.

And he laughed again. "They damn sure knew what they were doing when they got rid of it."

Years ago, when he was around fourteen, he'd been all hipped on the idea of going to India. He read books about people sitting on rocks, naked, in all kinds of weather, but mostly bad, naturally, and walking barefoot through hot coals and arriving at wisdom. I used to say that it sounded to me as though they were getting away from wisdom as fast as they could. I think he sort of looked down on me for that.

"Do you mind," he asked, "if we have the driver drive alongside the park? On the west side — I haven't seen the city in so long."

"Of course not," I said. I was afraid that I might sound as though I were humoring him, but I hoped he wouldn't take it that way.

So we drove along, between the green of the park and the stony, lifeless elegance of hotels and apartment buildings, toward the vivid, killing streets of our childhood. These streets hadn't changed, though housing projects jutted up out of them now like rocks in the middle of a boiling sea. Most of the houses in which we had grown up had vanished, as had the stores from which we had stolen, the basements in which we had first tried sex, the rooftops from which we had hurled tin cans and bricks. But houses exactly like the houses of our past yet dominated the landscape, boys exactly like the boys we once had been found themselves smothering in these houses, came down into the streets for light and air and found themselves encircled by disaster. Some escaped the trap, most didn't. Those who got out always left something of themselves behind, as some animals amputate a leg and leave it in the trap. It might be said, perhaps, that I had escaped, after all, I was a school teacher; or that Sonny had, he hadn't lived in Harlem for years. Yet, as the cab moved uptown through streets which seemed, with a rush, to darken with dark people, and as I covertly studied Sonny's face, it came to me that what we both were seeking through our separate cab windows was that part of ourselves which had been left behind. It's always at the hour of trouble and confrontation that the missing member aches.

We hit 110th Street and started rolling up Lenox Avenue. And I'd known this avenue all my life, but it seemed to me again, as it had seemed on the day I'd first heard about Sonny's trouble, filled with a hidden menace which was its very breath of life.

"We almost there," said Sonny.

"Almost." We were both too nervous to say anything more.

We live in a housing project. It hasn't been up long. A few days after it was up it seemed uninhabitably new, now, of course, it's already rundown. It looks like a parody of the good, clean, faceless life—God knows the people who live in it do their best to make it a parody. The beat-looking grass lying around isn't enough to make their lives green, the hedges will never hold out the streets, and they know it. The big windows fool no one, they aren't big enough to make space out of no space. They don't bother with the windows, they watch the TV screen instead. The playground is most popular with the children who don't play at jacks, or skip rope, or roller skate, or swing, and they can be found in it after dark. We moved in partly because it's not too far from where I teach, and partly for the kids; but it's really just like the houses in which Sonny and I grew up. The same things happen, they'll have the same things to remember. The moment Sonny and I started into the house I had the feeling that I was simply bringing him back into the danger he had almost died trying to escape.

Sonny has never been talkative. So I don't know why I was sure he'd be dying to talk to me when supper was over the first night. Everything went fine, the oldest boy remembered him, and the youngest boy liked him, and Sonny had remembered to bring something for each of them; and Isabel, who is really much nicer than I am, more open and giving, had gone to a lot of trouble about dinner and was genuinely glad to see him. And she's always been able to tease Sonny in a way that I haven't. It was nice to see her face so vivid again and to hear her laugh and watch her make Sonny laugh. She wasn't, or, anyway, she didn't seem to be, at all uneasy or embarrassed. She chatted as though there were no subject which had to be avoided and she got Sonny past his first, faint stiffness. And thank God she was there, for I was filled with that icy dread again. Everything I did seemed awkward to me, and everything I said sounded freighted with hidden meaning. I was trying to remember everything I'd heard about dope addiction and I couldn't help watching Sonny for signs. I wasn't doing it out of malice. I was trying to find out something about my brother. I was dying to hear him tell me he was safe.

"Safe!" my father grunted, whenever Mama suggested trying to move to a neighborhood which might be safer for children. "Safe, hell! Ain't no place safe for kids, nor nobody."

He always went on like this, but he wasn't, ever, really as bad as he sounded, not even on weekends, when he got drunk. As a matter of fact, he was always on the lookout for "something a little better," but he died before he found it. He died suddenly, during a drunken weekend in the middle of the war, when Sonny was fifteen. He and Sonny hadn't ever got on too well. And this was partly because Sonny was the apple of his father's eye. It was because he loved Sonny so much and was frightened for him, that he was always fighting with him. It doesn't do any good to fight with Sonny. Sonny just moves back, inside himself, where he can't be reached. But the principal reason that they never hit it off is that they were so much alike. Daddy was big and rough and loud-talking, just the opposite of Sonny, but they both had — that same privacy.

Mama tried to tell me something about this, just after Daddy died. I was home on leave from the army.

This was the last time I ever saw my mother alive. Just the same, this picture gets all mixed up in my mind with pictures I had of her when she was younger. The way I always see her is the way she used to be on a Sunday afternoon, say, when the old folks were talking after the big Sunday dinner. I always see her wearing pale blue. She'd be sitting on the sofa. And my father would be sitting in the easy chair, not far from her. And the living room would be full of church folks and relatives. There they sit, in chairs all around the living room, and the night is creeping up outside, but nobody knows it yet. You can see the darkness growing against the windowpanes and you hear the street noises every now and again, or maybe the jangling beat of a tambourine from one of the churches close by, but it's real quiet in the room. For a moment nobody's talking, but every face looks darkening, like the sky outside. And my mother rocks a little from the waist, and my father's eyes are closed. Everyone is looking at something a child can't see. For a minute they've forgotten the children. Maybe a kid is lying on the rug, half asleep. Maybe somebody's got a kid in his lap and is absent-mindedly stroking the kid's head. Maybe there's a kid, quiet and big-eyed, curled up in a big chair in the corner. The silence, the darkness coming, and the darkness in the faces frightens the child obscurely. He hopes that the hand which strokes his forehead will never stop — will never die. He hopes that there will never come a time when the old folks won't be sitting around the living room, talking about where they've come from, and what they've seen, and what's happened to them and their kinfolk.

But something deep and watchful in the child knows that this is bound to end, is already ending. In a moment someone will get up and turn on the light. Then the old folks will remember the children and they won't talk any more that day. And when light fills the room, the child is filled with darkness. He knows that everytime this happens he's moved just a little closer to that darkness outside. The darkness outside is what the old folks have been talking about. It's what they've come from. It's what they endure. The child knows that they won't talk any more because if he knows too much about what's happened to *them*, he'll know too much too soon, about what's going to happen to *him*.

The last time I talked to my mother, I remember I was restless. I wanted to get out and see Isabel. We weren't married then and we had a lot to straighten out between us.

There Mama sat, in black, by the window. She was humming an old church song, *Lord, you brought me from a long ways off.* Sonny was out somewhere. Mama kept watching the streets.

"I don't know," she said, "if I'll ever see you again, after you go off from here. But I hope you'll remember the things I tried to teach you."

"Don't talk like that," I said, and smiled. "You'll be here a long time yet."

She smiled, too, but she said nothing. She was quiet for a long time. And I said, "Mama, don't you worry about nothing. I'll be writing all the time, and you be getting the checks. . . ."

"I want to talk to you about your brother," she said, suddenly. "If anything happens to me he ain't going to have nobody to look out for him."

"Mama," I said, "ain't nothing going to happen to you *or* Sonny. Sonny's all right. He's a good boy and he's got good sense."

"It ain't a question of his being a good boy," Mama said, "nor of his having good sense. It ain't only the bad ones, nor yet the dumb ones that gets sucked under." She stopped, looking at me. "Your Daddy once had a brother," she said, and she smiled in a way that made me feel she was in pain. "You didn't never know that, did you?"

"No," I said, "I never knew that," and I watched her face.

"Oh, yes," she said, "your Daddy had a brother." She looked out of the window again. "I know you never saw your Daddy cry. But *I* did — many a time, through all these years."

I asked her, "What happened to his brother? How come nobody's ever talked about him?"

This was the first time I ever saw my mother look old.

"His brother got killed," she said, "when he was just a little younger than you are now. I knew him. He was a fine boy. He was maybe a little full of the devil, but he didn't mean nobody no harm."

Then she stopped and the room was silent, exactly as it had sometimes been on those Sunday afternoons. Mama kept looking out into the streets.

"He used to have a job in the mill," she said, "and, like all young folks, he just liked to perform on Saturday nights. Saturday nights, him and your father would drift around to different places, go to dances and things like that, or just sit around with people they knew, and your father's brother would sing, he had a fine voice, and play along with himself on his guitar. Well, this particular Saturday night, him and your father was coming home from some place, and they were both a little drunk and there was a moon that night, it was bright like day. Your father's brother was feeling kind of good, and he was whistling to himself, and he had his guitar slung over his shoulder. They was coming down a hill and beneath them was a road that turned off from the highway. Well, your father's brother, being always kind of frisky, decided to run down this hill, and he did, with that guitar banging and clanging behind him, and he ran across the road, and he was making water behind a tree. And your father was sort of amused at him and he was still coming down the hill, kind of slow. Then he heard a car motor and that same minute his brother stepped from behind the tree, into the road, in the moonlight. And he started to cross the road. And your father started to run down the hill, he says he don't know why. This car was full of white men. They was all drunk, and when they seen your father's brother they let out a great whoop and holler and they aimed the car straight at him. They was having fun, they just wanted to scare him, the way they do sometimes, you know. But they was drunk. And I guess the boy, being drunk, too, and scared, kind of lost his head. By the time he jumped it was too late. Your father says he heard his brother scream when the car rolled over him, and he heard the wood of that guitar when it give, and he heard them strings go flying, and he heard them white men shouting, and the car kept on a-going and it ain't stopped till this day. And, time your father got down the hill, his brother weren't nothing but blood and pulp."

Tears were gleaming on my mother's face. There wasn't anything I could say.

"He never mentioned it," she said, "because I never let him mention it before you children. Your Daddy was like a crazy man that night and for many a night thereafter. He says he never in his life seen anything as dark as that road after the lights of that car had gone away. Weren't nothing, weren't nobody on that road, just your Daddy and his brother and that busted guitar. Oh, yes. Your Daddy never did really get right again. Till the day he died he weren't sure but that every white man he saw was the man that killed his brother."

She stopped and took out her handkerchief and dried her eyes and looked at me.

"I ain't telling you all this," she said, "to make you scared or bitter or to make you hate nobody. I'm telling you this because you got a brother. And the world ain't changed."

I guess I didn't want to believe this. I guess she saw this in my face. She turned away from me, toward the window again, searching those streets.

"But I praise my Redeemer," she said at last, "that He called your Daddy home before me. I ain't saying it to throw no flowers at myself, but, I declare, it keeps me from feeling too cast down to know I helped your father get safely through this world. Your father always acted like he was the roughest, strongest man on earth. And everybody took him to be like that. But if he hadn't had *me* there—to see his tears!"

She was crying again. Still, I couldn't move. I said, "Lord, Lord, Mama, I didn't know it was like that."

"Oh, honey," she said, "there's a lot that you don't know. But you are going to find it out." She stood up from the window and came over to me. "You got to hold on to your brother," she said, "and don't let him fall, no matter what it looks like is happening to him and no matter how evil you gets with him. You going to be evil with him many a time. But don't you forget what I told you, you hear?"

"I won't forget," I said. "Don't you worry, I won't forget. I won't let nothing happen to Sonny."

My mother smiled as though she were amused at something she saw in my face. Then, "You may not be able to stop nothing from happening. But you got to let him know you's *there*."

Two days later I was married, and then I was gone. And I had a lot of things on my mind and I pretty well forgot my promise to Mama until I got shipped home on a special furlough for her funeral.

And, after the funeral, with just Sonny and me alone in the empty kitchen, I tried to find out something about him.

"What do you want to do?" I asked him.

"I'm going to be a musician," he said.

For he had graduated, in the time I had been away, from dancing to the juke box to finding out who was playing what, and what they were doing with it, and he had bought himself a set of drums.

"You mean, you want to be a drummer?" I somehow had the feeling that being a drummer might be all right for other people but not for my brother Sonny.

"I don't think," he said, looking at me very gravely, "that I'll ever be a good drummer. But I think I can play a piano."

I frowned. I'd never played the role of the older brother quite so seriously before, had scarcely ever, in fact, *asked* Sonny a damn thing. I sensed myself in the presence of something I didn't really know how to handle, didn't understand. So I made my frown a little deeper as I asked: "What kind of musician do you want to be?"

He grinned. "How many kinds do you think there are?"

"Be *serious*," I said.

He laughed, throwing his head back, and then looked at me. "I *am* serious."

"Well, then, for Christ's sake, stop kidding around and answer a serious question. I mean, do you want to be a concert pianist, you want to play classical music and all that, or — or what?" Long before I finished he was laughing again. "For Christ's *sake*, Sonny!"

He sobered, but with difficulty. "I'm sorry. But you sound so — *scared!*" and he was off again.

"Well, you may think it's funny now, baby, but it's not going to be so funny when you have to make your living at it, let me tell you *that*. I was furious because I knew he was laughing at me and I didn't know why.

"No," he said, very sober now, and afraid, perhaps, that he'd hurt me, "I don't want to be a classical pianist. That isn't what interests me. I mean" — he paused, looking hard at me, as though his eyes would help me to understand, and then gestured helplessly, as though perhaps his hand would help — "I mean, I'll have a lot of studying to do, and I'll have to study *everything*, but, I mean, I want to play *with* — jazz musicians." He stopped. "I want to play jazz," he said.

Well, the word had never before sounded as heavy, as real, as it sounded that afternoon in Sonny's mouth. I just looked at him and I was probably frowning a real frown by this time. I simply couldn't see why on earth he'd want to spend his time hanging around nightclubs, clowning around on bandstands, while people pushed each other around a dance floor. It seemed — beneath him, somehow. I had never thought about it before, had never been forced to, but I suppose I had always put jazz musicians in a class with what Daddy called "good-time people."

"Are you *serious?*"

"Hell, *yes,* I'm serious."

He looked more helpless than ever, and annoyed, and deeply hurt.

I suggested, helpfully: "You mean — like Louis Armstrong?"

His face closed as though I'd struck him. "No. I'm not talking about none of that old-time, down home crap."

"Well, look, Sonny, I'm sorry, don't get mad. I just don't altogether get it, that's all. Name somebody — you know, a jazz musician you admire."

"Bird."

"Who?"

"Bird! Charlie Parker! Don't they teach you nothing in the goddamn army?"

I lit a cigarette. I was surprised and then a little amused to discover that I was trembling. "I've been out of touch," I said. "You'll have to be patient with me. Now. Who's this Parker character?"

"He's just one of the greatest jazz musicians alive," said Sonny, sullenly, his hands in his pockets, his back to me. "Maybe *the* greatest," he added, bitterly, "that's probably why you never heard of him."

"All right," I said, "I'm ignorant. I'm sorry. I'll go out and buy all the cat's records right away, all right?"

"It don't," said Sonny, with dignity, "make any difference to me. I don't care what you listen to. Don't do me no favors."

I was beginning to realize that I'd never seen him so upset before. With another part of my mind I was thinking that this would probably turn out to be one of those things kids go through and that I shouldn't make it seem important by pushing it too hard. Still, I didn't think it would do any harm to ask: "Doesn't all this take a lot of time? Can you make a living at it?"

He turned back to me and half leaned, half sat, on the kitchen table. "Everything takes time," he said, "and — well, yes, sure, I can make a living at it. But what I don't seem to be able to make you understand is that it's the only thing I want to do."

"Well, Sonny," I said, gently, "you know people can't always do exactly what they *want* to do —"

"*No,* I don't know that," said Sonny, surprising me. "I think people *ought* to do what they want to do, what else are they alive for?"

"You getting to be a big boy," I said desperately, "it's time you started thinking about your future."

"I'm thinking about my future," said Sonny, grimly. "I think about it all the time."

I gave up. I decided, if he didn't change his mind, that we could always talk about it later. "In the meantime," I said, "you got to finish school." We had already decided that he'd have to move in with Isabel and her folks. I knew this wasn't the ideal arrangement because Isabel's folks are inclined to be dicty and they hadn't especially wanted Isabel to marry me. But I didn't know what else to do. "And we have to get you fixed up at Isabel's."

There was a long silence. He moved from the kitchen table to the window. "That's a terrible idea. You know it yourself."

"Do you have a *better* idea?"

He just walked up and down the kitchen for a minute. He was as tall as I was. He had started to shave. I suddenly had the feeling that I didn't know him at all.

He stopped at the kitchen table and picked up my cigarettes. Looking at me with a kind of mocking, amused defiance, he put one between his lips. "You mind?"

"You smoking already?"

He lit the cigarette and nodded, watching me through the smoke. "I just wanted to see if I'd have the courage to smoke in front of you." He grinned and blew a great cloud of smoke to the ceiling. "It was easy." He looked at my face. "Come on, now. I bet you was smoking at my age, tell the truth."

I didn't say anything but the truth was on my face, and he laughed. But now there was something very strained in his laugh. "Sure. And I bet that ain't all you was doing."

He was frightening me a little. "Cut the crap," I said. "We already decided that you was going to go and live at Isabel's. Now what's got into you all of a sudden?"

"*You* decided it," he pointed out. "*I* didn't decide nothing." He stopped in front of me, leaning against the stove, arms loosely folded. "Look, brother. I don't want to stay in Harlem no more, I really don't." He was very earnest. He looked at me, then over toward the kitchen window. There was something in his eyes I'd never seen before, some thoughtfulness, some worry all his own. He rubbed the muscle of one arm. "It's time I was getting out of here."

"Where do you want to *go,* Sonny?"

"I want to join the army. Or the navy, I don't care. If I say I'm old enough, they'll believe me."

Then I got mad. It was because I was so scared. "You must be crazy. You goddamn fool, what the hell do you want to go and join the *army* for?"

"I just told you. To get out of Harlem."

"Sonny, you haven't even finished *school.* And if you really want to be a musician, how do you expect to study if you're in the *army?*"

He looked at me, trapped, and in anguish. "There's ways. I might be able to work out some kind of deal. Anyway, I'll have the G.I. Bill when I come out."

"*If* you come out." We stared at each other. "Sonny, please. Be reasonable. I know the setup is far from perfect. But we got to do the best we can."

"I ain't learning nothing in school," he said. "Even when I go." He turned away from me and opened the window and threw his cigarette out into the narrow alley. I watched his back. "At least, I ain't learning nothing you'd want me to learn." He slammed the window so hard I thought the glass would fly out, and turned back to me. "And I'm sick of the stink of these garbage cans!"

"Sonny," I said, "I know how you feel. But if you don't finish school now, you're going to be sorry later that you didn't." I grabbed him by the shoulders. "And you only got another year. It ain't so bad. And I'll come back and I swear I'll help you do *whatever* you want to do. Just try to put up with it till I come back. Will you please do that? For me?"

He didn't answer and he wouldn't look at me.

"Sonny. You hear me?"

He pulled away. "I hear you. But you never hear anything *I* say."

I didn't know what to say to that. He looked out of the window and then back at me. "OK," he said, and sighed. "I'll try."

Then I said, trying to cheer him up a little, "They got a piano at Isabel's. You can practice on it."

And as a matter of fact, it did cheer him up for a minute. "That's right," he said to himself. "I forgot that." His face relaxed a little. But the worry, the thoughtfulness, played on it still, the way shadows play on a face which is staring into the fire.

But I thought I'd never hear the end of that piano. At first, Isabel would write me, saying how nice it was that Sonny was so serious about his music and how, as soon as he came in from school, or wherever he had been when he was supposed to be at school, he went straight to that piano and stayed there until suppertime. And, after supper, he went back to that piano and stayed there until everybody went to bed. He was at the piano all day Saturday and all day Sunday. Then he bought a record player and started playing records. He'd play one record over and over again, all day long sometimes, and he'd improvise along with it on the piano. Or he'd play one section of the record, one chord, one change, one progression, then he'd do it on the piano. Then back to the record. Then back to the piano.

Well, I really don't know how they stood it. Isabel finally confessed that it wasn't like living with a person at all, it was like living with sound. And the sound didn't make any sense to her, didn't make any sense to any of them—naturally. They began, in a way, to be afflicted by this presence that was living in their home. It was as though Sonny were some sort of god, or monster. He moved in an atmosphere which wasn't like theirs at all. They fed him and he ate, he washed himself, he walked in and out of their door; he certainly wasn't nasty or unpleasant or rude, Sonny isn't any of those things; but it was as though he were all wrapped up in some cloud, some fire, some vision all his own; and there wasn't any way to reach him.

At the same time, he wasn't really a man yet, he was still a child, and they had to watch out for him in all kinds of ways. They certainly couldn't throw him out. Neither did they dare to make a great scene about that piano because even they dimly sensed, as I sensed, from so many thousands of miles away, that Sonny was at that piano playing for his life.

But he hadn't been going to school. One day a letter came from the school board and Isabel's mother got it—there had, apparently, been other letters but Sonny had torn them up. This day, when Sonny came in, Isabel's mother showed him the letter and asked where he'd been spending his time. And she finally got it out of him that he'd been down in Greenwich Village, with musicians and other characters, in a white girl's apartment. And this scared her and she started to scream at him and what came up, once she began—though she denies it to this day—was what sacrifices they were making to give Sonny a decent home and how little he appreciated it.

Sonny didn't play the piano that day. By evening, Isabel's mother had calmed down but then there was the old man to deal with, and Isabel herself. Isabel says she did her best to be calm but she broke down and started crying. She says she just watched Sonny's face. She could tell, by watching him, what was happening with him. And what was happening was that they penetrated his cloud, they had reached him. Even if their fingers had been a thousand times more gentle than human fingers ever are, he could hardly help feeling that they had stripped him naked and were spitting on that nakedness. For he also had to see that his presence, that music, which was life or death to him, had been torture for them and that they had endured it, not at all for his sake, but only for mine. And Sonny couldn't take that. He can take it a little better today than he could then but he's still not very good at it and, frankly, I don't know anybody who is.

The silence of the next few days must have been louder than the sound of all the music ever played since time began. One morning, before she went to work, Isabel was in his room for something and she suddenly realized that all of his records were gone. And she knew for certain that he was gone. And he was. He went as far as the navy would carry him. He finally sent me a postcard from some place in Greece and that was the first I knew that Sonny was still alive. I didn't see him any more until we were both back in New York and the war had long been over.

He was a man by then, of course, but I wasn't willing to see it. He came by the house from time to time, but we fought almost every time we met. I didn't like the way he carried himself, loose and dreamlike all the time, and I didn't like his friends, and his music seemed to be merely an excuse for the life he led. It sounded just that weird and disordered.

Then we had a fight, a pretty awful fight, and I didn't see him for months. By and by I looked him up, where he was living, in a furnished room in the Village, and I tried to make it up. But there were lots of people in the room and Sonny just lay on his bed, and he wouldn't come downstairs with me, and he treated these other people as though they were his family and I weren't. So I got mad and then he got mad, and then I told him that he might just as well be dead as live the way he was living. Then he stood up and he told me not to worry about him any more in life, that he *was* dead as far as I was concerned. Then he pushed me to the door and the other people looked on as though nothing were happening, and he slammed the door behind me. I stood in the hallway, staring at the door. I heard somebody laugh in the room and then the tears came to my eyes. I started down the steps, whistling to keep from crying, I kept whistling to myself, *You going to need me, baby, one of these cold, rainy days.*

I read about Sonny's trouble in the spring. Little Grace died in the fall. She was a beautiful little girl. But she only lived a little over two years. She died of polio and she suffered. She had a slight fever for a couple of days, but it didn't seem like anything and we just kept her in bed. And we would certainly have called the doctor, but the fever dropped, she seemed to be all right. So we thought it had just been a cold. Then, one day, she was up, playing, Isabel was in the kitchen fixing lunch for the two boys when they'd come in from school, and she heard Grace fall down in the living room. When you have a lot of children you don't always start running when one of them falls, unless they start screaming or something. And, this time, Grace was quiet. Yet, Isabel says that when she heard that *thump* and then that silence, something happened in her to make her afraid. And she ran to the living room and there was little Grace on the floor, all twisted up, and the reason she hadn't screamed was that she couldn't get her breath. And when she did scream, it was the worst sound, Isabel says, that she'd ever heard in all her life, and she still hears it sometimes in her dreams. Isabel will sometimes wake me up with a low, moaning, strangled sound and I have to be quick to awaken her and hold her to me and where Isabel is weeping against me seems a mortal wound.

I think I may have written Sonny the very day that little Grace was buried. I was sitting in the living room in the dark, by myself, and I suddenly thought of Sonny. My trouble made his real.

One Saturday afternoon, when Sonny had been living with us, or, anyway, been in our house, for nearly two weeks, I found myself wandering aimlessly about the living room, drinking from a can of beer, and trying to work up the courage to search Sonny's room. He was out, he was usually out whenever I was home, and Isabel had taken the children to see their grandparents. Suddenly I was standing still in front of the living room window, watching Seventh Avenue. The idea of searching Sonny's room made me still. I scarcely dared to admit to myself what I'd be searching for. I didn't know what I'd do if I found it. Or if I didn't.

On the sidewalk across from me, near the entrance to a barbecue joint, some people were holding an old-fashioned revival meeting. The barbecue cook, wearing a dirty white apron, his conked hair reddish and metallic in the pale sun, and a cigarette between his lips, stood in the doorway, watching them. Kids and older people paused in their errands and stood there, along with some older men and a couple of very tough-looking women who watched everything that happened on the avenue, as though they owned it, or were maybe owned by it. Well, they were watching this, too. The revival was being carried on by three sisters in black, and a brother. All they had were their voices and their Bibles and a tambourine. The brother was testifying and while he testified two of the sisters stood together, seeming to say, amen, and the third sister walked around with the tambourine outstretched and a couple of people dropped coins into it. Then the brother's testimony ended and the sister who had been taking up the collection dumped the coins into her palm and transferred them to the pocket of her long black robe. Then she raised both hands, striking the tambourine against the air, and then against one hand, and she started to sing. And the two other sisters and the brother joined in.

It was strange, suddenly, to watch, though I had been seeing these street meetings all my life. So, of course, had everybody else down there. Yet, they paused and watched and listened and I stood still at the window. *"Tis the old ship of Zion,"* they sang, and the sister with the tambourine kept a steady, jangling beat, *"it has rescued many a thousand!"* Not a soul under the sound of their voices was hearing this song for the first time, not one of them had been rescued. Nor had they seen much in the way of rescue work being done around them. Neither did they especially believe in the holiness of the three sisters and the brother, they knew too much about them, knew where they lived, and how. The woman with the tambourine, whose voice dominated the air, whose face was bright with joy, was divided by very little from the woman who stood watching her, a cigarette between her heavy, chapped lips, her hair a cuckoo's nest, her face scarred and swollen from many beatings, and her black eyes glittering like coal. Perhaps they both knew this, which was why, when, as rarely, they addressed each other, they addressed each other as Sister. As the singing filled the air the watching, listening faces underwent a change, the eyes focusing on something within; the music seemed to soothe a poison out of them; and time seemed, nearly, to fall away from the sullen, belligerent, battered faces, as though they were fleeing back to their first condition, while dreaming of their last. The barbecue cook half shook his head and smiled, and dropped his cigarette and disappeared into his joint. A man fumbled in his pockets for change and stood holding it in his hand impatiently, as though he had just remembered a pressing appointment further up the avenue. He looked furious. Then I saw Sonny, standing on the edge of the crowd. He was carrying a wide, flat notebook with a green cover, and it made him look, from where I was standing, almost like a schoolboy. The coppery sun brought out the copper in his skin, he was very faintly smiling, standing very still.

Then the singing stopped, the tambourine turned into a collection plate again. The furious man dropped in his coins and vanished, so did a couple of the women, and Sonny dropped some change in the plate, looking directly at the woman with a little smile. He started across the avenue, toward the house. He has a slow, loping walk something like the way Harlem hipsters walk, only he's imposed on this his own half-beat. I had never really noticed it before.

I stayed at the window, both relieved and apprehensive. As Sonny disappeared from my sight, they began singing again. And they were still singing when his key turned in the lock.

"Hey," he said.

"Hey, yourself. You want some beer?"

"No. Well, maybe." But he came up to the window and stood beside me, looking out. "What a warm voice," he said.

They were singing *If I could only hear my mother pray again!*

"Yes," I said, "and she can sure beat that tambourine."

"But what a terrible song," he said, and laughed. He dropped his notebook on the sofa and disappeared into the kitchen. "Where's Isabel and the kids?"

"I think they went to see their grandparents. You hungry?"

"No." He came back into the living room with his can of beer. "You want to come some place with me tonight?"

I sensed, I don't know how, that I couldn't possibly say no. "Sure. Where?"

He sat down on the sofa and picked up his notebook and started leafing through it. "I'm going to sit in with some fellows in a joint in the Village."

"You mean, you're going to play, tonight?"

"That's right." He took a swallow of his beer and moved back to the window. He gave me a sidelong look. "If you can stand it."

"I'll try," I said.

He smiled to himself and we both watched as the meeting across the way broke up. The three sisters and the brother, heads bowed, were singing *God be with you till we meet again.* The faces around them were very quiet. Then the song ended. The small crowd dispersed. We watched the three women and the lone man walk slowly up the avenue.

"When she was singing before," said Sonny, abruptly, "her voice reminded me for a minute of what heroin feels like sometimes — when it's in your veins. It makes you feel sort of warm and cool at the same time. And distant. And — and sure." He sipped his beer, very deliberately not looking at me. I watched his face. "It makes you feel — in control. Sometimes you've got to have that feeling."

"Do you?" I sat down slowly in the easy chair.

"Sometimes." He went to the sofa and picked up his notebook again. "Some people do."

"In order," I asked, "to play?" And my voice was very ugly, full of contempt and anger.

"Well"—he looked at me with great, troubled eyes, as though, in fact, he hoped his eyes would tell me things he could never otherwise say—"they *think* so. And *if* they think so—!"

"And what do *you* think?" I asked.

He sat on the sofa and put his can of beer on the floor. "I don't know," he said, and I couldn't be sure if he were answering my question or pursuing his thoughts. His face didn't tell me. "It's not so much to *play*. It's to *stand* it, to be able to make it at all. On any level." He frowned and smiled: "In order to keep from shaking to pieces."

"But these friends of yours," I said, "they seem to shake themselves to pieces pretty goddamn fast."

"Maybe." He played with the notebook. And something told me that I should curb my tongue, that Sonny was doing his best to talk that I should listen. "But of course you only know the ones that've gone to pieces. Some don't—or at least they haven't *yet* and that's just about all *any* of us can say." He paused. "And then there are some who just live, really, in hell, and they know it and they see what's happening and they go right on. I don't know." He sighed, dropped the notebook folded his arms. "Some guys, you can tell from the way they play, they on something *all* the time. And you can see that, well, it makes something real for them. But of course," he picked up his beer from the floor and sipped it and put the can down again, "they want to, too, you've got to see that. Even some of them that say they don't—*some*, not all."

"And what about you?" I asked—I couldn't help it. "What about you? Do *you* want to?"

He stood up and walked to the window and remained silent for a long time. Then he sighed. "Me," he said. Then: "While I was downstairs before, on my way here, listening to that woman sing, it struck me all of a sudden how much suffering she must have had to go through—to sing like that. It's *repulsive* to think you have to suffer that much."

I said: "But there's no way not to suffer—is there, Sonny?"

"I believe not," he said and smiled, "but that's never stopped anyone from trying." He looked at me. "Has it?" I realized, with this mocking look, that there stood between us, forever, beyond the power of time or forgiveness, the fact that I had held silence—so long!—when he had needed human speech to help him. He turned back to the window. "No, there's no way not to suffer. But you try all kinds of ways to keep from drowning in it, to keep on top of it, and to make it seem—well, like *you*. Like you did something, all right, and now you're suffering for it. You know?" I said nothing. "Well you know," he said, impatiently, "why *do* people suffer? Maybe it's better to do something to give it a reason, *any* reason."

"But we just agreed," I said, "that there's no way not to suffer. Isn't it better, then, just to—take it?"

"But nobody just takes it," Sonny cried, "that's what I'm telling you! *Everybody* tries not to. You're just hung up on the *way* some people try—it's not *your* way!"

The hair on my face began to itch, my face felt wet. "That's not true," I said, "that's not true. I don't give a damn what other people do, I don't even care how they suffer. I just care how *you* suffer." And he looked at me. "Please believe me," I said, "I don't want to see you — die — trying not to suffer."

"I won't," he said, flatly, "die trying not to suffer. At least, not any faster than anybody else."

"But there's no need," I said, trying to laugh, "is there? in killing yourself."

I wanted to say more, but I couldn't. I wanted to talk about will power and how life could be — well, beautiful. I wanted to say that it was all within; but was it? or, rather, wasn't that exactly the trouble? And I wanted to promise that I would never fail him again. But it would all have sounded — empty words and lies.

So I made the promise to myself and prayed that I would keep it.

"It's terrible sometimes, inside," he said, "that's what's the trouble. You walk these streets, black and funky and cold, and there's not really a living ass to talk to, and there's nothing shaking, and there's no way of getting it out — that storm inside. You can't talk it and you can't make love with it, and when you finally try to get with it and play it, you realize *nobody's* listening. So *you've* got to listen. You got to find a way to listen."

And then he walked away from the window and sat on the sofa again, as though all the wind had suddenly been knocked out of him. "Sometimes you'll do *anything* to play, even cut your mother's throat." He laughed and looked at me. "Or your brother's." Then he sobered. "Or your own." Then: "Don't worry. I'm all right now and I think I'll *be* all right. But I can't forget — where I've been. I don't mean just the physical place I've been, I mean where I've *been*. And *what* I've been."

"What have you been, Sonny?" I asked.

He smiled — but sat sideways on the sofa, his elbow resting on the back his fingers playing with his mouth and chin, not looking at me. "I've been something I didn't recognize, didn't know I could be. Didn't know anybody could be." He stopped, looking inward, looking helplessly young, looking old. "I'm not talking about it now because I feel *guilty* or anything like that — maybe it would be better if I did, I don't know. Anyway, I can't really talk about it. Not to you, not to anybody," and now he turned and faced me. "Sometimes, you know, and it was actually when I was most *out* of the world, I felt that I was in it, that I was *with* it, really, and I could play or I didn't really have to *play*, it just came out of me, it was there. And I don't know how I played, thinking about it now, but I know I did awful things, those times, sometimes, to people. Or it wasn't that I *did* anything to them — it was that they weren't real." He picked up the beer can; it was empty; he rolled it between his palms: "And other times — well, I needed a fix, I needed to find a place to lean, I needed to clear a space to *listen* — and I couldn't find it, and I — went crazy, I did terrible things to *me*, I was terrible *for* me." He began pressing the beer can between his hands, I watched the metal begin to give. It glittered, as he played with it, like a knife, and I was afraid he would cut himself, but I said nothing. "Oh well. I can never tell you. I was all by myself at the bottom of something, stinking and sweating and crying and shaking, and I smelled it, you know? *my* stink, and I thought I'd die if I couldn't get away from it and yet, all the same, I knew that everything I was doing was just locking me in with it. And I didn't know," he paused, still flattening the beer can, "I didn't know, I still *don't* know, something kept telling me that maybe it was good to smell your own stink, but I didn't think that *that* was what I'd been trying to do — and — who can stand it?" and he abruptly dropped the ruined beer can, looking at me with a small, still smile, and then rose, walking to the window as though it were the lodestone rock. I watched his face, he watched the avenue. "I couldn't tell you when Mama died — but the reason I wanted to leave Harlem so bad was to get away from drugs. And then, when I ran away, that's what I was running from — really. When I came back, nothing had changed, *I* hadn't changed, I was just — older." And he stopped, drumming with his fingers on the windowpane. The sun had vanished, soon darkness would fall. I watched his face. "It can come again," he said, almost as though speaking to himself. Then he turned to me. "It can come again," he repeated. "I just want you to know that."

"All right," I said, at last. "So it can come again, All right."

He smiled, but the smile was sorrowful. "I had to try to tell you," he said.

"Yes," I said. "I understand that."

"You're my brother," he said, looking straight at me, and not smiling at all.

"Yes," I repeated, "yes. I understand that."

He turned back to the window, looking out. "All that hatred down there," he said, "all that hatred and misery and love. It's a wonder it doesn't blow the avenue apart."

We went to the only nightclub on a short, dark street, downtown. We squeezed through the narrow, chattering, jam-packed bar to the entrance of the big room, where the bandstand was. And we stood there for a moment, for the lights were very dim in this room and we couldn't see. Then, "Hello, boy," said a voice and an enormous black man, much older than Sonny or myself, erupted out of all that atmospheric lighting and put an arm around Sonny's shoulder. "I been sitting right here," he said, "waiting for you."

He had a big voice, too, and heads in the darkness turned toward us.

Sonny grinned and pulled a little away, and said, "Creole, this is my brother. I told you about him."

Creole shook my hand. "I'm glad to meet you, son," he said, and it was clear that he was glad to meet me *there*, for Sonny's sake. And he smiled, "You got a real musician in *your* family," and he took his arm from Sonny's shoulder and slapped him, lightly, affectionately, with the back of his hand.

"Well. Now I've heard it all," said a voice behind us. This was another musician, and a friend of Sonny's, a coal-black cheerful-looking man, built close to the ground. He immediately began confiding to me, at the top of his lungs, the most terrible things about Sonny, his teeth gleaming like a light-house and his laugh coming up out of him like the beginning of an earth-quake. And it turned out that everyone at the bar knew Sonny, or almost everyone; some were musicians, working there, or nearby, or not working, some were simply hangers-on, and some were there to hear Sonny play. I was introduced to all of them and they were all very polite to me. Yet, it was clear that, for them, I was only Sonny's brother. Here, I was in Sonny's world. Or, rather: his kingdom. Here, it was not even a question that his veins bore royal blood.

They were going to play soon and Creole installed me, by myself, at a table in a dark corner. Then I watched them, Creole, and the little black man, and Sonny, and the others, while they horsed around, standing just below the bandstand. The light from the bandstand spilled just a little short of them and, watching them laughing and gesturing and moving about, I had the feeling that they, nevertheless, were being most careful not to step into that circle of light too suddenly: that if they moved into the light too suddenly, without thinking, they would perish in flame. Then, while I watched, one of them, the small, black man, moved into the light and crossed the bandstand and started fooling around with his drums. Then — being funny and being, also, extremely ceremonious — Creole took Sonny by the arm and led him to the piano. A woman's voice called Sonny's name and a few hands started clapping. And Sonny, also being funny and being cere-monious, and so touched, I think, that he could have cried, but neither hid-ing it nor showing it, riding it like a man, grinned, and put both hands to his heart and bowed from the waist.

Creole then went to the bass fiddle and a lean, very bright-skinned brown man jumped up on the bandstand and picked up his horn. So there they were, and the atmosphere on the bandstand and in the room began to change and tighten. Someone stepped up to the microphone and announced them. Then there were all kinds of murmurs. Some people at the bar shushed others. The waitress ran around, frantically getting in the last orders, guys and chicks got closer to each other, and the lights on the bandstand, on the quartet, turned to a kind of indigo. Then they all looked different there. Cre-ole looked about him for the last time, as though he were making certain that all his chickens were in the coop, and then he — jumped and struck the fiddle. And there they were.

All I know about music is that not many people ever really hear it. And even then, on the rare occasions when something opens within, and the music enters, what we mainly hear, or hear corroborated, are personal, pri-vate, vanishing evocations. But the man who creates the music is hearing something else, is dealing with the roar rising from the void and imposing order on it as it hits the air. What is evoked in him, then, is of another order, more terrible because it has no words, and triumphant, too, for that same reason. And his triumph, when he triumphs, is ours. I just watched Sonny's face. His face was troubled, he was working hard, but he wasn't with it. And I had the feeling that, in a way, everyone on the bandstand was waiting for him, both waiting for him and pushing him along. But as I began to watch Creole, I realized that it was Creole who held them all back. He had them on a short rein. Up there, keeping the beat with his whole body, wailing on the fiddle, with his eyes half closed, he was listening to everything, but he was listening to Sonny. He was having a dialogue with Sonny. He wanted Sonny to leave the shoreline and strike out for the deep water. He was Sonny's witness that deep water and drowning were not the same thing — he had been there, and he knew. And he wanted Sonny to know. He was waiting for Sonny to do the things on the keys which would let Creole know that Sonny was in the water.

And, while Creole listened, Sonny moved, deep within, exactly like someone in torment. I had never before thought of how awful the relationship must be between the musician and his instrument. He has to fill it, this instrument, with the breath of life, his own. He has to make it do what he wants it to do. And a piano is just a piano. It's made out of so much wood and wires and little hammers and big ones, and ivory. While there's only so much you can do with it, the only way to find this out is to try; to try and make it do everything.

And Sonny hadn't been near a piano for over a year. And he wasn't on much better terms with his life, not the life that stretched before him now. He and the piano stammered, started one way, got scared, stopped; started another way, panicked, marked time, started again; then seemed to have found a direction, panicked again, got stuck. And the face I saw on Sonny I'd never seen before. Everything had been burned out of it, and, at the same time, things usually hidden were being burned in, by the fire and fury of the battle which was occurring in him up there.

Yet, watching Creole's face as they neared the end of the first set, I had the feeling that something had happened, something I hadn't heard. Then they finished, there was scattered applause, and then, without an instant's warning, Creole started into something else, it was almost sardonic, it was *Am I Blue*. And, as though he commanded, Sonny began to play. Something began to happen. And Creole let out the reins. The dry, low, black man said something awful on the drums, Creole answered, and the drums talked back. Then the horn insisted, sweet and high, slightly detached perhaps, and Creole listened, commenting now and then, dry, and driving, beautiful and calm and old. Then they all came together again, and Sonny was part of the family again. I could tell this from his face. He seemed to have found, right there beneath his fingers, a damn brand-new piano. It seemed that he couldn't get over it. Then, for awhile, just being happy with Sonny, they seemed to be agreeing with him that brand-new pianos certainly were a gas.

Then Creole stepped forward to remind them that what they were playing was the blues. He hit something in all of them, he hit something in me,
myself, and the music tightened and deepened, apprehension began to beat
the air. Creole began to tell us what the blues were all about. They were not
about anything very new. He and his boys up there were keeping it new, at
the risk of ruin, destruction, madness, and death, in order to find new ways
to make us listen. For, while the tale of how we suffer, and how we are delighted, and how we may triumph is never new, it always must be heard.
There isn't any other tale to tell, it's the only light we've got in all this darkness.

And this tale, according to that face, that body, those strong hands on
those strings, has another aspect in every country, and a new depth in every
generation. Listen, Creole seemed to be saying, listen. Now these are Sonny's
blues. He made the little black man on the drums know it, and the bright,
brown man on the horn. Creole wasn't trying any longer to get Sonny in the
water. He was wishing him Godspeed. Then he stepped back, very slowly,
filling the air with the immense suggestion that Sonny speak for himself.

Then they all gathered around Sonny and Sonny played. Every now and
again one of them seemed to say, amen. Sonny's fingers filled the air with
life, his life. But that life contained so many others. And Sonny went all the
way back, he really began with the spare, flat statement of the opening
phrase of the song. Then he began to make it his. It was very beautiful because it wasn't hurried and it was no longer a lament. I seemed to hear with
what burning he had made it his, with what burning we had yet to make it
ours, how we could cease lamenting. Freedom lurked around us and I understood, at last, that he could help us to be free if we would listen, that he
would never be free until we did. Yet, there was no battle in his face now. I
heard what he had gone through, and would continue to go through until
he came to rest in earth. He had made it his: that long line, of which we
knew only Mama and Daddy. And he was giving it back, as everything must
be given back, so that, passing through death, it can live forever. I saw my
mother's face again, and felt, for the first time, how the stones of the road
she had walked on must have bruised her feet. I saw the moonlit road where
my father's brother died. And it brought something else back to me, and carried me past it. I saw my little girl again and felt Isabel's tears again, and I
felt my own tears begin to rise. And I was yet aware that this was only a moment, that the world waited outside, as hungry as a tiger, and that trouble
stretched above us, longer than the sky.

Then it was over. Creole and Sonny let out their breath, both soaking
wet, and grinning. There was a lot of applause and some of it was real. In the
dark, the girl came by and I asked her to take drinks to the bandstand. There
was a long pause, while they talked up there in the indigo light and after
awhile I saw the girl put a Scotch and milk on top of the piano for Sonny. He
didn't seem to notice it, but just before they started playing again, he sipped
from it and looked toward me, and nodded. Then he put it back on top of

the piano. For me, then, as they began to play again, it glowed and shook above my brother's head like the very cup of trembling.

APPROACHING THE READING

1. The broad setting is Harlem in the 1950s. If you're not already familiar with Harlem, find it on a map and learn more about it. Is the story time-specific? Could it, or something like it, have happened last year? Why or why not?

2. What are the specific settings in the different parts of the story? How does each contribute to the story? Pick out a passage that evokes the flavor or atmosphere of a setting and explain why it does.

> Research this author in depth with cultural documents and multimedia resources on *LiterActive*.

3. Consider darkness as part of the cultural setting of the story. Explain what the speaker means by the two kinds of darkness. Be ready to discuss how darkness becomes a recurrent motif in the story.

4. Consider the role of music in the story and what meanings it might carry with it. Notice especially the narrator's reflections on music in the nightclub near the end. What suggested meanings for music emerge? Does the story use archetypes? If you believe it does, point them out and discuss their effect.

5. The glass of Scotch and milk appears only once, but it does so in a climactic position in the last paragraph. Could it be regarded as a symbol? The glass is referred to in the last three words of the story as a "cup of trembling." Those words echo two passages from the Bible, Isaiah 51:17 and 51:22. Look up these verses and consider what they contribute to the glass as a possible symbol and to the effect of the ending.

RESPONDING THROUGH WRITING

Journal Entries

1. Focus on the way settings are handled in two or three TV shows or movies. Pay attention to what was discussed in this chapter: setting as place broadly and specifically, setting in time, setting in social and cultural context. Consider uses and effects of setting: for atmosphere, characterization, symbol, and meaning. Then write a journal entry discussing ways that what you found can enhance your grasp of setting in literature.

> Research the authors in this chapter with LitLinks, or take a quiz on the stories with LitQuiz, at bedfordstmartins.com/approachinglit.

2. After reading James Baldwin's "Sonny's Blues" carefully, find ways to sharpen your visual images of Harlem. Look at photos of Harlem in a book like *Harlem: Lost and Found* (2002) by Michael Henry

Adams or in the Harlem section of a book of photos on New York City; or watch a movie set in Harlem, like *The Cotton Club* (1984). Write a journal entry discussing how such visual images affect the experience of reading the story. Does it make a significant difference or not?

3. Do the same for Alice Walker's "Everyday Use" (p. 101), researching its southern rural setting and discussing in your journal how bringing visual images to your reading changes the reading experience.

Literary Analysis Papers

4. Write a paper discussing the importance of setting in Toni Cade Bambara's "The Lesson" (p. 183), John Updike's "A & P" (p. 386), or Isabel Allende's "And of Clay Are We Created" (p. 407).

5. Write a paper discussing the relationship between settings and characters in Ralph Ellison's "Battle Royal" (p. 237), Flannery O'Connor's "A Good Man Is Hard to Find" (p. 341), "Swaddling Clothes" by Mishima Yukio (p. 438), or another story of your choice.

6. Write a paper on the literal and symbolic uses of music in Joyce Carol Oates's "Where Are You Going, Where Have You Been?" (p. 75) or James Baldwin's "Sonny's Blues" (p. 138).

Making Connections

7. After reading James Baldwin's "Sonny's Blues" twice, so you form your impressions of the story from reading, watch the fifteen-minute film version of it available at urbanentertainment.com (click on *Short Films,* then *Drama*). Write a short paper discussing the film's handling of setting and comparing the effect of reading the story and seeing the filmed version.

8. Write a paper exploring literal darkness and inner darkness in James Baldwin's "Sonny's Blues" (p. 138) and Ralph Ellison's "Battle Royal" (p. 237).

Cultural Criticism Papers

9. Do some reading on the cultural significance of hair and write a paper discussing various ways hair is important in Alice Walker's "Everyday Use" (p. 101) and Lan Samantha Chang's "The Eve of the Spirit Festival" (p. 228).

10. Write a paper discussing how characters encounter and deal with borders or boundaries that separate people from each other—either physical borders (such as borders between nations, streets dividing neighborhoods or areas, prison walls, the outsides of protective spaces like houses or cars) or social, economic, religious, or ethnic borders that separate people as being different from each other. You might consider using one or more of the following: Sandra Cisneros's "The House on Mango Street" (p. 91), James Baldwin's "Sonny's Blues" (p. 138), Ralph Ellison's "Battle Royal" (p. 237), Bharati Mukherjee's "Orbiting" (p. 315), or another story of your choice.

RESPONDING THROUGH THE ARTS

1. Pick out background music that you think is appropriate in evoking the atmosphere of a particular setting for one of the stories in Chapters 4 to 7, or another story of your choice. Write a journal entry or a short paper explaining your choice.

2. Draw or paint the setting(s) in Sandra Cisneros's "The House on Mango Street" (p. 91), William Faulkner's "A Rose for Emily" (p. 108), Ernest Hemingway's "Hills Like White Elephants" (p. 120), or another story of your choice. You could do a single picture showing the main setting for the story, or two or three that depict different settings, or you could illustrate different aspects of the main setting or the way it might look from various angles.

I like short sentences. They are forceful and can get you out of big trouble.

Annie Dillard

CHAPTER **7** **Style, Tone, and Irony**

The way things are said, their style and tone, matters—a lot. The way things are phrased and expressed can affect the meaning words convey (some people can talk their way out of anything, right?), and the tone of voice can decidedly alter the message. "Nice shirt!" can mean you love it or you hate it, depending on whether you say it enthusiastically about a friend's birthday present or mutter bitterly about a ragged T-shirt with an offensive slogan on the back. The same is true for a work of fiction. A work's style is important because it is interesting and enjoyable to read a distinctive style of writing, and because style helps shape tone, the "tone of voice" that affects how we take what is being said—whether what the narrator and characters say should be taken straightforwardly, or with a grain of salt, or the opposite way from which it is stated. This chapter focuses on some of the key elements that contribute to style and tone—and on the specific tone of irony—to help you be more alert to subtleties of fine writing as you listen to a work of literature.

As you read the following short story the first time, you'll probably focus more on what's happening and why than on the way it's said. Most readers listen more intently for style on a second reading. So read it a second time, paying close attention to the way things are phrased and expressed—to word choice, for example (listening for the sounds of words as well as determining their meaning), and to the way sentences are constructed. Think about whether the style seems to you appropriate and effective in conveying what happens to the central character and the feelings she experiences on hearing that her husband has died.

Kate Chopin 1851–1904

The Story of an Hour   [1894]

Knowing that Mrs. Mallard was afflicted with a heart trouble, great care was taken to break to her as gently as possible the news of her husband's death.

It was her sister Josephine who told her, in broken sentences; veiled hints that revealed in half concealing. Her husband's friend Richards was there, too, near her. It was he who had been in the newspaper office when intelligence of the railroad disaster was received, with Brently Mallard's name leading the list of "killed." He had only taken the time to assure himself of its truth by a second telegram, and had hastened to forestall any less careful, less tender friend in bearing the sad message.

She did not hear the story as many women have heard the same, with a paralyzed inability to accept its significance. She wept at once, with sudden, wild abandonment, in her sister's arms. When the storm of grief had spent itself she went away to her room alone. She would have no one follow her.

There stood, facing the open window, a comfortable, roomy armchair. Into this she sank, pressed down by a physical exhaustion that haunted her body and seemed to reach into her soul.

She could see in the open square before her house the tops of trees that were all aquiver with the new spring life. The delicious breath of rain was in the air. In the street below a peddler was crying his wares. The notes of a distant song which some one was singing reached her faintly, and countless sparrows were twittering in the eaves.

There were patches of blue sky showing here and there through the clouds that had met and piled one above the other in the west facing her window.

She sat with her head thrown back upon the cushion of the chair, quite motionless, except when a sob came up into her throat and shook her, as a child who has cried itself to sleep continues to sob in its dreams.

She was young, with a fair, calm face, whose lines bespoke repression and even a certain strength. But now there was a dull stare in her eyes, whose gaze was fixed away off yonder on one of those patches of blue sky. It was not a glance of reflection, but rather indicated a suspension of intelligent thought.

There was something coming to her and she was waiting for it, fearfully. What was it? She did not know; it was too subtle and elusive to name. But she felt it, creeping out of the sky, reaching toward her through the sounds, the scents, the color that filled the air.

Now her bosom rose and fell tumultuously. She was beginning to recognize this thing that was approaching to possess her, and she was striving to beat it back with her will — as powerless as her two white slender hands would have been.

When she abandoned herself a little whispered word escaped her slightly parted lips. She said it over and over under her breath: "free, free, free!" The vacant stare and the look of terror that had followed it went from her eyes. They stayed keen and bright. Her pulses beat fast, and the coursing blood warmed and relaxed every inch of her body.

She did not stop to ask if it were or were not a monstrous joy that held her. A clear and exalted perception enabled her to dismiss the suggestion as trivial.

She knew that she would weep again when she saw the kind, tender hands folded in death; the face that had never looked save with love upon her, fixed and gray and dead. But she saw beyond that bitter moment a long procession of years to come that would belong to her absolutely. And she opened and spread her arms out to them in welcome.

There would be no one to live for her during those coming years; she would live for herself. There would be no powerful will bending hers in that blind persistence with which men and women believe they have a right to impose a private will upon a fellow-creature. A kind intention or a cruel intention made the act seem no less a crime as she looked upon it in that brief moment of illumination.

And yet she had loved him — sometimes. Often she had not. What did it matter! What could love, the unsolved mystery, count for in face of this possession of self-assertion which she suddenly recognized as the strongest impulse of her being!

"Free! Body and soul free!" she kept whispering.

Josephine was kneeling before the closed door with her lips to the keyhole, imploring for admission. "Louise, open the door! I beg; open the door — you will make yourself ill. What are you doing, Louise? For heaven's sake open the door."

"Go away. I am not making myself ill." No; she was drinking in a very elixir of life through that open window.

Her fancy was running riot along those days ahead of her. Spring days, and summer days, and all sorts of days that would be her own. She breathed a quick prayer that life might be long. It was only yesterday she had thought with a shudder that life might be long.

She arose at length and opened the door to her sister's importunities. There was a feverish triumph in her eyes, and she carried herself unwittingly like a goddess of Victory. She clasped her sister's waist, and together they descended the stairs. Richards stood waiting for them at the bottom.

Some one was opening the front door with a latchkey. It was Brently Mallard who entered, a little travel-stained, composedly carrying his gripsack and umbrella. He had been far from the scene of accident, and did not even know there had been one. He stood amazed at Josephine's piercing cry; at Richards' quick motion to screen him from the view of his wife.

But Richards was too late.

When the doctors came they said she had died of heart disease — of joy that kills.

APPROACHING THE READING

1. Consider the word choice as an aspect of style. Chopin's language may sound a bit formal. Even in the 1890s, words such as *afflicted, intelligence, forestall, bespoke,* and *fancy,* although part of an educated person's vocabulary, were seldom used in everyday speech. Did you hear other words that struck you as distinctly formal? What would be the effect on the depiction of Mrs. Mallard's situation if the style were less formal?

2. Look also at sentence constructions in the story. Do they tend to be long or short? Are they mostly formal and "written" or casual and conversational? Do they read rapidly or more slowly and deliberately? Does the handling of sentences seem appropriate to the events and the characters involved in them?

   www

   Explore this author and story in depth, including images and cultural documents, with VirtuaLit Fiction at bedfordstmartins.com/approachinglit.

3. Think about comparisons used in the story: for example, of grief to a storm (para. 3) and the treatment of exhaustion as a spiritual emanation that presses Mrs. Mallard down, haunts her body, and reaches into her soul (para. 4). List several other examples. What do you think such comparisons add to the story? What would be changed or lost if the comparisons were omitted and the points stated only in straightforward terms?

4. Consider the handling of the two single-sentence paragraphs at the end. Ask yourself how the effect would be different if the two sentences were combined into a single paragraph. What is the advantage of the very short next-to-last paragraph?

The most striking thing about style in "The Story of an Hour" is its formality of word choice and sentence construction. The subject announced in the first sentence, "her husband's death," is one that must be treated seriously, of course. A formal style seems entirely appropriate — that the narrator refers to her as Mrs. Mallard rather than as Louise maintains a sense of dignity and respect. The formal, dignified style helps channel a reader's response as the story develops. It is surprising to learn that the fearful "something" that overcomes her is a sudden realization of release and freedom. If the unexpectedness of Mrs. Mallard's line "free, free, free!" would cause readers to laugh or even smile, the effect of the story would be destroyed. But the style guards against that possibility by suggesting that her response to her husband's death, as well as the death itself, must be taken very seriously.

The specific, detailed language of the style is important also as it affects the tone of the story. Our sympathy for Mrs. Mallard is aroused in the first two paragraphs, with the sudden death of her husband. It continues in the following paragraphs, as she seems devastated by the news. Then comes the twist: She isn't devastated, she's elated. The story risks losing our sympathy at that point, if it seems she didn't care about him. But through its handling of details the story seeks to shift our feelings to a different ground, not sympathy for her as a widow but empathy for her as a woman. The story goes on to say that, kind and loving though her husband had been toward her, his personality dominated their relationship, and she felt trapped. Instead of looking forward to her future, she dreaded what lay ahead. Our sympathy, thus, can turn to happiness for her when she spreads out her arms to welcome the "long procession of years to come that would belong to her absolutely." Only readers who respond to the tone actively, as it changes along the way, receive the full effect of the surprise ending: the sadness and regret that she didn't get to enjoy the new life of which she had a brief glimpse.

STYLE

In everyday speech, *style* is used in at least two important ways, as "that's a stylish suit" (it's attentive to the elements that are contemporary, "in," attractive, effective) and "that's their style of doing things" (their distinctive way or approach). Both uses apply when discussing literature, and they usually are closely related. **Style**, when applied to writing, is the manner in which a writer uses words, constructs sentences, incorporates nonliteral expressions, and handles rhythm, timing, and tone, all resulting in the effectiveness and individuality of a writer's work. The "Approaching the Reading" questions after "The Story of an Hour" are meant to direct your attention to some of the issues involved in style. In the pages that follow, we explore two aspects of style: style as effectiveness of expression and style as individuality of expression.

Style as Effectiveness of Expression

If your teacher asks you to discuss the style of a work, she or he wants you to describe how or explain why the words, sentences, and imaginative comparisons are effective in terms of what is being created: Is it done "with style," that is, with proper care and in ways appropriate to the content and purpose of the work? Such a question requires that you listen actively and attentively for at least three features: words, sentences, and imaginative comparisons.

Effectiveness always depends on appropriateness to a specific context. In expository writing, that means the appropriateness of the style to the writing's purpose: a formal style for a business letter or a research paper, an informal style for a personal letter or an essay describing your first day at college. In fiction, the style in the narrative passages must be appropriate to the narrator, and in dialogue it must fit the characters and the contexts in which they appear. A work of fiction usually has multiple styles, one for the narrative portions and different styles for the thoughts or words of different characters.

WORD CHOICE   Central to style is an author's diction. **Diction** in a narrow sense means word choice, but in a broader sense it refers to the overall character of language used in writing or speech and includes *vocabulary* (choice of words) and *syntax* (arrangement of words, their ordering, grouping, and placement within phrases, clauses, and sentences). We discuss vocabulary here and syntax a few pages later.

A writer can employ any of several types of diction, and the kind that predominates defines one aspect of a work's style. The words selected by a published author, or by you as a student writer, affect the way the work articulates the subject as well as the sound, rhythm, and feel of the writing. We already pointed to the formal diction in "The Story of an Hour," which seems to fit the strong, reserved character of Mrs. Mallard and the tight, careful plotting that sets up the surprise ending. Here are some other types of diction, though such a list can never be complete and exhaustive.

- *Simple words:* "When Miss Emily Grierson died, our whole town went to her funeral" ("A Rose for Emily," p. 108) — except for the names, all the words are everyday words, as is the language the narrator uses for objective description: "She was sick for a long time. When we saw her again, her hair was cut short, making her look like a girl" (p. 111). The diction in the first sentence of "Everyday Use" is similar: "I will wait for her in the yard that Maggie and I made so clean and wavy yesterday afternoon" (p. 101).
- *Complex words:* "But garages and cotton gins had *encroached* and *obliterated* even the *august* names of that neighborhood" ("A Rose for Emily," p. 108). When the narrator — obviously educated and formal — wants to convey an attitude toward something carefully and precisely, he turns to words derived from French or Latin, rather than to the simpler Anglo equivalents: New people and modern ways don't *edge in,* they *encroach* (trespass) where they don't belong; they don't just *wipe away* the *worthy* names, they *obliterate* (destroy violently) names that were *august* (awe-inspiring, deserving reverence and respect). Here is more such diction from later in the story: "With the crayon face of her father *musing profoundly* above the bier and the ladies *sibilant* and *macabre*" (p. 114).
- *Concrete words:* "She had *jeans* on and fancy *moccasins* and she carried a little *suitcase*" ("The Red Convertible," p. 69). Lyman's words describing Susy fit his usual emphasis on the down-to-earth when describing how things are. He relates the facts, rarely trying to provide abstract theories or explanations to explain them. Similarly, "the *hard clay* is *swept* clean as a *floor* and the *fine sand* around the *edges* lined with *tiny, irregular grooves*" ("Everyday Use," p. 101).
- *Abstract words:* "You just don't understand . . . your *heritage* . . . make *something* of yourself . . . *a new day*" ("Everyday Use," p. 107). Dee's vague, empty parting words of advice help bring out the irony that it is she, not her mother or sister, who needs deeper understanding.

Likewise, "on the rare *occasions* when *something* opens within, and the music enters, what we mainly hear, or hear corroborated, are *personal, private,* vanishing *evocations*" ("Sonny's Blues," p. 160).

- *Colloquialisms* (informal, conversational expressions): "*Don'tcha* know it's Sunday all day?" ("Where Are You Going, Where Have You Been?" p. 83). The slurred syllables are characteristic of speech, not written prose; the casual way Arnold Friend expresses himself helps us know more of what his character is like. Two other examples are "I'm an openminded *kinda* guy" ("Love in L.A.," p. 56), and "I *ain't learning nothing* in school" ("Sonny's Blues," p. 152).

- *Slang:* "A sweet broad soft-looking *can*" ("A & P," p. 386). Most of us wouldn't use the word *can* in a school paper, but it fits perfectly the breezy "with it" personality Sammy wants to project. Another example is the narrator's use of a slang term for heroin in "Sonny's Blues": "the first time Sonny had ever had *horse*" (p. 139).

- *Dignified, sophisticated terminology:* "A week later the mayor wrote her himself, offering to call or to send his car for her, and received in reply a note on paper of an archaic shape, in a thin, flowing calligraphy in faded ink, to the effect that she no longer went out at all" ("A Rose for Emily," p. 109) — the words convey the polite, formal, old-fashioned way the mayor and Miss Emily treat each other in what is a very delicate situation.

- *Technical terms:* "The milk in it *clabber* [thickly curdled and sour] by now" ("Everyday Use," p. 105) — the word is precise and informs us that the churn whose top Dee takes away as a keepsake is one still being used in the household. Also, "behind *jalousies* [a window, shade, or door of horizontal slats of glass, wood, or metal that can be adjusted for regulating air or light] closed upon the sun of Sunday afternoon" ("A Rose for Emily," p. 112).

As you read and reread a story, pause to notice the kinds of words, or the level of diction, being used and think about how word choice contributes to the work's effectiveness. Listen to the language of the character or the narrator. To be effective, the choice of words — like style generally — must be well suited to its purpose (formal, educated diction for an analytic paper; slangy, conversational diction for an e-mail message to a friend) and its context (diction in narrative passages appropriate to the narrator, and in dialogue fitting the characters and the situations in which they appear).

In many cases, diction becomes a part of characterization. In "The Red Convertible," for example, Lyman uses a lot of clichés — "The rest is history," "large as life," "But what are you going to do?" — and misuses them: "On to greener pastures, as they say." His choice of words sometimes is imprecise, as when he says that Susy "was *posed* alongside the road" or that ripping up the car "*just about* hurt me, I'll tell you." His handling of words, as he tells his story, shows that he is not polished and reveals at times how little he understands about such things as war and government: "By then I guess the whole war was *solved* in the government's mind."

SENTENCE STRUCTURE   Equally important to creating an effective style is **syntax**, the way phrases and sentences are put together. Writers can work with long sentences or short ones. They can structure and craft them tightly, using subordinate clauses and forcing one to read to the end of the sentence to grasp the meaning:

> All I know about music is that not many people ever really hear it. And even then, on the rare occasions when something opens within, and the music enters, what we mainly hear, or hear corroborated, are personal, private, vanishing evocations. ("Sonny's Blues," p. 160)

Or they can structure them loosely, using cumulative clauses, adding on phrases connected by commas or *and* or *but*:

> Connie sat with her eyes closed in the sun, dreaming and dazed with the warmth about her as if this were a kind of love, the caresses of love, and her mind slipped over onto thoughts of the boy she had been with the night before and how nice he had been, how sweet it always was, not the way someone like June would suppose but sweet, gentle, the way it was in movies and promised in songs. ("Where Are You Going, Where Have You Been?" p. 78)

Writers can create a narrator who uses grammatically correct form or one who treats grammar in a more casual, conversational manner.

Here too appropriateness is the key, suitability to the speaker and the occasion. Using incomplete sentences would hardly ever be effective in a scholarly article but might work well in a memoir; long, elegant, carefully shaped sentences would likely seem out of character for a streetwise gang leader but might be exactly right for a pompous clergyman. As with diction, the sentences used in the narrative parts of a story must suit the narrator, and those used in dialogue must be appropriate for the characters and the contexts using them. Lyman's sentences as he narrates "The Red Convertible" (p. 67), for example — mostly short and simple, or when long, made up of short phrases strung together — fit his character well.

Paying attention to differences in language and sentence structure helps you develop your ear, leading to greater appreciation and understanding of a work of literature and a more rewarding reading experience. What do you hear in the following passages, the opening paragraphs of two stories included later in this book?

> Young Goodman Brown came forth, at sunset, into the street of Salem village, but put his head back, after crossing the threshold, to exchange a parting kiss with his young wife. And Faith, as the wife was aptly named,

thrust her own pretty head into the street, letting the wind play with the pink ribbons of her cap, while she called to Goodman Brown. ("Young Goodman Brown," p. 252)

In walks these three girls in nothing but bathing suits. I'm in the third checkout slot, with my back to the door, so I don't see them until they're over by the bread. The one that caught my eye first was the one in the plaid green two-piece. She was a chunky kid, with a good tan and a sweet broad soft-looking can with those two crescents of white just under it, where the sun never seems to hit, at the top of the backs of her legs. I stood there with my hand on a box of HiHo crackers trying to remember if I rang it up or not. I ring it up again and the customer starts giving me hell. ("A & P," p. 386)

The diction of "Young Goodman Brown" — simple, clear, and constrained — and the precise, grammatically correct sentences suit the narrator's somber tone. The style is fitting for a story about a community that upholds rigid social and moral codes, or appears to uphold them, regardless of the internal conflict they engender in some citizens' hearts.

The diction and sentence structures of the second passage would feel terribly wrong if used for a story about Goodman Brown, but they suit Sammy, the first-person narrator of "A & P," perfectly. The style itself, the way Sammy tells his story, does a great deal to embody and express his character — the almost affectedly breezy, off-handed, "with-it" manner of "in walks," "two-piece," "can," and "giving me hell." The sentences are grammatical, yet structured in a loose, conversational way — quite a contrast to the terse, formal phrasings of "Young Goodman Brown."

RHYTHM   An important ingredient of prose style is **rhythm**, the pattern of flow and movement created by the choice of words and the arrangement of phrases and sentences. There is no set of precise labels to describe rhythm, so we are forced to borrow language from other arts, such as music. Thus we say that the rhythm of a piece of prose is, for example, fast, slow, syncopated, disjointed, smooth, halting, graceful, rough, or deliberate. Prose rhythm is affected particularly by the length and composition of sentences (everything said in the preceding section on sentence structures has an effect on rhythm), the use of pauses (punctuation) within the sentences, the use of repetitions, and the ease or difficulty in pronouncing the combinations of word sounds in the sentences. Long sentences with little punctuation might have a smooth and flowing rhythm, but the rhythm also could be almost breathless or fast or slow depending on how quickly or slowly the words can be spoken. Short sentences, or longer ones broken by punctuation into short phrases, may have a rough or choppy rhythm. If such sentences use a lot of short, single-syllable words, the rhythm may have a fast, even staccato-type rhythm. Listen for a smooth, graceful, almost wavelike rhythm in the following sentence from the opening paragraph of "Sonny's Blues":

I stared at it in the swinging lights of the subway car, and in the faces and bodies of the people, and in my own face, trapped in the darkness which roared outside. (p. 138)

Compare that with the faster, edgy, staccato rhythm of this sentence from "Where Are You Going, Where Have You Been?":

Her mother, who noticed everything and knew everything and who hadn't much reason any longer to look at her own face, always scolded Connie about it. (p. 75)

Actually, the possibilities for different types of prose rhythm are endless. The best approach as an active reader is to listen closely to the flow of the words, phrases, and sentences and describe as best you can the way they sound and feel as you read them aloud.

IMAGINATIVE USE OF LANGUAGE   Another factor contributing to style is the inclusion of comparisons, of nonliteral, or imaginative, expressions. The technical term for such usage is **figure of speech** — by definition, an unusual use of language that often associates or compares dissimilar things. In "The Story of an Hour" (p. 167), grief is compared to a storm in paragraph three, and the treatment of exhaustion, in paragraph four, is described as a spiritual emanation that presses Mrs. Mallard down, haunts her body, and reaches into her soul. Figures of speech are discussed in more detail in Part 3, "Approaching Poetry," because they are so central to understanding poems (see Chapter 13). But they also can be very significant in stories and plays, and recognizing expressions that are not to be taken literally can greatly enrich your reading. The title of "Hills Like White Elephants" contains a figure of speech — a surprising, imaginative comparison. And Lyman, in "The Red Convertible," uses figurative comparisons to convey more clearly the extremely difficult emotions and actions he needs to describe near the end of the story: "His face was totally white and hard. Then it broke, *like stones break all of a sudden when water boils up inside them*" (p. 73) and "I can tell his mood is *turning* again" (p. 74).

Style as Individuality of Expression

Another aspect of style is the way styles differ. The way one person develops a characteristic manner or approach ("that's his style of doing things") can be differentiated from another's. *Style* in this sense refers to the unique, individual manner in which almost anything can be carried out: singing, dancing, composing music, playing an instrument, making any visual art, designing buildings or bridges or clothes, walking, talking, playing a sport, wearing a hat, or relating to other people. A person who does something a lot develops a distinctive way of doing it, readily identifiable as hers or his by

an attentive and knowledgeable audience. Someone who knows art can recognize a painting as one done by Picasso because of distinctive characteristics in its style. Someone well versed in jazz can identify a piece by Miles
Davis because of unique features of its style.

The same is true of writers: Most authors have their own distinctive style
recognizable by readers familiar with their work. Although creative writers
must adjust their diction, sentence structures, and imaginative comparisons
to fit the particular characters and situations of each story, some characteristic attributes still show through. Preferences in word choice or sentence
and paragraph construction, ways of shaping phrases, uses of adjectives or
adverbs, attention to certain types of details, or combinations of sounds can
be constant in the background in spite of adaptations to specific characters
or contexts in the foreground.

A reader familiar with the works of William Faulkner would immediately identify the following sentence from "A Rose for Emily" as his from its
style (as well as the reference to Colonel Sartoris, who appears in other stories by Faulkner): "Alive, Miss Emily had been a tradition, a duty, and a care;
a sort of hereditary obligation upon the town, dating from that day in 1894
when Colonel Sartoris, the mayor — he who fathered the edict that no Negro
woman should appear on the streets without an apron — remitted her taxes,
the dispensation dating from the death of her father on into perpetuity"
(p. 109). The recognizable features include the educated, exact diction; the
long, languid sentences; phrases interrupting and words piled on to add even
more precision, to get a point or feeling or image exactly right. Even though
the narrator has his own sense of consciousness, Faulkner's personal style is
there as well — it can't help but be, for these are the structures and rhythms
in which Faulkner thought, imagined, talked, and wrote. You will find the
same characteristics, even more intensely, in the opening sentence of his
novel *Absalom, Absalom!* (1936):

> From a little after two o'clock until almost sundown of the long still hot
> weary dead September afternoon they sat in what Miss Coldfield still called
> the office because her father had called it that — a dim hot airless room with
> the blinds all closed and fastened for forty-three summers because when
> she was a girl someone had believed that light and moving air carried heat
> and that dark was always cooler, and which (as the sun shone fuller and
> fuller on that side of the house) became latticed with yellow slashes full of
> dust motes which Quentin thought of as being flecks of the dead old dried
> paint blown inward from the scaling blinds as wind might have blown them.

Contrast Faulkner's style with that of Ernest Hemingway, as in the
opening paragraph of "Hills Like White Elephants":

> The hills across the valley of the Ebro were long and white. On this side
> there was no shade and no trees and the station was between two lines of
> rails in the sun. Close against the side of the station there was the warm
> shadow of the building and a curtain, made of strings of bamboo beads,

hung across the open door into the bar, to keep out flies. The American and the girl with him sat at a table in the shade, outside the building. It was very hot and the express from Barcelona would come in forty minutes. It stopped at this junction for two minutes and went on to Madrid. (p. 120)

This passage is typical Hemingway, with its ordinary, largely concrete, diction and its mostly short, concise, simple but tightly knit sentences, or cumulative longer sentences made up of short phrases connected by *and* or just a comma. Notice these stylistic features again in another work, the opening paragraphs of "Soldier's Home" (1925):

> Krebs went to the war from a Methodist college in Kansas. There is a picture which shows him among his fraternity brothers, all of them wearing exactly the same height and style collar. He enlisted in the Marines in 1917 and did not return to the United States until the second division returned from the Rhine in the summer of 1919.
>
> There is a picture which shows him on the Rhine with two German girls and another corporal. Krebs and the corporal look too big for their uniforms. The German girls are not beautiful. The Rhine does not show in the picture.
>
> By the time Krebs returned to his home town in Oklahoma the greeting of heroes was over. He came back much too late. The men from the town who had been drafted had all been welcomed elaborately on their return. There had been a great deal of hysteria. Now the reaction had set in. People seemed to think it was rather ridiculous for Krebs to be getting back so late, years after the war was over.

Hemingway's style seems at first glance easy to copy, and many people have tried, but they quickly found out that it, like any distinctive style, is difficult to imitate because its roots lie deep within the whole personality and imagination of its originator.

Giving attention to the appropriateness of word choice, sentence structures, and imaginative expression can help you recognize and appreciate individuality of expression. This is another important component of active reading—making the effort to notice the way things are said rather than just passively taking in what is said. The more you read, and read carefully, the more you will appreciate the effectiveness of style and be able to differentiate one author's unique style from those of other authors.

TONE

When you listen to a story, it's important to pay attention to its **tone**, the "tone of voice" it projects, the attitude or "stance" it takes toward the characters and actions. Tone is a significant aspect of style, and of communication generally: It can add to, modify, or even invert the meaning of the words expressed. If someone says "Please close the door behind you," it makes a big difference if the words are spoken as a simple reminder or as an angry demand. Either way, the tone adds a lot that the words themselves don't say: In the former case, tone conveys respect, acceptance, and confidence; in the latter, rebuke, rejection, separation. Tone in a literary work similarly gets in, around, and behind the words to indicate the attitude the work takes toward the characters, setting, subject, or issues, or the attitude a character evinces toward an issue, situation, setting, or another character.

When we talk, our own tone is conveyed by the inflections in our voice. For a writer, spoken inflections, obviously, are not available, so tone must usually be indicated through style: word choice, ways of phrasing, and kinds of comparisons all can convey an attitude toward what is being described or discussed. Recall the way "The Story of an Hour" describes the beauty of the spring day and then compares Mrs. Mallard's sense of release and freedom to a living thing, "creeping out of the sky, reaching toward her through the sounds, the scents, the color that filled the air" and forcing itself on her (p. 167). The nature of the comparison, words such as "possess her" and "striving to beat it back," and her powerlessness to stop the approach of "this thing" create momentarily an ominous and threatening tone. That turns to relief when Mrs. Mallard accepts it willingly, and the fact that she has had this sense of freedom and release thrust on her unsought evokes sympathy for her, even though we might generally be unsympathetic toward a wife who feels relief at her spouse's death.

A story can convey a wide variety of attitudes toward characters and events. A predominant and important attitude is that of irony, so important, in fact, that it is discussed later in a section of its own. The best way to distinguish various kinds of tone is to look at some stories, mostly taken from Chapters 4 to 7, as specific examples.

"Where Are You Going, Where Have You Been?"   The story "Where Are You Going, Where Have You Been?" (p. 75) opens with a *comic* tone, expressing amusement at Connie's self-centeredness ("She was fifteen and she had a quick, nervous giggling habit of craning her neck to glance into mirrors") and poking fun at the romantic attitudes she has absorbed from movies and popular music: "And Connie paid close attention herself, bathed in a glow of slow-pulsed joy that seemed to rise mysteriously out of the music itself." But the tone gradually turns to *horror* ("She could see then that he wasn't a kid, he was much older—thirty, maybe more. At this knowledge her heart began to pound faster") and *sadness* ("She thought, I'm not going to see my mother again. She thought, I'm not going to sleep in my bed again") at what is happening.

"The House on Mango Street"   The overall tone conveyed in "The House on Mango Street" (p. 91) is *sympathy* with Esperanza and her family through its use of details about the kind of housing they put up with: "the third floor, the paint peeling, wooden bars Papa had nailed on the windows so we wouldn't fall out." But through comments on why the housing was the way it was ("The water pipes broke and the landlord wouldn't fix them because the house was too old") and the nun's disbelief that Esperanza lived where she did ("You live *there*?"), it also conveys a tone of subdued *anger at* or *frustration with* the social system that makes it impossible, or extremely difficult at least, for some families and groups to live in areas with adequate housing and living conditions.

"Hills Like White Elephants"   The tone of "Hills Like White Elephants" (p. 120) seems at first *objective* and *dispassionate*. But a good deal is going on through tones used by the characters — readers need to decide, for every line in the dialogue, what tone is being used. Jig's tones vary considerably. When the man says he's never seen a white elephant and Jig replies, "No, you wouldn't have," the tone clearly seems *scornful,* a put-down. When the man says he's known lots of people who have had the operation and Jig replies, "And afterward they were all so happy," the tone seems *ironic* (she means the opposite of what she is saying). When she says, "And if I do it you'll be happy and things will be like they were and you'll love me?" her tone seems *hopeful,* even full of longing. And when she says, "Then I'll do it. Because I don't care about me," the tone seems *serious,* even *resignedly sad.* That variety of tones shapes an attitude toward her: Although the narrator is objective, the story can strike us as being sympathetic toward her, and unsympathetic toward the man, partly because of the serious, *badgering* tone behind much of what he says, which treats her like an object to be manipulated ("I wouldn't have you do it if you didn't want to. But I know it's perfectly simple" and "I think it's the best thing to do. But I don't want you to do it if you don't really want to"), and because of his obvious attitude of concern only for himself ("That's the only thing that bothers us [me?]. It's the only thing that's made us [me?] unhappy").

"A & P"   When a story has a first-person speaker, there may be two levels of tone: the speaker's tone toward the subject and the story's tone toward the speaker. In "A & P" (p. 386), for example, Sammy tells his story with a *condescending* tone toward the "houseslaves" and with a *romantic idealization* of "Queenie" and her companions. The story's attitude toward Sammy is mostly *comic,* amused at his adolescent posturings, revealing them in a light, witty style. It is also partly *satiric,* joining Sammy in poking fun at the conventionality of life in a small New England town. The story does not take Sammy seriously until near the end when, perhaps for the first time in his life, he takes a stand on an issue and opposes prevailing opinion and the tone turns partly *serious,* as we admire what Sammy does, though we continue to be amused by the confusion about his motives (adherence to a genuine matter of principle? desire to seem a hero? need to follow through once you begin a gesture?).

The tone you hear in a literary work, then, can be serious, sober, solemn, playful, excited, impassioned, and a host of other possibilities as well as mixtures of them. As the examples above indicate, a work can have a single tone, but more often the tone is mixed, with two or more tones juxtaposed, or mingled, or played off each other. And tone, especially when it is complex, cannot always be easy to determine. When Jig in "Hills Like White Elephants" says "Everything tastes of licorice. Especially all the things you've waited so long for" (p. 121), the tone is difficult to assess: Is it wistful? Angry? Bitter? Wondering about tone, in a situation like that, is part of the richness and reward of being an active reader. Tone rarely can be summed up in a word or two. It needs to be described and discussed in a way that does justice to its full complexity.

IRONY

One of the more complex tones is **irony**, a way of expression in which the writer or speaker creates a discrepancy or incongruity between what is (reality) and what seems to be (appearance). Dealing with irony requires active reading because the words don't mean what they literally say. Therefore the reader has to be active in recognizing and processing the difference between what is said and what is meant. Irony appears in a variety of forms. The sections that follow describe the most important types of irony and indicate what to listen for to discern each type.

Verbal Irony

In **verbal irony**, what is said is the opposite of what is meant ("Beautiful day!" when the weather is miserable). The name *Arnold Friend,* in "Where Are You Going, Where Have You Been?" (p. 75), is an example, for Arnold is anything but a friend to Connie. You need to recognize the incongruity between the name and the person. Verbal irony requires listening for signals that what is said is not to be taken in a straightforward way — exaggerated and contradictory word choice, for example, or the sheer absurdity of what is said (it can't be straightforwardly true), or the cutting tone in which a word or phrase seems intended to be spoken. A specific form of verbal irony, **sarcasm**, is an especially direct, harsh, and cutting form ("Oh, no, these eggs are fine. I *prefer* them black and fused to the plate"). The narrator's put-down of Sonny's friend, "And how about you? You're pretty goddamn smart, I bet" (p. 141), is sarcastic. If we miss such signals, we risk misreading the work.

Dramatic Irony

Dramatic irony arises when a character says or does something that the reader or audience realizes has a meaning opposite to what the character intends. To detect dramatic irony, watch for occasions when characters don't realize the full implications of what they are saying or of what happens to them, and when you see more about it than they do. A famous example is the Greek tragedy *Oedipus Rex* (p. 1145), in which an oracle informs Oedipus that he will murder his father and marry his mother. As the story proceeds and we learn that Oedipus has indeed killed a man and has married a woman considerably older than himself, we begin to realize before he and the other characters do that what the oracle declared is true. Much of the power of the play comes from our growing horror as we watch Oedipus and his mother grasp what we already know, and our awareness that we can do nothing to change the outcome. Similarly, the last line of "The Story of an Hour" (p. 167) depends on dramatic irony: We know that Mrs. Mallard wasn't killed by joy at seeing her husband alive and well, but died from shock and disappointment instead. Also, be alert for the possibility of dramatic irony when a work of fiction uses an unreliable narrator, in cases where you are aware of more than the narrator is or the characters are.

Situational Irony

In **situational irony**, a result or situation turns out very differently from what was expected or hoped for. To notice situational irony, look for reversals—when something turns around from what it used to be, or what was expected, or what was desired. In many cases, such a reversal has ironic implications. In "Everyday Use," as Dee insists on being given the quilts her grandmother made, Mama recalls how she had "offered Dee (Wangero) a quilt when she went away to college. Then she had told me they were old-fashioned, out of style" (p. 107). Irony arises out of the changed situation, a change in Dee's attitude toward her heritage. And it's ironic when Dee accuses Mama of not appreciating her heritage when the situation has made clear that it's Dee who lacks such understanding. Unlike dramatic irony, in situational irony the reader does not necessarily know more than the characters and may be as surprised by what happens as the characters are.

www

Further explore style, tone, and irony, including interactive exercises, with VirtuaLit Fiction at bedfordstmartins.com/approachinglit.

That is the case with the unexpected double situational ironies in "The Story of an Hour" (p. 167). First, the "something" coming toward Mrs. Mallard, for which she waits fearfully, is not the sense of overwhelming loss and grief we expect her to feel; her reaction to the situation turns out to be the opposite. Second, the few moments in which Mrs. Mallard does experience a desire for life and an expectation of happiness end up being the result of a clerical error and, instead of the wonderful future she glimpsed, lead to her death.

☑ CHECKLIST on Style, Tone, and Irony

❑ Be especially attentive to style: word selection (diction), sentence construction, sentence rhythms, choice of nonliteral expressions, and handling of timing and tone.

❑ Consider the effectiveness (appropriateness) of the narrative style and the style used in characters' dialogue and thoughts, and, when applicable, how style differs in various parts of a story.

❑ Develop your ability to discern individuality of style — how one author's style differs from that of other authors, and how each author possesses a unique, individual manner of writing.

❑ Listen for tone, the attitude toward the subject implied in a literary work, the "tone of voice" that indicates how what is said should be taken — seriously, ironically, sympathetically, condescendingly. Does the tone convey humor, affection, anger, frustration, horror, grief, concern, scorn, bitterness (to name only a few possibilities)?

❑ Be alert for irony, an expression involving a discrepancy between appearance and reality, between what is said and what is intended. Identify the kind of irony being employed:

  • *Verbal irony:* A discrepancy between what is said and intended; saying the opposite of what is actually meant.
  • *Dramatic irony:* A discrepancy between what a reader or audience knows and what is known by a speaker or character; usually the reader or audience knows more than the speaker or character, or recognizes implications the speaker or character is not aware of.
  • *Situational irony:* A discrepancy between what is expected or what should be and what actually occurs; in it, a result or situation turns out very differently from what was anticipated or hoped for.

FURTHER READING

The following story is about a young African American girl growing up in Harlem, whose horizons are expanded in several ways through a visit to FAO Schwartz, one of the most famous (and expensive) toy stores in the world. Even on first reading, you'll notice that it depends heavily on its style and tone. As you reread it, listen for the way style helps create the voice. Pay attention to the diction, sentence length, sentence constructions (some of them nongrammatical), and rhythm. Listen for the tone, or actually the complex mixture of tones — the attitude of the speaker toward Miss Moore and toward the world at large, and the attitude of the story toward the speaker. And watch for ironies.

Toni Cade Bambara   1939–1995

The Lesson   [1972]

Back in the days when everyone was old and stupid or young and foolish and me and Sugar were the only ones just right, this lady moved on our block with nappy hair and proper speech and no makeup. And quite naturally we laughed at her, laughed the way we did at the junk man who went about his business like he was some big-time president and his sorry-ass horse his secretary. And we kinda hated her too, hated the way we did the winos who cluttered up our parks and pissed on our handball walls and stank up our hallways and stairs so you couldn't halfway play hide-and-seek without a goddamn gas mask. Miss Moore was her name. The only woman on the block with no first name. And she was black as hell, cept for her feet, which were fish-white and spooky. And she was always planning these boring-ass things for us to do, us being my cousin, mostly, who lived on the block cause we all moved North the same time and to the same apartment then spread out gradual to breathe. And our parents would yank our heads into some kinda shape and crisp up our clothes so we'd be presentable for travel with Miss Moore, who always looked like she was going to church, though she never did. Which is just one of things the grownups talked about when they talked behind her back like a dog. But when she came calling with some sachet she'd sewed up or some gingerbread she'd made or some book, why then they'd all be too embarrassed to turn her down and we'd get handed over all spruced up. She'd been to college and said it was only right that she should take responsibility for the young ones' education, and she not even related by marriage or blood. So they'd go for it. Specially Aunt Gretchen. She was the main gofer in the family. You got some ole dumb shit foolishness you want somebody to go for, you send for Aunt Gretchen. She been screwed into the go-along for so long, it's a blood-deep natural thing with her. Which is how she got saddled with me and Sugar and Junior in the first place while our mothers were in a la-de-da apartment up the block having a good ole time.

So this one day Miss Moore rounds us all up at the mailbox and it's puredee hot and she's knockin herself out about arithmetic. And school suppose to let up in summer I heard, but she don't never let up. And the starch in my pinafore scratching the shit outta me and I'm really hating this nappy-head bitch and her goddamn college degree. I'd much rather go to the pool or to the show where it's cool. So me and Sugar leaning on the mailbox being surly, which is a Miss Moore word. And Flyboy checking out what everybody brought for lunch. And Fat Butt already wasting his peanut-butter-and-jelly sandwich like the pig he is. And Junebug punchin on Q.T.'s arm for potato chips. And Rosie Giraffe shifting from one hip to the other waiting for somebody to step on her foot or ask her if she from Georgia so she can kick ass, preferably Mercedes'. And Miss Moore asking us do we know what money is, like we a bunch of retards. I mean real money, she say, like it's only poker chips or monopoly papers we lay on the grocer. So right away I'm tired of this and say so. And would much rather snatch Sugar and go to the Sunset and terrorize the West Indian kids and take their hair ribbons and their money too. And Miss Moore files that remark away for next week's lesson on brotherhood, I can tell. And finally I say we oughta get to the subway cause it's cooler and besides we might meet some cute boys. Sugar done swiped her mama's lipstick, so we ready.

So we heading down the street and she's boring us silly about what things cost and what our parents make and how much goes for rent and how money ain't divided up right in this country. And then she gets to the part about we all poor and live in the slums, which I don't feature. And I'm ready to speak on that, but she steps out in the street and hails two cabs just like that. Then she hustles half the crew in with her and hands me a five-dollar bill and tells me to calculate 10 percent tip for the driver. And we're off. Me and Sugar and Junebug and Flyboy hangin out the window and hollering to everybody, putting lipstick on each other cause Flyboy a faggot anyway, and making farts with our sweaty armpits. But I'm mostly trying to figure how to spend this money. But they all fascinated with the meter ticking and Junebug starts laying bets as to how much it'll read when Flyboy can't hold his breath no more. Then Sugar lays bets as to how much it'll be when we get there. So I'm stuck. Don't nobody want to go for my plan, which is to jump out at the next light and run off to the first bar-b-que we can find. Then the driver tells us to get the hell out cause we there already. And the meter reads eighty-five cents. And I'm stalling to figure out the tip and Sugar say give him a dime. And I decide he don't need it bad as I do, so later for him. But then he tries to take off with Junebug foot still in the door so we talk about his mama something ferocious. Then we check out that we on Fifth Avenue and everybody dressed up in stockings. One lady in a fur coat, hot as it is. White folks crazy.

"This is the place," Miss Moore say, presenting it to us in the voice she uses at the museum. "Let's look in the windows before we go in."

"Can we steal?" Sugar asks very serious like she's getting the ground rules squared away before she plays. "I beg your pardon," say Miss Moore, and we fall out. So she leads us around the windows of the toy store and me and Sugar screamin, "This is mine, that's mine, I gotta have that, that was made for me, I was born for that," till Big Butt drowns us out.

"Hey, I'm goin to buy that there."

"That there? You don't even know what it is, stupid."

"I do so," he say punchin on Rosie Giraffe. "It's a microscope."

"Whatcha gonna do with a microscope, fool?"

"Look at things."

"Like what, Ronald?" ask Miss Moore. And Big Butt ain't got the first notion. So here go Miss Moore gabbing about the thousands of bacteria in a drop of water and the somethinorother in a speck of blood and the million and one living things in the air around us is invisible to the naked eye. And what she say that for? Junebug go to town on that "naked" and we rolling. Then Miss Moore ask what it cost. So we all jam into the window smudgin it up and the price tag say $300. So then she ask how long'd take for Big Butt and Junebug to save up their allowances. "Too long," I say. "Yeh," adds Sugar, "outgrown it by that time." And Miss Moore say no, you never outgrow learning instruments. "Why, even medical students and interns and," blah, blah, blah. And we ready to choke Big Butt for bringing it up in the first damn place.

"This here costs four hundred eighty dollars," say Rosie Giraffe. So we pile up all over her to see what she pointin out. My eyes tell me it's a chunk of glass cracked with something heavy, and different-color inks dripped into the splits, then the whole thing put into a oven or something. But for $480 it don't make sense.

"That's a paperweight made of semi-precious stones fused together under tremendous pressure," she explains slowly, with her hands doing the mining and all the factory work.

"So what's a paperweight?" asks Rosie Giraffe.

"To weigh paper with, dumbbell," say Flyboy, the wise man from the East.

"Not exactly," say Miss Moore, which is what she say when you warm or way off too. "It's to weigh paper down so it won't scatter and make your desk untidy." So right away me and Sugar curtsy to each other and then to Mercedes who is more the tidy type.

"We don't keep paper on top of the desk in my class," say Junebug, figuring Miss Moore crazy or lyin one.

"At home, then," she say. "Don't you have a calendar and a pencil case and a blotter and a letter-opener on your desk at home where you do your homework?" And she know damn well what our homes look like cause she nosys around in them every chance she gets.

"I don't even have a desk," say Junebug. "Do we?"

"No. And I don't get no homework neither," say Big Butt.

"And I don't even have a home," say Flyboy like he do at school to keep the white folks off his back and sorry for him. Send this poor kid to camp posters, is his specialty.

"I do," says Mercedes. "I have a box of stationery on my desk and a picture of my cat. My godmother bought the stationery and the desk. There's a big rose on each sheet and the envelopes smell like roses."

"Who wants to know about your smelly-ass stationery," say Rosie Giraffe fore I can get my two cents in.

"It's important to have a work area all your own so that . . ."

"Will you look at this sailboat, please," say Flyboy, cuttin her off and pointin to the thing like it was his. So once again we tumble all over each other to gaze at this magnificent thing in the toy store which is just big enough to maybe sail two kittens across the pond if you strap them to the posts tight. We all start reciting the price tag like we in assembly. "Handcrafted sailboat of fiberglass at one thousand one hundred ninety-five dollars."

"Unbelievable," I hear myself say and am really stunned. I read it again for myself just in case the group recitation put me in a trance. Same thing. For some reason this pisses me off. We look at Miss Moore and she lookin at us, waiting for I dunno what.

"Who'd pay all that when you can buy a sailboat set for a quarter at Pop's, a tube of glue for a dime, and a ball of string for eight cents? It must have a motor and a whole lot else besides," I say. "My sailboat cost me about fifty cents."

"But will it take water?" say Mercedes with her smart ass.

"Took mine to Alley Pond Park once," say Flyboy. "String broke. Lost it. Pity."

"Sailed mine in Central Park and it keeled over and sank. Had to ask my father for another dollar."

"And you got the strap," laugh Big Butt. "The jerk didn't even have a string on it. My old man wailed on his behind."

Little Q.T. was staring hard at the sailboat and you could see he wanted it bad. But he too little and somebody'd just take it from him. So what the hell. "This boat for kids, Miss Moore?"

"Parents silly to buy something like that just to get all broke up," say Rosie Giraffe.

"That much money it should last forever," I figure.

"My father'd buy it for me if I wanted it."

"Your father, my ass," say Rosie Giraffe getting a chance to finally push Mercedes.

"Must be rich people shop here," say Q.T.

"You are a very bright boy," say Flyboy. "What was your first clue?" And he rap him on the head with the back of his knuckles, since Q.T. the only one he could get away with. Though Q.T. liable to come up behind you years later and get his licks in when you half expect it.

"What I want to know is," I says to Miss Moore though I never talk to her, I wouldn't give the bitch that satisfaction, "is how much a real boat costs? I figure a thousand'd get you a yacht any day."

"Why don't you check that out," she says, "and report back to the group?" Which really pains my ass. If you gonna mess up a perfectly good swim day least you could do is have some answers. "Let's go in," she say like she got something up her sleeve. Only she don't lead the way. So me and Sugar turn the corner to where the entrance is, but when we get there I kinda hang back. Not that I'm scared, what's there to be afraid of, just a toy store. But I feel funny, shame. But what I got to be shamed about? Got as much right to go in as anybody. But somehow I can't seem to get hold of the door, so I step away for Sugar to lead. But she hangs back too. And I look at her and she looks at me and this is ridiculous. I mean, damn, I have never ever been shy about doing nothing or going nowhere. But then Mercedes steps up and then Rosie Giraffe and Big Butt crowd in behind and shove, and next thing we all stuffed into the doorway with only Mercedes squeezing past us, smoothing out her jumper and walking right down the aisle. Then the rest of us tumble in like a glued-together jigsaw done all wrong. And people lookin at us. And it's like the time me and Sugar crashed into the Catholic church on a dare. But once we got in there and everything so hushed and holy and the candles and the bowin and the handkerchiefs on all the drooping heads, I just couldn't go through with the plan. Which was for me to run up to the altar and do a tap dance while Sugar played the nose flute and messed around in the holy water. And Sugar kept givin me the elbow. Then later teased me so bad I tied her up in the shower and turned it on and locked her in. And she'd be there till this day if Aunt Gretchen hadn't finally figured I was lyin about the boarder takin a shower.

Same thing in the store. We all walkin on tiptoe and hardly touchin the games and puzzles and things. And I watched Miss Moore who is steady watchin us like she waitin for a sign. Like Mama Drewery watches the sky and sniffs the air and takes note of just how much slant is in the bird formation. Then me and Sugar bump smack into each other, so busy gazing at the toys, 'specially the sailboat. But we don't laugh and go into our fat-lady bump-stomach routine. We just stare at that price tag. Then Sugar run a finger over the whole boat. And I'm jealous and want to hit her. Maybe not her, but I sure want to punch somebody in the mouth.

"Watcha bring us here for, Miss Moore?"

"You sound angry, Sylvia. Are you mad about something?" Givin me one of them grins like she tellin a grown-up joke that never turns out to be funny. And she's lookin very closely at me like maybe she plannin to do my portrait from memory. I'm mad, but I won't give her that satisfaction. So I slouch around the store bein very bored and say, "Let's go."

Me and Sugar at the back of the train watchin the tracks whizzin by large then small then gettin gobbled up in the dark. I'm thinkin about this tricky toy I saw in the store. A clown that somersaults on a bar then does chin-ups just cause you yank lightly at his leg. Cost $35. I could see me askin my mother for a $35 birthday clown. "You wanna who that costs what?" she'd say, cocking her head to the side to get a better view of the hole in my head. Thirty-five dollars could buy new bunk beds for Junior and Gretchen's boy. Thirty-five dollars and the whole household could go visit Granddaddy Nelson in the country. Thirty-five dollars would pay for the rent and the piano bill too. Who are these people that spend that much for performing clowns and $1,000 for toy sailboats? What kinda work they do and how they live and how come we ain't in on it? Where we are is who we are, Miss Moore always pointin out. But it don't necessarily have to be that way, she always adds then waits for somebody to say that poor people have to wake up and demand their share of the pie and don't none of us know what kind of pie she talkin about in the first damn place. But she ain't so smart cause I still got her four dollars from the taxi and she sure ain't gettin it. Messin up my day with this shit. Sugar nudges me in my pocket and winks.

Miss Moore lines us up in front of the mailbox where we started from, seem like years ago, and I got a headache for thinkin so hard. And we lean all over each other so we can hold up under the draggy-ass lecture she always finishes us off with at the end before we thank her for borin us to tears. But she just looks at us like she readin tea leaves. Finally she say, "Well, what did you think of F.A.O. Schwarz?"

Rosie Giraffe mumbles, "White folks crazy."

"I'd like to go there again when I get my birthday money," says Mercedes, and we shove her out the pack so she has to lean on the mailbox by herself.

"I'd like a shower. Tiring day," say Flyboy.

Then Sugar surprises me by sayin, "You know, Miss Moore, I don't think all of us here put together eat in a year what that sailboat costs." And Miss Moore lights up like somebody goosed her. "And?" she say, urging Sugar on. Only I'm standin on her foot so she don't continue.

"Imagine for a minute what kind of society it is in which some people can spend on a toy what it would cost to feed a family of six or seven. What do you think?"

"I think," say Sugar pushing me off her feet like she never done before, cause I whip her ass in a minute, "that this is not much of a democracy if you ask me. Equal chance to pursue happiness means an equal crack at the dough, don't it?" Miss Moore is besides herself and I am disgusted with Sugar's treachery. So I stand on her foot one more time to see if she'll shove me. She shuts up, and Miss Moore looks at me, sorrowfully I'm thinkin. And somethin weird is goin on, I can feel it in my chest.

"Anybody else learn anything today?" lookin dead at me. I walk away and Sugar has to run to catch up and don't even seem to notice when I shrug her arm off my shoulder.

"Well, we got four dollars anyway," she says.

"Uh hunh."

"We could go to Hascombs and get half a chocolate layer and then go to the Sunset and still have plenty money for potato chips and ice-cream sodas."

"Uh hunh."

"Race you to Hascombs," she say.

We start down the block and she gets ahead which is O.K. by me cause I'm goin to the West End and then over to the Drive to think this day through. She can run if she want to and even run faster. But ain't nobody gonna beat me at nuthin.

APPROACHING THE READING

1. Describe the style in "The Lesson." Consider the word choices, sentence structures, rhythm. How does the story establish the voice you listen to? What is Sylvia, the narrator of the story, like? Try sketching her character. In what ways does the style in and of itself help develop Sylvia's character?

2. Consider how the style reveals and helps create tone. Be ready to discuss the attitude Sylvia shows toward Miss Moore, the other kids, white people, the world in general. How did you feel about her in your first reading of the story? Did your feelings about her change or become more complex on rereading the story or as you thought back over it?

3. Is there evidence that Sylvia changes? If so, in what ways? Point out specific things that both cause and indicate a change (including stylistic ones, if any).

4. In what ways is the point of view important to the effect of the story? How would the story change if it had a different point of view? How would you describe the story's attitude toward Sylvia? How does it come through, given the use of the first-person point of view?

5. What lessons do the kids learn that day? Are they the ones Miss Moore intended them to learn? Why do you think so, or not? Does she have a teaching plan? It seems clear that Sugar is affected by what she experienced. Is Sylvia similarly affected, or does she resist it all? What sort of person would you predict she would turn out to be at your age, if the story followed her life further?

Here is another story about lessons an adult wants a young girl to learn and her resistance to them. In it too the style and tone are those of a girl with a definite "attitude." As you reread it, focus on word choice, sentence constructions, and rhythms, as you did for the previous story. Listen for tone—again, both the attitude of the speaker (toward her mother and the rest of the world) and the attitude of the story toward the speaker. Think about whether the girl ends up more or less like (and likeable than) Sylvia.

Amy Tan   b. 1952

Two Kinds   [1989]

My mother believed you could be anything you wanted to be in America. You could open a restaurant. You could work for the government and get good retirement. You could buy a house with almost no money down. You could become rich. You could become instantly famous.

"Of course you can be prodigy, too," my mother told me when I was nine. "You can be best anything. What does Auntie Lindo know? Her daughter, she is only best tricky."

America was where all my mother's hopes lay. She had come here in 1949 after losing everything in China: her mother and father, her family home, her first husband, and two daughters, twin baby girls. But she never looked back with regret. There were so many ways for things to get better.

*   *   *

We didn't immediately pick the right kind of prodigy. At first my mother thought I could be a Chinese Shirley Temple. We'd watch Shirley's old movies on TV as though they were training films. My mother would poke my arm and say, *"Ni kan"* — You watch. And I would see Shirley tapping her feet, or singing a sailor song, or pursing her lips into a very round O while saying, "Oh my goodness."

"Ni kan," said my mother as Shirley's eyes flooded with tears. "You already know how. Don't need talent for crying!"

Soon after my mother got this idea about Shirley Temple, she took me to a beauty training school in the Mission district and put me in the hands of a student who could barely hold the scissors without shaking. Instead of getting big fat curls, I emerged with an uneven mass of crinkly black fuzz. My mother dragged me off to the bathroom and tried to wet down my hair.

"You look like Negro Chinese," she lamented, as if I had done this on purpose.

The instructor of the beauty training school had to lop off these soggy clumps to make my hair even again. "Peter Pan is very popular these days," the instructor assured my mother. I now had hair the length of a boy's, with straight-across bangs that hung at a slant two inches above my eyebrows. I liked the haircut and it made me actually look forward to my future fame.

In fact, in the beginning, I was just as excited as my mother, maybe even more so. I pictured this prodigy part of me as many different images, trying each one on for size. I was a dainty ballerina girl standing by the curtains, waiting to hear the right music that would send me floating on my tiptoes. I was like the Christ child lifted out of the straw manger, crying with holy indignity. I was Cinderella stepping from her pumpkin carriage with sparkly cartoon music filling the air.

In all of my imaginings, I was filled with a sense that I would soon become *perfect*. My mother and father would adore me. I would be beyond reproach. I would never feel the need to sulk for anything.

But sometimes the prodigy in me became impatient. "If you don't hurry up and get me out of here, I'm disappearing for good," it warned. "And then you'll always be nothing."

Every night after dinner, my mother and I would sit at the Formica kitchen table. She would present new tests, taking her examples from stories of amazing children she had read in *Ripley's Believe It or Not,* or *Good Housekeeping, Reader's Digest,* and a dozen other magazines she kept in a pile in our bathroom. My mother got these magazines from people whose houses she cleaned. And since she cleaned many houses each week, we had a great assortment. She would look through them all, searching for stories about remarkable children.

The first night she brought out a story about a three-year-old boy who knew the capitals of all the states and even most of the European countries.

A teacher was quoted as saying the little boy could also pronounce the names of the foreign cities correctly.

"What's the capital of Finland?" my mother asked me, looking at the magazine story.

All I knew was the capital of California, because Sacramento was the name of the street we lived on in Chinatown. "Nairobi!" I guessed, saying the most foreign word I could think of. She checked to see if that was possibly one way to pronounce "Helsinki" before showing me the answer.

The tests got harder — multiplying numbers in my head, finding the queen of hearts in a deck of cards, trying to stand on my head without using my hands, predicting the daily temperatures in Los Angeles, New York, and London.

One night I had to look at a page from the Bible for three minutes and then report everything I could remember. "Now Jehoshaphat had riches and honor in abundance and . . . that's all I remember, Ma," I said.

And after seeing my mother's disappointed face once again, something inside of me began to die. I hated the tests, the raised hopes and failed expectations. Before going to bed that night, I looked in the mirror above the bathroom sink and when I saw only my face staring back — and that it would always be this ordinary face — I began to cry. Such a sad, ugly girl! I made high-pitched noises like a crazed animal, trying to scratch out the face in the mirror.

And then I saw what seemed to be the prodigy side of me — because I had never seen that face before. I looked at my reflection, blinking so I could see more clearly. The girl staring back at me was angry, powerful. This girl and I were the same. I had new thoughts, willful thoughts, or rather thoughts filled with lots of won'ts. I won't let her change me, I promised myself. I won't be what I'm not.

So now on nights when my mother presented her tests, I performed listlessly, my head propped on one arm. I pretended to be bored. And I was. I got so bored I started counting the bellows of the foghorns out on the bay while my mother drilled me in other areas. The sound was comforting and reminded me of the cow jumping over the moon. And the next day, I played a game with myself, seeing if my mother would give up on me before eight bellows. After a while I usually counted only one, maybe two bellows at most. At last she was beginning to give up hope.

Two or three months had gone by without any mention of my being a prodigy again. And then one day my mother was watching *The Ed Sullivan Show* on TV. The TV was old and the sound kept shorting out. Every time my mother got halfway up from the sofa to adjust the set, the sound would go back on and Ed would be talking. As soon as she sat down, Ed would go silent again. She got up, the TV broke into loud piano music. She sat down. Silence. Up and down, back and forth, quiet and loud. It was like a stiff embraceless dance between her and the TV set. Finally she stood by the set with her hand on the sound dial.

She seemed entranced by the music, a little frenzied piano piece with this mesmerizing quality, sort of quick passages and then teasing lilting ones before it returned to the quick playful parts.

"*Ni kan,*" my mother said, calling me over with hurried hand gestures, "Look here."

I could see why my mother was fascinated by the music. It was being pounded out by a little Chinese girl, about nine years old, with a Peter Pan haircut. The girl had the sauciness of a Shirley Temple. She was proudly modest like a proper Chinese child. And she also did this fancy sweep of a curtsy, so that the fluffy skirt of her white dress cascaded slowly to the floor like the petals of a large carnation.

In spite of these warning signs, I wasn't worried. Our family had no piano and we couldn't afford to buy one, let alone reams of sheet music and piano lessons. So I could be generous in my comments when my mother bad-mouthed the little girl on TV.

"Play note right, but doesn't sound good! No singing sound," complained my mother.

"What are you picking on her for?" I said carelessly. "She's pretty good. Maybe she's not the best, but she's trying hard." I knew almost immediately I would be sorry I said that.

"Just like you," she said. "Not the best. Because you not trying." She gave a little huff as she let go of the sound dial and sat down on the sofa.

The little Chinese girl sat down also to play an encore of "Anitra's Dance" by Grieg. I remember the song, because later on I had to learn how to play it.

Three days after watching *The Ed Sullivan Show*, my mother told me what my schedule would be for piano lessons and piano practice. She had talked to Mr. Chong, who lived on the first floor of our apartment building. Mr. Chong was a retired piano teacher and my mother had traded house-cleaning services for weekly lessons and a piano for me to practice on every day, two hours a day, from four until six.

When my mother told me this, I felt as though I had been sent to hell. I whined and then kicked my foot a little when I couldn't stand it anymore.

"Why don't you like me the way I am? I'm *not* a genius! I can't play the piano. And even if I could, I wouldn't go on TV if you paid me a million dollars!" I cried.

My mother slapped me. "Who ask you be genius?" she shouted. "Only ask you be your best. For you sake. You think I want you be genius? Hnnh! What for! Who ask you!"

"So ungrateful," I heard her mutter in Chinese. "If she had as much talent as she has temper, she would be famous now."

Mr. Chong, whom I secretly nicknamed Old Chong, was very strange, always tapping his fingers to the silent music of an invisible orchestra. He looked ancient in my eyes. He had lost most of the hair on top of his head and he wore thick glasses and had eyes that always looked tired and sleepy. But he must have been younger than I thought, since he lived with his mother and was not yet married.

I met Old Lady Chong once and that was enough. She had this peculiar smell like a baby that had done something in its pants. And her fingers felt like a dead person's, like an old peach I once found in the back of the refrigerator; the skin just slid off the meat when I picked it up.

I soon found out why Old Chong had retired from teaching piano. He was deaf. "Like Beethoven!" he shouted to me. "We're both listening only in our head!" And he would start to conduct his frantic silent sonatas.

Our lessons went like this. He would open the book and point to different things, explaining their purpose: "Key! Treble! Bass! No sharps or flats! So this is C major! Listen now and play after me!"

And then he would play the C scale a few times, a simple chord, and then, as if inspired by an old, unreachable itch, he gradually added more notes and running trills and a pounding bass until the music was really something quite grand.

I would play after him, the simple scale, the simple chord, and then I just played some nonsense that sounded like a cat running up and down on top of garbage cans. Old Chong smiled and applauded and then said, "Very good! But now you must learn to keep time!"

So that's how I discovered that Old Chong's eyes were too slow to keep up with the wrong notes I was playing. He went through the motions in half-time. To help me keep rhythm, he stood behind me, pushing down on my right shoulder for every beat. He balanced pennies on top of my wrists so I would keep them still as I slowly played scales and arpeggios. He had me curve my hand around an apple and keep that shape when playing chords. He marched stiffly to show me how to make each finger dance up and down, staccato like an obedient little soldier.

He taught me all these things, and that was how I also learned I could be lazy and get away with mistakes, lots of mistakes. If I hit the wrong notes because I hadn't practiced enough, I never corrected myself. I just kept playing in rhythm. And Old Chong kept conducting his own private reverie.

So maybe I never really gave myself a fair chance. I did pick up the basics pretty quickly, and I might have become a good pianist at that young age. But I was so determined not to try, not to be anybody different that I learned to play only the most ear-splitting preludes, the most discordant hymns.

Over the next year, I practiced like this, dutifully in my own way. And then one day I heard my mother and her friend Lindo Jong both talking in a loud bragging tone of voice so others could hear. It was after church, and I was leaning against the brick wall wearing a dress with stiff white petticoats. Auntie Lindo's daughter, Waverly, who was about my age, was standing farther down the wall about five feet away. We had grown up together and shared all the closeness of two sisters squabbling over crayons and dolls. In other words, for the most part, we hated each other. I thought she was snotty. Waverly Jong had gained a certain amount of fame as "Chinatown's Littlest Chinese Chess Champion."

"She bring home too many trophy," lamented Auntie Lindo that Sunday. "All day she play chess. All day I have no time do nothing but dust off her winnings." She threw a scolding look at Waverly, who pretended not to see her.

"You lucky you don't have this problem," said Auntie Lindo with a sigh to my mother.

And my mother squared her shoulders and bragged: "Our problem worser than yours. If we ask Jing-mei wash dish, she hear nothing but music. It's like you can't stop this natural talent."

And right then, I was determined to put a stop to her foolish pride.

A few weeks later, Old Chong and my mother conspired to have me play in a talent show which would be held in the church hall. By then, my parents had saved up enough to buy me a secondhand piano, a black Wurlitzer spinet with a scarred bench. It was the showpiece of our living room.

For the talent show, I was to play a piece called "Pleading Child" from Schumann's *Scenes from Childhood*. It was a simple, moody piece that sounded more difficult than it was. I was supposed to memorize the whole thing, playing the repeat parts twice to make the piece sound longer. But I dawdled over it, playing a few bars and then cheating, looking up to see what notes followed. I never really listened to what I was playing. I daydreamed about being somewhere else, about being someone else.

The part I liked to practice best was the fancy curtsy: right foot out, touch the rose on the carpet with a pointed foot, sweep to the side, left leg bends, look up and smile.

My parents invited all the couples from the Joy Luck Club to witness my debut. Auntie Lindo and Uncle Tin were there. Waverly and her two older brothers had also come. The first two rows were filled with children both younger and older than I was. The littlest ones got to go first. They recited simple nursery rhymes, squawked out tunes on miniature violins, twirled Hula Hoops, pranced in pink ballet tutus, and when they bowed or curtsied, the audience would sigh in unison, "Awww," and then clap enthusiastically.

When my turn came, I was very confident. I remember my childish excitement. It was as if I knew, without a doubt, that the prodigy side of me really did exist. I had no fear whatsoever, no nervousness. I remember thinking to myself, This is it! This is it! I looked out over the audience, at my mother's blank face, my father's yawn, Auntie Lindo's stiff-lipped smile, Waverly's sulky expression. I had on a white dress layered with sheets of lace, and a pink bow in my Peter Pan haircut. As I sat down I envisioned people jumping to their feet and Ed Sullivan rushing up to introduce me to everyone on TV.

And I started to play. It was so beautiful. I was so caught up in how lovely I looked that at first I didn't worry how I would sound. So it was a surprise to me when I hit the first wrong note and I realized something didn't sound quite right. And then I hit another and another followed that. A chill started at the top of my head and began to trickle down. Yet I couldn't stop playing, as though my hands were bewitched. I kept thinking my fingers would adjust themselves back, like a train switching to the right track. I played this strange jumble through two repeats, the sour notes staying with me all the way to the end.

When I stood up, I discovered my legs were shaking. Maybe I had just been nervous and the audience, like Old Chong, had seen me go through the right motions and had not heard anything wrong at all. I swept my right foot out, went down on my knee, looked up and smiled. The room was quiet, except for Old Chong, who was beaming and shouting, "Bravo! Bravo! Well done!" But then I saw my mother's face, her stricken face. The audience clapped weakly, and as I walked back to my chair, with my whole face quivering as I tried not to cry, I heard a little boy whisper loudly to his mother, "That was awful," and the mother whispered back, "Well, she certainly tried."

And now I realized how many people were in the audience, the whole world it seemed. I was aware of eyes burning into my back. I felt the shame of my mother and father as they sat stiffly throughout the rest of the show.

We could have escaped during intermission. Pride and some strange sense of honor must have anchored my parents to their chairs. And so we watched it all: the eighteen-year-old boy with a fake mustache who did a magic show and juggled flaming hoops while riding a unicycle. The breasted girl with white makeup who sang from *Madama Butterfly* and got honorable mention. And the eleven-year-old boy who won first prize playing a tricky violin song that sounded like a busy bee.

After the show, the Hsus, the Jongs, and the St. Clairs from the Joy Luck Club came up to my mother and father.

"Lots of talented kids," Auntie Lindo said vaguely, smiling broadly.

"That was somethin' else," said my father, and I wondered if he was referring to me in a humorous way, or whether he even remembered what I had done.

Waverly looked at me and shrugged her shoulders. "You aren't a genius like me," she said matter-of-factly. And if I hadn't felt so bad, I would have pulled her braids and punched her stomach.

But my mother's expression was what devastated me: a quiet, blank look that said she had lost everything. I felt the same way, and it seemed as if everybody were now coming up, like gawkers at the scene of an accident, to see what parts were actually missing. When we got on the bus to go home, my father was humming the busy-bee tune and my mother was silent. I kept thinking she wanted to wait until we got home before shouting at me. But when my father unlocked the door to our apartment, my mother walked in and then went to the back, into the bedroom. No accusations. No blame. And in a way, I felt disappointed. I had been waiting for her to start shouting, so I could shout back and cry and blame her for all my misery.

*   *   *

I assumed my talent-show fiasco meant I never had to play the piano again. But two days later, after school, my mother came out of the kitchen and saw me watching TV.

"Four clock," she reminded me as if it were any other day. I was stunned, as though she were asking me to go through the talent-show torture again. I wedged myself more tightly in front of the TV.

"Turn off TV," she called from the kitchen five minutes later.

I didn't budge. And then I decided. I didn't have to do what my mother said anymore. I wasn't her slave. This wasn't China. I had listened to her before and look what happened. She was the stupid one.

She came out from the kitchen and stood in the arched entryway of the living room. "Four clock," she said once again, louder.

"I'm not going to play anymore," I said nonchalantly. "Why should I? I'm not a genius."

She walked over and stood in front of the TV. I saw her chest was heaving up and down in an angry way.

"No!" I said, and I now felt stronger, as if my true self had finally emerged. So this was what had been inside me all along.

"No! I won't!" I screamed.

She yanked me by the arm, pulled me off the floor, snapped off the TV. She was frighteningly strong, half pulling, half carrying me toward the piano as I kicked the throw rugs under my feet. She lifted me up and onto the hard bench. I was sobbing by now, looking at her bitterly. Her chest was heaving even more and her mouth was open, smiling crazily as if she were pleased I was crying.

"You want me to be someone that I'm not!" I sobbed. "I'll never be the kind of daughter you want me to be!"

"Only two kinds of daughters," she shouted in Chinese. "Those who are obedient and those who follow their own mind! Only one kind of daughter can live in this house. Obedient daughter!"

"Then I wish I wasn't your daughter. I wish you weren't my mother," I shouted. As I said these things I got scared. It felt like worms and toads and slimy things crawling out of my chest, but it also felt good, as if this awful side of me had surfaced, at last.

"Too late change this," said my mother shrilly.

And I could sense her anger rising to its breaking point. I wanted to see it spill over. And that's when I remembered the babies she had lost in China, the ones we never talked about. "Then I wish I'd never been born!" I shouted. "I wish I were dead! Like them."

It was as if I had said the magic words. Alakazam! — and her face went blank, her mouth closed, her arms went slack, and she backed out of the room, stunned, as if she were blowing away like a small brown leaf, thin, brittle, lifeless.

*   *   *

It was not the only disappointment my mother felt in me. In the years that followed, I failed her so many times, each time asserting my own will, my right to fall short of expectations. I didn't get straight As. I didn't become class president. I didn't get into Stanford. I dropped out of college.

For unlike my mother, I did not believe I could be anything I wanted to be. I could only be me.

And for all those years, we never talked about the disaster at the recital or my terrible accusations afterward at the piano bench. All that remained unchecked, like a betrayal that was now unspeakable. So I never found a way to ask her why she had hoped for something so large that failure was inevitable.

And even worse, I never asked her what frightened me the most: Why had she given up hope?

For after our struggle at the piano, she never mentioned my playing again. The lessons stopped. The lid to the piano was closed, shutting out the dust, my misery, and her dreams.

So she surprised me. A few years ago, she offered to give me the piano, for my thirtieth birthday. I had not played in all those years. I saw the offer as a sign of forgiveness, a tremendous burden removed.

"Are you sure?" I asked shyly. "I mean, won't you and Dad miss it?"

"No, this your piano," she said firmly. "Always your piano. You only one can play."

"Well, I probably can't play anymore," I said. "It's been years."

"You pick up fast," said my mother, as if she knew this was certain. "You have natural talent. You could been genius if you want to."

"No I couldn't."

"You just not trying," said my mother. And she was neither angry nor sad. She said it as if to announce a fact that could never be disproved. "Take it," she said.

But I didn't at first. It was enough that she had offered it to me. And after that, every time I saw it in my parents' living room, standing in front of the bay windows, it made me feel proud, as if it were a shiny trophy I had won back.

Last week I sent a tuner over to my parents' apartment and had the piano reconditioned, for purely sentimental reasons. My mother had died a few months before and I had been getting things in order for my father, a little bit at a time. I put the jewelry in special silk pouches. The sweaters she had knitted in yellow, pink, bright orange—all the colors I hated—I put those in moth-proof boxes. I found some old Chinese silk dresses, the kind with little slits up the sides. I rubbed the old silk against my skin, then wrapped them in tissue and decided to take them home with me.

After I had the piano tuned, I opened the lid and touched the keys. It sounded even richer than I remembered. Really, it was a very good piano. Inside the bench were the same exercise notes with handwritten scales, the same secondhand music books with their covers held together with yellow tape.

I opened up the Schumann book to the dark little piece I had played at the recital. It was on the left-hand side of the page, "Pleading Child." It looked more difficult than I remembered. I played a few bars, surprised at how easily the notes came back to me.

And for the first time, or so it seemed, I noticed the piece on the right-hand side. It was called "Perfectly Contented." I tried to play this one as well. It had a lighter melody but the same flowing rhythm and turned out to be quite easy. "Pleading Child" was shorter but slower; "Perfectly Contented" was longer, but faster. And after I played them both a few times, I realized they were two halves of the same song.

APPROACHING THE READING

1. Describe Tan's style in "Two Kinds." Look closely at the style of the narrative passages, such as paragraphs 1, 9, and 19–20. Notice the word choices, sentence structures, rhythm. Think about how the narrator's style contributes to characterization — of her as a young girl and of her as a woman looking back at the events. Consider the style used for the mother. How does her broken English and incorporation of occasional Chinese phrases contribute to her characterization and to the effect of the story?

Research this author in depth with cultural documents and multimedia resources on *LiterActive*.

2. Consider the importance of various tones in the story. How is the attitude of the young girl toward her mother brought out? How does the attitude of the narrator toward her mother, on looking back at her, differ from her earlier attitude, and how is it brought out? Pick out examples of irony and of humor in the story. What do they contribute to its tone and overall effect?

3. Do you think the use of Shirley Temple in the story is effective or appropriate? What ironies can you think of in using her? What issues are involved in holding up a figure from one culture as a model for a person from another?

4. "And then you'll always be nothing," warns the prodigy side of the speaker (p. 190). What is ironic in this warning? How do this fear of failure and the often-required "make something of yourself" play out in this story? What are the cultural implications of these ideas? In what ways do they conflict with other ideas embedded in your or any culture?

5. Reflect on and be ready to comment on style and tone in the final paragraph. Why, for you, is the ending satisfying and effective, or unsatisfying and ineffective, or effective but not satisfying?

RESPONDING THROUGH WRITING

Journal Entries

1. In the course of a day, listen and watch for the word *style* in regard to anything—music, clothes, sports. Pay attention to radio, TV, advertisements, what you say, what you overhear other people saying, and so forth. Write a journal entry describing several styles you discover and discussing how ways the word is used elsewhere can help clarify its uses in literature.

   Research the authors in this chapter with LitLinks, or take a quiz on the stories with LitQuiz, at bedfordstmartins.com/ approachinglit.

2. Analyze a recording star in terms of style. Think not only about the music itself but also about everything else that goes into the making of the image, the style. Write a journal entry summarizing your conclusions and commenting on how this exercise can help clarify what style is and what style in writing means.

3. In your journal, list examples of irony that you notice during a day. Discuss how and why verbal irony in particular was used, and how it affected the people at whom it was directed.

Literary Analysis Papers

4. Choose a paragraph from one of the stories in this chapter and rewrite it in the style of a different author. Then write a short paper explaining why you chose the authors you did and in what ways the changes in style changed the nature and effect of the story as a whole.

5. Write a paper analyzing the relation of style, tone, and theme in James Joyce's "Eveline" (p. 280), Jamaica Kincaid's "Girl" (p. 283), or Patricia Grace's "Butterflies" (p. 420).

6. Write a paper discussing the importance of irony in John Updike's "A & P" (p. 386), Richard Wright's "The Man Who Was Almost a Man" (p. 395), or Bessie Head's "The Collector of Treasures" (p. 421).

Making Connections

7. Write a paper examining the connection between characterization and irony in Toni Cade Bambara's "The Lesson" (p. 183) and Amy Tan's "Two Kinds" (p. 189).

8. "The Lesson" and "Two Kinds" could be said to use style and tone to reveal another strong cultural reaction: identity and worth gained by refusal, rebellion, saying no. Think about other stories you've read that make a similar point. Write a paper in which you compare and contrast the development of this theme in at least two stories and relate it to your own experience.

Cultural Criticism Papers

9. Write a paper comparing and contrasting two stories about brothers, Louise Erdrich's "The Red Convertible" (p. 67) and James Baldwin's "Sonny's Blues" (p. 138), in handling of plot, point of view, and theme.

10. The narrator in Amy Tan's "Two Kinds" refers to "raised hopes and failed expectations" (p. 191). Think back to earlier stories that deal with the same topic. To what extent might the results be said to embody situational irony? Write a paper in which you discuss ways you see this "dark side of the American dream" playing out in one or more of these stories.

RESPONDING THROUGH THE ARTS

1. Ernest Hemingway's style has been compared to that of the cubist painters. As a way of responding to fiction through use of another art, do some research on cubism and read another story or two by Hemingway. Then pair up some passages from Hemingway with some cubist art and prepare a class presentation in which you explain how the art works are helpful in grasping his writing style.

2. Sylvia in Toni Cade Bambara's "The Lesson" (p. 183) comes through as a dynamic and fairly unforgettable character. Bring out the vitality and richness of her personality by preparing and delivering parts of what she says as a dramatic reading. Select several passages from the story that can be read aloud in about 6 to 7 minutes and that are particularly effective in capturing her character and relate to each other well (you may need to add some transitions to tie the passages together smoothly).

When you write you invite a reader to look in through a
window on everything.

William Stafford

Writing about Fiction

CHAPTER **8**

Writing papers about fiction is a well-established way of taking part in the ongoing conversation about literature described in Chapter 2. There's a natural progression from asking a friend or classmate about what happened in a story (Did the narrator really seal up Fortunato behind a masonry wall in the cellar? Did I get that right?) to discussing the story in class (What sort of person could do that, could have that attitude toward revenge?) to writing a paper on the disturbed personality of the narrator in "The Cask of Amontillado" (p. 359).

Chapters 4 to 7 helped equip you to read fiction actively and confidently. At the same time, they were preparing you to write about fiction effectively and with assurance. These chapters provided ways to "enter" a short story or novel and be able not only to understand all that is involved within a piece of fiction but also to talk and write about what makes it work, how its effects are achieved. The section on "Writing Short Papers" in Chapter 2 (pp. 32–45) provided you with general guidance for writing any literary paper. This chapter builds on that chapter by offering suggestions particularly applicable to writing about stories.

TOPICS

Topics for papers about fiction can be grouped into three categories: those focusing on what goes on *inside* the story, those focusing on what *surrounds* the story, and those focusing on what infuses but also goes *beyond* the story.

Looking Inside the Story

You can write a paper about what goes on inside the story, doing a literary analysis of it. *Analysis* is the process of separating something complex into its various elements as a way of studying its nature, determining its essential features, and examining their relationships to each other. One way of writing about a story is to focus on one or more of the technical elements used in creating it — for example, point of view, plot structure, characters and characterization, setting, symbols, style, tone, and irony. Another way is to focus on its theme, looking at how ideas, feelings, insights, issues, and implications relate to each other. Or you can focus on how technique and theme relate to each other to constitute an effective whole.

Literary analysis is not "tearing a story apart." Thinking of it that way is reductive and often diminishes our experience. Instead, analysis is somewhat like isolating a particular musician and discussing her or his role in a group's performance. Analysis draws our attention to aspects of a story we may have overlooked and leads us to reflect further on them. It involves not just separating a story into its constituent features but also examining the features themselves. Each feature is complex and can itself be explored and studied as a way of clarifying its contributions to the whole. Chapters 4 to 7 separated the elements of fiction, as indicated by chapter titles, and then examined those parts closely within the chapters. A literary analysis paper applies such a procedure to a particular work.

A thorough analysis of all techniques in a story of typical length is likely to take fifteen to twenty pages or more — longer than Introduction to Literature papers are usually expected to be. Trying to cover all aspects in fewer pages, however, is likely to result in thin, superficial, shallow coverage. Usually, therefore, in a literary analysis of a story you should select one or two features to analyze in detail, making only brief comments on other aspects if needed. You might do a character analysis, or an analysis of structure, or an analysis of prose style.

In selecting a feature for analysis, avoid the easy and obvious. Instead, look for what is fresh, unusual, subtle, or particularly thought-provoking about the story, or what it does best. Or you might focus on what is most difficult to understand or accept, or on what raises questions or problems. What you choose to write on does not have to be what is most central in or important to the story — very strong and interesting papers often focus on the handling of a small detail that has considerable significance or on a minor character who makes a major difference, such as the importance of Red Sammy in "A Good Man Is Hard to Find" (p. 341). Look for something that you find interesting to think and write about. When you do, there's a good chance someone else will find your piece interesting to read.

Alternatively, you can do a thematic analysis, that is, separate the thematic elements of a story and show how they relate to each other — how each character, or each scene, or each imaginative comparison and symbol contributes to the development of a theme. Thematic analysis works best for stories that use rich and complex thematic development, as, for example, a paper on the theme of suffering in James Baldwin's "Sonny's Blues" (p. 138).

Either a technical or a thematic analysis can involve not just what is in the story but also what is left out. Such omissions can be strategic gaps that force a reader to be actively involved in filling out the story or the inadvertent neglect or overlooking of things that reveal biases or incomplete understanding. Analyzing gaps of either type can make excellent topics for papers: the enormity of the gaps in "The Red Convertible" (p. 67), for example.

Many of the "Approaching the Reading" questions and topics following stories in Chapters 4 to 7 lead to topics for analytical papers. Also, many of the suggestions for writing at the end of these same chapters involve technical literary analyses. Here are some other possibilities.

1. Style in Richard Wright's "The Man Who Was Almost a Man" (p. 395), focusing particularly on the effectiveness of its use of dialect.
2. The handling of time in Kate Chopin's "The Story of an Hour" (p. 167), Helena María Viramontes's "The Moths" (p. 391), Naguib Mahfouz's "Half a Day" (p. 435), or another story of your choice. Try focusing on the way short stories frequently include an unusual moment in which time moves in a different way — faster or slower than usual — or stops briefly, forcing a character to a point of crisis or a crucial decision.
3. The effect of mixing fantasy with techniques of realism in Gabriel García Márquez's "A Very Old Man with Enormous Wings" (p. 415).
4. The handling of the parent-child conflict in Alice Walker's "Everyday Use" (p. 101), Lan Samantha Chang's "The Eve of the Spirit Festival" (p. 228), or Richard Wright's "The Man Who Was Almost a Man" (p. 395).
5. The relation of style, tone, and theme in James Joyce's "Eveline" (p. 280), Jamaica Kincaid's "Girl" (p. 283), or Patricia Grace's "Butterflies" (p. 420).
6. The relevance of the title in Toni Morrison's "Recitatif" (p. 300).

Looking at What Surrounds the Story

You can write a paper about the literary context surrounding a story, about its relations to other literary works. Connecting a story with another story, a novel, a poem, a play, or another author usually involves the rhetorical strategy of comparison and/or contrast. To *compare* things is to point out similarities between or among them; to *contrast* things is to focus on their differences. Note, however, that sometimes when *compare* is used alone, it is intended to mean "call attention to both similarities *and* differences." Be sure you're clear about how the word is meant if it's used in an assignment.

A paper comparing and/or contrasting two or more literary works can focus on any aspect of them: their subjects, plot events, characters, themes, points of view, settings, symbols, or styles. For such a paper to be effective, however, the works must have a good deal in common or share one especially important feature: Perhaps the stories are set in the same city or contain characters who fought in Vietnam or who live in the same decade. A character wearing a chartreuse dress in each story is not probably significant enough to build a compare/contrast paper around. These same principles apply to a contrast paper: If two things are totally different, with nothing in common, there's little value in pointing out the differences. And the similarities and differences should be something significant, something that really matters. Use the "So what?" principle many writing teachers suggest. Suppose both stories have a scene in the Empire State Building: So what? Does that make connecting them meaningful? Louise Erdrich's story "The Red Convertible" (p. 67) and Linda Hogan's poem "The History of Red" (p. 670) have a title word in common, but comparing and contrasting them probably would not be profitable. But comparing and contrasting the father-daughter relations in Judith Ortiz Cofer's "Not for Sale" (p. 134) and Lan Samantha Chang's "The Eve of the Spirit Festival" (p. 228) could prove helpful and illuminating.

A paper comparing and contrasting two works could use the first half to discuss one work and the second half to bring out similar points about the second. Two difficulties with that structure are keeping your reader interested in the first half, before the actual comparisons begin, and making sure the two halves are unified, so your paper doesn't end up coming across as two separate mini-papers on the same topic. A safer alternative is to outline the points of similarity and difference you want to cover and then discuss first the one work and then the other for each point. It is not necessary to give equal space to comparing and to contrasting. In some cases, it makes sense to treat similarities in more detail; in other cases, treating differences in more detail creates a stronger paper. Nor is it essential to give equal time to both works. One might be sketched out and the other treated in detail.

What is important is making sure your points, of whatever length, thoroughly and precisely develop and support your thesis (see pp. 35–36). And it's important that the thesis bring out a point about the significance of the comparisons and contrasts. "Judith Ortiz Cofer's 'Not for Sale' and Lan Samantha Chang's 'The Eve of the Spirit Festival' have several things in common as well as some that are different" is not an effective thesis. A more promising thesis is, "Although both 'Not for Sale' and 'The Eve of the Spirit Festival' describe tensions between immigrant fathers and their daughters in adapting to a new culture, differences in the ages and ethnic backgrounds of the daughters lead to significantly different outcomes for the two families."

Relating a story to other works doesn't have to involve comparison and contrast. Papers instead can explore how an author builds on or expands an

Comparison and/or contrast can be used, of course, within a story as well as between stories. One could write a paper, for example, comparing and contrasting Lyman and Henry in Louise Erdrich's "The Red Convertible" (p. 67) or Roberta and Twyla in Toni Morrison's "Recitatif" (p. 300), or contrasting the way Sylvia in Toni Cade Bambara's "The Lesson" (p. 183) acts and talks while outside and inside the toy store, using this as the basis for discussing the lesson she learns.

earlier work. Or they can discuss the way the artistry and ideas in one work are illuminated by details in another work, whether earlier or later, even if the author didn't consciously intend to make the connections you find. More narrowly, a paper can study the *influences* on an author: the effect or impact a writer, work, or group of writers has on another writer or work. To build an argument that a writer read other authors or works, had them in mind while writing, and was affected by them takes careful, thorough research and precise argumentation. Papers can also examine literary allusions. An **allusion** is a brief reference to a literary or an artistic work or to a historical figure, event, or object. The allusion is usually intended to place an author's work within, or alongside, the whole other context of the work that is evoked by the reference. Allusions to Walt Whitman's *Leaves of Grass* in Julia Alvarez's "Daughter of Invention" (p. 10), for example, carries into Alvarez's story the entire context of Whitman's themes of freedom, individualism, and self-reliance. Pointing out allusions and discussing what they add to a story often leads to a good topic for a paper.

Here are some topic suggestions, but the possibilities are almost endless. Picking out your own pairings and things to focus on is a valuable part of the discovery process.

1. Struggles with questions of identity and cultural borders in Louise Erdrich's "The Red Convertible" (p. 67) and James Baldwin's "Sonny's Blues" (p. 138).
2. Responses to abusive husbands by long-suffering wives in Zora Neale Hurston's "Sweat" (p. 263) and Bessie Head's "The Collector of Treasures" (p. 421).
3. Sonny and his brother in James Baldwin's "Sonny's Blues" (p. 138).
4. Cultures and understanding in Chinua Achebe's "Dead Men's Path" (p. 405) and Patricia Grace's "Butterflies" (p. 420).
5. Women and work in Tillie Olsen's "I Stand Here Ironing" (p. 353) and Katherine Anne Porter's "The Jilting of Granny Weatherall" (p. 364).
6. First-person plural points of view in William Faulkner's story "A Rose for Emily" (p. 108) and Edwin Arlington Robinson's poem "Richard Cory" (p. 552).

Looking Beyond the Story

You can also look beyond the techniques and literary context of the story and examine a story's relation to the cultural and social context that infuses it but that also connects the story to real-world issues all of us confront. Such topics involve the use of *cultural criticism.*

In general, cultural criticism is not usually focused on analysis of technique or connections to other literature or art forms. It is concerned instead with what a story conveys about social attitudes and relations generally and, more specifically, with issues regarding such things as social background, sex, class, ethnicity, power, and privilege. Authors write works of fiction at a specific time, surrounded by specific circumstances and attitudes. Even if the story does not refer directly to events or attitudes contemporary to the writing, those events and attitudes influence the writer and the story, consciously or unconsciously, whether she or he accepts and reflects prevailing attitudes or ignores, rejects, or challenges them.

Cultural critics direct our attention to such issues and clarify the relationship between the author and story and the cultural context in which they exist. Stories are generally set in a specific time (perhaps the same as that in which they are written, but often not), with specific circumstances imagined in the background, whether the story develops that background in detail or not. Cultural critics concentrate on the way a work embodies a cultural context, how the events, ideas, or attitudes in a story are influenced by the economic conditions, political situations, or social conventions that existed when it was written. But they also explore the way a work is a part of a culture and can influence, and perhaps change, the economic conditions, political situations, or social conventions of its time or later times.

Cultural criticism can, but doesn't have to, use the comparison/contrast method. You could, for example, write a paper comparing and/or contrasting social or cultural details in a story to those in a poem or a play or to the real-world conditions existing today. Cultural critics, however, do not limit themselves to literary works of the type included in this book. For them, such works are no more important or privileged than any other cultural artifact. They study popular culture from all times alongside what is considered classic literature or art, believing that popular culture reveals as much about a society as "high culture." If you take this approach, you might write a paper comparing what is going on in a classic story or novel with what is going on in a comic strip, Hollywood movie, television show, or popular work of "genre fiction" (a mystery or romance, for example).

Cultural criticism can also extend to particular approaches that are concerned with social attitudes and influences, such as feminist criticism and Marxist criticism, which are described in more detail in the appendix on theoretical approaches to literature (see p. 1479). Both are concerned with social power, particularly the indirect, unobvious, often ignored or unconscious kinds of power that underlie most societies — the patriarchal structures that have traditionally given men power over women and the ideologies used by the upper classes to maintain power over the lower classes. Feminist and Marxist critics focus on who has power and how they use it, and who doesn't have power and how they suffer as a result. Both provide helpful ways to open up literary texts, to see more in them, and, as a result, to gain fresh understandings of society and culture as well as of the work.

The last two writing suggestions in Chapters 4 to 7 involve cultural issues, and some of the "Approaching the Reading" questions following stories in Chapters 4 to 7 can lead to topics for cultural criticism papers. Here are some additional possibilities for topics, though you shouldn't limit yourself to them. Looking for cultural issues and framing questions that can be explored further is an important part of the learning process.

1. Misunderstandings between cultures in Jhumpa Lahiri's "Interpreter of Maladies" (p. 285).
2. The effect houses have on the people who live in them. Start by doing some reading on the social and economic implications of adequate housing; then apply what you find to Sandra Cisneros's "The House on Mango Street" (p. 91) and Alice Walker's "Everyday Use" (p. 101), and perhaps other stories in Chapters 4 to 7.
3. Racial stereotypes and racial tensions in Toni Morrison's "Recitatif" (p. 300).
4. The intricacies of ethnicities in Bharati Mukherjee's "Orbiting" (p. 315).
5. John Updike's "A & P" (p. 386) examined from a feminist approach.
6. The weight, in various senses, of everything U.S. military personnel in Vietnam carried, in Tim O'Brien's "The Things They Carried" (p. 327).

DEVELOPMENT

Once you've picked out a technique or question or problem or issue, you need to decide what to do with it, how to focus and develop it. The section "Writing Short Papers" in Chapter 2 (pp. 32–45) applies equally to papers on fiction, poetry, and drama. At this point it would be helpful to read or review the first four of the "Five Steps in the Writing Process" (pp. 33–38). Here we comment briefly on developing an argument specifically for a paper on fiction.

You must do more than just summarize or describe the story—that's seldom interesting or valuable for you or your reader. You need to develop a central idea of some originality, interest, and significance. In an argumentative paper, the central idea must be disputable, one about which there can be disagreement. Your job is to persuade readers that your views are sound and convincing. One way to bring out the argumentative nature of your topic is to mention and reply to other ways of looking at the issue, thus explaining why your way of approaching the matter is stronger than other ways.

A good strategy in reaching a disputable central idea is to begin asking questions about the technique or problem or issue. What is distinctive or unique or striking about the way the technique is handled? In what ways is that technique particularly important to the story? How does the technique relate to the theme? How is the problem or issue embodied in the plot, characters, or setting? Is the problem or issue embedded in a symbol? What are some broader implications of the problem or issue? What is controversial, or puzzling, or difficult about what the text seems to say about the issues raised in it?

It is often helpful to phrase your central idea as a question and then to use each of the paper's body paragraphs to develop a point answering part of the question. Develop each paragraph by elaborating the point, by supplying details and quotations to illustrate, support, and confirm the point, and by explaining how the illustration relates to the point being developed. Illustration and explanation need to go together. Details and quotations by themselves do not prove anything. Your explanations are needed to indicate what is important about the details and to tie them in to the whole fabric you are weaving in the paper. Likewise, explanations without details and quotations are not specific enough and are not anchored to the work. The key to a successful paper lies in its development and support of its ideas: explaining ideas so readers can understand them readily, and supporting them with details and quotations so readers have confidence that the points are well grounded and worth considering.

The way you start the paragraphs in the body of an argumentative paper is very important. Just as the thesis of your paper must state an idea, not just a fact, so should the first sentence of each paragraph. The opening sentence of a paragraph in an argumentative paper is a mini-thesis: It should state briefly the point or idea to be developed in that paragraph. If a paragraph starts with a statement of fact rather than with a statement of idea, the rest of the paragraph is likely to consist of summary and more factual statements and not explore an idea or develop an argument. The second sentence of the paragraph should expand on the point or idea stated briefly in the topic sentence, bringing out its significance and implications. The rest of the paragraph must develop and support the point or idea.

In supporting points in a paper about fiction, you can't talk about every paragraph in the story or novel, the way you can go line by line through a short poem. A solid paper is specific and goes into detail without summarizing the plot. One way to guard against too much summary is not using the plot as the outline for your paper. It's often better to organize the paper instead by topics or ideas, a series of techniques, or a series of points about your central idea.

Another way to be specific and detailed without summarizing is to focus on key passages. As we listen to and look at a story, we take the whole work into consideration as we seek to grasp its essence. In doing so, we usually find that a particular section — a sentence, a few sentences, a paragraph, a particular scene — seems to shed light on all the other parts of the story. Teacher-critic Benjamin De Mott calls such sections *key passages*. They are not something writers insert deliberately into a story as clues to readers but are simply parts of the story that appear particularly meaningful to an individual reader and to that reader's interpretation of the story. So, instead of trying to discuss every part of a story, focus on a key passage in depth, or perhaps two or three key passages, and use it or them to represent, connect with, and illuminate what is occurring in the work as a whole.

Some of the supporting illustrations in any literary paper must be quotations. You may be tempted to quote at length from a short story or novel to support a point or illustrate style or technique. At times, long quotations are unavoidable, but as a rule keep quotations short. Look in the long passage you want to quote for a key sentence or phrase or word and quote that instead of the whole passage. Often a carefully phrased introduction provides the context and reduces the need for a long quotation. For guidance on fitting quotations into your paragraphs and sentences, review the section on handling quotations (pp. 40–42) and the "Ten Guidelines for Formatting and Punctuating Quotations" (pp. 43–44). If your paper uses quotations only from stories included in this book, you do not need to add a bibliography page. Your teacher will take for granted that page numbers refer to this book (if you quote from more than one story, you may need to include the author's name with the page number—see p. 1394). When you include quotations from other sources or from stories you find in another book, you will need to include a bibliography page (see pp. 1396–1405).

When you've completed a draft of your paper, read or review the fifth step in the writing process, "Revising and Proofreading" (pp. 36–38), the "Five Guidelines for Making Literary Papers Effective" (pp. 39–43), and the "Ten Guidelines for Formatting and Punctuating Quotations" (pp. 43–44) from Chapter 2. Remember, titles of short stories are placed within quotation marks; titles of novels or collections of short stories are underlined or italicized:

> One of Alice Walker's stories is "The Flowers." It was published in her short story collection *In Love and Trouble: Stories of Black Women*.

A STUDENT WRITER AT WORK: ALICIA ABOOD ON THE WRITING PROCESS

Students in one of our Introduction to Literature classes were asked to write an analytical paper on Dagoberto Gilb's "Love in L.A." (p. 55). (If you don't remember the story, go back and reread it now.) The assignment was, "Write a two- to three-page paper analyzing the effectiveness of point of view, setting, or style in 'Love in L.A.'" We are going to follow one of our students, Alicia Abood, through the writing process in completing that assignment, using her own words as she retraces her steps.

On Finding a Topic

"I read 'Love in L.A.' for the first time while sitting in an airport termi-nal, waiting for my flight to board. At first, I read the piece silently to myself, and the second time I whispered it aloud. I refused to hold a pen in my hand so that I wouldn't be tempted to mark it up right away. I just read. I was im-mediately enticed by the sounds of the words in relation to what was hap-pening in the story. I found it intriguing that the language was rather sparse and delicate but still rich and full of texture — full of color and emotion. Considering the short length of the story, I was surprised by how much I could see and hear.

"After the initial reading, I put the story back into my backpack, and left it alone for a while. When I reread the piece two days later, I marked it up. I read it three times in a row — each time marking it up in different areas — noticing things that I hadn't noticed before. Several ideas for paper topics circulated in my head: how the title 'Love in L.A.' related to the plot and the language; the stance Gilb took on the theme of love and relationships; ele-ments of plot and/or elements of time in the story. I took a quick glance over the notes that I had made, and put the piece away again.

"When I brought the piece out after a week or so, I noticed that I was most captivated by particular elements of the diction in the piece: the verbs were strong and fulfilling, the similes were surprising and vibrant. At the end of the story, I made the comment that 'every single word feels like it needs to be here.' I felt compelled to write about the language."

On Narrowing and Focusing the Topic

"Having decided to focus on the effect of diction in Gilb's story, I went through a debate about how I wanted to present this issue in a paper. I was a little stuck on whether to confront one element like the use of verbs, or to confront a few elements like simile and imagery. I decided that the use of sound, verbs, and similes were the most captivating aspects of Gilb's story, but I was also curious about the dialogue. To maintain the focus and length of the paper, I had to cut out the discussion of dialogue completely.

"In terms of outline, I didn't do much. I made a very rough, skeleton-like outline as to how I would set up the paper but I 'outline' best through making lists. I made a list of the verbs that jumped out to me while reading the piece.

glimpsed	smack	fondled	clicked
stared	crawling	beamed	swelled
pounced	inhale	revved	

I wrote down the similes that I particularly enjoyed and silently dialogued to myself how these similes were effective to me personally and to the overall unity of the story."

On Turning the Topic into an Argumentative Thesis

"When beginning to physically put the piece into essay form, I spent too much time on the introduction. I always do that. It is evident that my starting introductions were weak, loose, and removed from the gut of the story. After a little frustration, I made myself just move on from the introduction and begin discussing the language — the sounds, verbs, and similes. For some odd reason I always have to have some sort of introduction *there* in my paper before I want to begin writing the rest. Even if it is weak, I want it there. It is an unfortunate habit to have, I suppose.

"I drafted a working thesis: Gilb's language in 'Love in L.A.' is particularly strong in its use of sound, similes, and active verbs. But I realized that, although it covered the topics I wanted to discuss, it didn't go anywhere, didn't have an argumentative slant. So I revised it to this: Gilb's handling of language — especially the sounds, the similes, and the verbs — lets us enter these characters' lives and the nature of love in L.A. That version gave me both an outline and an idea to develop as I discussed each technique and the various examples."

On Developing and Supporting the Thesis

"I really enjoyed writing this piece. I think part of my enjoyment stems from the amount of time that I spent reading the story in different settings, without doing much to it at all. I read it within the noisiness of the airport and a coffeehouse, but also within the confines of a library. There were lines, verbs, and similes that I really liked but had to leave out for the sake of space. Even though I had read the piece many times before I went to put down my thoughts on paper, I kept rereading it while in the essay writing process. I was often tempted to put another verb in, but I had to force myself to leave it alone. The practice of reading while writing did really help me to keep writing. Whenever I felt stuck, I'd just read the story again, and be reminded of a thought I wanted to add or a line I wanted to discuss. This story and writing project again reminded me that the catalyst behind writing an essay is reading the literature over and over again. Doing this kept me on my toes. Kept my thoughts going, moving, digressing, and returning.

"My initial plan was, because the story is short, to follow the order of events in the story and relate them to my three techniques. I liked the idea of tracing the plot through the paper. But I found that my first draft got too long, as I summarized too much of what was going on instead of focusing on language. And I found that my topic sentences were following the plot instead of focusing on my ideas. Here are the opening sentences of each paragraph in the body of that draft:

> The immediate attention to language from the start of the story places the reader in the backseat of Jake's car as he drives to work.

The language within the second paragraph shifts slightly in tone when Jake hits the vehicle in front of him.

When Jake discovers that the passenger inside of the Toyota he has hit is an attractive young woman, he doesn't hold back from displaying a persistent interest in her.

In the final paragraphs of the story Jake's character is further unveiled when he lies to Mariana by giving her the false impression that he is an actor.

Gilb effectively creates vivid verbs through the remainder of the story.

When I revised that draft, I combined some paragraphs, cut a lot of plot summary, and wrote topic sentences that named the technique discussed in that paragraph followed by a sentence that expands upon the topic and gives more detail about it. That kept me focused on my ideas and explanations of Gilb's ability to use language in exciting ways, instead of on following the plot. The new topic sentences were:

The importance of sound in the diction of the story is evident from the first sentence.

In addition to its sounds, language is important in a series of similes used to describe Jake and Mariana.

Along with sound and similes, the importance of language in the story comes out in its use of vivid verbs.

Within each paragraph I concentrated on giving several examples of the technique, explaining what about them was so striking that they were good illustrations of the technique, and attempting to convince readers that they were effective in the story and contributed to the development of the rather ironic "love" theme in the story. I tried to keep examples short and specific so they didn't take too much space and so I would keep myself focused on explaining and arguing, not just illustrating."

On Revising and Proofreading the Paper

"My first revisions were, as I described above, reorganizing the paper from following the plot to focusing on techniques and reshaping the thesis and topic sentences. I also did a lot of rearranging, to bring out the steps in my thinking more clearly, and a lot of cutting, to make the style more concise. Here is an example of the way I revised one paragraph (boldface for additions, strike-throughs for deletions):

In addition to the sounds of the language, the use of similes is an important technique in the story. Gilb uses a series of similes to describe the growing connection between Jake and Mariana (another kind

of love developing in L.A.). When Jake discovers that the passenger inside of the Toyota he has hit is an attractive young woman, **for example,** he **can't help feeling** ~~doesn't hold back from displaying a persistent~~ interest in her~~.~~: ~~To convey her impact on Jake, Gilb uses a simile:~~ "He inhaled her scent like it was clean air and straightened out his less than new but not unhip clothes." This comparison **to** ~~captures the attraction Jake feels toward this woman, Mariana. The refreshing image of~~ "clean air~~"~~ comes through powerfully ~~in this section of the story~~ because in previous paragraphs~~,~~ the highway traffic and Jake's unventilated car create~~s~~ a **stuffy** ~~tight~~ and claustrophobic feel. **Later, as they introduce themselves to each other,** ~~As the story continues, Gilb continues to use similes to more fully describe the impact that Mariana made on Jake's character. To describe the first time Jake and Mariana come into physical contact, Gilb writes~~ "They shook hands like she'd never done it before in her life." An apparent separation is created in this line, **contrasting** ~~as it causes the reader to think of~~ Jake's experienced and sly attitude **with** ~~next to~~ Mariana's young, naïve, and timid character.

"My final step was to proofread for slips in spelling, grammar, and punctuation (I tend to write fast and not pay much attention to agreement and apostrophes in the first draft). Also, at that point I inserted page numbers to go with the quoted words and phrases. If the story had been longer, I would have put them in as I wrote, but for this story it was easy to find them by going back. Because I used only one story, one that was included in our textbook, I didn't need to add a bibliography page."

SAMPLE PAPER

Alicia Abood
Professors Ridl and Schakel
English 105-04
October 8, 2003

Clips of Language:
The Effect of Diction in Dagoberto Gilb's "Love in L.A."

Short stories often use words to capture a small glimpse of time. That is certainly the case in Dagoberto Gilb's "Love in L.A." Gilb invites his readers into a snippet of time cut out of what feels like a cinematic slide-show. His carefully crafted diction helps to establish his characters and his sense of place, and entices the reader to linger on words and taste each sentence. Vivid images and catchy similes are rhythmically blended into

Thesis sentence.

each paragraph. Close attention to Gilb's diction will demonstrate that it is his handling of language--especially the sounds of the words, the use of similes, and the choice of strong verbs--that lets us enter a few moments in two characters' lives and offers us a glimpse into the nature of love in L.A.

Topic sentence, expansion of topic sentence.

The first way language becomes important in the story is through its handling of sound. Gilb chooses words carefully to make their sounds fit and reinforce their meaning and seem enjoyable for the reader. The importance of sound is evident from the first sentence: "Jake slouched in a clot of near motionless traffic" (55). The sounds of "slouched" and "clot" evoke the still, thick, and anguished moods that recur throughout the plot. Jake is "slouched" in traffic; moreover, he is "slouched" in and stuck with the terms of his lifestyle. He is vying for more before he even begins his day. As the opening paragraph continues, the speaker informs the audience that Jake is longing to upgrade from his '59 Buick to something newer and more stylish:

Block quotation (ellipses used to shorten it).

> It would have crushed velvet interior with electric controls for the LA summer, a nice warm heater and defroster . . . , a cruise control . . . , mellow speakers front and rear of course, [and] windows that hum closed. (55)

Verb tenses changed to the literary present.

The luxuries he dreams of for his vehicle extend to qualities he desires for his lifestyle. The very sounds of "crushed velvet interior," "cruise control," and "mellow speakers" convey notions of a free and easygoing daily regiment. He feels too mellow, in fact, and doesn't notice the car ahead until it's too late. Trying to avoid a crash, he "pounce[s] the brake pedal and steer[s] the front wheels away from the tiny brakelights but the smack [is] unavoidable" (55). The sound of "pounce" conveys an urgency that "steps on" would lack. The sound of "smack" echoes the actual impact of Jake's vehicle on the Toyota in front of him, and the way it jolts Jake back to reality. A few lines later, "smack" is repeated (55), emphasizing that the damage has been done and cannot be avoided. Jake's dreams, and the sounds of the words that describe them, suggest that one aspect of love in L.A. is a love of freedom and a good life.

Transition and topic sentence.

In addition to the sounds of the language, the use of similes is an important technique in the story. Gilb uses a series of similes to describe the growing connection between Jake and Mariana (another kind of love developing in L.A.). These similes, coming as they do through Jake's consciousness and showing his perspective, may indicate more about her impact on him than his on her. When Jake discovers that the passenger inside of the Toyota he has hit is an attractive young woman, for example, he can't help feeling interest in her: "He inhale[s] her scent like it was clean air and straighten[s] out his less than new but not unhip clothes"

Quotation introduced formally with a colon.

(56). This comparison to clean air comes through powerfully because in previous paragraphs the highway traffic and Jake's unventilated car create a stuffy and claustrophobic feel. Later, as they introduce themselves to each other, "They [shake] hands like she'd never done it before in her life" (56). An apparent separation is created in this line, contrasting Jake's experienced and sly attitude with Mariana's young, naïve, and timid character. Similes continue in the final paragraphs when Jake gives Mariana the false impression that he is an actor, "been in a couple of movies," and she "smile[s] like a fan" (57). The simile causes us to question whether she is falling for his lies, or whether Jake is just imagining that she is. When Jake says goodbye to Mariana, he initiates another handshake: "Her hand felt so warm and soft he felt like he'd been kissed" (57). Once again, this moment enforces the heightened sense of happiness that Jake feels when around Mariana. Similes throughout the story give a romantic aura to this snippet of time in which we see Jake and Mariana together.

Quotation integrated into sentence with a comma.

Quotation blended fully into sentence.

Along with sound and similes, the importance of language in the story comes out in its handling of verbs. Gilb chooses vivid, active verbs that bring out aspects of the characters and that energize the story for the reader. After Jake realizes that the scratch in the chrome of his own vehicle is hardly noticeable, for example, he "perk[s] up" (56). The word "perk" conveys a lifted and elevated spirit. The fact that Jake is most concerned with the appearance of his vehicle implies a certain self-centeredness. After apologizing for hitting her car, Jake "fondle[s]" the "wide dimple near the cracked taillight" (56). The use of the word "fondle" emphasizes the sensual and evocative (and again self-centered) emotions that Jake feels toward Mariana. In the final paragraph, his self-absorption is reiterated: "Back in his car he took a moment or two to feel both proud and sad about his performance" (57). (I know "performance" is not a verb, but he *was* performing.) Describing Jake's actions in terms of the way he performs further indicates that Jake is completely conscious of putting on a façade for Mariana in order to amplify his persona. When he notices that Mariana is writing down his license number and remembers that the plate is one he removed from a junkyard, it fuses the wavering, unsteadiness of Jake's lifestyle from the beginning and ending of the story. After he turns the ignition key, he revs the big engine and his sense of freedom swells as he drives away from the scene. The use of the verbs "revved" and "swelled" fill the ongoing sense of elation and accomplishment within Jake. He had pulled it off.

Development through elaboration, illustration, and explanation.

Gilb's language, particularly his use of sounds, similes, and verbs, carries the reader through the moments described in "Love in L.A." It starts with Jake dreaming about his need for an FM radio and ends, a few minutes later, as Jake drives back into the "now moving" traffic (57), with his

Conclusion, tying back to the introduction.

mind back to thinking about the FM radio for his car. Love in L.A., at least as this story portrays it, isn't deep and genuine but consists of a brief, hurried moment in a self-centered life. Gilb's writing resonates like a poem, as he steers his audience through the traffic and the minds of his characters. His poetic prose effectively weaves his audience in and out of a small yet significant slice of time.

A Collection of Stories

WEB: Research the authors in this collection with LitLinks, or take a quiz on the stories with LitQuiz, at bedfordstmartins.com/approachinglit.

Raymond Carver 1938–1988

Cathedral [1981]

This blind man, an old friend of my wife's, he was on his way to spend the night. His wife had died. So he was visiting the dead wife's relatives in Connecticut. He called my wife from his in-laws'. Arrangements were made. He would come by train, a five-hour trip, and my wife would meet him at the station. She hadn't seen him since she worked for him one summer in Seattle ten years ago. But she and the blind man had kept in touch. They made tapes and mailed them back and forth. I wasn't enthusiastic about his visit. He was no one I knew. And his being blind bothered me. My idea of blindness came from the movies. In the movies, the blind moved slowly and never laughed. Sometimes they were led by seeing-eye dogs. A blind man in my house was not something I looked forward to.

That summer in Seattle she had needed a job. She didn't have any money. The man she was going to marry at the end of the summer was in officers' training school. He didn't have any money, either. But she was in love with the guy, and he was in love with her, etc. She'd seen something in the paper: HELP WANTED — *Reading to Blind Man,* and a telephone number. She phoned and went over, was hired on the spot. She'd worked with this blind man all summer. She read stuff to him, case studies, reports, that sort of thing. She helped him organize his little office in the county social-service department. They'd become good friends, my wife and the blind man. How do I know these things? She told me. And she told me something else. On her last day in the office, the blind man asked if he could touch her face. She agreed to this. She told me he touched his fingers to every part of her face, her nose — even her neck! She never forgot it. She even tried to write a poem about it. She was always trying to write a poem. She wrote a poem or two every year, usually after something really important had happened to her.

217

When we first started going out together, she showed me the poem. In the poem, she recalled his fingers and the way they had moved around over her face. In the poem, she talked about what she had felt at the time, about what went through her mind when the blind man touched her nose and lips. I can remember I didn't think much of the poem. Of course, I didn't tell her that. Maybe I just don't understand poetry. I admit it's not the first thing I reach for when I pick up something to read.

Anyway, this man who'd first enjoyed her favors, the officer-to-be, he'd been her childhood sweetheart. So okay. I'm saying that at the end of the summer she let the blind man run his hands over her face, said goodbye to him, married her childhood etc., who was now a commissioned officer, and she moved away from Seattle. But they'd kept in touch, she and the blind man. She made the first contact after a year or so. She called him up one night from an Air Force base in Alabama. She wanted to talk. They talked. He asked her to send him a tape and tell him about her life. She did this. She sent the tape. On the tape, she told the blind man about her husband and about their life together in the military. She told the blind man she loved her husband but she didn't like it where they lived and she didn't like it that he was a part of the military-industrial thing. She told the blind man she'd written a poem and he was in it. She told him that she was writing a poem about what it was like to be an Air Force officer's wife. The poem wasn't finished yet. She was still writing it. The blind man made a tape. He sent her the tape. She made a tape. This went on for years. My wife's officer was posted to one base and then another. She sent tapes from Moody AFB, McGuire, McConnell, and finally Travis, near Sacramento, where one night she got to feeling lonely and cut off from people she kept losing in that moving-around life. She got to feeling she couldn't go it another step. She went in and swallowed all the pills and capsules in the medicine chest and washed them down with a bottle of gin. Then she got into a hot bath and passed out.

But instead of dying, she got sick. She threw up. Her officer — why should he have a name? he was the childhood sweetheart, and what more does he want? — came home from somewhere, found her, and called the ambulance. In time, she put it all on a tape and sent the tape to the blind man. Over the years, she put all kinds of stuff on tapes and sent the tapes off lickety-split. Next to writing a poem every year, I think it was her chief means of recreation. On one tape, she told the blind man she'd decided to live away from her officer for a time. On another tape, she told him about her divorce. She and I began going out, and of course she told her blind man about it. She told him everything, or so it seemed to me. Once she asked me if I'd like to hear the latest tape from the blind man. This was a year ago. I was on the tape, she said. So I said okay, I'd listen to it. I got us drinks and we settled down in the living room. We made ready to listen. First she inserted the tape into the player and adjusted a couple of dials. Then she pushed a lever. The tape squeaked and someone began to talk in this loud voice. She lowered the volume. After a few minutes of harmless chitchat, I heard my own name in the mouth of this stranger, this blind man I didn't even know! And then this: "From all you've said about him, I can only conclude —" But we were interrupted, a knock at the door, something, and we didn't ever get back to the tape. Maybe it was just as well. I'd heard all I wanted to.

Now this same blind man was coming to sleep in my house.

"Maybe I could take him bowling," I said to my wife. She was at the draining board doing scalloped potatoes. She put down the knife she was using and turned around.

"If you love me," she said, "you can do this for me. If you don't love me, okay. But if you had a friend, any friend, and the friend came to visit, I'd make him feel comfortable." She wiped her hands with the dish towel.

"I don't have any blind friends," I said.

"You don't have *any* friends," she said. "Period. Besides," she said, "goddamn it, his wife's just died! Don't you understand that? The man's lost his wife!"

I didn't answer. She'd told me a little about the blind man's wife. Her name was Beulah. Beulah! That's a name for a colored woman.

"Was his wife a Negro?" I asked.

"Are you crazy?" my wife said. "Have you just flipped or something?" She picked up a potato. I saw it hit the floor, then roll under the stove. "What's wrong with you?" she said. "Are you drunk?"

"I'm just asking," I said.

Right then my wife filled me in with more detail than I cared to know. I made a drink and sat at the kitchen table to listen. Pieces of the story began to fall into place.

Beulah had gone to work for the blind man the summer after my wife had stopped working for him. Pretty soon Beulah and the blind man had themselves a church wedding. It was a little wedding — who'd want to go to such a wedding in the first place? — just the two of them, plus the minister and the minister's wife. But it was a church wedding just the same. It was what Beulah had wanted, he'd said. But even then Beulah must have been carrying the cancer in her glands. After they had been inseparable for eight years — my wife's word, *inseparable* — Beulah's health went into a rapid decline. She died in a Seattle hospital room, the blind man sitting beside the bed and holding on to her hand. They'd married, lived and worked together, slept together — had sex, sure — and then the blind man had to bury her. All this without his having ever seen what the goddamned woman looked like. It was beyond my understanding. Hearing this, I felt sorry for the blind man for a little bit. And then I found myself thinking what a pitiful life this woman must have led. Imagine a woman who could never see herself as she was seen in the eyes of her loved one. A woman who could go on day after day and never receive the smallest compliment from her beloved. A woman whose husband could never read the expression on her face, be it misery or something better. Someone who could wear makeup or not — what difference to him? She could, if she wanted, wear green eye-shadow around one eye, a straight pin in her nostril, yellow slacks and purple shoes, no matter. And then to slip off into death, the blind man's hand on her hand, his blind eyes streaming tears—I'm imagining now—her last thought maybe this: that he never even knew what she looked like, and she on an express to the grave. Robert was left with a small insurance policy and half of a twenty-peso Mexican coin. The other half of the coin went into the box with her. Pathetic.

So when the time rolled around, my wife went to the depot to pick him up. With nothing to do but wait—sure, I blamed him for that—I was having a drink and watching the TV when I heard the car pull into the drive. I got up from the sofa with my drink and went to the window to have a look.

I saw my wife laughing as she parked the car. I saw her get out of the car and shut the door. She was still wearing a smile. Just amazing. She went around to the other side of the car to where the blind man was already starting to get out. This blind man, feature this, he was wearing a full beard! A beard on a blind man! Too much, I say. The blind man reached into the back seat and dragged out a suitcase. My wife took his arm, shut the car door, and, talking all the way, moved him down the drive and then up the steps to the front porch. I turned off the TV. I finished my drink, rinsed the glass, dried my hands. Then I went to the door.

My wife said, "I want you to meet Robert. Robert, this is my husband. I've told you all about him." She was beaming. She had this blind man by his coat sleeve.

The blind man let go of his suitcase and up came his hand.

I took it. He squeezed hard, held my hand, and then he let it go.

"I feel like we've already met," he boomed.

"Likewise," I said. I didn't know what else to say. Then I said, "Welcome. I've heard a lot about you." We began to move then, a little group, from the porch into the living room, my wife guiding him by the arm. The blind man was carrying his suitcase in his other hand. My wife said things like, "To your left here, Robert. That's right. Now watch it, there's a chair. That's it. Sit down right here. This is the sofa. We just bought this sofa two weeks ago."

I started to say something about the old sofa. I'd liked that old sofa. But I didn't say anything. Then I wanted to say something else, small-talk, about the scenic ride along the Hudson. How going *to* New York, you should sit on the right-hand side of the train, and coming *from* New York, the left-hand side.

"Did you have a good train ride?" I said. "Which side of the train did you sit on, by the way?"

"What a question, which side!" my wife said. "What's it matter which side?" she said.

"I just asked," I said.

"Right side," the blind man said. "I hadn't been on a train in nearly forty years. Not since I was a kid. With my folks. That's been a long time. I'd nearly forgotten the sensation. I have winter in my beard now," he said. "So I've been told, anyway. Do I look distinguished, my dear?" the blind man said to my wife.

"You look distinguished, Robert," she said. "Robert," she said. "Robert, it's just so good to see you."

My wife finally took her eyes off the blind man and looked at me. I had the feeling she didn't like what she saw. I shrugged.

I've never met, or personally known, anyone who was blind. This blind man was late forties, a heavy-set, balding man with stooped shoulders, as if he carried a great weight there. He wore brown slacks, brown shoes, a light-brown shirt, a tie, a sports coat. Spiffy. He also had this full beard. But he didn't use a cane and he didn't wear dark glasses. I'd always thought dark glasses were a must for the blind. Fact was, I wished he had a pair. At first glance, his eyes looked like anyone else's eyes. But if you looked close, there was something different about them. Too much white in the iris, for one thing, and the pupils seemed to move around in the sockets without his knowing it or being able to stop it. Creepy. As I stared at his face, I saw the left pupil turn in toward his nose while the other made an effort to keep in one place. But it was only an effort, for that eye was on the roam without his knowing it or wanting it to be.

I said, "Let me get you a drink. What's your pleasure? We have a little of everything. It's one of our pastimes."

"Bub, I'm a Scotch man myself," he said fast enough in this big voice.

"Right," I said. Bub! "Sure you are. I knew it."

He let his fingers touch his suitcase, which was sitting alongside the sofa. He was taking his bearings. I didn't blame him for that.

"I'll move that up to your room," my wife said.

"No, that's fine," the blind man said loudly. "It can go up when I go up."

"A little water with the Scotch?" I said.

"Very little," he said.

"I knew it," I said.

He said, "Just a tad. The Irish actor, Barry Fitzgerald? I'm like that fellow. When I drink water, Fitzgerald said, I drink water. When I drink whiskey, I drink whiskey." My wife laughed. The blind man brought his hand up under his beard. He lifted his beard slowly and let it drop.

I did the drinks, three big glasses of Scotch with a splash of water in each. Then we made ourselves comfortable and talked about Robert's travels. First the long flight from the West Coast to Connecticut, we covered that. Then from Connecticut up here by train. We had another drink concerning that leg of the trip.

I remembered having read somewhere that the blind didn't smoke because, as speculation had it, they couldn't see the smoke they exhaled. I thought I knew that much and that much only about blind people. But this blind man smoked his cigarette down to the nubbin and then lit another one. This blind man filled his ashtray and my wife emptied it.

When we sat down at the table for dinner, we had another drink. My wife heaped Robert's plate with cube steak, scalloped potatoes, green beans. I buttered him up two slices of bread. I said, "Here's bread and butter for you." I swallowed some of my drink. "Now let us pray," I said, and the blind man lowered his head. My wife looked at me, her mouth agape. "Pray the phone won't ring and the food doesn't get cold," I said.

We dug in. We ate everything there was to eat on the table. We ate like there was no tomorrow. We didn't talk. We ate. We scarfed. We grazed that table. We were into serious eating. The blind man had right away located his foods, he knew just where everything was on his plate. I watched with admiration as he used his knife and fork on the meat. He'd cut two pieces of meat, fork the meat into his mouth, and then go all out for the scalloped potatoes, the beans next, and then he'd tear off a hunk of buttered bread and eat that. He'd follow this up with a big drink of milk. It didn't seem to bother him to use his fingers once in a while, either.

We finished everything, including half a strawberry pie. For a few moments, we sat as if stunned. Sweat beaded on our faces. Finally, we got up from the table and left the dirty plates. We didn't look back. We took ourselves into the living room and sank into our places again. Robert and my wife sat on the sofa. I took the big chair. We had us two or three more drinks while they talked about the major things that had come to pass for them in the past ten years. For the most part, I just listened. Now and then I joined in. I didn't want him to think I'd left the room, and I didn't want her to think I was feeling left out. They talked of things that had happened to them — to them! — these past ten years. I waited in vain to hear my name on my wife's sweet lips: "And then my dear husband came into my life" — something like that. But I heard nothing of the sort. More talk of Robert. Robert had done a little of everything, it seemed, a regular blind jack-of-all-trades. But most recently he and his wife had had an Amway distributorship, from which, I gathered, they'd earned their living, such as it was. The blind man was also a ham radio operator. He talked in his loud voice about conversations he'd had with fellow operators in Guam, in the Philippines, in Alaska, and even in Tahiti. He said he'd have a lot of friends there if he ever wanted to go visit those places. From time to time, he'd turn his blind face toward me, put his hand under his beard, ask me something. How long had I been in my present position? (Three years.) Did I like my work? (I didn't.) Was I going to stay with it? (What were the options?) Finally, when I thought he was beginning to run down, I got up and turned on the TV.

My wife looked at me with irritation. She was heading toward a boil. Then she looked at the blind man and said, "Robert, do you have a TV?"

The blind man said, "My dear, I have two TVs. I have a color set and a black-and-white thing, an old relic. It's funny, but if I turn the TV on, and I'm always turning it on, I turn on the color set. It's funny, don't you think?"

I didn't know what to say to that. I had absolutely nothing to say to that. No opinion. So I watched the news program and tried to listen to what the announcer was saying.

"This is a color TV," the blind man said. "Don't ask me how, but I can tell."

"We traded up a while ago," I said.

The blind man had another taste of his drink. He lifted his beard, sniffed it, and let it fall. He leaned forward on the sofa. He positioned his ashtray on the coffee table, then put the lighter to his cigarette. He leaned back on the sofa and crossed his legs at the ankles.

My wife covered her mouth, and then she yawned. She stretched. She said, "I think I'll go upstairs and put on my robe. I think I'll change into something else. Robert, you make yourself comfortable," she said.

"I'm comfortable," the blind man said.

"I want you to feel comfortable in this house," she said.

"I am comfortable," the blind man said.

After she'd left the room, he and I listened to the weather report and then to the sports roundup. By that time, she'd been gone so long I didn't know if she was going to come back. I thought she might have gone to bed. I wished she'd come back downstairs. I didn't want to be left alone with a blind man. I asked him if he wanted another drink, and he said sure. Then I asked if he wanted to smoke some dope with me. I said I'd just rolled a number. I hadn't, but I planned to do so in about two shakes.

"I'll try some with you," he said.

"Damn right," I said. "That's the stuff."

I got our drinks and sat down on the sofa with him. Then I rolled us two fat numbers. I lit one and passed it. I brought it to his fingers. He took it and inhaled.

"Hold it as long as you can," I said. I could tell he didn't know the first thing.

My wife came back downstairs wearing her pink robe and her pink slippers.

"What do I smell?" she said.

"We thought we'd have us some cannabis," I said.

My wife gave me a savage look. Then she looked at the blind man and said, "Robert, I didn't know you smoked."

He said, "I do now, my dear. There's a first time for everything. But I don't feel anything yet."

"This stuff is pretty mellow," I said. "This stuff is mild. It's dope you can reason with," I said. "It doesn't mess you up."

"Not much it doesn't, bub," he said, and laughed.

My wife sat on the sofa between the blind man and me. I passed her the number. She took it and toked and then passed it back to me. "Which way is this going?" she said. Then she said, "I shouldn't be smoking this. I can hardly keep my eyes open as it is. That dinner did me in. I shouldn't have eaten so much."

"It was the strawberry pie," the blind man said. "That's what did it," he said, and he laughed his big laugh. Then he shook his head.

"There's more strawberry pie," I said.

"Do you want some more, Robert?" my wife said.

"Maybe in a little while," he said.

We gave our attention to the TV. My wife yawned again. She said, "Your bed is made up when you feel like going to bed, Robert. I know you must have had a long day. When you're ready to go to bed, say so." She pulled his arm. "Robert?"

He came to and said, "I've had a real nice time. This beats tapes, doesn't it?"

I said, "Coming at you," and I put the number between his fingers. He inhaled, held the smoke, and then let it go. It was like he'd been doing it since he was nine years old.

"Thanks, bub," he said. "But I think this is all for me. I think I'm beginning to feel it," he said. He held the burning roach out for my wife.

"Same here," she said. "Ditto. Me, too." She took the roach and passed it to me. "I may just sit here for a while between you two guys with my eyes closed. But don't let me bother you, okay? Either one of you. If it bothers you, say so. Otherwise, I may just sit here with my eyes closed until you're ready to go to bed," she said. "Your bed's made up, Robert, when you're ready. It's right next to our room at the top of the stairs. We'll show you up when you're ready. You wake me up now, you guys, if I fall asleep." She said that and then she closed her eyes and went to sleep.

The news program ended. I got up and changed the channel. I sat back down on the sofa. I wished my wife hadn't pooped out. Her head lay across the back of the sofa, her mouth open. She'd turned so that her robe had slipped away from her legs, exposing a juicy thigh. I reached to draw her robe back over her, and it was then that I glanced at the blind man. What the hell! I flipped the robe open again.

"You say when you want some strawberry pie," I said.

"I will," he said.

I said, "Are you tired? Do you want me to take you up to your bed? Are you ready to hit the hay?"

"Not yet," he said. "No, I'll stay up with you, bub. If that's all right. I'll stay up until you're ready to turn in. We haven't had a chance to talk. Know what I mean? I feel like me and her monopolized the evening." He lifted his beard and he let it fall. He picked up his cigarettes and his lighter.

"That's all right," I said. Then I said, "I'm glad for the company."

And I guess I was. Every night I smoked dope and stayed up as long as I could before I fell asleep. My wife and I hardly ever went to bed at the same time. When I did go to sleep, I had these dreams. Sometimes I'd wake up from one of them, my heart going crazy.

Something about the church and the Middle Ages was on the TV. Not your run-of-the-mill TV fare. I wanted to watch something else. I turned to the other channels. But there was nothing on them, either. So I turned back to the first channel and apologized.

"Bub, it's all right," the blind man said. "It's fine with me. Whatever you want to watch is okay. I'm always learning something. Learning never ends. It won't hurt me to learn something tonight. I got ears," he said.

We didn't say anything for a time. He was leaning forward with his head turned at me, his right ear aimed in the direction of the set. Very disconcerting. Now and then his eyelids drooped and then they snapped open again. Now and then he put his fingers into his beard and tugged, like he was thinking about something he was hearing on the television.

On the screen, a group of men wearing cowls was being set upon and tormented by men dressed in skeleton costumes and men dressed as devils. The men dressed as devils wore devil masks, horns, and long tails. This pageant was part of a procession. The Englishman who was narrating the thing said it took place in Spain once a year. I tried to explain to the blind man what was happening.

"Skeletons," he said. "I know about skeletons," he said, and he nodded.

The TV showed this one cathedral. Then there was a long, slow look at another one. Finally, the picture switched to the famous one in Paris, with its flying buttresses and its spires reaching up to the clouds. The camera pulled away to show the whole of the cathedral rising above the skyline.

There were times when the Englishman who was telling the thing would shut up, would simply let the camera move around over the cathedrals. Or else the camera would tour the countryside, men in fields walking behind oxen. I waited as long as I could. Then I felt I had to say something. I said, "They're showing the outside of this cathedral now. Gargoyles. Little statues carved to look like monsters. Now I guess they're in Italy. Yeah, they're in Italy. There's paintings on the walls of this one church."

"Are those fresco paintings, bub?" he asked, and he sipped from his drink.

I reached for my glass. But it was empty. I tried to remember what I could remember. "You're asking me are those frescoes?" I said. "That's a good question. I don't know."

The camera moved to a cathedral outside Lisbon. The differences in the Portuguese cathedral compared with the French and Italian were not that great. But they were there. Mostly the interior stuff. Then something occurred to me, and I said, "Something has occurred to me. Do you have any idea what a cathedral is? What they look like, that is? Do you follow me? If somebody says cathedral to you, do you have any notion what they're talking about? Do you know the difference between that and a Baptist church, say?"

He let the smoke dribble from his mouth. "I know they took hundreds of workers fifty or a hundred years to build," he said. "I just heard the man say that, of course. I know generations of the same families worked on a cathedral. I heard him say that, too. The men who began their life's work on them, they never lived to see the completion of their work. In that wise, bub, they're no different from the rest of us, right?" He laughed. Then his eyelids drooped again. His head nodded. He seemed to be snoozing. Maybe he was imagining himself in Portugal. The TV was showing another cathedral now. This one was in Germany. The Englishman's voice droned on. "Cathedrals," the blind man said. He sat up and rolled his head back and forth. "If you want the truth, bub, that's about all I know. What I just said. What I heard him say. But maybe you could describe one to me? I wish you'd do it. I'd like that. If you want to know, I really don't have a good idea."

I stared hard at the shot of the cathedral on the TV. How could I even begin to describe it? But say my life depended on it. Say my life was being threatened by an insane guy who said I had to do it or else.

I stared some more at the cathedral before the picture flipped off into the countryside. There was no use. I turned to the blind man and said, "To begin with, they're very tall." I was looking around the room for clues. "They reach way up. Up and up. Toward the sky. They're so big, some of them, they have to have these supports. To help hold them up, so to speak. These supports are called buttresses. They remind me of viaducts, for some reason. But maybe you don't know viaducts, either? Sometimes the cathedrals have devils and such carved into the front. Sometimes lords and ladies. Don't ask me why this is," I said.

He was nodding. The whole upper part of his body seemed to be moving back and forth.

"I'm not doing so good, am I?" I said.

He stopped nodding and leaned forward on the edge of the sofa. As he listened to me, he was running his fingers through his beard. I wasn't getting through to him, I could see that. But he waited for me to go on just the same. He nodded, like he was trying to encourage me. I tried to think what else to say. "They're really big," I said. "They're massive. They're built of stone. Marble, too, sometimes. In those olden days, when they built cathedrals, men wanted to be close to God. In those olden days, God was an important part of everyone's life. You could tell this from their cathedral-building. I'm sorry," I said, "but it looks like that's the best I can do for you. I'm just no good at it."

"That's all right, bub," the blind man said. "Hey, listen. I hope you don't mind my asking you. Can I ask you something? Let me ask you a simple question, yes or no. I'm just curious and there's no offense. You're my host. But let me ask if you are in any way religious? You don't mind my asking?"

I shook my head. He couldn't see that, though. A wink is the same as a nod to a blind man. "I guess I don't believe in it. In anything. Sometimes it's hard. You know what I'm saying?"

"Sure, I do," he said.

"Right," I said.

The Englishman was still holding forth. My wife sighed in her sleep. She drew a long breath and went on with her sleeping.

"You'll have to forgive me," I said. "But I can't tell you what a cathedral looks like. It just isn't in me to do it. I can't do any more than I've done."

The blind man sat very still, his head down, as he listened to me.

I said, "The truth is, cathedrals don't mean anything special to me. Nothing. Cathedrals. They're something to look at on late-night TV. That's all they are."

It was then that the blind man cleared his throat. He brought something up. He took a handkerchief from his back pocket. Then he said, "I get it, bub. It's okay. It happens. Don't worry about it," he said. "Hey, listen to me. Will you do me a favor? I got an idea. Why don't you find us some heavy paper? And a pen. We'll do something. We'll draw one together. Get us a pen and some heavy paper. Go on, bub, get the stuff," he said.

So I went upstairs. My legs felt like they didn't have any strength in them. They felt like they did after I'd done some running. In my wife's room, I looked around. I found some ballpoints in a little basket on her table. And then I tried to think where to look for the kind of paper he was talking about.

Downstairs, in the kitchen, I found a shopping bag with onion skins in the bottom of the bag. I emptied the bag and shook it. I brought it into the living room and sat down with it near his legs. I moved some things, smoothed the wrinkles from the bag, spread it out on the coffee table.

The blind man got down from the sofa and sat next to me on the carpet.

He ran his fingers over the paper. He went up and down the sides of the paper. The edges, even the edges. He fingered the corners.

"All right," he said. "All right, let's do her."

He found my hand, the hand with the pen. He closed his hand over my hand. "Go ahead, bub, draw," he said. "Draw. You'll see. I'll follow along with you. It'll be okay. Just begin now like I'm telling you. You'll see. Draw," the blind man said.

So I began. First I drew a box that looked like a house. It could have been the house I lived in. Then I put a roof on it. At either end of the roof, I drew spires. Crazy.

"Swell," he said. "Terrific. You're doing fine," he said. "Never thought anything like this could happen in your lifetime, did you, bub? Well, it's a strange life, we all know that. Go on now. Keep it up."

I put in windows with arches. I drew flying buttresses. I hung great doors. I couldn't stop. The TV station went off the air. I put down the pen and closed and opened my fingers. The blind man felt around over the paper. He moved the tips of his fingers over the paper, all over what I had drawn, and he nodded.

"Doing fine," the blind man said.

I took up the pen again, and he found my hand. I kept at it. I'm no artist. But I kept drawing just the same.

My wife opened up her eyes and gazed at us. She sat up on the sofa, her robe hanging open. She said, "What are you doing? Tell me, I want to know."

I didn't answer her.

The blind man said, "We're drawing a cathedral. Me and him are working on it. Press hard," he said to me. "That's right. That's good," he said.

"Sure. You got it, bub. I can tell. You didn't think you could. But you can, can't you? You're cooking with gas now. You know what I'm saying? We're going to really have us something here in a minute. How's the old arm?" he said. "Put some people in there now. What's a cathedral without people?"

My wife said, "What's going on? Robert, what are you doing? What's going on?"

"It's all right," he said to her. "Close your eyes now," the blind man said to me.

I did it. I closed them just like he said.

"Are they closed?" he said. "Don't fudge."

"They're closed," I said.

"Keep them that way," he said. He said, "Don't stop now. Draw."

So we kept on with it. His fingers rode my fingers as my hand went over the paper. It was like nothing else in my life up to now.

Then he said, "I think that's it. I think you got it," he said. "Take a look. What do you think?"

But I had my eyes closed. I thought I'd keep them that way for a little longer. I thought it was something I ought to do.

"Well?" he said. "Are you looking?"

My eyes were still closed. I was in my house. I knew that. But I didn't feel like I was inside anything.

"It's really something," I said.

CD-ROM: Research Raymond Carver in depth with cultural documents and multimedia resources on *LiterActive*.

Lan Samantha Chang   b. 1965

The Eve of the Spirit Festival   [1995]

After the Buddhist ceremony, when our mother's spirit had been chanted to a safe passage and her body cremated, Emily and I sat silently on our living room carpet. She held me in her arms; her long hair stuck to our wet faces. We sat as stiffly as temple gods except for the angry thump of my sister's heart against my cheek.

Finally she spoke. "It's Baba's fault," she said. "The American doctors would have fixed her."

I was six years old — I only knew that our father and mother had decided against an operation. And I had privately agreed, imagining the doctors tearing a hole in her body. As I thought of this, I felt a sudden sob pass through me.

"Don't cry, Baby," Emily whispered. "You're okay." I felt my tears dry to salt, my throat lock shut.

Then our father walked into the room.

He and Emily had grown close in the past few months. Emily was eleven, old enough to come along on his trips to the hospital. I had often stood in the neighbor's window and watched them leave for visiting hours, Emily's mittened hand tucked into his.

But now my sister refused to acknowledge him. She pushed the back of my head to turn me away from him also.

"First daughter—" he began.

"Go away, Baba," Emily said. Her voice shook. The evening sun glowed garnet red through the dark tent of her hair.

"You told me she would get better," I heard her say. "Now you're burning paper money for her ghost. What good will that do?"

"I am sorry," Baba said.

"I don't care."

Her voice burned. I squirmed beneath her hand, but she wouldn't let me look. It was something between her and Baba. I watched his black wingtip shoes retreat to the door. When he had gone, Emily let go of me. I sat up and looked at her; something had changed. Not in the lovely outlines of her face — our mother's face — but in her eyes, shadow-black, lost in unforgiveness.

They say the dead return to us. But we never saw our mother again, though we kept a kind of emptiness waiting in case she might come back. I listened always, seeking her voice, the lost thread of a conversation I'd been too young to have with her. I did not dare mention her to Emily. Since I could remember, my sister had kept her most powerful feelings private, sealed away. She rarely mentioned our mother, and soon my memories faded. I could not picture her. I saw only Emily's angry face, the late sun streaking red through her dark hair.

After the traditional forty-nine day mourning period, Baba did not set foot in the Buddhist temple. It was as if he had listened to Emily: what good did it do? Instead he focused on earthly ambitions, his research at the lab.

At that time he aspired beyond the position of lab instructor to the rank of associate professor, and he often invited his American colleagues over for "drinks." Emily and I were recruited to help with the preparations and serving. As we went about our tasks, we would sometimes catch a glimpse of our father, standing in the corner, watching the American men and studying to become one.

But he couldn't get it right — our parties had an air of cultural confusion. We served potato chips on laquered trays; Chinese landscapes bumped against watercolors of the Statue of Liberty, the Empire State Building.

Nor were Emily or I capable of helping him. I was still a child, and Emily said she did not care. Since my mother's death, she had rejected anything he held dear. She refused to study chemistry and spoke in American slang. Her rebellion puzzled me, it seemed so vehement and so arbitrary.

Now she stalked through the living room, platform shoes thudding on the carpet. "I hate this," she said, fiercely ripping another rag from a pair of old pajama bottoms. "Entertaining these jerks is a waste of time."

Some chemists from Texas were visiting his department and he had invited them over for cocktails.

"I can finish it," I said. "You just need to do the parts I can't reach."

"It's not the dusting," she said. "It's the way he acts around them. 'Herro, herro! Hi Blad, hi Warry! Let me take your coat! Howsa Giants game?'" she mimicked, in a voice that made me wince, a voice alive with cruelty and pain. "If he were smart he wouldn't invite people over on football afternoons in the first place."

"What do you mean?" I asked, startled. Brad Delmonte was our father's boss. I had noticed Baba reading the sports pages that morning — something he rarely did.

"Oh, forget it," Emily said. I felt as if she and I were utterly separate. Then she smiled. "You've got oil on your glasses, Claudia."

Baba walked in carrying two bottles of wine. "They should arrive in half an hour," he said, looking at his watch. "They won't be early. Americans are never early."

Emily looked away. "I'm going to Jodie's house," she said.

Baba frowned and straightened his tie. "I want you to stay while they're here. We might need something from the kitchen."

"Claudia can get it for them."

"She's barely tall enough to reach the cabinets."

Emily stood and clenched her dustcloth. "I don't care," she said. "I hate meeting the people you have over."

"They're successful American scientists. You'd be better off with them instead of running around with your teenage friends, these sloppy kids, these rich white kids who dress like beggars."

"You're nuts, Dad," Emily said — she had begun addressing him the way an American child does. "You're nuts if you think these bosses of yours are ever going to do anything for you or any of us." And she threw her dustcloth, hard, into our New York Giants wastebasket.

"Speak to me with respect."

"You don't deserve it!"

"You are staying in this apartment! That is an order!"

"I wish you'd died instead of Mama!" Emily cried. She darted past our father, her long braid flying behind her. He stared at her, his expression oddly slack, the way it had been in the weeks after the funeral. He stepped toward her, reached hesitantly at her flying braid, but she turned and saw him, cried out as if he had struck her, and ran out of the room. His hands dropped to his sides.

Emily refused to leave our bedroom. Otherwise that party was like so many others. The guests arrived late and left early. They talked about buying new cars and the Dallas Cowboys. I served pretzels and salted nuts.

Baba walked around emptying ashtrays and refilling drinks. I noticed that the other men also wore vests and ties, but that the uniform looked somehow different on my slighter, darker father.

"Cute little daughter you have there," said Baba's boss. He was a large bearded smoker with a sandy voice. He didn't bend down to look at me or the ashtray that I raised toward his big square hand.

I went into our room and found Emily sitting on one of our unmade twin beds. It was dusk. Through the window I could see that the dull winter sun had almost disappeared. I sat next to her on the bed. Until that day, I think, it was Emily who took care of me and not the other way around.

After a minute, she spoke. "I'm going to leave," she said. "As soon as I turn eighteen, I'm going to leave home and never come back!" She burst into tears. I reached for her shoulder but her thin, heaving body frightened me. She seemed too grown up to be comforted. I thought about the breasts swelling beneath her sweater. Her body had become a foreign place.

Perhaps Emily had warned me that she would someday leave in order to start me off on my own. I found myself avoiding her, as though her impending desertion would matter less if I deserted her first. I discovered a place to hide while she and my father fought, in the living room behind a painted screen. I would read a novel or look out the window. Sometimes they forgot about me — from the next room I would hear one of them break off an argument and say, "Where did Claudia go?" "I don't know," the other would reply. After a silence, they would start again.

One of these fights stands out in my memory. I must have been ten or eleven years old. It was the fourteenth day of the seventh lunar month: the eve of Guijie, the Chinese Spirit Festival, when the living are required to appease and provide for the ghosts of their ancestors. To the believing, the earth was thick with gathering spirits; it was safest to stay indoors and burn incense.

I seldom thought about the Chinese calendar, but every year on Guijie I wondered about my mother's ghost. Where was it? Would it still recognize me? How would I know when I saw it? I wanted to ask Baba, but I didn't dare. Baba had an odd attitude toward Guijie. On one hand, he had eschewed all Chinese customs since my mother's death. He was a scientist, he said; he scorned the traditional tales of unsatisfied spirits roaming the earth.

But I cannot remember a time when I was not made aware, in some way, of Guijie's fluctuating lunar date. That year the eve of the Spirit Festival fell on a Thursday, usually his night out with the men from his department. Emily and I waited for him to leave but he sat on the couch, calmly reading the *New York Times*.

I finished drying the dishes. Emily began to fidget. She had a date that night and had counted on my father's absence. She spent half an hour washing and combing her hair, trying to make up her mind. Finally she asked me to give her a trim. I knew she'd decided to go out.

"Just a little," she said. "The ends are scraggly." We spread some newspapers on the living room floor. Emily stood in the middle of the papers with her hair combed down her back, thick and glossy, black as ink. It hadn't really been cut since she was born. Since my mother's death I had taken over the task of giving it a periodic touch-up.

I hovered behind her with the shears, searching for the scraggly ends, but there were none.

My father looked up from his newspaper. "What are you doing that for? You can't go out tonight," he said.

"I have a date!"

My father put down his newspaper. I threw the shears onto a chair and fled to my refuge behind the screen.

Through a slit over the hinge I caught a glimpse of Emily near the foyer, slender in her denim jacket, her black hair flooding down her back, her delicate features contorted with anger. My father's hair was disheveled, his hands clenched at his sides. The newspapers had scattered over the floor.

"Dressing up in boys' clothes, with paint on your face—"

"This is nothing! My going out on a few dates is nothing! You don't know what you're talking about!"

"Don't shout." My father shook his finger. "The neighbors will hear you."

"Goddammit, Dad!" Her voice rose to a shriek. She stamped her feet to make the most noise possible.

"What happened to you?" he cried. "You used to be so much like her. Look at you—"

Though I'd covered my ears I could hear my sister's wail echo off the walls. The door slammed, and her footfalls vanished down the stairs.

Things were quiet for a minute. Then I heard my father walk toward my corner. My heart thumped with fear—usually he let me alone. I had to look up when I heard him move the screen away. He knelt down next to me. His hair was streaked with gray, and his glasses needed cleaning.

"What are you doing?" he asked.

I shook my head, nothing.

After a minute I asked him, "Is Guijie why you didn't go play bridge tonight, Baba?"

"No, Claudia," he said. He always called me by my American name. This formality, I thought, was an indication of how distant he felt from me. "I stopped playing bridge last week."

"Why?" We both looked toward the window, where beyond our reflections the Hudson River flowed.

"It's not important," he said.

"Okay."

But he didn't leave. "I'm getting old," he said after a moment. "Someone ten years younger was just promoted over me. I'm not going to try to keep up with them anymore."

It was the closest he had ever come to confiding in me. After a few more minutes he stood up and went into the kitchen. The newspapers rustled under his feet. For almost half an hour I heard him fumbling through the kitchen cabinets, looking for something he'd probably put there years ago. Eventually he came out, carrying a small brass urn and some matches. When Emily returned home after midnight, the apartment still smelled of the incense he had burned to protect her while she was gone.

I tried to be a good daughter. I stayed in every night and wore no make-up, I studied hard and got all A's, I did not leave home but went to college at NYU, right down the street. Jealously I guarded my small allotment of praise, clutching it like a pocket of precious stones. Emily snuck out of the apartment late at night; she wore high-heeled sandals with patched blue jeans; she twisted her long hair into graceful, complex loops and braids that belied respectability. She smelled of lipstick and perfume. Nothing I could ever achieve would equal my sister's misbehavior.

When Emily turned eighteen and did leave home, a part of my father disappeared. I wondered sometimes: where did it go? Did she take it with her? What secret charm had she carried with her as she vanished down the tunnel to the jet that would take her to college in California, steadily and without looking back, while my father and I watched silently from the window at the gate? The apartment afterwards became quite still — it was only the two of us, mourning and dreaming through pale-blue winter afternoons and silent evenings.

Emily called me, usually late at night after my father had gone to sleep. She sent me pictures of herself and people I didn't know, smiling on the sunny Berkeley campus. Sometimes after my father and I ate our simple meals or TV dinners I would go into our old room, where I had kept both of our twin beds, and take out Emily's pictures, trying to imagine what she must have been feeling, studying her expression and her swinging hair. But I always stared the longest at a postcard she'd sent me one winter break from northern New Mexico, a professional photo of a powerful, vast blue sky over faraway pink and sandy-beige mesas. The clarity and cleanness fascinated me. In a place like that, I thought, there would be nothing to search for, no reason to hide.

After college she went to work at a bank in San Francisco. I saw her once when she flew to Manhattan on business. She skipped a meeting to have lunch with me. She wore an elegant gray suit and had pinned up her hair.

"How's Dad?" she asked. I looked around, slightly alarmed. We were sitting in a bistro on the East Side, but I somehow thought he might over-hear us.

"He's okay," I said "We don't talk very much. Why don't you come home and see him?"

Emily stared at her water glass. "I don't think so."

"He misses you."

"I know. I don't want to hear about it."

"You hardly ever call him."

"There's nothing we can talk about. Don't tell him you saw me, promise?"

"Okay."

During my junior year at NYU, my father suffered a stroke. He was fifty-nine years old, and he was still working as a lab instructor in the chemistry department. One evening in early fall I came home from a class and found him on the floor, near the kitchen telephone. He was wearing his usual vest and tie. I called the hospital and sat down next to him. His wire-rimmed glasses lay on the floor a foot away. One-half of his face was frozen, the other half lined with sudden age and pain.

"They said they'll be right here," I said. "It won't be very long." I couldn't tell how much he understood. I smoothed his vest and straightened his tie. I folded his glasses. I knew he wouldn't like it if the ambulance workers saw him in a state of dishevelment. "I'm sure they'll be here soon," I said.

We waited. Then I noticed he was trying to tell me something. A line of spittle ran from the left side of his mouth. I leaned closer. After a while I made out his words: "Tell Emily," he said.

The ambulance arrived as I picked up the telephone to call California. That evening, at the hospital, what was remaining of my father left the earth.

Emily insisted that we not hold a Buddhist cremation ceremony. "I never want to think about that stuff again," she said. "Plus, all of his friends are Americans. I don't know who would come, except for us." She had reached New York the morning after his death. Her eyes were vague and her fingernails bitten down.

On the third day we scattered his ashes in the river. Afterward we held a small memorial service for his friends from work. We didn't talk much as we straightened the living room and dusted the furniture. It took almost three hours. The place was a mess. We hadn't had a party in years.

It was a warm cloudy afternoon, and the Hudson looked dull and sluggish from the living room window. I noticed that although she had not wanted a Buddhist ceremony, Emily had dressed in black and white according to Chinese mourning custom. I had asked the department secretary to put up a sign on the bulletin board. Eleven people came; they drank five bottles of wine. Two of his Chinese students stood in the corner, eating cheese and crackers.

Brad Delmonte, paunchy and no longer smoking, attached himself to Emily. "I remember you when you were just a little girl," I heard him say as I walked by with the extra crackers.

"I don't remember you," she said.

"You're still a cute little thing." She bumped his arm, and he spilled his drink.

Afterward we sat on the couch and surveyed the cluttered coffee table. It was past seven but we didn't talk about dinner.

"I'm glad they came," I said.

"I hate them." Emily looked at her fingernails. "I don't know whom I hate more: them, or him—for taking it."

"It doesn't matter anymore," I said.

"I suppose."

We watched the room grow dark.

"Do you know what?" Emily said. "It's the eve of the fifteenth day of the seventh lunar month."

"How do you know?" During college I had grown completely unaware of the lunar calendar.

"One of those chemistry nerds from Taiwan told me this afternoon."

I wanted to laugh, but instead I felt myself make a strange whimpering sound, squeezed out from my tight and hollow chest.

"Remember the time Dad and I had that big fight?" she said. "You know that now, in my grown-up life, I don't fight with anyone? I never had problems with anybody except him."

"No one cared about you as much as he did," I said.

"I don't want to hear about it." She twisted the end of her long braid. "He was a pain, and you know it. He got so strict after Mama died. It wasn't all my fault."

"I'm sorry," I said. But I was so angry with her that I felt my face turn red, my cheeks tingle in the dark. She'd considered our father a nerd as well, had squandered his love with such thoughtlessness that I could scarcely breathe to think about it. It seemed impossibly unfair that she had memories of my mother as well. Carefully I waited for my feelings to go away. Emily, I thought, was all I had.

But as I sat, a vision distilled before my eyes: the soft baked shades, the great blue sky of New Mexico. I realized that after graduation I could go wherever I wanted. A rusty door swung open and filled my mind with sweet freedom, fearful coolness.

"Let's do something," I said.

"What do you mean?"

"I want to do something."

"What did we used to do?" Emily looked down at the lock of hair in her hand. "Wait, I know."

We found newspapers and spread them on the floor. We turned on the lamps and moved the coffee table out of the way, brought the wineglasses to the sink. Emily went to the bathroom, and I searched for the shears a long time before I found them in the kitchen. I glimpsed the incense urn in a cabinet and quickly shut the door. When I returned to the living room it smelled of shampoo. Emily stood in the middle of the papers with her wet hair down her back, staring at herself in the reflection from the window. The lamplight cast circles under her eyes.

"I had a dream last night," she said. "I was walking down the street. I felt a tug. He was trying to reach me, trying to pull my hair."

"Just a trim?" I asked.

"No," she said. "Why don't you cut it."

"What do you mean?" I snipped a two-inch lock off the side.

Emily looked down at the hair on the newspapers. "I'm serious," she said. "Cut my hair. I want to see two feet of hair on the floor."

"Emily, you don't know what you're saying," I said. But a pleasurable, weightless feeling had come over me. I placed the scissors at the nape of her neck. "How about it?" I asked, and my voice sounded low and odd.

"*I don't care.*" An echo of the past. I cut. The shears went *snack.* A long black lock of hair hit the newspapers by my feet.

The Chinese say that our hair and our bodies are given to us from our ancestors, gifts that should not be tampered with. My mother herself had never done this. But after the first few moments I enjoyed myself, pressing the thick black locks through the shears, heavy against my thumb. Emily's hair slipped to the floor around us, rich and beautiful, lying in long graceful arcs over my shoes. She stood perfectly still, staring out the window. The Hudson River flowed behind our reflections, bearing my father's ashes through the night.

When I was finished, the back of her neck gleamed clean and white under a precise shining cap. "You missed your calling," Emily said. "You want me to do yours?"

My hair, browner and scragglier, had never been past my shoulders. I had always kept it short, figuring the ancestors wouldn't be offended by my tampering with a lesser gift. "No," I said. "But you should take a shower. Some of those small bits will probably itch."

"It's already ten o'clock. We should go to sleep soon anyway." Satisfied, she glanced at the mirror in the foyer. "I look like a completely different person," she said. She left to take her shower. I wrapped up her hair in the newspapers and went into the kitchen. I stood next to the sink for a long time before throwing the bundle away.

The past sees through all attempts at disguise. That night I was awakened by my sister's scream. I gasped and stiffened, grabbing a handful of blanket.

"*Claudia,*" Emily cried from the other bed. "Claudia, wake up!"

"What is it?"

"I saw Baba." She hadn't called our father Baba in years. "Over there, by the door. Did you see him?"

"No," I said. "I didn't see anything." My bones felt frozen in place. After a moment I opened my eyes. The full moon shone through the window, bathing our room in silver and shadow. I heard my sister sob and then fall silent. I looked carefully at the door, but I noticed nothing.

Then I understood that his ghost would never visit me. I was, one might say, the lucky daughter. But I lay awake until morning, waiting; part of me is waiting still.

Ralph Ellison   1914–1994

Battle Royal   [1952]

It goes a long way back, some twenty years. All my life I had been looking for something, and everywhere I turned someone tried to tell me what it was. I accepted their answers too, though they were often in contradiction and even self-contradictory. I was naïve. I was looking for myself and asking everyone except myself questions which I, and only I, could answer. It took me a long time and much painful boomeranging of my expectations to achieve a realization everyone else appears to have been born with: That I am nobody but myself. But first I had to discover that I am an invisible man!

And yet I am no freak of nature, nor of history. I was in the cards, other things having been equal (or unequal) eighty-five years ago. I am not ashamed of my grandparents for having been slaves. I am only ashamed of myself for having at one time been ashamed. About eighty-five years ago they were told that they were free, united with others of our country in everything pertaining to the common good, and, in everything social, separate like the fingers of the hand. And they believed it. They exulted in it. They stayed in their place, worked hard, and brought up my father to do the same. But my grandfather is the one. He was an odd old guy, my grandfather, and I am told I take after him. It was he who caused the trouble. On his deathbed he called my father to him and said, "Son, after I'm gone I want you to keep up the good fight. I never told you, but our life is a war and I have been a traitor all my born days, a spy in the enemy's country ever since I give up my gun back in the Reconstruction. Live with your head in the lion's mouth. I want you to overcome 'em with yeses, undermine 'em with grins, agree 'em to death and destruction, let 'em swoller you till they vomit or bust wide open." They thought the old man had gone out of his mind. He had been the meekest of men. The younger children were rushed from the room, the shades drawn and the flame of the lamp turned so low that it sputtered on the wick like the old man's breathing. "Learn it to the younguns," he whispered fiercely; then he died.

But my folks were more alarmed over his last words than over his dying. It was as though he had not died at all, his words caused so much anxiety. I was warned emphatically to forget what he had said and, indeed, this is the first time it has been mentioned outside the family circle. It had a tremendous effect upon me, however. I could never be sure of what he meant. Grandfather had been a quiet old man who never made any trouble, yet on his deathbed he had called himself a traitor and a spy, and he had spoken of his meekness as a dangerous activity. It became a constant puzzle which lay unanswered in the back of my mind. And whenever things went well for me I remembered my grandfather and felt guilty and uncomfortable. It was as though I was carrying out his advice in spite of myself. And to make it worse, everyone loved me for it. I was praised by the most lily-white men of the town. I was considered an example of desirable conduct — just as my grand-father had been. And what puzzled me was that the old man had defined it as *treachery*. When I was praised for my conduct I felt a guilt that in some way I was doing something that was really against the wishes of the white folks, that if they had understood they would have desired me to act just the opposite, that I should have been sulky and mean, and that that really would have been what they wanted, even though they were fooled and thought they wanted me to act as I did. It made me afraid that some day they would look upon me as a traitor and I would be lost. Still I was more afraid to act any other way because they didn't like that at all. The old man's words were like a curse. On my graduation day I delivered an oration in which I showed that humility was the secret, indeed, the very essence of progress. (Not that I believed this — how could I, remembering my grandfather? — I only be-lieved that it worked.) It was a great success. Everyone praised me and I was invited to give the speech at a gathering of the town's leading white citizens. It was a triumph for our whole community.

It was in the main ballroom of the leading hotel. When I got there I dis-covered that it was on the occasion of a smoker, and I was told that since I was to be there anyway I might as well take part in the battle royal to be fought by some of my schoolmates as part of the entertainment. The battle royal came first.

All of the town's big shots were there in their tuxedoes, wolfing down the buffet foods, drinking beer and whiskey and smoking black cigars. It was a large room with a high ceiling. Chairs were arranged in neat rows around three sides of a portable boxing ring. The fourth side was clear, revealing a gleaming space of polished floor. I had some misgivings over the battle royal, by the way. Not from a distaste for fighting, but because I didn't care too much for the other fellows who were to take part. They were tough guys who seemed to have no grandfather's curse worrying their minds. No one could mistake their toughness. And besides, I suspected that fighting a battle royal might detract from the dignity of my speech. In those pre-invisible days I vi-sualized myself as a potential Booker T. Washington. But the other fellows didn't care too much for me either, and there were nine of them. I felt supe-rior to them in my way, and I didn't like the manner in which we were all crowded together into the servants' elevator. Nor did they like my being there. In fact, as the warmly lighted floors flashed past the elevator we had words over the fact that I, by taking part in the fight, had knocked one of their friends out of a night's work.

We were led out of the elevator through a rococo hall into an anteroom and told to get into our fighting togs. Each of us was issued a pair of box-ing gloves and ushered out into the big mirrored hall, which we entered looking cautiously about us and whispering, lest we might accidentally be heard above the noise of the room. It was foggy with cigar smoke. And al-ready the whiskey was taking effect. I was shocked to see some of the most important men of the town quite tipsy. They were all there — bankers, lawyers, judges, doctors, fire chiefs, teachers, merchants. Even one of the more fashionable pastors. Something we could not see was going on up front. A clarinet was vibrating sensuously and the men were standing up and moving eagerly forward. We were a small tight group, clustered together, our bare upper bodies touching and shining with anticipatory sweat; while up front the big shots were becoming increasingly excited over something we still could not see. Suddenly I heard the school superintendent, who had told me to come, yell, "Bring up the shines, gentlemen! Bring up the little shines!"

We were rushed up to the front of the ballroom, where it smelled even more strongly of tobacco and whiskey. Then we were pushed into place. I almost wet my pants. A sea of faces, some hostile, some amused, ringed around us, and in the center, facing us, stood a magnificent blonde—stark naked. There was dead silence. I felt a blast of cold air chill me. I tried to back away, but they were behind me and around me. Some of the boys stood with lowered heads, trembling. I felt a wave of irrational guilt and fear. My teeth chattered, my skin turned to goose flesh, my knees knocked. Yet I was strongly attracted and looked in spite of myself. Had the price of looking been blindness, I would have looked. The hair was yellow like that of a circus kewpie doll, the face heavily powdered and rouged, as though to form an abstract mask, the eyes hollow and smeared a cool blue, the color of a baboon's butt. I felt a desire to spit upon her as my eyes brushed slowly over her body. Her breasts were firm and round as the domes of East Indian temples, and I stood so close as to see the fine skin texture and beads of pearly perspiration glistening like dew around the pink and erected buds of her nipples. I wanted at one and the same time to run from the room, to sink through the floor, or go to her and cover her from my eyes and the eyes of the others with my body; to feel the soft thighs, to caress her and destroy her, to love her and murder her, to hide from her, and yet to stroke where below the small American flag tattooed upon her belly her thighs formed a capital V. I had a notion that of all in the room she saw only me with her impersonal eyes.

And then she began to dance, a slow sensuous movement; the smoke of a hundred cigars clinging to her like the thinnest of veils. She seemed like a fair bird-girl girdled in veils calling to me from the angry surface of some gray and threatening sea. I was transported. Then I became aware of the clarinet playing and the big shots yelling at us. Some threatened us if we looked and others if we did not. On my right I saw one boy faint. And now a man grabbed a silver pitcher from a table and stepped close as he dashed ice water upon him and stood him up and forced two of us to support him as his head hung and moans issued from his thick bluish lips. Another boy began to plead to go home. He was the largest of the group, wearing dark red fighting trunks much too small to conceal the erection which projected from him as though in answer to the insinuating low-registered moaning of the clarinet. He tried to hide himself with his boxing gloves.

And all the while the blonde continued dancing, smiling faintly at the big shots who watched her with fascination, and faintly smiling at our fear. I noticed a certain merchant who followed her hungrily, his lips loose and drooling. He was a large man who wore diamond studs in a shirtfront which swelled with the ample paunch underneath, and each time the blonde swayed her undulating hips he ran his hand through the thin hair of his bald head and, with his arms upheld, his posture clumsy like that of an intoxicated panda, wound his belly in a slow and obscene grind. This creature was completely hypnotized. The music had quickened. As the dancer flung herself about with a detached expression on her face, the men began reaching out to touch her. I could see their beefy fingers sink into the soft flesh. Some of the others tried to stop them and she began to move around the floor in graceful circles, as they gave chase, slipping and sliding over the polished floor. It was mad. Chairs went crashing, drinks were spilt, as they ran laughing and howling after her. They caught her just as she reached a door, raised her from the floor, and tossed her as college boys are tossed at a hazing, and above her red, fixed-smiling lips I saw the terror and disgust in her eyes, almost like my own terror and that which I saw in some of the other boys. As I watched, they tossed her twice and her soft breasts seemed to flatten against the air and her legs flung wildly as she spun. Some of the more sober ones helped her to escape. And I started off the floor, heading for the anteroom with the rest of the boys.

Some were still crying and in hysteria. But as we tried to leave we were stopped and ordered to get into the ring. There was nothing to do but what we were told. All ten of us climbed under the ropes and allowed ourselves to be blindfolded with broad bands of white cloth. One of the men seemed to feel a bit sympathetic and tried to cheer us up as we stood with our backs against the ropes. Some of us tried to grin. "See that boy over there?" one of the men said. "I want you to run across at the bell and give it to him right in the belly. If you don't get him, I'm going to get you. I don't like his looks." Each of us was told the same. The blindfolds were put on. Yet even then I had been going over my speech. In my mind each word was as bright as flame. I felt the cloth pressed into place, and frowned so that it would be loosened when I relaxed.

But now I felt a sudden fit of blind terror. I was unused to darkness. It was as though I had suddenly found myself in a dark room filled with poisonous cottonmouths. I could hear the bleary voices yelling insistently for the battle royal to begin.

"Get going in there!"

"Let me at that big nigger!"

I strained to pick up the school superintendent's voice, as though to squeeze some security out of that slightly more familiar sound.

"Let me at those black sonsabitches!" someone yelled.

"No, Jackson, no!" another voice yelled. "Here, somebody, help me hold Jack."

"I want to get at that ginger-colored nigger. Tear him limb from limb," the first voice yelled.

I stood against the ropes trembling. For in those days I was what they called ginger-colored, and he sounded as though he might crunch me between his teeth like a crisp ginger cookie.

Quite a struggle was going on. Chairs were being kicked about and I could hear voices grunting as with a terrific effort. I wanted to see, to see more desperately than ever before. But the blindfold was tight as a thick skin-puckering scab and when I raised my gloved hands to push the layers of white aside a voice yelled, "Oh, no you don't, black bastard! Leave that alone!"

"Ring the bell before Jackson kills him a coon!" someone boomed in the sudden silence. And I heard the bell clang and the sound of the feet scuffling forward.

A glove smacked against my head. I pivoted, striking out stiffly as someone went past, and felt the jar ripple along the length of my arm to my shoulder. Then it seemed as though all nine of the boys had turned upon me at once. Blows pounded me from all sides while I struck out as best I could. So many blows landed upon me that I wondered if I were not the only blindfolded fighter in the ring, or if the man called Jackson hadn't succeeded in getting me after all.

Blindfolded, I could no longer control my motions. I had no dignity. I stumbled about like a baby or a drunken man. The smoke had become thicker and with each new blow it seemed to sear and further restrict my lungs. My saliva became like hot bitter glue. A glove connected with my head, filling my mouth with warm blood. It was everywhere. I could not tell if the moisture I felt upon my body was sweat or blood. A blow landed hard against the nape of my neck. I felt myself going over, my head hitting the floor. Streaks of blue light filled the black world behind the blindfold. I lay prone, pretending that I was knocked out, but felt myself seized by hands and yanked to my feet. "Get going, black boy! Mix it up!" My arms were like lead, my head smarting from blows. I managed to feel my way to the ropes and held on, trying to catch my breath. A glove landed in my mid-section and I went over again, feeling as though the smoke had become a knife jabbed into my guts. Pushed this way and that by the legs milling around me, I finally pulled erect and discovered that I could see the black, sweat-washed forms weaving in the smoky-blue atmosphere like drunken dancers weaving to the rapid drum-like thuds of blows.

Everyone fought hysterically. It was complete anarchy. Everybody fought everybody else. No group fought together for long. Two, three, four, fought one, then turned to fight each other, were themselves attacked. Blows landed below the belt and in the kidney, with the gloves open as well as closed, and with my eye partly opened now there was not so much terror. I moved carefully, avoiding blows, although not too many to attract attention, fighting from group to group. The boys groped about like blind, cautious crabs crouching to protect their mid-sections, their heads pulled in short against their shoulders, their arms stretched nervously before them, with their fists testing the smoke-filled air like the knobbed feelers of hyper-sensitive snails. In one corner I glimpsed a boy violently punching the air and heard him scream in pain as he smashed his hand against a ring post. For a second I saw him bent over holding his hand, then going down as a blow caught his unprotected head. I played one group against the other, slipping in and throwing a punch then stepping out of range while pushing the others into the melee to take the blows blindly aimed at me. The smoke was agonizing and there were no rounds, no bells at three minute intervals to relieve our exhaustion. The room spun round me, a swirl of lights, smoke, sweating bodies surrounded by tense white faces. I bled from both nose and mouth, the blood spattering upon my chest.

The men kept yelling, "Slug him, black boy! Knock his guts out!"

"Uppercut him! Kill him! Kill that big boy!"

Taking a fake fall, I saw a boy going down heavily beside me as though we were felled by a single blow, saw a sneaker-clad foot shoot into his groin as the two who had knocked him down stumbled upon him. I rolled out of range, feeling a twinge of nausea.

The harder we fought the more threatening the men became. And yet, I had begun to worry about my speech again. How would it go? Would they recognize my ability? What would they give me?

I was fighting automatically when suddenly I noticed that one after another of the boys was leaving the ring. I was surprised, filled with panic, as though I had been left alone with an unknown danger. Then I understood. The boys had arranged it among themselves. It was the custom for the two men left in the ring to slug it out for the winner's prize. I discovered this too late. When the bell sounded two men in tuxedoes leaped into the ring and removed the blindfold. I found myself facing Tatlock, the biggest of the gang. I felt sick at my stomach. Hardly had the bell stopped ringing in my ears than it clanged again and I saw him moving swiftly toward me. Thinking of nothing else to do I hit him smash on the nose. He kept coming, bringing the rank sharp violence of stale sweat. His face was a black blank of a face, only his eyes alive—with hate of me and aglow with a feverish terror from what had happened to us all. I became anxious. I wanted to deliver my speech and he came at me as though he meant to beat it out of me. I smashed him again and again, taking his blows as they came. Then on a sudden impulse I struck him lightly and as we clinched, I whispered, "Fake like I knocked you out, you can have the prize."

"I'll break your behind," he whispered hoarsely.

"For *them?*"

"For *me,* sonofabitch!"

They were yelling for us to break it up and Tatlock spun me half around with a blow, and as a joggled camera sweeps in a reeling scene, I saw the howling red faces crouching tense beneath the cloud of blue-gray smoke. For a moment the world wavered, unraveled, flowed, then my head cleared and Tatlock bounced before me. That fluttering shadow before my eyes was his jabbing left hand. Then falling forward, my head against his damp shoulder, I whispered,

"I'll make it five dollars more."

"Go to hell!"

But his muscles relaxed a trifle beneath my pressure and I breathed, "Seven?"

"Give it to your ma," he said, ripping me beneath the heart.

And while I still held him I butted him and moved away. I felt myself bombarded with punches. I fought back with hopeless desperation. I wanted to deliver my speech more than anything else in the world, because I felt that only these men could judge truly my ability, and now this stupid clown was ruining my chances. I began fighting carefully now, moving in to punch him and out again with my greater speed. A lucky blow to his chin and I had him going too — until I heard a loud voice yell, "I got my money on the big boy."

Hearing this, I almost dropped my guard. I was confused: Should I try to win against the voice out there? Would not this go against my speech, and was not this a moment for humility, for nonresistance? A blow to my head as I danced about sent my right eye popping like a jack-in-the-box and settled my dilemma. The room went red as I fell. It was a dream fall, my body languid and fastidious as to where to land, until the floor became impatient and smashed up to meet me. A moment later I came to. An hypnotic voice said FIVE emphatically. And I lay there, hazily watching a dark red spot of my own blood shaping itself into a butterfly, glistening and soaking into the soiled gray world of the canvas.

When the voice drawled TEN I was lifted up and dragged to a chair. I sat dazed. My eye pained and swelled with each throb of my pounding heart and I wondered if now I would be allowed to speak. I was wringing wet, my mouth still bleeding. We were grouped along the wall now. The other boys ignored me as they congratulated Tatlock and speculated as to how much they would be paid. One boy whimpered over his smashed hand. Looking up front, I saw attendants in white jackets rolling the portable ring away and placing a small square rug in the vacant space surrounded by chairs. Perhaps, I thought, I will stand on the rug to deliver my speech.

Then the M.C. called to us, "Come on up here boys and get your money."

We ran forward to where the men laughed and talked in their chairs, waiting. Everyone seemed friendly now.

"There it is on the rug," the man said. I saw the rug covered with coins of all dimensions and a few crumpled bills. But what excited me, scattered here and there, were the gold pieces.

"Boys, it's all yours," the man said. "You get all you grab."

"That's right, Sambo," a blond man said, winking at me confidentially.

I trembled with excitement, forgetting my pain. I would get the gold and the bills, I thought. I would use both hands. I would throw my body against the boys nearest me to block them from the gold.

"Get down around the rug now," the man commanded, "and don't any-one touch it until I give the signal."

"This ought to be good," I heard.

As told, we got around the square rug on our knees. Slowly the man raised his freckled hand as we followed it upward with our eyes.

I heard, "These niggers look like they're about to pray!"

Then, "Ready," the man said. "Go!"

I lunged for a yellow coin lying on the blue design of the carpet, touch-ing it and sending a surprised shriek to join those rising around me. I tried frantically to remove my hand but could not let go. A hot, violent force tore through my body, shaking me like a wet rat. The rug was electrified. The hair bristled up on my head as I shook myself free. My muscles jumped, my nerves jangled, writhed. But I saw that this was not stopping the other boys. Laughing in fear and embarrassment, some were holding back and scooping up the coins knocked off by the painful contortions of the others. The men roared above us as we struggled.

"Pick it up, goddamnit, pick it up!" someone called like a bass-voiced parrot. "Go on, get it!"

I crawled rapidly around the floor, picking up the coins, trying to avoid the coppers and to get greenbacks and the gold. Ignoring the shock by laugh-ing, as I brushed the coins off quickly, I discovered that I could contain the electricity—a contradiction, but it works. Then the men began to push us onto the rug. Laughing embarrassedly, we struggled out of their hands and kept after the coins. We were all wet and slippery and hard to hold. Suddenly I saw a boy lifted into the air, glistening with sweat like a circus seal, and dropped, his wet back landing flush upon the charged rug, heard him yell and saw him literally dance upon his back, his elbows beating a frenzied tat-too upon the floor, his muscles twitching like the flesh of a horse stung by many flies. When he finally rolled off, his face was gray and no one stopped him when he ran from the floor amid booming laughter.

"Get the money," the M.C. called. "That's good hard American cash!"

And we snatched and grabbed, snatched and grabbed. I was careful not to come too close to the rug now, and when I felt the hot whiskey breath de-scend upon me like a cloud of foul air I reached out and grabbed the leg of a chair. It was occupied and I held on desperately.

"Leggo, nigger! Leggo!"

The huge face wavered down to mine as he tried to push me free. But my body was slippery and he was too drunk. It was Mr. Colcord, who owned a chain of movie houses and "entertainment palaces." Each time he grabbed me I slipped out of his hands. It became a real struggle. I feared the rug more than I did the drunk, so I held on, surprising myself for a moment by trying to topple *him* upon the rug. It was such an enormous idea that I found my-self actually carrying it out. I tried not to be obvious, yet when I grabbed his leg, trying to tumble him out of the chair, he raised up roaring with laugh-ter, and, looking at me with soberness dead in the eye, kicked me viciously in the chest. The chair leg flew out of my hand and I felt myself going and rolled. It was as though I had rolled through a bed of hot coals. It seemed a whole century would pass before I would roll free, a century in which I was seared through the deepest levels of my body to the fearful breath within me and the breath seared and heated to the point of explosion. It'll all be over in a flash, I thought as I rolled clear. It'll all be over in a flash.

But not yet, the men on the other side were waiting, red faces swollen as though from apoplexy as they bent forward in their chairs. Seeing their fingers coming toward me I rolled away as a fumbled football rolls off the receiver's fingertips, back into the coals. That time I luckily sent the rug sliding out of place and heard the coins ringing against the floor and the boys scuffling to pick them up and the M.C. calling, "All right, boys, that's all. Go get dressed and get your money."

I was limp as a dish rag. My back felt as though it had been beaten with wires.

When we had dressed the M.C. came in and gave us each five dollars, except Tatlock, who got ten for being last in the ring. Then he told us to leave. I was not to get a chance to deliver my speech, I thought. I was going out into the dim alley in despair when I was stopped and told to go back. I returned to the ballroom, where the men were pushing back their chairs and gathering in groups to talk.

The M.C. knocked on a table for quiet. "Gentlemen," he said, "we almost forgot an important part of the program. A most serious part, gentlemen. This boy was brought here to deliver a speech which he made at his graduation yesterday . . ."

"Bravo!"

"I'm told that he is the smartest boy we've got out there in Greenwood. I'm told that he knows more big words than a pocket-sized dictionary."

Much applause and laughter.

"So now, gentlemen, I want you to give him your attention."

There was still laughter as I faced them, my mouth dry, my eye throbbing. I began slowly, but evidently my throat was tense, because they began shouting, "Louder! Louder!"

"We of the younger generation extol the wisdom of that great leader and educator," I shouted, "who first spoke these flaming words of wisdom: 'A ship lost at sea for many days suddenly sighted a friendly vessel. From the mast of the unfortunate vessel was seen a signal: "Water, water; we die of thirst!" The answer from the friendly vessel came back: "Cast down your bucket where you are." The captain of the distressed vessel, at last heeding the injunction, cast down his bucket, and it came up full of fresh sparkling water from the mouth of the Amazon River.' And like him I say, and in his words, 'To those of my race who depend upon bettering their condition in a foreign land, or who underestimate the importance of cultivating friendly relations with the Southern white man, who is his next-door neighbor, I would say: "Cast down your bucket where you are" — cast it down in making

friends in every manly way of the people of all races by whom we are surrounded . . .'"

I spoke automatically and with such fervor that I did not realize that the
men were still talking and laughing until my dry mouth, filling up with
blood from the cut, almost strangled me. I coughed, wanting to stop and go
to one of the tall brass, sand-filled spittoons to relieve myself, but a few of
the men, especially the superintendent, were listening and I was afraid. So I
gulped it down, blood, saliva and all, and continued. (What powers of en-
durance I had during those days! What enthusiasm! What a belief in the
rightness of things!) I spoke even louder in spite of the pain. But still they
talked and still they laughed, as though deaf with cotton in dirty ears. So I
spoke with greater emotional emphasis. I closed my ears and swallowed
blood until I was nauseated. The speech seemed a hundred times as long as
before, but I could not leave out a single word. All had to be said, each memorized nuance considered, rendered. Nor was that all. Whenever I uttered a
word of three or more syllables a group of voices would yell for me to repeat
it. I used the phrase "social responsibility" and they yelled:

"What's that word you say, boy?"

"Social responsibility," I said.

"What?"

"Social . . ."

"Louder."

". . . responsibility."

"More!"

"Respon—"

"Repeat!"

"—sibility."

The room filled with the uproar of laughter until, no doubt distracted by
having to gulp down my blood, I made a mistake and yelled a phrase I had
often seen denounced in newspaper editorials, heard debated in private.

"Social . . ."

"What?" they yelled.

". . . equality—"

The laughter hung smokelike in the sudden stillness. I opened my eyes,
puzzled. Sounds of displeasure filled the room. The M.C. rushed forward.
They shouted hostile phrases at me. But I did not understand.

A small dry mustached man in the front row blared out, "Say that
slowly, son!"

"What, sir?"

"What you just said!"

"Social responsibility, sir," I said.

"You weren't being smart, were you, boy?" he said, not unkindly.

"No, sir!"

"You sure that about 'equality' was a mistake?"

"Oh, yes, sir," I said. "I was swallowing blood."

"Well, you had better speak more slowly so we can understand. We mean to do right by you, but you've got to know your place at all times. All right, now, go on with your speech."

I was afraid. I wanted to leave but I wanted also to speak and I was afraid they'd snatch me down.

"Thank you, sir," I said, beginning where I had left off, and having them ignore me as before.

Yet when I finished there was a thunderous applause. I was surprised to see the superintendent come forth with a package wrapped in white tissue paper, and, gesturing for quiet, address the men.

"Gentlemen, you see that I did not overpraise this boy. He makes a good speech and some day he'll lead his people in the proper paths. And I don't have to tell you that that is important in these days and times. This is a good, smart boy, and so to encourage him in the right direction, in the name of the Board of Education I wish to present him a prize in the form of this . . ."

He paused, removing the tissue paper and revealing a gleaming calfskin brief case.

". . . in the form of this first-class article from Shad Whitmore's shop."

"Boy," he said, addressing me, "take this prize and keep it well. Consider it a badge of office. Prize it. Keep developing as you are and some day it will be filled with important papers that will help shape the destiny of your people."

I was so moved that I could hardly express my thanks. A rope of bloody saliva forming a shape like an undiscovered continent drooled upon the leather and I wiped it quickly away. I felt an importance that I had never dreamed.

"Open it and see what's inside," I was told.

My fingers a-tremble, I complied, smelling the fresh leather and finding an official-looking document inside. It was a scholarship to the state college for Negroes. My eyes filled with tears and I ran awkwardly off the floor.

I was overjoyed; I did not even mind when I discovered that the gold pieces I had scrambled for were brass pocket tokens advertising a certain make of automobile.

When I reached home everyone was excited. Next day the neighbors came to congratulate me. I even felt safe from grandfather, whose deathbed curse usually spoiled my triumphs. I stood beneath his photograph with my brief case in hand and smiled triumphantly into his stolid black peasant's face. It was a face that fascinated me. The eyes seemed to follow everywhere I went.

That night I dreamed I was at a circus with him and that he refused to laugh at the clowns no matter what they did. Then later he told me to open my brief case and read what was inside and I did, finding an official envelope stamped with the state seal; and inside the envelope I found another and another, endlessly, and I thought I would fall of weariness. "Them's years," he said. "Now open that one." And I did and in it I found an engraved document containing a short message in letters of gold. "Read it," my grandfather said. "Out loud!"

"To Whom It May Concern," I intoned. "Keep This Nigger-Boy Running."

I awoke with the old man's laughter ringing in my ears.

(It was a dream I was to remember and dream again for many years after. But at that time I had no insight into its meaning. First I had to attend college.)

CD-ROM: Research Ralph Ellison in depth with cultural documents and multimedia resources on *LiterActive*.

Diane Glancy b. 1941

Aunt Parnetta's Electric Blisters   [1990]

Some stories can be told only in the winter.
This is not one of them
because the fridge is for Parnetta
where it's always winter.

1.

Hey chekta! All this and now the refrigerator broke. Uncle Filo scratched the long gray hairs that hung in a tattered braid on his back. All that foot stomping and fancy dancing. Old warriors still at it. But when did it help? Aunt Parnetta asked. The fridge ran all through the cold winter when she could have set the milk and eggs in the snow. The fish and meat from the last hunt. The fridge had walked through the spring when she had her quilt and beading money. Now her pennyjar was empty and it was hot and the glossy white box broke. The coffin! If grandpa died, they could put him in it with his war ax and tomahawk. His old dog even. But how would she get a new fridge?

The repairman said he couldn't repair it. Whee choo tun. Filo loaded his shotgun and sent a bullet right through it. Well, he said, a man had to take revenge. Had to stand against civilization. He watched the summer sky for change as though the stars were white leaves across the hill. Would the stars fall? Would Filo have to rake them when cool weather came again? Filo coughed and scratched his shirt pocket as though something crawled deep within his breastbone. His heart maybe, if he ever found it.

Aunt Parnetta stood at the sink, soaking the sheets before she washed them.

"Dern't nothin' we dud ever werk?" Parnetta asked, poling the sheets with her stick.

"We bought that ferge back twenty yars," Filo told her. "And it nerked since then."

"Weld, derned," she answered. "Could have goned longer til the frost cobered us. Culb ha' set the milk ertside. But nowd. It weren't werk that far."

"Nope," Filo commented. "It weren't."

Parnetta looked at her beadwork. Her hands flopped at her sides. She couldn't have it done for a long time. She looked at the white patent-leathery box. Big enough for the both of them. For the cow if it died.

"Set it out in the backyard with the last one we had."

They drove to Tahlequah that afternoon, Filo's truck squirting dust and pinging rocks.

They parked in front of the hardware store on Muskogee Street. The regiments of stoves, fridges, washers, dryers, stood like white soldiers. The Yellow Hair Custer was there to command them. Little Big Horn. Whu chutah! The prices! Three hundred crackers.

"Some mord than thad," Filo surmised, his flannel shirt-collar tucked under itself, his braid sideways like a rattler on his back.

"Filo, I dern't think we shulb decide terday."

"No," the immediate answer stummed from his mouth like a roach from under the baseboard in the kitchen.

"We're just lookin'."

"Of course," said Custer.

They walked to the door leaving the stoves, washers, dryers, the televisions all blaring together, and the fridges lined up for battle.

Filo lifted his hand from the rattled truck.

"Surrender," Parnetta said. "Izend thad the way id always iz?"

The truck spurted and spattered and shook Filo and Aunt Parnetta before Filo got it backed into the street. The forward gear didn't buck as much as the backward.

When they got home, Filo took the back off the fridge and looked at the motor. It could move a load of hay up the road if it had wheels. Could freeze half the fish in the pond. The minute coils, the twisting intestines of the fridge like the hog he butchered last winter, also with a bullet hole in its head.

"Nothin' we dude nerks." Parnetta watched him from the kitchen window. "Everythin' against uz," she grumbled to herself.

Filo got his war feather from the shed, put it in his crooked braid. He stomped his feet, hooted. Filo, the medicine man, transcended to the spirit world for the refrigerator. He shook each kink and bolt. The spirit of cold itself. He whooped and warred in the yard for nearly half an hour.

"Not with a bullet hole in it," Parnetta shook her head and wiped the sweat from her face.

He got his wrench and hack saw, the axe and hammer. It was dead now for sure. Parnetta knew it at the sink. It was the thing that would be buried in the backyard. "Like most of us libed," Aunt Parnetta talked to herself. "Filled with our own workings, not doint what we shulb."

Parnetta hung the sheets in the yard, white and square as the fridge itself.

2.

The new refrigerator came in a delivery truck. It stood in the kitchen. Bought on time at a bargain. Cheapest in the store. Filo made sure of it. The interest over five years would be as much as the fridge. Aunt Parnetta tried to explain it to him. The men set the fridge where Parnetta instructed them. They adjusted and leveled the little hog feet. They gave Parnetta the packet of information, the guarantee. Then drove off in victory. The new smell of the gleaming white inside as though cleansed by cedar from the Keetowah fire.

Aunt Parnetta had Filo take her to the grocery store on the old road to Tahlequah. She loaded the cart with milk and butter. Frozen waffles. Orange juice. Anything that had to be kept cool. The fridge made noise, she thought, she would get used to it. But in the night, she heard the fridge. It seemed to fill her dreams. She had trouble going to sleep, even on the clean white sheets, and she had trouble staying asleep. The fridge was like a giant hog in the kitchen. Rutting and snorting all night. She got up once and unplugged it. Waking early the next morning to plug it in again before the milk and eggs got warm.

"That ferge bother yeu, Filo?" she asked.

"Nord."

Aunt Parnetta peeled her potatoes outside. She mended Filo's shirts under the shade tree. She didn't soak anything in the kitchen sink anymore, not even the sheets or Filo's socks. There just were things she had to endure, she grumped. That's the way it was.

When the grandchildren visited, she had them run in the kitchen for whatever she needed. They picnicked on the old watermelon table in the backyard. She put up the old teepee for them to sleep in.

"Late in the summer fer that?" Filo quizzed her.

"Nert. It waz nert to get homesick for the summer that's leabing us like the childurn." She gratified him with her keen sense. Parnetta could think up anything for what she wanted to do.

Several nights Filo returned to their bed with its geese-in-flight-over-the-swamp pattern quilt, but Aunt Parnetta stayed in the teepee under the stars.

"We bined muried thurdy yars. Git in the house," Filo said one night under the white leaves of the stars.

"I can't sleep cause of that wild hog in the kitchen," Aunt Parnetta said. "I tald yeu that."

"Hey chekta!" Filo answered her. "Why didn't yeu tell me so I knowd whad yeu said." Filo covered the white box of the fridge with the geese quilt and an old Indian blanket he got from the shed. "Werd yeu stayed out thar all winder?"

"Til the beast we got in thar dies."

"Hawly gizard," Filo spurted. "Thard be anuther twendy yars!"

Aunt Parnetta was comforted by the bedroom that night. Old Filo's snore after he made his snorting love to her. The gray and blue striped wallpaper with its watermarks. The stove pipe curling up to the wall like a hog tail. The bureau dresser with a little doily and her hairbrush. Pictures by their grandchildren. A turquoise coyote and a ghostly figure the boy told her was Running Wind.

She fell into a light sleep where the white stars blew down from the sky, flapping like the white sheets on the line. She nudged Filo to get his rake. He turned sharply against her. Parnetta woke and sat on the edge of the bed.

"Yeu wand me to cuber the furge wid something else?" Filo asked from his sleep.

"No," Aunt Parnetta answered him. "Nod unless id be the polar ice cap."

3.

Now it was an old trip to Minnesota when she was a girl. Parnetta saw herself in a plaid shirt and braids. Had her hair been that dark? Now it was streaked with gray. Everything was like a child's drawing. Exaggerated. The way dreams were sometimes. A sun in the left corner of the picture. The trail of chimney smoke from the narrow house. It was cold. So cold that everything creaked. She heard cars running late into the night. Early mornings, steam growled out of the exhaust. The pane of window-glass in the front door had been somewhere else. Old lettering showed up in the frost. Bones remembered their aches in the cold. Teeth, their hurt. The way Parnetta remembered every bad thing that happened. She dwelled on it.

The cold place was shriveled to the small upright rectangle in her chest, holding the fish her grandson caught in the river. That's where the cold place was. Right inside her heart. No longer pumping like the blinker lights she saw in town. She was the Minnesota winter she remembered as a child. The electricity it took to keep her cold! The energy. The moon over her like a ceiling light. Stars were holes where the rain came in. The dripping buckets. All of them like Parnetta. The hurrrrrrrrrr of the fridge. Off. On. All night. That white box. Wild boar! Think of it. She didn't always know why she was disgruntled. She just was. She saw herself as the fridge. A frozen fish stiff as a brick. The Great Spirit had her pegged. Could she find her heart, maybe, if she looked somewhere in her chest?

Hurrrrrrrr. Rat-tat-at-rat. Hurrr. The fridge came on again, and startled, she woke and teetered slightly on the edge of the bed while it growled.

But she was a stranger in this world. An Indian in a white man's land. "Even the furge's whate," Parnetta told the Great Spirit.

"Wasn't everybody a stranger and pilgrim?" The Great Spirit seemed to speak to her, or it was her own thoughts wandering in her head.

"No," Parnetta insisted. Some people were at home on this earth, moving with ease. She would ask the Great Spirit more about it later. When he finally yanked the life out of her like the pin in a grenade.

Suddenly Parnetta realized that she was always moaning like the fridge. Maybe she irritated the Great Spirit like the white box irritated her. Did she sound that way to anyone else? Was that the Spirit's revenge? She was stuck with the cheapest box in the store. In fact, in her fears, wasn't it a white boar that would tear into the room and eat her soon as she got good and asleep?

Hadn't she seen the worst in things? Didn't she weigh herself in the winter with her coat on? Sometimes wrapped in the blanket also?

"Filo?" She turned to him. But he was out cold. Farther away than Minnesota.

"No. Just think about it, Parnetta," her thoughts seemed to say. The Spirit had blessed her life. But inside the white refrigerator of herself — inside the coils, an ice river surged. A glacier mowed its way across a continent. Everything frozen for eons. In need of a Keetowah fire. Heat. The warmth of the Great Spirit. Filo was only a spark. He could not warm her. Even though he tried.

Maybe the Great Spirit had done her a favor. Hope like white sparks of stars glistened in her head. The electric blisters. TEMPORARY! She could shut up. She belonged to the Spirit. He had just unplugged her a minute. Took his shotgun right through her head.

The leaves growled and spewed white sparks in the sky. It was a volcano from the moon. Erupting in the heavens. Sending down its white sparklers like the pinwheels Filo used to nail on trees. It was the bright sparks of the Keetowah fire, the holy bonfire from which smaller fires burned, spreading the purification of the Great Spirit into each house. Into each hard, old pinecone heart.

Nathaniel Hawthorne 1804–1864
Young Goodman Brown   [1835]

Young Goodman° Brown came forth, at sunset, into the street of Salem village,° but put his head back, after crossing the threshold, to exchange a parting kiss with his young wife. And Faith, as the wife was aptly named, thrust her own pretty head into the street, letting the wind play with the pink ribbons of her cap, while she called to Goodman Brown.

"Dearest heart," whispered she, softly and rather sadly, when her lips were close to his ear, "pr'y thee, put off your journey until sunrise, and sleep in your own bed to-night. A lone woman is troubled with such dreams and such thoughts, that she's afeard of herself, sometimes. Pray, tarry with me this night, dear husband, of all nights in the year!"

Goodman: A man of ordinary status who was head of a household.   **Salem village:** Village in the Massachusetts Bay Colony.

"My love and my Faith," replied young Goodman Brown, "of all nights in the year, this one night must I tarry away from thee. My journey, as thou callest it, forth and back again, must needs be done 'twixt now and sunrise. What, my sweet, pretty wife, dost thou doubt me already, and we but three months married!"

"Then, God bless you!" said Faith, with the pink ribbons, "and may you find all well when you come back."

"Amen!" cried Goodman Brown. "Say thy prayers, dear Faith, and go to bed at dusk, and no harm will come to thee."

So they parted; and the young man pursued his way, until, being about to turn the corner by the meeting-house, he looked back, and saw the head of Faith still peeping after him, with a melancholy air, in spite of her pink ribbons.

"Poor little Faith!" thought he, for his heart smote him. "What a wretch am I, to leave her on such an errand! She talks of dreams, too. Methought, as she spoke, there was trouble in her face, as if a dream had warned her what work is to be done to-night. But, no, no! 'twould kill her to think it. Well; she's a blessed angel on earth; and after this one night, I'll cling to her skirts and follow her to Heaven."

With this excellent resolve for the future, Goodman Brown felt himself justified in making more haste on his present evil purpose. He had taken a dreary road, darkened by all the gloomiest trees of the forest, which barely stood aside to let the narrow path creep through, and closed immediately behind. It was all as lonely as could be; and there is this peculiarity in such a solitude, that the traveller knows not who may be concealed by the innumerable trunks and the thick boughs overhead; so that, with lonely footsteps, he may yet be passing through an unseen multitude.

"There may be a devilish Indian behind every tree," said Goodman Brown, to himself; and he glanced fearfully behind him, as he added, "What if the devil himself should be at my very elbow!"

His head being turned back, he passed a crook of the road, and looking forward again, beheld the figure of a man, in grave and decent attire, seated at the foot of an old tree. He arose, at Goodman Brown's approach, and walked onward, side by side with him.

"You are late, Goodman Brown," said he. "The clock of the Old South was striking as I came through Boston; and that is full fifteen minutes agone."°

"Faith kept me back awhile," replied the young man, with a tremor in his voice, caused by the sudden appearance of his companion, though not wholly unexpected.

It was now deep dusk in the forest, and deepest in that part of it where these two were journeying. As nearly as could be discerned, the second

---

full fifteen minutes agone: This mysterious figure apparently traveled the sixteen miles from Old South Church in Boston to woods outside Salem in a quarter of an hour.

traveller was about fifty years old, apparently in the same rank of life as Goodman Brown, and bearing a considerable resemblance to him, though perhaps more in expression than features. Still, they might have been taken for father and son. And yet, though the elder person was as simply clad as the younger, and as simple in manner too, he had an indescribable air of one who knew the world, and would not have felt abashed at the governor's dinnertable, or in King William's court,° were it possible that his affairs should call him thither. But the only thing about him, that could be fixed upon as remarkable, was his staff, which bore the likeness of a great black snake, so curiously wrought, that it might almost be seen to twist and wriggle itself, like a living serpent. This, of course, must have been an ocular deception, assisted by the uncertain light.

"Come, Goodman Brown!" cried his fellow-traveller, "this is a dull pace for the beginning of a journey. Take my staff, if you are so soon weary."

"Friend," said the other, exchanging his slow pace for a full stop, "having kept covenant by meeting thee here, it is my purpose now to return whence I came. I have scruples, touching the matter thou wot'st° of."

"Sayest thou so?" replied he of the serpent, smiling apart. "Let us walk on, nevertheless, reasoning as we go, and if I convince thee not, thou shalt turn back. We are but a little way in the forest, yet."

"Too far, too far!" exclaimed the goodman, unconsciously resuming his walk. "My father never went into the woods on such an errand, nor his father before him. We have been a race of honest men and good Christians, since the days of the martyrs.° And shall I be the first of the name of Brown, that ever took this path, and kept—"

"Such company, thou wouldst say," observed the elder person, interpreting his pause. "Well said, Goodman Brown! I have been as well acquainted with your family as with ever a one among the Puritans; and that's no trifle to say. I helped your grandfather, the constable, when he lashed the Quaker woman so smartly through the streets of Salem. And it was I that brought your father a pitch-pine knot, kindled at my own hearth, to set fire to an Indian village, in King Philip's war.° They were my good friends, both; and many a pleasant walk have we had along this path, and returned merrily after midnight. I would fain be friends with you, for their sake."

"If it be as thou sayest," replied Goodman Brown, "I marvel they never spoke of these matters. Or, verily, I marvel not, seeing that the least rumor of the sort would have driven them from New-England. We are a people of prayer, and good works, to boot, and abide no such wickedness."

King William's court: William III was king of England from 1689 to 1702, ruling jointly with his wife Mary II until her death in 1694. wot'st: Know. days of the martyrs: Period in England during the rule of a Catholic monarch, Mary I (1553–1558), when Protestants were persecuted and many ancestors of the New England Pilgrims lost their lives for their religious faith. King Philip's war: A bitter conflict (1675–1676) between the colonists and several New England tribes led by Metacomet, chief of the Wampanoag Indians, who was called King Philip by the colonists.

"Wickedness or not," said the traveller with the twisted staff, "I have a very general acquaintance here in New-England. The deacons of many a church have drunk the communion wine with me; the selectmen, of divers towns, make me their chairman; and a majority of the Great and General Court° are firm supporters of my interest. The governor and I, too—but these are state-secrets."

"Can this be so!" cried Goodman Brown, with a stare of amazement at his undisturbed companion. "Howbeit, I have nothing to do with the governor and council; they have their own ways, and are no rule for a simple husbandman,° like me. But, were I to go on with thee, how should I meet the eye of that good old man, our minister, at Salem village? Oh, his voice would make me tremble, both Sabbath-day and lecture-day!"°

Thus far, the elder traveller had listened with due gravity, but now burst into a fit of irrepressible mirth, shaking himself so violently, that his snake-like staff actually seemed to wriggle in sympathy.

"Ha! ha! ha!" shouted he, again and again; then composing himself, "Well, go on, Goodman Brown, go on; but pr'y thee, don't kill me with laughing!"

"Well, then, to end the matter at once," said Goodman Brown, considerably nettled, "there is my wife, Faith. It would break her dear little heart; and I'd rather break my own!"

"Nay, if that be the case," answered the other, "e'en go thy ways, Goodman Brown. I would not, for twenty old women like the one hobbling before us, that Faith should come to any harm."

As he spoke, he pointed his staff at a female figure on the path, in whom Goodman Brown recognized a very pious and exemplary dame, who had taught him his catechism, in youth, and was still his moral and spiritual adviser, jointly with the minister and Deacon Gookin.

"A marvel, truly, that Goody° Cloyse should be so far in the wilderness, at night-fall!" said he. "But, with your leave, friend, I shall take a cut through the woods, until we have left this Christian woman behind. Being a stranger to you, she might ask whom I was consorting with, and whither I was going."

"Be it so," said his fellow-traveller. "Betake you to the woods, and let me keep the path."

Accordingly, the young man turned aside, but took care to watch his companion, who advanced softly along the road, until he had come within a staff's length of the old dame. She, meanwhile, was making the best of her way, with singular speed for so aged a woman, and mumbling some indistinct words, a prayer, doubtless, as she went. The traveller put forth

---

Great and General Court: Colonial legislature. husbandman: Farmer. lecture-day: A weekday church service with a sermon. Goody: Short for Goodwife, a married woman of ordinary status (cf. "goodman"). Goody Cloyse and Goody Cory, along with Martha Carrier, were sentenced to death at the Salem witchcraft trials of 1692, at which Hawthorne's great-grandfather was a judge.

his staff, and touched her withered neck with what seemed the serpent's tail.

"The devil!" screamed the pious old lady.

"Then Goody Cloyse knows her old friend?" observed the traveller, confronting her, and leaning on his writhing stick.

"Ah, forsooth, and is it your worship, indeed?" cried the good dame. "Yea, truly is it, and in the very image of my old gossip,° Goodman Brown, the grandfather of the silly fellow that now is. But — would your worship believe it? — my broomstick hath strangely disappeared, stolen, as I suspect, by that unhanged witch, Goody Cory, and that, too, when I was all anointed with the juice of smallage and cinque-foil and wolf's-bane —"°

"Mingled with fine wheat and the fat of a new-born babe," said the shape of old Goodman Brown.

"Ah, your worship knows the receipt," cried the old lady, cackling aloud. "So, as I was saying, being all ready for the meeting, and no horse to ride on, I made up my mind to foot it; for they tell me, there is a nice young man to be taken into communion to-night. But now your good worship will lend me your arm, and we shall be there in a twinkling."

"That can hardly be," answered her friend. "I may not spare you my arm, Goody Cloyse, but here is my staff, if you will."

So saying, he threw it down at her feet, where, perhaps, it assumed life, being one of the rods which its owner had formerly lent to the Egyptian Magi.° Of this fact, however, Goodman Brown could not take cognizance. He had cast up his eyes in astonishment, and looking down again, beheld neither Goody Cloyse nor the serpentine staff, but his fellow-traveller alone, who waited for him as calmly as if nothing had happened.

"That old woman taught me my catechism!" said the young man; and there was a world of meaning in this simple comment.

They continued to walk onward, while the elder traveller exhorted his companion to make good speed and persevere in the path, discoursing so aptly, that his arguments seemed rather to spring up in the bosom of his auditor, than to be suggested by himself. As they went, he plucked a branch of maple, to serve for a walking-stick, and began to strip it of the twigs and little boughs, which were wet with evening dew. The moment his fingers touched them, they became strangely withered and dried up, as with a week's sunshine. Thus the pair proceeded, at a good free pace, until suddenly, in a gloomy hollow of the road, Goodman Brown sat himself down on the stump of a tree, and refused to go any farther.

"Friend," said he, stubbornly, "my mind is made up. Not another step will I budge on this errand. What if a wretched old woman do choose to go

---

gossip: Godfather or godmother, sponsor at a baptism. smallage . . . bane: "Smallage" is wild celery or water parsley; "cinque-foil" is a type of rose; "wolf's-bane" is aconite or monkshood. All are ingredients in a witch's brew. Egyptian Magi: Egyptian magicians who were able, like Aaron in the biblical account, to turn rods into serpents. See Exodus 7:11–12.

to the devil, when I thought she was going to Heaven! Is that any reason why I should quit my dear Faith, and go after her?"

"You will think better of this, by-and-by," said his acquaintance, composedly. "Sit here and rest yourself awhile; and when you feel like moving again, there is my staff to help you along."

Without more words, he threw his companion the maple stick, and was as speedily out of sight, as if he had vanished into the deepening gloom. The young man sat a few moments, by the road-side, applauding himself greatly, and thinking with how clear a conscience he should meet the minister, in his morning-walk, nor shrink from the eye of good old Deacon Gookin. And what calm sleep would be his, that very night, which was to have been spent so wickedly, but purely and sweetly now, in the arms of Faith! Amidst these pleasant and praiseworthy meditations, Goodman Brown heard the tramp of horses along the road, and deemed it advisable to conceal himself within the verge of the forest, conscious of the guilty purpose that had brought him thither, though now so happily turned from it.

On came the hoof-tramps and the voices of the riders, two grave old voices, conversing soberly as they drew near. These mingled sounds appeared to pass along the road, within a few yards of the young man's hiding-place; but owing, doubtless, to the depth of the gloom, at that particular spot, neither the travellers nor their steeds were visible. Though their figures brushed the small boughs by the way-side, it could not be seen that they intercepted, even for a moment, the faint gleam from the strip of bright sky, athwart which they must have passed. Goodman Brown alternately crouched and stood on tip-toe, pulling aside the branches, and thrusting forth his head as far as he durst, without discerning so much as a shadow. It vexed him the more, because he could have sworn, were such a thing possible, that he recognized the voices of the minister and Deacon Gookin, jogging along quietly, as they were wont to do, when bound to some ordination or ecclesiastical council. While yet within hearing, one of the riders stopped to pluck a switch.

"Of the two, reverend Sir," said the voice like the deacon's, "I had rather miss an ordination-dinner than to-night's meeting. They tell me that some of our community are to be here from Falmouth and beyond, and others from Connecticut and Rhode-Island; besides several of the Indian powows,° who, after their fashion, know almost as much deviltry as the best of us. Moreover, there is a goodly young woman to be taken into communion."

"Mighty well, Deacon Gookin!" replied the solemn old tones of the minister. "Spur up, or we shall be late. Nothing can be done, you know, until I get on the ground."

The hoofs clattered again, and the voices, talking so strangely in the empty air, passed on through the forest, where no church had ever been gathered, nor solitary Christian prayed. Whither, then, could these holy

---

powows: Medicine men.

men be journeying, so deep into the heathen wilderness? Young Goodman Brown caught hold of a tree, for support, being ready to sink down on the ground, faint and overburthened with the heavy sickness of his heart. He looked up to the sky, doubting whether there really was a Heaven above him. Yet, there was the blue arch, and the stars brightening in it.

"With Heaven above, and Faith below, I will yet stand firm against the devil!" cried Goodman Brown.

While he still gazed upward, into the deep arch of the firmament, and had lifted his hands to pray, a cloud, though no wind was stirring, hurried across the zenith, and hid the brightening stars. The blue sky was still visible, except directly overhead, where this black mass of cloud was sweeping swiftly northward. Aloft in the air, as if from the depths of the cloud, came a confused and doubtful sound of voices. Once, the listener fancied that he could distinguish the accents of town's-people of his own, men and women, both pious and ungodly, many of whom he had met at the communion-table, and had seen others rioting at the tavern. The next moment, so indistinct were the sounds, he doubted whether he had heard aught but the murmur of the old forest, whispering without a wind. Then came a stronger swell of those familiar tones, heard daily in the sunshine, at Salem village, but never, until now, from a cloud of night. There was one voice, of a young woman, uttering lamentations, yet with an uncertain sorrow, and entreating for some favor, which, perhaps, it would grieve her to obtain. And all the unseen multitude, both saints and sinners, seemed to encourage her onward.

"Faith!" shouted Goodman Brown, in a voice of agony and desperation; and the echoes of the forest mocked him, crying—"Faith! Faith!" as if bewildered wretches were seeking her, all through the wilderness.

The cry of grief, rage, and terror, was yet piercing the night, when the unhappy husband held his breath for a response. There was a scream, drowned immediately in a louder murmur of voices, fading into far-off laughter, as the dark cloud swept away, leaving the clear and silent sky above Goodman Brown. But something fluttered lightly down through the air, and caught on the branch of a tree. The young man seized it, and beheld a pink ribbon.

"My Faith is gone!" cried he, after one stupefied moment. "There is no good on earth; and sin is but a name. Come, devil! for to thee is this world given."

And maddened with despair, so that he laughed loud and long, did Goodman Brown grasp his staff and set forth again, at such a rate, that he seemed to fly along the forest-path, rather than to walk or run. The road grew wilder and drearier, and more faintly traced, and vanished at length, leaving him in the heart of the dark wilderness, still rushing onward, with the instinct that guides mortal man to evil. The whole forest was peopled with frightful sounds; the creaking of the trees, the howling of wild beasts, and the yell of Indians; while, sometimes, the wind tolled like a distant church-bell, and sometimes gave a broad roar around the traveller, as if all

Nature were laughing him to scorn. But he was himself the chief horror of the scene, and shrank not from its other horrors.

"Ha! ha! ha!" roared Goodman Brown, when the wind laughed at him. "Let us hear which will laugh loudest! Think not to frighten me with your deviltry! Come witch, come wizard, come Indian powow, come devil himself! and here comes Goodman Brown. You may as well fear him as he fear you!"

In truth, all through the haunted forest, there could be nothing more frightful than the figure of Goodman Brown. On he flew, among the black pines, brandishing his staff with frenzied gestures, now giving vent to an inspiration of horrid blasphemy, and now shouting forth such laughter, as set all the echoes of the forest laughing like demons around him. The fiend in his own shape is less hideous, than when he rages in the breast of man. Thus sped the demoniac on his course, until, quivering among the trees, he saw a red light before him, as when the felled trunks and branches of a clearing have been set on fire, and throw up their lurid blaze against the sky, at the hour of midnight. He paused, in a lull of the tempest that had driven him onward, and heard the swell of what seemed a hymn, rolling solemnly from a distance, with the weight of many voices. He knew the tune; it was a familiar one in the choir of the village meetinghouse. The verse died heavily away, and was lengthened by a chorus, not of human voices, but of all the sounds of the benighted wilderness, pealing in awful harmony together. Goodman Brown cried out; and his cry was lost to his own ear, by its unison with the cry of the desert.

In the interval of silence, he stole forward, until the light glared full upon his eyes. At one extremity of an open space, hemmed in by the dark wall of the forest, arose a rock, bearing some rude, natural resemblance either to an altar or a pulpit, and surrounded by four blazing pines, their tops aflame, their stems untouched, like candles at an evening meeting. The mass of foliage, that had overgrown the summit of the rock, was all on fire, blazing high into the night, and fitfully illuminating the whole field. Each pendent twig and leafy festoon was in a blaze. As the red light arose and fell, a numerous congregation alternately shone forth, then disappeared in shadow, and again grew, as it were, out of the darkness, peopling the heart of the solitary woods at once.

"A grave and dark-clad company!" quoth Goodman Brown.

In truth, they were such. Among them, quivering to-and-fro, between gloom and splendor, appeared faces that would be seen, next day, at the council-board of the province, and others which, Sabbath after Sabbath, looked devoutly heavenward, and benignantly over the crowded pews, from the holiest pulpits in the land. Some affirm, that the lady of the governor was there. At least, there were high dames well known to her, and wives of honored husbands, and widows, a great multitude, and ancient maidens, all of excellent repute, and fair young girls, who trembled, lest their mothers should espy them. Either the sudden gleams of light, flashing over the obscure field, bedazzled Goodman Brown, or he recognized a score of the church-members of Salem village, famous for their especial sanctity. Good old Deacon Gookin had arrived, and waited at the skirts of that venerable saint, his revered pastor. But, irreverently consorting with these grave, reputable, and pious people, these elders of the church, these chaste dames and dewy virgins, there were men of dissolute lives and women of spotted fame, wretches given over to all mean and filthy vice, and suspected even of horrid crimes. It was strange to see, that the good shrank not from the wicked, nor were the sinners abashed by the saints. Scattered, also, among their pale-faced enemies, were the Indian priests, or powows, who had often scared their native forest with more hideous incantations than any known to English witchcraft.

"But, where is Faith?" thought Goodman Brown; and, as hope came into his heart, he trembled.

Another verse of the hymn arose, a slow and mournful strain, such as the pious love, but joined to words which expressed all that our nature can conceive of sin, and darkly hinted at far more. Unfathomable to mere mortals is the lore of fiends. Verse after verse was sung, and still the chorus of the desert swelled between, like the deepest tone of a mighty organ. And, with the final peal of that dreadful anthem, there came a sound, as if the roaring wind, the rushing streams, the howling beasts, and every other voice of the unconverted wilderness, were mingling and according with the voice of guilty man, in homage to the prince of all. The four blazing pines threw up a loftier flame, and obscurely discovered shapes and visages of horror on the smoke-wreaths, above the impious assembly. At the same moment, the fire on the rock shot redly forth, and formed a glowing arch above its base, where now appeared a figure. With reverence be it spoken, the figure bore no slight similitude, both in garb and manner, to some grave divine of the New-England churches.

"Bring forth the converts!" cried a voice, that echoed through the field and rolled into the forest.

At the word, Goodman Brown stept forth from the shadow of the trees, and approached the congregation, with whom he felt a loathful brotherhood, by the sympathy of all that was wicked in his heart. He could have well nigh sworn, that the shape of his own dead father beckoned him to advance, looking downward from a smoke-wreath, while a woman, with dim features of despair, threw out her hand to warn him back. Was it his mother? But he had no power to retreat one step, nor to resist, even in thought, when the minister and good old Deacon Gookin seized his arms, and led him to the blazing rock. Thither came also the slender form of a veiled female, led between Goody Cloyse, that pious teacher of the catechism, and Martha Carrier, who had received the devil's promise to be queen of hell. A rampant hag was she! And there stood the proselytes, beneath the canopy of fire.

"Welcome, my children," said the dark figure, "to the communion of your race! Ye have found, thus young, your nature and your destiny. My children, look behind you!"

They turned; and flashing forth, as it were, in a sheet of flame, the fiend-worshippers were seen; the smile of welcome gleamed darkly on every visage.

"There," resumed the sable form, "are all whom ye have reverenced from youth. Ye deemed them holier than yourselves, and shrank from your own sin, contrasting it with their lives of righteousness, and prayerful aspirations heavenward. Yet, here are they all, in my worshipping assembly! This night it shall be granted you to know their secret deeds; how hoary-bearded elders of the church have whispered wanton words to the young maids of their households; how many a woman, eager for widow's weeds, has given her husband a drink at bed-time, and let him sleep his last sleep in her bosom; how beardless youths have made haste to inherit their fathers' wealth; and how fair damsels — blush not, sweet ones! — have dug little graves in the garden, and bidden me, the sole guest, to an infant's funeral. By the sympathy of your human hearts for sin, ye shall scent out all the places — whether in church, bed-chamber, street, field, or forest — where crime has been committed, and shall exult to behold the whole earth one stain of guilt, one mighty bloodspot. Far more than this! It shall be yours to penetrate, in every bosom, the deep mystery of sin, the fountain of all wicked arts, and which inexhaustibly supplies more evil impulses than human power — than my power, at its utmost! — can make manifest in deeds. And now, my children, look upon each other."

They did so; and, by the blaze of the hell-kindled torches, the wretched man beheld his Faith, and the wife her husband, trembling before that unhallowed altar.

"Lo! there ye stand, my children," said the figure, in a deep and solemn tone, almost sad, with its despairing awfulness, as if his once angelic nature could yet mourn for our miserable race. "Depending upon one another's hearts, ye had still hoped, that virtue were not all a dream. Now are ye undeceived! Evil is the nature of mankind. Evil must be your only happiness. Welcome, again, my children, to the communion of your race!"

"Welcome!" repeated the fiend-worshippers, in one cry of despair and triumph.

And there they stood, the only pair, as it seemed, who were yet hesitating on the verge of wickedness, in this dark world. A basin was hollowed, naturally, in the rock. Did it contain water, reddened by the lurid light? or was it blood? or, perchance, a liquid flame? Herein did the Shape of Evil dip his hand, and prepare to lay the mark of baptism upon their foreheads, that they might be partakers of the mystery of sin, more conscious of the secret guilt of others, both in deed and thought, than they could now be of their own. The husband cast one look at his pale wife, and Faith at him. What polluted wretches would the next glance shew them to each other, shuddering alike at what they disclosed and what they saw!

"Faith! Faith!" cried the husband. "Look up to Heaven, and resist the Wicked One!"

Whether Faith obeyed, he knew not. Hardly had he spoken, when he found himself amid calm night and solitude, listening to a roar of the wind, which died heavily away through the forest. He staggered against the rock and felt it chill and damp, while a hanging twig, that had been all on fire, besprinkled his cheek with the coldest dew.

The next morning, young Goodman Brown came slowly into the street of Salem village, staring around him like a bewildered man. The good old minister was taking a walk along the grave-yard, to get an appetite for breakfast and meditate his sermon, and bestowed a blessing, as he passed, on Goodman Brown. He shrank from the venerable saint, as if to avoid an anathema.° Old Deacon Gookin was at domestic worship, and the holy words of his prayer were heard through the open window. "What God doth the wizard pray to?" quoth Goodman Brown. Goody Cloyse, that excellent old Christian, stood in the early sunshine, at her own lattice, catechising a little girl, who had brought her a pint of morning's milk. Goodman Brown snatched away the child, as from the grasp of the fiend himself. Turning the corner by the meeting-house, he spied the head of Faith, with the pink ribbons, gazing anxiously forth, and bursting into such joy at sight of him, that she skipt along the street, and almost kissed her husband before the whole village. But, Goodman Brown looked sternly and sadly into her face, and passed on without a greeting.

Had Goodman Brown fallen asleep in the forest, and only dreamed a wild dream of a witch-meeting?

Be it so, if you will. But, alas! it was a dream of evil omen for young Goodman Brown. A stern, a sad, a darkly meditative, a distrustful, if not a desperate man, did he become, from the night of that fearful dream. On the Sabbath-day, when the congregation were singing a holy psalm, he could not listen, because an anthem of sin rushed loudly upon his ear, and drowned all the blessed strain. When the minister spoke from the pulpit, with power and fervid eloquence, and, with his hand on the open Bible, of the sacred truths of our religion, and of saint-like lives and triumphant deaths, and of future bliss or misery unutterable, then did Goodman Brown turn pale, dreading, lest the roof should thunder down upon the gray blasphemer and his hearers. Often, awakening suddenly at midnight, he shrank from the bosom of Faith, and at morning or eventide, when the family knelt down at prayer, he scowled, and muttered to himself, and gazed sternly at his wife, and turned away. And when he had lived long, and was borne to his grave, a hoary corpse, followed by Faith, an aged woman, and children and grandchildren, a goodly procession, besides neighbors, not a few, they carved no hopeful verse upon his tomb-stone; for his dying hour was gloom.

---

anathema: A thing accursed or consigned to damnation by an official decree of the church.

WEB: Explore Nathaniel Hawthorne and "Young Goodman Brown" in depth, including images and cultural documents, with VirtuaLit Fiction at bedfordstmartins.com/approachinglit.

Zora Neale Hurston   1891–1960

Sweat   [1926]

It was eleven o'clock of a Spring night in Florida. It was Sunday. Any other night, Delia Jones would have been in bed for two hours by this time. But she was a washwoman, and Monday morning meant a great deal to her. So she collected the soiled clothes on Saturday when she returned the clean things. Sunday night after church, she sorted them and put the white things to soak. It saved her almost a half day's start. A great hamper in the bedroom held the clothes that she brought home. It was so much neater than a number of bundles lying around.

She squatted on the kitchen floor beside the great pile of clothes, sorting them into small heaps according to color, and humming a song in a mournful key, but wondering through it all where Sykes, her husband, had gone with her horse and buckboard.

Just then something long, round, limp and black fell upon her shoulders and slithered to the floor beside her. A great terror took hold of her. It softened her knees and dried her mouth so that it was a full minute before she could cry out or move. Then she saw that it was the big bull whip her husband liked to carry when he drove.

She lifted her eyes to the door and saw him standing there bent over with laughter at her fright. She screamed at him.

"Sykes, what you throw dat whip on me like dat? You know it would skeer me — looks just like a snake, an' you knows how skeered Ah is of snakes."

"Course Ah knowed it! That's how come Ah done it." He slapped his leg with his hand and almost rolled on the ground in his mirth. "If you such a big fool dat you got to have a fit over a earth worm or a string, Ah don't keer how bad Ah skeer you."

"You aint got no business doing it. Gawd knows it's a sin. Some day Ah'm gointuh drop dead from some of yo' foolishness. 'Nother thing, where you been wid mah rig? Ah feeds dat pony. He aint fuh you to be drivin' wid no bull whip."

"You sho is one aggravatin' nigger woman!" he declared and stepped into the room. She resumed her work and did not answer him at once. "Ah done tole you time and again to keep them white folks' clothes outa dis house."

He picked up the whip and glared down at her. Delia went on with her work. She went out into the yard and returned with a galvanized tub and sat it on the washbench. She saw that Sykes had kicked all of the clothes together again, and now stood in her way truculently, his whole manner hoping, *praying,* for an argument. But she walked calmly around him and commenced to re-sort the things.

"Next time, Ah'm gointer kick 'em outdoors," he threatened as he struck a match along the leg of his corduroy breeches.

Delia never looked up from her work, and her thin, stooped shoulders sagged further.

"Ah aint for no fuss t'night, Sykes. Ah just come from taking sacrament at the church house."

He snorted scornfully. "Yeah, you just come from de church house on a Sunday night, but heah you is gone to work on them clothes. You ain't nothing but a hypocrite. One of them amen-corner Christians—sing, whoop, and shout, then come home and wash white folks clothes on the Sabbath."

He stepped roughly upon the whitest pile of things, kicking them helter-skelter as he crossed the room. His wife gave a little scream of dismay, and quickly gathered them together again.

"Sykes, you quit grindin' dirt into these clothes! How can Ah git through by Sat'day if Ah don't start on Sunday?"

"Ah don't keer if you never git through. Anyhow, Ah done promised Gawd and a couple of other men, Ah aint gointer have it in mah house. Don't gimme no lip neither, else Ah'll throw 'em out and put mah fist up side yo' head to boot."

Delia's habitual meekness seemed to slip from her shoulders like a blown scarf. She was on her feet; her poor little body, her bare knuckly hands bravely defying the strapping hulk before her.

"Looka heah, Sykes, you done gone too fur. Ah been married to you fur fifteen years, and Ah been takin' in washin' fur fifteen years. Sweat, sweat, sweat! Work and sweat, cry and sweat, pray and sweat!"

"What's that got to do with me?" he asked brutally.

"What's it got to do with you, Sykes? Mah tub of suds is filled yo' belly with vittles more times than yo' hands is filled it. Mah sweat is done paid for this house and Ah reckon Ah kin keep on sweatin' in it."

She seized the iron skillet from the stove and struck a defensive pose, which act surprised him greatly, coming from her. It cowed him and he did not strike her as he usually did.

"Naw you won't," she panted, "that ole snaggle-toothed black woman you runnin' with aint comin' heah to pile up on *mah* sweat and blood. You aint paid for nothin' on this place, and Ah'm gointer stay right heah till Ah'm toted out foot foremost."

"Well, you better quit gittin' me riled up, else they'll be totin' you out sooner than you expect. Ah'm so tired of you Ah don't know whut to do. Gawd! how Ah hates skinny wimmen!"

A little awed by this new Delia, he sidled out of the door and slammed the back gate after him. He did not say where he had gone, but she knew too well. She knew very well that he would not return until nearly daybreak also. Her work over, she went on to bed but not to sleep at once. Things had come to a pretty pass!

She lay awake, gazing upon the debris that cluttered their matrimonial trail. Not an image left standing along the way. Anything like flowers had long ago been drowned in the salty stream that had been pressed from her heart. Her tears, her sweat, her blood. She had brought love to the union and he had brought a longing after the flesh. Two months after the wedding, he had given her the first brutal beating. She had the memory of his numerous trips to Orlando with all of his wages when he had returned to her penniless, even before the first year had passed. She was young and soft then, but now she thought of her knotty, muscled limbs, her harsh knuckly hands, and drew herself up into an unhappy little ball in the middle of the big feather bed. Too late now to hope for love, even if it were not Bertha it would be someone else. This case differed from the others only in that she was bolder than the others. Too late for everything except her little home. She had built it for her old days, and planted one by one the trees and flowers there. It was lovely to her, lovely.

Somehow, before sleep came, she found herself saying aloud: "Oh well, whatever goes over the Devil's back, is got to come under his belly. Sometime or ruther, Sykes, like everybody else, is gointer reap his sowing." After that she was able to build a spiritual earthworks against her husband. His shells could no longer reach her. *Amen.* She went to sleep and slept until he announced his presence in bed by kicking her feet and rudely snatching the cover away.

"Gimme some kivah heah, an' git yo' damn foots over on yo' own side! Ah oughter mash you in yo' mouf fuh drawing dat skillet on me."

Delia went clear to the rail without answering him. A triumphant indifference to all that he was or did.

The week was as full of work for Delia as all other weeks, and Saturday found her behind her little pony, collecting and delivering clothes.

It was a hot, hot day near the end of July. The village men on Joe Clarke's porch even chewed cane listlessly. They did not hurl the cane-knots as usual. They let them dribble over the edge of the porch. Even conversation had collapsed under the heat.

"Heah come Delia Jones," Jim Merchant said, as the shaggy pony came 'round the bend of the road toward them. The rusty buckboard was heaped with baskets of crisp, clean laundry.

"Yep," Joe Lindsay agreed. "Hot or col', rain or shine, jes ez reg'lar ez de weeks roll roun' Delia carries 'em an' fetches 'em on Sat'day."

"She better if she wanter eat," said Moss. "Sykes Jones aint wuth de shot an' powder hit would tek tuh kill 'em. Not to *huh* he aint."

"He sho' aint," Walter Thomas chimed in. "It's too bad, too, cause she wuz a right pretty li'l trick when he got huh. Ah'd uh mah'ied huh mahseff if he hadnter beat me to it."

Delia nodded briefly at the men as she drove past.

"Too much knockin' will ruin *any* 'oman. He done beat huh 'nough tuh kill three women, let 'lone change they looks," said Elijah Moseley. "How Sykes kin stommuck dat big black greasy Mogul he's layin' roun' wid, gits me. Ah swear dat eight-rock couldn't kiss a sardine can Ah done thowed out de back do' 'way las' yeah."

"Aw, she's fat, thass how come. He's allus been crazy 'bout fat women," put in Merchant. "He'd a' been tied up wid one long time ago if he could a' found one tuh have him. Did Ah tell yuh 'bout him come sidlin' roun' *mah* wife — bringin' her a basket uh pee-cans outa his yard fuh a present? Yessir, mah wife! She tol' him tuh take 'em right straight back home, cause Delia works so hard ovah dat washtub she reckon everything on de place taste lak sweat an' soapsuds. Ah jus' wisht Ah'd a' caught 'im 'roun' dere! Ah'd a' made his hips ketch on fiah down dat shell road."

"Ah know he done it, too. Ah sees 'im grinnin' at every 'oman dat passes," Walter Thomas said. "But even so, he useter eat some mighty big hunks uh humble pie tuh git dat lil' 'oman he got. She wuz ez pritty ez a speckled pup! Dat wuz fifteen yeahs ago. He useter be so skeered uh losin' huh, she could make him do some parts of a husband's duty. Dey never wuz de same in de mind."

"There oughter be a law about him," said Lindsay. "He aint fit tuh carry guts tuh a bear."

Clarke spoke for the first time. "Taint no law on earth dat kin make a man be decent if it aint in 'im. There's plenty men dat takes a wife lak dey do a joint uh sugar-cane. It's round, juicy an' sweet when dey gits it. But dey squeeze an' grind, squeeze an' grind an' wring tell dey wring every drop uh pleasure dat's in 'em out. When dey's satisfied dat dey is wrung dry, dey treats 'em jes lak dey do a cane-chew. Dey thows 'em away. Dey knows whut dey is doin' while dey is at it, an' hates theirselves fuh it but they keeps on hangin' after huh tell she's empty. Den dey hates huh fuh bein' a cane-chew an' in de way."

"We oughter take Sykes an' dat stray 'oman uh his'n down in Lake Howell swamp an' lay on de rawhide till they cain't say 'Lawd a' mussy.' He allus wuz uh ovahbearin' niggah, but since dat white 'oman from up north done teached 'im how to run a automobile, he done got too biggety to live — an' we oughter kill 'im," Old Man Anderson advised.

A grunt of approval went around the porch. But the heat was melting their civic virtue and Elijah Moseley began to bait Joe Clarke.

"Come on, Joe, git a melon outa dere an' slice it up for yo' customers. We'se all sufferin' wid de heat. De bear's done got *me*!"

"Thass right, Joe, a watermelon is jes' whut Ah needs tuh cure de eppizudicks." Walter Thomas joined forces with Moseley. "Come on dere, Joe. We all is steady customers an' you aint set us up in a long time. Ah chooses dat long, bowlegged Floridy favorite."

"A god, an' be dough. You all gimme twenty cents and slice away," Clarke retorted. "Ah needs a col' slice m'self. Heah, everybody chip in. Ah'll lend y'all mah meat knife."

The money was quickly subscribed and the huge melon brought forth. At that moment, Sykes and Bertha arrived. A determined silence fell on the porch and the melon was put away again.

Merchant snapped down the blade of his jack-knife and moved toward the store door.

"Come on in, Joe, an' gimme a slab uh sow belly an' uh pound uh cof-fee — almost fuhgot 'twas Sat'day. Got to git on home." Most of the men left also.

Just then Delia drove past on her way home, as Sykes was ordering mag-nificently for Bertha. It pleased him for Delia to see.

"Git whutsoever yo' heart desires, Honey. Wait a minute, Joe. Give huh two botles uh strawberry soda-water, uh quart uh parched ground-peas, an a block uh chewin' gum."

With all this they left the store, with Sykes reminding Bertha that this was his town and she could have it if she wanted it.

The men returned soon after they left, and held their watermelon feast.

"Where did Sykes Jones git dat 'oman from nohow?" Lindsay asked.

"Ovah Apopka. Guess dey musta been cleanin' out de town when she lef'. She don't look lak a thing but a hunk uh liver wid hair on it."

"Well, she sho' kin squall," Dave Carter contributed. "When she gits ready tuh laff, she jes' opens huh mouf an' latches it back tuh de las' notch. No ole grandpa alligator down in Lake Bell aint got nothin' on huh."

Bertha had been in town three months now. Sykes was still paying her room rent at Della Lewis' — the only house in town that would have taken her in. Sykes took her frequently to Winter Park to "stomps." He still as-sured her that he was the swellest man in the state.

"Sho' you kin have dat lil' ole house soon's Ah kin git dat 'oman outa dere. Everything b'longs tuh me an' you sho' kin have it. Ah sho' 'bominates uh skinny 'oman. Lawdy, you sho' is got one portly shape on you! You kin git *anything* you wants. Dis is *mah* town an' you sho' kin have it."

Delia's work-worn knees crawled over the earth in Gethsemane° and up the rocks of Calvary many, many times during these months. She avoided the villagers and meeting places in her efforts to be blind and deaf. But Bertha nullified this to a degree, by coming to Delia's house to call Sykes out to her at the gate.

Delia and Sykes fought all the time now with no peaceful interludes. They slept and ate in silence. Two or three times Delia had attempted a timid friendliness, but she was repulsed each time. It was plain that the breaches must remain agape.

The sun had burned July to August. The heat streamed down like a mil-lion hot arrows, smiting all things living upon the earth. Grass withered, leaves browned, snakes went blind in shedding and men and dogs went mad. Dog days!

Delia came home one day and found Sykes there before her. She won-dered, but started to go on into the house without speaking, even though he was standing in the kitchen door and she must either stoop under his arm

___
Gethsemane: The garden in which Jesus agonized and prayed (Matthew 26:36–46) before being taken prisoner and crucified on a hill called Calvary (Luke 23:33).

or ask him to move. He made no room for her. She noticed a soap box beside the steps, but paid no particular attention to it, knowing that he must have brought it there. As she was stooping to pass under his outstretched arm, he suddenly pushed her backward, laughingly.

"Look in de box dere Delia, Ah done brung yuh somethin'!"

She nearly fell upon the box in her stumbling, and when she saw what it held, she all but fainted outright.

"Sykes! Sykes, mah Gawd! You take dat rattlesnake 'way from heah! You *gottuh*. Oh, Jesus, have mussy!"

"Ah aint gut tuh do nuthin' uh de kin'—fact is Ah aint got tuh do nothin' but die. Taint no use uh you puttin' on airs makin' out lak you skeered uh dat snake—he's gointer stay right heah tell he die. He wouldn't bite me cause Ah knows how tuh handle 'im. Nohow he wouldn't risk breakin' out his fangs 'gin *yo'* skinny laigs."

"Naw, now Sykes, don't keep dat thing 'roun' heah tuh skeer me tuh death. You knows Ah'm even feared uh earth worms. Thass de biggest snake Ah evah did see. Kill 'im Sykes, please."

"Doan ast me tuh do nothin' fuh yuh. Goin' 'roun' tryin' tuh be so damn astorperious. Naw, Ah aint gonna kill it. Ah think uh damn sight mo' uh him dan you! Dat's a nice snake an' anybody doan lak 'im kin jes' hit de grit."

The village soon heard that Sykes had the snake, and came to see and ask questions.

"How de hen-fire did you ketch dat six-foot rattler, Sykes?" Thomas asked.

"He's full uh frogs so he caint hardly move, thass how Ah eased up on 'm. But Ah'm a snake charmer an' knows how tuh handle 'em. Shux, dat aint nothin'. Ah could ketch one eve'y day if Ah so wanted tuh."

"Whut he needs is a heavy hick'ry club leaned real heavy on his head. Dat's de bes 'way tuh charm a rattlesnake."

"Naw, Walt, y'all jes' don't understand dese diamon' backs lak Ah do," said Sykes in a superior tone of voice.

The village agreed with Walter, but the snake stayed on. His box remained by the kitchen door with its screen wire covering. Two or three days later it had digested its meal of frogs and literally came to life. It rattled at every movement in the kitchen or the yard. One day as Delia came down the kitchen steps she saw his chalky-white fangs curved like scimitars hung in the wire meshes. This time she did not run away with averted eyes as usual. She stood for a long time in the doorway in a red fury that grew bloodier for every second that she regarded the creature that was her torment.

That night she broached the subject as soon as Sykes sat down to the table.

"Sykes, Ah wants you tuh take dat snake 'way fum heah. You done starved me an' Ah put up widcher, you done beat me an Ah took dat, but you done kilt all mah insides bringin' dat varmint heah."

Sykes poured out a saucer full of coffee and drank it deliberately before he answered her.

"A whole lot Ah keer 'bout how you feels inside uh out. Dat snake aint goin' no damn wheah till Ah gits ready fuh 'im tuh go. So fur as beatin' is concerned, yuh aint took near all dat you gointer take ef yuh stay 'roun' *me.*"

Delia pushed back her plate and got up from the table. "Ah hates you, Sykes," she said calmly. "Ah hates you tuh de same degree dat Ah useter love yuh. Ah done took an' took till mah belly is full up tuh mah neck. Dat's de reason Ah got mah letter fum de church an' moved mah membership tuh Woodbridge—so Ah don't haftuh take no sacrament wid yuh. Ah don't wantuh see yuh 'roun' me a-tall. Lay 'roun' wid dat 'oman all yuh wants tuh, but gwan 'way fum me an' mah house. Ah hates yuh lak uh suck-egg dog."

Sykes almost let the huge wad of corn bread and collard greens he was chewing fall out of his mouth in amazement. He had a hard time whipping himself up to the proper fury to try to answer Delia.

"Well, Ah'm glad you does hate me. Ah'm sho' tiahed uh you hangin' ontuh me. Ah don't want yuh. Look at yuh stringey ole neck! Yo' rawbony laigs an' arms is enough tuh cut uh man tuh death. You looks jes' lak de devvul's doll-baby tuh *me.* You cain't hate me no worse dan Ah hates you. Ah been hatin' *you* fuh years."

"Yo' ole black hide don't look lak nothin' tuh me, but uh passel uh wrinkled up rubber, wid yo' big ole yeahs flappin' on each side lak uh paih uh buzzard wings. Don't think Ah'm gointuh be run 'way fum mah house neither. Ah'm goin' tuh de white folks bout *you,* mah young man, de very nex' time you lay yo' han's on me. Mah cup is done run ovah." Delia said this with no signs of fear and Sykes departed from the house, threatening her, but made not the slightest move to carry out any of them.

That night he did not return at all, and the next day being Sunday, Delia was glad that she did not have to quarrel before she hitched up her pony and drove the four miles to Woodbridge.

She stayed to the night service—"love feast"—which was very warm and full of spirit. In the emotional winds her domestic trials were borne far and wide so that she sang as she drove homeward,

> Jurden water, black an' col'
> Chills de body, not de soul
> An' Ah wantah cross Jurden in uh calm time.

She came from the barn to the kitchen door and stopped.

"Whut's de mattah, ol' satan, you aint kickin' up yo' racket?" She addressed the snake's box. Complete silence. She went on into the house with a new hope in its birth struggles. Perhaps her threat to go to the white folks had frightened Sykes! Perhaps he was sorry! Fifteen years of misery and suppression had brought Delia to the place where she would hope *anything* that looked towards a way over or through her wall of inhibitions.

She felt in the match safe behind the stove at once for a match. There was only one there.

"Dat niggah wouldn't fetch nothin' heah tuh save his rotten neck, but he kin run thew whut Ah brings quick enough. Now he done toted off nigh on tuh haff uh box uh matches. He done had dat 'oman heah in mah house, too."

Nobody but a woman could tell how she knew this even before she struck the match. But she did and it put her into a new fury.

Presently she brought in the tubs to put the white things to soak. This time she decided she need not bring the hamper out of the bedroom; she would go in there and do the sorting. She picked up the pot-bellied lamp and went in. The room was small and the hamper stood hard by the foot of the white iron bed. She could sit and reach through the bedposts — resting as she worked.

"Ah wantah cross Jurden in uh calm time." She was singing again. The mood of the "love feast" had returned. She threw back the lid of the basket almost gaily. Then, moved by both horror and terror, she sprung back toward the door. *There lay the snake in the basket!* He moved sluggishly at first, but even as she turned round and round, jumped up and down in an insanity of fear, he began to stir vigorously. She saw him pouring his awful beauty from the basket upon the bed, then she seized the lamp and ran as fast as she could to the kitchen. The wind from the open door blew out the light and the darkness added to her terror. She sped to the darkness of the yard, slamming the door after her before she thought to set down the lamp. She did not feel safe even on the ground, so she climbed up in the hay barn.

There for an hour or more she lay sprawled upon the hay a gibbering wreck.

Finally she grew quiet, and after that, coherent thought. With this, stalked through her a cold, bloody rage. Hours of this. A period of introspection, a space of retrospection, then a mixture of both. Out of this an awful calm.

"Well, Ah done de bes' Ah could. If things aint right, Gawd knows taint mah fault."

She went to sleep — a twitchy sleep — and woke up to a faint gray sky. There was a loud hollow sound below. She peered out. Sykes was at the wood-pile, demolishing a wire-covered box.

He hurried to the kitchen door, but hung outside there some minutes before he entered, and stood some minutes more inside before he closed it after him.

The gray in the sky was spreading. Delia descended without fear now, and crouched beneath the low bedroom window. The drawn shade shut out the dawn, shut in the night. But the thin walls held back no sound.

"Dat ol' scratch is woke up now!" She mused at the tremendous whirr inside, which every woodsman knows, is one of the sound illusions. The rattler is a ventriloquist. His whirr sounds to the right, to the left, straight ahead, behind, close under foot — everywhere but where it is. Woe to him who guesses wrong unless he is prepared to hold up his end of the argument! Sometimes he strikes without rattling at all.

Inside, Sykes heard nothing until he knocked a pot lid off the stove while trying to reach the match safe in the dark. He had emptied his pockets at Bertha's.

The snake seemed to wake up under the stove and Sykes made a quick leap into the bedroom. In spite of the gin he had had, his head was clearing now.

"Mah Gawd!" he chattered, "ef Ah could on'y strack uh light!"

The rattling ceased for a moment as he stood paralyzed. He waited. It seemed that the snake waited also.

"Oh fuh de light! Ah thought he'd be too sick" — Sykes was muttering to himself when the whirr began again, closer, right underfoot this time. Long before this, Sykes' ability to think had been flattened down to primitive instinct and he leaped — onto the bed.

Outside Delia heard a cry that might have come from a maddened chimpanzee, a stricken gorilla. All the terror, all the horror, all the rage that man possibly could express, without a recognizable human sound.

A tremendous stir inside there, another series of animal screams, the intermittent whirr of the reptile. The shade torn violently down from the window, letting in the red dawn, a huge brown hand seizing the window stick, great dull blows upon the wooden floor punctuating the gibberish of sound long after the rattle of the snake had abruptly subsided. All this Delia could see and hear from her place beneath the window, and it made her ill. She crept over to the four-o'clocks and stretched herself on the cool earth to recover.

She lay there. "Delia, Delia!" She could hear Sykes calling in a most despairing tone as one who expected no answer. The sun crept on up, and he called. Delia could not move — her legs were gone flabby. She never moved, he called, and the sun kept rising.

"Mah Gawd!" she heard him moan. "Mah Gawd fum Heben!" She heard him stumbling about and got up from her flower-bed. The sun was growing warm. As she approached the door she heard him call out hopefully, "Delia, is dat you Ah heah?"

She saw him on his hands and knees as soon as she reached the door. He crept an inch or two toward her — all that he was able, and she saw his horribly swollen neck and his one open eye shining with hope. A surge of pity too strong to support bore her away from that eye that must, could not, fail to see the tubs. He would see the lamp. Orlando with its doctors was too far. She could scarcely reach the Chinaberry tree, where she waited in the growing heat while inside she knew the cold river was creeping up and up to extinguish that eye which must know by now that she knew.

Gish Jen b. 1956

Who's Irish?   [1999]

In China, people say mixed children are supposed to be smart, and definitely my granddaughter Sophie is smart. But Sophie is wild, Sophie is not like my daughter Natalie, or like me. I am work hard my whole life, and fierce besides. My husband always used to say he is afraid of me, and in our restaurant, busboys and cooks all afraid of me too. Even the gang members come for protection money, they try to talk to my husband. When I am there, they stay away. If they come by mistake, they pretend they are come to eat. They hide behind the menu, they order a lot of food. They talk about their mothers. Oh, my mother have some arthritis, need to take herbal medicine, they say. Oh, my mother getting old, her hair all white now.

I say, Your mother's hair used to be white, but since she dye it, it become black again. Why don't you go home once in a while and take a look? I tell them, Confucius say a filial son knows what color his mother's hair is.

My daughter is fierce too, she is vice president in the bank now. Her new house is big enough for everybody to have their own room, including me. But Sophie take after Natalie's husband's family, their name is Shea. Irish. I always thought Irish people are like Chinese people, work so hard on the railroad, but now I know why the Chinese beat the Irish. Of course, not all Irish are like the Shea family, of course not. My daughter tell me I should not say Irish this, Irish that.

How do you like it when people say the Chinese this, the Chinese that, she say.

You know, the British call the Irish heathen, just like they call the Chinese, she say.

You think the Opium War was bad, how would you like to live right next door to the British, she say.

And that is that. My daughter have a funny habit when she win an argument, she take a sip of something and look away, so the other person is not embarrassed. So I am not embarrassed. I do not call anybody anything either. I just happen to mention about the Shea family, an interesting fact: four brothers in the family, and not one of them work. The mother, Bess, have a job before she got sick, she was executive secretary in a big company. She is handle everything for a big shot, you would be surprised how complicated her job is, not just type this, type that. Now she is a nice woman with a clean house. But her boys, every one of them is on welfare, or so-called severance pay, or so-called disability pay. Something. They say they cannot find work, this is not the economy of the fifties, but I say, Even the black people doing better these days, some of them live so fancy, you'd be surprised. Why the Shea family have so much trouble? They are white people, they speak English. When I come to this country, I have no money and do not speak English. But my husband and I own our restaurant before he die. Free and clear, no mortgage. Of course, I understand I am just lucky, come from a country where the food is popular all over the world. I understand it is not the Shea family's fault they come from a country where everything is boiled. Still, I say.

She's right, we should broaden our horizons, say one brother, Jim, at Thanksgiving. Forget about the car business. Think about egg rolls.

Pad thai, say another brother, Mike. I'm going to make my fortune in pad thai. It's going to be the new pizza.

I say, You people too picky about what you sell. Selling egg rolls not good enough for you, but at least my husband and I can say, We made it. What can you say? Tell me. What can you say?

Everybody chew their tough turkey.

I especially cannot understand my daughter's husband John, who has no job but cannot take care of Sophie either. Because he is a man, he say, and that's the end of the sentence.

Plain boiled food, plain boiled thinking. Even his name is plain boiled: John. Maybe because I grew up with black bean sauce and hoisin sauce and garlic sauce, I always feel something is missing when my son-in-law talk.

But, okay: so my son-in-law can be man, I am baby-sitter. Six hours a day, same as the old sitter, crazy Amy, who quit. This is not so easy, now that I am sixty-eight, Chinese age almost seventy. Still, I try. In China, daughter take care of mother. Here it is the other way around. Mother help daughter, mother ask, Anything else I can do? Otherwise daughter complain mother is not supportive. I tell daughter, We do not have this word in Chinese, *supportive*. But my daughter too busy to listen, she has to go to meeting, she has to write memo while her husband go to the gym to be a man. My daughter say otherwise he will be depressed. Seems like all his life he has this trouble, depression.

No one wants to hire someone who is depressed, she say. It is important for him to keep his spirits up.

Beautiful wife, beautiful daughter, beautiful house, oven can clean itself automatically. No money left over, because only one income, but lucky enough, got the baby-sitter for free. If John lived in China, he would be very happy. But he is not happy. Even at the gym things go wrong. One day, he pull a muscle. Another day, weight room too crowded. Always something.

Until finally, hooray, he has a job. Then he feel pressure.

I need to concentrate, he say. I need to focus.

He is going to work for insurance company. Salesman job. A paycheck, he say, and at least he will wear clothes instead of gym shorts. My daughter buy him some special candy bars from the health-food store. They say THINK! on them, and are supposed to help John think.

John is a good-looking boy, you have to say that, especially now that he shave so you can see his face.

I am an old man in a young man's game, say John.

I will need a new suit, say John.

This time I am not going to shoot myself in the foot, say John.

Good, I say.

She means to be supportive, my daughter say. Don't start the send her back to China thing, because we can't.

Sophie is three years old American age, but already I see her nice Chinese side swallowed up by her wild Shea side. She looks like mostly Chinese. Beautiful black hair, beautiful black eyes. Nose perfect size, not so flat looks like something fell down, not so large looks like some big deal got stuck in wrong face. Everything just right, only her skin is a brown surprise to John's family. So brown, they say. Even John say it. She never goes in the sun, still she is that color, he say. Brown. They say, Nothing the matter with brown. They are just surprised. So brown. Nattie is not that brown, they say. They say, It seems like Sophie should be a color in between Nattie and John. Seems funny, a girl named Sophie Shea be brown. But she is brown, maybe her name should be Sophie Brown. She never go in the sun, still she is that color, they say. Nothing the matter with brown. They are just surprised.

The Shea family talk is like this sometimes, going around and around like a Christmas-tree train.

Maybe John is not her father, I say one day, to stop the train. And sure enough, train wreck. None of the brothers ever say the word *brown* to me again.

Instead, John's mother, Bess, say, I hope you are not offended.

She say, I did my best on those boys. But raising four boys with no father is no picnic.

You have a beautiful family, I say.

I'm getting old, she say.

You deserve a rest, I say. Too many boys make you old.

I never had a daughter, she say. You have a daughter.

I have a daughter, I say. Chinese people don't think a daughter is so great, but you're right. I have a daughter.

I was never against the marriage, you know, she say. I never thought John was marrying down. I always thought Nattie was just as good as white.

I was never against the marriage either, I say. I just wonder if they look at the whole problem.

Of course you pointed out the problem, you are a mother, she say. And now we both have a granddaughter. A little brown granddaughter, she is so precious to me.

I laugh. A little brown granddaughter, I say. To tell you the truth, I don't know how she came out so brown.

We laugh some more. These days Bess need a walker to walk. She take so many pills, she need two glasses of water to get them all down. Her favorite TV show is about bloopers, and she love her bird feeder. All day long, she can watch that bird feeder, like a cat.

I can't wait for her to grow up, Bess say. I could use some female company.

Too many boys, I say.

Boys are fine, she say. But they do surround you after a while.

You should take a break, come live with us, I say. Lots of girls at our house.

Be careful what you offer, say Bess with a wink. Where I come from, people mean for you to move in when they say a thing like that.

Nothing the matter with Sophie's outside, that's the truth. It is inside that she is like not any Chinese girl I ever see. We go to the park, and this is what she does. She stand up in the stroller. She take off all her clothes and throw them in the fountain.

Sophie! I say. Stop!

But she just laugh like a crazy person. Before I take over as baby-sitter, Sophie has that crazy-person sitter, Amy the guitar player. My daughter thought this Amy very creative—another word we do not talk about in China. In China, we talk about whether we have difficulty or no difficulty. We talk about whether life is bitter or not bitter. In America, all day long, people talk about creative. Never mind that I cannot even look at this Amy, with her shirt so short that her belly button showing. This Amy think Sophie should love her body. So when Sophie take off her diaper, Amy laugh. When Sophie run around naked, Amy say she wouldn't want to wear a diaper either. When Sophie go *shu-shu* in her lap, Amy laugh and say there are no germs in pee. When Sophie take off her shoes, Amy say bare feet is best, even the pediatrician say so. That is why Sophie now walk around with no shoes like a beggar child. Also why Sophie love to take off her clothes.

Turn around! say the boys in the park. Let's see that ass!

Of course, Sophie does not understand. Sophie clap her hands, I am the only one to say, No! This is not a game.

It has nothing to do with John's family, my daughter say. Amy was too permissive, that's all.

But I think if Sophie was not wild inside, she would not take off her shoes and clothes to begin with.

You never take off your clothes when you were little, I say. All my Chinese friends had babies, I never saw one of them act wild like that.

Look, my daughter say. I have a big presentation tomorrow.

John and my daughter agree Sophie is a problem, but they don't know what to do.

You spank her, she'll stop, I say another day.

But they say, Oh no.

In America, parents not supposed to spank the child.

It gives them low self-esteem, my daughter say. And that leads to problems later, as I happen to know.

My daughter never have big presentation the next day when the subject of spanking come up.

I don't want you to touch Sophie, she say. No spanking, period.

Don't tell me what to do, I say.

I'm not telling you what to do, say my daughter. I'm telling you how I feel.

I am not your servant, I say. Don't you dare talk to me like that.

My daughter have another funny habit when she lose an argument. She spread out all her fingers and look at them, as if she like to make sure they are still there.

My daughter is fierce like me, but she and John think it is better to explain to Sophie that clothes are a good idea. This is not so hard in the cold weather. In the warm weather, it is very hard.

Use your words, my daughter say. That's what we tell Sophie. How about if you set a good example.

As if good example mean anything to Sophie. I am so fierce, the gang members who used to come to the restaurant all afraid of me, but Sophie is not afraid.

I say, Sophie, if you take off your clothes, no snack.

I say, Sophie, if you take off your clothes, no lunch.

I say, Sophie, if you take off your clothes, no park.

Pretty soon we are stay home all day, and by the end of six hours she still did not have one thing to eat. You never saw a child stubborn like that.

I'm hungry! she cry when my daughter come home.

What's the matter, doesn't your grandmother feed you? My daughter laugh.

No! Sophie say. She doesn't feed me anything!

My daughter laugh again. Here you go, she say.

She say to John, Sophie must be growing.

Growing like a weed, I say.

Still Sophie take off her clothes, until one day I spank her. Not too hard, but she cry and cry, and when I tell her if she doesn't put her clothes back on I'll spank her again, she put her clothes back on. Then I tell her she is good girl, and give her some food to eat. The next day we go to the park and, like a nice Chinese girl, she does not take off her clothes.

She stop taking off her clothes, I report. Finally!

How did you do it? my daughter ask.

After twenty-eight years experience with you, I guess I learn something, I say.

It must have been a phase, John say, and his voice is suddenly like an expert.

His voice is like an expert about everything these days, now that he carry a leather briefcase, and wear shiny shoes, and can go shopping for a new car. On the company, he say. The company will pay for it, but he will be able to drive it whenever he want.

A free car, he say. How do you like that.

It's good to see you in the saddle again, my daughter say. Some of your family patterns are scary.

At least I don't drink, he say. He say, And I'm not the only one with scary family patterns.

That's for sure, say my daughter.

Everyone is happy. Even I am happy, because there is more trouble with Sophie, but now I think I can help her Chinese side fight against her wild side. I teach her to eat food with fork or spoon or chopsticks, she cannot just grab into the middle of a bowl of noodles. I teach her not to play with garbage cans. Sometimes I spank her, but not too often, and not too hard.

Still, there are problems. Sophie like to climb everything. If there is a railing, she is never next to it. Always she is on top of it. Also, Sophie like to hit the mommies of her friends. She learn this from her playground best friend, Sinbad, who is four. Sinbad wear army clothes every day and like to ambush his mommy. He is the one who dug a big hole under the play structure, a foxhole he call it, all by himself. Very hardworking. Now he wait in the foxhole with a shovel full of wet sand. When his mommy come, he throw it right at her.

Oh, it's all right, his mommy say. You can't get rid of war games, it's part of their imaginative play. All the boys go through it.

Also, he like to kick his mommy, and one day he tell Sophie to kick his mommy too.

I wish this story is not true.

Kick her, kick her! Sinbad say.

Sophie kick her. A little kick, as if she just so happened was swinging her little leg and didn't realize that big mommy leg was in the way. Still I spank Sophie and make Sophie say sorry, and what does the mommy say?

Really, it's all right, she say. It didn't hurt.

After that, Sophie learn she can attack mommies in the playground, and some will say, Stop, but others will say, Oh, she didn't mean it, especially if they realize Sophie will be punished.

This is how, one day, bigger trouble come. The bigger trouble start when Sophie hide in the foxhole with that shovel full of sand. She wait, and when I come look for her, she throw it at me. All over my nice clean clothes.

Did you ever see a Chinese girl act this way?

Sophie! I say. Come out of there, say you're sorry.

But she does not come out. Instead, she laugh. Naaah, naah-na, naaa-naaa, she say.

I am not exaggerate: millions of children in China, not one act like this.

Sophie! I say. Now! Come out now!

But she know she is in big trouble. She know if she come out, what will happen next. So she does not come out. I am sixty-eight, Chinese age almost seventy, how can I crawl under there to catch her? Impossible. So I yell, yell, yell, and what happen? Nothing. A Chinese mother would help, but

American mothers, they look at you, they shake their head, they go home. And, of course, a Chinese child would give up, but not Sophie.

I hate you! she yell. I hate you, Meanie!

Meanie is my new name these days.

Long time this goes on, long long time. The foxhole is deep, you cannot see too much, you don't know where is the bottom. You cannot hear too much either. If she does not yell, you cannot even know she is still there or not. After a while, getting cold out, getting dark out. No one left in the playground, only us.

Sophie, I say. How did you become stubborn like this? I am go home without you now.

I try to use a stick, chase her out of there, and once or twice I hit her, but still she does not come out. So finally I leave. I go outside the gate.

Bye-bye! I say. I'm go home now.

But still she does not come out and does not come out. Now it is dinnertime, the sky is black. I think I should maybe go get help, but how can I leave a little girl by herself in the playground? A bad man could come. A rat could come. I go back in to see what is happen to Sophie. What if she have a shovel and is making a tunnel to escape?

Sophie! I say.

No answer.

Sophie!

I don't know if she is alive. I don't know if she is fall asleep down there. If she is crying, I cannot hear her.

So I take the stick and poke.

Sophie! I say. I promise I no hit you. If you come out, I give you a lollipop.

No answer. By now I worried. What to do, what to do, what to do? I poke some more, even harder, so that I am poking and poking when my daughter and John suddenly appear.

What are you doing? What is going on? say my daughter.

Put down that stick! say my daughter.

You are crazy! say my daughter.

John wiggle under the structure, into the foxhole, to rescue Sophie.

She fell asleep, say John the expert. She's okay. That is one big hole.

Now Sophie is crying and crying.

Sophia, my daughter say, hugging her. Are you okay, peanut? Are you okay?

She's just scared, say John.

Are you okay? I say too. I don't know what happen, I say.

She's okay, say John. He is not like my daughter, full of questions. He is full of answers until we get home and can see by the lamplight.

Will you look at her? he yell then. What the hell happened?

Bruises all over her brown skin, and a swollen-up eye.

You are crazy! say my daughter. Look at what you did! You are crazy!

I try very hard, I say.

How could you use a stick? I told you to use your words!

She is hard to handle, I say.

She's three years old! You cannot use a stick! say my daughter.

She is not like any Chinese girl I ever saw, I say.

I brush some sand off my clothes. Sophie's clothes are dirty too, but at least she has her clothes on.

Has she done this before? ask my daughter. Has she hit you before?

She hits me all the time, Sophie say, eating ice cream.

Your family, say John.

Believe me, say my daughter.

A daughter I have, a beautiful daughter. I took care of her when she could not hold her head up. I took care of her before she could argue with me, when she was a little girl with two pigtails, one of them always crooked. I took care of her when we have to escape from China, I took care of her when suddenly we live in a country with cars everywhere, if you are not careful your little girl get run over. When my husband die, I promise him I will keep the family together, even though it was just two of us, hardly a family at all.

But now my daughter take me around to look at apartments. After all, I can cook, I can clean, there's no reason I cannot live by myself, all I need is a telephone. Of course, she is sorry. Sometimes she cry, I am the one to say everything will be okay. She say she have no choice, she doesn't want to end up divorced. I say divorce is terrible, I don't know who invented this terrible idea. Instead of live with a telephone, though, surprise, I come to live with Bess.

Imagine that. Bess make an offer and, sure enough, where she come from, people mean for you to move in when they say things like that. A crazy idea, go to live with someone else's family, but she like to have some female company, not like my daughter, who does not believe in company. These days when my daughter visit, she does not bring Sophie. Bess say we should give Nattie time, we will see Sophie again soon. But seems like my daughter have more presentation than ever before, every time she come she have to leave.

I have a family to support, she say, and her voice is heavy, as if soaking wet. I have a young daughter and a depressed husband and no one to turn to.

When she say no one to turn to, she mean me.

These days my beautiful daughter is so tired she can just sit there in a chair and fall asleep. John lost his job again, already, but still they rather hire a baby-sitter than ask me to help, even they can't afford it. Of course, the new baby-sitter is much younger, can run around. I don't know if Sophie these days is wild or not wild. She call me Meanie, but she like to kiss me too, sometimes. I remember that every time I see a child on TV. Sophie like to grab my hair, a fistful in each hand, and then kiss me smack on the nose. I never see any other child kiss that way.

The satellite TV has so many channels, more channels than I can count, including a Chinese channel from the Mainland and a Chinese channel from Taiwan, but most of the time I watch bloopers with Bess. Also, I watch the bird feeder — so many, many kinds of birds come. The Shea sons hang around all the time, asking when will I go home, but Bess tell them, Get lost.

She's a permanent resident, say Bess. She isn't going anywhere.

Then she wink at me, and switch the channel with the remote control.

Of course, I shouldn't say Irish this, Irish that, especially now I am become honorary Irish myself, according to Bess. Me! Who's Irish? I say, and she laugh. All the same, if I could mention one thing about some of the Irish, not all of them of course, I like to mention this: Their talk just stick. I don't know how Bess Shea learn to use her words, but sometimes I hear what she say a long time later. *Permanent resident. Not going anywhere.* Over and over I hear it, the voice of Bess.

James Joyce   1882–1941
Eveline   [1914]

She sat at the window watching the evening invade the avenue. Her head was leaned against the window curtains and in her nostril was the odour of dusty cretonne. She was tired.

Few people passed. The man out of the last house passed on his way home; she heard his footsteps clacking along the concrete pavement and afterwards crunching on the cinder path before the new red houses. One time there used to be a field there in which they used to play every evening with other people's children. Then a man from Belfast bought the field and built houses in it — not like their little brown houses but bright brick houses with shining roofs. The children of the avenue used to play together in that field — the Devines, the Waters, the Dunns, little Keogh the cripple, she and her brothers and sisters. Ernest, however, never played: he was too grown up. Her father used often to hunt them in out of the field with his blackthorn stick; but usually little Keogh used to keep *nix* and call out when he saw her father coming. Still they seemed to have been rather happy then. Her father was not so bad then; and besides, her mother was alive. That was a long time ago; she and her brothers and sisters were all grown up; her mother was dead. Tizzie Dunn was dead, too, and the Waters had gone back to England. Everything changes. Now she was going to go away like the others, to leave her home.

Home! She looked round the room, reviewing all its familiar objects which she had dusted once a week for so many years, wondering where on earth all the dust came from. Perhaps she would never see again those familiar objects from which she had never dreamed of being divided. And yet during all those years she had never found out the name of the priest whose yellowing photograph hung on the wall above the broken harmonium beside the coloured print of the promises made to Blessed Margaret Mary Alacoque. He had been a school friend of her father. Whenever he showed the photograph to a visitor her father used to pass it with a casual word:

"He is in Melbourne now."

She had consented to go away, to leave her home. Was that wise? She tried to weigh each side of the question. In her home anyway she had shelter and food; she had those whom she had known all her life about her. Of course she had to work hard, both in the house and at business. What would they say of her in the Stores when they found out that she had run away with a fellow? Say she was a fool, perhaps; and her place would be filled up by advertisement. Miss Gavan would be glad. She had always had an edge on her, especially whenever there were people listening.

"Miss Hill, don't you see these ladies are waiting?"

"Look lively, Miss Hill, please."

She would not cry many tears at leaving the Stores.

But in her new home, in a distant unknown country, it would not be like that. Then she would be married — she, Eveline. People would treat her with respect then. She would not be treated as her mother had been. Even now, though she was over nineteen, she sometimes felt herself in danger of her father's violence. She knew it was that that had given her the palpitations. When they were growing up he had never gone for her, like he used to go for Harry and Ernest, because she was a girl; but latterly he had begun to threaten her and say what he would do to her only for her dead mother's sake. And now she had nobody to protect her. Ernest was dead and Harry, who was in the church decorating business, was nearly always down somewhere in the country. Besides, the invariable squabble for money on Saturday nights had begun to weary her unspeakably. She always gave her entire wages — seven shillings — and Harry always sent up what he could but the trouble was to get any money from her father. He said she used to squander the money, that she had no head, that he wasn't going to give her his hard earned money to throw about the streets, and much more, for he was usually fairly bad on Saturday night. In the end he would give her the money and ask her had she any intention of buying Sunday's dinner. Then she had to rush out as quickly as she could and do her marketing, holding her black leather purse tightly in her hand as she elbowed her way through the crowds and returning home late under her load of provisions. She had hard work to keep the house together and to see that the two young children who had been left to her charge went to school regularly and got their meals regularly. It was hard work — a hard life — but now that she was about to leave it she did not find it a wholly undesirable life.

She was about to explore another life with Frank. Frank was very kind, manly, open-hearted. She was to go away with him by the night-boat to be his wife and to live with him in Buenos Ayres where he had a home waiting for her. How well she remembered the first time she had seen him; he was lodging in a house on the main road where she used to visit. It seemed a few weeks ago. He was standing at the gate, his peaked cap pushed back on his head and his hair tumbled forward over a face of bronze. Then they had come to know each other. He used to meet her outside the Stores every evening and see her home. He took her to see *The Bohemian Girl* and she felt elated as she sat in an unaccustomed part of the theatre with him. He was awfully fond of music and sang a little. People knew that they were courting and, when he sang about the lass that loves a sailor, she always felt pleasantly confused. He used to call her Poppens out of fun. First of all it had been an excitement for her to have a fellow and then she had begun to like him. He had tales of distant countries. He had started as a deck boy at a pound a month on a ship of the Allan Line going out to Canada. He told her the names of the ships he had been on and the names of the different services. He had sailed through the Straits of Magellan and he told her stories of the terrible Patagonians. He had fallen on his feet in Buenos Ayres, he said, and had come over to the old country just for a holiday. Of course, her father had found out the affair and had forbidden her to have anything to say to him.

"I know these sailor chaps," he said.

One day he had quarrelled with Frank and after that she had to meet her lover secretly.

The evening deepened in the avenue. The white of two letters in her lap grew indistinct. One was to Harry; the other was to her father. Ernest had been her favourite but she liked Harry too. Her father was becoming old lately, she noticed; he would miss her. Sometimes he could be very nice. Not long before, when she had been laid up for a day, he had read her out a ghost story and made toast for her at the fire. Another day, when their mother was alive, they had all gone for a picnic to the Hill of Howth. She remembered her father putting on her mother's bonnet to make the children laugh.

Her time was running out but she continued to sit by the window, leaning her head against the window curtain, inhaling the odour of dusty cretonne. Down far in the avenue she could hear a street organ playing. She knew the air. Strange that it should come that very night to remind her of the promise to her mother, her promise to keep the home together as long as she could. She remembered the last night of her mother's illness; she was again in the close dark room at the other side of the hall and outside she heard a melancholy air of Italy. The organ-player had been ordered to go away and given sixpence. She remembered her father strutting back into the sickroom saying:

"Damned Italians! coming over here!"

As she mused the pitiful vision of her mother's life laid its spell on the very quick of her being—that life of commonplace sacrifices closing in final craziness. She trembled as she heard again her mother's voice saying constantly with foolish insistence:

"Derevaun Seraun! Derevaun Seraun!"

She stood up in a sudden impulse of terror. Escape! She must escape! Frank would save her. He would give her life, perhaps love, too. But she wanted to live. Why should she be unhappy? She had a right to happiness. Frank would take her in his arms, fold her in his arms. He would save her.

She stood among the swaying crowd in the station at the North Wall. He held her hand and she knew that he was speaking to her, saying something about the passage over and over again. The station was full of soldiers with brown baggages. Through the wide doors of the sheds she caught a glimpse of the black mass of the boat, lying in beside the quay wall, with il-lumined portholes. She answered nothing. She felt her cheek pale and cold and, out of a maze of distress, she prayed to God to direct her, to show her what was her duty. The boat blew a long mournful whistle into the mist. If she went, to-morrow she would be on the sea with Frank, steaming towards Buenos Ayres. Their passage had been booked. Could she still draw back after all he had done for her? Her distress awoke a nausea in her body and she kept moving her lips in silent fervent prayer.

A bell clanged upon her heart. She felt him seize her hand:

"Come!"

All the seas of the world tumbled about her heart. He was drawing her into them: he would drown her. She gripped with both hands at the iron railing.

"Come!"

No! No! No! It was impossible. Her hands clutched the iron in frenzy. Amid the seas she sent a cry of anguish!

"Eveline! Evvy!"

He rushed beyond the barrier and called to her to follow. He was shouted at to go on but he still called to her. She set her white face to him, passive, like a helpless animal. Her eyes gave him no sign of love or farewell or recognition.

CD-ROM: Research James Joyce in depth with cultural documents and multimedia resources on *LiterActive*.

Jamaica Kincaid b. 1949

Girl
[1978]

Wash the white clothes on Monday and put them on the stone heap; wash the color clothes on Tuesday and put them on the clothesline to dry; don't walk barehead in the hot sun; cook pumpkin fritters in very hot sweet oil; soak your little cloths right after you take them off; when buying cotton to make yourself a nice blouse, be sure that it doesn't have gum on it, because that way it won't hold up well after a wash; soak salt fish overnight before you cook it; is it true that you sing benna in Sunday school?; always eat your food in such a way that it won't turn someone else's stomach; on Sundays try to walk like a lady and not like the slut you are so bent on becoming; don't sing benna in Sunday school; you mustn't speak to wharf-rat boys, not even to give directions; don't eat fruits on the street — flies will follow you; *but I don't sing benna on Sundays at all and never in Sunday school;* this is how to sew on a button; this is how to make a buttonhole for the button you have just sewed on; this is how to hem a dress when you see the hem coming down and so to prevent yourself from looking like the slut I know you are so bent on becoming; this is how you iron your father's khaki shirt so that it doesn't have a crease; this is how you iron your father's khaki pants so that they don't have a crease; this is how you grow okra — far from the house, because okra tree harbors red ants; when you are growing dasheen, make sure it gets plenty of water or else it makes your throat itch when you are eating it; this is how you sweep a corner; this is how you sweep a whole house; this is how you sweep a yard; this is how you smile to someone you don't like too much; this is how you smile to someone you don't like at all; this is how you smile to someone you like completely; this is how you set a table for tea; this is how you set a table for dinner; this is how you set a table for dinner with an important guest; this is how you set a table for lunch; this is how you set a table for breakfast; this is how to behave in the presence of men who don't know you very well, and this way they won't recognize immediately the slut I have warned you against becoming; be sure to wash every day, even if it is with your own spit; don't squat down to play marbles — you are not a boy, you know; don't pick people's flowers — you might catch something; don't throw stones at blackbirds, because it might not be a blackbird at all; this is how to make a bread pudding; this is how to make doukona; this is how to make pepper pot; this is how to make a good medicine for a cold; this is how to make a good medicine to throw away a child before it even becomes a child; this is how to catch a fish; this is how to throw back a fish you don't like, and that way something bad won't fall on you; this is how to bully a man; this is how a man bullies you; this is how to love a man, and if this doesn't work there are other ways, and if they don't work don't feel too bad about giving up; this is how to spit up in the air if you feel like it, and this is how to move quick so that it doesn't fall on you; this is how to make ends meet; always squeeze bread to make sure it's fresh; *but what if the baker won't let me feel the bread?;* you mean to say that after all you are really going to be the kind of woman who the baker won't let near the bread?

WEB: Explore Jamaica Kincaid and "Girl" in depth, including images and cultural documents, with VirtuaLit Fiction at bedfordstmartins.com/approachinglit.

Jhumpa Lahiri b. 1967

Interpreter of Maladies   [1999]

At the tea stall Mr. and Mrs. Das bickered about who should take Tina to the toilet. Eventually Mrs. Das relented when Mr. Das pointed out that he had given the girl her bath the night before. In the rearview mirror Mr. Kapasi watched as Mrs. Das emerged slowly from his bulky white Ambassador, dragging her shaved, largely bare legs across the back seat. She did not hold the little girl's hand as they walked to the rest room.

They were on their way to see the Sun Temple at Konarak. It was a dry, bright Saturday, the mid-July heat tempered by a steady ocean breeze, ideal weather for sightseeing. Ordinarily Mr. Kapasi would not have stopped so soon along the way, but less than five minutes after he'd picked up the family that morning in front of Hotel Sandy Villa, the little girl had complained. The first thing Mr. Kapasi had noticed when he saw Mr. and Mrs. Das, standing with their children under the portico of the hotel, was that they were very young, perhaps not even thirty. In addition to Tina they had two boys, Ronny and Bobby, who appeared very close in age and had teeth covered in a network of flashing silver wires. The family looked Indian but dressed as foreigners did, the children in stiff, brightly colored clothing and caps with translucent visors. Mr. Kapasi was accustomed to foreign tourists; he was assigned to them regularly because he could speak English. Yesterday he had driven an elderly couple from Scotland, both with spotted faces and fluffy white hair so thin it exposed their sunburnt scalps. In comparison, the tanned, youthful faces of Mr. and Mrs. Das were all the more striking. When he'd introduced himself, Mr. Kapasi had pressed his palms together in greeting, but Mr. Das squeezed hands like an American so that Mr. Kapasi felt it in his elbow. Mrs. Das, for her part, had flexed one side of her mouth, smiling dutifully at Mr. Kapasi, without displaying any interest in him.

As they waited at the tea stall, Ronny, who looked like the older of the two boys, clambered suddenly out of the back seat, intrigued by a goat tied to a stake in the ground.

"Don't touch it," Mr. Das said. He glanced up from his paperback tour book, which said "INDIA" in yellow letters and looked as if it had been published abroad. His voice, somehow tentative and a little shrill, sounded as though it had not yet settled into maturity.

"I want to give it a piece of gum," the boy called back as he trotted ahead.

Mr. Das stepped out of the car and stretched his legs by squatting briefly to the ground. A clean-shaven man, he looked exactly like a magnified version of Ronny. He had a sapphire blue visor, and was dressed in shorts, sneakers, and a T-shirt. The camera slung around his neck, with an impressive telephoto lens and numerous buttons and markings, was the only complicated thing he wore. He frowned, watching as Ronny rushed toward the goat, but appeared to have no intention of intervening. "Bobby, make sure that your brother doesn't do anything stupid."

"I don't feel like it," Bobby said, not moving. He was sitting in the front seat beside Mr. Kapasi, studying a picture of the elephant god taped to the glove compartment.

"No need to worry," Mr. Kapasi said. "They are quite tame." Mr. Kapasi was forty-six years old, with receding hair that had gone completely silver, but his butterscotch complexion and his unlined brow, which he treated in spare moments to dabs of lotus-oil balm, made it easy to imagine what he must have looked like at an earlier age. He wore gray trousers and a matching jacket-style shirt, tapered at the waist, with short sleeves and a large pointed collar, made of a thin but durable synthetic material. He had specified both the cut and the fabric to his tailor—it was his preferred uniform for giving tours because it did not get crushed during his long hours behind the wheel. Through the windshield he watched as Ronny circled around the goat, touched it quickly on its side, then trotted back to the car.

"You left India as a child?" Mr. Kapasi asked when Mr. Das had settled once again into the passenger seat.

"Oh, Mina and I were both born in America," Mr. Das announced with an air of sudden confidence. "Born and raised. Our parents live here now, in Assansol. They retired. We visit them every couple years." He turned to watch as the little girl ran toward the car, the wide purple bows of her sundress flopping on her narrow brown shoulders. She was holding to her chest a doll with yellow hair that looked as if it had been chopped, as a punitive measure, with a pair of dull scissors. "This is Tina's first trip to India, isn't it, Tina?"

"I don't have to go to the bathroom anymore," Tina announced.

"Where's Mina?" Mr. Das asked.

Mr. Kapasi found it strange that Mr. Das should refer to his wife by her first name when speaking to the little girl. Tina pointed to where Mrs. Das was purchasing something from one of the shirtless men who worked at the tea stall. Mr. Kapasi heard one of the shirtless men sing a phrase from a popular Hindi love song as Mrs. Das walked back to the car, but she did not appear to understand the words of the song, for she did not express irritation, or embarrassment, or react in any other way to the man's declarations.

He observed her. She wore a red-and-white-checkered skirt that stopped above her knees, slip-on shoes with a square wooden heel, and a close-fitting blouse styled like a man's undershirt. The blouse was decorated at chest-level with a calico appliqué in the shape of a strawberry. She was a short woman, with small hands like paws, her frosty pink fingernails painted to match her lips, and was slightly plump in her figure. Her hair, shorn only a little longer than her husband's, was parted far to one side. She was wearing large dark brown sunglasses with a pinkish tint to them, and carried a big straw bag, almost as big as her torso, shaped like a bowl, with a water bottle poking out of it. She walked slowly, carrying some puffed rice tossed with peanuts and chili peppers in a large packet made from newspapers. Mr. Kapasi turned to Mr. Das.

"Where in America do you live?"

"New Brunswick, New Jersey."

"Next to New York?"

"Exactly. I teach middle school there."

"What subject?"

"Science. In fact, every year I take my students on a trip to the Museum of Natural History in New York City. In a way we have a lot in common, you could say, you and I. How long have you been a tour guide, Mr. Kapasi?"

"Five years."

Mrs. Das reached the car. "How long's the trip?" she asked, shutting the door.

"About two and a half hours," Mr. Kapasi replied.

At this Mrs. Das gave an impatient sigh, as if she had been traveling her whole life without pause. She fanned herself with a folded Bombay film magazine written in English.

"I thought that the Sun Temple is only eighteen miles north of Puri," Mr. Das said, tapping on the tour book.

"The roads to Konarak are poor. Actually it is a distance of fifty-two miles," Mr. Kapasi explained.

Mr. Das nodded, readjusting the camera strap where it had begun to chafe the back of his neck.

Before starting the ignition, Mr. Kapasi reached back to make sure the cranklike locks on the inside of each of the back doors were secured. As soon as the car began to move the little girl began to play with the lock on her side, clicking it with some effort forward and backward, but Mrs. Das said nothing to stop her. She sat a bit slouched at one end of the back seat, not offering her puffed rice to anyone. Ronny and Tina sat on either side of her, both snapping bright green gum.

"Look," Bobby said as the car began to gather speed. He pointed with his finger to the tall trees that lined the road. "Look."

"Monkeys!" Ronny shrieked. "Wow!"

They were seated in groups along the branches, with shining black faces, silver bodies, horizontal eyebrows, and crested heads. Their long gray tails dangled like a series of ropes among the leaves. A few scratched themselves with black leathery hands, or swung their feet, staring as the car passed.

"We call them the hanuman," Mr. Kapasi said. "They are quite common in the area."

As soon as he spoke, one of the monkeys leaped into the middle of the road, causing Mr. Kapasi to brake suddenly. Another bounced onto the hood of the car, then sprang away. Mr. Kapasi beeped his horn. The children began to get excited, sucking in their breath and covering their faces partly with their hands. They had never seen monkeys outside of a zoo, Mr. Das explained. He asked Mr. Kapasi to stop the car so that he could take a picture.

While Mr. Das adjusted his telephoto lens, Mrs. Das reached into her straw bag and pulled out a bottle of colorless nail polish, which she proceeded to stroke on the tip of her index finger.

The little girl stuck out a hand. "Mine too. Mommy, do mine too."

"Leave me alone," Mrs. Das said, blowing on her nail and turning her body slightly. "You're making me mess up."

The little girl occupied herself by buttoning and unbuttoning a pinafore on the doll's plastic body.

"All set," Mr. Das said, replacing the lens cap.

The car rattled considerably as it raced along the dusty road, causing them all to pop up from their seats every now and then, but Mrs. Das continued to polish her nails. Mr. Kapasi eased up on the accelerator, hoping to produce a smoother ride. When he reached for the gearshift the boy in front accommodated him by swinging his hairless knees out of the way. Mr. Kapasi noted that this boy was slightly paler than the other children. "Daddy, why is the driver sitting on the wrong side in this car, too?" the boy asked.

"They all do that here, dummy," Ronny said.

"Don't call your brother a dummy," Mr. Das said. He turned to Mr. Kapasi. "In America, you know . . . it confuses them."

"Oh yes, I am well aware," Mr. Kapasi said. As delicately as he could, he shifted gears again, accelerating as they approached a hill in the road. "I see it on *Dallas,* the steering wheels are on the left-hand side."

"What's *Dallas?*" Tina asked, banging her now naked doll on the seat behind Mr. Kapasi.

"It went off the air," Mr. Das explained. "It's a television show."

They were all like siblings, Mr. Kapasi thought as they passed a row of date trees. Mr. and Mrs. Das behaved like an older brother and sister, not parents. It seemed that they were in charge of the children only for the day; it was hard to believe they were regularly responsible for anything other than themselves. Mr. Das tapped on his lens cap, and his tour book, dragging his thumbnail occasionally across the pages so that they made a scraping sound. Mrs. Das continued to polish her nails. She had still not removed her sunglasses. Every now and then Tina renewed her plea that she wanted her nails done, too, and so at one point Mrs. Das flicked a drop of polish on the little girl's finger before depositing the bottle back inside her straw bag.

"Isn't this an air-conditioned car?" she asked, still blowing on her hand. The window on Tina's side was broken and could not be rolled down.

"Quit complaining," Mr. Das said. "It isn't so hot."

"I told you to get a car with air-conditioning," Mrs. Das continued. "Why do you do this, Raj, just to save a few stupid rupees. What are you saving us, fifty cents?"

Their accents sounded just like the ones Mr. Kapasi heard on American television programs, though not like the ones on *Dallas.*

"Doesn't it get tiresome, Mr. Kapasi, showing people the same thing every day?" Mr. Das asked, rolling down his own window all the way. "Hey, do you mind stopping the car. I just want to get a shot of this guy."

   Mr. Kapasi pulled over to the side of the road as Mr. Das took a picture of a barefoot man, his head wrapped in a dirty turban, seated on top of a cart of grain sacks pulled by a pair of bullocks. Both the man and the bullocks were emaciated. In the back seat Mrs. Das gazed out another window, at the sky, where nearly transparent clouds passed quickly in front of one another.

   "I look forward to it, actually," Mr. Kapasi said as they continued on their way. "The Sun Temple is one of my favorite places. In that way it is a reward for me. I give tours on Fridays and Saturdays only. I have another job during the week."

   "Oh? Where?" Mr. Das asked.

   "I work in a doctor's office."

   "You're a doctor?"

   "I am not a doctor. I work with one. As an interpreter."

   "What does a doctor need an interpreter for?"

   "He has a number of Gujarati patients. My father was Gujarati, but many people do not speak Gujarati in this area, including the doctor. And so the doctor asked me to work in his office, interpreting what the patients say."

   "Interesting. I've never heard of anything like that," Mr. Das said.

   Mr. Kapasi shrugged. "It is a job like any other."

   "But so romantic," Mrs. Das said dreamily, breaking her extended silence. She lifted her pinkish brown sunglasses and arranged them on top of her head like a tiara. For the first time, her eyes met Mr. Kapasi's in the rearview mirror: pale, a bit small, their gaze fixed but drowsy.

   Mr. Das craned to look at her. "What's so romantic about it?"

   "I don't know. Something." She shrugged, knitting her brows together for an instant. "Would you like a piece of gum, Mr. Kapasi?" she asked brightly. She reached into her straw bag and handed him a small square wrapped in green-and-white-striped paper. As soon as Mr. Kapasi put the gum in his mouth a thick sweet liquid burst onto his tongue.

   "Tell us more about your job, Mr. Kapasi," Mrs. Das said.

   "What would you like to know, madame?"

   "I don't know," she shrugged, munching on some puffed rice and licking the mustard oil from the corners of her mouth. "Tell us a typical situation." She settled back in her seat, her head tilted in a patch of sun, and closed her eyes. "I want to picture what happens."

   "Very well. The other day a man came in with a pain in his throat."

   "Did he smoke cigarettes?"

   "No. It was very curious. He complained that he felt as if there were long pieces of straw stuck in his throat. When I told the doctor he was able to prescribe the proper medication."

   "That's so neat."

   "Yes," Mr. Kapasi agreed after some hesitation.

   "So these patients are totally dependent on you," Mrs. Das said. She spoke slowly, as if she were thinking aloud. "In a way, more dependent on you than the doctor."

"How do you mean? How could it be?"

"Well, for example, you could tell the doctor that the pain felt like a burning, not straw. The patient would never know what you had told the doctor, and the doctor wouldn't know that you had told the wrong thing. It's a big responsibility."

"Yes, a big responsibility you have there, Mr. Kapasi," Mr. Das agreed.

Mr. Kapasi had never thought of his job in such complimentary terms. To him it was a thankless occupation. He found nothing noble in interpreting people's maladies, assiduously translating the symptoms of so many swollen bones, countless cramps of bellies and bowels, spots on people's palms that changed color, shape, or size. The doctor, nearly half his age, had an affinity for bell-bottom trousers and made humorless jokes about the Congress party. Together they worked in a stale little infirmary where Mr. Kapasi's smartly tailored clothes clung to him in the heat, in spite of the blackened blades of a ceiling fan churning over their heads.

The job was a sign of his failings. In his youth he'd been a devoted scholar of foreign languages, the owner of an impressive collection of dictionaries. He had dreamed of being an interpreter for diplomats and dignitaries, resolving conflicts between people and nations, settling disputes of which he alone could understand both sides. He was a self-educated man. In a series of notebooks, in the evenings before his parents settled his marriage, he had listed the common etymologies of words, and at one point in his life he was confident that he could converse, if given the opportunity, in English, French, Russian, Portuguese, and Italian, not to mention Hindi, Bengali, Orissi, and Gujarati. Now only a handful of European phrases remained in his memory, scattered words for things like saucers and chairs. English was the only non-Indian language he spoke fluently anymore. Mr. Kapasi knew it was not a remarkable talent. Sometimes he feared that his children knew better English than he did, just from watching television. Still, it came in handy for the tours.

He had taken the job as an interpreter after his first son, at the age of seven, contracted typhoid—that was how he had first made the acquaintance of the doctor. At the time Mr. Kapasi had been teaching English in a grammar school, and he bartered his skills as an interpreter to pay the increasingly exorbitant medical bills. In the end the boy had died one evening in his mother's arms, his limbs burning with fever, but then there was the funeral to pay for, and the other children who were born soon enough, and the newer, bigger house, and the good schools and tutors, and the fine shoes and the television, and the countless other ways he tried to console his wife and to keep her from crying in her sleep, and so when the doctor offered to pay him twice as much as he earned at the grammar school, he accepted. Mr. Kapasi knew that his wife had little regard for his career as an interpreter. He knew it reminded her of the son she'd lost, and that she resented the other lives he helped, in his own small way, to save. If ever she referred to his position, she used the phrase "doctor's assistant," as if the process of interpretation were equal to taking someone's temperature, or changing a bedpan. She never asked him about the patients who came to the doctor's office, or said that his job was a big responsibility.

For this reason it flattered Mr. Kapasi that Mrs. Das was so intrigued by his job. Unlike his wife, she had reminded him of its intellectual challenges. She had also used the word "romantic." She did not behave in a romantic way toward her husband, and yet she had used the word to describe him. He wondered if Mr. and Mrs. Das were a bad match, just as he and his wife were. Perhaps they, too, had little in common apart from three children and a decade of their lives. The signs he recognized from his own marriage were there—the bickering, the indifference, the protracted silences. Her sudden interest in him, an interest she did not express in either her husband or her children, was mildly intoxicating. When Mr. Kapasi thought once again about how she had said "romantic," the feeling of intoxication grew.

He began to check his reflection in the rearview mirror as he drove, feeling grateful that he had chosen the gray suit that morning and not the brown one, which tended to sag a little in the knees. From time to time he glanced through the mirror at Mrs. Das. In addition to glancing at her face he glanced at the strawberry between her breasts, and the golden brown hollow in her throat. He decided to tell Mrs. Das about another patient, and another: the young woman who had complained of a sensation of raindrops in her spine, the gentleman whose birthmark had begun to sprout hairs. Mrs. Das listened attentively, stroking her hair with a small plastic brush that resembled an oval bed of nails, asking more questions, for yet another example. The children were quiet, intent on spotting more monkeys in the trees, and Mr. Das was absorbed by his tour book, so it seemed like a private conversation between Mr. Kapasi and Mrs. Das. In this manner the next half hour passed, and when they stopped for lunch at a roadside restaurant that sold fritters and omelette sandwiches, usually something Mr. Kapasi looked forward to on his tours so that he could sit in peace and enjoy some hot tea, he was disappointed. As the Das family settled together under a magenta umbrella fringed with white and orange tassels, and placed their orders with one of the waiters who marched about in tricornered caps, Mr. Kapasi reluctantly headed toward a neighboring table.

"Mr. Kapasi, wait. There's room here," Mrs. Das called out. She gathered Tina onto her lap, insisting that he accompany them. And so, together, they had bottled mango juice and sandwiches and plates of onions and potatoes deep-fried in graham-flour batter. After finishing two omelette sandwiches Mr. Das took more pictures of the group as they ate.

"How much longer?" he asked Mr. Kapasi as he paused to load a new roll of film in the camera.

"About half an hour more."

By now the children had gotten up from the table to look at more monkeys perched in a nearby tree, so there was a considerable space between Mrs. Das and Mr. Kapasi. Mr. Das placed the camera to his face and squeezed one eye shut, his tongue exposed at one corner of his mouth. "This looks funny. Mina, you need to lean in closer to Mr. Kapasi."

She did. He could smell a scent on her skin, like a mixture of whiskey and rosewater. He worried suddenly that she could smell his perspiration, which he knew had collected beneath the synthetic material of his shirt. He polished off his mango juice in one gulp and smoothed his silver hair with his hands. A bit of the juice dripped onto his chin. He wondered if Mrs. Das had noticed.

She had not. "What's your address, Mr. Kapasi?" she inquired, fishing for something inside her straw bag.

"You would like my address?"

"So we can send you copies," she said. "Of the pictures." She handed him a scrap of paper which she had hastily ripped from a page of her film magazine. The blank portion was limited, for the narrow strip was crowded by lines of text and a tiny picture of a hero and heroine embracing under a eucalyptus tree.

The paper curled as Mr. Kapasi wrote his address in clear, careful letters. She would write to him, asking about his days interpreting at the doctor's office, and he would respond eloquently, choosing only the most entertaining anecdotes, ones that would make her laugh out loud as she read them in her house in New Jersey. In time she would reveal the disappointment of her marriage, and he his. In this way their friendship would grow, and flourish. He would possess a picture of the two of them, eating fried onions under a magenta umbrella, which he would keep, he decided, safely tucked between the pages of his Russian grammar. As his mind raced, Mr. Kapasi experienced a mild and pleasant shock. It was similar to a feeling he used to experience long ago when, after months of translating with the aid of a dictionary, he would finally read a passage from a French novel, or an Italian sonnet, and understand the words, one after another, unencumbered by his own efforts. In those moments Mr. Kapasi used to believe that all was right with the world, that all struggles were rewarded, that all of life's mistakes made sense in the end. The promise that he would hear from Mrs. Das now filled him with the same belief.

When he finished writing his address Mr. Kapasi handed her the paper, but as soon as he did so he worried that he had either misspelled his name, or accidentally reversed the numbers of his postal code. He dreaded the possibility of a lost letter, the photograph never reaching him, hovering somewhere in Orissa, close but ultimately unattainable. He thought of asking for the slip of paper again, just to make sure he had written his address accurately, but Mrs. Das had already dropped it into the jumble of her bag.

They reached Konarak at two-thirty. The temple, made of sandstone, was a massive pyramid-like structure in the shape of a chariot. It was dedicated to the great master of life, the sun, which struck three sides of the edifice as it made its journey each day across the sky. Twenty-four giant wheels were carved on the north and south sides of the plinth. The whole thing was drawn by a team of seven horses, speeding as if through the heavens. As they approached, Mr. Kapasi explained that the temple had been built between

A.D. 1243 and 1255, with the efforts of twelve hundred artisans, by the great ruler of the Ganga dynasty, King Narasimhadeva the First, to commemorate his victory against the Muslim army.

"It says the temple occupies about a hundred and seventy acres of land," Mr. Das said, reading from his book.

"It's like a desert," Ronny said, his eyes wandering across the sand that stretched on all sides beyond the temple.

"The Chandrabhaga River once flowed one mile north of here. It is dry now," Mr. Kapasi said, turning off the engine.

They got out and walked toward the temple, posing first for pictures by the pair of lions that flanked the steps. Mr. Kapasi led them next to one of the wheels of the chariot, higher than any human being, nine feet in diameter.

"'The wheels are supposed to symbolize the wheel of life,'" Mr. Das read. "'They depict the cycle of creation, preservation, and achievement of realization.' Cool." He turned the page of his book. "'Each wheel is divided into eight thick and thin spokes, dividing the day into eight equal parts. The rims are carved with designs of birds and animals, whereas the medallions in the spokes are carved with women in luxurious poses, largely erotic in nature.'"

What he referred to were the countless friezes of entwined naked bodies, making love in various positions, women clinging to the necks of men, their knees wrapped eternally around their lovers' thighs. In addition to these were assorted scenes from daily life, of hunting and trading, of deer being killed with bows and arrows and marching warriors holding swords in their hands.

It was no longer possible to enter the temple, for it had filled with rubble years ago, but they admired the exterior, as did all the tourists Mr. Kapasi brought there, slowly strolling along each of its sides. Mr. Das trailed behind, taking pictures. The children ran ahead, pointing to figures of naked people, intrigued in particular by the Nagamithunas, the half-human, half-serpentine couples who were said, Mr. Kapasi told them, to live in the deepest waters of the sea. Mr. Kapasi was pleased that they liked the temple, pleased especially that it appealed to Mrs. Das. She stopped every three or four paces, staring silently at the carved lovers, and the processions of elephants, and the topless female musicians beating on two-sided drums.

Though Mr. Kapasi had been to the temple countless times, it occurred to him, as he, too, gazed at the topless women, that he had never seen his own wife fully naked. Even when they had made love she kept the panels of her blouse hooked together, the string of her petticoat knotted around her waist. He had never admired the backs of his wife's legs the way he now admired those of Mrs. Das, walking as if for his benefit alone. He had, of course, seen plenty of bare limbs before, belonging to the American and European ladies who took his tours. But Mrs. Das was different. Unlike the other women, who had an interest only in the temple, and kept their noses buried in a guidebook, or their eyes behind the lens of a camera, Mrs. Das had taken an interest in him.

Mr. Kapasi was anxious to be alone with her, to continue their private conversation, yet he felt nervous to walk at her side. She was lost behind her sunglasses, ignoring her husband's requests that she pose for another picture, walking past her children as if they were strangers. Worried that he might disturb her, Mr. Kapasi walked ahead, to admire, as he always did, the three life-sized bronze avatars of Surya, the sun god, each emerging from its own niche on the temple facade to greet the sun at dawn, noon, and evening. They wore elaborate headdresses, their languid, elongated eyes closed, their bare chests draped with carved chains and amulets. Hibiscus petals, offerings from previous visitors, were strewn at their gray-green feet. The last statue, on the northern wall of the temple, was Mr. Kapasi's favorite. This Surya had a tired expression, weary after a hard day of work, sitting astride a horse with folded legs. Even his horse's eyes were drowsy. Around his body were smaller sculptures of women in pairs, their hips thrust to one side.

"Who's that?" Mrs. Das asked. He was startled to see that she was standing beside him.

"He is the Astachala-Surya," Mr. Kapasi said. "The setting sun."

"So in a couple of hours the sun will set right here?" She slipped a foot out of one of her square-heeled shoes, rubbed her toes on the back of her other leg.

"That is correct."

She raised her sunglasses for a moment, then put them back on again. "Neat."

Mr. Kapasi was not certain exactly what the word suggested, but he had a feeling it was a favorable response. He hoped that Mrs. Das had understood Surya's beauty, his power. Perhaps they would discuss it further in their letters. He would explain things to her, things about India, and she would explain things to him about America. In its own way this correspondence would fulfill his dream, of serving as an interpreter between nations. He looked at her straw bag, delighted that his address lay nestled among its contents. When he pictured her so many thousands of miles away he plummeted, so much so that he had an overwhelming urge to wrap his arms around her, to freeze with her, even for an instant, in an embrace witnessed by his favorite Surya. But Mrs. Das had already started walking.

"When do you return to America?" he asked, trying to sound placid.

"In ten days."

He calculated: A week to settle in, a week to develop the pictures, a few days to compose her letter, two weeks to get to India by air. According to his schedule, allowing room for delays, he would hear from Mrs. Das in approximately six weeks' time.

The family was silent as Mr. Kapasi drove them back, a little past four-thirty, to Hotel Sandy Villa. The children had bought miniature granite versions of the chariot's wheels at a souvenir stand, and they turned them round in their hands. Mr. Das continued to read his book. Mrs. Das untangled Tina's hair with her brush and divided it into two little ponytails.

Mr. Kapasi was beginning to dread the thought of dropping them off. He was not prepared to begin his six-week wait to hear from Mrs. Das. As he stole glances at her in the rearview mirror, wrapping elastic bands around Tina's hair, he wondered how he might make the tour last a little longer. Ordinarily he sped back to Puri using a shortcut, eager to return home, scrub his feet and hands with sandalwood soap, and enjoy the evening newspaper and a cup of tea that his wife would serve him in silence. The thought of that silence, something to which he'd long been resigned, now oppressed him. It was then that he suggested visiting the hills at Udayagiri and Khandagiri, where a number of monastic dwellings were hewn out of the ground, facing one another across a defile. It was some miles away, but well worth seeing, Mr. Kapasi told them.

"Oh yeah, there's something mentioned about it in this book," Mr. Das said. "Built by a Jain king or something."

"Shall we go then?" Mr. Kapasi asked. He paused at a turn in the road. "It's to the left."

Mr. Das turned to look at Mrs. Das. Both of them shrugged.

"Left, left," the children chanted.

Mr. Kapasi turned the wheel, almost delirious with relief. He did not know what he would do or say to Mrs. Das once they arrived at the hills. Perhaps he would tell her what a pleasing smile she had. Perhaps he would compliment her strawberry shirt, which he found irresistibly becoming. Perhaps, when Mr. Das was busy taking a picture, he would take her hand.

He did not have to worry. When they got to the hills, divided by a steep path thick with trees, Mrs. Das refused to get out of the car. All along the path, dozens of monkeys were seated on stones, as well as on the branches of the trees. Their hind legs were stretched out in front and raised to shoulder level, their arms resting on their knees.

"My legs are tired," she said, sinking low in her seat. "I'll stay here."

"Why did you have to wear those stupid shoes?" Mr. Das said. "You won't be in the pictures."

"Pretend I'm there."

"But we could use one of these pictures for our Christmas card this year. We didn't get one of all five of us at the Sun Temple. Mr. Kapasi could take it."

"I'm not coming. Anyway, those monkeys give me the creeps."

"But they're harmless," Mr. Das said. He turned to Mr. Kapasi. "Aren't they?"

"They are more hungry than dangerous," Mr. Kapasi said. "Do not provoke them with food, and they will not bother you."

Mr. Das headed up the defile with the children, the boys at his side, the little girl on his shoulders. Mr. Kapasi watched as they crossed paths with a Japanese man and woman, the only other tourists there, who paused for a final photograph, then stepped into a nearby car and drove away. As the car disappeared out of view some of the monkeys called out, emitting soft whooping sounds, and then walked on their flat black hands and feet up the path. At one point a group of them formed a little ring around Mr. Das and the children. Tina screamed in delight. Ronny ran in circles around his father. Bobby bent down and picked up a fat stick on the ground. When he extended it, one of the monkeys approached him and snatched it, then briefly beat the ground.

"I'll join them," Mr. Kapasi said, unlocking the door on his side. "There is much to explain about the caves."

"No. Stay a minute," Mrs. Das said. She got out of the back seat and slipped in beside Mr. Kapasi. "Raj has his dumb book anyway." Together, through the windshield, Mrs. Das and Mr. Kapasi watched as Bobby and the monkey passed the stick back and forth between them.

"A brave little boy," Mr. Kapasi commented.

"It's not so surprising," Mrs. Das said.

"No?"

"He's not his."

"I beg your pardon?"

"Raj's. He's not Raj's son."

Mr. Kapasi felt a prickle on his skin. He reached into his shirt pocket for the small tin of lotus-oil balm he carried with him at all times, and applied it to three spots on his forehead. He knew that Mrs. Das was watching him, but he did not turn to face her. Instead he watched as the figures of Mr. Das and the children grew smaller, climbing up the steep path, pausing every now and then for a picture, surrounded by a growing number of monkeys.

"Are you surprised?" The way she put it made him choose his words with care.

"It's not the type of thing one assumes," Mr. Kapasi replied slowly. He put the tin of lotus-oil balm back in his pocket.

"No, of course not. And no one knows, of course. No one at all. I've kept it a secret for eight whole years." She looked at Mr. Kapasi, tilting her chin as if to gain a fresh perspective. "But now I've told you."

Mr. Kapasi nodded. He felt suddenly parched, and his forehead was warm and slightly numb from the balm. He considered asking Mrs. Das for a sip of water, then decided against it.

"We met when we were very young," she said. She reached into her straw bag in search of something, then pulled out a packet of puffed rice. "Want some?"

"No, thank you."

She put a fistful in her mouth, sank into the seat a little, and looked away from Mr. Kapasi, out the window on her side of the car. "We married when we were still in college. We were in high school when he proposed. We went to the same college, of course. Back then we couldn't stand the thought of being separated, not for a day, not for a minute. Our parents were best friends who lived in the same town. My entire life I saw him every weekend, either at our house or theirs. We were sent upstairs to play together while our parents joked about our marriage. Imagine! They never caught us at anything, though in a way I think it was all more or less a setup. The things we did those Friday and Saturday nights, while our parents sat downstairs drinking tea . . . I could tell you stories, Mr. Kapasi."

As a result of spending all her time in college with Raj, she continued, she did not make many close friends. There was no one to confide in about him at the end of a difficult day, or to share a passing thought or a worry. Her parents now lived on the other side of the world, but she had never been very close to them, anyway. After marrying so young she was overwhelmed by it all, having a child so quickly, and nursing, and warming up bottles of milk and testing their temperature against her wrist while Raj was at work, dressed in sweaters and corduroy pants, teaching his students about rocks and dinosaurs. Raj never looked cross or harried, or plump as she had become after the first baby.

Always tired, she declined invitations from her one or two college girlfriends, to have lunch or shop in Manhattan. Eventually the friends stopped calling her, so that she was left at home all day with the baby, surrounded by toys that made her trip when she walked or wince when she sat, always cross and tired. Only occasionally did they go out after Ronny was born, and even more rarely did they entertain. Raj didn't mind; he looked forward to coming home from teaching and watching television and bouncing Ronny on his knee. She had been outraged when Raj told her that a Punjabi friend, someone whom she had once met but did not remember, would be staying with them for a week for some job interviews in the New Brunswick area.

Bobby was conceived in the afternoon, on a sofa littered with rubber teething toys, after the friend learned that a London pharmaceutical company had hired him, while Ronny cried to be freed from his playpen. She made no protest when the friend touched the small of her back as she was about to make a pot of coffee, then pulled her against his crisp navy suit. He made love to her swiftly, in silence, with an expertise she had never known, without the meaningful expressions and smiles Raj always insisted on afterward. The next day Raj drove the friend to JFK. He was married now, to a Punjabi girl, and they lived in London still, and every year they exchanged Christmas cards with Raj and Mina, each couple tucking photos of their families into the envelopes. He did not know that he was Bobby's father. He never would.

"I beg your pardon, Mrs. Das, but why have you told me this information?" Mr. Kapasi asked when she had finally finished speaking, and had turned to face him once again.

"For God's sake, stop calling me Mrs. Das. I'm twenty-eight. You probably have children my age."

"Not quite." It disturbed Mr. Kapasi to learn that she thought of him as a parent. The feeling he had had toward her, that had made him check his reflection in the rearview mirror as they drove, evaporated a little.

"I told you because of your talents." She put the packet of puffed rice back into her bag without folding over the top.

"I don't understand," Mr. Kapasi said.

"Don't you see? For eight years I haven't been able to express this to anybody, not to friends, certainly not to Raj. He doesn't even suspect it. He thinks I'm still in love with him. Well, don't you have anything to say?"

"About what?"

"About what I've just told you. About my secret, and about how terrible it makes me feel. I feel terrible looking at my children, and at Raj, always terrible. I have terrible urges, Mr. Kapasi, to throw things away. One day I had the urge to throw everything I own out the window, the television, the children, everything. Don't you think it's unhealthy?"

He was silent.

"Mr. Kapasi, don't you have anything to say? I thought that was your job."

"My job is to give tours, Mrs. Das."

"Not that. Your other job. As an interpreter."

"But we do not face a language barrier. What need is there for an interpreter?"

"That's not what I mean. I would never have told you otherwise. Don't you realize what it means for me to tell you?"

"What does it mean?"

"It means that I'm tired of feeling so terrible all the time. Eight years, Mr. Kapasi, I've been in pain eight years. I was hoping you could help me feel better, say the right thing. Suggest some kind of remedy."

He looked at her, in her red plaid skirt and strawberry T-shirt, a woman not yet thirty, who loved neither her husband nor her children, who had already fallen out of love with life. Her confession depressed him, depressed him all the more when he thought of Mr. Das at the top of the path, Tina clinging to his shoulders, taking pictures of ancient monastic cells cut into the hills to show his students in America, unsuspecting and unaware that one of his sons was not his own. Mr. Kapasi felt insulted that Mrs. Das should ask him to interpret her common, trivial little secret. She did not resemble the patients in the doctor's office, those who came glassy-eyed and desperate, unable to sleep or breathe or urinate with ease, unable, above all, to give words to their pains. Still, Mr. Kapasi believed it was his duty to assist Mrs. Das. Perhaps he ought to tell her to confess the truth to Mr. Das. He would explain that honesty was the best policy. Honesty, surely, would help her feel better, as she'd put it. Perhaps he would offer to preside over the discussion, as a mediator. He decided to begin with the most obvious question, to get to the heart of the matter, and so he asked, "Is it really pain you feel, Mrs. Das, or is it guilt?"

She turned to him and glared, mustard oil thick on her frosty pink lips. She opened her mouth to say something, but as she glared at Mr. Kapasi some certain knowledge seemed to pass before her eyes, and she stopped. It crushed him; he knew at that moment that he was not even important enough to be properly insulted. She opened the car door and began walking up the path, wobbling a little on her square wooden heels, reaching into her straw bag to eat handfuls of puffed rice. It fell through her fingers, leaving a zigzagging trail, causing a monkey to leap down from a tree and devour the little white grains. In search of more, the monkey began to follow Mrs. Das. Others joined him, so that she was soon being followed by about half a dozen of them, their velvety tails dragging behind.

Mr. Kapasi stepped out of the car. He wanted to holler, to alert her in some way, but he worried that if she knew they were behind her, she would grow nervous. Perhaps she would lose her balance. Perhaps they would pull at her bag or her hair. He began to jog up the path, taking a fallen branch in his hand to scare away the monkeys. Mrs. Das continued walking, oblivious, trailing grains of puffed rice. Near the top of the incline, before a group of cells fronted by a row of squat stone pillars, Mr. Das was kneeling on the ground, focusing the lens of his camera. The children stood under the arcade, now hiding, now emerging from view.

"Wait for me," Mrs. Das called out. "I'm coming."

Tina jumped up and down. "Here comes Mommy!"

"Great," Mr. Das said without looking up. "Just in time. We'll get Mr. Kapasi to take a picture of the five of us."

Mr. Kapasi quickened his pace, waving his branch so that the monkeys scampered away, distracted, in another direction.

"Where's Bobby?" Mrs. Das asked when she stopped.

Mr. Das looked up from the camera. "I don't know. Ronny, where's Bobby?"

Ronny shrugged. "I thought he was right here."

"Where is he?" Mrs. Das repeated sharply. "What's wrong with all of you?"

They began calling his name, wandering up and down the path a bit. Because they were calling, they did not initially hear the boy's screams. When they found him, a little farther down the path under a tree, he was surrounded by a group of monkeys, over a dozen of them, pulling at his T-shirt with their long black fingers. The puffed rice Mrs. Das had spilled was scattered at his feet, raked over by the monkeys' hands. The boy was silent, his body frozen, swift tears running down his startled face. His bare legs were dusty and red with welts from where one of the monkeys struck him repeatedly with the stick he had given to it earlier.

"Daddy, the monkey's hurting Bobby," Tina said.

Mr. Das wiped his palms on the front of his shorts. In his nervousness he accidentally pressed the shutter on his camera; the whirring noise of the advancing film excited the monkeys, and the one with the stick began to beat Bobby more intently. "What are we supposed to do? What if they start attacking?"

"Mr. Kapasi," Mrs. Das shrieked, noticing him standing to one side. "Do something, for God's sake, do something!"

Mr. Kapasi took his branch and shooed them away, hissing at the ones that remained, stomping his feet to scare them. The animals retreated slowly, with a measured gait, obedient but unintimidated. Mr. Kapasi gathered Bobby in his arms and brought him back to where his parents and siblings were standing. As he carried him he was tempted to whisper a secret into the boy's ear. But Bobby was stunned, and shivering with fright, his legs bleeding slightly where the stick had broken the skin. When Mr. Kapasi delivered him to his parents, Mr. Das brushed some dirt off the boy's T-shirt and put the visor on him the right way. Mrs. Das reached into her straw bag to find a bandage which she taped over the cut on his knee. Ronny offered his brother a fresh piece of gum. "He's fine. Just a little scared, right, Bobby?" Mr. Das said, patting the top of his head.

"God, let's get out of here," Mrs. Das said. She folded her arms across the strawberry on her chest. "This place gives me the creeps."

"Yeah. Back to the hotel, definitely," Mr. Das agreed.

"Poor Bobby," Mrs. Das said. "Come here a second. Let Mommy fix your hair." Again she reached into her straw bag, this time for her hairbrush, and began to run it around the edges of the translucent visor. When she whipped out the hairbrush, the slip of paper with Mr. Kapasi's address on it fluttered away in the wind. No one but Mr. Kapasi noticed. He watched as it rose, carried higher and higher by the breeze, into the trees where the monkeys now sat, solemnly observing the scene below. Mr. Kapasi observed it too, knowing that this was the picture of the Das family he would preserve forever in his mind.

Toni Morrison b. 1931

Recitatif [1983]

My mother danced all night and Roberta's was sick. That's why we were taken to St. Bonny's. People want to put their arms around you when you tell them you were in a shelter, but it really wasn't bad. No big long room with one hundred beds like Bellevue. There were four to a room, and when Roberta and me came, there was a shortage of state kids, so we were the only ones assigned to 406 and could go from bed to bed if we wanted to. And we wanted to, too. We changed beds every night and for the whole four months we were there we never picked one out as our own permanent bed.

It didn't start out that way. The minute I walked in and the Big Bozo introduced us, I got sick to my stomach. It was one thing to be taken out of your own bed early in the morning — it was something else to be stuck in a strange place with a girl from a whole other race. And Mary, that's my mother, she was right. Every now and then she would stop dancing long enough to tell me something important and one of the things she said was that they never washed their hair and they smelled funny. Roberta sure did. Smell funny, I mean. So when the Big Bozo (nobody ever called her Mrs. Itkin, just like nobody ever said St. Bonaventure) — when she said, "Twyla, this is Roberta. Roberta, this is Twyla. Make each other welcome." I said, "My mother won't like you putting me in here."

"Good," said Bozo. "Maybe then she'll come and take you home."

How's that for mean? If Roberta had laughed I would have killed her, but she didn't. She just walked over to the window and stood with her back to us.

"Turn around," said the Bozo. "Don't be rude. Now Twyla. Roberta. When you hear a loud buzzer, that's the call for dinner. Come down to the first floor. Any fights and no movie." And then, just to make sure we knew what we would be missing, *"The Wizard of Oz."*

Roberta must have thought I meant that my mother would be mad about my being put in the shelter. Not about rooming with her, because as soon as Bozo left she came over to me and said, "Is your mother sick too?"

"No," I said. "She just likes to dance all night."

"Oh," she nodded her head and I liked the way she understood things so fast. So for the moment it didn't matter that we looked like salt and pepper standing there and that's what the other kids called us sometimes. We were eight years old and got F's all the time. Me because I couldn't remember what I read or what the teacher said. And Roberta because she couldn't read at all and didn't even listen to the teacher. She wasn't good at anything except jacks, at which she was a killer: pow scoop pow scoop pow scoop.

We didn't like each other all that much at first, but nobody else wanted to play with us because we weren't real orphans with beautiful dead parents in the sky. We were dumped. Even the New York City Puerto Ricans and the upstate Indians ignored us. All kinds of kids were in there, black ones, white ones, even two Koreans. The food was good, though. At least I thought so. Roberta hated it and left whole pieces of things on her plate: Spam, Salisbury steak — even jello with fruit cocktail in it, and she didn't care if I ate what she wouldn't. Mary's idea of supper was popcorn and a can of Yoo-Hoo. Hot mashed potatoes and two weenies was like Thanksgiving for me.

It really wasn't bad, St. Bonny's. The big girls on the second floor pushed us around now and then. But that was all. They wore lipstick and eyebrow pencil and wobbled their knees while they watched TV. Fifteen, sixteen, even, some of them were. They were put-out girls, scared runaways most of them. Poor little girls who fought their uncles off but looked tough to us, and mean. God did they look mean. The staff tried to keep them separate from the younger children, but sometimes they caught us watching them in the orchard where they played radios and danced with each other. They'd light out after us and pull our hair or twist our arms. We were scared of them, Roberta and me, but neither of us wanted the other one to know it. So we got a good list of dirty names we could shout back when we ran from them through the orchard. I used to dream a lot and almost always the orchard was there. Two acres, four maybe, of these little apple trees.

Hundreds of them. Empty and crooked like beggar women when I first came to St. Bonny's but fat with flowers when I left. I don't know why I dreamt about that orchard so much. Nothing really happened there. Nothing all that important, I mean. Just the big girls dancing and playing the radio. Roberta and me watching. Maggie fell down there once. The kitchen woman with legs like parentheses. And the big girls laughed at her. We should have helped her up, I know, but we were scared of those girls with lipstick and eyebrow pencil. Maggie couldn't talk. The kids said she had her tongue cut out, but I think she was just born that way: mute. She was old and sandy-colored and she worked in the kitchen. I don't know if she was nice or not. I just remember her legs like parentheses and how she rocked when she walked. She worked from early in the morning till two o'clock, and if she was late, if she had too much cleaning and didn't get out till two-fifteen or so, she'd cut through the orchard so she wouldn't miss her bus and have to wait another hour. She wore this really stupid little hat — a kid's hat with ear flaps — and she wasn't much taller than we were. A really awful little hat. Even for a mute, it was dumb — dressing like a kid and never saying anything at all.

"But what about if somebody tries to kill her?" I used to wonder about that. "Or what if she wants to cry? Can she cry?"

"Sure," Roberta said. "But just tears. No sounds come out."

"She can't scream?"

"Nope. Nothing."

"Can she hear?"

"I guess."

"Let's call her," I said. And we did.

"Dummy! Dummy!" She never turned her head.

"Bow legs! Bow legs!" Nothing. She just rocked on, the chin straps of her baby-boy hat swaying from side to side. I think we were wrong. I think she could hear and didn't let on. And it shames me even now to think there was somebody in there after all who heard us call her those names and couldn't tell on us.

We got along all right, Roberta and me. Changed beds every night, got F's in civics and communication skills and gym. The Bozo was disappointed in us, she said. Out of 130 of us state cases, 90 were under twelve. Almost all were real orphans with beautiful dead parents in the sky. We were the only ones dumped and the only ones with F's in three classes including gym. So we got along — what with her leaving whole pieces of things on her plate and being nice about not asking questions.

I think it was the day before Maggie fell down that we found out our mothers were coming to visit us on the same Sunday. We had been at the shelter twenty-eight days (Roberta twenty-eight and a half) and this was their first visit with us. Our mothers would come at ten o'clock in time for chapel, then lunch with us in the teachers' lounge. I thought if my dancing mother met her sick mother it might be good for her. And Roberta thought her sick mother would get a big bang out of a dancing one. We got excited about it and curled each other's hair. After breakfast we sat on the bed watching the road from the window. Roberta's socks were still wet. She washed them the night before and put them on the radiator to dry. They hadn't, but she put them on anyway because their tops were so pretty — scalloped in pink. Each of us had a purple construction-paper basket that we had made in craft class. Mine had a yellow crayon rabbit on it. Roberta's had eggs with wiggly lines of color. Inside were cellophane grass and just the jelly beans because I'd eaten the two marshmallow eggs they gave us. The Big Bozo came herself to get us. Smiling she told us we looked very nice and to come downstairs. We were so surprised by the smile we'd never seen before, neither of us moved.

"Don't you want to see your mommies?"

I stood up first and spilled the jelly beans all over the floor. Bozo's smile disappeared while we scrambled to get the candy up off the floor and put it back in the grass.

She escorted us downstairs to the first floor, where the other girls were lining up to file into the chapel. A bunch of grown-ups stood to one side. Viewers mostly. The old biddies who wanted servants and the fags who wanted company looking for children they might want to adopt. Once in a while a grandmother. Almost never anybody young or anybody whose face wouldn't scare you in the night. Because if any of the real orphans had young relatives they wouldn't be real orphans. I saw Mary right away. She had on those green slacks I hated and hated even more now because didn't she know we were going to chapel? And that fur jacket with the pocket linings so ripped she had to pull to get her hands out of them. But her face was pretty — like always, and she smiled and waved like she was the little girl looking for her mother — not me.

I walked slowly, trying not to drop the jelly beans and hoping the paper handle would hold. I had to use my last Chiclet because by the time I finished cutting everything out, all the Elmer's was gone. I am left-handed and the scissors never worked for me. It didn't matter, though; I might just as well have chewed the gum. Mary dropped to her knees and grabbed me, mashing the basket, the jelly beans, and the grass into her ratty fur jacket.

"Twyla, baby. Twyla, baby!"

I could have killed her. Already I heard the big girls in the orchard the next time saying, "Twyyyyyla, baby!" But I couldn't stay mad at Mary while she was smiling and hugging me and smelling of Lady Esther dusting powder. I wanted to stay buried in her fur all day.

To tell the truth I forgot about Roberta. Mary and I got in line for the traipse into chapel and I was feeling proud because she looked so beautiful even in those ugly green slacks that made her behind stick out. A pretty mother on earth is better than a beautiful dead one in the sky even if she did leave you all alone to go dancing.

I felt a tap on my shoulder, turned, and saw Roberta smiling. I smiled back, but not too much lest somebody think this visit was the biggest thing that ever happened in my life. Then Roberta said, "Mother, I want you to meet my roommate, Twyla. And that's Twyla's mother."

I looked up it seemed for miles. She was big. Bigger than any man and on her chest was the biggest cross I'd ever seen. I swear it was six inches long each way. And in the crook of her arm was the biggest Bible ever made.

Mary, simple-minded as ever, grinned and tried to yank her hand out of the pocket with the raggedy lining—to shake hands, I guess. Roberta's mother looked down at me and then looked down at Mary too. She didn't say anything, just grabbed Roberta with her Bible-free hand and stepped out of line, walking quickly to the rear of it. Mary was still grinning because she's not too swift when it comes to what's really going on. Then this light bulb goes off in her head and she says "That bitch!" really loud and us almost in the chapel now. Organ music whining; the Bonny Angels singing sweetly. Everybody in the world turned around to look. And Mary would have kept it up—kept calling names if I hadn't squeezed her hand as hard as I could. That helped a little, but she still twitched and crossed and uncrossed her legs all through service. Even groaned a couple of times. Why did I think she would come there and act right? Slacks. No hat like the grandmothers and viewers, and groaning all the while. When we stood for hymns she kept her mouth shut. Wouldn't even look at the words on the page. She actually reached in her purse for a mirror to check her lipstick. All I could think of was that she really needed to be killed. The sermon lasted a year, and I knew the real orphans were looking smug again.

We were supposed to have lunch in the teachers' lounge, but Mary didn't bring anything, so we picked fur and cellophane grass off the mashed jelly beans and ate them. I could have killed her. I sneaked a look at Roberta. Her mother had brought chicken legs and ham sandwiches and oranges and a whole box of chocolate-covered grahams. Roberta drank milk from a thermos while her mother read the Bible to her.

Things are not right. The wrong food is always with the wrong people. Maybe that's why I got into waitress work later—to match up the right people with the right food. Roberta just let those chicken legs sit there, but she did bring a stack of grahams up to me later when the visit was over. I think she was sorry that her mother would not shake my mother's hand. And I liked that and I liked the fact that she didn't say a word about Mary groaning all the way through the service and not bringing any lunch.

Roberta left in May when the apple trees were heavy and white. On her last day we went to the orchard to watch the big girls smoke and dance by the radio. It didn't matter that they said, "Twyyyyyla, baby." We sat on the ground and breathed. Lady Esther. Apple blossoms. I still go soft when I smell one or the other. Roberta was going home. The big cross and the big Bible was coming to get her and she seemed sort of glad and sort of not. I thought I would die in that room of four beds without her and I knew Bozo had plans to move some other dumped kid in there with me. Roberta promised to write every day, which was really sweet of her because she couldn't read a lick so how could she write anybody. I would have drawn pictures and sent them to her but she never gave me her address. Little by little she faded. Her wet socks with the pink scalloped tops and her big serious-looking eyes — that's all I could catch when I tried to bring her to mind.

I was working behind the counter at the Howard Johnson's on the Thruway just before the Kingston exit. Not a bad job. Kind of a long ride from Newburgh, but okay once I got there. Mine was the second night shift — eleven to seven. Very light until a Greyhound checked in for break-fast around six-thirty. At that hour the sun was all the way clear of the hills behind the restaurant. The place looked better at night — more like shelter — but I loved it when the sun broke in, even if it did show all the cracks in the vinyl and the speckled floor looked dirty no matter what the mop boy did.

It was August and a bus crowd was just unloading. They would stand around a long while: going to the john, and looking at gifts and junk-for-sale machines, reluctant to sit down so soon. Even to eat. I was trying to fill the coffee pots and get them all situated on the electric burners when I saw her. She was sitting in a booth smoking a cigarette with two guys smothered in head and facial hair. Her own hair was so big and wild I could hardly see her face. But the eyes. I would know them anywhere. She had on a powder-blue halter and shorts outfit and earrings the size of bracelets. Talk about lipstick and eyebrow pencil. She made the big girls look like nuns. I couldn't get off the counter until seven o'clock, but I kept watching the booth in case they got up to leave before that. My replacement was on time for a change, so I counted and stacked my receipts as fast as I could and signed off. I walked over to the booth, smiling and wondering if she would remember me. Or even if she wanted to remember me. Maybe she didn't want to be re-minded of St. Bonny's or to have anybody know she was ever there. I know I never talked about it to anybody.

I put my hands in my apron pockets and leaned against the back of the booth facing them.

"Roberta? Roberta Fisk?"

She looked up. "Yeah?"

"Twyla."

She squinted for a second and then said, "Wow."

"Remember me?"

"Sure. Hey. Wow."

"It's been a while," I said, and gave a smile to the two hairy guys.

"Yeah. Wow. You work here?"

"Yeah," I said. "I live in Newburgh."

"Newburgh? No kidding?" She laughed then a private laugh that in-cluded the guys but only the guys, and they laughed with her. What could I do but laugh too and wonder why I was standing there with my knees showing out from under that uniform. Without looking I could see the blue and white triangle on my head, my hair shapeless in a net, my ankles thick in white oxfords. Nothing could have been less sheer than my stockings.

There was this silence that came down right after I laughed. A silence it was her turn to fill up. With introductions, maybe, to her boyfriends or an invitation to sit down and have a Coke. Instead she lit a cigarette off the one she'd just finished and said, "We're on our way to the Coast. He's got an appointment with Hendrix." She gestured casually toward the boy next to her.

"Hendrix? Fantastic," I said. "Really fantastic. What's she doing now?"

Roberta coughed on her cigarette and the two guys rolled their eyes up at the ceiling.

"Hendrix. Jimi Hendrix, asshole. He's only the biggest — Oh, wow. Forget it."

I was dismissed without anyone saying goodbye, so I thought I would do it for her.

"How's your mother?" I asked. Her grin cracked her whole face. She swallowed. "Fine," she said. "How's yours?"

"Pretty as a picture," I said and turned away. The backs of my knees were damp. Howard Johnson's really was a dump in the sunlight.

James is as comfortable as a house slipper. He liked my cooking and I liked his big loud family. They have lived in Newburgh all of their lives and talk about it the way people do who have always known a home. His grandmother is a porch swing older than his father and when they talk about streets and avenues and buildings they call them names they no longer have. They still call the A & P Rico's because it stands on property once a mom and pop store owned by Mr. Rico. And they call the new community college Town Hall because it once was. My mother-in-law puts up jelly and cucumbers and buys butter wrapped in cloth from a dairy. James and his father talk about fishing and baseball and I can see them all together on the Hudson in a raggedy skiff. Half the population of Newburgh is on welfare now, but to my husband's family it was still some upstate paradise of a time long past. A time of ice houses and vegetable wagons, coal furnaces and children weeding gardens. When our son was born my mother-in-law gave me the crib blanket that had been hers.

But the town they remembered had changed. Something quick was in the air. Magnificent old houses, so ruined they had become shelter for squatters and rent risks, were bought and renovated. Smart IBM people moved out of their suburbs back into the city and put shutters up and herb gardens in their backyards. A brochure came in the mail announcing the opening of a Food Emporium. Gourmet food it said — and listed items the rich IBM crowd would want. It was located in a new mall at the edge of town and I drove out to shop there one day — just to see. It was late in June. After the tulips were gone and the Queen Elizabeth roses were open everywhere. I trailed my cart along the aisle tossing in smoked oysters and Robert's sauce and things I knew would sit in my cupboard for years. Only when I found some Klondike ice cream bars did I feel less guilty about spending James's fireman's salary so foolishly. My father-in-law ate them with the same gusto little Joseph did.

Waiting in the check-out line I heard a voice say, "Twyla!"

The classical music piped over the aisles had affected me and the woman leaning toward me was dressed to kill. Diamonds on her hand, a smart white summer dress. "I'm Mrs. Benson," I said.

"Ho. Ho. The Big Bozo," she sang.

For a split second I didn't know what she was talking about. She had a bunch of asparagus and two cartons of fancy water.

"Roberta!"

"Right."

"For heaven's sake. Roberta."

"You look great," she said.

"So do you. Where are you? Here? In Newburgh?"

"Yes. Over in Annandale."

I was opening my mouth to say more when the cashier called my attention to her empty counter.

"Meet you outside." Roberta pointed her finger and went into the express line.

I placed the groceries and kept myself from glancing around to check Roberta's progress. I remembered Howard Johnson's and looking for a chance to speak only to be greeted with a stingy "wow." But she was waiting for me and her huge hair was sleek now, smooth around a small, nicely shaped head. Shoes, dress, everything lovely and summery and rich. I was dying to know what happened to her, how she got from Jimi Hendrix to Annandale, a neighborhood full of doctors and IBM executives. Easy, I thought. Everything is so easy for them. They think they own the world.

"How long," I asked her. "How long have you been here?"

"A year. I got married to a man who lives here. And you, you're married too, right? Benson, you said."

"Yeah. James Benson."

"And is he nice?"

"Oh, is he nice?"

"Well, is he?" Roberta's eyes were steady as though she really meant the question and wanted an answer.

"He's wonderful, Roberta. Wonderful."

"So you're happy."

"Very."

"That's good," she said and nodded her head. "I always hoped you'd be happy. Any kids? I know you have kids."

"One. A boy. How about you?"

"Four."

"Four?"

She laughed. "Step kids. He's a widower."

"Oh."

"Got a minute? Let's have a coffee."

I thought about the Klondikes melting and the inconvenience of going all the way to my car and putting the bags in the trunk. Served me right for buying all that stuff I didn't need. Roberta was ahead of me.

"Put them in my car. It's right here."

And then I saw the dark blue limousine.

"You married a Chinaman?"

"No," she laughed. "He's the driver."

"Oh, my. If the Big Bozo could see you now."

We both giggled. Really giggled. Suddenly, in just a pulse beat, twenty years disappeared and all of it came rushing back. The big girls (whom we called gar girls — Roberta's misheard word for the evil stone faces described in a civics class) there dancing in the orchard, the ploppy mashed potatoes, the double weenies, the Spam with pineapple. We went into the coffee shop holding on to one another and I tried to think why we were glad to see each other this time and not before. Once, twelve years ago, we passed like strangers. A black girl and a white girl meeting in a Howard Johnson's on the road and having nothing to say. One in a blue and white triangle waitress hat — the other on her way to see Hendrix. Now we were behaving like sisters separated for much too long. Those four short months were nothing in time. Maybe it was the thing itself. Just being there, together. Two little girls who knew what nobody else in the world knew — how not to ask questions. How to believe what had to be believed. There was politeness in that reluctance and generosity as well. Is your mother sick too? No, she dances all night. Oh — and an understanding nod.

We sat in a booth by the window and fell into recollection like veterans.

"Did you ever learn to read?"

"Watch." She picked up the menu. "Special of the day. Cream of corn soup. Entrées. Two dots and a wriggly line. Quiche. Chef salad, scallops . . ."

I was laughing and applauding when the waitress came up.

"Remember the Easter baskets?"

"And how we tried to *introduce* them?"

"Your mother with that cross like two telephone poles."

"And yours with those tight slacks."

We laughed so loudly heads turned and made the laughter harder to suppress.

"What happened to the Jimi Hendrix date?"

Roberta made a blow-out sound with her lips.

"When he died I thought about you."

"Oh, you heard about him finally?"

"Finally. Come on, I was a small-town country waitress."

"And I was a small-town country dropout. God, were we wild. I still don't know how I got out of there alive."

"But you did."

"I did. I really did. Now I'm Mrs. Kenneth Norton."

"Sounds like a mouthful."

"It is."

"Servants and all?"

Roberta held up two fingers.

"Ow! What does he do?"

"Computers and stuff. What do I know?"

"I don't remember a hell of a lot from those days, but Lord, St. Bonny's is as clear as daylight. Remember Maggie? The day she fell down and those gar girls laughed at her?"

Roberta looked up from her salad and stared at me. "Maggie didn't fall," she said.

"Yes, she did. You remember."

"No, Twyla. They knocked her down. Those girls pushed her down and tore her clothes. In the orchard."

"I don't—that's not what happened."

"Sure it is. In the orchard. Remember how scared we were?"

"Wait a minute. I don't remember any of that."

"And Bozo was fired."

"You're crazy. She was there when I left. You left before me."

"I went back. You weren't there when they fired Bozo."

"What?"

"Twice. Once for a year when I was about ten, another for two months when I was fourteen. That's when I ran away."

"You ran away from St. Bonny's?"

"I had to. What do you want? Me dancing in that orchard?"

"Are you sure about Maggie?"

"Of course I'm sure. You've blocked it, Twyla. It happened. Those girls had behavior problems, you know."

"Didn't they, though. But why can't I remember the Maggie thing?"

"Believe me. It happened. And we were there."

"Who did you room with when you went back?" I asked her as if I would know her. The Maggie thing was troubling me.

"Creeps. They tickled themselves in the night."

My ears were itching and I wanted to go home suddenly. This was all very well but she couldn't just comb her hair, wash her face and pretend everything was hunky-dory. After the Howard Johnson's snub. And no apology. Nothing.

"Were you on dope or what that time at Howard Johnson's?" I tried to make my voice sound friendlier than I felt.

"Maybe, a little. I never did drugs much. Why?"

"I don't know; you acted sort of like you didn't want to know me then."

"Oh, Twyla, you know how it was in those days: black—white. You know how everything was."

But I didn't know. I thought it was just the opposite. Busloads of blacks and whites came into Howard Johnson's together. They roamed together then: students, musicians, lovers, protesters. You got to see everything at Howard Johnson's and blacks were very friendly with whites in those days. But sitting there with nothing on my plate but two hard tomato wedges wondering about the melting Klondikes it seemed childish remembering the slight. We went to her car, and with the help of the driver, got my stuff into my station wagon.

"We'll keep in touch this time," she said.

"Sure," I said. "Sure. Give me a call."

"I will," she said, and then just as I was sliding behind the wheel, she leaned into the window. "By the way. Your mother. Did she ever stop dancing?"

I shook my head. "No. Never."

Roberta nodded.

"And yours? Did she ever get well?"

She smiled a tiny sad smile. "No. She never did. Look, call me, okay?"

"Okay," I said, but I knew I wouldn't. Roberta had messed up my past somehow with that business about Maggie. I wouldn't forget a thing like that. Would I?

Strife came to us that fall. At least that's what the paper called it. Strife. Racial strife. The word made me think of a bird—a big shrieking bird out of 1,000,000,000 B.C. Flapping its wings and cawing. Its eye with no lid always bearing down on you. All day it screeched and at night it slept on the rooftops. It woke you in the morning and from the *Today* show to the eleven o'clock news it kept you an awful company. I couldn't figure it out from one day to the next. I knew I was supposed to feel something strong, but I didn't know what, and James wasn't any help. Joseph was on the list of kids to be transferred from the junior high school to another one at some far-out-of-the-way place and I thought it was a good thing until I heard it was a bad thing. I mean I didn't know. All the schools seemed dumps to me, and the fact that one was nicer looking didn't hold much weight. But the papers were full of it and then the kids began to get jumpy. In August, mind you. Schools weren't even open yet. I thought Joseph might be frightened to go over there, but he didn't seem scared so I forgot about it, until I found myself driving along Hudson Street out there by the school they were trying to integrate and saw a line of women marching. And who do you suppose was in line, big as life, holding a sign in front of her bigger than her mother's cross? MOTHERS HAVE RIGHTS TOO! —it said.

I drove on, and then changed my mind. I circled the block, slowed down, and honked my horn.

Roberta looked over and when she saw me she waved. I didn't wave back, but I didn't move either. She handed her sign to another woman and came over to where I was parked.

"Hi."

"What are you doing?"

"Picketing. What's it look like?"

"What for?"

"What do you mean, 'What for?' They want to take my kids and send them out of the neighborhood. They don't want to go."

"So what if they go to another school? My boy's being bussed too, and I don't mind. Why should you?"

"It's not about us, Twyla. Me and you. It's about our kids."

"What's more *us* than that?"

"Well, it is a free country."

"Not yet, but it will be."

"What the hell does that mean? I'm not doing anything to you."

"You really think that?"

"I know it."

"I wonder what made me think you were different."

"I wonder what made me think you were different."

"Look at them," I said. "Just look. Who do they think they are? Swarming all over the place like they own it. And now they think they can decide where my child goes to school. Look at them, Roberta. They're Bozos."

Roberta turned around and looked at the women. Almost all of them were standing still now, waiting. Some were even edging toward us. Roberta looked at me out of some refrigerator behind her eyes. "No, they're not. They're just mothers."

"And what am I? Swiss cheese?"

"I used to curl your hair."

"I hated your hands in my hair."

The women were moving. Our faces looked mean to them of course and they looked as though they could not wait to throw themselves in front of a police car, or better yet, into my car and drag me away by my ankles. Now they surrounded my car and gently, gently began to rock it. I swayed back and forth like a sideways yo-yo. Automatically I reached for Roberta, like the old days in the orchard when they saw us watching them and we had to get out of there, and if one of us fell the other pulled her up and if one of us was caught the other stayed to kick and scratch, and neither would leave the other behind. My arm shot out of the car window but no receiving hand was there. Roberta was looking at me sway from side to side in the car and her face was still. My purse slid from the car seat down under the dashboard. The four policemen who had been drinking Tab in their car finally got the message and strolled over, forcing their way through the women. Quietly, firmly they spoke. "Okay, ladies. Back in line or off the streets."

Some of them went away willingly; others had to be urged away from the car doors and the hood. Roberta didn't move. She was looking steadily at me. I was fumbling to turn on the ignition, which wouldn't catch because the gearshift was still in drive. The seats of the car were a mess because the swaying had thrown my grocery coupons all over it and my purse was sprawled on the floor.

"Maybe I am different now, Twyla. But you're not. You're the same little state kid who kicked a poor old black lady when she was down on the ground. You kicked a black lady and you have the nerve to call me a bigot."

The coupons were everywhere and the guts of my purse were bunched under the dashboard. What was she saying? Black? Maggie wasn't black.

"She wasn't black," I said.

"Like hell she wasn't, and you kicked her. We both did. You kicked a black lady who couldn't even scream."

"Liar!"

"You're the liar! Why don't you just go on home and leave us alone, huh?"

She turned away and I skidded away from the curb.

The next morning I went into the garage and cut the side out of the carton our portable TV had come in. It wasn't nearly big enough, but after a while I had a decent sign: red spray-painted letters on a white background — AND SO DO CHILDREN****. I meant just to go down to the school and tack it up somewhere so those cows on the picket line across the street could see it, but when I got there, some ten or so others had already assembled — protesting the cows across the street. Police permits and everything. I got in line and we strutted in time on our side while Roberta's group strutted on theirs. That first day we were all dignified, pretending the other side didn't exist. The second day there was name calling and finger gestures. But that was about all. People changed signs from time to time, but Roberta never did and neither did I. Actually my sign didn't make sense without Roberta's. "And so do children what?" one of the women on my side asked me. Have rights, I said, as though it was obvious.

Roberta didn't acknowledge my presence in any way and I got to thinking maybe she didn't know I was there. I began to pace myself in the line, jostling people one minute and lagging behind the next, so Roberta and I could reach the end of our respective lines at the same time and there would be a moment in our turn when we would face each other. Still, I couldn't tell whether she saw me and knew my sign was for her. The next day I went early before we were scheduled to assemble. I waited until she got there before I exposed my new creation. As soon as she hoisted her MOTHERS HAVE RIGHTS TOO I began to wave my new one, which said, HOW WOULD YOU KNOW? I know she saw that one, but I had gotten addicted now. My signs got crazier each day, and the women on my side decided that I was a kook. They couldn't make heads or tails out of my brilliant screaming posters.

I brought a painted sign in queenly red with huge black letters that said, IS YOUR MOTHER WELL? Roberta took her lunch break and didn't come back for the rest of the day or any day after. Two days later I stopped going too and couldn't have been missed because nobody understood my signs anyway.

It was a nasty six weeks. Classes were suspended and Joseph didn't go to anybody's school until October. The children — everybody's children — soon got bored with that extended vacation they thought was going to be so great.

They looked at TV until their eyes flattened. I spent a couple of mornings tutoring my son, as the other mothers said we should. Twice I opened a text from last year that he had never turned in. Twice he yawned in my face. Other mothers organized living room sessions so the kids would keep up. None of the kids could concentrate so they drifted back to *The Price Is Right* and *The Brady Bunch*. When the school finally opened there were fights once or twice and some sirens roared through the streets every once in a while. There were a lot of photographers from Albany. And just when ABC was about to send up a news crew, the kids settled down like nothing in the world had happened. Joseph hung my HOW WOULD YOU KNOW? sign in his bedroom. I don't know what became of AND SO DO CHILDREN****. I think my father-in-law cleaned some fish on it. He was always puttering around in our garage. Each of his five children lived in Newburgh and he acted as though he had five extra homes.

I couldn't help looking for Roberta when Joseph graduated from high school, but I didn't see her. It didn't trouble me much what she had said to me in the car. I mean the kicking part. I know I didn't do that, I couldn't do that. But I was puzzled by her telling me Maggie was black. When I thought about it I actually couldn't be certain. She wasn't pitch-black, I knew, or I would have remembered that. What I remember was the kiddie hat, and the semicircle legs. I tried to reassure myself about the race thing for a long time until it dawned on me that the truth was already there, and Roberta knew it. I didn't kick her; I didn't join in with the gar girls and kick that lady, but I sure did want to. We watched and never tried to help her and never called for help. Maggie was my dancing mother. Deaf, I thought, and dumb. Nobody inside. Nobody who would hear you if you cried in the night. Nobody who could tell you anything important that you could use. Rocking, dancing, swaying as she walked. And when the gar girls pushed her down, and started roughhousing, I knew she wouldn't scream, couldn't — just like me — and I was glad about that.

We decided not to have a tree, because Christmas would be at my mother-in-law's house, so why have a tree at both places? Joseph was at SUNY New Paltz and we had to economize, we said. But at the last minute, I changed my mind. Nothing could be that bad. So I rushed around town looking for a tree, something small but wide. By the time I found a place, it was snowing and very late. I dawdled like it was the most important purchase in the world and the tree man was fed up with me. Finally I chose one and had it tied onto the trunk of the car. I drove away slowly because the sand trucks were not out yet and the streets could be murder at the beginning of a snowfall. Downtown the streets were wide and rather empty except for a cluster of people coming out of the Newburgh Hotel. The one hotel in town that wasn't built out of cardboard and Plexiglas. A party, probably. The men huddled in the snow were dressed in tails and the women had on furs. Shiny things glittered from underneath their coats. It made me tired to look at them. Tired, tired, tired. On the next corner was a small diner with loops and loops of paper bells in the window. I stopped the car and went in. Just for a cup of coffee and twenty minutes of peace before I went home and tried to finish everything before Christmas Eve.

"Twyla?"

There she was. In a silvery evening gown and dark fur coat. A man and another woman were with her, the man fumbling for change to put in the cigarette machine. The woman was humming and tapping on the counter with her fingernails. They all looked a little bit drunk.

"Well. It's you."

"How are you?"

I shrugged. "Pretty good. Frazzled. Christmas and all."

"Regular?" called the woman from the counter.

"Fine," Roberta called back and then, "Wait for me in the car."

She slipped into the booth beside me. "I have to tell you something, Twyla. I made up my mind if I ever saw you again, I'd tell you."

"I'd just as soon not hear anything, Roberta. It doesn't matter now, anyway."

"No," she said. "Not about that."

"Don't be long," said the woman. She carried two regulars to go and the man peeled his cigarette pack as they left.

"It's about St. Bonny's and Maggie."

"Oh, please."

"Listen to me. I really did think she was black. I didn't make that up. I really thought so. But now I can't be sure. I just remember her as old, so old. And because she couldn't talk -- well, you know, I thought she was crazy. She'd been brought up in an institution like my mother was and like I thought I would be too. And you were right. We didn't kick her. It was the gar girls. Only them. But, well, I wanted to. I really wanted them to hurt her. I said we did it, too. You and me, but that's not true. And I don't want you to carry that around. It was just that I wanted to do it so bad that day -- wanting to is doing it."

Her eyes were watery from the drinks she'd had, I guess. I know it's that way with me. One glass of wine and I start bawling over the littlest thing.

"We were kids, Roberta."

"Yeah. Yeah. I know, just kids."

"Eight."

"Eight."

"And lonely."

"Scared, too."

She wiped her cheeks with the heel of her hand and smiled. "Well, that's all I wanted to say."

I nodded and couldn't think of any way to fill the silence that went from the diner past the paper bells on out into the snow. It was heavy now. I thought I'd better wait for the sand trucks before starting home.

"Thanks, Roberta."

"Sure."

"Did I tell you? My mother, she never did stop dancing."

"Yes. You told me. And mine, she never got well." Roberta lifted her hands from the tabletop and covered her face with her palms. When she took them away she really was crying. "Oh shit, Twyla. Shit, shit, shit. What the hell happened to Maggie?"

Bharati Mukherjee b. 1940

Orbiting [1988]

On Thanksgiving morning I'm still in my nightgown thinking of Vic when Dad raps on my apartment door. Who's he rolling joints for, who's he initiating now into the wonders of his inner space? What got me on Vic is remembering last Thanksgiving and his famous cranberry sauce with Grand Marnier, which Dad had interpreted as a sign of permanence in my life. A man who cooks like Vic is ready for other commitments. Dad cannot imagine cooking as self-expression. You cook *for* someone. Vic's sauce was a sign of his permanent isolation, if you really want to know.

Dad's come to drop off the turkey. It's a seventeen-pounder. Mr. Vitelli knows to reserve a biggish one for us every Thanksgiving and Christmas. But this November what with Danny in the Marines, Uncle Carmine having to be very careful after the bypass, and Vic taking off for outer space as well, we might as well have made do with one of those turkey rolls you pick out of the freezer. And in other years, Mr. Vitelli would not have given us a frozen bird. We were proud of that, our birds were fresh killed. I don't bring this up to Dad.

"Your mama took care of the thawing," Dad says. "She said you wouldn't have room in your Frigidaire."

"You mean Mom said Rindy shouldn't be living in a dump, right?" Mom has the simple, immigrant faith that children should do better than their parents, and her definition of better is comfortingly rigid. Fair enough — I believed it, too. But the fact is all I can afford is this third-floor studio with an art deco shower. The fridge fits under the kitchenette counter. The room has potential. I'm content with that. And I *like* my job even though it's selling, not designing, jewelry made out of seashells and semiprecious stones out of a boutique in Bellevue Plaza.

Dad shrugs. "You're an adult, Renata." He doesn't try to lower himself into one of my two deck chairs. He was a minor league catcher for a while and his knees went. The fake zebra-skin cushions piled as seats on the rug are out of the question for him. My futon bed folds up into a sofa, but the satin sheets are still lasciviously tangled. My father stands in a slat of sunlight, trying not to look embarrassed.

"Dad, I'd have come to the house and picked it up. You didn't have to make the extra trip out from Verona." A sixty-five-year-old man in wingtips and a Borsalino hugging a wet, heavy bird is so poignant I have to laugh.

"You wouldn't have gotten out of bed until noon, Renata." But Dad smiles. I know what he's saying. He's saying *he's* retired and *he* should be able to stay in bed till noon if he wants to, but he can't and he'd rather drive twenty miles with a soggy bird than read the *Ledger* one more time.

Grumbling and scolding are how we deMarcos express love. It's the North Italian way, Dad used to tell Cindi, Danny, and me when we were kids. Sicilians and Calabrians are emotional; we're contained. Actually, *he's* contained, the way Vic was contained for the most part. Mom's a Calabrian and she was born and raised there. Dad's very American, so Italy's a safe source of pride for him. I once figured it out: *his* father, Arturo deMarco, was a fifteen-week-old fetus when his mother planted her feet on Ellis Island. Dad, a proud son of North Italy, had one big adventure in his life, besides fighting in the Pacific, and that was marrying a Calabrian peasant. He made it sound as though Mom was a Korean or something, and their marriage was a kind of taming of the West, and that everything about her could be explained as a cultural deficiency. Actually, Vic could talk beautifully about his feelings. He'd brew espresso, pour it into tiny blue pottery cups and analyze our relationship. I should have listened. I mean really listened. I thought he was talking about us, but I know now he was only talking incessantly about himself. I put too much faith in mail-order nightgowns and bras.

"Your mama wanted me out of the house," Dad goes on. "She didn't used to be like this, Renata."

Renata and Carla are what we were christened. We changed to Rindy and Cindi in junior high. Danny didn't have to make such leaps, unless you count dropping out of Montclair State and joining the Marines. He was always Danny, or Junior.

I lug the turkey to the kitchen sink where it can drip away at a crazy angle until I have time to deal with it.

"Your mama must have told you girls I've been acting funny since I retired."

"No, Dad, she hasn't said anything about you acting funny." What she *has* said is do we think she ought to call Doc Brunetti and have a chat about Dad? Dad wouldn't have to know. He and Doc Brunetti are, or were, on the same church league bowling team. So is, or was, Vic's dad, Vinny Riccio.

"Your mama thinks a man should have an office to drive to every day. I sat at a desk for thirty-eight years and what did I get? Ask Doc, I'm too embarrassed to say." Dad told me once Doc — his real name was Frankie, though no one ever called him that — had been called Doc since he was six years old and growing up with Dad in Little Italy. There was never a time in his life when Doc wasn't Doc, which made his professional decision very easy. Dad used to say, no one ever called me Adjuster when I was a kid. Why didn't they call me something like Sarge or Teach? Then I would have known better.

I wish I had something breakfasty in my kitchen cupboard to offer him. He wants to stay and talk about Mom, which is the way old married people have. Let's talk about me means: What do you think of Mom? I'll take the turkey over means: When will Rindy settle down? I wish this morning I had bought the Goodwill sofa for ten dollars instead of letting Vic haul off the fancy deck chairs from Fortunoff's. Vic had flash. He'd left Jersey a long time before he actually took off.

"I can make you tea."

"None of that herbal stuff."

We don't talk about Mom, but I know what he's going through. She's just started to find herself. He's not burned out, he's merely stuck. I remember when Mom refused to learn to drive, wouldn't leave the house even to mail a letter. Her litany those days was: when you've spent the first fifteen years of your life in a mountain village, when you remember candles and gaslight and carrying water from a well, not to mention holding in your water at night because of wolves and the unlit outdoor privy, you *like* being housebound. She used those wolves for all they were worth, as though imaginary wolves still nipped her heels in the Clifton Mall.

Before Mom began to find herself and signed up for a class at Paterson, she used to nag Cindi and me about finding the right men. "Men," she said; she wasn't coy, never. Unembarrassed, she'd tell me about her wedding night, about her first sighting of Dad's "thing" ("Land ho!" Cindi giggled. "Thar she blows!" I chipped in.) and she'd giggle at our word for it, the common word, and she'd use it around us, never around Dad. Mom's peasant, she's earthy but never coarse. If I could get that across to Dad, how I admire it in men or in women, I would feel somehow redeemed of all my little mistakes with them, with men, with myself. Cindi and Brent were married on a cruise ship by the ship's captain. Tony, Vic's older brother, made a play for me my senior year. Tony's solid now. He manages a funeral home but he's invested in crayfish ponds on the side.

"You don't even own a dining table." Dad sounds petulant. He uses "even" a lot around me. Not just a judgment, but a comparative judgment. Other people have dining tables. *Lots* of dining tables. He softens it a bit, not wanting to hurt me, wanting more for me to judge him a failure. "We've always had a sit-down dinner, hon."

Okay, so traditions change. This year dinner's potluck. So I don't have real furniture. I eat off stack-up plastic tables as I watch the evening news. I drink red wine and heat a pita bread on the gas burner and wrap it around alfalfa sprouts or green linguine. The Swedish knockdown dresser keeps popping its sides because Vic didn't glue it properly. Swedish engineering, he said, doesn't need glue. Think of Volvos, he said, and Ingmar Bergman. He isn't good with directions that come in four languages. At least he wasn't.

"Trust me, Dad." This isn't the time to spring new lovers on him. "A friend made me a table. It's in the basement."

"How about chairs?" Ah, my good father. He could have said, friend? What friend?

Marge, my landlady, has all kinds of junky stuff in the basement. "Jorge and I'll bring up what we need. You'd strain your back, Dad." Shot knees, bad back: daily pain but nothing fatal. Not like Carmine.

"Jorge? Is that the new boyfriend?"

Shocking him makes me feel good. It would serve him right if Jorge were my new boyfriend. But Jorge is Marge's other roomer. He gives Marge Spanish lessons, and does the heavy cleaning and the yard work. Jorge has family in El Salvador he's hoping to bring up. I haven't met Marge's husband yet. He works on an offshore oil rig in some emirate with a funny name.

"No, Dad." I explain about Jorge.

"El Salvador!" he repeats. "That means 'the Savior.'" He passes on the information with a kind of awe. It makes Jorge's homeland, which he's shown me pretty pictures of, seem messy and exotic, at the very rim of human comprehension.

After Dad leaves, I call Cindi, who lives fifteen minutes away on Upper Mountainside Road. She's eleven months younger and almost a natural blonde, but we're close. Brent wasn't easy for me to take, not at first. He owns a discount camera and electronics store on Fifty-fourth in Manhattan. Cindi met him through Club Med. They sat on a gorgeous Caribbean beach and talked of hogs. His father is an Amish farmer in Kalona, Iowa. Brent, in spite of the obvious hairpiece and the gold chain, is a rebel. He was born Schwartzendruber, but changed his name to Schwartz. Now no one believes the Brent, either. They call him Bernie on the street and it makes everyone more comfortable. His father's never taken their buggy out of the county.

The first time Vic asked me out, he talked of feminism and holism and macrobiotics. Then he opened up on cinema and literature, and I was very impressed, as who wouldn't be? Ro, my current lover, is very different. He picked me up in an uptown singles bar that I and sometimes Cindi go to. He bought me a Cinzano and touched my breast in the dark. He was direct, and at the same time weirdly courtly. I took him home though usually I don't, at first. I learned in bed that night that the tall brown drink with the lemon twist he'd been drinking was Tab.

I went back on the singles circuit even though the break with Vic should have made me cautious. Cindi thinks Vic's a romantic. I've told her how it ended. One Sunday morning in March he kissed me awake as usual. He'd brought in the *Times* from the porch and was reading it. I made us some cinnamon rose tea. We had a ritual, starting with the real estate pages, passing remarks on the latest tacky towers. Not for us, we'd say, the view is terrible! No room for the servants, things like that. And our imaginary children's imaginary nanny. "Hi, gorgeous," I said. He is gorgeous, not strong, but showy. He said, "I'm leaving, babe. New Jersey doesn't do it for me anymore." I said, "Okay, so where're we going?" I had an awful job at the time, taking orders for MCI. Vic said, "I didn't say we, babe." So I asked, "You mean it's over? Just like that?" And he said, "Isn't that the best way? No fuss, no hang-ups." Then I got a little whiny. "But *why?*" I wanted to know.

But he was macrobiotic in lots of things, including relationships. Yin and yang, hot and sour, green and yellow. "You know, Rindy, there are *places*. You don't fall off the earth when you leave Jersey, you know. Places you see pictures of and read about. Different weathers, different trees, different everything. Places that get the Cubs on cable instead of the Mets." He was into that. For all the sophisticated things he liked to talk about, he was a very local boy. "Vic," I pleaded, "you're crazy. You need help." "I need help because I want to get out of Jersey? You gotta be kidding!" He stood up and for a moment I thought he would do something crazy, like destroy something, or hurt me. "Don't ever call me crazy, got that? And give me the keys to the van."

He took the van. Danny had sold it to me when the Marines sent him overseas. I'd have given it to him anyway, even if he hadn't asked.

"Cindi, I need a turkey roaster," I tell my sister on the phone.

"I'll be right over," she says. "The brat's driving me crazy."

"Isn't Franny's visit working out?"

"I could kill her. I think up ways. How does that sound?"

"Why not send her home?" I'm joking. Franny is Brent's twelve-year-old and he's shelled out a lot of dough to lawyers in New Jersey and Florida to work out visitation rights.

"Poor Brent. He feels so *divided*," Cindi says. "He shouldn't have to take sides."

I want her to ask who my date is for this afternoon, but she doesn't. It's important to me that she like Ro, that Mom and Dad more than tolerate him.

All over the country, I tell myself, women are towing new lovers home to meet their families. Vic is simmering cranberries in somebody's kitchen and explaining yin and yang. I check out the stuffing recipe. The gravy calls for cream and freshly grated nutmeg. Ro brought me six whole nutmegs in a Ziplock bag from his friend, a Pakistani, who runs a spice store in SoHo. The nuts look hard and ugly. I take one out of the bag and sniff it. The aroma's so exotic my head swims. On an impulse I call Ro.

The phone rings and rings. He doesn't have his own place yet. He has to crash with friends. He's been in the States three months, maybe less. I let it ring fifteen, sixteen, seventeen times.

Finally someone answers. "Yes?" The voice is guarded, the accent obviously foreign even though all I'm hearing is a one-syllable word. Ro has fled here from Kabul. He wants to take classes at NJIT and become an electrical engineer. He says he's lucky his father got him out. A friend of Ro's father, a man called Mumtaz, runs a fried chicken restaurant in Brooklyn in a neighborhood Ro calls "Little Kabul," though probably no one else has ever noticed. Mr. Mumtaz puts the legal immigrants to work as waiters out front. The illegals hide in a backroom as pluckers and gutters.

"Ro? I miss you. We're eating at three, remember?"

"Who is speaking, please?"

So I fell for the accent, but it isn't a malicious error. I *can* tell one Afghan tribe from another now, even by looking at them or by their names. I can make out some Pashto words. "Tell Ro it's Rindy. Please? I'm a friend. He wanted me to call this number."

"Not knowing any Ro."

"Hey, wait. Tell him it's Rindy deMarco."

The guy hangs up on me.

I'm crumbling cornbread into a bowl for the stuffing when Cindi honks half of "King Cotton" from the parking apron in the back. Brent bought her the BMW on the gray market and saved a bundle — once discount, always discount — then spent three hundred dollars to put in a horn that beeps a Sousa march. I wave a potato masher at her from the back window. She doesn't get out of the car. Instead she points to the pan in the back seat. I come down, wiping my hands on a dish towel.

"I should stay and help." Cindi sounds ready to cry. But I don't want her with me when Ro calls back.

"You're doing too much already, kiddo." My voice at least sounds comforting. "You promised one veg and the salad."

"I ought to come up and help. That or get drunk." She shifts the stick. When Brent bought her the car, the dealer threw in driving gloves to match the upholstery.

"Get Franny to shred the greens," I call as Cindi backs up the car. "Get her involved."

The phone is ringing in my apartment. I can hear it ring from the second-floor landing.

"Ro?"

"You're taking a chance, my treasure. It could have been any other admirer, then where would you be?"

"I don't have any other admirers." Ro is not a conventionally jealous man, not like the types I have known. He's totally unlike any man I have ever known. He wants men to come on to me. Lately when we go to a bar he makes me sit far enough from him so some poor lonely guy thinks I'm looking for action. Ro likes to swagger out of a dark booth as soon as someone buys me a drink. I go along. He comes from a macho culture.

"How else will I know you are as beautiful as I think you are? I would not want an unprized woman," he says. He is asking me for time, I know. In a few more months he'll know I'm something of a catch in my culture, or at least I've never had trouble finding boys. Even Brent Schwartzendruber has begged me to see him alone.

"I'm going to be a little late," Ro says. "I told you about my cousin Abdul, no?"

Ro has three or four cousins that I know of in Manhattan. They're all named Abdul something. When I think of Abdul, I think of a giant black man with goggles on, running down a court. Abdul is the teenage cousin whom immigration officials nabbed as he was gutting chickens in Mumtaz's backroom. Abdul doesn't have the right papers to live and work in this country, and now he's been locked up in a detention center on Varick Street. Ro's afraid Abdul will be deported back to Afghanistan. If that happens, he'll be tortured.

"I have to visit him before I take the DeCamp bus. He's talking nonsense. He's talking of starting a hunger fast."

"A hunger strike! God!" When I'm with Ro I feel I am looking at America through the wrong end of a telescope. He makes it sound like a police state, with sudden raids, papers, detention centers, deportations, and torture and death waiting in the wings. I'm not a political person. Last fall I wore the Ferraro button because she's a woman and Italian.

"Rindy, all night I've been up and awake. All night I think of your splendid breasts. Like clusters of grapes, I think. I am stroking and fondling your grapes this very minute. My talk gets you excited?"

I tell him to test me, please get here before three. I remind him he can't buy his ticket on the bus.

"We got here too early, didn't we?" Dad stands just outside the door to my apartment, looking embarrassed. He's in his best dark suit, the one he wears every Thanksgiving and Christmas. This year he can't do up the top button of his jacket.

"Don't be so formal, Dad." I give him a showy hug and pull him indoors so Mom can come in.

"As if your papa ever listens to me!" Mom laughs. But she sits primly on the sofa bed in her velvet cloak, with her tote bag and evening purse on her lap. Before Dad started courting her, she worked as a seamstress. Dad rescued her from a sweatshop. He married down, she married well. That's the family story.

"She told me to rush."

Mom isn't in a mood to squabble. I think she's reached the point of knowing she won't have him forever. There was Carmine, at death's door just a month ago. Anything could happen to Dad. She says, "Renata, look what I made! Crostolis." She lifts a cake tin out of her tote bag. The pan still feels warm. And for dessert, I know, there'll be a jar of super-thick, super-rich Death by Chocolate.

The story about Grandma deMarco, Dad's mama, is that every Thanksgiving she served two full dinners, one American with the roast turkey, candied yams, pumpkin pie, the works, and another with Grandpa's favorite pastas.

Dad relaxes. He appoints himself bartender. "Don't you have more ice cubes, sweetheart?"

I tell him it's good Glenlivet. He shouldn't ruin it with ice, just a touch of water if he must. Dad pours sherry in Vic's pottery espresso cups for his women. Vic made them himself, and I used to think they were perfect blue jewels. Now I see they're lumpy, uneven in color.

"Go change into something pretty before Carla and Brent come." Mom believes in dressing up. Beaded dresses lift her spirits. She's wearing a beaded green dress today.

I take the sherry and vanish behind a four-panel screen, the kind long-legged showgirls change behind in black and white movies while their moustached lovers keep talking. My head barely shows above the screen's top, since I'm no long-legged showgirl. My best points, as Ro has said, are my clusters of grapes. Vic found the screen at a country auction in the Adirondacks. It had filled the van. Now I use the panels as a bulletin board and I'm worried Dad'll spot the notice for the next meeting of Amnesty International, which will bother him. He will think the two words stand for draft dodger and communist. I was going to drop my membership, a legacy of Vic, when Ro saw it and approved. Dad goes to the Sons of Italy Anti-Defamation dinners. He met Frank Sinatra at one. He voted for Reagan last time because the Democrats ran an Italian woman.

Instead of a thirties lover, it's my moustached papa talking to me from the other side of the screen. "So where's this dining table?"

"Ro's got the parts in the basement. He'll bring it up, Dad."

I hear them whispering. "Bo? Now she's messing with a Southerner?" and "Shh, it's her business."

I'm just smoothing on my pantyhose when Mom screams for the cops. Dad shouts too, at Mom for her to shut up. It's my fault, I should have warned Ro not to use his key this afternoon.

I peek over the screen's top and see my lover the way my parents see him. He's a slight, pretty man with hazel eyes and a tufty moustache, so whom can he intimidate? I've seen Jews and Greeks, not to mention Sons of Italy, darker-skinned than Ro. Poor Ro resorts to his Kabuli pre-school manners.

"How do you do, madam! Sir! My name is Roashan."

Dad moves closer to Ro but doesn't hold out his hand. I can almost read his mind: *he speaks.* "Come again?" he says, baffled.

I cringe as he spells his name. My parents are so parochial. With each letter he does a graceful dip and bow. "Try it syllable by syllable, sir. Then it is not so hard."

Mom stares past him at me. The screen doesn't hide me because I've strayed too far in to watch the farce. "Renata, you're wearing only your camisole."

I pull my crew neck over my head, then kiss him. I make the kiss really sexy so they'll know I've slept with this man. Many times. And if he asks me, I will marry him. I had not known that till now. I think my mother guesses.

He's brought flowers: four long-stemmed, stylish purple blossoms in a florist's paper cone. "For you, madam." He glides over the dirty broadloom to Mom who fills up more than half the sofa bed. "This is my first Thanks-giving dinner, for which I have much to give thanks, no?"

"He was born in Afghanistan," I explain. But Dad gets continents wrong. He says, "We saw your famine camps on TV. Well, you won't starve this afternoon."

"They smell good," Mom says. "Thank you very much but you shouldn't spend a fortune."

"No, no, madam. What you smell good is my cologne. Flowers in New York have no fragrance."

"His father had a garden estate outside Kabul." I don't want Mom to think he's putting down American flowers, though in fact he is. Along with American fruits, meats, and vegetables. "The Russians bulldozed it," I add.

Dad doesn't want to talk politics. He senses, looking at Ro, this is not the face of Ethiopian starvation. "Well, what'll it be, Roy? Scotch and soda?" I wince. It's not going well.

"Thank you but no. I do not imbibe alcoholic spirits, though I have no objection for you, sir." My lover goes to the fridge and reaches down. He knows just where to find his Tab. My father is quietly livid, staring down at his drink.

In my father's world, grown men bowl in leagues and drink the best whiskey they can afford. Dad whistles "My Way." He must be under stress. That's his usual self-therapy: how would Francis Albert handle this?

"Muslims have taboos, Dad." Cindi didn't marry a Catholic, so he has no right to be upset about Ro, about us.

"Jews," Dad mutters. "So do Jews." He knows because catty-corner from Vitelli's is a kosher butcher. This isn't the time to parade new words before him, like *halal,* the Muslim kosher. An Italian-American man should be able to live sixty-five years never having heard the word, I can go along with that. Ro, fortunately, is cosmopolitan. Outside of pork and booze, he eats any-thing else I fix.

Brent and Cindi take forever to come. But finally we hear his MG squeal in the driveway. Ro glides to the front window; he seems to blend with the ficus tree and hanging ferns. Dad and I wait by the door.

"Party time!" Brent shouts as he maneuvers Cindi and Franny ahead of him up three flights of stairs. He looks very much the head of the family, a rich man steeply in debt to keep up appearances, to compete, to head off middle age. He's at that age—and Cindi's nowhere near that age—when people notice the difference and quietly judge it. I know these things from Cindi—I'd never guess it from looking at Brent. If he feels divided, as Cindi says he does, it doesn't show. Misery, anxiety, whatever, show on Cindi though; they bring her cheekbones out. When I'm depressed, my hair looks rough, my skin breaks out. Right now, I'm lustrous.

Brent does a lot of whooping and hugging at the door. He even hugs Dad who looks grave and funereal like an old-world Italian gentleman because of his outdated, pinched dark suit. Cindi makes straight for the fridge with her casserole of squash and browned marshmallow. Franny just stands in the middle of the room holding two biggish Baggies of salad greens and vinaigrette in an old Dijon mustard jar. Brent actually bought the mustard in Dijon, a story that Ro is bound to hear and not appreciate. Vic was mean enough last year to tell him that he could have gotten it for more or less the same price at the Italian specialty foods store down on Watchung Plaza. Franny doesn't seem to have her own winter clothes. She's wearing Cindi's car coat over a Dolphins sweatshirt. Her mother moved down to Florida the very day the divorce became final. She's got a Walkman tucked into the pocket of her cords.

"You could have trusted me to make the salad dressing at least," I scold my sister.

Franny gives up the Baggies and the jar of dressing to me. She scrutinizes us — Mom, Dad, me and Ro, especially Ro, as though she can detect something strange about him — but doesn't take off her earphones. A smirk starts twitching her tanned, feral features. I see what she is seeing. Asian men carry their bodies differently, even these famed warriors from the Khyber Pass. Ro doesn't stand like Brent or Dad. His hands hang kind of stiffly from the shoulder joints, and when he moves, his palms are tucked tight against his thighs, his stomach sticks out like a slightly pregnant woman's. Each culture establishes its own manly posture, different ways of claiming space. Ro, hiding among my plants, holds himself in a way that seems both too effeminate and too macho. I hate Franny for what she's doing to me. I am twenty-seven years old, I should be more mature. But I see now how wrong Ro's clothes are. He shows too much white collar and cuff. His shirt and his wool-blend flare-leg pants were made to measure in Kabul. The jacket comes from a discount store on Canal Street, part of a discontinued line of two-trousered suits. I ought to know, I took him there. I want to shake Franny or smash the earphones.

Cindi catches my exasperated look. "Don't pay any attention to her. She's unsociable this weekend. We can't compete with the Depeche Mode."

I intend to compete.

Franny, her eyes very green and very hostile, turns on Brent. "How come she never gets it right, Dad?"

Brent hi-fives his daughter, which embarrasses her more than anyone else in the room. "It's a Howard Jones, hon," Brent tells Cindi.

Franny, close to tears, runs to the front window where Ro's been hanging back. She has an ungainly walk for a child whose support payments specify weekly ballet lessons. She bores in on Ro's hidey hole like Russian artillery. Ro moves back to the perimeter of family intimacy. I have no way of helping yet. I have to set out the dips and Tostitos. Brent and Dad are talking sports, Mom and Cindi are watching the turkey. Dad's going on about the Knicks. He's in despair, so early in the season. He's on his second Scotch. I see Brent try. "What do you think, Roy?" He's doing his best to get my lover involved. "Maybe we'll get lucky, huh? We can always hope for a top draft pick. End up with Patrick Ewing!" Dad brightens. "That guy'll change the game. Just wait and see. He'll fill the lane better than Russell." Brent gets angry, since for some strange Amish reason he's a Celtics fan. So was Vic. "Bird'll make a monkey out of him." He looks to Ro for support.

Ro nods. Even his headshake is foreign. "You are undoubtedly correct, Brent," he says. "I am deferring to your judgment because currently I have not familiarized myself with these practices."

Ro loves squash, but none of my relatives have ever picked up a racket. I want to tell Brent that Ro's skied in St. Moritz, lost a thousand dollars in a casino in Beirut, knows where to buy Havana cigars without getting hijacked. He's sophisticated, he could make monkeys out of us all, but they think he's a retard.

Brent drinks three Scotches to Dad's two; then all three men go down to the basement. Ro and Brent do the carrying, negotiating sharp turns in the stairwell. Dad supervises. There are two trestles and a wide, splintery plywood top. "Try not to take the wall down!" Dad yells.

When they make it back in, the men take off their jackets to assemble the table. Brent's wearing a red lamb's wool turtleneck under his camel hair blazer. Ro unfastens his cuff links — they are 24-karat gold and his father's told him to sell them if funds run low — and pushes up his very white shirt sleeves. There are scars on both arms, scars that bubble against his dark skin, scars like lightning flashes under his thick black hair. Scar tissue on Ro is the color of freshwater pearls. I want to kiss it.

Cindi checks the turkey one more time. "You guys better hurry. We'll be ready to eat in fifteen minutes."

Ro, the future engineer, adjusts the trestles. He's at his best now. He's become quite chatty. From under the plywood top, he's holding forth on the Soviet menace in Kabul. Brent may actually have an idea where Afghanistan is, in a general way, but Dad is lost. He's talking of being arrested for handing out pro-American pamphlets on his campus. Dad stiffens at "arrest" and blanks out the rest. He talks of this "so-called leader," this "criminal" named Babrak Karmal and I hear other buzz-words like Kandahār and Pamir, words that might have been Polish to me a month ago, and I can see even Brent is slightly embarrassed. It's his first exposure to Third World passion. He thought only Americans had informed political opinion — other people staged coups out of spite and misery. It's an unwelcome revelation to him that a reasonably educated and rational man like Ro would die for things that he, Brent, has never heard of and would rather laugh about. Ro was tortured in jail. Franny has taken off her earphones. Electrodes, canes, freezing tanks. He leaves nothing out. Something's gotten into Ro.

Dad looks sick. The meaning of Thanksgiving should not be so explicit. But Ro's in a daze. He goes on about how — *inshallah* — his father, once a rich landlord, had stashed away enough to bribe a guard, sneak him out of this cell and hide him for four months in a tunnel dug under a servant's adobe hut until a forged American visa could be bought. Franny's eyes are wide, Dad joins Mom on the sofa bed, shaking his head. Jail, bribes, forged, what is this? I can read his mind. "For six days I must orbit one international airport to another," Ro is saying. "The main trick is having a valid ticket, that way the airline has to carry you, even if the country won't take you in. Colombo, Seoul, Bombay, Geneva, Frankfurt, I know too too well the transit lounges of many airports. We travel the world with our gym bags and prayer rugs, unrolling them in the transit lounges. The better airports have special rooms."

Brent tries to ease Dad's pain. "Say, buddy," he jokes, "you wouldn't be ripping us off, would you?"

Ro snakes his slender body from under the makeshift table. He hasn't been watching the effect of his monologue. "I am a working man," he says stiffly. I have seen his special permit. He's one of the lucky ones, though it might not last. He's saving for NJIT. Meantime he's gutting chickens to pay for room and board in Little Kabul. He describes the gutting process. His face is transformed as he sticks his fist into imaginary roasters and grabs for gizzards, pulls out the squishy stuff. He takes an Afghan dagger out of the pocket of his pants. You'd never guess, he looks like such a victim. "This," he says, eyes glinting. "This is all I need."

"Cool," Franny says.

"Time to eat," Mom shouts. "I made the gravy with the nutmeg as you said, Renata."

I lead Dad to the head of the table. "Everyone else sit where you want to."

Franny picks out the chair next to Ro before I can put Cindi there. I want Cindi to know him, I want her as an ally.

Dad tests the blade of the carving knife. Mom put the knife where Dad always sits when she set the table. He takes his thumb off the blade and pushes the switch. "That noise makes me feel good."

But I carry in the platter with the turkey and place it in front of Ro. "I want you to carve," I say.

He brings out his dagger all over again. Franny is practically licking his fingers. "You mean this is a professional job?"

We stare fascinated as my lover slashes and slices, swiftly, confidently, at the huge, browned, juicy breast. The dagger scoops out flesh.

Now I am the one in a daze. I am seeing Ro's naked body as though for the first time, his nicked, scarred, burned body. In his body, the blemishes seem embedded, more beautiful, like wood. I am seeing character made manifest. I am seeing Brent and Dad for the first time, too. They have their little scars, things they're proud of, football injuries and bowling elbows they brag about. Our scars are so innocent; they are invisible and come to us from rough-housing gone too far. Ro hates to talk about his scars. If I trace the puckered tissue on his left thigh and ask "How, Ro?" he becomes shy, dismissive: a pack of dogs attacked him when he was a boy. The skin on his back is speckled and lumpy from burns, but when I ask he laughs. A crazy villager whacked him with a burning stick for cheekiness, he explains. He's ashamed that he comes from a culture of pain.

The turkey is reduced to a drying, whitened skeleton. On our plates, the slices are symmetrical, elegant. I realize all in a rush how much I love this man with his blemished, tortured body. I will give him citizenship if he asks. Vic was beautiful, but Vic was self-sufficient. Ro's my chance to heal the world.

I shall teach him how to walk like an American, how to dress like Brent but better, how to fill up a room as Dad does instead of melting and blending but sticking out in the Afghan way. In spite of the funny way he holds himself and the funny way he moves his head from side to side when he wants to say yes, Ro is Clint Eastwood, scarred hero and survivor. Dad and Brent are children. I realize Ro's the only circumcised man I've slept with.

Mom asks, "Why are you grinning like that, Renata?"

Tim O'Brien b. 1946

The Things They Carried   [1986]

First Lieutenant Jimmy Cross carried letters from a girl named Martha, a junior at Mount Sebastian College in New Jersey. They were not love letters, but Lieutenant Cross was hoping, so he kept them folded in plastic at the bottom of his rucksack. In the late afternoon, after a day's march, he would dig his foxhole, wash his hands under a canteen, unwrap the letters, hold them with the tips of his fingers, and spend the last hour of light pretending. He would imagine romantic camping trips into the White Mountains in New Hampshire. He would sometimes taste the envelope flaps, knowing her tongue had been there. More than anything, he wanted Martha to love him as he loved her, but the letters were mostly chatty, elusive on the matter of love. She was a virgin, he was almost sure. She was an English major at Mount Sebastian, and she wrote beautifully about her professors and roommates and midterm exams, about her respect for Chaucer and her great affection for Virginia Woolf. She often quoted lines of poetry; she never mentioned the war, except to say, Jimmy, take care of yourself. The letters weighed 10 ounces. They were signed Love, Martha, but Lieutenant Cross understood that Love was only a way of signing and did not mean what he sometimes pretended it meant. At dusk, he would carefully return the letters to his rucksack. Slowly, a bit distracted, he would get up and move among his men, checking the perimeter, then at full dark he would return to his hole and watch the night and wonder if Martha was a virgin.

The things they carried were largely determined by necessity. Among the necessities or near-necessities were P-38 can openers, pocket knives, heat tabs, wristwatches, dog tags, mosquito repellent, chewing gum, candy, cigarettes, salt tablets, packets of Kool-Aid, lighters, matches, sewing kits,

Military Payment Certificates, C rations, and two or three canteens of water. Together, these items weighed between 15 and 20 pounds, depending upon a man's habits or rate of metabolism. Henry Dobbins, who was a big man, carried extra rations; he was especially fond of canned peaches in heavy syrup over pound cake. Dave Jensen, who practiced field hygiene, carried a toothbrush, dental floss, and several hotel-sized bars of soap he'd stolen on R&R° in Sydney, Australia. Ted Lavender, who was scared, carried tranquilizers until he was shot in the head outside the village of Than Khe in mid-April. By necessity, and because it was SOP,° they all carried steel helmets that weighed 5 pounds including the liner and camouflage cover. They carried the standard fatigue jackets and trousers. Very few carried underwear. On their feet they carried jungle boots—2.1 pounds—and Dave Jensen carried three pairs of socks and a can of Dr. Scholl's foot powder as a precaution against trench foot. Until he was shot, Ted Lavender carried six or seven ounces of premium dope, which for him was a necessity. Mitchell Sanders, the RTO,° carried condoms. Norman Bowker carried a diary. Rat Kiley carried comic books. Kiowa, a devout Baptist, carried an illustrated New Testament that had been presented to him by his father, who taught Sunday school in Oklahoma City, Oklahoma. As a hedge against bad times, however, Kiowa also carried his grandmother's distrust of the white man, his grandfather's old hunting hatchet. Necessity dictated. Because the land was mined and booby-trapped, it was SOP for each man to carry a steel-centered, nylon-covered flak jacket, which weighed 6.7 pounds, but which on hot days seemed much heavier. Because you could die so quickly, each man carried at least one large compress bandage, usually in the helmet band for easy access. Because the nights were cold, and because the monsoons were wet, each carried a green plastic poncho that could be used as a raincoat or groundsheet or makeshift tent. With its quilted liner, the poncho weighed almost two pounds, but it was worth every ounce. In April, for instance, when Ted Lavender was shot, they used his poncho to wrap him up, then to carry him across the paddy, then to lift him into the chopper that took him away.

They were called legs or grunts.

To carry something was to hump it, as when Lieutenant Jimmy Cross humped his love for Martha up the hills and through the swamps. In its intransitive form, to hump meant to walk, or to march, but it implied burdens far beyond the intransitive.

Almost everyone humped photographs. In his wallet, Lieutenant Cross carried two photographs of Martha. The first was a Kodacolor snapshot signed Love, though he knew better. She stood against a brick wall. Her eyes were gray and neutral, her lips slightly open as she stared straight-on at the

---

R&R: Rest and rehabilitation; a brief getaway from active service. **SOP:** Standard operating procedure. **RTO:** Radio and telephone operator.

camera. At night, sometimes, Lieutenant Cross wondered who had taken the picture, because he knew she had boyfriends, because he loved her so much, and because he could see the shadow of the picture-taker spreading out against the brick wall. The second photograph had been clipped from the 1968 Mount Sebastian yearbook. It was an action shot—women's volleyball—and Martha was bent horizontal to the floor, reaching, the palms of her hands in sharp focus, the tongue taut, the expression frank and competitive. There was no visible sweat. She wore white gym shorts. Her legs, he thought, were almost certainly the legs of a virgin, dry and without hair, the left knee cocked and carrying her entire weight, which was just over one hundred pounds. Lieutenant Cross remembered touching that left knee. A dark theater, he remembered, and the movie was *Bonnie and Clyde,* and Martha wore a tweed skirt, and during the final scene, when he touched her knee, she turned and looked at him in a sad, sober way that made him pull his hand back, but he would always remember the feel of the tweed skirt and the knee beneath it and the sound of the gunfire that killed Bonnie and Clyde, how embarrassing it was, how slow and oppressive. He remembered kissing her good night at the dorm door. Right then, he thought, he should've done something brave. He should've carried her up the stairs to her room and tied her to the bed and touched that left knee all night long. He should've risked it. Whenever he looked at the photographs, he thought of new things he should've done.

What they carried was partly a function of rank, partly of field specialty.

As a first lieutenant and platoon leader, Jimmy Cross carried a compass, maps, code books, binoculars, and a .45-caliber pistol that weighed 2.9 pounds fully loaded. He carried a strobe light and the responsibility for the lives of his men.

As an RTO, Mitchell Sanders carried the PRC-25 radio, a killer, 26 pounds with its battery.

As a medic, Rat Kiley carried a canvas satchel filled with morphine and plasma and malaria tablets and surgical tape and comic books and all the things a medic must carry, including M&M's° for especially bad wounds, for a total weight of nearly 20 pounds.

As a big man, therefore a machine gunner, Henry Dobbins carried the M-60, which weighed 23 pounds unloaded, but which was almost always loaded. In addition, Dobbins carried between 10 and 15 pounds of ammunition draped in belts across his chest and shoulders.

As PFCs or Spec 4s, most of them were common grunts and carried the standard M-16 gas-operated assault rifle. The weapon weighed 7.5 pounds unloaded, 8.2 pounds with its full 20-round magazine. Depending on numerous factors, such as topography and psychology, the riflemen carried anywhere from 12 to 20 magazines, usually in cloth bandoliers, adding on

M&M's: Medical supplies.

another 8.4 pounds at minimum, 14 pounds at maximum. When it was available, they also carried M-16 maintenance gear—rods and steel brushes and swabs and tubes of LSA oil—all of which weighed about a pound. Among the grunts, some carried the M-79 grenade launcher, 5.9 pounds unloaded, a reasonably light weapon except for the ammunition, which was heavy. A single round weighed 10 ounces. The typical load was 25 rounds. But Ted Lavender, who was scared, carried 34 rounds when he was shot and killed outside Than Khe, and he went down under an exceptional burden, more than 20 pounds of ammunition, plus the flak jacket and helmet and rations and water and toilet paper and tranquilizers and all the rest, plus the unweighed fear. He was dead weight. There was no twitching or flopping. Kiowa, who saw it happen, said it was like watching a rock fall, or a big sandbag or something—just boom, then down—not like the movies where the dead guy rolls around and does fancy spins and goes ass over teakettle— not like that, Kiowa said, the poor bastard just flat-fuck fell. Boom. Down. Nothing else. It was a bright morning in mid-April. Lieutenant Cross felt the pain. He blamed himself. They stripped off Lavender's canteens and ammo, all the heavy things, and Rat Kiley said the obvious, the guy's dead, and Mitchell Sanders used his radio to report one U.S. KIA° and to request a chopper. Then they wrapped Lavender in his poncho. They carried him out to a dry paddy, established security, and sat smoking the dead man's dope until the chopper came. Lieutenant Cross kept to himself. He pictured Martha's smooth young face, thinking he loved her more than anything, more than his men, and now Ted Lavender was dead because he loved her so much and could not stop thinking about her. When the dustoff arrived, they carried Lavender aboard. Afterward they burned Than Khe. They marched until dusk, then dug their holes, and that night Kiowa kept explaining how you had to be there, how fast it was, how the poor guy just dropped like so much concrete. Boom-down, he said. Like cement.

In addition to the three standard weapons—the M-60, M-16, and M-79—they carried whatever presented itself, or whatever seemed appropriate as a means of killing or staying alive. They carried catch-as-catch-can. At various times, in various situations, they carried M-14s and CAR-15s and Swedish Ks and grease guns and captured AK-47s and Chi-Coms and RPGs and Simonov carbines and black market Uzis and .38-caliber Smith & Wesson handguns and 66 mm LAWs and shotguns and silencers and blackjacks and bayonets and C-4 plastic explosives. Lee Strunk carried a slingshot; a weapon of last resort, he called it. Mitchell Sanders carried brass knuckles. Kiowa carried his grandfather's feathered hatchet. Every third or fourth man carried a Claymore antipersonnel mine—3.5 pounds with its firing device. They all carried fragmentation grenades—14 ounces each. They all carried at least one M-18 colored smoke grenade—24 ounces. Some carried CS

KIA: Killed in action.

or tear gas grenades. Some carried white phosphorus grenades. They carried all they could bear, and then some, including a silent awe for the terrible power of the things they carried.

In the first week of April, before Lavender died, Lieutenant Jimmy Cross received a good-luck charm from Martha. It was a simple pebble, an ounce at most. Smooth to the touch, it was a milky white color with flecks of orange and violet, oval-shaped, like a miniature egg. In the accompanying letter, Martha wrote that she had found the pebble on the Jersey shoreline, precisely where the land touched water at high tide, where things came together but also separated. It was this separate-but-together quality, she wrote, that had inspired her to pick up the pebble and to carry it in her breast pocket for several days, where it seemed weightless, and then to send it through the mail, by air, as a token of her truest feelings for him. Lieutenant Cross found this romantic. But he wondered what her truest feelings were, exactly, and what she meant by separate-but-together. He wondered how the tides and waves had come into play on that afternoon along the Jersey shoreline when Martha saw the pebble and bent down to rescue it from geology. He imagined bare feet. Martha was a poet, with the poet's sensibilities, and her feet would be brown and bare, the toenails unpainted, the eyes chilly and somber like the ocean in March, and though it was painful, he wondered who had been with her that afternoon. He imagined a pair of shadows moving along the strip of sand where things came together but also separated. It was phantom jealousy, he knew, but he couldn't help himself. He loved her so much. On the march, through the hot days of early April, he carried the pebble in his mouth, turning it with his tongue, tasting sea salt and moisture. His mind wandered. He had difficulty keeping his attention on the war. On occasion he would yell at his men to spread out the column, to keep their eyes open, but then he would slip away into daydreams, just pretending, walking barefoot along the Jersey shore, with Martha, carrying nothing. He would feel himself rising. Sun and waves and gentle winds, all love and lightness.

What they carried varied by mission.

When a mission took them to the mountains, they carried mosquito netting, machetes, canvas tarps, and extra bug juice.

If a mission seemed especially hazardous, or if it involved a place they knew to be bad, they carried everything they could. In certain heavily mined AOs,° where the land was dense with Toe Poppers and Bouncing Betties, they took turns humping a 28-pound mine detector. With its headphones and big sensing plate, the equipment was a stress on the lower back and shoulders, awkward to handle, often useless because of the shrapnel in the earth, but they carried it anyway, partly for safety, partly for the illusion of safety.

AOs: Areas of operations.

On ambush, or other night missions, they carried peculiar little odds and ends. Kiowa always took along his New Testament and a pair of moccasins for silence. Dave Jensen carried night-sight vitamins high in carotene. Lee Strunk carried his slingshot; ammo, he claimed, would never be a problem. Rat Kiley carried brandy and M&M's candy. Until he was shot, Ted Lavender carried the starlight scope, which weighed 6.3 pounds with its aluminum carrying case. Henry Dobbins carried his girlfriend's pantyhose wrapped around his neck as a comforter. They all carried ghosts. When dark came, they would move out single file across the meadows and paddies to their ambush coordinates, where they would quietly set up the Claymores and lie down and spend the night waiting.

Other missions were more complicated and required special equipment. In mid-April, it was their mission to search out and destroy the elaborate tunnel complexes in the Than Khe area south of Chu Lai. To blow the tunnels, they carried one-pound blocks of pentrite high explosives, four blocks to a man, 68 pounds in all. They carried wiring, detonators, and battery-powered clackers. Dave Jensen carried earplugs. Most often, before blowing the tunnels, they were ordered by higher command to search them, which was considered bad news, but by and large they just shrugged and carried out orders. Because he was a big man, Henry Dobbins was excused from tunnel duty. The others would draw numbers. Before Lavender died there were 17 men in the platoon, and whoever drew the number 17 would strip off his gear and crawl in headfirst with a flashlight and Lieutenant Cross's .45-caliber pistol. The rest of them would fan out as security. They would sit down or kneel, not facing the hole, listening to the ground beneath them, imagining cobwebs and ghosts, whatever was down there — the tunnel walls squeezing in — how the flashlight seemed impossibly heavy in the hand and how it was tunnel vision in the very strictest sense, compression in all ways, even time, and how you had to wiggle in — ass and elbows — a swallowed-up feeling — and how you found yourself worrying about odd things: Will your flashlight go dead? Do rats carry rabies? If you screamed, how far would the sound carry? Would your buddies hear it? Would they have the courage to drag you out? In some respects, though not many, the waiting was worse than the tunnel itself. Imagination was a killer.

On April 16, when Lee Strunk drew the number 17, he laughed and muttered something and went down quickly. The morning was hot and very still. Not good, Kiowa said. He looked at the tunnel opening, then out across a dry paddy toward the village of Than Khe. Nothing moved. No clouds or birds or people. As they waited, the men smoked and drank Kool-Aid, not talking much, feeling sympathy for Lee Strunk but also feeling the luck of the draw. You win some, you lose some, said Mitchell Sanders, and sometimes you settle for a rain check. It was a tired line and no one laughed.

Henry Dobbins ate a tropical chocolate bar. Ted Lavender popped a tranquilizer and went off to pee.

After five minutes, Lieutenant Jimmy Cross moved to the tunnel, leaned down, and examined the darkness. Trouble, he thought—a cave-in maybe. And then suddenly, without willing it, he was thinking about Martha. The stresses and fractures, the quick collapse, the two of them buried alive under all that weight. Dense, crushing love. Kneeling, watching the hole, he tried to concentrate on Lee Strunk and the war, all the dangers, but his love was too much for him, he felt paralyzed, he wanted to sleep inside her lungs and breathe her blood and be smothered. He wanted her to be a virgin and not a virgin, all at once. He wanted to know her. Intimate secrets: Why poetry? Why so sad? Why that grayness in her eyes? Why so alone? Not lonely, just alone—riding her bike across campus or sitting off by herself in the cafeteria—even dancing, she danced alone—and it was the aloneness that filled him with love. He remembered telling her that one evening. How she nodded and looked away. And how, later, when he kissed her, she received the kiss without returning it, her eyes wide open, not afraid, not a virgin's eyes, just flat and uninvolved.

Lieutenant Cross gazed at the tunnel. But he was not there. He was buried with Martha under the white sand at the Jersey shore. They were pressed together, and the pebble in his mouth was her tongue. He was smiling. Vaguely, he was aware of how quiet the day was, the sullen paddies, yet he could not bring himself to worry about matters of security. He was beyond that. He was just a kid at war, in love. He was twenty-four years old. He couldn't help it.

A few moments later Lee Strunk crawled out of the tunnel. He came up grinning, filthy but alive. Lieutenant Cross nodded and closed his eyes while the others clapped Strunk on the back and made jokes about rising from the dead.

Worms, Rat Kiley said. Right out of the grave. Fuckin' zombie.

The men laughed. They all felt great relief.

Spook city, said Mitchell Sanders.

Lee Strunk made a funny ghost sound, a kind of moaning, yet very happy, and right then, when Strunk made that high happy moaning sound, when he went *Ahhooooo,* right then Ted Lavender was shot in the head on his way back from peeing. He lay with his mouth open. The teeth were broken. There was a swollen black bruise under his left eye. The cheekbone was gone. Oh shit, Rat Kiley said, the guy's dead. The guy's dead, he kept saying, which seemed profound—the guy's dead. I mean really.

The things they carried were determined to some extent by superstition. Lieutenant Cross carried his good-luck pebble. Dave Jensen carried a rabbit's foot. Norman Bowker, otherwise a very gentle person, carried a thumb that had been presented to him as a gift by Mitchell Sanders. The thumb was dark brown, rubbery to the touch, and weighed four ounces at most. It had been cut from a VC corpse, a boy of fifteen or sixteen. They'd found him at the bottom of an irrigation ditch, badly burned, flies in his mouth and eyes.

The boy wore black shorts and sandals. At the time of his death he had been carrying a pouch of rice, a rifle, and three magazines of ammunition.

You want my opinion, Mitchell Sanders said, there's a definite moral here.

He put his hand on the dead boy's wrist. He was quiet for a time, as if counting a pulse, then he patted the stomach, almost affectionately, and used Kiowa's hunting hatchet to remove the thumb.

Henry Dobbins asked what the moral was.

Moral?

You know. *Moral.*

Sanders wrapped the thumb in toilet paper and handed it across to Norman Bowker. There was no blood. Smiling, he kicked the boy's head, watched the flies scatter, and said, It's like with that old TV show—Paladin. Have gun, will travel.

Henry Dobbins thought about it.

Yeah, well, he finally said. I don't see no moral.

There it *is*, man.

Fuck off.

They carried USO° stationery and pencils and pens. They carried Sterno, safety pins, trip flares, signal flares, spools of wire, razor blades, chewing tobacco, liberated joss sticks and statuettes of the smiling Buddha, candles, grease pencils, *The Stars and Stripes*, fingernail clippers, Psy Ops° leaflets, bush hats, bolos, and much more. Twice a week, when the resupply choppers came in, they carried hot chow in green mermite cans and large canvas bags filled with iced beer and soda pop. They carried plastic water containers, each with a two-gallon capacity. Mitchell Sanders carried a set of starched tiger fatigues for special occasions. Henry Dobbins carried Black Flag insecticide. Dave Jensen carried empty sandbags that could be filled at night for added protection. Lee Strunk carried tanning lotion. Some things they carried in common. Taking turns, they carried the big PRC-77 scrambler radio, which weighed 30 pounds with its battery. They shared the weight of memory. They took up what others could no longer bear. Often, they carried each other, the wounded or weak. They carried infections. They carried chess sets, basketballs, Vietnamese-English dictionaries, insignia of rank, Bronze Stars and Purple Hearts, plastic cards imprinted with the Code of Conduct. They carried diseases, among them malaria and dysentery. They carried lice and ringworm and leeches and paddy algae and various rots and molds. They carried the land itself—Vietnam, the place, the soil—a powdery orange-red dust that covered their boots and fatigues and faces. They carried the sky. The whole atmosphere, they carried it, the humidity, the monsoons, the stink of fungus and decay, all of it, they carried gravity. They moved like mules. By daylight they took sniper fire, at night they were mortared, but it

---

USO: United Service Organization.   **Psy Ops:** Psychological operations.

was not battle, it was just the endless march, village to village, without purpose, nothing won or lost. They marched for the sake of the march. They plodded along slowly, dumbly, leaning forward against the heat, unthinking, all blood and bone, simple grunts, soldiering with their legs, toiling up the hills and down into the paddies and across the rivers and up again and down, just humping, one step and then the next and then another, but no volition, no will, because it was automatic, it was anatomy, and the war was entirely a matter of posture and carriage, the hump was everything, a kind of inertia, a kind of emptiness, a dullness of desire and intellect and conscience and hope and human sensibility. Their principles were in their feet. Their calculations were biological. They had no sense of strategy or mission. They searched the villages without knowing what to look for, not caring, kicking over jars of rice, frisking children and old men, blowing tunnels, sometimes setting fires and sometimes not, then forming up and moving on to the next village, then other villages, where it would always be the same. They carried their own lives. The pressures were enormous. In the heat of early afternoon, they would remove their helmets and flak jackets, walking bare, which was dangerous but which helped ease the strain. They would often discard things along the route of march. Purely for comfort, they would throw away rations, blow their Claymores and grenades, no matter because by nightfall the resupply choppers would arrive with more of the same, then a day or two later still more, fresh watermelons and crates of ammunition and sunglasses and woolen sweaters — the resources were stunning — sparklers for the Fourth of July, colored eggs for Easter — it was the great American war chest — the fruits of science, the smokestacks, the canneries, the arsenals at Hartford, the Minnesota forests, the machine shops, the vast fields of corn and wheat — they carried like freight trains; they carried it on their backs and shoulders — and for all the ambiguities of Vietnam, all the mysteries and unknowns, there was at least the single abiding certainty that they would never be at a loss for things to carry.

After the chopper took Lavender away, Lieutenant Jimmy Cross led his men into the village of Than Khe. They burned everything. They shot chickens and dogs, they trashed the village well, they called in artillery and watched the wreckage, then they marched for several hours through the hot afternoon, and then at dusk, while Kiowa explained how Lavender died, Lieutenant Cross found himself trembling.

He tried not to cry. With his entrenching tool, which weighed five pounds, he began digging a hole in the earth.

He felt shame. He hated himself. He had loved Martha more than his men, and as a consequence Lavender was now dead, and this was something he would have to carry like a stone in his stomach for the rest of the war.

All he could do was dig. He used his entrenching tool like an ax, slashing, feeling both love and hate, and then later, when it was full dark, he sat at the bottom of his foxhole and wept. It went on for a long while. In part, he was grieving for Ted Lavender, but mostly it was for Martha, and for him-self, because she belonged to another world, which was not quite real, and because she was a junior at Mount Sebastian College in New Jersey, a poet and a virgin and uninvolved, and because he realized she did not love him and never would.

Like cement, Kiowa whispered in the dark. I swear to God—boom, down. Not a word.

I've heard this, said Norman Bowker.

A pisser, you know? Still zipping himself up. Zapped while zipping.

All right, fine. That's enough.

Yeah, but you had to see it, the guy just—

I *heard,* man. Cement. So why not shut the fuck *up?*

Kiowa shook his head sadly and glanced over at the hole where Lieu-tenant Jimmy Cross sat watching the night. The air was thick and wet. A warm dense fog had settled over the paddies and there was the stillness that precedes rain.

After a time Kiowa sighed.

One thing for sure, he said. The lieutenant's in some deep hurt. I mean that crying jag—the way he was carrying on—it wasn't fake or anything, it was real heavy-duty hurt. The man cares.

Sure, Norman Bowker said.

Say what you want, the man does care.

We all got problems.

Not Lavender.

No, I guess not, Bowker said. Do me a favor, though.

Shut up?

That's a smart Indian. Shut up.

Shrugging, Kiowa pulled off his boots. He wanted to say more, just to lighten up his sleep, but instead he opened his New Testament and arranged it beneath his head as a pillow. The fog made things seem hollow and unat-tached. He tried not to think about Ted Lavender, but then he was thinking how fast it was, no drama, down and dead, and how it was hard to feel any-thing except surprise. It seemed unchristian. He wished he could find some great sadness, or even anger, but the emotion wasn't there and he couldn't make it happen. Mostly he felt pleased to be alive. He liked the smell of the New Testament under his cheek, the leather and ink and paper and glue, whatever the chemicals were. He liked hearing the sounds of night. Even his fatigue, it felt fine, the stiff muscles and the prickly awareness of his own body, a floating feeling. He enjoyed not being dead. Lying there, Kiowa ad-mired Lieutenant Jimmy Cross's capacity for grief. He wanted to share the man's pain, he wanted to care as Jimmy Cross cared. And yet when he closed his eyes, all he could think was Boom-down, and all he could feel was the pleasure of having his boots off and the fog curling in around him and the damp soil and the Bible smells and the plush comfort of night.

After a moment Norman Bowker sat up in the dark.

What the hell, he said. You want to talk, *talk*. Tell it to me.

Forget it.

No, man, go on. One thing I hate, it's a silent Indian.

For the most part they carried themselves with poise, a kind of dignity. Now and then, however, there were times of panic, when they squealed or wanted to squeal but couldn't, when they twitched and made moaning sounds and covered their heads and said Dear Jesus and flopped around on the earth and fired their weapons blindly and cringed and sobbed and begged for the noise to stop and went wild and made stupid promises to themselves and to God and to their mothers and fathers, hoping not to die. In different ways, it happened to all of them. Afterward, when the firing ended, they would blink and peek up. They would touch their bodies, feeling shame, then quickly hiding it. They would force themselves to stand. As if in slow motion, frame by frame, the world would take on the old logic — absolute silence, then the wind, then sunlight, then voices. It was the burden of being alive. Awkwardly, the men would reassemble themselves, first in private, then in groups, becoming soldiers again. They would repair the leaks in their eyes. They would check for casualties, call in dustoffs, light cigarettes, try to smile, clear their throats and spit and begin cleaning their weapons. After a time someone would shake his head and say, No lie, I almost shit my pants, and someone else would laugh, which meant it was bad, yes, but the guy had obviously not shit his pants, it wasn't that bad, and in any case nobody would ever do such a thing and then go ahead and talk about it. They would squint into the dense, oppressive sunlight. For a few moments, perhaps, they would fall silent, lighting a joint and tracking its passage from man to man, inhaling, holding in the humiliation. Scary stuff, one of them might say. But then someone else would grin or flick his eyebrows and say, Roger-dodger, almost cut me a new asshole, *almost*.

There were numerous such poses. Some carried themselves with a sort of wistful resignation, others with pride or stiff soldierly discipline or good humor or macho zeal. They were afraid of dying but they were even more afraid to show it.

They found jokes to tell.

They used a hard vocabulary to contain the terrible softness. *Greased* they'd say. *Offed, lit up, zapped while zipping*. It wasn't cruelty, just stage presence. They were actors. When someone died, it wasn't quite dying, because in a curious way it seemed scripted, and because they had their lines mostly memorized, irony mixed with tragedy, and because they called it by other names, as if to encyst and destroy the reality of death itself. They kicked corpses. They cut off thumbs. They talked grunt lingo. They told stories about Ted Lavender's supply of tranquilizers, how the poor guy didn't feel a thing, how incredibly tranquil he was.

There's a moral here, said Mitchell Sanders.

They were waiting for Lavender's chopper, smoking the dead man's dope.

The moral's pretty obvious, Sanders said, and winked. Stay away from drugs. No joke, they'll ruin your day every time.

Cute, said Henry Dobbins.

Mind blower, get it? Talk about wiggy. Nothing left, just blood and brains.

They made themselves laugh.

There it is, they'd say. Over and over — there it is, my friend, there it is — as if the repetition itself were an act of poise, a balance between crazy and almost crazy, knowing without going, there it is, which meant be cool, let it ride, because Oh yeah, man, you can't change what can't be changed, there it is, there it absolutely and positively and fucking well *is*.

They were tough.

They carried all the emotional baggage of men who might die. Grief, terror, love, longing — these were intangibles, but the intangibles had their own mass and specific gravity, they had tangible weight. They carried shameful memories. They carried the common secret of cowardice barely restrained, the instinct to run or freeze or hide, and in many respects this was the heaviest burden of all, for it could never be put down, it required perfect balance and perfect posture. They carried their reputations. They carried the soldier's greatest fear, which was the fear of blushing. Men killed, and died, because they were embarrassed not to. It was what had brought them to the war in the first place, nothing positive, no dreams of glory or honor, just to avoid the blush of dishonor. They died so as not to die of embarrassment. They crawled into tunnels and walked point and advanced under fire. Each morning, despite the unknowns, they made their legs move. They endured. They kept humping. They did not submit to the obvious alternative, which was simply to close the eyes and fall. So easy, really. Go limp and tumble to the ground and let the muscles unwind and not speak and not budge until your buddies picked you up and lifted you into the chopper that would roar and dip its nose and carry you off to the world. A mere matter of falling, yet no one ever fell. It was not courage, exactly; the object was not valor. Rather, they were too frightened to be cowards.

By and large they carried these things inside, maintaining the masks of composure. They sneered at sick call. They spoke bitterly about guys who had found release by shooting off their own toes or fingers. Pussies, they'd say. Candyasses. It was fierce, mocking talk, with only a trace of envy or awe, but even so the image played itself out behind their eyes.

They imagined the muzzle against flesh. So easy: squeeze the trigger and blow away a toe. They imagined it. They imagined the quick, sweet pain, then the evacuation to Japan, then a hospital with warm beds and cute geisha nurses.

And they dreamed of freedom birds.

At night, on guard, staring into the dark, they were carried away by jumbo jets. They felt the rush of takeoff. *Gone!* they yelled. And then velocity—wings and engines—a smiling stewardess—but it was more than a plane, it was a real bird, a big sleek silver bird with feathers and talons and high screeching. They were flying. The weights fell off; there was nothing to bear. They laughed and held on tight, feeling the cold slap of wind and altitude, soaring, thinking *It's over, I'm gone!* —they were naked, they were light and free—it was all lightness, bright and fast and buoyant, light as light, a helium buzz in the brain, a giddy bubbling in the lungs as they were taken up over the clouds and the war, beyond duty, beyond gravity and mortification and global entanglements—*Sin loi!°* they yelled. *I'm sorry, motherfuckers, but I'm out of it, I'm goofed, I'm on a space cruise, I'm gone!* —and it was a restful, unencumbered sensation, just riding the light waves, sailing that big silver freedom bird over the mountains and oceans, over America, over the farms and great sleeping cities and cemeteries and highways and the golden arches of McDonald's, it was flight, a kind of fleeing, a kind of falling, falling higher and higher, spinning off the edge of the earth and beyond the sun and through the vast, silent vacuum where there were no burdens and where everything weighed exactly nothing—*Gone!* they screamed. *I'm sorry but I'm gone!* —and so at night, not quite dreaming, they gave themselves over to lightness, they were carried, they were purely borne.

On the morning after Ted Lavender died, First Lieutenant Jimmy Cross crouched at the bottom of his foxhole and burned Martha's letters. Then he burned the two photographs. There was a steady rain falling, which made it difficult, but he used heat tabs and Sterno to build a small fire, screening it with his body, holding the photographs over the tight blue flame with the tips of his fingers.

He realized it was only a gesture. Stupid, he thought. Sentimental, too, but mostly just stupid.

Lavender was dead. You couldn't burn the blame.

Besides, the letters were in his head. And even now, without photographs, Lieutenant Cross could see Martha playing volleyball in her white gym shorts and yellow T-shirt. He could see her moving in the rain.

When the fire died out, Lieutenant Cross pulled his poncho over his shoulders and ate breakfast from a can.

There was no great mystery, he decided.

In those burned letters Martha had never mentioned the war, except to say, Jimmy, take care of yourself. She wasn't involved. She signed the letters Love, but it wasn't love, and all the fine lines and technicalities did not matter. Virginity was no longer an issue. He hated her. Yes, he did. He hated her. Love, too, but it was a hard, hating kind of love.

The morning came up wet and blurry. Everything seemed part of everything else, the fog and Martha and the deepening rain.

He was a soldier, after all.

Sin loi: Vietnamese for "sorry."

Half smiling, Lieutenant Jimmy Cross took out his maps. He shook his head hard, as if to clear it, then bent forward and began planning the day's march. In ten minutes, or maybe twenty, he would rouse the men and they would pack up and head west, where the maps showed the country to be green and inviting. They would do what they had always done. The rain might add some weight, but otherwise it would be one more day layered upon all the other days.

He was realistic about it. There was that new hardness in his stomach. He loved her but he hated her.

No more fantasies, he told himself.

Henceforth, when he thought about Martha, it would be only to think that she belonged elsewhere. He would shut down the daydreams. This was not Mount Sebastian, it was another world, where there were no pretty poems or mid-term exams, a place where men died because of carelessness and gross stupidity. Kiowa was right. Boom-down, and you were dead, never partly dead.

Briefly, in the rain, Lieutenant Cross saw Martha's gray eyes gazing back at him.

He understood.

It was very sad, he thought. The things men carried inside. The things men did or felt they had to do.

He almost nodded at her, but didn't.

Instead he went back to his maps. He was now determined to perform his duties firmly and without negligence. It wouldn't help Lavender, he knew that, but from this point on he would comport himself as an officer. He would dispose of his good-luck pebble. Swallow it, maybe, or use Lee Strunk's slingshot, or just drop it along the trail. On the march he would impose strict field discipline. He would be careful to send out flank security, to prevent straggling or bunching up, to keep his troops moving at the proper pace and at the proper interval. He would insist on clean weapons. He would confiscate the remainder of Lavender's dope. Later in the day, perhaps, he would call the men together and speak to them plainly. He would accept the blame for what had happened to Ted Lavender. He would be a man about it. He would look them in the eyes, keeping his chin level, and he would issue the new SOPs in a calm, impersonal tone of voice, a lieutenant's voice, leaving no room for argument or discussion. Commencing immediately, he'd tell them, they would no longer abandon equipment along the route of march. They would police up their acts. They would get their shit together, and keep it together, and maintain it neatly and in good working order.

He would not tolerate laxity. He would show strength, distancing himself.

Among the men there would be grumbling, of course, and maybe worse, because their days would seem longer and their loads heavier, but Lieutenant Jimmy Cross reminded himself that his obligation was not to be loved but to lead. He would dispense with love; it was not now a factor. And if anyone quarreled or complained, he would simply tighten his lips and arrange his shoulders in the correct command posture. He might give a curt little nod. Or he might not. He might just shrug and say, Carry on, then they would saddle up and form into a column and move out toward the villages west of Than Khe.

CD-ROM: Research Tim O'Brien in depth with cultural documents and multimedia resources on *LiterActive*.

Flannery O'Connor 1925–1964

A Good Man Is Hard to Find   [1955]

The grandmother didn't want to go to Florida. She wanted to visit some of her connections in east Tennessee and she was seizing at every chance to change Bailey's mind. Bailey was the son she lived with, her only boy. He was sitting on the edge of his chair at the table, bent over the orange sports section of the *Journal*. "Now look here, Bailey," she said, "see here, read this," and she stood with one hand on her thin hip and the other rattling the newspaper at his bald head. "Here this fellow that calls himself The Misfit is aloose from the Federal Pen and headed toward Florida and you read here what it says he did to these people. Just you read it. I wouldn't take my children in any direction with a criminal like that aloose in it. I couldn't answer to my conscience if I did."

Bailey didn't look up from his reading so she wheeled around then and faced the children's mother, a young woman in slacks, whose face was as broad and innocent as a cabbage and was tied around with a green headkerchief that had two points on the top like rabbit's ears. She was sitting on the sofa, feeding the baby his apricots out of a jar. "The children have been to Florida before," the old lady said. "You all ought to take them somewhere else for a change so they would see different parts of the world and be broad. They never have been to east Tennessee."

The children's mother didn't seem to hear her but the eight-year-old boy, John Wesley, a stocky child with glasses, said, "If you don't want to go to Florida, why dontcha stay at home?" He and the little girl, June Star, were reading the funny papers on the floor.

"She wouldn't stay at home to be queen for a day," June Star said without raising her yellow head.

"Yes and what would you do if this fellow, The Misfit, caught you?" the grandmother asked.

"I'd smack his face," John Wesley said.

"She wouldn't stay at home for a million bucks," June Star said. "Afraid she'd miss something. She has to go everywhere we go."

"All right, Miss," the grandmother said. "Just remember that the next time you want me to curl your hair."

June Star said her hair was naturally curly.

The next morning the grandmother was the first one in the car, ready to go. She had her big black valise that looked like the head of a hippopotamus in one corner, and underneath it she was hiding a basket with Pitty Sing, the cat, in it. She didn't intend for the cat to be left alone in the house for three days because he would miss her too much and she was afraid he might brush against one of the gas burners and accidentally asphyxiate himself. Her son, Bailey, didn't like to arrive at a motel with a cat.

She sat in the middle of the back seat with John Wesley and June Star on either side of her. Bailey and the children's mother and the baby sat in front and they left Atlanta at eight forty-five with the mileage on the car at 55890. The grandmother wrote this down because she thought it would be interesting to say how many miles they had been when they got back. It took them twenty minutes to reach the outskirts of the city.

The old lady settled herself comfortably, removing her white cotton gloves and putting them up with her purse on the shelf in front of the back window. The children's mother still had on slacks and still had her head tied up in a green kerchief, but the grandmother had on a navy blue straw sailor hat with a bunch of white violets on the brim and a navy blue dress with a small white dot in the print. Her collars and cuffs were white organdy trimmed with lace and at her neckline she had pinned a purple spray of cloth violets containing a sachet. In case of an accident, anyone seeing her dead on the highway would know at once that she was a lady.

She said she thought it was going to be a good day for driving, neither too hot nor too cold, and she cautioned Bailey that the speed limit was fifty-five miles an hour and that the patrolmen hid themselves behind billboards and small clumps of trees and sped out after you before you had a chance to slow down. She pointed out interesting details of the scenery: Stone Mountain; the blue granite that in some places came up to both sides of the highway; the brilliant red clay banks slightly streaked with purple; and the various crops that made rows of green lace-work on the ground. The trees were full of silver-white sunlight and the meanest of them sparkled. The children were reading comic magazines and their mother had gone back to sleep.

"Let's go through Georgia fast so we won't have to look at it much," John Wesley said.

"If I were a little boy," said the grandmother, "I wouldn't talk about my native state that way. Tennessee has the mountains and Georgia has the hills."

"Tennessee is just a hillbilly dumping ground," John Wesley said, "and Georgia is a lousy state too."

"You said it," June Star said.

"In my time," said the grandmother, folding her thin veined fingers, "children were more respectful of their native states and their parents and everything else. People did right then. Oh look at the cute little picka-ninny!" she said and pointed to a Negro child standing in the door of a shack. "Wouldn't that make a picture, now?" she asked and they all turned and looked at the little Negro out of the back window. He waved.

"He didn't have any britches on," June Star said.

"He probably didn't have any," the grandmother explained. "Little nig-gers in the country don't have things like we do. If I could paint, I'd paint that picture," she said.

The children exchanged comic books.

The grandmother offered to hold the baby and the children's mother passed him over the front seat to her. She set him on her knee and bounced him and told him about the things they were passing. She rolled her eyes and screwed up her mouth and stuck her leathery thin face into his smooth bland one. Occasionally he gave her a faraway smile. They passed a large cot-ton field with five or six graves fenced in the middle of it, like a small island. "Look at the graveyard!" the grandmother said, pointing it out. "That was the old family burying ground. That belonged to the plantation."

"Where's the plantation?" John Wesley asked.

"Gone With the Wind," said the grandmother. "Ha. Ha."

When the children finished all the comic books they had brought, they opened the lunch and ate it. The grandmother ate a peanut butter sandwich and an olive and would not let the children throw the box and the paper napkins out the window. When there was nothing else to do they played a game by choosing a cloud and making the other two guess what shape it suggested. John Wesley took one the shape of a cow and June Star guessed a cow and John Wesley said, no, an automobile, and June Star said he didn't play fair, and they began to slap each other over the grandmother.

The grandmother said she would tell them a story if they would keep quiet. When she told a story, she rolled her eyes and waved her head and was very dramatic. She said once when she was a maiden lady she had been courted by a Mr. Edgar Atkins Teagarden from Jasper, Georgia. She said he was a very good-looking man and a gentleman and that he brought her a watermelon every Saturday afternoon with his initials cut in it, E. A. T. Well, one Saturday, she said, Mr. Teagarden brought the watermelon and there was nobody at home and he left it on the front porch and returned in his buggy to Jasper, but she never got the watermelon, she said, because a nigger boy ate it when he saw the initials, E. A. T.! This story tickled John Wesley's funny bone and he giggled and giggled but June Star didn't think it was any good. She said she wouldn't marry a man that just brought her a water-melon on Saturday. The grandmother said she would have done well to marry Mr. Teagarden because he was a gentleman and had bought Coca-Cola stock when it first came out and that he had died only a few years ago, a very wealthy man.

They stopped at The Tower for barbecued sandwiches. The Tower was a part stucco and part wood filling station and dance hall set in a clearing outside of Timothy. A fat man named Red Sammy Butts ran it and there were signs stuck here and there on the building and for miles up and down the highway saying, TRY RED SAMMY'S FAMOUS BARBECUE. NONE LIKE FAMOUS RED SAMMY'S! RED SAM! THE FAT BOY WITH THE HAPPY LAUGH. A VETERAN! RED SAMMY'S YOUR MAN!

Red Sammy was lying on the bare ground outside The Tower with his head under a truck while a gray monkey about a foot high, chained to a small chinaberry tree, chattered nearby. The monkey sprang back into the tree and got on the highest limb as soon as he saw the children jump out of the car and run toward him.

Inside, The Tower was a long dark room with a counter at one end and tables at the other and dancing space in the middle. They all sat down at a board table next to the nickelodeon and Red Sam's wife, a tall burnt-brown woman with hair and eyes lighter than her skin, came and took their order. The children's mother put a dime in the machine and played "The Tennessee Waltz," and the grandmother said that tune always made her want to dance. She asked Bailey if he would like to dance but he only glared at her. He didn't have a naturally sunny disposition like she did and trips made him nervous. The grandmother's brown eyes were very bright. She swayed her head from side to side and pretended she was dancing in her chair. June Star said play something she could tap to so the children's mother put in another dime and played a fast number and June Star stepped out onto the dance floor and did her tap routine.

"Ain't she cute?" Red Sam's wife said, leaning over the counter. "Would you like to come be my little girl?"

"No I certainly wouldn't," June Star said. "I wouldn't live in a broken-down place like this for a million bucks!" and she ran back to the table.

"Ain't she cute?" the woman repeated, stretching her mouth politely.

"Arn't you ashamed?" hissed the grandmother.

Red Sam came in and told his wife to quit lounging on the counter and hurry up with these people's order. His khaki trousers reached just to his hip bones and his stomach hung over them like a sack of meal swaying under his shirt. He came over and sat down at a table nearby and let out a combination sigh and yodel. "You can't win," he said. "You can't win," and he wiped his sweating red face off with a gray handkerchief. "These days you don't know who to trust," he said. "Ain't that the truth?"

"People are certainly not nice like they used to be," said the grandmother.

"Two fellers come in here last week," Red Sammy said, "driving a Chrysler. It was a old beat-up car but it was a good one and these boys looked all right to me. Said they worked at the mill and you know I let them fellers charge the gas they bought? Now why did I do that?"

"Because you're a good man!" the grandmother said at once.

"Yes'm, I suppose so," Red Sam said as if he were struck with this answer.

His wife brought the orders, carrying the five plates all at once without a tray, two in each hand and one balanced on her arm. "It isn't a soul in this green world of God's that you can trust," she said. "And I don't count nobody out of that, not nobody," she repeated, looking at Red Sammy.

"Did you read about that criminal, The Misfit, that's escaped?" asked the grandmother.

"I wouldn't be a bit surprised if he didn't attact this place right here," said the woman. "If he hears about it being here, I wouldn't be none surprised to see him. If he hears it's two cent in the cash register, I wouldn't be a tall surprised if he . . ."

"That'll do," Red Sam said. "Go bring these people their Co'-Colas," and the woman went off to get the rest of the order.

"A good man is hard to find," Red Sammy said. "Everything is getting terrible. I remember the day you could go off and leave your screen door unlatched. Not no more."

He and the grandmother discussed better times. The old lady said that in her opinion Europe was entirely to blame for the way things were now. She said the way Europe acted you would think we were made of money and Red Sam said it was no use talking about it, she was exactly right. The children ran outside into the white sunlight and looked at the monkey in the lacy chinaberry tree. He was busy catching fleas on himself and biting each one carefully between his teeth as if it were a delicacy.

They drove off again into the hot afternoon. The grandmother took cat naps and woke up every few minutes with her own snoring. Outside of Toombsboro she woke up and recalled an old plantation that she had visited in this neighborhood once when she was a young lady. She said the house had six white columns across the front and that there was an avenue of oaks leading up to it and two little wooden trellis arbors on either side in front where you sat down with your suitor after a stroll in the garden. She recalled exactly which road to turn off to get to it. She knew that Bailey would not be willing to lose any time looking at an old house, but the more she talked about it, the more she wanted to see it once again and find out if the little twin arbors were still standing. "There was a secret panel in this house," she said craftily, not telling the truth but wishing that she were, "and the story went that all the family silver was hidden in it when Sherman came through but it was never found . . ."

"Hey!" John Wesley said. "Let's go see it! We'll find it! We'll poke all the woodwork and find it! Who lives there? Where do you turn off at? Hey Pop, can't we turn off there?"

"We never have seen a house with a secret panel!" June Star shrieked. "Let's go to the house with the secret panel! Hey Pop, can't we go see the house with the secret panel!"

"It's not far from here, I know," the grandmother said. "It wouldn't take over twenty minutes."

Bailey was looking straight ahead. His jaw was as rigid as a horseshoe. "No," he said.

The children began to yell and scream that they wanted to see the house with the secret panel. John Wesley kicked the back of the front seat and June

Star hung over her mother's shoulder and whined desperately into her ear that they never had any fun even on their vacation, that they could never do what THEY wanted to do. The baby began to scream and John Wesley kicked the back of the seat so hard that his father could feel the blows in his kidney.

"All right!" he shouted and drew the car to a stop at the side of the road. "Will you all shut up? Will you all just shut up for one second? If you don't shut up, we won't go anywhere."

"It would be very educational for them," the grandmother murmured.

"All right," Bailey said, "but get this: this is the only time we're going to stop for anything like this. This is the one and only time."

"The dirt road that you have to turn down is about a mile back," the grandmother directed. "I marked it when we passed."

"A dirt road," Bailey groaned.

After they had turned around and were headed toward the dirt road, the grandmother recalled other points about the house, the beautiful glass over the front doorway and the candle-lamp in the hall. John Wesley said that the secret panel was probably in the fireplace.

"You can't go inside this house," Bailey said. "You don't know who lives there."

"While you all talk to the people in front, I'll run around behind and get in a window," John Wesley suggested.

"We'll all stay in the car," his mother said.

They turned onto the dirt road and the car raced roughly along in a swirl of pink dust. The grandmother recalled the times when there were no paved roads and thirty miles was a day's journey. The dirt road was hilly and there were sudden washes in it and sharp curves on dangerous embankments. All at once they would be on a hill, looking down over the blue tops of trees for miles around, then the next minute, they would be in a red depression with the dust-coated trees looking down on them.

"This place had better turn up in a minute," Bailey said, "or I'm going to turn around."

The road looked as if no one had traveled on it in months.

"It's not much farther," the grandmother said and just as she said it, a horrible thought came to her. The thought was so embarrassing that she turned red in the face and her eyes dilated and her feet jumped up, upsetting her valise in the corner. The instant the valise moved, the newspaper top she had over the basket under it rose with a snarl and Pitty Sing, the cat, sprang onto Bailey's shoulder.

The children were thrown to the floor and their mother, clutching the baby, was thrown out the door onto the ground; the old lady was thrown into the front seat. The car turned over once and landed right-side-up in a gulch off the side of the road. Bailey remained in the driver's seat with the cat—gray-striped with a broad white face and an orange nose—clinging to his neck like a caterpillar.

As soon as the children saw they could move their arms and legs, they scrambled out of the car, shouting, "We've had an ACCIDENT!" The grandmother was curled up under the dashboard, hoping she was injured so that Bailey's wrath would not come down on her all at once. The horrible thought she had had before the accident was that the house she had remembered so vividly was not in Georgia but in Tennessee.

Bailey removed the cat from his neck with both hands and flung it out the window against the side of a pine tree. Then he got out of the car and started looking for the children's mother. She was sitting against the side of the red gutted ditch, holding the screaming baby, but she only had a cut down her face and a broken shoulder. "We've had an ACCIDENT!" the children screamed in a frenzy of delight.

"But nobody's killed," June Star said with disappointment as the grandmother limped out of the car, her hat still pinned to her head but the broken front brim standing up at a jaunty angle and the violet spray hanging off the side. They all sat down in the ditch, except the children, to recover from the shock. They were all shaking.

"Maybe a car will come along," said the children's mother hoarsely.

"I believe I have injured an organ," said the grandmother, pressing her side, but no one answered her. Bailey's teeth were clattering. He had on a yellow sport shirt with bright blue parrots designed in it and his face was as yellow as the shirt. The grandmother decided that she would not mention that the house was in Tennessee.

The road was about ten feet above and they could see only the tops of the trees on the other side of it. Behind the ditch they were sitting in there were more woods, tall and dark and deep. In a few minutes they saw a car some distance away on top of a hill, coming slowly as if the occupants were watching them. The grandmother stood up and waved both arms dramatically to attract their attention. The car continued to come on slowly, disappeared around a bend and appeared again, moving even slower, on top of the hill they had gone over. It was a big black battered hearse-like automobile. There were three men in it.

It came to a stop just over them and for some minutes, the driver looked down with a steady expressionless gaze to where they were sitting, and didn't speak. Then he turned his head and muttered something to the other two and they got out. One was a fat boy in black trousers and a red sweat shirt with a silver stallion embossed on the front of it. He moved around on the right side of them and stood staring, his mouth partly open in a kind of loose grin. The other had on khaki pants and a blue striped coat and a gray hat pulled down very low, hiding most of his face. He came around slowly on the left side. Neither spoke.

The driver got out of the car and stood by the side of it, looking down at them. He was an older man than the other two. His hair was just beginning to gray and he wore silver-rimmed spectacles that gave him a scholarly look. He had a long creased face and didn't have on any shirt or undershirt. He had on blue jeans that were too tight for him and was holding a black hat and a gun. The two boys also had guns.

"We've had an ACCIDENT!" the children screamed.

The grandmother had the peculiar feeling that the bespectacled man was someone she knew. His face was as familiar to her as if she had known him all her life but she could not recall who he was. He moved away from the car and began to come down the embankment, placing his feet carefully so that he wouldn't slip. He had on tan and white shoes and no socks, and his ankles were red and thin. "Good afternoon," he said. "I see you all had you a little spill."

"We turned over twice!" said the grandmother.

"Oncet," he corrected. "We seen it happen. Try their car and see will it run, Hiram," he said quietly to the boy with the gray hat.

"What you got that gun for?" John Wesley asked. "Whatcha gonna do with that gun?"

"Lady," the man said to the children's mother, "would you mind calling them children to sit down by you? Children make me nervous. I want all you all to sit down right together there where you're at."

"What are you telling US what to do for?" June Star asked.

Behind them the line of woods gaped like a dark open mouth. "Come here," said their mother.

"Look here now," Bailey began suddenly, "we're in a predicament! We're in . . ."

The grandmother shrieked. She scrambled to her feet and stood staring. "You're The Misfit!" she said. "I recognized you at once!"

"Yes'm," the man said, smiling slightly as if he were pleased in spite of himself to be known, "but it would have been better for all of you, lady, if you hadn't of reckernized me."

Bailey turned his head sharply and said something to his mother that shocked even the children. The old lady began to cry and The Misfit reddened.

"Lady," he said, "don't you get upset. Sometimes a man says things he don't mean. I don't reckon he meant to talk to you thataway."

"You wouldn't shoot a lady, would you?" the grandmother said and removed a clean handkerchief from her cuff and began to slap at her eyes with it.

The Misfit pointed the toe of his shoe into the ground and made a little hole and then covered it up again. "I would hate to have to," he said.

"Listen," the grandmother almost screamed, "I know you're a good man. You don't look a bit like you have common blood. I know you must come from nice people!"

"Yes mam," he said, "finest people in the world." When he smiled he showed a row of strong white teeth. "God never made a finer woman than my mother and my daddy's heart was pure gold," he said. The boy with the red sweat shirt had come around behind them and was standing with his gun at his hip. The Misfit squatted down on the ground. "Watch them children, Bobby Lee," he said. "You know they make me nervous." He looked at the six of them huddled together in front of him and he seemed to be embarrassed as if he couldn't think of anything to say. "Ain't a cloud in the sky," he remarked, looking up at it. "Don't see no sun but don't see no cloud neither."

"Yes, it's a beautiful day," said the grandmother. "Listen," she said, "you shouldn't call yourself The Misfit because I know you're a good man at heart. I can just look at you and tell."

"Hush!" Bailey yelled. "Hush! Everybody shut up and let me handle this!" He was squatting in the position of a runner about to sprint forward but he didn't move.

"I pre-chate that, lady," The Misfit said and drew a little circle in the ground with the butt of his gun.

"It'll take a half a hour to fix this here car," Hiram called, looking over the raised hood of it.

"Well, first you and Bobby Lee get him and that little boy to step over yonder with you," The Misfit said, pointing to Bailey and John Wesley. "The boys want to ast you something," he said to Bailey. "Would you mind stepping back in them woods there with them?"

"Listen," Bailey began, "we're in a terrible predicament! Nobody realizes what this is," and his voice cracked. His eyes were as blue and intense as the parrots in his shirt and he remained perfectly still.

The grandmother reached up to adjust her hat brim as if she were going to the woods with him but it came off in her hand. She stood staring at it and after a second she let it fall on the ground. Hiram pulled Bailey up by the arm as if he were assisting an old man. John Wesley caught hold of his father's hand and Bobby Lee followed. They went off toward the woods and just as they reached the dark edge, Bailey turned and supporting himself against a gray naked pine trunk, he shouted, "I'll be back in a minute, Mamma, wait on me!"

"Come back this instant!" his mother shrilled but they all disappeared into the woods.

"Bailey Boy!" the grandmother called in a tragic voice but she found she was looking at The Misfit squatting on the ground in front of her. "I just know you're a good man," she said desperately. "You're not a bit common!"

"Nome, I ain't a good man," The Misfit said after a second as if he had considered her statement carefully, "but I ain't the worst in the world neither. My daddy said I was a different breed of dog from my brothers and sisters. 'You know,' Daddy said, 'it's some that can live their whole life out without asking about it and it's others has to know why it is, and this boy is one of the latters. He's going to be into everything!'" He put on his black hat and looked up suddenly and then away deep into the woods as if he were embarrassed again. "I'm sorry I don't have on a shirt before you ladies," he said, hunching his shoulders slightly. "We buried our clothes that we had on when we escaped and we're just making do until we can get better. We borrowed these from some folks we met," he explained.

"That's perfectly all right," the grandmother said. "Maybe Bailey has an extra shirt in his suitcase."

"I'll look and see terrectly," The Misfit said.

"Where are they taking him?" the children's mother screamed.

"Daddy was a card himself," The Misfit said. "You couldn't put anything over on him. He never got in trouble with the Authorities though. Just had the knack of handling them."

"You could be honest too if you'd only try," said the grandmother. "Think how wonderful it would be to settle down and live a comfortable life and not have to think about somebody chasing you all the time."

The Misfit kept scratching in the ground with the butt of his gun as if he were thinking about it. "Yes'm, somebody is always after you," he murmured.

The grandmother noticed how thin his shoulder blades were just behind his hat because she was standing up looking down on him. "Do you ever pray?" she asked.

He shook his head. All she saw was the black hat wiggle between his shoulder blades. "Nome," he said.

There was a pistol shot from the woods, followed closely by another. Then silence. The old lady's head jerked around. She could hear the wind move through the tree tops like a long satisfied insuck of breath. "Bailey Boy!" she called.

"I was a gospel singer for a while," The Misfit said. "I been most everything. Been in the arm service, both land and sea, at home and abroad, been twict married, been an undertaker, been with the railroads, plowed Mother Earth, been in a tornado, seen a man burnt alive oncet," and he looked up at the children's mother and the little girl who were sitting close together, their faces white and their eyes glassy; "I even seen a woman flogged," he said.

"Pray, pray," the grandmother began, "pray, pray . . ."

"I never was a bad boy that I remember of," The Misfit said in an almost dreamy voice, "but somewheres along the line I done something wrong and got sent to the penitentiary. I was buried alive," and he looked up and held her attention to him by a steady stare.

"That's when you should have started to pray," she said. "What did you do to get sent to the penitentiary that first time?"

"Turn to the right, it was a wall," The Misfit said, looking up again at the cloudless sky. "Turn to the left, it was a wall. Look up it was a ceiling, look down it was a floor. I forget what I done, lady. I set there and set there, trying to remember what it was I done and I ain't recalled it to this day. Oncet in a while, I would think it was coming to me, but it never come."

"Maybe they put you in by mistake," the old lady said vaguely.

"Nome," he said. "It wasn't no mistake. They had the papers on me."

"You must have stolen something," she said.

The Misfit sneered slightly. "Nobody had nothing I wanted," he said. "It was a head-doctor at the penitentiary said what I had done was kill my daddy but I known that for a lie. My daddy died in nineteen ought nineteen of the epidemic flu and I never had a thing to do with it. He was buried in the Mount Hopewell Baptist churchyard and you can go there and see for yourself."

"If you would pray," the old lady said, "Jesus would help you."

"That's right," The Misfit said.

"Well then, why don't you pray?" she asked trembling with delight suddenly.

"I don't want no hep," he said. "I'm doing all right by myself."

Bobby Lee and Hiram came ambling back from the woods. Bobby Lee was dragging a yellow shirt with bright blue parrots in it.

"Thow me that shirt, Bobby Lee," The Misfit said. The shirt came flying at him and landed on his shoulder and he put it on. The grandmother couldn't name what the shirt reminded her of. "No, lady," The Misfit said while he was buttoning it up, "I found out the crime don't matter. You can do one thing or you can do another, kill a man or take a tire off his car, because sooner or later you're going to forget what it was you done and just be punished for it."

The children's mother had begun to make heaving noises as if she couldn't get her breath. "Lady," he asked, "would you and that little girl like to step off yonder with Bobby Lee and Hiram and join your husband?"

"Yes, thank you," the mother said faintly. Her left arm dangled helplessly and she was holding the baby, who had gone to sleep, in the other. "Hep that lady up, Hiram," The Misfit said as she struggled to climb out of the ditch, "and Bobby Lee, you hold onto that little girl's hand."

"I don't want to hold hands with him," June Star said. "He reminds me of a pig."

The fat boy blushed and laughed and caught her by the arm and pulled her off into the woods after Hiram and her mother.

Alone with The Misfit, the grandmother found that she had lost her voice. There was not a cloud in the sky nor any sun. There was nothing around her but woods. She wanted to tell him that he must pray. She opened and closed her mouth several times before anything came out. Finally she found herself saying, "Jesus. Jesus," meaning, Jesus will help you, but the way she was saying it, it sounded as if she might be cursing.

"Yes'm," The Misfit said as if he agreed. "Jesus thown everything off balance. It was the same case with Him as with me except He hadn't committed any crime and they could prove I had committed one because they had the papers on me. Of course," he said, "they never shown me my papers. That's why I sign myself now. I said long ago, you get you a signature and sign everything you do and keep a copy of it. Then you'll know what you done and you can hold up the crime to the punishment and see do they match and in the end you'll have something to prove you ain't been treated right. I call myself The Misfit," he said, "because I can't make what all I done wrong fit what all I gone through in punishment."

There was a piercing scream from the woods, followed closely by a pistol report. "Does it seem right to you, lady, that one is punished a heap and another ain't punished at all?"

"Jesus!" the old lady cried. "You've got good blood! I know you wouldn't shoot a lady! I know you come from nice people! Pray! Jesus, you ought not to shoot a lady. I'll give you all the money I've got!"

"Lady," The Misfit said, looking beyond her far into the woods, "there never was a body that give the undertaker a tip."

There were two more pistol reports and the grandmother raised her head like a parched old turkey hen crying for water and called, "Bailey Boy, Bailey Boy!" as if her heart would break.

"Jesus was the only One that ever raised the dead," The Misfit continued, "and He shouldn't have done it. He thown everything off balance. If He did what He said, then it's nothing for you to do but thow away everything and follow Him, and if He didn't, then it's nothing for you to do but enjoy the few minutes you got left the best way you can—by killing somebody or burning down his house or doing some other meanness to him. No pleasure but meanness," he said and his voice had become almost a snarl.

"Maybe He didn't raise the dead," the old lady mumbled, not knowing what she was saying and feeling so dizzy that she sank down in the ditch with her legs twisted under her.

"I wasn't there so I can't say He didn't," The Misfit said. "I wisht I had of been there," he said, hitting the ground with his fist. "It ain't right I wasn't there because if I had of been there I would of known. Listen lady," he said in a high voice, "if I had of been there I would of known and I wouldn't be like I am now." His voice seemed about to crack and the grandmother's head cleared for an instant. She saw the man's face twisted close to her own as if he were going to cry and she murmured, "Why you're one of my babies. You're one of my own children!" She reached out and touched him on the shoulder. The Misfit sprang back as if a snake had bitten him and shot her three times through the chest. Then he put his gun down on the ground and took off his glasses and began to clean them.

Hiram and Bobby Lee returned from the woods and stood over the ditch, looking down at the grandmother who half sat and half lay in a puddle of blood with her legs crossed under her like a child's and her face smiling up at the cloudless sky.

Without his glasses, The Misfit's eyes were red-rimmed and pale and defenseless-looking. "Take her off and thow her where you thown the others," he said, picking up the cat that was rubbing itself against his leg.

"She was a talker, wasn't she?" Bobby Lee said, sliding down the ditch with a yodel.

"She would of been a good woman," The Misfit said, "if it had been somebody there to shoot her every minute of her life."

"Some fun!" Bobby Lee said.

"Shut up, Bobby Lee," The Misfit said. "It's no real pleasure in life."

CD-ROM: Research Flannery O'Connor in depth with cultural documents and multimedia resources on *LiterActive*.

Tillie Olsen   b. 1913

I Stand Here Ironing   [1961]

I stand here ironing, and what you asked me moves tormented back and forth with the iron.

"I wish you would manage the time to come in and talk with me about your daughter. I'm sure you can help me understand her. She's a youngster who needs help and whom I'm deeply interested in helping."

"Who needs help." . . . Even if I came, what good would it do? You think because I am her mother I have a key, or that in some way you could use me as a key? She has lived for nineteen years. There is all that life that has happened outside of me, beyond me.

And when is there time to remember, to sift, to weigh, to estimate, to total? I will start and there will be an interruption and I will have to gather it all together again. Or I will become engulfed with all I did or did not do, with what should have been and what cannot be helped.

She was a beautiful baby. The first and only one of our five that was beautiful at birth. You do not guess how new and uneasy her tenancy in her now-loveliness. You did not know her all those years she was thought homely, or see her poring over her baby pictures, making me tell her over and over how beautiful she had been — and would be, I would tell her — and was now, to the seeing eye. But the seeing eyes were few or nonexistent. Including mine.

I nursed her. They feel that's important nowadays. I nursed all the children, but with her, with all the fierce rigidity of first motherhood, I did like the books then said. Though her cries battered me to trembling and my breasts ached with swollenness, I waited till the clock decreed.

Why do I put that first? I do not even know if it matters, or if it explains anything.

She was a beautiful baby. She blew shining bubbles of sound. She loved motion, loved light, loved color and music and textures. She would lie on the floor in her blue overalls patting the surface so hard in ecstasy her hands and feet would blur. She was a miracle to me, but when she was eight months old I had to leave her daytimes with the woman downstairs to whom she was no miracle at all, for I worked or looked for work and for Emily's father, who "could no longer endure" (he wrote in his good-bye note) "sharing want with us."

I was nineteen. It was the pre-relief, pre-WPA world of the depression. I would start running as soon as I got off the streetcar, running up the stairs, the place smelling sour, and awake or asleep to startle awake, when she saw me she would break into a clogged weeping that could not be comforted, a weeping I can hear yet.

After a while I found a job hashing at night so I could be with her days, and it was better. But it came to where I had to bring her to his family and leave her.

It took a long time to raise the money for her fare back. Then she got chicken pox and I had to wait longer. When she finally came, I hardly knew her, walking quick and nervous like her father, looking like her father, thin, and dressed in a shoddy red that yellowed her skin and glared at the pock-marks. All the baby loveliness gone.

She was two. Old enough for nursery school they said, and I did not know then what I know now — the fatigue of the long day, and the lacerations of group life in the kinds of nurseries that are only parking places for children.

Except that it would have made no difference if I had known. It was the only place there was. It was the only way we could be together, the only way I could hold a job.

And even without knowing, I knew. I knew the teacher that was evil because all these years it has curdled into my memory, the little boy hunched in the corner, her rasp, "why aren't you outside, because Alvin hits you? that's no reason, go out, scaredy." I knew Emily hated it even if she did not clutch and implore "don't go Mommy" like the other children, mornings.

She always had a reason why we should stay home. Momma, you look sick. Momma, I feel sick. Momma, the teachers aren't there today, they're sick. Momma, we can't go, there was a fire there last night. Momma, it's a holiday today, no school, they told me.

But never a direct protest, never rebellion. I think of our others in their three-, four-year-oldness — the explosions, the tempers, the denunciations, the demands — and I feel suddenly ill. I put the iron down. What in me demanded that goodness in her? And what was the cost to her of such goodness?

The old man living in the back once said in his gentle way: "You should smile at Emily more when you look at her." What *was* in my face when I looked at her? I loved her. There were all the acts of love.

It was only with the others I remembered what he said, and it was the face of joy, and not of care or tightness or worry I turned to them — too late for Emily. She does not smile easily, let alone almost always as her brothers and sisters do. Her face is closed and sombre, but when she wants, how fluid. You must have seen it in her pantomimes, you spoke of her rare gift for comedy on the stage that rouses a laughter out of the audience so dear they applaud and applaud and do not want to let her go.

Where does it come from, that comedy? There was none of it in her when she came back to me that second time, after I had had to send her away again. She had a new daddy now to learn to love, and I think perhaps it was a better time.

Except when we left her alone nights, telling ourselves she was old enough.

"Can't you go some other time, Mommy, like tomorrow?" she would ask. "Will it be just a little while you'll be gone? Do you promise?"

The time we came back, the front door open, the clock on the floor in the hall. She rigid awake. "It wasn't just a little while. I didn't cry. Three times I called you, just three times, and then I ran downstairs to open the door so you could come faster. The clock talked loud. I threw it away, it scared me what it talked."

She said the clock talked loud again that night I went to the hospital to have Susan. She was delirious with the fever that comes before red measles, but she was fully conscious all the week I was gone and the week after we were home when she could not come near the new baby or me.

She did not get well. She stayed skeleton thin, not wanting to eat, and night after night she had nightmares. She would call for me, and I would rouse from exhaustion to sleepily call back: "You're all right, darling, go to sleep, it's just a dream," and if she still called, in a sterner voice, "now go to sleep, Emily, there's nothing to hurt you." Twice, only twice, when I had to get up for Susan anyhow, I went in to sit with her.

Now when it is too late (as if she would let me hold and comfort her like I do the others) I get up and go to her at once at her moan or restless stirring. "Are you awake, Emily? Can I get you something?" And the answer is always the same: "No, I'm all right, go back to sleep, Mother."

They persuaded me at the clinic to send her away to a convalescent home in the country where "she can have the kind of food and care you can't manage for her, and you'll be free to concentrate on the new baby." They still send children to that place. I see pictures on the society page of sleek young women planning affairs to raise money for it, or dancing at the affairs, or decorating Easter eggs or filling Christmas stockings for the children.

They never have a picture of the children so I do not know if the girls still wear those gigantic red bows and the ravaged looks on the every other Sunday when parents can come to visit "unless otherwise notified" — as we were notified the first six weeks.

Oh it is a handsome place, green lawns and tall trees and fluted flower beds. High up on the balconies of each cottage the children stand, the girls in their red bows and white dresses, the boys in white suits and giant red ties. The parents stand below shrieking up to be heard and the children shriek down to be heard, and between them the invisible wall "Not To Be Contaminated by Parental Germs or Physical Affection."

There was a tiny girl who always stood hand in hand with Emily. Her parents never came. One visit she was gone. "They moved her to Rose Cottage" Emily shouted in explanation. "They don't like you to love anybody here."

She wrote once a week, the labored writing of a seven-year-old. "I am fine. How is the baby. If I write my leter nicly I will have a star. Love." There never was a star. We wrote every other day, letters she could never hold or keep but only hear read — once. "We simply do not have room for children to keep any personal possessions," they patiently explained when we pieced one Sunday's shrieking together to plead how much it would mean to Emily, who loved so to keep things, to be allowed to keep her letters and cards.

Each visit she looked frailer. "She isn't eating," they told us.

(They had runny eggs for breakfast or mush with lumps, Emily said later, I'd hold it in my mouth and not swallow. Nothing ever tasted good, just when they had chicken.)

It took us eight months to get her released home, and only the fact that she gained back so little of her seven lost pounds convinced the social worker.

I used to try to hold and love her after she came back, but her body would stay stiff, and after a while she'd push away. She ate little. Food sickened her, and I think much of life too. Oh she had physical lightness and brightness, twinkling by on skates, bouncing like a ball up and down up and down over the jump rope, skimming over the hill; but these were momentary.

She fretted about her appearance, thin and dark and foreign-looking at a time when every little girl was supposed to look or thought she should look a chubby blonde replica of Shirley Temple. The doorbell sometimes rang for her, but no one seemed to come and play in the house or be a best friend. Maybe because we moved so much.

There was a boy she loved painfully through two school semesters. Months later she told me how she had taken pennies from my purse to buy him candy. "Licorice was his favorite and I brought him some every day, but he still liked Jennifer better'n me. Why, Mommy?" The kind of question for which there is no answer.

School was a worry to her. She was not glib or quick in a world where glibness and quickness were easily confused with ability to learn. To her overworked and exasperated teachers she was an overconscientious "slow learner" who kept trying to catch up and was absent entirely too often.

I let her be absent, though sometimes the illness was imaginary. How different from my now-strictness about attendance with the others. I wasn't working. We had a new baby, I was home anyhow. Sometimes, after Susan grew old enough, I would keep her home from school, too, to have them all together.

Mostly Emily had asthma, and her breathing, harsh and labored, would fill the house with a curiously tranquil sound. I would bring the two old dresser mirrors and her boxes of collections to her bed. She would select beads and single earrings, bottle tops and shells, dried flowers and pebbles, old postcards and scraps, all sorts of oddments; then she and Susan would play Kingdom, setting up landscapes and furniture, peopling them with action.

Those were the only times of peaceful companionship between her and Susan. I have edged away from it, that poisonous feeling between them, that terrible balancing of hurts and needs I had to do between the two, and did so badly, those earlier years.

Oh there are conflicts between the others too, each one human, needing, demanding, hurting, taking — but only between Emily and Susan, no, Emily toward Susan that corroding resentment. It seems so obvious on the surface, yet it is not obvious. Susan, the second child, Susan, golden- and curly-haired and chubby, quick and articulate and assured, everything in appearance and manner Emily was not; Susan, not able to resist Emily's precious things, losing or sometimes clumsily breaking them; Susan telling jokes and riddles to company for applause while Emily sat silent (to say to me later: that was *my* riddle, Mother, I told it to Susan); Susan, who for all the five years' difference in age was just a year behind Emily in developing physically.

I am glad for that slow physical development that widened the difference between her and her contemporaries, though she suffered over it. She was too vulnerable for that terrible world of youthful competition, of preening and parading, of constant measuring of yourself against every other, of envy, "If I had that copper hair," "If I had that skin. . . ." She tormented herself enough about not looking like the others, there was enough of the unsureness, the having to be conscious of words before you speak, the constant caring — what are they thinking of me? without having it all magnified by the merciless physical drives.

Ronnie is calling. He is wet and I change him. It is rare there is such a cry now. That time of motherhood is almost behind me when the ear is not one's own but must always be racked and listening for the child cry, the child call. We sit for a while and I hold him, looking out over the city spread in charcoal with its soft aisles of light. *"Shoogily,"* he breathes and curls closer. I carry him back to bed, asleep. *Shoogily.* A funny word, a family word, inherited from Emily, invented by her to say: *comfort.*

In this and other ways she leaves her seal, I say aloud. And startle at my saying it. What do I mean? What did I start to gather together, to try and make coherent? I was at the terrible, growing years. War years. I do not remember them well. I was working, there were four smaller ones now, there was not time for her. She had to help be a mother, and housekeeper, and shopper. She had to set her seal. Mornings of crisis and near hysteria trying to get lunches packed, hair combed, coats and shoes found, everyone to school or Child Care on time, the baby ready for transportation. And always the paper scribbled on by a smaller one, the book looked at by Susan then mislaid, the homework not done. Running out to that huge school where she was one, she was lost, she was a drop; suffering over the unpreparedness, stammering and unsure in her classes.

There was so little time left at night after the kids were bedded down. She would struggle over books, always eating (it was in those years she developed her enormous appetite that is legendary in our family) and I would be ironing, or preparing food for the next day, or writing V-mail to Bill, or tending the baby. Sometimes, to make me laugh, or out of her despair, she would imitate happenings or types at school.

I think I said once: "Why don't you do something like this in the school amateur show?" One morning she phoned me at work, hardly understandable through the weeping: "Mother, I did it. I won, I won; they gave me first prize; they clapped and clapped and wouldn't let me go."

Now suddenly she was Somebody, and as imprisoned in her difference as she had been in anonymity.

She began to be asked to perform at other high schools, even in colleges, then at city and statewide affairs. The first one we went to, I only recognized her that first moment when thin, shy, she almost drowned herself into the curtains. Then: Was this Emily? The control, the command, the convulsing and deadly clowning, the spell, then the roaring, stamping audience, unwilling to let this rare and precious laughter out of their lives.

Afterwards: You ought to do something about her with a gift like that — but without money or knowing how, what does one do? We have left it all to her, and the gift has as often eddied inside, clogged and clotted, as been used and growing.

She is coming. She runs up the stairs two at a time with her light graceful step, and I know she is happy tonight. Whatever it was that occasioned your call did not happen today.

"Aren't you ever going to finish the ironing, Mother? Whistler painted his mother in a rocker. I'd have to paint mine standing over an ironing board." This is one of her communicative nights and she tells me everything and nothing as she fixes herself a plate of food out of the icebox.

She is so lovely. Why did you want me to come in at all? Why were you concerned? She will find her way.

She starts up the stairs to bed. "Don't get me up with the rest in the morning." "But I thought you were having midterms." "Oh, those," she comes back in, kisses me, and says quite lightly, "in a couple of years when we'll all be atom-dead they won't matter a bit."

She has said it before. She *believes* it. But because I have been dredging the past, and all that compounds a human being is so heavy and meaningful in me, I cannot endure it tonight.

I will never total it all. I will never come in to say: She was a child seldom smiled at. Her father left me before she was a year old. I had to work her first six years when there was work, or I sent her home and to his relatives. There were years she had care she hated. She was dark and thin and foreign-looking in a world where the prestige went to blondeness and curly hair and dimples, she was slow where glibness was prized. She was a child of anxious, not proud, love. We were poor and could not afford for her the soil of easy growth. I was a young mother, I was a distracted mother. There were the other children pushing up, demanding. Her younger sister seemed all that she was not. There were years she did not want me to touch her. She kept too much in herself, her life was such she had to keep too much in herself. My wisdom came too late. She has much to her and probably nothing will come of it. She is a child of her age, of depression, of war, of fear.

Let her be. So all that is in her will not bloom — but in how many does it? There is still enough left to live by. Only help her to know — help make it so there is cause for her to know — that she is more than this dress on the ironing board, helpless before the iron.

Edgar Allan Poe   1809–1849

The Cask of Amontillado   [1846]

The thousand injuries of Fortunato I had borne as I best could; but when he ventured upon insult, I vowed revenge. You, who so well know the nature of my soul, will not suppose, however, that I gave utterance to a threat. *At length* I would be avenged; this was a point definitively settled — but the very definitiveness with which it was resolved precluded the idea of risk. I must not only punish, but punish with impunity. A wrong is unredressed when retribution overtakes its redresser. It is equally unredressed when the avenger fails to make himself felt as such to him who has done the wrong.

It must be understood that neither by word nor deed had I given Fortunato cause to doubt my good will. I continued, as was my wont, to smile in his face, and he did not perceive that my smile *now* was at the thought of his immolation.

He had a weak point — this Fortunato — although in other regards he was a man to be respected and even feared. He prided himself on his connoisseurship in wine. Few Italians have the true virtuoso spirit. For the most part their enthusiasm is adopted to suit the time and opportunity — to practise imposture upon the British and Austrian *millionaires.* In painting and gemmary Fortunato, like his countrymen, was a quack — but in the matter of old wines he was sincere. In this respect I did not differ from him materially; I was skilful in the Italian vintages myself, and bought largely whenever I could.

It was about dusk, one evening during the supreme madness of the carnival season, that I encountered my friend. He accosted me with excessive warmth, for he had been drinking much. The man wore motley. He had on a tight-fitting parti-striped dress, and his head was surmounted by the conical cap and bells. I was so pleased to see him that I thought I should never have done wringing his hand.

I said to him — "My dear Fortunato, you are luckily met. How remarkably well you are looking to-day! But I have received a pipe° of what passes for Amontillado, and I have my doubts."

"How?" said he. "Amontillado? A pipe? Impossible! And in the middle of the carnival!"

"I have my doubts," I replied; "and I was silly enough to pay the full Amontillado price without consulting you in the matter. You were not to be found, and I was fearful of losing a bargain."

"Amontillado!"

"I have my doubts."

"Amontillado!"

"And I must satisfy them."

---

pipe: A large keg or cask.

"Amontillado!"

"As you are engaged, I am on my way to Luchesi. If any one has a critical turn, it is he. He will tell me—"

"Luchesi cannot tell Amontillado from Sherry."

"And yet some fools will have it that his taste is a match for your own."

"Come, let us go."

"Whither?"

"To your vaults."

"My friend, no; I will not impose upon your good nature. I perceive you have an engagement. Luchesi—"

"I have no engagement;—come."

"My friend, no. It is not the engagement, but the severe cold with which I perceive you are afflicted. The vaults are insufferably damp. They are encrusted with nitre."

"Let us go, nevertheless. The cold is merely nothing. Amontillado! You have been imposed upon. And as for Luchesi, he cannot distinguish Sherry from Amontillado."

Thus speaking, Fortunato possessed himself of my arm. Putting on a mask of black silk, and drawing a *roquelaire*° closely about my person, I suffered him to hurry me to my palazzo.

There were no attendants at home; they had absconded to make merry in honor of the time. I had told them that I should not return until the morning, and had given them explicit orders not to stir from the house. These orders were sufficient, I well knew, to insure their immediate disappearance, one and all, as soon as my back was turned.

I took from their sconces two flambeaux, and giving one to Fortunato, bowed him through several suites of rooms to the archway that led into the vaults. I passed down a long and winding staircase, requesting him to be cautious as he followed. We came at length to the foot of the descent, and stood together on the damp ground of the catacombs of the Montresors.

The gait of my friend was unsteady, and the bells upon his cap jingled as he strode.

"The pipe," said he.

"It is farther on," said I; "but observe the white web-work which gleams from these cavern walls."

He turned towards me, and looked into my eyes with two filmy orbs that distilled the rheum of intoxication.

"Nitre?" he asked, at length.

"Nitre," I replied. "How long have you had that cough?"

"Ugh! ugh! ugh!—ugh! ugh! ugh!—ugh! ugh! ugh!—ugh! ugh! ugh!— ugh! ugh! ugh!"

My poor friend found it impossible to reply for many minutes.

"It is nothing," he said, at last.

---

roquelaire: A short cloak.

"Come," I said, with decision, "we will go back; your health is precious. You are rich, respected, admired, beloved; you are happy, as once I was. You are a man to be missed. For me it is no matter. We will go back; you will be ill, and I cannot be responsible. Besides, there is Luchesi —"

"Enough," he said; "the cough is a mere nothing; it will not kill me. I shall not die of a cough."

"True — true," I replied; "and, indeed, I had no intention of alarming you unnecessarily — but you should use all proper caution. A draught of this Medoc will defend us from the damps."

Here I knocked off the neck of a bottle which I drew from a long row of its fellows that lay upon the mould.

"Drink," I said, presenting him the wine.

He raised it to his lips with a leer. He paused and nodded to me familiarly, while his bells jingled.

"I drink," he said, "to the buried that repose around us."

"And I to your long life."

He again took my arm, and we proceeded.

"These vaults," he said, "are extensive."

"The Montresors," I replied, "were a great and numerous family."

"I forget your arms."

"A huge human foot d'or,° in a field azure; the foot crushes a serpent rampant whose fangs are imbedded in the heel."

"And the motto?"

"*Nemo me impune lacessit.*"°

"Good!" he said.

The wine sparkled in his eyes and the bells jingled. My own fancy grew warm with the Medoc. We had passed through walls of piled bones, with casks and puncheons intermingling, into the inmost recesses of the catacombs. I paused again, and this time I made bold to seize Fortunato by an arm above the elbow.

"The nitre!" I said; "see, it increases. It hangs like moss upon the vaults. We are below the river's bed. The drops of moisture trickle among the bones. Come, we will go back ere it is too late. Your cough —"

"It is nothing," he said; "let us go on. But first, another draught of the Medoc."

I broke and reached him a flaçon of De Grâve. He emptied it at a breath. His eyes flashed with a fierce light. He laughed and threw the bottle upwards with a gesticulation I did not understand.

I looked at him in surprise. He repeated the movement — a grotesque one.

"You do not comprehend?" he said.

"Not I," I replied.

"Then you are not of the brotherhood."

---

d'or: Of gold.   *Nemo me impune lacessit:* No one provokes me with impunity (Latin; the motto of the Order of the Thistle in Scotland and the national motto of Scotland).

"How?"

"You are not of the masons."

"Yes, yes," I said, "yes, yes."

"You? Impossible! A mason?"

"A mason," I replied.

"A sign," he said.

"It is this," I answered, producing a trowel from beneath the folds of my *roquelaire.*

"You jest," he exclaimed, recoiling a few paces. "But let us proceed to the Amontillado."

"Be it so," I said, replacing the tool beneath the cloak, and again offering him my arm. He leaned upon it heavily. We continued our route in search of the Amontillado. We passed through a range of low arches, descended, passed on, and descending again, arrived at a deep crypt, in which the foulness of the air caused our flambeaux rather to glow than flame.

At the most remote end of the crypt there appeared another less spacious. Its walls had been lined with human remains, piled to the vault overhead, in the fashion of the great catacombs of Paris. Three sides of this interior crypt were still ornamented in this manner. From the fourth the bones had been thrown down, and lay promiscuously upon the earth, forming at one point a mound of some size. Within the wall thus exposed by the displacing of the bones, we perceived a still interior recess, in depth about four feet, in width three, in height six or seven. It seemed to have been constructed for no especial use within itself, but formed merely the interval between two of the colossal supports of the roof of the catacombs, and was backed by one of their circumscribing walls of solid granite.

It was in vain that Fortunato, uplifting his dull torch, endeavored to pry into the depth of the recess. Its termination the feeble light did not enable us to see.

"Proceed," I said; "herein is the Amontillado. As for Luchesi—"

"He is an ignoramus," interrupted my friend, as he stepped unsteadily forward, while I followed immediately at his heels. In an instant he had reached the extremity of the niche, and finding his progress arrested by the rock, stood stupidly bewildered. A moment more and I had fettered him to the granite. In its surface were two iron staples, distant from each other about two feet, horizontally. From one of these depended a short chain, from the other a padlock. Throwing the links about his waist, it was but the work of a few seconds to secure it. He was too much astounded to resist. Withdrawing the key I stepped back from the recess.

"Pass your hand," I said, "over the wall; you cannot help feeling the nitre. Indeed it is *very* damp. Once more let me *implore* you to return. No? Then I must positively leave you. But I must first render you all the little attentions in my power."

"The Amontillado!" ejaculated my friend, not yet recovered from his astonishment.

"True," I replied; "the Amontillado."

As I said these words I busied myself among the pile of bones of which I have before spoken. Throwing them aside, I soon uncovered a quantity of building stone and mortar. With these materials and with the aid of my trowel, I began vigorously to wall up the entrance of the niche.

I had scarcely laid the first tier of the masonry when I discovered that the intoxication of Fortunato had in a great measure worn off. The earliest indication I had of this was a low moaning cry from the depth of the recess. It was *not* the cry of a drunken man. There was then a long and obstinate silence. I laid the second tier, and the third, and the fourth; and then I heard the furious vibrations of the chain. The noise lasted for several minutes, during which, that I might hearken to it with the more satisfaction, I ceased my labors and sat down upon the bones. When at last the clanking subsided, I resumed the trowel, and finished without interruption the fifth, the sixth, and the seventh tier. The wall was now nearly upon a level with my breast. I again paused, and holding the flambeaux over the mason-work, threw a few feeble rays upon the figure within.

A succession of loud and shrill screams, bursting suddenly from the throat of the chained form, seemed to thrust me violently back. For a brief moment I hesitated—I trembled. Unsheathing my rapier, I began to grope with it about the recess: but the thought of an instant reassured me. I placed my hand upon the solid fabric of the catacombs, and felt satisfied. I reapproached the wall. I replied to the yells of him who clamored. I re-echoed—I aided—I surpassed them in volume and in strength. I did this, and the clamorer grew still.

It was now midnight, and my task was drawing to a close. I had completed the eighth, the ninth, and the tenth tier. I had finished a portion of the last and the eleventh; there remained but a single stone to be fitted and plastered in. I struggled with its weight; I placed it partially in its destined position. But now there came from out the niche a low laugh that erected the hairs upon my head. It was succeeded by a sad voice, which I had difficulty in recognising as that of the noble Fortunato. The voice said—

"Ha! ha! ha!—he! he!—a very good joke indeed—an excellent jest. We will have many a rich laugh about it at the palazzo—he! he! he!—over our wine—he! he! he!"

"The Amontillado!" I said.

"He! he! he!—he! he! he!—yes, the Amontillado. But is it not getting late? Will not they be awaiting us at the palazzo, the Lady Fortunato and the rest? Let us be gone."

"Yes," I said, "let us be gone."

"For the love of God, Montresor!"

"Yes," I said, "for the love of God!"

But to these words I hearkened in vain for a reply. I grew impatient. I called aloud—

"Fortunato!"

No answer. I called again —

"Fortunato!"

No answer still. I thrust a torch through the remaining aperture and let it fall within. There came forth in return only a jingling of the bells. My heart grew sick — on account of the dampness of the catacombs. I hastened to make an end of my labor. I forced the last stone into its position; I plastered it up. Against the new masonry I re-erected the old rampart of bones. For the half of a century no mortal has disturbed them. *In páce requiescat!*°

In páce requiescat!: May he rest in peace!

CD-ROM: Research Edgar Allan Poe in depth with cultural documents and multimedia resources on *LiterActive*.

Katherine Anne Porter 1890–1980

The Jilting of Granny Weatherall   [1929]

She flicked her wrist neatly out of Doctor Harry's pudgy careful fingers and pulled the sheet up to her chin. The brat ought to be in knee breeches. Doctoring around the country with spectacles on his nose! "Get along now, take your schoolbooks and go. There's nothing wrong with me."

Doctor Harry spread a warm paw like a cushion on her forehead where the forked green vein danced and made her eyelids twitch. "Now, now, be a good girl, and we'll have you up in no time."

"That's no way to speak to a woman nearly eighty years old just because she's down. I'd have you respect your elders, young man."

"Well, Missy, excuse me." Doctor Harry patted her cheek. "But I've got to warn you, haven't I? You're a marvel, but you must be careful or you're going to be good and sorry."

"Don't tell me what I'm going to be. I'm on my feet now, morally speaking. It's Cornelia. I had to go to bed to get rid of her."

Her bones felt loose, and floated around in her skin, and Doctor Harry floated like a balloon around the foot of the bed. He floated and pulled down his waistcoat and swung his glasses on a cord. "Well, stay where you are, it certainly can't hurt you."

"Get along and doctor your sick," said Granny Weatherall. "Leave a well woman alone. I'll call for you when I want you. . . . Where were you forty years ago when I pulled through milk-leg and double pneumonia? You weren't even born. Don't let Cornelia lead you on," she shouted, because Doctor Harry appeared to float up to the ceiling and out. "I pay my own bills, and I don't throw my money away on nonsense!"

She meant to wave good-by, but it was too much trouble. Her eyes closed of themselves, it was like a dark curtain drawn around the bed. The pillow rose and floated under her, pleasant as a hammock in a light wind. She listened to the leaves rustling outside the window. No, somebody was swishing newspapers: no, Cornelia and Doctor Harry were whispering together. She leaped broad awake, thinking they whispered in her ear.

"She was never like this, *never* like this!" "Well, what can we expect?" "Yes, eighty years old. . . ."

Well, and what if she was? She still had ears. It was like Cornelia to whisper around doors. She always kept things secret in such a public way. She was always being tactful and kind. Cornelia was dutiful; that was the trouble with her. Dutiful and good: "So good and dutiful," said Granny, "that I'd like to spank her." She saw herself spanking Cornelia and making a fine job of it.

"What'd you say, Mother?"

Granny felt her face tying up in hard knots.

"Can't a body think, I'd like to know?"

"I thought you might want something."

"I do. I want a lot of things. First off, go away and don't whisper."

She lay and drowsed, hoping in her sleep that the children would keep out and let her rest a minute. It had been a long day. Not that she was tired. It was always pleasant to snatch a minute now and then. There was always so much to be done, let me see: tomorrow.

Tomorrow was far away and there was nothing to trouble about. Things were finished somehow when the time came; thank God there was always a little margin over for peace: then a person could spread out the plan of life and tuck in the edges orderly. It was good to have everything clean and folded away, with the hair brushes and tonic bottles sitting straight on the white embroidered linen: the day started without fuss and the pantry shelves laid out with rows of jelly glasses and brown jugs and white stone-china jars with blue whirligigs and words painted on them: coffee, tea, sugar, ginger, cinnamon, allspice: and the bronze clock with the lion on top nicely dusted off. The dust that lion could collect in twenty-four hours! The box in the attic with all those letters tied up, well, she'd have to go through that tomorrow. All those letters — George's letters and John's letters and her letters to them both — lying around for the children to find afterwards made her uneasy. Yes, that would be tomorrow's business. No use to let them know how silly she had been once.

While she was rummaging around she found death in her mind and it felt clammy and unfamiliar. She had spent so much time preparing for death there was no need for bringing it up again. Let it take care of itself now. When she was sixty she had felt very old, finished, and went around making farewell trips to see her children and grandchildren, with a secret in her mind: This is the very last of your mother, children! Then she made her will and came down with a long fever. That was all just a notion like a lot of other things, but it was lucky too, for she had once for all got over the idea of dying for a long time. Now she couldn't be worried. She hoped she had better sense now. Her father had lived to be one hundred and two years old and had drunk a noggin of strong hot toddy on his last birthday. He told the reporters it was his daily habit, and he owed his long life to that. He had made quite a scandal and was very pleased about it. She believed she'd just plague Cornelia a little.

"Cornelia! Cornelia!" No footsteps, but a sudden hand on her cheek. "Bless you, where have you been?"

"Here, Mother."

"Well, Cornelia, I want a noggin of hot toddy."

"Are you cold, darling?"

"I'm chilly, Cornelia. Lying in bed stops the circulation. I must have told you that a thousand times."

Well, she could just hear Cornelia telling her husband that Mother was getting a little childish and they'd have to humor her. The thing that most annoyed her was that Cornelia thought she was deaf, dumb, and blind. Little hasty glances and tiny gestures tossed around her and over her head saying, "Don't cross her, let her have her way, she's eighty years old," and she sitting there as if she lived in a thin glass cage. Sometimes Granny almost made up her mind to pack up and move back to her own house where nobody could remind her every minute that she was old. Wait, wait, Cornelia, till your own children whisper behind your back!

In her day she had kept a better house and had got more work done. She wasn't too old yet for Lydia to be driving eighty miles for advice when one of the children jumped the track, and Jimmy still dropped in and talked things over: "Now, Mammy, you've a good business head, I want to know what you think of this? . . ." Old. Cornelia couldn't change the furniture around without asking. Little things, little things! They had been so sweet when they were little. Granny wished the old days were back again with the children young and everything to be done over. It had been a hard pull, but not too much for her. When she thought of all the food she had cooked, and all the clothes she had cut and sewed, and all the gardens she had made—well, the children showed it. There they were, made out of her, and they couldn't get away from that. Sometimes she wanted to see John again and point to them and say, Well, I didn't do so badly, did I? But that would have to wait. That was for tomorrow. She used to think of him as a man, but now all the children were older than their father, and he would be a child beside her if she saw him now. It seemed strange and there was something wrong in the idea. Why, he couldn't possibly recognize her. She had fenced in a hundred acres once, digging the post holes herself and clamping the wires with just a negro boy to help. That changed a woman. John would be looking for a young woman with the peaked Spanish comb in her hair and the painted fan. Digging post holes changed a woman. Riding country roads in the winter when women had their babies was another thing: sitting up nights with sick horses and sick negroes and sick children and hardly ever losing one. John, I hardly ever lost one of them! John would see that in a minute, that would be something he could understand, she wouldn't have to explain anything!

It made her feel like rolling up her sleeves and putting the whole place to rights again. No matter if Cornelia was determined to be everywhere at once, there were a great many things left undone on this place. She would start tomorrow and do them. It was good to be strong enough for everything, even if all you made melted and changed and slipped under your hands, so that by the time you finished you almost forgot what you were working for. What was it I set out to do? she asked herself intently, but she could not remember. A fog rose over the valley, she saw it marching across the creek swallowing the trees and moving up the hill like an army of ghosts. Soon it would be at the near edge of the orchard, and then it was time to go in and light the lamps. Come in, children, don't stay out in the night air.

Lighting the lamps had been beautiful. The children huddled up to her and breathed like little calves waiting at the bars in the twilight. Their eyes followed the match and watched the flame rise and settle in a blue curve, then they moved away from her. The lamp was lit, they didn't have to be scared and hang on to mother any more. Never, never, never more. God, for all my life I thank Thee. Without Thee, my God, I could never have done it. Hail, Mary, full of grace.

I want you to pick all the fruit this year and see that nothing is wasted. There's always someone who can use it. Don't let good things rot for want of using. You waste life when you waste good food. Don't let things get lost. It's bitter to lose things. Now, don't let me get to thinking, not when I am tired and taking a little nap before supper. . . .

The pillow rose about her shoulders and pressed against her heart and the memory was being squeezed out of it: oh, push down the pillow, somebody: it would smother her if she tried to hold it. Such a fresh breeze blowing and such a green day with no threats in it. But he had not come, just the same. What does a woman do when she has put on the white veil and set out the white cake for a man and he doesn't come? She tried to remember. No, I swear he never harmed me but in that. He never harmed me but in that . . . and what if he did? There was the day, the day, but a whirl of dark smoke rose and covered it, crept up and over into the bright field where everything was planted so carefully in orderly rows. That was hell, she knew hell when she saw it. For sixty years she had prayed against remembering him and against losing her soul in the deep pit of hell, and now the two things were mingled in one and the thought of him was a smoky cloud from hell that moved and crept in her head when she had just got rid of Doctor Harry and was trying to rest a minute. Wounded vanity, Ellen, said a sharp voice in the top of her mind. Don't let your wounded vanity get the upper hand of you. Plenty of girls get jilted. You were jilted, weren't you? Then stand up to it. Her eyelids wavered and let in streamers of blue-gray light like tissue paper over her eyes. She must get up and pull the shades down or she'd never sleep. She was in bed again and the shades were not down. How could that happen? Better turn over, hide from the light, sleeping in the light gave you nightmares. "Mother, how do you feel now?" and a stinging wetness on her forehead. But I don't like having my face washed in cold water!

Hapsy? George? Lydia? Jimmy? No, Cornelia, and her features were swollen and full of little puddles. "They're coming, darling, they'll all be here soon." Go wash your face, child, you look funny.

Instead of obeying, Cornelia knelt down and put her head on the pillow. She seemed to be talking but there was no sound. "Well, are you tongue-tied? Whose birthday is it? Are you going to give a party?"

Cornelia's mouth moved urgently in strange shapes. "Don't do that, you bother me, daughter."

"Oh, no, Mother. Oh, no. . . ."

Nonsense. It was strange about children. They disputed your every word. "No what, Cornelia?"

"Here's Doctor Harry."

"I won't see that boy again. He just left five minutes ago."

"That was this morning, Mother. It's night now. Here's the nurse."

"This is Doctor Harry, Mrs. Weatherall. I never saw you look so young and happy!"

"Ah, I'll never be young again—but I'd be happy if they'd let me lie in peace and get rested."

She thought she spoke up loudly, but no one answered. A warm weight on her forehead, a warm bracelet on her wrist, and a breeze went on whispering, trying to tell her something. A shuffle of leaves in the everlasting hand of God, He blew on them and they danced and rattled. "Mother, don't mind, we're going to give you a little hypodermic." "Look here, daughter, how do ants get in this bed? I saw sugar ants yesterday." Did you send for Hapsy too?

It was Hapsy she really wanted. She had to go a long way back through a great many rooms to find Hapsy standing with a baby on her arm. She seemed to herself to be Hapsy also, and the baby on Hapsy's arm was Hapsy and himself and herself, all at once, and there was no surprise in the meeting. Then Hapsy melted from within and turned flimsy as gray gauze and the baby was a gauzy shadow, and Hapsy came up close and said, "I thought you'd never come," and looked at her very searchingly and said, "You haven't changed a bit!" They leaned forward to kiss, when Cornelia began whispering from a long way off, "Oh, is there anything you want to tell me? Is there anything I can do for you?"

Yes, she had changed her mind after sixty years and she would like to see George. I want you to find George. Find him and be sure to tell him I forgot him. I want him to know I had my husband just the same and my children and my house like any other woman. A good house too and a good husband that I loved and fine children out of him. Better than I hoped for even. Tell him I was given back everything he took away and more. Oh, no, oh, God, no, there was something else besides the house and the man and the children. Oh, surely they were not all? What was it? Something not given back. . . . Her breath crowded down under her ribs and grew into a monstrous frightening shape with cutting edges; it bored up into her head, and the agony was unbelievable: Yes, John, get the Doctor now, no more talk, my time has come.

When this one was born it should be the last. The last. It should have been born first, for it was the one she had truly wanted. Everything came in good time. Nothing left out, left over. She was strong, in three days she would be as well as ever. Better. A woman needed milk in her to have her full health.

"Mother, do you hear me?"

"I've been telling you —"

"Mother, Father Connolly's here."

"I went to Holy Communion only last week. Tell him I'm not so sinful as all that."

"Father just wants to speak to you."

He could speak as much as he pleased. It was like him to drop in and inquire about her soul as if it were a teething baby, and then stay on for a cup of tea and a round of cards and gossip. He always had a funny story of some sort, usually about an Irishman who made his little mistakes and confessed them, and the point lay in some absurd thing he would blurt out in the confessional showing his struggles between native piety and original sin. Granny felt easy about her soul. Cornelia, where are your manners? Give Father Connolly a chair. She had her secret comfortable understanding with a few favorite saints who cleared a straight road to God for her. All as surely signed and sealed as the papers for the new Forty Acres. Forever . . . heirs and assigns forever. Since the day the wedding cake was not cut, but thrown out and wasted. The whole bottom dropped out of the world, and there she was blind and sweating with nothing under her feet and the walls falling away. His hand had caught her under the breast, she had not fallen, there was the freshly polished floor with the green rug on it, just as before. He had cursed like a sailor's parrot and said, "I'll kill him for you." Don't lay a hand on him, for my sake leave something to God. "Now, Ellen, you must believe what I tell you. . . ."

So there was nothing, nothing to worry about any more, except sometimes in the night one of the children screamed in a nightmare, and they both hustled out shaking and hunting for the matches and calling, "There, wait a minute, here we are!" John, get the doctor now, Hapsy's time has come. But there was Hapsy standing by the bed in a white cap. "Cornelia, tell Hapsy to take off her cap. I can't see her plain."

Her eyes opened very wide and the room stood out like a picture she had seen somewhere. Dark colors with the shadows rising towards the ceiling in long angles. The tall black dresser gleamed with nothing on it but John's picture, enlarged from a little one, with John's eyes very black when they should have been blue. You never saw him, so how do you know how he looked? But the man insisted the copy was perfect, it was very rich and handsome. For a picture, yes, but it's not my husband. The table by the bed had a linen cover and a candle and a crucifix. The light was blue from Cornelia's silk lampshades. No sort of light at all, just frippery. You had to live forty years with kerosene lamps to appreciate honest electricity. She felt very strong and she saw Doctor Harry with a rosy nimbus around him.

"You look like a saint, Doctor Harry, and I vow that's as near as you'll ever come to it."

"She's saying something."

"I heard you, Cornelia. What's all this carrying-on?"

"Father Connolly's saying—"

Cornelia's voice staggered and bumped like a cart in a bad road. It rounded corners and turned back again and arrived nowhere. Granny stepped up in the cart very lightly and reached for the reins, but a man sat beside her and she knew him by his hands, driving the cart. She did not look in his face, for she knew without seeing, but looked instead down the road where the trees leaned over and bowed to each other and a thousand birds were singing a Mass. She felt like singing too, but she put her hand in the bosom of her dress and pulled out a rosary, and Father Connolly murmured Latin in a very solemn voice and tickled her feet. My God, will you stop that nonsense? I'm a married woman. What if he did run away and leave me to face the priest by myself? I found another a whole world better. I wouldn't have exchanged my husband for anybody except St. Michael himself, and you may tell him that for me with a thank you in the bargain.

Light flashed on her closed eyelids, and a deep roaring shook her. Cornelia, is that lightning? I hear thunder. There's going to be a storm. Close all the windows. Call the children in. . . . "Mother, here we are, all of us." "Is that you, Hapsy?" "Oh, no, I'm Lydia. We drove as fast as we could." Their faces drifted above her, drifted away. The rosary fell out of her hands and Lydia put it back. Jimmy tried to help, their hands fumbled together, and Granny closed two fingers around Jimmy's thumb. Beads wouldn't do, it must be something alive. She was so amazed her thoughts ran round and round. So, my dear Lord, this is my death and I wasn't even thinking about it. My children have come to see me die. But I can't, it's not time. Oh, I always hated surprises. I wanted to give Cornelia the amethyst set—Cornelia, you're to have the amethyst set, but Hapsy's to wear it when she wants, and, Doctor Harry, do shut up. Nobody sent for you. Oh, my dear Lord, do wait a minute. I meant to do something about the Forty Acres, Jimmy doesn't need it and Lydia will later on, with that worthless husband of hers. I meant to finish the altar cloth and send six bottles of wine to Sister Borgia for her dyspepsia. I want to send six bottles of wine to Sister Borgia, Father Connolly, now don't let me forget.

Cornelia's voice made short turns and tilted over and crashed. "Oh, Mother, oh, Mother, oh, Mother. . . ."

"I'm not going, Cornelia. I'm taken by surprise. I can't go."

You'll see Hapsy again. What about her? "I thought you'd never come." Granny made a long journey outward, looking for Hapsy. What if I don't find her? What then? Her heart sank down and down, there was no bottom to death, she couldn't come to the end of it. The blue light from Cornelia's lampshade drew into a tiny point in the center of her brain, it flickered and winked like an eye, quietly it fluttered and dwindled. Granny lay curled down within herself, amazed and watchful, staring at the point of light that was herself; her body was now only a deeper mass of shadow in an endless darkness and this darkness would curl around the light and swallow it up. God, give a sign!

For the second time there was no sign. Again no bridegroom and the priest in the house. She could not remember any other sorrow because this grief wiped them all away. Oh, no, there's nothing more cruel than this — I'll never forgive it. She stretched herself with a deep breath and blew out the light.

Nahid Rachlin   b. 1946

Departures   [1992]

I have no choice, I have to let him go, Farogh thought, as she went about making last-minute preparations for a farewell lunch for her son. But how can I really accept his going to a war that has killed and maimed hundreds of young men? Seventeen years of attachment, of interdependency, could be severed in an instant. Teheran was not the same. On every street at least one family had lost someone to the war. War was like a wild, blood-thirsty animal, merciless in its killing. Black flags indicating mourning hung on so many of the doors of houses. A fountain of red water, to symbolize blood, stood on Martyrdom Square, a few blocks away.

She spread a cloth on the living room rug and set plates and silverware on it. Then she put several bouquets of flowers she had picked from the courtyard on different spots of the cloth. The room was spacious with a high ceiling and two long, rectangular windows overlooking the courtyard. But the room, the whole house, had an empty, forlorn feel to it already, now that Ahmad was going away and might not come back to it for weeks, if ever. I must not let my thoughts get so carried away.

She went into the adjacent room and began to change. She took her blue dress with green floral designs on it out of the trunk in the corner of the room and put it on. Then she pulled her hair back with a tortoise-shell barrette. I should go and wake up Hassan, she thought. It is almost noon, but then he came home late from the rug shop last night. Let him sleep. He is no solace to me anyway. For the first time in years she thought of her old job, working as a pharmacist's assistant, and felt a pang of sadness that she had given it up. She used to like helping out the customers or talking with the other employees, two nice men, about drugs, world affairs. But Hassan had started to complain, "The house is a mess, we never have a proper meal." And then when she became pregnant with Ahmad he insisted, "You can't go to work like that, it makes me ashamed. I'm the man . . ." Maybe I had given in to him too easily, she thought regretfully. And now at my age, it would be hard to find employment. Jobs are scarce for women anyway.

Her eyes went to Ahmad's photograph in a silver frame on the mantle. Something about his eyes caught her attention. They reminded her of someone . . . Karim. They had the same eyes, dark and dreamy. What would her life have been like if she had married Karim instead of Hassan? Over the expanse of years, she could vividly see Karim — thin, tall, sensitive looking. She remembered meeting him one summer when both of their families had rented cottages in Darband. They had begun to talk by the stream that ran in front of the cottages. Then they would meet secretly behind the hill and walk together through cherry and quince orchards, holding hands, kissing. They had continued meeting for a while when they returned to the city. They would go to an afternoon movie in a far off neighborhood or to a distant park or a restaurant where no one would recognize them. A year later he left for America to study. He wrote letters to her in code but after a while they slowed down and then she did not hear from him again. Before he left he gave her a silver bracelet with a garnet stone on it. For years she had worn the bracelet. Then the stone fell off and got lost and the silver became dented and finally broke. Now she wore a row of thin, gold bracelets that Ahmad had given to her last year for her fortieth birthday. In the photograph Ahmad was standing in a boat on a lake with a pole in his hands. Curls of hair hung over his forehead. Farogh remembered sitting with Karim in a rowboat at dusk in Darband far away from where they were staying. His face was lit with lights reflected from cottages around the lake. Karim could have been Ahmad's father just as easily as Hassan, if judged by physical appearance. Did Ahmad really look that much like Karim or was that just how she recalled it? She wished she had a photograph of Karim, wished she could catch a glimpse of his face. She was only sixteen years old when Hassan's mother and sister came over to her parents' house to request that she marry her son. She had seen Hassan around the neighborhood — a fat, indolent looking man, fifteen years older than herself. She had tried to resist, but her parents had given her little choice. It suddenly seemed that Hassan had kept her in captivity all these years.

A few relatives had come over for lunch, to say goodbye to Ahmad — Hassan's mother and sister, her own nephews, nieces and cousins. The meal she had spent days preparing was lavish and colorful. Large platters were filled with a variety of rices and stews and salads she had garnished with fresh mint and tarragon leaves. The lacy tablecloth one of her daughters had knitted herself and sent to her went well with the silver utensils with floral designs embossed on them. The air was filled with the aroma of turmeric, saffron, dried lemon, pepper. Conversation, laughter, the clatter of dishes, created a lively chorus. Everyone was wearing their good clothes. Her nieces had shiny shoes on and wore ribbons in their hair. It was as if no one were aware that the country was torn by war. An alley cat with long, yellow hair found its way into the room. It stood by the cloth and mewed for food. Farogh put some meat and sauce in a platter and placed it before the cat. A sudden breeze outside made the wind chimes hanging on a hook on the door jangle.

Hassan was talking with others in a haughty manner, interrupting them with remarks like, "Let me explain," "I know what you're trying to say." He talked about life after death as if no one had ever heard of it — finding oneself in heaven: a vast garden redolent with fruit, flowers, streams flowing everywhere, angels with pink and blue wings flying in the air ready to be of service, some of them singing beautiful songs. Ahmad was lucky to be given the chance to fight in the war, he said. If he himself were a young man he would be eager to do so. She felt her cheeks flushing with anger. Didn't he see the danger hanging over Ahmad?

They were fussing over Ahmad now. Hassan's mother added food to his plate and said, "You won't get anything this good for a long time." Hassan kept leaning over and squeezing his arm affectionately. Ahmad's cousins glanced at him with adoring eyes — particularly Soosan, a pretty, fourteen-year-old girl, who had a crush on him. And Mohsen, a year younger than he and going to the same high school, always looked up to him as if he were an older brother. Then why aren't they as deeply upset as I am? She felt really apart from everyone. Then she thought, I have never been like all the others around me.

When she and her three sisters were growing up, she was the one, and the only one among them, who said, "Mother, why can't I go to the university?"

"University? How does that help you with diapering a baby?"

"Mother, why do some people die young?"

"How do I know, am I God?"

And then she was the only one who had resisted marrying the man selected for her. She had grown to like him (she even loved him at moments) but a part of her remained unconnected to him, to the life in this alley. Ahmad was her strongest bond . . . What good would it do to start an argument — Ahmad had to go no matter what.

Ahmad seemed strangely calm after weeks of turmoil and vacillation. At first he had tried to get himself exempted by pretending he could not hear in one ear but that had not worked. They had said, "You have one good ear . . ." Finally he was reconciled to going.

Ahmad's aunt, a gaunt looking woman, said, "Farogh, don't think so much, your hair is going to fall out."

"Yes, like my sister, one day her hair fell off in patches. She was very thoughtful too," Hassan's mother said. She was not wearing her artificial teeth and her mouth was sunken. She ate and spoke with difficulty.

Farogh tried to smile but she could not stop her thoughts jumping away from the scene. Her mind went to those days of growing up, the daily changes coming on herself and her sisters, bodily changes (when one of her breasts started budding while the other lagged behind), her sister Mehri growing taller and prettier, her oldest sister Narghes getting married, her face radiant behind the gauzy veil, sequins shining in her hair and dress. Her own first awareness that looking at a boy made her feel different. Then her mind drifted to those cool, fragrant orchards, the winding, hilly roads where she and Karim had taken walks and talked — two heedless adolescents. One evening she was wearing a pale blue dress with short ruffled sleeves, which she had a tailor make for her. Her hair, wavy and black, thicker than now, hung loose over her shoulders. She had been feeling very carefree. The other person, the person I was then, was so much more real than the one I am now. Hassan's creation, she thought.

The next day Farogh watched Ahmad polish his boots and put them on. He was already wearing his army clothes. He looked determined, even proud. Was that an act? As a boy he had been timid. He would stand and watch other boys in rough play without ever participating, she remembered. He was introspective, unlike his father. She went over to him and gave him several handkerchiefs on which she had embroidered his name. He put them in his already packed suitcase.

Hassan came into the room and the three of them waited for the honking of the army truck which was supposed to pick Ahmad up. Then the honking came. Ahmad shut his suitcase and picked it up and they all went outside. By the door Ahmad kissed each of them quickly.

"Write soon, will you?" she said.

"Of course," Ahmad said. But he seemed distracted, with a faraway look about him. He walked rapidly toward the truck which had parked on the avenue running perpendicular to the small alley.

Farogh turned to Hassan and for the first time she could see his composure was broken. But then he quickly looked away from her, shutting her out. She had flashes of herself alone in the house with Hassan, the two of them eating together and then going to bed and she had a sudden, aching wish that it were Hassan rather than Ahmad who was leaving, whose life was at risk.

After Ahmad's departure, she continued to feel the pain of that other departure, when Karim had left the country, for a bigger, freer world. He had said he would come back and apply what he had learned there, but of course he had not. He had written her a few letters from America the first year he was there, then they stopped abruptly. She had an impulse to write to him, to make some connection with him. She still had his address in an old address book. He was in the same place, his mother had said to her once in passing as they met in a line buying food. His mother had added, "He got married to an American girl, a mistake." She had not elaborated but now the remark made Farogh think: maybe he too looks back at those days. She took out a sheet of paper from a stationery box and began to write a letter to him. She hesitated. I am a married woman. But then, she thought, I need someone.

"... It's difficult for me to write this letter, it has been so many years ... Still, I remember all the walks we took together. I saw my son going to the army a few days ago and it was like that day I saw you leaving. You were the same age then as Ahmad is now. I hope you'll write back if you get this ..."

After she sealed the letter she stood and studied herself in the mirror as if she had not looked at her reflection for a long time. Her face was round, her features delicate. She was on the plump side. That and the roundness of her face made her look young for her age. She was attractive in a healthy, robust way. Odd, she thought, I've been living in hell since Ahmad left. It made her feel that she was not quite connected to her body.

She went out to mail the letter. She passed the burnt-out, boarded-up tea house, the sooty, grimy facade of an old hotel, but more than anything she was keenly aware of the black flags on the doors and the sound of prayers for the dead coming out from Noori Mosque. She paused by Jaafari's house. One of their sons had been wounded in the war and flown to Teheran to be treated at a hospital. Should I go in and ask about their son, she wondered. But the door was locked and there was a silence about it that was forbidding. She walked on, passing the house where the opium addict lived with his mother.

As she dropped the letter into the post office mailbox and heard the quiet thud of its hitting the bottom, a surge of happiness came over her, thinking of the letter traveling so far away—in a truck to the airport and then on the plane and from the plane in a truck again and finally landing at the address where Karim lived. Would his face light up at seeing her name or would he just be surprised?

Three weeks later she found a letter in the hallway which the mailman must have dropped in. It was an air-letter from America, she immediately noticed. She was startled by the sight. She realized she had not really expected an answer and so quickly. She opened it, her hand shaky. It was very brief, only a few lines.

"... I'm coming home for a five-day visit—that's all that my schedule will permit. From Sept. 1–5. Can you come to my mother's house and see me? ..." It was cool, detached. "That's all my schedule will permit," he had said. He had not asked to see her privately. She put the letter in a box, and put the box at the bottom of the trunk in the basement.

But as the date he had mentioned approached, she felt an urge to drop in at his mother's house and see him. Now she was grateful that Hassan stayed at his shop so late at night and slept most of the day, making him oblivious of the changes in her mood, swinging back and forth. On September first, as soon as she woke up, she thought of Karim. This is the first day of his arrival. I should wait a day or two before going over, she thought.

On the afternoon of September third, as soon as Hassan left for work she began to get ready to go over to Zeinab's house. She wondered what she should wear. Something that would not draw attention to itself, she decided. She put on an inconspicuous brown dress and her dark blue *chador*.

She was hesitant again when she reached the house but she forced herself to knock. Zeinab opened the door to her.

"Oh, Farogh Joon, how are you, how nice to see you."

"I have a favor to ask," Farogh said, feeling nervous. "If I could borrow a coupon for sugar."

"Of course. I owe you so many coupons, I'll be happy to help you out. By the way my son is here. He comes every year at this time, stays only a few days."

"Every year . . ." she said inaudibly. How odd, all these years he has come back here to this street a few blocks from my house and I had no idea. She had a sharp sense of having been betrayed. Then she thought, that's absurd . . .

"Have you had any word from Ahmad?"

"A couple of letters."

"Who is there?" Farogh heard a male voice. It was undeniably Karim's.

"It's Farogh," Zeinab said. "We're coming in." Then she turned to her, "Come and sit down for a while, I just had the samovar set up for tea."

Farogh followed Zeinab into the courtyard. A man, Karim, was sitting there on the rug in the shade of a plum tree, glancing at a book. He rose as she and Zeinab approached. "I don't know if I would have recognized you after so many years," he said.

She could not bring herself to say anything. He was so unfamiliar. He was older of course, with patches of gray showing in his hair, and there were lines on his face, but that was not what made him different. His eyes were not so much dreamy as wary now. And there was something stiff and alien in his manner and tone.

"Sit down, I'll bring up some cups," Zeinab said.

He sat down again and Farogh sat next to him on the rug, staring awkwardly at the yellow butterflies flitting in the parched bushes by the small, algae-covered pool.

"What have you been doing with yourself?" he asked.

"What does a wife and mother do?" she said formally, catching his tone. "Do you have any children?"

"No, not yet," he said. "I've been so busy with work. I've been teaching at UCLA."

The foreign word made her even more uncomfortable. "Do you write books?"

He chuckled. "I read them more than write them."

The samovar was hissing, giving out sparks, which hung in the air for an instant and then faded. Zeinab came up the kitchen stairs, carrying a tray containing cups and sugar. She sat down and began to pour tea for everyone. They started to drink slowly, quietly for a moment.

"I wish Karim would come and live here," Zeinab said, looking at her son and then at her. "He's past the age of being drafted."

He patted his mother on the back, in a patronizing way, it seemed to Farogh. His movements were controlled as if he had practiced them and he knew precisely what effect they would have on others. So then, was it intentional that his gaze on her was at once detached and scrutinizing, reflecting a certain skepticism that made her feel diminished? Time has really played tricks, changed everything, him, myself. She looked at him, still hoping to reach the person he had been and to then see a reflection of herself, the way she was at fifteen, but none of it came. "I should be going, I have a lot of errands to do before dark."

"Here is a coupon," Zeinab said, putting a piece of paper in her hand.

Farogh put it in her purse and got up. "I hope you have a good visit," she said to Karim.

He and his mother got up also and followed her to the outside door. At the door he said to her cryptically, "We were children . . ." Then he turned around and went inside.

"Come back again soon," Zeinab said and then went inside also.

The sun was about to set as Farogh walked back. A kite had gotten caught in the branches of a tree and children had collected around it, shaking it, trying to get the kite free. She had a mental picture of Ahmad when he was a child and would go up to the roof of their house to fly his kites — he had bought one, lantern-shaped and lit from the inside, from a fancy store in another neighborhood. She thought of other stages of his growing up too, of when his voice had started to become streaky and bristles of hair to grow on his face. How is he going to have changed when he comes back, when I see him next?

She watched the busy street, taking in as much of it as she could, as if it were a mirage that might slip away from her at any moment.

Leslie Marmon Silko   b. 1948

The Man to Send Rain Clouds   [1981]

They found him under a big cottonwood tree. His Levi jacket and pants were faded light blue so that he had been easy to find. The big cottonwood tree stood apart from a small grove of winterbare cottonwoods which grew in the wide, sandy arroyo. He had been dead for a day or more, and the sheep had wandered and scattered up and down the arroyo. Leon and his brother-in-law, Ken, gathered the sheep and left them in the pen at the sheep camp before they returned to the cottonwood tree. Leon waited under the tree while Ken drove the truck through the deep sand to the edge of the arroyo. He squinted up at the sun and unzipped his jacket — it sure was hot for this time of year. But high and northwest the blue mountains were still in snow. Ken came sliding down the low, crumbling bank about fifty yards down, and he was bringing the red blanket.

Before they wrapped the old man, Leon took a piece of string out of his pocket and tied a small gray feather in the old man's long white hair. Ken gave him the paint. Across the brown wrinkled forehead he drew a streak of white and along the high cheekbones he drew a strip of blue paint. He paused and watched Ken throw pinches of corn meal and pollen into the wind that fluttered the small gray feather. Then Leon painted with yellow under the old man's broad nose, and finally, when he had painted green across the chin, he smiled.

"Send us rain clouds, Grandfather." They laid the bundle in the back of the pickup and covered it with a heavy tarp before they started back to the pueblo.

They turned off the highway onto the sandy pueblo road. Not long after they passed the store and post office they saw Father Paul's car coming toward them. When he recognized their faces he slowed his car and waved for them to stop. The young priest rolled down the car window.

"Did you find old Teofilo?" he asked loudly.

Leon stopped the truck. "Good morning, Father. We were just out to the sheep camp. Everything is O.K. now."

"Thank God for that. Teofilo is a very old man. You really shouldn't allow him to stay at the sheep camp alone."

"No, he won't do that any more now."

"Well, I'm glad you understand. I hope I'll be seeing you at Mass this week — we missed you last Sunday. See if you can get old Teofilo to come with you." The priest smiled and waved at them as they drove away.

Louise and Teresa were waiting. The table was set for lunch, and the coffee was boiling on the black iron stove. Leon looked at Louise and then at Teresa.

"We found him under a cottonwood tree in the big arroyo near sheep camp. I guess he sat down to rest in the shade and never got up again." Leon walked toward the old man's bed. The red plaid shawl had been shaken and spread carefully over the bed, and a new brown flannel shirt and pair of stiff new Levi's were arranged neatly beside the pillow. Louise held the screen door open while Leon and Ken carried in the red blanket. He looked small and shriveled, and after they dressed him in the new shirt and pants he seemed more shrunken.

It was noontime now because the church bells rang the Angelus. They ate the beans with hot bread, and nobody said anything until after Teresa poured the coffee.

Ken stood up and put on his jacket. "I'll see about the gravediggers. Only the top layer of soil is frozen. I think it can be ready before dark."

Leon nodded his head and finished his coffee. After Ken had been gone for a while, the neighbors and clanspeople came quietly to embrace Teofilo's family and to leave food on the table because the gravediggers would come to eat when they were finished.

The sky in the west was full of pale yellow light. Louise stood outside with her hands in the pockets of Leon's green army jacket that was too big for her. The funeral was over, and the old men had taken their candles and medicine bags and were gone. She waited until the body was laid into the pickup before she said anything to Leon. She touched his arm, and he noticed that her hands were still dusty from the corn meal that she had sprinkled around the old man. When she spoke, Leon could not hear her.

"What did you say? I didn't hear you."

"I said that I had been thinking about something."

"About what?"

"About the priest sprinkling holy water for Grandpa. So he won't be thirsty."

Leon stared at the new moccasins that Teofilo had made for the ceremonial dances in the summer. They were nearly hidden by the red blanket. It was getting colder, and the wind pushed gray dust down the narrow pueblo road. The sun was approaching the long mesa where it disappeared during the winter. Louise stood there shivering and watching his face. Then he zipped up his jacket and opened the truck door. "I'll see if he's there."

Ken stopped the pickup at the church, and Leon got out; and then Ken drove down the hill to the graveyard where people were waiting. Leon knocked at the old carved door with its symbols of the Lamb. While he waited he looked up at the twin bells from the king of Spain with the last sunlight pouring around them in their tower.

The priest opened the door and smiled when he saw who it was. "Come in! What brings you here this evening?"

The priest walked toward the kitchen, and Leon stood with his cap in his hand, playing with the earflaps and examining the living room—the brown sofa, the green armchair, and the brass lamp that hung down from the ceiling by links of chain. The priest dragged a chair out of the kitchen and offered it to Leon.

"No thank you, Father. I only came to ask you if you would bring your holy water to the graveyard."

The priest turned away from Leon and looked out the window at the patio full of shadows and the dining-room windows of the nuns' cloister across the patio. The curtains were heavy, and the light from within faintly penetrated; it was impossible to see the nuns inside eating supper. "Why didn't you tell me he was dead? I could have brought the Last Rites anyway."

Leon smiled. "It wasn't necessary, Father."

The priest stared down at his scuffed brown loafers and the worn hem of his cassock. "For a Christian burial it was necessary."

His voice was distant, and Leon thought that his blue eyes looked tired.

"It's O.K. Father, we just want him to have plenty of water."

The priest sank down into the green chair and picked up a glossy missionary magazine. He turned the colored pages full of lepers and pagans without looking at them.

"You know I can't do that, Leon. There should have been the Last Rites and a funeral Mass at the very least."

Leon put on his green cap and pulled the flaps down over his ears. "It's getting late, Father. I've got to go."

When Leon opened the door Father Paul stood up and said, "Wait." He left the room and came back wearing a long brown overcoat. He followed Leon out the door and across the dim churchyard to the adobe steps in front of the church. They both stooped to fit through the low adobe entrance. And when they started down the hill to the graveyard only half of the sun was visible above the mesa.

The priest approached the grave slowly, wondering how they had managed to dig into the frozen ground; and then he remembered that this was New Mexico, and saw the pile of cold loose sand beside the hole. The people stood close to each other with little clouds of steam puffing from their faces. The priest looked at them and saw a pile of jackets, gloves, and scarves in the yellow, dry tumbleweeds that grew in the graveyard. He looked at the red blanket, not sure that Teofilo was so small, wondering if it wasn't some perverse Indian trick — something they did in March to ensure a good harvest — wondering if maybe old Teofilo was actually at sheep camp corraling the sheep for the night. But there he was, facing into a cold dry wind and squinting at the last sunlight, ready to bury a red wool blanket while the faces of his parishioners were in shadow with the last warmth of the sun on their backs.

His fingers were stiff, and it took him a long time to twist the lid off the holy water. Drops of water fell on the red blanket and soaked into dark icy spots. He sprinkled the grave and the water disappeared almost before it touched the dim, cold sand; it reminded him of something — he tried to remember what it was, because he thought if he could remember he might understand this. He sprinkled more water; he shook the container until it was empty, and the water fell through the light from sundown like August rain that fell while the sun was still shining, almost evaporating before it touched the wilted squash flowers.

The wind pulled at the priest's brown Franciscan robe and swirled away the corn meal and pollen that had been sprinkled on the blanket. They lowered the bundle into the ground, and they didn't bother to untie the stiff pieces of new rope that were tied around the ends of the blanket. The sun was gone, and over on the highway the eastbound lane was full of headlights. The priest walked away slowly. Leon watched him climb the hill, and when he had disappeared within the tall, thick walls, Leon turned to look up at the high blue mountains in the deep snow that reflected a faint red light from the west. He felt good because it was finished, and he was happy about the sprinkling of the holy water; now the old man could send them big thunderclouds for sure.

Virgil Suárez b. 1962

A Perfect Hotspot [1992]

This idea of selling ice cream during the summer seems ridiculous, pointless. I'd much rather be close to water. The waves. Where I can hear them tumble in and then roll out, and see the tiny bubbles left behind on the sand pop one by one. Or feel the undercurrents warm this time of year. Swimming. Watching the girls in bikinis with sand stuck to the backs of their thighs walk up and down the boardwalk. At this time of the morning, the surfers are out riding the waves.

Instead I'm inside an ice cream truck with my father, selling, cruising the streets. The pumps suck oil out of the ground rapidly with the creaking sounds of iron biting iron in a fenced lot at the end of the street. They look like giant rocking horses. Father turns at the corner, then, suddenly, he points to another ice cream truck.

"There's the competition," he says. "If the economy doesn't improve soon, these streets'll be full of them."

He's smoking, and the smoke floats back my way and chokes me. I can't stand it. Some of the guys on the swim team smoke. I don't understand how they can smoke and do their best when it's time for competition. I wouldn't smoke. To do so would be like cheating myself out of winning.

All morning he's been instructing me on how to sell ice cream.

"Tonio," he says now, "come empty your pockets."

I walk to the front of the truck, stick my hands deep into my pockets and grab a handful of coins — what we've made in change all morning. The coins fall, overlap and multiply against the sides of the grease-smudged, change box. I turn my pockets inside-out until the last coin falls. He picks out the pieces of lint and paper from the coins.

When he begins to explain the truck's quirks, "the little problems," as he calls the water leaks, burning oil, and dirty carburetor, I return to the back of the truck and sit down on top of the wood counter next to the window.

"Be always on the lookout for babies," father says. "The ones in pampers. They pop out of nowhere. Check your mirrors all the time."

A CAUTION CHILDREN cardboard sign hangs from the rearview mirror. Running over children is a deep fear that seems to haunt him.

All I need, I keep reminding myself, is to pass the CPR course, get certified, and look for a job as a beach lifeguard.

"Stop!" a kid screams, slamming the screen door of his house open. He runs to the grassy part next to the sidewalk. Father stops the truck. The kid's hand comes up over the edge of the window with a dollar bill forked between his little fingers.

"What do you want?" I say.

"A Froze Toe," he says, jumping up and down, dirt rings visible on his neck. He wets the corners of his mouth with his cherry, Kool-aid-stained tongue. I reach inside the freezer and bring out a bar. On its wrapper is the picture of an orange foot with a blue bubble gum ball on the big toe.

"See what else he wants," father says. "Make sure they always leave the dollar."

The kid takes his ice cream, and he smiles.

"What else?" I ask him.

He shrugs his shoulders, shakes his head, and bites the wrapper off. The piece of paper falls on the grass. I give him his change; he walks back to his house.

"Should always make sure they leave all the money they bring," father says. "They get it to spend it. That's the only way you'll make a profit. Don't steal their money, but exchange it for merchandise." His ears stick out from underneath his L.A. Dodgers cap. The short hair on the back of his head stands out.

I grin up at the rearview mirror, but he isn't looking.

"Want to split a Pepsi, Tonio?" he says.

"I'm not thirsty."

"Get me some water then."

The cold mist inside the freezer crawls up my hand. After he drinks and returns the bottle, I place it back with the ice cream.

"Close the freezer," he says, "before all the cold gets out and they melt."

If the cold were out I'd be at the natatorium doing laps.

On another street, a group of kids jumps and skips around a short man. The smallest of the kids hangs from the man's thigh. The man signals my father to stop, then walks up to the window. The kids scream excitedly.

"Want this one, daddy," one of the girls says.

"This one!" a boy says.

The smallest kid jumps, pointing his finger at the display my father has made with all the toys and candies.

"No, Jose," the man says, taking the kid by the wrist. "No candy."

The kid turns to look up at his father, not fully understanding, and then looks at me. His little lips tremble.

"Give me six Popsicles," the man says.

"I don't want no Pop—"

"Popsicles or nothing. I don't have money to buy you what you want."

"A Blue Ghost. I want a Blue Ghost."

"No, I said."

The smallest kid cries.

"Be quiet, Jose, or I'm going to tell the man to go away."

I put the six Popsicles on the counter.

"How much?" the man asks. The skin around his eyes is a darker brown than that of his nose and cheeks.

"A dollar-fifty," I say.

He digs inside his pockets and produces two wrinkled green balls which he throws on the counter. The two dollar bills roll. I unfold the bills, smooth them, and give them to father, who returns the man his change through the front window.

The man gives each kid a Popsicle, then walks away with his hands in his pockets. Jose, still crying, grabs his as he follows his father back to their house.

"He doesn't want to spend his beer money," father says, driving away from the curb.

After that, we have no more customers for hours. Ever since he brought the truck home two years ago, father has changed. Ice creams have become his world. According to father, appearance and cleanliness isn't important as long as the truck passes the Health Department inspection in order to obtain the sales license. The inside of the truck is a mess: paint flakes off, rust hides between crevices, the freezer lids hold layer upon layer of dirt and melted ice cream. Here I'll have to spend the rest of my summer, I think, among the strewn Doritos, Munchos, and the rest of the merchandise.

The outside of the truck had been painted by father's friend, Gaspar, before mother died. I remember how Gaspar drank beer after beer while he painted the crown over the κ in KING OF ICE CREAM and assured mother, who never missed one of my swim meets and who always encouraged me to become the best swimmer I could be, that I was going to make it all right in the end.

Father lives this way, I know, out of loneliness. He misses mother as much as I do.

I count the passing of time by how many ice creams I sell. It isn't anything like swimming laps. Doing laps involves the idea of setting and breaking new limits.

"How much do you think we have?" my father asks. The visor of his cap tilts upward.

"I don't know." I hate the metallic smell money leaves on my fingers.

"Any idea?"

"No."

"A couple of months on your own and you'll be able to guess approximately how much you make."

A couple of months, I think, and I'll be back in high school. Captain of the varsity swim team. A customer waits down the street.

"Make the kill fast," father says.

A barefooted woman holding a child to her breast comes to the window. She has dirty fingernails, short and uneven, as if she bites them all the time. Make the kill fast, I think.

Ice creams on the counter, I tell her, "Two dollars."

She removes the money out of her brassiere and hands it to me, then she walks away. She has yellow blisters on the back of each heel.

After that, he begins to tell me the story of the wild dog. When he was a kid, a wild bitch came down from the hills and started killing my grandfather's chickens. "Seeing the scattered feathers," father says, "made your grandfather so angry I thought his face would burst because it'd turned so red."

"Anyway," he continues, "the wild dog kept on killing chickens."

Not only my grandfather's, but other farmers' as well. The other farmers were scared because they thought the wild dog was a witch. One morning, my grandfather got my father out of bed early and took him up to the hills behind the house with a jar of poison. A farmer had found the bitch's litter. My grandfather left my father in charge of anointing the poison all over the puppies fur so that when the mother came back, if he hadn't shot it by then, she'd die the minute she licked her young. My father didn't want to do it, but my grandfather left him in command while he went after the wild dog to shoot it. The dog disappeared and the puppies licked each other to death.

When he finishes telling me the story, father looks at the rearview mirror and grins, then he drives on. He turns up the volume in the music box and now *Raindrops Keep Falling On My Head* blares out of the speakers. The old people'll complain, he says, because the loud music hurts their eardrums, but the louder the music, the more people'll hear it, and more ice creams'll get sold.

Farther ahead, another kid stops us. The kid has his tongue out. His eyes seem to be too small for his big face. Though he seems old, he still drools. He claps his small hands quickly.

"Does he have money?" father asks.

"Can't see."

The kid walks over to the truck and hangs from the edge of the window.

"Get him away from the truck," father says, then to the kid, "Hey, move away!"

"Come on," I tell the kid, "you might fall and hurt yourself."

"Wan icleam," the kid says.

"We'll be back in a little while," father tells him.

"Wan icleam!" He doesn't let go. "Wan icleam!"

"Move back!" father shouts. "Tonio, get him away from the truck."

I try to unstick the kid's pudgy fingers from the metal edge of the window, but he won't let go. His saliva falls on my hands.

"Wan icleam!"

I reach over to one of the shelves to get a penny candy for him so that I can bait him into letting go, but father catches me.

"Don't you dare," he says.

He opens the door and comes around the back to the kid, pulling him away from the truck to the sidewalk where he sets the kid down, and returns.

"Can't give your merchandise away," he says. "You can't make a profit that way, Tonio."

The kid runs after us shouting, waving his arms. I grab a handful of candies and throw them out the window to the sidewalk, where they fall on the grass and scatter.

The sun sets slowly, and, descending, it spreads Popsicle orange on the sky. Darkness creeps on the other side of the city.

If I don't get a job as a lifeguard, I think, then I'm going to travel southeast and visit the islands.

"How are the ice creams doing?" father asks. "Are they softening?"

I check by squeezing a bar and say, "I think we should call it a day."

"Tonio," he says. He turns off the music, makes a left turn to the main street, and heads home. "Why didn't you help me with that kid? You could have moved him. What will happen when you're here by yourself?"

"Couldn't do it."

"Here," he says, giving me the change box. "Take it inside when we get home."

"I'll get it when we get there."

He puts the blue box back down on top of the stand he built over the motor. Cars speed by. The air smells heavy with exhaust and chemical fumes. In the distance, columns of smoke rise from factory smokestacks.

He turns into the driveway, drives the truck all the way to the front of the garage, and parks underneath the long branches of the avocado tree.

"Take the box inside," he says, turning off the motor. He steps down from the truck and connects the freezer to the extension cord coming out of the kitchen window.

I want to tell him that I won't come out tomorrow.

"Come on, Tonio. Bring the box in."

"You do it," I say.

"What's the matter, son?"

"I'd rather you do it."

"Like you'd rather throw all my merchandise out of the window," he says, growing red in the face. "I saw you."

He walks toward me, and I sense another argument coming. Father stops in front of me and gives me a wry smile. "Dreamers like you," he says, "learn the hard way."

He turns around, picks up the change box, and says, "I'm putting the truck up for sale. From now on you're on your own, you hear. I'm not forcing you to do something you don't want to."

I don't like the expressionless look on his face when usually, whenever he got angry at me, his face would get red and sweaty.

He unlocks the kitchen door and enters the house.

I jump out of the truck, lock the door, and walk around our clapboard house to the patio. Any moment now, I think, father'll start slamming doors inside and throwing things around. He'll curse. I lean against the wall and feel the glass of the window behind me when it starts to tremble.

John Updike   b. 1932

A & P°   [1961]

In walks these three girls in nothing but bathing suits. I'm in the third checkout slot, with my back to the door, so I don't see them until they're over by the bread. The one that caught my eye first was the one in the plaid green two-piece. She was a chunky kid, with a good tan and a sweet broad soft-looking can with those two crescents of white just under it, where the sun never seems to hit, at the top of the backs of her legs. I stood there with my hand on a box of HiHo crackers trying to remember if I rang it up or not. I ring it up again and the customer starts giving me hell. She's one of these cash-register-watchers, a witch about fifty with rouge on her cheek-bones and no eyebrows, and I know it made her day to trip me up. She'd been watching cash registers for fifty years and probably never seen a mistake before.

By the time I got her feathers smoothed and her goodies into a bag—she gives me a little snort in passing, if she'd been born at the right time they would have burned her over in Salem—by the time I get her on her way the girls had circled around the bread and were coming back, without a push-cart, back my way along the counters, in the aisle between the checkouts and the Special bins. They didn't even have shoes on. There was this chunky one, with the two-piece—it was bright green and the seams on the bra were still sharp and her belly was still pretty pale so I guessed she just got it (the suit)—there was this one, with one of those chubby berry-faces, the lips all bunched together under her nose, this one, and a tall one, with black hair that hadn't quite frizzed right, and one of these sunburns right across under the eyes, and a chin that was too long—you know, the kind of girl other girls think is very "striking" and "attractive" but never quite makes it, as they very well know, which is why they like her so much—and then the third one, that wasn't quite so tall. She was the queen. She kind of led them, the other two peeking around and making their shoulders round. She didn't

---

A & P: Grocery stores operated by the Great Atlantic & Pacific Tea Company, which was founded in New York City in 1859 and is currently headquartered in Montvale, New Jersey.

look around, not this queen, she just walked straight on slowly, on these long white prima-donna legs. She came down a little hard on her heels, as if she didn't walk in her bare feet that much, putting down her heels and then letting the weight move along to her toes as if she was testing the floor with every step, putting a little deliberate extra action into it. You never know for sure how girls' minds work (do you really think it's a mind in there or just a little buzz like a bee in a glass jar?) but you got the idea she had talked the other two into coming in here with her, and now she was showing them how to do it, walk slow and hold yourself straight.

She had on a kind of dirty-pink—beige maybe, I don't know—bathing suit with a little nubble all over it and, what got me, the straps were down. They were off her shoulders looped loose around the cool tops of her arms, and I guess as a result the suit had slipped a little on her, so all around the top of the cloth there was this shining rim. If it hadn't been there you wouldn't have known there could have been anything whiter than those shoulders. With the straps pushed off, there was nothing between the top of the suit and the top of her head except just *her,* this clean bare plane of the top of her chest down from the shoulder bones like a dented sheet of metal tilted in the light. I mean, it was more than pretty.

She had sort of oaky hair that the sun and salt had bleached, done up in a bun that was unravelling, and a kind of prim face. Walking into the A & P with your straps down, I suppose it's the only kind of face you *can* have. She held her head so high her neck, coming up out of those white shoulders, looked kind of stretched, but I didn't mind. The longer her neck was, the more of her there was.

She must have felt in the corner of her eye me and over my shoulder Stokesie in the second slot watching, but she didn't tip. Not this queen. She kept her eyes moving across the racks, and stopped, and turned so slow it made my stomach rub the inside of my apron, and buzzed to the other two, who kind of huddled against her for relief, and then they all three of them went up the cat-and-dog-food-breakfast-cereal-macaroni-rice-raisins-seasonings-spreads-spaghetti-soft-drinks-crackers-and-cookies aisle. From the third slot I look straight up this aisle to the meat counter, and I watched them all the way. The fat one with the tan sort of fumbled with the cookies, but on second thought she put the package back. The sheep pushing their carts down the aisle—the girls were walking against the usual traffic (not that we have one-way signs or anything)—were pretty hilarious. You could see them, when Queenie's white shoulders dawned on them, kind of jerk, or hop, or hiccup, but their eyes snapped back to their own baskets and on they pushed. I bet you could set off dynamite in an A & P and the people would by and large keep reaching and checking oatmeal off their lists and muttering "Let me see, there was a third thing, began with A, asparagus, no, ah, yes, applesauce!" or whatever it is they do mutter. But there was no doubt, this jiggled them. A few houseslaves in pin curlers even looked around after pushing their carts past to make sure what they had seen was correct.

You know, it's one thing to have a girl in a bathing suit down on the beach, where what with the glare nobody can look at each other much anyway, and another thing in the cool of the A & P, under the fluorescent lights, against all those stacked packages, with her feet paddling along naked over our checkerboard green-and-cream rubber-tile floor.

"Oh Daddy," Stokesie said beside me. "I feel so faint."

"Darling," I said. "Hold me tight." Stokesie's married, with two babies chalked up on his fuselage already, but as far as I can tell that's the only difference. He's twenty-two, and I was nineteen this April.

"Is it done?" he asks, the responsible married man finding his voice. I forgot to say he thinks he's going to be manager some sunny day, maybe in 1990 when it's called the Great Alexandrov and Petrooshki Tea Company or something.

What he meant was, our town is five miles from a beach, with a big summer colony out on the Point, but we're right in the middle of town, and the women generally put on a shirt or shorts or something before they get out of the car into the street. And anyway these are usually women with six children and varicose veins mapping their legs and nobody, including them, could care less. As I say, we're right in the middle of town, and if you stand at our front doors you can see two banks and the Congregational church and the newspaper store and three real-estate offices and about twenty-seven old freeloaders tearing up Central Street because the sewer broke again. It's not as if we're on the Cape; we're north of Boston and there's people in this town haven't seen the ocean for twenty years.

The girls had reached the meat counter and were asking McMahon something. He pointed, they pointed, and they shuffled out of sight behind a pyramid of Diet Delight peaches. All that was left for us to see was old McMahon patting his mouth and looking after them sizing up their joints. Poor kids, I began to feel sorry for them, they couldn't help it.

Now here comes the sad part of the story, at least my family says it's sad, but I don't think it's so sad myself. The store's pretty empty, it being Thursday afternoon, so there was nothing much to do except lean on the register and wait for the girls to show up again. The whole store was like a pinball machine and I didn't know which tunnel they'd come out of. After a while they come around out of the far aisle, around the light bulbs, records at discount of the Caribbean Six or Tony Martin Sings or some such gunk you wonder they waste the wax on, sixpacks of candy bars, and plastic toys done up in cellophane that fall apart when a kid looks at them anyway. Around they come, Queenie still leading the way, and holding a little gray jar in her hand. Slots Three through Seven are unmanned and I could see her wondering between Stokes and me, but Stokesie with his usual luck draws an old party in baggy gray pants who stumbles up with four giant cans of pineapple juice (what do these bums *do* with all that pineapple juice? I've often asked myself) so the girls come to me. Queenie puts down the jar and I take it into my fingers icy cold. Kingfish Fancy Herring Snacks in Pure Sour Cream: 49¢. Now her hands are empty, not a ring or a bracelet, bare as God made them, and I wonder where the money's coming from. Still with that prim look she lifts a folded dollar bill out of the hollow at the center of her nubbled pink top. The jar went heavy in my hand. Really, I thought that was so cute.

Then everybody's luck begins to run out. Lengel comes in from haggling with a truck full of cabbages on the lot and is about to scuttle into that door marked MANAGER behind which he hides all day when the girls touch his eye. Lengel's pretty dreary, teaches Sunday school and the rest, but he doesn't miss that much. He comes over and says, "Girls, this isn't the beach."

Queenie blushes, though maybe it's just a brush of sunburn I was noticing for the first time, now that she was so close. "My mother asked me to pick up a jar of herring snacks." Her voice kind of startled me, the way voices do when you see the people first, coming out so flat and dumb yet kind of tony, too, the way it ticked over "pick up" and "snacks." All of a sudden I slid right down her voice into her living room. Her father and the other men were standing around in ice-cream coats and bow ties and the women were in sandals picking up herring snacks on toothpicks off a big glass plate and they were all holding drinks the color of water with olives and sprigs of mint in them. When my parents have somebody over they get lemonade and if it's a real racy affair Schlitz in tall glasses with "They'll Do It Every Time" cartoons stencilled on.

"That's all right," Lengel said. "But this isn't the beach." His repeating this struck me as funny, as if it had just occurred to him, and he had been thinking all these years the A & P was a great big dune and he was the head lifeguard. He didn't like my smiling — as I say he doesn't miss much — but he concentrates on giving the girls that sad Sunday-school-superintendent stare.

Queenie's blush is no sunburn now, and the plump one in plaid, that I liked better from the back — a really sweet can — pipes up, "We weren't doing any shopping. We just came in for the one thing."

"That makes no difference," Lengel tells her, and I could see from the way his eyes went that he hadn't noticed she was wearing a two-piece before. "We want you decently dressed when you come in here."

"We *are* decent," Queenie says suddenly, her lower lip pushing, getting sore now that she remembers her place, a place from which the crowd that runs the A & P must look pretty crummy. Fancy Herring Snacks flashed in her very blue eyes.

"Girls, I don't want to argue with you. After this come in here with your shoulders covered. It's our policy." He turns his back. That's policy for you. Policy is what the kingpins want. What the others want is juvenile delinquency.

All this while, the customers had been showing up with their carts but, you know, sheep, seeing a scene, they had all bunched up on Stokesie, who shook open a paper bag as gently as peeling a peach, not wanting to miss a word. I could feel in the silence everybody getting nervous, most of all Lengel, who asks me, "Sammy, have you rung up their purchase?"

I thought and said "No" but it wasn't about that I was thinking. I go through the punches, 4, 9, GROC, TOT—it's more complicated than you think, and after you do it often enough, it begins to make a little song, that you hear words to, in my case "Hello (*bing*) there, you (*gung*) hap-py *pee-pul* (*splat*)!"—the *splat* being the drawer flying out. I uncrease the bill, tenderly as you may imagine, it just having come from between the two smoothest scoops of vanilla I had ever known were there, and pass a half and a penny into her narrow pink palm, and nestle the herrings in a bag and twist its neck and hand it over, all the time thinking.

The girls, and who'd blame them, are in a hurry to get out, so I say "I quit" to Lengel quick enough for them to hear, hoping they'll stop and watch me, their unsuspected hero. They keep right on going, into the electric eye; the door flies open and they flicker across the lot to their car, Queenie and Plaid and Big Tall Goony-Goony (not that as raw material she was so bad), leaving me with Lengel and a kink in his eyebrow.

"Did you say something, Sammy?"

"I said I quit."

"I thought you did."

"You didn't have to embarrass them."

"It was they who were embarrassing us."

I started to say something that came out "Fiddle-de-doo." It's a saying of my grandmother's, and I know she would have been pleased.

"I don't think you know what you're saying," Lengel said.

"I know you don't," I said. "But I do." I pull the bow at the back of my apron and start shrugging it off my shoulders. A couple customers that had been heading for my slot begin to knock against each other, like scared pigs in a chute.

Lengel sighs and begins to look very patient and old and gray. He's been a friend of my parents for years. "Sammy, you don't want to do this to your Mom and Dad," he tells me. It's true, I don't. But it seems to me that once you begin a gesture it's fatal not to go through with it. I fold the apron, "Sammy" stitched in red on the pocket, and put it on the counter, and drop the bow tie on top of it. The bow tie is theirs, if you've ever wondered. "You'll feel this for the rest of your life," Lengel says, and I know that's true, too, but remembering how he made that pretty girl blush makes me so scrunchy inside I punch the No Sale tab and the machine whirs "pee-pul" and the drawer splats out. One advantage to this scene taking place in summer, I can follow this up with a clean exit, there's no fumbling around getting your coat and galoshes, I just saunter into the electric eye in my white shirt that my mother ironed the night before, and the door heaves itself open, and outside the sunshine is skating around on the asphalt.

I look around for my girls, but they're gone, of course. There wasn't anybody but some young married screaming with her children about some candy they didn't get by the door of a powder-blue Falcon station wagon. Looking back in the big windows, over the bags of peat moss and aluminum lawn furniture stacked on the pavement, I could see Lengel in my place in the slot, checking the sheep through. His face was dark gray and his back stiff, as if he'd just had an injection of iron, and my stomach kind of fell as I felt how hard the world was going to be to me hereafter.

CD-ROM: Research John Updike in depth with cultural documents and multimedia resources on *LiterActive*.

Helena María Viramontes b. 1954

The Moths   [1985]

I was fourteen years old when Abuelita requested my help. And it seemed only fair. Abuelita had pulled me through the rages of scarlet fever by placing, removing and replacing potato slices on the temples of my forehead; she had seen me through several whippings, an arm broken by a dare jump off Tío Enrique's toolshed, puberty, and my first lie. Really, I told Amá, it was only fair.

Not that I was her favorite granddaughter or anything special. I wasn't even pretty or nice like my older sisters and I just couldn't do the girl things they could do. My hands were too big to handle the fineries of crocheting or embroidery and I always pricked my fingers or knotted my colored threads time and time again while my sisters laughed and called me bull hands with their cute waterlike voices. So I began keeping a piece of jagged brick in my sock to bash my sisters or anyone who called me bull hands. Once, while we all sat in the bedroom, I hit Teresa on the forehead, right above her eyebrow and she ran to Amá with her mouth open, her hand over her eye while blood seeped between her fingers. I was used to the whippings by then.

I wasn't respectful either. I even went so far as to doubt the power of Abuelita's slices, the slices she said absorbed my fever. "You're still alive, aren't you?" Abuelita snapped back, her pasty gray eye beaming at me and burning holes in my suspicions. Regretful that I had let secret questions drop out of my mouth, I couldn't look into her eyes. My hands began to fan out, grow like a liar's nose until they hung by my side like low weights. Abuelita made a balm out of dried moth wings and Vicks and rubbed my hands, shaped them back to size and it was the strangest feeling. Like bones melting. Like sun shining through the darkness of your eyelids. I didn't mind helping Abuelita after that, so Amá would always send me over to her.

In the early afternoon Amá would push her hair back, hand me my sweater and shoes, and tell me to go to Mama Luna's. This was to avoid another fight and another whipping, I knew. I would deliver one last direct shot on Marisela's arm and jump out of our house, the slam of the screen door burying her cries of anger, and I'd gladly go help Abuelita plant her wild lilies or jasmine or heliotrope or cilantro or hierbabuena in red Hills Brothers coffee cans. Abuelita would wait for me at the top step of her porch holding a hammer and nail and empty coffee cans. And although we hardly spoke, hardly looked at each other as we worked over root transplants, I always felt her gray eye on me. It made me feel, in a strange sort of way, safe and guarded and not alone. Like God was supposed to make you feel.

On Abuelita's porch, I would puncture holes in the bottom of the coffee cans with a nail and a precise hit of a hammer. This completed, my job was to fill them with red clay mud from beneath her rose bushes, packing it softly, then making a perfect hole, four fingers round, to nest a sprouting avocado pit, or the spidery sweet potatoes that Abuelita rooted in mayonnaise jars with toothpicks and daily water, or prickly chayotes that produced vines that twisted and wound all over her porch pillars, crawling to the roof, up and over the roof, and down the other side, making her small brick house look like it was cradled within the vines that grew pear-shaped squashes ready for the pick, ready to be steamed with onions and cheese and butter. The roots would burst out of the rusted coffee cans and search for a place to connect. I would then feed the seedlings with water.

But this was a different kind of help, Amá said, because Abuelita was dying. Looking into her gray eye, then into her brown one, the doctor said it was just a matter of days. And so it seemed only fair that these hands she had melted and formed found use in rubbing her caving body with alcohol and marihuana, rubbing her arms and legs, turning her face to the window so that she could watch the Bird of Paradise blooming or smell the scent of clove in the air. I toweled her face frequently and held her hand for hours. Her gray wiry hair hung over the mattress. Since I could remember, she'd kept her long hair in braids. Her mouth was vacant and when she slept, her eyelids never closed all the way. Up close, you could see her gray eye beaming out the window, staring hard as if to remember everything. I never kissed her. I left the window open when I went to the market.

Across the street from Jay's Market there was a chapel. I never knew its denomination, but I went in just the same to search for candles. I sat down on one of the pews because there were none. After I cleaned my fingernails, I looked up at the high ceiling. I had forgotten the vastness of these places, the coolness of the marble pillars and the frozen statues with blank eyes. I was alone. I knew why I had never returned.

That was one of Apá's biggest complaints. He would pound his hands on the table, rocking the sugar dish or spilling a cup of coffee and scream that if I didn't go to mass every Sunday to save my goddamn sinning soul, then I had no reason to go out of the house, period. Punto final. He would grab my arm and dig his nails into me to make sure I understood the importance of catechism. Did he make himself clear? Then he strategically directed his anger at Amá for her lousy ways of bringing up daughters, being disrespectful and unbelieving, and my older sisters would pull me aside and tell me if I didn't get to mass right this minute, they were all going to kick the holy shit out of me. Why am I so selfish? Can't you see what it's doing to Amá, you idiot? So I would wash my feet and stuff them in my black Easter shoes that shone with Vaseline, grab a missal and veil, and wave good-bye to Amá.

I would walk slowly down Lorena to First to Evergreen, counting the cracks on the cement. On Evergreen I would turn left and walk to Abuelita's. I liked her porch because it was shielded by the vines of the chayotes and I could get a good look at the people and car traffic on Evergreen without them knowing. I would jump up the porch steps, knock on the screen door as I wiped my feet and call Abuelita? mi Abuelita? As I opened the door and stuck my head in, I would catch the gagging scent of toasting chile on the placa. When I entered the sala, she would greet me from the kitchen, wringing her hands in her apron. I'd sit at the corner of the table to keep from being in her way. The chiles made my eyes water. Am I crying? No, Mama Luna, I'm sure not crying. I don't like going to mass, but my eyes watered anyway, the tears dropping on the tablecloth like candle wax. Abuelita lifted the burnt chiles from the fire and sprinkled water on them until the skins began to separate. Placing them in front of me, she turned to check the menudo. I peeled the skins off and put the flimsy, limp looking green and yellow chiles in the molcajete and began to crush and crush and twist and crush the heart out of the tomato, the clove of garlic, the stupid chiles that made me cry, crushed them until they turned into liquid under my bull hand. With a wooden spoon, I scraped hard to destroy the guilt, and my tears were gone. I put the bowl of chile next to a vase filled with freshly cut roses. Abuelita touched my hand and pointed to the bowl of menudo that steamed in front of me. I spooned some chile into the menudo and rolled a corn tortilla thin with the palms of my hands. As I ate, a fine Sunday breeze entered the kitchen and a rose petal calmly feathered down to the table.

I left the chapel without blessing myself and walked to Jay's. Most of the time Jay didn't have much of anything. The tomatoes were always soft and the cans of Campbell soups had rusted spots on them. There was dust on the tops of cereal boxes. I picked up what I needed: rubbing alcohol, five cans of chicken broth, a big bottle of Pine Sol. At first Jay got mad because I thought I had forgotten the money. But it was there all the time, in my back pocket.

When I returned from the market, I heard Amá crying in Abuelita's kitchen. She looked up at me with puffy eyes. I placed the bags of groceries on the table and began putting the cans of soup away. Amá sobbed quietly. I never kissed her. After a while, I patted her on the back for comfort. Finally: "¿Y mi Amá?"° she asked in a whisper, then choked again and cried into her apron.

Abuelita fell off the bed twice yesterday, I said, knowing that I shouldn't have said it and wondering why I wanted to say it because it only made

"¿Y mi Amá?": "And my Mama?"

Amá cry harder. I guess I became angry and just so tired of the quarrels and beatings and unanswered prayers and my hands just there hanging help-lessly by my side. Amá looked at me again, confused, angry, and her eyes were filled with sorrow. I went outside and sat on the porch swing and watched the people pass. I sat there until she left. I dozed off repeating the words to myself like rosary prayers: when do you stop giving when do you start giving when do you . . . and when my hands fell from my lap, I awoke to catch them. The sun was setting, an orange glow, and I knew Abuelita was hungry.

There comes a time when the sun is defiant. Just about the time when moods change, inevitable seasons of a day, transitions from one color to an-other, that hour or minute or second when the sun is finally defeated, finally sinks into the realization that it cannot with all its power to heal or burn, exist forever, there comes an illumination where the sun and earth meet, a final burst of burning red orange fury reminding us that although endings are inevitable, they are necessary for rebirths, and when that time came, just when I switched on the light in the kitchen to open Abuelita's can of soup, it was probably then that she died.

The room smelled of Pine Sol and vomit and Abuelita had defecated the remains of her cancerous stomach. She had turned to the window and tried to speak, but her mouth remained open and speechless. I heard you, Abuelita, I said, stroking her cheek, I heard you. I opened the windows of the house and let the soup simmer and overboil on the stove. I turned the stove off and poured the soup down the sink. From the cabinet I got a tin basin, filled it with lukewarm water and carried it carefully to the room. I went to the linen closet and took out some modest bleached white towels. With the sacredness of a priest preparing his vestments, I unfolded the towels one by one on my shoulders. I removed the sheets and blankets from her bed and peeled off her thick flannel nightgown. I toweled her puzzled face, stretching out the wrinkles, removing the coils of her neck, toweled her shoulders and breasts. Then I changed the water. I returned to towel the creases of her stretch-marked stomach, her sporadic vaginal hairs, and her sagging thighs. I removed the lint from between her toes and noticed a mapped birthmark on the fold of her buttock. The scars on her back which were as thin as the life lines on the palms of her hands made me realize how little I really knew of Abuelita. I covered her with a thin blanket and went into the bathroom. I washed my hands, and turned on the tub faucets and watched the water pour into the tub with vitality and steam. When it was full, I turned off the water and undressed. Then, I went to get Abuelita.

She was not as heavy as I thought and when I carried her in my arms, her body fell into a V, and yet my legs were tired, shaky, and I felt as if the distance between the bedroom and bathroom was miles and years away. Amá, where are you?

I stepped into the bathtub one leg first, then the other. I bent my knees slowly to descend into the water slowly so I wouldn't scald her skin. There,

there, Abuelita, I said, cradling her, smoothing her as we descended, I heard you. Her hair fell back and spread across the water like eagle's wings. The water in the tub overflowed and poured onto the tile of the floor. Then the moths came. Small, gray ones that came from her soul and out through her mouth fluttering to light, circling the single dull light bulb of the bathroom. Dying is lonely and I wanted to go to where the moths were, stay with her and plant chayotes whose vines would crawl up her fingers and into the clouds; I wanted to rest my head on her chest with her stroking my hair, telling me about the moths that lay within the soul and slowly eat the spirit up; I wanted to return to the waters of the womb with her so that we would never be alone again. I wanted. I wanted my Amá. I removed a few strands of hair from Abuelita's face and held her small light head within the hollow of my neck. The bathroom was filled with moths, and for the first time in a long time I cried, rocking us, crying for her, for me, for Amá, the sobs emerging from the depths of anguish, the misery of feeling half born, sobbing until finally the sobs rippled into circles and circles of sadness and relief. There, there, I said to Abuelita, rocking us gently, there, there.

Richard Wright 1908–1960

The Man Who Was Almost a Man [1961]

Dave struck out across the fields, looking homeward through paling light. Whut's the use talkin wid em niggers in the field? Anyhow, his mother was putting supper on the table. Them niggers can't understan nothing. One of these days he was going to get a gun and practice shooting, then they couldn't talk to him as though he were a little boy. He slowed, looking at the ground. Shucks, Ah ain scareda them even ef they are biggern me! Aw, Ah know whut Ahma do. Ahm going by ol Joe's sto n git that Sears Roebuck catlog n look at them guns. Mebbe Ma will lemme buy one when she gits mah pay from ol man Hawkins. Ahma beg her t gimme some money. Ahm ol ernough to hava gun. Ahm seventeen. Almost a man. He strode, feeling his long loose-jointed limbs. Shucks, a man oughta hava little gun aftah he done worked hard all day.

He came in sight of Joe's store. A yellow lantern glowed on the front porch. He mounted steps and went through the screen door, hearing it bang behind him. There was a strong smell of coal oil and mackerel fish. He felt very confident until he saw fat Joe walk in through the rear door, then his courage began to ooze.

"Howdy, Dave! Whutcha want?"

"How yuh, Mistah Joe? Aw, Ah don wanna buy nothing. Ah jus wanted t see ef yuhd lemme look at tha catlog erwhile."

"Sure! You wanna see it here?"

"Nawsuh. Ah wans t take it home wid me. Ah'll bring it back termorrow when Ah come in from the fiels."

"You plannin on buying something?"

"Yessuh."

"Your ma lettin you have your own money now?"

"Shucks. Mistah Joe, Ahm gittin t be a man like anybody else!"

Joe laughed and wiped his greasy white face with a red bandanna.

"Whut you plannin on buyin?"

Dave looked at the floor, scratched his head, scratched his thigh, and smiled. Then he looked up shyly.

"Ah'll tell yuh, Mistah Joe, ef yuh promise yuh won't tell."

"I promise."

"Waal, Ahma buy a gun."

"A gun? Whut you want with a gun?"

"Ah wanna keep it."

"You ain't nothing but a boy. You don't need a gun."

"Aw, lemme have the catlog, Mistah Joe. Ah'll bring it back."

Joe walked through the rear door. Dave was elated. He looked around at barrels of sugar and flour. He heard Joe coming back. He craned his neck to see if he were bringing the book. Yeah, he's got it. Gawddog, he's got it!

"Here, but be sure you bring it back. It's the only one I got."

"Sho, Mistah Joe."

"Say, if you wanna buy a gun, why don't you buy one from me? I gotta gun to sell."

"Will it shoot?"

"Sure it'll shoot."

"Whut kind is it?"

"Oh, it's kinda old . . . a left-hand Wheeler. A pistol. A big one."

"Is it got bullets in it?"

"It's loaded."

"Kin Ah see it?"

"Where's your money?"

"Whut yuh wan fer it?"

"I'll let you have it for two dollars."

"Just two dollahs? Shucks, Ah could buy tha when Ah git mah pay."

"I'll have it here when you want it."

"Awright, suh. Ah be in fer it."

He went through the door, hearing it slam again behind him. Ahma git some money from Ma n buy me a gun! Only two dollahs! He tucked the thick catalogue under his arm and hurried.

"Where yuh been, boy?" His mother held a steaming dish of black-eyed peas.

"Aw, Ma, Ah jus stopped down the road t talk wid the boys."

"Yuh know bettah t keep suppah waitin."

He sat down, resting the catalogue on the edge of the table.

"Yuh git up from there and git to the well n wash yosef! Ah ain feedin no hogs in mah house!"

She grabbed his shoulder and pushed him. He stumbled out of the room, then came back to get the catalogue.

"Whut this?"

"Aw, Ma, it's jusa catlog."

"Who yuh git it from?"

"From Joe, down at the sto."

"Waal, thas good. We kin use it in the outhouse."

"Naw, Ma." He grabbed for it. "Gimme ma catlog, Ma."

She held onto it and glared at him.

"Quit hollerin at me! Whut's wrong wid yuh? Yuh crazy?"

"But Ma, please. It ain mine! It's Joe's! He tol me t bring it back t im termorrow."

She gave up the book. He stumbled down the back steps, hugging the thick book under his arm. When he had splashed water on his face and hands, he groped back to the kitchen and fumbled in a corner for the towel. He bumped into a chair; it clattered to the floor. The catalogue sprawled at his feet. When he had dried his eyes he snatched up the book and held it again under his arm. His mother stood watching him.

"Now, ef yuh gonna act a fool over that ol book, Ah'll take it n burn it up."

"Naw, Ma, please."

"Wall, set down n be still!"

He sat down and drew the oil lamp close. He thumbed page after page, unaware of the food his mother set on the table. His father came in. Then his small brother.

"Whutcha got there, Dave?" his father asked.

"Jusa catlog," he answered, not looking up.

"Yeah, here they is!" His eyes glowed at blue-and-black revolvers. He glanced up, feeling sudden guilt. His father was watching him. He eased the book under the table and rested it on his knees. After the blessing was asked, he ate. He scooped up peas and swallowed fat meat without chewing. Buttermilk helped to wash it down. He did not want to mention money before his father. He would do much better by cornering his mother when she was alone. He looked at his father uneasily out of the edge of his eye.

"Boy, how come yuh don quit foolin wid tha book n eat yo suppah?"

"Yessuh."

"How you n ol man Hawkins gitten erlong?"

"Suh?"

"Can't yuh hear? Why don yuh lissen? Ah ast yu how wuz yuh n ol man Hawkins gittin erlong?"

"Oh, swell, Pa. Ah plows mo lan than anybody over there."

"Waal, yuh oughta keep yo mind on whut yuh doin."

"Yessuh."

He poured his plate full of molasses and sopped it up slowly with a chunk of cornbread. When his father and brother had left the kitchen, he still sat and looked again at the guns in the catalogue, longing to muster courage enough to present his case to his mother. Lawd, ef Ah only had tha pretty one! He could almost feel the slickness of the weapon with his fingers. If he had a gun like that he would polish it and keep it shining so it would never rust. N Ah'd keep it loaded, by Gawd!

"Ma?" His voice was hesitant.

"Hunh?"

"Ol man Hawkins give yuh mah money yit?"

"Yeah, but ain no usa yuh thinking bout throwin nona it erway. Ahm keepin tha money sos yuh kin have cloes t go to school this winter."

He rose and went to her side with the open catalogue in his palms. She was washing dishes, her head bent low over a pan. Shyly he raised the book. When he spoke, his voice was husky, faint.

"Ma, Gawd knows Ah wans one of these."

"One of whut?" she asked, not raising her eyes.

"One of these," he said again, not daring even to point. She glanced up at the page, then at him with wide eyes.

"Nigger, is yuh gone plumb crazy?"

"Aw, Ma—"

"Git outta here! Don yuh talk t me bout no gun! Yuh a fool!"

"Ma, Ah kin buy one fer two dollahs."

"Not ef Ah knows it, yuh ain!"

"But yuh promised me one—"

"Ah don care whut Ah promised! Yuh ain nothing but a boy yit!"

"Ma, ef yuh lemme buy one Ah'll *never* ast yuh fer nothing no mo."

"Ah tol yuh t git outta here! Yuh ain gonna toucha penny of tha money fer no gun! Thas how come Ah has Mistah Hawkins t pay yo wages t me, cause Ah knows yuh ain got no sense."

"But, Ma, we needa gun. Pa ain got no gun. We needa gun in the house. Yuh kin never tell whut might happen."

"Now don yuh try to maka fool outta me, boy! Ef we did hava gun, yuh wouldn't have it!"

He laid the catalogue down and slipped his arm around her waist.

"Aw, Ma, Ah done worked hard alla summer n ain ast yuh fer nothin, is Ah, now?"

"Thas whut yuh spose t do!"

"But Ma, Ah wans a gun. Yuh kin lemme have two dollahs outta mah money. Please, Ma. I kin give it to Pa . . . Please, Ma! Ah loves yuh, Ma."

When she spoke her voice came soft and low.

"Whut yu wan wida gun, Dave? Yuh don need no gun. Yuh'll git in trouble. N ef yo pa jus thought Ah let yuh have money t buy a gun he'd hava fit."

"Ah'll hide it, Ma. It ain but two dollahs."

"Lawd, chil, whut's wrong wid yuh?"

"Ain nothin wrong, Ma. Ahm almos a man now. Ah wans a gun."

"Who gonna sell yuh a gun?"

"Ol Joe at the sto."

"N it don cos but two dollahs?"

"Thas all, Ma. Jus two dollahs. Please, Ma."

She was stacking the plates away; her hands moved slowly, reflectively. Dave kept an anxious silence. Finally, she turned to him.

"Ah'll let yuh git tha gun ef yuh promise me one thing."

"Whut's tha, Ma?"

"Yuh bring it straight back t me, yuh hear? It be fer Pa."

"Yessum! Lemme go now, Ma."

She stooped, turned slightly to one side, raised the hem of her dress, rolled down the top of her stocking, and came up with a slender wad of bills.

"Here," she said. "Lawd knows yuh don need no gun. But yer pa does. Yuh bring it right back t me, yuh hear? Ahma put it up. Now ef yuh don, Ahma have yuh pa lick yuh so hard yuh won fergit it."

"Yessum."

He took the money, ran down the steps, and across the yard.

"Dave! Yuuuuuh Daaaaave!"

He heard, but he was not going to stop now. "Naw, Lawd!"

The first movement he made the following morning was to reach under his pillow for the gun. In the gray light of dawn he held it loosely, feeling a sense of power. Could kill a man with a gun like this. Kill anybody, black or white. And if he were holding his gun in his hand, nobody could run over him; they would have to respect him. It was a big gun, with a long barrel and a heavy handle. He raised and lowered it in his hand, marveling at its weight.

He had not come straight home with it as his mother had asked; instead he had stayed out in the fields, holding the weapon in his hand, aiming it now and then at some imaginary foe. But he had not fired it; he had been afraid that his father might hear. Also he was not sure he knew how to fire it.

To avoid surrendering the pistol he had not come into the house until he knew that they were all asleep. When his mother had tiptoed to his bedside late that night and demanded the gun, he had first played possum; then he had told her that the gun was hidden outdoors, that he would bring it to her in the morning. Now he lay turning it slowly in his hands. He broke it, took out the cartridges, felt them, and then put them back.

He slid out of bed, got a long strip of old flannel from a trunk, wrapped the gun in it, and tied it to his naked thigh while it was still loaded. He did not go in to breakfast. Even though it was not yet daylight, he started for Jim

Hawkins' plantation. Just as the sun was rising he reached the barns where the mules and plows were kept.

"Hey! That you, Dave?"

He turned. Jim Hawkins stood eying him suspiciously.

"What're yuh doing here so early?"

"Ah didn't know Ah wuz gittin up so early, Mistah Hawkins. Ah wuz fixin t hitch up ol Jenny n take her t the fiels."

"Good. Since you're so early, how about plowing that stretch down by the woods?"

"Suits me, Mistah Hawkins."

"O.K. Go to it!"

He hitched Jenny to a plow and started across the fields. Hot dog! This was just what he wanted. If he could get down by the woods, he could shoot his gun and nobody would hear. He walked behind the plow, hearing the traces creaking, feeling the gun tied tight to his thigh.

When he reached the woods, he plowed two whole rows before he decided to take out the gun. Finally, he stopped, looked in all directions, then untied the gun and held it in his hand. He turned to the mule and smiled.

"Know whut this is, Jenny? Naw, yuh wouldn know! Yuhs jusa ol mule! Anyhow, this is a gun, n it kin shoot, by Gawd!"

He held the gun at arm's length. Whut t hell, Ahma shoot this thing! He looked at Jenny again.

"Lissen here, Jenny! When Ah pull this ol trigger, Ah don wan yuh t run n acka fool now!"

Jenny stood with head down, her short ears pricked straight. Dave walked off about twenty feet, held the gun far out from him at arm's length, and turned his head. Hell, he told himself, Ah ain afraid. The gun felt loose in his fingers; he waved it wildly for a moment. Then he shut his eyes and tightened his forefinger. Bloom! A report half deafened him and he thought his right hand was torn from his arm. He heard Jenny whinnying and galloping over the field, and he found himself on his knees, squeezing his fingers hard between his legs. His hand was numb; he jammed it into his mouth, trying to warm it, trying to stop the pain. The gun lay at his feet. He did not quite know what had happened. He stood up and stared at the gun as though it were a living thing. He gritted his teeth and kicked the gun. Yuh almos broke mah arm! He turned to look for Jenny; she was far over the fields, tossing her head and kicking wildly.

"Hol on there, ol mule!"

When he caught up with her she stood trembling, walling her big white eyes at him. The plow was far away; the traces had broken. Then Dave stopped short, looking, not believing. Jenny was bleeding. Her left side was red and wet with blood. He went closer. Lawd, have mercy! Wondah did Ah shoot this mule? He grabbed for Jenny's mane. She flinched, snorted, whirled, tossing her head.

"Hol on now! Hol on."

Then he saw the hole in Jenny's side, right between the ribs. It was round, wet, red. A crimson stream streaked down the front leg, flowing fast. Good Gawd! Ah wuzn't shootin at tha mule. He felt panic. He knew he had to stop that blood, or Jenny would bleed to death. He had never seen so much blood in all his life. He chased the mule for half a mile, trying to catch her. Finally she stopped, breathing hard, stumpy tail half arched. He caught her mane and led her back to where the plow and gun lay. Then he stooped and grabbed handfuls of damp black earth and tried to plug the bullet hole. Jenny shuddered, whinnied, and broke from him.

"Hol on! Hol on now!"

He tried to plug it again, but blood came anyhow. His fingers were hot and sticky. He rubbed dirt into his palms, trying to dry them. Then again he attempted to plug the bullet hole, but Jenny shied away, kicking her heels high. He stood helpless. He had to do something. He ran at Jenny; she dodged him. He watched a red stream of blood flow down Jenny's leg and form a bright pool at her feet.

"Jenny . . . Jenny," he called weakly.

His lips trembled. She's bleeding t death! He looked in the direction of home, wanting to go back, wanting to get help. But he saw the pistol lying in the damp black clay. He had a queer feeling that if he only did something, this would not be; Jenny would not be there bleeding to death.

When he went to her this time, she did not move. She stood with sleepy, dreamy eyes; and when he touched her she gave a low-pitched whinny and knelt to the ground, her front knees slopping in blood.

"Jenny . . . Jenny . . ." he whispered.

For a long time she held her neck erect; then her head sank, slowly. Her ribs swelled with a mighty heave and she went over.

Dave's stomach felt empty, very empty. He picked up the gun and held it gingerly between his thumb and forefinger. He buried it at the foot of a tree. He took a stick and tried to cover the pool of blood with dirt—but what was the use? There was Jenny lying with her mouth open and her eyes walled and glassy. He could not tell Jim Hawkins he had shot his mule. But he had to tell something. Yeah, Ah'll tell em Jenny started gittin wil n fell on the joint of the plow. . . . But that would hardly happen to a mule. He walked across the field slowly, head down.

It was sunset. Two of Jim Hawkins' men were over near the edge of the woods digging a hole in which to bury Jenny. Dave was surrounded by a knot of people, all of whom were looking down at the dead mule.

"I don't see how in the world it happened," said Jim Hawkins for the tenth time.

The crowd parted and Dave's mother, father, and small brother pushed into the center.

"Where Dave?" his mother called.

"There he is," said Jim Hawkins.

His mother grabbed him.

"Whut happened, Dave? Whut yuh done?"

"Nothin."

"C mon, boy, talk," his father said.

Dave took a deep breath and told the story he knew nobody believed.

"Waal," he drawled. "Ah brung ol Jenny down here sos Ah could do mah plowin. Ah plowed bout two rows, just like yuh see." He stopped and pointed at the long rows of upturned earth. "Then somethin musta been wrong wid ol Jenny. She wouldn ack right a-tall. She started snortin n kickin her heels. Ah tried t hol her, but she pulled erway, rearin n goin in. Then when the point of the plow was stickin up in the air, she swung erroun n twisted herself back on it . . . She stuck herself n started t bleed. N fo Ah could do anything, she wuz dead."

"Did you ever hear of anything like that in all your life?" asked Jim Hawkins.

There were white and black standing in the crowd. They murmured. Dave's mother came close to him and looked hard into his face. "Tell the truth, Dave," she said.

"Looks like a bullet hole to me," said one man.

"Dave, whut yuh do wid the gun?" his mother asked.

The crowd surged in, looking at him. He jammed his hands into his pockets, shook his head slowly from left to right, and backed away. His eyes were wide and painful.

"Did he hava gun?" asked Jim Hawkins.

"By Gawd, Ah tol yuh tha wuz a gun wound," said a man, slapping his thigh.

His father caught his shoulders and shook him till his teeth rattled.

"Tell whut happened, yuh rascall! Tell whut . . ."

Dave looked at Jenny's stiff legs and began to cry.

"Whut yuh do wid tha gun?" his mother asked.

"Whut wuz he doin wida gun?" his father asked.

"Come on and tell the truth," said Hawkins. "Ain't nobody going to hurt you . . ."

His mother crowded close to him.

"Did yuh shoot tha mule, Dave?"

Dave cried, seeing blurred white and black faces.

"Ahh ddinn gggo tt sshooot hher . . . Ah ssswear ffo Gawd Ahh ddin. . . . Ah wuz a-tryin t sssee ef the old gggun would sshoot —"

"Where yuh git the gun from?" his father asked.

"Ah got it from Joe, at the sto."

"Where yuh git the money?"

"Ma give it t me."

"He kept worryin me, Bob. Ah had t. Ah tol im t bring the gun right back t me . . . It was fer yuh, the gun."

"But how yuh happen to shoot that mule?" asked Jim Hawkins.

"Ah wuzn shootin at the mule, Mistah Hawkins. The gun jumped when Ah pulled the trigger . . . N fo Ah knowed anythin Jenny was there a-bleedin."

Somebody in the crowd laughed. Jim Hawkins walked close to Dave and looked into his face.

"Well, looks like you have bought you a mule, Dave."

"Ah swear fo Gawd, Ah didn go t kill the mule, Mistah Hawkins!"

"But you killed her!"

All the crowd was laughing now. They stood on tiptoe and poked heads over one another's shoulders.

"Well, boy, looks like yuh done bought a dead mule! Hahaha!"

"Ain tha ershame."

"Hohohohoho."

Dave stood, head down, twisting his feet in the dirt.

"Well, you needn't worry about it, Bob," said Jim Hawkins to Dave's father. "Just let the boy keep on working and pay me two dollars a month."

"Whut yuh wan fer yo mule, Mistah Hawkins?"

Jim Hawkins screwed up his eyes.

"Fifty dollars."

"Whut yuh do wid tha gun?" Dave's father demanded.

Dave said nothing.

"Yuh wan me t take a tree n beat yuh till yuh talk!"

"Nawsuh!"

"Whut yuh do wid it?"

"Ah throwed it erway."

"Where?"

"Ah . . . Ah throwed it in the creek."

"Waal, c mon home. N firs thing in the mawnin git to tha creek n fin tha gun."

"Yessuh."

"Whut yuh pay fer it?"

"Two dollahs."

"Take tha gun n git yo money back n carry it t Mistah Hawkins, yuh hear? N don fergit Ahma lam you black bottom good fer this! Now march yosef on home, suh!"

Dave turned and walked slowly. He heard people laughing. Dave glared, his eyes welling with tears. Hot anger bubbled in him. Then he swallowed and stumbled on.

That night Dave did not sleep. He was glad that he had gotten out of killing the mule so easily, but he was hurt. Something hot seemed to turn over inside him each time he remembered how they had laughed. He tossed on his bed, feeling his hard pillow. N Pa says he's gonna beat me . . . He remembered other beatings, and his back quivered. Naw, naw, Ah sho don

wan im t beat me tha way no mo. Dam em all! Nobody ever gave him anything. All he did was work. They treat me like a mule, n then they beat me.
He gritted his teeth. N Ma had t tell on me.

Well, if he had to, he would take old man Hawkins that two dollars. But
that meant selling the gun. And he wanted to keep that gun. Fifty dollars for
a dead mule.

He turned over, thinking how he had fired the gun. He had an itch to
fire it again. Ef other men kin shoota gun, by Gawd, Ah kin! He was still, listening. Mebbe they all sleepin now. The house was still. He heard the soft
breathing of his brother. Yes, now! He would go down and get that gun and
see if he could fire it! He eased out of bed and slipped into overalls.

The moon was bright. He ran almost all the way to the edge of the
woods. He stumbled over the ground, looking for the spot where he had
buried the gun. Yeah, here it is. Like a hungry dog scratching for a bone, he
pawed it up. He puffed his black cheeks and blew dirt from the trigger and
barrel. He broke it and found four cartridges unshot. He looked around; the
fields were filled with silence and moonlight. He clutched the gun stiff and
hard in his fingers. But, as soon as he wanted to pull the trigger, he shut his
eyes and turned his head. Naw, Ah can't shoot wid mah eyes closed n mah
head turned. With effort he held his eyes open; then he squeezed. *Blooooom!*
He was stiff, not breathing. The gun was still in his hands. Dammit, he'd
done it! He fired again. *Blooooom!* He smiled. *Bloooom! Blooooom! Click,
click.* There! It was empty. If anybody could shoot a gun, he could. He put
the gun into his hip pocket and started across the fields.

When he reached the top of a ridge he stood straight and proud in the
moonlight, looking at Jim Hawkins' big white house, feeling the gun sagging
in his pocket. Lawd, ef Ah had just one mo bullet Ah'd taka shot at tha
house. Ah'd like t scare ol man Hawkins jusa little . . . Jusa enough t let im
know Dave Saunders is a man.

To his left the road curved, running to the tracks of the Illinois Central.
He jerked his head, listening. From far off came a faint *hoooof-hoooof;
hoooof-hoooof; hoooof-hoooof.* . . . He stood rigid. Two dollahs a mont. Les
see now . . . Tha means it'll take bout two years. Shucks! Ah'll be dam!

He started down the road, toward the tracks. Yeah, here she comes! He
stood beside the track and held himself stiffly. Here she comes, erroun the
ben . . . C mon, yuh slow poke! C mon! He had his hand on his gun; something quivered in his stomach. Then the train thundered past, the gray and
brown box cars rumbling and clinking. He gripped the gun tightly; then
he jerked his hand out of his pocket. Ah betcha Bill wouldn't do it! Ah
betcha . . . The cars slid past, steel grinding upon steel. Ahm ridin yuh
ternight, so hep me Gawd! He was hot all over. He hesitated just a moment;
then he grabbed, pulled atop of a car, and lay flat. He felt his pocket; the gun
was still there. Ahead the long rails were glinting in the moonlight, stretching away, away to somewhere, somewbere where he could be a man . . .

STORIES FROM AROUND THE WORLD

Chinua Achebe   Nigeria, b. 1930

Dead Men's Path   [1973]

Michael Obi's hopes were fulfilled much earlier than he had expected. He was appointed headmaster of Ndume Central School in January 1949. It had always been an unprogressive school, so the Mission authorities decided to send a young and energetic man to run it. Obi accepted this responsibility with enthusiasm. He had many wonderful ideas and this was an opportunity to put them into practice. He had had sound secondary school education which designated him a "pivotal teacher" in the official records and set him apart from the other headmasters in the mission field. He was outspoken in his condemnation of the narrow views of these older and often less-educated ones.

"We shall make a good job of it, shan't we?" he asked his young wife when they first heard the joyful news of his promotion.

"We shall do our best," she replied. "We shall have such beautiful gardens and everything will be just *modern* and delightful . . ." In their two years of married life she had become completely infected by his passion for "modern methods" and his denigration of "these old and superannuated people in the teaching field who would be better employed as traders in the Onitsha market." She began to see herself already as the admired wife of the young headmaster, the queen of the school.

The wives of the other teachers would envy her position. She would set the fashion in everything . . . Then, suddenly, it occurred to her that there might not be other wives. Wavering between hope and fear, she asked her husband, looking anxiously at him.

"All our colleagues are young and unmarried," he said with enthusiasm which for once she did not share. "Which is a good thing," he continued.

"Why?"

"Why? They will give all their time and energy to the school."

Nancy was downcast. For a few minutes she became sceptical about the new school; but it was only for a few minutes. Her little personal misfortune could not blind her to her husband's happy prospects. She looked at him as he sat folded up in a chair. He was stoop-shouldered and looked frail. But he sometimes surprised people with sudden bursts of physical energy. In his present posture, however, all his bodily strength seemed to have retired behind his deep-set eyes, giving them an extraordinary power of penetration. He was only twenty-six, but looked thirty or more. On the whole, he was not unhandsome.

"A penny for your thoughts, Mike," said Nancy after a while, imitating the woman's magazine she read.

"I was thinking what a grand opportunity we've got at last to show these people how a school should be run."

Ndume School was backward in every sense of the word. Mr. Obi put his whole life into the work, and his wife hers too. He had two aims. A high standard of teaching was insisted upon, and the school compound was to be turned into a place of beauty. Nancy's dream-gardens came to life with the coming of the rains, and blossomed. Beautiful hibiscus and allamanda hedges in brilliant red and yellow marked out the carefully tended school compound from the rank neighbourhood bushes.

One evening as Obi was admiring his work he was scandalized to see an old woman from the village hobble right across the compound, through a marigold flower-bed and the hedges. On going up there he found faint signs of an almost disused path from the village across the school compound to the bush on the other side.

"It amazes me," said Obi to one of his teachers who had been three years in the school, "that you people allowed the villagers to make use of this foot-path. It is simply incredible." He shook his head.

"The path," said the teacher apologetically, "appears to be very important to them. Although it is hardly used, it connects the village shrine with their place of burial."

"And what has that got to do with the school?" asked the headmaster.

"Well, I don't know," replied the other with a shrug of the shoulders. "But I remember there was a big row some time ago when we attempted to close it."

"That was some time ago. But it will not be used now," said Obi as he walked away. "What will the Government Education Officer think of this when he comes to inspect the school next week? The villagers might, for all I know, decide to use the schoolroom for a pagan ritual during the inspection."

Heavy sticks were planted closely across the path at the two places where it entered and left the school premises. These were further strengthened with barbed wire.

Three days later the village priest of *Ani* called on the headmaster. He was an old man and walked with a slight stoop. He carried a stout walking-stick which he usually tapped on the floor, by way of emphasis, each time he made a new point in his argument.

"I have heard," he said after the usual exchange of cordialities, "that our ancestral footpath has recently been closed . . ."

"Yes," replied Mr. Obi. "We cannot allow people to make a highway of our school compound."

"Look here, my son," said the priest bringing down his walking-stick, "this path was here before you were born and before your father was born.

The whole life of this village depends on it. Our dead relatives depart by it and our ancestors visit us by it. But most important, it is the path of children coming in to be born . . ."

Mr. Obi listened with a satisfied smile on his face.

"The whole purpose of our school," he said finally, "is to eradicate just such beliefs as that. Dead men do not require footpaths. The whole idea is just fantastic. Our duty is to teach your children to laugh at such ideas."

"What you say may be true," replied the priest, "but we follow the practices of our fathers. If you re-open the path we shall have nothing to quarrel about. What I always say is: let the hawk perch and let the eagle perch." He rose to go.

"I am sorry," said the young headmaster. "But the school compound cannot be a thoroughfare. It is against our regulations. I would suggest your constructing another path, skirting our premises. We can even get our boys to help in building it. I don't suppose the ancestors will find the little detour too burdensome."

"I have no more words to say," said the old priest, already outside.

Two days later a young woman in the village died in childbed. A diviner was immediately consulted and he prescribed heavy sacrifices to propitiate ancestors insulted by the fence.

Obi woke up next morning among the ruins of his work. The beautiful hedges were torn up not just near the path but right round the school, the flowers trampled to death and one of the school buildings pulled down . . . That day, the white Supervisor came to inspect the school and wrote a nasty report on the state of the premises but more seriously about the "tribal-war situation developing between the school and the village, arising in part from the misguided zeal of the new headmaster."

Isabel Allende   Chile, b. 1942

And of Clay Are We Created   [1984]

Translated by Margaret Sayers Peden

They discovered the girl's head protruding from the mudpit, eyes wide open, calling soundlessly. She had a First Communion name, Azucena. Lily. In that vast cemetery where the odor of death was already attracting vultures from far away, and where the weeping of orphans and wails of the injured filled the air, the little girl obstinately clinging to life became the symbol of the tragedy. The television cameras transmitted so often the unbearable image of the head budding like a black squash from the clay that there was no one who did not recognize her and know her name. And every time we saw her on the screen, right behind her was Rolf Carlé, who had gone there on assignment, never suspecting that he would find a fragment of his past, lost thirty years before.

First a subterranean sob rocked the cotton fields, curling them like waves of foam. Geologists had set up their seismographs weeks before and knew that the mountain had awakened again. For some time they had predicted that the heat of the eruption could detach the eternal ice from the slopes of the volcano, but no one heeded their warnings; they sounded like the tales of frightened old women. The towns in the valley went about their daily life, deaf to the moaning of the earth, until that fateful Wednesday night in November when a prolonged roar announced the end of the world, and walls of snow broke loose, rolling in an avalanche of clay, stones, and water that descended on the villages and buried them beneath unfathomable meters of telluric vomit. As soon as the survivors emerged from the paralysis of that first awful terror, they could see that houses, plazas, churches, white cotton plantations, dark coffee forests, cattle pastures — all had disappeared. Much later, after soldiers and volunteers had arrived to rescue the living and try to assess the magnitude of the cataclysm, it was calculated that beneath the mud lay more than twenty thousand human beings and an indefinite number of animals putrefying in a viscous soup. Forests and rivers had also been swept away, and there was nothing to be seen but an immense desert of mire.

When the station called before dawn, Rolf Carlé and I were together. I crawled out of bed, dazed with sleep, and went to prepare coffee while he hurriedly dressed. He stuffed his gear in the green canvas backpack he always carried, and we said goodbye, as we had so many times before. I had no presentiments. I sat in the kitchen, sipping my coffee and planning the long hours without him, sure that he would be back the next day.

He was one of the first to reach the scene, because while other reporters were fighting their way to the edges of that morass in jeeps, bicycles, or on foot, each getting there however he could, Rolf Carlé had the advantage of the television helicopter, which flew him over the avalanche. We watched on our screens the footage captured by his assistant's camera, in which he was up to his knees in muck, a microphone in his hand, in the midst of a bedlam of lost children, wounded survivors, corpses, and devastation. The story came to us in his calm voice. For years he had been a familiar figure in newscasts, reporting live at the scene of battles and catastrophes with awesome tenacity. Nothing could stop him, and I was always amazed at his equanimity in the face of danger and suffering; it seemed as if nothing could shake his fortitude or deter his curiosity. Fear seemed never to touch him, although he had confessed to me that he was not a courageous man, far from it. I believe that the lens of the camera had a strange effect on him; it was as if it transported him to a different time from which he could watch events without actually participating in them. When I knew him better, I came to realize that this fictive distance seemed to protect him from his own emotions.

Rolf Carlé was in on the story of Azucena from the beginning. He filmed the volunteers who discovered her, and the first persons who tried to reach her; his camera zoomed in on the girl, her dark face, her large desolate eyes, the plastered-down tangle of her hair. The mud was like quicksand around her, and anyone attempting to reach her was in danger of sinking. They threw a rope to her that she made no effort to grasp until they shouted to her to catch it; then she pulled a hand from the mire and tried to move, but immediately sank a little deeper. Rolf threw down his knapsack and the rest of his equipment and waded into the quagmire, commenting for his assistant's microphone that it was cold and that one could begin to smell the stench of corpses.

"What's your name?" he asked the girl, and she told him her flower name. "Don't move, Azucena," Rolf Carlé directed, and kept talking to her, without a thought for what he was saying, just to distract her, while slowly he worked his way forward in mud up to his waist. The air around him seemed as murky as the mud.

It was impossible to reach her from the approach he was attempting, so he retreated and circled around where there seemed to be firmer footing. When finally he was close enough, he took the rope and tied it beneath her arms, so they could pull her out. He smiled at her with that smile that crinkles his eyes and makes him look like a little boy; he told her that everything was fine, that he was here with her now, that soon they would have her out. He signaled the others to pull, but as soon as the cord tensed, the girl screamed. They tried again, and her shoulders and arms appeared, but they could move her no farther; she was trapped. Someone suggested that her legs might be caught in the collapsed walls of her house, but she said it was not just rubble, that she was also held by the bodies of her brothers and sisters clinging to her legs.

"Don't worry, we'll get you out of here," Rolf promised. Despite the quality of the transmission, I could hear his voice break, and I loved him more than ever. Azucena looked at him, but said nothing.

During those first hours Rolf Carlé exhausted all the resources of his ingenuity to rescue her. He struggled with poles and ropes, but every tug was an intolerable torture for the imprisoned girl. It occurred to him to use one of the poles as a lever but got no result and had to abandon the idea. He talked a couple of soldiers into working with him for a while, but they had to leave because so many other victims were calling for help. The girl could not move, she barely could breathe, but she did not seem desperate, as if an ancestral resignation allowed her to accept her fate. The reporter, on the other hand, was determined to snatch her from death. Someone brought him a tire, which he placed beneath her arms like a life buoy, and then laid a plank near the hole to hold his weight and allow him to stay closer to her. As it was impossible to remove the rubble blindly, he tried once or twice to dive toward her feet, but emerged frustrated, covered with mud, and spitting gravel. He concluded that he would have to have a pump to drain the water, and radioed a request for one, but received in return a message that there was no available transport and it could not be sent until the next morning.

"We can't wait that long!" Rolf Carlé shouted, but in the pandemonium no one stopped to commiserate. Many more hours would go by before he accepted that time had stagnated and reality had been irreparably distorted.

A military doctor came to examine the girl, and observed that her heart was functioning well and that if she did not get too cold she could survive the night.

"Hang on, Azucena, we'll have the pump tomorrow," Rolf Carlé tried to console her.

"Don't leave me alone," she begged.

"No, of course I won't leave you."

Someone brought him coffee, and he helped the girl drink it, sip by sip. The warm liquid revived her and she began telling him about her small life, about her family and her school, about how things were in that little bit of world before the volcano had erupted. She was thirteen, and she had never been outside her village. Rolf Carlé, buoyed by a premature optimism, was convinced that everything would end well: the pump would arrive, they would drain the water, move the rubble, and Azucena would be transported by helicopter to a hospital where she would recover rapidly and where he could visit her and bring her gifts. He thought, She's already too old for dolls, and I don't know what would please her; maybe a dress. I don't know much about women, he concluded, amused, reflecting that although he had known many women in his lifetime, none had taught him these details. To pass the hours he began to tell Azucena about his travels and adventures as a newshound, and when he exhausted his memory, he called upon imagination, inventing things he thought might entertain her. From time to time she dozed, but he kept talking in the darkness, to assure her that he was still there and to overcome the menace of uncertainty.

That was a long night.

Many miles away, I watched Rolf Carlé and the girl on a television screen. I could not bear the wait at home, so I went to National Television, where I often spent entire nights with Rolf editing programs. There, I was near his world, and I could at least get a feeling of what he lived through during those three decisive days. I called all the important people in the city, senators, commanders of the armed forces, the North American ambassador, and the president of National Petroleum, begging them for a pump to remove the silt, but obtained only vague promises. I began to ask for urgent help on radio and television, to see if there wasn't *someone* who could help us. Between calls I would run to the newsroom to monitor the satellite transmissions that periodically brought new details of the catastrophe. While reporters selected scenes with most impact for the news report, I searched for footage that featured Azucena's mudpit. The screen reduced the disaster to a single plane and accentuated the tremendous distance that separated me from Rolf Carlé; nonetheless, I was there with him. The child's every suffering hurt me as it did him; I felt his frustration, his impotence. Faced with the impossibility of communicating with him, the fantastic idea came to me that if I tried, I could reach him by force of mind and in that way give him encouragement. I concentrated until I was dizzy — a frenzied and futile activity. At times I would be overcome with compassion and burst out crying; at other times, I was so drained I felt as if I were staring through a telescope at the light of a star dead for a million years.

I watched that hell on the first morning broadcast, cadavers of people and animals awash in the current of new rivers formed overnight from the melted snow. Above the mud rose the tops of trees and the bell towers of a church where several people had taken refuge and were patiently awaiting rescue teams. Hundreds of soldiers and volunteers from the Civil Defense were clawing through rubble searching for survivors, while long rows of ragged specters awaited their turn for a cup of hot broth. Radio networks announced that their phones were jammed with calls from families offering shelter to orphaned children. Drinking water was in scarce supply, along with gasoline and food. Doctors, resigned to amputating arms and legs without anesthesia, pled that at least they be sent serum and painkillers and antibiotics; most of the roads, however, were impassable, and worse were the bureaucratic obstacles that stood in the way. To top it all, the clay contaminated by decomposing bodies threatened the living with an outbreak of epidemics.

Azucena was shivering inside the tire that held her above the surface. Immobility and tension had greatly weakened her, but she was conscious and could still be heard when a microphone was held out to her. Her tone was humble, as if apologizing for all the fuss. Rolf Carlé had a growth of beard, and dark circles beneath his eyes; he looked near exhaustion. Even from that enormous distance I could sense the quality of his weariness, so different from the fatigue of other adventures. He had completely forgotten the camera; he could not look at the girl through a lens any longer. The pictures we were receiving were not his assistant's but those of other reporters who had appropriated Azucena, bestowing on her the pathetic responsibility of embodying the horror of what had happened in that place. With the first light Rolf tried again to dislodge the obstacles that held the girl in her tomb, but he had only his hands to work with; he did not dare use a tool for fear of injuring her. He fed Azucena a cup of the cornmeal mush and bananas the Army was distributing, but she immediately vomited it up. A doctor stated that she had a fever, but added that there was little he could do: antibiotics were being reserved for cases of gangrene. A priest also passed by and blessed her, hanging a medal of the Virgin around her neck. By evening a gentle, persistent drizzle began to fall.

"The sky is weeping," Azucena murmured, and she, too, began to cry.

"Don't be afraid," Rolf begged "You have to keep your strength up and be calm. Everything will be fine. I'm with you, and I'll get you out somehow."

Reporters returned to photograph Azucena and ask her the same questions, which she no longer tried to answer. In the meanwhile, more television and movie teams arrived with spools of cable, tapes, film, videos, precision lenses, recorders, sound consoles, lights, reflecting screens, auxiliary motors, cartons of supplies, electricians, sound technicians, and cameramen: Azucena's face was beamed to millions of screens around the world. And all the while Rolf Carlé kept pleading for a pump. The improved technical facilities bore results, and National Television began receiving sharper pictures and clearer sound; the distance seemed suddenly compressed, and I had the horrible sensation that Azucena and Rolf were by my side, separated from me by impenetrable glass. I was able to follow events hour by hour; I knew everything my love did to wrest the girl from her prison and help her endure her suffering; I overheard fragments of what they said to one another and could guess the rest; I was present when she taught Rolf to pray, and when he distracted her with the stories I had told him in a thousand and one nights beneath the white mosquito netting of our bed.

When darkness came on the second day, Rolf tried to sing Azucena to sleep with old Austrian folk songs he had learned from his mother, but she was far beyond sleep. They spent most of the night talking, each in a stupor of exhaustion and hunger, and shaking with cold. That night, imperceptibly, the unyielding floodgates that had contained Rolf Carlé's past for so many years began to open, and the torrent of all that had lain hidden in the deepest and most secret layers of memory poured out, leveling before it the obstacles that had blocked his consciousness for so long. He could not tell it all to Azucena; she perhaps did not know there was a world beyond the sea or time previous to her own; she was not capable of imagining Europe in the years of the war. So he could not tell her of defeat, nor of the afternoon the Russians had led them to the concentration camp to bury prisoners dead from starvation. Why should he describe to her how the naked bodies piled like a mountain of firewood resembled fragile china? How could he tell this dying child about ovens and gallows? Nor did he mention the night that he had seen his mother naked, shod in stiletto-heeled red boots, sobbing with humiliation. There was much he did not tell, but in those hours he relived for the first time all the things his mind had tried to erase. Azucena had surrendered her fear to him and so, without wishing it, had obliged Rolf to confront his own. There, beside that hellhole of mud, it was impossible for Rolf to flee from himself any longer, and the visceral terror he had lived as a boy suddenly invaded him. He reverted to the years when he was the age of Azucena, and younger, and, like her, found himself trapped in a pit without escape, buried in life, his head barely above ground; he saw before his eyes the boots and legs of his father, who had removed his belt and was whipping it in the air with the never-forgotten hiss of a viper coiled to strike. Sorrow flooded through him, intact and precise, as if it had lain always in his mind, waiting. He was once again in the armoire where his father locked him to punish him for imagined misbehavior, there where for eternal hours he had crouched with his eyes closed, not to see the darkness, with his hands over his ears, to shut out the beating of his heart, trembling, huddled like a cornered animal. Wandering in the mist of his memories he found his sister Katharina, a sweet, retarded child who spent her life hiding, with the hope that her father would forget the disgrace of her having been born. With Katharina, Rolf crawled beneath the dining room table, and with her hid there under the long white tablecloth, two children forever embraced, alert to footsteps and voices. Katharina's scent melded with his own sweat, with aromas of cooking, garlic, soup, freshly baked bread, and the unexpected odor of putrescent clay. His sister's hand in his, her frightened breathing, her silk hair against his cheek, the candid gaze of her eyes. Katharina . . . Katharina materialized before him, floating on the air like a flag, clothed in the white tablecloth, now a winding sheet, and at last he could weep for her death and for the guilt of having abandoned her. He understood then that all his exploits as a reporter, the feats that had won him such recognition and fame, were merely an attempt to keep his most ancient fears at bay, a stratagem for taking refuge behind a lens to test whether reality was more tolerable from that perspective. He took excessive risks as an exercise of courage, training by day to conquer the monsters that tormented him by night. But he had come face to face with the moment of truth; he could not continue to escape his past. He *was* Azucena; he was buried in the clayey mud; his terror was not the distant emotion of an almost forgotten childhood, it was a claw sunk in his throat. In the flush of his tears he saw his mother, dressed in black and clutching her imitation-crocodile pocketbook to her bosom, just as he had last seen her on the dock when she had come to put him on the boat to South America. She had not come to dry his tears, but to tell him to pick up a shovel: the war was over and now they must bury the dead.

"Don't cry. I don't hurt anymore. I'm fine," Azucena said when dawn came.

"I'm not crying for you," Rolf Carlé smiled. "I'm crying for myself. I hurt all over."

The third day in the valley of the cataclysm began with a pale light filtering through storm clouds. The President of the Republic visited the area in his tailored safari jacket to confirm that this was the worst catastrophe of the century; the country was in mourning; sister nations had offered aid; he had ordered a state of siege; the Armed Forces would be merciless, anyone caught stealing or committing other offenses would be shot on sight. He added that it was impossible to remove all the corpses or count the thousands who had disappeared; the entire valley would be declared holy ground, and bishops would come to celebrate a solemn mass for the souls of the victims. He went to the Army field tents to offer relief in the form of vague promises to crowds of the rescued, then to the improvised hospital to offer a word of encouragement to doctors and nurses worn down from so many hours of tribulations. Then he asked to be taken to see Azucena, the little girl the whole world had seen. He waved to her with a limp statesman's hand,

and microphones recorded his emotional voice and paternal tone as he told her that her courage had served as an example to the nation. Rolf Carlé interrupted to ask for a pump, and the President assured him that he personally would attend to the matter. I caught a glimpse of Rolf for a few seconds kneeling beside the mudpit. On the evening news broadcast, he was still in the same position; and I, glued to the screen like a fortuneteller to her crystal ball, could tell that something fundamental had changed in him. I knew somehow that during the night his defenses had crumbled and he had given in to grief; finally he was vulnerable. The girl had touched a part of him that he himself had no access to, a part he had never shared with me. Rolf had wanted to console her, but it was Azucena who had given him consolation.

I recognized the precise moment at which Rolf gave up the fight and surrendered to the torture of watching the girl die. I was with them, three days and two nights, spying on them from the other side of life. I was there when she told him that in all her thirteen years no boy had ever loved her and that it was a pity to leave this world without knowing love. Rolf assured her that he loved her more than he could ever love anyone, more than he loved his mother, more than his sister, more than all the women who had slept in his arms, more than he loved me, his life companion, who would have given anything to be trapped in that well in her place, who would have exchanged her life for Azucena's, and I watched as he leaned down to kiss her poor forehead, consumed by a sweet, sad emotion he could not name. I felt how in that instant both were saved from despair, how they were freed from the clay, how they rose above the vultures and helicopters, how together they flew above the vast swamp of corruption and laments. How, finally, they were able to accept death. Rolf Carlé prayed in silence that she would die quickly, because such pain cannot be borne.

By then I had obtained a pump and was in touch with a general who had agreed to ship it the next morning on a military cargo plane. But on the night of that third day, beneath the unblinking focus of quartz lamps and the lens of a hundred cameras, Azucena gave up, her eyes locked with those of the friend who had sustained her to the end. Rolf Carlé removed the life buoy, closed her eyelids, held her to his chest for a few moments, and then let her go. She sank slowly, a flower in the mud.

You are back with me, but you are not the same man. I often accompany you to the station and we watch the videos of Azucena again; you study them intently, looking for something you could have done to save her, something you did not think of in time. Or maybe you study them to see yourself as if in a mirror, naked. Your cameras lie forgotten in a closet; you do not write or sing; you sit long hours before the window, staring at the mountains. Beside you, I wait for you to complete the voyage into yourself, for the old wounds to heal. I know that when you return from your nightmares, we shall again walk hand in hand, as before.

Gabriel García Márquez   Colombia, b. 1928

A Very Old Man with Enormous Wings   [1955]
A Tale for Children

Translated by Gregory Rabassa

On the third day of rain they had killed so many crabs inside the house that Pelayo had to cross his drenched courtyard and throw them into the sea, because the newborn child had a temperature all night and they thought it was due to the stench. The world had been sad since Tuesday. Sea and sky were a single ash-gray thing and the sands of the beach, which on March nights glimmered like powdered light, had become a stew of mud and rotten shellfish. The light was so weak at noon that when Pelayo was coming back to the house after throwing away the crabs, it was hard for him to see what it was that was moving and groaning in the rear of the courtyard. He had to go very close to see that it was an old man, a very old man, lying face down in the mud, who, in spite of his tremendous efforts, couldn't get up, impeded by his enormous wings.

Frightened by that nightmare, Pelayo ran to get Elisenda, his wife, who was putting compresses on the sick child, and he took her to the rear of the courtyard. They both looked at the fallen body with mute stupor. He was dressed like a ragpicker. There were only a few faded hairs left on his bald skull and very few teeth in his mouth, and his pitiful condition of a drenched great-grandfather had taken away any sense of grandeur he might have had. His huge buzzard wings, dirty and half-plucked, were forever entangled in the mud. They looked at him so long and so closely that Pelayo and Elisenda very soon overcame their surprise and in the end found him familiar. Then they dared speak to him, and he answered in an incomprehensible dialect with a strong sailor's voice. That was how they skipped over the inconvenience of the wings and quite intelligently concluded that he was a lonely castaway from some foreign ship wrecked by the storm. And yet, they called in a neighbor woman who knew everything about life and death to see him, and all she needed was one look to show them their mistake.

"He's an angel," she told them. "He must have been coming for the child, but the poor fellow is so old that the rain knocked him down."

On the following day everyone knew that a flesh-and-blood angel was held captive in Pelayo's house. Against the judgment of the wise neighbor woman, for whom angels in those times were the fugitive survivors of a celestial conspiracy, they did not have the heart to club him to death. Pelayo watched over him all afternoon from the kitchen, armed with his bailiff's club, and before going to bed he dragged him out of the mud and locked him up with the hens in the wire chicken coop. In the middle of the night, when the rain stopped, Pelayo and Elisenda were still killing crabs. A short time

afterward the child woke up without a fever and with a desire to eat. Then
they felt magnanimous and decided to put the angel on a raft with fresh
water and provisions for three days and leave him to his fate on the high
seas. But when they went out into the courtyard with the first light of dawn,
they found the whole neighborhood in front of the chicken coop having fun
with the angel, without the slightest reverence, tossing him things to eat
through the openings in the wire as if he weren't a supernatural creature but
a circus animal.

Father Gonzaga arrived before seven o'clock, alarmed at the strange
news. By that time onlookers less frivolous than those at dawn had already
arrived and they were making all kinds of conjectures concerning the captive's future. The simplest among them thought that he should be named
mayor of the world. Others of sterner mind felt that he should be promoted
to the rank of five-star general in order to win all wars. Some visionaries
hoped that he could be put to stud in order to implant on earth a race of
winged wise men who could take charge of the universe. But Father Gonzaga, before becoming a priest, had been a robust woodcutter. Standing by
the wire, he reviewed his catechism in an instant and asked them to open
the door so that he could take a close look at that pitiful man who looked
more like a huge decrepit hen among the fascinated chickens. He was lying
in a corner drying his open wings in the sunlight among the fruit peels and
breakfast leftovers that the early risers had thrown him. Alien to the imper-
tinences of the world, he only lifted his antiquarian eyes and murmured
something in his dialect when Father Gonzaga went into the chicken coop
and said good morning to him in Latin. The parish priest had his first suspicion of an imposter when he saw that he did not understand the language of
God or know how to greet His ministers. Then he noticed that seen close up
he was much too human: he had an unbearable smell of the outdoors, the
back side of his wings was strewn with parasites and his main feathers had
been mistreated by terrestrial winds, and nothing about him measured up to
the proud dignity of angels. Then he came out of the chicken coop and in a
brief sermon warned the curious against the risks of being ingenuous. He
reminded them that the devil had the bad habit of making use of carnival
tricks in order to confuse the unwary. He argued that if wings were not the
essential element in determining the difference between a hawk and an airplane, they were even less so in the recognition of angels. Nevertheless, he
promised to write a letter to his bishop so that the latter would write to his
primate so that the latter would write to the Supreme Pontiff in order to get
the final verdict from the highest courts.

His prudence fell on sterile hearts. The news of the captive angel spread
with such rapidity that after a few hours the courtyard had the bustle of a
marketplace and they had to call in troops with fixed bayonets to disperse
the mob that was about to knock the house down. Elisenda, her spine all
twisted from sweeping up so much marketplace trash, then got the idea of
fencing in the yard and charging five cents admission to see the angel.

The curious came from far away. A traveling carnival arrived with a flying acrobat who buzzed over the crowd several times, but no one paid any attention to him because his wings were not those of an angel but, rather, those of a sidereal° bat. The most unfortunate invalids on earth came in search of health: a poor woman who since childhood had been counting her heartbeats and had run out of numbers; a Portuguese man who couldn't sleep because the noise of the stars disturbed him; a sleepwalker who got up at night to undo the things he had done while awake; and many others with less serious ailments. In the midst of that shipwreck disorder that made the earth tremble, Pelayo and Elisenda were happy with fatigue, for in less than a week they had crammed their rooms with money and the line of pilgrims waiting their turn to enter still reached beyond the horizon.

The angel was the only one who took no part in his own act. He spent his time trying to get comfortable in his borrowed nest, befuddled by the hellish heat of the oil lamps and sacramental candles that had been placed along the wire. At first they tried to make him eat some mothballs, which, according to the wisdom of the wise neighbor woman, were the food prescribed for angels. But he turned them down, just as he turned down the papal lunches that the penitents brought him, and they never found out whether it was because he was an angel or because he was an old man that in the end he ate nothing but eggplant mush. His only supernatural virtue seemed to be patience. Especially during the first days, when the hens pecked at him, searching for the stellar parasites that proliferated in his wings, and the cripples pulled out feathers to touch their defective parts with, and even the most merciful threw stones at him, trying to get him to rise so they could see him standing. The only time they succeeded in arousing him was when they burned his side with an iron for branding steers, for he had been motionless for so many hours that they thought he was dead. He awoke with a start, ranting in his hermetic language and with tears in his eyes, and he flapped his wings a couple of times, which brought on a whirlwind of chicken dung and lunar dust and a gale of panic that did not seem to be of this world. Although many thought that his reaction had been one not of rage but of pain, from then on they were careful not to annoy him, because the majority understood that his passivity was not that of a hero taking his ease but that of a cataclysm in repose.

Father Gonzaga held back the crowd's frivolity with formulas of maidservant inspiration while awaiting the arrival of a final judgment on the nature of the captive. But the mail from Rome showed no sense of urgency. They spent their time finding out if the prisoner had a navel, if his dialect had any connection with Aramaic, how many times he could fit on the head of a pin, or whether he wasn't just a Norwegian with wings. Those meager letters might have come and gone until the end of time if a providential event had not put an end to the priest's tribulations.

---

sidereal: Coming from the stars.

It so happened that during those days, among so many other carnival attractions, there arrived in town the traveling show of the woman who had been changed into a spider for having disobeyed her parents. The admission to see her was not only less than the admission to see the angel, but people were permitted to ask her all manner of questions about her absurd state and to examine her up and down so that no one would ever doubt the truth of her horror. She was a frightful tarantula the size of a ram and with the head of a sad maiden. What was most heartrending, however, was not her outlandish shape but the sincere affliction with which she recounted the details of her misfortune. While still practically a child she had sneaked out of her parents' house to go to a dance, and while she was coming back through the woods after having danced all night without permission, a fearful thunderclap rent the sky in two and through the crack came the lightning bolt of brimstone that changed her into a spider. Her only nourishment came from the meatballs that charitable souls chose to toss into her mouth. A spectacle like that, full of so much human truth and with such a fearful lesson, was bound to defeat without even trying that of a haughty angel who scarcely deigned to look at mortals. Besides, the few miracles attributed to the angel showed a certain mental disorder, like the blind man who didn't recover his sight but grew three new teeth, or the paralytic who didn't get to walk but almost won the lottery, and the leper whose sores sprouted sunflowers. Those consolation miracles, which were more like mocking fun, had already ruined the angel's reputation when the woman who had been changed into a spider finally crushed him completely. That was how Father Gonzaga was cured forever of his insomnia and Pelayo's courtyard went back to being as empty as during the time it had rained for three days and crabs walked through the bedrooms.

The owners of the house had no reason to lament. With the money they saved they built a two-story mansion with balconies and gardens and high netting so that crabs wouldn't get in during the winter, and with iron bars on the windows so that angels wouldn't get in. Pelayo also set up a rabbit warren close to town and gave up his job as bailiff for good, and Elisenda bought some satin pumps with high heels and many dresses of iridescent silk, the kind worn on Sunday by the most desirable women in those times. The chicken coop was the only thing that didn't receive any attention. If they washed it down with creolin and burned tears of myrrh inside it every so often, it was not in homage to the angel but to drive away the dungheap stench that still hung everywhere like a ghost and was turning the new house into an old one. At first, when the child learned to walk, they were careful that he not get too close to the chicken coop. But then they began to lose their fears and got used to the smell, and before the child got his second teeth he'd gone inside the chicken coop to play, where the wires were falling apart. The angel was no less standoffish with him than with other mortals, but he tolerated the most ingenious infamies with the patience of a dog who had no illusions. They both came down with chicken pox at the same time.

The doctor who took care of the child couldn't resist the temptation to listen to the angel's heart, and he found so much whistling in the heart and so many sounds in his kidneys that it seemed impossible for him to be alive. What surprised him most, however, was the logic of his wings. They seemed so natural on that completely human organism that he couldn't understand why other men didn't have them too.

When the child began school it had been some time since the sun and rain had caused the collapse of the chicken coop. The angel went dragging himself about here and there like a stray dying man. They would drive him out of the bedroom with a broom and a moment later find him in the kitchen. He seemed to be in so many places at the same time that they grew to think that he'd been duplicated, that he was reproducing himself all through the house, and the exasperated and unhinged Elisenda shouted that it was awful living in that hell full of angels. He could scarcely eat and his antiquarian eyes had also become so foggy that he went about bumping into posts. All he had left were the bare cannulae° of his last feathers. Pelayo threw a blanket over him and extended him the charity of letting him sleep in the shed, and only then did they notice that he had a temperature at night, and was delirious with the tongue twisters of an old Norwegian. That was one of the few times they became alarmed, for they thought he was going to die and not even the wise neighbor woman had been able to tell them what to do with dead angels.

And yet he not only survived his worst winter, but seemed improved with the first sunny days. He remained motionless for several days in the farthest corner of the courtyard, where no one would see him, and at the beginning of December some large, stiff feathers began to grow on his wings, the feathers of a scarecrow, which looked more like another misfortune of decrepitude. But he must have known the reason for those changes, for he was quite careful that no one should notice them, that no one should hear the sea chanteys that he sometimes sang under the stars. One morning Elisenda was cutting some bunches of onions for lunch when a wind that seemed to come from the high seas blew into the kitchen. Then she went to the window and caught the angel in his first attempts at flight. They were so clumsy that his fingernails opened a furrow in the vegetable patch and he was on the point of knocking the shed down with the ungainly flapping that slipped on the light and couldn't get a grip on the air. But he did manage to gain altitude. Elisenda let out a sigh of relief, for herself and for him, when she saw him pass over the last houses, holding himself up in some way with the risky flapping of a senile vulture. She kept watching him even when she was through cutting the onions and she kept on watching until it was no longer possible for her to see him, because then he was no longer an annoyance in her life but an imaginary dot on the horizon of the sea.

---

cannulae: The tubelike quills by which feathers are attached to a body.

Patricia Grace   New Zealand, b. 1937

Butterflies   [1987]

The grandmother plaited her granddaughter's hair and then she said, "Get your lunch. Put it in your bag. Get your apple. You come straight back after school, straight home here. Listen to the teacher," she said. "Do what she say."

Her grandfather was out on the step. He walked down the path with her and out on to the footpath. He said to a neighbor, "Our granddaughter goes to school. She lives with us now."

"She's fine," the neighbor said. "She's terrific with her two plaits in her hair."

"And clever," the grandfather said. "Writes every day in her book."

"She's fine," the neighbor said.

The grandfather waited with his granddaughter by the crossing and then he said, "Go to school. Listen to the teacher. Do what she say."

When the granddaughter came home from school her grandfather was hoeing round the cabbages. Her grandmother was picking beans. They stopped their work.

"You bring your book home?" the grandmother asked.

"Yes."

"You write your story?"

"Yes."

"What's your story?"

"About the butterflies."

"Get your book, then. Read your story."

The granddaughter took her book from her schoolbag and opened it.

"I killed all the butterflies," she read. "This is me and this is all the butterflies."

"And your teacher like your story, did she?"

"I don't know."

"What your teacher say?"

"She said butterflies are beautiful creatures. They hatch out and fly in the sun. The butterflies visit all the pretty flowers, she said. They lay their eggs and then they die. You don't kill butterflies, that's what she said."

The grandmother and grandfather were quiet for a long time, and their granddaughter, holding the book, stood quite still in the warm garden.

"Because you see," the grandfather said, "your teacher, she buy all her cabbages from the supermarket and that's why."

Bessie Head   Botswana, 1937–1986

The Collector of Treasures   [1977]

The long-term central state prison in the south was a whole day's journey away from the villages of the northern part of the country. They had left the village of Puleng at about nine that morning and all day long the police truck droned as it sped southwards on the wide, dusty cross-country track-road. The everyday world of ploughed fields, grazing cattle, and vast expanses of bush and forest seemed indifferent to the hungry eyes of the prisoner who gazed out at them through the wire mesh grating at the back of the police truck. At some point during the journey, the prisoner seemed to strike at some ultimate source of pain and loneliness within her being and, overcome by it, she slowly crumpled forward in a wasted heap, oblivious to everything but her pain. Sunset swept by, then dusk, then dark and still the truck droned on, impersonally, uncaring.

At first, faintly on the horizon, the orange glow of the city lights of the new independence town of Gaborone, appeared like an astonishing phantom in the overwhelming darkness of the bush, until the truck struck tarred roads, neon lights, shops and cinemas, and made the bush a phantom amidst a blaze of light. All this passed untimed, unwatched by the crumpled prisoner; she did not stir as the truck finally droned to a halt outside the prison gates. The torchlight struck the side of her face like an agonizing blow. Thinking she was asleep, the policeman called out briskly:

"You must awaken now. We have arrived."

He struggled with the lock in the dark and pulled open the grating. She crawled painfully forward, in silence.

Together, they walked up a short flight of stairs and waited awhile as the man tapped lightly, several times, on the heavy iron prison door. The night-duty attendant opened the door a crack, peered out and then opened the door a little wider for them to enter. He quietly and casually led the way to a small office, looked at his colleague and asked: "What do we have here?"

"It's the husband murder case from Puleng village," the other replied, handing over a file.

The attendant took the file and sat down at a table on which lay open a large record book. In a big, bold scrawl he recorded the details: Dikeledi Mokopi. Charge: Man-slaughter. Sentence: Life. A night-duty wardress appeared and led the prisoner away to a side cubicle, where she was asked to undress.

"Have you any money on you?" the wardress queried, handing her a plain, green cotton dress which was the prison uniform. The prisoner silently shook her head.

"So, you have killed your husband, have you?" the wardress remarked, with a flicker of humor. "You'll be in good company. We have four other women here for the same crime. It's becoming the fashion these days. Come with me," and she led the way along a corridor, turned left and stopped at an iron gate which she opened with a key, waited for the prisoner to walk in ahead of her and then locked it with the key again. They entered a small, immensely high-walled courtyard. On one side were toilets, showers, and a cupboard. On the other, an empty concrete quadrangle. The wardress walked to the cupboard, unlocked it and took out a thick roll of clean-smelling blankets which she handed to the prisoner. At the lower end of the walled courtyard was a heavy iron door which led to the cell. The wardress walked up to this door, banged on it loudly and called out: "I say, will you women in there light your candle?"

A voice within called out: "All right," and they could hear the scratch-scratch of a match. The wardress again inserted a key, opened the door and watched for a while as the prisoner spread out her blankets on the floor. The four women prisoners already confined in the cell sat up briefly, and stared silently at their new companion. As the door was locked, they all greeted her quietly and one of the women asked: "Where do you come from?"

"Puleng," the newcomer replied, and seemingly satisfied with that, the light was blown out and the women lay down to continue their interrupted sleep. And as though she had reached the end of her destination, the new prisoner too fell into a deep sleep as soon as she had pulled her blankets about her.

The breakfast gong sounded at six the next morning. The women stirred themselves for their daily routine. They stood up, shook out their blankets and rolled them up into neat bundles. The day-duty wardress rattled the key in the lock and let them out into the small concrete courtyard so that they could perform their morning toilet. Then, with a loud clatter of pails and plates, two male prisoners appeared at the gate with breakfast. The men handed each woman a plate of porridge and a mug of black tea and they settled themselves on the concrete floor to eat. They turned and looked at their new companion and one of the women, a spokesman for the group said kindly:

"You should take care. The tea has no sugar in it. What we usually do is scoop the sugar off the porridge and put it into the tea."

The woman, Dikeledi, looked up and smiled. She had experienced such terror during the awaiting-trial period that she looked more like a skeleton than a human being. The skin creaked tautly over her cheeks. The other woman smiled, but after her own fashion. Her face permanently wore a look of cynical, whimsical humor. She had a full, plump figure. She introduced herself and her companions: "My name is Kebonye. Then that's Otsetswe, Galeboe, and Monwana. What may your name be?"

"Dikeledi Mokopi."

"How is it that you have such a tragic name," Kebonye observed. "Why did your parents have to name you *tears*?"

"My father passed away at that time and it is my mother's tears that I am named after," Dikeledi said, then added: "She herself passed away six years later and I was brought up by my uncle."

Kebonye shook her head sympathetically, slowly raising a spoonful of porridge to her mouth. That swallowed, she asked next:

"And what may your crime be?"

"I have killed my husband."

"We are all here for the same crime," Kebonye said, then with her cynical smile asked: "Do you feel any sorrow about the crime?"

"Not really," the other woman replied.

"How did you kill him?"

"I cut off all his special parts with a knife," Dikeledi said.

"I did it with a razor," Kebonye said. She sighed and added: "I have had a troubled life."

A little silence followed while they all busied themselves with their food, then Kebonye continued musingly:

"Our men do not think that we need tenderness and care. You know, my husband used to kick me between the legs when he wanted that. I once aborted with a child, due to this treatment. I could see that there was no way to appeal to him if I felt ill, so I once said to him that if he liked he could keep some other woman as well because I couldn't manage to satisfy all his needs. Well, he was an education-officer and each year he used to suspend about seventeen male teachers for making school girls pregnant, but he used to do the same. The last time it happened the parents of the girl were very angry and came to report the matter to me. I told them: 'You leave it to me. I have seen enough.' And so I killed him."

They sat in silence and completed their meal, then they took their plates and cups to rinse them in the wash-room. The wardress produced some pails and a broom. Their sleeping quarters had to be flushed out with water; there was not a speck of dirt anywhere, but that was prison routine. All that was left was an inspection by the director of the prison. Here again Kebonye turned to the newcomer and warned:

"You must be careful when the chief comes to inspect. He is mad about one thing—attention! Stand up straight! Hands at your sides! If this is not done you should see how he stands here and curses. He does not mind anything but that. He is mad about that."

Inspection over, the women were taken through a number of gates to an open, sunny yard, fenced in by high, barbed-wire where they did their daily work. The prison was a rehabilitation center where the prisoners produced goods which were sold in the prison store; the women produced garments of cloth and wool; the men did carpentry, shoe-making, brick-making, and vegetable production.

Dikeledi had a number of skills—she could knit, sew, and weave baskets. All the women at present were busy knitting woollen garments; some were learners and did their work slowly and painstakingly. They looked at Dikeledi with interest as she took a ball of wool and a pair of knitting needles and rapidly cast on stitches. She had soft, caressing, almost boneless, hands of strange power—work of a beautiful design grew from those hands. By mid-morning she had completed the front part of a jersey and they all stopped to admire the pattern she had invented in her own head.

"You are a gifted person," Kebonye remarked, admiringly.

"All my friends say so," Dikeledi replied smiling. "You know, I am the woman whose thatch does not leak. Whenever my friends wanted to thatch their huts, I was there. They would never do it without me. I was always busy and employed because it was with these hands that I fed and reared my children. My husband left me after four years of marriage but I managed well enough to feed those mouths. If people did not pay me in money for my work, they paid me with gifts of food."

"It's not so bad here," Kebonye said. "We get a little money saved for us out of the sale of our work, and if you work like that you can still produce money for your children. How many children do you have?"

"I have three sons."

"Are they in good care?"

"Yes."

"I like lunch," Kebonye said, oddly turning the conversation. "It is the best meal of the day. We get samp and meat and vegetables."

So the day passed pleasantly enough with chatter and work and at sunset the women were once more taken back to the cell for lock-up time. They unrolled their blankets and prepared their beds, and with the candle lit continued to talk a while longer. Just as they were about to retire for the night, Dikeledi nodded to her new-found friend, Kebonye:

"Thank you for all your kindness to me," she said, softly.

"We must help each other," Kebonye replied, with her amused, cynical smile. "This is a terrible world. There is only misery here."

And so the woman Dikeledi began phase three of a life that had been ashen in its loneliness and unhappiness. And yet she had always found gold amidst the ash, deep loves that had joined her heart to the hearts of others. She smiled tenderly at Kebonye because she knew already that she had found another such love. She was the collector of such treasures.

There were really only two kinds of men in the society. The one kind created such misery and chaos that he could be broadly damned as evil. If one watched the village dogs chasing a bitch on heat, they usually moved around in packs of four or five. As the mating progressed one dog would attempt to gain dominance over the festivities and oust all the others from the bitch's vulva. The rest of the hapless dogs would stand around yapping and snapping in its face while the top dog indulged in a continuous spurt of orgasms, day and night until he was exhausted. No doubt, during that Herculean feat, the dog imagined he was the only penis in the world and that there had to be a scramble for it. That kind of man lived near the animal level and behaved just the same. Like the dogs and bulls and donkeys, he also accepted no responsibility for the young he procreated and like the dogs and bulls and donkeys, he also made females abort. Since that kind of man was in the majority in the society, he needed a little analyzing as he was responsible for the complete breakdown of family life. He could be analyzed over three time-spans. In the old days, before the colonial invasion of Africa, he was a man who lived by the traditions and taboos outlined for all the people by the forefathers of the tribe. He had little individual freedom to assess whether these traditions were compassionate or not — they demanded that he comply and obey the rules, without thought. But when the laws of the ancestors are examined, they appear on the whole to have been vast, external disciplines for the good of the society as a whole, with little attention given to individual preferences and needs. The ancestors made so many errors and one of the most bitter-making things was that they relegated to men a superior position in the tribe, while women were regarded, in a congenital sense, as being an inferior form of human life. To this day, women still suffered from all the calamities that befell an inferior form of human life. The colonial era and the period of migratory mining labor to South Africa was a further affliction visited on this man. It broke the hold of the ancestors. It broke the old, traditional form of family life and for long periods a man was separated from his wife and children while he worked for a pittance in another land in order to raise the money to pay his British Colonial poll-tax. British Colonialism scarcely enriched his life. He then became "the boy" of the white man and a machine-tool of the South African mines. African independence seemed merely one more affliction on top of the afflictions that had visited this man's life. Independence suddenly and dramatically changed the pattern of colonial subservience. More jobs became available under the new government's localization program and salaries sky-rocketed at the same time. It provided the first occasion for family life of a new order, above the childlike discipline of custom, the degradation of colonialism. Men and women, in order to survive, had to turn inwards to their own resources. It was the man who arrived at this turning point, a broken wreck with no inner resources at all. It was as though he was hideous to himself and in an effort to flee his own inner emptiness, he spun away from himself in a dizzy kind of death dance of wild destruction and dissipation.

One such man was Garesego Mokopi, the husband of Dikeledi. For four years prior to independence, he had worked as a clerk in the district administration service, at a steady salary of R50.00° a month. Soon after independence his salary shot up to R200.00 per month. Even during his lean days he had had a taste for womanizing and drink; now he had the resources for a real spree. He was not seen at home again and lived and slept around the village, from woman to woman. He left his wife and three sons — Banabothe, the eldest, aged four; Inalame, aged three; and the youngest, Motsomi, aged one — to their own resources. Perhaps he did so because she was the boring, semi-literate traditional sort, and there were a lot of exciting new women around. Independence produced marvels indeed.

R50.00: 50 rands. The rand is the basic monetary unit of South Africa.

There was another kind of man in the society with the power to create himself anew. He turned all his resources, both emotional and material, towards his family life and he went on and on with his own quiet rhythm, like a river. He was a poem of tenderness.

One such man was Paul Thebolo and he and his wife, Kenalepe, and their three children, came to live in the village of Puleng in 1966, the year of independence. Paul Thebolo had been offered the principalship of a primary school in the village. They were allocated an empty field beside the yard of Dikeledi Mokopi, for their new home.

Neighbors are the center of the universe to each other. They help each other at all times and mutually loan each other's goods. Dikeledi Mokopi kept an interested eye on the yard of her new neighbors. At first, only the man appeared with some workmen to erect the fence, which was set up with incredible speed and efficiency. The man impressed her immediately when she went around to introduce herself and find out a little about the newcomers. He was tall, large-boned, slow-moving. He was so peaceful as a person that the sunlight and shadow played all kinds of tricks with his eyes, making it difficult to determine their exact color. When he stood still and looked reflective, the sunlight liked to creep into his eyes and nestle there; so sometimes his eyes were the color of shade, and sometimes light brown.

He turned and smiled at her in a friendly way when she introduced herself and explained that he and his wife were on transfer from the village of Bobonong. His wife and children were living with relatives in the village until the yard was prepared. He was in a hurry to settle down as the school term would start in a month's time. They were, he said, going to erect two mud huts first and later he intended setting up a small house of bricks. His wife would be coming around in a few days with some women to erect the mud walls of the huts.

"I would like to offer my help too," Dikeledi said. "If work always starts early in the morning and there are about six of us, we can get both walls erected in a week. If you want one of the huts done in woman's thatch, all my friends know that I am the woman whose thatch does not leak."

The man smilingly replied that he would impart all this information to his wife, then he added charmingly that he thought she would like his wife when they met. His wife was a very friendly person; everyone liked her.

Dikeledi walked back to her own yard with a high heart. She had few callers. None of her relatives called for fear that since her husband had left her she would become dependent on them for many things. The people who called did business with her; they wanted her to make dresses for their children or knit jerseys for the winter time and at times when she had no orders at all, she made baskets which she sold. In these ways she supported herself and the three children but she was lonely for true friends.

All turned out as the husband had said—he had a lovely wife. She was fairly tall and thin with a bright, vivacious manner. She made no effort to conceal that normally, and every day, she was a very happy person. And all turned out as Dikeledi had said. The work-party of six women erected the mud walls of the huts in one week; two weeks later, the thatch was complete. The Thebolo family moved into their new abode and Dikeledi Mokopi moved into one of the most prosperous and happy periods of her life. Her life took a big, wide upward curve. Her relationship with the Thebolo family was more than the usual friendly exchange of neighbors. It was rich and creative.

It was not long before the two women had going one of those deep, affectionate, sharing-everything kind of friendships that only women know how to have. It seemed that Kenalepe wanted endless amounts of dresses made for herself and her three little girls. Since Dikeledi would not accept cash for these services — she protested about the many benefits she received from her good neighbors — Paul Thebolo arranged that she be paid in household goods for these services so that for some years Dikeledi was always assured of her basic household needs — the full bag of corn, sugar, tea, powdered milk, and cooking oil. Kenalepe was also the kind of woman who made the whole world spin around her; her attractive personality attracted a whole range of women to her yard and also a whole range of customers for her dressmaking friend, Dikeledi. Eventually, Dikeledi became swamped with work, was forced to buy a second sewing-machine and employ a helper. The two women did everything together — they were forever together at weddings, funerals, and parties in the village. In their leisure hours they freely discussed all their intimate affairs with each other, so that each knew thoroughly the details of the other's life.

"You are a lucky someone," Dikeledi remarked one day, wistfully. "Not everyone has the gift of a husband like Paul."

"Oh yes," Kenalepe said happily. "He is an honest somebody." She knew a little of Dikeledi's list of woes and queried: "But why did you marry a man like Garesego? I looked carefully at him when you pointed him out to me near the shops the other day and I could see at one glance that he is a butterfly."

"I think I mostly wanted to get out of my uncle's yard," Dikeledi replied. "I never liked my uncle. Rich as he was, he was a hard man and very selfish. I was only a servant there and pushed about. I went there when I was six years old when my mother died, and it was not a happy life. All his children despised me because I was their servant. Uncle paid for my education for six years, then he said I must leave school. I longed for more because as you know, education opens up the world for one. Garesego was a friend of my uncle and he was the only man who proposed for me. They discussed it between themselves and then my uncle said: 'You'd better marry Garesego because you're just hanging around here like a chain on my neck.' I agreed, just to get away from that terrible man. Garesego said at that time that he'd rather be married to my sort than the educated kind because those women were stubborn and wanted to lay down the rules for men. Really, I did not ever protest when he started running about. You know what the other women do. They chase after the man from one hut to another and beat up the girlfriends. The man just runs into another hut, that's all. So you don't really win. I wasn't going to do anything like that. I am satisfied I have children. They are a blessing to me."

"Oh, it isn't enough," her friend said, shaking her head in deep sympathy. "I am amazed at how life imparts its gifts. Some people get too much. Others get nothing at all. I have always been lucky in life. One day my parents will visit—they live in the south—and you'll see the fuss they make over me. Paul is just the same. He takes care of everything so that I never have a day of worry . . ."

The man Paul, attracted as wide a range of male friends as his wife. They had guests every evening; illiterate men who wanted him to fill in tax forms or write letters for them, or his own colleagues who wanted to debate the political issues of the day—there was always something new happening every day now that the country had independence. The two women sat on the edge of these debates and listened with fascinated ears, but they never participated. The following day they would chew over the debates with wise, earnest expressions.

"Men's minds travel widely and boldly," Kenalepe would comment. "It makes me shiver the way they freely criticize our new government. Did you hear what Petros said last night? He said he knew all those bastards and they were just a lot of crooks who would pull a lot of dirty tricks. Oh dear! I shivered so much when he said that. The way they talk about the government makes you feel in your bones that this is not a safe world to be in, not like the old days when we didn't have governments. And Lentswe said that ten percent of the population in England really control all the wealth of the country, while the rest live at starvation level. And he said communism would sort all this out. I gathered from the way they discussed this matter that our government is not in favor of communism. I trembled so much when this became clear to me . . ." She paused and laughed proudly. "I've heard Paul say this several times: 'The British only ruled us for eighty years.' I wonder why Paul is so fond of saying that?"

And so a completely new world opened up for Dikeledi. It was so impossibly rich and happy that, as the days went by, she immersed herself more deeply in it and quite overlooked the barrenness of her own life. But it hung there like a nagging ache in the mind of her friend, Kenalepe.

"You ought to find another man," she urged one day, when they had one of their personal discussions. "It's not good for a woman to live alone."

"And who would that be?" Dikeledi asked, disillusioned. "I'd only be bringing trouble into my life whereas now it is all in order. I have my eldest son at school and I can manage to pay the school fees. That's all I really care about."

"I mean," said Kenalepe, "we are also here to make love and enjoy it!"

"Oh I never really cared for it," the other replied. "When you experience the worst of it, it just puts you off altogether."

"What do you mean by that?" Kenalepe asked, wide-eyed.

"I mean it was just jump on and jump off and I used to wonder what it was all about. I developed a dislike for it."

"You mean Garesego was like that!" Kenalepe said, flabbergasted. "Why, that's just like a cock hopping from hen to hen. I wonder what he is doing with all those women. I'm sure they are just after his money and so they flatter him . . ." She paused and then added earnestly. "That's really all the more reason you should find another man. Oh, if you knew what it was really like, you would long for it, I can tell you! I sometimes think I enjoy that side of life far too much. Paul knows a lot about all that. And he always has some new trick with which to surprise me. He has a certain way of smiling when he has thought up something new and I shiver a little and say to myself: 'Ha, what is Paul going to do tonight!'"

Kenalepe paused and smiled at her friend, slyly.

"I can loan Paul to you if you like," she said, then raised one hand to block the protest on her friend's face. "I would do it because I have never had a friend like you in my life before whom I trust so much. Paul had other girls you know, before he married me, so it's not such an uncommon thing to him. Besides, we used to make love long before we got married and I never got pregnant. He takes care of that side too. I wouldn't mind loaning him because I am expecting another child and I don't feel so well these days . . ."

Dikeledi stared at the ground for a long moment, then she looked up at her friend with tears in her eyes.

"I cannot accept such a gift from you," she said, deeply moved. "But if you are ill I will wash for you and cook for you."

Not put off by her friend's refusal of her generous offer, Kenalepe mentioned the discussion to her husband that very night. He was so taken off-guard by the unexpectedness of the subject that at first he looked slightly astonished, and burst out into loud laughter and for such a lengthy time that he seemed unable to stop.

"Why are you laughing like that?" Kenalepe asked, surprised.

He laughed a bit more, then suddenly turned very serious and thoughtful and was lost in his own thoughts for some time. When she asked him what he was thinking he merely replied: "I don't want to tell you everything. I want to keep some of my secrets to myself."

The next day Kenalepe reported this to her friend.

"Now whatever does he mean by that? I want to keep some of my secrets to myself?"

"I think," Dikeledi said smiling, "I think he has a conceit about being a good man. Also, when someone loves someone too much, it hurts them to say so. They'd rather keep silent."

Shortly after this Kenalepe had a miscarriage and had to be admitted to hospital for a minor operation. Dikeledi kept her promise "to wash and cook" for her friend. She ran both their homes, fed the children and kept everything in order. Also, people complained about the poorness of the hospital diet and each day she scoured the village for eggs and chicken, cooked them, and took them to Kenalepe every day at the lunch-hour.

One evening Dikeledi ran into a snag with her routine. She had just dished up supper for the Thebolo children when a customer came around with an urgent request for an alteration on a wedding dress. The wedding was to take place the next day. She left the children seated around the fire eating and returned to her own home. An hour later, her own children asleep and settled, she thought she would check the Thebolo yard to see if all was well there. She entered the children's hut and noted that they had put themselves to bed and were fast asleep. Their supper plates lay scattered and unwashed around the fire. The hut which Paul and Kenalepe shared was in darkness. It meant that Paul had not yet returned from his usual evening visit to his wife. Dikeledi collected the plates and washed them, then poured the dirty dishwater on the still-glowing embers of the outdoor fire. She piled the plates one on top of the other and carried them to the third additional hut which was used as a kitchen. Just then Paul Thebolo entered the yard, noted the lamp and movement in the kitchen hut and walked over to it. He paused at the open door.

"What are you doing now, Mma-Banabothe?" he asked, addressing her affectionately in the customary way by the name of her eldest son, Banabothe.

"I know quite well what I am doing," Dikeledi replied happily. She turned around to say that it was not a good thing to leave dirty dishes standing overnight but her mouth flew open with surprise. Two soft pools of cool liquid light were in his eyes and something infinitely sweet passed between them; it was too beautiful to be love.

"You are a very good woman, Mma-Banabothe," he said softly.

It was the truth and the gift was offered like a nugget of gold. Only men like Paul Thebolo could offer such gifts. She took it and stored another treasure in her heart. She bowed her knee in the traditional curtsey and walked quietly away to her own home.

Eight years passed for Dikeledi in a quiet rhythm of work and friendship with the Thebolo's. The crisis came with the eldest son, Banabothe. He had to take his primary school leaving examination at the end of the year. This serious event sobered him up considerably as like all boys he was very fond of playtime. He brought his books home and told his mother that he would like to study in the evenings. He would like to pass with a "Grade A" to please her. With a flushed and proud face Dikeledi mentioned this to her friend, Kenalepe.

"Banabothe is studying every night now," she said. "He never really cared for studies. I am so pleased about this that I bought him a spare lamp and removed him from the children's hut to my own hut where things will be peaceful for him. We both sit up late at night now. I sew on buttons and fix hems and he does his studies . . ."

She also opened a savings account at the post office in order to have some standby money to pay the fees for his secondary education. They were rather high — R85.00. But in spite of all her hoarding of odd cents, towards the end of the year, she was short on R20.00 to cover the fees. Midway during the Christmas school holidays the results were announced. Banabothe passed with a "Grade A." His mother was almost hysterical in her joy at his achievement. But what to do? The two youngest sons had already started primary school and she would never manage to cover all their fees from her resources. She decided to remind Garesego Mokopi that he was the father of the children. She had not seen him in eight years except as a passer-by in the village. Sometimes he waved but he had never talked to her or enquired about her life or that of the children. It did not matter. She was a lower form of human life. Then this unpleasant something turned up at his office one day, just as he was about to leave for lunch. She had heard from village gossip, that he had eventually settled down with a married woman who had a brood of children of her own. He had ousted her husband, in a typical village sensation of brawls, curses, and abuse. Most probably the husband did not care because there were always arms outstretched towards a man, as long as he looked like a man. The attraction of this particular woman for Garesego Mokopi, so her former lovers said with a snicker, was that she went in for heady forms of love-making like biting and scratching.

Garesego Mokopi walked out of his office and looked irritably at the ghost from his past, his wife. She obviously wanted to talk to him and he walked towards her, looking at his watch all the while. Like all the new "success men," he had developed a paunch, his eyes were blood-shot, his face was bloated, and the odor of the beer and sex from the previous night clung faintly around him. He indicated with his eyes that they should move around to the back of the office block where they could talk in privacy.

"You must hurry with whatever you want to say," he said impatiently. "The lunch-hour is very short and I have to be back at the office by two."

Not to him could she talk of the pride she felt in Banabothe's achievement, so she said simply and quietly: "Garesego, I beg you to help me pay Banabothe's fees for secondary school. He has passed with a 'Grade A' and as you know, the school fees must be produced on the first day of school or else he will be turned away. I have struggled to save money the whole year but I am short by R20.00."

She handed him her post office savings book, which he took, glanced at and handed back to her. Then he smiled, a smirky know-all smile, and thought he was delivering her a blow in the face.

"Why don't you ask Paul Thebolo for the money?" he said. "Everyone knows he's keeping two homes and that you are his spare. Everyone knows about that full bag of corn he delivers to your home every six months so why can't he pay the school fees as well?"

She neither denied this, nor confirmed it. The blow glanced off her face which she raised slightly, in pride. Then she walked away.

As was their habit, the two women got together that afternoon and Dikeledi reported this conversation with her husband to Kenalepe who tossed back her head in anger and said fiercely: "The filthy pig himself! He thinks every man is like him, does he? I shall report this matter to Paul, then he'll see something."

And indeed Garesego did see something but it was just up his alley. He was a female prostitute in his innermost being and like all professional prostitutes, he enjoyed publicity and sensation—it promoted his cause. He smiled genially and expansively when a madly angry Paul Thebolo came up to the door of his house where he lived with *his* concubine. Garesego had been through a lot of these dramas over those eight years and he almost knew by rote the dialogue that would follow.

"You bastard!" Paul Thebolo spat out. "Your wife isn't my concubine, do you hear?"

"Then why are you keeping her in food?" Garesego drawled. "Men only do that for women they fuck! They never do it for nothing."

Paul Thebolo rested one hand against the wall, half dizzy with anger, and he said tensely: "You defile life, Garesego Mokopi. There's nothing else in your world but defilement. Mma-Banabothe makes clothes for my wife and children and she will never accept money from me so how else must I pay her?"

"It only proves the story both ways," the other replied, vilely. "Women do that for men who fuck them."

Paul Thebolo shot out the other hand, punched him soundly in one grinning eye and walked away: Who could hide a livid, swollen eye? To every surprised enquiry, he replied with an injured air:

"It was done by my wife's lover, Paul Thebolo."

It certainly brought the attention of the whole village upon him, which was all he really wanted. Those kinds of men were the bottom rung of government. They secretly hungered to be the President with all eyes on them. He worked up the sensation a little further. He announced that he would pay the school fees of the child of his concubine, who was also to enter secondary school, but not the school fees of his own child, Banabothe. People half liked the smear on Paul Thebolo; he was too good to be true. They delighted in making him a part of the general dirt of the village, so they turned on Garesego and scolded: "Your wife might be getting things from Paul Thebolo but it's beyond the purse of any man to pay the school fees of his own children as well as the school fees of another man's children. Banabothe wouldn't be there had you not procreated him, Garesego, so it is your duty to care for him. Besides, it's your fault if your wife takes another man. You left her alone all these years."

So that story was lived with for two weeks, mostly because people wanted to say that Paul Thebolo was a part of life too and as uncertain of his morals as they were. But the story took such a dramatic turn that it made all the men shudder with horror. It was some weeks before they could find the courage to go to bed with women; they preferred to do something else.

Garesego's obscene thought processes were his own undoing. He really believed that another man had a stake in his hen-pen and like any cock, his hair was up about it. He thought he'd walk in and re-establish his own claim to it and so, after two weeks, once the swelling in his eye had died down, he espied Banabothe in the village and asked him to take a note to his mother. He said the child should bring a reply. The note read: "Dear Mother, I am coming home again so that we may settle our differences. Will you prepare a meal for me and some hot water that I might take a bath. Gare."

Dikeledi took the note, read it and shook with rage. All its overtones were clear to her. He was coming home for some sex. They had had no differences. They had not even talked to each other.

"Banabothe," she said. "Will you play nearby? I want to think a bit then I will send you to your father with the reply."

Her thought processes were not very clear to her. There was something she could not immediately touch upon. Her life had become holy to her during all those years she had struggled to maintain herself and the children. She had filled her life with treasures of kindness and love she had gathered from others and it was all this that she wanted to protect from defilement by an evil man. Her first panic-stricken thought was to gather up the children and flee the village. But where to go? Garesego did not want a divorce, she had left him to approach her about the matter, she had desisted from taking any other man. She turned her thoughts this way and that and could find no way out except to face him. If she wrote back, don't you dare put foot in the yard I don't want to see you, he would ignore it. Black women didn't have that kind of power. A thoughtful, brooding look came over her face. At last, at peace with herself, she went into her hut and wrote a reply: "Sir, I shall prepare everything as you have said. Dikeledi."

It was about midday when Banabothe sped back with the reply to his father. All afternoon Dikeledi busied herself making preparations for the appearance of her husband at sunset. At one point Kenalepe approached the yard and looked around in amazement at the massive preparations, the large iron water pot full of water with a fire burning under it, the extra cooking pots on the fire. Only later Kenalepe brought the knife into focus. But it was only a vague blur, a large kitchen knife used to cut meat and Dikeledi knelt at a grinding-stone and sharpened it slowly and methodically. What was in focus then was the final and tragic expression on the upturned face of her friend. It threw her into confusion and blocked their usual free and easy feminine chatter. When Dikeledi said: "I am making some preparations for Garesego. He is coming home tonight," Kenalepe beat a hasty retreat to her own home terrified. They knew they were involved because when she mentioned this to Paul he was distracted and uneasy for the rest of the day. He kept on doing upside-down sorts of things, not replying to questions, absent-mindedly leaving a cup of tea until it got quite cold, and every now and again he stood up and paced about, lost in his own thoughts. So deep was their sense of disturbance that towards evening they no longer made a pretence of talking. They just sat in silence in their hut. Then, at about nine o'clock, they heard those wild and agonized bellows. They both rushed out together to the yard of Dikeledi Mokopi.

He came home at sunset and found everything ready for him as he had requested, and he settled himself down to enjoy a man's life. He had brought a pack of beer along and sat outdoors slowly savouring it while every now and then his eye swept over the Thebolo yard. Only the woman and children moved about the yard. The man was out of sight. Garesego smiled to himself, pleased that he could crow as loud as he liked with no answering challenge.

A basin of warm water was placed before him to wash his hands and then Dikeledi served him his meal. At a separate distance she also served the children and then instructed them to wash and prepare for bed. She noted that Garesego displayed no interest in the children whatsoever. He was entirely wrapped up in himself and thought only of himself and his own comfort. Any tenderness he offered the children might have broken her and swerved her mind away from the deed she had carefully planned all that afternoon. She was beneath his regard and notice too for when she eventually brought her own plate of food and sat near him, he never once glanced at her face. He drank his beer and cast his glance every now and again at the Thebolo yard. Not once did the man of the yard appear until it became too dark to distinguish anything any more. He was completely satisfied with that. He could repeat the performance every day until he broke the mettle of the other cock again and forced him into angry abuse. He liked that sort of thing.

"Garesego, do you think you could help me with Banabothe's school fees?" Dikeledi asked at one point.

"Oh, I'll think about it," he replied casually.

She stood up and carried buckets of water into the hut, which she poured into a large tin bath that he might bathe himself, then while he took his bath she busied herself tidying up and completing the last of the household chores. Those done, she entered the children's hut. They played hard during the day and they had already fallen asleep with exhaustion. She knelt down near their sleeping mats and stared at them for a long while, with an extremely tender expression. Then she blew out their lamp and walked to her own hut. Garesego lay sprawled across the bed in such a manner that indicated he only thought of himself and did not intend sharing the bed with anyone else. Satiated with food and drink, he had fallen into a deep, heavy sleep the moment his head touched the pillow. His concubine had no doubt taught him that the correct way for a man to go to bed, was naked. So he lay, unguarded and defenseless, sprawled across the bed on his back.

The bath made a loud clatter as Dikeledi removed it from the room, but still he slept on, lost to the world. She re-entered the hut and closed the door. Then she bent down and reached for the knife under the bed which she had merely concealed with a cloth. With the precision and skill of her hardworking hands, she grasped hold of his genitals and cut them off with one stroke. In doing so, she slit the main artery which ran on the inside of the groin. A massive spurt of blood arched its way across the bed. And Gare-sego bellowed. He bellowed his anguish. Then all was silent. She stood and watched his death anguish with an intent and brooding look, missing not one detail of it. A knock on the door stirred her out of her reverie. It was the boy, Banabothe. She opened the door and stared at him, speechless. He was trembling violently.

"Mother," he said, in a terrified whisper. "Didn't I hear father cry?"

"I have killed him," she said, waving her hand in the air with a gesture that said — well, that's that. Then she added sharply: "Banabothe, go and call the police."

He turned and fled into the night. A second pair of footsteps followed hard on his heels. It was Kenalepe running back to her own yard, half out of her mind with fear. Out of the dark Paul Thebolo stepped towards the hut and entered it. He took in every detail and then he turned and looked at Dikeledi with such a tortured expression that for a time words failed him. At last he said: "You don't have to worry about the children, Mma-Banabothe. I'll take them as my own and give them all a secondary school education."

Naguib Mahfouz   Egypt, b. 1911

Half a Day   [1989]

Translated by Denys Johnson-Davies

I proceeded alongside my father, clutching his right hand, running to keep up with the long strides he was taking. All my clothes were new: the black shoes, the green school uniform, and the red tarboosh.° My delight in my new clothes, however, was not altogether unmarred, for this was no feast day but the day on which I was to be cast into school for the first time.

My mother stood at the window watching our progress, and I would turn toward her from time to time, as though appealing for help. We walked along a street lined with gardens; on both sides were extensive fields planted with crops, prickly pears, henna trees, and a few date palms.

"Why school?" I challenged my father openly. "I shall never do anything to annoy you."

"I'm not punishing you," he said, laughing. "School's not a punishment. It's the factory that makes useful men out of boys. Don't you want to be like your father and brothers?"

---

tarboosh: A cloth or felt cap with a tassel worn by Muslim men.

I was not convinced. I did not believe there was really any good to be had in tearing me away from the intimacy of my home and throwing me into this building that stood at the end of the road like some huge, high-walled fortress, exceedingly stern and grim.

When we arrived at the gate we could see the courtyard, vast and crammed full of boys and girls. "Go in by yourself," said my father, "and join them. Put a smile on your face and be a good example to others."

I hesitated and clung to his hand, but he gently pushed me from him. "Be a man," he said. "Today you truly begin life. You will find me waiting for you when it's time to leave."

I took a few steps, then stopped and looked but saw nothing. Then the faces of boys and girls came into view. I did not know a single one of them, and none of them knew me. I felt I was a stranger who had lost his way. But glances of curiosity were directed toward me, and one boy approached and asked, "Who brought you?"

"My father," I whispered.

"My father's dead," he said quite simply.

I did not know what to say. The gate was closed, letting out a pitiable screech. Some of the children burst into tears. The bell rang. A lady came along, followed by a group of men. The men began sorting us into ranks. We were formed into an intricate pattern in the great courtyard surrounded on three sides by high buildings of several floors; from each floor we were over-looked by a long balcony roofed in wood.

"This is your new home," said the woman. "Here too there are mothers and fathers. Here there is everything that is enjoyable and beneficial to knowledge and religion. Dry your tears and face life joyfully."

We submitted to the facts, and this submission brought a sort of con-tentment. Living beings were drawn to other living beings, and from the first moments my heart made friends with such boys as were to be my friends and fell in love with such girls as I was to be in love with, so that it seemed my misgivings had had no basis. I had never imagined school would have this rich variety. We played all sorts of different games: swings, the vaulting horse, ball games. In the music room we chanted our first songs. We also had our first introduction to language. We saw a globe of the Earth, which revolved and showed the various continents and countries. We started learning the numbers. The story of the Creator of the universe was read to us, we were told of His present world and of His Hereafter, and we heard examples of what He said. We ate delicious food, took a little nap, and woke up to go on with friendship and love, play and learning.

As our path revealed itself to us, however, we did not find it as totally sweet and unclouded as we had presumed. Dust-laden winds and unex-pected accidents came about suddenly, so we had to be watchful, at the ready, and very patient. It was not all a matter of playing and fooling around. Rivalries could bring about pain and hatred or give rise to fighting.

And while the lady would sometimes smile, she would often scowl and scold. Even more frequently she would resort to physical punishment.

In addition, the time for changing one's mind was over and gone and there was no question of ever returning to the paradise of home. Nothing lay ahead of us but exertion, struggle, and perseverance. Those who were able took advantage of the opportunities for success and happiness that presented themselves amid the worries.

The bell rang announcing the passing of the day and the end of work. The throngs of children rushed toward the gate, which was opened again. I bade farewell to friends and sweethearts and passed through the gate. I peered around but found no trace of my father, who had promised to be there. I stepped aside to wait. When I had waited for a long time without avail, I decided to return home on my own. After I had taken a few steps, a middle-aged man passed by, and I realized at once that I knew him. He came toward me, smiling, and shook me by the hand, saying, "It's a long time since we last met — how are you?"

With a nod of my head, I agreed with him and in turn asked, "And you, how are you?"

"As you can see, not all that good, the Almighty be praised!"

Again he shook me by the hand and went off. I proceeded a few steps, then came to a startled halt. Good Lord! Where was the street lined with gardens? Where had it disappeared to? When did all these vehicles invade it? And when did all these hordes of humanity come to rest upon its surface? How did these hills of refuse come to cover its sides? And where were the fields that bordered it? High buildings had taken over, the street surged with children, and disturbing noises shook the air. At various points stood conjurers showing off their tricks and making snakes appear from baskets. Then there was a band announcing the opening of a circus, with clowns and weight lifters walking in front. A line of trucks carrying central security troops crawled majestically by. The siren of a fire engine shrieked, and it was not clear how the vehicle would cleave its way to reach the blazing fire. A battle raged between a taxi driver and his passenger, while the passenger's wife called out for help and no one answered. Good God! I was in a daze. My head spun. I almost went crazy. How could all this have happened in half a day, between early morning and sunset? I would find the answer at home with my father. But where was my home? I could see only tall buildings and hordes of people. I hastened on to the crossroads between the gardens and Abu Khoda. I had to cross Abu Khoda to reach my house, but the stream of cars would not let up. The fire engine's siren was shrieking at full pitch as it moved at a snail's pace, and I said to myself, "Let the fire take its pleasure in what it consumes." Extremely irritated, I wondered when I would be able to cross. I stood there a long time, until the young lad employed at the ironing shop on the corner came up to me. He stretched out his arm and said gallantly, "Grandpa, let me take you across."

Mishima Yukio   Japan, 1925–1970

Swaddling Clothes   [1955]

Translated by Ivan Morris

He was always busy, Toshiko's husband. Even tonight he had to dash off to an appointment, leaving her to go home alone by taxi. But what else could a woman expect when she married an actor — an attractive one? No doubt she had been foolish to hope that he would spend the evening with her. And yet he must have known how she dreaded going back to their house, unhomely with its Western-style furniture and with the bloodstains still showing on the floor.

Toshiko had been oversensitive since girlhood: that was her nature. As the result of constant worrying she never put on weight, and now, an adult woman, she looked more like a transparent picture than a creature of flesh and blood. Her delicacy of spirit was evident to her most casual acquaintance.

Earlier that evening, when she had joined her husband at a night club, she had been shocked to find him entertaining friends with an account of "the incident." Sitting there in his American-style suit, puffing at a cigarette, he had seemed to her almost a stranger.

"It's a fantastic story," he was saying, gesturing flamboyantly as if in an attempt to outweigh the attractions of the dance band. "Here this new nurse for our baby arrives from the employment agency, and the very first thing I noticed about her is her stomach. It's enormous as if she had a pillow stuck under her kimono! No wonder, I thought, for I soon saw that she could eat more than the rest of us put together. She polished off the contents of our rice bin like that. . . ." He snapped his fingers. "'Gastric dilation' — that's how she explained her girth and her appetite. Well, the day before yesterday we heard groans and moans coming from the nursery. We rushed in and found her squatting on the floor, holding her stomach in her two hands, and moaning like a cow. Next to her our baby lay in his cot, scared out of his wits and crying at the top of his lungs. A pretty scene, I can tell you!"

"So the cat was out of the bag?" suggested one of their friends, a film actor like Toshiko's husband.

"Indeed it was! And it gave me the shock of my life. You see, I'd completely swallowed that story about 'gastric dilation.' Well, I didn't waste any time. I rescued our good rug from the floor and spread a blanket for her to lie on. The whole time the girl was yelling like a stuck pig. By the time the doctor from the maternity clinic arrived, the baby had already been born. But our sitting room was a pretty shambles!"

"Oh, that I'm sure of!" said another of their friends, and the whole company burst into laughter.

Toshiko was dumbfounded to hear her husband discussing the horrifying happening as though it were no more than an amusing incident which they chanced to have witnessed. She shut her eyes for a moment and all at once she saw the newborn baby lying before her: on the parquet floor the infant lay, and his frail body was wrapped in bloodstained newspapers.

Toshiko was sure that the doctor had done the whole thing out of spite. As if to emphasize his scorn for his mother who had given birth to a bastard under such sordid conditions, he had told his assistant to wrap the baby in some loose newspapers, rather than proper swaddling. This callous treatment of the newborn child had offended Toshiko. Overcoming her disgust at the entire scene, she had fetched a brand-new piece of flannel from her cupboard and, having swaddled the baby in it, had laid him carefully in an armchair.

This all had taken place in the evening after her husband had left the house. Toshiko had told him nothing of it, fearing that he would think her oversoft, oversentimental; yet the scene had engraved itself deeply in her mind. Tonight she sat silently thinking back on it, while the jazz orchestra brayed and her husband chatted cheerfully with his friends. She knew that she would never forget the sight of the baby, wrapped in stained newspapers and lying on the floor — it was a scene fit for a butchershop. Toshiko, whose own life had been spent in solid comfort, poignantly felt the wretchedness of the illegitimate baby.

I am the only person to have witnessed its shame, the thought occurred to her. The mother never saw her child lying there in its newspaper wrappings, and the baby itself of course didn't know. I alone shall have to preserve that terrible scene in my memory. When the baby grows up and wants to find out about his birth, there will be no one to tell him, so long as I preserve silence. How strange that I should have this feeling of guilt! After all, it was I who took him up from the floor, swathed him properly in flannel, and laid him down to sleep in the armchair.

They left the night club and Toshiko stepped into the taxi that her husband had called for her. "Take this lady to Ushigomé," he told the driver and shut the door from the outside. Toshiko gazed through the window at her husband's smiling face and noticed his strong, white teeth. Then she leaned back in the seat, oppressed by the knowledge that their life together was in some way too easy, too painless. It would have been difficult for her to put her thoughts into words. Through the rear window of the taxi she took a last look at her husband. He was striding along the street toward his Nash car, and soon the back of his rather garish tweed coat had blended with the figures of the passersby.

The taxi drove off, passed down a street dotted with bars and then by a theatre, in front of which the throngs of people jostled each other on the pavement. Although the performance had only just ended, the lights had already been turned out and in the half dark outside it was depressingly obvious that the cherry blossoms decorating the front of the theatre were merely scraps of white paper.

Even if that baby should grow up in ignorance of the secret of his birth, he can never become a respectable citizen, reflected Toshiko, pursuing the same train of thoughts. Those soiled newspaper swaddling clothes will be the symbol of his entire life. But why should I keep worrying about him so much? Is it because I feel uneasy about the future of my own child? Say twenty years from now, when our boy will have grown up into a fine, carefully educated young man, one day by a quirk of fate he meets that other boy, who then will also have turned twenty. And say that the other boy, who has been sinned against, savagely stabs him with a knife. . . .

It was a warm, overcast April night, but thoughts of the future made Toshiko feel cold and miserable. She shivered on the back seat of the car. No, when the time comes I shall take my son's place, she told herself suddenly. Twenty years from now I shall be forty-three. I shall go to that young man and tell him straight out about everything — about his newspaper swaddling clothes, and about how I went and wrapped him in flannel.

The taxi ran along the dark wide road that was bordered by the park and by the Imperial Palace moat. In the distance Toshiko noticed the pinpricks of light which came from the blocks of tall office buildings.

Twenty years from now that wretched child will be in utter misery. He will be living a desolate, hopeless, poverty-stricken existence — a lonely rat. What else could happen to a baby who has had such a birth? He'll be wandering through the streets by himself, cursing his father, loathing his mother.

No doubt Toshiko derived a certain satisfaction from her somber thoughts: she tortured herself with them without cease. The taxi approached Hanzomon and drove past the compound of the British Embassy. At that point the famous rows of cherry trees were spread out before Toshiko in all their purity. On the spur of the moment she decided to go and view the blossoms by herself in the dark night. It was a strange decision for a timid and unadventurous young woman, but then she was in a strange state of mind and she dreaded the return home. That evening all sorts of unsettling fancies had burst open in her mind.

She crossed the wide street — a slim, solitary figure in the darkness. As a rule when she walked in the traffic Toshiko used to cling fearfully to her companion, but tonight she darted alone between the cars and a moment later had reached the long narrow park that borders the Palace moat. Chidorigafuchi, it is called — the Abyss of the Thousand Birds.

Tonight the whole park had become a grove of blossoming cherry trees. Under the calm cloudy sky the blossoms formed a mass of solid whiteness. The paper lanterns that hung from wires between the trees had been put out; in their place electric light bulbs, red, yellow, and green, shone dully beneath the blossoms. It was well past ten o'clock and most of the flower-viewers had gone home. As the occasional passersby strolled through the park, they would automatically kick aside the empty bottles or crush the waste paper beneath their feet.

Newspapers, thought Toshiko, her mind going back once again to those happenings. Bloodstained newspapers. If a man were ever to hear of that piteous birth and know that it was he who had lain there, it would ruin his entire life. To think that I, a perfect stranger, should from now on have to keep such a secret—the secret of a man's whole existences. . . .

Lost in these thoughts, Toshiko walked on through the park. Most of the people still remaining there were quiet couples; no one paid her any attention. She noticed two people sitting on a stone bench beside the moat, not looking at the blossoms, but gazing silently at the water. Pitch black it was, and swathed in heavy shadows. Beyond the moat the somber forest of the Imperial Palace blocked her view. The trees reached up, to form a solid dark mass against the night sky. Toshiko walked slowly along the path beneath the blossoms hanging heavily overhead.

On a stone bench, slightly apart from the others, she noticed a pale object—not, as she had at first imagined, a pile of cherry blossoms, nor a garment forgotten by one of the visitors to the park. Only when she came closer did she see that it was a human form lying on the bench. Was it, she wondered, one of those miserable drunks often to be seen sleeping in public places? Obviously not, for the body had been systematically covered with newspapers, and it was the whiteness of those papers that had attracted Toshiko's attention. Standing by the bench, she gazed down at the sleeping figure.

It was a man in a brown jersey who lay there, curled up on layers of newspapers, other newspapers covering him. No doubt this had become his normal night residence now that spring had arrived. Toshiko gazed down at the man's dirty, unkempt hair, which in places had become hopelessly matted. As she observed the sleeping figure wrapped in its newspapers, she was inevitably reminded of the baby who had lain on the floor in its wretched swaddling clothes. The shoulder of the man's jersey rose and fell in the darkness in time with his heavy breathing.

It seemed to Toshiko that all her fears and premonitions had suddenly taken concrete form. In the darkness the man's pale forehead stood out, and it was a young forehead, though carved with wrinkles of long poverty and hardship. His khaki trousers had been slightly pulled up; on his sockless feet he wore a pair of battered gym shoes. She could not see his face and suddenly had an overmastering desire to get one glimpse of it.

She walked to the head of the bench and looked down. The man's head was half buried in his arms, but Toshiko could see that he was surprisingly young. She noticed the thick eyebrows and the fine bridge of his nose. His slightly open mouth was alive with youth.

But Toshiko had approached too close. In the silent night the newspaper bedding rustled, and abruptly the man opened his eyes. Seeing the young woman standing directly beside him, he raised himself with a jerk, and his eyes lit up. A second later a powerful hand reached out and seized Toshiko by her slender wrist.

She did not feel in the least afraid and made no effort to free herself. In a flash the thought had struck her, Ah, so the twenty years have already gone by! The forest of the Imperial Palace was pitch dark and utterly silent.

Salman Rushdie   India, b. 1947

The Prophet's Hair   [1994]

Early in the year 19 —, when Srinagar was under the spell of a winter
so fierce it could crack men's bones as if they were glass, a young man
upon whose cold-pinked skin there lay, like a frost, the unmistakable sheen
of wealth was to be seen entering the most wretched and disreputable part
of the city, where the houses of wood and corrugated iron seemed perpetually on the verge of losing their balance, and asking in low, grave tones
where he might go to engage the services of a dependably professional burglar. The young man's name was Atta, and the rogues in that part of town
directed him gleefully into ever darker and less public alleys, until in a yard
wet with the blood of a slaughtered chicken he was set upon by two men
whose faces he never saw, robbed of the substantial bank-roll which he had
insanely brought on his solitary excursion, and beaten within an inch of
his life.

Night fell. His body was carried by anonymous hands to the edge of the
lake, whence it was transported by shikara across the water and deposited,
torn and bleeding, on the deserted embankment of the canal which led to
the gardens of Shalimar. At dawn the next morning a flower-vendor was
rowing his boat through water to which the cold of the night had given the
cloudy consistency of wild honey when he saw the prone form of young
Atta, who was just beginning to stir and moan, and on whose now deathly
pale skin the sheen of wealth could still be made out dimly beneath an actual layer of frost.

The flower-vendor moored his craft and by stooping over the mouth of
the injured man was able to learn the poor fellow's address, which was
mumbled through lips that could scarcely move; whereupon, hoping for
a large tip, the hawker rowed Atta home to a large house on the shores of
the lake, where a beautiful but inexplicably bruised young woman and her
distraught, but equally handsome mother, neither of whom, it was clear
from their eyes, had slept a wink from worrying, screamed at the sight of
their Atta — who was the elder brother of the beautiful young woman — lying
motionless amidst the funereally stunted winter blooms of the hopeful
florist.

The flower-vendor was indeed paid off handsomely, not least to ensure
his silence, and plays no further part in our story. Atta himself, suffering
terribly from exposure as well as a broken skull, entered a coma which
caused the city's finest doctors to shrug helplessly. It was therefore all the
more remarkable that on the very next evening the most wretched and disreputable part of the city received a second unexpected visitor. This was

Huma, the sister of the unfortunate young man, and her question was the same as her brother's, and asked in the same low, grave tones:

"Where may I hire a thief?"

The story of the rich idiot who had come looking for a burglar was already common knowledge in those insalubrious gullies, but this time the young woman added: "I should say that I am carrying no money, nor am I wearing any jewelery items. My father has disowned me and will pay no ransom if I am kidnapped; and a letter has been lodged with the Deputy Commissioner of Police, my uncle, to be opened in the event of my not being safe at home by morning. In that letter he will find full details of my journey here, and he will move Heaven and Earth to punish my assailants."

Her exceptional beauty, which was visible even through the enormous welts and bruises disfiguring her arms and forehead, coupled with the oddity of her inquiries, had attracted a sizable group of curious onlookers, and because her little speech seemed to them to cover just about everything, no one attempted to injure her in any way, although there were some raucous comments to the effect that it was pretty peculiar for someone who was trying to hire a crook to invoke the protection of a high-up policeman uncle.

She was directed into ever darker and less public alleys until finally in a gully as dark as ink an old woman with eyes which stared so piercingly that Huma instantly understood she was blind motioned her through a doorway from which darkness seemed to be pouring like smoke. Clenching her fists, angrily ordering her heart to behave normally, Huma followed the old woman into the gloom-wrapped house.

The faintest conceivable rivulet of candlelight trickled through the darkness; following this unreliable yellow thread (because she could no longer see the old lady), Huma received a sudden sharp blow to the shins and cried out involuntarily, after which she at once bit her lip, angry at having revealed her mounting terror to whoever or whatever waited before her, shrouded in blackness.

She had, in fact, collided with a low table on which a single candle burned and beyond which a mountainous figure could be made out, sitting cross-legged on the floor. "Sit, sit," said a man's calm, deep voice, and her legs, needing no more flowery invitation, buckled beneath her at the terse command. Clutching her left hand in her right, she forced her voice to respond evenly:

"And you, sir, will be the thief I have been requesting?"

Shifting its weight very slightly, the shadow-mountain informed Huma that all criminal activity originating in this zone was well organized and also centrally controlled, so that all requests for what might be termed freelance work had to be channelled through this room.

He demanded comprehensive details of the crime to be committed, including a precise inventory of items to be acquired, also a clear statement of all financial inducements being offered with no gratuities excluded, plus, for filing purposes only, a summary of the motives for the application.

At this, Huma, as though remembering something, stiffened both in body and resolve and replied loudly that her motives were entirely a matter for herself; that she would discuss details with no one but the thief himself; but that the rewards she proposed could only be described as "lavish."

"All I am willing to disclose to you, sir, since it appears that I am on the premises of some sort of employment agency, is that in return for such lavish rewards I must have the most desperate criminal at your disposal, a man for whom life holds no terrors, not even the fear of God.

"The worst of fellows, I tell you — nothing less will do!"

At this a paraffin storm-lantern was lighted, and Huma saw facing her a grey-haired giant down whose left cheek ran the most sinister of scars, a cicatrice in the shape of the letter *sín* in the Nastaliq script. She was gripped by the insupportably nostalgic notion that the bogeyman of her childhood nursery had risen up to confront her, because her ayah had always forestalled any incipient acts of disobedience by threatening Huma and Atta: "You don't watch out and I'll send that one to steal you away — that Sheikh Sín, the Thief of Thieves!"

Here, grey-haired but unquestionably scarred, was the notorious criminal himself — and was she out of her mind, were her ears playing tricks, or had he truly just announced that, given the stated circumstances, he himself was the only man for the job?

Struggling hard against the newborn goblins of nostalgia, Huma warned the fearsome volunteer that only a matter of extreme urgency and peril would have brought her unescorted into these ferocious streets.

"Because we can afford no last-minute backings-out," she continued, "I am determined to tell you everything, keeping back no secrets whatsoever. If, after hearing me out, you are still prepared to proceed, then we shall do everything in our power to assist you, and to make you rich."

The old thief shrugged, nodded, spat. Huma began her story.

Six days ago, everything in the household of her father, the wealthy moneylender Hashim, had been as it always was. At breakfast her mother had spooned khichri lovingly on to the moneylender's plate; the conversation had been filled with those expressions of courtesy and solicitude on which the family prided itself.

Hashim was fond of pointing out that while he was not a godly man he set great store by "living honorably in the world." In that spacious lakeside residence, all outsiders were greeted with the same formality and respect, even those unfortunates who came to negotiate for small fragments of

Hashim's large fortune, and of whom he naturally asked an interest rate of over seventy percent, partly, as he told his khichri-spooning wife, "to teach these people the value of money; let them only learn that, and they will be cured of this fever of borrowing borrowing all the time — so you see that if my plans succeed, I shall put myself out of business!"

In their children, Atta and Huma, the moneylender and his wife had successfully sought to inculcate the virtues of thrift, plain dealing and a healthy independence of spirit. On this, too, Hashim was fond of congratulating himself.

Breakfast ended; the family members wished one another a fulfilling day. Within a few hours, however, the glassy contentment of that household, of that life of porcelain delicacy and alabaster sensibilities, was to be shattered beyond all hope of repair.

The moneylender summoned his personal shikara and was on the point of stepping into it when, attracted by a glint of silver, he noticed a small vial floating between the boat and his private quay. On an impulse, he scooped it out of the glutinous water.

It was a cylinder of tinted glass cased in exquisitely wrought silver, and Hashim saw within its walls a silver pendant bearing a single strand of human hair.

Closing his fist around this unique discovery, he muttered to the boatman that he'd changed his plans, and hurried to his sanctum, where, behind closed doors, he feasted his eyes on his find.

There can be no doubt that Hashim the moneylender knew from the first that he was in possession of the famous relic of the Prophet Muhammad, that revered hair whose theft from its shrine at Hazratbal mosque the previous morning had created an unprecedented hue and cry in the valley.

The thieves — no doubt alarmed by the pandemonium, by the procession through the streets of endless ululating crocodiles of lamentation, by the riots, the political ramifications and by the massive police search which was commanded and carried out by men whose entire careers now hung upon the finding of this lost hair — had evidently panicked and hurled the vial into the gelatine bosom of the lake.

Having found it by a stroke of great good fortune, Hashim's duty as a citizen was clear: the hair must be restored to its shrine, and the state to equanimity and peace.

But the moneylender had a different notion.

All around him in his study was the evidence of his collector's mania. There were enormous glass cases full of impaled butterflies from Gulmarg, three dozen scale models in various metals of the legendary cannon Zamzama, innumerable swords, a Naga spear, ninety-four terracotta camels of

the sort sold on railway station platforms, many samovars, and a whole zo-
ology of tiny sandalwood animals, which had originally been carved to serve
as children's bathtime toys.

"And after all," Hashim told himself, "the Prophet would have disapproved mightily of this relic-worship. He abhorred the idea of being deified!
So, by keeping this hair from its distracted devotees, I perform — do I not? —
a finer service than I would by returning it! Naturally, I don't want it for its
religious value . . . I'm a man of the world, of this world. I see it purely as a
secular object of great rarity and blinding beauty. In short, it's the silver vial
I desire, more than the hair.

"They say there are American millionaires who purchase stolen art masterpieces and hide them away — they would know how I feel. I must, must
have it!"

Every collector must share his treasures with one other human being,
and Hashim summoned — and told — his only son Atta, who was deeply per-
turbed but, having been sworn to secrecy, only spilled the beans when the
troubles became too terrible to bear.

The youth excused himself and left his father alone in the crowded solitude of his collections. Hashim was sitting erect in a hard, straight-backed
chair, gazing intently at the beautiful vial.

It was well known that the moneylender never ate lunch, so it was not
until evening that a servant entered the sanctum to summon his master to
the dining-table. He found Hashim as Atta had left him. The same, and not
the same — for now the moneylender looked swollen, distended. His eyes
bulged even more than they always had, they were red-rimmed, and his
knuckles were white.

He seemed to be on the point of bursting! As though, under the influence of the misappropriated relic, he had filled up with some spectral fluid
which might at any moment ooze uncontrollably from his every bodily
opening.

He had to be helped to the table, and then the explosion did indeed take
place.

Seemingly careless of the effect of his words on the carefully constructed
and fragile constitution of the family's life, Hashim began to gush, to spume
long streams of awful truths. In horrified silence, his children heard their father turn upon his wife, and reveal to her that for many years their marriage
had been the worst of his afflictions. "An end to politeness!" he thundered.
"An end to hypocrisy."

Next, and in the same spirit, he revealed to his family the existence of a
mistress; he informed them also of his regular visits to paid women. He told
his wife that, far from being the principal beneficiary of his will, she would
receive no more than the eighth portion which was her due under Islamic

law. Then he turned upon his children, screaming at Atta for his lack of academic ability — "A dope! I have been cursed with a dope!" — and accusing his daughter of lasciviousness, because she went around the city barefaced, which was unseemly for any good Muslim girl to do. She should, he commanded, enter purdah forthwith.

Hashim left the table without having eaten and fell into the deep sleep of a man who has got many things off his chest, leaving his children stunned, in tears, and the dinner going cold on the sideboard under the gaze of an anticipatory bearer.

At five o'clock the next morning the moneylender forced his family to rise, wash and say their prayers. From then on, he began to pray five times daily for the first time in his life, and his wife and children were obliged to do likewise.

Before breakfast, Huma saw the servants, under her father's direction, constructing a great heap of books in the garden and setting fire to it. The only volume left untouched was the Qur'an, which Hashim wrapped in a silken cloth and placed on a table in the hall. He ordered each member of his family to read passages from this book for at least two hours per day. Visits to the cinema were forbidden. And if Atta invited male friends to the house, Huma was to retire to her room.

By now, the family had entered a state of shock and dismay; but there was worse to come.

That afternoon, a trembling debtor arrived at the house to confess his inability to pay the latest installment of interest owed, and made the mistake of reminding Hashim, in somewhat blustering fashion, of the Qur'an's strictures against usury. The moneylender flew into a rage and attacked the fellow with one of his large collection of bullwhips.

By mischance, later the same day a second defaulter came to plead for time, and was seen fleeing Hashim's study with a great gash in his arm, because Huma's father had called him a thief of other men's money and had tried to cut off the wretch's right hand with one of the thirty-eight kukri knives hanging on the study walls.

These breaches of the family's unwritten laws of decorum alarmed Atta and Huma, and when, that evening, their mother attempted to calm Hashim down, he struck her on the face with an open hand. Atta leapt to his mother's defense and he, too, was sent flying.

"From now on," Hashim bellowed, "there's going to be some discipline around here!"

The moneylender's wife began a fit of hysterics which continued throughout that night and the following day, and which so provoked her husband that he threatened her with divorce, at which she fled to her room, locked the door and subsided into a raga of sniffling. Huma now lost her composure, challenged her father openly, and announced (with that same independence of spirit which he had encouraged in her) that she would wear no cloth over her face; apart from anything else, it was bad for the eyes.

On hearing this, her father disowned her on the spot and gave her one week in which to pack her bags and go.

By the fourth day, the fear in the air of the house had become so thick that it was difficult to walk around. Atta told his shock-numbed sister: "We are descending to gutter-level — but I know what must be done."

That afternoon, Hashim left home accompanied by two hired thugs to extract the unpaid dues from his two insolvent clients. Atta went immediately to his father's study. Being the son and heir, he possessed his own key to the moneylender's safe. This he now used, and removing the little vial from its hiding-place, he slipped it into his trouser pocket and re-locked the safe door.

Now he told Huma the secret of what his father had fished out of Lake Dal, and exclaimed: "Maybe I'm crazy — maybe the awful things that are happening have made me cracked — but I am convinced there will be no peace in our house until this hair is out of it."

His sister at once agreed that the hair must be returned, and Atta set off in a hired shikara to Hazratbal mosque. Only when the boat had delivered him into the throng of the distraught faithful which was swirling around the desecrated shrine did Atta discover that the relic was no longer in his pocket. There was only a hole, which his mother, usually so attentive to household matters, must have overlooked under the stress of recent events.

Atta's initial surge of chagrin was quickly replaced by a feeling of profound relief.

"Suppose," he imagined, "that I had already announced to the mullahs that the hair was on my person! They would never have believed me now — and this mob would have lynched me! At any rate, it has gone, and that's a load off my mind." Feeling more contented than he had for days, the young man returned home.

Here he found his sister bruised and weeping in the hall; upstairs, in her bedroom, his mother wailed like a brand-new widow. He begged Huma to tell him what had happened, and when she replied that their father, returning from his brutal business trip, had once again noticed a glint of silver between boat and quay, had once again scooped up the errant relic, and was consequently in a rage to end all rages, having beaten the truth out of her — then Atta buried his face in his hands and sobbed out his opinion, which was that the hair was persecuting them, and had come back to finish the job.

It was Huma's turn to think of a way out of their troubles.

While her arms turned black and blue and great stains spread across her forehead, she hugged her brother and whispered to him that she was determined to get rid of the hair *at all costs* — she repeated this last phrase several times.

"The hair," she then declared, "was stolen from the mosque; so it can be stolen from this house. But it must be a genuine robbery, carried out by a bona-fide thief, not by one of us who are under the hair's thrall — by a thief so desperate that he fears neither capture nor curses."

Unfortunately, she added, the theft would be ten times harder to pull off now that their father, knowing that there had already been one attempt on the relic, was certainly on his guard.

"Can you do it?"

Huma, in a room lit by candle and storm-lantern, ended her account with one further question: "What assurances can you give that the job holds no terrors for you still?"

The criminal, spitting, stated that he was not in the habit of providing references, as a cook might, or a gardener, but he was not alarmed so easily, certainly not by any children's djinni of a curse. Huma had to be content with this boast, and proceeded to describe the details of the proposed burglary.

"Since my brother's failure to return the hair to the mosque, my father has taken to sleeping with his precious treasure under his pillow. However, he sleeps alone, and very energetically; only enter his room without waking him, and he will certainly have tossed and turned quite enough to make the theft a simple matter. When you have the vial, come to my room," and here she handed Sheikh Sín a plan of her home, "and I will hand over all the jewelery owned by my mother and myself. You will find . . . it is worth . . . that is, you will be able to get a fortune for it . . ."

It was evident that her self-control was weakening and that she was on the point of physical collapse.

"Tonight," she burst out finally. "You must come tonight!"

No sooner had she left the room than the old criminal's body was convulsed by a fit of coughing: he spat blood into an old vanaspati can. The great Sheikh, the "Thief of Thieves," had become a sick man, and every day the time drew nearer when some young pretender to his power would stick a dagger in his stomach. A lifelong addiction to gambling had left him almost as poor as he had been when, decades ago, he had started out in this line of work as a mere pickpocket's apprentice; so in the extraordinary commission he had accepted from the moneylender's daughter he saw his opportunity of amassing enough wealth at a stroke to leave the valley for ever, and acquire the luxury of a respectable death which would leave his stomach intact.

As for the Prophet's hair, well, neither he nor his blind wife had ever had much to say for prophets — that was one thing they had in common with the moneylender's thunderstruck clan.

It would not do, however, to reveal the nature of this, his last crime, to his four sons. To his consternation, they had all grown up to be hopelessly devout men, who even spoke of making the pilgrimage to Mecca some day. "Absurd!" their father would laugh at them. "Just tell me how you will go?" For, with a parent's absolutist love, he had made sure they were all provided with a lifelong source of high income by crippling them at birth, so that, as they dragged themselves around the city, they earned excellent money in the begging business.

The children, then, could look after themselves.

He and his wife would be off soon with the jewel-boxes of the money-lender's women. It was a timely chance indeed that had brought the beautiful bruised girl into his corner of the town.

That night, the large house on the shore of the lake lay blindly waiting, with silence lapping at its walls. A burglar's night: clouds in the sky and mists on the winter water. Hashim the moneylender was asleep, the only member of his family to whom sleep had come that night. In another room, his son Atta lay deep in the coils of his coma with a blood-clot forming on his brain, watched over by a mother who had let down her long greying hair to show her grief, a mother who placed warm compresses on his head with gestures redolent of impotence. In a third bedroom Huma waited, fully dressed, amidst the jewel-heavy caskets of her desperation.

At last a bulbul sang softly from the garden below her window and, creeping downstairs, she opened a door to the bird, on whose face there was a scar in the shape of the Nastaliq letter *sín*.

Noiselessly, the bird flew up the stairs behind her. At the head of the staircase they parted, moving in opposite directions along the corridor of their conspiracy without a glance at one another.

Entering the moneylender's room with professional ease, the burglar, Sín, discovered that Huma's predictions had been wholly accurate. Hashim lay sprawled diagonally across his bed, the pillow untenanted by his head, the prize easily accessible. Step by padded step, Sín moved towards the goal.

It was at this point that, in the bedroom next door, young Atta sat bolt upright in his bed, giving his mother a great fright, and without any warning — prompted by goodness knows what pressure of the blood-clot upon his brain — began screaming at the top of his voice:

"Thief! Thief! Thief!"

It seems probable that his poor mind had been dwelling, in these last moments, upon his own father; but it is impossible to be certain, because having uttered these three emphatic words the young man fell back upon his pillow and died.

At once his mother set up a screeching and a wailing and a keening and a howling so earsplittingly intense that they completed the work which

Atta's cry had begun — that is, her laments penetrated the walls of her husband's bedroom and brought Hashim wide awake.

Sheikh Sín was just deciding whether to dive beneath the bed or brain the moneylender good and proper when Hashim grabbed the tiger-striped swordstick which always stood propped up in a corner beside his bed, and rushed from the room without so much as noticing the burglar who stood on the opposite side of the bed in the darkness. Sín stooped quickly and removed the vial containing the Prophet's hair from its hiding-place.

Meanwhile Hashim had erupted into the corridor, having unsheathed the sword inside his cane. In his right hand he held the weapon and was waving it about dementedly. His left hand was shaking the stick. A shadow came rushing towards him through the midnight darkness of the passageway and, in his somnolent anger, the moneylender thrust his sword fatally through its heart. Turning up the light, he found that he had murdered his daughter, and under the dire influence of this accident he was so overwhelmed by remorse that he turned the sword upon himself, fell upon it and so extinguished his life. His wife, the sole surviving member of the family, was driven mad by the general carnage and had to be committed to an asylum for the insane by her brother, the city's Deputy Commissioner of Police.

Sheikh Sín had quickly understood that the plan had gone awry.

Abandoning the dream of the jewel-boxes when he was but a few yards from its fulfilment, he climbed out of Hashim's window and made his escape during the appalling events described above. Reaching home before dawn, he woke his wife and confessed his failure. It would be necessary, he whispered, for him to vanish for a while. Her blind eyes never opened until he had gone.

The noise in the Hashim household had roused their servants and even managed to awaken the night-watchman, who had been fast asleep as usual on his charpoy by the street-gate. They alerted the police, and the Deputy Commissioner himself was informed. When he heard of Huma's death, the mournful officer opened and read the sealed letter which his niece had given him, and instantly led a large detachment of armed men into the light-repellent gullies of the most wretched and disreputable part of the city.

The tongue of a malicious cat-burglar named Huma's fellow-conspirator; the finger of an ambitious bank-robber pointed at the house in which he lay concealed; and although Sín managed to crawl through a hatch in the attic and attempt a roof-top escape, a bullet from the Deputy Commissioner's own rifle penetrated his stomach and brought him crashing messily to the ground at the feet of Huma's enraged uncle.

From the dead thief's pocket rolled a vial of tinted glass, cased in filigree silver.

*   *   *

The recovery of the Prophet's hair was announced at once on All-India Radio. One month later, the valley's holiest men assembled at the Hazratbal mosque and formally authenticated the relic. It sits to this day in a closely guarded vault by the shores of the loveliest of lakes in the heart of the valley which was once closer than any other place on earth to Paradise.

But before our story can properly be concluded, it is necessary to record that when the four sons of the dead Sheikh awoke on the morning of his death, having unwittingly spent a few minutes under the same roof as the famous hair, they found that a miracle had occurred, that they were all sound of limb and strong of wind, as whole as they might have been if their father had not thought to smash their legs in the first hours of their lives. They were, all four of them, very properly furious, because the miracle had reduced their earning powers by 75 percent, at the most conservative estimate; so they were ruined men.

Only the Sheikh's widow had some reason for feeling grateful, because although her husband was dead she had regained her sight, so that it was possible for her to spend her last days gazing once more upon the beauties of the valley of Kashmir.

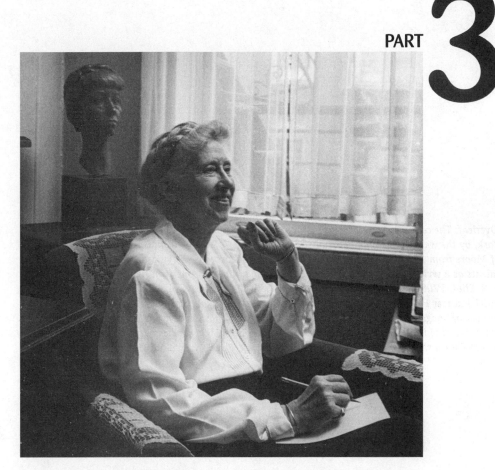

Approaching
POETRY

Overleaf: The celebrated poet Marianne Moore, photographed in 1953 in Brooklyn, New York, by the well-known photojournalist Esther Bobley. A Gaston Lachaise bust sculpture of Moore from 1921 can be seen in the background. Moore was recognized early on for her talents as a writer, and she earned the support of many major American figures including T. S. Eliot, William Carlos Williams, and Elizabeth Bishop. Her Collected Poems *won the 1951 Pulitzer Prize for Poetry along with the National Book Award. Moore is known for her use of imagery of the natural world in her poems and has written that poetry "is the art of creating imaginary gardens with real toads." (See p. 694 for her poem "Poetry" and p. 1447 for a short biography.)* Reprinted by permission of the Estate of Esther Bubley.

Poetry is a conversation with the world; poetry is a conversation with the words on the page in which you allow those words to speak back to you; and poetry is a conversation with yourself.

Naomi Shihab Nye

Reading Poetry

Why would a person feel suddenly compelled to write a poem? Very few if any of us who are not fiction writers or playwrights decide one day to sit down and write a novel or a play. And yet time and time again, people who do not consider themselves poets write poems. After the events of September 11, 2001, thousands of poems were written, sent, stored away, stuck in a wallet or purse, pasted in a scrapbook. Students took time out from their usual classroom studies and wrote a poem. Parents sent their poems to their children away at school or gone from the nest. Poems expressed by "non-poets" showed up on Web sites and subway walls, in newsletters, within in-house publications, during school announcements, and in memos, letters, and e-mails. People from every walk of life wrote and expressed their reactions, what they were feeling. Why do people write poetry? What does that show about them? About us? And what does that suggest about the nature and value of poetry — about what poetry is and what poetry does?

WHAT IS POETRY?

We can usually tell someone what a novel, a play, or an essay is, but a poem can be baffling to explain. It can't be defined as writing that has meter: A lot of poetry is nonmetrical. It's not confined to writing that rhymes: Poetry doesn't always use rhyme. Though most poetry is written in lines, prose poems don't have line divisions. Much poetry uses figurative language and is intense and emotional — but the same is true for powerful prose. Whatever characteristics one tries to apply are never typical of all poetry or exclusive to poetry alone. So, what is this thing we call poetry?

Those who we'd think ought to know usually offer personal responses: e. e. cummings said that poetry is "dancing on your own grave." Ezra Pound purportedly said it is "what poets write." Emily Dickinson described poetry by its effect: "If I read a book [and] it makes my whole body so cold no fire ever can warm me, I know THAT is poetry. If I feel physically as if the top of my head were taken off, I know THAT is poetry. These are the only ways I know it. Is there any other way?"

What Does Poetry Do?

Maybe a better way to approach the question "What is poetry?" is to ask "What does poetry do?" Poetry comes from some deep impulse that needs expression; it arises when no other form of expression is sufficient under the circumstances. The poem comes from a sense of urgency; it feels it must be "let out," shared, given, offered up. It has about it a sense of wonder. Lucille Clifton once said, "Poetry began when somebody walked off a savanna or out of a cave and looked up at the sky with wonder and said, 'Ah-h-h!' *That* was the first poem. The urge toward 'Ah-h-h' is very human, it's in everybody." Every day, each of us feels that impulse, and we go "Ah-h-h!" or "Wow!" or "Oh no!" or simply sigh.

Poetry often crosses, or even eliminates, boundaries. We are all citizens in the culture of joy, pain, anger, love, fear, despair, hope. Every one of us carries the emotions of every other one of us. Our situations and stories and conflicts may differ, but the news from the heart comes to each of us. And though we can't claim "I know just how you feel," we can say with confidence, "I, too, have known that feeling."

And poetry gives voice. For many of us in our day-to-day lives, voices come at us — from the news media, sales pitches, movies, and general information overload. It often seems our voices are not heard. Poetry offers a chance to speak, and speak from the deepest part of our selves: We feel liberated and in touch with our selves. The words are our words, the rhythms are our rhythms, the clumsiness and sophistication of phrasings are ours, the sounds, the tones, even the attempts to be artful are authentic.

Former Poet Laureate Rita Dove has stated, "[I want] to help people see that poetry is not something above them or somehow distant; it's part of their very lives. I would like to remind people that we *have* an interior life — even if we don't talk about it because it's not expedient, because it's not cool, because it's potentially embarrassing — and without that interior life, we are shells, we are nothing." Is that also why, under a sense of urgency, many feel the impulse to express themselves in poetry? Do they suddenly experience that connection to their inner lives? Do thoughts and feelings rise up and ask, even demand, to be expressed, and expressed in their own voice?

WHY READ POETRY?

Poetry gives the poet a voice, but why do others read poetry? People read poetry to hear that what they themselves are moved by and want to express is something others do too. They read poetry to relish an artist's craftsmanship; to experience the beauty of the words and sounds and pictures through which a poem expresses emotions and ideas or tells a story; to feel life with greater intensity and to open themselves to wider and more inclusive experiences; to feel connected to many things that they are pulled away from, things they cherish and need in their lives. People read poetry to recover what they have lost or to hold on to what they have, to be challenged, to be shaken, to be comforted.

Traditionally poetry has been classified in three major types: *narrative,* poems that tell stories; *dramatic,* plays written in verse or shorter poems that use techniques from drama, such as dialogue; and *lyric,* usually shorter poems characterized by imagination, melody, and intensity of feelings, all combined to create a unified effect. Other less central types include poetry of ideas (verse essays), satiric poetry, and light verse. Most of the poetry in this book is lyric poetry. **Lyric** poems tend to focus on an event, experience, idea, reaction, or feeling that has impressed the poet deeply, rendering it in such sharp, concrete detail, with an imaginative approach and a musical use of language, that readers often feel that the experience, and the poem, are actually their own.

One of the principles in choosing poems for this book was to provide examples of many different poetic styles, approaches, and types. Some poems and some kinds of poetry you will like better than others, but we hope that you give them all a chance and remain open to the variety of cultures and experiences they embody.

ACTIVE READING: Poetry

The essence of poetry is elusive. There is no one way to pin it down. Although that may be intimidating, it is also part of the appeal, part of the seductiveness of poetry. We enter the world of a poem, every poem, not really knowing what to expect. And whenever we enter something new—whether an unfamiliar city, or a new job, or a new relationship—we tend to feel uncertain. We have to look around. We have to be attentive. Here are some suggestions for reading poetry with an active imagination.

- *Look and listen.* Be attentive to everything in and about the poem. Start with its shape, the way the poem appears on the page. Listen to its sounds—the way it sounds when it's read aloud, the rhythms, the word sounds, and the combinations of sounds. Look for what it helps you see — the mental pictures called up by some of the words.

- *Watch the words.* After shape and sounds, start paying attention to what the words say — not what the whole poem *means,* but what the words *say.* Don't be overly eager to figure out what a poem "means," especially some deep, "hidden" meaning. When you walk through a wood, you don't keep saying, "What does that tree mean?" or "What does that stone mean?" You accept them for what they are. So it should be with poetry: Look at the words, listen for what they say, and understand them as best you can. And if at first you don't understand all that much, don't worry — there are many things in a poem that you can experience even before you "understand" it.

- *Read straight through.* Go straight through a poem the first time you read it. If you wonder about a word or want to savor a line, stop only briefly. Then keep going. Get a feel for the poem without worrying about what you don't know or understand.

- *Interact with the work.* Reading a poem differs from reading a newspaper or an e-mail message or a textbook. You usually read those to glean some information or ideas. Many poems, of course, also contain information and ideas. But they can do other things: They can lead us to feel intensely, to experience deeply, to perceive freshly, to extend our understanding of experiences different from our own, and to affirm our own ideas, feelings, and experiences.

REREADING: Poetry

Rereading is just as important for poetry as for fiction, perhaps more so. Reread until you've internalized parts of the poem. Focus on something different each time you go back. If you're open to the poem, it will give and give. Here are some suggestions for rereading.

- *Slow down.* You have to slow down to read a poem. You can't speed-read a poem any more than you can speed-listen to your favorite recordings. So slow down and listen: Listen for, and to, the poem.

- *Read aloud.* Many poems are meant to be heard. Their sounds and rhythms need to be read aloud. In poet Robert Pinsky's phrase, you should "say the poem" so the poem comes out from within you as you vocalize the poem and feel the words, phrases, and rhythms in your mouth, the way you did as a kid when you kept saying certain words over and over just because they felt good. Hide if you are worried that someone will laugh at you.

- *Hear the "music."* Poems work with what is often called the musicality of language, by blending the sounds and rhythms of words and word connections. It's not unlike a song lyric together with its music, but in this case the poem is aspiring to music through the sounds and rhythms of language.

- *Focus on what catches your attention.* Make sure what you focus on is something *in* the poem, not an impression you have formed. You might be drawn to a particular image, how it alters your usual perception of something. Maybe you like the sounds of the language or the way the rhythm shifts or remains regular in every line. Maybe the poem is funny or poignant or both. You don't have to have a masterful grasp of the whole poem to notice things within it or wonder about it or begin talking about it. Paying passionate attention to what is actually in a poem is a wise way to start.

- *Follow the sentences.* The sentences in the poem may be broken up into lines, but they are still sentences. Get their sense correct. If the order of words in a sentence is inverted, it's important to pay attention to cues that identify what is subject and what is object. If a poet uses incomplete sentences, "fragments," try to figure out the purpose behind them. After working out where sentences start and stop, focus on the lines: Begin noticing what the line divisions and line breaks add to the experience of the sentence.

- *Ask questions.* You can, of course, ask what a poem means, but you don't need to start with that question. Try instead asking questions such as, What is going on in this poem? What is this poem doing? Why am I drawn to that phrase or line? What is the poem connecting me with or challenging me about? How is the poem shifting my usual way of perceiving things and leading me to reconsider the ways I've thought and felt?

The imagery of one line exudes a sparkling fountain of energy that fills your spirit.

Jimmy Santiago Baca

CHAPTER 10 Words and Images

Perhaps you are hesitant about your ability to understand a poem, or even have the feeling that a poem is in some code you have to break or that only the poet or your teacher can comprehend it. Or perhaps you think that poetry can "just mean anything." With prose, we usually gain understanding by reading whole units of focused meaning (sentences and paragraphs). But poems are often not written that way, and maybe that's a reason why we feel poems are difficult to grasp. Poems ask you to look both at and within lines and sentences, to focus your attention on particular words and particular images in them.

To comprehend a poem, then, requires attention to its words. That's obvious enough. How can you read without looking at the words? But when you read poetry, you not only have to look at words but also need to pay closer attention than you usually would. **Diction**, the choice and arrangement of words, is an important aspect of style, whether in prose (see p. 171) or poetry. And, like fiction, but more so, you need not only to look for the "meaning" of words with your mind but also to respond to many words with your senses. This chapter's aim is to enable you to enjoy and appreciate poetry more fully by enjoying and appreciating words and images more fully.

Like most writers, poets love words — their look, their sounds, their textures, the associations clustered around them, what they evoke, their power. Poets roll words around on their tongues and in their minds, experimenting with different combinations, playing with them, listening to the results. They care about their meanings, and the uses and abuses of those meanings. They look for ways to put their feelings or ideas into exactly the right words, ones with the right sounds and textures and meanings. So, even though this chapter focuses on words — on their denotations and connotations and the images many of them create — in one sense all the chapters in this book are about the precise and imaginative use of words.

Poets work with words in three ways: to report ("It was a moonless night"), to describe ("It was so dark we couldn't see the tree right outside our window"), and to provide a new or fresh way of perceiving ("It was so dark outside the window that it made us feel as if the night were anonymous"). All three are found in the opening lines of Robert Hayden's "Those Winter Sundays" (p. 462). The speaker reports: "Sundays too my father got up early." He describes: "cracked hands that ached / from labor in the weekday weather." And he gives us a fresh way of perceiving: "hear the cold splintering, breaking." Watching for those uses as you continue reading poetry can help you be alert to and responsive to the denotations and connotations words convey.

DENOTATION

In focusing attention on words, it's important to realize that words have two dimensions, denotation and connotation. **Denotation** refers to what words mean, to their dictionary definitions. It may seem obvious that, in reading, we need to pay attention to what the words mean; but sometimes it takes effort, and at times you will probably need to use different dictionaries. In other kinds of reading, the context may convey adequately the general meaning of an unfamiliar word, but in reading poetry, approximate meanings aren't enough. And sometimes in poetry the secondary, less familiar meanings of a word may be as important as, or more important than, the first meaning.

It is usually easier to understand the denotations of words in poems written in your own time and from your own culture. Because they are connected to something you are familiar with, you can count on having a vocabulary pretty much in common with that of the poet. But even in these cases, it may help to check in a dictionary for any key words you're not certain about.

Denotations pose a bigger problem when you read poems from the past or from a culture different from your own. You already know you need to look up unfamiliar words. Much trickier are words that look familiar but seem unusual in the context of the poem. In some cases, often in poems written several centuries ago, word meanings have changed or previous meanings are no longer used. A desk dictionary may indicate such changes, but a better resource is the *Oxford English Dictionary,* often called the *OED.* It is a historical dictionary found in most libraries and online through many libraries. It gives you what words meant in earlier times as well as now, and it shows, through illustrative quotes, when each meaning was in use and, if it is no longer current, when that usage ceased.

Consider the following lines from Shakespeare's *Julius Caesar,* where Portia asks Brutus what has been bothering him.

Is Brutus sick? And is it physical
To walk unbraced and suck up the humors
Of the dank morning? (2.1.262)

Both *physical* and *humor* are familiar words, but none of our current uses seems to fit these lines. Looking in an ordinary desk dictionary won't help, but using the *OED* does. If you look up *physical,* under definition 5b, you find, "Beneficial to health; curative, remedial" (if this seems odd, think of the word *physician*). In this case, you can be sure you have found the right meaning because the line from *Julius Caesar* is quoted as an illustration of this definition. If you look up *humor* (it appears under the British spelling *humour*), the first entry fits — "Moisture; damp exhalation; vapour" — and again the passage from *Julius Caesar* is given as an example. The last example cited for this usage is from 1697 — this is the latest example of this usage that has been found in print. By then that meaning may already have disappeared from spoken language, or it may have lingered in speech a bit longer; in any case, it died out completely around 1700, so present-day dictionaries do not bother to include it (not even as an "archaic" usage).

The denotations of words in the following poem probably seem straightforward and clear, even from your first reading. But spend some time looking up words that you're unfamiliar with or that look important and perhaps might mean more than the context conveys (perhaps the words *banked, chronic, austere,* and *offices;* and what about *blueblack*?). Remember too that denotation involves not just the meaning of individual words but the meaning of words combined with other words: Think about the meaning of "chronic angers" and "love's austere and lonely offices."

Robert Hayden   1913–1980

Those Winter Sundays   [1962]

Sundays too my father got up early
and put his clothes on in the blueblack cold,
then with cracked hands that ached
from labor in the weekday weather made
banked fires blaze. No one ever thanked him.   5

I'd wake and hear the cold splintering, breaking.
When the rooms were warm, he'd call,
and slowly I would rise and dress,
fearing the chronic angers of that house,

Speaking indifferently to him,   10
who had driven out the cold

and polished my good shoes as well.
What did I know, what did I know
of love's austere and lonely offices?

APPROACHING THE READING

1. In addition to "important" words such as *banked, chronic, austere, offices,* and *blueblack,* pay attention to easily overlooked "little" words such as *those* in the title and *too* in line 1. Why do they matter? Discuss their effect and impact.

2. What is suggested in line 9 by the phrase "chronic angers of that house"? Why did the son speak "indifferently" to his father? What does word choice indicate about relationships in the family?

3. What do the last five words of the poem mean and say? Are they an effective ending? What is the effect of the repetition in line 13? How is what the speaker now knows different from what he thought as a child?

This poem is masterful in the ways its diction subtly and seamlessly enriches the poem. One could readily argue that the success of this poem in all its elements and effects is the result of Hayden's accomplished use of diction. Notice the beautifully muted combinations of words, each of which reveals a profound intelligence quietly coming to life-changing realizations throughout the poem: "Sundays too" rather than "Even on Sunday"; "The blueblack cold" — the words and order mysteriously convey both how the cold felt to the father and how the son came to recognize the depth and continuity of the father's responsibility; "banked" starts the fifth line and rhymes with "thanked" at the end of the line, gently emphasizing the contrast between duty fulfilled and a lack of gratitude. "Chronic angers" (l. 9) is striking in combining a technical word, *chronic,* with a prosaic one, *angers.* The result leads us to realize and imagine the atmosphere the speaker grew up within. And the unusual combination of the word *love* with *austere, lonely,* and *offices* provokes us to reflect on and reconsider what real love is.

CONNOTATION

Of course, words are more than their dictionary definitions. Words also have **connotations**, the shared or communal overtones and associations they carry in addition to their dictionary meanings. Two words may have almost the same denotation but very different connotations; the associations a reader connects with them could make one suitable and the other unsuitable in a certain situation. For example, in "Those Winter Sundays," "working in the weekday weather" means almost the same thing, denotatively, as "labor in the weekday weather." But Hayden uses *labor* in line 4 probably because its connotations suggest work of a harder and more fatiguing kind than *working* does, and that's what Hayden wants to say about his father.

Connotations are shaped by cultures and sets of belief, and to feel what "most readers" feel requires being able to share their context. For example, denotatively, the word *mother* means "a woman who has borne a child"; for many people, *mother* connotes tenderness, support, caring. For those whose mothers abused them, however, the word *mother* would not have the "common" connotation, and it could be difficult for such readers to respond to it imaginatively. Also, the word can be used as a denigrating term, as in "you mother." Viewing connotations as the same for everybody assumes a large degree of similarity of experience among readers, and today's society is so diverse that a common effect in language is less usual than it was in the past. It's very important to recognize that connotation is complex and problematic, and that it is crucial in determining how any of us as readers experience a poem.

Most poets search for the word that has exactly the right meaning, sound, and feeling, and then depend on you as reader to weigh denotations and connotations carefully. The words in the following poem seem very carefully chosen. As you read it, pay particular attention to the words — to what the denotations of familiar and unfamiliar words and the connotations of simple, ordinary words contribute to the poem's meaning and effect.

Gwendolyn Brooks 1917–2000

The Bean Eaters   [1960]

They eat beans mostly, this old yellow pair.
Dinner is a casual affair.
Plain chipware on a plain and creaking wood,
Tin flatware.

Two who are Mostly Good.   5
Two who have lived their day,
But keep on putting on their clothes
And putting things away.

And remembering . . .
Remembering, with twinklings and twinges,   10
As they lean over the beans in their rented back room that is full of
    beads and receipts and dolls and cloths, tobacco crumbs, vases
    and fringes.

APPROACHING THE READING

1. Look up any words whose denotations are not clear to you.

2. What words are particularly important for their connotations?

Research this author in depth with cultural documents and multimedia resources on *LiterActive*.

3. Brooks chooses the words she does for both denotations and connotations. Consider why they are appropriate for this couple, their daily lives, the setting, and their circumstances. How do Brooks's words reveal the speaker and poet's empathy?

4. Pick out some uses of diction that seem particularly striking or important and explain why you feel that they are.

The denotations of words in "The Bean Eaters" are likely clear to you. You might look up *flatware* (utensils, such as knives, forks, and spoons) or *chipware* (though you are not likely to find it in a dictionary; it appears to be a term Brooks coined for beat-up china). You can probably figure out most of the words, including *chipware,* from the context. More important to this poem, however, are the words' connotations.

What beans are, denotatively, is not the crucial thing; what they suggest and what we associate them with is. The feeling or association generated by a word depends to some extent on the background and experiences of the readers. Brooks probably expects that readers will associate beans with being inexpensive and ordinary. Given those connotations, it seems safe to conclude that this couple's eating beans suggests *mostly* that they are poor. *Yellow* may factually, denotatively, describe the color of their skin, but equally important are the feelings of age, health, and fragility that many people associate with the word *yellow.* The facts of what chipware and tin flatware are do not solely create their effect as words in the poem; the way we perceive them as inexpensive, utilitarian products does.

Denotatively, "rented back room" simply states that the room the couple lives in is not in the front of the building and is owned by someone else. But the connotations are meaningful. Back rooms are cheaper (and less desirable) than front rooms. Presumably, Brooks's couple is renting a room because they cannot afford to own a house, and a back room because they cannot afford even to rent a front room.

Finally, the things listed in the last line are more important to the couple — and to us — for the feelings they evoke than for what they are in and of themselves. This old pair lives more in the past than in the present, and memories cluster with "twinklings and twinges" around the objects that fill the room. Perhaps you have more — or other — connotations for the words in the poem. Bring them into the reading of it and discuss how they differ from those we present here. Also, think about what part your background plays in your response to the poem. (Be aware, however, that connotations are different from the "personal associations" a word or image carries for a particular individual because of an experience connected with it — "sailboats always make me think of people who own them and how they got the money to buy them" — though such personal associations do contribute to the way connotations affect us.)

IMAGES

Our earliest knowledge of the world comes through the senses. Babies become acquainted with objects by looking at them, touching them, putting them in their mouths; everything to them is wonderfully sensate and interesting. As poet W. S. Merwin has said, "A child picks up a fallen leaf and doesn't say, what is it good for? To the child, a leaf is what it is, full of color." The senses remain crucial sources of knowledge for us as adults as well, but as we get older, we become accustomed to the things we encounter and cease to find amazement in ordinary things. One of the beauties of poetry is that it reconnects us to the world of our senses and thus to a world of wonder.

As child or adult, we experience the things around us through mental representations or "mental images." An image is formed in the mind as we look at a tree or hear a band play. Light rays fall on the retina or sound waves on the ear drum, sending messages to the brain that constructs them into images — mental representations — of sight or sound. Images are formed in the mind by viewing external objects or hearing a live band, or by reading the words "enormous oak tree" or "the percussion section of the Rockford High School marching band."

In literature, an **image** is a word or group of words that calls up a sensory representation, a mental picture of an object or action that can be known by one or more of the senses. An image is a specific detail in a story, poem, or play that triggers in our minds a mental representation of a sight, sound, touch, taste, or smell. Poetry relies heavily on images. To comprehend and *experience* what is going on in poems and therefore to enjoy reading them, being attentive to images is vital. Try focusing on images in the following poem, which describes the sights and sounds of night at a lakeshore cottage and is full of sensory detail.

Maxine Kumin b. 1925

The Sound of Night   [1961]

And now the dark comes on, all full of chitter noise.
Birds huggermugger crowd the trees,
the air thick with their vesper cries,
and bats, snub seven-pointed kites,

skitter across the lake, swing out,   5
squeak, chirp, dip, and skim on skates
of air, and the fat frogs wake and prink
wide-lipped, noisy as ducks, drunk
on the boozy black, gloating chink-chunk.

And now on the narrow beach we defend ourselves from dark.   10
The cooking done, we build our firework
bright and hot and less for outlook
than for magic, and lie in our blankets
while night nickers around us. Crickets
chorus hallelujahs; paws, quiet   15
and quick as raindrops, play on the stones
expertly soft, run past and are gone;
fish pulse in the lake; the frogs hoarsen.

Now every voice of the hour — the known, the supposed, the strange,
the mindless, the witted, the never seen —   20
sing, thrum, impinge, and rearrange
endlessly; and debarred from sleep we wait
for the birds, importantly silent,
for the crease of first eye-licking light,
for the sun, lost long ago and sweet.   25
By the lake, locked black away and tight,
we lie, day creatures, overhearing night.

APPROACHING THE READING

1. This poet clearly loves to explore the possibilities of language. Pick out examples of unusual uses of language and consider if they are effective. Look up words that aren't familiar. Does each seem the right word for the place it's used?

2. Kumin seems especially to like verbs. Notice examples of active, energetic verbs. Consider whether they are effective in creating mental images.

3. Pick out words and phrases that create mental images of the way things look, sound, and feel.

The diction of this poem aims to bring to life a scene for readers to recall or create in their imaginations. Its emphasis is not on an intellectual meaning or an abstract idea, but on evoking not only what you see at the lake but especially what you hear. Because nouns are not as effective in describing sounds, the poem emphasizes verbs, such as "skitter," "squeak, chirp, dip, and skim," and "prink" in the first stanza. Look for other examples in stanzas two and three. Notice also that the verbs are present tense, giving the scene immediacy, a perpetual quality. This is not a scene from the past, which is over and gone, but a scene that continues to go on, in fact (somewhere, for someone) as well as in the memory of the speaker, and now in you the reader. Memories come to life through images. Realizing this gives us a solid sense of the remarkable power of images, of imagistic language.

The power of concrete detail is at the heart of William Carlos Williams's short and much-discussed poem, "The Red Wheelbarrow."

William Carlos Williams 1883–1963

The Red Wheelbarrow   [1923]

so much depends
upon

a red wheel
barrow

glazed with rain   5
water

beside the white
chickens.

APPROACHING THE READING

1. Pick out words in the poem that help create sensory impressions in your mind (its images). Approximately what percentage of the words is imagistic?

2. Try sketching the scene on paper or visualizing it clearly in your mind. Consider what it would look like as a still-life painting in an art gallery. Even though this poem is highly visual, why might a sketch or painting fail to "capture" the poem?

3. What do you think is the "so much" that "depends" (l. 1)? Why does it "depend"?

Some readers distrust or overlook the literal effects of Williams's images and search for "deeper meanings." The opening line of "The Red Wheelbarrow" seems to invite digging for deeper meaning — if "so much depends" on the objects mentioned, we had better figure out what they *really* mean. But the line more likely asserts the importance of images as themselves: So much depends on sensuously experiencing and respecting and realizing the value of things as themselves, on *really* using our senses, on experiencing

---

☑ CHECKLIST on Words and Images

❏ Pay careful attention to denotations—the pertinent dictionary definitions of words in a poem.

❏ Use a desk dictionary and specialized dictionaries (such as the *Oxford English Dictionary*) for finding useful and sometimes surprising denotations.

❏ Be open to the connotations of words in poetry—the overtones or associations that become connected with a word through repeated uses.

❏ Respond with your senses, intellect, and emotions to images (words representing sensory experience or objects that can be known by one or more of the senses) and to sense images (mental representations of sensory experience) in a poem.

---

the world with our senses alert and sensitive. As you did in answering "Approaching the Reading" question 2, imagine the scene Williams describes as a still-life painting. Still lifes celebrate concrete detail, and that's a good place to start with much poetry as well.

We call these sense-centered words on a page "images," but in a way they are only potential images; they are the means for calling up sights, sounds, smells, tastes, and tactile sensations in each reader's mind. If you have spent your summers at a lake cottage, images of that location probably come to your mind as you read Kumin's "The Sound of Night." If you've never spent a night on a lakeshore, your mental images probably are influenced by pictures of such scenes or by movies or TV shows with such a setting. The important thing for you as a reader is to let such images form in your mind as you read, encourage them by giving them time to form. The clearer the images in your mind are, the more fully you will enjoy the poem.

> **www**
> Further explore words and images, including interactive exercises, with VirtuaLit Poetry at bedfordstmartins.com/approachinglit.

Writers help by supplying specific details and precise images that use concrete language rather than abstract language (see p. 171). If you hear, "Think of a dog," you may visualize a spaniel, poodle, mutt, or whatever you choose. *Dog* is general. You make up the particular dog. However, if you hear, "Don't imagine a golden retriever," such is the power of images that, even though you're told not to, you can't help visualizing a fairly large dog with a thick golden coat and feathering on its neck, legs, and tail (provided that you know what a golden retriever looks like).

Some people are convinced that all poetry is indirect and symbolic—even a "code." They think that reading poetry means finding hidden meanings, as if poets think of meanings and then hide them. These readers often distrust or even overlook the literal and search instead for "deeper meanings." But an image is, first and foremost, simply itself. Poems do use symbols, and much of what was said about symbols in fiction (pp. 127–33) applies as well to poetry. But remember that a symbol is initially "an image that is exactly what it is." True, an image may suggest further meanings, but it doesn't "turn into" something else. It is always itself. And it always retains its literal meaning. Because imagery is so rich a part of poetry, one starting point in reading poems is to look at — *and trust* — the literal, to realize, appreciate, and enjoy the images for what they are and for what they do as themselves.

FURTHER READING

A culture is deeply imbedded in its language. You learned about your own culture partly through its words. To begin to learn about a different culture, a key step is to learn its language. Words are important to your individual identity as well: To some extent, you are the kind of words you use.

Because language is so important to all of us, it's not surprising that poets often write poems that talk about language. In the following poem, look for what it says about words, and for the way it uses words and sounds to consider the effect of words on culture and relationships between different ethnic groups.

Allison Joseph   b. 1967

On Being Told I Don't Speak Like a Black Person   [1999]

Emphasize the "h," you hignorant ass,
was what my mother was told
when colonial-minded teachers
slapped her open palm with a ruler
in that Jamaican schoolroom.   5
Trained in England, they tried
to force their pupils to speak
like Eliza Doolittle° after
her transformation, fancying themselves
British as Henry Higgins,°   10
despite dark, sun-ripened skin.
Mother never lost her accent,

8–10. Eliza Doolittle . . . Henry Higgins: Flower-girl with a strong Cockney (working class) accent in George Bernard Shaw's play *Pygmalion* and the musical based on it, *My Fair Lady.* Henry Higgins, a linguistics professor, takes on the challenge of teaching her how to speak (and act and dress) like a proper British lady.

though, the music of her voice
charming everyone, an infectious lilt
I can imitate, not duplicate.   15
No one in the States told her
to eliminate the accent,
my high school friends adoring
the way her voice would lift
when she called me to the phone —   20
A-ll-i-son, it's friend Cathy.
Why don't you sound like her,
they'd ask. I didn't sound
like anyone or anything,
no grating New Yorker nasality,   25
no fastidious British mannerisms
like the ones my father affected
when he wanted to sell someone
something. And I didn't sound
like a Black American,   30
college acquaintances observed,
sure they knew what a black person
was supposed to sound like.
Was I supposed to sound lazy,
dropping syllables here and there   35
not finishing words but
slurring their final letters
so each sentence joined
the next, sliding past the listener?
Were certain words off limits,   40
too erudite for someone whose skin
came with a natural tan?
I asked them what they meant
and they stuttered, blushed,
said *you know, Black English,*   45
applying a term from that
semester's text. *Does everyone*
in your family speak alike,
I'd ask, and they'd say *don't*
take this the wrong way,   50
nothing personal.

Now I realize there's nothing
more personal than speech,
that I don't have to defend
how I speak, how any person,   55
black, white, chooses to speak.
Let us speak. Let us talk

with the sounds of our mothers
and fathers still reverberating
in our minds, wherever our mothers   60
or fathers come from:
Arkansas, Belize, Alabama,
Brazil, Aruba, Arizona.
Let us simply speak
to one another,   65
listen and prize the inflections,
never assuming how any person will sound
until his mouth opens, until her
mouth opens, greetings welcome
in any language.   70

APPROACHING THE READING

1. Most of the language of the poem is straightforward. Look up any words you aren't familiar with. Pick out a few phrases you like, with especially effective or interesting diction, and be prepared to explain why.

2. The speaker mentions that her acquaintances seemed sure they knew what a black person is supposed to sound like. What does she mean by that? Reflect on the cultural assumptions that lie behind such certainty.

3. The speaker says in lines 52–55 that "there's nothing / more personal than speech, / that I don't have to defend / how I speak." Think about your own speech. In what ways is it yours? When do you feel you have to defend your speech or even abandon or change or modify it?

Forming images in your imagination is easiest with poems from familiar settings such as from our own neighborhood or culture. It becomes more challenging with poems from places or cultures we are less familiar with — but such poems provide opportunities to expand our range of knowledge and imaginative experience.

The following poem is packed with specific images that, combined, create a larger image — of a Los Angeles neighborhood, with the sights and sounds and smells of an evening in early fall just as the moon emerges, casting a yellow glow over the entire scene. The details will trigger sharp images if you are familiar with the foods, shops, games, plants, and architecture in the poem. The images will be less crisp if you don't recognize "*yaoya*" (a vegetable stand or seller), "a loaf from Langendorf" (bread from a well-known bakery in California), or "jacaranda" (a tropical tree of the catalpa family, with showy clusters of flowers, usually purplish), but the overall effect of the poem is still very evocative.

Garrett Kaoru Hongo   b. 1951

Yellow Light   [1982]

One arm hooked around the frayed strap
of a tar-black patent-leather purse,
the other cradling something for dinner:
fresh bunches of spinach from a J-Town *yaoya*,
sides of a split Spanish mackerel from Alviso's,   5
maybe a loaf of Langendorf; she steps
off the hissing bus at Olympic and Fig,
begins the three-block climb up the hill,
passing gangs of schoolboys playing war,
Japs against Japs, Chicanas chalking sidewalks   10
with the holy double-yoked crosses of hopscotch,
and the Korean grocer's wife out for a stroll
around this neighborhood of Hawaiian apartments
just starting to steam with cooking
and the anger of young couples coming home   15
from work, yelling at kids, flicking on
TV sets for the Wednesday Night Fights.

If it were May, hydrangeas and jacaranda
flowers in the streetside trees would be
blooming through the smog of late spring.   20
Wisteria in Masuda's front yard would be
shaking out the long tresses of its purple hair.
Maybe mosquitoes, moths, a few orange butterflies
settling on the lattice of monkey flowers
tangled in chain-link fences by the trash.   25

But this is October, and Los Angeles
seethes like a billboard under twilight.
From used-car lots and the movie houses uptown,
long silver sticks of light probe the sky.
From the Miracle Mile, whole freeways away,   30
a brilliant fluorescence breaks out
and makes war with the dim squares
of yellow kitchen light winking on
in all the side streets of the Barrio.

She climbs up the two flights of flagstone   35
stairs to 201-B, the spikes of her high heels
clicking like kitchen knives on a cutting board,
props the groceries against the door,

fishes through memo pads, a compact,
empty packs of chewing gum, and finds her keys.   40

The moon then, cruising from behind
a screen of eucalyptus across the street,
covers everything, everything in sight,
in a heavy light like yellow onions.

APPROACHING THE READING

1. Look up any words that you don't recognize or aren't sure of.

2. As an exercise on imagery, circle nouns and underline verbs that evoke sensory impressions — sights, sounds, smells, tastes, touch. Notice how much of the language in the poem is devoted to the senses.

3. Draw a square box around words the poem uses to make images sharper or clearer for the reader — for example, adjectives that make nouns more specific ("the *frayed* strap / of a *tar-black, patent-leather* purse"), or comparisons that make images easier to imagine ("clicking *like* kitchen knives on a cutting board").

4. What is the point or theme of the poem? What does it all add up to?

> When discussing or writing about literature, the word **imagery** is used in two ways: (1) It can mean all language in a literary work collectively that refers to a sensory experience or to objects that can be known by one or more of the senses in a poem — "The rich imagery in the first stanza of 'Those Winter Sundays' establishes a strong empathy with the father," for example. (2) It can mean a related pattern of imaginative comparisons and allusions running through an entire literary work or a portion of one — for example, "Notice the juxtaposition of Christian imagery with Nazi holocaust imagery in Charles Simic's 'Begotten of the Spleen'" (p. 728).

Much of the imagery in "Yellow Light" is of nature and sounds in an October night. Here is another autumn poem full of nature imagery — an elderly man reflects on the crop of apples he has just finished picking and on his life, which is nearing its end. As you read it, pay special attention to its use of connotations and to the way its words create images appealing to various senses.

Robert Frost 1874–1963

After Apple-Picking   [1914]

My long two-pointed ladder's sticking through a tree
Toward heaven still,
And there's a barrel that I didn't fill
Beside it, and there may be two or three
Apples I didn't pick upon some bough.   5
But I am done with apple-picking now.
Essence of winter sleep is on the night,
The scent of apples: I am drowsing off.
I cannot rub the strangeness from my sight
I got from looking through a pane of glass   10
I skimmed this morning from the drinking trough
And held against the world of hoary grass.
It melted, and I let it fall and break.
But I was well
Upon my way to sleep before it fell,   15
And I could tell
What form my dreaming was about to take.
Magnified apples appear and disappear,
Stem end and blossom end,
And every fleck of russet showing clear.   20
My instep arch not only keeps the ache,
It keeps the pressure of a ladder-round.
I feel the ladder sway as the boughs bend.
And I keep hearing from the cellar bin
The rumbling sound   25
Of load on load of apples coming in.
For I have had too much
Of apple-picking: I am overtired
Of the great harvest I myself desired.
There were ten thousand thousand fruit to touch,   30
Cherish in hand, lift down, and not let fall.
For all
That struck the earth,
No matter if not bruised or spiked with stubble,
Went surely to the cider-apple heap   35
As of no worth.
One can see what will trouble
This sleep of mine, whatever sleep it is.
Were he not gone,
The woodchuck could say whether it's like his   40
Long sleep, as I describe its coming on,
Or just some human sleep.

APPROACHING THE READING

1. In this poem, descriptive images convey what the speaker experienced at a particular time of year. Notice how they do this. What things has the speaker experienced that have occupied him so totally that they even fill his dreams?

2. Look for images invoking various senses. What do they contribute to the poem? What do you make of the contrast between the richly sensuous detail and the speaker's matter-of-fact tone?

3. Consider word choice in the poem. How does the diction help give us a sense of what the speaker is like? Notice the words "Toward heaven" (l. 2). How would the poem be affected if the line read "toward the sky" instead?

4. Review the discussion of archetypes in Chapter 6 (pp. 131–32). Do some of the images in this poem also function as archetypes? If you think they do, point out examples and explain their effect in the poem. How do they contribute to what the poem adds up to?

Nature also is important in the following two poems, but the focus of each is on a relationship involving vulnerable, hurting individuals: the strong friendship of two young girls — one who is blind, the other who misses her father — in the first, and the deep love of a woman for a sister who is repeatedly wounded by men in the second. Consider how denotations, connotations, and images are important in each.

Anita Endrezze b. 1952

The Girl Who Loved the Sky   [1992]

Outside the second grade room,
the jacaranda tree blossomed
into purple lanterns, the papery petals
drifted, darkening the windows.
Inside, the room smelled like glue.   5
The desks were made of yellowed wood,
the tops littered with eraser rubbings,
rulers, and big fat pencils.
Colored chalk meant special days.
The walls were covered with precise   10
bright tulips and charts with shiny stars
by certain names. There, I learned

how to make butter by shaking a jar
until the pale cream clotted
into one sweet mass. There, I learned   15
that numbers were fractious beasts
with dens like dim zeros. And there,
I met a blind girl who thought the sky
tasted like cold metal when it rained
and whose eyes were always covered   20
with the bruised petals of her lids.

She loved the formless sky, defined
only by sounds, or the cool umbrellas
of clouds. On hot, still days
we listened to the sky falling   25
like chalk dust. We heard the noon
whistle of the pig-mash factory,
smelled the sourness of home-bound men.

I had no father; she had no eyes;
we were best friends. The other girls   30
drew shaky hopscotch squares
on the dusty asphalt, talked about
pajama parties, weekend cookouts,
and parents who bought sleek-finned cars.
Alone, we sat in the canvas swings,   35
our shoes digging into the sand, then pushing,
until we flew high over their heads,
our hands streaked with red rust
from the chains that kept us safe.

I was born blind, she said, an act of nature.   40
Sure, I thought, like birds born
without wings, trees without roots.
I didn't understand. The day she moved
I saw the world clearly: the sky
backed away from me like a departing father.   45
I sat under the jacaranda, catching
the petals in my palm, enclosing them
until my fist was another lantern
hiding a small and bitter flame.

APPROACHING THE READING

1. Notice the rich sensory texture of this poem. Find examples of words that
   evoke each of the five senses — sight, hearing, smell, taste, and touch. Why is
   sensory imagery so important to this poem?

2. We get to know the speaker and her friend partly through the poem's images, through the kinds of things they notice and experience. Describe what both girls are like, grounding your response in the poem's details.

3. Discuss the nature of the girls' friendship. What makes it solid, touching, vulnerable? How do certain images help convey it?

4. Reread the final stanza of the poem on the effect of the experience on the narrator. Explain how images help get her points across. How fully did the speaker understand the experience then? What indication is there that the poet, in looking back, has a different understanding of it now?

Louise Erdrich b. 1954

A Love Medicine   [1984]

Still it is raining lightly
in Wahpeton. The pickup trucks
sizzle beneath the blue neon
bug traps of the dairy bar.

Theresa goes out in green halter and chains   5
that glitter at her throat.
This dragonfly, my sister,
she belongs more than I
to this night of rising water.

The Red River swells to take the bridge.   10
She laughs and leaves her man in his Dodge.
He shoves off to search her out.
He wears a long rut in the fog.

And later, at the crest of the flood,
when the pilings are jarred from their sockets   15
and pitch into the current,
she steps against the fistwork of a man.
She goes down in wet grass
and his boot plants its grin
among the arches of her face.   20

Now she feels her way home in the dark.
The white-violet bulbs of the streetlamps
are seething with insects,
and the trees lean down aching and empty.
The river slaps at the dike works, insistent.   25

*   *   *

I find her curled up in the roots of a cottonwood.
I find her stretched out in the park, where all night
the animals are turning in their cages.
I find her in a burnt-over ditch, in a field
that is gagging on rain,   30
sheets of rain sweep up down
to the river held tight against the bridge.

We see that now the moon is leavened and the water,
as deep as it will go,
stops rising. Where we wait for the night to take us   35
the rain ceases. *Sister, there is nothing*
I would not do.

APPROACHING THE READING

1. Focus on the images in the poem to see how they alone convey the movement of the poem: the people involved, what happens, location, weather, time of day. The poem begins with a narrative. What differences in effect might there be if the story were told as a short story in prose?

2. What is a "love medicine"? Does the title seem appropriate? How does it fit the rest of the poem?

3. What is the speaker suggesting in the next-to-last stanza where the sharp, distinct images evoke the multiple places she finds her sister? Describe the mix of feelings the speaker has toward her sister. What specifics in the poem support your response?

Research this author in depth with cultural documents and multimedia resources on *LiterActive*.

4. What are the relationships between what's happening in the outer world described through the poem's images and what happens to the sister and to the speaker? What do you make of the last sentence: *"Sister, there is nothing /*
I would not do."

5. Why are the insect images appropriate in this poem? Might they serve as symbols (see p. 127) as well as images? If so, explain.

Verbal images in literature are similar to the visual images created by a painter or photographer. It is not surprising, therefore, that poets often write poems inspired by or in response to paintings or other works of visual art. Read the following poem and look carefully at the print that inspired it on page 481. Notice the way Cathy Song's poem is filled with images attempting to reproduce details from the print and to fill in parts of the scene that are only implicit in the print.

Cathy Song b. 1955

Girl Powdering Her Neck   [1983]

from a ukiyo-e° print by Utamaro°

The light is the inside
sheen of an oyster shell,
sponged with talc and vapor,
moisture from a bath.

A pair of slippers   5
are placed outside
the rice-paper doors.
She kneels at a low table
in the room,
her legs folded beneath her   10
as she sits on a buckwheat pillow.

Her hair is black
with hints of red,
the color of seaweed
spread over rocks.   15

Morning begins the ritual
wheel of the body,
the application of translucent skins.
She practices pleasure:
the pressure of three fingertips   20
applying powder.
Fingerprints of pollen
some other hand will trace.

The peach-dyed kimono
patterned with maple leaves   25
drifting across the silk,
falls from right to left
in a diagonal, revealing
the nape of her neck

---

ukiyo-e: Japanese for "pictures of the floating world" — prints and paintings from Edo (Tokyo) in the seventeenth to nineteenth centuries, depicting everyday urban life, particularly its pleasures, such as the theater and beautiful women. The print referred to here is an example of *bijinga* (pictures of beautiful women), one of the most popular types of ukiyo-e.   **Utamaro:** Utamaro Kitagawa (1753–1806), one of the leading ukiyo-e artists, known especially for his work in bijinga.

Utamaro Kitagawa (1753–1806), Girl Powdering Her Neck.
Musée des Arts Asiatiques-Guimet, Paris, France. Réunion des Musées Nationaux/Art Resource, NY.

and the curve of a shoulder   30
like the slope of a hill
set deep in snow in a country
of huge white solemn birds.
Her face appears in the mirror,
a reflection in a winter pond,   35
rising to meet itself.

She dips a corner of her sleeve
like a brush into water
to wipe the mirror;
she is about to paint herself.   40
The eyes narrow
in a moment of self-scrutiny.
The mouth parts
as if desiring to disturb
the placid plum face;   45
break the symmetry of silence.
But the berry-stained lips,
stenciled into the mask of beauty,
do not speak.

Two chrysanthemums   50
touch in the middle of the lake
and drift apart.

APPROACHING THE READING

1. Compare the images in the poem with the reproduction of the Utamaro print. Notice which details are in the print and which are extensions created by bringing to life the setting and actions implicit in the print.

2. Imagery of movement is significant within this poem. It has a dance-like quality, which captures the "ritual" (l. 16) the woman is engaged in. What is the significance of that ritual? How do the images of the poem convey it? Is it culture-specific to eighteenth-century Japan? Do cultures today have similar rituals?

3. Ukiyo-e art is celebrated for its sensuous qualities, as this print illustrates well. Reproductions are readily available on the Internet: Do a search for "ukiyo-e" and look for similar qualities in other examples. In what ways do the images of Song's poem capture and evoke such sensuousness? Pick out specific examples and explain how the words and images achieve it.

4. Reread the last stanza. How does it relate to the rest of the poem? Explain why you might see these lines as taking on a symbolic quality.

RESPONDING THROUGH WRITING

Journal Entries

1. As an exercise on language, write in your journal lists of words that you notice during an entire day: unfamiliar words, moving words, words that sound beautiful, words that look good, and so on. At the end of the day and a few days later, look back over the list and run through the words using your memory and imagination. Jot some notes about experiences, feelings, and associations some of the words bring back to you: It may give you a new sense of the power and importance words have.

Research the authors in this chapter with LitLinks at bedfordstmartins.com/ approachinglit.

2. Choose a nonpoetic text — a letter, an advertisement, a magazine article, or an editorial, for example — and look closely at its handling of language. Discuss in your journal how the denotations and connotations of the words are or are not manipulated.

3. Images — visual and verbal — are enormously important for the advertising industry. In your journal, list some examples of how advertisers use words and pictures to imprint images in your mind and to stimulate your imagination, to get you to notice and remember their products. Write some reflections on some ways advertisers use the same techniques as poets, though with a different purpose in mind.

Literary Analysis Papers

4. Find two poems on a similar subject. Look closely at the words used in both. Write a paper in which you discuss differences of language in the two poems and the effects those differences create.

5. Write a paper discussing a poem's imagery by thinking of the poem in terms of cinematography. See the poem as film. Note where in the poem you would use crucial camera angles, shots, close-ups, pans, and so forth. Help your reader see the poem as a film. Explain why you decided to film it as you did.

6. Write a paper on the use of imagery in capturing and conveying the atmosphere of a season: autumn, for example, in John Keats's "To Autumn" (p. 677), or the harvest season (June) in Gary Soto's "The Elements of San Joaquin" (p. 729), or spring in William Carlos Williams's "Spring and All" (p. 753).

Making Connections

7. Write a paper comparing and contrasting what two or more poems about words say about language (perhaps including the cultural implications of language) and the diction they use to communicate it. Some poems you

might consider are Allison Joseph's "On Being Told I Don't Speak Like a Black Person" (p. 470), Gary Miranda's "Love Poem" (p. 693), and Alberto Ríos's "Nani" (p. 713).

8. Write a paper comparing and contrasting the expressions of love in Elizabeth Barrett Browning's "How do I love thee? Let me count the ways" (p. 617) and Gary Miranda's "Love Poem" (p. 693). Consider the extent to which each relies on images and how the effect of each differs.

Cultural Criticism Papers

9. Write a paper discussing a poem, or several poems, that treat the importance of language and cultural separation and acceptance, such as Allison Joseph's "On Being Told I Don't Speak Like a Black Person" (p. 470), Rosemary Catacalos's "David Talamántez on the Last Day of Second Grade" (p. 620), or Alberto Ríos's "Nani" (p. 713). Try to include some discussion of why poetry is an appropriate form for exploring this topic.

10. Write a paper on the use of imagery to present a situation graphically in poems of political protest—as for example, Ana Doina's "The Extinct Homeland—A Conversation with Czeslaw Milosz" (p. 636), Carolyn Forché's "The Colonel" (p. 650), or Sonia Sanchez's "An Anthem" (p. 717).

RESPONDING THROUGH THE ARTS

1. Create a set of drawings representing or illustrating Anita Endrezze's "The Girl Who Loved the Sky" (p. 476), e. e. cummings's "in Just-" (p. 629), Luis Rodriguez's "Running to America" (p. 714), or another poem of your choice.

2. Write a poem consisting mostly of images. Do your best not to convey any ideas or feelings outright. Try to embody the experience entirely in images, the way Maxine Kumin does in "The Sound of Night (p. 466)."

Poetic speech is a way of sounding in order to hear that voice.
And once you hear it, everything else is like dishwater.
Li-Young Lee

Voice, Tone, and Sound

We said in Chapter 3 that stories did not originate as something to be read: People listened to stories being told long before they read them. The same is true of poems. Even today, when poems are written down, most poems are not meant just to be read; they are also meant to be heard. In fiction and narrative poetry, you listen with your mind's ear to a storyteller, a first- or third-person narrator. In nonnarrative poetry, you hear the imagined voice of a **speaker**, of someone "speaking" the poem, either the poet directly or a character who expresses views or feelings the poet may or may not share. This chapter aims to develop your ability to listen for the voice of the speaker (or narrator), or the voice of the poem, and to help you hear the sounds and rhythms that create the musicality of poetry and are an important part of that voice.

Because of the importance of voice and sounds, it is helpful to read poems aloud at least once, if not several times, and to listen to someone else read them. Attending to the sounds and rhythms brings out aspects of the poem that you otherwise might overlook. As you read aloud, don't rush: Reading too fast distorts the rhythms and blurs the words and sounds. Pay attention to punctuation—full stop at a period or semicolon, brief pause at a comma—and decide on the pitch (inflection) that fits the meaning—downturn, upturn, or level. When lines end with no punctuation, lengthen the last sound with level pitch to signal the movement to a new line. It might feel uncomfortable at first, but soon you may find yourself enjoying what can happen when you read aloud. It can also influence your silent reading, putting you in touch with a voice in your head.

VOICE

In a first-person poem, a key question to ask is whether the *I* speaking in the poem is a voice very similar to that of the author or is a character different from the author. Just as you should not assume that the *I* in a story is identical to the author, you shouldn't automatically assume that the *I* in a poem is the author. Thomas Hardy, for example, wrote a poem in which the *I* is a dead man; Gerald Stern wrote a poem in which the *I* is a dead dog.

Pay attention to the speaker in the following poem as he recalls his father and expresses his love for what is now lost. Watch for indications of what the *I* is like—character traits and attitudes. And listen for indications of whether the voice you hear represents that of the author or of a character separate and different from the author.

Li-Young Lee   b. 1957
Eating Alone   [1986]

I've pulled the last of the year's young onions.
The garden is bare now. The ground is cold,
brown and old. What is left of the day flames
in the maples at the corner of my
eye. I turn, a cardinal vanishes.   5
By the cellar door, I wash the onions,
then drink from the icy metal spigot.

Once, years back, I walked beside my father
among the windfall pears. I can't recall
our words. We may have strolled in silence. But   10
I still see him bend that way—left hand braced
on knee, creaky—to lift and hold to my
eye a rotten pear. In it, a hornet
spun crazily, glazed in slow, glistening juice.

It was my father I saw this morning   15
waving to me from the trees. I almost
called to him, until I came close enough
to see the shovel, leaning where I had
left it, in the flickering, deep green shade.

White rice steaming, almost done. Sweet green peas   20
fried in onions. Shrimp braised in sesame
oil and garlic. And my own loneliness.
What more could I, a young man, want.

APPROACHING THE READING

1. Focus on the *I* who speaks the poem. Does anything suggest that the *I* is different from, or distanced from, the author of the poem?

2. Describe the voice you hear as you listen to the poem. What personal qualities and attributes come through what is said?

3. How does the last stanza of the poem relate to the previous three stanzas? What is the meaning of the last line?

4. How does the title affect your sense of the voice of the poem?

5. In what ways does hearing the poem's voice enrich your experience of the poem? What would be lost if you did not hear the voice?

In the text of "Eating Alone," there seems to be no reason for thinking the *I* is significantly different from the author, and biographical information about the author (including the biographical sketch on p. 1442) confirms basic similarities between the speaker and the poem. The voice we hear appears to be Li-Young Lee's voice. Or, perhaps we should say, his voice as a poet in this poem. What we're really considering when we talk about **voice** is authorial presence, not as a biographical personality but as the sense conveyed by a poem of an intelligence and moral sensibility that has invented, arranged, and expressed the elements and ideas in a particular manner. For a poem in which the *I* is close to the poet, the *I* supplies the voice we listen to; for a poem in which the *I* is different from the poet, to consider the poet's presence we need to listen for the voice of the poem, which is likely to be somewhat different from the speaker's voice.

From the beginning of "Eating Alone," the person speaking seems low-keyed, matter-of-fact, unemotional. He is very observant, someone who notices the appearance of the now-barren earth, the brilliant sunset shining through the leaves of a maple tree, the flight of a cardinal. Clearly this person is in touch with his surroundings. The voice in the second stanza sounds soft, sensitive, perhaps pensive, as he recalls a particular moment, years ago, with his father, who seems no longer to be living. The moment was memorable not for what they said to each other but for the particular way his father bent over to pick up a rotting pear and showed him a hornet circling drunkenly in its hollowed-out center. From his father, it seems, the speaker learned the attentiveness to nature demonstrated in the first stanza.

The third stanza makes clear that the speaker is not in fact unemotional: He felt a great deal of emotion when he thought he saw his father, but then realized what he saw was actually a shovel in flickering light. But the voice we hear restrains that deep emotion, understates it, which may end up making it sound all the stronger. The understated emotion is carried over to the final stanza, in the details of an excellent meal, fit for a festive, shared occasion, in contrast to the speaker's "loneliness."

The word *loneliness* and the final line raise key questions about voice, questions of the kind that each reader must think through for herself or himself. What kind of voice says the words "my own loneliness"? Is it a depressing, isolated loneliness brought on by his feeling lost without his father? Is it an accepted loneliness, in which he misses his father's physical presence but is consoled by a sense of the father's continuing presence because of his memories? Or could it be a mixture of the two, or something else?

Similarly, what kind of voice says the last line, "What more could I, a young man, want"? Is the voice heavy with irony? (There's a lot more I could want, starting with having my father back!) Or does it express the genuine consolations that are found in good food and the flood of memories associated with the food and with other experiences? The title brings those questions about the voice into focus: Is eating alone a sad, solitary activity for the speaker? Does he actually feel lonely as he eats alone? When do being alone and not being lonely coincide? When do they not?

It is important when working with a poem to allow for complexity of emotion. Our feelings are always "mixed," meaning complex, even contradictory. A poem — an effective, honest poem — is never emotionally simplistic. Notice, too, that in the previous paragraphs, whenever the voice is described we support the description with specific details from the poem itself. Nothing is stated and then followed up by an ungrounded impression or a phrase such as "that's how it feels to me." Each description is linked to a concrete passage, part of the poem.

As you read the following poem about a rather different father-son relationship from that in "Eating Alone," watch for any indications that the *I* speaking in the poem does not represent the author's voice. Notice character traits of the speaker and be able to describe what the speaker is like as a person.

Charles Bukowski   1920-1994

my old man   [1977]

16 years old
during the depression
I'd come home drunk
and all my clothing —
shorts, shirts, stockings —   5
suitcase, and pages of
short stories
would be thrown out on the
front lawn and about the
street.   10

          *   *   *

my mother would be
waiting behind a tree:
"Henry, Henry, don't
go in . . . he'll
kill you, he's read   15
your stories . . ."

"I can whip his
ass . . ."

"Henry, please take
this . . . and   20
find yourself a room."

but it worried him
that I might not
finish high school
so I'd be back   25
again.

one evening he walked in
with the pages of
one of my short stories
(which I had never submitted   30
to him)
and he said, "this is
a great short story."
I said, "o.k.,"
and he handed it to me   35
and I read it.
it was a story about
a rich man
who had a fight with
his wife and had   40
gone out into the night
for a cup of coffee
and had observed
the waitress and the spoons
and forks and the   45
salt and pepper shakers
and the neon sign
in the window
and then had gone back
to his stable   50
to see and touch his
favorite horse
who then

kicked him in the head
and killed him.   55

somehow
the story held
meaning for him
though
when I had written it   60
I had no idea
of what I was
writing about.

so I told him,
"o.k., old man, you can   65
have it."
and he took it
and walked out
and closed the door.
I guess that's   70
as close
as we ever got.

APPROACHING THE READING

1. Describe the voice you hear in the poem. Is it the voice of the poet directly, of a character expressing views or feelings the poet shares, or of a character distinct from the poet?

2. How would you characterize the father and the son? Do you sympathize with either? Why or why not?

3. Why do you think the father likes the story?

4. Why do you think Henry wrote the story? He says he had no idea of what he was writing about.

5. Why do you think the poet included the story? How does it fit the voice of the poem?

This is a first-person poem, and the fact that the *I* is a writer can make it seem that the voice in this poem, like that in "Eating Alone," is pretty much the same as the author's. But the mother calls the speaker (narrator, actually, since this is a poem telling a story) "Henry," which suggests that the *I* may be a character different from the author. In that case, we need to listen for the voice of the poem behind Henry's words and attitudes.

In this poem, thinking in terms of point of view (see p. 94) helps. We hear everything from Henry's point of view. What happens and what is said would sound quite different from the father's perspective. Perhaps we can hear the voice of the poem — its authorial presence, the intelligence and moral sensibility that has invented, arranged, and expressed the elements and ideas — if we listen for both perspectives and consider whether the poem might be indicating some degree of disapproval of the son's attitude. If so, that could affect how we think about several key issues in the poem.

> Some books use the term **persona** for the first-person narrator through whom an author speaks or the speaker whose voice is heard in a lyric poem. They assume that one can never hear the author directly in a written work, even when he or she uses *I*, that the author always, inevitably talks through a mask the way actors did in Greek plays (which is where the term *persona* came from). This book does not make that assumption, though it stresses that an *I* should never automatically be equated with the author.

Dramatic Monologue

One poetic form in which the *I* is not the author is the **dramatic monologue**. In dramatic monologues, there is only one speaker, a character overheard in a dramatic moment, usually addressing another character or characters who do not speak. The speaker's words reveal what is going on in the scene and bring out significant aspects of what the speaker is like. You can, therefore, figure out who is speaking, to whom, and on what occasion, and the substance and tone of what she or he is saying. See, for example, Robert Browning's "My Last Duchess" (p. 511). (If the character is speaking to her- or himself, the poem is using interior monologue — see p. 98; that is probably the case in T. S. Eliot's "The Love Song of J. Alfred Prufrock" — p. 645.)

TONE

When you are hearing a voice, an important aspect of what you are hearing is its tone. **Tone** was defined in Chapter 7 (p. 177) as the attitude or "stance" toward the subject and toward the reader or audience implied in a work. As we said there, tone can be, for example, serious, playful, exaggerated, understated, poignant, distanced, formal, informal, ironic, blunt, or a complex mixture of more than one of these.

Tone is as important in poems as it is in stories. Poems can have a single tone, but usually the tone is not singular and straightforward; it cannot be summed up in a word or two. More often two or more tones mix and play off or with each other. In "my old man" (p. 488), for example, one needs to consider Henry's tone — his attitude toward his father and perhaps toward life in general — and the tone of the poem toward Henry. Here is another poem about a son's memories of his father. Listen carefully for its voice and tone. Pay attention to the diction, connotations, and images. Does the father-son relationship seem closer to that of "Eating Alone" or that of "my old man"?

Theodore Roethke 1908–1963

My Papa's Waltz   [1948]

The whiskey on your breath
Could make a small boy dizzy;
But I hung on like death:
Such waltzing was not easy.

We romped until the pans   5
Slid from the kitchen shelf;
My mother's countenance
Could not unfrown itself.

The hand that held my wrist
Was battered on one knuckle;   10
At every step you missed
My right ear scraped a buckle.

You beat time on my head
With a palm caked hard by dirt,
Then waltzed me off to bed   15
Still clinging to your shirt.

APPROACHING THE READING

1. Consider the voice in the poem. Is the *I* a character narrating the episode or the voice of the poet?

www   Explore this author and poem in depth, including images and cultural documents, with VirtuaLit Poetry at bedfordstmartins.com/approachinglit.

2. Unlike "Eating Alone" (p. 486) and "my old man" (p. 488), which address the reader, this poem addresses *you*, the father. How does that affect the voice of the poem?

3. Be ready to discuss the age of the speaker whose voice we hear — his age now and at the time of the event — and what you think he felt then and feels now. What difference does it make to the way we hear the voice whether the father is living or has died?

4. Discuss the effect of the word *papa* on the tone of the poem. Substitute *daddy* or *father* or *old man*. What happens?

5. Discuss the effect of the word *waltz* on the tone of the poem. Substitute *romps* or *craziness*. What happens?

"My Papa's Waltz" affects readers in different ways. For some the poem describes a troubled relationship or dysfunctional home. The word *whiskey* suggests for them that the father has a drinking problem; the mother's disapproval suggests that the father and mother have a difficult relationship. *Battered* indicates that the father abuses his son and perhaps his wife. The simile "I hung on like death" in line 3 suggests a home in which fear pervades the atmosphere. For these readers, the poem has a dark tone, perhaps a tragic one, as a little boy — too young to be aware of what he's doing — puts up with his father's frightening romps because he is forced to physically and desperately tries to gain his father's love and approval.

Other readers discern a different tone in the poem. For them words such as *waltz* and *romped* convey a lighter tone — a waltz is a graceful, flowing, lyrical dance that suggests joy and celebration (though, of course, the poet could be using the word ironically). The father described is a physical laborer (his hands are battered and caked with dirt) who has a couple of drinks with his buddies after work on a Friday. Feeling good, he frolics with his son, and being a bit tipsy, he's wilder than he probably should be, creating disorder in the kitchen, and rougher than he should be, thus scraping the boy's ear and tapping on his head more enthusiastically than he should. The romp is scary for the small boy ("dizzy," "like death," "clinging") — but excitingly scary; most kids enjoy being frightened a bit (a carnival ride that doesn't scare you isn't worth spending money on). For these readers, the poem describes a speaker looking back at his childhood, thinking of a father who may no longer be alive, recalling a happy memory, a memory that evinces his father's affection (people generally waltz with people they love) and his own positive response to his father (one can cling out of love as well as fear).

Assessing tone is a central part of the total interpretation of a literary work. As in all interpretation, it's not simple or straightforward. Every aspect of the work can come to bear on tone. It's important always to be alert for indicators of tone. Some are the same as in fiction — word choice, ways of phrasing, repetitions, understatement, overstatement, a particular figure of speech. Others — such as the handling of sounds and rhythm — are more particular to poetry. And as "My Papa's Waltz" makes clear, tone is not an objective detail on which all readers must agree. Readers can read tones differently, and discussions about tone often form a vital part of conversations about literature, with each side pointing to aspects that lead them to respond to the work the way they do.

IRONY

Irony is as important in poetry as it is in stories. Review the discussion of irony in Chapter 7 (pp. 180–81), especially — for poetry — verbal irony and sarcasm. Then try out your ear for irony as you read the following poem. Pay attention especially to word choice, exaggerations, and incongruities.

Marge Piercy b. 1936

Barbie Doll   [1973]

This girlchild was born as usual
and presented dolls that did pee-pee
and miniature GE stoves and irons
and wee lipsticks the color of cherry candy.
Then in the magic of puberty, a classmate said: 5
You have a great big nose and fat legs.

She was healthy, tested intelligent,
possessed strong arms and back,
abundant sexual drive and manual dexterity.
She went to and fro apologizing.   10
Everyone saw a fat nose on thick legs.

She was advised to play coy,
exhorted to come on hearty,
exercise, diet, smile and wheedle.
Her good nature wore out   15
like a fan belt.
So she cut off her nose and her legs
and offered them up.

In the casket displayed on satin she lay
with the undertaker's cosmetics painted on,   20
a turned-up putty nose,
dressed in a pink and white nightie.
Doesn't she look pretty? everyone said.
Consummation at last.
To every woman a happy ending.   25

APPROACHING THE READING

1. What effect on tone do words such as *girlchild*, *pee-pee*, *wee*, and *cherry candy* have? How did they strike you the first time you read them?

2. What do you think the speaker means by the "magic" of puberty in line 5? How does the wording of line 6 connect with it? What tone do you think the two lines convey?

3. At what point in the poem did you realize this poem critiques prevailing social attitudes?

4. Point out several examples of irony in the poem.

This poem is narrated by an unidentified, third-person observer, not the poet in first person and not a character involved in the action. The voice may well be that of the poet, but it has a heavily ironic tone. In such cases, of course, it is important to distinguish between the voice of the speaker (who seems to say the events have a happy ending) and the voice of the poem (which means the opposite).

The title and opening lines can seem straightforward initially, with words such as "girlchild" and "did pee-pee" creating a childlike simplicity. However, a deeper seriousness begins to emerge in line 6: "You have a great big nose and fat legs." The middle stanzas develop the contrast between what this young woman was and the Barbie Doll and supermodel expectations society imposes on women. Phrasings such as "went to and fro apologizing" (l. 10) and "a fat nose on thick legs" (l. 11) and the comparison "wore out / like a fan belt" (ll. 15-16) are signals that the voice is not to be heard as straightforward. Line 17 is certainly not straightforward: "So she cut off her nose and her legs" is the speaker's ironic way of saying that, unable to cope with what she perceived as society's expectations, she committed suicide.

The ironies intensify in the final paragraph. In her coffin, thanks to the undertakers' skills, she looks like a Barbie doll and everyone now, when she can't hear them, says how pretty she looks. The poem's voice continues to intensify as the final lines convey the author's sentiments: "Consummation at last" (l. 24) is highly ironic in that her consummation — completion, fulfillment, perfection — is found only after death. The most common use of *consummation* — the completion of a marriage by sexual intercourse — makes the irony even stronger since she did not feel sexually attractive when she was living, and perhaps did not seem so to young men, with their society-shaped expectations. In the final line — "To every woman a happy ending" — the ironic voice turns sarcastic.

As you read a poem, always be alert for signals that what is said is not to be taken in a literal way: word choice, the sheer absurdity of what is said, the way a thought is phrased, the sounds and rhythms in which it is expressed. Recognition of irony is crucial to good reading. But it's not just identifying irony that's important. Active reading of a poem, like active reading of other literature, involves the whole person — intellect, senses, emotions, ideas, and values. Responding to any kind of tone is crucial to enjoying a poem fully and meaningfully.

The rest of this chapter, along with the chapters that follow, goes on to discuss specific techniques and elements poets draw from when they compose a poem. As we focus on sounds, metaphors, rhythm, and form, however, it is important that you continue to listen for, and to, the voices in poems. Listen to the variety of voices, from different times, different experiences, and different cultures. Listen for and to the variety of things they give voice to in their poems. *Hear* the poems and *hear* what the poems are saying.

SOUND

Sound is one of the great pleasures of life and of poetry. Hearing poetry also involves paying attention to the sounds of the combinations of words, syllables, and even individual letters, listening to the sounds in the poem as well as the sound of the poem. Fine writers have "good ears." They attend to sounds of words as well as combinations of sounds, listening for the way sound and rhythm work together to create the poem's "music," all of which contribute to the voice of a poem. Rhythm is treated later in the book, in Chapter 14. Here we focus on the effects of repeating or contrasting syllable sounds, vowel sounds, and consonant sounds. To gain the full experience of effective writing, a reader needs to hear not only the words but also the repetitions, connections, contrasts, and combinations of vowels, consonants, and syllables that form the words.

The following poem is about an African American driver being stopped by a police officer. Listen for the sounds made by the words and phrases — repetitions of words, parallel constructions, felicitous phrasings, echoes of vowel and consonant sounds, and rhyming words as well as the sound of the speaker's voice. Think about the ways the sounds help convey the meaning.

Sekou Sundiata b. 1948

Blink Your Eyes   [1995]

Remembering Sterling A. Brown°

I was on my way to see my woman
but the Law said I was on my way
thru a red light red light red light
and if you saw my woman
you could understand,   5
I was just being a man
It wasn't about no light
it was about my ride
and if you saw my ride
you could dig that too, you dig?   10
Sunroof stereo radio black leather

Sterling A. Brown: Brown (1901–1989) was an African American poet and a longtime professor at Howard University. See his poem "Riverbank Blues" (p. 616) and biographical sketch (p. 1420).

bucket seats sit low you know,
the body's cool, but the tires are worn.
Ride when the hard time come, ride
when they're gone, in other words   15
the light was green.

I could wake up in the morning
without a warning
and my world could change:
blink your eyes.   20
All depends, all depends on the skin,
all depends on the skin you're living in.

Up to the window comes the Law
with his hand on his gun
what's up? what's happening?   25
I said I guess
that's when I really broke the law.
He said *a routine, step out the car*
a routine, assume the position.
Put your hands up in the air   30
you know the routine, like you just don't care.
License and registration.
Deep was the night and the light
from the North Star on the car door, déjà vu
we've been through this before,   35
why did you stop me?
Somebody had to stop you.
I watch the news, you always lose.
You're unreliable, that's undeniable.
This is serious, you could be dangerous.   40

I could wake up in the morning
without a warning
and my world could change:
blink your eyes.
All depends, all depends on the skin,   45
all depends on the skin you're living in.

New York City, they got laws
Can't no bruthas drive outdoors,
in certain neighborhoods, on particular streets
near and around certain types of people.   50
They got laws.
All depends, all depends on the skin,
all depends on the skin you're living in.

APPROACHING THE READING

1. As you listen to the *I* in this poem, does it seem like you are hearing the voice of the author directly, a character speaking for the author, or a character different from the author?

2. Is there an overall tone in the poem, or do different types of tone appear in different parts? What would you say is the tone of the repeated phrase "all depends on the skin you're living in"?

3. Read the first stanza of the poem aloud. Pay close attention to the sounds of the syllables, words, and phrases in those lines (not sounds they describe, but the sounds you hear as you say them aloud). Find examples of repeated consonant sounds and vowel sounds, of words repeated rhythmically, of words that rhyme. Reflect on the "feel" and tone the sounds create.

A significant portion of the effect of "Blink Your Eyes" arises from the sounds—the rhymes, the repetitions, the echoes of vowels and consonants that create a saucy aura and reinforce the poem's ironies. The poem describes an experience of racial profiling: Encountering such racism has the potential to change one's world in the blink of an eye. Even though the speaker voices the poem as an event in his past, he is still able to remember the innocence of his excited anticipation of driving to see his lover. We can feel that throughout the poem's opening section with its vivid picture of how "cool" his car was, as conveyed by the images, and how hip he was, as conveyed by the sounds and rhythms of the words he uses. Then he runs a red light and everything changes. He is not treated the way one is supposed to be treated for such an infraction, and he realizes there are two different worlds with two different ways of enforcing the law, that it "all depends on the skin you're living in." The subject turns more serious after line 23, but the use of rhyme, the repetition of phrases, and the echoes of vowels and consonants continue, to keep the poem from turning dark and bitter.

Close examination of techniques of sound can become technical and abstract, and risks making you want to back away. Yet, only by looking closely can we see exactly how the effects we appreciate are created. We ask you to focus on just four important types of sound technique: alliteration, assonance, repetition, and rhyme. We use examples from "Blink Your Eyes" to illustrate them.

Alliteration

One kind of sound is **alliteration**, the repetition of identical consonant sounds in words relatively near one another (in the same line or adjacent lines usually). Alliteration is most common at the beginnings of words or syllables, especially the beginnings of stressed syllables (*"green as grass"*), though it sometimes can occur within words and syllables as well (*"golden baggage"*). But in every case the sound must be stressed sufficiently that it is heard clearly. Throughout this chapter, the pronunciation is what matters, not the letters. "Call the *k*id in the *c*enter" does alliterate, but the last *g* in *baggage* just above does not.

> Sunroof stereo radio black leather
> bucket seats sit low you know.

Alliteration is used sometimes just because it sounds appealing, as it does in these lines. But it also calls attention to words and gives them greater emphasis, links words together and gets us to connect their meanings, and makes phrases more memorable.

A variant on alliteration is **consonance**, the use of words whose consonant sounds are the same but whose vowels are different. In perfect examples, all the consonants are alike: *live, love; chitter, chatter; reader, rider*; or, in Romeo's words, "I'll *l*oo*k* to *l*i*k*e, if *l*oo*k*ing *l*i*k*ing move" (*Romeo and Juliet* 1.4.98). The more usual examples of consonance are words in which the consonants following the main vowels are identical: *dive, love; swatter, chitter; sound, bond*. Line 5 of "Blink Your Eyes" (p. 496) employs consonance: "you coul*d* understan*d*"; likewise, lines 7–8: "It wasn'*t* abou*t* no ligh*t* / it was abou*t* my ride."

   Thus, alliteration is the repetition of *initial* consonant sounds; consonance is the repetition of *final* consonant sounds.

Assonance

Another kind of sound, **assonance**, is the repetition of identical vowel sounds in words whose consonants differ. It too can be initial, within a line or perhaps adjacent lines ("*u*nder the *u*mbrella"), though internal is more usual ("tr*ee* by l*ea*f," "tr*ee* and tr*ea*t"). Its strongest effect is a subtle musical quality that often reinforces the tone of a poem, adds gradations to its feel, and contributes to levels of meaning by making connections and adding emphasis. Listen for the assonance in lines 14–16 from "Blink Your Eyes." Then reread them, thinking about its effects.

> Ride when the hard time come, ride
> when they're gone, in other words
> the light was green.

Repetition

Repetition is the reuse of a word, group of words, line, or lines later in the same poem, but close enough so readers remember the earlier use and hear the later one as an echo. The lines "All depends, all depends on the skin, / all depends on the skin you're living in" repeat "all depends" and "all depends on the skin" for rhythmic effect and to build up to the climactic key phrase "on the skin you're living in." These two lines are repeated three times in the poem, which gives them added emphasis. Because these lines occur at the end of a stanza (or section), they could be called a **refrain**.

Rhyme

You are probably familiar with rhyme from songs, jingles, nursery rhymes, and some poems. Rhyme is often thought of, wrongly, as a defining characteristic of poetry. It is, in fact, only one of many kinds of sound that can appear in a poem and is not an essential one: Many poems do not rhyme. **Rhyme** is the repetition of the final vowel sound and all following consonant sounds in two or more words that have differing consonant sounds preceding the vowel, as in the words *air* and *care* in lines 30–31 from "Blink Your Eyes":

> *Put your hands up in the* air
> *you know the routine, like you just don't* care.

Rhyme leads to various effects. In the lines above, the rhymes become a bitter comic device, used to ridicule the officer who has stopped and racially profiled the speaker without any valid reason. In other situations, rhyme emphasizes important words; it creates a connection or a bonding; it tightens the organization and strengthens unity; it contains meaning; it provides a sense of completion, or termination, to lines, stanzas, and whole poems; and it pleases the ear in its musicality and expectation or surprise. If well written — and well read — rhyme does not distract us from the poem itself but blends with everything else in the poem. When reading a poem aloud, make sure to say the rhyming words in a way that enables a listener to hear the rhymes as echoes of sound, without letting them "steal the show."

Rhyme is described according to several categories: exact or approximate, end or internal, single or double.

EXACT OR APPROXIMATE   The definition given above is for **exact rhyme**, in which the vowel and the consonant sounds following the vowel are the same: br*ight* and n*ight, art* and h*eart,* "*I watch the* news, *you always* lose."

Approximate rhyme, or **slant rhyme**, is a form of rhyme in which words contain similar sounds but do not rhyme perfectly (usually involving assonance or, more frequently, consonance): d*eep* and f*eet;* rhyme and writhe; g*ate* and m*at;* *a*ll and st*o*le, wi*ll,* or ha*le.*

END OR INTERNAL   **End rhyme** involves rhyming words that occur at the ends of lines, such as *air* and *care:*

> *Put your hands up in the* air
> *you know the routine, like you just don't* care.

In **internal rhyme**, two or more words within a line, or within lines near each other, rhyme with each other, or words within lines rhyme with words at the ends:

> *I watch the* news, *you always* lose.
> *You're* unreliable, *that's* undeniable.

SINGLE OR DOUBLE   **Single rhyme** involves only the final, stressed syllable in rhyming words: *west* and *vest,* a*way* and to*day.*

> All depends, all depends on the *skin,*
> all depends on the skin you're living *in.*

In **double rhyme** the accented, rhyming syllable is followed by one or more identical, unstressed syllables: *thrill*ing and *kill*ing, *marry* and *tarry,* un*reli*able and un*deni*able.

> I could wake up in the *morn*ing
> without a *warn*ing.

Unless specified otherwise, *rhyme* used alone means exact, end, single rhyme.

> Single rhyme used to be called **masculine rhyme** (because it was considered "strong" and "forceful"), and double rhyme was called **feminine rhyme** (because it was regarded as "weaker" than single rhyme). These labels generally are no longer used because of their sexist overtones.

The pattern of end rhymes in a poem or stanza, that is, its recurring sequence, is called its **rhyme scheme**. The pattern is usually described by assigning a letter to each word sound, the same word sounds having the same letter. For poems in stanzas, the pattern is usually the same for each stanza. In that case, you need to mark the rhyme scheme only once. Thus the rhyme scheme of Samuel Hazo's "For Fawzi in Jerusalem" (p. 665) is *abcba.*

There has long been debate among students of language about the suggestive quality of sounds themselves. Attempts have been made to associate individual vowel and consonant sounds with specific feelings or meanings:

high vowels (ē, ĭ,), for example, with excitement (scream, giddy); low vowels (ou, oo) with power or gloominess; the nasal consonants (m, n, ng) with warm, positive associations (mother); sn with usually unpleasant things (snake, sneer); and st with strong, stable, energetic things. Those attempts have been countered with claims that meanings are being read into the sounds, rather than the sounds shaping meaning. In either case, something meaningful and interesting is being created or elicited by sound.

Beyond the notion that vowels and consonants can be associated with a feeling or meaning is the concept of **onomatopoeia**, words whose pronunciation suggests their meaning. Samuel Johnson, in the eighteenth century, described it this way: "Every language has some words framed to exhibit the noises which they express, as *thump, rattle, growl, hiss.*" Onomatopoeia, at its best, involves not just individual words but entire passages that carry their meaning in their sounds. Listen to these lines from "The Princess" by Alfred, Lord Tennyson: "The moan of doves in immemorial elms, / And murmuring of innumerable bees." Reread Maxine Kumin's "The Sound of Night" (p. 466) and notice her effective use of onomatopoetic language such as "chitter noise," "huggermugger crowd," "skitter across," and "squeak, chirp, dip, and skim."

✅ CHECKLIST on Voice, Tone, and Sound

❑ Listen for the voice of the speaker, if the speaker and poet are almost the same, or for the voice of the speaker and the voice of the poem if they are different. In either case, listen for the intelligence and sensibility that has invented, arranged, and expressed the elements and ideas in a particular manner.

❑ Listen for the tone: the tone of voice or attitude toward the subject or situation in the poem (playful, serious, ironic, cheerful, pessimistic, sorrowful, and so forth).

❑ Listen for irony: an expression involving a discrepancy or incongruity between appearance and reality, between what is said and what is intended. In poetry, verbal irony (saying what is nearly opposite of what is meant) is used most often, though situational irony (things turning out not as hoped or expected) is frequent as well.

❑ Listen for and respond to patterns of sound, such as alliteration (repetition of initial consonant sounds), consonance (repetition of all consonant sounds or of final consonant sounds), assonance (repetition of identical vowel sounds), rhyme (repetition of the accented vowel sound of a word and all succeeding sounds), onomatopoeia (words whose pronunciation suggests their meaning), and repetitions (of words, phrases, or lines).

The important thing to notice is that sounds in a poem do generally seem to fit the meanings being expressed. Alexander Pope illustrated that point in his poem *An Essay on Criticism* (1711) by suggesting differences in the sounds of the words used to describe a gentle breeze and a fierce storm: "Soft is the strain when Zephyr gently blows" and "The hoarse, rough verse shou'd like the Torrent roar." For an active reader of poetry, therefore, listening attentively to the sounds of words and syllables is a step toward understanding the meaning those words are creating.

> **www**
>
> Further explore voice, tone, and sound, including interactive exercises, with VirtuaLit Poetry at bedfordstmartins.com/ approachinglit.

FURTHER READING

Poetry provides many people — published and unpublished authors — a way to "give voice to" things they are not able to express, or to express adequately, any other way. As you read the poems below, in addition to paying attention to voice and sounds, listen for and keep in mind what the poet is giving voice to. In the following two poems, former soldiers wrestle with their feelings about World War I and the Vietnam war.

Wilfred Owen   1893–1918

Dulce et Decorum Est   [1920]

Bent double, like old beggars under sacks,
Knock-kneed, coughing like hags, we cursed through sludge,
Till on the haunting flares we turned our backs
And towards our distant rest began to trudge.
Men marched asleep. Many had lost their boots   5
But limped on, blood-shod. All went lame; all blind;
Drunk with fatigue; deaf even to the hoots
Of tired, outstripped Five-Nines° that dropped behind.

Gas! GAS! Quick, boys! — An ecstasy of fumbling,
Fitting the clumsy helmets just in time;   10
But someone still was yelling out and stumbling
And flound'ring like a man in fire or lime . . .
Dim, through the misty panes° and thick green light,
As under a green sea, I saw him drowning.

*   *   *

---

8. Five-Nines: 5.9-inch caliber shells.   **13. misty panes:** Of a gas mask.

In all my dreams, before my helpless sight,   15
He plunges at me, guttering, choking, drowning.

If in some smothering dreams you too could pace
Behind the wagon that we flung him in,
And watch the white eyes writhing in his face,
His hanging face, like a devil's sick of sin;   20
If you could hear, at every jolt, the blood
Come gargling from the froth-corrupted lungs,
Obscene as cancer, bitter as the cud
Of vile, incurable sores on innocent tongues, —
My friend, you would not tell with such high zest   25
To children ardent for some desperate glory,
The old Lie: Dulce et decorum est
Pro patria mori.°

27–28. **Dulce . . . mori:** It is sweet and fitting / to die for one's country (Horace, *Odes* 3.12.13).

APPROACHING THE READING

1. Summarize what the speaker is describing and reflecting on in the poem, what he is "giving voice to." If you are uncertain about any sections or lines, ask questions about them.

2. Describe the speaker/voice of the poem. The poem looks back at the incident it describes. (From how much later, do you think? Does it matter?) What difference does it make to have it told from a later point? How do you think the distance in time has affected the speaker?

Research this author in depth with cultural documents and multimedia resources on *LiterActive*.

3. Consider the speaker's use of second person beginning in line 17. On the original draft of the poem, a dedication "To Jessie Pope" is scratched out and replaced with "To a certain Poetess." Jessie Pope published patriotic poems in a popular London newspaper during World War I. Neither dedication was included in published versions of "Dulce et Decorum Est." How does knowledge of the dedication affect your reading of the poem? Should "you" and "My friend" be limited to Jessie Pope?

4. Pick out uses of alliteration, assonance, and rhyme. What do such sound techniques contribute to the effect of the poem? Specifically, what tone is achieved by rhyming "glory" with the Latin word for "to die"?

Yosef Komunyakaa   b. 1947

Facing It   [1988]

My black face fades,
hiding inside the black granite.
I said I wouldn't,
dammit: No tears.
I'm stone. I'm flesh.   5
My clouded reflection eyes me
like a bird of prey, the profile of night
slanted against morning. I turn
this way — the stone lets me go.
I turn that way — I'm inside   10
the Vietnam Veterans Memorial
again, depending on the light
to make a difference.
I go down the 58,022 names,
half-expecting to find   15
my own in letters like smoke.
I touch the name Andrew Johnson;
I see the booby trap's white flash.
Names shimmer on a woman's blouse
but when she walks away   20
the names stay on the wall.
Brushstrokes flash, a red bird's
wings cutting across my stare.
The sky. A plane in the sky.
A white vet's image floats   25
closer to me, then his pale eyes
look through mine. I'm a window.
He's lost his right arm
inside the stone. In the black mirror
a woman's trying to erase names: 30
No, she's brushing a boy's hair.

APPROACHING THE READING

1. Characterize the speaker of the voice you hear in the poem. What can you
   tell about the speaker's experiences and feelings?

2. How does the title fit the poem and the speaker? How does the last line fit?

3. Discuss the tone of the poem and point to specific details or techniques that
   help shape it.

4. If you have not visited the Vietnam Veterans Memorial in Washington, D.C., look at pictures of it and read about it (you can do both on the Web or in books). Talk to someone who has seen it, if you can. Reflect on how all this helps you visualize and experience the poem more fully.

5. Pick out examples of sound techniques such as alliteration, assonance, rhyme. What do such sound techniques contribute to the effect of the poem?

In the following two poems, poets give voice to a different kind of concern—the pains one experiences in growing up. In the first, a young girl sitting alone in a waiting room comes to a sudden sense of her identity. In the second, an adolescent expresses the frustrations of waiting ("hanging fire") between youth and adulthood. Each has a strong voice—listen for it and for the use of sounds in creating its effect.

Elizabeth Bishop   1911–1979

In the Waiting Room   [1976]

In Worcester, Massachusetts,
I went with Aunt Consuelo
to keep her dentist's appointment
and sat and waited for her
in the dentist's waiting room.   5
It was winter. It got dark
early. The waiting room
was full of grown-up people,
arctics and overcoats,
lamps and magazines.   10
My aunt was inside
what seemed like a long time
and while I waited I read
the *National Geographic*
(I could read) and carefully   15
studied the photographs:
the inside of a volcano,
black, and full of ashes;
then it was spilling over
in rivulets of fire.   20
Osa and Martin Johnson°

---

21. **Osa and Martin Johnson:** Husband-and-wife explorers and naturalists.

dressed in riding breeches,
laced boots, and pith helmets.
A dead man slung on a pole
— "Long Pig,"° the caption said. 25
Babies with pointed heads
wound round and round with string;
black, naked women with necks
wound round and round with wire
like the necks of light bulbs. 30
Their breasts were horrifying.
I read it right straight through.
I was too shy to stop.
And then I looked at the cover:
the yellow margins, the date. 35
Suddenly, from inside,
came an *oh!* of pain
— Aunt Consuelo's voice —
not very loud or long.
I wasn't at all surprised; 40
even then I knew she was
a foolish, timid woman.
I might have been embarrassed,
but wasn't. What took me
completely by surprise 45
was that it was *me:*
my voice, in my mouth.
Without thinking at all
I was my foolish aunt,
I — we — were falling, falling, 50
our eyes glued to the cover
of the *National Geographic,*
February, 1918.

I said to myself: three days
and you'll be seven years old. 55
I was saying it to stop
the sensation of falling off
the round, turning world
into cold, blue-black space.
But I felt: you are an *I,* 60
you are an *Elizabeth,*
you are one of *them.*
Why should you be one, too?

———————

25. **Long Pig:** Polynesian cannibals' name for a human carcass.

I scarcely dared to look
to see what it was I was.
I gave a sidelong glance   65
—I couldn't look any higher—
at shadowy gray knees,
trousers and skirts and boots
and different pairs of hands   70
lying under the lamps.
I knew that nothing stranger
had ever happened, that nothing
stranger could ever happen.
Why should I be my aunt,   75
or me, or anyone?
What similarities—
boots, hands, the family voice
I felt in my throat, or even
the *National Geographic*   80
and those awful hanging breasts—
held us all together
or made us all just one?
How—I didn't know any
word for it—how "unlikely" . . .   85
How had I come to be here,
like them, and overhear
a cry of pain that could have
got loud and worse but hadn't?

The waiting room was bright   90
and too hot. It was sliding
beneath a big black wave,
another, and another.

Then I was back in it.
The War was on. Outside,   95
in Worcester, Massachusetts,
were night and slush and cold,
and it was still the fifth
of February, 1918.

APPROACHING THE READING

1. Bishop was born in 1911, making her the same age as Elizabeth in the poem.
   Does that indicate that the speaker's and the poet's voice are one and the
   same? If so, what difference does it make in your reading? If they are not the
   same, what difference does that make?

2. Describe the speaker's voice. The speaker experiences a wide range of feelings. What about that makes the voice's consistency particularly interesting? In what ways would the poem change, be different, and have a different effect if it were written in the voice of a child?

3. What happens to Elizabeth? Why does looking at the cover and the date elicit such a profound reaction from her?

4. One could say that the poem itself is about finding one's voice. Point out specific passages that support this and explain how they do.

Research this author in depth with cultural documents and multimedia resources on *LiterActive*.

5. Bishop is a master of the subtleties of sound. Notice how in any line there is at least one particular "sound effect." How does this realization affect your reading of and response to the poem?

Audre Lorde 1934–2002
Hanging Fire

[1978]

I am fourteen
and my skin has betrayed me
the boy I cannot live without
still sucks his thumb
in secret   5
how come my knees are
always so ashy
what if I die
before morning
and momma's in the bedroom   10
with the door closed.

I have to learn how to dance
in time for the next party
my room is too small for me
suppose I die before graduation   15
they will sing sad melodies
but finally
tell the truth about me
There is nothing I want to do
and too much   20
that has to be done
and momma's in the bedroom
with the door closed.

           *   *   *

Nobody even stops to think
about my side of it   25
I should have been on Math Team
my marks were better than his
why do I have to be
the one
wearing braces   30
I have nothing to wear tomorrow
will I live long enough
to grow up
and momma's in the bedroom
with the door closed.   35

APPROACHING THE READING

1. Describe the speaker by focusing on her voice alone. What in the poem supports what you describe? Is this the voice of a fourteen-year-old? Why or
   why not?

2. Think about the sudden shifts of subject and tone throughout the poem. Do
   you find them effective or ineffective? What is the effect of the lack of punctuation except for the period at the end of each stanza?

3. Consider the title. What is its connection to the poem? What effect does it
   have on your reading of the poem?

4. Take the list of sound techniques and find examples of as many as you can
   in the poem. Most of the effects are unassuming and easily overlooked.
   Why, though, do they play an important role in the poem?

5. What do you make of the narrator's emphasizing that "momma's in the
   bedroom / with the door closed" (ll. 10–11, 22–23, 34–35)?

The following poem is based on events that occurred in the life of Al-
fonso II, Duke of Ferrara in sixteenth-century northern Italy. The speaker is
the Duke. He is giving a guest a personal guided tour of his palace and
pauses to show him a portrait of his previous wife painted by a fictitious but
supposedly famous painter, Frà (that is, "brother," or monk) Pandolf. Ferrara's first wife, Lucrezia, died in 1561 at age seventeen after three years of
marriage. We overhear what he says about the painting and about her. From
that we are left to determine what he is like, what she was like, who the
guest is, and why the Duke says what he does.

Robert Browning 1812–1889

My Last Duchess [1842]

Ferrara

That's my last Duchess painted on the wall,
Looking as if she were alive. I call
That piece a wonder, now: Frà Pandolf's hands
Worked busily a day, and there she stands.
Will't please you sit and look at her? I said   5
"Frà Pandolf" by design, for never read
Strangers like you that pictured countenance,
The depth and passion of its earnest glance,
But to myself they turned (since none puts by
The curtain I have drawn for you, but I)   10
And seemed as they would ask me, if they durst,
How such a glance came there; so, not the first
Are you to turn and ask thus. Sir, 'twas not
Her husband's presence only, called that spot
Of joy into the Duchess' cheek: perhaps   15
Frà Pandolf chanced to say "Her mantle laps
Over my lady's wrist too much," or "Paint
Must never hope to reproduce the faint
Half-flush that dies along her throat": such stuff
Was courtesy, she thought, and cause enough   20
For calling up that spot of joy. She had
A heart—how shall I say?—too soon made glad,
Too easily impressed; she liked whate'er
She looked on, and her looks went everywhere.
Sir, 'twas all one! My favour at her breast,   25
The dropping of the daylight in the West,
The bough of cherries some officious fool
Broke in the orchard for her, the white mule
She rode with round the terrace—all and each
Would draw from her alike the approving speech,   30
Or blush, at least. She thanked men,—good! but thanked
Somehow—I know not how—as if she ranked
My gift of a nine-hundred-year-old name
With anybody's gift. Who'd stoop to blame
This sort of trifling? Even had you skill   35
In speech—(which I have not)—to make your will
Quite clear to such an one, and say, "Just this
Or that in you disgusts me; here you miss,
Or there exceed the mark"—and if she let

Herself be lessoned so, nor plainly set   40
Her wits to yours, forsooth, and made excuse,
— E'en then would be some stooping; and I choose
Never to stoop. Oh sir, she smiled, no doubt,
Whene'er I passed her; but who passed without
Much the same smile? This grew; I gave commands;   45
Then all smiles stopped together. There she stands
As if alive. Will't please you rise? We'll meet
The company below, then. I repeat,
The Count your master's known munificence
Is ample warrant that no just pretense   50
Of mine for dowry will be disallowed;
Though his fair daughter's self, as I avowed
At starting, is my object. Nay, we'll go
Together down, sir. Notice Neptune, though,
Taming a sea-horse, thought a rarity,   55
Which Claus of Innsbruck° cast in bronze for me!

---

56. **Claus of Innsbruck:** A fictional sculptor.

APPROACHING THE READING

1. In a dramatic monologue, you listen to the voice of a character speaking in a setting and situation. What are they like in this poem? Who is the Duke talking to in the poem? Try thinking in terms of "a person who . . ." Some dramatic movement and action takes place. Summarize what's going on.

2. The point of a dramatic monologue is that the speaker's voice and what it says reveal his or her character. What sort of person is the Duke? Point out the details that lead you to your conclusions about him.

Research this author in depth with cultural documents and multimedia resources on *LiterActive*.

3. What the Duke says also reveals all that we can know about the Duchess. What sort of person was she? What happened to her?

4. Consider tone in the poem. What is the Duke's attitude toward the Duchess? What is the poem's attitude toward the Duke?

5. This is a good poem for reviewing the techniques of sound. Look for examples of alliteration and assonance; think about what they contribute to the effect of the poem. The poem is written in couplets, two consecutive lines of poetry with the same end rhyme, though the rhyme is not so obvious because of the use of run-on lines (see p. 565). What does the rhyme add to the poem? How would its effect be different if it did not rhyme or if the rhyme was more obvious?

RESPONDING THROUGH WRITING

Journal Entries

1. Reflect on the variety of voices we hear during an average day. Often we're bombarded with voices: from radios or TVs, at home, on the street, on a bus, in class. The list could go on and on. To some we give close attention; others we pretty much ignore. In your journal, write a list of voices you notice during a morning or even an hour. Note which ones you pay attention to and which you don't. Of the ones you do pay attention to, reflect on what matters about the quality of each voice — whether it's interesting, engaging, honest, pleasant, appealing, and so on.

2. The same techniques for word sounds discussed in this chapter are also very important in the world of advertising. As you read or hear advertisements during a day or a few hours, keep track of techniques you notice (alliteration, assonance, repetition, rhyme, and so forth). Jot notes describing the effects the techniques achieve.

   www

   Research the authors in this chapter with LitLinks at bedfordstmartins.com/approachinglit.

3. Take a poem and change some of the diction (words) to alter the tone. Write a journal entry describing what you did and why the effect of the poem now is different.

Literary Analysis Papers

4. Write a paper on voice and tone, or tracing shifts in tone in Robert Hayden's "Those Winter Sundays" (p. 462), Elizabeth Bishop's "In the Waiting Room" (p. 506), Agha Shahid Ali's "I Dream It Is Afternoon When I Return to Delhi" (p. 597), Eavan Boland's "The Pomegranate" (p. 613), Gary Soto's "The Elements of San Joaquin" (p. 729), or another poem of your choice.

5. Write a paper discussing techniques of sound and their effect in Robert Browning's "My Last Duchess" (p. 511), Leslie Marmon Silko's "Prayer to the Pacific" (p. 529), Samuel Taylor Coleridge's "Kubla Khan" (p. 623), Samuel Hazo's "For Fawzi in Jerusalem" (p. 665), Alberto Ríos's "Nani" (p. 713), or another poem of your choice.

6. Write a paper discussing the character of the speaker in T. S. Eliot's "The Love Song of J. Alfred Prufrock" (p. 645). The poem is usually regarded as a dramatic monologue, but readers differ on whether it uses interior monologue. If you think it does, show how that contributes to characterization and the effect of the poem.

Making Connections

7. Write a paper in which you compare and/or contrast a musical composition with the musicality of Cathy Song's "Girl Powdering Her Neck" (p. 480),

Sekou Sundiata's "Blink Your Eyes" (p. 496), Lucille Clifton's "at the cemetery, walnut grove plantation, south carolina, 1989" (p. 573), or another poem of your choice.

8. Compare and contrast voice, tone, and purpose in two poems dealing with fences, as, for example, Lorna Dee Cervantes's "Freeway 280" (p. 575), Robert Frost's "Mending Wall" (p. 651), or Luis Rodriguez's "Running to America" (p. 714).

Cultural Criticism Papers

9. Research racial profiling and talk to people who have experienced it. Write a paper discussing Sekou Sundiata's "Blink Your Eyes" (p. 496) in light of what you discover.

10. Talk to a war veteran. Listen to the way the person talks about the experiences as well as to what she or he says. Write a paper discussing similarities and/or differences between the person's way of "voicing" the experience and that in Wilfred Owen's "Dulce et Decorum Est" (p. 503) or Yosef Komunyakaa's "Facing It" (p. 505).

RESPONDING THROUGH THE ARTS

1. Compose a piece of music that evokes the tones of Maxine Kumin's "The Sound of Night" (p. 466), Samuel Hazo's "For Fawzi in Jerusalem" (p. 665), Gary Miranda's "Love Poem" (p. 693), or another poem of your choice.

2. If you're not into composing music, pick out a piece of music that captures the tones of one of the poems mentioned in question 5 on page 513 or of another poem of your choice. Write a journal entry explaining why you chose it.

That's something which is not always recognized, the freeing
effect of a lot of traditional techniques. Richard Wilbur

Form and Type

Think of the effect when a well-designed Internet site appears on the screen — how it catches your eye, grabs your attention, and makes you want to explore the site further. We notice such effective uses of shape or layout every day all around us. The same quality, the immediate impression made by form, is true also of poetry: The impact of visual design, along with internal design, is often part of its appeal. The word *form* is used for "design" in both internal and external construction. **Form** can refer to external structure, the way the poem looks on the page — which may relate to the type of poem it is (to its "genre") and to what the poem is dealing with. It can refer also to the inner structure that arranges, organizes, or connects the various elements in a work. Every poem has form, in both senses. This chapter helps you see poems more distinctly and completely by discussing the role of form and of poetic types, as well as what form may mean, embody, express, or reveal in a given poem.

In some cases, poets start out with an external form in mind and work to blend the words of the poem with this form. It may be an "inherited" form related to or demanded by the type, or "genre," of poem the poet wants to write — perhaps a haiku or a sonnet or a villanelle. In other cases, instead of starting with a form in mind, poets begin with an image, feeling, experience, or idea, or with a few words or lines. The writing itself leads to or creates the form, both the inner arrangement and external shape. The form, therefore, is a result of working with the other elements of poetry.

LINES

Perhaps the most obvious aspect of the external shape of a poem involves its division into **lines**. Most poems are written in lines, and each line normally holds something of significance to the whole poem. Lines offer additional opportunities for effect. In prose, the layout on the page is controlled by margins. Poets, however, control the beginnings and ends of lines — positions that can confer added attention, anticipation, and emphasis. Each line also creates a rhythm, what Ezra Pound called "the musical phrase."

Lines can interplay with sentences, becoming units of rhythm discovered or decided on within a sentence. Lineation invites you to read line by line, feeling the musicality with each; but you also need to read "past" the lines to follow the meaning of the sentences. This superimposing of lines on sentences also directs our attention to words that might get passed over. Watch for this in the following poem.

Gwendolyn Brooks   1917–2000

We Real Cool   [1960]

The Pool Players.
Seven at the Golden Shovel.

We real cool. We
Left school. We

Lurk late. We
Strike straight. We

Sing sin. We   5
Thin gin. We

Jazz June. We
Die soon.

APPROACHING THE READING

1. Read the poem aloud, pausing at the end of each line by holding onto or lengthening the "We" with a level pitch. Don't let your voice drop because the sentence continues in the next line.

2. What is the effect of dividing the sentences into two lines?

3. What is the effect of starting each new sentence at the end of each line?

4. Notice the cumulative effect of the various things the pool players at the Golden Shovel boast about doing. What poetic devices are used to unify and build the intensity of the lines?

Research this author in depth with cultural documents and multimedia resources on *LiterActive*.

5. What is the effect of having a deliberate rhyme scheme (see p. 501), even a typical end rhyme format? How is it affected by the addition of the repeated "We" at the line's end?

The unusual line breaks create anticipation and a jazzlike rhythm; they place emphasis on both the subjects and predicates of the sentences; and they lead to the isolated and unsettling last line. Test the effect of the poem's line breaks and the importance of its form by reading it this way:

We real cool.
We left school.

We lurk late.
We strike straight.

We sing sin.
We thin gin.

We jazz June.
We die soon.

The words are the same, but it is not the same poem. Changing the form of a poem gives it a different effect and makes it a different work. Form is integral to poetry, as it is to all art.

Part of the pleasure for us as readers is that we can respond to the rhythms of lines, can notice and feel how certain words get emphasized by their position in the line, can appreciate the interplay between line and sentence, and can recognize and experience the role of each line in the life of a poem. Notice and feel the rhythms and emphases in the lines as they are used in varying ways throughout the rest of this chapter.

Not all poems are separated into lines: **Prose poems** are a notable exception. The prose poem works with all the elements of poetry except line. It is often written in common paragraph form. It is a hybrid form, drawing together some of the best aspects of both prose and poetry, creating new possibilities out of the challenges presented by the way it fuses the two forms. For an example of a prose poem, see Carolyn Forché's "The Colonel" (p. 650).

STANZAS

Another thing you may notice as you look at certain poems is the presence of stanzas. A **stanza** is a grouping of poetic lines into a section, either according to a given form—each section having the same number of lines and the same arrangement of line lengths, meter, and rhyme—or according to shifts in thought, moment, setting, effect, voice, time, and so on, creating units comparable to paragraphs in prose. The word *stanza* derives from the Italian word for "room," so one could say that stanzas are "rooms" into which some poems are divided. In some poems, all the "rooms" look alike; in other poems, they differ from each other.

Stanza shapes can be *invented,* that is, individually created, unique to a particular poem. The poet may plan out such a stanza form before beginning to write or create it in the process of writing. Look again at "We Real Cool" (p. 516). Probably no other poem in existence has stanzas just like these. Perhaps the first stanza found its own form, without conscious attention to it; perhaps Brooks initially wrote

> We real cool.
> We left school.

and then realized the powerful effect of ending the lines with "We." If so, at that point Brooks began consciously thinking about the form and making the other stanzas fit the form she had "found" for the first one.

Many stanza patterns, however, are not invented but *inherited:* handed down through the centuries, from one generation of poets to another, often with a prescribed meter and sometimes a set rhyme scheme. The most frequently used inherited stanza forms, in the past and today, are four-line stanzas called **quatrains**. One variety of quatrain, the **ballad stanza**, has a long history, used in traditional ballads for many centuries. The ballad stanza is a simple but easily adaptable form—four-line stanzas rhyming *abcb* with eight syllables in the first and third lines, six in the second and fourth. Perhaps it is easier to visualize in diagram form (each square equals one syllable):

Look for that structure in the following poem (in some of its lines you will find an extra syllable—that's typical of the form).

Countee Cullen   1903–1946

Incident   [1925]

for Eric Walrond°

Once riding in old Baltimore,
    Heart-filled, head-filled with glee,
I saw a Baltimorean
    Keep looking straight at me.

Now I was eight and very small,   5
    And he was no whit bigger,
And so I smiled, but he poked out
    His tongue, and called me, "Nigger."

I saw the whole of Baltimore
    From May until December;   10
Of all the things that happened there
    That's all that I remember.

Eric Walrond: Walrond (1898–1966) was a writer and activist in the New York literary community from the early 1920s.

APPROACHING THE READING

1. Notice that each stanza is made up of one sentence. What is the effect of the spaces after lines 4 and 8 that divide the poem into three stanzas? How would the poem read differently if it were a single unit of twelve lines, without stanza breaks? Explain.

2. Each sentence is divided into four lines. On the one hand, we need to read past the lines and grasp the meaning of the sentence as a whole. But we also should give attention to the lines as units. What is the effect of the division into lines? What is lost when you read straight through without such divisions?

Traditionally, ballad stanzas were used for narrative poems, often tragic stories with a melancholy tone. Cullen's use of the form seems appropriate: Like the early folk ballads, it tells a sad story, with a distinctly melancholy tone. A great deal of the poem's emotional power is generated by its form. The stanzas divide the incident into three distinct segments, each building to a climax. The lines help control the rhythm, leading us to pause after each line and focus on each statement individually, letting its point sink in. And the words at the end of the second and fourth lines in each stanza receive strong emphasis, from their position in the stanzas and from the rhyme. The poem opens with an "old world" sense of decorum conveying the child's natural excitement, void of any apprehension. Then comes the "incident" and we move to the speaker's later realization: that no matter how much positive experience he accumulates, it is the impact of cruelty that is remembered. The word *incident* usually carries a connotation of inconsequence. The irony of Cullen's title is certainly bitter.

> Other stanza forms are used less frequently. Some well-known inherited examples are described in the Glossary (pp. 1502–20). Look, for example, at **Chaucerian stanza**, **ottava rima**, **Spenserian stanza**, and **terza rima**.

In addition to inheriting stanza patterns, poems can inherit patterns for the entire poems. The poet may plan from the beginning to use an inherited form, perhaps setting out to write a poem in a preset pattern such as a sestina or a sonnet. The poet may feel the traditional form is most appropriate for the subject. Or the poet may want to participate in a centuries-old poetic tradition, to refresh an inherited form, to embody meaning within the form, or to meet the challenge of working within the form's requirements. The opportunities offered by a prescribed form can lead a writer's imagination to come up with something it likely would not have without the "pressure" of the form. Or the poet may think about an inherited form while writing — may start with a subject or images but no particular form in mind, and then discover that an effective way the poem can develop is as a sonnet, as a sestina, as couplets, or as a variation on a particular form. In such cases, the poet discovers that the material "needs" or perhaps even "demands" that form, or the poet may realize that the form may be the perfect "fit" for that poem.

SONNETS

Some inherited forms have become well known as types of poems significant in their own right. The one you are likely to encounter most often is the **sonnet**. These fourteen-line poems originally were lyrical love poems, but they came to be used also for meditations on death and nature. Poets now use the sonnet form for all subjects. In English, they are usually written in lines of ten syllables each, the odd ones unstressed (traditionally indicated by ˘) and the even ones stressed (´) — more on this can be found in Chapter 14 (pp. 568–70) and the appendix on scansion (p. 1469). You could visualize a typical sonnet as a grid of 140 squares in fourteen lines and ten columns. The poet must fit one syllable into each square, with those in the even-numbered columns usually being stressed, those in the odd-numbered columns unstressed, and the final syllables fitting a given rhyme scheme. Sonnets in English typically fall into two types, differentiated by the structure of their development and their rhyme schemes.

English (or Shakespearean) Sonnet

The **English sonnet** is formed of three quatrains (four-line units, typically rhyming *abab cdcd efef*) and a couplet (two rhyming lines), as in the following diagram:

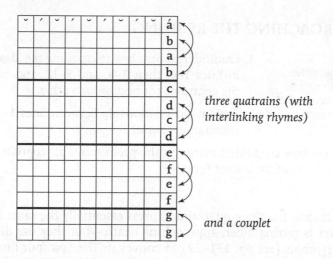

three quatrains (with interlinking rhymes)

and a couplet

Usually the subject is introduced in the first quatrain, expanded or restated in different terms in the second, and expanded further or restated again in the third; the couplet adds a logical, pithy conclusion or a surprising twist. See, for example, this sonnet by William Shakespeare. Shakespeare is known today as one of the great playwrights of all time; but in the 1590s he also wrote a good deal of lyric poetry, including 154 sonnets, all in the form that now bears his name.

William Shakespeare   1564–1616

That time of year thou mayst in me behold   [1609]

That time of year thou mayst in me behold
When yellow leaves, or none, or few, do hang
Upon those boughs which shake against the cold,
Bare ruined choirs,° where late° the sweet birds sang.   *choirstalls; lately*

In me thou seest the twilight of such day   5
As after sunset fadeth in the west,
Which by and by black night doth take away,
Death's second self, that seals up all in rest.
In me thou seest the glowing of such fire
That on the ashes of his youth doth lie,   10
As the deathbed whereon it must expire,
Consumed with that which it was nourished by.
    This thou perceiv'st, which makes thy love more strong,
    To love that well which thou must leave ere long.

APPROACHING THE READING

Research this author in depth with cultural documents and multimedia resources on *LiterActive*.

1. Outline the poem by summarizing the idea developed in lines 1–4, then 5–8, and 9–12, and explain how the quatrains connect to each other.

2. Explain the relationship between lines 1–12 and the concluding couplet.

3. Consider how the subject matter of the poem seems appropriate to the traditional uses of the sonnet form.

In this case, the three quatrains express essentially the same idea — that the speaker is getting older, approaching death — but they use different archetypal symbols (see pp. 131–32) to convey it: The first four lines describe old age in terms of late autumn, with few leaves left on the branches; lines 5–8 describe the approach of death in terms of twilight, with darkness — which closely resembles death — approaching; and lines 9–12 compare the speaker's stage in life to a bed of coals, what is left of a fire that earlier had burned brightly, consuming the firewood that nourished it. The pithy conclusion in lines 13–14 clarifies that the "thou" is not us, the readers, but someone who cares about him and who loves him not less as he grows older and less "lovely" but more because it is clear that they do not have all that much time left together.

Here is another sonnet in Shakespearean form, written in response to a summer of antiblack violence in several cities, particularly Chicago. McKay said later that the poem did not refer directly to blacks and whites.

Claude McKay   1890–1948

If we must die   [1919]

If we must die, let it not be like hogs
Hunted and penned in an inglorious spot,
While round us bark the mad and hungry dogs,
Making their mock at our accursed lot.
If we must die, O let us nobly die,   5
So that our precious blood may not be shed
In vain; then even the monsters we defy
Shall be constrained to honor us though dead!
O kinsmen! we must meet the common foe!
Though far outnumbered let us show us brave,   10
And for their thousand blows deal one deathblow!
What though before us lies the open grave?
Like men we'll face the murderous, cowardly pack,
Pressed to the wall, dying, but fighting back!

APPROACHING THE READING

1. Outline the movement of the poem's inspiring challenge to the speaker's comrades, quatrain by quatrain, as we did with the Shakespeare sonnet above. Note the way sentences are used to structure the four sections of the poem.

2. Consider the appropriateness of using a traditional sonnet for the poem's subject. Is it effective to use a prescribed form for an emotional declamation?

3. Imagine the poem without meter, rhyme, and these specific line breaks. In what ways might that be more effective? In what ways does its actual form contribute to its effect? What things might it lose if it were written in a freer form?

Whether intended or not, much of this poem's power comes from the juxtaposition of the passionate voice expressing intense feeling with this most traditional and exact of verse forms. One can ask if the form adds to and amplifies what is being said, if it is a way to reveal the speaker's ability to balance passion and reason, or if the form depicts a confining of the speaker, something the voice is being constrained by, something the voice wants to break down. Notice how the intensity of feeling alters the traditional form: The third quatrain does not repeat or expand the subject of the first two quatrains; instead, it makes explicit what was implied in the

"If we must die" quatrains—we must fight back aggressively, even if it means dying in the attempt. The closing couplet is not a pithy summary or surprising twist, but a trumpet-like call to action. Perhaps the intensity of feelings being expressed in the poem forced this African American writer to break from the traditional pattern handed down from sonneteers in the past.

Italian (or Petrarchan) Sonnet

The **Italian sonnet** is composed of an **octave** (an eight-line unit), rhyming *abbaabba,* and a **sestet** (a six-line unit), often rhyming *cdecde* or *cdcdcd,* though variations are frequent.

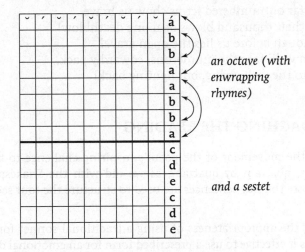

an octave (with enwrapping rhymes)

and a sestet

The octave usually develops an idea or question or problem; then the poem pauses or "turns," and the sestet completes the idea, answers the question, or resolves the difficulty. See, for example, Gary Miranda's "Love Poem" (p. 693) and the following poem.

Gerard Manley Hopkins 1844–1889

God's Grandeur   [*1877;* 1918]

The world is charged with the grandeur of God.
  It will flame out, like shining from shook foil;°   *shaken gold foil*
  It gathers to a greatness, like the ooze of oil°   *from olives*
Crushed. Why do men then now not reck° his rod?°   *recognize; discipline*
Generations have trod, have trod, have trod;   5

And all is seared with trade; bleared, smeared with toil;
And wears man's smudge and shares man's smell: the soil
Is bare now, nor can foot feel, being shod.

And, for° all this, nature is never spent;   *despite*
There lives the dearest freshness deep down things;   10
And though the last lights off the black West went
Oh, morning, at the brown brink eastward, springs —
Because the Holy Ghost over the bent
World broods with warm breast and with ah! bright wings.

APPROACHING THE READING

1. Summarize the idea developed in lines 1–4 and 5–8 and clarify the connection between the two quatrains.

2. Explain the relationship between lines 1–8 and the concluding sestet.

3. Consider the difference in effect between a Shakespearean division of 1–12 and 13–14 and the Italian division of 1–8 and 9–14.

Hopkins converted to Roman Catholicism in 1866, in his early twenties; he was ordained a priest in 1877. After his conversion, almost all of his poetry was religious: "God's Grandeur" combines adoration of the divine with an expression of environmental concerns. Hopkins uses the traditional structure of an Italian sonnet to organize the points he wants to get across.

The opening quatrain affirms that the natural world, in its great beauty, is filled with — loaded to capacity with — God's glory. It should be unmissable — it should flash in our eyes the way sunlight shines off a piece of gold foil; it collects around us the way olive oil emerges as olives are crushed. Yet, people ignore God by neglecting their responsibility to the world God created. The second quatrain images that neglect: For generations people have focused on trade, industry, and self-advancement. That they are out of touch with nature is signaled by shoes: No longer do we feel the soil and thus care about its condition.

The sestet is set off by a space, as if the speaker pauses to draw a big breath and then give vent to an outburst of praise and affirmation: No matter what human beings do to the earth, they will never eliminate God from it. Even if they destroy all human life, put out the "last lights," and leave the planet in darkness, God's presence will be there still, arising as the light of a new day. The poem concludes by comparing God's constant, caring presence to a mother bird brooding over her newborn chicks, but with the bright wings of an angel.

The tight, orderly traditional form of the sonnet seems fitting for a poem conveying a sense of orderliness — that God has a plan for the world itself that humans should not violate. The rhythms and sounds are intensified by their confinement in a compressed space: The energy of the poem seems to burst out as the reader opens the poem. Here is another example of a sonnet in Italian form, developing a very different subject. See if you think using the sonnet form leads to some of the same kind of intensity and power.

Helene Johnson   1907–1995

Sonnet to a Negro in Harlem   [1927]

You are disdainful and magnificent —
Your perfect body and your pompous gait,
Your dark eyes flashing solemnly with hate,
Small wonder that you are incompetent
To imitate those whom you so despise —   5
Your shoulders towering high above the throng,
Your head thrown back in rich, barbaric song,
Palm trees and mangoes stretched before your eyes.
Let others toil and sweat for labor's sake
And wring from grasping hands their meed° of gold.   *reward* 10
Why urge ahead your supercilious feet?
Scorn will efface each footprint that you make.
I love your laughter arrogant and bold.
You are too splendid for this city street.

APPROACHING THE READING

1. Notice the way the subject is adapted to the structure, with its turn after the octave. Summarize what is said in lines 1–8, in 9–12, and then in 13–14. In what ways are the form and its handling appropriate and effective?

2. In this sonnet, sentences do not coincide with the quatrains — the poem seems to be playing off against the form as well as adopting it. Is that appropriate and effective for the content?

3. Like McKay in "If we must die" (p. 523), Johnson employs a form from the white literary tradition. What ironies do you see in that? Could she be said to be claiming the form for her race as well as her purposes? Does anything in the poem support saying that?

This poem is as much about the speaker and cultural perceptions as it is about the person it is written to. Notice how the speaker "spins" what the culture usually judges negatively, revealing its embodiment as "magnificent." The speaker celebrates the man's attitude and, by implication, criticizes the cultural mores as well as what causes the man's behavior. The easy "either/or" of what is proper and improper is shown to be both false and controlling.

> There are many other inherited types of poem. Some of the well-known examples are described in the Glossary (pp. 1502–20). Look, for example, at **haiku**, **sestina**, and **villanelle**.

BLANK VERSE AND COUPLETS

There are also inherited patterns for nonstanzaic verse. These specify line lengths and sometimes sequences of rhyme, but not any specific separation into similar groupings of lines. The best known among these patterns is **blank verse** (unrhymed iambic pentameter—see pp. 568 and 570), the most widely used verse form of English poetry. Shakespeare's plays, Milton's *Paradise Lost* and *Paradise Regained,* Wordsworth's *Prelude,* and countless other long poems were composed in blank verse because it is well suited to narrative and dialogue. Here are the inspiring closing lines from Alfred, Lord Tennyson's poem "Ulysses" (p. 739), in which the old adventurer Ulysses (Odysseus) seeks to inspire his aging comrades to leave the safety and comfort of their homes and join him in another, perhaps final, adventure, sailing westward through the Strait of Gibraltar and into the unknown sea:

> Though much is taken, much abides; and though
> We are not now that strength which in old days
> Moved earth and heaven, that which we are, we are—
> One equal temper of heroic hearts,
> Made weak by time and fate, but strong in will
> To strive, to seek, to find, and not to yield.

Iambic is often considered the "natural" meter of English. When we talk or write in English, we often fall into loose iambics that can be divided into groups about ten syllables long. Many say that is the primary reason it is so widely used.

Another important inherited form, **couplets** (two lines rhyming), can be grouped into stanzas (as in A. E. Housman's "To an Athlete Dying Young"—p. 672), but more often they are strung out in extended, nonstanzaic passages. They provide a simple pattern, like blank verse, but because of the rhyme, the emphasis is different. Other poems in couplets include Robert Browning's "My Last Duchess" (p. 511), Gwendolyn Brooks's "We Real Cool" (p. 516), and Angelina Weld Grimké's "A Winter Twilight"

(p. 550). In seventeenth- and eighteenth-century England, the **heroic couplet** (couplets in iambic pentameter with a full stop, usually, at the end of the second line) was widely used for short and long poems. See, for example, Anne Bradstreet's "To My Dear and Loving Husband" (p. 615) and Jonathan Swift's "A Description of the Morning" (p. 737). Couplets also are used as parts of other forms, as, for example, the concluding lines of the English sonnet.

FREE VERSE

Many twentieth-century poets do not use inherited or preplanned forms, preferring to work without a blueprint for a poem's form. They allow the entire poem to "find" its own shape. The poem may emerge from the poet's imagination and skillful intuition in the form that it needs, or the form may develop in the process of writing and revising. In either case, the poet's attention is focused primarily on other things — on images, sounds, rhythms — and the poet allows forms to develop, consciously shaping them as they are discovered or letting them result from attention to line, line break, rhythm, and so forth.

Such poems traditionally have been called **free verse** because they are free of predetermined metrical and stanzaic patterns. The term *free verse* is misleading, however, if it is interpreted to mean "anything goes," that form and the other elements don't matter. Some books use the term **open form** to avoid such misunderstanding. Either term is usually acceptable. Just remember that no matter how "free" a poem appears, it *does have form*. Every poem does.

Unlike metrical or stanzaic poetry, free verse does not rely on organized structural repetition (like those of meter, rhyme, stanza, or identical syllable counts) to achieve form and coherence. Instead, it relies on connected images and sounds, parallelism in phrasing, and handlings of lines, spaces, rhythms, indentations, gaps, and timing. For the beginning poet, writing in open form may look easier than writing in inherited forms. However, each approach requires an ability to work with the elements of poetry. Each is challenging when one is aware of the complexities of writing any poem well. Each is easy only if done carelessly.

Consider the ways the following poem, though it is free of predetermined metrical and stanzaic patterns, does have form, and reflect on how its form contributes to the effect of what it is saying.

Leslie Marmon Silko   b. 1948

Prayer to the Pacific   [1981]

I traveled to the ocean
    distant
        from my southwest land of sandrock
      to the moving blue water
    Big as the myth of origin.   5

Pale
pale water in the yellow-white light of
      sun   floating west
        to China
    where ocean herself was born.   10
Clouds that blow across the sand are wet.

Squat in the wet sand and speak to the Ocean:
   I return to you   turquoise   the red coral you sent us,
      sister spirit of Earth.
Four round stones in my pocket   I carry back the ocean   15
    to suck and to taste.

Thirty thousand years ago
    Indians came riding across the ocean
    carried by giant sea turtles.
Waves were high that day   20
   great sea turtles waded   slowly out
        from the gray sundown sea.

Grandfather Turtle rolled in the sand   four times
    and disappeared
      swimming into the sun.   25

And so   from that time
   immemorial,
      as the old people say,
rain clouds drift from the west
      gift from the ocean.   30

Green leaves in the wind
Wet earth on my feet
   swallowing raindrops
     clear from China.

APPROACHING THE READING

1. Examine the form of the poem carefully, focusing on its visual appearance. Consider how the structure affects your reading of the poem, how the lines' placement creates a kind of choreography of movement for your eyes. How is this structure essential to the timing, energy, and rhythm within the poem?

2. Follow the way sentences run through several lines. Discuss what the juxtaposition of lines with sentences adds to the effect of the poem.

3. Why does the speaker go to the seashore to offer a prayer to the Pacific? In what ways is the form appropriate to the speaker and to the prayer being offered?

The most striking formal feature of this poem is the attractiveness of its layout on the page. To look at the poem is like observing a work of visual art, with its clear attention to composition, design, and proportion. There is a kinetic sense to Silko's poem, the way the lines move through our eyes and into our actual physical nature. As we follow the movement of the lines, we can feel in our bodies the energy, oceanic rhythm, and "flow" of the poem. Along with such visual appeal, the poem's division into lines and its arrangement on the page indicate how it should be read—which lines go together, where pauses amplify its impact, what particular words should be emphasized. The poem describes the speaker's journey to the seaside to offer a prayer to the ocean—by dropping four round stones into its waters. It is a prayer of gratitude for the gift in the past of the ocean carrying the speaker's ancestors to these shores on giant turtles and for the gift in the present of carrying clouds with much-needed rain across the waters to the land the speaker inhabits. The use of open, seemingly organic, form to evoke a trust in the natural world feels appropriate to the Native American myths it recounts, certainly more appropriate than to use an inherited verse form from another culture, such as those discussed earlier in this chapter.

INTERNAL FORM

In addition to shape, or external form, a poem also has an *internal form,* the inner arrangement or organization of its parts and content. The variety of techniques and arrangements used by poets is extensive; we list here some of the most important ones.

Parallelism

This key organizing technique is used in conjunction with other ways of handling of inner form. **Parallelism** can be considered in two ways: (1) When elements of equal weight within phrases, sentences, or paragraphs are expressed in a similar grammatical order and structure. It can appear within a line or pair of lines: "And he was always quietly arrayed, / And he was always human when he talked" — Edwin Arlington Robinson's "Richard Cory" (p. 552); or, more noticeably, it can appear as a series of parallel items, as in Langston Hughes's "Harlem" (p. 546). (2) When two consecutive lines in open form are related by the second line's repeating, expanding on, or contrasting with the idea of the first, as, for example, in the poems of Walt Whitman (pp. 748–52).

Juxtaposition

This important organizational technique is also used in conjunction with other ways of handling inner form. **Juxtaposition** is the placement of things (often very different things) side by side or close together for comparison or contrast or to create something new from the union, without necessarily making them grammatically parallel. See, for example, how Victor Hernandez Cruz's "Problems with Hurricanes" (p. 628) juxtaposes the seriousness of an honorable death during a hurricane (drowning or being hurled by the wind against a mountain) with the ludicrous danger of dying dishonorably from being smashed by a mango, banana, or plantain.

Looking for juxtapositions can be an effective and interesting starting point in trying to "get hold" of a poem (or story or play). Juxtaposition is not always present, but it often is, and often with an ironic twist. Juxtaposition usually has the effect of placing you between paired items, so that you must work through the oppositions, perhaps reconciling them, perhaps being left with an inherent tension or reaching to the wonderful strangeness of what is created.

Narrative

One of the most basic approaches to structure is **narrative**, a poet recounting an event as a sequence of actions and details, as in Jimmy Santiago Baca's "Family Ties" (p. 601) or Robert Morgan's "Mountain Bride" (p. 695). There are also *long* narrative poems, stories cast in poetic form, from Homer on down to the present.

Description

Another basic approach is description. The poem's images are arranged in an order that focuses the reader's attention most effectively. These poems are often unified by the way specific images connect throughout the poem, much like a tapestry. See, among many examples, Garrett Kaoru Hongo's "Yellow Light" (p. 473) and Gary Soto's "The Elements of San Joaquin" (p. 729).

Logical Pattern

Materials can be arranged in a logical pattern of development. This could be in the form of a logical argument, like the three-part attempt at persuasion in Andrew Marvell's "To His Coy Mistress" (p. 688), or of logical explanation, like the "wonderings" in Cornelius Eady's "My Mother, If She Had Won Free Dance Lessons" (p. 642).

Question-Answer

Poems can raise a question (explicitly or implicitly) and work toward an answer (which also can be stated or implied). Emily Dickinson's "I'm Nobody! Who are you?" (p. 578) raises a deep, perennial question and explores it playfully, but seriously. Langston Hughes's "Harlem" (p. 546) is a series of questions with an implied answer phrased as a final question, and the title of Ai's "Why Can't I Leave You?" (p. 596) raises a question that the rest of the poem seeks to answer.

Problem-Response

Some poems raise or suggest a problem and develop or imply a solution. Victor Hernández Cruz's "Problems with Hurricanes" (p. 628) uses this structure in a whimsical way, while Samuel Hazo's "For Fawzi in Jerusalem" (p. 665) explores long-term problems that seem to have no solution.

Meditative Movement

Some poems are arranged as meditations, often moving from a reflection on a physical place or object or a scene visualized mentally to personal or spiritual perceptions, as in Lucille Clifton's "at the cemetery, walnut grove plantation, south carolina, 1989" (p. 572) or James Wright's "A Blessing" (p. 539).

Association

Poems can be arranged through association, moving from word or image or idea or other element to another word, image, idea, or other element connected to it on the basis of free associations, as in Amiri Baraka's "AM/TRAK" (p. 602) and Jayne Cortez's "Into This Time" (p. 626).

Lists (or Catalogs) and Litanies

Lists and litanies may be the most common use of form (we all construct them). Poets employ them by laying out a series of details, often referred to as a catalog. Lists can create range, rhythm, intensity, and texture. For a poem structured as a litany, a ceremonial form of prayer using a series of invocations and repeated responses, see Joy Harjo's "She Had Some Horses" (p. 537). Catalogs also can structure parts of a poem, as in the last line of Gwendolyn Brooks's "The Bean Eaters" (p. 464).

Circular Form

Poems frequently employ a circular form, that is, they verbally or otherwise relate the end to the beginning, the way Anita Endrezze's "The Girl Who Loved the Sky" (p. 476) begins and ends with imagery of "lanterns," and Mary Tall Mountain's "Matmiya" (p. 738) at the end circles back to the opening line "I see you sitting," and Seamus Heaney's "Digging" (p. 667) returns at the end to the poem's opening lines, "Between my finger and my thumb / The squat pen rests."

www

Further explore form and type, including interactive exercises, with VirtuaLit Poetry at bedfordstmartins.com/approachinglit.

Poetic Types That Impose Structure

A number of traditional types of poetry, such as **epic**, **ballad**, **epigram**, song, and hymn, carry with them expectations of what the poem should include and sometimes how it should be organized. An epic, for example, must

---

☑ CHECKLIST on Form and Type

❑ Notice the role form plays in a poem and the effect it has on your experience of reading the poem.

❑ Watch for the handlings of lines and consider the various ways they affect a poem's appearance, rhythm, and emphasis, and the way they interact with sentences.

❑ Be aware of both a poem's external form (the way the poem looks on the page) and its inner form (the artistic design or structure that arranges, organizes, or connects the various elements).

❑ For poems in stanzas, consider the effectiveness and appropriateness of the form selected for the poem. If the poet introduces a variation in the form once established, consider what the changes convey in meaning, tone, and effect.

❑ Watch for inherited forms (such as the English sonnet, the Italian sonnet, ballad stanza, couplets, and blank verse) and consider the kind of creativity and imaginativeness that writing such poetry entails.

❑ Watch for poetry written as free verse (lacking such repeated features as rhyme, meter, or stanza, but using unity of pattern, such as visual structures, parallelism, or rhythm) and consider the kind of creativity and craft that writing such poetry requires.

open *in medias res* (see p. 58) and include such features as a formal state-ment of theme; an invocation to a deity; catalogs of warriors, ships, and armies; and a journey to the underworld.

Combinations of the Above

Almost any of the structures described above can be used with another or others to create fresh and interesting combinations. See what combina-tions you can find in, for example, Nikki Giovanni's "Nikka-Rosa" (below) and Heather McHugh's "What He Thought" (p. 684).

FURTHER READING

Consider form in the following poems, asking such questions as these: How would you describe the structuring of the poem? Is it an inherited or invented structure? In what ways is the form appropriate for the poem? In what ways does the form itself carry, add to, or intensify the meaning or ef-fect of the poem? In what ways is the form aesthetically satisfying? The first two poems are about memories of earlier days and the people in them, each with a distinct handling of lines and sentences.

Nikki Giovanni   b. 1943

Nikka-Rosa   [1968]

childhood rememberances are always a drag
if you're Black
you always remember things like living in Woodlawn°
with no inside toilet
and if you become famous or something   5
they never talk about how happy you were to have your mother
all to yourself and
how good the water felt when you got your bath from one of those
big tubs that folk in chicago barbecue in
and somehow when you talk about home   10
it never gets across how much you
understood their feelings
as the whole family attended meetings about Hollydale°
and even though you remember

---

3. **Woodlawn:** A suburb of Cincinnati.   13. **Hollydale:** An all-black housing development in which Giovanni's father invested money.

your biographers never understand   15
your father's pain as he sells his stock
and another dream goes
and though you're poor it isn't poverty that
concerns you
and though they fought a lot   20
it isn't your father's drinking that makes any difference
but only that everybody is together and you
and your sister have happy birthdays and very good christmasses
and I really hope no white person ever has cause to write about me
because they never understand Black love is Black wealth and they'll 25
probably talk about my hard childhood and never understand that
all the while I was quite happy

APPROACHING THE READING

1. An important structural feature of the poem is the mixture of long lines and short lines. Consider the effect of both and the effect of using varying lengths.

2. Pick out contrasts the poem builds around: of past and present, white culture and black culture. Note ways the poem's structure brings them out.

3. Reflect on the effects of eliminating both punctuation and capitalization from the poem. Did you have difficulty following sentences without such conventional signals? Might there be a political, social, or cultural reason in addition to the effect on tone and rhythm?

David Mura b. 1952

Grandfather-in-Law   [1989]

It's nothing really, and really, it could have been worse, and of course,
    he's now several years dead,
and his widow, well, if oftentimes she's somewhat distracted, overly
    cautious when we visit —
after all, Boston isn't New York — she seems, for some reason, enor-
    mously proud that there's now a writer in the family,
and periodically, sends me clippings about the poet laureate, Thoreau,
    Anne Sexton's daughter, Lowell, New England literary lore —
in which I fit, if I fit at all, simply because I write in English — as if
    color of skin didn't matter anymore.
Still, years ago, during my first visit to Boston, when we were all
    asleep,   5

he, who used to require that my wife memorize lines of Longfellow or
    Poe and recite them on the phone,
so that, every time he called, she ran outdoors and had to be coaxed
    back, sometimes with threats, to talk to Pops
(though she remembers too his sly imitations of Lincoln, ice cream at
    Brighams, burgers and fries, all the usual grandfatherly treats),
he, who for some reason was prejudiced against Albanians — where
    on earth did he find them I wondered —   10
who, in the thirties, would vanish to New York, catch a show, buy a
    suit, while up north,
the gas and water bills pounded the front door (his spendthrift ways
    startled me with my grandfather's resemblance),
who for over forty years came down each morning, "How's the old
    goat?" with a tie only his wife could knot circling his neck,
he slipped into my wife's room — we were unmarried at the time —
    and whispered so softly she thought
he almost believed she was really asleep, and was saying this like a
    wish or spell, some bohunk miscalculated Boston sense of duty: 15
"Don't make a mistake with your life, Susie. Don't make a
    mistake . . ."
Well. The thing that gets me now, despite the dangling rantings I've
    let go, is that, at least at that time,
he was right: There was, inside me, some pressing, raw unpeeled per-
    sistence, some libidinous desire for dominance
that, in the scribbled first drafts of my life, seemed to mark me as
    wastrel and rageful, bound to be unfaithful,
to destroy, in some powerful, nuclear need, fissioned both by child-
    hood and racism, whatever came near —   20
And I can't help but feel, forgiving him now, that if she had listened,
    if she had been awake,
if this flourishing solace, this muscled-for-happiness, shared by us
    now, had never awakened,
he would have become for me a symbol of my rage and self-destruction,
    another raw, never healing wound,
and not this silenced grandfatherly presence, a crank and scoundrel,
    red-necked Yankee who created the delicate seed of my wife, my
    child.

APPROACHING THE READING

1. The most notable formal feature of the poem is the use of long, prose-like
   lines. What effect do they create — in terms of the speaker, the overall situation, the tone, your role as reader?

2. Give some attention to the interplay of lines and sentences. What is the effect of the long, rambling sentences — on character, on tone, on rhythm?

3. Consider the inner arrangement of the poem. How does it bring out the conflicts between generations and its resolution? How does the idea of forgiveness in line 21 fit in?

Here are three poems about animals. Each poet has worked carefully, and in distinctive ways, with her or his poem's form. As with the previous poems, think about whether the form is appropriate for the poem; ways the form carries, adds, or intensifies the meaning of the poem; ways the form is aesthetically satisfying; and ways the form affects your reading.

Joy Harjo   b. 1951

She Had Some Horses   [1983]

She had some horses.

She had horses who were bodies of sand.
She had horses who were maps drawn of blood.
She had horses who were skins of ocean water.
She had horses who were the blue air of sky.   5
She had horses who were fur and teeth.
She had horses who were clay and would break.
She had horses who were splintered red cliff.

She had some horses.

She had horses with long, pointed breasts.
She had horses with full, brown thighs.   10
She had horses who laughed too much.
She had horses who threw rocks at glass houses.
She had horses who licked razor blades.

She had some horses.   15

She had horses who danced in their mothers' arms.
She had horses who thought they were the sun and their
bodies shone and burned like stars.
She had horses who waltzed nightly on the moon.
She had horses who were much too shy, and kept quiet   20
in stalls of their own making.

She had some horses.

She had horses who liked Creek Stomp Dance songs.
She had horses who cried in their beer.
She had horses who spit at male queens who made   25
them afraid of themselves.

She had horses who said they weren't afraid.
She had horses who lied.
She had horses who told the truth, who were stripped
bare of their tongues.   30

She had some horses.

She had horses who called themselves, "horse."
She had horses who called themselves, "spirit," and kept
their voices secret and to themselves.
She had horses who had no names.   35
She had horses who had books of names.

She had some horses.

She had horses who whispered in the dark, who were afraid to speak.
She had horses who screamed out of fear of the silence, who
carried knives to protect themselves from ghosts.   40
She had horses who waited for destruction.
She had horses who waited for resurrection.

She had some horses.

She had horses who got down on their knees for any saviour.
She had horses who thought their high price had saved them.   45
She had horses who tried to save her, who climbed in her
bed at night and prayed as they raped her.

She had some horses.

She had some horses she loved.
She had some horses she hated.   50

These were the same horses.

APPROACHING THE READING

1. This poem is in one of the oldest of forms, the litany. Read it aloud, feeling the rhythms of its lines and inner arrangement. Consider what the rhythm and repetition of litany contribute to the impact, effect, and power of the poem.

2. Describe how the external form struck you when you first saw it. Was it inviting? Why or why not?

3. The poem uses other techniques for inner arrangement along with the list or litany. Pick out at least three.

4. What do you make of the last three lines?

5. Harjo has said that she has been asked the most about this poem and has the least to say about it. Speculate on why you think each is the case.

James Wright   1927–1980

A Blessing   [1963]

Just off the highway to Rochester, Minnesota,
Twilight bounds softly forth on the grass.
And the eyes of those two Indian ponies
Darken with kindness.
They have come gladly out of the willows   5
To welcome my friend and me.
We step over the barbed wire into the pasture
Where they have been grazing all day, alone.
They ripple tensely, they can hardly contain their happiness
That we have come.   10
They bow shyly as wet swans. They love each other.
There is no loneliness like theirs.
At home once more,
They begin munching the young tufts of spring in the darkness.
I would like to hold the slenderer one in my arms,   15
For she has walked over to me
And nuzzled my left hand.
She is black and white,
Her mane falls wild on her forehead,
And the light breeze moves me to caress her long ear   20
That is delicate as the skin over a girl's wrist.
Suddenly I realize
That if I stepped out of my body I would break
Into blossom.

APPROACHING THE READING

1. The form of the poem relies on lineation. Consider the effects of the longer and shorter lines, and of the variation between longer and shorter.

2. What techniques of inner arrangement do you find in the poem? Do you feel any are particularly effective? Why?

3. What mood is evoked by the images throughout the poem?

4. Why do you think the speaker refers to this experience as a blessing? What are the denotations and connotations of "blessing"? Do any of them fit this poem?

5. Explain what is suggested by the last three lines.

Galway Kinnell b. 1927

Saint Francis and the Sow   [1980]

The bud
stands for all things,
even for those things that don't flower,
for everything flowers, from within, of self-blessing;
though sometimes it is necessary   5
to reteach a thing its loveliness,
to put a hand on its brow
of the flower
and retell it in words and in touch
it is lovely   10
until it flowers again from within, of self-blessing;
as Saint Francis
put his hand on the creased forehead
of the sow, and told her in words and in touch
blessings of earth on the sow, and the sow   15
began remembering all down her thick length,
from the earthen snout all the way
through the fodder and slops to the spiritual curl of the tail,
from the hard spininess spiked out from the spine
down through the great broken heart   20
to the blue milken dreaminess spurting and shuddering
from the fourteen teats into the fourteen mouths sucking and
     blowing beneath them:
the long, perfect loveliness of sow.

APPROACHING THE READING

1. The form of the poem, like the previous one, relies on lineation. Consider the different effects of the longer and shorter lines on sound, rhythm, emphasis.

2. The first nine lines of the poem are fairly direct and less lyrical than those that follow, which heighten in lyrical intensity. Do you think this is effective?

3. To what extent is this poem, like the last one, about "blessing"? Consider similarities and differences in what "blessing" means in each.

4. People often say, "beauty is in the eye of the beholder." Is that what this poem is about? Or is it a critique challenging that idea?

RESPONDING THROUGH WRITING

Journal Entries

1. Choose a poem and change the way it is divided into lines. Then write in your journal about what you discovered from these changes.

2. Be on the lookout for **found poetry**, that is, prose found in newspapers, magazines, advertisements, textbooks, or elsewhere in everyday life that contains elements of poetry, such as meter, effective rhythm, phrasings that can be divided into lines, imaginative uses of language and sound, and so on. For an example, see the opening lines of T. S. Eliot's "Journey of the Magi" (p. 643), which Eliot borrowed from a sermon and divided into lines. Collect a dozen examples for your journal, dividing them carefully into poetic lines. Comment briefly on what this revealed to you about choices poets make about line divisions and about their effect.

Research the authors in this chapter with *LitLinks* at bedfordstmartins.com/ approachinglit.

3. In your journal, describe and discuss briefly the inner arrangements of the following poems: Elizabeth Bishop's "The Fish" (p. 608), Robert Frost's "Mending Wall" (p. 651), Richard Lovelace's "To Lucasta, Going to the Wars" (p. 683), Cheryl Savageau's "Bones — A City Poem" (p. 719), Charles Simic's "Begotten of the Spleen" (p. 728), and Mary Tall Mountain's "Matmiya" (p. 738).

Literary Analysis Papers

4. For one of the following poems, write a paper describing its form and discussing the effectiveness and appropriateness of its distinctive handling of lines: Charles Bukowski's "my old man" (p. 488), Rosemary Catacalos's "David Talamántez on the Last Day of Second Grade" (p. 620), Allen Ginsberg's "A Supermarket in California" (p. 656), Dwight Okita's "In Response to Executive Order 9066" (p. 698), or Wendy Rose's "Loo-Wit" (p. 715).

5. The form of Peter Blue Cloud's "Rattle" (p. 610), with different things going on in parallel columns, makes unusual demands of a reader. Write a paper discussing what is going on in the poem and how form contributes to its effectiveness.

6. Write a paper explicating a sonnet with emphasis on the way its structure fits and brings out its subject and theme. Use a traditional sonnet such as John Milton's "When I consider how my light is spent" (p. 692) or Edmund Spenser's "One day I wrote her name upon the strand" (p. 735), or use a sonnet that seems surprising to see in that form, such as, for example, Gary Miranda's "Love Poem" (p. 693) or Vijay Seshadri's "The Refugee" (p. 720).

Making Connections

7. Write a paper assessing the appeal and effectiveness of villanelle as a form by discussing how it works in two poems, Dylan Thomas's "Do not go gentle into that good night" (p. 741) and John Yau's "Chinese Villanelle" (p. 757).

8. Write a paper comparing the free verse form used in two of the following poems and discussing for each how the invented form fits and accentuates the poem's subject and theme: Lucille Clifton's "at the cemetery, walnut grove plantation, south carolina, 1989" (p. 573), Gerald Barrax's "Dara" (p. 607), Cornelius Eady's "My Mother, If She Had Won Free Dance Lessons" (p. 642), or Linda Hogan's "The History of Red" (p. 670).

Cultural Criticism Papers

9. Write a paper discussing the cultural implications of poetic form. Look at examples of poems in traditional forms by poets from outside the conventional Anglo-American heritage, such as Claude McKay's "If we must die" (p. 523) or "America" (p. 686), Helene Johnson's "Sonnet to a Negro in Harlem" (p. 526), Vijay Seshadri's "The Refugee" (p. 720), or John Yau's "Chinese Villanelle" (p. 757). Discuss whether it seems appropriate and effective for these poets to use these forms for these subjects. Would it be more appropriate and effective for them to write free verse poetry? Also discuss if their use of those literary forms could be viewed as a way of crossing borders and making connections between different cultures.

10. Write a paper in which you discuss how the form of a particular poem, or of several poems, is appropriate for and an embodiment of the culture the poem emerges from. Think, for example, of "She Had Some Horses" by Joy Harjo (p. 537), how the litany connects with the idea of the chant.

RESPONDING THROUGH THE ARTS

1. A good way to learn about how a sonnet works is to try writing one (English or Italian). Use contemporary diction, the language you speak. Remember, you are "inheriting" the *form* from the past, not the past's language. Then write a short description of what trying it was like.

2. Try writing a free verse poem working with an important event in your personal life. Take advantage of what you have learned about line, line breaks, and form to add to the impact of your poem. Then write a paragraph about why you decided to do what you did with each of those elements.

M etaphor has interested me more as a way of knowledge, a
way of grasping something. I like to . . . use the metaphor as a
way to discover something about the nature of reality.

Charles Simic

Figurative
Language

CHAPTER 13

When Romeo says, "But, soft, what light through yonder window
breaks? / It is the east, and Juliet is the sun," the hearer or reader of Shakespeare's *Romeo and Juliet* knows perfectly well that Romeo doesn't think
Juliet actually is the sun. He may be lovesick, but he's not loony. The ability
almost all of us have to process language lets us understand, almost instan-
taneously, that Romeo is comparing Juliet to, or identifying her with, the
sun. Romeo is making imaginative, not logical, sense. He is using a **figure of
speech** or **figurative language**, that is, a shift from standard or customary
usage of words to achieve a special effect or particular meaning. He is trying
to pack lots of meaning into a few words: that Juliet's beauty dazzles like the
sun, that Juliet is the center of his life the way the sun is the center of our
solar system. An important part of comprehending poetry is being able to
recognize when language is to be taken "figuratively" instead of at face
value, and what its figurativeness conveys.

From the dozens of specific types of figurative language available to writers, you need to know and recognize only about half a dozen. It helps to be
able to call them by name. Some people grimace when they are asked to
learn the particular vocabulary of poetry. But think about it. When you are
talking about a sound system, you might use the terms *Dolby* or *amplifier*. If
you can assume that your listener understands these terms, you don't need
to take the time to explain them. Similarly, attaching names to figures helps
in getting to know them and provides a useful, shared shorthand when talking about a poem. Knowing the terms makes it easier to communicate.
Equally or even more important than using the correct label is being able to
describe what the figure's role is and how it functions in the poem and in
your reading. That is the focus in this chapter.

SIMILE

To help someone understand something—how you felt as a first-year college student, for example—you might use a *comparison:* "When I walked into my first class, my mind seemed as blank as the paper in my notebook." Writers of fiction, poetry, and drama often use comparisons that are unexpected and imaginative (thus, figurative). Figurative comparisons occur when we discover that two things we thought were entirely dissimilar actually have attributes in common or when the comparison leads us to a new way of perceiving or considering something. The comparison stretches our ideas about perception and about experiences of the things compared ("I've never thought about or seen it that way before"). The following lines may do this for you.

Julie Moulds   b. 1962

From "Wedding Iva"   [1995]

When he held her
she became
white and armless
like a goddess
or a bowling pin.

At first you may see a similarity in a rather conventional way: the comparison to a goddess. However, when you look more closely, you realize that the woman feels "armless" like a goddess. You may wonder to yourself, how is she being held? Our assumption that being compared to a goddess is positive is brought into tension. Then comes the surprise of the last line which shifts the comparison to a startlingly dissimilar object, a bowling pin. You may now see the embrace, the comparison to a goddess, and the way the woman feels in an uncommon way that challenges your common perceptions.

Reread Anita Endrezze's poem "The Girl Who Loved the Sky" (p. 476). Endrezze uses comparisons to get across how a blind girl experiences the world, especially how she conceives the sky she cannot see: "I met a blind girl who thought the sky / tasted like cold metal when it rained." What is the taste of cold metal? Is its taste different in the rain? How can the sky have taste at all? The blind girl uses her imagination to grasp what the sky is like since she can't see it. Endrezze helps us experience that imaginative process by giving us language that stretches our imaginations to a point where our rational minds can't grasp or put into logical terms what the words are expressing. And yet we intuitively understand it.

Actually, figurative language isn't limited to literary writers. All of us use it all the time: "I worked like a dog," "tough as nails." In fact, much of language by its very nature is figurative. Almost all of the words we use, except ones that identify concrete objects or actions such as *cup* or *kick,* involve figures. Often the figures go unnoticed. You are reading this section to comprehend it. *Comprehend,* in that context, is figurative: Its root is the Latin word *hendere,* "to grasp or hold with the thumb." That physical action has been extended imaginatively to include "grasping" or "taking hold of" an idea or concept.

We don't notice or react to most of the figures we use in everyday language because they have become either too familiar or stale. Some originally inventive figures (a river bed, a table leg) have been absorbed into the language to such an extent that, though they still are figures, we seldom think of them as figurative. And yet even these, when you look again at them as figures, may surprise you.

Surprising comparisons, using direct, explicit signal words such as *like, as, than,* or *similar to,* are called **similes** (from the Latin word for "similar"). Direct comparisons are usually the easiest figures to notice because they carry the signal word with them. But only surprising, unexpected comparisons are similes. The comparison discussed above from Anita Endrezze's "The Girl Who Loved the Sky" was a simile. So is this, a few lines further: "On hot, still days / we listened to the sky falling / like chalk dust." The comparison is definitely surprising: It takes very keen hearing to catch the sound of chalk dust falling; one would have to be even more alert to hear the sound of the sky falling. Similes appear again later in the poem:

> I was born blind, she said, an act of nature.
> Sure, I thought, like birds born
> without wings, trees without roots.

Here the speaker's comparisons bring out her anger at her friend's fate, but also her failure to understand that her friend, though she cannot see physically, is not rendered helpless the way a bird without wings would be. And,

> The day she moved
> I saw the world clearly: the sky
> backed away from me like a departing father.

The simile connects two great losses in the speaker's world — her father's absence and her friend's departure — and those losses, at this point anyhow, come to define the way she views her world. On the other hand, Endrezze's line "the room smells like glue" is not a simile: It is not surprising and not imaginative (the room smells the way glue smells or smells of glue because glue is used in the room). Comparisons between similar things (squid tastes like chicken; his eyes are like his father's) are straightforward analogy, not similes and not figurative.

The following poem uses a series of six comparisons to suggest the effect of having the attainment of one's hopes and aspirations delayed indefinitely. Watch for them as you read and notice how the sixth is different from the first five.

Langston Hughes   1902–1967

Harlem   [1951]

What happens to a dream deferred?

Does it dry up
like a raisin in the sun?
Or fester like a sore —
And then run?   5
Does it stink like rotten meat?
Or crust and sugar over —
like a syrupy sweet?

Maybe it just sags
like a heavy load.   10

Or does it explode?

APPROACHING THE READING

1. Explain why each of the comparisons is effective and meaningful.

Research this author in depth with cultural documents and multimedia resources on *LiterActive*.

2. How is the comparison in the final line different from the other five? How does that difference increase its power as well as the impact of the whole poem?

3. The poem refers to any dreams, but especially to the "American dream." If you are not familiar with the term, look it up. Relate it to the title of the poem and consider the bitter ironies that reading evokes.

In response to the question raised in the opening line, Hughes's poem poses further questions, suggesting a number of possible answers. These follow-up questions rely on similes to intensify their points. Read the lines without the similes and notice what happens: "What happens to a dream deferred? Does it dry up or fester? Does it stink, or crust and sugar over? Maybe it just sags." The points make sense. Dreams can dry up if their fulfillment keeps getting put off and the dreamer loses hope of ever achieving or receiving what she or he dreams about. But the points by themselves lack emotional impact; they aren't memorable. Much of the poem's power derives from the comparisons, the way they amplify the points, their appropriateness and the variety of applications they invite. For example, a dream deferred can be compared to a raisin drying up in the sun because as a once-juicy raisin dries up it shrivels, becomes smaller and smaller, and looks withered and unappealing. Try doing the same for the other comparisons.

METAPHOR

"All the world is like a stage." "All the world is a stage." Sense the difference? The former is a simile; the latter is a **metaphor**, a figure of speech in which two things usually thought to be dissimilar are treated as if they were the same, the same because they have characteristics in common. The word *metaphor* is derived from the Greek *metaphora,* "carry (*phor*) across (*meta*)." In a metaphor, characteristics of one thing are "carried across" to another, from the thing used to illustrate ("stage") to the subject being illustrated ("world").

Metaphors are basic to poetry and are widely used in fiction and drama as well. Shakespeare's character Jaques asserts, "All the world's a stage," in the comedy *As You Like It.* Without even thinking about it, we may treat this as a comparison ("the world is *like* a stage," with people playing roles, making entrances and exits, and so on). The line, however, does not say that the world is *like* a stage, but that it *is* a stage. Common sense and logic, of course, claim that the world is not part of a theater. But the figure says it is. Here metaphor opens our minds to see what they may not have seen before. A metaphor can break down a barrier and carry us into a world in which, through our imaginations, we discover transformations and uncommon relationships, sometimes even new "realities" and ways of experiencing.

Metaphors are easiest to recognize when *is* or *are* or some other linking word is present, as in "All the world is a stage." More difficult to recognize and explain are **implied metaphors**, in which the *to be* verb is omitted and the comparison may be implied, or "buried," rather than stated directly. "A car thief is a dirty dog" is direct metaphor. "Some dirty dog stole my car" contains an implied metaphor: The key term ("car thief") is implied, and you must supply it to complete the equation involved. Look again at "Harlem." Notice how it relies on a shift from similes in lines 2–10 to the implied metaphor of line 11: *"Or does it explode?"* The reader must supply the object that describes the ultimate effect of having dreams deferred: the possibility of frustration exploding into riot? defeat? revolution? despair? The fact that the poem doesn't use the word it refers to but has the reader think of it makes the conclusion more interactive and its impact all the stronger.

In "The Girl Who Loved the Sky" (p. 476), Endrezze uses both explicit and implied metaphors. "I learned / that numbers were fractious beasts" is an explicit metaphor: Math is like a beast that lives in a den, something wild, threatening, and hard to manage. The comparison conveys her feelings vividly. "The bruised petals of her lids" is implied, or buried, metaphor: The blind girl's eyelids apparently are dark, and this line compares them, even equates them, to the purple petals of the jacaranda tree outside the classroom. Similarly, the final lines of the poem also use metaphor: "until my fist was another lantern / hiding a small and bitter flame." Her fist is not a lantern, but the figure equates it with one; and her fist, like her heart, holds not a literal flame but petals and memories that remind her how the world takes from her those she loves, leaving her lonely and angry.

Read the following poem in which the speaker reflects on a southern African city at night and expresses his affection for it, despite its many problems. It is filled with figurative language, especially similes and implied metaphors. Watch for the way the figures pack the poem with meaning, beyond what literal equivalents could convey.

Dennis Brutus   b. 1924

Nightsong: City   [1963]

Sleep well, my love, sleep well:
the harbour lights glaze over restless docks,
police cars cockroach through the tunnel streets;

from the shanties creaking iron-sheets
violence like a bug-infested rag is tossed   5
and fear is immanent as sound in the wind-swung bell;

the long day's anger pants from sand and rocks;
but for this breathing night at least,
my land, my love, sleep well.

APPROACHING THE READING

1. The poem starts off as if it were a love poem addressed to a person. At what point do you realize that line one is figurative and the "love" it refers to is the city the speaker calls home? What leads you to that realization?

2. In line 3, the author uses a noun (*cockroach*) as a verb and turns it into a vivid metaphor. Explain how it works figuratively and whether you think it is effective, explaining why.

3. Line 4 takes us to a shantytown and helps us see houses with sheet-metal walls and roofs and hear the sounds as they creak in the wind. The follow-

ing two lines use similes to convey the violence and fear that pervade the area. Explain the comparisons and discuss their effectiveness.

4. Pick out the metaphors in lines 7 and 8 and, after reading the next section, the personification in line 9, and explain what each contributes to the poem.

The poem starts out with "Sleep well, my love." The title might signal that this song in the night is addressed to a city; but it could signal that the city is the setting for a nightsong to someone. It might be only after reading it a second time or looking back from the end of the poem that you realize that "my love" is the city the speaker loves. Saying that a city can "sleep" compares it to, or identifies it with, a living creature — an animal (metaphor) or a human being (see the next section on personification). The latter seems to fit best: The words of the first line sound like ones the speaker would offer at night to someone cherished. It may come as a surprise that the words are spoken to a city, but of course that shows how much he cares about it.

In this poem, the figurative comparisons add distinctness and vivid immediacy to the appearance of the city at night (harbor lights make the docks look shiny, the way a glaze does when applied to pottery or china; police cars dart around between rows of high-rise buildings with the quickness and agility of a cockroach). And they intensify the emotional impact of the descriptions of life in the city: violence pervades the shantytowns the way bugs infest a rag, fear is as present through the city as the sound of a bell, and the anger that fills the days "pants" everywhere like a fierce animal. But for the moment, the speaker wants to forget all that. For this one living, "breathing" night, he hopes his beloved city rests quietly and sleeps well.

PERSONIFICATION

Personification is a figure of speech in which something nonhuman is given some attributes of a person or is treated as if it has human characteristics or takes human actions. Sometimes abstract qualities are treated as if they are human. In Patricia Goedicke's lines, "Speak to me, Trouble, / Tell me how to move" (p. 559), for example, trouble does not have a voice; it is treated as if it is human. In other cases, concrete things are given human characteristics: in the phrase "a brilliant fluorescence breaks out / and makes war with the dim squares / of yellow kitchen light," from "Yellow Light" (p. 473), "fluorescence" is being given, briefly, the human attribute of warring. And in "the sky / backed away from me like a departing father," from "The Girl Who Loved the Sky" (p. 476), the sky is made human for a moment, able to walk away from the speaker as her father did.

Personification is sometimes defined incorrectly as treating something not living in terms of being alive rather than specifically being human. For example, in Shakespeare's *Romeo and Juliet,* Juliet, fearful of being drugged and buried in a vault, expresses fear of the tomb's "foul mouth [that] no healthsome air breathes in" (4.3.34). "Mouth" here is metaphor, not personification, since animals as well as humans have mouths and breathe through them.

A particular type of personification is **apostrophe**, that is, addressing someone not present or something ordinarily not spoken to as if present or capable of understanding, as when Macbeth says "Time, thou anticipatest my dread exploits" (4.1.144). Dennis Brutus uses apostrophe as well when his speaker in "Nightsong: City" talks to the city as if it could hear and understand.

Watch in the following poem for places where something nonliving is spoken of as if it is alive. Then decide which of these exemplify personification and consider what such personifications contribute to the effect of the poem.

Angelina Weld Grimké 1880–1958

A Winter Twilight [1923]

A silence slipping around like death,
Yet chased by a whisper, a sigh, a breath;
One group of trees, lean, naked and cold,
Inking their crest 'gainst a sky green-gold;
One path that knows where the corn flowers were;   5
Lonely, apart, unyielding, one fir;
And over it softly leaning down,
One star that I loved ere the fields went brown.

APPROACHING THE READING

1. What examples do you find of nonliving things treated as if alive? Point out ones that are personification — where the living attributes apply only to humans — and ones that are metaphors — where the connection could also apply to animals.

2. Consider the effect of personifications in the poem. What do they contribute that a comparison to something nonhuman wouldn't?

You may have heard someone speak of how a painting "brings a scene to life." That could be said of "A Winter Twilight" as well. The poem creates a picture, almost a verbal landscape painting. And, as with a painting, it slows everything to a stop, arrests this one moment, suspending it in time so that we can truly experience it. An irony in our lives is that actual life experiences go by so fast that we can't experience them fully. We need the arts to give us the chance to stop and really take in what otherwise goes by and is lost.

This poet wants not only to see the scene — she wants to bring alive its feeling and aura. She does so through metaphors and personifications comparing landscape features to living things. That this is a quiet scene is evoked by the way silence "slips around" in it, as an animal or a person would, and the way it is "chased by a whisper." For the trees to be "naked" treats them as living beings, as persons really since that word generally is applied only to humans. Similarly, the path comes alive through personification (since it "knows" where the corn flowers are), as does the "lonely" fir tree (a word usually reserved for a human conscious reaction to feeling cut off from what matters).

A winter scene can seem dead and lifeless, and the poem is acutely aware of death, mentioning it in the opening line; but that very awareness heightens the way the figures of speech bring out the life present even in a "barren" landscape. The poem closes with a sense of the intimacy of life and death: The star is given the living attribute of "leaning down," but this is a star the speaker loved (past tense — does she or he no longer love it?) before the fields "went brown" (died? lost their appeal and desirability?).

METONYMY AND SYNECDOCHE

Another figure of speech that, like metaphor, talks about one thing in terms of another is **metonymy**, a figure of speech in which the name of one thing is substituted for that of something closely associated with it. Like similes and metaphors, metonymies are used every day. When you hear a news reporter say, "The White House announced today . . . ," you've encountered a metonymy: "White House" invites you to visualize a familiar image closely associated with the president that substitutes for the staff members who issued the announcement. When the speaker in "The Girl Who Loved the Sky" (p. 476) says her friend "had no eyes," she does not mean that the girl's eye sockets were empty; she substitutes "eyes" for what is closely associated with eyes, "sight," because the word *eyes* is more concrete and vivid than the abstract word *sight*.

A subset of metonymy is **synecdoche**, a special kind of metonymy in which a part of a thing is substituted for the whole of which it is a part. When someone says to you, "Give me a hand," she or he actually wants help not just from your hands but also from the rest of you. Likewise, the familiar phrases "many mouths to feed" or "let's count noses" use synecdoche.

When the two girls in "The Girl Who Loved the Sky" are swinging and flying (note the metaphor — riding in a swing is something like flying) high over the other girls' heads, "heads" is synecdoche, a part substituted for the whole because it is the highest part of their bodies.

Recognizing metonymies and synecdoches helps you appreciate the way little things can have greater importance than they seem to at first. Robert Frost said, "If I must be classified as a poet, I might be called a Synecdochist, for I prefer the synecdoche in poetry," that figure of speech in which "a little thing touches a larger thing." Instead of starting with huge, complex themes and issues, Frost often uses local, everyday experiences as subjects, trusting our minds will be led to "a larger thing." Read his poem "Mending Wall" (p. 651) and think about how it embodies Frost's idea.

Look in the following poem for examples of nonliteral expression, figures of various sorts, including metonymy and synecdoche. Consider how the figures work (what is compared to what or what is substituted for what), and why the use of figures is effective and contributes to the poem's overall effect.

Edwin Arlington Robinson 1869–1935

Richard Cory   [1897]

Whenever Richard Cory went down town,
We people on the pavement looked at him:
He was a gentleman from sole to crown,
Clean favored, and imperially slim.

And he was always quietly arrayed,   5
And he was always human when he talked;
But still he fluttered pulses when he said,
"Good-morning," and he glittered when he walked.

And he was rich — yes, richer than a king —
And admirably schooled in every grace: 10
In fine, we thought that he was everything
To make us wish that we were in his place.

So on we worked, and waited for the light,
And went without the meat, and cursed the bread;
And Richard Cory, one calm summer night,   15
Went home and put a bullet through his head.

APPROACHING THE READING

1. Pick out examples of metonymy and synecdoche and explain how they work (what is being substituted for what). What do they contribute to the effect of the poem?

2. Describe the speaker. What is the effect of using *we* for the speaker instead of *I*? Could one say that "We people on the pavement" is a kind of synecdoche? Explain.

3. Pick out examples of other figures of speech and explain how they work and what they bring to the poem. Also point out examples of irony (see p. 493). Consider how both figures and irony bring out the "point" of the poem.

Robinson's poem seems a good example of Frost's point about being a synecdochist: The poem has lots of little things that touch larger things. One person speaks the poem but uses the pronoun *we*, thus attempting to suggest that what he felt was true for the whole population of the town. The poem focuses on "little" details—the way Richard Cory dresses, talks (even the way he says so little a thing as "Good-morning" makes hearts beat

Here are three other figures of speech that you will frequently encounter:

- **Paradox:** A figure of speech in which a statement initially seeming self-contradictory or absurd turns out to make good sense when seen in another light. In Shakespeare's *Much Ado about Nothing,* for example, when the Friar says to Hero, "Come, lady, die to live," he is using paradox. By pretending to die, she may regain the reputation she has lost through false slander. A subset of paradox is **oxymoron**, a self-contradictory combination of words or phrases, such as "O brawling love! O loving hate! . . . Feather of lead, bright smoke, cold fire, sick health!" in Shakespeare's *Romeo and Juliet.*
- **Hyperbole:** Exaggeration, or overstatement; a figure of speech in which something is stated more strongly than is warranted. Hyperbole is often used to make a point emphatically, as when Hamlet protests that he loved Ophelia much more than her brother did: "Forty thousand brothers / Could not with all their quantity of love / Make up my sum" (5.1.272–74).
- **Understatement:** A figure of speech that expresses something in an unexpectedly restrained way. Paradoxically, to deemphasize through understatement can be a way of emphasizing, of making people react with "there must be more to it than that." When Mercutio in *Romeo and Juliet,* after being stabbed by Tybalt, calls his wound "a scratch, a scratch" (3.1.92), he is understating, for the wound is serious. He calls for a doctor in the next line and dies a few minutes later.

faster), and walks. The townspeople long for any little thing to improve their lives, "light" substituting for "better days" because they see only dark despair around them and get by on almost nothing ("bread" substituted for "bare essentials") because they can't afford anything more ("meat" substituted for luxuries of any sort). Meanwhile Richard Cory, whose life seems so large, who seems to have so much, in a huge example of situational irony, ends his life with a little thing, a bullet through the head. Robinson could have told the story without figures of speech, but the use of synecdoches especially, with their emphasis on parts and small aspects, seems perfect for a poem that contrasts having a lot and having very little.

TWO OTHER OBSERVATIONS ABOUT FIGURES

No sharp lines divide figures of speech from one another. Read the following poem about a driver coming upon a deer that an earlier driver had struck and killed. Watch for the way it relies on images and figures for its effect, and for the way some figures could be labeled and explained in different ways.

William Stafford   1914–1995

Traveling through the Dark   [1962]

Traveling through the dark I found a deer
dead on the edge of the Wilson River road.
It is usually best to roll them into the canyon:
that road is narrow; to swerve might make more dead.

By glow of the tail-light I stumbled back of the car   5
and stood by the heap, a doe, a recent killing;
she had stiffened already, almost cold.
I dragged her off; she was large in the belly.

My fingers touching her side brought me the reason —
her side was warm; her fawn lay there waiting,   10
alive, still, never to be born.
Beside that mountain road I hesitated.

The car aimed ahead its lowered parking lights;
under the hood purred the steady engine.
I stood in the glare of the warm exhaust turning red;   15
around our group I could hear the wilderness listen.

I thought hard for us all — my only swerving —
then pushed her over the edge into the river.

APPROACHING THE READING

1. Pick out several figures of speech, identify them, and explain how they work. Which ones could be labeled as more than one type of figure? Explain why or how.

2. Consider why images seem appropriate in the first twelve lines and figures in the last six.

3. The figures supply a large part of the poetic impact of the poem. However, there are other poetic aspects that come through the use of alliteration and assonance, along with some slant rhyme (see pp. 498–500). Mark examples of such sound techniques. Think about how they cooperate with the figurative language to develop the theme of the poem.

The first twelve lines of the poem are narrative, describing what happened. They rely on images, without any figures. Lines 13–18 reflect on the experience and use a good deal of figurative language, such as bringing the car to life by having it purr like a harmless cat (though ironically it was a similar car that killed the deer) and making the wilderness not just a living thing but one that listens and presumably understands. And the word *swerve,* which is used in a literal sense in line 4, comes back in a figurative sense in line 17 as the speaker momentarily avoids doing what he must before proceeding to do it.

The poem illustrates two important characteristics of figurative language. First, a figure often fits into more than one category. "I could hear the wilderness listen," for example, stands either as metonymy ("wilderness" being substituted for the creatures and the natural habitat in it) or as personification ("wilderness" given humanlike ability to understand, not just hear). In this and most cases, applying labels to figures is a means to an end: It alerts you to their presence, helps you talk and write about them, and helps clarify the nature of the imaginative action you experience as you read them.

> **www**
> Further explore figurative language, including interactive exercises, with VirtuaLit Poetry at bedfordstmartins.com/approachinglit.

In addition to being aware that figures overlap with each other, keep in mind that figures of speech occur *within* poems, not *as* poems. Some people attempt to treat entire poems as figures of speech. After reading "Traveling through the Dark," they may say, "On the surface it's about a man finding a deer on the road, but what it's *really* about is our journey through life and the difficult decisions we face along the way." They substitute an abstract "meaning" for the concrete images of the poem. The poem is *really* about a deer on the road, though it may *also* (as opposed to *really*) be about life's journey. This book discusses images before figures because of the importance of grounding the experience in images and of letting the action or description be first and always itself.

> ☑ **CHECKLIST on Figurative Language**
>
> ❏ Notice any figurative language and the way it works imaginatively, especially these five types:
>
> - Simile: the expression of a direct similarity, using words such as *like, as,* or *than,* between two things usually regarded as dissimilar
> - Metaphor: treating two things usually thought to be dissimilar as if they are the same and have characteristics in common
> - Personification: treating something nonhuman as if it has human characteristics or takes human actions
> - Metonymy: substituting the name of one thing for that of something closely associated with it
> - Synecdoche: substituting a part of something for the whole of it
>
> ❏ Consider how the choice of a figure affects the concept being developed.

FURTHER READING

Here are two more poems that, like "Traveling through the Dark," explore aspects of nature. Read each, and then reread them, looking for language that can't be taken literally. Pick out several figures of speech and be ready to explain what is imaginative about them and what they contribute to the effect of the poem. The first poem explores several fresh, unusual, and striking ways of thinking about tornados. In the second, the speaker uses images of winter and snow in surprising ways to relate to and comfort her dying grandmother.

Thylias Moss   b. 1954

Tornados   [1991]

Truth is, I envy them
not because they dance; I out jitterbug them
as I'm shuttled through and through legs
strong as looms, weaving time. They
do black more justice than I, frenzy   5
of conductor of philharmonic and electricity, hair
on end, result of the charge when horns and strings release
the pent up Beethoven and Mozart. Ions played

instead of notes. The movement
is not wrath, not hormone swarm because   10

I saw my first forming above the church a surrogate
steeple. The morning of my first baptism and
salvation already tangible, funnel for the spirit
coming into me without losing a drop, my black
guardian angel come to rescue me before all the words   15

get out, *I looked over Jordan and what did I see coming for*
to carry me home.° *Regardez,*° it all comes back, even the first   *look*
grade French, when the tornado stirs up the past, bewitched spoon
lost in its own spin, like a roulette wheel that won't
be steered, like the world. They drove me underground,   20
tornado watches and warnings, atomic bomb drills. Adult
storms so I had to leave the room. Truth is

the tornado is a perfect nappy curl, tightly wound,
spinning wildly when I try to tamper with its nature, shunning
the hot comb and pressing oil even though if absolutely straight   25
I'd have the longest hair in the world. Bouffant tornadic
crown taking the royal path on a trip to town, stroll down
Tornado Alley where it intersects Memory Lane. Smoky spirit-
clouds, shadows searching for what cast them.

16–17. I looked . . . home: Lines from a Negro spiritual, "Swing Low, Sweet Chariot."

APPROACHING THE READING

1. The poem starts off with an imaginative comparison: a tornado *dancing*. In
   what way does that verb seem appropriate for a tornado? How does it help
   you perceive of a familiar thing in a fresh way?

2. Look for other imaginative comparisons that describe tornados from various angles and help you see and appreciate them in new and different ways.

3. The speaker begins by saying she envies tornados. This "envy" is actually a
   longing. What do you think the speaker longs for? Why does she, do you
   think?

4. The poem employs a type of meditational movement in which the speaker
   remembers experiences with tornados. Pick out several figurative references
   to memory. What is it about tornados that makes them an appropriate link
   to the past for her?

Judith Ortiz Cofer b. 1952

Cold as Heaven   [1995]

Before there is a breeze again
before the cooling days of Lent, she may be gone.
My grandmother asks me to tell her
again about the snow.
We sit on her white bed   5
in this white room, while outside
the Caribbean sun winds up the world
like an old alarm clock. I tell her
about the enveloping blizzard I lived through
that made everything and everyone the same;   10
how we lost ourselves in drifts so tall
we fell through our own footprints;
how wrapped like mummies in layers of wool
that almost immobilized us, we could only
take hesitant steps like toddlers   15
toward food, warmth, shelter.
I talk winter real for her,
as she would once conjure for me to dream
at sweltering siesta time,
cool stone castles in lands far north.   20
Her eyes wander to the window,
to the teeming scene of children
pouring out of a yellow bus, then to the bottle
dripping minutes through a tube
into her veins. When her eyes return to me,   25
I can see she's waiting to hear more
about the purifying nature of ice,
how snow makes way for a body,
how you can make yourself an angel
by just lying down and waving your arms   30
as you do when you say
good-bye.

APPROACHING THE READING

1. Consider weather in the poem. How does literal weather fit in the poem? In what ways is weather metaphorical? Why are both essential for the poem to have the deepest impact?

2. Pick out uses of simile, metaphor, metonymy, and synecdoche. What do they add to the poem's meaning and effect?

3. Discuss the relationship between the granddaughter and grandmother. How would you describe the tone (attitude of the speaker toward her grandmother's death and toward herself)? Point out figures that express what both are feeling.

4. Explain the implications of the simile in the poem's title. Consider the contrasts between cold and heat. What does snow convey in the poem? What does the speaker mean in line 17 by saying, "I talk winter real for her"?

The following two poems are about young persons struggling with situations and feelings they find difficult. Watch for ways images and figures bring out the concerns of each poem and the way the persons involved seek resolution.

Patricia Goedicke b. 1931

My Brother's Anger   [1992]

And here they are again, the duffel bags of sadness,
Shouldering their way into the house like a football team.

Mute, muscular, swollen,
Straining at the seams

Their small eyes look up   5
Waiting for me to open them.

Friends, how can I help you?

I want to pick you up, to cradle you in my arms
But I am too heavy myself.

Can't anyone tie his own shoes?   10

Speak to me, Trouble,
Tell me how to move.

My brother's anger is a helmet.

My sister's voice is a cracked flute
Talking to itself underwater.   15

What can I offer but a sieve?

Shoving yesterday in a closet
I make small talk, smile

Rush around trying to hang up coats

*   *   *

But all over the house there are these dull   20
Enormous sacks of pain.

Stumbling over other people's leftover lumber

I keep trying to embrace them,
Battering my head against weathered flanks . . .

Every day more suicides   25
Among the living, more hangovers

Among the dead.

I throw myself down on the floor
Right in front of them

But it's no use: these slab-sided sorrows   30
Have taken up permanent residence

And will not be comforted.

APPROACHING THE READING

1. The first two lines are dense with figurative language and need careful explanation. "Duffel bags of sadness" is an implied metaphor—what is being
   compared to what? Explain the simile comparing the "they" in line 1 to a
   football team.

2. Work your way through the poem, pointing out and explaining other similes, metaphors, and metonymies. What do they reveal about what the
   speaker's brother and sister are dealing with? How do they bring out what
   the speaker is feeling and trying to do for her siblings?

3. How do the poem's figures affect the tone of the poem? How does the
   poem's form help you feel what the speaker is experiencing?

4. Explain line 16, "What can I offer but a sieve?" Look up *sieve* to be sure
   you're clear about its denotations. Explain how it how it works as a figure
   and how it is being used in the poem.

Julia Alvarez   b. 1950

How I Learned to Sweep   [1996]

My mother never taught me sweeping.
One afternoon she found me watching
t.v. She eyed the dusty floor
boldly, and put a broom before
me, and said she'd like to be able   5

to eat her dinner off that table,
and nodded at my feet, then left.
I knew right off what she expected
and went at it. I stepped and swept;
the t.v. blared the news; I kept   10
my mind on what I had to do,
until in minutes, I was through.
Her floor was as immaculate
as a just-washed dinner plate.
I waited for her to return   15
and turned to watch the President,
live from the White House, talk of war:
in the Far East our soldiers were
landing in their helicopters
into jungles their propellers   20
swept like weeds seen underwater
while perplexing shots were fired
from those beautiful green gardens
into which these dragonflies
filled with little men descended.   25
I got up and swept again
as they fell out of the sky.
I swept all the harder when
I watched a dozen of them die.
as if their dust fell through the screen   30
upon the floor I had just cleaned.
She came back and turned the dial;
the screen went dark. *That's beautiful,*
she said, and ran her clean hand through
my hair, and on, over the window-   35
sill, coffee table, rocker, desk,
and held it up — I held my breath —
That's beautiful, she said, impressed,
she hadn't found a speck of death.

APPROACHING THE READING

1. Explain what is going on in lines 1–14, 15–25, and 26–39, and how the three
   sections relate to each other. Pick out similes, metaphors, and metonymies
   that clarify each section. How does the occasional use of rhyme contribute
   to the poem?

2. Is the title itself a metonymy? What is the mother teaching the speaker?
   What is the speaker learning?

3. Look again at the last line. One expects to read "speck of dust," or "dirt." In
   what ways is the substitution of "death" meaningful?

RESPONDING THROUGH WRITING

Journal Entries

www

Research the authors in this chapter with LitLinks at bedfordstmartins.com/approachinglit.

1. Look for similes as you read your favorite magazine, look at advertisements in magazines or on billboards, or watch commercials on TV. List several examples in your journal and comment on why use of similes makes for effective advertising.

2. As a journal entry, finish this line: "Waiting for you is like _____."
   Come up with three different similes, each having the effect of "stretching your reader's perception." Try to push each one further than the one before. For example:

   like waiting for summer

   like listening to a scratched CD

   like Thursday

   Then, choose a subject and write several different figures for it. For example:

   Love is like _____.

   Love is _____.

   Love _____.

   Write a paragraph in which you discuss the varied effects the different figures create.

3. Watch and/or listen to several comedians. Write a journal entry discussing their uses of paradox, overstatement, and understatement.

Literary Analysis Papers

4. Select a poem with striking use of figures, such as Geoffrey Hill's elegy "In Memory of Jane Fraser" (p. 669) or Andrew Marvell's love poem "To His Coy Mistress" (p. 688). Write a paper in which you discuss what the poem's figures suggest, what they help you realize, and how they affect your perceptions.

5. Many English poems from the early seventeenth century used surprising, far-fetched metaphors referred to as *conceits*. In a short paper, describe conceits and discuss how they function in John Donne's "A Valediction: Forbidding Mourning" (p. 638), which affirms that a strong love transcends distance and separation.

6. Go back to one of the poems in chapters 10–12 that relies heavily on figurative language, such as Robert Hayden's "Those Winter Sundays" (p. 462), Louise Erdrich's "A Love Medicine" (p. 478), or William Shakespeare's "That time of year thou mayst in me behold" (p. 521). Write a paper discussing the effect of figurative language in the poem.

Making Connections

7. Write a paper comparing and contrasting two or more poems dealing with fame, considering the way they create paradox and irony through the use of figures. Some poems to look at are Percy Bysshe Shelley's "Ozymandias" (p. 721) and Edmund Spenser's "One day I wrote her name upon the strand" (p. 735).

8. Write a paper comparing some poems about weather. You might start with Thylias Moss's "Tornados" (p. 556) and Judith Ortiz Cofer's "Cold as Heaven" (p. 558), and look for others, such as Victor Hernández Cruz's "Problems with Hurricanes" (p. 628), David Hernandez's "The Butterfly Effect" (p. 668), and James Welch's "Christmas Comes to Moccasin Flat" (p. 746). Consider how weather is used in them literally, figuratively, and symbolically.

Cultural Criticism Papers

9. Write a paper discussing the use of figures and archetypes in A. E. Housman's "To an Athlete Dying Young" (p. 672). Discuss how the poem's ideas relate to the present-day emphasis on superstar athletes and athletics.

10. Choose a poem written in a particular cultural or ethnic context on a theme most people experience. Then write a paper that discusses what would perhaps be different in the poem had it been written from a different cultural perspective. You could consider how images, rhythms, diction, tone, or figurative language might differ from the original.

RESPONDING THROUGH THE ARTS

1. Come up with a screenplay for William Stafford's "Traveling through the Dark" (p. 554). Include camera shots for each moment, explain why you chose each shot, and include a discussion of how you would convey the figurative language.

2. Find or compose music for one or more of the poems and write a paragraph explaining why you think the music is an appropriate "score" for the poem.

There's poetry in the language I speak. There's poetry, therefore,
in my culture, and in this place.
                                    Sekou Sundiata

CHAPTER 14 Rhythm and Meter

Our lives are rich with rhythms: the regular rhythms of sunrise and sunset, the change of seasons, the waves on the shore, the beats of our heart, even the routines in our lives—holidays, trash days, final exam week, income tax time. Life also has irregular rhythms that are, paradoxically, rhythmical: the syncopations of the city, the stutter step of a basketball player, the anxious cadence of our speech under stress and uncertainty, people dropping by, and the infamous pop quiz. We need rhythms and live by them, regardless of whether we are aware of them. The same can be said of poetry: Every poem has rhythm, and experiencing a poem fully requires being attentive to its rhythms. This chapter focuses on the ways rhythms, regular and irregular, contribute to a poem's impact and meanings and on ways to help you hear and feel these rhythms more accurately and more intensely.

RHYTHM

All careful writing has **rhythm**, the patterned "movement" created by words and their arrangement. Poetry in particular emphasizes it. Rhythm is somewhat difficult to describe. Because no set of precise descriptive labels is available, we turn to metaphorical language. We say that rhythm is, for example, fast, slow, syncopated, disjointed, smooth, halting, graceful, rough, deliberate, frenzied, or a mixture of any or all of these. The rhythms in a poem are affected by the way the poet handles various features.

Line Length

Short lines can have one effect, long lines another, though the effect varies from poem to poem. Usually short lines create a faster rhythm and longer lines a slower rhythm, but that's not always the case. Compare the rapid rhythms in the short lines of "my old man" (p. 488) with the slower ones of "In the Waiting Room" (p. 506), and the fairly rapid long lines of "Grandfather-in-Law" (p. 535) with the slower ones of "God's Grandeur" (p. 524).

Line Endings

Lines without end punctuation are said to "run on" into the next line (**run-on lines**; also called **enjambment**), which tends toward a faster, smoother pace from line to line. Lines with end punctuation, especially periods and semicolons (**end-stopped lines**), often slow down. Notice the difference in rhythm between lines 1–2 (end-stopped) and lines 3–4 (run-on) of the third stanza of "Richard Cory" (p. 552):

> And he was rich — yes, richer than a king —
> And admirably schooled in every grace:
> In fine, we thought that he was everything
> To make us wish that we were in his place.

Lines broken at unexpected or irregular places create a jolt and break up the rhythmic flow; line breaks at expected or "natural" places create a gentle shift carrying the rhythm along smoothly.

Pauses

Pauses (or lack of them) within lines can affect their pace and smoothness. A **pause**, called a **caesura** and usually indicated by punctuation, tends to break up the flow of a line, slow it down a bit, perhaps make it "jagged" or "halting." Lack of pauses can propel a line and make it either flowing and graceful or hurried, even frenetic. Compare the first three lines, broken by pauses, with the unbroken last line of the final stanza of "Richard Cory":

> So on we worked, and waited for the light,
> And went without the meat, and cursed the bread;
> And Richard Cory, one calm summer night,
> Went home and put a bullet through his head. (p. 552)

How would placing a comma after "home" in the last line change the effect?

Spaces

Leaving gaps within, at the beginning or end of, or between lines can slow up the movement, even stop it altogether, or indicate which words to group together; crowding things together can speed up a rhythm. (Note the various uses of spacing in "Buffalo Bill 's" on p. 566.)

Word Choice and Combinations of Sounds

Words that are easy to say together can create a steady, smooth, harmonious pace in a line; those hard to say can make it "jagged" or "harsh" or "tired" or simply slow and deliberate. Notice the difference between the way sounds slide into each other and are easy to say in the five-word line "Clean favored, and imperially slim," from the first stanza in "Richard Cory," and the way the nine words in the last line, "Went home and put a bullet through his head," force us to enunciate each separately and distinctly. The sounds don't flow together but come from different parts of the mouth, which takes longer to get them out.

It is important to realize that different rhythms may be appropriate for the same experience. For example, a frantic or a calm rhythm may be appropriate for a poem about a traffic accident, depending on what the poet wants you to experience.

The following poem celebrates a hero of the old American West. As you read it, notice the effects of line lengths, line endings, pauses within lines (or lack of them), spaces, word choices, and combinations of sounds.

e. e. cummings   1894–1962

Buffalo Bill 's   [1923]

```
Buffalo Bill 's
defunct
          who used to
          ride a watersmooth-silver
                                   stallion                          5
and break onetwothreefourfive pigeonsjustlikethat
                                             Jesus

he was a handsome man
                       and what i want to know is
how do you like your blueeyed boy                                  10
Mister Death
```

APPROACHING THE READING

Research this author in depth with cultural documents and multimedia resources on *LiterActive*.

1. Try reading the poem aloud, respecting line divisions by pausing briefly at the ends of lines (but without letting your voice drop the way it does at the end of a sentence) and reading "onetwothreefourfive" as nearly like one word as possible. Listen for how all this affects pace and rhythm.

2. Then read for meaning. What is the effect on meaning to put individual words on separate lines, to break lines and situate words at unexpected places, and to jam several words together? Write a brief statement of your interpretation of the poem's theme.

To help focus on the effect of gaps, spaces, line divisions, and line groupings, listen to the poem the way it could have been written — in six lines, using conventional punctuation, and a fairly regular beat:

> Buffalo Bill's defunct, who used to ride
> A water-smooth silver stallion and break
> One, two, three, four, five pigeons, just like that.
> Jesus, he was a handsome man.
> And what I want to know is,
> How do you like your blue-eyed boy, Mister Death?

Notice how cummings's form of the poem creates a rhythm entirely different from this version written in six conventional lines. The rhythm definitely affects the meaning. A line break invites you to pause briefly after "Buffalo Bill 's," to linger on the name and give it emphasis as well as creating a moment of anticipation. Without the line break, the emphasis would fall on "defunct," instead of each line receiving emphasis. The pause in the middle of the infinitive "to ride" shifts meaning from "used to *ride*" to "who *used to*," which reinforces the meaning of "defunct" (used to, but does so no more). This break once again sets up an anticipation. What did he "used to" do? "Ride," then, at the beginning of the line answers the question and its positioning emphasizes the poignancy of loss.

Emphasis falls next on "a watersmooth-silver" and on "stallion" as a single-word line emphatic in both rhythm and meaning. Jamming the words "onetwothreefourfive" and "pigeonsjustlikethat" together creates a quick staccato rhythm that echoes the rapid firing of a revolver. The rhythm slows with "Jesus" set off in a line of its own far to the right: Its position far to the right requires a pause, not unlike the exhaled sigh one expresses when saying "Jesus" in this manner, but so does the extra space between it and the next line of text. The next three phrases also are slower and more reflective. Their similarity in length (six, seven, and eight syllables) creates a rhythmical similarity that makes the short, abrupt last line surprising in rhythm as well as in meaning and tone.

Because rhythm is not fixed, your involvement as a reader is crucial. How long a word is to be "held," how much stress is to be put on a syllable, how short a short line is and how long a long line is, and how much pause there is in a pause are effects you create or decide on.

METER

As part of their rhythm, poems can have a regular "beat." You're already familiar with beat: When you listen to certain types of music, you are probably struck by or react to the beat. You may say or hear someone else say, "I love the beat of that song. The words are OK, but it's the beat that really hits me."

A beat in poetry arises from the contrast of louder (stressed or accented) and softer (unstressed or unaccented) syllables. Poetry with a steady beat, or measured pulse, is said to have **meter**, a regularized beat created by a repeating pattern of accents, syllables, or both. The most widely used type of meter in English (called *accentual-syllabic*) takes into account both the number of stresses and the number of syllables per line. If you're unsure about syllables and accents for a particular word, check a dictionary: It divides words into syllables and indicates where the stress is put.

> The process of picking out a poem's meter by marking stressed and unstressed syllables is called **scansion**. For a fuller and more technical discussion of meter and scansion, see the appendix on scansion (pp. 1469–78).

The basis of accentual-syllabic meter is the repetition of metrical "feet." A **foot** is a two- or three-syllable metrical unit made up (usually) of one stressed and one or two unstressed syllables. As these combinations of stressed plus unstressed syllables (*da DA,* or *da da DA*) are repeated, a regular pattern or beat (*da DA da DA da DA,* or *da da DA da da DA*) becomes established in your ear; you unconsciously expect to continue to hear it, and you notice variations from the "norm."

There are terms, or names, for these feet. The *da DA* feet, called **iambs**, create iambic meter. Listen for it in this line:

i AM bic ME ter GOES like THIS.

Now listen for it in the opening lines of Claude McKay's sonnet "America" (p. 686):

AlTHOUGH she FEEDS me BREAD of BITterNESS,
And SINKS inTO my THROAT her TIger's TOOTH,
STEALing my BREATH of LIFE, i WILL conFESS
i LOVE this CULtured HELL that TESTS my YOUTH!

Iambic is by far the most frequently used foot. The other feet are often used for variation in mostly iambic poems, though sometimes they are found as the dominant foot in an entire poem.

The inversion of the iambic foot is the **trochee** (*DA da*), which forms a trochaic meter (again, listen for it):

TRO chees PUT the AC cent FIRST

In the third line quoted above from "America," "STEALing" is a trochaic foot, used as a **substitution** (a different kind of foot put in place of the one normally demanded by the meter). Substitutions add variety, emphasize the dominant foot by contrasting with it, and often coincide with a switch in meaning. Here the substitution makes "stealing" more emphatic and foregrounds its meaning.

Listen for trochaic feet in this stanza from the introduction to William Blake's (mostly cheerful) *Songs of Innocence*:

PIPing DOWN the VALleys WILD,
PIPing SONGS of PLEASant GLEE,
ON a CLOUD i SAW a CHILD,
AND he LAUGHing SAID to ME:

"PIPE a SONG aBOUT a LAMB."
SO i PIPED with MERry CHEER.

Stresses are never equally strong; that is one way of attaining rhythmic variety even in lines that are metrically regular. Thus, in the third line, CLOUD and CHILD get more stress than ON and SAW. Some syllables (AND in the fourth line, SO in line 6) are given a light stress mainly because we expect, from the pattern established, that they *should* be stressed (likewise the "into" in the McKay passage above). You may have noticed that these lines have four stressed syllables but only three unstressed syllables; the fourth trochee in each line is incomplete, lacking its unstressed syllable, which is replaced by a mandatory pause: All the lines are end-stopped. This is another way to do something unusual with, and add variety to, a metrical poem.

Two other feet add an unstressed syllable to the feet described above: an **anapest** adds one to an iamb (*da da DA*), and a **dactyl** adds one to a trochee (*DA da da*). Whole poems in these meters are unusual; they are typically used for substitutions in predominantly iambic or trochaic poems. Here, however, are the final lines from a poem mostly in anapestic meter, also by William Blake, "The Chimney Sweeper" (p. 610), which appeared in his more pessimistic *Songs of Experience*. The poem describes the awful lives of small boys forced to climb up chimneys and clean out the soot. The lilting anapests create a sharply ironic contrast with the content, as Tom receives comfort from a dream about heaven he had the night before:

Though the MORNing was COLD, Tom was HAPpy and WARM;
So if ALL do their DUty, they NEED not fear HARM.

One other important foot, the **spondee**, has two stressed syllables (*DA DA*), with no unstressed syllables, as in GOOD NIGHT and RAGE, RAGE in these lines from a poem by Dylan Thomas pleading to his father not to accept death passively and quietly (p. 741):

> Do NOT go GENtle INto THAT GOOD NIGHT.
> RAGE, RAGE aGAINST the DYing OF the LIGHT.

Many other feet have been given names, but knowing these five (iamb, trochee, anapest, dactyl, spondee) will enable you to describe the basic meter and variations from it in most poems — and describing them will help you hear them more clearly.

The other thing to notice in poems in traditional meters involves the length of the lines. Line lengths are measured by the number of feet in each line and are labeled with names derived from Greek roots; for example,

monometer = a line with one foot

dimeter = a line with two feet

trimeter = a line with three feet

tetrameter = a line with four feet

pentameter = a line with five feet

hexameter = a line with six feet (and so on)

The line we used above ("iAMbic MEter GOES like THIS") is *iambic tetrameter*. The description identifies the predominant foot (here, iamb) and the predominant line length (four feet) in a poem — that is, the ones used the majority of the time.

The following poem by a late nineteenth-century African American poet expresses the conflict experienced for persons of color forced to conform to societal expectations of behavior and attitude. Try picking out the meter in the poem by noting the syllables stressed in each line.

Paul Laurence Dunbar   1872–1906

We Wear the Mask   [1896]

We wear the mask that grins and lies,
It hides our cheeks and shades our eyes, —
This debt we pay to human guile;
With torn and bleeding hearts we smile,
And mouth with myriad subtleties.   5

*   *   *

Why should the world be over-wise,
In counting all our tears and sighs?
Nay, let them only see us, while
    We wear the mask.

We smile, but, O great Christ, our cries   10
To thee from tortured souls arise.
We sing, but oh the clay is vile
Beneath our feet, and long the mile;
But let the world dream otherwise,
    We wear the mask!   15

APPROACHING THE READING

1. Hearing a regular beat in the first few lines should be fairly easy: All the words have one syllable, and important words alternate with less important ones. Label the predominant meter and the predominant line length. Do you find any variations (substitutions) from the predominant feet? If so, point them out.

2. Label the metrical foot and length of lines 9 and 15. What is the effect of changing from the longer lines to which our ears have become accustomed to a shorter line?

3. Notice the interplay between rhythmic devices and meter. The meter provides a very regular beat, but pauses and variance in line endings break up the rhythm and keep the beat from dominating the poem. Point out examples, especially from lines 8–15.

4. In what sense could writing a poem on this topic in a traditional meter be thought of as an example of wearing a mask?

In this poem, the meter stands out; it is almost glaringly regular. Here and there a spondee may be substituted for one of the predominant iambs, depending on where a reader decides to place particular emphasis. "We" might well be stressed equally with the verb following it in lines 1, 9, 10, 12, and 15, in order to emphasize the *people* who are forced to present a false image to others while hiding their authentic self: "WE WEAR," "WE SMILE," "WE SING." A poem that calls attention to the mask also lifts it off, enabling us to realize that it is a mask, that it is a lie (line 1), and, ironically, that it is a form of resistance at the same time it is a mark of servitude.

One could even ask, in that regard, if the use of meter in Dunbar's poem serves also as a mask. In the late nineteenth century, meter was still expected in poetry. Only a few poets, such as Walt Whitman, wrote nonmetrical poems, and Whitman was regarded warily as a radical. An African

American poet had to use meter to have her or his work be read widely and not be dismissed as unskilled. But it must have created some tension to write in the cadences of white educated society instead of the cadences and rhythms sung by workers in the fields or when they gathered in the evenings. So Dunbar wrote in meter, probably to have his verse accepted but also perhaps because its strict, almost excessive regularity might suggest that the metrical form is a mask, a lie, a form not freely chosen but forced on him.

What does paying attention to meter gain you? It can help you hear more clearly a central rhythmic feature in a metrical poem, its regular beat and the irregular alterations in that beat. Poems written in meter usually have a dominant foot, that is, one used the majority of the time. Once you get accustomed to the meter, your ear becomes attuned to that foot, begins to expect it, and notices when a different foot is substituted and alters the "sameness." Such substitution is an important means of controlling emphasis as well as adding variety.

www

Further explore rhythm and meter, including interactive exercises, with VirtuaLit Poetry at bedfordstmartins.com/approachinglit.

☑ CHECKLIST on Rhythm and Meter

❑ Listen for and respond to the rhythms of poems.

❑ Note formal structures that affect rhythm (such as line length, line endings, pauses, word choice, combinations of sound).

❑ Listen for the difference between poems with metrical (written in meter with a regular beat, such as "Richard Cory" — p. 552) and nonmetrical verse (such as "Cold as Heaven" — p. 558).

❑ Listen for the recurring beat in metrical poems and be able to identify the most important traditional metrical feet: iamb (da DA), trochee (DA da), anapest (da da DA), dactyl (DA da da), and spondee (DA DA).

FURTHER READING

Here are two poems about remembrance — about whether people are remembered after their deaths for what they have been and done. The first reflects on a visit to a southern plantation and on what the tour guide points out (and doesn't point out). In the second, the speaker reflects on family members who have died and confronts the fact that his life too is passing, with whatever that implies for him. Listen for rhythm in each — how the handling of lines, line endings and groupings, combinations of words and sounds and pauses all lead you to speed up, slow down, pause, and adjust your timing.

Lucille Clifton   b. 1936

at the cemetery, walnut grove plantation, south carolina, 1989

[1991]

among the rocks
at walnut grove
your silence drumming
in my bones,
tell me your names.   5

nobody mentioned slaves
and yet the curious tools
shine with your fingerprints.
nobody mentioned slaves
but somebody did this work   10
who had no guide, no stone,
who moulders under rock.

tell me your names,
tell me your bashful names
and i will testify.   15

the inventory lists ten slaves
but only men were recognized.

among the rocks
at walnut grove
some of these honored dead   20
were dark
some of these dark
were slaves
some of these slaves
were women   25
some of them did this
honored work.
tell me your names
foremothers, brothers,
tell me your dishonored names.   30
here lies
here lies
here lies
here lies
hear   35

APPROACHING THE READING

1. This begins as a poem of address: The speaker addresses the dead slaves. Consider whether the rhythms of the poem fit or enhance the addressing. Why is this way of writing on this subject effective?

2. Select groups of two or three lines anywhere in the poem and mark the stressed syllables (see the appendix on scansion [pp. 1469–78] for the traditional method of doing so). Is there a regular beat all the time, or some of the time, or never? If there is a regular beat at all, comment on how it contributes to the rhythm and effect of the poem.

3. Describe the rhythm of the last five lines. Is the list effective? What is the effect of the serious pun as the last line?

4. "Tell me your names," the speaker says, "and I will testify" (ll. 13, 15). What does "testify" denote and connote here? In what sense is the poem itself a testimony? In what sense does it have the rhythms of testimony? Can the speaker testify even though she receives no response to her request in line 13?

Joseph Awad   b. 1929

Autumnal   [1988]

Death, it is all about us lately.
Uncle Joe buried just three weeks.
Now Leo gone. And Richard gone.
It is the season. The insistent years,
Like winds that tear away the autumn leaves,   5
Wear us down, resigned to go more gentle.
Even the hidden how, the grim unknown
Of hour or place, wakefulness or pain,
Intimidate us less each autumn. Now
Disquiet whispers with a different question;   10
Whether, before the frost, we will have done
Whatever the work we were created for.
Was it for one supreme heroic deed,
Pivotal, that might reshape the world?
Or the accumulating labors, day by day,   15
That make an exemplary life? Perhaps
My *raison d'être*° is given in this instant —   *reason for existing*
Looking up to see you smiling,
Leaning, in autumn roselight from the window,
To put your hand upon my drooping shoulder.   20

Is it the knowing I alone was born —
Of all Arabia's lovers, I alone —
To sing the secret of this living moment,
That fills my windswept spirit with such peace,
And so much praise?   25

APPROACHING THE READING

1. Consider how sentences and line divisions affect rhythm in the poem. Describe the poem's rhythm. Why do you think it is appropriate for the subject and tone of the poem? How does it help develop subject and tone?

2. Compare the handling of sentences and caesuras in lines 1–16 with the way they are handled in lines 17–25. Describe the difference and explain how each fits and enhances the thought in that section of the poem.

3. Reflect on the phrase "before the frost" (l. 11). Explain how it ties into the title's archetypal implications (see pp. 131–32). How do the rhythms of the poem seem appropriate for an "autumnal" poem?

Here are two more remembrance poems. These two deal with the desire to go home again and the difficulty of doing so. In the first, the speaker returns to the urban scene she once wanted to get away from, with the hope that by going there she will get in touch with a part of her identity. In the second, the speaker returns to the small town from which he had to escape and finds that it hasn't changed and still isn't the right place for him. Listen for the rhythm in each poem and for how the rhythm fits with and contributes to the meaning and effect.

Lorna Dee Cervantes   b. 1954

Freeway 280   [1981]

Las casitas° near the gray cannery,   *little houses*
nestled amid wild abrazos° of climbing roses   *bear hugs*
and man-high red geraniums
are gone now. The freeway conceals it
all beneath a raised scar.   5

But under the fake windsounds of the open lanes,
in the abandoned lots below, new grasses sprout,
wild mustard remembers, old gardens
come back stronger than they were,

trees have been left standing in their yards.   10
Albaricoqueros, cerezos, nogales° . . .   *apricot, cherry, walnut trees*
Viejitas° come here with paper bags to gather greens.   *old women*
Espinaca, verdolagas, yerbabuena° . . .   *spinach, purslane, mint*

I scramble over the wire fence
that would have kept me out.   15
Once, I wanted out, wanted the rigid lanes
to take me to a place without sun,
without the smell of tomatoes burning
on swing shift in the greasy summer air.

Maybe it's here   20
en los campos extraños de esta ciudad°   *in the strange fields of this city*
where I'll find it, that part of me
mown under
like a corpse
or a loose seed.   25

APPROACHING THE READING

1. The poem starts with description of a scene, juxtaposing the way it was before, as the speaker looks back, and the way it is now. Listen to the rhythms
   in the first two sections of the poem. How do they fit the subject and tone?
   Why does the speaker use Spanish words part of the time? In what ways do
   they fit the subject and tone? The rhythm?

2. Listen to the rhythm of each line in stanzas 3 and 4, as well as the rhythm of
   the whole poem. The speaker says that in the past she "wanted out" (l. 16)?
   Why? What is the speaker's attitude now? What was it before? How does
   the rhythm fit and reinforce what she is saying?

3. Where does this poem have meter? Be ready to talk about how the meter interacts with, or becomes a part of, the rhythm, and how the meter shapes or
   contributes to intensity, emphasis, meaning, and implications.

4. Consider the comparisons to a corpse or a loose seed in the short closing
   lines. Why does the speaker see the comparison differently now? How does
   the rhythm of the three short concluding lines fit the poem?

5. How does the title fit the poem? Why that as title?

Jim Barnes b. 1933

Return to La Plata, Missouri   [1982]

The warping bandstand reminds you of the hard rage
you felt in the heart of the town the day you said goodbye
to the park, silver jet, and cicadas dead in the sage.

The town is basic red, although it browns. A cry
of murder, rape, or wrong will always bend the night   5
hard into the broken grass. You listen close for sighs

of lovers on the ground. The darkness gathers light
and throws it down: something glows that you cannot name,
something fierce, abstract, given time and space you might

on a journey leave behind, a stone to carve your fame   10
on, or a simple word like *love*. The sun is down
or always going down in La Plata, the same

sun. Same too the child's cry that turns the mother's frown
brittle as chalk or the town's face against the moon.
Same too the moan of dog and diesel circling the town   15

in an air so heavy with cloud that there is little room
for breath or moon. Strange: in a town so country, so
foreign, you never hear a song nor see a loom

pattern dark threads into a history you would know
and would not know. You think you see one silver star.   20
But the town offers only itself, and you must go.

APPROACHING THE READING

1. This poem is filled with memories of past experiences, with transformations, and with contrasts of appearance and reality. Notice the rhythms as
   you look for examples: Stanza 1 is one long, mostly unbroken sentence; the
   other stanzas mix short and longer sentences, but generally with breaks or
   pauses (never, however, at the end of a stanza). What does that change contribute to the rhythm?

2. The speaker is observing, noticing, concluding. What is the effect of his
   using *you* instead of *I* in describing the experience? Does the use of second
   person affect the rhythm? What is the "something" in line 8 that you cannot name?

3. Notice the external form and the use of rhyme. What do they contribute to
   the rhythm and the overall impact of the poem?

4. Mark the stressed syllables in the first stanza. Is there a regular beat all the time, or some of the time, or never? If there is a regular beat at all, comment on how it contributes to the rhythm and to the effect of the stanza. Do the same for another stanza to see if the result is the same.

5. Where should the emphasis in the last line fall—on "you," or "must," or "go"? Which best fits the meaning and the rhythm? What point is being made in the last two sentences?

The following four poems extend the theme of identity touched on in the last two poems. Decide which of them is/are written in meter and which is/are nonmetrical. Watch for how their handling of rhythm, metrical or nonmetrical, contributes to the effect and meaning of each poem.

A. K. Ramanujan 1929–1993

Self-Portrait   [1966]

I resemble everyone
but myself, and sometimes see
in shop-windows,
   despite the well-known laws
   of optics,   5
the portrait of a stranger,
date unknown,
often signed in a corner
by my father.

Emily Dickinson 1830–1886

I'm Nobody! Who are you?   [c. 1861; 1891]

I'm Nobody! Who are you?
Are you – Nobody – Too?
Then there's a pair of us?
Don't tell! they'd advertise – you know!

How dreary – to be – Somebody!   5
How public – like a Frog –
To tell one's name – the livelong June –
To an admiring Bog!

Simon J. Ortiz b. 1941

Speaking [1977]

I take him outside
under the trees,
have him stand on the ground.
We listen to the crickets,
cicadas, million years old sound.   5
Ants come by us.
I tell them,
"This is he, my son.
This boy is looking at you.
I am speaking for him."   10

The crickets, cicadas,
the ants, the millions of years
are watching us,
hearing us.
My son murmurs infant words,   15
speaking, small laughter
bubbles from him.
Tree leaves tremble.
They listen to this boy
speaking for me.   20

Georgia Douglas Johnson 1880–1966

Wishes [1927]

I'm tired of pacing the petty round of the ring of the thing I know —
I want to stand on the daylight's edge and see where the sunsets go.

I want to sail on a swallow's tail and peep through the sky's blue glass.
I want to see if the dreams in me shall perish or come to pass.

I want to look through the moon's pale crook and gaze on the
      moon-man's face.   5
I want to keep all the tears I weep and sail to some unknown place.

APPROACHING THE READING

1. Read each poem aloud. Listen for a regular beat; if you hear one, mark
   stressed syllables in several lines to help decide if the poem is in meter.

2. If the lines are metrical, label the predominant foot and line and listen for how the meter interacts with and becomes a part of the rhythm. Consider how the meter shapes or contributes to intensity, emphasis, meaning, and implications.

3. If the lines are not metrical, consider how the rhythm seems appropriate to and helps develop the subject, tone, and theme.

4. For each poem, write a brief statement of theme and a brief explanation of how rhythm contributes to the way the poem works.

RESPONDING THROUGH WRITING

Journal Entries

1. Review the discussion of prose rhythms in Chapter 7 (pp. 174–75). Then read a poem written in long, prose-like lines, such as David Mura's "Grandfather-in-Law" (p. 535), Allen Ginsberg's "A Supermarket in California" (p. 656), and Etheridge Knight's "Hard Rock Returns to Prison from the Hospital for the Criminal Insane" (p. 676). In your journal, discuss ways rhythms in prose and rhythms in poetry are similar and different (and are created in similar and different ways).

2. Fill in the following sentence: I got up this morning and _____, then I _____, and then I _____. Now break it into rhythmic units, writing each unit as a line of poetry. Try dividing it in other places. In your journal, discuss how rhythm and emphasis change as a result of different breaks, and reflect on the kinds of aesthetic decisions a writer has to make about where to divide lines.

 Research the authors in this chapter with LitLinks at bedfordstmartins.com/ approachinglit.

3. Nursery rhymes and children's poetry are often written in meter. Choose two or three examples, write a few lines of each in your journal, mark the stressed syllables, and label the metric foot and line length. Then perhaps write a paper examining the handling of meter in a nursery rhyme or children's poem — or more than one of them — and discussing why meter is an effective technique in verse for children.

Literary Analysis Papers

4. Write a paper on the interaction between rhythm, line divisions, and theme in Heather McHugh's "What He Thought" (p. 684).

5. Write a paper discussing what one of the following poems says about rhythm, and discuss the way the poem uses rhythm to convey what it says (or, alternatively, compare and contrast the two poems): Lawson Fusao Inada's "Plucking Out a Rhythm" (p. 673) and Ishmael Reed's "Poetry Makes Rhythm in Philosophy" (p. 709).

6. Write a paper discussing the interaction of meter and rhythm in Wilfred Owen's "Dulce et Decorum Est" (p. 503), Samuel Taylor Coleridge's "Kubla Khan" (p. 623), Andrew Marvell's "To His Coy Mistress" (p. 688), Dudley Randall's "Ballad of Birmingham" (p. 708), or Dylan Thomas's "Do not go gentle into that good night" (p. 741).

Making Connections

7. Rhythm is important in poems about music. Write a paper discussing the handling of rhythm in one of the following poems about jazz and jazz musicians, or comparing and contrasting such handling in two or more of them: Amiri Baraka's "AM/TRAK" (p. 602), Jayne Cortez's "Into This Time" (p. 626), Christopher Gilbert's "Horizontal Cosmology" (p. 654), Kazuko Shiraishi's "Dedicated to the Late John Coltrane" (p. 724), or Quincy Troupe's "Snake-Back Solo 2" (p. 742). Or, write a paper discussing the rhythms in Sterling A. Brown's blues poem, "Riverbank Blues" (p. 616).

8. Rhythm is also important in poems about dance. Write a paper discussing the handling of rhythm in one of the following poems about dance, or comparing and contrasting such handling in two or more of them: Theodore Roethke's "My Papa's Waltz" (p. 492), Cornelius Eady's "My Mother, If She Had Won Free Dance Lessons" (p. 642), or Al Young's "A Dance for Ma Rainey" (p. 759).

Cultural Criticism Papers

9. Select a protest poem, such as William Blake's "The Chimney Sweeper" (p. 610), Rosemary Catacalos's "David Talamántez on the Last Day of Second Grade" (p. 620), or Carolyn Forché's "The Colonel" (p. 650). Discuss how the rhythms of the poem intertwine with its tone to articulate its political or social message forcefully.

10. Write a paper discussing the social or economic implications of "Richard Cory" (p. 552) and include how the poem's use of meter and rhythm contributes to the impact of the moments throughout the poem.

RESPONDING THROUGH THE ARTS

1. Try your hand at choreographing a poem or at creating a rhythmic accompaniment to a poem.

2. Abstract expressionism in the visual arts often reveals feeling and energy. Pick a poem and create an abstract drawing, painting, sculpture, or collage that evokes what you think the poem is trying to express.

In the writing process, the more a thing cooks the better.

Doris Lessing

CHAPTER 15 **Writing about Poetry**

We write about poetry for the same reasons we write about fiction—to participate in an ongoing conversation about things that interest, provoke, excite, or puzzle us about the literary works we read. After asking a friend or classmate about the meaning of a line (What's the point behind Marge Piercy's "Barbie Doll" cutting off her nose and legs and "offer[ing] them up"?) and participating in class discussion of the poem (What does it show about attitudes toward women that she was "advised to play coy, / exhorted to come on hearty, / exercise, diet, smile and wheedle"? Would men be told things like that?), you might decide to write a paper on "Marge Piercy's Critique of Social Attitudes toward Women in 'Barbie Doll.'"

Chapters 10–14 helped prepare you to read poetry with increasing sensitivity, alertness, and confidence, and also prepared you to write about poetry. Each chapter provided ways to move into a poem and to enlarge your experience of the variety of things happening in it: in subject matter, formal elements, the range of effects, and the techniques through which the effects are achieved. The section on short papers in Chapter 2 (pp. 32–45) provided you with general guidance for essays on literature. Also notice that some of the suggestions in Chapter 8 on writing about fiction can be carried over to your writing about poetry. This chapter examines what is different about poetry and the particular challenges it poses.

TOPICS

The difference starts with preparation. To write effectively about a particular poem, it's wise to live with it for a while. Even though a poem is usually a shorter piece to read than a story, spend a similar amount of time exploring a poem as you would a short story. If possible, spread the time you spend with it over at least a week. Read the poem two or three times a day, sometimes aloud, sometimes — if you can arrange it — listening to someone else read it. Each time you read the poem, focus on a different aspect — one time on the speaker and voice, another on images, another on rhythm, and so on. Photocopy the poem and mark it up; jot notes that you can come back to later. By doing this, the poem becomes part of you (you'll probably even be able to recite parts or all of it from memory).

Papers about poetry, like those about fiction, can focus on what goes on *inside* the work, what *surrounds* the work, and what goes *beyond* the work. But in each case, papers on poetry take a slightly different slant from that taken toward fiction.

Looking Inside the Poem

You can do a literary analysis of a poem, writing about what goes on inside it. The process is similar to the way you analyze a story (read or review pp. 202–3). It involves separating out the elements of a poem as a way of studying its nature and the relationships of its central features to each other, the way figurative language relates to tone and theme, for example. A literary analysis of a poem might focus on one of the technical features covered in Chapters 10–14 — diction, imagery, sounds, figures, rhythm, meter — clarifying how the technique is used and relating that feature to the effect, or theme, of the poem. Thus, you might explore the use of similes and metaphors for describing the "tremendous fish" in Elizabeth Bishop's "The Fish" (p. 608). Integrating the feature with the poem as a whole is crucial. Your analysis should not isolate a feature from the rest of the work; instead, looking closely at one aspect should be a way toward seeing the entire poem more clearly and fully.

Select for your analysis a feature, or two or three features, that are striking, unusual, complex, or subtle, are difficult to understand or accept, or raise questions or problems. The subject doesn't have to be a major or central aspect — a minor feature, like the handling of lines and space in e. e. cummings's "pity this busy monster,manunkind" (p. 630), could result in a good paper. Look for something that you will find interesting to think and write about. Be careful to avoid just summarizing the poem by restating what it's about in other words. Your paper needs to make a point about the feature and its relation to the whole poem — it needs to have a thesis (see p. 35). And be sure that your point is not one that is obvious to someone on first or even second reading of the poem. That's another reason why it's important to live with the poem before you begin to write on it. Its subtleties and complexities can then sink into your mind and you can write from a more thoughtful understanding of it.

A literary analysis of a short poem often takes the form of **explication**. Explication involves looking closely at the work, opening it up line by line, clarifying how diction, images, figurative language, symbols, sounds, rhythm, form, and allusions contribute toward shaping the poem's meaning and effect. An insightful explication helps the reader understand and enjoy a poem more completely. Close reading focuses especially on ambiguities, complexities, gaps, what's left unsaid, and interrelationships within a text. It requires being very attentive to specific words and phrases, considering their effects (perhaps considering why the effects of alternate words would be different), discussing the impact and meaning of ambiguities and subtleties, and explaining how these elements work together (as they will in an effective poem) toward a particular purpose or theme. For poems up to twenty or thirty lines, you may be able to explicate the entire poem in a four- or five-page paper; for longer poems, you may need to write a longer paper or explicate only a key passage (see pp. 208–9) and relate it to the whole poem.

One way of organizing an explication paper is to go through the poem from beginning to end, line by line (or by groups of lines), clarifying how techniques and features in the lines create their meaning or effect. In using a line-by-line approach, be careful not to slide into just restating what the poem is about in different words. Make sure you have a unifying principle in your paper, for example, following a technique (such as the use of images, or of a certain kind of images, or of related figures of speech) through the poem. Doing this avoids having the paper lapse into being merely a series of disconnected paragraphs. The paragraphs should build on each other to develop the central point (thesis) of the paper. How you handle topic sentences (the first sentence of each paragraph, setting up the topic, or main point, of that paragraph) and transition between paragraphs are important in achieving a unified paper.

Alternatively, an explication paper can be organized topically. That is, one paragraph might discuss the poem's use of images, another its use of figures, and others its tone, use of sound techniques, and rhythm. Each paragraph should include examples from different parts of the poem, chosen so that somewhere in the paper nearly every line is discussed (though not necessarily in the order they appear in the poem). Each paragraph needs to explain how the element it covers contributes to building the total effect of the poem. This approach is less likely to slide into summarizing what the poem is about than the line-by-line approach, but it requires decisions about what features should be chosen for the different paragraphs and about which lines or phrases should be used for illustrations at various points, to make sure all parts of the poem receive attention. Here, too, unity is important: Without a unifying principle, this approach also can result in disconnected mini-essays. Building each paragraph on the one before and using effective topic sentences and transitions are important.

Some of the "Approaching the Reading" questions and topics following poems in Chapters 10–14 make good topics for analytical or explication papers. Also, many of the suggestions for writing at the end of each chapter involve literary analyses and could be turned into explication topics. Here are some sample topics, out of hundreds of possibilities using poems from this book alone:

1. An analysis of the denotations and connotations of "red" in the vision of history in Linda Hogan's "The History of Red" (p. 670).
2. An analysis of the interaction of form and feeling in Li-Young Lee's "Visions and Interpretations" (p. 680).
3. An analysis of the varied implications of "digging" in Seamus Heaney's "Digging" (p. 667).
4. An explication focused on the role of personification and metaphor in Emily Dickinson's "Because I could not stop for Death" (p. 635).
5. An explication clarifying the interrelation of far-fetched analogies and argument in John Donne's love poem "A Valediction: Forbidding Mourning" (p. 638).
6. An explication dealing with diction and meaning in Michael S. Harper's "Nightmare Begins Responsibility" (p. 664).

Looking at What Surrounds the Poem

A second approach to writing a poetry paper is to work with the literary context surrounding a poem and its connections to other literary works. Poems, like stories, are surrounded by other poems, as well as by stories, novels, and plays, all of which form a meaningful interactive network. A poem can relate to other works in that network by similarities and differences between them, and a literary paper can compare and/or contrast a poem with another poem, a novel, a story, or a play (read or review the pointers about comparison/contrast on pp. 203–5). Possibilities for topics are almost endless. Picking out your own pairings and things to focus on can be enjoyable and can lead you to see things you otherwise might not realize.

A comparison/contrast paper can discuss any aspects of the works, but the works must have a good deal in common or share one especially important feature. If two things are totally different, with nothing in common, there's little value in pointing out the differences. A paper comparing and contrasting Reza Baraheni's "Autumn in Tehran" (p. 772) and Elizabeth Bishop's "The Fish" (p. 608) would have little value because the two have almost nothing in common. And the similarities and differences should be something of significance, something that really matters. Both "Autumn in Tehran" and Joseph Awad's "Autumnal" (p. 574) use imagery of autumn and are written by poets of Middle Eastern origins. So what? Does that make connecting them meaningful?

And it's important that your discussion of the similarities and differences makes a point worth considering. Simply noticing and presenting the similarities and differences seldom, if ever, results in an effective paper. Your paper should have an argumentative thesis that unifies the discussion and brings out its significance. You might, for example, consider comparing and contrasting Joseph Awad's "Autumnal" (p. 574) and William Shakespeare's "That time of year thou mayst in me behold" (p. 521). A paper with a thesis sentence stating that "Autumnal" and "That time of year" have interesting similarities in technique and meaning is off to a good start. Much better is something like, "Although 'Autumnal' and 'That time of year' are similar in their use of archetypal symbols to affirm their devotion to a loved one, Awad's poem goes a step beyond Shakespeare's in the significant way it leads the reader to explore the meaning of life."

Literary works relate to each other also through the use of **allusions**, brief references to a literary or an artistic work or to a historical figure, event, or object, intended usually to place one's work within, or alongside, the whole other context of the work that is evoked by the reference. Allusions become a way works talk to each other, part of the great literary conversation we've mentioned a number of times. It is exciting to notice such communication between poems and to write about it; and the more poetry you read, the more such conversations you will notice. T. S. Eliot, for example, was keenly aware of working within the whole Western literary tradition and packed his poems with allusions to other works. Writing a paper on the use of literary and biblical allusions in T. S. Eliot's "The Love Song of J. Alfred Prufrock" (p. 645) would be challenging but also exciting and rewarding. Poems that draw on ancient myths or retell them are also interesting to study. Writing a paper on a poem that retells a classical myth, examining how the poem retells the original story—what it retains, what it changes, how it adjusts the emphasis—can prove interesting and informative, as, for example, W. H. Auden's handling of the Icarus myth in "Musée des Beaux Arts" (p. 600) and Eavan Boland's use of the myth of Demeter and Persephone in "The Pomegranate" (p. 613).

A significant part of the literary relationships of some poems is their sharing of traditional literary forms, ones used again and again by earlier poets, perhaps for hundreds of years. By writing in such a form, a poet enters the "world" of the sonnet or the blues, the chant, the villanelle, or whatever form is chosen and makes her or his contribution to that ongoing tradition. Poets often find it meaningful and exciting to feel that, by writing in a traditional form, they are facing the same challenges and feeling the same satisfactions that such writers as William Shakespeare, Bashō, Langston Hughes, and many other great writers have before them. You could write a paper about a poet's handling of a traditional form, as, for example, the use and adaptation of a traditional sonnet form in Gary Miranda's "Love Poem"

(p. 693) or Vijay Seshadri's "The Refugee" (p. 720), considering the appropriateness of the form to the content and the effect of the way the form is handled. Keep in mind that just demonstrating that a poem adheres to the conventions of its type is seldom interesting or valuable. Your paper will be effective and helpful when you write about how an author employs a traditional form in a new or unusual or subtle or particularly meaningful way. To point out both what is traditional and what is unexpected, and to evaluate the effectiveness of the innovations, can result in an enjoyable and enlightening paper.

Here are some possible topics for papers dealing with the literary contexts of poems, though, of course, there are countless additional possibilities:

1. Compare and contrast Lucille Clifton's "at the cemetery, walnut grove plantation, south carolina, 1989" (p. 573) and Thomas Gray's "Elegy Written in a Country Churchyard" (p. 660).
2. Compare and contrast the handling of the loss of innocence or "coming of age" theme in Elizabeth Bishop's "In the Waiting Room" (p. 506) and Julia Alvarez's "How I Learned to Sweep" (p. 560).
3. Compare and contrast the themes of Michael S. Harper's "Nightmare Begins Responsibility" (p. 664) and Ben Jonson's "On My First Son" (p. 674).
4. Discuss the use of biblical and holocaust allusions in Charles Simic's "Begotten of the Spleen" (p. 728).
5. Analyze how Dudley Randall's "Ballad of Birmingham" (p. 708) follows and adapts the ballad tradition, bringing in "Sir Patrick Spens" (p. 598) as an example of the traditional ballad.
6. Compare and contrast Dylan Thomas's use of the villanelle form in "Do not go gentle into that good night" (p. 741) with John Yau's in "Chinese Villanelle" (p. 757). The paper might discuss how a villanelle "works," how it affects and appeals to poets and to readers. It also might consider what a "Chinese" villanelle is and the possible influence of Chinese literature on Yau's poem.

Looking Beyond the Poem

You can also look beyond the techniques and literary context of a poem and write about its relation to its cultural and social context and to the real-world issues it deals with. Poetry, like fiction, responds well to cultural criticism (review the discussion of cultural approaches to fiction, pp. 206–7). Narrative poetry lends itself to the same critical approach as fiction. Stories, whether in fiction or narrative poetry, often show characters acting within a cultural situation. Thus, a paper might discuss and evaluate the implications of what they do and say—the exploitation of young boys in William Blake's "The Chimney Sweeper" (p. 610), for example. But applying cultural criticism to lyric poetry requires a different approach. Lyric poems tend not to depict an action but to express, explore, or reflect on a reaction, dwelling on a particular moment, idea, situation, feeling, or event, as in the speaker's reflections on the exploitation of slaves in Lucille Clifton's "at the cemetery, walnut grove plantation, south carolina, 1989" (p. 578). A paper on a lyric poem, instead of examining how a character acts, is likely to focus on the poet's or speaker's or poem's response to a cultural issue or situation — as a critique of, an answer to, a relating to, or a reply or reaction to it. Thus, a cultural criticism paper might explore the ideas of homeland and exile in Ana Doina's "The Extinct Homeland — A Conversation with Czeslaw Milosz" (p. 636), including its use of an implied dialogue with Milosz (see his poem on p. 691 and the biographical sketch on p. 1446).

Obviously topics for cultural criticism papers can range very widely. The last two writing suggestions in Chapters 10–14 involve cultural issues. Some of the "Approaching the Reading" questions following poems in Chapters 10–14 can also lead to topics for cultural criticism papers. Just as for all paper topics, a cultural criticism paper needs to make a point. Simply describing a social or cultural attitude or context will not be especially interesting or useful. You need a thesis that unifies your paper and states the position or hypothesis it is advancing. Here are some sample topic ideas, though the list goes on and on:

1. William Blake's critique of social conditions in "The Chimney Sweeper" (p. 610).
2. Rosemary Catacalos's critique of teachers and education in "David Talamántez on the Last Day of Second Grade" (p. 620).
3. The critique of cultural misunderstandings and tensions in Samuel Hazo's "For Fawzi in Jerusalem" (p. 665) or Dwight Okita's "In Response to Executive Order 9066" (p. 698).
4. Compare and contrast the tensions faced by young people attempting to find a place in U.S. society in Sandra Castillo's poem "Exile" (p. 618) and Julia Alvarez's short story "Daughter of Invention" (p. 10).
5. The repression of women as explored in Taslima Nasrin's "Things Cheaply Had" (p. 780) and Dahlia Ravikovitch's "Clockwork Doll" (p. 782).
6. The critique of country in Claude McKay's "If we must die" (p. 523) and "America" (p. 686).

DEVELOPMENT

Once you've picked out a technique or question or problem or issue, you need to decide what to do with it, how to focus and develop it. The section on "Writing Short Papers" in Chapter 2 (pp. 32–45) applies to papers on poetry as well as fiction and drama. Review the first four of the "Five Steps in the Writing Process" (pp. 33–36) if you need to. Here we comment briefly on developing an argument specifically for a paper on poetry.

Many of the steps in developing an argumentative paper on poetry are the same as for a paper dealing with fiction. You need to avoid just summarizing or describing what the poem says. Assume the reader of your paper has read the poem and understands what it's about. You need to develop a central idea that clarifies or illuminates a significant aspect of the poem's technique, meaning, or context, literary or cultural. The central idea must be one about which there can be disagreement for the paper to be argumentative. Your task is to show readers that your views are sound and convincing.

As with papers on fiction, a good strategy in reaching a disputable central idea is to begin asking questions about the technique or problem or issue. And the same kinds of questions apply: What is distinctive or unique or striking about the way the technique is handled? In what ways is that technique particularly important to the poem? How does the technique relate to the theme? How is the problem or issue you're looking at embodied in the voice, diction, images, figures, or form? Is the problem or issue embedded in a symbol? What are some broader implications of the problem or issue you are focusing on? What is controversial or puzzling or difficult about what the text seems to say about the issues raised in it?

As with papers on fiction, it can be helpful to phrase your central idea as a question and then to use the body of the paper for a series of paragraphs, each paragraph developing a point answering part of the question. And as in a paper on fiction, the paragraphs need to begin with a topic sentence and to be developed by elaborating the point; by supplying details and quotations to illustrate, support, and confirm the point; and by explaining what we should notice in the illustrations and how the illustrations relate to the points being developed. Illustration and explanation need to go together in any literary paper. The key to a successful paper lies in its development and support of its ideas: explaining ideas so readers understand them readily and supporting them with details and quotations so readers have confidence that the points are well grounded and worth considering.

One key difference in a paper on poetry is that you can discuss every line in a short poem. That means you'll need to decide how to organize the paper's development. You can work your way through the poem line by line. That works best if you organize your discussion by making two or three major points about the poem and divide up the lines to discuss some of them under each point. It's important for the paper to follow an outline *you* devise, rather than one that follows the outline the poet created in the poem. Or, instead of working your way down the poem, taking lines in order, you can create an outline based on points you want to cover (perhaps three different techniques or three different ideas in the poem) and then develop the points by drawing illustrations from anywhere in the poem they happen to appear.

Supporting illustrations in any literary paper must include quotations. For general advice on fitting quotations into your paragraphs and sentences, review the section on "Handling Quotations" (pp. 40–42) and the "Ten

Guidelines for Formatting and Punctuating Quotations" (pp. 43–44). Keep quotations short by focusing on key lines or phrases or words. A carefully phrased introduction usually provides the context and reduces the need for long quotations. If your paper uses quotations only from poems included in this book, you do not need to add a bibliography page. Your teacher will take for granted that you are using the text in this book. When you include quotations from other sources or from poems you find in another book, you need to include a bibliography page (see pp. 1396–1405).

When writing a paper about one or two short poems (up to two pages, let's say), provide your reader with a copy of the poem (photocopied or typed out) on separate sheets after the title page. If it's a very short poem (up to fourteen lines, perhaps), provide a photocopy or type the poem below

FIVE TIPS FOR QUOTING POETRY

Because of the line divisions in poetry, some conventions for dealing with quotations are unique to poetry. Here are five tips on handling quotations of poetry:

1. In quoting poetry, retain the spelling, punctuation, and capitalization of the original (except that the final punctuation mark may be dropped if the sentence does not end at the quotation mark — see p. 44).
2. Cite the line numbers for the lines quoted in parentheses at the end of the passage.
3. If you quote fewer than four lines of poetry, blend them into your sentence in prose form, with the lines separated by a slash:

    The opening lines of "Love Poem" are "A kind of slant: the way a ball will glance / off the end of a bat when you swing for the fence."

    Indicating line divisions is important because line breaks are a significant formal feature in a poem. This applies only to poetry written in lines; slashes are not used to indicate wrap breaks in prose. This means, of course, that you must be able to distinguish poetry from prose, or long free verse lines that wrap at the right margins from shorter lines that are intentionally divided.
4. If you quote four or more lines of poetry, type them into the paper as a block quotation with each on a separate line. Make sure you type them exactly as they appear in the poem. Indent the passage at least one inch, or center the passage on the page if you prefer. Double-space between the lines. If you begin the quotation in the middle of a poetic line, place the first word approximately where it occurs in the poem, not at the left-hand margin. (For an example, see p. 594.)
5. If you omit a word or words from within a line you're quoting, indicate this by including an ellipsis (see p. 44). Usually ellipses are not needed at the beginning or end of quotations. If you omit a complete line or more than one line, indicate this by adding a row of spaced periods as long as the lines in the passage you are quoting.

the title of the paper. (If you type it, check it carefully against the original to make sure it's accurate.) Insert line numbers every fifth line — write them in if you use a photocopy that lacks them — so you can refer to the poem by line number.

When you've completed a draft of your paper, read or review the fifth step in the writing process, "Revising and Proofreading" (pp. 36–38), the "Five Guidelines for Making Literary Papers Effective" (pp. 39–43), and the "Ten Guidelines for Formatting and Punctuating Quotations" (pp. 43–44) from Chapter 2. Remember, titles of poems are placed within quotation marks, except for book-length poems such as John Milton's *Paradise Lost,* which should be underlined or italicized.

A STUDENT WRITER AT WORK: DAN CARTER ON THE WRITING PROCESS

In one of our Introduction to Literature classes, we suggested this topic: Write a paper on the handling of form and content in a sonnet of your choice — the appropriateness of making the content fit the form or the effectiveness of adapting the form to fit the content. Dan Carter chose to write on Gary Miranda's "Love Poem" (p. 693). Here's what Dan told us about the way he went about writing the paper.

"I enjoy approaching a poem when it is clear that the author is doing something purposefully unique. 'Love Poem' by Gary Miranda immediately struck me as unusual in its choice of the sonnet form. I thought immediately that this is not a standard sonnet, and I wanted to understand what was going on in it. I chose this poem also because there is a lot going on in it. And just because I like it. I enjoy the sounds and the bouncing, sometimes awkward movement of the lines and I enjoy the simplicity and honesty of its message. I began asking myself, 'how did Miranda accomplish this effect of simplicity and love?' and 'how does the poem convey those effects?' I could sense a richness and subtlety under the surface of the verse, and I decided I wanted to do an explication of the poem to bring that out, but not a line-by-line reading.

"By the time I had read the poem a number of times, I had a list of half a dozen things I could use in my paper: diction (the games played with denotation, connotations, multiple meanings); images (active and visual, especially); adaptation of the traditional Italian sonnet form (same rhyme scheme, but using several slant rhymes instead of only exact rhymes); related to that, what the poem does with meter (line 1 in iambic pentameter, line 2 in anapestic trimeter, the rest mostly not metrical, though some phrases are); the title; the use of sound (alliteration, assonance, etc.); the use of figures; the choice of dynamic verbs.

"I eventually narrowed the list to the things I found most interesting: the form, the title, the images, and the sounds. But because of its overall effect of honesty, I didn't want to overanalyze the poem. It stands as a wonderful little poem without much analyzing, so I fought against the temptation to go overboard. I wanted to allow the poem to speak for itself, by working with aspects that the poem lent itself to. In preparing for this paper I was really interested in the poem and what was going on in it, so the essay flowed out easily when I sat down to write because I was expressing things I had already thought through extensively just because I found aspects of it so fascinating."

SAMPLE PAPER

Dan Carter
Professors Ridl and Schakel
English 105-04
November 3, 2003

A Slant on the Standard Love Sonnet

Love Poem

Text of short poem typed in.

A kind of slant: the way a ball will glance
off the end of a bat when you swing for the fence
and miss--that is, if you could watch that once,
up close and in slow motion; or the chance
meanings, not even remotely intended, that dance   5
at the edge of words, like sparks. Bats bounce
just so off the edges of the dark at a moment's
notice, as swallows do off sunlight. Slants

like these have something to do with why *angle*
is one of my favorite words, whenever it chances   10
to be a verb; and with why the music I single
out tonight--eighteenth-century dances--
made me think just now of you untangling
blueberries, carefully, from their dense branches. (p. 693)

There is no meter, no lofty conceits, no stunning imagery, no confessions of undying commitment, and no assurance that the beloved's glory will live forever in the poet's verse. Why, then, does Gary Miranda entitle his work "Love Poem" and include several basic elements of a traditional sonnet? My initial reaction after the first reading was that the speaker was either being light-hearted or avoiding the topic of his "love" altogether. Upon a more thorough examination, however, there is a great deal of sincerity and love to be found in its verses. But this poem does not approach the traditional form in a predictable way. There are no references to the beloved's beauty, or roses, or spring, or anything except . . . picking blueberries?! The speaker spends a significant portion of the verse discussing "slants." Fittingly, that is precisely what this poem is: a slant on our preconceived notion of what a "love poem" should be. Despite the absence of standard love poetry elements, various aspects of the poem such as the form, the title, the images, and the innumerable things that Miranda does with sound reveal that the speaker has composed a rather eloquent and sincere sonnet to the one he loves.

Argumentative thesis.

    The first aspects of this poem (and really any poem for that matter) that catch the attention of the reader are the title and the form--"Love Poem," sonnet. Both establish specific expectations. We expect a fairly consistent meter, a certain rhyming pattern, and flowery imagery ("Shall I compare thee to a summer's day?"). But those expectations are not fulfilled. Instead, the poem thrusts three very different images upon the reader in the first eight lines: a ball glancing off the end of a bat; the "chance meanings" of words (lines 4-5); and the aerial movement of swallows and bats (the same word used in line 2, but by chance having a different meaning here). These all can be placed neatly under the heading "A kind of slant" that the speaker himself provides in the very first phrase (line 1). The effect of bringing these three distinct images together and linking them as different types of slants is, in a way, metaphorical. The reader now associates together a baseball being tipped "off the end of a bat," the dancing meanings that weighted words carry, and the zigzagging motion of two flying animals. The speaker has defined "slant" on his own terms.

Transition sentence.

Topic sentence followed by lots of specific details.

Quotation blended into sentence.

    The traditional form of the Italian sonnet includes a turn between lines 8 and 9. Miranda surprises the reader by starting the turn before the last word of line 8, again making the poem slant:

> Slants
> like these have something to do with why *angle*
> is one of my favorite words, whenever it chances
> to be a verb.
>
> (lines 8-11)

Block quotation of poetry.

Slants--and the images associated with them, specifically, in this case, the abrupt diving of bats and swallows--hold immense meaning for the speaker and the word "favorite" forcefully implies that because of this meaning, he enjoys these types of slants. The way Miranda has repeated his chosen word "slant" also provides an excellent example of the use of sound in "Love Poem."

There is no meter in "Love Poem" (another deviation/slant from the traditional form), which leaves the sounds to carry the flow of the poem. In the first three lines alone we see the repetition of the "an" and "nce" sounds ("slant," "glance," "fence," and "once"). There is also a fair amount of alliteration ("way/will," "ball/bat," "for/fence," "watch/once") and . . . surprise!!! *slant* rhyme: "glance/fence/once." Throughout the poem the words "slant," "chance," "edge," and "dance" are used twice and are important to the speaker. "Edge," for instance, is another way of conveying what this poem is doing: riding the "edge," so to speak, of traditional form. By repeating these words it is as if the speaker is trying to aid the reader in finding the crucial words by repeating, multiple times, the sounds in them; "angle" and "untangling" are two more notable examples. The sound games found in "Love Poem" also include the following: assonance ("close/slow/motion"); consonance ("ball/will"); end rhyme ("chances/dances"); and internal rhyme ("sparks/dark"). The way in which all of these sounds push and pull the tempo and feeling of the verse create the unique flow of the poem.

The sestet is made up of two parallel "with why" clauses. If we skip the first one we just discussed and go directly to the second, this is the result:

Use of brief, concise quotations.

Slants

Ellipses indicate words omitted from line; row of dots indicates omission of one or more complete lines.

like these have something to do with . . .
. . . .
. . . why the music I single
out tonight--eighteenth-century dances--
made me think just now of you untangling
blueberries, carefully, from their dense branches.

(lines 8-9, 11-14)

The reader is finally privy to why the speaker included the three "slant" images in the beginning of the poem. If we visually observe the style of an eighteenth-century dance with all of its intricacies and formalities, we notice, well . . . slants (there is an excellent scene that displays this in the BBC movie of *Pride and Prejudice,* 1987). The speaker has now deftly defined these dances as a fourth slant. These complicated angles remind the speaker of his beloved "untangling / blueberries, carefully, from their dense branches." While this may not seem as effective as comparing her to a rose or a summer's day, the speaker makes his sincerity known. Apparently, his love is great enough to adore the simple image of her plucking blueberries. Not only that, but also this memory, or image (from near or far), is so precious as to merit surfacing during music--and perhaps, by default, the other three "slants." Miranda thus also captures the universal phenomenon of music producing nostalgia.

When we view the poem in this way, the function of the form and the meaning of the title become more obvious. The poem is not typical. But the title and the sonnet form aid the reader in discovering the love that is written between the lines. It is interesting to note as well that Miranda brings about in the poem many things that the speaker dwells on. For instance, the very first phrase, "A kind of slant," is an excellent description of the poem itself; it is a slant, an angle, and a variation on the traditional sonnet. Miranda also "angles" love and sincerity into the poem and the speaker includes words and phrases (loosely, the entire poem) that have "chance meanings." It is these types of chance meanings that make him think of his beloved at all. These layers add to the richness of the poem, tangling it up and making it memorable, just like the blueberry's dense branches.

Good wrap-up sentence.

A Collection of Poems

WEB: Research the authors in this collection with LitLinks at bedfordstmartins.com/approachinglit.

Ai   b. 1947

Why Can't I Leave You?   [1973]

You stand behind the old black mare,
dressed as always in that red shirt,
stained from sweat, the crying of the armpits,
that will not stop for anything,
stroking her rump, while the barley goes unplanted.   5
I pick up my suitcase and set it down,
as I try to leave you again.
I smooth the hair back from your forehead.
I think with your laziness and the drought too,
you'll be needing my help more than ever.   10
You take my hands, I nod
and go to the house to unpack,
having found another reason to stay.

I undress, then put on my white lace slip
for you to take off, because you like that   15
and when you come in, you pull down the straps
and I unbutton your shirt.
I know we can't give each other any more
or any less than what we have.
There is safety in that, so much   20
that I can never get past the packing,
the begging you to please, if I can't make you happy,
come close between my thighs
and let me laugh for you from my second mouth.

Agha Shahid Ali 1949–2001

I Dream It Is Afternoon When I Return to Delhi   [1987]

At Purana Qila I am alone, waiting
for the bus to Daryaganj. I see it coming,
but my hands are empty.
"Jump on, jump on," someone shouts,
"I've saved this change for you   5
for years. Look!"
A hand opens, full of silver rupees.
"Jump on, jump on." The voice doesn't stop.
There's no one I know. A policeman,
handcuffs silver in his hands,   10
asks for my ticket.

I jump off the running bus,
sweat pouring from my hair.
I run past the Doll Museum, past
headlines on the Times of India   15
building, PRISONERS BLINDED IN A BIHAR
JAIL, HARIJAN VILLAGES BURNED BY LANDLORDS.
Panting, I stop in Daryaganj,
outside Golcha Cinema.

Sunil is there, lighting   20
a cigarette, smiling. I say,
"It must be ten years, you haven't changed,
it was your voice on the bus!"
He says, "The film is about to begin,
I've bought an extra ticket for you,"   25
and we rush inside:

Anarkali is being led away,
her earrings lying on the marble floor.
Any moment she'll be buried alive.
"But this is the end," I turn   30
toward Sunil. He is nowhere.
The usher taps my shoulder, says
my ticket is ten years old.

Once again my hands are empty.
I am waiting, alone, at Purana Qila.   35
Bus after empty bus is not stopping.
Suddenly, beggar women with children
are everywhere, offering
me money, weeping for me.

Anonymous

Sir Patrick Spens   [1765]

The king sits in Dumferling town,
   Drinking the blude-reid° wine;   blood-red
"O whar will I get guid sailor,
   To sail this ship of mine?"

Up and spak an eldern° knicht,°   elderly/knight   5
   Sat at the king's richt° knee;   right
"Sir Patrick Spens is the best sailor
   That sails upon the sea."

The king has written a braid° letter   broad (clear)
   And signed it wi' his hand,   10
And sent it to Sir Patrick Spens,
   Was walking on the sand.

The first line that Sir Patrick read,
   A loud lauch° lauched he;   laugh
The next line that Sir Patrick read,   15
   The tear blinded his ee.°   eye

"O wha° is this has done this deed,   who
   This ill deed done to me,
To send me out this time o' the year,
   To sail upon the sea?   20

"Mak haste, mak haste, my mirry men all,
   Our guid ship sails the morn."
"O say na° sae,° my master dear,   not/so
   For I fear a deadly storm.

"Late, late yestre'en I saw the new moon   25
   Wi' the auld moon in hir arm,
And I fear, I fear, my dear master,
   That we will come to harm."

O our Scots nobles were richt laith°   loath
   To weet° their cork-heeled shoon,°   wet/shoes 30
But lang or° a' the play were played   before
   Their hats they swam aboon.°   above

O lang, lang may their ladies sit,
   Wi' their fans into their hand,
Or ere they see Sir Patrick Spens   35
   Come sailing to the land.

*   *   *

O lang, lang may the ladies stand
   Wi' their gold kems° in their hair,   *combs*
Waiting for their ain° dear lords,   *own*
   For they'll see them na mair.°   *more* 40

Half o'er, half o'er to Aberdour
   It's fifty fadom° deep,   *fathoms*
And there lies guid Sir Patrick Spens
   Wi' the Scots lords at his feet.

Susan Atefat-Peckham   1970–2004

Dates   [2001]

Three days and they wrapped
his washed body in muslin,
no lumbering sounds of coffins
carried, only the white ripple
of cloth. I sat back where all   5
women sat, staring from behind
a wooden net, carved and set
aside. The others swayed
as if crows under the mirrored
dome of the mosque webbed   10
in their chadors, breathing cloth
in and out of their wailing,
in and out. Their black heads
bobbed against the carved light
of the wooden boundary, the roar   15
and echo of men beating themselves
downstairs, pounding their chests
tightly, fists on flesh, to the rhythm
of a prayer for the dead.

A woman stood and held a tray,   20
the edges of her chador clenched
in her teeth and wrapped so tightly
around her face that it cut angles
into her cheeks. She offered us
a silver tray of fruit as chanting   25
grew, beating grew, that fleshy
rhythm. And the woman
with dates walked the aisles
offering the shriveled skin
and its sweet stench on a silver tray,   30

making her way from one woman
to the next. Somewhere under
Iranian earth, seamless cloth lay
on its side, a turned face frozen
under a concrete canopy, legs bent   35
toward Mecca. She lowered the tray.
I reached for a date, and my mouth
watered to taste its sugar.

W. H. Auden   1907–1973

Musée des Beaux Arts°   [1940]

About suffering they were never wrong,
The Old Masters: how well they understood
Its human position; how it takes place
While someone else is eating or opening a window or just
    walking dully along;

Musée des Beaux Arts: The painting *Landscape with the Fall of Icarus* (below), on which the
poem is based, is in the Musées Royaux des Beaux-Arts in Brussels.

Pieter Brueghel the Elder (c. 1525–1569), Landscape with the Fall of Icarus, *1558*.
Musée d'Art Ancien, Musées Royaux des Beaux-Arts, Brussels. © Bridgeman-Giraudon/Art Resource, NY.

How, when the aged are reverently, passionately waiting   5
For the miraculous birth, there always must be
Children who did not specially want it to happen, skating
On a pond at the edge of the wood:
They never forgot
That even the dreadful martyrdom must run its course   10
Anyhow in a corner, some untidy spot
Where the dogs go on with their doggy life and the torturer's horse
Scratches its innocent behind on a tree.

In Breughel's *Icarus,* for instance: how everything turns away
Quite leisurely from the disaster; the ploughman may   15
Have heard the splash, the forsaken cry,
But for him it was not an important failure; the sun shone
As it had to on the white legs disappearing into the green
Water; and the expensive delicate ship that must have seen
Something amazing, a boy falling out of the sky,   20
Had somewhere to get to and sailed calmly on.

Jimmy Santiago Baca   b. 1952

Family Ties   [1989]

Mountain barbecue.
They arrive, young cousins singly,
older aunts and uncles in twos and threes,
like trees. I play with a new generation
of children, my hands in streambed silt   5
of their lives, a scuba diver's hands, dusting
surface sand for buried treasure.
Freshly shaved and powdered faces
of uncles and aunts surround taco
and tamale tables. Mounted elk head on wall,   10
brass rearing horse cowboy clock
on fireplace mantle. Sons and daughters
converse round beer and whiskey table.
Tempers ignite on land grant issues.
Children scurry round my legs.   15
Old bow-legged men toss horseshoes on lawn,
other farmhands from Mexico sit on a bench,
broken lives repaired for this occasion.
I feel no love or family tie here. I rise
to go hiking, to find abandoned rock cabins   20

in the mountains. We come to a grass clearing,
my wife rolls her jeans up past ankles,
wades ice cold stream, and I barefooted,
carry a son in each arm and follow.
We cannot afford a place like this.   25
At the party again, I eat bean and chile
burrito, and after my third glass of rum,
we climb in the car and my wife drives
us home. My sons sleep in the back,
dream of the open clearing,   30
they are chasing each other with cattails
in the sunlit pasture, giggling,
as I stare out the window
at no trespassing signs white flashing past.

Amiri Baraka   b. 1934

AM/TRAK   [1969]

1

Trane.
Trane.
History Love Scream Oh
Trane, Oh
Trane, Oh   5
Scream History Love
Trane

2

Begin on by a Philly night club
or the basement of a cullut chuhch
walk the bars my man for pay   10
honk the night lust of money
oh
blow—
scream history love

Rabbit, Cleanhead, Diz   15
Big Maybelle. Trees in the shining night forest

                    *   *   *

Oh
blow
love, history

Alcohol we submit to thee   20
3x's consume our lives
our livers quiver under yr poison hits
eyes roll back in stupidness
The navy, the lord, niggers,
the streets   25
all converge a shitty symphony
of screams
    to come
      dazzled invective
Honk Honk Honk, "I am here   30
to love
it." Let me be fire-mystery
air feeder beauty."

Honk
Oh   35
scream — Miles
comes.

3

Hip band alright
sum up life in the slick
street part of the   40
world, oh,
blow,
if you cd
nigger
man   45

Miles wd stand back and negative check
oh, he dug him — Trane
But Trane clawed at the limits of cool
slandered sanity
with his tryin to be born   50
raging
shit
    Oh
    blow,
yeh go do it   55

honk, scream
uhuh yeh — history
      love
      blue clipped moments
      of intense feeling.   60
"Trane you blows too long."
Screaming niggers drop out yr solos
Bohemian nights, the "heavyweight champ"
smacked him
in the face   65
his eyes sagged like a spent
dick, hot vowels escaped the metal clone of his soul
fucking saxophone
tell us shit tell us tell us!

4

There was nothing left to do but   70
be where monk cd find him
that crazy
mother fucker
      duh duh-duh duh-duh duh
      duh duh   75
      duh duh-duh duh-duh duh
      duh duh
      duh duh-duh duh-duh duh
      duh duh
      duh Duuuuuuuuuuhhhhhh   80
Can you play this shit? (Life asks
Come by and listen

& at the 5 Spot Bach, Mulatto ass Beethoven
& even Duke, who has given America its hip tongue
checked   85
checked
Trane stood and dug
Crazy monk's shit
Street gospel intellectual mystical survival codes
Intellectual street gospel funk modes   90
Tink a ling put downs of dumb shit
pink pink a cool bam groove note air breath
a why I'm here
a why I aint
  & who is you-ha-you-ha-you-ha   95
Monk's shit
Blue Cooper 5 Spot

was the world busting
on piano bass drums & tenor

This was Coltrane's College. A Ph motherfuckin d   100
sitting at the feet, elbows
& funny grin
Of Master T Sphere
too cool to be a genius
he was instead   105
Thelonious
with Comrades Shadow
on tubs, lyric Wilbur
who hipped us to electric futures
& the monster with the horn.   110

5

From the endless sessions
money lord hovers oer us
capitalism beats our ass
dope & juice wont change it
Trane, blow, oh scream   115
yeh, anyway.

There then came down in the ugly streets of us
inside the head & tongue
of us
a man   120
black blower of the now
The vectors from all sources — slavery, renaissance
bop charlie parker,
nigger absolute super-sane screams against reality
course through him   125
AS SOUND!
"Yes, it says
this is now in you screaming
recognize the truth
recognize reality   130
& even check me (Trane)
who blows it
Yes it says
Yes &
Yes again   Convulsive multi orgasmic   135
             Art
             Protest

        *   *   *

& finally, brother, you took you were
(are we gathered to dig this?
electric wind find us finally   140
on red records of the history of ourselves)

The cadre came together
the inimitable 4 who blew the pulse of then, exact
The flame the confusion the love of
whatever the fuck there was   145
    to love
Yes it says
blow, oh honk-scream (bahhhhhhh - wheeeeeeee)

(If Don Lee thinks I am imitating him in this poem,
this is only payback for his imitating me — we   150
are brothers, even if he is a backward cultural nationalist
motherfucker — Hey man only socialism brought by revolution
can win)

        Trane was the spirit of the 60's
        He was Malcolm X in New Super Bop Fire   155
        Baaahhhhh
        Wheeeeeee . . . Black Art!!!

Love
History
    On The Bar Tops of Philly   160
in the Monkish College of Express
in the cool Grottoes of Miles Davis Funnytimery
Be
Be
Be reality   165
Be reality alive in motion in flame to change (You Knew It!)
                        to change!!
        (All you reactionaries listening
        Fuck you, Kill you
        get outta here!!!)   170
Jimmy Garrison, bass, McCoy Tyner, piano, Captain Marvel Elvin
on drums, the number itself — the precise saying
all of it in it afire aflame talking saying being doing meaning

Meditations
Expressions   175
A Love Supreme
(I lay in solitary confinement, July 67
    Tanks rolling thru Newark
    & whistled all I knew of Trane
    my knowledge heartbeat   180
    & he was *dead*

they
said.

And yet last night I played *Meditations*
& it told me what to do   185
Live you crazy mother
fucker!
Live!
   & organize
   yr shit   190
   as rightly
   burning!

Gerald Barrax   b. 1933

Dara   [1984]

When they start pulling you out
The anesthesiologist tells me I may look.
I stand and look over the tent
That hides your mother's body from herself.
I look and see   5
The slick wet head, deceptively black,
That will dry to your nappy red.
Tugs at you. Cuts. Cuts.
I understand your fear, reluctance.
You had clung so tightly   10
Inside, attached so uncertainly to the womb
Against the tide of blood that threatened to sweep you away
Down the toilet where she sat, head bowed,
Watching the flood.
Bargaining for you (Yes, with that promise she keeps)   15
With the god she might as easily have cursed.
Except that it might be you who paid.
Cuts. Cuts. Your mother's flesh, muscle, fat, blood.
They tug and tug now
After you had held so tightly   20
In that micro-ocean, your gray eyes shut
In desperation, clinging to your only hope,
Yourself, imitating her position, her purpose,
Hugging and bowing into yourself,
Into your own stubborn strength,   25
Curving your feet so tightly against you
They would need casting,
The tide flowing, seeming to drain, leech you

Fair black child
You are free,   30
Out, I tell her, second daughter,
Dara. The Beautiful One, last
Child (before they close her)
Is free.

Elizabeth Bishop   1911–1979

The Fish   [1946]

I caught a tremendous fish
and held him beside the boat
half out of water, with my hook
fast in a corner of his mouth.
He didn't fight.   5
He hadn't fought at all.
He hung a grunting weight,
battered and venerable
and homely. Here and there
his brown skin hung in strips   10
like ancient wallpaper,
and its pattern of darker brown
was like wallpaper:
shapes like full-blown roses
stained and lost through age.   15
He was speckled with barnacles,
fine rosettes of lime,
and infested
with tiny white sea-lice,
and underneath two or three   20
rags of green weed hung down.
While his gills were breathing in
the terrible oxygen
— the frightening gills,
fresh and crisp with blood,   25
that can cut so badly —
I thought of the coarse white flesh
packed in like feathers,
the big bones and the little bones,
the dramatic reds and blacks   30
of his shiny entrails,
and the pink swim-bladder
like a big peony.

I looked into his eyes
which were far larger than mine   35
but shallower, and yellowed,
the irises backed and packed
with tarnished tinfoil
seen through the lenses
of old scratched isinglass.°   *transparent sheet of mica*   40
They shifted a little, but not
to return my stare.
— It was more like the tipping
of an object toward the light.
I admired his sullen face,   45
the mechanism of his jaw,
and then I saw
that from his lower lip
— if you could call it a lip —
grim, wet, and weaponlike,   50
hung five old pieces of fish-line,
or four and a wire leader
with the swivel still attached,
with all their five big hooks
grown firmly in his mouth.   55
A green line, frayed at the end
where he broke it, two heavier lines,
and a fine black thread
still crimped from the strain and snap
when it broke and he got away.   60
Like medals with their ribbons
frayed and wavering,
a five-haired beard of wisdom
trailing from his aching jaw.
I stared and stared   65
and victory filled up
the little rented boat,
from the pool of bilge
where oil had spread a rainbow
around the rusted engine   70
to the bailer rusted orange,
the sun-cracked thwarts,
the oarlocks on their strings,
the gunnels — until everything
was rainbow, rainbow, rainbow!   75
And I let the fish go.

WEB: Explore Elizabeth Bishop and "The Fish" in depth, including images and cultural
documents, with VirtuaLit Poetry at bedfordstmartins.com/approachinglit.

William Blake 1757–1827

The Chimney Sweeper [1789]

When my mother died I was very young,
And my father sold me while yet my tongue
Could scarcely cry "'weep! 'weep! 'weep! 'weep!"
So your chimneys I sweep, and in soot I sleep.

There's little Tom Dacre, who cried when his head 5
That curled like a lamb's back, was shaved; so I said,
"Hush, Tom! never mind it, for when your head's bare,
You know that the soot cannot spoil your white hair."

And so he was quiet, and that very night,
As Tom was asleeping, he had such a sight! 10
That thousands of sweepers, Dick, Joe, Ned, and Jack,
Were all of them locked up in coffins of black;

And by came an Angel who had a bright key,
And he opened the coffins and set them all free.
Then down a green plain, leaping, laughing, they run, 15
And wash in a river, and shine in the Sun.

Then naked and white, all their bags left behind,
They rise upon clouds, and sport in the wind;
And the Angel told Tom, if he'd be a good boy,
He'd have God for his father, and never want joy. 20

And so Tom awoke, and we rose in the dark,
And got with our bags and our brushes to work.
Though the morning was cold, Tom was happy and warm;
So if all do their duty, they need not fear harm.

CD-ROM: Research William Blake in depth with cultural documents and multimedia resources on
LiterActive.

Peter Blue Cloud b. 1935

Rattle [1978]

When a new world is born, the old
turns itself inside out, to cleanse
and prepare for a new beginning.
It is
told by some that the stars are

Let us shake
the rattle
to call back
a rattlesnake
to dream back 5

small holes piercing the great
intestine
of a sleeping creature. The earth is
a hollow gourd and earthquakes are
gas rumblings and restless dreaming
of the sleeping creature.
       What
sleeping plant sings the seed
shaken in the globe of a rattle,
the quick breath of the singer warms
and awakens the seed to life.

    The old man rolled fibres of
milkweed across his thigh, softly
speaking to grandchildren, slowly
saying
the thanksgiving to a sacred plant.

His left hand coiled the string as it
grew, thin and very strong; as he
explained the strength of a unity
of threads combined.
       He took his
small basket of cocoons and poured
grains of coarse sand, poured from
his hand the coarse sand like a
funnel
of wind, a cone between hand and
cocoon.

    Then, seven by seven, he bound
these nests to a stick with the
string,
and took the sap of white blood
of the plant, and with a finger,
rubbed
the encircling string.
       And waited, holding
the rattle to the sun for drying. And
when
he shook the first sound, the
children
sucked in their breaths and felt
strange
stirrings in their minds and
stomachs.

the dancers.

When the wind
sweeps earth
there is fullness   10
of sound,
we are given
a beat
to dance by
and drum   15
now joins us

and flutes
are like gentle
birds and
   20
crickets on
   branches,
swaying trees.
The fan of
winged hawks   25
brush clouds like
streaks of
white clay upon
a field
of blue sky   30

water base.
The seeds in

the pod
of a plant   35

are children
of the sun

of earth   40
that we sing
we are

a rainfall voice
   45
a plumed

and sacred bird

And when he sang the first song of
many,
the leaves of the cottonwood joined
in,
and desert winds shifted sand.
                    And the
children closed their eyes, the better
        to hear tomorrow.

What sleeping plant sings the seed
in the gourd of night within the
hollow moon, the ladder going down,
down into the core of this good earth
leads to stars and wheeling suns
and
planets beyond count.
                    What sound
is that in the moist womb of the sea;
the softly swaying motion in a
multitude of sleeping seeds.
                    Maybe it
is rattlesnake, the medicine singer.
                    And
it is gourd, cocoon, seed pod, hollow
horn,
shell of snapping turtle, bark of
birch,
hollowed cedar, intestines of
creatures,
    rattle
is an endless element in sound and
vibration, singing the joys of
awakening,
shushing like the dry stalks of corn
in wind, the cradle songs of night.
    Hail-heavy wind bending upon
a roof of elm bark,
                the howling song
of a midwinter blizzard heard by
a people sitting in circle close to
the fire. The fire is the sun, is the
burning core of Creation's seed,
sputtering
and seeking the womb of life.

we are   50

shadows come back

to protect
the tiny seedlings   55
we are
a memory in

single dance
which is all
dancing forever.   60
We are eyes
looking about

for the children
do they   65
run and play
our echos
our former joys
in today?
Let us shake   70
the rattle
for the ancients

who dwell
                                    75
upon this land

whose spirits
joined to ours
guide us   80

and direct us
that we
may ever walk
a harmony   85
that our songs
be clear.
Let us shake
the rattle
for the fliers   90

and swimmers

*   *   *

When someone asked Coyote, why
is there loneliness, and what is the
reason and meaning of loneliness:
Coyote
took an empty gourd and began
shaking
it, and he shook it for a long time.
          Then
he took a single pebble and put it
into the gourd, and again began to
shake the gourd for many days, and
the pebble was indeed loneliness.
          Again
Coyote paused to put a handful of
pebbles into the gourd.
          And the sound
now had a wholeness and a meaning
beyond questioning.

for the trees
and mushrooms
for tall grasses   95

blessed by

a snake's passage
for insects   100
keeping the balance,
and winds
which bring rain
and rivers
going to sea   105
and all
things of Creation.
Let us
shake the rattle
    always, forever.   110

Eavan Boland b. 1944

The Pomegranate   [1994]

The only legend I have ever loved is
The story of a daughter lost in hell.
And found and rescued there.
Love and blackmail are the gist of it.
Ceres° and Persephone the names.   5
And the best thing about the legend is
I can enter it anywhere. And have.
As a child in exile in
A city of fogs and strange consonants,
I read it first and at first I was   10
An exiled child in the crackling dusk of
The underworld, the stars blighted. Later

---

5. **Ceres:** Roman name of Demeter, the goddess of crops and harvest. Her daughter Persephone was kidnapped by Pluto (or Hades) and taken to the underworld. Demeter, grieving and angry, refused to let seeds germinate or crops grow. To save the human race from extinction, Zeus finally ordered Pluto to release Persephone. Pluto told her she was free to leave but tricked her by offering a pomegranate seed; anyone who eats food in the underworld must return there. Zeus therefore arranged a compromise: Persephone would spend a third of each year in the land of the dead with Pluto (winter, when Demeter went into mourning); but she would be with her mother for the other two-thirds of each year (spring and summer).

I walked out in a summer twilight
Searching for my daughter at bedtime.
When she came running I was ready   15
To make any bargain to keep her.
I carried her back past whitebeams.
And wasps and honey-scented buddleias.
But I was Ceres then and I knew
Winter was in store for every leaf   20
On every tree on that road.
Was inescapable for each one we passed.
And for me.
It is winter
And the stars are hidden.   25
I climb the stairs and stand where I can see
My child asleep beside her teen magazines,
Her can of Coke, her plate of uncut fruit.
The pomegranate! How did I forget it?
She could have come home and been safe   30
And ended the story and all
Our heartbroken searching but she reached
Out a hand and plucked a pomegranate.
She put out her hand and pulled down
The French sound for apple° and   *pomme* 35
The noise of stone° and the proof   *granite*
That even in the place of death,
At the heart of legend, in the midst
Of rocks full of unshed tears
Ready to be diamonds by the time   40
The story was told, a child can be
Hungry. I could warn her. There is still a chance.
The rain is cold. The road is flint-coloured.
The suburb has cars and cable television.
The veiled stars are above ground.   45
It is another world. But what else
Can a mother give her daughter but such
Beautiful rifts in time?
If I defer the grief I will diminish the gift.
The legend must be hers as well as mine.   50
She will enter it. As I have.
She will wake up. She will hold
The papery, flushed skin in her hand.
And to her lips. I will say nothing.

Anne Bradstreet c. 1612–1672

To My Dear and Loving Husband   [1678]

If ever two were one, then surely we.
If ever man were loved by wife, then thee;
If ever wife was happy in a man,
Compare with me, ye women, if you can.
I prize thy love more than whole mines of gold,   5
Or all the riches that the East doth hold.
My love is such that rivers cannot quench,
Nor ought but love from thee give recompense.
Thy love is such I can no way repay;
The heavens reward thee manifold, I pray.   10
Then while we live, in love let's so persever,
That when we live no more we may live ever.

Gwendolyn Brooks   1917–2000

the mother   [1945]

Abortions will not let you forget.
You remember the children you got that you did not get,
The damp small pulps with a little or with no hair,
The singers and workers that never handled the air.
You will never neglect or beat   5
Them, or silence or buy with a sweet.
You will never wind up the sucking-thumb
Or scuttle off ghosts that come.
You will never leave them, controlling your luscious sigh,
Return for a snack of them, with gobbling mother-eye.   10

I have heard in the voices of the wind the voices of my dim killed
    children.
I have contracted. I have eased
My dim dears at the breasts they could never suck.
I have said, Sweets, if I sinned, if I seized
Your luck   15
And your lives from your unfinished reach,
If I stole your births and your names,
Your straight baby tears and your games,
Your stilted or lovely loves, your tumults, your marriages, aches,
    and your deaths,

If I poisoned the beginnings of your breaths,   20
Believe that even in my deliberateness I was not deliberate.
Though why should I whine,
Whine that the crime was other than mine? —
Since anyhow you are dead.
Or rather, or instead,   25
You were never made.
But that too, I am afraid,
Is faulty: oh, what shall I say, how is the truth to be said?
You were born, you had body, you died.
It is just that you never giggled or planned or cried.   30

Believe me, I loved you all.
Believe me, I knew you, though faintly, and I loved, I loved you
All.

CD-ROM: Research Gwendolyn Brooks in depth with cultural documents and multimedia resources on *LiterActive*.

Sterling A. Brown   1901–1989

Riverbank Blues   [1932]

A man git his feet set in a sticky mudbank,
A man git dis yellow water in his blood,
No need for hopin', no need for doin',
Muddy streams keep him fixed for good.

Little Muddy, Big Muddy, Moreau and Osage,   5
Little Mary's, Big Mary's, Cedar Creek,
Flood deir muddy water roundabout a man's roots,
Keep him soaked and stranded and git him weak.

Lazy sun shinin' on a little cabin,
Lazy moon glistenin' over river trees;   10
Ole river whisperin', lappin' 'gainst de long roots:
"Plenty of rest and peace in these. . . ."

Big mules, black loam, apple and peach trees,
But seems lak de river washes us down
Past de rich farms, away from de fat lands,   15
Dumps us in some ornery riverbank town.

Went down to the river, sot me down an' listened,
Heard de water talkin' quiet, quiet lak an' slow:

"Ain' no need fo' hurry, take yo' time, take yo' time. . . ."
Heard it sayin' — "Baby, hyeahs de way life go. . . ."   20

Dat is what it tole me as I watched it slowly rollin',
But somp'n way inside me rared up an' say,
"Better be movin' . . . better be travelin' . . .
Riverbank'll git you ef you stay. . . ."

Towns are sinkin' deeper, deeper in de riverbank,   25
Takin' on de ways of deir sulky Ole Man —
Takin' on his creepy ways, takin' on his evil ways,
"Bes' git way, a long way . . . whiles you can.

"Man got his sea too lak de Mississippi
Ain't got so long for a whole lot longer way,   30
Man better move some, better not git rooted
Muddy water fool you, ef you stay. . . ."

Elizabeth Barrett Browning 1806–1861

How do I love thee?
Let me count the ways   [1850]

How do I love thee? Let me count the ways.
I love thee to the depth and breadth and height
My soul can reach, when feeling out of sight
For the ends of Being and ideal Grace.
I love thee to the level of everyday's   5
Most quiet need, by sun and candlelight.
I love thee freely, as men strive for Right;
I love thee purely, as they turn from Praise.
I love thee with the passion put to use
In my old griefs, and with my childhood's faith.   10
I love thee with a love I seemed to lose
With my lost saints — I love thee with the breath,
Smiles, tears, of all my life! — and, if God choose,
I shall but love thee better after death.

Sandra M. Castillo   b. 1962

Exile   [2001]

And you wonder how you could have decided
what to take with you for the rest of your life,
                    what to leave behind.
                    — *Dionisio Martínez°*

i.

We are gitanas,
con barajas y collares,°
thinking ourselves nomads,
Hungarians, bohemians
because sometimes, our adventures define us   5
as much as our props.
Or so we think, my cousin Norma and I,
as we go door to door along East 4th Avenue,
a street we are not supposed to be on,
using candy as our pretext,   10
our costumes as our shields,
thinking we are who we want to be
on this, my first Halloween, 1970.

ii.

Pale and thin,
he stands in the middle of that icebox,   15
where voices cling, like dishes or silverware,
like the unintelligible sounds of English,
of my voice, our trays slamming into one another,
falling on that cold-white cafeteria floor,
the green mush of American food on my lap,   20
on his blue v-neck sweater
because I turned to look for him,
Francisco Insignari,
the first boy I consciously liked.

iii.

It is my third year in Miami;   25
I am in the 5th grade and Mr. Powers,

Dionisio Martínez: Cuban-American poet, born 1956.   **1–2. gitanas, con barajas y collares:**
Gypsies, with cards (for reading fortunes) and necklaces.

my angry American teacher, is telling us about Nixon,
showing us the influence of suggestion,
the persuasion of danger,
asking us who should be president   30
by countering Gonzalo, the new boy,
who alone raises his hand for McGovern,
for a change he never got
before speech and America
because he just doesn't know   35
Mr. Powers.

iv.

Our classroom is called a Pod,
and we rotate to the sound of a bell.
Mr. Shuker gives us word puzzles
from *The Miami Herald,*   40
Miss Christie, bride games:
"something borrowed, something blue,
something old, something new,"
except on Fridays,
when we speak and listen off index cards   45
and have assigned cafeteria seats:
Gerardo Legra, Michael Algair,
Danny Rogers, Maria Murgia and I.

And we sit in silence,
our conversation on our laps,   50
our napkins in our mouths,
for we are graded on our manners,
the silence we share.

v.

The first time I hear the word,
I think about breakfast: 55
tortilla, Cuban style,
with onions and French fries,
on Cuban bread from the bakery on East 10th.

It was what my father made for us
on those days he played weekend cook,   60
but there was an extra syllable
that didn't make me think of Veronica,
slow dancing with Orlando's sister
to *Me & Mrs. Jones,* "Mrs. Jones, Mrs. Jones . . ."
though the boys gathered around her,   65

taunting her with what I knew couldn't be
breakfast.

vi.

Already hip at twelve,
Claro wears otherness
like a worn leather jacket I look for   70
down the humid, yellow halls
of Carol City Junior High,
where we are divided into shifts:
7 A.M. to 12, 12:30 to 5:30 P.M.
where, in dark corners,   75
he finds amor propio°
with my closest girlfriends,
too eager to part their lips
to his popularity and my amazement,
because he knows   80
he is my first obsession.

---

76. amor propio: Too much interest in love.

Rosemary Catacalos   b. 1944

David Talamántez on the Last Day
of Second Grade   [1996]

San Antonio, Texas 1988

David Talamántez, whose mother is at work, leaves his mark
    everywhere in the schoolyard,
tosses pages from a thick sheaf of lined paper high in the air one
    by one, watches them

catch on the teachers' car bumpers, drift into the chalky narrow shade
    of the water fountain.
One last batch, stapled together, he rolls tight into a makeshift horn
    through which he shouts

David! and *David, yes!* before hurling it away hard and darting across
    Brazos Street against   5
the light, the little sag of head and shoulders when, safe on the other
    side, he kicks a can

*   *   *

in the gutter and wanders toward home. David Talamántez believes
  birds are warm blooded,
the way they are quick in the air and give out long strings of complicated music, different

all the time, not like cats and dogs. For this he was marked down in
  Science, and for putting
his name in the wrong place, on the right with the date instead of
  on the left with Science   10

Questions, and for not skipping a line between his heading and
  answers. The X's for wrong
things are big, much bigger than David Talamántez's tiny writing.
  Write larger, his teacher says

in red ink across the tops of many pages. *Messy!* she says on others
  where he's erased
and started over, erased and started over. Spelling, Language Expression, Sentences Using

the Following Words. *Neck. I have a neck name. No!* 20's, 30's.
  Think again! He's good   15
in Art, though, makes 70 on Reading Station Artist's Corner, where
  he's traced and colored

an illustration from *Henny Penny.* A goose with red-and-white
  striped shirt, a hen in a turquoise
dress. Points off for the birds, cloud and butterfly he's drawn in free-
  hand. *Not in the original*

picture! Twenty-five points off for writing nothing in the blank after
  This is my favorite scene
in the book because. . . . There's a page called Rules. *Listen! Always
  working! Stay in your seat!*   20

Raise your hand before you speak! No fighting! Be quiet! Rules copied
  from the board, no grade,
only a huge red checkmark. Later there is a test on Rules. *Listen!
  Alay ercng! Sast in ao snet!*

Rars aone bfo your spek! No finagn! Be cayt! He gets 70 on Rules,
  10 on Spelling. An old man
stoops to pick up a crumpled drawing of a large family crowded
  around a table, an apartment

with bars on the windows in Alazán Courts, a huge sun in one
  corner saying, *To mush noys!*   25
After correcting the spelling, the grade is 90. *Nice details!* And
  there's another mark, on this paper

*   *   *

and all the others, the one in the doorway of La Rosa Beauty Shop,
    the one that blew under
the pool table at La Tenampa, the ones older kids have wadded up like
    big spit balls, the ones run

over by cars. On every single page David Talamántez has crossed out
    the teacher's red numbers
and written in giant letters, blue ink, *Yes! David, yes!*   30

Marilyn Chin   b. 1955

Turtle Soup   [1987]

for Ben Huang

You go home one evening tired from work,
and your mother boils you turtle soup.
Twelve hours hunched over the hearth
(who knows what else is in that cauldron).

You say, "Ma, you've poached the symbol of long life;   5
that turtle lived four thousand years, swam
the Wei, up the Yellow, over the Yangtze.
Witnessed the Bronze Age, the High Tang,
grazed on splendid sericulture."
(So, she boils the life out of him.)   10

"All our ancestors have been fools.
Remember Uncle Wu who rode ten thousand miles
to kill a famous Manchu and ended up
with his head on a pole? Eat, child,
its liver will make you strong."   15

"Sometimes you're the life, sometimes the sacrifice."
Her sobbing is inconsolable.
So, you spread that gentle napkin
over your lap in decorous Pasadena.

Baby, some high priestess has got it wrong.   20
The golden decal on the green underbelly
says "Made in Hong Kong."

Is there nothing left but the shell
and humanity's strange inscriptions,
the songs, the rites, the oracles?   25

Samuel Taylor Coleridge   1772–1834

Kubla Khan   [*c. 1797–1798;* 1813]
Or, A Vision in a Dream. A Fragment°

In Xanadu did Kubla Khan
A stately pleasure dome decree:°
Where Alph,° the sacred river, ran
Through caverns measureless to man
    Down to a sunless sea.   5
So twice five miles of fertile ground
With walls and towers were girdled round:
And there were gardens bright with sinuous rills,
Where blossomed many an incense-bearing tree;
And here were forests ancient as the hills,   10
Enfolding sunny spots of greenery.

But oh! that deep romantic chasm which slanted
Down the green hill athwart a cedarn cover!
A savage place! as holy and enchanted
As e'er beneath a waning moon was haunted   15
By woman wailing for her demon lover!
And from this chasm, with ceaseless turmoil seething,
As if this earth in fast thick pants were breathing,
A mighty fountain momently was forced:
Amid whose swift half-intermitted burst   20
Huge fragments vaulted like rebounding hail,
Or chaffy grain beneath the thresher's flail:
And 'mid these dancing rocks at once and ever
It flung up momently the sacred river.
Five miles meandering with a mazy motion   25
Through wood and dale the sacred river ran,
Then reached the caverns measureless to man,
And sank in tumult to a lifeless ocean:
And 'mid this tumult Kubla heard from far
Ancestral voices prophesying war!   30
    The shadow of the dome of pleasure

Or, a Vision . . . A Fragment: Coleridge stated in a preface that this poem composed itself in his mind during "a profound sleep" (actually an opium-induced reverie); that he began writing it down immediately upon waking but was interrupted by a caller; and that when he returned to his room an hour later he could not complete it.   **1–2. In . . . decree:** "In Xanadu did Cublai Can build a stately Palace, encompassing sixteene miles of plaine ground with a wall" (Samuel Purchas, *Purchas his Pilgrimage* [1613]). The historical Kublai Khan (1215–1294) was the founder of the Yüan dynasty of China and overlord of the Mongol Empire.   **3. Alph:** Probably derived from the name of the River Alpheus in southern Greece, which according to mythology ran under the sea and emerged at Syracuse (Italy) in the fountain of Arethusa.

Floated midway on the waves;
Where was heard the mingled measure
From the fountain and the caves.
It was a miracle of rare device,   35
A sunny pleasure dome with caves of ice!

A damsel with a dulcimer
In a vision once I saw:
It was an Abyssinian maid,
And on her dulcimer she played,   40
Singing of Mount Abora.°
Could I revive within me
Her symphony and song,
To such a deep delight 'twould win me,
That with music loud and long,   45
I would build that dome in air,
That sunny dome! those caves of ice!
And all who heard should see them there,
And all should cry, Beware! Beware!
His flashing eyes, his floating hair!   50
Weave a circle round him thrice,
And close your eyes with holy dread,
For he on honey-dew hath fed,
And drunk the milk of Paradise.

39–41. Abyssinian . . . Abora: See *Paradise Lost* 4.280-82: "where Abassin Kings their issue
Guard, / Mount Amara, though this by some supposed / True Paradise under the Ethiop Line."

Billy Collins   b. 1941

Marginalia   [1998]

Sometimes the notes are ferocious,
skirmishes against the author
raging along the borders of every page
in tiny black script.
If I could just get my hands on you,   5
Kierkegaard,° or Conor Cruise O'Brien,°
they seem to say,
I would bolt the door and beat some logic into your head.

*   *   *

---

6. Kierkegaard: Søren Kierkegaard (1813-1855), Danish philosopher and theologian; **Conor
Cruise O'Brien:** Irish statesman and writer, born 1917.

Other comments are more offhand, dismissive—
"Nonsense." "Please!" "HA!!"—   10
that kind of thing.
I remember once looking up from my reading,
my thumb as a bookmark,
trying to imagine what the person must look like
who wrote "Don't be a ninny"   15
alongside a paragraph in *The Life of Emily Dickinson.*

Students are more modest
needing to leave only their splayed footprints
along the shore of the page.
One scrawls "Metaphor" next to a stanza of Eliot's.°   20
Another notes the presence of "Irony"
fifty times outside the paragraphs of *A Modest Proposal.*°

Or they are fans who cheer from the empty bleachers,
hands cupped around their mouths.
"Absolutely," they shout   25
to Duns Scotus° and James Baldwin.°
"Yes." "Bull's-eye." "My man!"
Check marks, asterisks, and exclamation points
rain down along the sidelines.

And if you have managed to graduate from college   30
without ever having written "Man vs. Nature"
in a margin, perhaps now
is the time to take one step forward.

We have all seized the white perimeter as our own
and reached for a pen if only to show   35
we did not just laze in an armchair turning pages;
we pressed a thought into the wayside,
planted an impression along the verge.

Even Irish monks in their cold scriptoria
jotted along the borders of the Gospels   40
brief asides about the pains of copying,
a bird singing near their window,
or the sunlight that illuminated their page—
anonymous men catching a ride into the future
on a vessel more lasting than themselves.   45

                    *   *   *

---

20. Eliot's: T. S. Eliot (1888–1965), American-born poet (see pp. 643, 645, 1427).   **22. A**
Modest Proposal: Satiric essay (1729) by Jonathan Swift (see p. 737).   **26. Duns Scotus:**
John Duns Scotus (1265?–1308), Scottish scholastic theologian; **James Baldwin:** (1924–
1987), American poet and novelist (see pp. 138 and 1418).

And you have not read Joshua Reynolds,°
they say, until you have read him
enwreathed with Blake's° furious scribbling.

Yet the one I think of most often,
the one that dangles from me like a locket,   50
was written in the copy of *Catcher in the Rye*°
I borrowed from the local library
one slow, hot summer.
I was just beginning high school then,
reading books on a davenport in my parents' living room,   55
and I cannot tell you
how vastly my loneliness was deepened,
how poignant and amplified the world before me seemed,
when I found on one page

a few greasy looking smears   60
and next to them, written in soft pencil —
by a beautiful girl, I could tell,
whom I would never meet —
"Pardon the egg salad stains, but I'm in love."

---

46. Joshua Reynolds: Sir Joshua Reynolds (1723–1792), English painter and critic.   **48. Blake's:** William Blake (1757–1827), English poet and artist.   **51. *Catcher in the Rye:*** Novel (1951) by J. D. Salinger (b. 1919).

Jayne Cortez b. 1936

Into This Time   [1991]

for Charles Mingus°

Into this time
of steel feathers blowing from hearts
into this turquoise flame time in the mouth
into this sonic boom time in the conch
into this musty stone-fly time sinking into   5
the melancholy buttocks of dawn
sinking into lacerated whelps
into gun holsters
into breast bones
into a manganese field of uranium nozzles   10
into a nuclear tube full of drunk rodents

Charles Mingus: (1929–1979), an innovative American jazz bassist.

into the massive vein of one interval
into one moment's hair plucked down into
the timeless droning fixed into
long pauses   15
fixed into a lash of ninety-eight minutes screeching into
the internal heat of an ice ball melting time into
a configuration of commas on strike
into a work force armed with a calendar of green wings
into a collection of nerves   20
into magnetic mucus
into tongueless shrines
into water pus of a silver volcano
into the black granite face of Morelos°
into the pigeon toed dance of Mingus   25
into a refuge of air bubbles
into a cylinder of snake whistles
into clusters of slow spiders
into spade fish skulls
into rosin coated shadows of women wrapped in live iguanas   30
into coins into crosses into St. Martin De Porres°
into the pain of this place changing pitches beneath
fingers swelling into
night shouts
into day trembles   35
into month of precious bloods flowing into
this fiesta of sadness year
into this city of eternal spring
into this solo
on the road of young bulls   40
on the street of lost children
on the avenue of dead warriors
on the frisky horse tail fuzz zooming
into ears of every madman
stomping into every new composition   45
everyday of the blues
penetrating into this time

This time of loose strings in low tones
pulling boulders of Olmec heads into the sun
into tight wires uncoiling from body of a strip teaser on the table   50
into half-tones wailing between snap and click
of two castanets smoking into
scales jumping from tips of sacrificial flints

24. Morelos: José Maria Morelos (1765–1815), a Mexican revolutionary leader. 31. Martin De Porres: A seventeenth-century Peruvian saint.

into frogs yodeling across grieving cults
yodeling up into word stuffed smell of flamingo stew   55
into wind packed fuel of howling dog throats slit into
this January flare of aluminum dust falling into
laminated stomach of a bass violin rubbed into red ashes
rubbed into the time sequence of
this time of salmonella leaking from eyeballs of a pope   60
into this lavender vomit time in the chest into
this time plumage of dried bats in the brain into
this wallowing time weed of invisible wakes on cassettes into
this off-beat time syncopation in a leopard skin suit
into this radiated protrusion of time in the desert into   65
this frozen cheek time of dead infants in the cellar
into this time flying with the rotten bottoms of used tuxedos
into this purple   brown   grey   gold minus zero time trilling into
a lime stone crusted Yucatan belching
into fifty six medallions shaking   70
into armadillo drums thumping
into tambourines of fetishes rattling
into an oil slick of poverty symbols flapping
into flat-footed shuffle of two birds advancing
into back spine of luminous impulses tumbling   75
into metronomes of colossal lips ticking
into a double zigzag of callouses splitting
into foam of electric snow flashing into this time
of steel feathers blowing from hearts
into this turquoise flame time in the mouth into   80
this sonic boom time in the conch
into this musty stone fly time sinking into
the melancholy buttocks of dawn

Victor Hernández Cruz   b. 1949

Problems with Hurricanes   [1991]

A campesino looked at the air
And told me:
With hurricanes it's not the wind
or the noise or the water.
I'll tell you he said: 5
it's the mangoes, avocados
Green plantains and bananas
flying into town like projectiles.

*   *   *

How would your family
feel if they had to tell   10
The generations that you
got killed by a flying
Banana.

Death by drowning has honor
If the wind picked you up   15
and slammed you
Against a mountain boulder
This would not carry shame
But
to suffer a mango smashing   20
Your skull
or a plantain hitting your
Temple at 70 miles per hour
is the ultimate disgrace.

The campesino takes off his hat—   25
As a sign of respect
towards the fury of the wind
And says:
Don't worry about the noise
Don't worry about the water   30
Don't worry about the wind—
If you are going out
beware of mangoes
And all such beautiful
sweet things.   35

e. e. cummings 1894–1962

in Just-   [1923]

in Just-
spring   when the world is mud-
luscious the little
lame balloonman

whistles   far   and wee   5

and eddieandbill come
running from marbles and
piracies and it's
spring

     *   *   *

when the world is puddle-wonderful   10

the queer
old balloonman whistles
far   and   wee
and bettyandisbel come dancing

from hop-scotch and jump-rope and   15

it's
spring
and
    the

            goat-footed   20

balloonMan   whistles
far
and
wee

e. e. cummings

pity this busy monster,manunkind   [1944]

pity this busy monster,manunkind,

not. Progress is a comfortable disease:
your victim(death and life safely beyond)

plays with the bigness of his littleness
— electrons deify one razorblade   5
into a mountainrange;lenses extend

unwish through curving wherewhen till unwish
returns on its unself.

                        A world of made
is not a world of born — pity poor flesh   10

and trees,poor stars and stones,but never this
fine specimen of hypermagical

ultraomnipotence. We doctors know

a hopeless case if — listen:there's a hell
of a good universe next door;let's go   15

CD-ROM: Research e. e. cummings in depth with cultural documents and multimedia resources on
LiterActive.

Keki N. Daruwalla   b. 1937

Pestilence   [1970]

pairs of padded feet
        are behind me
astride me
          in front of me
the footpaths are black feet   5
converging on the town

brown shoulders   black shoulders
shoulders round as orbs
muscles smooth as river-stones
        glisten   10
till a dry wind scourges
the sweat from off their backs

they are palanquin-bearers of a different sort
on the string-beds they carry
no henna-smeared brides.   15
prone upon them are frail bodies
frozen bodies   delirious bodies
some drained of fever and sap
some moving   others supine
transfixed under the sun   20

the hospital-floors are marble-white
black bodies dirty them
nurses in white habits
unicef jeeps with white bonnets
doctors with white faces receive them   25
"who says they have cholera?
they are down with diarrhoea
who says it is cholera?
it is gastro-enteritis
who says they have cholera?"   30

the land's visage is unmarked
soot-brown   soot-green
       soot-grey
mongrels tail the ambulance
till dust and gasoline-fumes   35
choke them off

but memory like a crane-arm
unloads its ploughed-up rubble
ancient visitations is what one recalls

the sweep of black feet   40
          towards the ghats
dying villages
the land   surplus once again
as after a flood
migrations as only birds have known   45
forgotten cattle dying at the stakes
— someone left them untethered

this is miniature by contrast
but the image lingers
string-beds creaking   50
over padded feet
and when of a sudden
cholera turns to death
the feet keep up their padded progress
only the string-bed is exchanged   55
for a plank

Kamala Das b. 1934

In Love   [1965]

Of what does the burning mouth
Of sun, burning in today's
Sky remind me . . . oh, yes, his
Mouth, and . . . his limbs like pale and
Carnivorous plants reaching   5
Out for me, and the sad lie
Of my unending lust. Where
Is room, excuse or even
Need for love, for, isn't each
Embrace a complete thing, a   10
Finished jigsaw, when mouth on
Mouth, I lie, ignoring my poor
Moody mind, while pleasure
With deliberate gaiety
Trumpets harshly into the   15
Silence of the room. . . . At noon
I watch the sleek crows flying
Like poison on wings — and at
Night, from behind the Burdwan
Road, the corpse-bearers cry "Bol   20
Hari Bol," a strange lacing

For moonless nights, while I walk
The verandah sleepless, a
Million questions awake in
Me, and all about him, and   25
This skin-communicated
Thing that I dare not yet in
His presence call our love.

Toi Derricotte   b. 1941

A Note on My Son's Face   [1989]

I

Tonight, I look, thunderstruck
at the gold head of my grandchild.
Almost asleep, he buries his feet
between my thighs;
his little straw eyes   5
close in the near dark.
I smell the warmth of his raw
slightly foul breath, the new death
waiting to rot inside him.
Our breaths equalize our heartbeats;   10
every muscle of the chest uncoils,
the arm bones loosen in the nest
of nerves. I think of the peace
of walking through the house,
pointing to the name of this, the name of that,   15
an educator of a new man.

Mother. Grandmother. Wise
Snake-woman who will show the way;
Spider-woman whose black tentacles
hold him precious. Or will tear off his head,   20
her teeth over the little husband,
the small fist clotted in trust at her breast.

This morning, looking at the face of his father,
I remembered how, an infant, his face was too dark,
nose too broad, mouth too wide.   25
I did not look in that mirror
and see the face that could save me
from my own darkness.
Did he, looking in my eye, see
what I turned from: 30

my own dark grandmother
bending over gladioli in the field,
her shaking black hand defenseless
at the shining cock of flower?

I wanted that face to die,   35
to be reborn in the face of a white child.

I wanted the soul to stay the same,
for I loved to death,
to damnation and God-death,
the soul that broke out of me.   40
I crowed: My Son! My Beautiful!
But when I peeked in the basket,
I saw the face of a black man.

Did I bend over his nose
and straighten it with my fingers   45
like a vine growing the wrong way?
Did he feel my hand in malice?

Generations we prayed and fucked
for this light child,
the shining god of the second coming;   50
we bow down in shame
and carry the children of the past
in our wallets, begging forgiveness.

II

A picture in a book,
a lynching.   55
The bland faces of men who watch
a Christ go up in flames, smiling,
as if he were a hooked
fish, a felled antelope, some
wild thing tied to boards and burned.   60
His charring body
gives off light — a halo
burns out of him.
His face scorched featureless;
the hair matted to the scalp   65
like feathers.
One man stands with his hand on his hip,
another with his arm
slung over the shoulder of a friend,
as if this moment were large enough   70
to hold affection.

III

How can we wake
from a dream
we are born into,
that shines around us,   75
the terrible bright air?

Having awakened,
having seen our own bloody hands,
how can we ask forgiveness,
bring before our children the real   80
monster of their nightmares?

The worst is true.
Everything you did not want to know.

Emily Dickinson   1830–1886

Because I could not stop for Death   [c. 1863; 1890]

Because I could not stop for Death –
He kindly stopped for me –
The Carriage held but just Ourselves –
And Immortality.

We slowly drove – He knew no haste   5
And I had put away
My labor and my leisure too,
For His Civility –

We passed the School, where Children strove
At Recess – in the Ring –   10
We passed the Fields of Gazing Grain –
We passed the Setting Sun –

Or rather – He passed Us –
The Dews drew quivering and chill –
For only Gossamer, my Gown –   15
My Tippet° – only Tulle° –   *scarf/silk net*

We paused before a House that seemed
A Swelling of the Ground –
The Roof was scarcely visible –
The Cornice – in the Ground –   20

Since then – 'tis Centuries – and yet
Feels shorter than the Day
I first surmised the Horses' Heads
Were toward Eternity –

Emily Dickinson

Much Madness is divinest Sense

[*c. 1862;* 1890]

Much Madness is divinest Sense –
To a discerning Eye –
Much Sense – the starkest Madness –
'Tis the Majority
In this, as All, prevail –   5
Assent – and you are sane –
Demur – you're straightway dangerous –
And handled with a Chain –

CD-ROM: Research Emily Dickinson in depth with cultural documents and multimedia resources on *LiterActive.*

Ana Doina   b. 1955

The Extinct Homeland –
A Conversation with Czeslaw Milosz°

[2001]

Tell me, as you would in the middle of the night
When we face only night, the ticking of a watch,
The whistle of an express train, tell me
Whether you really think that this world
Is your home?
                    — *"An Appeal" by Czeslaw Milosz*

Home? Somewhere we belong? The metaphor
which includes us in its landscape? The place
that always takes us in, gives us context
is part of our texture? A land where, no matter
how scorched the soil, our roots can still grow?   5
Where all that we should, could, would have been
realized? There is no home for us, Czeslaw.
There is no homeland. Not anymore, not anywhere.

I wish I could learn to live with the malady
of an elsewhere, with the "hidden certainty"   10
that trees grow taller, and sunset's peacock tail
opens more intense colors over *other* horizons, or else
quit trying to understand *here* in comparison with *there*

Czeslaw Milosz: Polish-born poet, born 1911 (see pp. 691 and 1446).

as if I never am where I am, as if I never embody
my own presence.   15

I wish I could cease to crave a pathway
to a physical place I come from, or go to,
and like nomads who don't know where
they have started their exile, I could accept
oblivion as enough of a homeland.   20

Czeslaw, you've been at this game
far longer than I, tell me, is elsewhere real?
Or did I create a lucid paradise of what exists
only in memory? Obsessive, like the negative
of an otherwise ordinary picture. Do I,   25
haunted by the need for symmetry — a known beginning
to a perceivable end — hold real what I choose to keep
alive and harmonious through my story? Do I,
asking for the benefit of nostalgia — this hallucination
whose life is hunger and thirst — break bread   30
with a Fata Morgana?°

Homeland — its cannibal mouth, open
like a graveyard, threatened to swallow me. I too
ran away from my civilization foolishly thinking
I would be able to escape it, and emerge   35
from the narrow cocoon of my flight like a butterfly
who has no memory of the caterpillar. But no land
lets itself be eradicated without leaving behind ruins
or fossils. And no new round is comparable
to what becomes sweeter through memory. Homeland —   40
inscrutable, freed from its bitterness, turns into a garden
while the present, always a temporary ark, is no salvation,
only a journey without a known destination.

I must have been kneaded out of a clay that doesn't stick
to the potter's hands and is not one with the rest of the earth,   45
and just like wisdom words don't keep the breath of the wise,
my life once undone from its originating landscape cannot
be tied to a place anymore. Nor to the sword-laden history
whose blood throbs in my temples, nor to an ancestral oath
which still awakens forgotten passions when I bite   50
the bitter bread of a past ethnic pride. Not even to a generic
alley between columnar poplars. All I have are images
voices, faces of people and angels — memorized.

---

31. **Fata Morgana:** Mirage.

A homeland that neither lives, nor dies, but stays
crystallized like a picture.   55

All there is is a harsh saddle I haven't yet broken in
and the promise of a mythology that doesn't remember
people trudging out of burning pasts, a mythology
that doesn't describe fog-encircled forests and rolling hills,
but a calling, a thirst.   60

Exiled I make a vow to be what I don't know
to a land I haven't inherited, while the old homeland,
the one that becomes extinct in the distance, survives
only in my mouth, in the flavors I long for,
in the mother tongue I teach to my children.   65

There is no homeland. I am its preexisting condition.
I am the great-grandmother of someone who will not
remember the exact place I came from, or why
I needed to run away from the ancestral land, or how
I worshiped. I am my own myth, the first memory, nebulous   70
like any beginning.

John Donne 1572–1631

A Valediction: Forbidding Mourning   [1633]

As virtuous men pass mildly away,
    And whisper to their souls, to go,
Whilst some of their sad friends do say:
    "The breath goes now," and some say, "No";

So let us melt, and make no noise,   5
    No tear-floods, nor sigh-tempests move;
'Twere profanation of our joys
    To tell the laity our love.

Moving of th' earth brings harms and fears,
    Men reckon what it did and meant;   10
But trepidation of the spheres,
    Though greater far, is innocent.°

                    *   *   *

9–12. Moving . . . innocent: Earthquakes cause damage and were taken as portending further changes or dangers. Trepidation (an oscillating motion of the eighth or ninth sphere, in the Ptolemaic cosmological system) is greater than an earthquake, but not harmful or ominous.

Dull sublunary° lovers' love   *under the moon; hence, inconstant*
    (Whose soul is sense) cannot admit
Absence, because it doth remove   15
    Those things which elemented° it.   *composed*

But we, by a love so much refined
    That our selves know not what it is,
Inter-assurèd of the mind,
    Care less, eyes, lips, and hands to miss.   20

Our two souls therefore, which are one,
    Though I must go, endure not yet
A breach, but an expansion,
    Like gold to airy thinness beat.

If they be two, they are two so   25
    As stiff twin compasses° are two;   *drawing compasses*
Thy soul, the fixed foot, makes no show
    To move, but doth, if th' other do.

And though it in the center sit,
    Yet when the other far doth roam,   30
It leans, and hearkens after it,
    And grows erect, as that comes home.

Such wilt thou be to me, who must,
    Like th' other foot, obliquely run;
Thy firmness makes my circle just,   35
    And makes me end where I begun.

Mark Doty b. 1953

Tiara   [1991]

Peter died in a paper tiara
cut from a book of princess paper dolls;
he loved royalty, sashes

and jewels. *I don't know,*
he said, when he woke in the hospice,   5
I was watching the Bette Davis film festival

on Channel 57 and then —
At the wake, the tension broke
when someone guessed

       *   *   *

the casket closed because
he was *in there in a big wig
and heels,* and someone said,

*You know he's always late,
he probably isn't here yet —
he's still fixing his makeup.*

And someone said he asked for it.
Asked for it —
when all he did was go down

into the salt tide
of wanting as much as he wanted,
giving himself over so drunk

or stoned it almost didn't matter who,
though they were beautiful,
stampeding into him in the simple,

ravishing music of their hurry.
I think heaven is perfect stasis
poised over the realms of desire,

where dreaming and waking men lie
on the grass while wet horses
roam among them, huge fragments

of the music we die into
in the body's paradise.
Sometimes we wake not knowing

how we came to lie here,
or who has crowned us with these temporary,
precious stones. And given

the world's perfectly turned shoulders,
the deep hollows blued by longing,
given the irreplaceable silk

of horses rippling in orchards,
fruit thundering and chiming down,
given the ordinary marvels of form

and gravity, what could he do,
what could any of us ever do
but ask for it?

Rita Dove b. 1952

The Satisfaction Coal Company   [1986]

1

What to do with a day.
Leaf through *Jet*. Watch T.V.
Freezing on the porch
but he goes anyhow, snow too high
for a walk, the ice treacherous.   5
Inside, the gas heater takes care of itself;
he doesn't even notice being warm.

Everyone says he looks great.
Across the street a drunk stands smiling
at something carved in a tree.   10
The new neighbor with the floating hips
scoots out to get the mail
and waves once, brightly,
storm door clipping her heel on the way in.

2

Twice a week he had taken the bus down Glendale hill   15
to the corner of Market. Slipped through
the alley by the canal and let himself in.
Started to sweep
with terrible care, like a woman
brushing shine into her hair,   20
same motion, same lullaby.
No curtains — the cop on the beat
stopped outside once in the hour
to swing his billy club and glare.

It was better on Saturdays   25
when the children came along:
he mopped while they emptied
ashtrays, clang of glass on metal
then a dry scutter. Next they counted
nailheads studding the leather cushions.   30
Thirty-four! they shouted,
that was the year and
they found it mighty amusing.

But during the week he noticed more —
lights when they gushed or dimmed   35

at the Portage Hotel, the 10:32
picking up speed past the B & O switchyard,
floorboards trembling and the explosive
kachook kachook kachook kachook
and the oiled rails ticking underneath.   40

3

They were poor then but everyone had been poor.
He hadn't minded the sweeping,
just the thought of it — like now
when people ask him what he's thinking
and he says *I'm listening*.   45

Those nights walking home alone,
the bucket of coal scraps banging his knee,
he'd hear a roaring furnace
with its dry, familiar heat. Now the nights
take care of themselves — as for the days,   50
there is the canary's sweet curdled song,
the wino smiling through his dribble.
Past the hill, past the gorge
choked with wild sumac in summer,
the corner has been upgraded.   55
Still, he'd like to go down there someday
to stand for a while, and get warm.

Cornelius Eady b. 1954

My Mother, If She Had Won Free
Dance Lessons   [1986]

Would she have been a person
With a completely different outlook on life?
There are times when I visit
And find her settled on a chair
In our dilapidated house,   5
The neighborhood crazy lady
Doing what the neighborhood crazy lady is supposed to do,
Which is absolutely nothing

And I wonder as we talk our sympathetic talk,
Abandoned in easy dialogue,   10
I, the son of the crazy lady,

Who crosses easily into her point of view
As if yawning
Or taking off an overcoat.
Each time I visit   15
I walk back into our lives

And I wonder, like any child who wakes up one day to find themself
Abandoned in a world larger than their
    Bad dreams,
I wonder as I see my mother sitting there,   20
Landed to the right-hand window in the living room,
Pausing from time to time in the endless loop of our dialogue
To peek for rascals through the
Venetian blinds,

I wonder a small thought.   25
I walk back into our lives.
Given the opportunity,
How would she have danced?
Would it have been as easily

As we talk to each other now,   30
The crazy lady
And the crazy lady's son,
As if we were old friends from opposite coasts
Picking up the thread of a long conversation,

Or two ballroom dancers   35
Who only know
One step?

What would have changed
If the phone had rung like a suitor,
If the invitation had arrived in the mail   40
Like Jesus, extending a hand?

T. S. Eliot   1888–1965

Journey of the Magi   [1927]

"A cold coming we had of it,
Just the worst time of the year
For a journey, and such a long journey:
The ways deep and the weather sharp,
The very dead of winter."   5
And the camels galled, sore-footed, refractory,

Lying down in the melting snow.
There were times we regretted
The summer palaces on slopes, the terraces,
And the silken girls bringing sherbet.   10
Then the camel men cursing and grumbling
And running away, and wanting their liquor and women,
And the night-fires going out, and the lack of shelters,
And the cities hostile and the towns unfriendly
And the villages dirty and charging high prices: 15
A hard time we had of it.
At the end we preferred to travel all night,
Sleeping in snatches,
With the voices singing in our ears, saying
That this was all folly.   20

    Then at dawn we came down to a temperate valley,
Wet, below the snow line, smelling of vegetation;
With a running stream and a water-mill beating the darkness,
And three trees on the low sky,
And an old white horse galloped away in the meadow.   25
Then we came to a tavern with vine-leaves over the lintel,
Six hands at an open door dicing for pieces of silver,
And feet kicking the empty wine-skins.
But there was no information, and so we continued
And arrived at evening, not a moment too soon   30
Finding the place; it was (you may say) satisfactory.

    All this was a long time ago, I remember,
And I would do it again, but set down
This set down
This: were we led all that way for   35
Birth or Death? There was a Birth, certainly,
We had evidence and no doubt. I had seen birth and death,
But had thought they were different; this Birth was
Hard and bitter agony for us, like Death, our death.
We returned to our places, these Kingdoms,   40
But no longer at ease here, in the old dispensation,
With an alien people clutching their gods.
I should be glad of another death.

T. S. Eliot

The Love Song of J. Alfred Prufrock   [1917]

*S'io credesse che mia risposta fosse
A persona che mai tornasse al mondo,
Questa fiamma staria senza piu scosse.
Ma perciocche giammai di questo fondo
Non torno vivo alcun, s'i'odo il vero,
Senza tema d'infamia ti rispondo.°*

Let us go then, you and I,
When the evening is spread out against the sky
Like a patient etherised upon a table;
Let us go, through certain half-deserted streets,
The muttering retreats   5
Of restless nights in one-night cheap hotels
And sawdust restaurants with oyster-shells:
Streets that follow like a tedious argument
Of insidious intent
To lead you to an overwhelming question . . .   10
Oh, do not ask, "What is it?"
Let us go and make our visit.

    In the room the women come and go
Talking of Michelangelo.

    The yellow fog that rubs its back upon the window-panes,   15
The yellow smoke that rubs its muzzle on the window-panes
Licked its tongue into the corners of the evening,
Lingered upon the pools that stand in drains,
Let fall upon its back the soot that falls from chimneys,
Slipped by the terrace, made a sudden leap,   20
And seeing that it was a soft October night,
Curled once about the house, and fell asleep.

    And indeed there will be time
For the yellow smoke that slides along the street,
Rubbing its back upon the window-panes;   25
There will be time, there will be time

Epigraph: "If I thought that my answer were being made to someone who would ever return to earth, this flame would remain without further movement; but since no one has ever returned alive from this depth, if what I hear is true, I answer you without fear of infamy" (Dante, *Inferno* 27.61–66). Dante encounters Guido de Montefeltro in the eighth circle of hell, where souls are trapped within flames (tongues of fire) as punishment for giving evil counsel. Guido tells Dante details about his evil life only because he assumes that Dante is on his way to an even deeper circle in hell and will never return to earth and be able to repeat what he has heard.

To prepare a face to meet the faces that you meet;
There will be time to murder and create,
And time for all the works and days° of hands
That lift and drop a question on your plate;   30
Time for you and time for me,
And time yet for a hundred indecisions,
And for a hundred visions and revisions,
Before the taking of a toast and tea.

    In the room the women come and go   35
Talking of Michelangelo.

    And indeed there will be time
To wonder, "Do I dare?" and, "Do I dare?"
Time to turn back and descend the stair,
With a bald spot in the middle of my hair—   40
[They will say: "How his hair is growing thin!"]
My morning coat, my collar mounting firmly to the chin,
My necktie rich and modest, but asserted by a simple pin—
[They will say: "But how his arms and legs are thin!"]
Do I dare   45
Disturb the universe?
In a minute there is time
For decisions and revisions which a minute will reverse.

    For I have known them all already, known them all:—
Have known the evenings, mornings, afternoons,   50
I have measured out my life with coffee spoons;
I know the voices dying with a dying fall°
Beneath the music from a farther room.
    So how should I presume?

    And I have known the eyes already, known them all—   55
The eyes that fix you in a formulated phrase,
And when I am formulated, sprawling on a pin,
When I am pinned and wriggling on the wall,
Then how should I begin
To spit out all the butt-ends of my days and ways?   60
    And how should I presume?

    And I have known the arms already, known them all—
Arms that are braceleted and white and bare

---

29. works and days: *Works and Days* is the title of a didactic poem about farming by the Greek poet Hesiod (eighth century B.C.E.) that includes instruction about doing each task at the proper time. **52. a dying fall:** An allusion to Shakespeare's *Twelfth Night* (1.1.4): "That strain [of music] again! It had a dying fall" (a cadence that falls away).

[But in the lamplight, downed with light brown hair!]
Is it perfume from a dress   65
That makes me so digress?
Arms that lie along a table, or wrap about a shawl.
    And should I then presume?
    And how should I begin?

*   *   *

Shall I say, I have gone at dusk through narrow streets   70
And watched the smoke that rises from the pipes
Of lonely men in shirt-sleeves, leaning out of windows? . . .

    I should have been a pair of ragged claws
Scuttling across the floors of silent seas.

*   *   *

And the afternoon, the evening, sleeps so peacefully!   75
Smoothed by long fingers,
Asleep . . . tired . . . or it malingers,
Stretched on the floor, here beside you and me.
Should I, after tea and cakes and ices,
Have the strength to force the moment to its crisis?   80
But though I have wept and fasted, wept and prayed,
Though I have seen my head [grown slightly bald] brought in upon
   a platter,°
I am no prophet — and here's no great matter;
I have seen the moment of my greatness flicker,
And I have seen the eternal Footman hold my coat, and snicker,   85
And in short, I was afraid.

    And would it have been worth it, after all,
After the cups, the marmalade, the tea,
Among the porcelain, among some talk of you and me,
Would it have been worth while,   90
To have bitten off the matter with a smile,
To have squeezed the universe into a ball
To roll it toward some overwhelming question,
To say: "I am Lazarus,° come from the dead,
Come back to tell you all, I shall tell you all" —   95
If one, settling a pillow by her head,

---

82. head . . . platter: As a reward for dancing before King Herod, Salome, his stepdaughter, asked for the head of John the Baptist to be presented to her on a platter (Matthew 14:1–12; Mark 6:17–28).   **94. Lazarus:** Either the beggar Lazarus, who in Luke 16:19–31 did not return from the dead, or Jesus' friend Lazarus, who did (John 11:1–44).

Should say: "That is not what I meant at all.
That is not it, at all."

And would it have been worth it, after all,
Would it have been worth while,   100
After the sunsets and the dooryards and the sprinkled streets,
After the novels, after the teacups, after the skirts that trail along
     the floor—
And this, and so much more?—
It is impossible to say just what I mean!
But as if a magic lantern threw the nerves in patterns on a screen: 105
Would it have been worth while
If one, settling a pillow or throwing off a shawl,
And turning toward the window, should say:
     "That is not it at all,
     That is not what I meant, at all."   110

                    *   *   *

No! I am not Prince Hamlet, nor was meant to be;
Am an attendant lord, one that will do
To swell a progress,° start a scene or two,
Advise the prince; no doubt, an easy tool,
Deferential, glad to be of use,   115
Politic, cautious, and meticulous;
Full of high sentence,° but a bit obtuse;   *sententiousness*
At times, indeed, almost ridiculous—
Almost, at times, the Fool.

     I grow old . . . I grow old . . .   120
I shall wear the bottoms of my trousers rolled.°   *turned up, with cuffs*

     Shall I part my hair behind? Do I dare to eat a peach?
I shall wear white flannel trousers, and walk upon the beach.
I have heard the mermaids singing, each to each.

     I do not think that they will sing to me.   125

     I have seen them riding seaward on the waves
Combing the white hair of the waves blown back
When the wind blows the water white and black.

     We have lingered in the chambers of the sea
By sea-girls wreathed with seaweed red and brown   130
Till human voices wake us, and we drown.

---

113. progress: Ceremonial journey made by a royal court.

Martín Espada   b. 1957

The Saint Vincent de Paul Food Pantry Stomp   [1990]

Madison, Wisconsin, 1980

Waiting for the carton of food
given with Christian suspicion
even to agency-certified charity cases
like me,
thin and brittle   5
as uncooked linguini,
anticipating the factory-damaged cans
of tomato soup, beets, three-bean salad
in a welfare cornucopia,
I spotted a squashed dollar bill   10
on the floor, and with
a Saint Vincent de Paul food pantry stomp
pinned it under my sneaker,
tied my laces meticulously,
and stuffed the bill in my sock   15
like a smuggler of diamonds,
all beneath the plaster statue wingspan
of Saint Vinnie,
who was unaware
of the dance   20
named in his honor
by a maraca shaker
in the salsa band
of the unemployed.

Sandra María Esteves   b. 1948

A la Mujer Borrinqueña°   [1980]

My name is Maria Christina
I am a Puerto Rican woman born in el barrio°

Our men . . . they call me negra° because they love me
and in turn I teach them to be strong

*   *   *

A la Mujer Borrinqueña: "To the woman of Puerto Rico." *Borinquen* is the Taíno Indian name for Puerto Rico.   **2. el barrio:** The neighborhood (ethnic enclave).   **3. negra:** Black — dark skinned.

I respect their ways   5
inherited from our proud ancestors
I do not tease them with eye catching clothes
I do not sleep with their brothers and cousins
although I've been told that this is a liberal society
I do not poison their bellies with instant chemical foods   10
our table holds food from earth and sun

My name is Maria Christina
I speak two languages broken into each other
but my heart speaks the language of people
born in oppression   15

I do not complain about cooking for my family
because abuela° taught me that woman is the master of fire
I do not complain about nursing my children
because I determine the direction of their values

I am the mother of a new age of warriors   20
I am the child of a race of slaves
I teach my children how to respect their bodies
so they will not o.d. under the stairway's shadow of shame
I teach my children to read and develop their minds
so they will understand the reality of oppression   25
I teach them with discipline . . . and love
so they will become strong and full of life

My eyes reflect the pain
of that which has shamelessly raped me
        but my soul reflects the strength of my culture   30
My name is Maria Christina
I am a Puerto Rican woman born in el barrio
Our men . . . they call me negra because they love me
and in turn I teach them to be strong.

---

17. **abuela:** Grandmother.

Carolyn Forché b. 1950

The Colonel   [1981]

What you have heard is true. I was in his house. His wife carried a tray of coffee and sugar. His daughter filed her nails, his son went out for the night. There were daily papers, pet dogs, a pistol on the cushion beside him. The moon swung bare on its black cord over the house. On the television was a cop show. It was in English. Broken bottles were embedded in the walls around the house to scoop the kneecaps from a man's legs or cut his hands to lace. On the windows there were gratings like those in liquor stores. We had dinner, rack of lamb, good wine, a gold bell was on the table for calling the maid. The maid brought green mangoes, salt, a type of bread. I was asked how I enjoyed the country. There was a brief commercial in Spanish. His wife took everything away. There was some talk then of how difficult it had become to govern. The parrot said hello on the terrace. The colonel told it to shut up, and pushed himself from the table. My friend said to me with his eyes: say nothing. The colonel returned with a sack used to bring groceries home. He spilled many human ears on the table. They were like dried peach halves. There is no other way to say this. He took one of them in his hands, shook it in our faces, dropped it into a water glass. It came alive there. I am tired of fooling around he said. As for the rights of anyone, tell your people they can go fuck themselves. He swept the ears to the floor with his arm and held the last of his wine in the air. Something for your poetry, no? he said. Some of the ears on the floor caught this scrap of his voice. Some of the ears on the floor were pressed to the ground.

Robert Frost   1874–1963

Mending Wall   [1914]

Something there is that doesn't love a wall,
That sends the frozen-ground-swell under it
And spills the upper boulders in the sun,
And makes gaps even two can pass abreast.
The work of hunters is another thing: 5
I have come after them and made repair
Where they have left not one stone on a stone,
But they would have the rabbit out of hiding,
To please the yelping dogs. The gaps I mean,
No one has seen them made or heard them made,   10
But at spring mending-time we find them there.
I let my neighbor know beyond the hill;
And on a day we meet to walk the line
And set the wall between us once again.
We keep the wall between us as we go.   15
To each the boulders that have fallen to each.
And some are loaves and some so nearly balls
We have to use a spell to make them balance:
"Stay where you are until our backs are turned!"

We wear our fingers rough with handling them.   20
Oh, just another kind of outdoor game,
One on a side. It comes to little more:
There where it is we do not need the wall:
He is all pine and I am apple orchard.
My apple trees will never get across   25
And eat the cones under his pines, I tell him.
He only says, "Good fences make good neighbors."
Spring is the mischief in me, and I wonder
If I could put a notion in his head:
"*Why* do they make good neighbors? Isn't it   30
Where there are cows? But here there are no cows.
Before I built a wall I'd ask to know
What I was walling in or walling out,
And to whom I was like to give offense.
Something there is that doesn't love a wall,   35
That wants it down." I could say "Elves" to him,
But it's not elves exactly, and I'd rather
He said it for himself. I see him there,
Bringing a stone grasped firmly by the top
In each hand, like an old-stone savage armed.   40
He moves in darkness as it seems to me,
Not of woods only and the shade of trees.
He will not go behind his father's saying,
And he likes having thought of it so well
He says again, "Good fences make good neighbors."   45

Robert Frost

The Road Not Taken   [1916]

Two roads diverged in a yellow wood,
And sorry I could not travel both
And be one traveler, long I stood
And looked down one as far as I could
To where it bent in the undergrowth;   5

Then took the other, as just as fair,
And having perhaps the better claim,
Because it was grassy and wanted wear;
Though as for that, the passing there
Had worn them really about the same,   10

*   *   *

And both that morning equally lay
In leaves no step had trodden black.
Oh, I kept the first for another day!
Yet knowing how way leads on to way,
I doubted if I should ever come back.   15

I shall be telling this with a sigh
Somewhere ages and ages hence:
Two roads diverged in a wood, and I —
I took the one less traveled by,
And that has made all the difference.   20

CD-ROM: Research Robert Frost in depth with cultural documents and multimedia resources on
LiterActive.

Richard Garcia   b. 1941

Why I Left the Church   [1993]

Maybe it was
because the only time
I hit a baseball
it smashed the neon cross
on the church across   5
the street. Even
twenty-five years later
when I saw Father Harris
I would wonder
if he knew it was me.   10
Maybe it was the demon-stoked
rotisseries of purgatory
where we would roast
hundreds of years
for the smallest of sins.   15
Or was it the day
I wore my space helmet
to catechism? Clear plastic
with a red-and-white
inflatable rim.   20
Sister Mary Bernadette
pointed toward the door
and said, "Out! Come back
when you're ready."
I rose from my chair   25

and kept rising
toward the ceiling
while the children
screamed and Sister
kept crossing herself.   30
The last she saw of me
was my shoes disappearing
through cracked plaster.
I rose into the sky and beyond.
It is a good thing   35
I am wearing my helmet,
I thought as I floated
and turned in the blackness
and brightness of outer space,
my body cold on one side and hot   40
on the other. It would
have been very quiet
if my blood had not been
rumbling in my ears so loud.
I remember thinking,   45
Maybe I will come back
when I'm ready.
But I won't tell
the other children
what it was like.   50
I'll have to make something up.

Christopher Gilbert   b. 1949

Horizontal Cosmology   [1984]

1. The Backyard

Suddenly this voice is calling
when I go to the backyard.
The garden leaves cut the wind to singing
and their bodies, the perfect green
instruments for what they do.   5

The tree next door whose leaves
are phrases falling
where the wind is blowing,

the arpeggio of the Charlie Parker° tune —
an impossible flight of notes.   10
And I'm humming to myself.

I will work the day out here, singing.
It makes me a gift with myself.
Something to make the yard bigger.
My hands fall at my sides, octaves apart,   15
How far? Clear enough for my friends
who look for me to feel between them.

4. Saxophone

My bell is Charlie Parker's
hatband. So few of you who
come to touch me understand   20
my feeling,
only this black voice.
I am a temple and he comes
to speak through me. I am the dream
lip because   25
I say what you're afraid of
facing, *Living is intense.*

I am bad from note to note
like god's nostril, I connect
living to what lies ahead   30
by breath.
You want to know how to feel
in this world, the technology
bigger than the ear? Listen,
I can't tell you what to hear.   35
I have no message waiting
for you: you must be-
hold enough to play.

---

9. **Charlie Parker:** (1920–1955), known as "Bird," American jazz saxophonist.

Allen Ginsberg 1926–1997

A Supermarket in California   [1956]

What thoughts I have of you tonight, Walt Whitman, for I walked down the sidestreets under the trees with a headache self-conscious looking at the full moon.

In my hungry fatigue, and shopping for images, I went into the neon fruit supermarket, dreaming of your enumerations!

What peaches and what penumbras! Whole families shopping at night! Aisles full of husbands! Wives in the avocados, babies in the tomatoes! — and you, García Lorca,° what were you doing down by the watermelons?

I saw you, Walt Whitman, childless, lonely old grubber, poking among the meats in the refrigerator and eyeing the grocery boys.

I heard you asking questions of each: Who killed the pork chops? What price bananas? Are you my Angel?   5

I wandered in and out of the brilliant stacks of cans following you, and followed in my imagination by the store detective.

We strode down the open corridors together in our solitary fancy tasting artichokes, possessing every frozen delicacy, and never passing the cashier.

Where are we going, Walt Whitman? The doors close in an hour. Which way does your beard point tonight?

(I touch your book and dream of our odyssey in the supermarket and feel absurd.)

Will we walk all night through solitary streets? The trees add shade to shade, lights out in the houses, we'll both be lonely.   10

Will we stroll dreaming of the lost America of love past blue automobiles in driveways, home to our silent cottage?

Ah, dear father, graybeard, lonely old courage-teacher, what America did you have when Charon° quit poling his ferry and you got out on a smoking bank and stood watching the boat disappear on the black waters of Lethe?°

Berkeley, 1955

---

3. García Lorca: (1899–1936), Spanish surrealist poet and playwright. **12. Charon:** The boatman in Greek mythology who carried the dead across the river Styx to Hades; **Lethe:** River of Forgetfulness in Hades.

Diane Glancy b. 1941

Battery   [2001]

. . . north of Waco, exit I35 on Loop 340 east,
take Elk Road left 3–4 miles to a water tower°

I pass a sign, *ATF FBI KNOW HOW TO LIE*
spray-painted on the side of a metal shed,
a cottonfield like a salvage yard for angels,
then there's nothing but fields broken into by the sky,
trees squatting to the land,   5
a trough of weeds leaning in the wind.

A few miles, a fork in the road, a blue tank,
I drive on but turn around
and go back to a man mowing the ditch grass.
He can't hear but I find him willing to turn off his motor.   10
He says, *turn left at the blue water-tank not tower*
go half a mile.

I drive by a hand-painted sign,
don't stop don't even slow down,
and at a shadow of a tree across the road turn around,   15
but another car comes and seems to slow and I drive on,
disappointed at my hesitancy to walk in,

but settle for another kind of seeing,
a daunted sideways glance
like the runover of a plane trying to make a fogdrop in a field. 20

But there is nothing to see,
the sunken desks of land,
a pond, a few shacks, a burned-out schoolbus,
another sign something like a burst of yellow on blue
though I can't be sure,   25
a woman stands in the yard, her hand on her waist
caught in the bare wind of her mind.

I don't know what to say in the fervor of religion,
what words he must have preached when he ran into the stars
like a hubcap scraping a median strip,   30
the sparks, *wow,* when you know you're being seen

---

north . . . tower: Directions to Mount Carmel ranch a few miles outside Waco, Texas, where several ATF (Bureau of Alcohol, Tobacco and Firearms) agents were killed on February 28, 1993, as they raided the Branch Davidian religious cult. Its leader, David Koresh (l. 35), and seventy-five others died when the compound burned down after a fifty-one-day siege by the FBI.

like in one of those gas-station restrooms on the highway,
you know they watch you through some hole.

The grass mower said the woman was probably
the wife of the original founder whom David Koresh ran off,   35
not sweetly playing his harp as David rushed Saul,
but the impounding voice of God,
Noah build a compound it's going to rain,
or the fiery voice of Nebuchadnezzar,° *heat the furnace seven times.*

His followers must have talked behind their backs,   40
he's playing his harmonica, making it up as he goes.

The mower said they've been here for years,
living at first along a ravine in tents like pigs,
the usual story: *a group of them,*
the mower said, *waiting for the end of the world,*   45
fire or water. It would be both.

He must have gone crazy from rejection and failure
in the world, he just couldn't fit,
but he could father children,
he could instruct them as he thought God would   50
and there was the sweetest smell of that cut grass.

He tried out the words he brought back from stars
in their green skirts and electric heads.
He could even hear the sermon of the cosmos
when God stepped out with women,   55
his myriad of believers, and David was a part.
He would have many wives too.
It seems to be the way with men when they can get away with it,
as many as they want.

All his life he'd been a stem pulled from the apple,   60
now he'd ride the Milky Way on that trail of black smoke,
that cloud-burst from firetrucks
flashing bright as Texas in the sungorged field.

The angels must have torn up their wings getting here,
an afternoon's burnout from finding the place: 65
Elk Road, blue water-tower left,
there's a sudden burst imploding,
orange-flaked pieces of gunshot from the sun
and the end of the world in the fiery mouth of God.

---

39. Nebuchadnezzar: King of Babylon who threw three Israelites into a fiery furnace because
they refused to worship him (Daniel 3).

Louise Glück   b. 1943

Parable of Flight   [1996]

A flock of birds leaving the side of the mountain.
Black against the spring evening, bronze in early summer,
rising over blank lake water.

Why is the young man disturbed suddenly,
his attention slipping from his companion?   5
His heart is no longer wholly divided; he's trying to think
how to say this compassionately.

Now we hear the voices of the others, moving through the library
toward the veranda, the summer porch; we see them
taking their usual places on the various hammocks and chairs,   10
the white wood chairs of the old house, rearranging
the striped cushions.

Does it matter where the birds go? Does it even matter
what species they are?
They leave here, that's the point,   15
first their bodies, then their sad cries.
And from that moment, cease to exist for us.

You must learn to think of our passion that way.
Each kiss was real, then
each kiss left the face of the earth.   20

Ray González   b. 1952

Praise the Tortilla, Praise the Menudo,
Praise the Chorizo   [1994]

I praise the tortilla in honor of El Panzón,
who hit me in school every day and made me see
how the bruises on my arms looked like
the brown clouds on my mother's tortillas.
I praise the tortilla because I know   5
they can fly into our hands like
eager flesh of the one we love,
those soft yearnings we delight in biting
as we tear the tortilla and wipe the plate clean.

                    *   *   *

I praise the menudo° as visionary food that it is,   10
the tripas y posole° tight flashes of color
we see as the red caldo° smears across our notebooks
like a vision we have not had in years,
our lives going down like the empty bowl
of menudo exploding in our stomachs   15
with the chili piquin° of our poetic dreams.

I praise the chorizo° and smear it
across my face and hands,
the dayglow brown of it painting me
with the desire to find out   20
what happened to la familia,
why the chorizo sizzled in the pan
and covered the house with a smell
of childhood we will never have again,
the chorizo burrito hot in our hands,   25
as we ran out to play and show the vatos°
it's time to cut the chorizo,
tell it like it is before la manteca° runs down
our chins and drips away.

---

10. menudo: Mexican soup made with hominy and tripe; said to have special powers.   11. tripas y posole: Tripe and hominy.   12. caldo: Soup.   16. chili piquin: Type of pepper, added to menudo or other soups.   17. chorizo: Mexican sausage.   26. vatos: Guys.   28. la manteca: Lard or grease.

Thomas Gray   1716–1771

Elegy Written in a Country Churchyard   [1751]

The curfew° tolls the knell of parting day,   *evening bell*
    The lowing herd wind slowly o'er the lea,
The plowman homeward plods his weary way,
    And leaves the world to darkness and to me.

Now fades the glimmering landscape on the sight,   5
    And all the air a solemn stillness holds,
Save where the beetle wheels his droning flight,
    And drowsy tinklings lull the distant folds;

Save that from yonder ivy-mantled tower
    The moping owl does to the moon complain   10
Of such, as wandering near her secret bower,
    Molest her ancient solitary reign.

                    *   *   *

Beneath those rugged elms, that yew tree's shade,
   Where heaves the turf in many a moldering heap,
Each in his narrow cell forever laid,   15
   The rude forefathers° of the hamlet sleep.   *humble ancestors*

The breezy call of incense-breathing morn,
   The swallow twittering from the straw-built shed,
The cock's shrill clarion, or the echoing horn,°   *(of a hunter)*
   No more shall rouse them from their lowly bed.   20

For them no more the blazing hearth shall burn,
   Or busy housewife ply her evening care;
No children run to lisp their sire's return,
   Or climb his knees the envied kiss to share.

Oft did the harvest to their sickle yield,   25
   Their furrow oft the stubborn glebe° has broke;   *soil*
How jocund did they drive their team afield!
   How bowed the woods beneath their sturdy stroke!

Let not Ambition mock their useful toil,
   Their homely joys, and destiny obscure;   30
Nor Grandeur hear with a disdainful smile
   The short and simple annals of the poor.

The boast of heraldry,° the pomp of power,   *noble ancestry*
   And all that beauty, all that wealth e'er gave,
Awaits alike the inevitable hour.   35
   The paths of glory lead but to the grave.

Nor you, ye proud, impute to these the fault,
   If memory o'er their tomb no trophies° raise, *memorials*
Where through the long-drawn aisle and fretted° vault *ornamented*
   The pealing anthem swells the note of praise.   40

Can storied° urn or animated° bust   *decorated/lifelike*
   Back to its mansion call the fleeting breath?
Can Honor's voice provoke° the silent dust,   *call forth*
   Or Flattery soothe the dull cold ear of Death?

Perhaps in this neglected spot is laid   45
   Some heart once pregnant with celestial fire;
Hands that the rod of empire might have swayed,
   Or waked to ecstasy the living lyre.

But Knowledge to their eyes her ample page
   Rich with the spoils of time did ne'er unroll;   50
Chill Penury repressed their noble rage,
   And froze the genial current of the soul.

       *   *   *

Full many a gem of purest ray serene,
    The dark unfathomed caves of ocean bear:
Full many a flower is born to blush unseen,   55
    And waste its sweetness on the desert air.

Some village Hampden, that with dauntless breast
    The little tyrant of his fields withstood;
Some mute inglorious Milton here may rest,
    Some Cromwell° guiltless of his country's blood.   60

The applause of listening senates to command,
    The threats of pain and ruin to despise,
To scatter plenty o'er a smiling land,
    And read their history in a nation's eyes,

Their lot forbade: nor° circumscribed alone   *not* 65
    Their growing virtues, but their crimes confined;
Forbade to wade through slaughter to a throne,
    And shut the gates of mercy on mankind,

The struggling pangs of conscious truth to hide,
    To quench the blushes of ingenuous shame,   70
Or heap the shrine of Luxury and Pride
    With incense kindled at the Muse's flame.

Far from the madding crowd's ignoble strife,
    Their sober wishes never learned to stray;
Along the cool sequestered vale of life   75
    They kept the noiseless tenor of their way.

Yet even these bones from insult to protect
    Some frail memorial° still erected nigh,   *simple tombstone*
With uncouth rhymes and shapeless sculpture decked,
    Implores the passing tribute of a sigh.   80

Their name, their years, spelt by the unlettered Muse,
    The place of fame and elegy supply:
And many a holy text around she strews,
    That teach the rustic moralist to die.

For who to dumb Forgetfulness a prey,   85
    This pleasing anxious being e'er resigned,
Left the warm precincts of the cheerful day,
    Nor cast one longing lingering look behind?

On some fond breast the parting soul relies,
    Some pious drops° the closing eye requires;   *tears* 90

57–60. Hampden, Cromwell: John Hampden (1594–1643) refused to pay a special tax imposed in 1636 and led a defense of the people's rights in Parliament. Oliver Cromwell (1599–1658) was a rebel leader in the English Civil War.

Even from the tomb the voice of Nature cries,
    Even in our ashes live their wonted fires.

For thee,° who mindful of the unhonored dead   *(the poet himself)*
    Dost in these lines their artless tale relate;
If chance, by lonely contemplation led,   95
    Some kindred spirit shall inquire thy fate,

Haply° some hoary-headed swain° may say,   *perhaps/elderly shepherd*
    "Oft have we seen him° at the peep of dawn   *the poet*
Brushing with hasty steps the dews away
    To meet the sun upon the upland lawn.   100

"There at the foot of yonder nodding beech
    That wreathes its old fantastic roots so high,
His listless length at noontide would he stretch,
    And pore upon the brook that babbles by.

"Hard by yon wood, now smiling as in scorn,   105
    Muttering his wayward fancies he would rove,
Now drooping, woeful wan, like one forlorn,
    Or crazed with care, or crossed in hopeless love.

"One morn I missed him on the customed hill,
    Along the heath and near his favorite tree;   110
Another° came, nor yet beside the rill,   *(another day)*
    Nor up the lawn, nor at the wood was he;

"The next with dirges due in sad array
    Slow through the churchway path we saw him borne.
Approach and read (for thou canst read) the lay,   115
    Graved on the stone beneath yon aged thorn."

The Epitaph

Here rests his head upon the lap of Earth
    A youth to fortune and to Fame unknown.
Fair Science° frowned not on his humble birth,   *learning*
    And Melancholy marked him for her own.   120

Large was his bounty, and his soul sincere,
    Heaven did a recompense as largely send:
He gave to Misery all he had, a tear,
    He gained from Heaven ('twas all he wished) a friend.

No farther seek his merits to disclose,   125
    Or draw his frailties from their dread abode
(There they alike in trembling hope repose),
    The bosom of his Father and his God.

Kimiko Hahn b. 1955

When You Leave   [1989]

This sadness could only be a color
if we call it *momoiro,* Japanese

for *peach-color,* as in the first story
Mother told us: It is the color of the hero's skin

when the barren woman discovered him   5
inside a peach floating down the river.

And of the banner and gloves she sewed
when he left her to battle the horsemen, then found himself

torn, like fruit off a tree. Even when he met a monkey
dog and bird he could not release   10

the color he saw when he closed his eyes.
        In his boat
the lap of the waves against the hold

was too intimate as he leaned back to sleep.
        He wanted   15
to leave all thoughts of peach behind him —

the fruit that brought him to her
and she, the one who opened the color forever.

Michael S. Harper b. 1938

Nightmare Begins Responsibility   [1975]

I place these numbed wrists to the pane
watching white uniforms whisk over
him in the tube-kept
prison
fear what they will do in experiment   5
watch my gloved stickshifting gasolined hands
breathe *boxcar-information-please* infirmary tubes
distrusting white-pink mending paperthin
silkened end hairs, distrusting tubes
shrunk in his *trunk-skincapped*   10
shaven head, in thighs
distrusting-white-hands-picking-baboon-light
on this son who will not make his second night

of this wardstrewn intensive airpocket
where his father's asthmatic   15
hymns of *night-train, train done gone*
his mother can only know that he has flown
up into essential calm unseen corridor
going boxscarred home, *mamaborn, sweetsonchild*
gonedowntown into *researchtestingwarehousebatteryacid*   20
*mama-son-done-gone/*me telling her 'nother
train tonight, no music, no breathstroked
heartbeat in my infinite distrust of them:

and of my distrusting self
white-doctor-who-breathed-for-him-all-night   25
say it for two sons gone,
say nightmare, say it loud
panebreaking heartmadness:
nightmare begins responsibility.

Samuel Hazo   b. 1928

For Fawzi in Jerusalem   [1968]

Leaving a world too old to name
and too undying to forsake,
I flew the cold, expensive sea
toward Columbus' mistake
where life could never be the same   5

for me. In Jerash° on the sand
I saw the colonnades of Rome
bleach in the sun like skeletons.
Behind a convalescent home,
armed soldiers guarded no man's land   10

between Jordanians and Jews.
Opposing sentries frowned and spat.
Fawzi, you mocked in Arabic
this justice from Jehoshophat°
before you shined my Pittsburgh shoes   15

        *   *   *

---

6. Jerash: The ancient city of Gerasa, twenty-two miles north of Amman in present-day Jordan. Called Jerash by the Romans who rebuilt it in 65 C.E., it is the best-preserved Palestinian city of Roman times.   **14. Jehoshophat:** Hebrew king of Judah (c. 873–849 B.C.E.), the first to make a treaty with the neighboring kingdom of Israel.

for nothing. Why you never kept
the coins I offered you is still
your secret and your victory.
Saying you saw marauders kill
your father while Beershebans° wept   20

for mercy in their holy war,
you told me how you stole to stay
alive. You must have thought I thought
your history would make me pay
a couple of piastres more   25

than any shine was worth — and I
was ready to — when you said, "No,
I never take. I never want
America to think I throw
myself on you. I never lie."   30

I watched your young but old man's stare
demand the sword to flash again
in blood and flame from Jericho°
and leave the bones of these new men
of Judah bleaching in the air   35

like Roman stones upon the plain
of Jerash. Then you faced away.
Jerusalem, Jerusalem,
I asked myself if I could pray
for peace and not recall the pain   40

you spoke. But what could praying do?
Today I live your loss in no
man's land but mine, and every time
I talk of fates not just but so,
Fawzi, my friend, I think of you.   45

---

20. Beershebans: Inhabitants of Beersheba, a city in southern Israel. Given to the Arabs in the partition of Palestine (1948), it was retaken by Israel in the Arab-Israeli war of 1948. **33. Jericho:** Ancient city in biblical Palestine, in the Jordan valley north of the Dead Sea, captured from the Canaanites by Joshua and destroyed (Joshua 6:1–21).

Seamus Heaney   b. 1939

Digging   [1966]

Between my finger and my thumb
The squat pen rests; snug as a gun.

Under my window, a clean rasping sound
When the spade sinks into gravelly ground:
My father, digging. I look down   5

Till his straining rump among the flowerbeds
Bends low, comes up twenty years away
Stooping in rhythm through potato drills
Where he was digging.

The coarse boot nestled on the lug, the shaft   10
Against the inside knee was levered firmly.
He rooted out tall tops, buried the bright edge deep
To scatter new potatoes that we picked
Loving their cool hardness in our hands.

By God, the old man could handle a spade.   15
Just like his old man.

My grandfather cut more turf in a day
Than any other man on Toner's bog.
Once I carried him milk in a bottle
Corked sloppily with paper. He straightened up   20
To drink it, then fell to right away
Nicking and slicing neatly, heaving sods
Over his shoulder, going down and down
For the good turf. Digging.

The cold smell of potato mould, the squelch and slap   25
Of soggy peat, the curt cuts of an edge
Through living roots awaken in my head.
But I've no spade to follow men like them.

Between my finger and my thumb
The squat pen rests.   30
I'll dig with it.

George Herbert   1593–1633

The Pulley   [1633]

When God at first made man,
Having a glass of blessings standing by,
"Let us," said he, "pour on him all we can.
Let the world's riches, which dispersèd lie,
    Contract into a span."   5

So strength first made a way;
Then beauty flowed, then wisdom, honor, pleasure.
When almost all was out, God made a stay,
Perceiving that, alone of all his treasure,
    Rest in the bottom lay.   10

"For if I should," said he,
"Bestow this jewel also on my creature,
He would adore my gifts instead of me,
And rest in Nature, not the God of Nature;
    So both should losers be.   15

"Yet let him keep the rest,
But keep them with repining restlessness.
Let him be rich and weary, that at least,
If goodness lead him not, yet weariness
    May toss him to my breast."   20

David Hernandez   b. 1971

The Butterfly Effect   [2003]

If a butterfly flapping its wings in Beijing
could cause a hurricane off the coast of Florida,
so could a deck of cards shuffled at a picnic.
So could the clapping hands of a father
watching his son rounding the bases,   5
the wind sculpting his baggy pants.
So could a woman reading a book of poems,
a tiny current from a turned page
slipping out the open window, nudging
a passing breeze: an insignificant event   10
that could snowball months later into a monsoon
at a coastal village halfway around the world.

Palm trees bowing on the shore.
Grass huts disintegrating like blown dandelions.

Hard to believe, but when I rewind my life,   15
starting from a point when my heart
was destroyed, I see the dominoes rising,
how that storm was just a gale weeks earlier,
a gust days before that. Finally I see
where it all began: I say hello to a woman   20
sitting alone at the bar, a tattoo butterfly
perched on her ankle, ready to wreak havoc.

Robert Herrick 1591–1674

To the Virgins, to Make Much of Time   [1648]

Gather ye rosebuds while ye may,
    Old time is still a-flying;
And this same flower that smiles today
    Tomorrow will be dying.

The glorious lamp of heaven, the sun,   5
    The higher he's a-getting,
The sooner will his race be run,
    And nearer he's to setting.

That age is best which is the first,
    When youth and blood are warmer;   10
But being spent, the worse, and worst
    Times still succeed the former.

Then be not coy, but use your time,
    And while ye may, go marry;
For having lost but once your prime,   15
    You may forever tarry.

Geoffrey Hill b. 1932

In Memory of Jane Fraser   [1959]

When snow like sheep lay in the fold
And winds went begging at each door,
And the far hills were blue with cold,
And a cold shroud lay on the moor,

*   *   *

She kept the siege. And every day   5
We watched her brooding over death
Like a strong bird above its prey.
The room filled with the kettle's breath.

Damp curtains glued against the pane
Sealed time away. Her body froze   10
As if to freeze us all, and chain
Creation to a stunned repose.

She died before the world could stir.
In March the ice unloosed the brook
And water ruffled the sun's hair.   15
Dead cones upon the alder shook.

Linda Hogan   b. 1947

The History of Red   [1993]

First
there was some other order of things
never spoken
but in dreams of darkest creation.

Then there was black earth,   5
lake, the face of light on water.
Then the thick forest all around
that light,
and then the human clay
whose blood we still carry   10
rose up in us
who remember caves with red bison
painted in their own blood,
after their kind.

A wildness   15
swam inside our mothers,
desire through closed eyes,
a new child
wearing the red, wet mask of birth,
delivered into this land   20
already wounded,
stolen and burned
beyond reckoning.

                    *   *   *

Red is this yielding land
turned inside out
by a country of hunters
with iron, flint and fire.   25
Red is the fear
that turns a knife back
against men, holds it at their throats,
and they cannot see the claw on the handle,   30
the animal hand
that haunts them
from some place inside their blood.

So that is hunting, birth,
and one kind of death.   35
Then there was medicine, the healing of wounds.
Red was the infinite fruit
of stolen bodies.
The doctors wanted to know
what invented disease   40
how wounds healed
from inside themselves
how life stands up in skin,
if not by magic.   45

They divined the red shadows of leeches
that swam in white bowls of water;
they believed stars
in the cup of sky,
They cut the wall of skin   50
to let
what was bad escape
but they were reading the story of fire
gone out
and that was science.   55

As for the animal hand on death's knife,
knives have as many sides
as the red father of war
who signs his name
in the blood of other men.   60

And red was the soldier
who crawled
through a ditch
of human blood in order to live.
It was the canal of his deliverance.   65
It is his son who lives near me.

Red is the thunder in our ears
when we meet.
Love, like creation,
is some other order of things.   70

Red is the share of fire
I have stolen
from root, hoof, fallen fruit.
And this was hunger.

Red is the human house   75
I come back to at night
swimming inside the cave of skin
that remembers bison.
In that round nation
of blood   80
we are all burning,
red, inseparable fires
the living have crawled
and climbed through
in order to live   85
so nothing will be left
for death at the end.

This life in the fire, I love it,
I want it,
this life.   90

A. E. Housman   1859–1936

To an Athlete Dying Young   [1896]

The time you won your town the race
We chaired you through the market-place;
Man and boy stood cheering by,
And home we brought you shoulder-high.

To-day, the road all runners come,   5
Shoulder-high we bring you home,
And set you at your threshold down,
Townsman of a stiller town.

Smart lad, to slip betimes away
From fields where glory does not stay   10
And early though the laurel grows
It withers quicker than the rose.

*   *   *

Eyes the shady night has shut
Cannot see the record cut,° *broken*
And silence sounds no worse than cheers 15
After earth has stopped the ears:

Now you will not swell the rout
Of lads that wore their honours out,
Runners whom renown outran
And the name died before the man. 20

So set, before its echoes fade,
The fleet foot on the sill of shade,
And hold to the low lintel up
The still-defended challenge-cup.

And round that early-laurelled head 25
Will flock to gaze the strengthless dead,
And find unwithered on its curls
The garland briefer than a girl's.

Lawson Fusao Inada b. 1938

Plucking Out a Rhythm [1971]

Start with a simple room —
a dullish color —
and draw the one shade down.
Hot plate. Bed.
Little phonograph in a corner. 5

Put in a single figure —
medium weight and height —
but oversize, as a child might.

The features must be Japanese.

Then stack a black pompadour on, 10
and let the eyes
slide behind a night of glass.

The figure is in disguise:

slim green suit
for posturing on a bandstand, 15
the turned-up shoes of Harlem . . .

Then start the music playing —
thick jazz, strong jazz —

       *   *   *

and notice that the figure
comes to life: 20

sweating, growling
over an imaginary bass —
plucking out a rhythm —
as the music rises and the room is full,
exuding with that rhythm . . .   25

Then have the shade flap up
and daylight catch him
frozen in that pose

as it starts to snow —
thick snow, strong snow —   30

blowing in the window
while the music quiets,
the room is slowly covered,

and the figure is completely
out of sight.   35

Ben Jonson   1572–1637

On My First Son   [1616]

Farewell, thou child of my right hand,° and joy;
    My sin was too much hope of thee, loved boy:
Seven years thou'wert lent to me, and I thee pay,
    Exacted by thy fate, on the just day.
O could I lose all father now! for why   5
    Will man lament the state he should envy,
To have so soon 'scaped world's and flesh's rage,
    And, if no other misery, yet age?
Rest in soft peace, and asked, say, "Here doth lie
    Ben Jonson his best piece of poetry."   10
For whose sake henceforth all his° vows be such   *(the father's)*
    As what he loves may never like° too much.

---

1. child . . . hand: A literal translation of the Hebrew name "Benjamin." The boy, named for his father, was born in 1596 and died on his birthday ("the just day") in 1603.   **12. like:** Archaic meaning both "want" and "please."

A. Van Jordan   b. 1965

The Journey of Henry "Box" Brown   [2001]

Perhaps Henry Brown remembered Golgotha,°
the taunt of the trail, the inevitable end —
the enviable end — the sting of vinegar doused eyes,
much like his own urine drenched skin, or
he remembered those who pined in bondage,   5
those who longed for the freedom of either his box,
the carpenter's geometric womb, the nails
pulled straight from hands to hold
the walls together till his new life,
or the voice, as if from above, in his head   10
which whispered, "Go and get a box,
and put yourself in it," that voice which dreamt
him through white hands, through bounds
his black face could not cross; first,
to the express office, the box placed on its end,   15
so he started with his head downwards —
as if he were on the verge of life —
the crate marked "This Side Up
With Care," but no one cared and no one
bent to break his falls or to stop the blood   20
from rushing to his temple —
two hours on his head, veins strained, eyes
bulged, death's breath held —
then, three o'clock in the morning, a depot,
now with the box directed right side up,   25
to the home of a friend in Philadelphia
whose trembling voice — imagine,
on the outside and his voice trembled —
asked, *Is all right within?* to which Henry,
in a trumpeted tone, replied, *All right.*   30

---

1. Golgotha: Place where Jesus was crucified.

John Keats 1795–1821

Ode on a Grecian Urn [1820]

1

Thou still unravished bride of quietness,
  Thou foster child of silence and slow time,
Sylvan historian, who canst thus express
  A flowery tale more sweetly than our rhyme:
What leaf-fringed legend haunts about thy shape   5
  Of deities or mortals, or of both,
    In Tempe or the dales of Arcady?°
  What men or gods are these? What maidens loath?
What mad pursuit? What struggle to escape?
    What pipes and timbrels? What wild ecstasy?   10

2

Heard melodies are sweet, but those unheard
  Are sweeter; therefore, ye soft pipes, play on;
Not to the sensual ear,° but, more endeared,
  Pipe to the spirit ditties of no tone:
Fair youth, beneath the trees, thou canst not leave   15
  Thy song, nor ever can those trees be bare;
    Bold lover, never, never canst thou kiss,
Though winning near the goal — yet, do not grieve;
    She cannot fade, though thou hast not thy bliss,
  Forever wilt thou love, and she be fair!   20

3

Ah, happy, happy boughs! that cannot shed
  Your leaves, nor ever bid the spring adieu;
And, happy melodist, unwearièd,
  Forever piping songs forever new;
More happy love! more happy, happy love!   25
  Forever warm and still to be enjoyed,
    Forever panting, and forever young;
All breathing human passion far above,
  That leaves a heart high-sorrowful and cloyed,
    A burning forehead, and a parching tongue.   30

---

7. **Tempe, Arcady:** Tempe, a valley in Greece, and Arcadia ("Arcady"), a region of ancient Greece, represent ideal pastoral landscapes. **13. Not . . . ear:** Not to the ear of the senses, but to the imagination.

4

Who are these coming to the sacrifice?
    To what green altar, O mysterious priest,
Lead'st thou that heifer lowing at the skies,
    And all her silken flanks with garlands dressed?
What little town by river or sea shore,   35
    Or mountain-built with peaceful citadel,
        Is emptied of this folk, this pious morn?
And, little town, thy streets forevermore
    Will silent be; and not a soul to tell
        Why thou art desolate, can e'er return.   40

5

O Attic° shape! Fair attitude! with brede°
    Of marble men and maidens overwrought,
With forest branches and the trodden weed;
    Thou, silent form, dost tease us out of thought
As doth eternity: Cold Pastoral!   45
    When old age shall this generation waste,
        Thou shalt remain, in midst of other woe
Than ours, a friend to man, to whom thou say'st,
    "Beauty is truth, truth beauty,"° — that is all
        Ye know on earth, and all ye need to know.   50

---

41. Attic: Greek, specifically Athenian; **brede:** Interwoven pattern.   **49. Beauty . . . beauty:** The quotation marks around this phrase were found in its earliest printing, an 1820 volume of poetry by Keats, but not in a printing later that year or in written transcripts. This discrepancy has led to considerable critical controversy concerning the last two lines. Critics disagree whether "Beauty is truth, truth beauty" is spoken by the urn (and thus perhaps expressing a limited perspective not to be taken at face value) or by the speaker in the poem, or whether the last two lines in their entirety are said by the urn (some recent editors enclose both lines in quotation marks to make this explicit) or by the speaker.

John Keats

To Autumn   [1820]

I

Season of mists and mellow fruitfulness,
    Close bosom-friend of the maturing sun;
Conspiring with him how to load and bless
    With fruit the vines that round the thatch-eves run;
To bend with apples the mossed cottage-trees,   5

And fill all fruit with ripeness to the core;
    To swell the gourd, and plump the hazel shells
With a sweet kernel; to set budding more,
    And still more, later flowers for the bees,
    Until they think warm days will never cease,   10
        For Summer has o'er-brimmed their clammy cells.

II

Who hath not seen thee oft amid thy store?
    Sometimes whoever seeks abroad may find
Thee sitting careless on a granary floor,
    Thy hair soft-lifted by the winnowing wind;   15
Or on a half-reaped furrow sound asleep,
    Drowsed with the fume of poppies, while thy hook°   *scythe*
        Spares the next swath and all its twinèd flowers:
And sometimes like a gleaner thou dost keep
    Steady thy laden head across a brook;   20
    Or by a cider-press, with patient look,
        Thou watchest the last oozings hours by hours.

III

Where are the songs of Spring? Aye, where are they?
    Think not of them, thou hast thy music too, —
While barrèd clouds bloom the soft-dying day,   25
    And touch the stubble-plains with rosy hue;
Then in a wailful choir the small gnats mourn
    Among the river sallows,° borne aloft   *willows*
        Or sinking as the light wind lives or dies;
And full-grown lambs loud bleat from hilly bourn;°   *region* 30
    Hedge-crickets sing; and now with treble soft
    The red-breast whistles from a garden-croft;
        And gathering swallows twitter in the skies.

CD-ROM: Research John Keats in depth with cultural documents and multimedia resources on *LiterActive*.

Etheridge Knight   1931–1991

Hard Rock Returns to Prison from the
Hospital for the Criminal Insane   [1968]

Hard Rock / was / "known not to take no shit
From nobody," and he had the scars to prove it:
Split purple lips, lumbed ears, welts above
His yellow eyes, and one long scar that cut
Across his temple and plowed through a thick   5
Canopy of kinky hair.

The WORD / was / that Hard Rock wasn't a mean nigger
Anymore, that the doctors had bored a hole in his head,
Cut out part of his brain, and shot electricity
Through the rest. When they brought Hard Rock back,   10
Handcuffed and chained, he was turned loose,
Like a freshly gelded stallion, to try his new status.
And we all waited and watched, like a herd of sheep,
To see if the WORD was true.

As we waited we wrapped ourselves in the cloak   15
Of his exploits: "Man, the last time, it took eight
Screws° to put him in the Hole."° "Yeah, remember when he
Smacked the captain with his dinner tray?" "He set
The record for time in the Hole — 67 straight days!"
"Ol Hard Rock! man, that's one crazy nigger."   20
And then the jewel of a myth that Hard Rock had once bit
A screw on the thumb and poisoned him with syphilitic spit.

The testing came, to see if Hard Rock was really tame.
A hillbilly called him a black son of a bitch
And didn't lose his teeth, a screw who knew Hard Rock   25
From before shook him down and barked in his face.
And Hard Rock did *nothing*. Just grinned and looked silly,
His eyes empty like knot holes in a fence.

And even after we discovered that it took Hard Rock
Exactly 3 minutes to tell you his first name,   30
We told ourselves that he had just wised up,
Was being cool; but we could not fool ourselves for long,
And we turned away, our eyes on the ground. Crushed.
He had been our Destroyer, the doer of things
We dreamed of doing but could not bring ourselves to do,   35

---

17. Screws: Guards; **the Hole:** Solitary confinement.

The fears of years, like a biting whip,
Had cut deep bloody grooves
Across our backs.

Li-Young Lee b. 1957

Visions and Interpretations   [1986]

Because this graveyard is a hill,
I must climb up to see my dead,
stopping once midway to rest
beside this tree.

It was here, between the anticipation   5
of exhaustion, and exhaustion,
between vale and peak,
my father came down to me

and we climbed arm in arm to the top.
He cradled the bouquet I'd brought,   10
and I, a good son, never mentioned his grave,
erect like a door behind him.

And it was here, one summer day, I sat down
to read an old book. When I looked up
from the noon-lit page, I saw a vision   15
of a world about to come, and a world about to go.

Truth is, I've not seen my father
since he died, and, no, the dead
do not walk arm in arm with me.

If I carry flowers to them, I do so without their help,   20
the blossoms not always bright, torch-like,
but often heavy as sodden newspaper.

Truth is, I came here with my son one day,
and we rested against this tree,
and I fell asleep, and dreamed   25

a dream which, upon my boy waking me, I told.
Neither of us understood.
Then we went up.

Even this is not accurate.
Let me begin again: 30

*   *   *

Between two griefs, a tree.
Between my hands, white chrysanthemums, yellow chrysanthemums.

The old book I finished reading
I've since read again and again.

And what was far grows near,   35
and what is near grows more dear,

and all of my visions and interpretations
depend on what I see,

and between my eyes is always
the rain, the migrant rain.   40

Philip Levine   b. 1928

What Work Is   [1991]

We stand in the rain in a long line
waiting at Ford Highland Park. For work.
You know what work is — if you're
old enough to read this you know what
work is, although you may not do it.   5
Forget you. This is about waiting,
shifting from one foot to another.
Feeling the light rain falling like mist
into your hair, blurring your vision
until you think you see your own brother   10
ahead of you, maybe ten places.
You rub your glasses with your fingers,
and of course it's someone else's brother,
narrower across the shoulders than
yours but with the same sad slouch, the grin   15
that does not hide the stubbornness,
the sad refusal to give in to
rain, to the hours wasted waiting,
to the knowledge that somewhere ahead
a man is waiting who will say, "No,   20
we're not hiring today," for any
reason he wants. You love your brother,
now suddenly you can hardly stand
the love flooding you for your brother,
who's not beside you or behind or   25
ahead because he's home trying to

sleep off a miserable night shift
at Cadillac so he can get up
before noon to study his German.
Works eight hours a night so he can sing   30
Wagner, the opera you hate most,
the worst music ever invented.
How long has it been since you told him
you loved him, held his wide shoulders,
opened your eyes wide and said those words,   35
and maybe kissed his cheek? You've never
done something so simple, so obvious,
not because you're too young or too dumb,
not because you're jealous or even mean
or incapable of crying in   40
the presence of another man, no,
just because you don't know what work is.

Timothy Liu   b. 1965

Thoreau   [1995]

My father and I have no place to go.
His wife will not let us in the house —
afraid of catching AIDS. She thinks
sleeping with men is more than a sin,
my father says, as we sit on the curb   5
in front of someone else's house.
Sixty-four years have made my father
impotent. Silver roots, faded black dye
mottling his hair make him look
almost comical, as if his shame   10
belonged to me. Last night we read
Thoreau in a steak house down the road
and wept: *If a man does not keep pace*
with his companions, let him travel
to the music that he hears, however   15
measured or far away. The orchards
are gone, his village near Shanghai
bombed by the Japanese, the groves
I have known in Almaden — apricot,
walnut, peach and plum — hacked down.   20

Richard Lovelace 1618–1657

To Lucasta, Going to the Wars   [1649]

Tell me not, Sweet, I am unkind,
  That from the nunnery
Of thy chaste breast and quiet mind
  To war and arms I fly.

True, a new mistress now I chase,   5
  The first foe in the field;
And with a stronger faith embrace
  A sword, a horse, a shield.

Yet this inconstancy is such
  As you too shall adore;   10
I could not love thee, dear, so much,
  Loved I not honor more.

Robert Lowell 1917–1978

Skunk Hour   [1963]

for Elizabeth Bishop°

Nautilus Island's hermit
heiress still lives through winter in her Spartan cottage;
her sheep still graze above the sea.
Her son's a bishop. Her farmer
is first selectman in our village;   5
she's in her dotage.

Thirsting for
the hierarchic privacy
of Queen Victoria's century,
she buys up all   10
the eyesores facing her shore,
and lets them fall.

The season's ill—
we've lost our summer millionaire,
who seemed to leap from an L. L. Bean   15

Elizabeth Bishop: American poet (1911–1979); see the poems on pages 506 and 608 and the
biographical sketch on page 1419.

catalogue. His nine-knot yawl
was auctioned off to lobstermen.
A red fox stain covers Blue Hill.

And now our fairy
decorator brightens his shop for fall;   20
his fishnet's filled with orange cork,
orange, his cobbler's bench and awl;
there is no money in his work,
he'd rather marry.

One dark night,   25
my Tudor Ford climbed the hill's skull;
I watched for love-cars. Lights turned down,
they lay together, hull to hull,
where the graveyard shelves on the town. . . .
My mind's not right.   30

A car radio bleats,
"Love, O careless Love. . . ." I hear
my ill-spirit sob in each blood cell,
as if my hand were at its throat. . . .
I myself am hell;   35
nobody's here—

only skunks, that search
in the moonlight for a bite to eat.
They march on their soles up Main Street:
white stripes, moonstruck eyes' red fire   40
under the chalk-dry and spar spire
of the Trinitarian Church.

I stand on top
of our back steps and breathe the rich air—
a mother skunk with her column of kittens swills the garbage pail.   45
She jabs her wedge-head in a cup
of sour cream, drops her ostrich tail,
and will not scare.

Heather McHugh   b. 1948

What He Thought   [1994]

We were supposed to do a job in Italy
and, full of our feeling for
ourselves (our sense of being
Poets from America) we went

from Rome to Fano, met
the mayor, mulled
a couple matters over (what's
cheap date, they asked us; what's
flat drink). Among Italian literati   5

we could recognize our counterparts:
the academic, the apologist,
the arrogant, the amorous,
the brazen and the glib — and there was one   10

administrator (the conservative), in suit
of regulation gray, who like a good tour guide
with measured pace and uninflected tone narrated   15
sights and histories the hired van hauled us past.
Of all, he was most politic and least poetic,
so it seemed. Our last few days in Rome
(when all but three of the New World Bards had flown)   20
I found a book of poems this
unprepossessing one had written: it was there
in the *pensione* room (a room he'd recommended)
where it must have been abandoned by
the German visitor (was there a bus of *them*?)   25
to whom he had inscribed and dated it a month before.
I couldn't read Italian, either, so I put the book
back into the wardrobe's dark. We last Americans

were due to leave tomorrow. For our parting evening then
our host chose something in a family restaurant, and there   30
we sat and chatted, sat and chewed,
till, sensible it was our last
big chance to be poetic, make
our mark, one of us asked
                         "What's poetry?   35
Is it the fruits and vegetables and
marketplace of Campo dei Fiori, or
the statue there?" Because I was

the glib one, I identified the answer
instantly, I didn't have to think — "The truth   40
is both, it's both," I blurted out. But that
was easy. That was easiest to say. What followed
taught me something about difficulty,
for our underestimated host spoke out,
all of a sudden, with a rising passion, and he said: 45

The statue represents Giordano Bruno,
brought to be burned in the public square

because of his offense against
authority, which is to say
the Church. His crime was his belief   50
the universe does not revolve around
the human being: God is no
fixed point or central government, but rather is
poured in waves through all things. All things
move. "If God is not the soul itself, He is   55
the soul of the soul of the world." Such was
his heresy. The day they brought him
forth to die, they feared he might
incite the crowd (the man was famous
for his eloquence). And so his captors   60
placed upon his face
an iron mask, in which

he could not speak. That's
how they burned him. That is how
he died: without a word, in front   65
of everyone.
     And poetry —
        (we'd all
put down our forks by now, to listen to
the man in gray; he went on   70
softly) —
     poetry is what

he thought, but did not say.

Claude McKay   1890–1948

America   [1922]

Although she feeds me bread of bitterness,
And sinks into my throat her tiger's tooth,
Stealing my breath of life, I will confess
I love this cultured hell that tests my youth!
Her vigor flows like tides into my blood,   5
Giving me strength erect against her hate.
Her bigness sweeps my being like a flood.
Yet as a rebel fronts a king in state,
I stand within her walls with not a shred
Of terror, malice, not a word of jeer.   10
Darkly I gaze into the days ahead,

And see her might and granite wonders there,
Beneath the touch of Time's unerring hand,
Like priceless treasures sinking in the sand.

Clarence Major   b. 1936

Young Woman   [1974]

Young woman — dark lovely angry —
old people are spending their last days
deep in your life. Your work is not a lark.
You serve them tea.
Yet they do not trust you.   5
You empty their piss pots,
and joy drains from your bosom.
I see you burn trash and eat sardines
from the can. You stand on the outhouse
throwing grain at excited chickens.   10
What kind of lady can you become?
Whores in the Valley knew your Indian mother,
the gambling drunks in town
were cheated by your black father.
Who are you? Where can you live?   15
Remember your grandfather's mule?
Left it to your father. Lost in a crap game.
The young mothers on the hill whisper your name.
Husbands are wild and helpless!
Still I love you —   20
and want to marry you
and to take you with me to Denver.

Christopher Marlowe   1564–1593

The Passionate Shepherd to His Love   [1599]

Come live with me and be my love,
And we will all the pleasures prove
That valleys, groves, hills, and fields,
Woods, or steepy mountain yields.

And we will sit upon the rocks,   5
Seeing the shepherds feed their flocks,

By shallow rivers, to whose falls
Melodious birds sing madrigals.

And I will make thee beds of roses
And a thousand fragrant posies,
A cap of flowers, and a kirtle°   10
Embroidered all with leaves of myrtle.   *skirt, outer petticoat*

A gown made of the finest wool
Which from our pretty lambs we pull,
Fair lined slippers for the cold,   15
With buckles of the purest gold.

A belt of straw and ivy buds,
With coral clasps and amber studs,
And if these pleasures may thee move,
Come live with me, and be my love.   20

The shepherd swains shall dance and sing
For thy delight each May morning.
If these delights thy mind may move,
Then live with me and be my love.

Andrew Marvell   1621–1678

To His Coy° Mistress   [*c. 1650;* 1681]

   Had we but world enough, and time,
This coyness, lady, were no crime.
We would sit down, and think which way
To walk, and pass our long love's day.
Thou by the Indian Ganges' side   5
Shouldst rubies find; I by the tide
Of Humber would complain.° I would
Love you ten years before the Flood,
And you should, if you please, refuse
Till the conversion of the Jews.°   10
My vegetable° love should grow   *living and growing*
Vaster than empires, and more slow;

Coy: In the seventeenth century, "coy" could carry its older meaning, "shy," or its modern sense of "coquettish."   **5–7. Indian Ganges', Humber:** The Ganges River in India, with its distant, romantic associations, contrasts with the Humber River, running through Hull in northeast England, Marvell's home town.   **10. conversion . . . Jews:** An occurrence foretold, in some traditions, as one of the concluding events of human history.

An hundred years should go to praise
Thine eyes, and on thy forehead gaze;
Two hundred to adore each breast,   15
But thirty thousand to the rest;
An age at least to every part,
And the last age should show your heart.
For, lady, you deserve this state,°   *dignity*
Nor would I love at lower rate.   20
    But at my back I always hear
Time's wingèd chariot hurrying near;
And yonder all before us lie
Deserts of vast eternity.
Thy beauty shall no more be found,   25
Nor, in thy marble vault, shall sound
My echoing song; then worms shall try
That long-preserved virginity,
And your quaint honor turn to dust,
And into ashes all my lust: 30
The grave's a fine and private place,
But none, I think, do there embrace.
    Now therefore, while the youthful hue
Sits on thy skin like morning dew,
And while thy willing soul transpires°   *breathes forth* 35
At every pore with instant fires,°   *urgent passion*
Now let us sport us while we may,
And now, like amorous birds of prey,
Rather at once our time devour
Than languish in his slow-chapped° power.   40
Let us roll all our strength and all
Our sweetness up into one ball,
And tear our pleasures with rough strife
Thorough° the iron gates of life;   *through*
Thus, though we cannot make our sun   45
Stand still,° yet we will make him run.

---

40. slow-chapped: Slow-jawed, devouring slowly.   **45–46. make our sun stand still:** An allusion to Joshua 10:12. In answer to Joshua's prayer, God made the sun stand still, to prolong the day and give the Israelites more time to defeat the Amorites.

WEB: Explore Andrew Marvell and "To His Coy Mistress" in depth, including images and cultural documents, with VirtuaLit Poetry at bedfordstmartins.com/approachinglit.

Orlando Ricardo Menes b. 1958

Letter to Mirta Yáñez°   [2001]

I read *Some Place in Ruins,*°
your recent book of poems, and that title
seems incredibly ironic —
photograph of a Greek temple
on the cover — for our Old Habana   5
lies in tropical ruins; you should instead
put that colonial house
at Jesús María number 13
where my mother lived as a little girl
(abode of the ghost   10
Don Melitón, in life a Galician
shopkeeper)
or the Golgothas° of rubble
I saw walking toward the Cathedral
on Obispo Street,   15
surrounded by trash and skeletal animals
(like the black dog
with the hairless tail that ate
a mango pit).
An old black woman   20
on Angel Hill begged me for money
to buy orange juice,
I gave her the last dollar in my pocket.

Perhaps some of her street names
could be interpreted   25
as omens
since Cuba crosses Anguish
and also Poor Rock.
My gray Habana,
covered with scars and wrinkles,   30
breath of death,
so poorly plastered and nailed together
you will soon collapse,
your only solace
ill-remembered memories.   35
I know you were
voluptuously beautiful,
painted with colors

Mirta Yáñez: (b. 1947), Cuban poet, essayist, and fiction writer. **1.** *Some . . . Ruins:* *Algún lugar en ruinas* (1997).   **13. Golgothas:** Golgotha was where Jesus was crucified.

of guava, papaya, and guanábana,
sassy, proud, impetuous   40
with carnal delights,
praised with *piropos*
(flirtatious remarks)
more vulgar than sophisticated.
The world   45
has scarcely noticed
your destruction,
invisible behind bars
of sugar cane.

Czeslaw Milosz b. 1911

It Was Winter   [1964]

Winter came as it does in this valley.
After eight dry months rain fell
And the mountains, straw-colored, turned green for a while.
In the canyons where gray laurels
Graft their stony roots to granite,   5
Streams must have filled the dried-up creek beds.
Ocean winds churned the eucalyptus trees,
And under clouds torn by a crystal of towers
Prickly lights were glowing on the docks.

This is not a place where you sit under a café awning   10
On a marble piazza, watching the crowd,
Or play the flute at a window over a narrow street
While children's sandals clatter in the vaulted entryway.

They heard of a land, empty and vast,
Bordered by mountains. So they went, leaving behind crosses   15
Of thorny wood and traces of campfires.
As it happened, they spent winter in the snow of a mountain pass,
And drew lots and boiled the bones of their companions;
And so afterward a hot valley where indigo could be grown
Seemed beautiful to them. And beyond, where fog   20
Heaved into shoreline coves, the ocean labored.

Sleep: rocks and capes will lie down inside you,
War councils of motionless animals in a barren place,
Basilicas of reptiles, a frothy whiteness.
Sleep on your coat, while your horse nibbles grass   25
And an eagle gauges a precipice.
When you wake up, you will have the parts of the world.

West, an empty conch of water and air.
East, always behind you, the voided memory of snow-covered fir.
And extending from your outspread arms   30
Nothing but bronze grasses, north and south.

We are poor people, much afflicted.
We camped under various stars,
Where you dip water with a cup from a muddy river
And slice your bread with a pocketknife.   35
This is the place; accepted, not chosen.
We remembered that there were streets and houses where we came
     from,
So there had to be houses here, a saddler's signboard,
A small veranda with a chair. But empty, a country where
The thunder beneath the rippled skin of the earth,   40
The breaking waves, a patrol of pelicans, nullified us.
As if our vases, brought here from another shore,
Were the dug-up spearheads of some lost tribe
Who fed on lizards and acorn flour.

And here I am walking the eternal earth.   45
Tiny, leaning on a stick.
I pass a volcanic park, lie down at a spring,
Not knowing how to express what is always and everywhere:
The earth I cling to is so solid
Under my breast and belly that I feel grateful   50
For every pebble, and I don't know whether
It is my pulse or the earth's that I hear,
When the hems of invisible silk vestments pass over me,
Hands, wherever they have been, touch my arm,
Or small laughter, once, long ago over wine,   55
With lanterns in the magnolias, for my house is huge.

John Milton 1608–1674

When I consider how my light is spent   [c. 1652; 1673]

When I consider how my light is spent°
     Ere half my days, in this dark world and wide,
     And that one talent which is death to hide
     Lodged with me useless, though my soul more bent
To serve therewith my Maker, and present   5

___
1. **When . . . spent:** Milton went blind in 1652. Lines 1–2 allude to Matthew 25:1–13; line 3, to Matthew 25:14–30; and line 11, to Matthew 11:30.

My true account, lest he returning chide.
"Doth God exact day-labor, light denied?"
I fondly° ask; but patience to prevent   *foolishly*
That murmur, soon replies, "God doth not need
Either man's work or his own gifts; who best   10
Bear his mild yoke, they serve him best. His state
Is kingly. Thousands at his bidding speed
And post o'er land and ocean without rest:
They also serve who only stand and wait."

Gary Miranda   b. 1938

Love Poem   [1978]

A kind of slant: the way a ball will glance
off the end of a bat when you swing for the fence
and miss — that is, if you could watch that once,
up close and in slow motion; or the chance
meanings, not even remotely intended, that dance   5
at the edge of words, like sparks. Bats bounce
just so off the edges of the dark at a moment's
notice, as swallows do off sunlight. Slants

like these have something to do with why *angle*
is one of my favorite words, whenever it chances   10
to be a verb; and with why the music I single
out tonight — eighteenth-century dances —
made me think just now of you untangling
blueberries, carefully, from their dense branches.

Janice Mirikitani   b. 1942

For a Daughter Who Leaves   [2001]

More than gems in my comb box shaped by the
God of the Sea, I prize you, my daughter . . .
                    — Lady Otomo, 8th century, Japan

A woman weaves
her daughter's wedding
slippers that will carry
her steps into a new life.
The mother weeps alone   5
into her jeweled sewing box

slips red thread
around its spool,
the same she used to stitch
her daughter's first silk jacket   10
embroidered with turtles
that would bring luck, long life.
She remembers all the steps
taken by her daughter's
unbound quick feet: 15
dancing on the stones
of the yard among yellow
butterflies and white breasted sparrows.
And she grew, legs strong
body long, mind   20
independent.
Now she captures all eyes
with her hair combed smooth
and her hips gently
swaying like bamboo.   25
The woman
spins her thread
from the spool of her heart,
knotted to her daughter's
departing   30
wedding slippers.

Marianne Moore   1887–1972

Poetry   [1921]

I, too, dislike it: there are things that are important beyond all this fiddle.
    Reading it, however, with a perfect contempt for it, one discovers in
    it after all, a place for the genuine.
        Hands that can grasp, eyes
        that can dilate, hair that can rise   5
            if it must, these things are important not because a

high-sounding interpretation can be put upon them but because they are
    useful. When they become so derivative as to become unintelligible,
    the same thing may be said for all of us, that we
        do not admire what   10
        we cannot understand: the bat
            holding on upside down or in quest of something to

*   *   *

eat, elephants pushing, a wild horse taking a roll, a tireless wolf under
   a tree, the immovable critic twitching his skin like a horse that
                feels a flea, the base-
   ball fan, the statistician —   15
      nor is it valid
        to discriminate against "business documents and

school-books"; all these phenomena are important. One must make
                    a distinction
   however: when dragged into prominence by half poets, the result
                    is not poetry,
   nor till the poets among us can be   20
      "literalists of
      the imagination" — above
        insolence and triviality and can present

for inspection, "imaginary gardens with real toads in them," shall
                   we have
   it. In the meantime, if you demand on the one hand,   25
   the raw material of poetry in
      all its rawness and
      that which is on the other hand
        genuine, you are interested in poetry.

Robert Morgan b. 1944

Mountain Bride   [1979]

They say Revis found a flatrock
on the ridge just
perfect for a natural hearth,
and built his cabin with a stick

and clay chimney right over it.   5
On their wedding night he lit
the fireplace to dry away the mountain
chill of late spring, and flung on

applewood to dye
the room with molten color while   10
he and Martha that was a Parrish
warmed the sheets between the tick

stuffed with leaves and its feather
cover. Under that wide hearth

a nest of rattlers,   15
they'll knot a hundred together,

had wintered and were coming awake.
The warming rock
flushed them out early.
It was she   20

who wakened to their singing near
the embers and roused him to go look.
Before he reached the fire
more than a dozen struck

and he died yelling her to stay   25
on the big four-poster.
Her uncle coming up the hollow
with a gift bearham two days later

found her shivering there
marooned above a pool   30
of hungry snakes,
and the body beginning to swell.

Duane Niatum   b. 1938

First Spring   [1980; rev. 2004]

Drifting off the wheel of a past
looking like a redskin American gothic,
I stare through forty-one years
of rain-pelted windows and bear
with modest grace, diminished nerves,   5
narrowing light, half-formed figures:
memories floating in purgatory.

Renting a small house, the first
in fifteen years, I admire each hour
the diffidence of elders walking by,   10
from a tavern down the street,
their snow-cave eyes, hands
dancing like puppets. When a former love calls,
having abandoned another, I say, —

> *Sorry, sorry, I'm too busy*   15
> *with the friends still left.*
> *I'll call you.*

*   *   *

The lie of copper skids along my tongue.
Why tell her they're the sparrows at the feeder,
bees in the lilacs, roses, and plum trees,   20
books on the shelves and everywhere,
paintings on the walls, sculptures in the corners,
wind at the door and on the roof?

    It is called giving your body
    a river to jump in to,   25
    it is called giving your brain cells
    a field to get planted in.
    It is called standing on your head
    before the women you lost,
    sleeping in the embers of your name.   30

Naomi Shihab Nye b. 1952

The Small Vases from Hebron°   [1998]

Tip their mouths open to the sky.
Turquoise, amber,
the deep green with fluted handle,
pitcher the size of two thumbs,
tiny lip and graceful waist.   5

Here we place the smallest flower
which could have lived invisibly
in loose soil beside the road,
sprig of succulent rosemary,
bowing mint.   10

They grow deeper in the center of the table.

Here we entrust the small life,
thread, fragment, breath.
And it bends. It waits all day.
As the bread cools and the children   15
open their gray copybooks
to shape the letter that looks like
a chimney rising out of a house.

    *   *   *

Hebron: An ancient city in the West Bank area of Israel; a sacred place for both Muslims and
Jews and a focus of tension between Israelis and Palestinians since the 1967 Arab-Israeli war.

And what do the headlines say?

Nothing of the smaller petal   20
perfectly arranged inside the larger petal
or the way tinted glass filters light.
Men and boys, praying when they died,
fall out of their skins.
The whole alphabet of living,   25
heads and tails of words,
sentences, the way they said,
"Ya'Allah!" when astonished,
or "ya'ani" for "I mean" —
a crushed glass under the feet   30
still shines.
But the child of Hebron sleeps
with the thud of her brothers falling
and the long sorrow of the color red.

Dwight Okita   b. 1958

In Response to Executive Order 9066:   [1983]
All Americans of Japanese Descent Must Report
to Relocation Centers

Dear Sirs:
Of course I'll come. I've packed my galoshes
and three packets of tomato seeds. Denise calls them
love apples. My father says where we're going
they won't grow.   5

I am a fourteen-year-old girl with bad spelling
and a messy room. If it helps any, I will tell you
I have always felt funny using chopsticks
and my favorite food is hot dogs.
My best friend is a white girl named Denise —   10
we look at boys together. She sat in front of me
all through grade school because of our names:
O'Connor, Ozawa. I know the back of Denise's head very well.

I tell her she's going bald. She tells me I copy on tests.
We're best friends.   15

I saw Denise today in Geography class.
She was sitting on the other side of the room.
"You're trying to start a war," she said, "giving secrets

away to the Enemy, Why can't you keep your big
mouth shut?"   20

I didn't know what to say.
I gave her a packet of tomato seeds
and asked her to plant them for me, told her
when the first tomato ripened
she'd miss me.   25

Mary Oliver b. 1935

Goldenrod   [1992]

On roadsides,
    in fall fields,
        in rumpy bunches,
            saffron and orange and pale gold,

in little towers,   5
    soft as mash,
        sneeze-bringers and seed-bearers,
            full of bees and yellow beads and perfect flowerlets

and orange butterflies.
    I don't suppose   10
        much notice comes of it, except for honey,
            and how it heartens the heart with its

blank blaze.
    I don't suppose anything loves it except, perhaps,
        the rocky voids   15
            filled by its dumb dazzle.

For myself,
    I was just passing by, when the wind flared
        and the blossoms rustled,
            and the glittering pandemonium   20

leaned on me.
    I was just minding my own business
        when I found myself on their straw hillsides,
            citron and butter-colored,

and was happy, and why not?   25
    Are not the difficult labors of our lives
        full of dark hours?
            And what has consciousness come to anyway, so far,

*   *   *

that is better than these light-filled bodies?
>   All day   30
>   on their airy backbones
>   they toss in the wind,

they bend as though it was natural and godly to bend,
>   they rise in a stiff sweetness,
>   in the pure peace of giving   35
>   one's gold away.

Michael Ondaatje   b. 1943

Biography   [1979]

The dog scatters her body in sleep,
paws, finding no ground, whip at air,
the unseen eyeballs reel deep, within.
And waking — crouches,
tacked to humility all day,   5
children ride her, stretch,
display the black purple lips,
pull hind legs to dance;
unaware that she
tore bulls apart, loosed   10
heads of partridges,
dreamt blood.

Ricardo Pau-Llosa   b. 1954

Years of Exile   [2001]

After the paintings of Humberto Calzada°

The water enters the old ballroom
and the once bedroom, seeps across
the erstwhile chessboard floor
where rumors made their way.
The squares once mapped   5
the tinted flights of sun
that stained-glass half-wheels wrote,

Humberto Calzada: (b. 1944), Cuban American painter.

pages in the metronome diary of an age.
These testaments only seemed random,
stretched lights falling like   10
premeditated leaves
against the staring wall
or upon the lurid waist of the piano.

And then the water came.
The first arrival left   15
a pale ghost on the tiles.
Later more water came and more
so that no one could show
the uninvited flood the door,
which was half drowned.   20
The glass wheels turned
their voices on the murk.

And we waited for the new day
when losses would turn to stories.
We would laugh, we knew it, about   25
the swallowed rooms, the stabbed
recollections where gilded curtains
and danzones swayed.

But the years knew better.
We have learned to love   30
the cracks on the ceiling,
a nose away. We stare into them now
that we have learned to float and have become
the Sistine chroniclers of our shrinkings.
We create, we are free   35
now that we have lost count of everything.

Gustavo Pérez Firmat   b. 1949

José Canseco Breaks Our Hearts Again   [2001]

Out for the season, what's new.
31 homers, best in the AL, 71 RBIs,
and a herniated disk.

David had asked me to tape the home-run derby
and now he says not to bother.   5
Stupid me, I worry that with Canseco

                    *   *   *

laid up, my son and I will not have something to talk about.
José has missed one-third of his career,
over 500 games, or he'd have 600 homers by now.

I think of all the sentences   10
David and I could have said to each other
if José's back did not keep giving out on us.

(He had to be Cuban, that impossible man-child,
delicate as an orchid beneath the rippling chest.)

I'll keep my fingers crossed for next season   15
when José, like a certain country I know,
will break our hearts again.

Wang Ping   b. 1957

Opening the Face   [2003]

She comes in,
thread between her teeth,
the "lady of wholesome fortune,"
two sons, three daughters,
husband in government service,   5
parents-in-law healthy and content,
surrounded by laughing grandchildren.
Mother paid her gold to open
my face on my wedding day.

"Sit still," she orders, twining   10
the cotton thread to test its strength.
"It hurts, but nothing like footbinding,
or the hardship of a newlywed."
She pulls it through her teeth,
lines it against my forehead.   15
Wet, cold, it furrows into the skin,
into the roots of my virgin down.
The uprooted hair hisses
after the twanging thread.

"Don't make a sound, girl," she whispers   20
to my drenched face, "not until you bear him a son,
not until you have grandchildren."
She holds her breath as she scrapes
between the eyebrows and lashes, opens
her mouth again when she reaches for the cheek.   25
"What's ten, twenty, or even thirty years?

We came to this world with nothing but
patience. You have high cheekbones
and a big nose, signs of a man-killer,
but compensated by a round chin.   30
Just keep your mouth shut, eyes open.
There, there," she leans closer, wiping
beads of tears from my eyelashes.

        I turn to the light, my face
        a burning field.   35

"Now you're ready for the big day."
Her fingers trace along my cheekbones.
"Your face clean and open.
I'll cover it with a red scarf.
The only person who can lift   40
the veil is your groom. All other eyes
are evil eyes. Remember, remember."

She puts on her shoes.
"Ah, one more thing," she leans to my ear,
her breath steaming with pickled mustard greens,   45
yellow rice wine, its bitter sweetness
from years of fermentation in a sealed jar
deep underground. Her secret
tickles the inside of my ear.
"When he sleeps, put your shoes   50
in his boots and let them sit overnight.
It'll keep him under your thumb, forever."

Robert Pinsky b. 1940

Shirt   [1990]

The back, the yoke, the yardage. Lapped seams,
The nearly invisible stitches along the collar
Turned in a sweatshop by Koreans or Malaysians

Gossiping over tea and noodles on their break
Or talking money or politics while one fitted   5
This armpiece with its overseam to the band

Of cuff I button at my wrist. The presser, the cutter,
The wringer, the mangle. The needle, the union,
The treadle, the bobbin. The code. The infamous blaze

     *   *   *

At the Triangle Factory° in nineteen-eleven.   *(in New York City)*   10
One hundred and forty-six died in the flames
On the ninth floor, no hydrants, no fire escapes —

The witness in a building across the street
Who watched how a young man helped a girl to step
Up to the windowsill, then held her out   15

Away from the masonry wall and let her drop.
And then another. As if he were helping them up
To enter a streetcar, and not eternity.

A third before he dropped her put her arms
Around his neck and kissed him. Then he held   20
Her into space, and dropped her. Almost at once

He stepped to the sill himself, his jacket flared
And fluttered up from his shirt as he came down,
Air filling up the legs of his gray trousers —

Like Hart Crane's Bedlamite, "shrill shirt ballooning."   25
Wonderful how the pattern matches perfectly
Across the placket and over the twin bar-tacked

Corners of both pockets, like a strict rhyme
Or a major chord. Prints, plaids, checks,
Houndstooth, Tattersall, Madras. The clan tartans   30

Invented by mill-owners inspired by the hoax of Ossian,°
To control their savage Scottish workers, tamed
By a fabricated heraldry: MacGregor,

Bailey, MacMartin. The kilt, devised for workers
To wear among the dusty clattering looms.   35
Weavers, carders, spinners. The loader,

The docker, the navvy. The planter, the picker, the sorter
Sweating at her machine in a litter of cotton
As slaves in calico headrags sweated in fields:

George Herbert,° your descendant is a Black   40
Lady in South Carolina, her name is Irma
And she inspected my shirt. Its color and fit

*   *   *

---

31. Ossian: Legendary Gaelic poet, hero of a cycle of traditional tales and poems that place him in the third century C.E. The hoax involved Scottish author James Macpherson (1736–1796), who published two epic poems that he said were translations of works written by Ossian but were in fact mostly composed by Macpherson himself.   **40. George Herbert:** (1593–1633), English metaphysical poet. See pp. 668 and 1435.

And feel and its clean smell have satisfied
Both her and me. We have culled its cost and quality
Down to the buttons of simulated bone,   45

The buttonholes, the sizing, the facing, the characters
Printed in black on neckband and tail. The shape,
The label, the labor, the color, the shade. The shirt.

Sylvia Plath   1932–1963

Daddy   [1962]

You do not do, you do not do
Any more, black shoe
In which I have lived like a foot
For thirty years, poor and white,
Barely daring to breathe or Achoo.   5

Daddy, I have had to kill you.
You died before I had time —
Marble-heavy, a bag full of God,
Ghastly statue with one grey toe
Big as a Frisco seal   10

And a head in the freakish Atlantic
Where it pours bean green over blue
In the waters off beautiful Nauset.
I used to pray to recover you.
Ach, du.°   Oh, you (German)   15

In the German tongue, in the Polish town
Scraped flat by the roller
Of wars, wars, wars.
But the name of the town is common.
My Polack friend   20

Says there are a dozen or two.
So I never could tell where you
Put your foot, your root,
I never could talk to you.
The tongue stuck in my jaw.   25

It stuck in a barb wire snare.
Ich, ich, ich, ich,°   I (German)
I could hardly speak.

I thought every German was you.
And the language obscene   30

An engine, an engine
Chuffing me off like a Jew.
A Jew to Dachau, Auschwitz, Belsen.°
I began to talk like a Jew.
I think I may well be a Jew.   35

The snows of the Tyrol,° the clear beer of Vienna
Are not very pure or true.
With my gypsy ancestress and my weird luck
And my Taroc pack and my Taroc pack
I may be a bit of a Jew.   40

I have always been scared of *you*,
With your Luftwaffe,° your gobbledygoo.
And your neat moustache
And your Aryan eye, bright blue.
Panzer°-man, panzer-man, O You—   45

Not God but a swastika
So black no sky could squeak through.
Every woman adores a Fascist,
The boot in the face, the brute
Brute heart of a brute like you.   50

You stand at the blackboard, daddy,
In the picture I have of you,
A cleft in your chin instead of your foot
But no less a devil for that, no not
Any less the black man who   55

Bit my pretty red heart in two.
I was ten when they buried you.
At twenty I tried to die
And get back, back, back to you.
I thought even the bones would do.   60

But they pulled me out of the sack,
And they stuck me together with glue.
And then I knew what to do.
I made a model of you,
A man in black with a Meinkampf° look   65

                  *   *   *

---

33. Dachau, Auschwitz, Belsen: Nazi concentration camps.   **36. the Tyrol:** An alpine region in western Austria and northern Italy.   **42. Luftwaffe:** The Nazi air force in World War II. **45. Panzer:** An armored unit in the German army in World War II.   **65.** *Mein Kampf: My Struggle,* the title of Adolf Hitler's autobiography.

And a love of the rack and the screw.
And I said I do, I do.
So daddy, I'm finally through.
The black telephone's off at the root,
The voices just can't worm through.   70

If I've killed one man, I've killed two —
The vampire who said he was you
And drank my blood for a year,
Seven years, if you want to know.
Daddy, you can lie back now.   75

There's a stake in your fat black heart
And the villagers never liked you.
They are dancing and stamping on you.
They always *knew* it was you.
Daddy, daddy, you bastard, I'm through.   80

Sylvia Plath

Metaphors   [1960]

I'm a riddle in nine syllables,
An elephant, a ponderous house,
A melon strolling on two tendrils.
O red fruit, ivory, fine timbers!
This loaf's big with its yeasty rising.   5
Money's new-minted in this fat purse.
I'm a means, a stage, a cow in calf.
I've eaten a bag of green apples,
Boarded the train there's no getting off.

CD-ROM: Research Sylvia Plath in depth with cultural documents and multimedia resources on
LiterActive.

Sir Walter Ralegh   1552–1618

The Nymph's Reply to the Shepherd   [1600]

If all the world and love were young,
And truth in every shepherd's tongue,
These pretty pleasures might me move
To live with thee and be thy love.

                    *   *   *

Time drives the flocks from field to fold   5
When rivers rage and rocks grow cold,
And Philomel° becometh dumb;   *nightingale*
The rest complains of cares to come.

The flowers do fade, and wanton fields
To wayward winter reckoning yields;   10
A honey tongue, a heart of gall,
Is fancy's spring, but sorrow's fall.

Thy gowns, thy shoes, thy beds of roses,
Thy cap, thy kirtle,° and thy posies   *skirt, outer petticoat*
Soon break, soon wither, soon forgotten —   15
In folly ripe, in reason rotten.

Thy belt of straw and ivy buds
Thy coral clasps and amber studs,
All these in me no means can move
To come to thee and be thy love.   20

But could youth last and love still breed,
Had joys no date° nor age no need,   *ending*
Then these delights my mind might move
To live with thee and be thy love.

Dudley Randall   1914–2000

Ballad of Birmingham   [1969]
On the Bombing of a Church in Birmingham, Alabama, 1963

"Mother dear, may I go downtown
Instead of out to play,
And march the streets of Birmingham
In a Freedom March today?"

"No, baby, no, you may not go,   5
For the dogs are fierce and wild,
And clubs and hoses, guns and jails
Aren't good for a little child."

"But, mother, I won't be alone.
Other children will go with me,   10
And march the streets of Birmingham
To make our country free."

"No, baby, no, you may not go,
For I fear those guns will fire.

But you may go to church instead   15
And sing in the children's choir."

She has combed and brushed her night-dark hair,
And bathed rose petal sweet,
And drawn white gloves on her small brown hands,
And white shoes on her feet.   20

The mother smiled to know her child
Was in the sacred place,
But that smile was the last smile
To come upon her face.

For when she heard the explosion,   25
Her eyes grew wet and wild.
She raced through the streets of Birmingham
Calling for her child.

She clawed through bits of glass and brick,
Then lifted out a shoe.   30
"Oh, here's the shoe my baby wore,
But, baby, where are you?"

Ishmael Reed   b. 1938

Poetry Makes Rhythm in Philosophy   [1978]

Maybe it was the Bichot
Beaujolais, 1970
But in an a.m. upstairs on
Crescent Ave. I had a conversation
with K.C. Bird   5

   We were discussing
rhythm and I said
"Rhythm makes everything move
the seasons swing
it backs up the elements
Like walking Paul-Chamber's fingers"   10

   "My worthy constituent"
Bird said, "The Universe is a
spiralling Big Band in a
polka-dotted speakeasy,
effusively generating new light   15
every one-night stand"

                    *   *   *

We agreed that nature can't
do without rhythm but rhythm can
get along without nature   20

This rhythm, a stylized Spring
conducted by a blue-collared man
in Keds and denims
(His Williamsville swimming pool
shaped like a bass clef)   25
in Baird Hall
on Sunday afternoons
Admission Free!

All *harrumphs!* must be
checked in at   30
the door

I wanted to spin
Bennie Moten's
"It's Hard to Laugh or Smile"
but the reject wouldn't automate   35
and the changer refused to drop
"Progress," you know

Just as well
because Bird vanished

A steel band had   40
entered the room

Adrienne Rich   b. 1929

Diving into the Wreck   [1973]

First having read the book of myths,
and loaded the camera,
and checked the edge of the knife-blade,
I put on
the body-armor of black rubber   5
the absurd flippers
the grave and awkward mask.
I am having to do this
not like Cousteau° with his

---

9. **Cousteau:** Jacques-Yves Cousteau (1910–1997), French underwater explorer, photographer, and author.

assiduous team   10
aboard the sun-flooded schooner
but here alone.

There is a ladder,
The ladder is always there
hanging innocently   15
close to the side of the schooner.
We know what it is for,
we who have used it.
Otherwise
it's a piece of maritime floss   20
some sundry equipment.

I go down.
Rung after rung and still
the oxygen immerses me
the blue light   25
the clear atoms
of our human air.
I go down.
My flippers cripple me,
I crawl like an insect down the ladder   30
and there is no one
to tell me when the ocean
will begin.

First the air is blue and then
it is bluer and then green and then   35
black I am blacking out and yet
my mask is powerful
it pumps my blood with power
the sea is another story
the sea is not a question of power   40
I have to learn alone
to turn my body without force
in the deep element.

And now: it is easy to forget
what I came for   45
among so many who have always
lived here
swaying their crenellated° fans
between the reefs

---

48. crenellated: Notched; *crenels* are the open spaces between the solid portions of a
battlement.

and besides   50
you breathe differently down here.

I came to explore the wreck.
The words are purposes.
The words are maps.
I came to see the damage that was done   55
and the treasures that prevail.
I stroke the beam of my lamp
slowly along the flank
of something more permanent
than fish or weed   60

the thing I came for:
the wreck and not the story of the wreck
the thing itself and not the myth
the drowned face° always staring
toward the sun   65
the evidence of damage
worn by salt and sway into this threadbare beauty
the ribs of the disaster
curving their assertion
among the tentative haunters.   70

This is the place.
And I am here, the mermaid whose dark hair
streams black, the merman in his armored body
We circle silently
about the wreck   75
we dive into the hold.
I am she: I am he

whose drowned face sleeps with open eyes
whose breasts still bear the stress
whose silver, copper, vermeil° cargo lies   80
obscurely inside barrels
half-wedged and left to rot
we are the half-destroyed instruments
that once held to a course
the water-eaten log   85
the fouled compass

We are, I am, you are
by cowardice or courage

---

64. **drowned face:** The ornamental female figurehead on the prow of an old sailing ship.
80. **vermeil:** Gilded silver, bronze, or copper.

the one who find our way
back to this scene   90
carrying a knife, a camera
a book of myths
in which
our names do not appear.

Alberto Ríos b. 1952

Nani°   [1982]

Sitting at her table, she serves
the sopa de arroz° to me   *rice soup*
instinctively, and I watch her,
the absolute *mamá,* and eat words
I might have had to say more   5
out of embarrassment. To speak,
now-foreign words I used to speak,
too, dribble down her mouth as she serves
me albondigas.° No more   *meatballs*
than a third are easy to me.   10
By the stove she does something with words
and looks at me only with her
back. I am full. I tell her
I taste the mint, and watch her speak
smiles at the stove. All my words   15
make her smile. Nani never serves
herself, she only watches me
with her skin, her hair. I ask for more.

I watch the *mamá* warming more
tortillas for me. I watch her   20
fingers in the flame for me.
Near her mouth, I see a wrinkle speak
of a man whose body serves
the ants like she serves me, then more words
from more wrinkles about children, words   25
about this and that, flowing more
easily from these other mouths. Each serves
as a tremendous string around her,
holding her together. They speak

Nani: Diminutive for "grandmother."

nani was this and that to me   30
and I wonder just how much of me
will die with her, what were the words
I could have been, was. Her insides speak
through a hundred wrinkles, now, more
than she can bear, steel around her,   35
shouting, then, What is this thing she serves?

She asks me if I want more.
I own no words to stop her.
Even before I speak, she serves.

Luis Rodriguez   b. 1954

Running to America   [2001]

They are night shadows
Violating borders.
Fingers curled through chain-link fences,
Hiding from infra-red eyes,
Dodging 30-30 bullets,   5
They leave familiar smells,
Warmth and sounds,
As ancient as the trampled stones.

Running to America.

There is a woman in her finest   10
Border-crossing wear:
A purple blouse from an older sister,
A pair of worn shoes
From a church bazaar,
A tattered coat from a former lover.   15

There is a child dressed in black,
Fear sparkling from dark Indian eyes,
Clinging to a headless Barbie doll.

And the men, some hardened, quiet,
Others young and loud—   20
You see something like this in prisons.

Soon they will cross on their bellies,
Kissing black earth,
Then run to America.

Wendy Rose b. 1948

Loo-Wit°   [1985]

The way they do
this old woman
no longer cares
what others think
but spits her black tobacco   5
any which way
stretching full length
from her bumpy bed.
Finally up
she sprinkles ashes   10
on the snow,
cold buttes
promise nothing
but the walk
of winter.   15
Centuries of cedar
have bound her
to earth,
huckleberry ropes
lay prickly   20
on her neck.
Around her
machinery growls,
snarls and ploughs
great patches   25
of her skin.
She crouches
in the north,
her trembling
the source   30
of dawn.
Light appears
with the shudder
of her slopes,
the movement   35
of her arm.
Blackberries unravel,
stones dislodge;

Loo-Wit: "Loo-wit" is the name by which the Cowlitz People know Mt. St. Helens — "lady of fire." [Poet's note.]

it's not as if
they weren't warned.   40

She was sleeping
but she heard the boot scrape,
the creaking floor,
felt the pull of the blanket
from her thin shoulder.   45
With one free hand
she finds her weapons
and raises them high;
clearing the twigs from her throat
she sings, she sings,   50
shaking the sky
like a blanket about her
Loo-wit sings and sings and sings!

Benjamin Alire Sáenz   b. 1954

Elegy Written on a Blue Gravestone
(To You, the Archaeologist)   [2001]

                        What history is:
a mound of gathered rocks. In time the rocks will
melt, will turn to dunes of sand, will blanket everything
you fought your wars to keep. All that work and worry;
the countless sleepless nights; the house you built   5
and loved (thirty years of paying right on time);
the perfect car that lasted forty years, the ring
you gave your wife, the clothes you bought your sons.
All buried now, those things (the worries, too).
Remember this: everything will die except the desert   10
sands. Everything will fade except the ashes of the
earth we filtered through a smelter's lonely tower.
The smelter, too, has died. And one day, soon, the tower
will be dust (not unlike your car; not unlike your
house; not unlike your wife). All debris and ashes.   15

                        Pick up a spade. Roll up your sleeves
and dig. Wipe the sweat from your brow. Then dig deeper,
deeper still. You cannot stop. You're a worker now.
Pray to God to find the heart you lost here long ago.
You need it now. Pray. Dig. Laugh (if you can) at   20
the blatant irony: to end your days doing what you
hated. Fated to become an archaeologist.

                *   *   *

See this artifact? Laid with crude cement and painted
blue. Deep as moaning from a mourner. Deep as scars
on Jesus' arms and feet. A gravestone, a marker, not   25
granite, not marble, a common monument befitting
the class and taste of the deceased (or the survivors).
The inexpensive cross with corpus (bought retail
at a shut-down shop on Stanton Street). History
is buying and selling. History's an aisle of icons.   30
History's a birth, it's a funeral. History's a rose
made of plastic. History's a grave with no date.
History is broken cement. History's a litany
of questions: How many minds wasted at the plant?
How many bones fractured? Broken? Mended? How   35
many hearts shattered like a cheap ceramic cup?
Find the pieces, archaeologist! Reconstruct the
hearts! Remember this: these ruins guard their
solitude. They've fought their wars, and fight them
still. Ask anything you like.   40
You will not make them speak.

        A son or son-in-law, in grief,
designed this monument. A daughter picked the paint.
They thought their work would make the world remember.
There was a day: this painted blue cement was God   45
in heaven's envy. Not now. No longer. That day is
dead. The wind and rain, the ceaseless sun, the endless
days. The work, the dust, the drought. It's broken
now, this stone that praised a life. It's broken now.
The earth will break us all.   50

Sonia Sanchez b. 1934

An Anthem   [1987]

for the ANC and Brandywine Peace Community

Our vision is our voice
we cut through the country
where madmen goosestep in tune to Guernica.°

        *   *   *

---

3. Guernica: A town in northern Spain that was destroyed in 1937 by insurgents in the Spanish civil war, aided by German planes; the indiscriminate killing of women and children
aroused world opinion, and the bombing of Guernica made it a symbol of fascist brutality.

we are people made of fire
we walk with ceremonial breaths   5
we have condemned talking mouths.

we run without legs
we see without eyes
loud laughter breaks over our heads.

give me courage so I can spread   10
it over my face and mouth.

we are secret rivers
with shaking hips and crests
come awake in our thunder
so that our eyes can see behind trees.   15

for the world is split wide open
and you hide your hands behind your backs
for the world is broken into little pieces
and you beg with tin cups for life.

are we not more than hunger and music?   20
are we not more than harlequins and horns?

are we not more than color and drums?
are we not more than anger and dance?

give me courage so I can spread it
over my face and mouth.   25

we are the shakers
walking from top to bottom in a day
we are like Shango°
involving ourselves in acts
that bring life to the middle   30
of our stomachs

we are coming towards you madmen
shredding your death talk
standing in front with mornings around our waist
we have inherited our prayers from   35
the rain
our eyes from the children of Soweto.°

red rain pours over the land
and our fire mixes with the water.

give me courage so I can spread   40
it over my face and mouth.

---

28. Shango: One of the gods of the Yoruba tribe of western Nigeria. He is lord of lightning, thunder, rain, and testicular fertility.   **37. Soweto:** Group of segregated townships inhabited by blacks near Johannesburg, South Africa; scene of a 1976 uprising against the policies of apartheid.

Cheryl Savageau   b. 1950

Bones – A City Poem   [1992]

forget the great blue heron flying low
   over the marsh, its footprints
   still fresh in the sand

forget the taste of wild mushrooms
   and where to find them   5

forget lichen-covered pines
   and iceland moss

forget the one-legged duck
   and the eggs of the snapping turtle
   laid in the bank   10

forget the frog found in the belly of a bass

forget the cove testing its breath
   against the autumn morning

forget the down-filled nest
   and the snake swimming at midday   15

forget the bullhead lilies
   and the whiskers
   of the pout

forget walking on black ice
   beneath the sky hunter's bow   20

forget the living waters
   of Quinsigamond

forget how to find the Pole star and why

forget the eyes of the red fox
   the hornets that made their home   25
   in the skull of a cow

forget waking to hear the call of the loon

forget that raccoons are younger brothers
   to the bear

forget that you are walking   30
   on the bones of your grandmothers

Vijay Seshadri   b. 1954

The Refugee   [1996]

He feels himself at his mind's borders moving
down the fifteen rows of laid-out soil
and out to the fence where the mulch heaps spoil
beside the rust-scabbed, dismantled swing
and the visions that disturb him sometimes spring   5
up from a harmless garden-hose coil:
the jackbooted armies dripping spoors of oil
that slick the leaf and crap the wing. . . .

He sees each rifle as we who see him,
in the crystal blizzard of a century's static,   10
try to reach him with our two-bit magic.
But he escapes us to roam in the garden:
too clear to look through or distant to ask;
pinned like a flower on the genocidal past.

William Shakespeare   1564–1616

My mistress' eyes are nothing like the sun   [1590s; 1609]

My mistress' eyes are nothing like the sun;
Coral is far more red than her lips' red;
If snow be white, why then her breasts are dun;°   *dull grayish brown*
If hairs be wires, black wires grow on her head.
I have seen roses damasked,° red and white,   *variegated*   5
But no such roses see I in her cheeks;
And in some perfumes is there more delight
Than in the breath that from my mistress reeks.
I love to hear her speak, yet well I know
That music hath a far more pleasing sound.   10
I grant I never saw a goddess go;°   *walk*
My mistress, when she walks, treads on the ground.
    And yet, by heaven, I think my love as rare
    As any she° belied° with false compare.   *woman/misrepresented*

CD-ROM: Research William Shakespeare in depth with cultural documents and multimedia
resources on *LiterActive.*

Percy Bysshe Shelley 1792–1822

Ozymandias°   [1818]

I met a traveler from an antique land
Who said: Two vast and trunkless legs of stone
Stand in the desert. . . . Near them, on the sand,
Half sunk, a shattered visage lies, whose frown,
And wrinkled lip, and sneer of cold command,   5
Tell that its sculptor well those passions read
Which yet survive, stamped on these lifeless things,
The hand that mocked them, and the heart that fed:
And on the pedestal these words appear:
"My name is Ozymandias, king of kings: 10
Look on my works, ye Mighty, and despair!"
Nothing beside remains. Round the decay
Of that colossal wreck, boundless and bare
The lone and level sands stretch far away.

Ozymandias: The Greek name for Ramses II of Egypt (thirteenth century B.C.E.), who erected the largest statue in Egypt as a memorial to himself.

Percy Bysshe Shelley

Ode to the West Wind   [1820]

1

O wild West Wind, thou breath° of Autumn's being,
Thou, from whose unseen presence the leaves dead
Are driven, like ghosts from an enchanter fleeing,

Yellow, and black, and pale, and hectic red,
Pestilence-stricken multitudes: O thou,   5
Who chariotest to their dark wintry bed

The wingèd seeds, where they lie cold and low,
Each like a corpse within its grave, until
Thine azure sister of the Spring shall blow

        *   *   *

---

1. breath: In many ancient languages, the words for *breath, wind, soul,* and *inspiration* are the same or closely related: in Latin, *spiritus.* Shelley uses this to interconnect nature and artistic inspiration (poetry) in his poem.

Her clarion o'er the dreaming earth, and fill   10
(Driving sweet buds like flocks to feed in air)
With living hues and odors plain and hill:

Wild Spirit, which art moving everywhere;
Destroyer and preserver; hear, oh, hear!

2

Thou on whose stream, mid the steep sky's commotion,   15
Loose clouds like earth's decaying leaves are shed,
Shook from the tangled boughs of Heaven and Ocean,

Angels of rain and lightning: there are spread
On the blue surface of thine airy surge,
Like the bright hair uplifted from the head   20

Or some fierce Maenad,° even from the dim verge
Of the horizon to the zenith's height,
The locks of the approaching storm. Thou dirge

Of the dying year, to which this closing night
Will be the dome of a vast sepulcher,   25
Vaulted with all thy congregated might

Of vapors, from whose solid atmosphere
Black rain, and fire, and hail will burst: oh, hear!

3

Thou who didst waken from his summer dreams
The blue Mediterranean, where he lay,   30
Lulled by the coil of his crystàlline streams,

Beside a pumice isle in Baiae's bay,°
And saw in sleep old palaces° and towers
Quivering within the wave's intenser day,

All overgrown with azure moss and flowers   35
So sweet, the sense faints picturing them! Thou
For whose path the Atlantic's level powers

Cleave themselves into chasms, while far below
The sea-blooms and the oozy woods which wear
The sapless foliage of the ocean, know   40

           *   *   *

---

21. Maenad: A female votary of Dionysus, Greek god of wine and vegetation, who took part in the wild, orgiastic rites that characterize his worship.   **32. pumice:** Porous volcanic stone; **Baiae's bay:** West of Naples, Italy.   **33. old palaces:** Villas built by the Roman emperors.

Thy voice, and suddenly grow gray with fear,
And tremble and despoil themselves: oh, hear!

4

If I were a dead leaf thou mightest bear;
If I were a swift cloud to fly with thee;
A wave to pant beneath thy power, and share   45

The impulse of thy strength, only less free
Than thou, O uncontrollable! If even
I were as in my boyhood, and could be

The comrade of thy wanderings over Heaven,
As then, when to outstrip thy skyey speed   50
Scarce seemed a vision; I would ne'er have striven

As thus with thee in prayer in my sore need.
Oh, lift me as a wave, a leaf, a cloud!
I fall upon the thorns of life! I bleed!

A heavy weight of hours has chained and bowed   55
One too like thee: tameless, and swift, and proud.

5

Make me thy lyre,° even as the forest is:
What if my leaves are falling like its own!
The tumult of thy mighty harmonies

Will take from both a deep, autumnal tone,   60
Sweet though in sadness. Be thou, Spirit fierce,
My spirit! Be thou me, impetuous one!

Drive my dead thoughts over the universe
Like withered leaves to quicken a new birth!
And, by the incantation of this verse,   65

Scatter, as from an unextinguished hearth
Ashes and sparks, my words among mankind!
Be through my lips to unawakened earth

The trumpet of a prophecy! O Wind,
If Winter comes, can Spring be far behind?   70

---

57. lyre: An Aeolian harp, whose strings produce a sequence of rising and falling harmonies as
air blows over them.

Kazuko Shiraishi   b. 1931

Dedicated to the Late John Coltrane°   [1970]

Suddenly
He went to heaven
John Coltrane

In several ways
You were drastic about living   5
Out of your beauty
Beyond any meaning
A blue rain began to fall
People
Sit cross-legged on the richness of meaning   10
And like beggars grab the rice of sound
Eating, they weep goldly
Uncontrollably in misery

Coltrane
You have entered through   15
A hole in heaven

Because you died
On earth, again, one huge
Soundless hole has opened
People   20
Crawl to the edge of that pit
Missing him and his sounds
They clutch his thrown away shirts
Or album covers
Yearning sadly, loving him   25
They groan, get angry, and cry

Kulu Sé Mama°
Kulu Sé Mama

Coltrane
With your extremely heavy   30
And short pilgrimage
Full of fleeting eternity
Spirit traveling
You were mainly blowing thoughts
Thoughts are eyes, wind   35

John Coltrane: (1926–1967), a well-known jazz saxophonist.   **27. *Kulu Sé Mama*:** Title track
of a John Coltrane album.

Cascades of spicy sweat
Streaming down your forehead
Thought is an otter's scream
The sexual legs of chickens
Killed by your old lady   40
Boiling in a pot
Women's pubic hair
Alice or Aisha
Thoughts are the faceless songs
Of pink stars   45
Squirming in the sky
Of every woman's womb

Hot, dark summer afternoon
Coltrane
Your "Olé"   50
So full of romanticism and power
Now we don't have your "Olé" of love
For a little while, about as long as forever,
We won't receive your
"Olé"   55

On this earth
In this human hot arena
In the bullring
Cicadas are crying now
Hot, dark summer   60
Sits by itself
No bulls, no glory
Only shadows and memory
You in my memory
Coltrane, your music   65

People see the colors of your sounds
So passionately
They listen with ears of dread
To the ordeal of your sounds

For forty-one years   70
In your very busy history
The sun often rose and sank
Orange sun, African sun, American sun
The taste of human sun
Rose and set hundreds and thousands of times   75
In a black, soul room
You are sunbathing
That dude the sun shines brightly

On your silent back
That dude the sun often cried   80
And became the sweat of blinding music
Diving into a saxophone blown by you
He cried out loud and free

Brilliant blue
Even the orange sun   85
Against those black, desperate cheeks
Has begun to cry incoherently
Coltrane almost became a sky
He became a cascade of will
Carrying the sounds   90
He made them fall
Pouring them out
We know the monsoon
In John's long lasting solo
The blazing rain continues   95

We are often beaten with the rainfall of sound
We are numbed
To the deepest room of our hearts
We are soaked through
The door breaks, the mast snaps   100
The chairs float away
Then we regain that certain consciousness

Which is volition
Which is desire
It is the cosmos announcing   105
The trivial existence of humans
Alone, carrying his saxophone
He takes giant steps
Walking through the cosmos
Though his stride helps us see the blue   110
Unstable vertebrae of earth
His expression was mostly invisible
Sometimes he mysteriously, shyly
Buried his face in a cloud

John, wandering Coltrane   115
Even though you are no longer on earth
I, we remember you when you were
All of a sudden
We recall you wandering for awhile
In the season without answers   120

With your face hidden
In that opaque cloud

While flowing slowly down the river of agony
You met the fish of pleasure
You met love   125
You met woman, son, friend, God
You met music and its Holy Spirit
Then you became the Holy Spirit
You became the music itself

On earth, from now on   130
A long, hot, dark summer continues
Even though you died
Even though your transient life ended

On earth
In whatever cold struggle   135
Hot passions and determinations
Are smoldering
Humans are walking on the day

John Coltrane
Your day, that day which was once alive   140
That day which met 'someday'
That day which dissolved the next moment

Coltrane
In the way I love you
I love the days you lived through   145
I love the season of those days
Which you survived for forty-one years
Your music, your voice
Your glory and rage
Your love and conviction   150
Your God, your Holy Spirit
Your cosmos with East and West
Its desperation and grief

All those I love and warm
And meditate upon   155
May your spirit rest in peace
Our beloved John Coltrane
A tremendous saxophone player

For the strong, black soul
Of Saint Coltrane   160
In heaven

Charles Simic   b. 1938

Begotten of the Spleen°   [1980; rev. 1999]

The Virgin Mother° walked barefoot
Among the land mines.
She carried an old man in her arms
Like a howling babe.

The earth was an old people's home.   5
Judas was the night nurse,
Emptying bedpans into the river Jordan,
Tying people on a dog chain.

The old man had two stumps for legs.
St. Peter came pushing a cart   10
Loaded with flying carpets.
They were not flying carpets.

They were piles of bloody diapers.
The Magi° stood around
Cleaning their nails with bayonets.   15
The old man gave little Mary Magdalene°

A broke piece of a mirror.
She hid in the church outhouse.
When she got thirsty she licked
the steam off the glass.   20

That leaves Joseph.° Poor Joseph,
Standing naked in the snow.
He only had a rat
To load his suitcases on.

The rat wouldn't run into its hole.   25
Even when the lights came on —
And the lights came on:
The floodlights in the guard towers.

Spleen: The seat or source in a person either of high spirit, courage, and resolute mind or of ill-nature, ill-humor, and irritable or peevish temper.   **1. The Virgin Mother:** Mary, the mother of Jesus.   **14. Magi:** The wise men from the East who visited the baby Jesus.   **16. Mary Magdalene:** A follower of Jesus who was present at his crucifixion and burial and who went to the tomb on Easter Sunday to anoint his body.   **21. Joseph:** The husband of Mary, the mother of Jesus.

Gary Soto b. 1952

The Elements of San Joaquin   [1977; rev. 1995]

for César Chávez°

Field

The wind sprays pale dirt into my mouth
The small, almost invisible scars
On my hands.

The pores in my throat and elbows
Have taken in a seed of dirt of their own.   5

After a day in the grape fields near Rolinda
A fine silt, washed by sweat,
Has settled into the lines
On my wrists and palms.

Already I am becoming the valley,   10
A soil that sprouts nothing.
For any of us.

Wind

A dry wind over the valley
Peeled mountains, grain by grain,
To small slopes, loose dirt   15
Where red ants tunnel.

The wind strokes
The skulls and spines of cattle
To white dust, to nothing,

Covers the spiked tracks of beetles,   20
Of tumbleweed, of sparrows
That pecked the ground for insects.

Evenings, when I am in the yard weeding,
The wind picks up the breath of my armpits
Like dust, swirls it   25
Miles away

    * * *

César Chávez: (1927–1993), Hispanic American labor leader and activist known for creating
the United Farm Workers and for leading a nationwide boycott of California table grapes in
1968 as part of an effort to achieve labor contracts for field workers.

And drops it
On the ear of a rabid dog,
And I take on another life.

Wind

When you got up this morning the sun   30
Blazed an hour in the sky,

A lizard hid
Under the curled leaves of manzanita°
And winked its dark lids.

Later, the sky grayed,   35
And the cold wind you breathed
Was moving under your skin and already far
From the small hives of your lungs.

Stars

At dusk the first stars appear.
Not one eager finger points toward them.   40
A little later the stars spread with the night
And an orange moon rises
To lead them, like a shepherd, toward dawn.

Sun

In June the sun is a bonnet of light
Coming up,   45
Little by little,
From behind a skyline of pine.

The pastures sway with fiddle-neck,
Tassels of foxtail.

At Piedra   50
A couple fish on the river's edge,
Their shadows deep against the water.
Above, in the stubbled slopes,
Cows climb down
As the heat rises   55
In a mist of blond locusts,
Returning to the valley.

---

33. manzanita: An evergreen shrub or small tree found in arid regions of the western United
States.

Rain

When autumn rains flatten sycamore leaves,
The tiny volcanos of dirt
Ants raised around their holes,   60
I should be out of work.

My silverware and stack of plates will go unused
Like the old, my two good slacks
Will smother under a growth of lint
And smell of the old dust   65
That rises
When the closet door opens or closes.

The skin of my belly will tighten like a belt
And there will be no reason for pockets.

Harvest

East of the sun's slant, in the vineyard that never failed,   70
A wind crossed my face, moving the dust
And a portion of my voice a step closer to a new year.

The sky went black in the ninth hour of rolling trays,
And in the distance ropes of rain dropped to pull me
From the thick harvest that was not mine.   75

Fog

If you go to your window
You will notice a fog drifting in.

The sun is no stronger than a flashlight.
Not all the sweaters
Hung in closets all summer   80

Could soak up this mist. The fog:
A mouth nibbling everything to its origin,
Pomegranate trees, stolen bicycles,

The string of lights at a used-car lot,
A Pontiac with scorched valves.   85

In Fresno the fog is passing
The young thief prying a window screen,
Graying my hair that falls
And goes unfound, my fingerprints
Slowly growing a fur of dust —   90

*   *   *

One hundred years from now
There should be no reason to believe
I lived.

Daybreak

In this moment when the light starts up
In the east and rubs   95
The horizon until it catches fire,

We enter the fields to hoe,
Row after row, among the small flags of onion,
Waving off the dragonflies
That ladder the air.   100

And tears the onions raise
Do not begin in your eyes but in ours,
In the salt blown
From one blister into another;

They begin in knowing   105
You will never waken to bear
The hour timed to a heart beat,
The wind pressing us closer to the ground.

When the season ends,
And the onions are unplugged from their sleep,   110
We won't forget what you failed to see,
And nothing will heal
Under the rain's broken fingers.

CD-ROM: Research Gary Soto in depth with cultural documents and multimedia resources on
LiterActive.

Wole Soyinka   b. 1934

Flowers for My Land   [1972]

From a distant
Shore they cry, Where
Are all the flowers gone?
I cannot tell
The gardens here are furrowed still and bare.   5

Death alike
We sow. Each novel horror
Whets inhuman appetites

I do not
Dare to think these bones will bloom tomorrow   10

Garlands
Of scavengers weigh
Heavy on human breasts
Such
Are flowers that fill the garden of decay   15

Seeking:
Voices of rain in sunshine
Blue kites on ivory-cloud
Towers
Smell of passing hands on mountain flowers   20

I saw:
Four steel kites, riders
On shrouded towers
Do you think
Their arms are spread to scatter mountain flowers?   25

Seeking: Truth
Seeds split and browse
In ordure, corruption. From
Beds of worms
Ivory towers uphold the charnel-house   30

I know
Of flowers unseen, and they
Distil beatific dawns
But tares
Withhold possession of our mangled lawns   35

Visions pall
Realities invade
Our innermost sanctuaries
Oil erupts
Upon the altar, casts an evil shade   40

Hooded hands
Knock upon our doors
We say, let them have place
And offer
Ours in hope to make a common cause   45

It cannot be!
Hands of slag, fingers
Of spike, they press to full
Possession.
Creepers, climbers thrive beneath their rule   50

*   *   *

Slogans
Louder than empty barrels
And more barren, a rattle
In cups of beggary
Monkeys in livery dance to barrel organs   55

Break who can
The yet encroaching ring
Their hands are tainted, their breath
Withers all
They feed their thoughts upon the bounty of death   60

I traced
A dew-lane on the sun-
flower leaf; a hailstone
Burning, blew
A trap-door on my lane for falling through   65

These buds
That burst upon our prayers
Diffuse an equal essence
Will for ill
As others their atomic efflorescence   70

Alienates
Of heart from land, outcasts
Of toadstool blooms, the coral
Is a grim
Historic flower, a now and future moral   75

Come, let us
With that mangled kind
Make pact, no less
Against the lesser
Leagues of death, and mutilators of the mind.   80

Take Justice
In your hands who can
Or dare. Insensate sword
Of Power
Outherods Herod and the law's outlawed   85

Sun-beacons
On every darkened shore
Orphans of the world
Ignite! Draw
Your fuel of pain from earth's sated core.   90

Edmund Spenser 1552–1599

One day I wrote her name upon the strand   [1595]

One day I wrote her name upon the strand,
But came the waves and washèd it away:
Again I wrote it with a second hand,
But came the tide, and made my pains his prey.
"Vain man," said she, "that dost in vain assay,   5
A mortal thing so to immortalize,
For I myself shall like to this decay,
And eek° my name be wipèd out likewise."   *also*
"Not so," quod° I, "let baser things devise,   *quoth (said)*
To die in dust, but you shall live by fame: 10
My verse your virtues rare shall eternize,
And in the heavens write your glorious name.
Where whenas death shall all the world subdue,
Our love shall live, and later life renew."

Wallace Stevens 1879–1955

The Emperor of Ice-Cream   [1923]

Call the roller of big cigars,
The muscular one, and bid him whip
In kitchen cups concupiscent curds.
Let the wenches dawdle in such dress
As they are used to wear, and let the boys   5
Bring flowers in last month's newspapers.
Let be be finale of seem.
The only emperor is the emperor of ice-cream.

Take from the dresser of deal,
Lacking the three glass knobs, that sheet   10
On which she embroidered fantails once
And spread it so as to cover her face.
If her horny feet protrude, they come
To show how cold she is, and dumb.
Let the lamp affix its beam.   15
The only emperor is the emperor of ice-cream.

Virgil Suárez b. 1962

Las tendederas/Clotheslines   [1999]

The day my mother stood in the kitchen
    & cooked all the turtle meat from the turtles
        I helped my father kill & she screamed

when the sizzling chunks started to jump
    & we rushed in to check on what was up   5
        & my father told her that it was okay,

that turtle meat always did that when fried
    & then we got back to the slaughter of the pig
        my father had bartered a dozen rabbits for

& when we finally cornered it at the end   10
    of the walkway by the side of the house,
        next to the chicken coop, it squealed & set

the chickens all aflutter & a cloud of dust
    rose, a combination of dirt & dung
        & my father got something in his eyes   15

& he laughed & I sneezed & sneezed
    & when the chickens settled down the pig
        snuck by us & ran back to the patio,

knocking on its way the stick holding up
    my mother's clothesline & all the laundry   20
        drying fell on the dirt & the pig trampled

it & it made my father so angry he took
    the wire from the clothesline, looped it over
        the pig's neck & when the pig stood still

my father reeled it in & with a broom handle   25
    he applied a tourniquet to the pig
        & with a final squeal it dropped on its front

knees, choked by the wire which cut so deep
    blood spurted onto everything, mainly
        my mother's washed clothes; the pig stood   30

still long enough for my father to plunge
    a knife into its heart. There we stood, my
        father & I, out of breath, he with bloodied

*   *   *

arms & myself with the pangs of excitement
 loose in my chest. Amazed by the slaughter   35
  of so many animals in one afternoon, I stood

there quiet, caught in the splendor of my mother's
 once-white laundry. My father put the clothesline
  back & one by one I picked all the garments

from the ground & carried them to my mother.   40
 With a cigarette in his mouth, my father leaned
  against the door frame, a satisfied look on his face,

a smile on his lips. This was Havana in 1968
 & I have never seen my father more content.
  Now when I travel the open roads of the U.S.,   45

I look across the expanse of peoples' yards
 & when I see clotheslines, laundry-heavy & bowed,
  swaying in the breeze & the fact that someone

worked so hard at putting it up & out, I think
 about how much debris time & distance   50
  have kicked up into my eyes.

Jonathan Swift   1667–1745

A Description of the Morning   [1709]

Now hardly here and there a hackney-coach
Appearing, showed the ruddy morn's approach.
Now Betty from her master's bed had flown,
And softly stole to discompose her own;
The slip-shod 'prentice from his master's door   5
Had pared the dirt and sprinkled round the floor.
Now Moll had whirled her mop with dext'rous airs,
Prepared to scrub the entry and the stairs.
The youth with broomy stumps° began to trace   *worn broom*
The kennel-edge,° where wheels had worn the place.   *gutter* 10
The small-coal man° was heard with cadence deep,   *coal vendor*
Till drowned in shriller notes of chimney-sweep:
Duns° at his lordship's gate began to meet;   *debt collectors*
And brickdust Moll° had screamed through half the street

---

14. brickdust Moll: Woman selling powdered brick.

The turnkey now his flock returning sees,   15
Duly let out a-nights to steal for fees:
The watchful bailiffs take their silent stands,
And schoolboys lag with satchels in their hands.

Mary Tall Mountain   b. 1918

Matmiya   [1981]

for my Grandmother

I see you sitting
Implanted by roots
Coiled deep from your thighs.
Roots, flesh red, centuries pale.
Hairsprings wound tight   5
Through fertile earthscapes
Where each layer feeds the next
Into depths immutable.

Though you must rise, must
Move large and slow   10
When it is time, O my
Gnarled mother-vine, ancient
As vanished ages,
Your spirit remains
Nourished,   15
Nourishing me.

I see your figure wrapped in skins
Curved into a mound of earth
Holding your rich dark roots.
Matmiya,   20
I see you sitting.

Alfred, Lord Tennyson   1809–1892

Ulysses°   [1833]

It little profits that an idle king,
By this still hearth, among these barren crags,
Matched with an agèd wife, I mete and dole
Unequal laws° unto a savage race,
That hoard, and sleep, and feed, and know not me.   5

I cannot rest from travel; I will drink
Life to the lees. All times I have enjoyed
Greatly, have suffered greatly, both with those
That loved me, and alone; on shore, and when
Through scudding drifts° the rainy Hyades°   10
Vexed the dim sea. I am become a name;
For always roaming with a hungry heart
Much have I seen and known — cities of men
And manners, climates, councils, governments,
Myself not least, but honored of them all —   15
And drunk delight of battle with my peers,
Far on the ringing plains of windy Troy.
I am a part of all that I have met;
Yet all experience is an arch wherethrough
Gleams that untraveled world whose margin fades   20
Forever and forever when I move.
How dull it is to pause, to make an end,
To rust unburnished, not to shine in use!
As though to breathe were life! Life piled on life
Were all too little, and of one to me   25
Little remains; but every hour is saved
From that eternal silence, something more,
A bringer of new things; and vile it were

Ulysses (the Roman form of Odysseus): The hero of Homer's epic *The Odyssey,* which tells the story of Odysseus's adventures on his voyage back to his home, the little island of Ithaca, after he and the other Greek heroes had defeated Troy. It took Odysseus ten years to reach Ithaca, the small, rocky island of which he was king, where his wife (Penelope) and son (Telemachus) had been waiting for him. Upon his return he defeated the suitors who had been trying to marry the faithful Penelope, and he resumed the kingship and his old ways of life. Here Homer's story ends, but in Canto 26 of the *Inferno* Dante extended the story: Odysseus eventually became restless and dissatisfied with his settled life and decided to return to the sea and sail west, into the unknown sea, and seek whatever adventures he might find there. Tennyson's poem amplifies the speech delivered in Dante's poem as Ulysses challenges his men to accompany him on this new voyage.   **3–4. mete . . . race:** Administer inadequate (unequal to what is needed) laws to a still somewhat lawless race.   **10. scudding drifts:** Wind-driven spray; **Hyades:** Five stars in the constellation Taurus whose rising was assumed would be followed by rain.

For some three suns° to store and hoard myself,   *years*
And this gray spirit yearning in desire   30
To follow knowledge like a sinking star,
Beyond the utmost bound of human thought.

    This is my son, mine own Telemachus,
To whom I leave the scepter and the isle —
Well-loved of me, discerning to fulfill   35
This labor, by slow prudence to make mild
A rugged people, and through soft degrees
Subdue them to the useful and the good.
Most blameless is he, centered in the sphere
Of common duties, decent not to fail   40
In offices of tenderness, and pay
Meet adoration to my household gods,
When I am gone. He works his work, I mine.

    There lies the port; the vessel puffs her sail;
There gloom the dark, broad seas. My mariners,   45
Souls that have toiled, and wrought, and thought with me —
That ever with a frolic welcome took
The thunder and the sunshine, and opposed
Free hearts, free foreheads — you and I are old;
Old age hath yet his honor and his toil.   50
Death closes all; but something ere the end,
Some work of noble note, may yet be done,
Not unbecoming men that strove with Gods.
The lights begin to twinkle from the rocks;
The long day wanes; the slow moon climbs; the deep   55
Moans round with many voices. Come, my friends,
'Tis not too late to seek a newer world.
Push off, and sitting well in order smite
The sounding furrows; for my purpose holds
To sail beyond the sunset, and the baths°   60
Of all the western stars, until I die.
It may be that the gulfs will wash us down;
It may be we shall touch the Happy Isles,°
And see the great Achilles,° whom we knew.
Though much is taken, much abides; and though   65
We are not now that strength which in old days
Moved earth and heaven, that which we are, we are —

---

60. **baths:** The outer river or ocean surrounding the flat earth, in Greek cosmology, into which the stars descended upon setting.   63. **Happy Isles:** The Islands of the Blessed, or Elysian Fields, in Greek myth, which lay in the western seas beyond the Strait of Gibraltar and were the abode of heroes after death.   64. **Achilles:** The hero of the Greeks, and Odysseus's comrade, in Homer's *Iliad*.

One equal temper of heroic hearts,
Made weak by time and fate, but strong in will
To strive, to seek, to find, and not to yield.   70

Dylan Thomas 1914–1953

Do not go gentle into that good night   [1952]

Do not go gentle into that good night,
Old age should burn and rave at close of day;
Rage, rage against the dying of the light.

Though wise men at their end know dark is right,
Because their words had forked no lightning they   5
Do not go gentle into that good night.

Good men, the last wave by, crying how bright
Their frail deeds might have danced in a green bay,
Rage, rage against the dying of the light.

Wild men who caught and sang the sun in flight,   10
And learn, too late, they grieved it on its way,
Do not go gentle into that good night.

Grave men, near death, who see with blinding sight
Blind eyes could blaze like meteors and be gay,
Rage, rage against the dying of the light.   15

And you, my father, there on the sad height,
Curse, bless, me now with your fierce tears, I pray.
Do not go gentle into that good night.
Rage, rage against the dying of the light.

CD-ROM: Research Dylan Thomas in depth with cultural documents and multimedia resources on
LiterActive.

Jean Toomer 1894–1967

Face   [1923]

Hair—
silver-gray,
like streams of stars,
Brows —
recurved canoes   5

quivered by the ripples blown by pain,
Her eyes —
mist of tears
condensing on the flesh below
And her channeled muscles   10
are cluster grapes of sorrow
purple in the evening sun
nearly ripe for worms.

Quincy Troupe   b. 1943

Snake-Back Solo 2   [1979]

for Louis Armstrong, Steve Cannon, Miles Davis, & Eugene Redmond

with the music up high, boogalooin'
bass down way way low
up & under, eye come slidin' on in, mojoin'
on in, spacin' on in on a riff full of rain
riffin' on in full of rain & pain   5
spacin' on in on a sound
like coltrane°

& my metaphor is a blues
hot pain-dealin' blues, is a blues
axin' guitar voices, whiskey broken, niggah   10
deep in the heart, is a blues in a glass filled with rain
is a blues in the dark
slurred voices of straight bourbon
is a blues, dagger stuck off in the heart
of night, moanin' like bessie smith°   15
is a blues filling up, glooming under
the wings of darkness, is a blues
is a blues, a blues

& looking through the heart
a dream can become a raindrop window to see through   20
can become a window, to see through this moment
to see yourself hanging around the dark
to see through this moment
& see yourself as a river catching rain there
feeding time there with your movement   25

---

7. **coltrane:** John Coltrane (1926–1967), a well-known jazz saxophonist.   15. **bessie smith:**
Bessie Smith (1894–1937), an influential classic blues singer of the 1920s.

to wash time clean as a window
to see through to the other side
while outside windows, flames trigger
the deep explosion; time steals rivers that move on
& stay where they are, inside yourself, moving   30
soon there will be daylight
breaking the darkness
to point the way home, soon there will be
voices breaking music, to come on home by
down & upriver, breaking the darkness   35
to come on home by, stroking with the music
swimming upriver
the sound of louie armstrong
swinging upriver, carrying river boats
upstream, on the back of his honky-tonk jazz rhythms   40
licks of vibratos climbing up from new orleans, close heat & rain
swimming upriver, up the river of mud & rain
satchmo° breaking the darkness, his cornet speaking
flames bouncing off the river's back
at sunset, snake river's back, big muddy, mississippi   45
up from naw'leans, to east st. louis, illinois
cross river from st. louis
to come on home by, upriver now
the music swims, breaking silence to land
in miles dewey davis's° horn, then leap off again   50
& fly up in space to create
new music in time with place
to create new music in time with this place
to pass it on, pass it on
pass it on, into space   55

where eye catch it now, inside myself
inside this poem eye am (w)riting here
where eye am soloing, now
soloing of rivers catching rains & dreams & sunsets
solo of 'trane tracks screaming through the night, stark   60
a dagger in the heart
solo of bird° spreading wings for the wind
to lift up by, solo of miles, pied piper, prince of darkness
river rain voice now, eye solo at the root of the flower
leaning against promises of shadows   65
solo of bones leering beneath the river's snake-back

---

43. satchmo: Louis "Satchmo" Armstrong (1901–1971), American jazz trumpeter.   **50. miles dewey davis:** Miles Davis (1926–1991), jazz trumpet player, composer, and bandleader.
62. bird: Charlie "Bird" Parker (1920–1955), jazz saxophonist and composer.

solo of trees cut down by double-bladed axes
river rain voice now eye solo
of the human condition, solo of the matrix
mojoin' new blues, river rain voice   70
now, eye solo   solo
solo now to become the wings & eyes of an owl
to see through this darkness, eye solo now
to become a simple skybreak shattering darkness
to become lightning's jagged-sword-like thunder   75
eye solo now to become, to become
eye solo now to become

with the music up high
up way, way high, boogalooin' bass down
way, way low   80
up & under, eye come slidin' on in, mojoin' on in
spacin' on in on a poetic riff full of rain
river riff full of rain & trains & dreams
lookin' through ajax°-clean windows
eye come slidin' on through   85
these blues metaphors
riffin' on in through rain & pain
ridin' on a tongue of poetic flame
leanin' & glidin', eye solo   solo
loopin' & flyin' eye solo now   solo   90

---

84. **ajax:** A brand name for household cleaning products.

Gerald Vizenor b. 1934

Shaman Breaks   [1988]

1

colonists
unearth their wealth
and tease
the old stone man
over the breaks   5

moths batter
the cold windows
their light
is not our day

*   *   *

leaves abide the seasons   10
the last crows
smarten the poplars

2

tourists
discover their ruins
and mimic   15
the old stone woman
over the breaks

nasturtiums
dress the barbed wire
fences down   20
down to the wild sea

magnolias
bloom under a whole moon
words fall apart

3

soldiers   25
bleach the landscapes
hound the shamans

wild stories
break from the stones

Derek Walcott   b. 1930

Sea Grapes   [1976]

That sail which leans on light,
tired of islands,
a schooner beating up the Caribbean

for home, could be Odysseus,°
home-bound on the Aegean;   5
that father and husband's

*   *   *

4. **Odysseus:** For background, see page 739. Princess Nausicaa (line 8) fell in love with Odysseus when he was carried by a storm to Phaiacia; he could have married her and stayed there, but he chose to go home (responsibility) rather than to enjoy an indulgent life with her (obsession). Odysseus blinded Polyphemus (line 16), a giant one-eyed Cyclops, who held him prisoner; as Odysseus escaped, Polyphemus threw great rocks in front of his boat to wash it back to shore. The *Odyssey* was written in hexameter verse (line 17).

longing, under gnarled sour grapes, is
like the adulterer hearing Nausicaa's name
in every gull's outcry.

This brings nobody peace. The ancient war   10
between obsession and responsibility
will never finish and has been the same

for the sea-wanderer or the one on shore
now wriggling on his sandals to walk home,
since Troy sighed its last flame,   15

and the blind giant's boulder heaved the trough
from whose groundswell the great hexameters come
to the conclusions of exhausted surf.

The classics can console. But not enough.

James Welch b. 1940

Christmas Comes to Moccasin Flat   [1976]

Christmas comes like this: Wise men
unhurried, candles bought on credit (poor price
for calves), warriors face down in wine sleep.
Winds cheat to pull heat from smoke.

Friends sit in chinked cabins, stare out   5
plastic windows and wait for commodities.
Charlie Blackbird, twenty miles from church
and bar, stabs his fire with flint.

When drunks drain radiators for love
or need, chiefs eat snow and talk of change,   10
an urge to laugh pounding their ribs.
Elk play games in high country.

Medicine Woman, clay pipe and twist tobacco,
calls each blizzard by name and predicts
five o'clock by spitting at her television.   15
Children lean into her breath to beg a story:

Something about honor and passion,
warriors back with meat and song,
a peculiar evening star, quick vision of birth.
Blackbird feeds his fire. Outside, a quick 30 below. 20

Roberta Hill Whiteman   b. 1947

The White Land   [1984]

When Orion° straddled his apex of sky,
over the white land we lingered loving.
The River Eridanus° flickered, foretelling
tropical waves and birds arrayed
in feathers of sunset, but we didn't waste   5
that prickling dark.

Not a dog barked our arrival before dawn.
Only in sleep did I drift vagabond
and suffer the patterns that constantly state
time has no time. Fate is a warlord.   10
That morning I listened to your long breath
for decades.

That morning you said bears
fell over the white land. Leaving their lair
in thick polar fur, they roused our joy   15
by leaving no footprint. Fat ones fell headlong,
but most of them danced, then without quarrel,
balanced on branches.

I couldn't breathe in the roar of that plane,
flying me back to a wooded horizon.   20
Regular rhythms bridge my uneven sleep.
What if the wind in the white land keeps you?
The dishwater's luminous; a truck
grinds down the street.

---

1. Orion: Prominent constellation located on the celestial equator.   **3. River Eridanus:** Large
southern constellation stretching southwest from Orion, identified with a river because of its
long winding shape.

Walt Whitman   1819–1892

From Song of Myself   [*1855;* 1891–1892]°

1

I celebrate myself, and sing myself,
And what I assume you shall assume,
For every atom belonging to me as good belongs to you.

I loafe and invite my soul,
I lean and loafe at my ease observing a spear of summer grass.   5

My tongue, every atom of my blood, form'd from this soil, this air,
Born here of parents born here from parents the same, and their
    parents the same,
I, now thirty-seven years old in perfect health begin,
Hoping to cease not till death.

Creeds and schools in abeyance,   10
Retiring back a while suffced at what they are, but never forgotten,
I harbor for good or bad, I permit to speak at every hazard,
Nature without check with original energy.

7

Has any one supposed it lucky to be born?
I hasten to inform him or her it is just as lucky to die, and I know it.

I pass death with the dying and birth with the new-wash'd babe,
    and am not contain'd between my hat and boots,
And peruse manifold objects, no two alike and every one good,
The earth good and the stars good, and their adjuncts all good.   135

I am not an earth nor an adjunct of an earth,
I am the mate and companion of people, all just as immortal and
    fathomless as myself,
(They do not know how immortal, but I know.)

Every kind for itself and its own, for me mine male and female,
For me those that have been boys and that love women,   140
For me the man that is proud and feels how it stings to be slighted,

---

Date: The poem was first published in 1855 as an untitled section of *Leaves of Grass*. It was a rough, rude, and vigorous example of antebellum American cultural politics and free verse experimentation. The version excerpted here, from the sixth edition (1891–1892), is much longer, more carefully crafted, and more conventionally punctuated.

For me the sweet-heart and old maid, for me mothers and the
    mothers of mothers,
For me lips that have smiled, eyes that have shed tears,
For me children and the begetters of children.

Undrape! you are not guilty to me, nor stale nor discarded,   145
I see through the broadcloth and gingham whether or no,
And am around, tenacious, acquisitive, tireless, and cannot be
    shaken away.

21

I am the poet of the Body and I am the poet of the Soul,
The pleasures of heaven are with me and the pains of hell are
    with me,
The first I graft and increase upon myself, the latter I translate into
    a new tongue.

I am the poet of the woman the same as the man,   425
And I say it is as great to be a woman as to be a man,
And I say there is nothing greater than the mother of men.

I chant the chant of dilation or pride,
We have had ducking and deprecating about enough,
I show that size is only development.   430

Have you outstript the rest? are you the President?
It is a trifle, they will more than arrive there every one, and still
    pass on.

I am he that walks with the tender and growing night,
I call to the earth and sea half-held by the night.

Press close bare-bosom'd night — press close magnetic nourishing
    night!   435
Night of south winds — night of the large few stars!
Still nodding night — mad naked summer night.

Smile O voluptuous cool-breath'd earth!
Earth of the slumbering and liquid trees!
Earth of departed sunset — earth of the mountains misty-topt!   440
Earth of the vitreous pour of the full moon just tinged with blue!
Earth of shine and dark mottling the tide of the river!
Earth of the limpid gray of clouds brighter and clearer for my sake!
Far-swooping elbow'd earth — rich apple-blossom'd earth!
Smile, for your lover comes.   445

Prodigal, you have given me love — therefore I to you give love!
O unspeakable passionate love.

24

Walt Whitman, a kosmos, of Manhattan the son,
Turbulent, fleshy, sensual, eating, drinking and breeding,
No sentimentalist, no stander above men and women or apart
    from them,
No more modest than immodest.   500

Unscrew the locks from the doors!
Unscrew the doors themselves from their jambs!

Whoever degrades another degrades me,
And whatever is done or said returns at last to me.

Through me the afflatus° surging and surging, through me the
    current and index.   505

I speak the pass-word primeval, I give the sign of democracy,
By God! I will accept nothing which all cannot have their counter-
    part of on the same terms.

Through me many long dumb voices,
Voices of the interminable generations of prisoners and slaves,
Voices of the diseas'd and despairing and of thieves and dwarfs,   510
Voices of cycles of preparation and accretion,
And of the threads that connect the stars, and of wombs and of
    the father-stuff,
And of the rights of them the others are down upon.

47

I am the teacher of athletes,
He that by me spreads a wider breast than my own proves the
    width of my own,   1235
He most honors my style who learns under it to destroy the teacher.

The boy I love, the same becomes a man not through derived power,
    but in his own right,
Wicked rather than virtuous out of conformity or fear,
Fond of his sweetheart, relishing well his steak,
Unrequited love or a slight cutting him worse than sharp steel cuts, 1240
First-rate to ride, to fight, to hit the bull's eye, to sail a skiff, to sing
    a song or play on the banjo,
Preferring scars and the beard and faces pitted with small-pox over
    all latherers,
And those well-tann'd to those that keep out of the sun.

*   *   *

---

505. **afflatus:** Inspiration, from Latin meaning "to blow on."

I teach straying from me, yet who can stray from me?
I follow you whoever you are from the present hour,   1245
My words itch at your ears till you understand them.

I do not say these things for a dollar or to fill up the time while I
    wait for a boat,
(It is you talking just as much as myself, I act as the tongue of you,
Tied in your mouth, in mine it begins to be loosen'd.)

I swear I will never again mention love or death inside a house,   1250
And I swear I will never translate myself at all, only to him or her
    who privately stays with me in the open air.

If you would understand me go to the heights or water-shore,
The nearest gnat is an explanation, and a drop or motion of waves
    a key,
The maul, the oar, the hand-saw, second my words.

No shutter'd room or school can commune with me,   1255
But roughs and little children better than they.

The young mechanic is closest to me, he knows me well,
The woodman that takes his axe and jug with him shall take me
    with him all day,
The farm-boy ploughing in the field feels good at the sound of my
    voice,
In vessels that sail my words sail, I go with fishermen and seamen
    and love them.   1260

The soldier camp'd or upon the march is mine,
On the night ere the pending battle many seek me, and I do not fail
    them,
On that solemn night (it may be their last) those that know me
    seek me.

My face rubs to the hunter's face when he lies down alone in his
    blanket,
The driver thinking of me does not mind the jolt of his wagon,   1265
The young mother and old mother comprehend me,
The girl and the wife rest the needle a moment and forget where
    they are,
They and all would resume what I have told them.

52

The spotted hawk swoops by and accuses me, he complains of my
    gab and my loitering.

*   *   *

I too am not a bit tamed, I too am untranslatable,
I sound my barbaric yawp over the roofs of the world.

The last scud of day holds back for me,
It flings my likeness after the rest and true as any on the shadow'd
    wilds,   1335
It coaxes me to the vapor and the dusk.

I depart as air, I shake my white locks at the runaway sun,
I effuse my flesh in eddies, and drift it in lacy jags.

I bequeath myself to the dirt to grow from the grass I love,
If you want me again look for me under your boot-soles.   1340

You will hardly know who I am or what I mean,
But I shall be good health to you nevertheless,
And filter and fibre your blood.

Failing to fetch me at first keep encouraged,
Missing me one place search another,   1345
I stop somewhere waiting for you.

CD-ROM: Research Walt Whitman in depth with cultural documents and multimedia resources on
LiterActive.

Richard Wilbur   b. 1921

Love Calls Us to the Things of This World   [1956]

    The eyes open to a cry of pulleys,
And spirited from sleep, the astounded soul
Hangs for a moment bodiless and simple
As false dawn.
                Outside the open window
The morning air is all awash with angels.   5

    Some are in bed-sheets, some are in blouses,
Some are in smocks: but truly there they are.
Now they are rising together in calm swells
Of halcyon feeling, filling whatever they wear
With the deep joy of their impersonal breathing;   10

    Now they are flying in place, conveying
The terrible speed of their omnipresence, moving
And staying like white water; and now of a sudden
They swoon down into so rapt a quiet

That nobody seems to be there.
The soul shrinks   15

    From all that it is about to remember,
From the punctual rape of every blessèd day,
And cries,
        "Oh, let there be nothing on earth but laundry,
Nothing but rosy hands in the rising steam
And clear dances done in the sight of heaven."   20

    Yet, as the sun acknowledges
With a warm look the world's hunks and colors,
The soul descends once more in bitter love
To accept the waking body, saying now
In a changed voice as the man yawns and rises,   25

    "Bring them down from their ruddy gallows;
Let there be clean linen for the backs of thieves;
Let lovers go fresh and sweet to be undone,
And the heaviest nuns walk in a pure floating
Of dark habits,
        keeping their difficult balance."   30

William Carlos Williams   1883–1963

Spring and All   [1923]

By the road to the contagious hospital°
under the surge of the blue
mottled clouds driven from the
northeast—a cold wind. Beyond, the
waste of broad, muddy fields   5
brown with dried weeds, standing and fallen

patches of standing water
the scattering of tall trees

All along the road the reddish
purplish, forked, upstanding, twiggy   10
stuff of bushes and small trees
with dead, brown leaves under them
leafless vines—

        *   *   *

---

1. **contagious hospital:** A hospital for the treatment of contagious diseases.

Lifeless in appearance, sluggish
dazed spring approaches — 15

They enter the new world naked,
cold, uncertain of all
save that they enter. All about them
the cold, familiar wind —

Now the grass, tomorrow 20
the stiff curl of wildcarrot leaf

One by one objects are defined —
It quickens: clarity, outline of leaf

But now the stark dignity of
entrance — Still, the profound change 25
has come upon them: rooted, they
grip down and begin to awaken

Nellie Wong   b. 1934

Grandmother's Song   [1977]

Grandmothers sing their song
Blinded by the suns' rays
Grandchildren for whom they long
For pomelo°-golden days   *grapefruit*

Blinded by the sun's rays   5
Gold bracelets, opal rings
For pomelo-golden days
Tiny fingers, ancient things

Gold bracelets, opal rings
Sprinkled with Peking dust   10
Tiny fingers, ancient things
So young they'll never rust

Sprinkled with Peking dust
To dance in fields of mud
So young they'll never rust   15
Proud as if of royal blood

To dance in fields of mud
Or peel shrimp for pennies a day
Proud as if of royal blood
Coins and jade to put away   20

*   *   *

Or peel shrimp for pennies a day
Seaweed washes up the shore
Coins and jade to put away
A camphor chest is home no more

Seaweed washes up the shore   25
Bound feet struggle to loosen free
A camphor chest is home no more
A foreign tongue is learned at three

Bound feet struggle to loosen free
Grandchildren for whom they long   30
A foreign tongue is learned at three
Grandmothers sing their song

William Wordsworth 1770–1850

The world is too much with us   [1807]

The world is too much with us; late and soon,
Getting and spending, we lay waste our powers;
Little we see in Nature that is ours;
We have given our hearts away, a sordid boon!°   *gift*
This Sea that bares her bosom to the moon,   5
The winds that will be howling at all hours,
And are up-gathered now like sleeping flowers,
For this, for everything, we are out of tune;
It moves us not. — Great God! I'd rather be
A Pagan suckled in a creed outworn;   10
So might I, standing on this pleasant lea,°   *open meadow*
Have glimpses that would make me less forlorn;
Have sight of Proteus° rising from the sea;
Or hear old Triton° blow his wreathèd° horn.

---

13. Proteus: In Greek mythology, a sea god who could change his own form or appearance at will.   **14. Triton:** A Greek sea god with the head and upper body of a man and the tail of a fish, usually pictured as playing on a conch-shell trumpet; **wreathèd:** Curved.

Sir Thomas Wyatt   1503–1542

They flee from me   [from an undated manuscript]

They flee from me, that sometime did me seek,
With naked foot stalking in my chamber.
I have seen them, gentle, tame, and meek,
That now are wild, and do not remember
That sometime they put themselves in danger   5
To take bread at my hand; and now they range,
Busily seeking with a continual change.

Thanked be fortune it hath been otherwise,
Twenty times better; but once in special,
In thin array, after a pleasant guise,°   *manner of dress*   10
When her loose gown from her shoulders did fall,
And she me caught in her arms long and small,°   *slender*
Therewithall sweetly did me kiss
And softly said, "Dear heart,° how like you this?"

It was no dream, I lay broad waking.   15
But all is turned, thorough° my gentleness,   *through*
Into a strange fashion of forsaking;
And I have leave to go, of° her goodness,   *out of (motivated by)*
And she also to use newfangleness.
But since that I so kindly° am served,   20
I fain would know what she hath deserved.

---

14. Dear heart (pun): Heart, and hart (deer).   **20. kindly** (pun): Graciously (ironic), and
"in kind"; i.e., in a way typical of female nature.

John Yau   b. 1950

Chinese Villanelle   [1979]

I have been with you, and I have thought of you
Once the air was dry and drenched with light
I was like a lute filling the room with description

We watched glum clouds reject their shape
We dawdled near a fountain, and listened   5
I have been with you, and I have thought of you

Like a river worthy of its gown
And like a mountain worthy of its insolence . . .
Why am I like a lute left with only description

How does one cut an axe handle with an axe   10
What shall I do to tell you all my thoughts
When I have been with you, and thought of you

A pelican sits on a dam, while a duck
Folds its wings again; the song does not melt
I remember you looking at me without description   15

Perhaps a king's business is never finished,
Though "perhaps" implies a different beginning
I have been with you, and I have thought of you
Now I am a lute filled with this wandering description

William Butler Yeats   1865–1939

The Lake Isle of Innisfree   [1892]

I will arise and go now, and go to Innisfree,
And a small cabin build there, of clay and wattles made:
Nine bean-rows will I have there, a hive for the honey-bee,
And live alone in the bee-loud glade.

And I shall have some peace there, for peace comes dropping slow,   5
Dropping from the veils of the morning to where the cricket sings;
There midnight's all a glimmer, and noon a purple glow,
And evening full of the linnet's wings.

I will arise and go now, for always night and day
I hear lake water lapping with low sounds by the shore;   10
While I stand on the roadway, or on the pavements grey,
I hear it in the deep heart's core.

William Butler Yeats

The Second Coming°   [1921]

Turning and turning in the widening gyre
The falcon cannot hear the falconer;
Things fall apart; the centre cannot hold;
Mere anarchy is loosed upon the world,
The blood-dimmed tide is loosed, and everywhere   5
The ceremony of innocence is drowned;
The best lack all conviction, while the worst
Are full of passionate intensity.

Surely some revelation is at hand;
Surely the Second Coming is at hand.   10
The Second Coming! Hardly are those words out
When a vast image out of *Spiritus Mundi*°
Troubles my sight: somewhere in sands of the desert
A shape with lion body and the head of a man,
A gaze blank and pitiless as the sun,   15
Is moving its slow thighs, while all about it
Reel shadows of the indignant desert birds.
The darkness drops again; but now I know
That twenty centuries of stony sleep
Were vexed to nightmare by a rocking cradle,   20
And what rough beast, its hour come round at last,
Slouches towards Bethlehem to be born?

The Second Coming: Alludes to Matthew 24:3–44, on the return of Christ at the end of the present age. Yeats viewed history as a series of 2,000-year cycles (imaged as gyres, cone-shaped motions). The birth of Christ in Bethlehem brought to an end the cycle that ran from the Babylonians through the Greeks and Romans. The approach of the year 2000, then, anticipated for Yeats the end of another era (the Christian age). Yeats wrote this poem shortly after the Russian Revolution of 1917 (lines 4–8), which may have confirmed his sense of imminent change and of a new beginning of an unpredictable nature (Yeats expected the new era to be violent and despotic).   **12. *Spiritus Mundi*:** Latin, "the spirit of the universe." Yeats believed in a Great Memory, a universal storehouse of symbolic images from the past. Individuals, drawing on it for images, are put in touch with the soul of the universe.

CD-ROM: Research William Butler Yeats in depth with cultural documents and multimedia resources on *LiterActive*.

Al Young b. 1939

A Dance for Ma Rainey°   [1969]

I'm going to be just like you, Ma
Rainey this monday morning
clouds puffing up out of my head
like those balloons
that float above the faces of white people   5
in the funnypapers

I'm going to hover in the corners
of the world, Ma
& sing from the bottom of hell
up to the tops of high heaven   10
& send out scratchless waves of yellow
& brown & that basic black honey
misery

I'm going to cry so sweet
& so low   15
& so dangerous,
Ma,
that the message is going to reach you
back in 1922
where you shimmer   20
snaggle-toothed
perfumed &
powdered
in your bauble beads

hair pressed & tied back   25
throbbing with that sick pain
I know
& hide so well
that pain that blues
jives the world with   30
aching to be heard
that downness
that bottomlessness
first felt by some stolen delta nigger
swamped under with redblooded american agony;   35
reduced to the sheer shit
of existence

Ma Rainey: Gertrude "Ma" Rainey (1886–1939), American singer known as the "Mother of the Blues."

that bred
& battered us all,
Ma,   40
the beautiful people
our beautiful brave black people
who no longer need to jazz
or sing to themselves in murderous vibrations
or play the veins of their strong tender arms   45
with needles
to prove we're still here

Ray A. Young Bear   b. 1950

From the Spotted Night   [1990]

In the blizzard
while chopping wood
the mystical whistler
beckons my attention.
Once there were longhouses   5
here. A village.
In the abrupt spring floods
swimmers retrieved our belief.
So their spirit remains.
From the spotted night   10
distant jets transform
into fireflies who float
towards me like incandescent
snowflakes.
The leather shirt   15
which is suspended
on a wire hanger
above the bed's headboard
is humanless; yet when one
stands outside the house,   20
the strenuous sounds
of dressers and boxes
being moved can be heard.
We believe someone wears
the shirt and rearranges   25
the heavy furniture,
although nothing
is actually changed.
Unlike the Plains Indian shirts

which repelled lead bullets,   30
ricocheting from them
in fiery sparks,
this shirt is the means;
this shirt *is* the bullet.

READING POEMS IN TRANSLATION

American humorist James Thurber was approached once by a French-man who said to him, "I've read you both in English and in French, and frankly, I prefer the translation." Thurber replied, "Yes, I know. I always lose something in the original."

What is the difference between the original and the translated version of any work? We often hear that something is, in the words of the popular 2003 film, "lost in translation." According to Robert Frost, in an often-quoted line, "Poetry is what gets lost in translation." Or is something gained? One thing is certain: The debate over translations of works has been going on for ages, and there is no end in sight to the discussion.

What are some of the issues? Some say that literary texts should be read only in the language in which they were originally written. They argue that "capturing" or recreating a work of art through translation is impossible. The only way to read and understand and truthfully experience and appreciate a work of literary art is to learn the language it was written in.

Provocative political agendas can be connected to the work of translation. Some people argue that unless one is from or deeply immersed in the culture underlying the original work, one has no right translating. Others say that one at least must be fluent in the language of the original; not to be is at the very least an act of disrespect. And yet translations are made by people who hardly know the language, who rely heavily on a lexicon.

Another danger claimed for translation is that the translator can readily commit an act of cultural appropriation or impose her or his own cultural influences or beliefs on those of the original, twisting the meaning, intent, or effect. Yet others ask, how else, without translation and without learning every language on earth, can we enrich and expand our own lives in the ways offered by reading works from other cultures?

Therefore, translations do exist, even abound. Each year new versions of the *Divine Comedy* or *Beowulf* or the poetry of Rumi or Neruda are rendered in English. *Are* they the same as the originals? Better? Misrepresentations? Improvements on past translations? None of the above?

If you were to translate a literary work, for example, how would you go about it? Would you translate it literally? If so, how would you handle the complexity of imagery? Images are often "culture-bound" so that translating *snow* into the equivalent word in another language, or vice versa, may not come even close to what the implications are in the original. And what about the nuances of tone? You know that the way one word or phrase hits you may differ from the way it strikes someone else. How does one translate tone?

If you were translating a poem rather than prose, imagine how much more complex the issues would be given line length, line breaks, how crucial rhythms are to every line, how one image that is also a metaphor could suggest something very different in another language, how symbols vary from culture to culture. Prose allows a bit more room for communicating its meaning through context; however, one slight change in a poem could alter the entire work. In theory, that could be said also for prose, but in the most practical sense, this kind of loss of nuance or meaning or implication is more likely to affect the reading and resulting interpretation in a poem.

Almost anyone would agree that translation is an act of enormous responsibility that requires great skill, for it is very easy to distort or mislead or misinform. What, then, are the parameters? What liberties, if any, can the translator take? What about interpretation? What does a translator do if it is clear that the particular wording could lead to an interpretation not justified by the original? What if the translator believes that the best word in English is not the equivalent word because the equivalent word does not carry the tone or associations or sound or impact of the original? What if *sassafras* is, in the mind of the translator, a more effective image, closer to the original than the literal *palm tree*? Or in a drama, what if the characters' use of slang or a political metaphor or way of praising or cursing another character can't be translated literally? What then?

Translation is indeed fraught with complexities and issues. It might be useful and instructive for you to try translating a work of literature, and then to write in your journal about the issues you ran into, the decisions you discovered you had to make, and the dilemmas you found yourself facing.

What is lost then in translation? Likely a lot. What is gained? Likely a valuable opportunity to enter into worlds other than our own, something very important for sure. Or maybe there are even those rare times, as Thurber said, when what is lost was in the original and what was gained was in the translation.

JORGE LOUIS BORGES: A CASE STUDY ON TRANSLATION

To explore translation further we turn to the Argentinean poet Jorge Luis Borges. From earliest childhood, Borges was bilingual, learning English before learning Spanish. He grew up in the prosperous neighborhood Palmero in a large house with an extensive library. In 1914, Borges's parents moved to Geneva, where he learned French and German and received his BA from the Collège of Geneva. After World War I, the family lived in Spain, where Borges became a member of an avant-garde literary group and his first poem, "Hymn to the Sea," in the style of Walt Whitman, was published in the magazine *Grecia*.

In 1921, Borges settled in Buenos Aires and started his career as a writer by publishing poems and essays and cofounding the literary journals *Proa* and *Sur,* the latter of which became Argentina's most important literary journal. From 1937 to 1946, he worked at a branch of the Buenos Aires Municipal Library, and between 1946 and 1955, he lectured widely and increasingly became a public figure. From 1955 until 1973, Borges served as director of the National Library in Buenos Aires, during which time his eyesight failed; by 1970 he was almost completely blind. He also was a professor of literature at the University of Buenos Aires, teaching there from 1955 to 1970.

Borges was a prolific writer — of short stories, poetry, essays, screenplays, literary criticism, prologues, and reviews. He also edited numerous anthologies. His ideas were deeply influenced by such thinkers as the eighteenth-century Irish philosopher George Berkeley, who held that there is no material substance and that the sensible world consists wholly of ideas, which exist only as long as they are perceived. In the end, however, Borges did accept reality, because he accepted his own reality. Many of Borges's works explore universal themes through such images as the circular labyrinth, used as a metaphor for the ultimate futility of searching for meaning in life, the double (or the "other"), and the mirror, which reflects but does not assimilate (i.e., it conveys a specious reality). Although he achieved international fame as a literary figure and was nominated for the Nobel Prize, Borges never received the distinction of becoming a Nobel Laureate.

In addition to his writing, Borges translated European literature into Spanish. His mother was a translator by profession, so he became aware of the difficulties faced by a translator from his early years, and he wrote about them frequently in his essays. His basic position was that translation is impossible. One cannot duplicate the original text but only give an approximation of it. To attempt to translate the spirit of an original text is such an enormous undertaking that it's taken for granted that the effort will fail. But to translate literally, word for word, requires such extraordinary precision that it is doomed to failure too. The most important thing, he held, is to make a judgment call on what details to include and what to leave out, and to attempt to capture the syntactical movement, the flow, of the original. In the end, a translation cannot be a copy of the original. A translation can stimulate curiosity about the original, but it cannot substitute for the original.

To illustrate those difficulties we turn to "El otro tigre" ("The Other Tiger"), a poem by Borges that includes many images central to his life and works: libraries, books, poetry, and labyrinths. In the twilight, the thought of a living, powerful tiger makes the bookshelves of the library recede into the distance, creating a contrast between books — with their sense of history, their cultural justification of human existence — and the immediacy of the tiger — which has no past, which lives only in the present guided by unerring instincts to its prey. And yet this tiger is not immediate, not a real tiger. The speaker's thought brings up a tiger only as a symbol in a poem, one created with words and pieced together from what the speaker has read about tigers in books (as the epigraph says, craft creates a semblance, a likeness, not the real thing). The speaker realizes this, yet he wants more, wants a third tiger, different from a living tiger in the jungle and a poetic symbol made up from books. The speaker wants the "other tiger," the essential, mythological tiger (the Platonic idea of tiger) that exists behind both the literary symbol and the living tiger. Through the tiger, he reaches for reality.

We include two versions of the poem. First is the poem in Spanish, for those of you able to enjoy it in the original language. If you do not read Spanish, try to find someone who can read the poem aloud to you, so you can hear the sounds and rhythms of the original, even though you don't know the meanings of the words. The original text is followed by an English translation by Alastair Reid. This is the authorized translation of the poem — that is, the "official" translation, one approved by the Borges estate as rendering the poem in the way the estate believes is most authentic.

Jorge Luis Borges   Argentina, 1899–1986

El otro tigre   [1960]

And the craft createth a semblance.
   — *Morris,* Sigurd the Volsung *(1876)*

Pienso en un tigre. La penumbra exalta
La vasta Biblioteca laboriosa
Y parece alejar los anaqueles;
Fuerte, inocente, ensangrentado y nuevo,
Él irá por su selva y su mañana   5
Y marcará su rastro en la limosa
Margen de un río cuyo nombre ignora
(En su mundo no hay nombres ni pasado
Ni porvenir, sólo un instante cierto.)
Y salvará las bárbaras distancias   10
Y husmeará en el trenzado laberinto
De los olores el olor del alba
Y el olor deleitable del venado;
Entre las rayas del bambú descifro
Sus rayas y presiento la osatura   15
Baja la piel espléndida que vibra.
En vano se interponen los convexos
Mares y los desiertos del planeta;
Desde esta casa de un remoto puerto

De América del Sur, te sigo y sueño,   20
Oh tigre de las márgenes del Ganges.

Cunde la tarde en mi alma y reflexiono
Que el tigre vocativo de mi verso
Es un tigre de símbolos y sombras,
Una serie de tropos literarios   25
Y de memorias de la enciclopedia
Y no el tigre fatal, la aciaga joya
Que, bajo el sol o la diversa luna,
Va cumpliendo en Sumatra o en Bengala
Su rutina de amor, de ocio y de muerte.   30
Al tigre de los símbolos he opuesto
El verdadero, el de caliente sangre,
El que diezma la tribu de los búfalos
Y hoy, 3 de agosto del 59,
Alarga en la pradera una pausada   35
Sombra, pero ya el hecho de nombrarlo
Y de conjeturar su circunstancia
Lo hace ficción del arte y no criatura
Viviente de las que andan por la tierra.

Un tercer tigre buscaremos. Ésta   40
Será como los otros una forma
De mi sueño, un sistema de palabras
Humanas y no el tigre vertebrado
Que, más allá de las mitologías,
Pisa la tierra. Bien lo sé, pero algo   45
Me impone esta aventura indefinida,
Insensata y antigua, y persevero
En buscar por el tiempo de la tarde
El otro tigre, el que no está en el verso.

Jorge Luis Borges

The Other Tiger   [1960]

Translated by Alastair Reid

And the craft createth a semblance.
    — *Morris*, Sigurd the Volsung *(1876)*

I think of a tiger. The fading light enhances
the vast complexities of the Library
and seems to set the bookshelves at a distance;

powerful, innocent, bloodstained, and new-made,
it will prowl through its jungle and its morning   5
and leave its footprint on the muddy edge
of a river with a name unknown to it
(in its world, there are no names, nor past, nor future,
only the sureness of the present moment)
and it will cross the wilderness of distance   10
and sniff out in the woven labyrinth
of smells the smell peculiar to morning
and the scent on the air of deer, delectable.
Behind the lattice of bamboo, I notice
its stripes, and I sense its skeleton   15
under the magnificence of the quivering skin.
In vain the convex oceans and the deserts
spread themselves across the earth between us;
from this one house in a far-off seaport
in South America, I dream you, follow you,   20
oh tiger on the fringes of the Ganges.

Evening spreads in my spirit and I keep thinking
that the tiger I am calling up in my poem
is a tiger made of symbols and of shadows,
a set of literary images,   25
scraps remembered from encyclopedias,
and not the deadly tiger, the fateful jewel
that in the sun or the deceptive moonlight
follows its paths, in Bengal or Sumatra,
of love, of indolence, of dying.   30
Against the tiger of symbols I have set
the real one, the hot-blooded one
that savages a herd of buffalo,
and today, the third of August, '59,
its patient shadow moves across the plain,   35
but yet, the act of naming it, of guessing
what is its nature and its circumstance
creates a fiction, not a living creature,
not one of those that prowl on the earth.

Let us look for a third tiger. This one   40
will be a form in my dream like all the others,
a system, an arrangement of human language,
and not the flesh-and-bone tiger
that, out of reach of all mythologies,
paces the earth. I know all this; yet something   45
drives me to this ancient, perverse adventure,

> foolish and vague, yet still I keep on looking
> throughout the evening for the other tiger,
> the other tiger, the one not in this poem.

This translation conveys faithfully both the meaning of the Spanish text and the spirit of the poem. The translator knows Borges's work intimately and makes choices that are appropriate for the way he understands Borges's thinking and imagination. Because this is a verse translation, the translator, in addition to striving for textual accuracy, wants the translation to read well as a poem in English. When you read it, you should be carried by its rhythms, catch the way lineation groups words together and separates them from other phrases, and notice the emphasis created by line breaks and word placements.

Translators must always choose between staying close to the meaning of the original, even when that requires sacrificing stylistic elements in the translation, and achieving a readable, attractive translation, even if that means taking liberties with the meaning of the original. The Reid translation makes the first choice; an anonymous (and unauthorized) translation that can be found on many Web sites makes the second. You might do a search for the latter translation (under "Borges Other Tiger") and then compare it with the original (even if you don't know much Spanish) and with the Reid translation. It begins, "A tiger comes to mind," a wording that is not as close to the Spanish as Reid's. "I think" is an active verb and suggests something that can be conscious and deliberate; "comes to mind" is passive and suggests something that is not controllable but just happens. These differences can have significant implications. In the unauthorized version line 3 is translated as "seems to set the bookshelves back in gloom." Here, the original sense of having the bookshelves seem to move away from the speaker is replaced by having them seem more difficult to see because of darkness. The wording in this case sacrifices preciseness of meaning for the sake of alliteration ("seems to set the bookshelves back in gloom").

You can see from these examples some of the reasons it is so difficult to experience a poem through a translation. Not only can the words of one language not duplicate those of another, but the translator also is constantly forced to make choices between alternative results and effects — choices you can't be aware of if you don't know the original language well (and if you did, it is unlikely that you would be reading the translation). If you want to analyze a translated poem, try to find out something about the translator's approach: How faithful is the translation to the original in meaning and style? Does the translator capture the spirit and flavor of the original, as well as the meanings of its words? Check reviews of the translation, or ask your instructor for guidance on how the translation is regarded by experts. Translations found on the Internet should be used with care. They may be excellent; but they may not be.

Although translations have great value, allowing us to enter into worlds we would not be able to access by any other means, they need to be used cautiously and alertly, with full awareness of their possible drawbacks as well as their potential benefits.

Borges often wrote about tigers: They form a recurring motif and are a central symbol in his work. To place "The Other Tiger" in a wider context, and to provide further examples of translation, we include two more pieces by Borges. First is the Spanish text and then an English translation by Kenneth Krabbenhoft of a brief prose passage from *Atlas* (1984), a book containing pictures by Maria Kodama, whom Borges married two years later, and text by Borges recording their travels together. In one of the book's pictures, Borges is surrounded by living tigers that he is caressing. Following that is Alastair Reid's translation of another Borges poem, "El oro de los tigres" ("The Gold of the Tigers").

Jorge Luis Borges
Mi último tigre   [1984]

En mi vida siempre hubo tigres. Tan entretejida está la lectura con los otros hábitos de mis días que verdaderamente no sé si mi primer tigre fue el tigre de un grabado o aquel, ya muerto, cuyo terco ir y venir por la jaula yo seguía como hechizado del otro lado do los barrotes de hierro. A mi padre le gustaban las enciclopedias; yo las juzgaba, estoy seguro, por las imágenes de tigres que me ofrecían. Recuerdo ahora los de Montaner y Simón (un blanco tigre siberiano y un tigre de Bengala) y otro, cuidadosamente dibujado a pluma y saltando, en el que había algo de río. A esos tigres visuales se agregaron los tigres hechos de palabras: la famosa hoguera de Blake (*Tyger, tyger, burning bright*) y la definición de Chesterton: *Es un emblema de terrible elegancia.* Cuando leí, de niño, los Jungle Books, no dejó de apenarme que Shere Khan fuera el villano de la fábula, no el amigo del héroe. Querría recordar, y no puedo, un sinuoso tigre trazado por el pincel de un chino, que no había visto nunca un tigre, pero que sin duda había visto el arquetipo del tigre. Ese tigre platónico puede buscarse en el libro de Anita Berry, *Art for Children*. Se preguntará muy razonablemente ¿por qué tigres y no leopardos o jaguares? Sólo puedo contestar que las manchas me desagradan y no las rayas. Si yo escribiera *leopardo* en lugar de tigre el lector intuiría inmediatamente que estoy mintiendo. A esos tigres de la vista y del verbo he agregado otro que me fue revelado por nuestro amigo Cuttini, en el curioso jardín zoológico cuyo nombre es Mundo Animal y que se abstiene de prisones.

Ese último tigre es de carne y hueso. Con evidente y aterrada felicidad llegué a ese tigre, cuya lengua lamió mi cara, cuya garra indiferente o cariñosa se demoró en mi cabeza, y que, a diferencia de sus precursores, olía y pesaba. No diré que ese tigre que me asombró es más real que los otros, ya que una encina no es más real que las formas de un sueño, pero quiero agradecer aquí a nuestro amigo, ese tigre de carne y hueso que percibieron mis sentidos esa mañana y cuya imagen vuelve como vuelven los tigres de los libros.

Jorge Luis Borges

My Last Tiger [1984]

Translated by Kenneth Krabbenhoft

There have always been tigers in my life. Reading is so woven into all my daily habits that I really don't know if my first tiger was the tiger I saw in a print or the one — now dead — that paced back and forth stubbornly in its cage while I looked on as if enchanted from the other side of the iron bars. My father liked encyclopedias; I rated them — of this I am sure — according to the pictures of tigers they provided. I am remembering now the pictures in the encyclopedia of Montaner y Simón (a white Siberian tiger and a Bengal tiger) and, in another book, a meticulous pen and ink drawing of a tiger in mid-leap; there was something in him like a river. These visual tigers were soon joined by tigers made out of words: Blake's famous fire ("Tyger, tyger, burning bright . . ."), also Chesterton's definition, "an emblem of terrible elegance." When as a child I read *The Jungle Books* I could not help regretting that Shere Khan was the villain of the story, and not the hero's friend. I would like to recall, though I am unable to do so, a sinuous tiger painted by the brush of a Chinese artist who had never seen a tiger, although he had certainly seen the tiger's archetype. This Platonic tiger can be found in Anita Berry's *Art for Children*. One might reasonably ask: why tigers instead of leopards or jaguars? I can only answer that spots are not pleasing to me, while stripes are. If I were to write *leopard* instead of tiger the reader would immediately sense that I was lying. To those tigers of sight and word I have added another, one that was shown to me by our friend Cuttini in that strange zoo called Animal World, a zoo without cages or bars.

This last tiger is made of flesh and blood. In a show of terrified happiness, I went up to this tiger. Its tongue licked my face and its claws — distracted or caressing — rested on my head. Unlike its predecessors, it had smell and weight. I do not claim that this tiger, which frightened me, is more real than the others, since an oak tree is no more real than the figures in a dream. But I want to thank our friend, the flesh and blood tiger that my senses perceived that morning, whose image comes back to me like those tigers in books.

Jorge Luis Borges

The Gold of the Tigers

[1972]

Translated by Alastair Reid

Up to the moment of the yellow sunset,
how many times will I have cast my eyes on
the sinewy-bodied tiger of Bengal
to-ing and fro-ing on its paced-out path
behind the labyrinthine iron bars,   5
never suspecting them to be a prison.
Afterwards, other tigers will appear:
the blazing tiger of Blake, burning bright;
and after that will come the other golds —
the amorous gold shower disguising Zeus,   10
the gold ring which, on every ninth night,
gives light to nine rings more, and these, nine more,
and there is never an end.
All the other overwhelming colors,
in company with the years, kept leaving me,   15
and now alone remains
the amorphous light, the inextricable shadow
and the gold of the beginning.
O sunsets, O tigers, O wonders
of myth and epic,   20
O gold more dear to me, gold of your hair
which these hands long to touch.

POEMS IN TRANSLATION

Anna Akhmatova   Russia, 1889–1966

The Song of the Last Meeting

[1911]

Translated by Judith Hemschemeyer

Then helplessly my breast grew cold,
But my steps were light.
I pulled the glove for my left hand
Onto my right.

There seemed to be many steps,   5
But I knew — there were only three!

The whisper of autumn in the maples
Was pleading: "Die with me!"

I am betrayed by my doleful,
Fickle, evil fate.   10
I answered: "Darling, darling!
I too. I will die with you . . ."

This is the song of the last meeting.
I glanced at the dark house.
Candles were burning only in the bedroom,   15
With an indifferent-yellow flame.

September 29, 1911
Tsarskoye Selo

Yehuda Amichai   Israel, b. 1924

Wildpeace   [1971]

Translated by Chana Bloch and Stephen Mitchell

Not the peace of a cease-fire,
not even the vision of the wolf and the lamb,
but rather
as in the heart when the excitement is over
and you can talk only about a great weariness.   5
I know that I know how to kill,
that makes me an adult.
And my son plays with a toy gun that knows
how to open and close its eyes and say Mama.
A peace   10
without the big noise of beating swords into ploughshares,
without words, without
the thud of the heavy rubber stamp: let it be
light, floating, like lazy white foam.
A little rest for the wounds —   15
who speaks of healing?
(And the howl of the orphans is passed from one generation
to the next, as in a relay race:
the baton never falls.)

Let it come   20
like wildflowers,
suddenly, because the field
must have it: wildpeace.

Reza Baraheni   Iran, b. 1935

Autumn in Tehran   [1993]

Translated by the poet

at first   a puzzling whisper   started   in the wind   and in the leaves
    seeming young and green
then the sick sneezes came   from carefree street kids   who lay in
    bed a few days later
defining such people's eyes   suits only minds in love with music
as the wind blew it whirled deep tears within weakened eyes   of
    retired old men in the parks
as if an eternal mourning had rained on their cheeks   5
the women hurried   the queue became restless   they were shivering
in the wind   the leaves seeming young and green   eyeless and
    drenched   watched the women
piece by piece they consoled the women   in   grammarless, stammer-
    ing tongues
down deserted alleys   young women in love   drove their shoulders
    into the cavities of their lovers' chests
— it suddenly got cold   I'm cold   aren't you cold?   aren't you? —   10
— no, I'm still hot   hot from your kisses   kisses   still   still
then a blatant crow flew in the horizon   drew its dagger at the
    swallows
and savaged the routes of the air with the convex dagger of its beak
the crow screamed: here comes the season of scorched space   I am
    your emperor!
the looting of the branches began in the evening   15
as though there was no end to it
it poured down in the sparkling of rain and wind   in the street
    lights
millions of small, wet and colourful balancing scales   descended
    from the sky
men with bare heads, having no umbrellas   walked with newspapers
    over their heads
the night drove freshets from the bright north   down the world's
    dark souths   20
and the next day   world streets were filled with water
and the fresh perfume of the season rose   from the retreats of
    leaves
a strange siesta gripped the world and carried it off
in the anguished hour   the arrow of the haggard autumn man's
    stick   drove into death's running stream

*   *   *

and the next day   in Darakeh,°   when a young woman showed me
    the sun   that had just spread on death's color feast   I wept   25
I was not used to the death of so many worlds
the sun came from every side and every angle
and launched a huge ship of leaves off the coast of the Alborz°
    precipice   down the seas of my eyes
the eyes wept blood   with the colors of the leaves
[season! you obstinate season in the home of dreams!   dream!
    obstinate dream in the seasons of water!   yellow leaves   falling
    on my shoulders   when I am no more!]   30
I wept—without grasping the meaning of this mass of decay   this
    expansion of volumes—
beheaded   my lovely peacocks   floated down the waves
and a duplicitous parrot   mimicked the sun   from a hidden sky
I wept   without grasping their meaning

who?   who is that coming on the flanks   lonely   burning
    wavering?   35
the queen of this Shaman?   This Ozan's° lover?
no! no!
cover the height of the young leaf   in the cloak of dying love!
bury it!
throw the dust of the body to the wind and water!   40
I was not used to the death of so many worlds
unable to grasp the meaning of all this!

---

25. Darakeh: Village on the northwestern part of Tehran, famous for its beauty, its tea-houses and restaurants, a visiting place of students, writers, and intellectuals of the capital Tehran. Ironically, it overlooks the horrendous Evin prison, where many intellectuals have been shot by both the previous Monarchist and the present Islamic regime in Iran. [Poet's note.]   **28. Alborz:** The mountain on the north of Tehran. [Poet's note.]   **36. Ozan:** Ozan means "poet" in Azeri Turkish, the language spoken in the northwestern part of Iran, as well as by half of the population of Tehran, the capital of Iran. [Poet's note.]

Julia de Burgos   Puerto Rico, 1914–1953

Returning   [1947]

Translated by Dwight García and Margarite Fernández Olmos

    Indefinitely,
extended like shadows and waves,
sunburnt in salt and foam and impossible skulls,
my sadness grows sadder;
this orbitless sadness which is mine   5

since the world became mine,
since darkness blazed my name,
since the first cause for all tears
came to be my own.

It's as if I'd like to love   10
and the wind doesn't let me.
It's as if I'd like to return
and yet can't discover why, nor where to.
It's as if I'd like to follow the course of the waters
yet all thirst is gone.   15

Indefinitely . . .

A word so mine;
ghostly specter of my specter!

There's no longer a voice,
or tears,   20
or distant sprigs of grain.
No more shipwrecks,
or echoes,
not even anguish;
silence itself is dead!   25

What say you, my soul, should I flee?
Where could I go where I would not be
shadowing my own shadow?

Bei Dao   China, b. 1949

Night: Theme and Variations   [1981]

Translated by Bonnie S. McDougall

Here the roads converge
parallel beams of light
are a longwinded but abruptly interrupted dialogue
suffused with the drivers' pungent smoke
and rough muttered curses   5
railings have replaced the queues
the lamplight seeping out from between cracks in the doorboards
is cast with the cigarette butts onto the roadside
for nimble feet to tread on
an old man's forgotten walking stick against a billboard   10

looks as if it were ready to go
the stone waterlily has withered
in the fountain tall buildings slowly topple
the rising moon suddenly strikes
the hour again and again   15
arousing ancient Time inside the palace wall
the sundial calibrates errors as it turns
waiting for the grand rite of the dawn
brocade dress ribbons stand up rustling in the wind
brushing away the dust from the stone steps   20
the shadow of a tramp slinks past the wall
red and green neon lights blaze for him
and keep him from sleeping all night
a lost cat scurries up a bench
gazing down at the smoke-soft gleam of the waves   25
but the mercury vapour-lamp rudely opening the curtain
to peer at the secrets that others store
disturbs the dream wakens the lonely
behind a small door
a hand gently draws the catch   30
as if pulling a rifle bolt

Faiz Ahmed Faiz   Pakistan, 1911–1984

A Prison Daybreak   [1952]

Translated by Agha Shahid Ali

Night wasn't over
when the moon stood beside my bed
and said, "You've drunk your sleep to the dregs,
your share of that wine is finished for this night."

My eyes tore themselves from a dream of passion —   5
they said farewell to my lover's image, still
lingering in the night's stagnant waters
that were spread, like a sheet, over the earth.
Silver whirlpools began their dervish dance
as lotuses of stars fell from the moon's hands.   10
Some sank. Some rose to the surface,
floated, and opened their petals.
Night and daybreak had fallen desperately
into each other's arms.

                    *   *   *

In the courtyard,   15
the prisoners emerged slowly
from a backdrop of gloom. They were shining,
for the dew of sleep had washed, for that moment,
all grief for their country from their eyes,
all agony of separation from their lovers.   20

But there's a drum, far off. A siren wails.
The famished guards, their faces pale,
begin their reluctant rounds, in step
with stifled screams from torture rooms.
The cries of those who'll be broken on the rack awake   25
just as light breezes intoxicated with sleep awake.
Poison awakes. Nothing in the world is asleep.
A door opens in the distance, another is shut.
A chain rasps, then shrieks.
A knife opens a lock's heart, far off,   30
and a window begins to break its head,
like a madman, against the wind.

So it is the enemies of life awake
and crush the delicate spirit
that keeps me company in my barren despair   35
while the prisoners and I wait, all day and night,
for a rebel prince of legends to come
with burning arrows, ready to pierce
these tyrant hearts of stone and steel.

Nazim Hikmet   Turkey, 1902–1963

Letters from a Man in Solitary   [1938]

Translated by Randy Blasing and Mutlu Konuk

1

I carved your name on my watchband
with my fingernail.
Where I am, you know,
I don't have a pearl-handled jackknife
(they won't give me anything sharp)   5
                or a plane tree with its head in the clouds.
Trees may grow in the yard,
but I'm not allowed
                        to see the sky overhead . . .

How many others are in this place?   10
I don't know.
I'm alone far from them,
they're all together far from me.
To talk to anyone besides myself
                    is forbidden.   15
So I talk to myself.
But I find my conversation so boring,
        my dear wife, that I sing songs.
And what do you know,
that awful, always off-key voice of mine   20
            touches me so
                    that my heart breaks.
And just like the barefoot orphan
        lost in the snow
in those old sad stories, my heart   25
— with moist blue eyes
and a little red runny nose —
            wants to snuggle up in your arms.
It doesn't make me blush
            that right now   30
                I'm this weak,
                    this selfish,
                        this *human* simply.

No doubt my state can be explained
physiologically, psychologically, etc.   35
Or maybe it's
            this barred window,
                this earthen jug,
                        these four walls,
            which for months have kept me from hearing   40
            another human voice.

It's five o'clock, my dear.
Outside,
            with its dryness,
                    eerie whispers,   45
                        mud roof,
and lame, skinny horse
        standing motionless in infinity
— I mean, it's enough to drive the man inside crazy with grief —
outside, with all its machinery and all its art,   50
a plains night comes down red on treeless space.

                        *   *   *

Again today, night will fall in no time.
A light will circle the lame, skinny horse.
And the treeless space, in this hopeless landscape
stretched out before me like the body of a hard man,   55
will suddenly be filled with stars.
We'll reach the inevitable end once more,
which is to say the stage is set
again today for an elaborate nostalgia.
Me,   60
the man inside,
once more I'll exhibit my customary talent,
and singing an old-fashioned lament
in the reedy voice of my childhood,
once more, by God, it will crush my unhappy heart   65
to hear you inside my head,
so far
away, as if I were watching you
                              in a smoky, broken mirror . . .

2

It's spring outside, my dear wife, spring.   70
Outside on the plain, suddenly the smell
of fresh earth, birds singing, etc.
It's spring, my dear wife,
the plain outside sparkles . . .
And inside the bed comes alive with bugs,   75
                    the water jug no longer freezes,
and in the morning sun floods the concrete . . .
The sun —
every day till noon now
it comes and goes   80
from me, flashing off
                    and on . . .
And as the day turns to afternoon, shadows climb the walls,
the glass of the barred window catches fire,
                              and it's night outside,   85
                              a cloudless spring night . . .
And inside this is spring's darkest hour.
In short, the demon called freedom,
with its glittering scales and fiery eyes,
possesses the man inside   90
                    especially in spring . . .
I know this from experience, my dear wife,
                    from experience . . .

3

Sunday today.
Today they took me out in the sun for the first time.   95
And I just stood there, struck for the first time in my life
                    by how far away the sky is,
                    how blue
                    and how wide.
Then I respectfully sat down on the earth.   100
I leaned back against the wall.
For a moment no trap to fall into,
no struggle, no freedom, no wife.
Only earth, sun, and me . . .
I am happy.   105

Miroslav Holub   Czech Republic, b. 1923

Elementary School Field Trip
to the Dinosaur Exhibit   [1996]

Translated by David Young and Miroslav Holub

Jurassic
roar.

Answered by
St. Georges
or Rambos.   5

Only one
glum little boy,
evidently blind,
is lifted to the Triceratops
to breathlessly run his hand   10
up and down the skull,
over the bony collar,
the horns above the eyes,
the skin-folds on the neck,

the boy's face   15
is insanely blank,
but the hand already knows
that nothing is in the mind
that hasn't been in the senses,
that giants are pinkish-gray   20
like Händel's Concerto Grosso

that life is just a step aside
just like mother
always said.

Triceratops,   25
Abel's younger brother.

Dark in there, in
the midbrain:
the last dinosaur
meeting the last man.   30

Taslima Nasrin Bangladesh, b. 1962

Things Cheaply Had   [1991]

Translated from the Bengali by Carolyne Wright,
Mohammad Nurul Hada, and Taslima Nasrin

In the market nothing can be had as cheap as women.
If they get a small bottle of *alta*° for their feet
            they spend three nights sleepless for sheer joy.
If they get a few bars of soap to scrub their skin
            and some scented oil for their hair   5
they become so submissive that they scoop out
            chunks of their flesh
to be sold in the flea market twice a week.
If they get a jewel for their nose
            they lick feet for seventy days or so,   10
a full three and a half months
            if it's a single striped sari.°

Even the mangy cur of the house barks now and then,
and over the mouths of women cheaply had
            there's a lock   15
    a golden lock.

---

2. alta: Lac-dye, a red liquid with which South Asian women decorate the borders of their feet on ceremonial occasions, such as weddings and dance performances. Alta is more in vogue among Hindus, but Bangladeshi women also use it, and it can be seen on the feet of Muslim heroines and harem women in Moghul miniature paintings. [Translator's note.]   **12. sari:** A garment worn chiefly by women in India and Pakistan consisting of a long cloth wrapped around the body with one end draped over one shoulder or the head.

Pablo Neruda   Chile, 1904–1973

The Dead Woman   [1959]

Translated by Donald D. Walsh

If suddenly you do not exist,
if suddenly you are not living,
I shall go on living.

I do not dare,
I do not dare to write it,   5
if you die.

I shall go on living.

Because where a man has no voice,
there, my voice.

Where blacks are beaten,   10
I can not be dead.
When my brothers go to jail
I shall go with them.

When victory,
not my victory   15
but the great victory
arrives,
even though I am mute I must speak:
I shall see it come even though I am blind.

No, forgive me.   20
If you are not living,
if you, beloved, my love,
if you
have died,
all the leaves will fall on my breast,   25
it will rain upon my soul night and day,
the snow will burn my heart,
I shall walk with cold and fire and death and snow,
my feet will want to march toward where you sleep,
but   30
I shall go on living,
because you wanted me to be, above all things,
untamable,
and, love, because you know that I am not just one man
but all men.   35

Octavio Paz   Mexico, 1914–1998

The Street   [1938–1946]

Translated by Muriel Rukeyser

A long and silent street.
I walk in blackness and I stumble and fall
and rise, and I walk blind, my feet
stepping on silent stones and dry leaves.
Someone behind me also stepping on stones, leaves: 5
if I slow down, he slows;
if I run, he runs. I turn: nobody.
Everything dark and doorless.
Turning and turning among these corners
which lead forever to the street   10
where nobody waits for, nobody follows me,
where I pursue a man who stumbles
and rises and says when he sees me: nobody

Dahlia Ravikovitch   Israel, b. 1936

Clockwork Doll   [1959]

Translated by Chana Bloch and Ariel Bloch

That night, I was a clockwork doll
and I whirled around, this way and that,
and I fell on my face and shattered to bits
and they tried to fix me with all their skill.

Then I was a proper doll once again   5
and I did what they told me, poised and polite.
But I was a doll of a different sort,
an injured twig that dangles from a stem.

And then I went to dance at the ball,
but they left me alone with the dogs and cats   10
though my steps were measured and rhythmical.

And I had blue eyes and golden hair
and a dress all the colors of garden flowers,
and a trimming of cherries on my straw hat.

Masaoka Shiki   Japan, 1867–1902

Haiku   [1891–1899]

Translated by Burton Watson

1891 Summer

In cleft on cleft,
on rock face after rock face —
wild azaleas

1892 Summer

From the firefly
in my hands,
cold light

1893 Spring

Deserted temple
where the bell's been stolen —
cherries just opening

1893 Spring

Under my sandal soles
the sweet smell
of meadow grasses

1895 Spring

A train goes by,
its smoke curling
around the new tree leaves

1899 Summer

I think I'll die
eating apples,
in the presence of peonies

Wislawa Szymborska   Poland, b. 1923

The End and the Beginning   [1993]

Translated by Stanislaw Barańczak and Clare Cavanagh

After every war
someone has to tidy up.
Things won't pick
themselves up, after all.

Someone has to shove   5
the rubble to the roadsides
so the carts loaded with corpses
can get by.

Someone has to trudge
through sludge and ashes,   10
through the sofa springs,
the shards of glass,
the bloody rags.

Someone has to lug the post
to prop the wall,   15
someone has to glaze the window,
set the door in its frame.

No sound bites, no photo opportunities,
and it takes years.
All the cameras have gone   20
to other wars.

The bridges need to be rebuilt,
the railroad stations, too.
Shirtsleeves will be rolled
to shreds.   25

Someone, broom in hand,
still remembers how it was.
Someone else listens, nodding
his unshattered head.
But others are bound to be bustling nearby   30
who'll find all that
a little boring.

From time to time someone still must
dig up a rusted argument
from underneath a bush   35
and haul it off to the dump.

*   *   *

Those who knew
what this was all about
must make way for those
who know little.   40
And less than that.
And at last nothing less than nothing.

Xu Gang   China, b. 1945

Red Azalea on the Cliff   [1982]

Translated by Fang Dai, Dennis Ding, and Edward Morin

Red azalea, smiling
From the cliffside at me,
You make my heart shudder with fear!
A body could smash and bones splinter in the canyon —
Beauty, always looking on at disaster.   5

But red azalea on the cliff,
That you comb your twigs even in a mountain gale
Calms me down a bit.
Of course you're not wilfully courting danger,
Nor are you at ease with whatever happens to you.   10
You're merely telling me: beauty is nature.

Would anyone like to pick a flower
To give to his love
Or pin to his own lapel?
On the cliff there is no road   15
And no azalea grows where there is a road.
If someone actually reached that azalea,
Then an azalea would surely bloom in his heart.

Red azalea on the cliff,
You smile like the Yellow Mountains,   20
Whose sweetness encloses slyness,
Whose intimacy embraces distance.
You remind us all of our first love.
Sometimes the past years look
Just like the azalea on the cliff.   25

May 1982
Yellow Mountain
Revised at Hangzhou

Those who knew
what this was all about
must make way for those
who knew little,
and less than that.
And at last, nothing less than nothing.

Xu Gang, China b.1945

Red Azalea on the Cliff

Translated by Fang Dai, Dennis Ding, and Edward Morin

Red azalea, smiling
from the cliffside at me,
you make my heart shudder with fear!
A body could smash and bones splinter in the canyon—
Beauty, always looking on at disaster.

But red azalea on the cliff,
That rosecomb you hang over in momentum ... said
Calms me down a bit.
Of course you're not infinity counting danger
Nor are you at ease with whatever happens to you.
You're merely telling me: beauty is nature.

Would anyone like to pick a flower
To give to his love,
Or pin to his own lapel?
On the cliff there is no road
And no azalea grows where there is a road.
If someone actually reached that azalea
Then nirvana would surely bloom being heard.

Red azalea on the cliff,
you smile like the yellow Mountains,
Whose sweetness ripples on ...
Whose intimacy embraces distance.
You remind us all of a girl first love
Sometimes the past wins to look
That life is precious on the cliff.

Mar 1982
Yellow Mountain
Renmin at Hongzhou

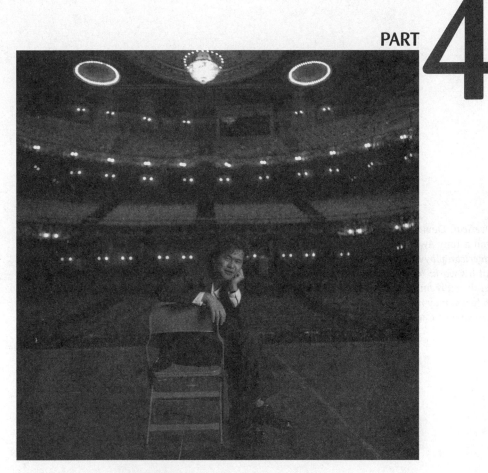

Approaching DRAMA

Overleaf: David Henry Hwang visiting a Seattle theater production of M. Butterfly, *which won a Tony Award for Best Play in 1988 and established him as a major contemporary American playwright. In an interview he describes the common thread that runs throughout his work: "One of the most important themes . . . is the fluidity of identity. You can think you're one person, but in a different social context you can be transformed into somebody you may not recognize, somebody completely different." (See page 1438 for a short biography.)* Copyright © Michael Romanos.

Live performance is still the most organic of all the media.
Because it's not done with machines or editing, it's got all the
imperfections, all the mistakes, and all the magic of real talent.

John Leguizamo

Reading Drama

"The play's the thing," said Hamlet many centuries ago, and it still is today. Drama has captured the minds, hearts, and imaginations of people since the times of the ancient Greeks. In drama, then and now, people and actions "come to life" in a form that entertains and challenges. As we laugh, cry, fear, hope, and despair with the characters of a drama, our own hopes, dreams, and fears are touched and our own lives enriched and enlarged. And that happens not only by attending a production, but by reading a play as well. Duplicating the complex, interactive experience that live theater creates may be impossible when reading a play; but you can approximate it by holding that live experience as the ideal, trying to achieve imaginatively as much of it as possible as you bring the characters and actions to life in the home theater of your mind.

WHAT IS DRAMA?

Drama is one of the oldest forms of verbal art. From earliest times, people have enjoyed pretending, or "acting something out." This "let's pretend" became more highly developed as people planned and organized their playacting for the benefit and entertainment of an audience, composing words to say and instructions on how to move about. Such acting is recognized for its value to entertain, educate, and enlighten.

Drama has deep connections to religion: Greek tragedy grew out of the worship of Dionysus, Passover reenacts the flight of the Israelites from Egypt, and the Catholic Mass is a dramatic enactment of the sacrificial death of Christ. Drama enables an audience to participate, vicariously, in some of the deeply meaningful archetypal or mythic events in cultural history. Drama is a basic form of verbal art, and performance was a viable way to present one's work before the printing press made wide dissemination of texts possible. Thus a study of literature is not complete without including written plays.

Drama differs from fiction and poetry because it includes physical activity. The word *drama* derives from the Greek word meaning "to do, act, or perform." From the time of the Greeks, *drama* was used to describe literary works that could be acted out or performed — either one such work ("a Shakespearean drama") or a group of such works ("Elizabethan drama"). The word *play* (from an Old English word meaning "to be active and engaged") is also used for dramatic works, but it is a narrower term than *drama*. A **play** is a drama intended for performance before a theatrical audience. All plays are dramas, but some dramas are not plays. **Closet dramas**, for example, are meant to be read as literary works, not acted out in theaters.

Watching "live action" on the stage differs from watching film, video, or television — it demands a different use of imagination and intellect. At a play, the viewer constantly makes decisions about who or what to pay particular attention to, whether to focus in on one character's expressions or "pan out" to take in the entire stage. Trying to notice everything important and not to miss key words, glances, or gestures, in addition to responding emotionally to characters and situations, can be exhausting as well as exhilarating. In film, you watch what the camera watches; the decisions you would make when watching a dramatic stage production are made by the camera's eye.

Live theater also has a kind of "suspense of production" that film lacks. An actor risks missing a line or tripping during an entrance. Mistakes lead to another "take" in filming or are edited out, but in live theater they're evident for all to see. Actors live with the anxiety of potential embarrassment and enjoy the challenge of either coming through flawlessly or recovering beautifully from a slip. But audience members feel some anxiety too. They don't want to see actors embarrassed or the effect of the performance damaged, so in the back of their minds is the hope everything will go well (and a twinge of fear that it won't). There is no such anxiety in watching a film — we know all the slips, at least those that were caught, have been edited away. And the audience at a live theater, by responding emotionally and imaginatively to the action on stage, makes a contribution to performance. Actors in live theater are aware of and energized by an involved, appreciative audience. A mutual synergy develops between actors and audience that leads to a deeper experience for both.

There is no question about it: All that a performance involves cannot be duplicated in reading a play. But awareness of what happens in a real theater enhances one's reading of a play. Reading a play well does take a lot of imaginative participation. Does it require more than fiction or poetry? Such comparisons aren't helpful, in the end. An active reader pours her- or himself into whatever reading is at hand. Drama, like all literature, demands a lot of a reader, but the rewards are well worth it.

WHY READ DRAMA?

Plays can be hard to read. One reason for this is that the majority of plays are not meant primarily to be read. The heart of drama is *impersonation* — plays usually are written to be seen and heard as dramatic productions. When we read a play, we assume that there is value in treating a play as a literary work. In reading a play, we concentrate on the words, not on the performance; the words embody the pure play, the play as written rather than as cut and rearranged and interpreted for a particular performance, the part that lasts and remains the same. Reading allows us to pause and reflect, to go back and look at earlier lines, to do the kind of close analysis of structure, characters, and style we've been doing for stories and poems.

One of the most exciting types of theaters is the theater of your mind and imagination. Here you can stage, direct, and perform whatever play you are reading. Reading the texts of plays has long been regarded as an enjoyable and valuable thing to do. But we need to recognize from the start that this kind of reading differs from reading stories and poems. Imagining a play requires particular reading skills and approaches.

ACTIVE READING: Drama

A play is a "dramatic work": that is, it doesn't *tell* a story and doesn't have a narrator the way narrative does. A play *acts out* a story, bringing the people and events to life, imaginatively, on a stage. The text of a play looks different from the way a story or a poem looks on the page.

- *Consider the cast.* The first thing you see is the cast of characters, the *dramatis personae* (the "persons of the drama"), a list of the people who appear in the drama. The same list is included in the program when you attend a theater performance, with the names of the actors who play the roles.

   A good starting point for reading (or watching) a play is to go through the list carefully, trying to remember the names of the characters and their relationships with each other. When reading a play with a large cast of characters, such as a play by Shakespeare, some people jot down names and diagram their relationships on a slip of paper for easy reference.

- *Pay attention to stage directions.* After listing the cast of characters, the printed play may offer some "stage directions," a description of what the playwright visualizes for the scenery on the stage and perhaps the age and appearance of the characters and the way they are dressed, sometimes even a personality characteristic. These are intended, of course, as guidelines for the director, set designer, and costume designer in planning how to produce the work on the stage. When reading a play, you need to fill these roles yourself and imagine the actors, their stage movements, the set design, and the costumes.

You are likely to find more extensive stage directions in a modern play than in one by Sophocles or Shakespeare. A dramatist always writes to fit the facilities available at the time (the kind of theater, scenery, and stage machinery). The scenery Sophocles or Shakespeare could count on was less elaborate than what came later, so they often wrote directions into the text. For example, many Elizabethan plays were acted in open-air theaters during the afternoon, so to indicate darkness Shakespeare has a character say that it's dark and has him or her carry a lantern. The directions included in modern plays vary widely. Some playwrights go into extensive detail illustrating everything from the color of the walls to the type of table sitting in a corner of a room, to the lighting and atmosphere they think is appropriate. Others may offer the sparest generalizations: "a room, some furniture."

- *Use your imagination.* Your imagination functions differently for a play than for a story or poem. The texts of stories, because they are meant to be read, include descriptions to help along your imagination ("the short, heavy man with stringy brown hair plodded up the dimly lighted staircase"). A play assumes you are seeing the character on the stage, so it doesn't provide the same description. In watching a play, the role of the imagination is to accept the pretense that the actor really is the character and that what you see on the stage really is a kitchen or a forest. One of the challenges in reading a play is picturing the scene and characters in your mind. Stage directions help you to visualize the characters and action in your imagination.

- *Read the lines.* After the stage directions come the lines of the play itself, the script the actors memorize as they prepare to perform the play on the stage, together with further stage directions for particular actions (including entrances and exits). What you see on the page is the name of the character, followed by words indicating what the character says or does. In reading the text of a play, first look at the name of the speaker — notice who and what the character is; then go on to what the character says. As you keep reading, use your intellect and imagination to connect the speeches to each other. Watch for interactions between characters and for the ways the diction varies among characters. Just as when you read a story, you will come to experience the characters extending and developing as they reply to what other characters say.

- *Imagine the action.* The characters will expand and develop also as you imagine their movements as they would take place on the stage: people arriving and leaving, meeting each other, moving at various paces and with particular styles of movement and gestures, embracing or assaulting each other, using props, and interacting with the set. Remember always that this is a drama: You are observing the characters on the stage of your imagination as they act out a scene of considerable importance in the life of at least one of them.

REREADING: Drama

To experience a play fully, you need to read it more than once. As with a story or poem, during the first reading you primarily concentrate on what's going on. Only on the second or third time through do you begin to appreciate fully what the work offers. Many of the suggestions for rereading fiction and poetry (pp. 52–53 and 458–59) apply to rereading drama as well. We comment here on how they apply particularly to rereading a play.

- *The second time you read a play, slow down.* The first time through you usually read fast because you want to find out what happens to the characters as they deal with a dramatic situation. You probably don't pay close attention to the way characters are expressing themselves or to the subtleties embedded in their speeches. Like poets and story writers, dramatists write carefully — each phrase is thoughtfully shaped and every word counts. On second reading, linger on speeches to enjoy the style, to catch the nuances that reveal subtleties in character, and to notice details that foreshadow later events that you now realize are significant.

- *Pay attention to little things.* The second time through, you can be more alert for easily overlooked details, things most readers do not notice the first time, and to the subtlety of techniques the author uses. (The same thing is true of watching a play. Seeing it a second time — like watching a movie a second or third or tenth time — helps you to appreciate it more fully.) You notice new things during subsequent readings — especially little things, like a gesture or an item on a table in act 1 that turns out to be significant in act 3. What may appear at first reading to be merely a set or stage direction, on rereading, is recognized to be of wider significance and thus is experienced more meaningfully.

- *Be selective about parts to reread, if you have to.* Because of the length of a three- or five-act play, it may be difficult to find the time to reread it. In some cases (if you need to write a long paper studying the play thoroughly, for example), you'll need to find the time for a complete rereading. In other cases, if you can't reread the entire play, at least reread scenes and passages that are crucial to revealing character traits or plot development.

- *Remember the reading strategies we gave you for fiction and poetry.* Pay attention to the title; look up things that aren't familiar; research people, times, and places that relate to the plot; notice the opening and closing lines; reflect on what the characters are like and what motivates them, on the organization of the plot, and on the significance of the actions and events.

- *Read some parts aloud.* Dramatic dialogue is meant to be heard. Reading sections of the play aloud, working to interpret the expression, rhythms, and tone effectively, will help you hear other parts more clearly and meaningfully in your mind's ear as you read silently. And it can be fun. Divide up the parts among a few of your friends and see what happens.

Action is eloquence. **William Shakespeare**

CHAPTER **17** **Character, Conflict, and Dramatic Action**

Almost everyone enjoys watching stories acted out. Even if you don't attend live theater all that often, you probably watch television or movies. Television producers certainly recognize this appeal and place enormous importance on garnering huge audiences. Advertisers know it and tap into those shows that have the highest ratings, all because we love to watch everything from soaps to sitcoms to serious drama. There's something compelling about watching a skilled actor or actress entering a role and bringing a character to life, making us laugh at comic characters and empathize with tragic ones. Reading scripts can never substitute for watching an excellent performance: The script was meant for performance, after all. But reading plays has its own rewards, and learning to do it well is worth some effort. Whether you're watching or reading a play, the essential core is the same: character, conflict, and dramatic action. Drama usually focuses on characters, the created persons who appear or are referred to in a play. Those characters come to life primarily through conflict. And the conflict is presented through dramatic action on a stage, whether in a theater or in the imagination. You have already worked with conflict and character earlier in this book (see pp. 59–60 and 63–66). Returning to them in this chapter will help you get at characterization and development of conflict through dialogue and dramatic action, the distinctive methods used by drama.

"Active Reading: Drama" (pp. 791–92) offered guidelines for reading a play. Practice applying them to *Florence* (p. 795), a short, one-act play by an important African American woman dramatist of the mid-twentieth century, Alice Childress. Look first at the list of characters: There are four, with

794

no descriptions to clarify anything about them. You have to figure out who they are from what they say and do and what is said about them.

The play takes place in "a very small town in the South" in "the present." The latter raises a problem: The play was first performed in 1950, when the segregated conditions like those described in the description of the opening scene still existed — separate waiting areas and rest rooms for whites and blacks. If you read "the present" and think, "Oh, early twenty-first century," it will be confusing because such physical conditions are not found today. If you attend a performance of this play next week, it is likely that in the program handed you as you enter "the present" would be changed to "the early 1950s" to make the historical details clearer for the audience.

The text provides a detailed but very straightforward description of the set, or "scene," of the play. The basics are easy to visualize: a waiting room divided into the area for whites and the area for blacks, with a single set of doors for entering the set at the back of the stage ("upstage" in theater lingo; the front, closest to the audience, is "downstage") and two restroom doors on each side, for black men and black women in the wall to the audience's left ("stage right"), and for white men and white women in the wall to the audience's right ("stage left").

The stage directions provide help for visualizing the action of the opening of the play and the first two characters, Mama and Marge. From there on you need to imagine the rest of the action and character development from reading dialogue and stage directions (in parentheses, italicized). As you read, pay attention to who is speaking; watch for what is happening in the present, especially conflicts that emerge; piece together what has happened in the past, what led up to the present situation; watch for past (perhaps continuing) conflicts; notice places where you need to "read between the lines," where you perhaps understand things the characters don't; and figure out what each character is like from what they say and do (including the important absent character for whom the play is named, Florence).

Alice Childress   1920–1994

Florence   [1950]

CHARACTERS

MARGE
MAMA
PORTER
MRS. CARTER

PLACE

A very small town in the South.

TIME

The present.

SCENE: A railway station waiting room. The room is divided in two sections by a low railing. Upstage center is a double door which serves as an entrance to both sides of the room. Over the doorway stage right is a sign "Colored," over the doorway stage left is another sign "White." Stage right are two doors . . . one marked "Colored men" . . . the other "Colored women." Stage left two other doorways are "White ladies" and "White gentlemen." There are two benches, one on each side. The room is drab and empty looking. Through the double doors upstage center can be seen a gray lighting which gives the effect of an early evening and open platform.

At rise of curtain the stage remains empty for about twenty seconds . . . A middle aged Negro woman enters, looks offstage . . . then crosses to the "Colored" side and sits on the bench. A moment later she is followed by a young Negro woman about twenty-one years old. She is carrying a large new cardboard suitcase and a wrapped shoebox. She is wearing a shoulder strap bag and a newspaper protrudes from the flap. She crosses to the "Colored" side and rests the suitcase at her feet as she looks at her mother with mild annoyance.

MARGE: You didn't have to get here so early, mama. Now you got to wait!

MAMA: If I'm goin' someplace . . . I like to get there in plenty time. You don't have to stay.

MARGE: You shouldn't wait 'round here alone.

MAMA: I ain't scared. Ain't a soul going to bother me.

MARGE: I got to get back to Ted. He don't like to be in the house by himself. (*She picks up the bag and places it on the bench by Mama.*)

MAMA: You'd best go back. (*smiles*) You know I think he misses Florence.

MARGE: He's just a little fellow. He needs his mother. You make her come home! She shouldn't be way up there in Harlem. She ain't got nobody there.

MAMA: You know Florence don't like the South.

MARGE: It ain't what we like in this world! You tell her that.

MAMA: If Mr. Jack ask about the rent, you tell him we gonna be a little late on account of the trip.

MARGE: I'll talk with him. Don't worry so about everything. (*places suitcase on floor*) What you carryin', mama . . . bricks?

MAMA: If Mr. Jack won't wait . . . write to Rudley. He oughta send a little somethin'.

MARGE: Mama . . . Rudley ain't got nothin' fo himself. I hate to ask him to give us.

MAMA: That's your brother! If push come to shove, we got to ask.

MARGE (*places box on bench*): Don't forget to eat your lunch . . . and try to get a seat near the window so you can lean on your elbow and get a little rest.

MAMA: Hmmmm . . . mmmph. Yes.

MARGE: Buy yourself some coffee when the man comes through. You'll need something hot and you can't go to the diner.

MAMA: I know that. You talk like I'm a northern greenhorn.

MARGE: You got handkerchiefs?

MAMA: I got everything, Marge.

MARGE (*wanders upstage to the railing division line*): I know Florence is real bad off or she wouldn't call on us for money. Make her come home. She ain't gonna get rich up there and we can't afford to do for her.

MAMA: We talked all of that before.

MARGE (*touches rail*): Well, you got to be strict on her. She got notions a Negro woman don't need.

MAMA: But she was in a real play. Didn't she send us twenty-five dollars a week?

MARGE: For two weeks.

MAMA: Well the play was over.

MARGE (*crosses to Mama and sits beside her*): It's not money, Mama. Sarah wrote us about it. You know what she said Florence was doin'. Sweepin' the stage!

MAMA: She was *in* the play!

MARGE: Sure she was in it! Sweepin'! Them folks ain't gonna let her be no actress. You tell her to wake up.

MAMA: I . . . I . . . think.

MARGE: Listen, Mama . . . She won't wanna come. We know that . . . but she gotta!

MAMA: Maybe we shoulda told her to expect me. It's kind of mean to just walk in like this.

MARGE: I bet she's livin' terrible. What's the matter with her? Don't she know we're keepin' her son?

MAMA: Florence don't feel right 'bout down here since Jim got killed.

MARGE: Who does? I should be the one goin' to get her. You tell her she ain't gonna feel right in no place. Mama, honestly! She must think she's white!

MAMA: Florence is brownskin.

MARGE: I don't mean that. I'm talkin' about her attitude. Didn't she go to Strumley's down here and ask to be a salesgirl? (*rises*) Now ain't that somethin'? They don't hire no Colored folks.

MAMA: Others beside Florence been talkin' about their rights.

MARGE: I know it . . . but there's things we can't do cause they ain't gonna let us. (*She wanders over to the "White" side of the stage.*) Don't feel a damn bit different over here than it does on our side. (*silence*)

MAMA: Maybe we shoulda just sent her the money this time. This one time.

MARGE (*coming back to the "Colored" side*): Mama! Don't you let her cash that check for nothin' but to bring her back home.

MAMA: I know.

MARGE (*restless . . . fidgets with her hair . . . patting it in place*): I oughta go now.

MAMA: You best get back to Ted. He might play with the lamp.

MARGE: He better not let me catch him! If you got to go to the ladies' room take your grip.

MAMA: I'll be alright. Make Ted get up on time for school.

MARGE (*kisses her quickly and gives her the newspaper*): Here's something to read. So long, Mama.

MAMA: G'bye, Margie baby.

MARGE (*goes to door . . . stops and turns to her mother*): You got your smelling salts?

MAMA: In my pocketbook.

MARGE (*wistfully*): Tell Florence I love her and miss her too.

Porter can be heard singing in the distance.

MAMA: Sure.

MARGE (*reluctant to leave*): Pin that check in your bosom, Mama. You might fall asleep and somebody'll rob you.

MAMA: I got it pinned to me. (*feels for the check which is in her blouse*)

MARGE (*almost pathetic*): Bye, Ma.

Mama sits for a moment looking at her surroundings. She opens the paper and begins to read.

PORTER (*offstage*): Hello, Marge. What you doin' down here?

MARGE: I came to see Mama off.

PORTER: Where's she going?

MARGE: She's in there; she'll tell you. I got to get back to Ted.

PORTER: Bye now . . . Say, wait a minute, Marge.

MARGE: Yes?

PORTER: I told Ted he could have some of my peaches and he brought all them Brandford boys and they picked 'em all. I wouldn't lay a hand on him but I told him I was gonna tell you.

MARGE: I'm gonna give it to him!

PORTER (*enters and crosses to white side of waiting room. He carries a pail of water and a mop. He is about fifty years old. He is obviously tired but not lazy.*): Every peach off my tree!

MAMA: There wasn't but six peaches on that tree.

PORTER (*smiles . . . glances at Mama as he crosses to the "White" side and begins to mop*): How d'ye do, Mrs. Whitney . . . you going on a trip?

MAMA: Fine, I thank you. I'm going to New York.

PORTER: Wish it was me. You gonna stay?

MAMA: No, Mr. Brown. I'm bringing Florence . . . I'm visiting Florence.

PORTER: Tell her I said hello. She's a fine girl.

MAMA: Thank you.

PORTER: My brother Bynum's in Georgia now.

MAMA: Well now, that's nice.

PORTER: Atlanta.

MAMA: He goin' to school?

PORTER: Yes'm. He saw Florence in a Colored picture. A moving picture.

MAMA: Do tell! She didn't say a word about it.

PORTER: They got Colored moving picture theaters in Atlanta.

MAMA: Yes. Your brother going to be a doctor?

PORTER (*with pride*): No. He writes things.

MAMA: Oh.

PORTER: My son is goin' back to Howard next year.

MAMA: Takes an awful lot of goin' to school to be anything. Lot of money leastways.

PORTER (*thoughtfully*): Yes'm, it sure do.

MAMA: That sure was a nice church sociable the other night.

PORTER: Yes'm. We raised 87 dollars.

MAMA: That's real nice.

PORTER: I won your cake at the bazaar.

MAMA: The chocolate one?

PORTER (*as he wrings mop*): Yes'm . . . was light as a feather. That old train is gonna be late this evenin'. It's number 42.

MAMA: I don't mind waitin'.

PORTER (*lifts pail, tucks mop handle under his arm. He looks about in order to make certain no one is around and leans over and addresses Mama in a confidential tone*): Did you buy your ticket from that Mr. Daly?

MAMA (*in a low tone*): No. Marge bought it yesterday.

PORTER (*leaning against railing*): That's good. That man is real mean. Especially if he thinks you're goin' north. (*He starts to leave . . . then turns back to Mama*) If you go to the rest room, use the Colored men's . . . the other one is out of order.

MAMA: Thank you, sir.

MRS. CARTER (*a white woman . . . well dressed, wearing furs and carrying a small, expensive overnight bag breezes in . . . breathless . . . flustered and smiling. She addresses the Porter as she almost collides with him*): Boy! My bags are out there. The taxi driver just dropped them. Will they be safe?

PORTER: Yes, mam. I'll see after them.

MRS. CARTER: I thought I'd missed the train.

PORTER: It's late, mam.

MRS. CARTER (*crosses to bench on the "White" side and rests her bag*): Fine! You come back here and get me when it comes. There'll be a tip in it for you.

PORTER: Thank you, mam. I'll be here. (*as he leaves*) Miss Whitney, I'll take care of your bag too.

MAMA: Thank you, sir.

MRS. CARTER (*wheels around . . . notices Mama*): Oh . . . Hello there . . .

MAMA: Howdy, mam. (*She opens her newspaper and begins to read.*)

MRS. CARTER (*paces up and down rather nervously. She takes a cigarette from her purse, lights it and takes a deep draw. She looks at her watch and then speaks to Mama across the railing*): Have you any idea how late the train will be?

MAMA: No, mam. (*starts to read again*)

MRS. CARTER: I can't leave this place fast enough. Two days of it and I'm bored to tears. Do you live here?

MAMA (*rests paper on her lap*): Yes, mam.

MRS. CARTER: Where are you going?

MAMA: New York City, mam.

MRS. CARTER: Good for you! You can stop "maming" me. My name is Mrs. Carter. I'm not a southerner really. (*takes handkerchief from her purse and covers her nose for a moment*) My God! Disinfectant! This is a frightful place. My brother's here writing a book. Wants atmosphere. Well, he's got it. I'll never come back here ever.

MAMA: That's too bad, mam . . . Mrs. Carter.

MRS. CARTER: That's good. I'd die in this place. Really die. Jeff . . . Mr. Wiley . . . my brother . . . He's tied in knots, a bundle of problems . . . positively in knots.

MAMA (*amazed*): That so, mam?

MRS. CARTER: You don't have to call me mam. It's so southern. Mrs. Carter! These people are still fighting the Civil War. I'm really a New Yorker now. Of course, I was born here . . . in the South I mean. Memphis. Listen . . . am I annoying you? I've simply got to talk to someone.

MAMA (*places her newspaper on the bench*): No, Mrs. Carter. It's perfectly alright.

MRS. CARTER: Fine! You see Jeff has ceased writing. Stopped! Just like that! (*snaps fingers*)

MAMA (*turns to her*): That so?

MRS. CARTER: Yes. The reviews came out on his last book. Poor fellow.

MAMA: I'm sorry, mam . . . Mrs. Carter. They didn't like his book?

MRS. CARTER: Well enough . . . but Jeff's . . . well, Mr. Wiley is a genius. He says they missed the point! Lost the whole message! Did you read . . . do you . . . have you heard of *Lost My Lonely Way*?

MAMA: No, mam. I can't say I have.

MRS. CARTER: Well, it doesn't matter. It's profound. Real . . . you know. (*stands at the railing upstage*) It's about your people.

MAMA: That's nice.

MRS. CARTER: Jeff poured his complete self into it. Really delved into the heart of the problem, pulled no punches! He hardly stopped for his meals . . . And of course I wasn't here to see that he didn't overdo. He suffers so with his characters.

MAMA: I guess he wants to do his best.

MRS. CARTER: Zelma! . . . That's his heroine . . . Zelma! A perfect character.

MAMA (*interested . . . coming out of her shell eagerly*): She was colored, mam?

MRS. CARTER: Oh yes! . . . But of course you don't know what it's about do you?

MAMA: No, miss . . . Would you tell me?

MRS. CARTER (*leaning on the railing*): Well . . . she's almost white, see? Really you can't tell except in small ways. She wants to be a lawyer . . . and . . . and . . . well, there she is full of complexes and this deep shame you know.

MAMA (*excitedly but with curiosity*): Do tell! What shame has she got?

MRS. CARTER (*takes off her fur neckpiece and places it on bench with overnight bag*): It's obvious! This lovely creature . . . intelligent, ambitious, and well . . . she's a Negro!

MAMA (*waiting eagerly*): Yes'm, you said that . . .

MRS. CARTER: Surely you understand? She's constantly hating herself. Just before she dies she says it! . . . Right on the bridge . . .

MAMA (*genuinely moved*): How sad. Ain't it a shame she had to die?

MRS. CARTER: It was inevitable . . . couldn't be any other way!

MAMA: What did she say on the bridge?

MRS. CARTER: Well . . . just before she jumped . . .

MAMA (*slowly straightening*): You mean she killed *herself*?

MRS. CARTER: Of course. Close your eyes and picture it!

MAMA (*turns front and closes her eyes tightly with enthusiasm*): Yes'm.

MRS. CARTER (*center stage on "White" side*): Now. . .! She's standing on the bridge in the moonlight . . . Out of her shabby purse she takes a mirror . . . and by the light of the moon she looks at her reflection in the glass.

MAMA (*clasps her hands together gently*): I can see her just as plain.

MRS. CARTER (*sincerely*): Tears roll down her cheeks as she says . . . almost! almost white . . . but I'm black! I'm a Negro! and then . . . (*turns to Mama*) she jumps and drowns herself!

MAMA (*opens her eyes and speaks quietly*): Why?

MRS. CARTER: She can't face it! Living in a world where she almost belongs but not quite. (*drifts upstage*) Oh it's so . . . so . . . tragic.

MAMA (*carried away by her convictions . . . not anger . . . she feels challenged. She rises*): That ain't so! Not one bit it ain't!

MRS. CARTER (*surprised*): But it is!

MAMA (*during the following she works her way around the railing until she crosses over about one foot to the "White" side and is face to face with Mrs. Carter*): I know it ain't! Don't my friend Essie Kitredge daughter look just like a German or somethin'? She didn't kill herself! She's teachin' the third grade in the colored school right here. Even the bus drivers ask her to sit in the front seats cause they think she's white! . . . an' . . . an' . . . she just says as clear as you please . . . "I'm sittin' where my people got to sit by law. I'm a Negro woman!"

MRS. CARTER (*uncomfortable and not knowing why*): . . . But there you have it. The exception makes the rule. That's proof!

MAMA: No such thing! My cousin Hemsly's as white as you! . . . an' . . . an' he never . . .

MRS. CARTER (*flushed with anger . . . yet lost . . . because she doesn't know why*): Are you losing your temper? (*weakly*) Are you angry with me?

MAMA (*stands silently trembling as she looks down and notices she is on the wrong side of the railing. She looks up at the "White Ladies Room" sign and slowly works her way back to the "Colored" side. She feels completely lost*): No, mam. Excuse me please. (*with bitterness*) I just meant Hemsly works in the colored section of the shoe store . . . He never once wanted to kill his self! (*She sits down on the bench and fumbles for her newspaper. Silence.*)

MRS. CARTER (*caught between anger and reason . . . she laughs nervously*): Well! Let's not be upset by this. It's entirely my fault you know. This whole thing is a completely controversial subject. (*silence*) If it's too much for Jeff . . . well naturally I shouldn't discuss it with you. (*approaching railing*) I'm sorry. Let *me* apologize.

MAMA (*keeps her eyes on the paper*): No need for that, mam. (*silence*)

MRS. CARTER (*painfully uncomfortable*): I've drifted away from . . . What started all of this?

MAMA (*no comedy intended or allowed on this line*): Your brother, mam.

MRS. CARTER (*trying valiantly to brush away the tension*): Yes . . . Well, I had to come down and sort of hold his hand over the reviews. He just thinks too much . . . and studies. He knows the Negro so well that sometimes our friends tease him and say he almost *seems* like . . . well you know . . .

MAMA (*tightly*): Yes'm.

MRS. CARTER (*slowly walks over to the "Colored" side near the top of the rail*): You know I try but it's really difficult to understand you people. However . . . I keep trying.

MAMA (*still tight*): Thank you, mam.

MRS. CARTER (*retreats back to "White" side and begins to prove herself*): Last week . . . Why do you know what I did? I sent a thousand dollars to a Negro college for scholarships.

MAMA: That was right kind of you.

MRS. CARTER (*almost pleading*): I know what's going on in your mind . . . and what you're thinking is wrong. I've . . . I've . . . eaten with Negroes.

MAMA: Yes, mam.

MRS. CARTER (*trying to find a straw*): . . . And there's Malcom! If it weren't for the guidance of Jeff he'd never written his poems. Malcom is a Negro.

MAMA (*freezing*): Yes, mam.

MRS. CARTER (*gives up, crosses to her bench, opens her overnight bag and takes out a book and begins to read. She glances at Mama from time to time. Mama is deeply absorbed in her newspaper. Mrs. Carter closes her book with a bang . . . determined to penetrate the wall Mama has built around her*): Why are you going to New York?

MAMA (*almost accusingly*): I got a daughter there.

MRS. CARTER: I lost my son in the war. (*silence . . . Mama is ill at ease.*) Your daughter . . . what is she doing . . . studying?

MAMA: No'm, she's trying to get on stage.

MRS. CARTER (*pleasantly*): Oh . . . a singer?

MAMA: No, mam. She's . . .

MRS. CARTER (*warmly*): You people have such a gift. I love spirituals . . . "Steal Away," "Swing Low, Sweet Chariot."

MAMA: They are right nice. But Florence wants to act. Just say things in plays.

MRS. CARTER: A dramatic actress?

MAMA: Yes, that's what it is. She been in a colored moving picture, and a big show for two weeks on Broadway.

MRS. CARTER: The dear, precious child! . . . But this is funny . . . no! it's pathetic. She must be bitter . . . *really* bitter. Do you know what I do?

MAMA: I can't rightly say.

MRS. CARTER: I'm an actress! A dramatic actress . . . And I haven't really worked in six months . . . And I'm pretty well-known . . . And everyone knows Jeff. I'd like to work. Of course, there are my committees, but you see, they don't need me. Not really . . . not even Jeff.

MAMA: Now that's a shame.

MRS. CARTER: Now your daughter . . . you must make her stop before she's completely unhappy. Make her stop!

MAMA: Yes'm . . . why?

MRS. CARTER: I have the best of contacts and *I've* only done a few *broadcasts* lately. Of course, I'm not counting the things I just wouldn't do. Your daughter . . . make her stop.

MAMA: A drama teacher told her she has real talent.

MRS. CARTER: A drama teacher! My dear woman, there are loads of unscrupulous whites up there that just hand out opinions for . . .

MAMA: This was a colored gentleman down here.

MRS. CARTER: Oh well! . . . And she went up there on the strength of that? This makes me very unhappy. (*puts book away in case, and snaps lock. Silence*)

MAMA (*getting an idea*): Do you really, truly feel that way, mam?

MRS. CARTER: I do. Please . . . I want you to believe me.

MAMA: Could I ask you something?

MRS. CARTER: Anything.

MAMA: You won't be angry, mam?

MRS. CARTER (*remembering*): I won't. I promise you.

MAMA (*gathering courage*): Florence is proud . . . but she's having it hard.

MRS. CARTER: I'm sure she is.

MAMA: Could you help her out some, mam? Knowing all the folks you do . . . maybe . . .

MRS. CARTER (*rubs the outside of the case*): Well . . . it isn't that simple . . . but . . . you're very sweet. If only I could . . .

MAMA: Anything you did, I feel grateful. I don't like to tell it, but she can't even pay her rent and things. And she's used to my cooking for her . . . I believe my girl goes hungry sometime up there . . . and yet she'd like to stay so bad.

MRS. CARTER (*looks up, resting case on her knees*): How can I refuse? You seem like a good woman.

MAMA: Always lived as best I knew how and raised my children up right. We got a fine family, mam.

MRS. CARTER: And I've no family at all. I've got to! It's clearly my duty. Jeff's books . . . guiding Malcom's poetry . . . It isn't enough . . . oh I know it isn't. Have you ever heard of Melba Rugby?

MAMA: No, mam. I don't know anybody much . . . except right here.

MRS. CARTER (*brightening*): She's in California, but she's moving East again . . . hates California.

MAMA: Yes'm.

MRS. CARTER: A most versatile woman. Writes, directs, acts . . . everything!

MAMA: That's nice, mam.

MRS. CARTER: Well, she's uprooting herself and coming back to her first home . . . New York . . . to direct "Love Flowers" . . . it's a musical.

MAMA: Yes'm.

MRS. CARTER: She's grand . . . helped so many people . . . and I'm sure she'll help your . . . what's her name.

MAMA: Florence.

MRS. CARTER (*turns back to bench, opens bag, takes out a pencil and an address book*): Yes, Florence. She'll have to *make* a place for her.

MAMA: Bless you, mam.

MRS. CARTER (*holds handbag steady on rail as she uses it to write on*): Now let's see . . . the best thing to do would be to give you the telephone number . . . since you're going there.

MAMA: Yes'm.

MRS. CARTER (*writing address on paper*): Your daughter will love her . . . and if she's a deserving girl . . .

MAMA (*looking down as Mrs. Carter writes*): She's a good child. Never a bit of trouble. Except about her husband, and neither one of them could help that.

MRS. CARTER (*stops writing, raises her head questioning*): Oh?

MAMA: He got killed at voting time. He was a good man.

MRS. CARTER (*embarrassed*): I guess that's worse than losing him in the war.

MAMA: We all got our troubles passing through here.

MRS. CARTER (*gives her the address*): Tell your dear girl to call this number about a week from now.

MAMA: Yes, mam.

MRS. CARTER: Her experience won't matter with Melba. I know she'll understand. I'll call her too.

MAMA: Thank you, mam.

MRS. CARTER: I'll just tell her . . . no heavy washing or ironing . . . just light cleaning and a little cooking . . . does she cook?

MAMA: Mam? (*slowly backs away from Mrs. Carter and sits down on bench*)

MRS. CARTER: Don't worry, that won't matter to Melba. (*silence. Moves around the rail to "Colored" side, leans over Mama*) I'd take your daughter myself, but I've got Binnie. She's been with me for years, and I just can't let her go . . . can I?

MAMA (*looks at Mrs. Carter closely*): No, mam.

MRS. CARTER: Of course she must be steady. I couldn't ask Melba to take a fly-by-night. (*touches Mama's arm*) But she'll have her own room and bath, and above all . . . security.

MAMA (*reaches out, clutches Mrs. Carter's wrist almost pulling her off balance*): Child!

MRS. CARTER (*frightened*): You're hurting my wrist.

MAMA (*looks down, realizes how tight she's clutching her, and releases her wrist*): I mustn't hurt you, must I.

MRS. CARTER (*backing away rubbing her wrist*): It's all right.

MAMA (*rises*): You better get over on the other side of that rail. It's against the law for you to be over here with me.

MRS. CARTER (*frightened and uncomfortable*): If you think so.

MAMA: I don't want to break the law.

MRS. CARTER (*keeps her eye on Mama as she drifts around railing to bench on her side. Gathers overnight bag*): I know I must look like a fright. The train should be along soon. When it comes, I won't see you until New York. These silly laws. (*silence*) I'm going to powder my nose. (*exits into "White ladies" room*)

Porter singing offstage.

Mama sits quietly, staring in front of her . . . then looks at the address for a moment . . . tears the paper into little bits and lets them flutter to the floor. She opens the suitcase, takes out notebook, an envelope and a pencil. She writes a few words on the paper.

PORTER (*enters with broom and dust pan*): Number 42 will be coming along in nine minutes. (*When Mama doesn't answer him, he looks up and watches her. She reaches in her bosom, unpins the check, smooths it out, places it in the envelope with the letter. She closes the suitcase.*) I said the train's coming. Where's the lady?

MAMA: She's in the *ladies'* room. You got a stamp?

PORTER: No. But I can get one out of the machine. Three for a dime.

MAMA (*hands him the letter*): Put one on here and mail it for me.

PORTER (*looks at it*): Gee . . . you writing Florence when you're going to see her?

MAMA (*picks up the shoebox and puts it back on the bench*): You want a good lunch? It's chicken and fruit.

PORTER: Sure . . . thank you . . . but you won't . . .

MAMA (*rises, paces up and down*): I ain't gonna see Florence for a long time. Might be never.

PORTER: How's that, Mrs. Whitney?

MAMA: She can be anything in the world she wants to be! That's her right. Marge can't make her turn back, Mrs. Carter can't make her turn back. *Lost My Lonely Way!* That's a book! People killing theyselves 'cause they look white but be black. They just don't know do they, Mr. Brown?

PORTER: Whatever happened don't you fret none. Life is too short.

MAMA: Oh, I'm gonna fret plenty! You know what I wrote Florence?

PORTER: No, mam. But you don't have to tell me.

MAMA: I said "Keep trying.". . . . Oh, I'm going home.

PORTER: I'll take your bag. (*picks up bag and starts out*) Come on, Mrs. Whitney. (*Porter exits*)

Mama moves around to "White" side, stares at sign over door. She starts to knock on "White Ladies" door, but changes her mind. As she turns to leave, her eye catches the railing; she approaches it gently, touches it, turns, exits. Stage is empty for about six or seven seconds. Sound of train whistle is heard in the distance. Slow curtain.

CURTAIN

APPROACHING THE READING

1. Describe the main characters — Marge, Mama, Mrs. Carter, and Florence. Which of the characters do you feel drawn to? What techniques are used to draw you to them? Which characters do you dislike? What techniques are used to turn you against them?

2. What is it that makes Mama decide not to go to New York? Is her decision convincing, in terms of what you learn of her character and situation?

3. List several key conflicts in the play. What issues do those conflicts raise? What are you left thinking about as you leave the play (as you exit from the theater of the mind where you watched the play)?

4. Why do you think the play is named for a character who doesn't appear in the play? What does that suggest about issues that are important in the play?

5. This play is over fifty years old. Is it "dated" in terms of the issues it raises and the way they are dramatized, or are the issues it raises and the techniques it uses still relevant? What value is there in reading a play that shows us historical conditions that no longer exist?

CHARACTER

As in fiction, some of the first questions to ask about a play are likely to involve the characters. Who are they? What are they like? Why do they act and feel they way they do?

Many of the terms you used earlier for understanding characters in fiction apply to drama as well. Some of the terms actually originated with drama. **Protagonist** originally meant the actor who played the first part, or leading role, in classical Greek tragedy. That usage has been expanded to mean the most important character in a work of fiction or drama. Sometimes the term **hero** is used instead, especially for premodern tragedies; but the protagonists of modern tragedies, like Willy Loman in *Death of a Salesman* (p. 980), often are not "heroic." The corresponding term **antagonist** (the rival or opponent or enemy of the protagonist), though it goes back to a Greek word etymologically, was not applied to Greek drama. In *Florence*, Mama is the protagonist, Mrs. Carter the antagonist. Drama, like fiction, has major characters who are developed in some depth, like Mama and Mrs. Porter (tragedies and other serious drama often aim at developing one or two key characters in much greater depth than these), and minor characters, like Marge and the Porter, who carry out a function but are not given much detail or individuality (these often are called **stock characters** — see p. 66). The terms **round** and **flat** originated in discussion of fiction but also apply to drama, as do the terms **dynamic** and **static** (pp. 65–66). It could be argued that none of the characters in *Florence* deserve to be called round; the length of the play does not allow development in depth.

Some of the techniques that help you watch the development of characters in fiction apply to drama also. The technique of *telling* (p. 64) is less important in drama than in fiction because rarely do dramas have narrators who stand outside the action and comment on it — exceptions are the chorus in Greek tragedies and the omniscient Stage Manager in Thornton Wilder's *Our Town*. More often one character gives a description of another (who may or may not be present), but this description may be highly subjective, even quite inaccurate; it may tell us more about the speaker than about the character being discussed. *Entering* a character's thoughts is less frequent in drama than in fiction (p. 65), but it does occur in some instances. In a **soliloquy**, for example, a speaker alone on the stage reveals to the audience what is going through her or his mind. (Shakespeare uses soliloquies frequently. Hamlet's famous "To be or not to be" speech is one example.) And in some cases, in drama as well in fiction, the names given to characters reveal aspects of what they are like, as, for example, Willy *Loman* in *Death of a Salesman* (p. 980).

DIALOGUE

Of special importance for developing character in drama are *saying* and *showing*. These techniques are important in fiction as well (p. 64), but they stand out in drama because of the distinctive methods through which drama is presented: **dialogue** and *dramatic action*. Drama, like fiction and poetry, is made up of words, and the words in a play are primarily used for dialogue. Characters talking to each other is the fundamental method used in drama. In drama, almost everything starts from and relies on dialogue. The only exception is when a chorus or narrator (like the older Tom in Tennessee Williams's *The Glass Menagerie*) comments on what is happening, but the playwright still often tries to include the chorus or narrator among the characters, making that voice seem like part of the dialogue.

From what the characters say to each other, the audience or reader must piece the story together, including details about relevant events in the past and foreshadowings of what may occur in the future. Through what Mama and Marge say to each other in the opening scene, we are provided needed **exposition**: where Florence is, some indication of what she is like, what her present needs are, why Marge thinks she should return. Dialogue also provides the primary means for becoming familiar with the characters: What they say and to whom, and how they say it, reveal things about the characters and help us understand the conflict and motivations. What Marge says in the opening scene makes clear that Marge and Florence have quite different views about what attitudes and expectations are proper for an African American to hold. And Mrs. Carter's hypocrisy comes out, for example, as she contrasts herself with southerners—"These people are still fighting the Civil War. I'm really a New Yorker now" (p. 800)—but reveals her racist views by assuming that someone with light skin has the tragic fate of "living in a world where she almost belongs but not quite" (p. 801).

Also, through dialogue we gain insight into the issues the play is exploring. Marge brings up the issue of rights when she says Florence went "to Strumley's down here and ask[ed] to be a salesgirl. . . . They don't hire no Colored folks" (p. 797). (At the same time, we gain insight into Florence's character.) This ties in with the matter of stereotyping, which becomes evident when Mrs. Carter assumes that if Florence is trying to get on stage, she must be a singer and, later in her reply, when Mama asks her to help Florence: "I'll just tell her . . . no heavy washing or ironing . . . just light cleaning and a little cooking." This dialogue gives us insight into Mrs. Carter's character: Mrs. Carter automatically thinks of African Americans as having a natural aptitude for singing and of housework as the work appropriate for an African American woman. When we watch a play, we need to listen closely to the words of the dialogue; reading a play requires the same attentiveness, and a great deal of imaginativeness as well.

Style (p. 170) and **tone** (pp. 177, 491) contribute in a significant way to dialogue in drama. Aspects of style that we discussed earlier in the book apply here as well, and appropriateness remains the key factor: Word choice and sentence structure (see pp. 171–74) need to fit the character using the words and expressing the sentences. Figures of speech (see pp. 175 and 543) must be suitable to the character selecting them. A good playwright is able to create stylistic differences in the dialogue of various characters as an aspect of characterization. In *Florence,* such differences are most obvious between Mama, with her dialect, and Mrs. Carter. But notice also how the Porter's use of short sentences and simple diction sets his dialogue apart from Mama's. The imagery (choice of images and figures—see p. 466) also contributes to characterization. The subjects of the images often fall into a pattern that reveals things about a character or reflects on a situation (such as the animal, often even bestial, imagery that runs through the speeches of Iago in Shakespeare's *Othello*—see, for example, 1.1.47, 88–89, 112–14, 117; 1.3.312–13, 386; 2.1.166, 292; 2.3.42; and 3.3.403–4). And tone is important to determine in individual speeches as well as in a play as a whole. **Irony** is particularly important, especially **dramatic irony**, because playwrights often find it effective to let the audience know more than the characters do. The audience has the satisfaction of being "in the know" about things and seeing future implications in what a character says and does at a given point in the action. (Irony is so important that you should review it on pp. 180–81.)

One of the pleasures in reading a play is imagining how the dialogue would sound on stage—what tones of voice, pace, sound, and inflections fit each character. Should the actor shout or whisper "Shut up!"? How does she or he express anger or grief or bewilderment, or all three at once? What words should be emphasized? If you have ever acted or known an actor, you've likely experienced how many ways there are to say something seemingly as simple as "Where have you been?" In reading a play, we get to be the actors, experimenting with each line to decide how to express it most effectively and get across its meaning most completely, including what it reveals about the speaker.

Creating convincing dialogue is a challenge for playwrights: The discussions, arguments, questions, outbursts, seductions, and compliments must seem natural and appropriate to the speakers and "realistic" for their time and setting. At the same time, they must be carefully crafted to make every speech, even every word, count toward all the different things the dialogue needs to accomplish (for example, advancing the plot, revealing character, engaging the audience, focusing the conflict). Because watching or reading a play requires such close attention to the words of the dialogue, some people find it helpful to read a plot summary first. Knowing the broad plot outline can help you to pick up the signals and subtleties the words are conveying.

CONFLICT

In drama, characters are most often found in a situation involving **conflict**, a struggle or confrontation between opposing characters or a character and opposing forces. Conflict is important to drama first because it usually creates action on the stage — whether external and physical or internal and psychological — and thus creates the kind of excitement, suspense, and tension we associate with the word *drama*. Even outside the theater, we hear *drama* used that way, as, for example, in describing a news story about a dramatic standoff as police attempt to rescue hostages from a convenience store where a robber is holding them at gunpoint. Second, conflict is important because the nature of the conflict, the issues involved, and the way it is handled generally bring out aspects of character: The essence and the depths of a person come out as she or he confronts a challenging situation.

The kinds of conflict in drama range as widely as those in fiction, but the same three broad categories discussed in Chapter 4 (pp. 59–60) are useful here as well.

Physical Conflict

Physical conflict involves a struggle between a character or group of characters and another character or group of characters, or humans struggling against nature. There is little physical conflict in *Florence,* though when Mama crosses over to the "white" side of the waiting room and refutes Mrs. Carter heatedly, it is close to a physical confrontation, as is the later incident when she clutches Mrs. Carter's wrist tightly without realizing it.

Social Conflict

Social conflict occurs in personal or societal relationships or values. We see in *Florence* a personal conflict between Marge and Florence, with the latter's side reported by exchanges between Mama and Marge. And there is a personal conflict between Mama and Mrs. Carter over the latter's attitudes toward blacks. The major conflicts of the play, however, are social. The set itself presents the audience with the dominant conflict, the segregation of blacks enforced by whites. That conflict is evident throughout the play in the racist views expressed by Mrs. Carter.

Internal or Psychological Conflict

Internal or psychological conflict involves a struggle within a character, as she or he wrestles with competing moral claims or a difficult decision. A crucial incident of inner conflict in *Florence* occurs near the end of the play, after Mrs. Carter goes to the white ladies' room. Mama, the stage directions tell us, "sits quietly, staring in front of her" (p. 805), wrestling with an inner conflict: Marge told her to "make [Florence] come home" and to "be strict on her" (p. 797). If Mama goes home instead of going to Harlem, Marge will be deeply upset. Yet the confrontation with Mrs. Carter has changed how Mama thinks about Florence and her aspirations. Clearly, she struggles, inwardly, over what she should do.

Chapter 4 points out that watching for conflicts is a good way to get to the crucial issues in a work of fiction. That is even more true for a play. Identifying areas of conflict as you watch or read a play, or as you watch a movie or television show, usually takes you directly to the heart of its action and significance.

DRAMATIC ACTION

Some dramatic productions do not use action on a stage. In reader's theater, for example, actors typically perch on stools and read their parts to each other and the audience. In most theater productions, however, actors move about on stage "acting out" what is going on. The characters enter and exit; they walk from one side of the stage to the other, they hide behind a sofa or trip on an electric cord and fall flat. They slap one another, have a sword fight, or shoot each other. They carry props, set the table, open a window. They pace, faint, fall back into a chair.

Dramatic action is almost always a fundamental aspect of drama— movement on stage is a vital aspect of keeping the audience's interest and attention. Conflict in drama often becomes a part of the play's dramatic action: As characters differ, argue, quarrel, challenge each other, and find solutions to their problems or difficulties, what occurs on the stage becomes interesting and compelling. A play in which the characters stroll around the stage agreeing with each other is not going to get off the page and accepted for any theater. Therefore, another challenge for you as the reader of a play is using your imagination to visualize the action of a play while reading the text. The dramatic action needs to be seen, on stage or in the mind's theater, for the play to be complete.

In some cases, the script of the play supplies guidelines for what actions should accompany the words, either in stage directions or in the lines themselves. Thus the resolution of Mama's inner conflict is conveyed near the end of the play through dramatic action, as she looks at the slip of paper Mrs. Carter gave her and then "tears the paper into little bits and lets them flutter to the floor" (p. 805). For the most part, however, the actors and directors are left to decide how the characters should move on stage (called "blocking" in theater parlance) and what gestures they should use. This is a crucial part of their joint interpretation of what is going on and how the characters react. As a reader, you are both director and actor, so you get to use your intelligence to try to understand the characters fully enough so that you can picture their actions, gestures, and expressions on the imaginary stage of your mind.

A key part of any action is timing: When the text is acted out on stage, the pace depends on variations in the intensity of different moments. Words almost always take more time to say aloud than to read silently, and some lines need to be spoken more slowly than others. Action on the stage occurs during lines, between lines, or while no one is speaking. Actions can be large—a sword fight—or smaller—as a character walking across the stage, looking out a window, or searching in a desk drawer. Both large and small actions can be significant. Sometimes characters come on stage, do something, and leave without saying any words at all. Sometimes pauses occur between sentences or between words in a speech, as one character looks angrily at another or ponders on what another character has just said. In a play, as in life, pauses or silences often say as much as or even more than words do. For such reasons, a scene that takes five minutes to read might take ten minutes to act out. Here too it is important for you the reader to imagine the pace at which things are taking place, especially where the script does not include specific indications.

The situation depicted in *Florence* occurred over fifty years ago, and laws, customs, and attitudes, and even the words people use, have changed a great deal since then. But we believe the play is still worth reading and has something relevant to say—about a mother's faith in her daughter and her willingness to give her daughter the chance to pursue a dream, for one thing. There is also something valuable about a work that takes us back to earlier times and helps us see "firsthand" what conditions were like then. Knowing history helps us clarify, understand, and define our present.

www
Further explore character and conflict, including interactive exercises, with VirtuaLit Drama at bedfordstmartins.com/approachinglit.

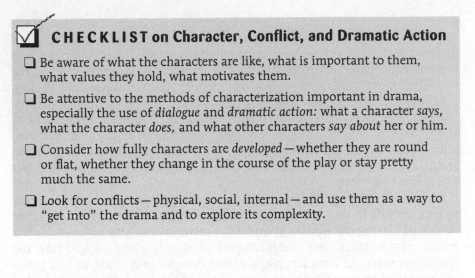

CHECKLIST on Character, Conflict, and Dramatic Action

❑ Be aware of what the characters are like, what is important to them, what values they hold, what motivates them.

❑ Be attentive to the methods of characterization important in drama, especially the use of *dialogue* and *dramatic action:* what a character *says,* what the character *does,* and what other characters *say about* her or him.

❑ Consider how fully characters are *developed* — whether they are round or flat, whether they change in the course of the play or stay pretty much the same.

❑ Look for conflicts — physical, social, internal — and use them as a way to "get into" the drama and to explore its complexity.

FURTHER READING

The following short, contemporary play has a tone very different from that found in *Florence.* The plot and tone are closer to those of a TV sitcom. As you read it, notice the characters and the way they are developed through dialogue, conflicts, and dramatic action. There are three characters: Amadeus Waddlington (Ama); Belinda Stafford (BigB); and Miles Morgan. The location of Bellmore College is not indicated, nor is the time at which the action takes place.

Caleen Sinnette Jennings   b. 1950

Classyass   [2002]

CHARACTERS

AMA: or Amadeus. Black college freshman.
BIGB: or Belinda. Black woman, 20, dressed like a street person.
MILES: White college senior and radio station manager.

A small room that serves as a modest campus radio studio at Bellmore College. Ama speaks into the mic with a suave broadcaster's voice.

AMA: Okay you Bellmore boneheads, that was Tchaikovsky's *1812 Overture,* bet those cannons busted a couple of you dozers. Perfect for 3:47 a.m. on a cold, rainy Thursday in finals week. It's the end of the time at the end of the line. Study on, people. Bang out papers. Cram the facts. Justify that exorbitant tuition and make Bellmore College proud. I'M FEELING Y'ALL! Especially those of you studying for Calc 801 with Professor

Cobb. Call me if you have a clue about question #3 on page 551. You're listening to "Casual Classics," because you don't have to be uptight and white to love classical music. This is WBMR, the radio station of Bellmore College. Miles Morgan is your station manager. Ama here. That's Amadeus Waddlington, with you 'til 6 a.m. Guzzle that warm Red Bull and cold Maxwell House. Here's music to squeeze your brains by. It's Dvořák's *New World Symphony* comin' atcha. (*He puts on the CD, grabs a beer and a huge textbook, and sprawls out on the floor. A bold knock interrupts him. He shouts.*) Go to hell, Miles. I like *New World*! (*Another knock.*) Okay, okay. I'll play Beethoven's *Symphony #1* next. Lots of strings, okay? (*Persistent knocking.*) Damn!

(*Ama strides to the door and opens it. BigB strides in, carrying shopping bag and waving several faxes.*)

BIGB: You messed up, boy!

AMA: Excuse me?

BIGB: And your smart-assed faxes made it worse!

AMA: Do I know you?

BIGB (*examining the mic and CDs*): I want a public apology.

AMA: Don't touch that! Listen, whoever you are . . .

BIGB: Whomever!

AMA: Whatever!

BIGB: You ain't got a clue who I am.

AMA: A fabulous person, no doubt, but you've got to go. This is a classical music show and I've got a killer calculus final tomorrow.

BIGB: Color me compassionate. You're shorter than I thought. But I figured right about you being a dumbass. I told you right here . . .

(*BigB shows Ama the faxes and he realizes who she is.*)

AMA: Oh my God . . . you're . . . BigB! I thought you were . . .

BIGB: . . . a brother, I know, 'cause I ain't hearing none of your bullshit. Well, I thought you was a white boy, and I was right.

AMA: Look, I don't know what you want . . .

BIGB: How long I been faxing you, moron? You said the "Gloria" was by Fauré . . .

AMA: . . . As I told you one thousand faxes ago, "Gloria" is by Poulenc and when I played it, I said Poulenc . . .

BIGB: . . . Fauré!

AMA: . . . Poulenc!

BIGB: I know what I heard, you arrogant shithead.

AMA: Does that BigB stand for "bitch" or "borderline psychotic"?

BIGB: I ain't even 'pressed by you trottin' out them tired SAT joints. I'm down at the Palmer Street Shelter, which you knew by the headin' on the fax, and you just figured I didn't know shit about classical music.

AMA: BigB, I'm truly flattered that you even listen, but you don't . . .

BIGB: My crew at the shelter want to come up here and kick yo ass.

AMA: Whoa, whoa there. I'm sorry about our misunderstanding, okay?

BIGB: And that s'posed to float my boat?

AMA: Let's be calm, B?

BIGB: BigB to you, and I know you ain't s'posed to be drinkin' beer up in here.

AMA: You never saw that.

BIGB: Now I got two things on ya. This gonna be what they call an interesting evening. (*Thumbing through his calculus book.*) This the shit probably got your brain too messed up to know your Poulenc from your Fauré. (*She sips Ama's beer.*)

AMA: Don't do that. Suppose I have a social disease?

BIGB: Ha! Bet you still a cherry.

AMA: Suppose YOU have a social disease?

BIGB: I'll just call your Dean and tell him I caught it sippin' outta your freshman-ass beer can.

AMA: What do you want from me?

BIGB: You made me look stupid in front of my crew.

AMA: Look, I'm just a nerd playing dead white men's music. Why do you even listen to my show?

BIGB: So a sister like me ain't s'posed to be a classical music affectionado.

AMA: The word's "afficionado" . . .

BIGB: Boy, I'm feelin' better 'n better about bustin' yo ass.

AMA: This is like something out of Scorsese. If I apologize for the thing I DID NOT DO, will you go?

BIGB: Maybe. Or maybe I'll stay and watch you work awhile.

AMA: It's against the rules.

BIGB: Lots of things against the rules, freshman boy. Don't mean they ain't delicious to do.

AMA: If my station manager comes in . . .

BIGB: Tell him I'm studyin' witcha, that we putting the "us" in calculus.

AMA: Well, you don't exactly look like a student.

BIGB: Well, you don't exactly look like a asshole, but you the poster boy. Where you get "Ama" from anyway?

AMA: Wolfgang *Amadeus* Mozart. My dad's a classical musician.

BIGB: Oh yeah? Where he play at?

AMA: He sells insurance. No major symphony'll hire him.

BIGB: I know that's right. Oughta be called "sym-phoney," like phoney baloney, right?

AMA (*patronizingly*): That's very clever, BigB, but I've got a lot of work to do. How about I give you and your people at the shelter a, what do you call it, a "shout out." Right in the middle of Dvořák. How would you like that? (*Ama goes to the mic but BigB stops him.*)

BIGB: How you gonna interrupt *New World Symphony* and mess up everybody's flow? You crazy, Amadeus Waddlington. You also a lucky bastard. BigB like you. She gonna take it easy on you.

AMA: Why does your use of the third person chill my blood?

BIGB: Take me to dinner and we cool.

AMA: What?

BIGB: Over there to the Purple Pheasant, where the President of Bellmore College eat at!

AMA: . . . Are you crazy? I don't have that kind of . . .

BIGB: . . . an' buy me a present . . .

AMA: . . . a present? I'm broke!

BIGB: . . . somethin', how they say it, "droll." Yeah, "droll" and "ironic"! Like a CD of "Dialogues of the Carmelites" by *POULENC*. I can see you 'n me sittin' up in the Purple Pheasant, chucklin' over our little in-joke, sippin' a half-ass California *pinot grigio*.

AMA: Who the hell writes your material?

BIGB: And pick me up in a shiny new car.

AMA: Hello? Freshmen aren't allowed to have cars.

BIGB: Beg, borrow or steal, my brother, but you better have yo ass waiting for me at the shelter tomorrow night at 7:30. And don't shit in your khakis. My boys'll watch your back in the 'hood.

AMA: You're delusional.

BIGB: Oh, you insultin' BigB, now? You don't wanna be seen with her?

AMA: I'd love to be seen with her . . . you! I'd give my right arm to have the whole town and the President of Bellmore see me escort you into the Purple Pheasant. Hell, I'd even invite my parents. But I'm a scholarship student with five bucks to my name.

BIGB (*sniffing him*): Ya wearing cashmere and ya reek of Hugo Boss. Don't even try to play me, boy.

AMA: Maxed out credit cards, BigB. I'm just a half-ass, wannabe freshman with a little gig, trying to make some headway with Mr. Mastercard. I'll apologize on air. I'll stamp your name on my forehead, I'll run naked down the quad and bark like a dog . . .

BIGB: . . . anything but take me out. You're a snob, Amadeus Waddlington. You a broke-ass, cashmere-wearin', shit-talkin' loser who don't know his Poulenc from his Fauré . . . (*BigB finishes off Ama's beer.*) . . . and drinks lite beer! My crew was right. Ya need a beat down.

AMA: BigB, please . . .

BIGB: See, I be down at the shelter, diggin' on ya voice early in the mornin'. People say you ain't shit, but you gotta way a soundin' all mellow an' sexy. And when you spank that Rachmaninoff, oh yeah, baby! So when you screw up the Poulenc I send a friendly fax to point out yo error and help yo ass out . . .

AMA: And I appreciate . . .

BIGB: But you had to get up in my grill wit that, "what-do-you-know-about-classical-music-you-stupid-ass-homeless-crackhead" kind of attitude. (*She starts to leave.*) Well, Palmer Street crew will be very happy to whup yo behind.

AMA (*stopping her*): I didn't mean to give you attitude. I'm sorry. I'm broke, I swear! I'll show you my bills, I'll show you my bank statements. Isn't there anything else I can do, BigB? Please!

(*Pause. BigB looks Ama up and down, to his great discomfort.*)

BIGB: Kiss me.

AMA: What did you say?

BIGB: I'm gettin' somethin' outta this deal. Kiss me.

AMA: But . . .

BIGB: Not one a them air flybys, neither. Gimme some tongue!

AMA: Oh God.

BIGB (*she advances on him*): Lay it on me, Amadeus Waddlington. Kiss me or kiss yo ass goodbye.

AMA (*backing away, near tears*): This isn't Scorsese, it's John Woo.

BIGB: Come on classyass, pucker up!

(*BigB tackles Ama and plants a long, deep kiss on him. When she lets him go, Ama steps back, looks at her, touches his mouth, and faints. BigB kneels calmly beside him. Her entire demeanor changes. Her voice is rich, cultured, her grammar impeccable. She sits him up and gives him a few light slaps.*)

Hey! Hey. Ama? Damn it, Amadeus Waddlington, wake up!

(*Miles Morgan enters drinking a beer.*)

MILES: Who are you, and what the hell did you do to Waddlington?

BIGB: He fainted. Get something cold.

(*Miles pours cold beer on Ama's head. Ama comes to.*)

BIGB: Have you sufficiently recuperated, Mr. Waddlington?

MILES (*to BigB*): Hey, you look familiar . . . where do I know you from? . . . in the paper . . . from the shelter. You're . . . Man you sure look . . . different! Oh my God . . . You're not going to tell your father about the beer, are you? I'm a fifth-year senior trying to graduate . . .

BIGB: Just make sure he's okay.

(*Miles bends down to Ama who grabs him by the collar. They whisper urgently, while BigB thumbs through the CDs and eavesdrops, greatly amused.*)

AMA: Oh God. Oh God! I kissed her!

MILES: Way to go, man!

AMA: I'm gonna die!

MILES: She's that good, huh? Bet she's a knockout under all that stuff she's wearing. You all going to a costume party or something?

AMA: Don't you get it, Miles? I kissed her!

MILES: Lucky bastard! Kickin' it with Dean Stafford's daughter.

AMA (*after a beat*): What did you say?

MILES: That's Belinda Stafford, Dean Stafford's youngest daughter! She dropped out of Bellmore to work at the shelter. It was all in the papers and everything.

BIGB (*handing him money*): Thanks for the beer and the amusement, Mr. Waddlington.

AMA: Is this true? Are you really. . . ?

BIGB (*removing her dirty garments and putting them in a bag*): I work night shifts at the Palmer Street Shelter. You can imagine that some of the women find it hard to sleep. Your music and your incredibly boring commentary usually do the trick. Everything was fine until you responded so rudely to my fax. You assumed because it came from the shelter . . .

AMA: No . . . I just . . . I didn't . . .

BIGB: You're an arrogant, ill-informed elitist, Amadeus Waddlington. I've known guys like you all my life. It broke Daddy's heart when I dropped out of Bellmore, but your faxes reminded me exactly why I did it. So, I decided to teach you a lesson. You're not going to die from my kiss, but I hope you won't forget what it felt like to think that you were. (*She scatters the faxes over his head and starts to exit.*)

MILES: Now, uh, Ms. Stafford, you wouldn't mention this to your father . . .

BIGB: I've got people without winter coats on my mind.

AMA (*rushes to her*): BigB, I mean Belinda, I mean, Ms. Stafford, please wait. I get a lot of shit from people about this show and I thought you were just another brother hassling me. I don't have an attitude about the shelter because I've got too many poor folks in my own family. I'm sorry about the vibe. Can I make it up to you? Maybe put in some hours at the shelter?

BIGB: If you think you can hack it. I picked out some CDs for you to play. My people sleep well to Debussy. I'll be checkin' you! (*She puts on her headphones as she exits.*)

MILES: And you won't mention this to . . . (*Miles exits calling after Belinda. Ama suddenly remembers he's on air. He runs to the mic.*)

AMA: Yo, my people, was that dope? Bet the *New World Symphony* woke yo asses up! Hey, I'm still waiting to speak to anybody with a clue to #3 on page 551 in Cobb's calculus class. Anybody? It's 3:59 on WBMR the voice of Bellmore College. I'm Amadeus Waddlington and this is "Casual Classics," because you don't have to be uptight and white to love classical music. You don't have to be a snob either. I wanna give a shout out to my girl BigB. I think I'm in love, people. Yo, B, I apologize. "Gloria" was, is, and always will be Poulenc. I dig the lesson . . . (*He touches his lips.*) . . . and I dig the way you taught it. I'll be down to lend a hand, you better believe that. And for the folks listening at the Palmer Street Shelter, here's a little Debussy to soothe you to sleep. Better times ahead, my people. Better times ahead.

(*Lights dim as sounds of Debussy come up.*)

END OF PLAY

APPROACHING THE READING

1. Describe the main characters and summarize their character traits. Are they round or flat, dynamic or static? Explain why you think so.

2. Explain how dialogue is used to fill in the background for what happens in the play.

3. List several conflicts in the play and label what kind of conflict each is.

4. What does the play "add up to"? (How would you describe its theme?)

5. Explain the significance of the play's title.

RESPONDING THROUGH WRITING

Journal Entries

1. Record two or more dialogues you have overheard or been involved in. Write a journal entry that discusses why the real-life dialogue seems artificial on the page and why the artful dialogue from a play seems real.

Research the authors in this chapter with LitLinks, or take a quiz on the plays with LitQuiz, at bedfordstmartins.com/approachinglit.

2. Write a journal entry in which you discuss what makes the dialogue of one character in Alice Childress's *Florence* (p. 795) or Caleen Sinnette Jennings's *Classyass* (p. 812) distinct from that of another character.

3. In your journal, make a list of the conflicts in Caleen Sinnette Jennings's *Classyass* (p. 812), indicating their types, and a list of the dramatic actions that occur in the play. Write a brief comment on the extent to which conflicts and dramatic actions coincide.

Literary Analysis Papers

4. Write out the first page of Ernest Hemingway's dialogue-filled story "Hills Like White Elephants" (p. 120) the way it would look if it were a play instead of a short story, using Alice Childress's *Florence* (p. 795) as a model. Then compare the two versions. Write a paper discussing how it would be different, or not much different, to read "Hills Like White Elephants" if it was written as a play rather than as a short story.

5. Write a paper exploring the personal and social conflicts, and the use of irony in developing them, in Caleen Sinnette Jennings's *Classyass* (p. 812).

6. Write a paper in which you support the analysis of a character in Alice Childress's *Florence* or in another play by focusing on what the character does. Pay special attention to what might be taken to be minor or trivial gestures, actions, or movements.

Making Connections

7. Write a paper comparing and contrasting two characters in Alice Childress's *Florence* (p. 795) whom we do not see, Florence and Jeff. What is each one like? Why is each character important in *Florence*?

8. Write a paper comparing and contrasting the methods of characterization in Alice Childress's *Florence* (p. 795) and in Caleen Sinette Jennings's *Classyass* (p. 812).

Cultural Criticism Papers

9. Plays sometimes "dramatize" issues by calling attention to them, even if the things mentioned aren't the direct focus of the play. Write a paper clarifying and discussing a number of social issues and practices alluded to in Alice Childress's *Florence* (p. 795). Show how they fill in the overall picture of conditions African Americans faced before the civil rights movement of the 1960s (for example, separate facilities, employment, and voting).

10. Alice Childress's *Florence* (p. 795) raises issues of gender discrimination as well as racial discrimination. Write a paper discussing *Florence* from a feminist perspective (see pp. 1492–94).

RESPONDING THROUGH THE ARTS

1. Design or describe costumes for characters from one of the plays in this chapter. Explain why the costume design, style, color, and so forth are appropriate for the character.

2. Compose a song in which there is a conflict and a dialogue between two people. Think about hip-hop, country, blues, rock, or any other type of music that interests you.

I wished to create a form which, in itself as a form, would literally be the process of Willy Loman's way of mind.

Arthur Miller

CHAPTER 18 **Setting and Structure**

Think of the place shown each week in your favorite TV show. If it's an ongoing series, the action likely takes place in the same building, street, or room every week, and you come to know those made-up places, those "sets" (the backdrops and properties constructed for staging a scene in a play or film), almost as well as the kitchen in your own house. For years, one of the most popular shows on television, *Cheers,* took place almost completely in a Boston pub. The set of that imaginary neighborhood pub became so familiar that tourists visiting Boston expect to find and walk into the real Cheers. Dramatic actions by characters occur in a location that is almost always significant and that is represented by a stage set. Reading as well as watching a play must include thoughtful consideration of sets and setting, and of the way the dramatic action occurring in them is structured and connected in a meaningful way to them. Setting and structure in fiction are discussed earlier in this book. This chapter examines their significance for drama and the distinctive ways they are handled in a play.

SETTING

The **setting** of a play — where, when, and in what circumstances the action occurs — is just as important in drama as it is in fiction. Significant aspects of setting include the *place* of the action (in broad terms such as region, country, or city, and in narrow terms such as neighborhood, street, or building), the *time* at which the action occurs (the century, year, season, day, hour), and the *cultural context* of the action (social and historical circumstances that characterize the time and place). Each of these is discussed at length in Chapter 6. (Reviewing pages 119–27 will prepare you to consider the importance of setting in drama.)

Sets are an important aspect of setting in plays, movies, and TV, an aspect not present in fiction because it lacks the performance dimension of drama. The **set** is the physical set-up on the stage, including the background (backdrop), structures, properties (all movable articles, such as furniture and objects handled by the actors), and lighting. Set is often the first thing you encounter when watching a play in a theater, but imagining how the play might be set is also an important part of staging the play in the theater of your mind. Set depends to a great extent on the nature of the theater in which a play is produced and the kind of stage used in it. These, and their influence on the writer and reader of drama, are discussed in the next chapter. Here, we cover the broad points regarding the relation of setting and stage set.

Remember that setting is always a larger concept than set: The entire setting of a play cannot appear on stage. A play's setting may be Los Angeles, for example, but only one city street and one store might appear on the stage. Plays written before the mid-1800s indicate their setting but offer little guidance on how specific sets are to be designed. Thus William Shakespeare tells us that the overall setting of *Othello* is "Venice and Cyprus" (p. 1054). But directions for individual scenes are nothing more than "A street in Venice" "The Venetian Senate Chamber," and "The castle grounds" (pp. 1054, 1062, 1093). The particular backdrop and props to use on the stage are left to the discretion of the acting company, so you as the reader have great freedom to imagine how those should look.

Modern playwrights, on the other hand, in addition to indicating the setting of a play, often give detailed instructions on how to construct the set. Here, for example, are the stage directions for Henrik Ibsen's *A Doll House:*

> A comfortable room, tastefully but not expensively furnished. A door to the right in the back wall leads to the entryway; another to the left leads to Helmer's study. Between these doors, a piano. Midway in the left-hand wall a door, and further back a window. Near the window a round table with an armchair and a small sofa. In the right-hand wall, toward the rear, a door, and nearer the foreground a porcelain stove with two armchairs and a rocking chair beside it. Between the stove and the side door, a small table. Engravings on the walls. An étagère with china figures and other small art objects; a small bookcase with richly bound books; the floor carpeted; a fire burning in the stove. It is a winter day. (p. 926)

Unlike earlier playwrights, who considered it their role to produce a text and leave the decisions about production to an acting company, most modern playwrights are concerned about the production as well as the text and therefore provide their visions on how the stage appears, how characters are dressed, and even, in some cases, what they look like ("Happy is tall, powerfully made. Sexuality is like a visible color on him, or a scent that many women have discovered" — *Death of a Salesman,* p. 985). Such instructions offer guidance not only to set and costume designers but also to readers of drama, who are given a host of detailed images to help them as they attempt to picture the set, characters, and action in their minds.

As you read the following one-act play, notice the way Susan Glaspell spells out how to construct the set and how characters should appear. Concentrate on visualizing the play in your mind as fully and sharply as you can. Also consider the importance of its rural, isolated setting — how it contributes to what has happened, and does happen, and to our reaction to it all. The play falls into the enjoyable genre of the mystery story, as law officers attempt to solve a murder case. But it also explores matters of human interest and of moral and legal importance. As you read, pay attention to the handling of dialogue and action, to the ways characters are revealed and developed, and to the conflicts presented.

Susan Glaspell   1882–1948

Trifles   [1916]

CHARACTERS

GEORGE HENDERSON (County Attorney)
HENRY PETERS (Sheriff)
LEWIS HALE, a neighboring farmer
MRS. PETERS
MRS. HALE

SCENE: *The kitchen in the now abandoned farmhouse of John Wright, a gloomy kitchen, and left without having been put in order — unwashed pans under the sink, a loaf of bread outside the bread-box, a dish-towel on the table — other signs of incompleted work. At the rear the outer door opens and the Sheriff comes in followed by the County Attorney and Hale. The Sheriff and Hale are men in middle life, the County Attorney is a young man; all are much bundled up and go at once to the stove. They are followed by the two women — the Sheriff's wife first; she is a slight wiry woman, a thin nervous face. Mrs. Hale is larger and would ordinarily be called more comfortable looking, but she is disturbed now and looks fearfully about as she enters. The women have come in slowly, and stand close together near the door.*

COUNTY ATTORNEY (*rubbing his hands*): This feels good. Come up to the fire, ladies.
MRS. PETERS (*after taking a step forward*): I'm not — cold.
SHERIFF (*unbuttoning his overcoat and stepping away from the stove as if to mark the beginning of official business*): Now, Mr. Hale, before we move things about, you explain to Mr. Henderson just what you saw when you came here yesterday morning.

COUNTY ATTORNEY: By the way, has anything been moved? Are things just as you left them yesterday?

SHERIFF (*looking about*): It's just the same. When it dropped below zero last night I thought I'd better send Frank out this morning to make a fire for us — no use getting pneumonia with a big case on, but I told him not to touch anything except the stove — and you know Frank.

COUNTY ATTORNEY: Somebody should have been left here yesterday.

SHERIFF: Oh — yesterday. When I had to send Frank to Morris Center for that man who went crazy — I want you to know I had my hands full yesterday. I knew you could get back from Omaha by today and as long as I went over everything here myself —

COUNTY ATTORNEY: Well, Mr. Hale, tell just what happened when you came here yesterday morning.

HALE: Harry and I had started to town with a load of potatoes. We came along the road from my place and as I got here I said, "I'm going to see if I can't get John Wright to go in with me on a party telephone." I spoke to Wright about it once before and he put me off, saying folks talked too much anyway, and all he asked was peace and quiet — I guess you know about how much he talked himself; but I thought maybe if I went to the house and talked about it before his wife, though I said to Harry that I didn't know as what his wife wanted made much difference to John —

COUNTY ATTORNEY: Let's talk about that later, Mr. Hale. I do want to talk about that, but tell now just what happened when you got to the house.

HALE: I didn't hear or see anything; I knocked at the door, and still it was all quiet inside. I knew they must be up, it was past eight o'clock. So I knocked again, and I thought I heard somebody say, "Come in." I wasn't sure, I'm not sure yet, but I opened the door — this door (*indicating the door by which the two women are still standing*) and there in that rocker — (*pointing to it*) sat Mrs. Wright.

(*They all look at the rocker.*)

COUNTY ATTORNEY: What — was she doing?

HALE: She was rockin' back and forth. She had her apron in her hand and was kind of — pleating it.

COUNTY ATTORNEY: And how did she — look?

HALE: Well, she looked queer.

COUNTY ATTORNEY: How do you mean — queer?

HALE: Well, as if she didn't know what she was going to do next. And kind of done up.

COUNTY ATTORNEY: How did she seem to feel about your coming?

HALE: Why, I don't think she minded — one way or other. She didn't pay much attention. I said, "How do, Mrs. Wright it's cold, ain't it?" And she said, "Is it?" — and went on kind of pleating at her apron. Well, I was surprised; she didn't ask me to come up to the stove, or to set down, but just sat there, not even looking at me, so I said, "I want to see John." And then she — laughed. I guess you would call it a laugh. I thought of

Harry and the team outside, so I said a little sharp: "Can't I see John?" "No," she says, kind o' dull like. "Ain't he home?" says I. "Yes," says she, "he's home." "Then why can't I see him?" I asked her, out of patience. "'Cause he's dead," says she. *"Dead?"* says I. She just nodded her head, not getting a bit excited, but rockin' back and forth. "Why — where is he?" says I, not knowing what to say. She just pointed upstairs — like that (*himself pointing to the room above*) I got up, with the idea of going up there. I walked from there to here — then I says, "Why, what did he die of?" "He died of a rope round his neck," says she, and just went on pleatin' at her apron. Well, I went out and called Harry. I thought I might — need help. We went upstairs and there he was lyin' —

COUNTY ATTORNEY: I think I'd rather have you go into that upstairs, where you can point it all out. Just go on now with the rest of the story.

HALE: Well, my first thought was to get that rope off. It looked . . . (*stops, his face twitches*) . . . but Harry, he went up to him, and he said, "No, he's dead all right, and we'd better not touch anything." So we went back down stairs. She was still sitting that same way. "Has anybody been notified?" I asked. "No," says she unconcerned. "Who did this, Mrs. Wright?" said Harry. He said it business-like — and she stopped pleatin' of her apron. "I don't know," she says. "You don't *know?*" says Harry. "No," says she. "Weren't you sleepin' in the bed with him?" says Harry. "Yes," says she, "but I was on the inside." "Somebody slipped a rope round his neck and strangled him and you didn't wake up?" says Harry. "I didn't wake up," she said after him. We must 'a looked as if we didn't see how that could be, for after a minute she said, "I sleep sound." Harry was going to ask her more questions but I said maybe we ought to let her tell her story first to the coroner, or the sheriff, so Harry went fast as he could to Rivers' place, where there's a telephone.

COUNTY ATTORNEY: And what did Mrs. Wright do when she knew that you had gone for the coroner?

HALE: She moved from that chair to this one over here (*pointing to a small chair in the corner*) and just sat there with her hands held together and looking down. I got a feeling that I ought to make some conversation, so I said I had come in to see if John wanted to put in a telephone, and at that she started to laugh, and then she stopped and looked at me — scared. (*the County Attorney, who has had his notebook out, makes a note*) I dunno, maybe it wasn't scared. I wouldn't like to say it was. Soon Harry got back, and then Dr. Lloyd came, and you, Mr. Peters, and so I guess that's all I know that you don't.

COUNTY ATTORNEY (*looking around*): I guess we'll go upstairs first — and then out to the barn and around there. (*to the Sheriff*) You're convinced that there was nothing important here — nothing that would point to any motive.

SHERIFF: Nothing here but kitchen things.

(*The County Attorney, after again looking around the kitchen, opens the door of a cupboard closet. He gets up on a chair and looks on a shelf. Pulls his hand away, sticky.*)

COUNTY ATTORNEY: Here's a nice mess.

(*The women draw nearer.*)

MRS. PETERS (*to the other woman*): Oh, her fruit; it did freeze. (*to the Lawyer*) She worried about that when it turned so cold. She said the fire'd go out and her jars would break.

SHERIFF: Well, can you beat the women! Held for murder and worryin' about her preserves.

COUNTY ATTORNEY: I guess before we're through she may have something more serious than preserves to worry about.

HALE: Well, women are used to worrying over trifles.

(*The two women move a little closer together.*)

COUNTY ATTORNEY (*with the gallantry of a young politician*): And yet, for all their worries, what would we do without the ladies? (*the women do not unbend. He goes to the sink, takes a dipperful of water from the pail and pouring it into a basin, washes his hands. Starts to wipe them on the roller-towel, turns it for a cleaner place*) Dirty towels! (*kicks his foot against the pans under the sink*) Not much of a housekeeper, would you say, ladies?

MRS. HALE (*stiffly*): There's a great deal of work to be done on a farm.

COUNTY ATTORNEY: To be sure. And yet (*with a little bow to her*) I know there are some Dickson county farmhouses which do not have such roller towels.

(*He gives it a pull to expose its length again.*)

MRS. HALE: Those towels get dirty awful quick. Men's hands aren't always as clean as they might be.

COUNTY ATTORNEY: Ah, loyal to your sex, I see. But you and Mrs. Wright were neighbors. I suppose you were friends, too.

MRS. HALE (*shaking her head*): I've not seen much of her of late years. I've not been in this house — it's more than a year.

COUNTY ATTORNEY: And why was that? You didn't like her?

MRS. HALE: I liked her all well enough. Farmers' wives have their hands full, Mr. Henderson. And then —

COUNTY ATTORNEY: Yes — ?

MRS. HALE (*looking about*): It never seemed a very cheerful place.

COUNTY ATTORNEY: No — it's not cheerful. I shouldn't say she had the home-making instinct.

MRS. HALE: Well, I don't know as Wright had, either.

COUNTY ATTORNEY: You mean that they didn't get on very well?

MRS. HALE: No, I don't mean anything. But I don't think a place'd be any cheerfuller for John Wright's being in it.

COUNTY ATTORNEY: I'd like to talk more of that a little later. I want to get the lay of things upstairs now.

(*He goes to the left, where three steps lead to a stair door.*)

SHERIFF: I suppose anything Mrs. Peters does'll be all right. She was to take in some clothes for her, you know, and a few little things. We left in such a hurry yesterday.

COUNTY ATTORNEY: Yes, but I would like to see what you take, Mrs. Peters, and keep an eye out for anything that might be of use to us.

MRS. PETERS: Yes, Mr. Henderson.

(*The women listen to the men's steps on the stairs, then look about the kitchen.*)

MRS. HALE: I'd hate to have men coming into my kitchen, snooping around and criticising.

(*She arranges the pans under sink which the Lawyer had shoved out of place.*)

MRS. PETERS: Of course it's no more than their duty.

MRS. HALE: Duty's all right, but I guess that deputy sheriff that came out to make the fire might have got a little of this on. (*gives the roller towel a pull*) Wish I'd thought of that sooner. Seems mean to talk about her for not having things slicked up when she had to come away in such a hurry.

MRS. PETERS (*who has gone to a small table in the left rear corner of the room, and lifted one end of a towel that covers a pan*): She had bread set.

(*Stands still.*)

MRS. HALE (*eyes fixed on a loaf of bread beside the breadbox, which is on a low shelf at the other side of the room. Moves slowly toward it*): She was going to put this in there. (*picks up loaf, then abruptly drops it. In manner of returning to familiar things*) It's a shame about her fruit. I wonder if it's all gone. (*gets up on the chair and looks*) I think there's some here that's all right, Mrs. Peters. Yes—here; (*holding it toward the window*) this is cherries, too. (*looking again*) I declare I believe that's the only one. (*gets down, bottle in her hand. Goes to the sink and wipes it off on the outside*) She'll feel awful bad after all her hard work in the hot weather. I remember the afternoon I put up my cherries last summer.

(*She puts the bottle on the big kitchen table, center of the room. With a sigh, is about to sit down in the rocking-chair. Before she is seated realizes what chair it is; with a slow look at it, steps back. The chair which she has touched rocks back and forth.*)

MRS. PETERS: Well, I must get those things from the front room closet. (*she goes to the door at the right, but after looking into the other room, steps back*) You coming with me, Mrs. Hale? You could help me carry them.

(*They go in the other room; reappear, Mrs. Peters carrying a dress and skirt, Mrs. Hale following with a pair of shoes.*)

MRS. PETERS: My, it's cold in there.

(*She puts the clothes on the big table, and hurries to the stove.*)

MRS. HALE (*examining the skirt*): Wright was close. I think maybe that's why she kept so much to herself. She didn't even belong to the Ladies Aid. I suppose she felt she couldn't do her part, and then you don't enjoy things when you feel shabby. She used to wear pretty clothes and be lively, when she was Minnie Foster, one of the town girls singing in the choir. But that — oh, that was thirty years ago. This all you was to take in?

MRS. PETERS: She said she wanted an apron. Funny thing to want, for there isn't much to get you dirty in jail, goodness knows. But I suppose just to make her feel more natural. She said they was in the top drawer in this cupboard. Yes, here. And then her little shawl that always hung behind the door. (*opens stair door and looks*) Yes, here it is.

(*Quickly shuts door leading upstairs.*)

MRS. HALE (*abruptly moving toward her*): Mrs. Peters?

MRS. PETERS: Yes, Mrs. Hale?

MRS. HALE: Do you think she did it?

MRS. PETERS (*in a frightened voice*): Oh, I don't know.

MRS. HALE: Well, I don't think she did. Asking for an apron and her little shawl. Worrying about her fruit.

MRS. PETERS (*starts to speak, glances up, where footsteps are heard in the room above. In a low voice*): Mr. Peters says it looks bad for her. Mr. Henderson is awful sarcastic in a speech and he'll make fun of her sayin' she didn't wake up.

MRS. HALE: Well, I guess John Wright didn't wake when they was slipping that rope under his neck.

MRS. PETERS: No, it's strange. It must have been done awful crafty and still. They say it was such a — funny way to kill a man, rigging it all up like that.

MRS. HALE: That's just what Mr. Hale said. There was a gun in the house. He says that's what he can't understand.

MRS. PETERS: Mr. Henderson said coming out that what was needed for the case was a motive; something to show anger, or — sudden feeling.

MRS. HALE (*who is standing by the table*): Well, I don't see any signs of anger around here. (*she puts her hand on the dish towel which lies on the table, stands looking down at table, one half of which is clean, the other half messy*) It's wiped to here. (*makes a move as if to finish work, then turns and looks at loaf of bread outside the breadbox. Drops towel. In that voice of coming back to familiar things.*) Wonder how they are finding things upstairs. I hope she had it a little more red-up° there. You know, it seems kind of *sneaking.* Locking her up in town and then coming out here and trying to get her own house to turn against her!

MRS. PETERS: But Mrs. Hale, the law is the law.

MRS. HALE: I s'pose 'tis. (*unbuttoning her coat*) Better loosen up your things, Mrs. Peters. You won't feel them when you go out.

(*Mrs. Peters takes off her fur tippet,° goes to hang it on hook at back of room, stands looking at the under part of the small corner table.*)

---

red-up: Orderly; picked up.   **tippet:** A shoulder cape.

MRS. PETERS: She was piecing a quilt.

(*She brings the large sewing basket and they look at the bright pieces.*)

MRS. HALE: It's log cabin pattern. Pretty, isn't it? I wonder if she was goin' to quilt it or just knot it?

(*Footsteps have been heard coming down the stairs. The Sheriff enters followed by Hale and the County Attorney.*)

SHERIFF: They wonder if she was going to quilt it or just knot it!

(*The men laugh, the women look abashed.*)

COUNTY ATTORNEY (*rubbing his hands over the stove*): Frank's fire didn't do much up there, did it? Well, let's go out to the barn and get that cleared up.

(*The men go outside.*)

MRS. HALE (*resentfully*): I don't know as there's anything so strange, our takin' up our time with little things while we're waiting for them to get the evidence. (*she sits down at the big table smoothing out a block with decision*) I don't see as it's anything to laugh about.

MRS. PETERS (*apologetically*): Of course they've got awful important things on their minds.

(*Pulls up a chair and joins Mrs. Hale at the table.*)

MRS. HALE (*examining another block*): Mrs. Peters, look at this one. Here, this is the one she was working on, and look at the sewing! All the rest of it has been so nice and even. And look at this! It's all over the place! Why, it looks as if she didn't know what she was about!

(*After she has said this they look at each other, then start to glance back at the door. After an instant Mrs. Hale has pulled at a knot and ripped the sewing.*)

MRS. PETERS: Oh, what are you doing, Mrs. Hale?

MRS. HALE (*mildly*): Just pulling out a stitch or two that's not sewed very good. (*threading a needle*) Bad sewing always made me fidgety.

MRS. PETERS (*nervously*): I don't think we ought to touch things.

MRS. HALE: I'll just finish up this end. (*suddenly stopping and leaning forward*) Mrs. Peters?

MRS. PETERS: Yes, Mrs. Hale?

MRS. HALE: What do you suppose she was so nervous about?

MRS. PETERS: Oh—I don't know. I don't know as she was nervous. I sometimes sew awful queer when I'm just tired. (*Mrs. Hale starts to say something, looks at Mrs. Peters, then goes on sewing*) Well I must get these things wrapped up. They may be through sooner than we think. (*putting apron and other things together*) I wonder where I can find a piece of paper, and string.

MRS. HALE: In that cupboard, maybe.

MRS. PETERS (*looking in cupboard*): Why, here's a bird-cage. (*holds it up*) Did she have a bird, Mrs. Hale?

MRS. HALE: Why, I don't know whether she did or not — I've not been here for so long. There was a man around last year selling canaries cheap, but I don't know as she took one; maybe she did. She used to sing real pretty herself.

MRS. PETERS (*glancing around*): Seems funny to think of a bird here. But she must have had one, or why would she have a cage? I wonder what happened to it.

MRS. HALE: I s'pose maybe the cat got it.

MRS. PETERS: No, she didn't have a cat. She's got that feeling some people have about cats — being afraid of them. My cat got in her room and she was real upset and asked me to take it out.

MRS. HALE: My sister Bessie was like that. Queer, ain't it?

MRS. PETERS (*examining the cage*): Why, look at this door. It's broke. One hinge is pulled apart.

MRS. HALE (*looking too*): Looks as if someone must have been rough with it.

MRS. PETERS: Why, yes.

(*She brings the cage forward and puts it on the table.*)

MRS. HALE: I wish if they're going to find any evidence they'd be about it. I don't like this place.

MRS. PETERS: But I'm awful glad you came with me, Mrs. Hale. It would be lonesome for me sitting here alone.

MRS. HALE: It would, wouldn't it? (*dropping her sewing*) But I tell you what I do wish, Mrs. Peters. I wish I had come over sometimes when *she* was here. I — (*looking around the room*) — wish I had.

MRS. PETERS: But of course you were awful busy, Mrs. Hale — your house and your children.

MRS. HALE: I could've come. I stayed away because it weren't cheerful — and that's why I ought to have come. I — I've never liked this place. Maybe because it's down in a hollow and you don't see the road. I dunno what it is, but it's a lonesome place and always was. I wish I had come over to see Minnie Foster sometimes. I can see now — (*shakes her head*)

MRS. PETERS: Well, you mustn't reproach yourself, Mrs. Hale. Somehow we just don't see how it is with other folks until — something comes up.

MRS. HALE: Not having children makes less work — but it makes a quiet house, and Wright out to work all day, and no company when he did come in. Did you know John Wright, Mrs. Peters?

MRS. PETERS: Not to know him; I've seen him in town. They say he was a good man.

MRS. HALE: Yes — good; he didn't drink, and kept his word as well as most, I guess, and paid his debts. But he was a hard man, Mrs. Peters. Just to pass the time of day with him — (*shivers*) Like a raw wind that gets to the bone. (*pauses, her eye falling on the cage*) I should think she would 'a wanted a bird. But what do you suppose went with it?

MRS. PETERS: I don't know, unless it got sick and died.

(*She reaches over and swings the broken door, swings it again, both women watch it.*)

MRS. HALE: You weren't raised round here, were you? (*Mrs. Peters shakes her head*) You didn't know — her?

MRS. PETERS: Not till they brought her yesterday.

MRS. HALE: She — come to think of it, she was kind of like a bird herself — real sweet and pretty, but kind of timid and — fluttery. How — she — did — change. (*silence; then as if struck by a happy thought and relieved to get back to everyday things*) Tell you what, Mrs. Peters, why don't you take the quilt in with you? It might take up her mind.

MRS. PETERS: Why, I think that's a real nice idea, Mrs. Hale. There couldn't possibly be any objection to it, could there? Now, just what would I take? I wonder if her patches are in here — and her things.

(*They look in the sewing basket.*)

MRS. HALE: Here's some red. I expect this has got sewing things in it. (*brings out a fancy box*) What a pretty box. Looks like something somebody would give you. Maybe her scissors are in here. (*Opens box. Suddenly puts her hand to her nose*) Why — (*Mrs. Peters bends nearer, then turns her face away*) There's something wrapped up in this piece of silk.

MRS. PETERS: Why, this isn't her scissors.

MRS. HALE (*lifting the silk*): Oh, Mrs. Peters — it's —

(*Mrs. Peters bends closer.*)

MRS. PETERS: It's the bird.

MRS. HALE (*jumping up*): But, Mrs. Peters — look at it! It's neck! Look at its neck! It's all — other side *to*.

MRS. PETERS: Somebody — wrung — its — neck.

(*Their eyes meet. A look of growing comprehension, of horror. Steps are heard outside. Mrs. Hale slips box under quilt pieces, and sinks into her chair. Enter Sheriff and County Attorney. Mrs. Peters rises.*)

COUNTY ATTORNEY (*as one turning from serious things to little pleasantries*): Well ladies, have you decided whether she was going to quilt it or knot it?

MRS. PETERS: We think she was going to — knot it.

COUNTY ATTORNEY: Well, that's interesting, I'm sure. (*seeing the birdcage*) Has the bird flown?

MRS. HALE (*putting more quilt pieces over the box*): We think the — cat got it.

COUNTY ATTORNEY (*preoccupied*): Is there a cat?

(*Mrs. Hale glances in quick covert way at Mrs. Peters.*)

MRS. PETERS: Well, not *now*. They're superstitious, you know. They leave.

COUNTY ATTORNEY (*to Sheriff Peters, continuing an interrupted conversation*): No sign at all of anyone having come from the outside. Their own rope. Now let's go up again and go over it piece by piece. (*they start upstairs*) It would have to have been someone who knew just the —

(*Mrs. Peters sits down. The two women sit there not looking at one another, but as if peering into something and at the same time holding back. When they talk now it is in the manner of feeling their way over strange ground, as if afraid of what they are saying, but as if they can not help saying it.*)

MRS. HALE: She liked the bird. She was going to bury it in that pretty box.

MRS. PETERS (*in a whisper*): When I was a girl — my kitten — there was a boy took a hatchet, and before my eyes — and before I could get there — (*covers her face an instant*) If they hadn't held me back I would have — (*catches herself, looks upstairs where steps are heard, falters weakly*) — hurt him.

MRS. HALE (*with a slow look around her*): I wonder how it would seem never to have had any children around. (*pause*) No, Wright wouldn't like the bird — a thing that sang. She used to sing. He killed that, too.

MRS. PETERS (*moving uneasily*): We don't know who killed the bird.

MRS. HALE: I knew John Wright.

MRS. PETERS: It was an awful thing was done in this house that night, Mrs. Hale. Killing a man while he slept, slipping a rope around his neck that choked the life out of him.

MRS. HALE: His neck. Choked the life out of him.

(*Her hand goes out and rests on the bird-cage.*)

MRS. PETERS (*with rising voice*): We don't know who killed him. We don't *know*.

MRS. HALE (*her own feeling not interrupted*): If there'd been years and years of nothing, then a bird to sing to you, it would be awful — still, after the bird was still.

MRS. PETERS (*something within her speaking*): I know what stillness is. When we homesteaded in Dakota, and my first baby died — after he was two years old, and me with no other then —

MRS. HALE (*moving*): How soon do you suppose they'll be through, looking for the evidence?

MRS. PETERS: I know what stillness is. (*pulling herself back*) The law has got to punish crime, Mrs. Hale.

MRS. HALE (*not as if answering that*): I wish you'd seen Minnie Foster when she wore a white dress with blue ribbons and stood up there in the choir and sang. (*a look around the room*) Oh, I *wish* I'd come over here once in a while! That was a crime! That was a crime! Who's going to punish that?

MRS. PETERS (*looking upstairs*): We mustn't — take on.

MRS. HALE: I might have known she needed help! I know how things can be — for women. I tell you, it's queer, Mrs. Peters. We live close together and we live far apart. We all go through the same things — it's all just a different kind of the same thing. (*brushes her eyes, noticing the bottle of fruit, reaches out for it*) If I was you, I wouldn't tell her her fruit was gone. Tell her it *ain't*. Tell her it's all right. Take this in to prove it to her. She — she may never know whether it was broke or not.

MRS. PETERS (*takes the bottle, looks about for something to wrap it in; takes petticoat from the clothes brought from the other room, very nervously begins winding this around the bottle. In a false voice*): My, it's a good thing the men couldn't hear us. Wouldn't they just laugh! Getting all stirred up over a little thing like a — dead canary. As if that could have anything to do with — with — wouldn't they *laugh!*

(*The men are heard coming down stairs.*)

MRS. HALE (*under her breath*): Maybe they would — maybe they wouldn't.

COUNTY ATTORNEY: No, Peters, it's all perfectly clear except a reason for doing it. But you know juries when it comes to women. If there was some definite thing. Something to show — something to make a story about — a thing that would connect up with this strange way of doing it —

(*The women's eyes meet for an instant. Enter Hale from outer door.*)

HALE: Well, I've got the team around. Pretty cold out there.

COUNTY ATTORNEY: I'm going to stay here a while by myself. (*to the Sheriff*) You can send Frank out for me, can't you? I want to go over everything. I'm not satisfied that we can't do better.

SHERIFF: Do you want to see what Mrs. Peters is going to take in?

(*The Lawyer goes to the table, picks up the apron, laughs.*)

COUNTY ATTORNEY: Oh, I guess they're not very dangerous things the ladies have picked out. (*Moves a few things about, disturbing the quilt pieces which cover the box. Steps back*) No, Mrs. Peters doesn't need supervising. For that matter, a sheriff's wife is married to the law. Ever think of it that way, Mrs. Peters?

MRS. PETERS: Not — just that way.

SHERIFF (*chuckling*): Married to the law. (*moves toward the other room*) I just want you to come in here a minute, George. We ought to take a look at these windows.

COUNTY ATTORNEY (*scoffingly*): Oh, windows!

SHERIFF: We'll be right out, Mr. Hale.

(*Hale goes outside. The Sheriff follows the County Attorney into the other room. Then Mrs. Hale rises, hands tight together, looking intensely at Mrs. Peters, whose eyes make a slow turn, finally meeting Mrs. Hale's. A moment Mrs. Hale holds her, then her own eyes point the way to where the box is concealed. Suddenly Mrs. Peters throws back quilt pieces and tries to put the box in the bag she is wearing. It is too big. She opens box, starts to take bird out, cannot touch it, goes to pieces, stands there helpless. Sound of a knob turning in the other room. Mrs. Hale snatches the box and puts it in the pocket of her big coat. Enter County Attorney and Sheriff.*)

COUNTY ATTORNEY (*facetiously*): Well, Henry, at least we found out that she was not going to quilt it. She was going to — what is it you call it, ladies?

MRS. HALE (*her hand against her pocket*): We call it — knot it, Mr. Henderson.

CURTAIN

APPROACHING THE READING

1. Summarize the plot and explain the significance of details in it (the mess in the kitchen, the jam and jam jars, the quilting and the way Mrs. Wright was doing it, the bird and birdcage, the choice of a rope as weapon, and so on). If you feel you would have difficulty explaining the plot to a friend, go back to the play and look at it again in terms of the above, or ask questions about it in class.

2. Examine the way the story is presented as a mystery play. Do you notice situations or lines that are conventional in detective stories you've read or seen in movies or on television? Find uses of foreshadowing in the play and explain whether you find these uses effective or ineffective.

   Explore this author and play in depth, including images and cultural documents, with VirtuaLit Drama at bedfordstmartins.com/approachinglit.

3. List several conflicts, and several types of conflict, in the play. Which conflicts focus your attention on issues that seem important in the play? List several such issues.

4. Reflect on the characters: Who are the major characters, what is important to them, what motivates them, how do they change (if they do) and why? How does your impression of them change? Who are the minor characters, and what are their roles and significance?

5. Unlike *Florence* (p. 795), this play does not indicate the time in which the action takes place. It was written in 1916. If you were directing a production of the play, would you give it a setting in the past (perhaps "Time: the early 1900s") or in the present? Why? How would that decision affect costuming, set design, props, and so on? What difference, if any, would that decision have on the central issues explored in the play?

We won't discuss here the characters, conflicts, and themes of *Trifles*. Instead, we direct your attention to matters concerning setting and structure. Very little is indicated about setting in the broad sense. The stage directions place the play in a farmhouse, but they do not indicate what state or region of the country. Perhaps the setting is a farm in the Midwest since Glaspell was born and raised in Iowa and worked for a short time as a journalist in Des Moines. But she moved to the Northeast more than a decade before she wrote *Trifles,* and its setting could just as easily be rural New England.

The text indicates that the location of the farmhouse is isolated and depressing. As Mrs. Hale says, "I—I've never liked this place. Maybe because it's down in a hollow and you don't see the road. I dunno what it is, but it's a lonesome place and always was" (p. 829). Such isolation is important to the play: Mrs. Wright lacks contact with other people, sees neither neighbors nor friends. Her only source of companionship is a husband who rarely talks to or interacts with others.

Glaspell was more specific about set than setting. The set is the kitchen of the Wrights' home, and the detailed stage directions give a reader lots of help in imagining how the room appears (gloomy, probably sparsely furnished, in a state of considerable disorder, with a door to outside in the rear wall) and what the room contains (a breadbox, a sink with dirty pots and pans under it, a stove, and a table).

In this play, Glaspell scatters additional stage directions throughout the text. We learn later that the room contains a cupboard, a rocking chair, a small table in the left rear corner with a large sewing basket under it, a small chair in another corner, a roller towel on the wall near the sink, and a low shelf on which the breadbox rests. The stove is a wood-burning cooking stove, and the kitchen table is large, sits in the center of the room, and probably has chairs around it. There is at least one window, a door at the right into another room, and steps at the left leading to a door behind, which are the stairs to the second floor. The text indicates that the sink does not have running water — next to it is a pail, presumably for bringing in water from a well outside, and there's a basin in the sink for washing.

A stage designer who wants to create a historically authentic set for the play would do research into early twentieth-century kitchen furnishings and either make or find pieces that approximate what Glaspell describes as the "ideal" set for this play. You as a reader probably won't be able to spend that kind of time on furnishing your mental theater in historically correct detail. But you don't need to. The set in your mind as you stage *Trifles* will differ from the set of an acting company, of course; but it's important to realize that the sets of different productions will differ too. The way each stage designer envisions Glaspell's directions is individual and unique — just as the way you visualize it will be. Some stage designers will attempt to recreate authentic early twentieth-century details, while others will give it a more timeless feel and not try for historical "correctness." Reading a set, and reading a play, is like all other kinds of reading. There is no single set design, or a single interpretation of a text, that all readers must seek to attain. Instead, we should decide what is appropriate for the drama itself and relish the diversity and enrichment that results when others see things differently from the way we do.

STRUCTURE

The structuring of a play, like that of a poem, involves external form as well as internal form. The external form starts with such features as the list of characters, the stage directions, the division of the text into speeches headed by tags identifying the characters, the stage directions guiding the actor on such things as action, tone, or expression.

External form includes the division of longer plays into acts and scenes that help you, as a viewer or reader, to follow the play by dividing it into segments that are easier to grasp than the whole at once. An **act** is a major division of a drama, a significant section of the action. In performance, the end of an act is signaled by an intermission, or by the lowering of the stage curtain. In reading, the text is usually marked as act 1, act 2, and so forth. Often playwrights structure the action so as to leave the audience in suspense at the end of an act, eager for the action to resume. Roman plays were divided into five acts, following Aristotle's belief that Greek plays fell into five parts that reflected steps in the internal development of a play (more on that to follow). Elizabethan playwrights, including Shakespeare, followed the Roman pattern, as did European dramatists generally until Ibsen began to modify it. Modern and contemporary plays are often divided into two or three acts, corresponding with the intermissions usual in performances.

Scenes are minor divisions in a drama—a single act may be divided into scenes, or a one-act play might consist of several scenes. Often a new scene jumps ahead to a different time or moves to a different location. Scene changes are signaled in different ways: the stage may empty while the curtain remains raised, or the lights may go out, or the scenery may be reconfigured. Sometimes locations are identified for the audience in the printed program. But it is left to the imagination of the reader or viewer to bridge such gaps by making the needed connections or by supplying information that is only hinted at. Many modern dramatists divide their plays only into scenes, without division into acts, though a production may label the part before the intermission as "act 1" and the part following as "act 2."

The internal structure of a play centers on **plot**, the structural pattern by which it is organized and developed. The plot in drama involves many of the same issues as plot in fiction. *Beginnings:* starting **in medias res**, for example, making use of **exposition** to explain things that occurred before the initial action of the play, and making use of **flashbacks** to clarify events prior to the beginning of the play. *Middles:* using conflicts, suspense, gaps, foreshadowings, and repetitions to increase plot "complications" and build to a climax. *Endings:* resolving (or in some cases not resolving) the mysteries, problems, or tensions that have developed in the beginning and middle and tying up loose ends to create a sense of finality. All of these terms and techniques are discussed thoroughly in pages 54–63. Reviewing those pages will prepare you for studying plot in drama.

Some theorists hold that the internal structure of a play involves a natural dramatic rhythm that develops in five divisions or steps, which some scholars believe correspond with the traditional five-act structure of a play.

- *Introduction or exposition:* The introduction, or exposition, occurs early in the play, usually as one or more characters deliver speeches providing information required for following the action of the play: introducing characters, filling in prior action and the background from which the central conflict will develop, establishing setting and tone.

- *Complication:* **Complication** is the rising action of the play; entanglements caused by the central conflict are set in motion.
- *Crisis or climax:* The **crisis** is the turning point in the action, the point at which the protagonist's situation turns for the better or worse. **Climax** is the point at which a significant emotional response is elicited. It does not always coincide with the moment of crisis.
- *Reversal:* Reversal is the falling action of a play, the depiction of the change in fortune experienced by the protagonist.
- *Catastrophe and resolution, or dénouement:* The term **catastrophe**, used mostly for tragedy, depicts the action, the unhappy ending, that results from parts 3 and 4. **Resolution**, or restoration of order, usually follows the catastrophe. **Dénouement** (French for "unknotting") is often used for the final unraveling of the plot complications in a comedy, though the unknotting at the end turns into a tying up of loose ends.

These steps can be diagrammed as a pyramid, with action rising until it reaches a peak at the climax or crisis, then falling as implications of earlier events are worked out. The diagram is often referred to as "Freytag's Pyramid" because it was developed by Gustav Freytag in the mid-1800s. Some scholars believe the five steps correspond to, and perhaps gave rise to, the traditional five-act structure of a play. But they can be applied to a one-act play as well. Follow along as we apply the above terms to *Trifles:* The first few pages of *Trifles* are the *introduction,* with Mr. Hale providing the necessary background (exposition) as he describes his encounter with Mrs. Wright the previous morning. The *complication* develops as the men seek a possible motive that would support their suspicion that Mrs. Wright killed her husband, and as the women begin to see what Mrs. Wright's life was like and to sympathize increasingly with her. The *climax* arrives when the women find the dead canary and reach a conclusion about who committed the crime. The *reversal* comes as the women struggle with whether they are obliged to inform the men about such a trifle as a dead bird and help them grasp its implications. The *resolution* comes as the ladies decide to conceal the box with the dead bird and not assist the men in their investigation of the crime.

Compression and Contrast

Dramatic works are shaped also by use of two key structural principles: compression and contrast. The first, *compression,* is necessary because although a work of fiction can extend to any length to tell its story, a playwright usually works under fairly strict time constraints. Audiences generally expect a play to last no more than three hours. There are plays that run four or five hours and some even for days, but those are the exceptions, and many playgoers may avoid them unless reviews say they are extraordinarily gripping and worthwhile. Playwrights, therefore, are usually aware of time and use techniques that enable them to compress their material economically. Being aware of such techniques can help you in understanding how a play and a play's structure works and why some things have to be handled so as to fit the constraints of time.

To compress their material, playwrights tend to start close to the most exciting or significant scene (see "Beginnings," p. 835). *Trifles,* for example, opens the morning after Mr. Wright dies because the play is most concerned with the motivation for the murder and the way Mrs. Hale and Mrs. Peters come to regard that motivation. In reading or watching plays, you need to get used to arriving in the middle of a conversation and to use what is said to figure out what happened earlier. Often it is said that dramatic action occurs only in the present: What occurs on the stage is always "now." Even when a flashback is acted out, as in *The Death of a Salesman* (p. 980), we see the past events occurring as we watch, as if they were happening now. Events that are not acted out are narrated through exposition, the way Mr. Hale fills in his experiences of the previous day. Playwrights also compress by using exposition to clarify information that the audience needs to know about earlier events and by using foreshadowing to alert us about things to watch for in what follows (see "Beginnings," p. 835). And they compress material by organizing events into moments, or scenes (p. 835).

Playwrights can achieve compression through the use of **symbols**, images or actions or characters that are first and fundamentally themselves in the play but also embody an abstract idea. Symbols are discussed at length on pages 127–33. What Chapter 6 says about symbols applies equally to drama. The same types of symbols (private, literary, conventional, traditional, and archetypal) are used in drama, and the same formal devices convey to a reader or viewer that an image, action, or character may be symbolic: repetition, description, placement in noticeable positions (title, beginning, ending, climactic scene), or a sense of weightiness or significance beyond the literal function in the work. The birdcage in *Trifles,* for example, is a literal object in the story, but it also suggests qualities of the relationship between Mr. and Mrs. Wright. Mrs. Wright used to enjoy singing and, like the bird, her song was stifled by Mr. Wright. She, like the bird, lived in a cage, trapped and broken figuratively in spirit, the way the bird's neck was broken literally. Symbols help achieve compression because the symbols — objects, character types, or actions — are seen on stage by the audience and require few words and little time to convey their meaning. The viewer, or the reader watching the play imaginatively, has the opportunity to recognize the symbol and to take part in discerning its appropriateness and meaning.

Contrast is important to playwrights both as a means of compression and as a way to establish relationships in a play. Dramatists regularly establish parallels or contrasts between two or more situations, characters, actions, or symbols to get us to notice things about each that we might miss without the pairing. Often parallel items reinforce a point or theme or serve as a means of repetition, a valuable technique for creating emphasis, while contrasts direct our attention to differences and distinctions more clearly and

www
Further explore setting and structure, including interactive exercises, with VirtuaLit Drama at bedfordstmartins.com/approachinglit.

forcefully. In *Trifles*, the stillness in the house Mrs. Peters experienced after losing a child enabled her to empathize with the similar stillness Mrs. Wright must have felt after the death of the canary. The principal contrast of the play is between the women and the men, with their different approaches, outlooks, and attitudes. The term **foil** is used for a character who stands in contrast to another character and thus calls attention to distinctive features of the second character or to significant differences between the two. Marge can be taken as a foil to the unseen Florence in Alice Childress's play (p. 795).

☑ CHECKLIST on Setting and Structure

❑ Be attentive to setting, in terms of place, time, and historical, social, and cultural context, and to the effects of setting in a play.

❑ Be attentive to stage directions provided by the playwright, and use descriptions of set, props, costumes, stage movements, and character descriptions to sharpen your images as you visualize the plays.

❑ Be alert for symbols of different kinds (literary, conventional, traditional, and archetypal) and the various ways they can contribute to a play.

❑ Notice the structuring of plot in a play: its handling of beginning, middle, and ending; its use of gaps, flashbacks, suspense, foreshadowing, and repetition; and its use of compression and contrasts.

❑ Know the traditional five-part dramatic pattern (introduction, complication, climax, reversal, and resolution) and test to see if Freytag's Pyramid applies to a particular play.

FURTHER READING

Trifles illustrates a traditional drama, conventional in structure and technique. The following short, one-act play is unconventional and experimental. It involves two characters, a single setting, and little dramatic action. In it we watch two characters as they attempt to connect with one another. But there's a twist: If the character does not connect or slips up, she or he backtracks and tries again. The play does not have conventional scene divisions; instead, each time a character misspeaks, a bell rings to signal a breakdown, and the two characters back up a line or two and try a different version. After the thirty-eighth time — well, see for yourself what happens.

David Ives   b. 1950

Sure Thing   [1988]

This play is for Jason Buzas

Betty, a woman in her late twenties, is reading at a café table. An empty chair is opposite her. Bill, same age, enters.

BILL: Excuse me. Is this chair taken?
BETTY: Excuse me?
BILL: Is this taken?
BETTY: Yes it is.
BILL: Oh. Sorry.
BETTY: Sure thing.

(*A bell rings softly.*)

BILL: Excuse me. Is this chair taken?
BETTY: Excuse me?
BILL: Is this taken?
BETTY: No, but I'm expecting somebody in a minute.
BILL: Oh. Thanks anyway.
BETTY: Sure thing.

(*A bell rings softly.*)

BILL: Excuse me. Is this chair taken?
BETTY: No, but I'm expecting somebody very shortly.
BILL: Would you mind if I sit here till he or she or it comes?
BETTY (*glances at her watch*): They do seem to be pretty late. . . .
BILL: You never know who you might be turning down.
BETTY: Sorry. Nice try, though.
BILL: Sure thing.

(*Bell.*)

Is this seat taken?
BETTY: No it's not.
BILL: Would you mind if I sit here?
BETTY: Yes I would.
BILL: Oh.

(*Bell.*)

Is this chair taken?
BETTY: No it's not.
BILL: Would you mind if I sit here?
BETTY: No. Go ahead.
BILL: Thanks. (*He sits. She continues reading.*) Everyplace else seems to be taken.
BETTY: Mm-hm.

BILL: Great place.
BETTY: Mm-hm.
BILL: What's the book?
BETTY: I just wanted to read in quiet, if you don't mind.
BILL: No. Sure thing.

(*Bell.*)

BILL: Everyplace else seems to be taken.
BETTY: Mm-hm.
BILL: Great place for reading.
BETTY: Yes, I like it.
BILL: What's the book?
BETTY: *The Sound and the Fury.*
BILL: Oh. Hemingway.

(*Bell.*)

What's the book?
BETTY: *The Sound and the Fury.*
BILL: Oh. Faulkner.
BETTY: Have you read it?
BILL: Not . . . actually. I've sure read *about* it, though. It's supposed to be great.
BETTY: It is great.
BILL: I hear it's great. (*Small pause.*) Waiter?

(*Bell.*)

What's the book?
BETTY: *The Sound and the Fury.*
BILL: Oh. Faulkner.
BETTY: Have you read it?
BILL: I'm a Mets fan, myself.

(*Bell.*)

BETTY: Have you read it?
BILL: Yeah, I read it in college.
BETTY: Where was college?
BILL: I went to Oral Roberts University.

(*Bell.*)

BETTY: Where was college?
BILL: I was lying. I never really went to college. I just like to party.

(*Bell.*)

BETTY: Where was college?
BILL: Harvard.

BETTY: Do you like Faulkner?

BILL: I love Faulkner. I spent a whole winter reading him once.

BETTY: I've just started.

BILL: I was so excited after ten pages that I went out and bought everything else he wrote. One of the greatest reading experiences of my life. I mean, all that incredible psychological understanding. Page after page of gorgeous prose. His profound grasp of the mystery of time and human existence. The smells of the earth . . . What do you think?

BETTY: I think it's pretty boring.

(Bell.)

BILL: What's the book?

BETTY: *The Sound and the Fury.*

BILL: Oh! Faulkner!

BETTY: Do you like Faulkner?

BILL: I love Faulkner.

BETTY: He's incredible.

BILL: I spent a whole winter reading him once.

BETTY: I was so excited after ten pages that I went out and bought everything else he wrote.

BILL: All that incredible psychological understanding.

BETTY: And the prose is so gorgeous.

BILL: And the way he's grasped the mystery of time —

BETTY: — and human existence. I can't believe I've waited this long to read him.

BILL: You never know. You might not have liked him before.

BETTY: That's true.

BILL: You might not have been ready for him. You have to hit these things at the right moment or it's no good.

BETTY: That's happened to me.

BILL: It's all in the timing. *(Small pause.)* My name's Bill, by the way.

BETTY: I'm Betty.

BILL: Hi.

BETTY: Hi. *(Small pause.)*

BILL: Yes I thought reading Faulkner was . . . a great experience.

BETTY: Yes. *(Small pause.)*

BILL: *The Sound and the Fury* . . . *(Another small pause.)*

BETTY: Well. Onwards and upwards. *(She goes back to her book.)*

BILL: Waiter — ?

(Bell.)

You have to hit these things at the right moment or it's no good.

BETTY: That's happened to me.

BILL: It's all in the timing. My name's Bill, by the way.

BETTY: I'm Betty.

BILL: Hi.

BETTY: Hi.

BILL: Do you come in here a lot?

BETTY: Actually I'm just in town for two days from Pakistan.

BILL: Oh. Pakistan.

(*Bell.*)

My name's Bill, by the way.

BETTY: I'm Betty.

BILL: Hi.

BETTY: Hi.

BILL: Do you come in here a lot?

BETTY: Every once in a while. Do you?

BILL: Not so much anymore. Not as much as I used to. Before my nervous breakdown.

(*Bell.*)

Do you come in here a lot?

BETTY: Why are you asking?

BILL: Just interested.

BETTY: Are you really interested, or do you just want to pick me up?

BILL: No, I'm really interested.

BETTY: Why would you be interested in whether I come in here a lot?

BILL: I'm just . . . getting acquainted.

BETTY: Maybe you're only interested for the sake of making small talk long enough to ask me back to your place to listen to some music, or because you've just rented this great tape for your VCR, or because you've got some terrific unknown Django Reinhardt record, only all you really want to do is fuck — which you won't do very well — after which you'll go into the bathroom and pee very loudly, then pad into the kitchen and get yourself a beer from the refrigerator without asking me whether I'd like anything, and then you'll proceed to lie back down beside me and confess that you've got a girlfriend named Stephanie who's away at medical school in Belgium for a year, and that you've been involved with her — *off and on* — in what you'll call a very "intricate" relationship, for the past *seven YEARS.* None of which *interests* me, mister!

BILL: Okay.

(*Bell.*)

Do you come in here a lot?

BETTY: Every other day, I think.

BILL: I come in here quite a lot and I don't remember seeing you.

BETTY: I guess we must be on different schedules.

BILL: Missed connections.

BETTY: Yes. Different time zones.

BILL: Amazing how you can live right next door to somebody in this town and never even know it.

BETTY: I know.

BILL: City life.

BETTY: It's crazy.

BILL: We probably pass each other in the street every day. Right in front of this place, probably.

BETTY: Yep.

BILL (*looks around*): Well the waiters here sure seem to be in some different time zone. I can't seem to locate one anywhere. . . . Waiter! (*He looks back.*) So what do you — (*He sees that she's gone back to her book.*)

BETTY: I beg pardon?

BILL: Nothing. Sorry.

(*Bell.*)

BETTY: I guess we must be on different schedules.

BILL: Missed connections.

BETTY: Yes. Different time zones.

BILL: Amazing how you can live right next door to somebody in this town and never even know it.

BETTY: I know.

BILL: City life.

BETTY: It's crazy.

BILL: You weren't waiting for somebody when I came in, were you?

BETTY: Actually I was.

BILL: Oh. Boyfriend?

BETTY: Sort of.

BILL: What's a sort-of boyfriend?

BETTY: My husband.

BILL: Ah-ha.

(*Bell.*)

You weren't waiting for somebody when I came in, were you?

BETTY: Actually I was.

BILL: Oh. Boyfriend?

BETTY: Sort of.

BILL: What's a sort-of boyfriend?

BETTY: We were meeting here to break up.

BILL: Mm-hm . . .

(*Bell.*)

What's a sort-of boyfriend?

BETTY: My lover. Here she comes right now!

(*Bell.*)

BILL: You weren't waiting for somebody when I came in, were you?

BETTY: No, just reading.

BILL: Sort of a sad occupation for a Friday night, isn't it? Reading here, all by yourself?

BETTY: Do you think so?

BILL: Well sure. I mean, what's a good-looking woman like you doing out alone on a Friday night?

BETTY: Trying to keep away from lines like that.

BILL: No, listen —

(*Bell.*)

You weren't waiting for somebody when I came in, were you?

BETTY: No, just reading.

BILL: Sort of a sad occupation for a Friday night, isn't it? Reading here all by yourself?

BETTY: I guess it is, in a way.

BILL: What's a good-looking woman like you doing out alone on a Friday night anyway? No offense, but . . .

BETTY: I'm out alone on a Friday night for the first time in a very long time.

BILL: Oh.

BETTY: You see, I just recently ended a relationship.

BILL: Oh.

BETTY: Of rather long standing.

BILL: I'm sorry. (*Small pause.*) Well listen, since reading by yourself is such a sad occupation for a Friday night, would you like to go elsewhere?

BETTY: No . . .

BILL: Do something else?

BETTY: No thanks.

BILL: I was headed out to the movies in a while anyway.

BETTY: I don't think so.

BILL: Big chance to let Faulkner catch his breath. All those long sentences get him pretty tired.

BETTY: Thanks anyway.

BILL: Okay.

BETTY: I appreciate the invitation.

BILL: Sure thing.

(*Bell.*)

You weren't waiting for somebody when I came in, were you?

BETTY: No, just reading.

BILL: Sort of a sad occupation for a Friday night, isn't it? Reading here all by yourself?

BETTY: I guess I was trying to think of it as existentially romantic. You know — cappuccino, great literature, rainy night . . .

BILL: That only works in Paris. We *could* hop the late plane to Paris. Get on a Concorde. Find a café . . .
BETTY: I'm a little short on plane fare tonight.
BILL: Darn it, so am I.
BETTY: To tell you the truth, I was headed to the movies after I finished this section. Would you like to come along? Since you can't locate a waiter?
BILL: That's a very nice offer, but . . .
BETTY: Uh-huh. Girlfriend?
BILL: Two, actually. One of them's pregnant, and Stephanie —

(*Bell.*)

BETTY: Girlfriend?
BILL: No, I don't have a girlfriend. Not if you mean the castrating bitch I dumped last night.

(*Bell.*)

BETTY: Girlfriend?
BILL: Sort of. Sort of.
BETTY: What's a sort-of girlfriend?
BILL: My mother.

(*Bell.*)

I just ended a relationship, actually.
BETTY: Oh.
BILL: Of rather long standing.
BETTY: I'm sorry to hear it.
BILL: This is my first night out alone in a long time. I feel a little bit at sea, to tell you the truth.
BETTY: So you didn't stop to talk because you're a Moonie, or you have some weird political affiliation — ?
BILL: Nope. Straight-down-the-ticket Republican.

(*Bell.*)

Straight-down-the-ticket Democrat.

(*Bell.*)

Can I tell you something about politics?

(*Bell.*)

I like to think of myself as a citizen of the universe.

(*Bell.*)

I'm unaffiliated.
BETTY: That's a relief. So am I.

BILL: I vote my beliefs.

BETTY: Labels are not important.

BILL: Labels are not important, exactly. Take me, for example. I mean, what does it matter if I had a two-point at —

(*Bell.*)

three-point at —

(*Bell.*)

four-point at college? Or if I did come from Pittsburgh —

(*Bell.*)

Cleveland —

(*Bell.*)

Westchester County?

BETTY: Sure.

BILL: I believe that a man is what he is.

(*Bell.*)

A person is what he is.

(*Bell.*)

A person is . . . what they are.

BETTY: I think so too.

BILL: So what if I admire Trotsky?

(*Bell.*)

So what if I once had a total-body liposuction?

(*Bell.*)

So what if I don't have a penis?

(*Bell.*)

So what if I spent a year in the Peace Corps? I was acting on my convictions.

BETTY: Sure.

BILL: You just can't hang a sign on a person.

BETTY: Absolutely. I'll bet you're a Scorpio.

(*Many bells ring.*)

Listen, I was headed to the movies after I finished this section. Would you like to come along?

BILL: That sounds like fun. What's playing?

BETTY: A couple of the really early Woody Allen movies.

BILL: Oh.

BETTY: You don't like Woody Allen?

BILL: Sure. I like Woody Allen.

BETTY: But you're not crazy about Woody Allen.

BILL: Those early ones kind of get on my nerves.

BETTY: Uh-huh.

(Bell.)

BILL: Y'know I was headed to the —

BETTY (simultaneously): I was thinking about —

BILL: I'm sorry.

BETTY: No, go ahead.

BILL: I was going to say that I was headed to the movies in a little while, and . . .

BETTY: So was I.

BILL: The Woody Allen festival?

BETTY: Just up the street.

BILL: Do you like the early ones?

BETTY: I think anybody who doesn't ought to be run off the planet.

BILL: How many times have you seen *Bananas*?

BETTY: Eight times.

BILL: Twelve. So are you still interested (*Long pause.*)

BETTY: Do you like Entenmann's crumb cake . . . ?

BILL: Last night I went out at two in the morning to get one. Did you have an Etch-a-Sketch as a child?

BETTY: Yes! And do you like Brussels sprouts? (*Pause.*)

BILL: No, I think they're disgusting.

BETTY: They *are* disgusting!

BILL: Do you still believe in marriage in spite of current sentiments against it?

BETTY: Yes.

BILL: And children?

BETTY: Three of them.

BILL: Two girls and a boy.

BETTY: Harvard, Vassar, and Brown.

BILL: And will you love me?

BETTY: Yes.

BILL: And cherish me forever?

BETTY: Yes.

BILL: Do you still want to go to the movies?

BETTY: Sure thing.

BILL AND BETTY (*together*): Waiter!

BLACKOUT

APPROACHING THE READING

1. The text describes the immediate setting as a café but says nothing about where it is located. What assumptions do you make as you read about the broader setting of the play? How does your having to do this affect your reading and add to or detract from the play?

2. Describe the dramatic structure of the play. Could you argue that, experimental as it is, it still has a traditional introduction, complication, climax, reversal, and resolution, or something corresponding to them? If so, explain. If not, describe the distinctions.

3. It has been said that *Sure Thing* includes a variety of characters and a wide range of emotions. How can there be a "variety of characters" in a two-person play?

4. Which character would you call the protagonist? Which the antagonist? Describe both characters. Do you think either changes or grows in the course of the play? If so, how?

5. Does the play's unorthodox form affect how you engage with the characters and the issues explored in the play? Be ready to discuss the basis of its appeal and effect.

RESPONDING THROUGH WRITING

Journal Entries

1. Write a journal entry listing ways the structuring of Susan Glaspell's *Trifles* (p. 822) both corresponds to and doesn't correspond to a popular TV detective drama. Do the same for David Ives's *Sure Thing* (p. 839) but use a popular TV sitcom instead.

2. In your journal, write a list of stage movements in Susan Glaspell's *Trifles* (p. 822), both those noted in the stage directions and those suggested by the text, and comment on their significance. Note especially what is indicated by the way characters are positioned in relation to one another.

www
Research the authors in this chapter with LitLinks, or take a quiz on the plays with LitQuiz, at bedfordstmartins.com/ approachinglit.

3. Write a journal entry listing various uses of irony in Susan Glaspell's *Trifles* (p. 822) and commenting on their importance to the effect and meaning of the play.

Literary Analysis Papers

4. Write a paper analyzing the means of characterization in Susan Glaspell's *Trifles* (p. 822) and the relation of characters to the play's theme. Include the two key characters who do not appear on the stage, Mr. and Mrs. Wright.

5. Write a paper discussing the role of symbolism and its relation to theme in Susan Glaspell's *Trifles* (p. 822).

6. Write a paper examining the dramatic structure of David Ives's *Sure Thing* (p. 839) and its contribution to the theme and effect of the play.

Making Connections

7. Write a paper comparing and contrasting the way Susan Glaspell's *Trifles* (p. 822) and Bessie Head's "The Collector of Treasures" (p. 421) handle the motif of a wife killing a tyrannical husband. Focus on setting in both (similarities and differences) and ways both works draw the audience's or reader's sympathy away from the husband and toward the wife in a social context where male primacy was assumed.

8. Compare and contrast Susan Glaspell's *Trifles* (p. 822) to a contemporary TV detective program, focusing on generic conventions they have in common and ones they do not share.

Cultural Criticism Papers

9. Write a paper discussing Susan Glaspell's *Trifles* (p. 822) from a feminist point of view (see pp. 1492–94).

10. Write a paper discussing the appeal of detective stories (in books, on TV, in movies and plays), including Susan Glaspell's *Trifles* (p. 822), as a cultural phenomenon. What is it about our culture that makes such stories popular? Try to find out if that popularity extends to other cultures and include that in your consideration.

RESPONDING THROUGH THE ARTS

1. Instead of just reading a play, try directing one. Find two willing (fellow student) actors, a table, and two chairs, and begin rehearsing for a performance of David Ives's *Sure Thing* (p. 839).

2. Do one or a group of diagrams to show how you would design the set and properties for a production of Susan Glaspell's *Trifles* (p. 822).

The printed script of a play is hardly more than an architect's blueprint of a house not yet built or built and destroyed.
                                    Tennessee Williams

CHAPTER **19 Theaters and Their Influence**

Chapters 17 and 18 focus on the elements of drama that need attention as you read a play—the handling of character, dialogue, dramatic action, setting, and structure. For drama, however, we need to go a step beyond the elements because most plays are written for public performance, not for private reading like stories or poems are. Playwrights nearly always write with specific stage structures and theatrical conventions in mind, usually the theaters and practices of their day—that is, as they write a play, their imaginations shape things in terms of the kind of theater the play will be performed in. For you to read plays from different periods knowledgeably, you need some information about the ways theaters have varied through history. This chapter provides a quick historical survey of theaters, focusing on four important eras of drama in Western culture: ancient Greece, Elizabethan England, late nineteenth-century England and America, and the late twentieth century.

In looking at theaters in this chapter, our focus is not their influence on dramatic performances, but their influence on how playwrights imagined the way their plays would be acted as they wrote them. We consider not just the shape of the buildings and stages, but also the conventions used on those stages, some common to all theaters, some growing out of a specific kind of theater. **Conventions** are assumptions shared by playwrights and audiences about how an imagined action on the stage can be accepted as real and believable. Conventions rely on what the nineteenth-century poet and critic Samuel Taylor Coleridge called a "willing suspension of disbelief"—that is, a willingness not to question the truth, accuracy, or probability of what occurs in a work so that one can enter and enjoy the work as if it were real. Thus, for example, if an actor on an Elizabethan stage (where lighting could not be controlled) says it is so dark he can't even see his hand in front of his face, the playwright and audience accept that as true, even though the audience can see the actor clearly on the stage. Awareness of the theaters, stages, and conventions that playwrights needed to consider is helpful in understanding a play as you read it and in visualizing the acting out of the play in the theater of your mind.

THE GREEK THEATER

Ancient Greek drama was performed in a large, open-air stadium designed for the annual celebrations in Athens of the festival of Dionysus, the Greek god of fertility. At the center of the structure was the circular "orchestra," or "dancing place" where the chorus moved from side to side and chanted their lines. On it was an altar used for the religious ceremonies, of which the drama was a part. Circling two-thirds of the orchestra was the *theatron* or "seeing place" — tiers of wood or stone seats for the audience rose up a hillside and created a bowl large enough to hold 15,000 people. Comparing that to the size of theaters today — 1,500 to 2,000 seats is large — gives some indication of how important these ceremonies were in Athenian culture.

Closing off the circle was the *skene* (literally, the "hut"), a wooden building where actors changed masks or costumes. Three doors opened onto the *proskenion*, a long, narrow area that served as the main acting area (the term *proscenium*, for the apron or forestage of a modern theater, came from

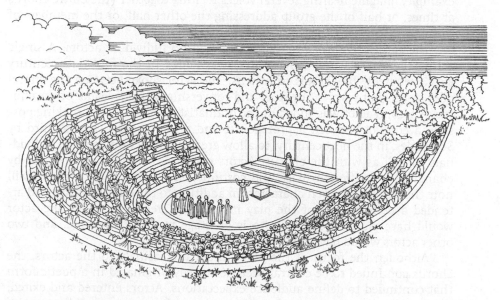

Sketch of the classical Greek theater

the Greek word). The actors moved back and forth between the *proskenion* and the orchestra; the roof of the *skene* was also used as an acting area, for example, to suggest a cliff or the place of the gods.

Performing in such a huge theater made it impossible to rely on subtle voice inflections, slight gestures, or facial expressions. Actors wore large masks to identify their characters, perhaps with megaphonic mouthpieces to enlarge their voices; they used exaggerated gestures so even those seated at the top of the *theatron* could see them. In reading a Greek play, therefore, you should not visualize the kind of intimate, realistic space and feel that we've become accustomed to in nineteenth- and twentieth-century drama. Think, rather, of a stately style of acting, with the flowing movements of a dance company and the dignity of a formal religious celebration. Visualizing it as a kind of ballet or pageant without music comes closer to its spirit than imagining it as realistic drama.

In visualizing the actors, you also need to separate yourself from your memories of modern theatrical performances. The earliest Dionysian religious celebrations used only a chorus of ten to twelve men dressed in goat skins (our word *tragedy* derives from the Greek word for "goat song") chanting in unison, with no individual speakers. Their material was not dialogue but a long, formal poem (an **ode**) written in sections called **strophe**, **antistrophe**, and **epode**. The chorus chanted the strophe on one side of the orchestra, moved across to the other side in a dance-like pattern for the antistrophe, and then moved again for the epode, if the play included epodes. The choral lyric continued to be a convention of later Greek drama as well: When you read speeches by the chorus in *Oedipus Rex* (p. 1145), for example, imagine hearing several voices reciting together (the entire chorus at times, or half of the group addressing the other half, or the members of the chorus conversing with the leader of the chorus).

The earliest Dionysian celebrations had no individual actors. A single actor (the Greek word is *hypocrites*) was added in the mid-sixth century B.C.E., reputedly by Thespis of Athens. The actor spoke between the choral odes, acting out parts in the story and conversing with the leader of the chorus. A second actor was added by the dramatist Aeschylus, thus making possible a conflict between a protagonist and an antagonist, and a third by Sophocles, in the next century, to allow greater interaction between individuals as well as with the chorus. Actors could play more than one role by changing to a different mask and costume. As you read *Oedipus,* you will note the cast list of seven characters in addition to the chorus. If you had attended a performance of the play in ancient Greece, probably one actor would have played Oedipus, who is on stage much of the time, and two other actors would have covered the other six roles.

Although the focus of the play shifted increasingly to the actors, the chorus continued to be central because tragedy originated in a poetic form that continued to define audience expectations. Actors entered and exited, but the chorus was present throughout the performance, providing a continuous point of reference for the audience and serving as an intermediary with the audience, sometimes addressing it directly. The chorus at times stood outside the action to provide background information, listen in on what characters said, comment on or react to what was said or done, or point out the moral at the end. At other times, the chorus interacted with the characters, giving them advice or warning against falling into a mistake. Sometimes the chorus, seeming rather dense, did not "get" what was going on and required more explanation from the characters — thus enlightening the audience as well.

The chorus helps in visualizing the play in that its presence reminds us that this is a staged play. In Greek drama, little action occurs on the stage. The actors deliver speeches that describe important actions (such as Oedipus relating how, years before, he fought with and killed the stranger who forced him off the road, and the second messenger describing what happens to Jocasta and Oedipus near the end of the play). The conflict that does occur on stage is verbal and emotional sparring (like the angry exchange between Oedipus and Teiresias), not a physical clash. Violence was never shown on the Greek stage; when it was part of the plot, it occurred in the past or appeared offstage and was reported to the audience.

Scenery and props were minimal and conventional — painted scenery to suggest a building, rocks, or trees was introduced in the mid-fifth century B.C.E. The immediate setting of *Oedipus* is in front of the King's palace, which may have required no scenery — the *skene* with its doors could serve as backdrop. No scene changes occur in *Oedipus* — the action on stage happens in one place and in "real time," that is, the events dramatized in the play take as long to occur as the acting of the play itself (there are no breaks in the action). The compression of time this requires, having all the necessary characters arrive or be available during this two-hour period, is one of the conventions accepted by the audience. Aristotle, writing about drama in the generation after Sophocles, praised *Oedipus* for its unity of time, place, and action. Though *Oedipus* was held up widely as an ideal of dramatic structure, critics since the mid-1700s have agreed that an audience's imagination has no difficulty accepting changes of time and place, though unity of action is still regarded as important.

THE ELIZABETHAN THEATER

The majority of William Shakespeare's plays were written for and performed in theaters adapted from courtyards at inns, where traveling acting companies performed as they went from town to town before permanent theaters were built (and where, in later years, plays were presented during times of plague when the theaters were closed and those who could left the city for the countryside). In 1599, the Lord Chamberlain's Company, to which Shakespeare belonged — he was an actor in it as well as writing plays

Sketch of the Elizabethan theater

for it—opened a new theater, the Globe. It was typical of theaters of the time, circular or octagonal structures with the center open to the sky. The audience was seated in several balconies on three sides, nearly surrounding the actors, who performed mostly on a "thrust stage," extending out into and partially encircled by the audience. The stage was covered to protect the actors from rain. The theaters could hold up to 3,000 patrons, but the closeness of audience to stage, coupled with patrons standing in the "pit" around the stage and even leaning on the edge of the stage, created an intimacy impossible in the large Greek theaters.

At the back of the thrust stage was the wall separating the stage from the backstage "tiring house," or dressing room. Two doors in the wall were used for entrances and exits. An upper gallery, normally used to seat wealthy patrons, was sometimes employed as an additional acting area (as when Brabantio appears at his window in the first scene of *Othello* — p. 1054). Most of the action, however, took place toward the front of the thrust stage, with those standing in the pit crowded around three sides. The closeness of the audience permits one of the striking effects in *Othello* — the soliloquies of Iago (see, for example, pp. 1072 and 1080). Alone on the stage, he steps forward and talks directly to the audience, some of whom in Shakespeare's day were only a few feet away from him.

As you read *Othello*, you will find fairly long speeches, with most of the play written in blank verse (see p. 527). Poetry was used because almost all serious literature at the time was written in verse: epics, ballads, and elegies as well as lyric poetry. Poetic drama is a convention of Elizabethan theater: It's not realistic that a soldier on a battlefield would talk in iambic pentameter, but the audience accepted it by suspending their disbelief. And Shakespeare could count on members of the audience to be good listeners, on the whole, able to follow speeches packed with meaning and to catch some intricate word plays. He could also count on excellent actors in his company, such as Richard Burbage and Will Kempe, being able to deliver such speeches effectively.

Elizabethan playwrights generally used stories already familiar to the audience: Originality was in the development of character and the freshness of expression, not in the creation of new stories. Thus the audience could concentrate on the way ideas were expressed, rather than on following an unfamiliar plot. Today, those reading a Shakespeare play for the first time, especially if they aren't familiar with his language, sometimes listen to a recorded or filmed production of the play — not to watch the action but to follow in the text and hear how the lines should be expressed and emphasized.

Unlike Greek plays, Elizabethan dramas showed a great deal of action on the stage, including violent action: Brabantio's followers draw swords against Othello's men in 1.2.58–61, though they don't use them, and Cassio fights Roderigo and wounds Montano in 2.3.127–34. Murders and suicides, which occurred offstage in Greek plays, are shown onstage in Elizabethan drama.

The Elizabethan theater used very little scenery. It relied on the convention that the words of the actors would supply the spectators as much as they needed to imagine where the action was occurring and the details of the scene. Thus, act 2 of *Othello* opens with Montano's line, "What from the cape can you discern at sea?" (p. 1073), which informs the audience that the scene has shifted from Venice, in act 1, to the seaside — presumably on Cyprus, to which Othello was sent in the previous scene. The lines following provide verbal images of the fierce storm the audience cannot see: "it is a high-wrought flood [steep waves]. / I cannot 'twixt the heaven and the main [sea] / Descry a sail" (2.1.2–4). Because performances were held midafternoon in an open-air structure, little could be done with lights. If actors carried torches (as in act 1) or called for a light (5.1.30), the audience knew it was dark. In other cases, words told the spectators what to imagine ("The sun begins to gild the western sky" — Shakespeare, *Two Gentlemen of Verona* 5.1.1).

But performances in Shakespeare's day were not limited to public theaters like the Globe. Acting companies also did indoor performances, sometimes at Court for the monarch and courtiers, sometimes in the banqueting halls of noble families, sometimes at private theaters such as the Blackfriars and the Whitefriars. These acting places replicated the open-air theaters as much as possible, with a thrust stage and "tiring house" backdrop with doors. More could be done with scenery and props indoors; costumes and scenery became quite spectacular for "masques," pageant-like entertainments with some elements similar to present-day opera and some to musical comedy.

By half a century after Shakespeare's death, the indoor theater had become dominant, with candles providing illumination. A "proscenium arch" with its front curtain divided the forestage from the rear stage. The area behind the arch was not used for acting, however, as it was in the following century. The rear stage was used mostly for scenery painted on rows of large flat canvases ("flats") that could be changed easily by sliding them back and forth. The action took place mainly on the forestage, which was not a thrust stage but extended across the theater from wall to wall. The audience was seated in front of the stage, not surrounding it as before. This created a sense of separation of the actors from the audience, in contrast to the intimacy of the Elizabethan theater, and laid the basis for the modern theater that developed in the mid-1800s.

THE MODERN THEATER

A major theatrical change occurred in the mid-1800s when the action of a play moved behind the proscenium arch and the forestage was pretty much eliminated. Thus, what had been called the rear stage (now referred to just as the "stage") became the main acting area. The result was the "box set." Playwrights began writing for a stage that they thought of as a box behind the arch. They visualized the box as an actual room and instructed stage designers to build it with real windows and doors that could open and close, and realistic carpets and furniture. Instead of action taking place in front of artificial, painted flats, action took place within what looked like a room in an actual house. Three walls of the room were visible to the audience; the fourth wall, of course, was not. The major convention of the modern theater was the "invisible fourth wall" through which the audience

Sketch of the box set decorated with wall and window hangings

could see into the room, though the actors treated it as if the wall was present and couldn't be crossed.

That was the stage Henrik Ibsen had in mind as he wrote the stage directions for *A Doll House:*

> A comfortable room, tastefully but not expensively furnished. A door to the right in the back wall leads to the entryway; another to the left leads to Helmer's study. Between these doors, a piano. Midway in the left-hand wall a door, and further back a window. Near the window a round table with an armchair and a small sofa. In the right-hand wall, toward the rear, a door, and nearer the foreground a porcelain stove with two armchairs and a rocking chair beside it. Between the stove and the side door, a small table. Engravings on the walls. An étagère with china figures and other small art objects; a small bookcase with richly bound books; the floor carpeted; a fire burning in the stove. It is a winter day. (p. 926)

The desired effect was a high degree of "realism," making the play as close to real life as possible. This was aided by improvements in lighting: Candles had been replaced by gas lamps, which later were replaced by electric lights. The Elizabethan bare stage and the painted flats of its successor required a great deal of imaginative involvement by the audience. An audience watching *Othello* had to imagine the street in Venice, the council chamber in Venice, and the sea shore, streets, and palace chambers on Cyprus, with minimal scenery and props to assist them. Realistic drama lessened the amount of imagining the audience had to do. The ideal would be for audience members attending a performance of *A Doll House* to forget they were in a theater and feel that they were watching real people deal with real-life situations.

Because the set filled the stage and was difficult to move, the entire play takes place in the Helmers' living room. Nora, the protagonist of the play, is on stage much of the time. Mrs. Linde, Dr. Rank, and Krogstad visit her in that room; her scenes with her husband are there as well. A key scene — Nora dancing her tarantella — occurs in the Stenborgs' apartment directly above the room shown on stage; but that scene is reported by Torvald. In the twentieth century, large theaters developed revolving platforms on stage that, by rotations between scenes, presented two or three realistic, box stage sets. But nineteenth-century theaters were far from such technology, so playwrights had to accept unity of place, writing to fit the entire play into one location.

The modern theater was well suited to, or perhaps was necessitated by, the plays of Ibsen and his contemporaries, especially Ibsen's "problem plays," which explored problems that ordinary people in real life faced. *A Doll House* explores the real-life problem of a husband who treats his wife like a doll, his "little songbird," his possession, and does not give her the space and opportunity to develop her own separate identity. It is also psychologically realistic in the way Nora comes to understand the importance of personal integrity in her life and in human relations generally. The realistic appearance of the stage was well suited to the realistic tone of the plays performed on it.

Of course, realistic theater relied as heavily on conventions as its predecessors: The spectators knew they were in a theater. They knew the actor was not the character, the gun did not have real bullets, and no one onstage really died when she or he was "shot." Nineteenth-century realistic drama also required the imaginative participation of its audience, just as plays of the Elizabethan era and the century following it did, especially empathetic imagination and willingness to suspend disbelief. For us as readers of those dramas, visualizing them is easier when we know the kind of stage and stage conventions authors had in mind as they wrote and the kind of effect they sought to create for their audiences.

Most theaters of the early and mid-twentieth century continued to have a proscenium arch. But dramatists and the theater as a whole have moved away from the realism of the late 1800s and early 1900s. In late modern and contemporary theater — both in the plays written now and the productions of earlier plays — it is assumed that people in the audience know that they are watching a performance and that the set is an artistic construction that requires the imaginative participation of the audience. The set is rarely limited to one room or space. Playwrights, as they write, no longer envisage a lifelike room in a box set, with all action occurring within that one space.

Arthur Miller's conception of the set for *Death of a Salesman* (p. 980) illustrates the postmodern, nonrealistic approach. Miller had a proscenium stage in mind: The stage directions begin with "The curtain rises." But what we see on the stage as the curtain rises is not one room from the inside, but the house from the outside: "Before us is the Salesman's house. . . . As more light appears, we see a solid vault of apartment houses around the small, fragile-seeming home" (p. 981). The outer and inner walls of the house are invisible (perhaps only the bottom couple of feet of the walls, outlining the rooms), which allows us to see into the rooms — not just one room, as in the box set, but into several rooms:

> The kitchen at center seems actual enough, for there is a kitchen table with three chairs, and a refrigerator. But no other fixtures are seen. At the back of the kitchen there is a draped entrance, which leads to the living room. To the right of the kitchen, on a level raised two feet, is a bedroom furnished only with a brass bedstead and a straight chair. . . .
>
> Behind the kitchen, on a level raised six and a half feet, is the boys' bedroom, at present barely visible. Two beds are dimly seen, and at the back of the room a dormer window. . . . At the left a stairway curves up to it from the kitchen.
>
> The entire setting is wholly or, in some places, partially transparent. The roofline of the house is one-dimensional; under and over it we see the apartment buildings. (p. 981)

The set is not cut off at the proscenium arch, but extends to and makes important use of the forestage: "Before the house lies an apron, curving beyond the forestage into the orchestra. This forward area serves as the back yard as well as the locale of all Willy's imaginings and of his city scenes" (p. 981). Thus the actors and audience are not separated by the proscenium arch, as they are in Ibsen's theater, but the action reaches out toward or into the audience. Because action is not contained within a box set, the play could readily be adapted to a theater without a proscenium arch. It is easy to imagine staging it on a contemporary thrust stage (see p. 861), for example — what Miller describes as being behind the arch is placed at the rear of the thrust stage. It does not seem well suited, however, for the contemporary arena theater or "theater-in-the-round" (p. 861).

The set is used both to describe the space and to create atmosphere: ("Only the blue light of the sky falls upon the house and forestage; the surrounding area shows an angry glow of orange. . . . An air of the dream clings to the place, a dream rising out of reality" (p. 981). It is used also to separate past events from action taking place in the present:

> Whenever the action is in the present the actors observe the imaginary wall-lines, entering the house only through its doors at the left. But in the scenes of the past these boundaries are broken, and characters enter or leave a room by stepping "through" a wall onto the forestage. (p. 981)

The audience, of course, does not read this explanation: They are required to catch this through alert, active observation of what occurs on stage.

The set allows Miller to do things the realistic box set does not permit. For example, he does not have to contrive ways to have all the action take place in a single room. We can visualize, and the audience can see, Biff and Happy talking in their bedroom and overhearing Willy talk to himself in the kitchen below. He is not limited to action in the present: Because walls and rooms are suggestive rather than realistic, flashbacks can be acted out, not just recounted as exposition the way Ibsen was forced to do. And Miller is not limited in location. Ibsen, using a realistic room as set, had to report what went on in the flat above that room. Miller does not need to rely on reports. Events that occurred years ago in a Boston hotel room are acted out on the forestage, not just reported, as in Ibsen's play.

Death of a Salesman portrays a man living in the past as well as, or as much as, in the present. It explores how a man who formerly found his identity in his older son and his work can know who he is in the present when he has lost both son and work. The stage Miller uses, conceived with flexibility and suggestiveness, enables him to dramatize his story in ways that a realistic box stage doesn't allow.

THE CONTEMPORARY THEATER

Theater in the mid- to late 1900s moved still further away from realism in text and stagecraft. Many contemporary theaters reach out to the audience not just through the imagination but physically, by thrusting the stage out into the audience (returning to the Elizabethan theater's way of bringing the action close to the audience) or by placing the stage in the center of the theater, with the audience surrounding it on all sides. The arena theater, or "theater-in-the-round," eliminates the sense of separation created by the proscenium arch or the forestage and rearstage areas of the thrust stage. It gives actors the chance to enter and exit through the audience, using the same aisles as the audience. Some plays even have a character initially seated in the audience who later rises and joins in the action — eliminating still further the sense of distance between actors and audience.

A thrust stage or theater-in-the-round cannot, of course, create rooms with real walls. Sets and props usually are simple and minimal or impressionistic and symbolic rather than realistically detailed. Playwrights and stage designers often think in terms of platforms connected by ramps and stairways to allow multiple locations. Modern equipment produces lighting effects undreamed of even a few decades ago. All of this means that playwrights today are free to imagine a far greater variety of spaces and uses for them as they write. Playwrights are less confined to a particular kind of theater than were their counterparts in earlier centuries.

August Wilson's *Fences* (p. 1186) was written with the variety and flexibility of contemporary theaters in mind. The stage directions do not limit it

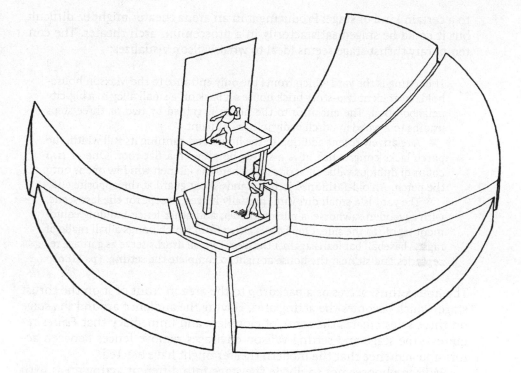

Sketches of the contemporary thrust stage (above) and contemporary arena stage (below)

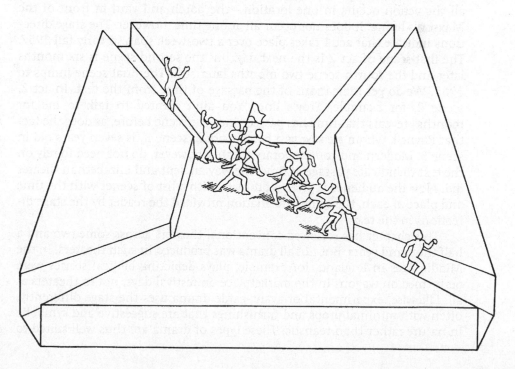

to a certain kind of stage: Producing it in an arena theater might be difficult, but it could be staged satisfactorily in a proscenium arch theater. The contemporary thrust stage seems ideal to what Wilson visualizes:

> The setting is the yard which fronts the only entrance to the Maxson household, an ancient two-story brick house set back off a small alley in a big-city neighborhood. The entrance to the house is gained by two or three steps leading to a wooden porch badly in need of paint.
>
> A relatively recent addition to the house and running its full width, the porch lacks congruence. It is a sturdy porch with a flat roof. One or two chairs of dubious value sit at one end where the kitchen window opens onto the porch. An old-fashioned icebox stands silent guard at the opposite end.
>
> The yard is a small dirt yard, partially fenced, except for the last scene, with a wooden sawhorse, a pile of lumber, and other fence-building equipment set off to the side. Opposite is a tree from which hangs a ball made of rags. A baseball bat leans against the tree. Two oil drums serve as garbage receptacles and sit near the house at right to complete the setting. (p. 1186)

The house, thus, serves as a backdrop to the area in front of it on the thrust stage, which becomes the acting area. Having the audience around the stage on three sides creates the sense of closeness and immediacy that *Fences* requires — the stage and setting Wilson envisages remove fences between actors and audience that the modern theater might have erected.

Wilson chooses not to divide the stage into different acting areas with platforms and ramps or stairs connecting them. He shapes the play so that all the action occurs in one location — the porch and yard in front of the Maxson's home. It does not occur all at one time, however. The stage directions indicate that act 1 takes place over a two-week span in early fall 1957. The first scene of act 2 is the next day, but the second scene is six months later and the fourth scene two months later still. The final scene jumps to 1965. We do get indications of the passage of time from the text: In act 2, scene 2, for example, Troy's line "You ain't wanted to talk to me for months" reveals that time has passed since the scene before, as does the fact that Raynell, whom we saw as a baby in act 2, scene 3, is seven years old in scene 5. Modern and contemporary theater, however, do not need to rely on the text to indicate passage of time, the way ancient and Elizabethan theater did. Now the audience is given a program with a list of scenes with the time and place of each, the same information provided the reader by the stage directions in the text.

This chapter has reviewed conventional theaters across some two and a half thousand years. But not all drama was produced in such theaters. In the Middle Ages in England, for example, plays depicting biblical stories were performed on wagons in the marketplace on festival days, not in theaters at all. Likewise, experimental or avant-garde drama uses the stage differently, often with minimal props and furnishings that are suggestive and symbolic in nature rather than realistic. These types of drama are thus well suited to theater-in-the-round or a thrust stage. The two plays included in this chapter illustrate: Neither was intended for performance as "legitimate" theater. The first, *Los Vendidos* (p. 864), experiments with places for staging plays. Its author, Luis Valdez, says that, as he wrote it, he did not have in mind the "white western Europe (gabacho) proscenium theatre." He intended it to be performed in bare halls or even on the streets, not by professional actors but by workers and other ordinary people. In the second, *Mambo Mouth* (p. 874), John Leguizamo experiments with unconventional staging in conventional theaters. Instead of dramatizing a story, the play has a single actor depicting a series of characters who appear individually on the stage and deliver a monologue. Very little is required in terms of stage set and props, and the play can be staged in any kind of theater.

Whatever the era, the configuration of theater and stage, and the theatrical conventions in use at the time, influence the way a playwright conceives and visualizes a play. But it's equally clear that playwrights influence theater design. The changes in theaters and stages discussed in this chapter occurred in part as playwrights conceived plays that could not be performed to full advantage in the spaces provided by currently existing theaters. Such plays led first to modifications of the existing spaces and later to new theaters with redesigned spaces for both stage and audience. Because the theater is a dynamic, growing, responsive world, such changes in theaters and the plays presented in them will continue in the future.

> **www**
> Further explore theaters and their influence, including interactive exercises, with VirtuaLit Drama at bedfordstmartins.com/approachinglit.

☑ CHECKLIST on Theaters and Their Influence

❑ Be aware of the different types of theaters used in different eras and the types of stages used in each:
  - the Greek outdoor amphitheaters with their orchestra and *proskenion*
  - the Elizabethan open-air circular (or octagonal) theaters and indoor theaters, both with thrust stage
  - the modern rectangular indoor theaters with proscenium and realistic box sets
  - contemporary thrust stage and arena stage theaters

❑ Be attentive to how different kinds of theaters and stages influence the way playwrights envision plays as they write.

❑ Be alert to how awareness of the theaters for which plays were written helps readers "watch" the plays in the theater of their minds.

❑ Consider, when reading a play, what type of theater may have influenced how it was written, and think about what the effects would be of staging it in other types of theaters with different types of stages.

FURTHER READING

Here are two satiric comedies that illustrate experimental ways of staging plays, a trend that continues in the theater world today. The first, *Los Vendidos,* is set in 1960s Los Angeles. As you read and visualize it, try to see it not in one of the theaters discussed in this chapter but in a bare hall or on the streets, the kind of "ordinary life" context Luis Valdez has in mind for his works.

Luis Valdez   b. 1940

Los Vendidos   [1967]

CHARACTERS

HONEST SANCHO
MISS JIMENEZ
FARM WORKER
PACHUCO
REVOLUCIONARIO
MEXICAN-AMERICAN

FIRST PERFORMANCE

Brown Beret junta, Elysian Park, East Los Angeles.

Los Vendidos°

SCENE: *Honest Sancho's Used Mexican Lot and Mexican Curio Shop. Three models are on display in Honest Sancho's shop: to the right, there is a Revolucionario, complete with sombrero, carrilleras,° and carabina 30-30.° At center, on the floor, there is the Farm Worker, under a broad straw sombrero. At stage left is the Pachuco,° filero° in hand.*

Honest Sancho is moving among his models, dusting them off and preparing for another day of business.

SANCHO: Bueno, bueno, mis monos, vamos a ver a quien vendemos ahora, ¿no?° (*To audience*) Quihubo!° I'm Honest Sancho and this is my shop. Antes fui contratista pero ahora logré tener mi negocito.° All I need now is a customer. (*A bell rings offstage.*) Ay, a customer!

Los Vendidos: The sellouts, the traitors.   **carrilleras:** Cartridge belts.   **carabina 30-30:** A rifle, and the name of a famous song of the Revolution.   **Pachuco:** Chicano slang for 1940s zoot suiter.   **filero:** switchblade.   **Bueno, bueno, . . . ahora, ¿no?:** Well, well, my monkeys, let's see whom we can sell today, okay?   **Quihubo:** Hello.   **Antes fui . . . negocito:** I used to be a contractor, but now I've succeeded in having my little business.

SECRETARY (*entering*): Good morning, I'm Miss Jimenez from —

SANCHO: ¡Ah, una chicana! Welcome, welcome Señorita Jiménez.

SECRETARY (*Anglo pronunciation*): JIM-enez.

SANCHO: ¿Que?°

SECRETARY: My name is Miss JIM-enez. Don't you speak English? What's wrong with you?

SANCHO: Oh, nothing, Señorita JIM-enez. I'm here to help you.

SECRETARY: That's better. As I was starting to say, I'm a secretary from Governor Reagan's office, and we're looking for a Mexican type for the administration.

SANCHO: Well, you come to the right place, lady. This is Honest Sancho's Used Mexican lot, and we got all types here. Any particular type you want?

SECRETARY: Yes, we were looking for somebody suave —

SANCHO: Suave.

SECRETARY: Debonair.

SANCHO: De buen aire.

SECRETARY: Dark.

SANCHO: Prieto.

SECRETARY: But of course not too dark.

SANCHO: No muy prieto.

SECRETARY: Perhaps, beige.

SANCHO: Beige, just the tone. Así como cafecito con leche,° ¿no?

SECRETARY: One more thing. He must be hardworking.

SANCHO: That could only be one model. Step right over here to the center of the shop, lady. (*They cross to the Farm Worker.*) This is our standard farm worker model. As you can see, in the words of our beloved Senator George Murphy, he is "built close to the ground." Also take special notice of his 4-ply Goodyear huaraches, made from the rain tire. This wide-brimmed sombrero is an extra added feature — keeps off the sun, rain, and dust.

SECRETARY: Yes, it does look durable.

SANCHO: And our farmworker model is friendly. Muy amable.° Watch. (*Snaps his fingers.*)

FARM WORKER (*lifts up head*): Buenos dias, señorita.° (*His head drops.*)

SECRETARY: My, he's friendly.

SANCHO: Didn't I tell you? Loves his patrones!° But his most attractive feature is that he's hardworking. Let me show you. (*Snaps fingers. Farm Worker stands.*)

FARM WORKER: ¡El jale!° (*He begins to work.*)

SANCHO: As you can see, he is cutting grapes.

SECRETARY: Oh, I wouldn't know.

¿Que?: What?   **Así como . . . leche:** Like coffee with milk.   **Muy amable:** Very friendly.
Buenos dias, señorita: Good day, young lady.   **patrones:** Bosses.   **El jale:** The job.

SANCHO: He also picks cotton. (*Snap. Farm Worker begins to pick cotton.*)

SECRETARY: Versatile isn't he?

SANCHO: He also picks melons. (*Snap. Farm Worker picks melons.*) That's his slow speed for late in the season. Here's his fast speed. (*Snap. Farm Worker picks faster.*)

SECRETARY: ¡Chihuahua!° . . . I mean, goodness, he sure is a hard worker.

SANCHO (*pulls the Farm Worker to his feet*): And that isn't the half of it. Do you see these little holes on his arms that appear to be pores? During those hot sluggish days in the field, when the vines or the branches get so entangled it's almost impossible to move, these holes emit a certain grease that allows our model to slip and slide right through the crop with no trouble at all.

SECRETARY: Wonderful. But is he economical?

SANCHO: Economical? Señorita, you are looking at the Volkswagen of Mexicans. Pennies a day is all it takes. One plate of beans and tortillas will keep him going all day. That, and chile. Plenty of chile. Chile jalapenos, chile verde, chile colorado. But, of course, if you do give him chile (*Snap. Farm Worker turns left face. Snap. Farm Worker bends over.*), then you have to change his oil filter once a week.

SECRETARY: What about storage?

SANCHO: No problem. You know these new farm labor camps our Honorable Governor Reagan has built out by Parlier or Raisin City? They were designed with our model in mind. Five, six, seven, even ten in one of those shacks will give you no trouble at all. You can also put him in old barns, old cars, riverbanks. You can even leave him out in the field overnight with no worry!

SECRETARY: Remarkable.

SANCHO: And here's an added feature: every year at the end of the season, this model goes back to Mexico and doesn't return, automatically, until next Spring.

SECRETARY: How about that. But tell me, does he speak English?

SANCHO: Another outstanding feature is that last year this model was programmed to go out on STRIKE! (*Snap.*)

FARM WORKER: ¡HUELGA! ¡HUELGA! Hermanos, sálganse de esos filos.° (*Snap. He stops.*)

SECRETARY: No! Oh no, we can't strike in the State Capitol.

SANCHO: Well, he also scabs. (*Snap.*)

FARM WORKER: Me vendo barato, ¿y qué?° (*Snap.*)

SECRETARY: That's much better, but you didn't answer my question. Does he speak English?

SANCHO: Bueno . . . no, pero° he has other —

¡Chihuahua!: Oh, my!   ¡HUELGA! ¡HUELGA! . . . esos filos: STRIKE! STRIKE! Brothers, leave those rows.   Me vendo . . . qué?: I sell myself cheaply, so what?   Bueno . . . no, pero: Well, no, but . . .

SECRETARY: No.

SANCHO: Other features.

SECRETARY: NO! He just won't do!

SANCHO: Okay, okay pues.° We have other models.

SECRETARY: I hope so. What we need is something a little more sophisticated.

SANCHO: Sophisti — ¿que?

SECRETARY: An urban model.

SANCHO: Ah, from the city! Step right back. Over here in this corner of the shop is exactly what you're looking for. Introducing our new 1969 Johnny Pachuco model! This is our fast-back model. Streamlined. Built for speed, low-riding, city life. Take a look at some of these features. Mag shoes, dual exhausts, green chartreuse paint-job, dark-tint windshield, a little poof on top. Let me just turn him on. (*Snap. Johnny walks to stage center with a pachuco bounce.*)

SECRETARY: What was that?

SANCHO: That, señorita, was the Chicano shuffle.

SECRETARY: Okay, what does he do?

SANCHO: Anything and everything necessary for city life. For instance, survival: he knife fights. (*Snap. Johnny pulls out switchblade and swings at Secretary.*)

Secretary screams.

SANCHO: He dances. (*Snap.*)

JOHNNY (*singing*): "Angel Baby, my Angel Baby . . ." (*Snap.*)

SANCHO: And here's a feature no city model can be without. He gets arrested, but not without resisting, of course. (*Snap.*)

JOHNNY: En la madre, la placa.° I didn't do it! I didn't do it! (*Johnny turns and stands up against an imaginary wall, legs spread out, arms behind his back.*)

SECRETARY: Oh no, we can't have arrests! We must maintain law and order.

SANCHO: But he's bilingual!

SECRETARY: Bilingual?

SANCHO: Simón que yes.° He speaks English! Johnny, give us some English. (*Snap.*)

JOHNNY (*comes downstage*): Fuck you!

SECRETARY (*gasps*): Oh! I've never been so insulted in my whole life!

SANCHO: Well, he learned it in your school.

SECRETARY: I don't care where he learned it.

SANCHO: But he's economical!

SECRETARY: Economical?

SANCHO: Nickels and dimes. You can keep Johnny running on hamburgers, Taco Bell tacos, Lucky Lager beer, Thunderbird wine, yesca — °

SECRETARY: Yesca?

---

pues: Agh (a pause). **En la . . . placa:** Son of a bitch, the police. **Simón que yes:** Yes. **yesca:** Marijuana.

SANCHO: Mota.°
SECRETARY: Mota?
SANCHO: Leños° . . . marijuana. (*Snap, Johnny inhales on an imaginary joint.*)
SECRETARY: That's against the law!
JOHNNY (*big smile, holding his breath*): Yeah.
SANCHO: He also sniffs glue. (*Snap. Johnny inhales glue, big smile.*)
JOHNNY: Tha's too much man, ése.°
SECRETARY: No, Mr. Sancho, I don't think this —
SANCHO: Wait a minute, he has other qualities I know you'll love. For example, an inferiority complex. (*Snap.*)
JOHNNY (*to Sancho*): You think you're better than me, huh ése? (*Swings switchblade.*)
SANCHO: He can also be beaten and he bruises, cut him and he bleeds, kick him and he — (*He beats, bruises and kicks Pachuco.*) would you like to try it?
SECRETARY: Oh, I couldn't.
SANCHO: Be my guest. He's a great scapegoat.
SECRETARY: No, really.
SANCHO: Please.
SECRETARY: Well, alright. Just once. (*She kicks Pachuco.*) Oh, he's so soft.
SANCHO: Wasn't that good? Try again.
SECRETARY (*kicks Pachuco*): Oh, he's so wonderful! (*She kicks him again.*)
SANCHO: Okay, that's enough, lady. You ruin the merchandise. Yes, our Johnny Pachuco model can give you many hours of pleasure. Why, the L.A.P.D. just bought 20 of these to train their rookies cops on.° And talk about maintenance. Señorita, you are looking at an entirely self-supporting machine. You're never going to find our Johnny Pachuco model on the relief rolls. No, sir, this model knows how to liberate.
SECRETARY: Liberate?
SANCHO: He steals. (*Snap. Johnny rushes the Secretary and steals her purse.*)
JOHNNY: ¡Dame esa bolsa, vieja!° (*He grabs the purse and runs. Snap by Sancho. He stops.*)

Secretary runs after Johnny and grabs purse away from him, kicking him as she goes.

SECRETARY: No, no, no! We can't have any *more* thieves in the State Administration. Put him back.
SANCHO: Okay, we still got other models. Come on, Johnny, we'll sell you to some old lady. (*Sancho takes Johnny back to his place.*)
SECRETARY: Mr. Sancho, I don't think you quite understand what we need. What we need is something that will attract the women voters. Something more traditional, more romantic.

Mota: Marijuana. **Leños:** Firewood. **ése:** Dude, guy. **the L.A.P.D. . . . rookie cops on:** Alluding to the Zoot Suit Riots in Los Angeles, 1941–1943. **¡Dame esa bolsa, vieja!:** Gimme that bag, old lady!

SANCHO: Ah, a lover. (*He smiles meaningfully.*) Step right over here, señorita. Introducing our standard Revolucionario and/or Early California Bandit type. As you can see he is well-built, sturdy, durable. This is the International Harvester of Mexicans.

SECRETARY: What does he do?

SANCHO: You name it, he does it. He rides horses, stays in the mountains, crosses deserts, plains, rivers, leads revolutions, follows revolutions, kills, can be killed, serves as a martyr, hero, movie star — did I say movie star? Did you ever see *Viva Zapata?*° *Viva Villa? Villa Rides? Pancho Villa Returns? Pancho Villa Goes Back? Pancho Villa Meets Abbott and Costello —* °

SECRETARY: I've never seen any of those.

SANCHO: Well, he was in all of them. Listen to this. (*Snap.*)

REVOLUCIONARIO (*scream*): ¡VIVA VILLAAAAA!

SECRETARY: That's awfully loud.

SANCHO: He has a volume control. (*He adjusts volume. Snap.*)

REVOLUCIONARIO (*mousey voice*): ¡viva villa!

SECRETARY: That's better.

SANCHO: And even if you didn't see him in the movies, perhaps you saw him on TV. He makes commercials. (*Snap.*)

REVOLUCIONARIO: Is there a Frito Bandito in your house?

SECRETARY: Oh yes, I've seen that one!

SANCHO: Another feature about this one is that he is economical. He runs on raw horsemeat and tequila!

SECRETARY: Isn't that rather savage?

SANCHO: Al contrario,° it makes him a lover. (*Snap.*)

REVOLUCIONARIO (*to Secretary*): ¡Ay, mamasota, cochota, ven pa'ca!° (*He grabs Secretary and folds her back — Latin-lover style.*)

SANCHO (*Snap. Revolucionario goes back upright*): Now wasn't that nice?

SECRETARY: Well, it was rather nice.

SANCHO: And finally, there is one outstanding feature about this model I KNOW the ladies are going to love: he's a GENUINE antique! He was made in Mexico in 1910!

SECRETARY: Made in Mexico?

SANCHO: That's right. Once in Tijuana, twice in Guadalajara, three times in Cuernavaca.

SECRETARY: Mr. Sancho, I thought he was an American product.

SANCHO: No, but —

SECRETARY: No, I'm sorry. We can't buy anything but American-made products. He just won't do.

Viva Zapata: Title of a romantic 1952 movie that tells the story of Mexican rebel Emiliano Zapata, starring Marlon Brando and Anthony Quinn, directed by Elia Kazan, produced by Darryl F. Zanuck; the screenplay was written by John Steinbeck. *Viva* means "long live." **Viva Villa, . . . Costello:** Parody names of movies. **Al contrario:** On the contrary. **¡Ay, mamasota, cochota, ven pa'ca!:** Hey, big sexy mamma, come here.

SANCHO: But he's an antique!

SECRETARY: I don't care. You still don't understand what we need. It's true we need Mexican models such as these, but it's more important that he be *American.*

SANCHO: American?

SECRETARY: That's right, and judging from what you've shown me, I don't think you have what we want. Well, my lunch hour's almost over, I better —

SANCHO: Wait a minute! Mexican but American?

SECRETARY: That's correct.

SANCHO: Mexican but . . . (*A sudden flash.*) AMERICAN! Yeah, I think we've got exactly what you want. He just came in today! Give me a minute. (*He exits. Talks from backstage.*) Here he is in the shop. Let me just get some papers off. There. Introducing our new 1970 Mexican-American! Ta-ra-ra-ra-ra-ra-RA-RAAA!

Sancho brings out the Mexican-American model, a clean-shaven middle-class type in a business suit, with glasses.

SECRETARY (*impressed*): Where have you been hiding this one?

SANCHO: He just came in this morning. Ain't he a beauty? Feast your eyes on him! Sturdy US STEEL frame, streamlined, modern. As a matter of fact, he is built exactly like our Anglo models except that he comes in a variety of darker shades: naughahide, leather, or leatherette.

SECRETARY: Naugahyde.

SANCHO: Well, we'll just write that down. Yes, señorita, this model represents the apex of American engineering! He is bilingual, college educated, ambitious! Say the word "acculturate" and he accelerates. He is intelligent, well-mannered, clean — did I say clean? (*Snap. Mexican-American raises his arm.*) Smell.

SECRETARY (*smells*): Old Sobaco,° my favorite.

SANCHO (*snap. Mexican-American turns toward Sancho*): Eric? (*To Secretary*) We call him Eric Garcia. (*To Eric*) I want you to meet Miss JIM-enez, Eric.

MEXICAN-AMERICAN: Miss JIM-enez, I am delighted to make your acquaintance. (*He kisses her hand.*)

SECRETARY: Oh, my, how charming!

SANCHO: Did you feel the suction? He has seven especially engineered suction cups right behind his lips. He's a charmer all right!

SECRETARY: How about boards, does he function on boards?

SANCHO: You name them, he is on them. Parole boards, draft boards, school boards, taco quality control boards, surf boards, two-by-fours.

SECRETARY: Does he function in politics?

SANCHO: Señorita, you are looking at a political MACHINE. Have you ever heard of the OEO, EOC, COD, WAR ON POVERTY? That's our model! Not only that, he makes political speeches.

Sobaco: Underarm.

SECRETARY: May I hear one?

SANCHO: With pleasure. (*Snap.*) Eric, give us a speech.

MEXICAN-AMERICAN: Mr. Congressman, Mr. Chairman, members of the board, honored guests, ladies and gentlemen. (*Sancho and Secretary applaud.*) Please, please. I come before you as a Mexican-American to tell you about the problems of the Mexican. The problems of the Mexican stem from one thing and one thing alone: he's stupid. He's uneducated. He needs to stay in school. He needs to be ambitious, forward-looking, harder working. He needs to think American, American, American, AMERICAN, AMERICAN, AMERICAN. GOD BLESS AMERICA! GOD BLESS AMERICA! GOD BLESS AMERICA!! (*He goes out of control.*)

Sancho snaps frantically and the Mexican-American finally slumps forward, bending at the waist.

SECRETARY: Oh my, he's patriotic too!

SANCHO: Sí, señorita, he loves his country. Let me just make a little adjustment here. (*Stands Mexican-American up.*)

SECRETARY: What about upkeep? Is he economical?

SANCHO: Well, no, I won't lie to you. The Mexican-American costs a little bit more, but you get what you pay for. He's worth every extra cent. You can keep him running on dry martinis, Langendorf bread . . .

SECRETARY: Apple pie?

SANCHO: Only Mom's. Of course, he's also programmed to eat Mexican food on ceremonial functions, but I must warn you: an overdose of beans will plug up his exhaust.

SECRETARY: Fine! There's just one more question: HOW MUCH DO YOU WANT FOR HIM?

SANCHO: Well, I tell you what I'm gonna do. Today and today only, because you've been so sweet, I'm gonna let you steal this model from me! I'm gonna let you drive him off the lot for the simple price of — let's see, taxes and license included — $15,000.

SECRETARY: Fifteen thousand DOLLARS? For a MEXICAN!

SANCHO: Mexican? What are you talking, lady? This is a Mexican-AMERICAN! We had to melt down two pachucos, a farm worker, and three gavachos° to make this model! You want quality, but you gotta pay for it! This is no cheap run-about. He's got class!

SECRETARY: Okay, I'll take him.

SANCHO: You will?

SECRETARY: Here's your money.

SANCHO: You mind if I count it?

SECRETARY: Go right ahead.

SANCHO: Well, you'll get your pink slip in the mail. Oh, do you want me to wrap him up for you? We have a box in the back.

---

gavachos: White boys.

SECRETARY: No, thank you. The Governor is having a luncheon this afternoon, and we need a brown face in the crowd. How do I drive him?

SANCHO: Just snap your fingers. He'll do anything you want.

Secretary snaps. Mexican-American steps forward.

MEXICAN-AMERICAN: RAZA QUERIDA, ¡VAMOS LEVANTANDO ARMAS PARA LIBERARNOS DE ESTOS DESGRACIADOS GABACHOS QUE NOS EXPLOTAN! VAMOS —°

SECRETARY: What did he say?

SANCHO: Something about lifting arms, killing white people, etc.

SECRETARY: But he's not suppose to say that!

SANCHO: Look, lady, don't blame me for bugs from the factory. He's your Mexican-American; you bought him, now drive him off the lot!

SECRETARY: But he's broken!

SANCHO: Try snapping another finger.

Secretary snaps. Mexican-American comes to life again.

MEXICAN-AMERICAN: ¡ESTA GRAN HUMANIDAD HA DICHO BASTA! ¡Y SE HA PUESTO EN MARCHA! ¡BASTA! ¡BASTA! ¡VIVA LA RAZA! ¡VIVA LA CAUSA! ¡VIVA LA HUELGA! ¡VIVAN LOS BROWN BERETS! ¡VIVA LOS ESTUDIANTES! ¡CHICANO POWER!°

The Mexican-American turns toward the Secretary, who gasps and backs up. He keeps turning toward the Pachuco, Farm Worker, and Revolucionario, snapping his fingers and turning each of them on, one by one.

PACHUCO (*snap. To Secretary*): I'm going to get you, baby! ¡Viva La Raza!

FARM WORKER (*snap. To Secretary*): ¡Viva la huelga! ¡Viva la huelga! ¡VIVA LA HUELGA!

REVOLUCIONARIO (*snap. To Secretary*): ¡Viva la revolucion! ¡VIVA LA REVOLUCION!

The three models join together and advance toward the Secretary who backs up and runs out of the shop screaming. Sancho is at the other end of the shop holding his money in his hand. All freeze. After a few seconds of silence, the Pachuco moves and stretches, shaking his arms and loosening up. The Farm Worker and Revolucionario do the same. Sancho stays where he is, frozen to his spot.

JOHNNY: Man, that was a long one, ése. (*Others agree with him.*)

FARM WORKER: How did we do?

RAZA QUERIDA, . . . NOS EXPLOTAN! VAMOS: Beloved people, let's take up arms to liberate ourselves from those damned whites that exploit us! Let's go.   **¡ESTA GRAN . . . ¡CHICANO POWER!:** This great mass of humanity has said enough! And it begins to march! Enough! Enough! Long live the people! Long live the Cause! Long live the strike! Long live the Brown Berets! Long live the students! Chicano Power!

JOHNNY: Perty good, look all that lana,° man! (*He goes over to Sancho and removes the money from his hand. Sancho stays where he is.*)

REVOLUCIONARIO: En la madre,° look at all the money.

JOHNNY: We keep this up, we're going to be rich.

FARM WORKER: They think we're machines.

REVOLUCIONARIO: Burros.

JOHNNY: Puppets.

MEXICAN-AMERICAN: The only thing I don't like is — how come I always got to play the goddamn Mexican-American?

JOHNNY: That's what you get for finishing high school.

FARM WORKER: How about our wages, ése?

JOHNNY: Here it comes right now. $3,000 for you, $3,000 for you, $3,000 for you, and $3,000 for me. The rest we put back into the business.

MEXICAN-AMERICAN: Too much, man. Heh, where you vatos° going tonight?

FARM WORKER: I'm going over to Concha's. There's a party.

JOHNNY: Wait a minute, vatos. What about our salesman? I think he needs an oil job.

REVOLUCIONARIO: Leave him to me.

The Pachuco, Farm Worker, and Mexican-American exit, talking loudly about their plans for the night. The Revolucionario goes over to Sancho, removes his derby hat and cigar, lifts him up, and throws him over his shoulder. Sancho hangs loose, lifeless.

REVOLUCIONARIO (*to audience*): He's the best model we got! ¡Ajua!°   (*Exit.*)

FIN

---

lana: Money.   En la madre: Son of a bitch.   vatos: Guys.   ¡Ajua!: (exclamation)

APPROACHING THE READING

1. Write a brief summary of what goes on in the play and the point of it all.

2. Valdez called works like *Los Vendidos* "actos" instead of "plays." Actos, he said, are written collectively, developed through improvisation by a group. Their aim, he said, is to "inspire the audience to social action. Illuminate specific points about social problems. Satirize the opposition. Show or hint at a solution. Express what people are feeling." To what extent do you feel *Los Vendidos* achieves those aims?

3. Who or what is being satirized in the play? Identify several satiric targets. Point out several comic techniques.

4. If you are Anglo, are you offended by the play and its attacks on the dominant culture? Why or why not? Do you find it entertaining? If you are Latino, do you find parts of it offensive? Do you find it entertaining?

5. What stereotypes of Mexican Americans are used in *Los Vendidos*? At the end of the play, what image of Mexican Americans is depicted? How does it compare with the stereotypes?

6. The play contains a number of phrases and speeches in Spanish. Do they add to the play, or would it be preferable to have them in English instead?

Mambo Mouth, like *Los Vendidos*, is a satire on racial and ethnic stereotypes in American culture. But it is very different in form and approach. It is a one-man show consisting of a series of monologues by seven characters, including Agamemnon, a stuck-up woman-bashing talk-show host; Loco Louie, a crazy and horny teen; Angel Garcia, in jail for hitting his wife because he claims she cheated on him and they got in a little argument; Pepe, an illegal immigrant trying to convince the guard he is of another race; and Manny the Fanny, an outgoing woman who tells one of her friends a story about how she got revenge on her man. As you read Pepe's monologue below, imagine the speaker as a fully developed individual and his role as part of a whole play commenting on the way cultures deal with ethnic and racial difference.

John Leguizamo b. 1964

From Mambo Mouth: A Savage Comedy   [1988]

Pepe

(*The stage is dark. A backstage light reveals the silhouette of a man wearing jeans and a T-shirt standing in a doorway.*)

PEPE: Excuse me, ése,° I just got this gift certificate in the mail saying that I was entitled to gifts and prizes and possibly money if I came to La Guardia Airport? (*Comes downstage.*) Oh sure, the name is Pepe. Pepe Vásquez. (*Panics.*) Orale,° what are you doing? You're making a big mistake! (*Lights up. Pepe stands center stage, holding a grille of prison bars in front of his face.*)

I'm not Mexican! I'm Swedish! No, you've never seen me before. Sure I look familiar — all Swedish people look alike. (*Gibberish in Swedish accent.*) Uta Häagen, Häagen Däazen, Frusen Glädjé, Nina Häagen. . . .

Okay. Did I say Swedish? I meant Irish — yeah, black Irish! (*Singsongy Irish accent.*) Toy ti-toy ti-toy. Oh, Lucky Charms, they're magically deli-

---

ése: Dude, guy.   Orale: What's up?

cious! Pink hearts, green clovers, yellow moons. What time is it? Oh, Jesus, Joseph, and Mary! It's cabbage and corned beef time — let me go!

Okay. (*Confessional.*) You got me. I'm not Swedish and I'm not Irish. You probably guessed it already — I'm Israeli! Mazel tov, bubeleh (*Jackie Mason schtick.*) Come on, kineahora, open up the door. I'll walk out, you'll lock the door, you won't miss me, I'll send you a postcard. . . .

Orale, gabacho pendejo.° I'm American, man. I was born right here in Flushing. Well, sure I sound Mexican. I was raised by a Mexican nanny. Doesn't everybody have a Maria Consuelo?

As a matter of fact, I got proof right here that I'm American. I got two tickets to the Mets game. Yeah, Gooden's pitching. Come on, I'm late.

Orale, ése.° Is it money? It's always money. (*Conspiratorially.*) Well, I got a lot of money. I just don't have it on me. But I know where to get it.

Orale, ése. Tell me, where did your people come from? Santo Domingo? Orale, we're related! We're cousins! Tell me, what's your last name? Rivera? Rivera! That's my mother's maiden name! What a coinky dinky. Hermano, cousin, brother, primo, por favor dejeme ir que somos de la mismita sangre. Los latinos debemos ser unidos y jamás seremos vencidos.°

Oh, you don't understand, huh? You're a coconut. (*Angry.*) Brown on the outside, but white on the inside. Why don't you do something for your people for a change and let me out of here?

Okay, I'm sorry, cuz. (*Apologetic.*) Come here. Mira, mijito,° I got all my family here. I got my wife and daughter. And my daughter, she's in the hospital. She's a preemie with double pneumonia and asthma. And if you deport me, who's gonna take care of my little chucawala?

Come on, ése. It's not like I'm stealing or living off of you good people's taxes. I'm doing the shit jobs that Americans don't want. (*Anger builds again.*) Tell me, who the hell wants to work for two twenty-five an hour picking toxic pesticide-coated grapes? I'll give you a tip: Don't eat them.

Orale, you Americans act like you own this place, but we were here first. That's right, the Spaniards were here first. Ponce de León, Cortés, Vásquez, Cabeza de Vaca. If it's not true, then how come your country has all our names? Florida, California, Nevada, Arizona, Las Vegas, Los Angeles, San Bernardino, San Antonio, Santa Fe, Nueva York!

Orale, gabacho pendejo: What's up, dumb whitey? **Orale, ése:** What's up, guy? **primo, por favor . . . vencidos:** Cuz, please let me go, we are of the same blood. Latinos united, we'll never be divided. **Mira, mijito:** Look, my daughter.

Tell you what I'm going to do. I'll let you stay if you let me go.

What are you so afraid of? I'm not a threat. I'm just here for the same reason that all your people came here for—in search of a better life, that's all.

(*Leans away from grille, then comes back outraged.*) Okay, go ahead and send me back. But who's going to clean for you? Because if we all stopped cleaning and said "adiós," we'd still be the same people, but you'd be dirty! Who's going to pick your chef salads? And who's going to make your guacamole? You need us more than we need you. 'Cause we're here revitalizing the American labor force!

Go ahead and try to keep us back. Because we're going to multiply and multiply (*thrusts hips*) so uncontrollably till we push you so far up, you'll be living in Canada! Oh, scary monsters, huh? You might have to learn a second language. Oh, the horror!

But don't worry, we won't deport you. We'll just let you clean our toilets. Yeah, we don't even hold grudges—we'll let you use rubber gloves.

Orale, I'm gonna miss you white people.

(*Lights down.*)

APPROACHING THE READING

1. Write a brief synopsis of what Pepe says. How would you summarize a work constructed from a series of monologues?

2. What types of theatrical setting or stage do you think would be most effective for this play?

Research this author in depth, including images and cultural documents, with VirtuaLit Drama at bedfordstmartins.com/approachinglit.

3. Think about how various people might respond to this type of comedy. How can what is "savage" be funny?

4. Consider the title. What is implied by "mouth" and calling it a "mambo mouth"? What is suggested by the subtitle "A Savage Comedy"?

RESPONDING THROUGH WRITING

Journal Entries

1. Attend a performance of a play at a professional theater, a college performance, or a community theater. Note the kind of stage and the way the play is adapted to it. Write a journal entry discussing the appropriateness of the play for the stage and the effectiveness of the company's adaptation to and use of the space available.

2. Write a journal entry comparing and contrasting a television screen to the invisible fourth wall of a modern theater. To what extent does the television set of a sitcom, for example, have similarities to the stage sketched on page 857? In what ways is television quite different, thus eliciting effects that are quite different?

Research the authors in this chapter with LitLinks, or take a quiz on the plays with LitQuiz, at bedfordstmartins.com/approachinglit.

3. Write a journal entry describing how you would produce Pepe's monologue from John Leguizamo's *Mambo Mouth:* What kind of stage would you prefer? What kind of set would you design? What props would you use? What stage movements would you suggest? What else should you consider?

Literary Analysis Papers

4. Write a paper discussing the kind of theater the author of Alice Childress's *Florence* (p. 795) or Susan Glaspell's *Trifles* (p. 822) had in mind as she wrote. How did that theater influence the way the play was crafted and the way its themes and effects are conveyed?

5. The dedication to John Leguizamo's *Mambo Mouth* (p. 874) reads, "This book is for all the Latino people who have had a hard time holding on to a dream and just made do." Write a paper examining how that dedication fits and illuminates the play.

6. Some modern playwrights make use of antirealistic techniques to create an "alienation effect" in their plays. An alienation effect is achieved by any device that works against realism, such as distorting the time sequence, breaking through the "fourth wall," or having actors wear masks or speak directly to the audience. Such techniques alienate (or separate) the audience from the play and prevent them from identifying closely with the characters and action, so they will pay more attention to the play's political or social message. Write a paper in which you discuss possible alienation effects in John Leguizamo's *Mambo Mouth* (p. 874).

Making Connections

7. Compare and contrast ways Luis Valdez's *Los Vendidos* (p. 864) and John Leguizamo's *Mambo Mouth* (p. 874) use dramatic conventions and satiric techniques to force their audiences (and readers) to confront social problems and conditions the audience (and readers) might prefer to ignore.

8. Compare and contrast the explorations of racial stereotyping in Alice Childress's *Florence* (p. 795), Caleen Sinnette Jennings's *Classyass* (p. 812), and Luis Valdez's *Los Vendidos* (p. 864) in terms of the themes each play is developing (how stereotyping relates to the play as a whole) and the tone and emphasis used in each case.

Cultural Criticism Papers

9. Write a paper examining the cultural implications of theaters as buildings and as institutions. You might consider, for example, the implications of using a traditional theater, on the one hand, and Luis Valdez's decision to do his plays in a factory or on the street, on the other. Think about who would attend (including the cost of tickets), what social aura surrounds attendance at a performance, and what kind of support (financial and otherwise) a production requires.

10. Write a paper discussing ways in which the satiric attacks on racial and ethnic stereotypes in American culture and the exploration of other social and political issues in Luis Valdez's *Los Vendidos* (p. 864) and John Leguizamo's *Mambo Mouth* (p. 874) are similar. Then discuss ways they are different, for example, in focus, tone, emphasis, or technique.

RESPONDING THROUGH THE ARTS

1. Draw a set of sketches on how the setting of the same play — perhaps Alice Childress's *Florence* (p. 795), Susan Glaspell's *Trifles* (p. 822), or August Wilson's *Fences* (p. 1186) — could be designed for a proscenium arch stage, a contemporary thrust stage, and (if feasible) a contemporary arena stage.

2. Design a poster for one or more of the plays you've read.

Dramatic Types and Their Effects

Before you go to a movie, you want to know whether it's a romantic comedy, a horror show, an action film, or a serious drama. You gear up mentally and psychologically for the kind of film you expect to see. If you are told that a movie is a comedy but it turns out to be a psychodrama thriller, you probably will feel frustrated, want your money back, or find it hard to suddenly switch your mood, even if ordinarily you like psychodrama thrillers. Because of the way expectations affect us in going to movies, or in reading (or watching) drama, it helps to be aware of the traditional dramatic classifications — not for the sake of categorizing plays but to help in recognizing the effects different types of plays aim to achieve. And recognizing their effects helps us better understand why people, from earliest times onward, have found plays appealing, provocative, and satisfying. Classical drama had only two clearly differentiated types (or **genres**): comedy and tragedy. From the Middle Ages on, other types appeared: mystery plays, morality plays, tragicomedy, romance, masques, heroic drama, sentimental drama, problem plays, avant-garde plays, and the catch-all form "serious drama." All of these, although their effects are very different, derive from and are adaptations of the original two.

Knowing the characteristics of comedy and tragedy specifically and of the other key influential dramatic types, and knowing something about the way the genres developed, will help you recognize the effects of plays as you watch, read, study, and write about them. Familiarity with dramatic genres is also useful because their influence lives on, beyond the theatrical world, in the ways they have shaped the conventions of movies and television programs in our day.

TRAGEDY

A **tragedy** in literary usage is a play or work characterized by serious and significant actions that often lead to a disastrous result for the protagonist. Until the 1700s, tragedies were usually, or mostly, written in poetry, and usually in an elevated and dignified literary style. Their tone is correspondingly sober and weighty. Although the central character comes to a tragic end, tragedies usually conclude with a restoration of order and an expectation of a brighter future for those who survive.

Aristotle, discussing literature in his *Poetics* (c. 330 B.C.E.), described tragedy as raising fear and pity in its audience and as having the effect of a *catharsis,* which has usually been translated as "purgation" or "purification." What he meant by this is widely disputed, but a common summation is as follows. The play first raises emotions: Members of the audience pity the hero and feel fear lest they encounter a fate similar to the hero's. But the artistic handling of the conclusion releases and quiets those emotions, as order is restored and the hero faces her or his destiny with fortitude, thus affirming the courage and dignity of humankind. In Aristotle's view, such raising and releasing of emotion has a healthy effect, psychologically and physically: The audience goes away feeling not dejected but relieved.

Aristotle's account was based on Greek drama, the only drama he knew. Some literary historians claim that Aristotle's theories fit later tragedy equally well, that Aristotle got at the essence of the form. But after the Greeks, tragedy took many different forms and, though Aristotle's formula may apply broadly to them all, we think it is wiser to treat each individually and to recognize the value of how their specific effects vary. Here is a selective survey, beginning with the Greeks and ending with modern tragedy.

Greek Tragedy

The word *tragedy* comes from the Greek word *tragōidía,* or "goat-song," likely connected to the sacrifice of goats as part of an annual festival honoring the god Dionysus. The festival included an ode, or *dithyramb,* chanted by a chorus, lamenting the death of Dionysus. The Greek dramatist Thespis is usually given credit for transforming the content of the *dithyramb* from a hymn honoring the god to tragic stories about famous heroes and for first introducing an actor to the stage and initiating dialogue between the actor and the chorus (see pp. 852–53).

Because the subject of tragedy was drawn overwhelmingly from myth, which told stories of heroes and gods, the protagonists of Greek tragedies are persons of high rank or great importance. In keeping with his analysis, Aristotle said the hero should be neither superhumanly good, for a calamity falling on such a person is too hard to accept, nor thoroughly evil, for the downfall of such a person is deserved and therefore does not elicit pity. The tragic hero suffers a change in fortune from prosperity to adversity as a result of a mistake, an error in judgment, a frailty. Aristotle's word for this is *hamartia*. *Hamartia* is not the same as having a character flaw. Some critics explain all tragedies in terms of a "tragic flaw" in the hero and cite Aristotle as their source; but the supposed flaws are not always defects or faults, but rather central or defining aspects of the character. As we read or watch, we are always led to ask what causes the tragedy, what leads to the downfall; watching for an error or misstep (*hamartia*) is preferable to looking for a defect in character (tragic flaw).

In *Oedipus Rex* (p. 1145), the protagonist is a good but not perfect man. Because he has a quick temper, some critics fix on that as a character flaw that leads to his downfall. Doing so, however, shifts attention away from what for the Greeks would have been a more significant issue. True, his temper prevents him from learning the truth sooner and aggravates his suffering later. But his downfall stems not from his temper but from an error in judgment (*hamartia*). Oedipus, having heard from a drunken man that Polybos is not his father, visits an oracle to learn the truth. He is told that he will kill his father and marry his mother, and so Oedipus decides to leave Corinth to escape this fate. That is his fatal error in judgment: The Greeks believed in fate and so knew to accept and endure it; attempting to avoid it was futile.

By attempting to escape his fate, Oedipus ironically fulfills it: He kills a man whose chariot forced him off a road near Thebes and later marries the Queen of Thebes. As the story unfolds, scene by scene, Oedipus learns that, in fleeing Corinth to distance himself from his supposed parents, he fulfilled what the oracle foretold regarding his actual parents. The play makes effective use of dramatic irony (see p. 808): Readers or those viewing the play realize the truth before Oedipus does and thus watch with horror as he moves step by step toward the awful realization that will destroy his life. If Aristotle is right, the reader or audience member feels a great sense of pity for Oedipus and Jocasta, and a sense of fear that if these basically good and decent people could experience such a tragic series of events, what can prevent the same sort of thing happening to anyone else? But the audience also experiences relief ("purgation") — relief that Oedipus accepts the outcome with courage and dignity, as we hope we would, and relief that order is restored in Thebes. The blight and plagues that afflict the city at the beginning of the play are lifted, and the new king, Creon, who replaces Oedipus, gives promise of prosperity in the future.

Medieval Tragedy

Tragedy in the Middle Ages focused on one aspect of Aristotle's formula — the change of fortune experienced by the protagonist. But medieval tragedy did not emphasize the *hamartia* that, in the Greek plays, accounts for the change. Works written during this period reflect the medieval belief in *mutability* or constant change. Fortune is like a wheel that keeps turning:

Those at the top of the wheel should resist pride or complacency because inevitably their fortunes will decline and they will reach bottom. During the Middle Ages, plays were used mostly in religious festivals. Medieval tragedy appears exclusively in narrative, not dramatic, form. The series of stories recounted by the Monk in Geoffrey Chaucer's *The Canterbury Tales* (c. 1386–1400) are the best-known examples: stories about the decline and fall—whether deserved or not—of persons of high status, who have a great deal to lose. The effect of such works is not so much to create and release fear and pity as to teach a lesson: They warn the great not to take their happiness for granted, and reassure those of lower status that greatness is not without its dangers and costs.

Renaissance Tragedy

England during the reigns of Elizabeth I (1558–1603) and James I (1603–1625) witnessed an outpouring of splendidly written drama and an increase in theatrical activity: It was one of the greatest periods for drama in history. Dramatists such as Thomas Kyd, Christopher Marlowe, Ben Jonson, Francis Beaumont, John Fletcher, John Webster, and, of course, William Shakespeare wrote during this time, and theaters such as the Curtain, the Rose, the Globe, and the Fortune (see p. 854) drew large audiences from across the social classes. The film *Shakespeare in Love* (1998), directed by John Madden and starring Gwyneth Paltrow and Joseph Fiennes, offers a lively, imaginative reenactment of the theater scene at the time.

Tragedies from this era tend to deal with the results of evil in the world. Often they show how a misstep or an association with an antagonist harboring evil intentions results in a consequence that far exceeds what the protagonist seems to deserve. Or they show the destruction of an innocent victim caught in an evil web not of her or his own making. The protagonists continue to be persons of high status and importance (whose actions affect many people) or, at least, from the upper ranks of society. Unlike classical tragedy, with its unified seriousness of tone, Elizabethan tragedy mixes lighter scenes (influenced by characters and scenes popular in medieval tragedy, such as ranting tyrants) with the serious ones, often elaborating the serious action thematically in comic form. It's interesting to note that the serious scenes are usually written in poetry, befitting their characters' elevated status and dignity; the humorous scenes, and other scenes involving characters from the lower classes, are often written in the less "elevated" and dignified medium of prose.

Elizabethan tragedy appears in several subtypes. One popular variety is *revenge tragedy* in which an avenger who seeks to exact revenge for a death of a relative or comrade dies in achieving that aim. Revenge tragedy was influenced by drama of the Roman era, especially the five-act closet dramas of Seneca, which are filled with violence, supernatural agents, and lengthy declamatory speeches. In Senecan plays, as in Greek plays, horrifying events take place off stage. But Elizabethan playwrights—unaware that Seneca's plays were meant to be recited, not acted out—brought them on stage, creating performances full of action and violence (sometimes called "tragedies of blood"). The best-known tragedy of this type is Shakespeare's *Hamlet* (c. 1599–1601): The play, in fact, was referred to as "the Revenge of Hamlet, Prince of Denmark" when the publisher entered it in the Stationer's Register for future publication.

Another popular subtype, *tragedy of passion,* occurs when characters die as a result of excessively passionate reactions or relationships. Psychological and ethical thinking since the Greeks, and still influential in and beyond the Renaissance, held that unchecked passions posed great danger to individuals and society. It was crucial that one use reason to keep the passions in check, to restrain them and maintain a proper balance of reason and emotions. Unrestrained passion, an unbalanced life, was a recipe for disaster. Shakespeare's *Romeo and Juliet* (c. 1594–1596) illustrates this subtype: Love at first sight and the hasty marriage of the young persons grow out of their intense emotions and lead to their unfortunate and untimely deaths.

A third subtype, *tragedy of fate,* depicts characters who cannot escape the doom that fortune has in store for them. *Romeo and Juliet* fits this category as well. From the opening lines, in which Romeo and Juliet are referred to as "star-crossed lovers," their doom seems inescapable. This fate, however, is not the same as the divine inevitability of the Greeks but an inexplicable, inescapable destiny. Chance, accident, and coincidence play a major role: The audience is left with a sense of sympathy for the young lovers, and a sense of regret, even frustration, because with only slight changes in timing or communication at any number of points, the catastrophe would have been avoided.

In still another subtype, *tragedy of character,* disastrous results grow out of an individual's character traits—not necessarily weaknesses or flaws but often strengths and virtues that are carried too far or applied unwisely. Shakespeare's great tragedies (*Hamlet, Othello, King Lear, Macbeth*) develop protagonists of great depth and complexity. Careful reading and reflection are required to understand such characters well (perhaps "fully" can never be achieved) and to grasp the various acts, decisions, and influences that lead to their catastrophes. Attempting to reduce the reasons for what happens to a "tragic flaw" risks oversimplifying works of great subtlety and sophistication.

That is the case for the Shakespeare play included in this book. *Othello* (p. 1054) is a tragedy of character. Both the protagonist—Othello—and the antagonist—Iago—are complex characters who are developed in great depth. It takes a good deal of rereading and reflection for most readers to gain an understanding of Othello and Iago, and even then they know there is more to be learned and considered. Some critics have tried to explain Othello in terms of a "tragic flaw," but most regard this as oversimplifying. Othello is too fascinatingly complicated to sum up in a simple formula.

Modern Tragedy

Tragedy was not a major form among playwrights (and audiences) during the 1700s and 1800s. Witty comedies of manners were popular at the time, and spectacular performances of serious plays, full of bright, colorful costumes and set designs, served to deflect attention from the words and story. When theaters did stage a tragedy, they usually revived Shakespearean plays, but most eighteenth- and nineteenth-century audiences preferred happy endings. In fact, the text of Shakespeare's *King Lear* used throughout the 1700s and early 1800s was a revised version with a happy ending.

The early 1700s did revive one form of tragedy, *domestic tragedy,* which had been a minor but lively and popular subgenre during and following the Elizabethan era, and this revival affected the future course of the genre. Before the 1700s, almost all tragedies were written in verse and featured a protagonist of noble rank whose death had a major impact on her or his society or nation. Domestic tragedy in the 1700s, however, was written in prose with an ordinary person as its protagonist, not a person of high rank or great importance. George Lillo's *The London Merchant: or, The History of George Barnwell* (1731), for example, deals with an apprentice who, under the influence of his mistress, robs his employer and murders his uncle, but repents of his misdeeds before his execution. Its tone is sentimental, or tenderly emotional. Its effect is first to elicit revulsion at what George does but then to permit relief and gratitude that he repents.

Modern tragedies, dating from the mid-1900s, also involve middle-class characters but do not use the sentimental emotions characteristic of domestic drama. Most are written in prose, though a few — such as T. S. Eliot's *Murder in the Cathedral* (1935) — are in verse. Modern tragedies generally present ordinary people encountering forces (economic, social, political, or personal) far beyond their control. They are destroyed but often not defeated by them. The protagonist is more likely to be a tragic victim than a classic tragic hero. In its effects, modern tragedy elicits pity, as sympathetic understanding, and fear, as awareness that what happens to the protagonist could happen to any of us. But modern tragedy typically does not create the sense of awe or horror evoked by classical tragedy and by some Elizabethan tragedy; thus some argue that it has a lessened sense of release and purgation.

Arthur Miller's *Death of a Salesman* (p. 980) provides a good example in its treatment of the life of an ordinary salesman (what he is selling is never identified). Nearing retirement age, Willy Loman is no longer able to travel as he has for thirty-six years. He has never achieved great financial success and has always struggled to make ends meet. He finds satisfaction and meaning chiefly through the lives of his sons, especially the older, Biff, who was a successful athlete in high school. Something that occurred between them continues as a barrier for fifteen years. *Death of a Salesman* avoids sentimentality and rises to tragic seriousness by treating Willy's life as representative of the struggle of ordinary people with values and economic forces of society that they cannot cope with, let alone control.

COMEDY

The most basic definition of **comedy** is a story with a happy ending. No matter what the characters go through, if the ending is happy, the play is a comedy. All's well that ends well. The tone of comedy is lighter than that of tragedy and its style less elevated; it is usually written in prose. It uses wit and humor to evoke smiles and laughter from its readers and audience. Even though comedy has a realistic strain, dealing with ordinary people in their everyday activities, the events of a comedy often include exaggeration and unrealistic circumstances, with characters turning things upside down, breaking rules, reversing normal relationships, and falling into incongruous situations. Comedies celebrate life, with all the disorder, misunderstandings, and confusion that often accompany it; beginning in disorder, comedies end with restoration of order, and often conclude with a dance, marriage, or celebration of some kind symbolizing harmony and happiness.

Comedy, like tragedy, emerged from Greek religious ceremonies, particularly from Dionysian fertility rites. The word *comedy* derives from the Greek word *kômos,* meaning "revel" or "merry-making"; in early comedies the revelry involved explicit sexuality. Although later Greek comedies became less blatantly sexual, they retained the earthy, physical qualities of their Dionysian origins. Comedy continues to emphasize the physical or sensuous nature of humans; their ridiculousness, weaknesses and foibles; their physical relationships; and their outrageous behaviors and foolish misunderstandings.

Satiric Comedy

Greek drama initiated two major strains of comedy that have remained influential through the centuries. The earlier strain was **Old Comedy**, represented by the satiric works of Aristophanes (c. 450–385 B.C.E.), predecessor of later satiric comedy playwrights. Satiric comedy ridicules political policies, social practices, or philosophical ideas by poking fun at those who deviate from the standards upheld by common sense or by the author. Behind satiric comedy is the hope that the exposure of flaws and follies will result in improving society, though in practice the only result may be amusement for those observing the ridicule. Modern satiric comedy is illustrated in this book by Luis Valdez's *Los Vendidos* (p. 864), with its wide-ranging ridicule of such things as racial stereotypes, tokenism, used car salesmen, government officials, and much more. The effect of satiric comedy depends on the perspective of those reading or viewing it: Those who are the butt of the satiric attack may feel uncomfortable or embarrassed or angry or insulted. But the form assumes that such victims are a minority and that the majority will approve of the attack; for them the effect is likely to be delight and amusement.

Comedy of Manners

Old Comedy was replaced by **New Comedy**, originated by the Greek playwright Menander (c. 342–292 B.C.E.) and developed further by the Roman dramatists Plautus (c. 254–184 B.C.E.) and Terence (c. 190–159 B.C.E.). New Comedy concerns the obstacles faced by young lovers and the unpredictable changes of fortune they encounter, and pokes fun at the foibles and attitudes of the lovers as well as those around them. New Comedy developed into the later form called the *comedy of manners,* which laughs at the behavior and conventions of members of the upper classes, at their vanities and self-centeredness, their social interactions, their follies and intrigues.

Among the best examples of the New Comedy tradition are the late seventeenth and early eighteenth comedies of William Wycherley (1640–1715), Sir George Etherege (1635–1692), and William Congreve (1670–1729), which treat love as a game or contest involving sophisticated lovers, jealous spouses, and conniving rivals. These plays are characterized by sparkling dialogue, with clever conversations and quick, witty responses — amusing and refreshing in effect. The closest thing to a comedy of manners in this book is *Classyass* (p. 812), with its rapid-fire dialogue, ridicule of Ama's stereotyping of people at the Shelter, and teasing possibility of a relationship between Ama and BigB.

Romantic Comedy

Another Elizabethan subtype, *romantic comedy,* also was influenced by the Greeks, but by Greek prose romances rather than by Greek drama. Romantic comedy typically involves young lovers who face obstacles to fulfilling their relationship (perhaps parental opposition, a competing lover, their own differences, poverty, separation because of war or travel, or coincidences that prevent them from joining together). After facing numerous complications and encountering several near disasters, all of which make a favorable outcome seem impossible, the lovers at last are united and their union is accepted.

Shakespeare wrote a number of well-known works in this form, including *A Midsummer Night's Dream* (c. 1595), *Much Ado about Nothing* (1598–1599), *As You Like It* (1598–1600), *Twelfth Night* (1600–1602), and *All's Well That Ends Well* (c. 1601–1605). Hollywood movies and TV comedies continue the tradition today. In effect, romantic comedies are entertaining and enjoyable, and at their best — as in the Shakespearean examples — they achieve thematic depth and insight as well.

Other Types of Comedy

Two other comic subtypes are comedy of situation and sentimental comedy. *Comedy of situation,* which focuses on ingenuity of plot more than on exploration of character, relies on accidents, coincidences, disguises, mistaken identities, chaos, and confusion. An example of the type is Shakespeare's early play *The Comedy of Errors* (c. 1589–1594), an imitation of Roman comedy, especially that of Plautus. You can recognize its influence any time you tune into a television sitcom. In *sentimental comedy,* a scoundrel reforms in the last act and turns into a model citizen, or a model hero withstands a variety of difficulties and trials and, in a melodramatic happy ending, is rewarded. This is "feel good" comedy, leading the audience to feel first concern and sympathy, then relief and exhilaration. Perhaps the best example of this type is Richard Steele's *The Conscious Lovers* (1722).

THREE OTHER DRAMATIC TYPES

The subgenres of tragedy and comedy discussed above show that these two central forms of drama are not fixed and unchanging, in form or effect. As playwrights encountered new social and political situations and changing cultural attitudes, they responded by adapting the traditional genres and developing new subgenres with effects different from the previous ones. In addition to developing subgenres of tragedy and comedy, playwrights made more radical adaptations. These types, although they clearly grow out of comedy and tragedy, are sufficiently different from them in form and effect to be discussed as distinct minor genres, rather than as additional subgenres. Three are particularly worth attention.

Tragicomedy

Tragicomedy emerged in Elizabethan drama, with its mixed influences of classical and medieval works. Elizabethan tragedies included comic scenes, unlike classical tragedy with its consistency and unity of tone. Tragicomedy takes this a step further: Its plot is appropriate to tragedy until the final act, when it turns out to have an unexpectedly happy ending. The tone and style of tragicomedy are serious, and the expected outcome is disaster or death; but somehow at the end the disaster is averted and order and harmony prevail. (Tragicomedy is not the same as dark comedy, which mixes a humorous tone with serious and potentially tragic events, often with an unhappy outcome.)

Problem Play

A **problem play** is a serious work that dramatizes a real-life, usually contemporary, social, political, or ethical problem. Although in a broad sense it covers all drama dealing with problems of human life, it is used more narrowly for the "drama of ideas" that emerged in the late 1800s in the work, for example, of Norwegian playwright Henrik Ibsen (1828–1906), Irish playwright George Bernard Shaw (1856–1950), and English playwright John Galsworthy (1867–1933).

Ibsen's play *A Doll House* (p. 926) dramatizes the problem of the status of women in marital relationships. Nora Helmer lives figuratively in a doll house, an isolated and unreal world where she plays with her children and indulges her pompous, self-important husband. She demonstrates the stereotypical womanly traits of helplessness, obedience, and resourcefulness in using feminine wiles to achieve her goals. She doesn't question her life — it's what she expected when she moved from the protection of her father to that of her husband, who becomes a surrogate father figure.

Questions begin to arise, however, when Nora moves into a bigger world, the adult, real, "male" world of careers and responsibility. Once she steps outside the doll house, can she ever return to her former life and role? The rest of the play depicts the personal and marital conflicts she encounters and reveals in stark terms the legal, social, and economic problems women like Nora faced during the nineteenth century.

"Serious Drama"

The word *drama,* in addition to meaning a literary work intended for performance or the whole body of such works, is also used for any particularly striking or interesting event or series of events that involve conflict and tension. In literature or theater today, *drama* is often used, instead of *tragedy,* for a play that is not a comedy and does not have a tragic ending, but that deals with serious events involving such conflict and tension. August Wilson's *Fences* (p. 1186) is an example. So too are many of the works by twentieth-century playwrights Bertolt Brecht and Samuel Beckett. You may have noticed that many video stores have sections labeled "comedy," "action," and "drama" — not tragedy.

This chapter makes clear that drama is dynamic and flexible, constantly developing and adapting its forms and effects to different social, political, and cultural situations. A question like "What is the effect of drama?" needs to be narrowed and qualified before it can be answered. Different types of drama, and even different subtypes, convey different effects. Both satiric comedy and romantic comedy have happy endings, but in tone and effect they are very different. Tragedy of fate and domestic tragedy both end unhappily, but their effects on a reader or audience are totally dissimilar. Such adaptation of and experimentation with genre forms continues today, as illustrated by some of the plays included in this book. *Sure Thing* (p. 839), *Mambo Mouth* (p. 874), and *The Cuban*

www

Further explore dramatic types and their effects, including interactive exercises, with VirtuaLit Drama at bedfordstmartins .com/approachinglit.

Swimmer (p. 890) do not fit neatly into the categories described in this chapter, but in their adaptation of elements from earlier types, they are typical of the diversity in form, tone, and effect found in contemporary drama. To participate fully in the kinds of experiences drama offers, you must be alert and responsive to such differences. Drama has so much to offer that your effort will be richly rewarded.

☑ **CHECKLIST on Dramatic Types and Their Effects**

❑ Be able to describe tragedy as a play or other literary work in an elevated and dignified style and with a sober, weighty tone that depicts serious and significant actions leading to a disastrous result for the protagonist. Be able to describe too its overall effects on readers and audiences.

❑ Be able to characterize the different forms of tragedy that developed historically — Greek tragedy, medieval tragedy, renaissance tragedy, domestic tragedy, and modern tragedy — and their distinctive effects on readers and audiences.

❑ Be able to describe comedy as a play or other work in a light style that makes use of wit and humor; that depicts the actions of ordinary people in everyday activities; that, despite potentially disastrous confusion, difficulties, reversals, misunderstandings, and disorders, turns out satisfactorily; and that has a happy ending. Be able to describe too its overall effects on readers and audiences.

❑ Be able to characterize the important subtypes of comedy — satiric comedy, comedy of manners, and romantic comedy — and the distinctive effects they have on readers and audiences.

❑ Be able to describe other significant dramatic types — tragicomedy, problem plays, and "serious drama" — and the effects they have on readers and audiences.

❑ Be able, when you read a play, to identify elements in it that place it in one or another of these genres.

FURTHER READING

The two short, contemporary plays that follow illustrate the kind of experimentation with genre typical of contemporary drama. Scenes 1–4 of *The Cuban Swimmer* are mostly comic, including satire on high-pressure athletics and the media, comedy of manners, and lots of verbal wit. But watch for a change in tone and manner in the remainder of the play and consider how the author is trying for different, unanticipated effects in them.

Milcha Sanchez-Scott b. 1955

The Cuban Swimmer   [1984]

CHARACTERS

MARGARITA SUÁREZ, the swimmer

EDUARDO SUÁREZ, her father,
   the coach

SIMÓN SUÁREZ, her brother

AÍDA SUÁREZ, her mother

ABUELA, her grandmother

VOICE OF MEL MUNSON

VOICE OF MARY BETH WHITE

VOICE OF RADIO OPERATOR

Live conga drums can be used to punctuate the action of the play.

TIME
Summer.

PLACE
The Pacific Ocean between San Pedro and Catalina Island.

Scene 1

Pacific Ocean. Midday. On the horizon, in perspective, a small boat enters upstage left, crosses to upstage right and exits. Pause. Lower on the horizon, the same boat, in larger perspective, enters upstage right, crosses and exits upstage left. Blackout.

Scene 2

Pacific Ocean. Midday. The swimmer, Margarita Suárez, is swimming. On the boat following behind her are her father, Eduardo Suárez, holding a megaphone, and Simón, her brother, sitting on top of the cabin with his shirt off, punk sunglasses on, binoculars hanging on his chest.

EDUARDO (*leaning forward, shouting in time to Margarita's swimming*): Uno, dos, uno, dos. Y uno, dos° . . . keep your shoulders parallel to the water.

SIMÓN: I'm gonna take these glasses off and look straight into the sun.

EDUARDO (*through megaphone*): Muy bien, muy bien° . . . but punch those arms in, baby.

SIMÓN (*looking directly at the sun through binoculars*): Come on, come on, zap me. Show me something. (*He looks behind at the shoreline and ahead at the sea.*) Stop! Stop, Papi! Stop! (*Aída Suárez and Abuela, the swimmer's mother and grandmother, enter running from the back of the boat.*)

AÍDA and ABUELA: Qué? Qué es?°

AÍDA: Es un shark?°

Uno, dos, uno, dos. Y uno, dos: One, two, one, two. And one, two.   **Muy Bien, muy bien:** Very good, very good.   **Qué? Qué es?:** What is it?   **Es un shark?:** Is it a shark?

EDUARDO: Eh?

ABUELA: *Que es un* shark *dicen?*° (*Eduardo blows whistle. Margarita looks up at the boat.*)

SIMÓN: No, Papi, no shark, no shark. We've reached the halfway mark.

ABUELA (*looking into the water*): *A dónde está?*°

AÍDA: It's not in the water.

ABUELA: Oh no? Oh no?

AÍDA: No! *A poco*° do you think they're gonna have signs in the water to say you are halfway to Santa Catalina? No. It's done very scientific. *A ver, hijo,*° explain it to your grandma.

SIMÓN: Well, you see Abuela° — (*He points behind.*) There's San Pedro. (*He points ahead.*) And there's Santa Catalina. Looks halfway to me. (*Abuela shakes her head and is looking back and forth, trying to make the decision, when suddenly the sound of a helicopter is heard.*)

ABUELA (*looking up*): *Virgencita de la Caridad del Cobre. Qué es eso?*° (*Sound of helicopter gets closer. Margarita looks up.*)

MARGARITA: Papi, Papi! (*A small commotion on the boat, with everybody pointing at the helicopter above. Shadows of the helicopter fall on the boat. Simón looks up at it through binoculars.*) Papi — *qué es?* What is it?

EDUARDO (*through megaphone*): Uh . . . uh . . . uh *un momentico . . . mi hija.*° . . . Your papi's got everything under control, understand? Uh . . . you just keep stroking. And stay . . . uh . . . close to the boat.

SIMÓN: Wow, Papi! We're on TV man! Holy Christ, we're all over the fucking U.S.A.! It's Mel Munson and Mary Beth White!

AÍDA: *Por Dios!*° Simón, don't swear. And put on your shirt. (*Aída fluffs her hair, puts on her sunglasses and waves to the helicopter. Simón leans over the side of the boat and yells to Margarita.*)

SIMÓN: Yo, Margo! You're on TV, man.

EDUARDO: Leave your sister alone. Turn on the radio.

MARGARITA: Papi! *Qué está pasando?*°

ABUELA: *Que es la televisión dicen?* (*She shakes her head.*) *Porque como yo no puedo ver nada sin mis espejuelos.*° (*Abuela rummages through the boat, looking for her glasses. Voices of Mel Munson and Mary Beth White are heard over the boat's radio.*)

MEL'S VOICE: As we take a closer look at the gallant crew of La Havana . . . and there . . . yes, there she is . . . the little Cuban swimmer from Long Beach, California, nineteen-year-old Margarita Suárez. The unknown swimmer is our Cinderella entry . . . a bundle of tenacity, battling her

---

Que es un shark *dicen?*: Did they say a shark?   *A dónde está?*: Where is it?   *A poco:* Next.
A ver, hijo: Let's see, son.   **Abuela:** Grandmother.   *Virgencita de la Caridad del Cobre. Qué es eso?*: Virgin of Charity! What is that?   *un momentico . . . mi hija:* Just a second, my daughter.
Por Dios!: For God's sake!   *Qué está pasando?:* What's happening?   *Que es la televisión dicen? . . . Porque como yo no puedo ver nada sin mis espejuelos:* Did they say television? Because I can't see anything without my glasses.

way through the choppy, murky waters of the cold Pacific to reach the Island of Romance . . . Santa Catalina . . . where should she be the first to arrive, two thousand dollars and a gold cup will be waiting for her.

AÍDA: Doesn't even cover our expenses.

ABUELA: *Qué dice?*°

EDUARDO: Shhhh!

MARY BETH'S VOICE: This is really a family effort, Mel, and—

MEL'S VOICE: Indeed it is. Her trainer, her coach, her mentor is her father, Eduardo Suárez. Not a swimmer himself, it says here, Mr. Suárez is head usher of the Holy Name Society and the owner-operator of Suárez Treasures of the Sea and Salvage Yard. I guess it's one of those places . . .

MARY BETH'S VOICE: If I might interject a fact here, Mel, assisting in this swim is Mrs. Suárez who is a former Miss Cuba.

MEL'S VOICE: And a beautiful woman in her own right. Let's try and get a closer look. (*Helicopter sound gets louder. Margarita, frightened, looks up again.*)

MARGARITA: Papi!

EDUARDO (*through megaphone*): *Mi hija,* don't get nervous . . . it's the press. I'm handling it.

AÍDA: I see how you're handling it.

EDUARDO (*through megaphone*): Do you hear? Everything is under control. Get back into your rhythm. Keep your elbows high and kick and kick and kick and kick . . .

ABUELA (*finds her glasses and puts them on*): *Ay sí, es la televisión*° . . . (*She points to helicopter.*) *Qué lindo mira*° . . . (*She fluffs her hair, gives a big wave.*) *Alo América! Viva mi Margarita, viva todo los Cubanos en los Estados Unidos!*°

AÍDA: *Ay por Dios,*° Cecilia, the man didn't come all this way in his helicopter to look at you jumping up and down, making a fool of yourself.

ABUELA: I don't care. I'm proud.

AÍDA: He can't understand you anyway.

ABUELA: *Viva* . . . (*She stops.*) *Simón, comó se dice viva?*°

SIMÓN: Hurray.

ABUELA: Hurray for *mi* Margarita *y* for all the Cubans living *en* the United States, *y un abrazo*° . . . Simón, *abrazo* . . .

SIMÓN: A big hug.

ABUELA: *Sí,* a big hug to all my friends in Miami, Long Beach, Union City, except for my son Carlos who lives in New York in sin! He lives . . . (*She crosses herself.*) in Brooklyn with a Puerto Rican woman in sin! *No decente* . . .

SIMÓN: Decent.

Qué dice?: What do you say?   *Ay sí, es la televisión:* Ah, yes, it is the television.   *Qué lindo mira:* It looks beautiful.   *Aló América! Viva mi Margarita, viva todo los Cubanos en los Estados Unidos!:* Hello America! Long live my Margarita, long live all the Cubans in the United States! *Ay por Dios:* Oh, for God's sake.   *cómo se dice viva?:* How do you say [translate] "viva"? *y un abrazo:* And a hug.

ABUELA: Carlos, *no decente*. This family, *decente*.

AÍDA: Cecilia, *por Dios*.

MEL'S VOICE: Look at that enthusiasm. The whole family has turned out to cheer little Margarita on to victory! I hope they won't be too disappointed.

MARY BETH'S VOICE: She seems to be making good time, Mel.

MEL'S VOICE: Yes, it takes all kinds to make a race. And it's a testimonial to the all-encompassing fairness . . . the greatness of this, the Wrigley Invitational Women's Swim to Catalina, where among all the professionals there is still room for the amateurs . . . like these, the simple people we see below us on the ragtag La Havana, taking their long-shot chance to victory. *Vaya con Dios!*° (*Helicopter sound fading as family, including Margarita, watch silently. Static as Simón turns radio off. Eduardo walks to bow of boat, looks out on the horizon.*)

EDUARDO (*to himself*): Amateurs.

AÍDA: Eduardo, that person insulted us. Did you hear, Eduardo? That he called us a simple people in a ragtag boat? Did you hear . . . ?

ABUELA (*clenching her fist at departing helicopter*): Mal-Rayo los parta!°

SIMÓN (*same gesture*): Asshole! (*Aída follows Eduardo as he goes to side of boat and stares at Margarita.*)

AÍDA: This person comes in his helicopter to insult your wife, your family, your daughter . . .

MARGARITA (*pops her head out of the water*): Papi?

AÍDA: Do you hear me, Eduardo? I am not simple.

ABUELA: Sí.

AÍDA: I am complicated.

ABUELA: Sí, *demasiada complicada*.°

AÍDA: Me and my family are not so simple.

SIMÓN: Mom, the guy's an asshole.

ABUELA (*shaking her fist at helicopter*): Asshole!

AÍDA: If my daughter was simple she would not be in that water swimming.

MARGARITA: Simple? Papi . . . ?

AÍDA: *Ahora,*° Eduardo, this is what I want you to do. When we get to Santa Catalina I want you to call the TV station and demand *un* apology.

EDUARDO: *Cállete mujer! Aquí mando yo.*° I will decide what is to be done.

MARGARITA: Papi, tell me what's going on.

EDUARDO: Do you understand what I am saying to you, Aída?

SIMÓN (*leaning over side of boat, to Margarita*): Yo Margo! You know that Mel Munson guy on TV? He called you a simple amateur and said you didn't have a chance.

ABUELA (*leaning directly behind Simón*): Mi hija, insultó a la familia. Desgraciado!°

Vaya con Dios!: Go with God['s blessing].   *Mal-Rayo los parta!:* May a bad lightning bolt strike you! [i.e., To hell with you!]   *Sí, demasiada complicada:* Yes, too complicated.   *Ahora:* Now.   *Cállete mujer! Aquí mando yo:* Shut up, woman! I give the orders here.   *Mi hija, insultó a la familia. Desgraciado!:* My daughter, he insulted the family. Disgraceful person!

AÍDA (*leaning in behind Abuela*): He called us peasants! And your father is not doing anything about it. He just knows how to yell at me.

EDUARDO (*through megaphone*): Shut up! All of you! Do you want to break her concentration? Is that what you are after? Eh? (*Abuela, Aída and Simón shrink back. Eduardo paces before them.*) Swimming is rhythm and concentration. You win a race *aquí.*° (*Pointing to his head.*) Now . . . (*To Simón.*) you, take care of the boat, Aída y Mama . . . do something. Anything. Something practical. (*Abuela and Aída get on knees and pray in Spanish.*) Hija, give it everything, eh? . . . *por la familia.*° Uno . . . dos. . . . You must win. (*Simón goes into cabin. The prayers continue as lights change to indicate bright sunlight, later in the afternoon.*)

Scene 3

Tableau for a couple of beats. Eduardo on bow with timer in one hand as he counts strokes per minute. Simón is in the cabin steering, wearing his sunglasses, baseball cap on backwards. Abuela and Aída are at the side of the boat, heads down, hands folded, still muttering prayers in Spanish.

AÍDA and ABUELA (*crossing themselves*): *En el nombre del Padre, del Hijo y del Espíritu Santo amén.*°

EDUARDO (*through megaphone*): You're stroking seventy-two!

SIMÓN (*singing*): Mama's stroking, Mama's stroking seventy-two . . .

EDUARDO (*through megaphone*): You comfortable with it?

SIMÓN (*singing*): Seventy-two, seventy-two, seventy-two for you.

AÍDA (*looking at the heavens*): Ay, Eduardo, *ven acá,*° we should be grateful that *Nuestro Señor*° gave us such a beautiful day.

ABUELA (*crosses herself*): *Sí, gracias a Dios.*°

EDUARDO: She's stroking seventy-two, with no problem. (*He throws a kiss to the sky.*) It's a beautiful day to win.

AÍDA: *Qué hermoso!*° So clear and bright. Not a cloud in the sky. *Mira! Mira!*° Even rainbows on the water . . . a sign from God.

SIMÓN (*singing*): Rainbows on the water . . . you in my arms . . .

ABUELA and EDUARDO (*looking the wrong way*): *Dónde?*°

AÍDA (*pointing toward Margarita*): There, dancing in front of Margarita, leading her on . . .

EDUARDO: Rainbows on . . . *Ay coño!*° It's an oil slick! You . . . you . . . (*To Simón.*) Stop the boat. (*Runs to bow, yelling.*) Margarita! Margarita! (*On the next stroke, Margarita comes up all covered in black oil.*)

---

aquí: Here.   *por la familia:* For the sake of the family.   *En el nombre del Padre, del Hijo y del Espíritu Santo amén:* In the name of the Father, the Son, and the Holy Ghost, Amen.   *ven acá:* Come here.   *Nuestro Señor:* God [literally, Our Lord].   *Sí, gracias a Dios:* Yes, thanks be to God.   *Qué hermoso!:* How handsome!   *Mira!:* Look.   *Dónde?:* Where?   *Ay coño!:* Dammit!

MARGARITA: Papi! Papi! (*Everybody goes to the side and stares at Margarita, who stares back. Eduardo freezes.*)

AÍDA: *Apúrate* Eduardo, move . . . what's wrong with you . . . *no me oíste,°* get my daughter out of the water.

EDUARDO (*softly*): We can't touch her. If we touch her, she's disqualified.

AÍDA: But I'm her mother.

EDUARDO: Not even by her own mother. Especially by her own mother . . . You always want the rules to be different for you, you always want to be the exception. (*To Simón*) And you . . . you didn't see it, eh? You were playing again?

SIMÓN: Papi, I was watching . . .

AÍDA (*interrupting*): *Pues,°* do something Eduardo. You are the big coach, the monitor.

SIMÓN: Mentor! Mentor!

EDUARDO: How can a person think around you? (*He walks off to bow, puts head in hands.*)

ABUELA (*looking over side*): *Mira como todos los°* little birds are dead. (*She crosses herself.*)

AÍDA: Their little wings are glued to their sides.

SIMÓN: Christ, this is like the La Brea tar pits.

AÍDA: They can't move their little wings.

ABUELA: *Esa niña tiene que moverse.°*

SIMÓN: Yeah Margo, you gotta move, man. (*Abuela and Simón gesture for Margarita to move. Aída gestures for her to swim.*)

ABUELA: *Anda niña, muévete.°*

AÍDA: Swim, *hija,* swim or the *aceite°* will stick to your wings.

MARGARITA: Papi?

ABUELA (*taking megaphone*): Your papi say "move it!" (*Margarita with difficulty starts moving.*)

ABUELA, AÍDA and SIMÓN (*laboriously counting*): Uno, dos . . . uno, dos . . . anda . . . uno, dos.

EDUARDO (*running to take megaphone from Abuela*): Uno, dos . . . (*Simón races into cabin and starts the engine. Abuela, Aída and Eduardo count together.*)

SIMÓN (*looking ahead*): Papi, it's over there!

EDUARDO: Eh?

SIMÓN (*pointing ahead and to* R.): It's getting clearer over there.

EDUARDO (*through megaphone*): Now pay attention to me. Go to the right. (*Simón, Abuela, Aída and Eduardo all lean over side. They point ahead and to right, except Abuela, who points to left.*)

FAMILY (*shouting together*): *Para yá! Para yá!°* (*Lights go down on boat. A special light on Margarita, swimming through the oil, and on Abuela, watching her.*)

Apúrate . . . no me oíste: Hurry up! . . . didn't you hear me? *Pues:* Well. *Mira como todos los . . . :* Look how all the . . . *Esa niña tiene que moverse:* That girl has to move. *Anda niña, muévete:* Come on, girl, move! *aceite:* Oil. *Para yá:* Over there.

ABUELA: *Sangre de mi sangre,*° you will be another to save us. *En Bolondron,* where your great-grandmother Luz Suárez was born, they say one day it rained blood. All the people, they run into their houses. They cry, they pray, *pero*° your great-grandmother Luz she had *cojones*° like a man. She run outside. She look straight at the sky. She shake her fist. And she say to the evil one, "*Mira . . . (Beating her chest.) coño, Diablo, aquí estoy si me quieres.*"° And she open her mouth, and she drunk the blood.

(*Blackout.*)

Scene 4

Lights up on boat. Aída and Eduardo are on deck watching Margarita swim.
    We hear the gentle, rhythmic lap, lap, lap, of the water, then the sound of inhaling and exhaling as Margarita's breathing becomes louder. Then Margarita's heartbeat is heard, with the lapping of the water and the breathing under it. These sounds continue beneath the dialogue to the end of the scene.

AÍDA: *Dios mío.*° Look how she moves through the water . . .
EDUARDO: You see, it's very simple. It is a matter of concentration.
AÍDA: The first time I put her in water she came to life, she grew before my eyes. She moved, she smiled, she loved it more than me. She didn't want my breast any longer. She wanted the water.
EDUARDO: And of course, the rhythm. The rhythm takes away the pain and helps the concentration. (*Pause. Aída and Eduardo watch Margarita.*)
AÍDA: Is that my child, or a seal. . . .
EDUARDO: Ah a seal, the reason for that is that she's keeping her arms very close to her body. She cups her hands and then she reaches and digs, reaches and digs.
AÍDA: To think that a daughter of mine . . .
EDUARDO: It's the training, the hours in the water. I used to tie weights around her little wrists and ankles.
AÍDA: A spirit, an ocean spirit, must have entered my body when I was carrying her.
EDUARDO (*to Margarita*): Your stroke is slowing down. (*Pause. We hear Margarita's heartbeat with the breathing under, faster now.*)
AÍDA: Eduardo, that night, the night on the boat . . .
EDUARDO: Ah, the night on the boat again . . . the moon was . . .
AÍDA: The moon was full. We were coming to America . . . *Qué romantico.*°
    (*Heartbeat and breathing continue.*)

Sangre de mi sangre: Blood of my blood.   *pero:* But.   *cojones:* Balls [nerve].   *Mira . . . coño, Diablo, aquí estoy si me quieres:* Look . . . shit, hell [or Devil], here I am if you want me.   *Dios mío:* My God.   *Qué romantico:* How romantic.

EDUARDO: We were cold, afraid, with no money, and on top of everything, you were hysterical, yelling at me, tearing at me with your nails. (*Opens his shirt, points to the base of his neck.*) Look, I still bear the scars . . . telling me that I didn't know what I was doing . . . saying that we were going to die . . .

AÍDA: You took me, you stole me from my home . . . you didn't give me a chance to prepare. You just said we have to go now, now! Now, you said. You didn't let me take anything. I left everything behind . . . I left everything behind.

EDUARDO: Saying that I wasn't good enough, that your father didn't raise you so that I could drown you in the sea.

AÍDA: You didn't let me say even a goodbye. You took me, you stole me, you tore me from my home.

EDUARDO: I took you so we could be married.

AÍDA: That was in Miami. But that night on the boat, Eduardo. . . . We were not married, that night on the boat.

EDUARDO: *No pasó nada!°* Once and for all get it out of your head, it was cold, you hated me and we were afraid. . . .

AÍDA: *Mentiroso!°*

EDUARDO: A man can't do it when he is afraid.

AÍDA: Liar! You did it very well.

EDUARDO: I did?

AÍDA: *Sí.* Gentle. You were so gentle and then strong . . . my passion for you so deep. Standing next to you . . . I would ache . . . looking at your hands I would forget to breathe, you were irresistible.

EDUARDO: I was?

AÍDA: You took me into your arms, you touched my face with your fingertips . . . you kissed my eyes . . . *la esquina de la boca y°* . . .

EDUARDO: *Sí, sí,* and then . . .

AÍDA: I look at your face on top of mine, and I see the lights of Havana in your eyes. That's when you seduced me.

EDUARDO: Shhh, they're gonna hear you. (*Lights go down. Special on Aída.*)

AÍDA: That was the night. A woman doesn't forget those things . . . and later that night was the dream . . . the dream of a big country with fields of fertile land and big, giant things growing. And there by a green, slimy pond I found a giant pea pod and when I opened it, it was full of little, tiny baby frogs. (*Aída crosses herself as she watches Margarita. We hear louder breathing and heartbeat.*)

MARGARITA: Santa Teresa. Little Flower of God, pray for me. San Martín de Porres, pray for me. Santa Rosa de Lima, *Virgencita de la Caridad del Cobre,°* pray for me . . . Mother pray for me.

No pasó nada!: Nothing happened.   *Mentiroso!:* Liar!   *la esquina de la boca y:* The corner of the mouth.   *Virgencita de la Caridad del Cobre:* Copper Virgin of Charity.

Scene 5

Loud howling of wind is heard, as lights change to indicate unstable weather, fog and mist. Family on deck, braced and huddled against the wind. Simón is at the helm.

AÍDA: *Ay Dios mío, qué viento.*°

EDUARDO (*through megaphone*): Don't drift out . . . that wind is pushing you out. (*To Simón*) You! Slow down. Can't you see your sister is drifting out?

SIMÓN: It's the wind, Papi.

AÍDA: Baby, don't go so far. . . .

ABUELA (*to heaven*): *Ay Gran Poder de Dios, quita este maldito viento.*°

SIMÓN: Margo! Margo! Stay close to the boat.

EDUARDO: Dig in. Dig in hard. . . . Reach down from your guts and dig in.

ABUELA (*to heaven*): *Ay Virgen de la Caridad del Cobre, por lo más tú quieres a pararla.*°

AÍDA (*putting her hand out, reaching for Margarita*): Baby, don't go far. (*Abuela crosses herself. Action freezes. Lights get dimmer, special on Margarita. She keeps swimming, stops, starts again, stops, then, finally exhausted, stops altogether. The boat stops moving.*)

EDUARDO: What's going on here? Why are we stopping?

SIMÓN: Papi, she's not moving! Yo Margo! (*The family all run to the side.*)

EDUARDO: *Hija!* . . . *Hijita!*° You're tired, eh?

AÍDA: *Por supuesto*° she's tired. I like to see you get in the water, waving your arms and legs from San Pedro to Santa Catalina. A person isn't a machine, a person has to rest.

SIMÓN: Yo, Mama! Cool out, it ain't fucking brain surgery.

EDUARDO (*to Simón*): Shut up, you. (*Louder to Margarita.*) I guess your mother's right for once, huh? . . . I guess you had to stop, eh? . . . Give your brother, the idiot . . . a chance to catch up with you.

SIMÓN (*clowning like Mortimer Snurd*): Dum dee dum dee dum ooops, ah shucks. . . .

EDUARDO: I don't think he's Cuban.

SIMÓN (*like Ricky Ricardo*): Oye Lucy! I'm home! Ba ba lu!

EDUARDO (*joins in clowning, grabbing Simón in a headlock*): What am I gonna do with this idiot, eh? I don't understand this idiot. He's not like us, Margarita. (*Laughing.*) You think if we put him into your bathing suit with a cap on his head . . . (*He laughs hysterically.*) you think anyone would know . . . huh? Do you think anyone would know? (*Laughs.*)

SIMÓN (*vamping*): *Ay, mi amor.*° Anybody looking for tits would know. (*Eduardo slaps Simón across the face, knocking him down. Aída runs to Simón's aid. Abuela holds Eduardo back.*)

Ay Dios mío, qué viento: Oh my God, what wind!   *Ay Gran Poder de Dios, quita este maldito viento:* Oh great power of God, keep the cursed winds away!   *por lo más tú quieres a pararla:* By as much as you want to stop her.   *Hija! . . . Hijita!:* Daughter . . . little daughter.   *Por supuesto:* Of course.   *Ay, mi amor:* Oh, my love.

MARGARITA: *Mía culpa! Mía culpa!*°

ABUELA: *Qué dices hija?*°

MARGARITA: Papi, it's my fault, it's all my fault. . . . I'm so cold, I can't move. . . . I put my face in the water . . . and I hear them whispering . . . laughing at me. . . .

AÍDA: Who is laughing at you?

MARGARITA: The fish are all biting me . . . they hate me . . . they whisper about me. She can't swim, they say. She can't glide. She has no grace. . . . Yellowtails, bonita, tuna, man-o'-war, snub-nose sharks, los baracudas . . . they all hate me . . . only the dolphins care . . . and sometimes I hear the whales crying . . . she is lost, she is dead. I'm so numb, I can't feel. Papi! Papi! Am I dead?

EDUARDO: *Vamos,*° baby, punch those arms in. Come on . . . do you hear me?

MARGARITA: Papi . . . Papi . . . forgive me. . . . (*All is silent on the boat. Eduardo drops his megaphone, his head bent down in dejection. Abuela, Aída, Simón all leaning over the side of the boat. Simón slowly walks away.*)

AÍDA: *Mi hija, qué tienes?*°

SIMÓN: Oh Christ, don't make her say it. Please don't make her say it.

ABUELA: Say what? *Qué cosa?*°

SIMÓN: She wants to quit, can't you see she's had enough?

ABUELA: *Mira, para eso. Esta niña*° is turning blue.

AÍDA: *Oyeme, mi hija.*° Do you want to come out of the water?

MARGARITA: Papi?

SIMÓN (*to Eduardo*): She won't come out until *you* tell her.

AÍDA: Eduardo . . . answer your daughter.

EDUARDO: *Le dije*° to concentrate . . . concentrate on your rhythm. Then the rhythm would carry her . . . ay it's a beautiful thing, Aída. It's like yoga, like meditation, the mind over matter . . . the mind controlling the body . . . that's how the great things in the world have been done. I wish you . . . I wish my wife could understand.

MARGARITA: Papi?

SIMÓN (*to Margarita*): Forget him.

AÍDA (*imploring*): Eduardo, *por favor.*°

EDUARDO (*walking in circles*): Why didn't you let her concentrate? Don't you understand, the concentration, the rhythm is everything. But no, you wouldn't listen. (*Screaming to the ocean.*) Goddam Cubans, why, God, why do you make us go everywhere with our families? (*He goes to back of boat.*)

AÍDA (*opening her arms*): Mi hija, ven,° come to Mami. (*Rocking.*) Your mami knows. (*Abuela has taken the training bottle, puts it in a net. She and Simón lower it to Margarita.*)

Mía culpa!: It's my fault.   *Qué dices hija?:* What are you saying, daughter?   *Vamos:* Let's go. *Mi hija, qué tienes?:* Daughter, what's the matter?   *Qué cosa?:* What?   *Mira, para eso. Esta niña . . . :* Look, stop this. The girl . . .   *Oyeme, mi hija:* Listen to me, daughter.   *Le dije:* I told her.   *por favor:* Please.   *Mi hija, ven:* Come, daughter.

SIMÓN: Take this. Drink it. (*As Margarita drinks, Abuela crosses herself.*)

ABUELA: *Sangre de mi sangre.°* (*Music comes up softly. Margarita drinks, gives the bottle back, stretches out her arms, as if on a cross. Floats on her back. She begins a graceful backstroke. Lights fade on boat as special lights come up on Margarita. She stops. Slowly turns over and starts to swim, gradually picking up speed. Suddenly as if in pain she stops, tries again, then stops in pain again. She becomes disoriented and falls to the bottom of the sea. Special on Margarita at the bottom of the sea.*)

MARGARITA: *Ya no puedo°* . . . I can't . . . A person isn't a machine . . . *es mi culpa* . . . Father forgive me . . . Papi! Papi! One, two. *Uno, dos.* (*Pause.*) Papi! *A dónde estás?* (*Pause.*) One, two, one, two. Papi! Ay Papi! Where are you . . . ? Don't leave me. . . . Why don't you answer me? (*Pause. She starts to swim, slowly.*) *Uno, dos, uno, dos.* Dig in, dig in. (*Stops swimming.*) *Por favor,* Papi! (*Starts to swim again.*) One, two, one, two. Kick from your hip, kick from your hip. (*Stops swimming. Starts to cry.*) Oh God, please. . . . (*Pause.*) Hail Mary, full of grace . . . dig in, dig in . . . the Lord is with thee. . . . (*She swims to the rhythm of her Hail Mary.*) Hail Mary, full of grace . . . dig in, dig in, . . . the Lord is with thee . . . dig in, dig in. . . . Blessed art thou among women. . . . Mommie it hurts. You let go of my hand. I'm lost. . . . And blessed is the fruit of thy womb, now and at the hour of our death. Amen. I don't want to die, I don't want to die. (*Margarita is still swimming. Blackout. She is gone.*)

Scene 6

Lights up on boat, we hear radio static. There is a heavy mist. On deck we see only black outline of Abuela with shawl over her head. We hear the voices of Eduardo, Aída, and Radio Operator.

EDUARDO'S VOICE: La Havana! Coming from San Pedro. Over.

RADIO OPERATOR'S VOICE: Right. DT6-6, you say you've lost a swimmer.

AÍDA'S VOICE: Our child, our only daughter . . . listen to me. Her name is Margarita Inez Suárez, she is wearing a black one-piece bathing suit cut high in the legs with a white racing stripe down the sides, a white bathing cap with goggles and her whole body covered with a . . . with a . . .

EDUARDO'S VOICE: With lanolin and paraffin.

AÍDA'S VOICE: Sí . . . *con* lanolin and paraffin. (*More radio static. Special on Simón, on the edge of the boat.*)

SIMÓN: Margo! Yo Margo! (*Pause*) Man don't do this. (*Pause.*) Come on. . . . Come on. . . . (*Pause.*) God, why does everything have to be so hard? (*Pause.*) Stupid. You know you're not supposed to die for this. Stupid. It's his dream and he can't even swim. (*Pause.*) Punch those arms in. Come home. Come home. I'm your little brother. Don't forget what Mama

---

Sangre de mi sangre: Blood of my blood.   **Ya no puedo:** I can't take it anymore.

said. You're not supposed to leave me behind. *Vamos,* Margarita, take your little brother, hold his hand tight when you cross the street. He's so little. (*Pause.*) Oh Christ, give us a sign. . . . I know! I know! Margo, I'll send you a message . . . like mental telepathy. I'll hold my breath, close my eyes and I'll bring you home. (*He takes a deep breath; a few beats.*) This time I'll beep . . . I'll send out sonar signals like a dolphin. (*He imitates dolphin sounds. The sound of real dolphins takes over from Simón, then fades into sound of Abuela saying the Hail Mary in Spanish, as full lights come up slowly.*)

Scene 7

Eduardo coming out of cabin, sobbing, Aída holding him. Simón anxiously scanning the horizon. Abuela looking calmly ahead.

EDUARDO: *Es mi culpa, sí, es mi culpa.°* (*He hits his chest.*)
AÍDA: *Ya, ya viejo°* . . . it was my sin . . . I left my home.
EDUARDO: Forgive me, forgive me. I've lost our daughter, our sister, our granddaughter, *mi carne, mi sangre, mis ilusiones.°* (*To heaven.*) *Dios mío* take me . . . take me, I say . . . Goddammit, take me!
SIMÓN: I'm going in.
AÍDA and EDUARDO: No!
EDUARDO (*grabbing and holding Simón, speaking to heaven*): God, take me, not my children. They are my dreams, my illusions . . . and not this one, this one is my mystery . . . he has my secret dreams. In him are the parts of me I cannot see. (*Eduardo embraces Simón. Radio static becomes louder.*)
AÍDA: I . . . I think I see her.
SIMÓN: No it's just a seal.
ABUELA (*looking out with binoculars*): *Mi nietacita, dónde estás?°* (*She feels her heart.*) I don't feel the knife in my heart . . . my little fish is not lost. (*Radio crackles with static. As lights dim on boat, voices of Mel and Mary Beth are heard over the radio.*)
MEL'S VOICE: Tragedy has marred the face of the Wrigley Invitational Women's Race to Catalina. The Cuban swimmer, little Margarita Suárez, has reportedly been lost at sea. Coast Guard and divers are looking for her as we speak. Yet in spite of this tragedy the race must go on because . . .
MARY BETH'S VOICE (*interrupting loudly*): Mel!
MEL'S VOICE (*startled*): What!
MARY BETH'S VOICE: Ah . . . excuse me, Mel . . . we have a winner. We've just received word from Catalina that one of the swimmers is just fifty yards from the breakers . . . it's oh, it's Margarita Suárez! (*Special on family in cabin listening to radio.*)

Es mi culpa, sí, es mi culpa: It's my fault, yes, it's my fault.   *Ya, ya viejo:* Yes, yes, old man.
mi carne, mi sangre, mis ilusiones: My flesh, my blood, my dreams.   *Mi nietacita, dónde estás?:* My granddaughter, where are you?

MEL'S VOICE: What? I thought she died! (*Special on Margarita, taking off bathing cap, trophy in hand, walking on the water.*)

MARY BETH'S VOICE: Ahh . . . unless . . . unless this is a tragic. . . . No . . . there she is, Mel. Margarita Suárez! The only one in the race wearing a black bathing suit cut high in the legs with a racing stripe down the side. (*Family cheering, embracing.*)

SIMÓN (*screaming*): Way to go, Margo!

MEL'S VOICE: This is indeed a miracle! It's a resurrection! Margarita Suárez with a flotilla of boats to meet her, is now walking on the waters, through the breakers . . . onto the beach, with crowds of people cheering her on. What a jubilation! This is a miracle! (*Sound of crowds cheering. Pinspot on Abuela.*)

ABUELA: *Sangre de mi sangre* you will be another to save us, . . . to say to the evil one, *Coño Diablo, aqui estoy si me quieres.*° (*Lights and cheering fade. Blackout.*)

END OF PLAY

Coño Diablo, aqui estoy si me quieres: Hell, dammit, I am here if you want me.

APPROACHING THE READING

1. In scenes 1–4, pick out examples of various types of comedy such as witty dialogue, satiric comedy, and parody. Explain what they contribute to the play and their cumulative effect.

2. Summarize what happens in scenes 5–6. How are these scenes different from scenes 1–4? What is the effect of the change from scenes 1–4 to scenes 5–6?

3. Explain what happens in scene 7, how it fits the play, and how it helps shape our response to the play.

4. How would you describe the play's theme, what it "all adds up to"?

As the Crow Flies draws humor from miscommunications, cultural misunderstandings, characters talking past each other, and witty dialogue. But watch also for places where the dialogue turns more serious and be ready to account for the closing scene.

David Henry Hwang   b. 1957

As the Crow Flies   [1986]

CHARACTERS

HANNAH, a black woman in her 60s.
MRS. CHAN, a Chinese woman in her 70s, sometimes called Popo
    (Grandma).
P. K., a Chinese man in his 70s, sometimes called Gung Gung
    (Grandfather).
SANDRA, a black woman in her 40s.

TIME AND PLACE

The living room of an upper middle-class home. The present.

*A living room in an upper middle-class home, owned by Mrs. Chan, a Chinese
woman in her seventies, and her husband, P. K. Up right, a door leads out to the front
driveway. Stage left is a door leading to the rest of the house. Mrs. Chan sits in a large
chair, center stage, looking downstage out into a garden. Around her, Hannah, a black
woman in her late sixties, cleans. She has been their cleaning woman for over a decade.*

HANNAH: I guess I never told you this before, Mrs. Chan, but I think the time
    is right now. See, I'm really two different folks. You've been knowin' me
    as Hannah Carter, 'cuz when I'm over here cleanin', that's who I am.
    But at night, or when I'm outside and stuff, I turn into Sandra Smith.
    (*Beat*) Is that all clear?

CHAN: Um. Yeah.

HANNAH: You got all that?

CHAN: When you are here, you are Hannah Carter —

HANNAH: Right.

CHAN: And, then, you go outside, and you are . . . someone . . . someone . . .

HANNAH: Sandra Smith.

CHAN: Um. Okay.

Pause.

HANNAH: You don't have any questions 'bout that?

CHAN: Hannah Carter, Sandra Smith — I understand.

HANNAH: Well, you know how you can tell the two apart?

CHAN: No. Because I have not seen Sandra — Sandra . . .

HANNAH: Smith. Well, when I'm Sandra Smith, see, I look different. First of
    all, I'm a lot younger.

CHAN: Good.

HANNAH: And, you know, since I'm younger, well, guess I'm looser, too. What
    I mean by that, is, when I talk, well, I use different words. Young words.
    And, Mrs. Chan, since I'm younger, my hair color's a lot different too.
    And I don't clean floors. 'Cuz young people nowadays, they don't clean

floors. They stay up around the clock, and make themselves into lazy good-for-nothings, and drink a lot, and dance themselves into a state. Young people — just don't know what's got into them. But whatever it is, the same thing's gotten into Sandra Smith. (*Pause*) You don't think this is all a little strange?

CHAN: No.

HANNAH: Well, that's the first time . . . I remember when I told Mrs. Washburn about Sandra Smith — she just fell right over.

CHAN: So what? So you have two different people.

HANNAH: That's right. Living inside me.

CHAN: So what? My uncle had six!

HANNAH: Six people?

CHAN: Maybe even seven. Who can keep count?

HANNAH: Seven? All in one guy?

CHAN: Way back in China — my second uncle — he had seven, maybe even eight, people — inside here. I don't . . . is hard to remember all their name.

HANNAH: I can believe that.

CHAN: Chan Yup Lee — he was, uh, I think, the businessman. He runs Uncle's import-export association. Good man. Very stingy. I like him. Then, I think there was another: ah, C. Y. Sing — he is the family man. Then, one man, Fat-Fingers Lew. Introduce this sport — what is the name? Ball goes through big hoop.

HANNAH: Basketball?

CHAN: Yes, yes — introduce that to our village. Then, there is Big Ear Tong — collects debt for C. Y.'s company. Never talks, only fight. Then, also, one who has been to America — Morty Fong. He all the time warns us about Communists. And, then, oh, maybe two or three others that I hardly ever meet.

HANNAH: This is all one guy?

CHAN: Mmmmm.

HANNAH: Isn't that somethin'?

CHAN: No.

HANNAH: Huh?

CHAN: Whatever you can tell me — man with six persons inside, man with three heads, man who sees a flying ghost, a sitting ghost, a ghost disguise to look like his dead wife — none of these are so unusual.

HANNAH: No?

CHAN: I have lived a long time.

HANNAH: Well, so have I, Mrs. Chan, so have I. And I'm still scared of Sandra Smith.

CHAN: Scare? Why scare? Happens all the time.

HANNAH: I don't want Sandra comin' round to any of my houses that I clean.

CHAN: Aaah — do not worry.

HANNAH: Whaddya mean? Sandra's got no respect for authority.

CHAN: Do not worry. She will not come into any house.

HANNAH: What makes you so sure?

CHAN: You have to know how ghosts think. You say, Sandra appears out-doors. Therefore, she is the outside ghost. She cannot come inside.

HANNAH: Yeah? They got rules like that? In ghost-land?

CHAN: Yes — there are rules everyplace! Have you ever been someplace where there were none?

HANNAH: Well, no, but —

CHAN: You see? Ghosts cannot kill a man if there is a goldfish in the room. They will think the fish is gold, and take it instead. They cannot enter a house if there is a raised step in the doorway. Ghosts do not look, so they trip over it instead.

HANNAH: These ghosts don't sound like they got a lot on the ball.

CHAN: Some ghosts, they are smart. But most ghosts, they are like most people. When alive, they were stupid. After death, they remain the same.

HANNAH: Well, I don't think Sandra's got much respect for those rules. That's probably why she showed up at Mrs. Washburn's.

CHAN: Inside the house?

HANNAH: 'Fraid so.

CHAN: Oh. Mrs. Washburn — does she have a goldfish?

HANNAH: No, no — I don't think so.

CHAN: There — you see?

HANNAH: Anyway, Mrs. Chan, I just thought I oughta tell you about her, on account of what happened to Mrs. Washburn. I been working for all you people ten, sometimes twenty years. All my clients — they're gettin' up there. We're all startin' to show our age. Can't compete with the young girls no more.

CHAN: I never try — even when I was one.

HANNAH: Well, the older I get, the more I see of Sandra, so I just thought I oughta be warnin' you.

CHAN: I am not afraid of Sandra Smith.

HANNAH: Well, good then. Good for you.

CHAN: She comes here, I will fight her. Not like these Americans. So stupid. Never think of these things. Never think of ghost. Never think of death. Never prepare for anything. Always think, life goes on and on, forever. And so, always, it ends.

HANNAH: Okay. Glad to hear it. Guess I'll go take the slime off the shower walls.

Hannah exits, into the house. Chan just stares downstage, from her chair. Silence. P. K. enters from the driveway, golf clubs slung over his shoulder.

P. K.: Hi, Popo!

CHAN: Hello.

P. K.: Do you have a beer?

CHAN: Look in 'frigerator.

P. K.: Just return from a good game of golf!

CHAN: Ah! What are you talking about?

P. K.: Eighteen holes, Popo!

CHAN: Ai! You cannot remember anything anymore!

P. K.: So? I remember that I go to golf!

CHAN: How can this be? You do not drive!

P. K.: What do you mean? I drive the Eldorado.

CHAN: You cannot drive the Eldorado.

P. K.: I do!

CHAN: Hanh! We sell it many years ago!

P. K.: What?

CHAN: Yes! Remember? We sell it! To John, your nephew.

P. K.: Huh? How much did he pay?

CHAN: Who cares?

P. K.: I want to know!

CHAN: I always tell you, John buys the car; you always ask me, how much does he pay?

P. K.: It is important! It is worth — lots of money!

CHAN: Ah, not so much money.

P. K.: No! Lots!

CHAN: Not after Humphrey breaks the back window by trying to lower top while driving.

P. K.: Yes! I tell Humphrey — cannot lower while driving. He says, "Of course! Can! This is a luxury car!" How come we sell the car?

CHAN: Ah! You cannot remember anything!

P. K.: No. Gung Gung cannot remember anything anymore.

CHAN: We sell, because you can no longer drive.

P. K.: I can! I can!

CHAN: You cannot pass the test.

P. K.: Can Humphrey pass the test?

CHAN: Of course! Of course, he passes it.

P. K.: How can? He is the one who lowers top while driving!

CHAN: Gung Gung! Because he is young, so he can pass the test!

P. K.: Young, but not so smart.

CHAN: Stupid.

P. K.: Sometimes, stupid.

CHAN: Stupid does not matter. Many stupid people drive.

Pause.

P. K.: So I did not go to golf?

CHAN: No! How can you go to golf? You cannot go anyplace.

P. K. (*Points to clubs*): Then, what are these?

CHAN: You just put them on your shoulder, then walk outside. Two hour later, you return.

P. K.: Where did I go?

CHAN: I don't know! You tell me!

P. K.: I cannot remember anything, anymore. I thought that I go to play eighteen hole golf. But there is no golf course. So perhaps I walk into those hills. Maybe I shoot a few balls in the hills. Maybe I sink a putt into a gopher hole.

Pause.

CHAN: Gung Gung.
P. K.: Yes, Popo?
CHAN: I saw a ghost today.
P. K.: Popo! A ghost?
CHAN: Yes — a warning ghost.
P. K.: Which is this?
CHAN: They warn that another ghost will soon come. Bigger. More dangerous. Fatter.
P. K.: Oh! Popo! Why do they send this warning ghost?
CHAN: Because, they are stupid! This is how, they become dead to begin with. Because when they were living, they were too stupid to listen to the warning ghost!
P. K.: Popo! Will you die? (*He starts to cry*) What will Gung Gung do without you?
CHAN: No.
P. K.: Without Popo, I will be completely all lost.
CHAN: No, Gung Gung.
P. K.: I will walk around all day, not know where I am going, not know where I come from, only saying, "Popo? Where is Popo? Where is — ?"
CHAN: No! Will you listen to me? You ask the question, then you will not listen to the answer! Talk, talk, talk! If I die, leave you alone, I would be lucky!
P. K.: You mean, you will not die?
CHAN: No, I will not die.
P. K.: How can this be?
CHAN: They are stupid enough to send the warning ghost. This is how I know, they will not defeat me.
P. K.: But, when the ghost come, no one can resist.
CHAN: Who says this?
P. K.: Ummm . . .
CHAN: See? Maybe, Gung Gung, *you* cannot resist.
P. K.: No. I cannot resist.
CHAN: But you have no responsibilities. I have. I have responsibility. I cannot leave you alone, Gung Gung. And also, I must watch the grandchildren grow to adults.
P. K.: Yes — this would be good.
CHAN: So, you see, I cannot die.
P. K.: This makes me so happy.
CHAN: I will defeat the ghost.

P. K.: Yes! Popo! You can do it! Popo is very smart!

CHAN: Yeah, yeah, yeah, we all know this already.

P. K.: I am fortunate to marry such a smart wife.

CHAN: Not smart. Smart is not enough.

P. K.: More than smart.

CHAN: Fight. Fight is more important. I am willing to fight. I like to fight.

Pause.

P. K.: Why do I carry these golf clubs?

CHAN: I do not know! You ask so many times already!

P. K.: Oh — I suppose — I must go to golf.

Pause.

CHAN: Yes — you must go to golf.

P. K.: Okay. I will leave now. Take the Eldorado. Bye, Popo.

CHAN: Bye, Gung Gung.

P. K.: You will have a cold can of beer in the 'frigerator, for when I return?

CHAN: I will, Gung Gung. I will.

P. K. starts to exit out the upstage door.

Gung Gung!

P. K.: Yes, Popo?

CHAN: Have a good game, okay, Gung Gung?

P. K.: I will have a good game, okay, Popo. (*He exits*)

CHAN: I arrive in America one day, June 16, 1976. Many times, I have come here before, to visit children, but on this day, I arrive to stay. All my friends, all the Chinese in the Philippine, they tell me, "We thought you are stupid when you send all your children to America. We even feel sorry for you, that you will grow old all alone — no family around you." This is what they tell me.

    The day I arrive in America, I do not feel sorry. I do not miss the Philippine, I do not look forward live in America. Just like, I do not miss China, when I leave it many years ago — go live in Philippine. Just like, I do not miss Manila, when Japanese take our home during wartime, and we are all have to move to Baguio, and live in haunted house. It is all same to me. Go, one home to the next, one city to another, nation to nation, across ocean big and small.

    We are born traveling. We travel — all our lives. I am not looking for a home. I know there is none. The day I was marry, my mother put many gold bracelets on my arm, and so many necklaces that the back of my head grows sore. "These," she tells me. "These are for the times when you will have to run."

The upstage door opens. Hannah is standing there, dressed as Sandra Smith. Sandra wears a bright orange fright wig and a tight dress, sports huge sunglasses, and swings a small purse.

SANDRA: Well, hello there! Howdy, howdy, howdy!

CHAN: Hi.

SANDRA: Say, you seen Hannah? Hannah Carter? I understand she works here on Wednesdays.

CHAN: I think, she just leave.

SANDRA: Oh, well, that's a shame. I usually don't get to visit where she works. We were supposed to go for dinner at Chicken on Fire, but, looks like we're just not connecting. Damn! Always happens, whenever I try to meet her at one of these houses.

CHAN: So, would you like to go home, now?

SANDRA: Mmmm. Guess I could, but I wouldn't mind enjoying some of your hospitality.

CHAN: What is this, hospitality?

SANDRA: You know. What you show your guests.

CHAN: We do not have guests here! Only relatives, and, ah, servants.

SANDRA: Well, what do you do when someone comes over?

CHAN: They tell me what they want. Then, they leave.

SANDRA: No time to socialize?

CHAN: What is, socialize?

SANDRA: You know. You're not gonna offer me a tea, coffee, cake, Sanka?

CHAN: No.

SANDRA: I can't hardly believe this house.

CHAN: People—they are like cats. If you feed them, they will always return.

SANDRA: What ever happened to old-fashioned manners?

CHAN: My manners—they are very old. We act like this for centuries.

SANDRA: My name's Sandra. Sandra Smith.

CHAN: This is no surprise. Are you finish, now? Hannah is not here.

SANDRA: No—I can see that. (*Pause*) You know, I've known Hannah—well, ever since she was a little girl. She wasn't very pretty. No one in Louisville paid much attention to her. Yeah, she's had five husbands and all, okay, that's true, but my personal guess is that most of 'em married her because she was a hard-working woman who could bring home the bacon week after week. Certain men will hold their noses for a free lunch. Hannah thinks the same thing, though she hardly ever talks about it. How can she think anything else when all five of them left her as soon as they got a whiff of some girl with pipe cleaners for legs? Hard for her to think she's much more than some mule, placed on this earth to work her back. She spends most of her life wanderin' from one beautiful house to the next, knowing intimately every detail, but never layin' down her head in any of 'em. She's what they call a good woman. Men know it, rich folks know it. Everyplace is beautiful, 'cept the place where she lives. Home is a dark room, she knows it well, knows its limits. She knows she can't travel nowhere without returnin' to that room once the sun goes down. Home is fixed, it does not move, even as the rest of the world circles 'round and 'round, picking up speed.

CHAN: You are a ghost.

SANDRA: I have a good time, if that's what you mean.

CHAN: I was warned that you would come.

SANDRA: By Hannah? She's always tellin' people about me. Like I was some kinda celebrity or somethin'.

CHAN: I fight ghosts. I chase them.

SANDRA: Can't chase anything, unless you get it runnin' from ya first.

CHAN: In Baguio, we live in a haunted house.

SANDRA: In where?

CHAN: Baguio. In the Philippine.

SANDRA: I never been there.

CHAN: During the war, we live in a haunted house. I chase the ghost out, with pots and pan. So, I know I can defeat them.

SANDRA: Hannah — she lives in a haunted house right now.

CHAN: Yes — haunted with you.

SANDRA: I show her how to make her life a little easier. Someone's gotta do it, after all her sixty-some-odd years. How 'bout you? Anything I can help you with?

CHAN: Ha! I do not need a thing!

SANDRA: I'm not sure if I believe that, Mrs. . . . Mrs. . . . whatever. Hannah sees you sittin' here, day after day —

CHAN: I am old! Of course I sit!

SANDRA: — starin' out into that garden —

CHAN: So?

SANDRA: First off, it's mostly dirt.

CHAN: This way, easier to take care of.

SANDRA: But you stare like there's somethin' out there.

CHAN: Yes! The sun is out there!

SANDRA: Lookin' at the sun, Mrs. — ma'am? Gotta be careful you don't burn your eyeballs out.

CHAN: I only look outside because — sky, clouds, sun — they are all there — interesting to watch.

SANDRA: Real pretty, huh?

CHAN: Yes. Sometimes pretty.

SANDRA: Looks like home.

CHAN: What is this? All the time, you talk about home, home, home?

SANDRA: Just like you do.

CHAN: I never talk about home. Barely talk at all.

SANDRA: You think, you keep your lips buttoned, that means all your secrets are safe inside? If they're strong enough, things make themselves known, one way or another. Hannah knows, she's not stupid. She'd never tell anyone but me. But me, I'd tell anybody. (Pause) Want me to tell you?

CHAN: Tell me what?

SANDRA: What you're lookin' at out there?

Pause.

CHAN: I can defeat you. I defeat ghost before.

SANDRA: Honey, it's not a fight no more. I've been around fifteen years. I already know you. You know me. We see the same thing. Out there. (*Pause*) There's a crow sitting on a window sill. And two kids who chase it down a steep ravine. Their path grows darker and darker, but the crow continues, and the kids don't tire, even when the blisters start to show on their feet. Mud, sleet, rain, and snow, all try to make the kids give up the chase. The crow caws — mountains fall in its wake, but still the children continue. And then it becomes dark, so dark, and the crow throws disasters at their feet. Floods, droughts, wars. The children see nothing, now. They follow the crow only by the catastrophes it leaves in its path. Where there is famine, the crow must have been. Where there are earthquakes, it has rested. They run on faith now, passing through territories uncharted, following the sound of their suffering. And it is in this way that they pass through their lives. Hardly noticing that they've entered. Without stopping to note its passing. Just following a crow, with single dedication, forgetting how they started, or why they're chasing, or even what may happen if they catch it. Running without pause or pleasure, past the point of their beginning.

Over the next section, Mrs. Chan's dress slowly rises into the air. She wears a white slip beneath. She stands up from the chair, for the first time in the play, and walks over to Sandra.

I see it in the distance.

CHAN: It is waiting for me.

SANDRA: I cannot stop my running.

CHAN: I cannot rest, even for a second.

SANDRA: There's a field out in the distance.

CHAN: There's a wooden gate in that field.

SANDRA: There is a crow sitting on that gate.

CHAN: It caws.

SANDRA: It caws.

CHAN: And disaster comes.

SANDRA: Once again.

CHAN: Nothing new.

SANDRA: Nothing blue.

CHAN: Only the scent of home.

SANDRA: I don't know why I follow it.

CHAN: I don't care to know.

SANDRA: Not now.

CHAN: Not here.

SANDRA: Not ever. Perhaps someday.
CHAN: Maybe to remember.
SANDRA: Why I run.
CHAN: Why I chase.
SANDRA: Until I am so—
CHAN: So tired.
SANDRA: Another disaster.
CHAN: Another lonely child.
SANDRA: We follow the scent of home.

Sandra removes her wig, glasses, tight dress. She too wears a white slip. She is Hannah again. Mrs. Chan moves towards the door. Hannah ever so slowly lowers herself into Mrs. Chan's chair. Hannah sits in it, beams.

HANNAH: Ooooh. Nice home, Mrs. Chan.
CHAN: I see it.
HANNAH: So do I, so do I.
CHAN: I see all the way past those mountains.
HANNAH: Welcome home, Mrs. Chan.
CHAN: Welcome home, Hannah.

Mrs. Chan exits through the garden. Hannah looks around her like a kid with a new toy. Upstage, P. K. enters with golf clubs. He cannot see Hannah in the chair.

P. K.: Hi, Popo! (*Pause*) Where is my beer?

Hannah closes her eyes, a smile on her face.

You leave a beer in the 'frigerator? (*Pause*) Popo? Popo?

P. K. is walking towards the chair as lights fade to black.

END OF PLAY

APPROACHING THE READING

1. Point out types of humor and comedy in the play.

2. Look for a point in the play where the tone turns more serious. After that point the comedy continues, but how does its effect change?

3. How does the title relate to the play? Be ready to discuss the meaning of the final two pages, with their focus on a crow.

4. What is going on at the end of the play? Is this comedy, tragedy, fantasy, or something else? Explain.

5. What is the overall effect of the play, considering both its comic and its serious aspects?

RESPONDING THROUGH WRITING

Journal Entries

1. Write a journal entry in which you fit the short plays in Chapters 17–19 (*Florence, Classyass, Trifles, Sure Thing, Los Vendidos,* and *Mambo Mouth*) into the dramatic types discussed in this chapter. If they don't fit one category, combine categories or develop new ones that seem most appropriate.

www

Research the authors in this chapter with LitLinks at bedfordstmartins.com/ approachinglit.

2. Jot a list of your favorite (or currently popular) TV shows. Place them into the type categories described in this chapter or into other categories not discussed here.

3. Note any "dramas" you see during a day. List and categorize them. Take one or more of them and turn them into scenes. Keep in mind that you probably will need to fictionalize somewhat to make a scene effective and believable.

Literary Analysis Papers

4. The discussion topics after Milcha Sanchez-Scott's *The Cuban Swimmer* (p. 890) suggest that different sections of the play employ different types or subtypes with different tones and effects. Write a paper that examines scenes 1–4, then 5–6, and then 7, discussing the changing types and effects in the play, and how it is a unified work nonetheless.

5. Write a paper discussing what such aspects as swimming, the swimmer, the ocean, and the followers in Milcha Sanchez-Scott's *The Cuban Swimmer* (p. 890) suggest on levels other than the literal.

6. Consider the different dramatic types or subtypes (or tones, at least) used in David Henry Hwang's *As the Crow Flies* (p. 903). Write a paper discussing the effect created in different parts of the play and the effect of the play as a whole.

Making Connections

7. Compare and contrast the way both Milcha Sanchez-Scott's *The Cuban Swimmer* (p. 890) and David Henry Hwang's *As the Crow Flies* (p. 903) mix realism and the fantastic (something visionary and mystical inserts itself into an everyday world setting). Explore the purpose and effect in each work. Explore too how realism and the mystical differ but also how they help clarify the other and make it easier to understand.

8. Compare and contrast the handling of ethnic parents with American dreams for the children in Amy Tan's "Two Kinds" (p. 189) and Milcha Sanchez-Scott's *The Cuban Swimmer* (p. 890).

Cultural Criticism Papers

9. Write a paper discussing why an author wishing to explore a contemporary culturally sensitive or complex subject might turn to comedy instead of one of the other available types (as the authors of *Classyass, Los Vendidos, Mambo Mouth, The Cuban Swimmer,* and *As the Crow Flies* have done).

10. Write a paper discussing how reading Milcha Sanchez-Scott's *The Cuban Swimmer* (p. 890) or David Henry Hwang's *As the Crow Flies* (p. 903) from a particular cultural context might affect a reader's response.

RESPONDING THROUGH THE ARTS

1. When plays are staged in a theater, the director often includes some music as the lights go down and the curtain rises. When plays are filmed, they often make even more use of background music. As a way of responding to drama through the arts, select some pieces of music that you think would be effective introductory or background music for a comedy, a tragedy, and a problem play. Look for pieces that fit the tone and time setting of the play.

2. Design a set for a comedy and for a tragedy (or serious drama). Write a brief discussion of the differences in them and why you handled them differently.

Writing has been to me like a bath from which I have risen feeling cleaner, healthier, and freer.

Henrik Ibsen

Writing about Drama

Drama enters the ongoing conversation about literature most often through performances of plays. People attend a play and then talk about what they experienced, especially with others who saw the same production. Writing extends the conversation in the form of drama reviews in newspapers, periodicals, and on the Web. This chapter, however, does not focus on writing (or talking) about drama on the stage — about whether the director's interpretation is satisfactory, how well the actors and actresses played their roles, and how effective the sets and costumes were. Instead it discusses how to write effectively about plays when they are read as literature (which has been our emphasis throughout the drama section). We concentrate not on the way a particular production handled the play, but on the way a reader interacts with a text's presentation of an action, characters, and setting.

The suggestions offered in "Writing Short Papers" in Chapter 2 (pp. 32–45) apply to writing about drama, as they do to any literary paper. And much that is covered in Chapters 8 and 15 on writing about fiction and poetry carries over to writing about drama as well. This chapter adds to those chapters by offering suggestions particularly applicable to writing about plays.

TOPICS

As in Chapters 8 and 15, the discussion of topics for papers about drama are grouped into three categories: those focusing on what goes on *inside* the play, those focusing on what *surrounds* the play, and those focusing on what infuses but also goes *beyond* the play.

Looking Inside the Play

Analyses of what goes on inside a play, technically and thematically, work well for drama. Chapters 17 and 18 introduce the central techniques and strategies of drama, to equip you to read plays attentively and sensitively and to write about them knowledgeably. Your papers can isolate and examine any one of the key dramatic techniques discussed in Chapters 17 and 18. You can examine the strategies used for *compressing* and *structuring* material to hold the audience's attention and interest and to build in dramatic intensity to an effective climax (the way Arthur Miller manages to contract the action in *Death of a Salesman* [p. 980] into a span of about twenty-four hours). You can discuss the use of *conflict,* both as a structural and dramatic technique, and as a way of focusing on theme (for example, how the conflict between Iago and Cassio becomes a unifying structural pattern in *Othello* [p. 1054]). You can analyze *characters* and *characterization:* Bring out the subtleties and complexities of the characters, especially if you fill in the things that are implied rather than stated, and clarify the techniques through which the characters are developed (the influence of sports and competition on the character of Troy Maxson in *Fences* [p. 1186], for example). You can focus on the use of *contrast* within a play, showing how it uses structural juxtapositions of people, actions, images, and ideas to develop characters, dramatic tensions, and themes (the function of Mrs. Linde as a foil to Nora Helmer in *A Doll House* [p. 926], for example).

When you write about a play, do not fall into simply summarizing the story. Assume your reader knows what happens but needs help in understanding fully *why* it happens, along with the broader significance and implications of what happens, and the artistry involved in bringing all of that out. Trying to cover thoroughly every, or even one, aspect of a full-length play is difficult in a short paper. Select a single feature to analyze in detail, and perhaps focus that even further by limiting your in-depth analysis to one act or scene.

Be sure also that your paper has a discussible, disputable point to make about its subject. A paper on drama, like any paper on literature, needs an argumentative thesis — not "This paper discusses the role of athletics in Troy Maxson's life," but "Troy Maxson's attitudes toward his wife and son, and toward life in general, are shaped by his experiences as a baseball player." As with writing on the other genres, avoid the easy and obvious. Get to know the play well, or the part of it you decide to examine closely, so you recognize and bring out to your reader what is particularly skillful, intriguing, impressive, or thought-provoking about it, or what is difficult, questionable, or problematic in it. Look for a subject that interests or excites you; this will help you convey that excitement to your reader.

A topic possibility unique to drama is a paper in which you take on the role of directing a play. In this sort of paper, you need to explain how you as director interpret the play and why, and how you want your cast to present the characters. You could describe how you would stage the play — what kind of set, props, costumes, lighting, sound, and music you would use, and what kind of stage movement (called "blocking") and action you would want. The decisions you make and descriptions you give will clarify the way you read and interpret the play. This kind of paper, like any of the others suggested in this chapter, needs a thesis that makes an arguable point about the play. It also must discuss and illustrate whatever points you use to develop and support that thesis.

One can also approach an analysis paper on drama by explication (see p. 584) of a key passage (see p. 208) in the play. Explication works best for plays that are poetic in style and use meter and lines or rely heavily on figurative language, like parts of many Shakespearean plays, or that are particularly packed with meaning central to the work as a whole. You cannot, of course, explicate an entire play, even a short play. The challenge is to identify a speech or short section of dialogue that is complex in its use of language, rich in implications, and crucial in the overall development of the play — one that is central to the development of a character's motives or an important theme, as, for example, these lines in which Othello wrestles with whether to believe Iago or to trust his wife:

> This fellow's of exceeding honesty,
> And knows all qualities, with a learned spirit
> Of human dealings. If I do prove her haggard,
> Though that her jesses were my dear heartstrings,
> I'd whistle her off and let her down the wind
> To prey at fortune. Haply, for I am black
> And have not those soft parts of conversation
> That chamberers have, or for I am declined
> Into the vale of years — yet that's not much —
> She's gone. I am abused, and my relief
> Must be to loathe her. O curse of marriage,
> That we can call these delicate creatures ours,
> And not their appetites! I had rather be a toad
> And live upon the vapor of a dungeon
> Than keep a corner in the thing I love
> For others' uses.
>
> (*Othello* 3.3.258–273)

Your goal is to demonstrate to your reader the importance of the passage. Open up its subtleties, ambiguities, and complexities (clarifying words such as "haggard," "jesses," "Haply," and figures of speech such as "whistle her off and let her down the wind," and images such as "I had rather be a toad" as expanded in the three lines following). Show the relationship of the passage to the rest of the play (how does it help us understand why Othello can be so easily convinced that Desdemona has been unfaithful to him, and how does Iago take advantage of what is shown here in deceiving Othello?).

Looking closely at the diction, images, figurative language, rhythm, sounds, and style of a specific passage provides a focal point from which the overall strategies, techniques, and themes of the play are illuminated.

Some of the "Approaching the Reading" questions and topics that follow plays in Chapters 17–20 provide topics for analytical papers. Also, many of the suggestions for writing at the end of each chapter involve literary analysis. Here are some sample topics, though the possibilities for analysis of techniques in drama are endless:

1. The dramatic and social roles of the chorus in Sophocles's *Oedipus Rex* (p. 1145).
2. The use and effect of Emilia as a foil to Desdemona in William Shakespeare's *Othello* (p. 1054).
3. The influence exerted by imagery of building and planting in Arthur Miller's *Death of a Salesman* (p. 980), of dolls in Henrik Ibsen's *A Doll House* (p. 926), or of baseball in August Wilson's *Fences* (p. 1186).
4. Relate the four-line epigraph at the beginning of *Fences* (p. 1186) to the play as a whole.
5. The use and effect of foreshadowing in *A Doll House* (p. 926).
6. Explicate one of the following passages and relate the passage in some way to the play as a whole: Teiresias's speech in *Oedipus Rex,* lines 191–214 (p. 1156); Othello's monologue in *Othello* 5.2.1–22 (p. 1133); Helmer's "calm yourself and collect your thoughts speech" in *A Doll House* (p. 975); Willy's speech about Dave Singleman in *Death of a Salesman* (p. 1020); or Rose's big speech in *Fences* (p. 1238).

Looking at What Surrounds the Play

You could also write a paper about the literary context surrounding a play, about its relations to other literary works — comparisons and contrasts (see p. 203), or the influence of literary traditions, or the use of allusions (see p. 205). To be successful, such a paper requires finding connections that are meaningful and significant. Test your ideas by asking "So what?" (see p. 204), and use the topic only if you can answer in a thoughtful way.

Part of what surrounds and affects a play is its theatrical context: What other plays were being performed at the time, what types of plays did audiences prefer, what kind of theater was being used, what actors and actresses were available? What other writers were doing at the time is important for fiction and poetry as well, of course, but it is particularly influential for drama, given its nature as a form intended for public performance. Shakespeare was very much aware of the plays of Christopher Marlowe and other contemporary dramatists, as the film *Shakespeare in Love* illustrates vividly in its fictionalized account. Equally interesting and important is how plays from the past influenced a later play or playwright. When Arthur Miller thought about *Death of a Salesman,* was he influenced by George Lillo's *The*

London Merchant (1731) and the tradition of domestic tragedy that led up to it? You could write a paper discussing how an aspect of the theatrical context — the physical layout of the theater and the stage (see Chapter 19) or the success of a rival writer — influenced or affected a play or playwright, though doing so likely will require some outside research. A paper could, for example, explore whether the success of Thomas Kyd's revenge play *The Spanish Tragedy* (c. 1585–1587), and perhaps an early version of the Hamlet story, might have motivated Shakespeare to write his *Hamlet* (c. 1600).

Here are some ideas for topics, though the possibilities for comparing and connecting are almost endless:

1. Compare and contrast the influence of fathers on sons in Arthur Miller's *Death of a Salesman* (p. 980) and August Wilson's *Fences* (p. 1186).
2. Compare and contrast attitudes toward ethnicity in Gish Jen's "Who's Irish" (p. 272) and John Leguizamo's *Mambo Mouth* (p. 874), or in *Mambo Mouth* and Luis Valdez's *Los Vendidos* (p. 864).
3. Compare and contrast the mixture of realistic and fantastic details in Gabriel García Márquez's "A Very Old Man with Enormous Wings" (p. 415) and Milcha Sanchez-Scott's *The Cuban Swimmer* (p. 890).
4. Compare and contrast the conception of tragedy in Sophocles's *Oedipus Rex* (p. 1145) and William Shakespeare's *Othello* (p. 1054), or in *Oedipus* and Arthur Miller's *Death of a Salesman* (p. 980).
5. Compare and contrast Shakespeare as poet and poetic dramatist by looking closely at a passage from *Othello* (p. 1054) (perhaps 1.3.247–258 or 3.3.155–161 or 5.2.340–356) and a Shakespearean sonnet (pp. 521 or 720).
6. Compare and contrast the film version of a play with its written text — perhaps the 1995 version of *Othello* starring Laurence Fishburne as Othello and Kenneth Branagh as Iago, or the 1985 version of *Death of a Salesman* starring Dustin Hoffman. Does the movie stick close to the text or take considerable liberties? Is the result effective and satisfying or a disappointment? What things can the play do that the film version cannot, and what is the film able to do that the play can't?

Looking Beyond the Play

You can look beyond the techniques and literary context of a play and write about its relation to its cultural and social context and to the real-world issues it deals with. Plays, like stories, often reflect contemporary social conditions and examine attitudes toward sex, class, ethnicity, power, and privilege. Even if the play does not refer directly to events or attitudes contemporary to the writing, those events and attitudes — consciously or unconsciously — influence the writer. The result could be a play that reflects prevailing attitudes or one that ignores, rejects, or challenges them. A paper might assess the implications of capitalism and economic competition on

Death of a Salesman (p. 980), for example, or racial attitudes in Elizabethan England on *Othello* (p. 1054).

Cultural criticism concentrates on the way a work embodies a cultural context, how the events, ideas, or attitudes in a play were influenced by the economic conditions, political situation, or social conventions existing when it was written; but cultural criticism also explores the way a work is a part of a culture and influences, and perhaps changes, the economic conditions, political situation, or social conventions of its time or later times. Such a paper might investigate whether *A Doll House* (p. 926) had a direct influence on changing attitudes toward women in the period following its appearance, or if Ibsen's *Ghosts* (1881), which deals directly with the topic of congenital venereal disease and created quite a scandal, had an effect on future public awareness and attitudes toward sexuality.

Just as for all paper topics, a paper that engages in cultural criticism needs to make a point. Simply describing a social or cultural attitude or context is not especially interesting or useful. You need to write a thesis that unifies your paper and advances an argumentative position that the paper explores further. "This paper shows that Shakespeare's *Othello* contains a great deal of racist language" is not a thesis because it presents only a statement of fact, not an argumentative proposition. A true thesis sentence would be this: "Although Othello contains a great deal of racist language, the play as a whole offers a complex and balanced exploration of the subject of racism."

Topics for cultural criticism papers range widely. The last two writing suggestions in Chapters 17–20 involve cultural issues. Some of the "Approaching the Reading" topics following plays in those chapters also lead to topics for cultural criticism papers. Here are some more sample topic ideas, though the list could go on and on:

1. The effect of Othello's military background and training on his concept of identity, his attitudes, and his actions in Shakespeare's *Othello* (p. 1054).
2. Compare and contrast the birdcage in Susan Glaspell's *Trifles* (p. 822) and the doll house in Henrik Ibsen's *A Doll House* (p. 926) as feminist metaphors.
3. Compare and contrast the definition and cultural implications of *hero* in Sophocles' *Oedipus Rex* (p. 1145) and Shakespeare's *Othello* (p. 1054) with those in Arthur Miller's *Death of a Salesman* (p. 980) and August Wilson's *Fences* (p. 1186).
4. Compare and contrast the importance and social implications of sports in Arthur Miller's *Death of a Salesman* (p. 980) and August Wilson's *Fences* (p. 1186).
5. The use and effect of racial stereotypes and racial tensions in Shakespeare's *Othello* (p. 1054).
6. Compare and contrast the pursuit of the American dream in Arthur Miller's *Death of a Salesman* (p. 980) and August Wilson's *Fences* (p. 1186).

DEVELOPMENT

Once you've picked out a technique, question, problem, or issue, you need to decide what to do with it, how to focus and develop it. The section on "Writing Short Papers" in Chapter 2 (pp. 32–45) applies to papers on drama as well as to those on fiction and poetry. Review the first four of the "Five Steps in the Writing Process" (pp. 33–36) if you need to. Here we comment briefly on developing an argument specifically for a paper on drama.

Many of the steps in developing an argumentative paper on drama are the same as those outlined earlier for papers on fiction and poetry. Avoid plot summaries — assume the reader of your paper has read the play and understands what it's about. Develop a central idea that clarifies or illuminates a significant aspect of the play's technique, meaning, or context, literary or cultural. The central idea must be one about which there can be disagreement for the paper to be argumentative. Your task is to show readers that your views are sound and convincing.

As with papers on fiction or poetry, asking questions is a good way to hone in on an argumentative central idea. And the same kinds of questions apply: What is distinctive or unique or striking about the way a technique is handled? In what ways is that technique used in the play? How does that technique relate to the theme? How is the problem or issue you're looking at brought out through characters, dialogue, conflicts, and contrasts? Does the play include symbols? If so, what are they, and how are they used in the play? What is controversial, or puzzling, or difficult about what the text seems to say about the issues raised in it?

As we've suggested before, phrasing your central idea as a question and then using the paragraphs in the body of the paper to answer the question can help you organize the paper. It's generally best not to use plot as the outline for your paper since you can't cover everything about a full-length play in a short paper. Organize instead by topics or ideas — two or three techniques used by the playwright, or a series of points about your central idea. Each paragraph should have a topic sentence that states the paragraph's central idea. You should then elaborate on that idea, supporting it with details and illustrations and explaining how the details and illustrations support and clarify the ideas. Because you can't deal with the entire play, you can focus on an important scene or a crucial speech, examining it thoroughly and relating it to the rest of the play, or you can focus on key passages in the play (see p. 208), particular sections — a sentence, a few sentences, a paragraph, a particular scene — that seem to shed light on all the other parts of the play.

As for fiction and poetry, your illustrations must include quotations. If your paper uses quotations only from plays included in this book, you do not need to add a bibliography page. Your teacher will take for granted that you are using the text in this book. When you include quotations from other sources, or from plays you find in another book, you need to include a Works Cited page (see pp. 1396–1405).

Make the quotations you use short, pointed, and economical. Focus on key lines, phrases, or words whenever possible instead of typing out extended passages. Often a careful lead-in phrase or introductory sentence or two can clarify the context and point you are leading up to, and thus reduce the need for a long quotation. For general advice on fitting quotations into your paragraphs and sentences, review the sections on handling quotations (pp. 40–42) and the "Ten Guidelines for Formatting and Punctuating Quotations" (pp. 43–44). Much of what is said on those pages applies to quoting from a play. But quoting from a play poses some special challenges. Here are five tips on handling quotations of drama:

1. Handle prose passages from one speech in a play as you do quotations from any other prose. Merge quotations of four lines or fewer into your sentence; format longer passages as block quotations (see pp. 43–44).
2. Handle passages from one speech in a play written in verse as you do quotations from poetry. Merge quotations of one to three lines into your sentence, using slashes to indicate line divisions; format passages of four lines or more as block quotations (see pp. 43–44).
3. Format passages quoting from more than one speech as block quotations. Indent the first line one inch; type the character's name in capitals, followed by a colon and then by the text of the speech; indent following lines in the same speech another half-inch. For example:

> Although Mrs. Carter thinks of herself as open and accepting, her unconscious racism begins to appear as she talks about her brother's novel:
>
>> MRS. CARTER (*leaning on the railing*): Well . . . she's almost white, see? Really you can't tell except in small ways. She wants to be a lawyer . . . and . . . and . . . well, there she is full of complexes and this deep shame you know.
>>
>> MAMA (*excitedly but with curiosity*): Do tell! What shame has she got?
>>
>> MRS. CARTER (*takes off her fur neckpiece and places it on bench with overnight bag*): It's obvious! This lovely creature . . . intelligent, ambitious, and well . . . she's a Negro! (p. 800)

4. For plays written in verse and divided into acts and scenes, identify passages by giving their act, scene, and line numbers in parentheses after the quotation. Use Arabic numbers even if the original uses Roman numerals, separated by periods. This is especially helpful for older plays that have been reprinted many times. A page number isn't much help if you have a different edition from the one used in someone's paper. Thus a citation of the "To be or not to be" speech in the first scene of the third act of *Hamlet* would appear as "(3.1.57–89)." Include the title of the

play if other plays are cited in the paper. Give the edition from which you are quoting in a footnote or bibliography.

5. For plays written in prose, cite passages by page number in parentheses after the quotation. Give the edition from which you are quoting in a footnote or bibliography.

A STUDENT WRITER AT WORK: CALEB SHENG ON THE WRITING PROCESS

In a recent Introduction to Literature class, we assigned a paper on an aspect of theme or dramatic technique in one of the short plays in Chapters 17–20. A student in the class, Caleb Sheng, chose to do his paper on Alice Childress's *Florence*. Here's what he told us about the way he went about writing the paper.

"The most difficult part of writing this paper was deciding on a topic. When I was given this assignment, the criteria for choosing a subject were very broad. Beyond an analysis of technique or theme within the play, the assignment gave few specifications as to the content of the paper. As is often the case with me, this open-ended paper left me with a blank page and a scrambling mind.

"I first had to decide on a play. I chose *Florence* because it has a traditional form, which seemed to me easier to deal with than an experimental form, and because its subject appealed to me. Though it's fairly old, it deals with underlying issues that continue to be relevant. I read the play several times. I thought of writing on Florence's pursuit of her dreams (they seem impossible to attain — is it better to try and fail, or to be sensible and realistic?) or of doing a character study of Mama and the way her encounter with Mrs. Carter leads her to change her mind about going to New York.

"As I reread and thought about the text, I began paying attention to Marge and Mrs. Carter. I noticed similarities and contrasts between them and started jotting notes (about concern for or support of siblings; taking chances or not doing so; responsibility; stereotypical roles and attitudes). The area they had in common that most intrigued me was the attitude towards race shown by both, ways they were similar and different. And within that area, the qualities of identity and independence appeared increasingly to be central to the concerns explored in the play. I decided to write on that as a contrast paper, on the way both had wrong attitudes about racial assimilation, but wrong in nearly opposite ways."

SAMPLE PAPER

Caleb Sheng
Professors Ridl and Schakel
English 105-04
December 1, 2003

Identity and Independence in Alice Childress's <u>Florence</u>

As the United States has become increasingly diverse, the issue of inclusivity, of how to create a society that embraces a diversity of cultures, has become of greater and greater importance. Alice Childress's short play <u>Florence</u> includes an exploration of this issue. The thematic progress of racial assimilation into society is embodied in two characters, Marge and Mrs. Carter. They exhibit dual facets of the same problem: misconceptions about the qualities of identity and independence. While Mrs. Carter represents the tragic ignorance of mainstream society, Marge mirrors the equally tragic attitude of the minority mentality. Both mindsets, though different in approach, are equally imprisoning.

Thesis sentence.

For Marge, independence is vital. In fact, she would rather her family face uncertain hardship than implore her brother for financial assistance: "Rudley ain't got nothin' fo himself. I hate to ask him to give us" (p. 796). What is bothersome to her about Florence is not her desire for independence, but her means of pursuing it--her desire for mainstream types of accomplishment, something for which Marge feels minorities are not to aspire: "She got notions a Negro woman don't need" (p. 797). To yearn for this is to claim presumptuously an equal footing with others and thus reject the societal separation of identities: "She must think she's white!" (p. 797). Why must one try to be like another in order to achieve happiness or success? To Marge, independence as an African American is a matter of plain self-sufficiency, not one of alteration or adaptation.

Quotation introduced formally with colon.

Builds argument with assertions and illustrations.

However much she may extol autonomy, though, Marge is obstinately unwilling to try and achieve an independence of identity. She regards efforts to achieve equality and civil rights as presumptuous:

Block quotation; inserted ellipses in brackets to show that later ellipsis is part of original text.

> MARGE: I'm talkin' about her attitude. Didn't she
> go to Strumley's down here and ask to be
> a salesgirl? [. . .] They don't hire no Col-
> ored folks.
> MAMA: Others besides Florence been talkin' about their
> rights.
> MARGE: I know it . . . but there's things we can't do
> cause they ain't gonna let us.
> (p. 797)

Marge is entrenched in the role that society has assigned her and does her best not only to fulfill it, but also to enforce it on those who waver from theirs. It follows then that Florence's efforts to grow outside of the socially permissible bounds of her designated identity indirectly threaten the security that Marge tries to maintain through her acquiescence to this cultural imposition. Marge is concerned partly that Florence might fail and thus subject her to ridicule from both whites and blacks. To Marge, Florence is wrong to give individuality a traitorous preference over identity with the black community.

Mrs. Carter, on the other hand, presents a contrasting side of the crisis. She earnestly seeks to portray a comprehension of the African American identity and an acceptance of their independence. She seems to identify with her brother, when she says he "knows the Negro so well that sometimes our friends tease him and say he almost <u>seems</u> like [one]" (p. 802). It is apparent, however, that her understanding of blacks is very limited and her acceptance of them incomplete. Her assumption that a person would kill herself because she's "almost white" but, tragically, "a Negro" (p. 800), and her stereotyping of blacks as good singers and suitable only for housework shows how far she has to go. Still distanced from her black neighbors by an entrenched obstructionism, Mrs. Carter is unable to fathom the true transplantation and transformation of the minority identity and is therefore incapable of properly identifying and interacting with "your people" (p. 800).

Transition and topic sentence.

Quotation blended into sentence.

When Florence abandons the aforementioned allegiances in pursuit of her aspirations, she depends on mainstream society to accept her with a rewarding benevolence that does justice to her risk. Unfortunately, it appears that, though members of the minority have separated themselves from societal conventions, the white majority adheres to them not deliberately but unconsciously: "I'll just tell her . . . no heavy washing or ironing . . . just light cleaning and a little cooking" (p. 804). The failure of one majority to move with the minority leaves those like Florence at an impasse: having deserted their former identities, they are prevented from moving fully into new ones.

Transition and topic sentence.

Political emancipation has not yet begotten cultural enlightenment. Both from within and without, Florence is beset by the symptoms of a deficient societal transition to the contemporary issue of equality. Hope is grim in this paradox, where an exit from cultural identity does not necessarily ensure an entry into social independence. And, until there is a sufficient awareness of true identity and independence on the part of others, the only recourse for individuals like Florence is to "keep trying" (p. 805).

Conclusion.

A Collection of Plays

WEB: Research the authors in this collection with LitLinks, or take a quiz on the plays with LitQuiz, at bedfordstmartins.com/approachinglit.

Henrik Ibsen   1828–1906

A Doll House°   [1879]

Translated by Rolf Fjelde

THE CHARACTERS

TORVALD HELMER, a lawyer	THE HELMERS' THREE SMALL CHILDREN
NORA, his wife	ANNE-MARIE, their nurse
DR. RANK	HELENE, a maid
MRS. LINDE	A DELIVERY BOY
NILS KROGSTAD, a bank clerk	

The action takes place in Helmer's residence.

ACT I

(*A comfortable room, tastefully but not expensively furnished. A door to the right in the back wall leads to the entryway; another to the left leads to Helmer's study. Between these doors, a piano. Midway in the left-hand wall a door, and further back a window. Near the window a round table with an armchair and a small sofa. In the right-hand wall, toward the rear, a door, and nearer the foreground a porcelain stove with two armchairs and a rocking chair beside it. Between the stove and the side door, a small table. Engravings on the walls. An étagère° with china figures and other small art objects; a small bookcase with richly bound books; the floor carpeted; a fire burning in the stove. It is a winter day.*)

A Doll House: Fjelde explains, in the foreword to his translation, that he translates the title as "A Doll House" instead of "A Doll's House" to avoid the suggestion that it is the house of the doll, Nora. Rather, he believes, Ibsen meant that both Torvald and Nora are living in an unreal, "let's pretend" situation.   **s.d. étagère:** A cabinet with a number of shelves.

(A bell rings in the entryway; shortly after we hear the door being unlocked. Nora comes into the room, humming happily to herself; she is wearing street clothes and carries an armload of packages, which she puts down on the table to the right. She has left the hall door open, and through it a Delivery Boy is seen holding a Christmas tree and a basket, which he gives to the Maid who let them in.)

NORA: Hide the tree well, Helene. The children mustn't get a glimpse of it till this evening, after it's trimmed. *(To the Delivery Boy, taking out her purse.)* How much?

DELIVERY BOY: Fifty, ma'am.

NORA: There's a crown. No, keep the change. *(The Boy thanks her and leaves. Nora shuts the door. She laughs softly to herself while taking off her street things. Drawing a bag of macaroons from her pocket, she eats a couple, then steals over and listens at her husband's study door.)* Yes, he's home. *(Hums again as she moves to the table right.)*

HELMER *(from the study)*: Is that my little lark twittering out there?

NORA *(busy opening some packages)*: Yes, it is.

HELMER: Is that my squirrel rummaging around?

NORA: Yes!

HELMER: When did my squirrel get in?

NORA: Just now. *(Putting the macaroon bag in her pocket and wiping her mouth.)* Do come in, Torvald, and see what I've bought.

HELMER: Can't be disturbed. *(After a moment he opens the door and peers in, pen in hand.)* Bought, you say? All that there? Has the little spendthrift been out throwing money around again?

NORA: Oh, but Torvald, this year we really should let ourselves go a bit. It's the first Christmas we haven't had to economize.

HELMER: But you know we can't go squandering.

NORA: Oh yes, Torvald, we can squander a little now. Can't we? Just a tiny, wee bit. Now that you've got a big salary and are going to make piles and piles of money.

HELMER: Yes — starting New Year's. But then it's a full three months till the raise comes through.

NORA: Pooh! We can borrow that long.

HELMER: Nora! *(Goes over and playfully takes her by the ear.)* Are your scatter-brains off again? What if today I borrowed a thousand crowns, and you squandered them over Christmas week, and then on New Year's Eve a roof tile fell on my head, and I lay there —

NORA *(putting her hand on his mouth)*: Oh! Don't say such things!

HELMER: Yes, but what if it happened — then what?

NORA: If anything so awful happened, then it just wouldn't matter if I had debts or not.

HELMER: Well, but the people I'd borrowed from?

NORA: Them? Who cares about them! They're strangers.

HELMER: Nora, Nora, how like a woman! No, but seriously, Nora, you know what I think about that. No debts! Never borrow! Something of freedom's lost — and something of beauty, too — from a home that's founded on borrowing and debt. We've made a brave stand up to now, the two of us; and we'll go right on like that the little while we have to.

NORA (*going toward the stove*): Yes, whatever you say, Torvald.

HELMER (*following her*): Now, now, the little lark's wings mustn't droop. Come on, don't be a sulky squirrel. (*Taking out his wallet.*) Nora, guess what I have here.

NORA (*turning quickly*): Money!

HELMER: There, see. (*Hands her some notes.*) Good grief, I know how costs go up in a house at Christmastime.

NORA: Ten — twenty — thirty — forty. Oh, thank you, Torvald; I can manage no end on this.

HELMER: You really will have to.

NORA: Oh yes, I promise I will! But come here so I can show you everything I bought. And so cheap! Look, new clothes for Ivar here — and a sword. Here a horse and a trumpet for Bob. And a doll and a doll's bed here for Emmy; they're nothing much, but she'll tear them to bits in no time anyway. And here I have dress material and handkerchiefs for the maids. Old Anne-Marie really deserves something more.

HELMER: And what's in that package there?

NORA (*with a cry*): Torvald, no! You can't see that till tonight!

HELMER: I see. But tell me now, you little prodigal, what have you thought of for yourself?

NORA: For myself? Oh, I don't want anything at all.

HELMER: Of course you do. Tell me just what — within reason — you'd most like to have.

NORA: I honestly don't know. Oh, listen, Torvald —

HELMER: Well?

NORA (*fumbling at his coat buttons, without looking at him*): If you want to give me something, then maybe you could — you could —

HELMER: Come on, out with it.

NORA (*hurriedly*): You could give me money, Torvald. No more than you think you can spare; then one of these days I'll buy something with it.

HELMER: But Nora —

NORA: Oh, please, Torvald darling, do that! I beg you, please. Then I could hang the bills in pretty gilt paper on the Christmas tree. Wouldn't that be fun?

HELMER: What are those little birds called that always fly through their fortunes?

NORA: Oh yes, spendthrifts; I know all that. But let's do as I say, Torvald; then I'll have time to decide what I really need most. That's very sensible, isn't it?

HELMER (*smiling*): Yes, very — that is, if you actually hung onto the money I give you, and you actually used it to buy yourself something. But it goes for the house and for all sorts of foolish things, and then I only have to lay out some more.

NORA: Oh, but Torvald—

HELMER: Don't deny it, my dear little Nora. (*Putting his arm around her waist.*) Spendthrifts are sweet, but they use up a frightful amount of money. It's incredible what it costs a man to feed such birds.

NORA: Oh, how can you say that! Really, I save everything I can.

HELMER (*laughing*): Yes, that's the truth. Everything you can. But that's nothing at all.

NORA (*humming, with a smile of quiet satisfaction*): Hm, if you only knew what expenses we larks and squirrels have, Torvald.

HELMER: You're an odd little one. Exactly the way your father was. You're never at a loss for scaring up money; but the moment you have it, it runs right out through your fingers; you never know what you've done with it. Well, one takes you as you are. It's deep in your blood. Yes, these things are hereditary, Nora.

NORA: Ah, I could wish I'd inherited many of Papa's qualities.

HELMER: And I couldn't wish you anything but just what you are, my sweet little lark. But wait; it seems to me you have a very—what should I call it?—a very suspicious look today—

NORA: I do?

HELMER: You certainly do. Look me straight in the eye.

NORA (*looking at him*): Well?

HELMER (*shaking an admonitory finger*): Surely my sweet tooth hasn't been running riot in town today, has she?

NORA: No. Why do you imagine that?

HELMER: My sweet tooth really didn't make a little detour through the confectioner's?

NORA: No, I assure you, Torvald—

HELMER: Hasn't nibbled some pastry?

NORA: No, not at all.

HELMER: Not even munched a macaroon or two?

NORA: No, Torvald, I assure you, really—

HELMER: There, there now. Of course I'm only joking.

NORA (*going to the table, right*): You know I could never think of going against you.

HELMER: No, I understand that; and you *have* given me your word. (*Going over to her.*) Well, you keep your little Christmas secrets to yourself, Nora darling. I expect they'll come to light this evening, when the tree is lit.

NORA: Did you remember to ask Dr. Rank?

HELMER: No. But there's no need for that, it's assumed he'll be dining with us. All the same, I'll ask him when he stops by here this morning. I've ordered some fine wine. Nora, you can't imagine how I'm looking forward to this evening.

NORA: So am I. And what fun for the children, Torvald!

HELMER: Ah, it's so gratifying to know that one's gotten a safe, secure job, and with a comfortable salary. It's a great satisfaction, isn't it?

NORA: Oh, it's wonderful!

HELMER: Remember last Christmas? Three whole weeks before, you shut yourself in every evening till long after midnight, making flowers for the Christmas tree, and all the other decorations to surprise us. Ugh, that was the dullest time I've ever lived through.

NORA: It wasn't at all dull for me.

HELMER (*smiling*): But the outcome *was* pretty sorry, Nora.

NORA: Oh, don't tease me with that again. How could I help it that the cat came in and tore everything to shreds.

HELMER: No, poor thing, you certainly couldn't. You wanted so much to please us all, and that's what counts. But it's just as well that the hard times are past.

NORA: Yes, it's really wonderful.

HELMER: Now I don't have to sit here alone, boring myself, and you don't have to tire your precious eyes and your fair little delicate hands —

NORA (*clapping her hands*): No, is it really true, Torvald, I don't have to? Oh, how wonderfully lovely to hear! (*Taking his arm.*) Now I'll tell you just how I've thought we should plan things. Right after Christmas — (*The doorbell rings.*) Oh, the bell. (*Straightening the room up a bit.*) Somebody would have to come. What a bore!

HELMER: I'm not at home to visitors, don't forget.

MAID (*from the hall doorway*): Ma'am, a lady to see you —

NORA: All right, let her come in.

MAID (*to Helmer*): And the doctor's just come too.

HELMER: Did he go right to my study?

MAID: Yes, he did.

(*Helmer goes into his room. The Maid shows in Mrs. Linde, dressed in traveling clothes, and shuts the door after her.*)

MRS. LINDE (*in a dispirited and somewhat hesitant voice*): Hello, Nora.

NORA (*uncertain*): Hello —

MRS. LINDE: You don't recognize me.

NORA: No, I don't know — but wait, I think — (*Exclaiming.*) What! Kristine! Is it really you?

MRS. LINDE: Yes, it's me.

NORA: Kristine! To think I didn't recognize you. But then, how could I? (*More quietly.*) How you've changed, Kristine!

MRS. LINDE: Yes, no doubt I have. In nine — ten long years.

NORA: Is it so long since we met! Yes, it's all of that. Oh, these last eight years have been a happy time, believe me. And so now you've come in to town, too. Made the long trip in the winter. That took courage.

MRS. LINDE: I just got here by ship this morning.

NORA: To enjoy yourself over Christmas, of course. Oh, how lovely! Yes, enjoy ourselves, we'll do that. But take your coat off. You're not still cold? (*Helping her.*) There now, let's get cozy here by the stove. No, the easy chair there! I'll take the rocker here. (*Seizing her hands.*) Yes, now you have your old look again; it was only in that first moment. You're a bit more pale, Kristine — and maybe a bit thinner.

MRS. LINDE: And much, much older, Nora.

NORA: Yes, perhaps a bit older; a tiny, tiny bit; not much at all. (*Stopping short; suddenly serious.*) Oh, but thoughtless me, to sit here, chattering away. Sweet, good Kristine, can you forgive me?

MRS. LINDE: What do you mean, Nora?

NORA (*softly*): Poor Kristine, you've become a widow.

MRS. LINDE: Yes, three years ago.

NORA: Oh, I knew it, of course; I read it in the papers. Oh, Kristine, you must believe me; I often thought of writing you then, but I kept postponing it, and something always interfered.

MRS. LINDE: Nora dear, I understand completely.

NORA: No, it was awful of me, Kristine. You poor thing, how much you must have gone through. And he left you nothing?

MRS. LINDE: No.

NORA: And no children?

MRS. LINDE: No.

NORA: Nothing at all, then?

MRS. LINDE: Not even a sense of loss to feed on.

NORA (*looking incredulously at her*): But Kristine, how could that be?

MRS. LINDE (*smiling wearily and smoothing her hair*): Oh, sometimes it happens, Nora.

NORA: So completely alone. How terribly hard that must be for you. I have three lovely children. You can't see them now; they're out with the maid. But now you must tell me everything —

MRS. LINDE: No, no, no, tell me about yourself.

NORA: No, you begin. Today I don't want to be selfish. I want to think only of you today. But there is something I must tell you. Did you hear of the wonderful luck we had recently?

MRS. LINDE: No, what's that?

NORA: My husband's been made manager in the bank, just think!

MRS. LINDE: Your husband? How marvelous!

NORA: Isn't it? Being a lawyer is such an uncertain living, you know, especially if one won't touch any cases that aren't clean and decent. And of course Torvald would never do that, and I'm with him completely there. Oh, we're simply delighted, believe me! He'll join the bank right after New Year's and start getting a huge salary and lots of commissions. From now on we can live quite differently — just as we want. Oh, Kristine, I feel so light and happy! Won't it be lovely to have stacks of money and not a care in the world?

MRS. LINDE: Well, anyway, it would be lovely to have enough for necessities.

NORA: No, not just for necessities, but stacks and stacks of money!

MRS. LINDE (*smiling*): Nora, Nora, aren't you sensible yet? Back in school you were such a free spender.

NORA (*with a quiet laugh*): Yes, that's what Torvald still says. (*Shaking her finger.*) But "Nora, Nora" isn't as silly as you all think. Really, we've been in no position for me to go squandering. We've had to work, both of us.

MRS. LINDE: You too?

NORA: Yes, at odd jobs — needlework, crocheting, embroidery, and such — (*casually*) and other things too. You remember that Torvald left the department when we were married? There was no chance of promotion in his office, and of course he needed to earn more money. But that first year he drove himself terribly. He took on all kinds of extra work that kept him going morning and night. It wore him down, and then he fell deathly ill. The doctors said it was essential for him to travel south.

MRS. LINDE: Yes, didn't you spend a whole year in Italy?

NORA: That's right. It wasn't easy to get away, you know. Ivar had just been born. But of course we had to go. Oh, that was a beautiful trip, and it saved Torvald's life. But it cost a frightful sum, Kristine.

MRS. LINDE: I can well imagine.

NORA: Four thousand, eight hundred crowns it cost. That's really a lot of money.

MRS. LINDE: But it's lucky you had it when you needed it.

NORA: Well, as it was, we got it from Papa.

MRS. LINDE: I see. It was just about the time your father died.

NORA: Yes, just about then. And, you know, I couldn't make that trip out to nurse him. I had to stay here, expecting Ivar any moment, and with my poor sick Torvald to care for. Dearest Papa, I never saw him again, Kristine. Oh, that was the worst time I've known in all my marriage.

MRS. LINDE: I know how you loved him. And then you went off to Italy?

NORA: Yes. We had the means now, and the doctors urged us. So we left a month after.

MRS. LINDE: And your husband came back completely cured?

NORA: Sound as a drum!

MRS. LINDE: But — the doctor?

NORA: Who?

MRS. LINDE: I thought the maid said he was a doctor, the man who came in with me.

NORA: Yes, that was Dr. Rank — but he's not making a sick call. He's our closest friend, and he stops by at least once a day. No, Torvald hasn't had a sick moment since, and the children are fit and strong, and I am, too. (*Jumping up and clapping her hands.*) Oh, dear God, Kristine, what a lovely thing to live and be happy! But how disgusting of me — I'm talking of nothing but my own affairs. (*Sits on a stool close by Kristine, arms resting across her knees.*) Oh, don't be angry with me! Tell me, is it really true that you weren't in love with your husband? Why did you marry him, then?

MRS. LINDE: My mother was still alive, but bedridden and helpless—and I had my two younger brothers to look after. In all conscience, I didn't think I could turn him down.

NORA: No, you were right there. But was he rich at the time?

MRS. LINDE: He was very well off, I'd say. But the business was shaky, Nora. When he died, it all fell apart, and nothing was left.

NORA: And then—?

MRS. LINDE: Yes, so I had to scrape up a living with a little shop and a little teaching and whatever else I could find. The last three years have been like one endless workday without a rest for me. Now, it's over, Nora. My poor mother doesn't need me, for she's passed on. Nor the boys, either; they're working now and can take care of themselves.

NORA: How free you must feel—

MRS. LINDE: No—only unspeakably empty. Nothing to live for now. (*Standing up anxiously.*) That's why I couldn't take it any longer out in that desolate hole. Maybe here it'll be easier to find something to do and keep my mind occupied. If I could only be lucky enough to get a steady job, some office work—

NORA: Oh, but Kristine, that's so dreadfully tiring, and you already look so tired. It would be much better for you if you could go off to a bathing resort.

MRS. LINDE (*going toward the window*): I have no father to give me travel money, Nora.

NORA (*rising*): Oh, don't be angry with me.

MRS. LINDE (*going to her*): Nora dear, don't you be angry with me. The worst of my kind of situation is all the bitterness that's stored away. No one to work for, and yet you're always having to snap up your opportunities. You have to live; and so you grow selfish. When you told me the happy change in your lot, do you know I was delighted less for your sakes than for mine?

NORA: How so? Oh, I see. You think maybe Torvald could do something for you.

MRS. LINDE: Yes, that's what I thought.

NORA: And he will, Kristine! Just leave it to me; I'll bring it up so delicately—find something attractive to humor him with. Oh, I'm so eager to help you.

MRS. LINDE: How very kind of you, Nora, to be so concerned over me—doubly kind, considering you really know so little of life's burdens yourself.

NORA: I—? I know so little—?

MRS. LINDE (*smiling*): Well, my heavens—a little needlework and such—Nora, you're just a child.

NORA (*tossing her head and pacing the floor*): You don't have to act so superior.

MRS. LINDE: Oh?

NORA: You're just like the others. You all think I'm incapable of anything serious —

MRS. LINDE: Come now —

NORA: That I've never had to face the raw world.

MRS. LINDE: Nora dear, you've just been telling me all your troubles.

NORA: Hm! Trivial! (*Quietly.*) I haven't told you the big thing.

MRS. LINDE: Big thing? What do you mean?

NORA: You look down on me so, Kristine, but you shouldn't. You're proud that you worked so long and hard for your mother.

MRS. LINDE: I don't look down on a soul. But it is true: I'm proud — and happy, too — to think it was given to me to make my mother's last days almost free of care.

NORA: And you're also proud thinking of what you've done for your brothers.

MRS. LINDE: I feel I've a right to be.

NORA: I agree. But listen to this, Kristine — I've also got something to be proud and happy for.

MRS. LINDE: I don't doubt it. But whatever do you mean?

NORA: Not so loud. What if Torvald heard! He mustn't, not for anything in the world. Nobody must know, Kristine. No one but you.

MRS. LINDE: But what is it, then?

NORA: Come here. (*Drawing her down beside her on the sofa.*) It's true — I've also got something to be proud and happy for. I'm the one who saved Torvald's life.

MRS. LINDE: Saved — ? Saved how?

NORA: I told you about the trip to Italy. Torvald never would have lived if he hadn't gone south —

MRS. LINDE: Of course; your father gave you the means —

NORA (*smiling*): That's what Torvald and all the rest think, but —

MRS. LINDE: But — ?

NORA: Papa didn't give us a pin. I was the one who raised the money.

MRS. LINDE: You? That whole amount?

NORA: Four thousand, eight hundred crowns. What do you say to that?

MRS. LINDE: But Nora, how was it possible? Did you win the lottery?

NORA (*disdainfully*): The lottery? Pooh! No art to that.

MRS. LINDE: But where did you get it from then?

NORA (*humming, with a mysterious smile*): Hmm, tra-la-la-la.

MRS. LINDE: Because you couldn't have borrowed it.

NORA: No? Why not?

MRS. LINDE: A wife can't borrow without her husband's consent.

NORA (*tossing her head*): Oh, but a wife with a little business sense, a wife who knows how to manage —

MRS. LINDE: Nora, I simply don't understand —

NORA: You don't have to. Whoever said I *borrowed* the money? I could have gotten it other ways. (*Throwing herself back on the sofa.*) I could have gotten it from some admirer or other. After all, a girl with my ravishing appeal —

MRS. LINDE: You lunatic.

NORA: I'll bet you're eaten up with curiosity, Kristine.

MRS. LINDE: Now listen here, Nora — you haven't done something indiscreet?

NORA (*sitting up again*): Is it indiscreet to save your husband's life?

MRS. LINDE: I think it's indiscreet that without his knowledge you —

NORA: But that's the point: He mustn't know! My Lord, can't you understand? He mustn't ever know the close call he had. It was to *me* the doctors came to say his life was in danger — that nothing could save him but a stay in the south. Didn't I try strategy then! I began talking about how lovely it would be for me to travel abroad like other young wives; I begged and I cried; I told him please to remember my condition, to be kind and indulge me; and then I dropped a hint that he could easily take out a loan. But at that, Kristine, he nearly exploded. He said I was frivolous, and it was his duty as man of the house not to indulge me in whims and fancies — as I think he called them. Aha, I thought, now you'll just have to be saved — and that's when I saw my chance.

MRS. LINDE: And your father never told Torvald the money wasn't from him?

NORA: No, never. Papa died right about then. I'd considered bringing him into my secret and begging him never to tell. But he was too sick at the time — and then, sadly, it didn't matter.

MRS. LINDE: And you've never confided in your husband since?

NORA: For heaven's sake, no! Are you serious? He's so strict on that subject. Besides — Torvald, with all his masculine pride — how painfully humiliating for him if he ever found out he was in debt to me. That would just ruin our relationship. Our beautiful, happy home would never be the same.

MRS. LINDE: Won't you ever tell him?

NORA (*thoughtfully, half smiling*): Yes — maybe sometime years from now, when I'm no longer so attractive. Don't laugh! I only mean when Torvald loves me less than now, when he stops enjoying my dancing and dressing up and reciting for him. Then it might be wise to have something in reserve — (*Breaking off.*) How ridiculous! That'll never happen — Well, Kristine, what do you think of my big secret? I'm capable of something too, hm? You can imagine, of course, how this thing hangs over me. It really hasn't been easy meeting the payments on time. In the business world there's what they call quarterly interest and what they call amortization, and these are always so terribly hard to manage. I've had to skimp a little here and there, wherever I could, you know. I could hardly spare anything from my house allowance, because Torvald has to live well. I couldn't let the children go poorly dressed; whatever I got for them, I felt I had to use up completely — the darlings!

MRS. LINDE: Poor Nora, so it had to come out of your own budget, then?

NORA: Yes, of course. But I was the one most responsible, too. Every time Torvald gave me money for new clothes and such, I never used more than half; always bought the simplest, cheapest outfits. It was a godsend that everything looks so well on me that Torvald never noticed. But it did weigh me down at times, Kristine. It *is* such a joy to wear fine things. You understand.

MRS. LINDE: Oh, of course.

NORA: And then I found other ways of making money. Last winter I was lucky enough to get a lot of copying to do. I locked myself in and sat writing every evening till late in the night. Ah, I was tired so often, dead tired. But still it was wonderful fun, sitting and working like that, earning money. It was almost like being a man.

MRS. LINDE: But how much have you paid off this way so far?

NORA: That's hard to say, exactly. These accounts, you know, aren't easy to figure. I only know that I've paid out all I could scrape together. Time and again I haven't known where to turn. (*Smiling.*) Then I'd sit here dreaming of a rich old gentleman who had fallen in love with me—

MRS. LINDE: What! Who is he?

NORA: Oh, really! And that he'd died, and when his will was opened, there in big letters it said, "All my fortune shall be paid over in cash, immediately, to that enchanting Mrs. Nora Helmer."

MRS. LINDE: But Nora dear—who *was* this gentleman?

NORA: Good grief, can't you understand? The old man never existed; that was only something I'd dream up time and again whenever I was at my wits' end for money. But it makes no difference now; the old fossil can go where he pleases for all I care; I don't need him or his will—because now I'm free. (*Jumping up.*) Oh, how lovely to think of that, Kristine! Carefree! To know you're carefree, utterly carefree; to be able to romp and play with the children, and to keep up a beautiful, charming home—everything just the way Torvald likes it! And think, spring is coming, with big blue skies. Maybe we can travel a little then. Maybe I'll see the ocean again. Oh yes, it *is* so marvelous to live and be happy!

(*The front doorbell rings.*)

MRS. LINDE (*rising*): There's the bell. It's probably best that I go.

NORA: No, stay. No one's expected. It must be for Torvald.

MAID (*from the hall doorway*): Excuse me, ma'am—there's a gentleman here to see Mr. Helmer, but I didn't know—since the doctor's with him—

NORA: Who is the gentleman?

KROGSTAD (*from the doorway*): It's me, Mrs. Helmer.

(*Mrs. Linde starts and turns away toward the window.*)

NORA (*stepping toward him, tense, her voice a whisper*): You? What is it? Why do you want to speak to my husband?

KROGSTAD: Bank business—after a fashion. I have a small job in the investment bank, and I hear now your husband is going to be our chief—

NORA: In other words, it's—

KROGSTAD: Just dry business, Mrs. Helmer. Nothing but that.

NORA: Yes, then please be good enough to step into the study. (*She nods indifferently as she sees him out by the hall door, then returns and begins stirring up the stove.*)

MRS. LINDE: Nora — who was that man?

NORA: That was a Mr. Krogstad — a lawyer.

MRS. LINDE: Then it really was him.

NORA: Do you know that person?

MRS. LINDE: I did once — many years ago. For a time he was a law clerk in our town.

NORA: Yes, he's been that.

MRS. LINDE: How he's changed.

NORA: I understand he had a very unhappy marriage.

MRS. LINDE: He's a widower now.

NORA: With a number of children. There now, it's burning. (*She closes the stove door and moves the rocker a bit to one side.*)

MRS. LINDE: They say he has a hand in all kinds of business.

NORA: Oh? That may be true; I wouldn't know. But let's not think about business. It's so dull.

(*Dr. Rank enters from Helmer's study.*)

RANK (*still in the doorway*): No, no, really — I don't want to intrude, I'd just as soon talk a little while with your wife. (*Shuts the door, then notices Mrs. Linde.*) Oh, beg pardon. I'm intruding here too.

NORA: No, not at all. (*Introducing him.*) Dr. Rank, Mrs. Linde.

RANK: Well now, that's a name much heard in this house. I believe I passed the lady on the stairs as I came.

MRS. LINDE: Yes, I take the stairs very slowly. They're rather hard on me.

RANK: Uh-hm, some touch of internal weakness?

MRS. LINDE: More overexertion, I'd say.

RANK: Nothing else? Then you're probably here in town to rest up in a round of parties?

MRS. LINDE: I'm here to look for work.

RANK: Is that the best cure for overexertion?

MRS. LINDE: One has to live, Doctor.

RANK: Yes, there's a common prejudice to that effect.

NORA: Oh, come on, Dr. Rank — you really do want to live yourself.

RANK: Yes, I really do. Wretched as I am, I'll gladly prolong my torment indefinitely. All my patients feel like that. And it's quite the same, too, with the morally sick. Right at this moment there's one of those moral invalids in there with Helmer —

MRS. LINDE (*softly*): Ah!

NORA: Who do you mean?

RANK: Oh, it's a lawyer, Krogstad, a type you wouldn't know. His character is rotten to the root — but even he began chattering all-importantly about how he had to *live*.

NORA: Oh? What did he want to talk to Torvald about?

RANK: I really don't know. I only heard something about the bank.

NORA: I didn't know that Krog — that this man Krogstad had anything to do with the bank.

RANK: Yes, he's gotten some kind of berth down there. (*To Mrs. Linde.*) I don't know if you also have, in your neck of the woods, a type of person who scuttles about breathlessly, sniffing out hints of moral corruption, and then maneuvers his victim into some sort of key position where he can keep an eye on him. It's the healthy these days that are out in the cold.

MRS. LINDE: All the same, it's the sick who most need to be taken in.

RANK (*with a shrug*): Yes, there we have it. That's the concept that's turning society into a sanatorium.

(*Nora, lost in her thoughts, breaks out into quiet laughter and claps her hands.*)

RANK: Why do you laugh at that? Do you have any real idea of what society is?

NORA: What do I care about dreary old society? I was laughing at something quite different — something terribly funny. Tell me, Doctor — is everyone who works in the bank dependent now on Torvald?

RANK: Is that what you find so terribly funny?

NORA (*smiling and humming*): Never mind, never mind! (*Pacing the floor.*) Yes, that's really immensely amusing: that we — that Torvald has so much power now over all those people. (*Taking the bag out of her pocket.*) Dr. Rank, a little macaroon on that?

RANK: See here, macaroons! I thought they were contraband here.

NORA: Yes, but these are some that Kristine gave me.

MRS. LINDE: What? I — ?

NORA: Now, now, don't be afraid. You couldn't possibly know that Torvald had forbidden them. You see, he's worried they'll ruin my teeth. But hmp! Just this once! Isn't that so, Dr. Rank? Help yourself! (*Puts a macaroon in his mouth.*) And you too, Kristine. And I'll also have one, only a little one — or two, at the most. (*Walking about again.*) Now I'm really tremendously happy. Now's there's just one last thing in the world that I have an enormous desire to do.

RANK: Well! And what's that?

NORA: It's something I have such a consuming desire to say so Torvald could hear.

RANK: And why can't you say it?

NORA: I don't dare. It's quite shocking.

MRS. LINDE: Shocking?

RANK: Well, then it isn't advisable. But in front of us you certainly can. What do you have such a desire to say so Torvald could hear?

NORA: I have such a huge desire to say — to hell and be damned!

RANK: Are you crazy?

MRS. LINDE: My goodness, Nora!

RANK: Go on, say it. Here he is.

NORA (*hiding the macaroon bag*): Shh, shh, shh!

(*Helmer comes in from his study, hat in hand, overcoat over his arm.*)

NORA (*going toward him*): Well, Torvald dear, are you through with him?

HELMER: Yes, he just left.

NORA: Let me introduce you — this is Kristine, who's arrived here in town.

HELMER: Kristine — ? I'm sorry, but I don't know —

NORA: Mrs. Linde, Torvald dear. Mrs. Kristine Linde.

HELMER: Of course. A childhood friend of my wife's, no doubt?

MRS. LINDE: Yes, we knew each other in those days.

NORA: And just think, she made the long trip down here in order to talk with you.

HELMER: What's this?

MRS. LINDE: Well, not exactly —

NORA: You see, Kristine is remarkably clever in office work, and so she's terribly eager to come under a capable man's supervision and add more to what she already knows —

HELMER: Very wise, Mrs. Linde.

NORA: And then when she heard that you'd become a bank manager — the story was wired out to the papers — then she came in as fast as she could and — Really, Torvald, for my sake you can do a little something for Kristine, can't you?

HELMER: Yes, it's not at all impossible. Mrs. Linde, I suppose you're a widow?

MRS. LINDE: Yes.

HELMER: Any experience in office work?

MRS. LINDE: Yes, a good deal.

HELMER: Well, it's quite likely that I can make an opening for you —

NORA (*clapping her hands*): You see, you see!

HELMER: You've come at a lucky moment, Mrs. Linde.

MRS. LINDE: Oh, how can I thank you?

HELMER: Not necessary. (*Putting his overcoat on.*) But today you'll have to excuse me —

RANK: Wait, I'll go with you. (*He fetches his coat from the hall and warms it at the stove.*)

NORA: Don't stay out long, dear.

HELMER: An hour; no more.

NORA: Are you going too, Kristine?

MRS. LINDE (*putting on her winter garments*): Yes, I have to see about a room now.

HELMER: Then perhaps we can all walk together.

NORA (*helping her*): What a shame we're so cramped here, but it's quite impossible for us to —

MRS. LINDE: Oh, don't even think of it! Good-bye, Nora dear, and thanks for everything.

NORA: Good-bye for now. Of course you'll be back this evening. And you too, Dr. Rank. What? If you're well enough? Oh, you've got to be! Wrap up tight now.

(*In a ripple of small talk the company moves out into the hall; children's voices are heard outside on the steps.*)

NORA: There they are! There they are! (*She runs to open the door. The children come in with their nurse, Anne-Marie.*) Come in, come in! (*Bends down and kisses them.*) Oh, you darlings—! Look at them, Kristine. Aren't they lovely!

RANK: No loitering in the draft here.

HELMER: Come, Mrs. Linde—this place is unbearable now for anyone but mothers.

(*Dr. Rank, Helmer, and Mrs. Linde go down the stairs. Anne-Marie goes into the living room with the children. Nora follows, after closing the hall door.*)

NORA: How fresh and strong you look. Oh, such red cheeks you have! Like apples and roses. (*The children interrupt her throughout the following.*) And it was so much fun? That's wonderful. Really? You pulled both Emmy and Bob on the sled? Imagine, all together! Yes, you're a clever boy, Ivar. Oh, let me hold her a bit, Anne-Marie. My sweet little doll baby! (*Takes the smallest from the nurse and dances with her.*) Yes, yes, Mama will dance with Bob as well. What? Did you throw snowballs? Oh, if I'd only been there! No, don't bother, Anne-Marie—I'll undress them myself. Oh yes, let me. It's such fun. Go in and rest; you look half frozen. There's hot coffee waiting for you on the stove. (*The nurse goes into the room to the left. Nora takes the children's winter things off, throwing them about, while the children talk to her all at once.*) Is that so? A big dog chased you? But it didn't bite? No, dogs never bite little, lovely doll babies. Don't peek in the packages, Ivar! What is it? Yes, wouldn't you like to know. No, no, it's an ugly something. Well? Shall we play? What shall we play? Hide-and-seek? Yes, let's play hide-and-seek. Bob must hide first. I must? Yes, let me hide first. (*Laughing and shouting, she and the children play in and out of the living room and the adjoining room to the right. At last Nora hides under the table. The children come storming in, search, but cannot find her, then hear her muffled laughter, dash over to the table, lift the cloth up and find her. Wild shouting. She creeps forward as if to scare them. More shouts. Meanwhile, a knock at the hall door; no one has noticed it. Now the door half opens, and Krogstad appears. He waits a moment; the game goes on.*)

KROGSTAD: Beg pardon, Mrs. Helmer—

NORA (*with a strangled cry, turning and scrambling to her knees*): Oh! What do you want?

KROGSTAD: Excuse me. The outer door was ajar; it must be someone forgot to shut it—

NORA (*rising*): My husband isn't home, Mr. Krogstad.

KROGSTAD: I know that.

NORA: Yes — then what do you want here?

KROGSTAD: A word with you.

NORA: With — ? (*To the children, quietly.*) Go in to Anne-Marie. What? No, the strange man won't hurt Mama. When he's gone, we'll play some more. (*She leads the children into the room to the left and shuts the door after them. Then, tense and nervous:*) You want to speak to me?

KROGSTAD: Yes, I want to.

NORA: Today? But it's not yet the first of the month —

KROGSTAD: No, it's Christmas Eve. It's going to be up to you how merry a Christmas you have.

NORA: What is it you want? Today I absolutely can't —

KROGSTAD: We won't talk about that till later. This is something else. You do have a moment to spare, I suppose?

NORA: Oh yes, of course — I do, except —

KROGSTAD: Good. I was sitting over at Olsen's Restaurant when I saw your husband go down the street —

NORA: Yes?

KROGSTAD: With a lady.

NORA: Yes. So?

KROGSTAD: If you'll pardon my asking: Wasn't that lady a Mrs. Linde?

NORA: Yes.

KROGSTAD: Just now come into town?

NORA: Yes, today.

KROGSTAD: She's a good friend of yours?

NORA: Yes, she is. But I don't see —

KROGSTAD: I also knew her once.

NORA: I'm aware of that.

KROGSTAD: Oh? You know all about it. I thought so. Well, then let me ask you short and sweet: Is Mrs. Linde getting a job in the bank?

NORA: What makes you think you can cross-examine me, Mr. Krogstad — you, one of my husband's employees? But since you ask, you might as well know — yes, Mrs. Linde's going to be taken on at the bank. And I'm the one who spoke for her, Mr. Krogstad. Now you know.

KROGSTAD: So I guessed right.

NORA (*pacing up and down*): Oh, one does have a tiny bit of influence, I should hope. Just because I am a woman, don't think it means that — When one has a subordinate position, Mr. Krogstad, one really ought to be careful about pushing somebody who — hm —

KROGSTAD: Who has influence?

NORA: That's right.

KROGSTAD (*in a different tone*): Mrs. Helmer, would you be good enough to use your influence on my behalf?

NORA: What? What do you mean?

KROGSTAD: Would you please make sure that I keep my subordinate position in the bank?

NORA: What does that mean? Who's thinking of taking away your position?

KROGSTAD: Oh, don't play the innocent with me. I'm quite aware that your friend would hardly relish the chance of running into me again; and I'm also aware now whom I can thank for being turned out.

NORA: But I promise you—

KROGSTAD: Yes, yes, yes, to the point: There's still time, and I'm advising you to use your influence to prevent it.

NORA: But Mr. Krogstad, I have absolutely no influence.

KROGSTAD: You haven't? I thought you were just saying—

NORA: You shouldn't take me so literally. I! How can you believe that I have any such influence over my husband?

KROGSTAD: Oh, I've known your husband from our student days. I don't think the great bank manager's more steadfast than any other married man.

NORA: You speak insolently about my husband, and I'll show you the door.

KROGSTAD: The lady has spirit.

NORA: I'm not afraid of you any longer. After New Year's, I'll soon be done with the whole business.

KROGSTAD (restraining himself): Now listen to me, Mrs. Helmer. If necessary, I'll fight for my little job in the bank as if it were life itself.

NORA: Yes, so it seems.

KROGSTAD: It's not just a matter of income; that's the least of it. It's something else—All right, out with it! Look, this is the thing. You know, just like all the others, of course, that once, a good many years ago, I did something rather rash.

NORA: I've heard rumors to that effect.

KROGSTAD: The case never got into court; but all the same, every door was closed in my face from then on. So I took up those various activities you know about. I had to grab hold somewhere; and I dare say I haven't been among the worst. But now I want to drop all that. My boys are growing up. For their sakes, I'll have to win back as much respect as possible here in town. That job in the bank was like the first rung in my ladder. And now your husband wants to kick me right back down in the mud again.

NORA: But for heaven's sake, Mr. Krogstad, it's simply not in my power to help you.

KROGSTAD: That's because you haven't the will to—but I have the means to make you.

NORA: You certainly won't tell my husband that I owe you money?

KROGSTAD: Hm—what if I told him that?

NORA: That would be shameful of you. (Nearly in tears.) This secret—my joy and my pride—that he should learn it in such a crude and disgusting way—learn it from you. You'd expose me to the most horrible unpleasantness—

KROGSTAD: Only unpleasantness?

NORA (vehemently): But go on and try. It'll turn out the worse for you, because then my husband will really see what a crook you are, and then you'll never be able to hold your job.

KROGSTAD: I asked if it was just domestic unpleasantness you were afraid of?

NORA: If my husband finds out, then of course he'll pay what I owe at once, and then we'd be through with you for good.

KROGSTAD (*a step closer*): Listen, Mrs. Helmer—you've either got a very bad memory, or else no head at all for business. I'd better put you a little more in touch with the facts.

NORA: What do you mean?

KROGSTAD: When your husband was sick, you came to me for a loan of four thousand, eight hundred crowns.

NORA: Where else could I go?

KROGSTAD: I promised to get you that sum—

NORA: And you got it.

KROGSTAD: I promised to get you that sum, on certain conditions. You were so involved in your husband's illness, and so eager to finance your trip, that I guess you didn't think out all the details. It might just be a good idea to remind you. I promised you the money on the strength of a note I drew up.

NORA: Yes, and that I signed.

KROGSTAD: Right. But at the bottom I added some lines for your father to guarantee the loan. He was supposed to sign down there.

NORA: Supposed to? He did sign.

KROGSTAD: I left the date blank. In other words, your father would have dated his signature himself. Do you remember that?

NORA: Yes, I think—

KROGSTAD: Then I gave you the note for you to mail to your father. Isn't that so?

NORA: Yes.

KROGSTAD: And naturally you sent it at once—because only some five, six days later you brought me the note, properly signed. And with that, the money was yours.

NORA: Well, then; I've made my payments regularly, haven't I?

KROGSTAD: More or less. But—getting back to the point—those were hard times for you then, Mrs. Helmer.

NORA: Yes, they were.

KROGSTAD: Your father was very ill, I believe.

NORA: He was near the end.

KROGSTAD: He died soon after?

NORA: Yes.

KROGSTAD: Tell me, Mrs. Helmer, do you happen to recall the date of your father's death? The day of the month, I mean.

NORA: Papa died the twenty-ninth of September.

KROGSTAD: That's quite correct; I've already looked into that. And now we come to a curious thing—(*taking out a paper*) which I simply cannot comprehend.

NORA: Curious thing? I don't know—

KROGSTAD: This is the curious thing: that your father co-signed the note for your loan three days after his death.

NORA: How — ? I don't understand.

KROGSTAD: Your father died the twenty-ninth of September. But look. Here your father dated his signature October second. Isn't that curious, Mrs. Helmer? (*Nora is silent.*) Can you explain it to me? (*Nora remains silent.*) It's also remarkable that the words "October second" and the year aren't written in your father's hand, but rather in one that I think I know. Well, it's easy to understand. Your father forgot perhaps to date his signature, and then someone or other added it, a bit sloppily, before anyone knew of his death. There's nothing wrong in that. It all comes down to the signature. And there's no question about *that,* Mrs. Helmer. It really *was* your father who signed his own name here, wasn't it?

NORA (*after a short silence, throwing her head back and looking squarely at him*): No, it wasn't. *I* signed Papa's name.

KROGSTAD: Wait, now — are you fully aware that this is a dangerous confession?

NORA: Why? You'll soon get your money.

KROGSTAD: Let me ask you a question — why didn't you send the paper to your father?

NORA: That was impossible. Papa was so sick. If I'd asked him for his signature, I also would have had to tell him what the money was for. But I couldn't tell him, sick as he was, that my husband's life was in danger. That was just impossible.

KROGSTAD: Then it would have been better if you'd given up the trip abroad.

NORA: I couldn't possibly. The trip was to save my husband's life. I couldn't give that up.

KROGSTAD: But didn't you ever consider that this was a fraud against me?

NORA: I couldn't let myself be bothered by that. You weren't any concern of mine. I couldn't stand you, with all those cold complications you made, even though you knew how badly off my husband was.

KROGSTAD: Mrs. Helmer, obviously you haven't the vaguest idea of what you've involved yourself in. But I can tell you this: It was nothing more and nothing worse that I once did — and it wrecked my whole reputation.

NORA: You? Do you expect me to believe that you ever acted bravely to save your wife's life?

KROGSTAD: Laws don't inquire into motives.

NORA: Then they must be very poor laws.

KROGSTAD: Poor or not — if I introduce this paper in court, you'll be judged according to law.

NORA: This I refuse to believe. A daughter hasn't a right to protect her dying father from anxiety and care? A wife hasn't a right to save her husband's life? I don't know much about laws, but I'm sure that somewhere in the books these things are allowed. And you don't know anything about it — you who practice the law? You must be an awful lawyer, Mr. Krogstad.

KROGSTAD: Could be. But business — the kind of business we two are mixed up in — don't you think I know about that? All right. Do what you want now. But I'm telling you *this:* If I get shoved down a second time, you're going to keep me company. (*He bows and goes out through the hall.*)

NORA (*pensive for a moment, then tossing her head*): Oh, really! Trying to frighten me! I'm not so silly as all that. (*Begins gathering up the children's clothes, but soon stops.*) But—? No, but that's impossible! I did it out of love.

THE CHILDREN (*in the doorway, left*): Mama, that strange man's gone out the door.

NORA: Yes, yes, I know it. But don't tell anyone about the strange man. Do you hear? Not even Papa!

THE CHILDREN: No, Mama. But now will you play again?

NORA: No, not now.

THE CHILDREN: Oh, but Mama, you promised.

NORA: Yes, but I can't now. Go inside; I have too much to do. Go in, go in, my sweet darlings. (*She herds them gently back in the room and shuts the door after them. Settling on the sofa, she takes up a piece of embroidery and makes some stitches, but soon stops abruptly.*) No! (*Throws the work aside, rises, goes to the hall door and calls out.*) Helene! Let me have the tree in here. (*Goes to the table, left, opens the table drawer, and stops again.*) No, but that's utterly impossible!

MAID (*with the Christmas tree*): Where should I put it, ma'am?

NORA: There. The middle of the floor.

MAID: Should I bring anything else?

NORA: No, thanks. I have what I need.

(*The Maid, who has set the tree down, goes out.*)

NORA (*absorbed in trimming the tree*): Candles here—and flowers here. That terrible creature! Talk, talk, talk! There's nothing to it at all. The tree's going to be lovely. I'll do anything to please you Torvald. I'll sing for you, dance for you—

(*Helmer comes in from the hall, with a sheaf of papers under his arm.*)

NORA: Oh! You're back so soon?

HELMER: Yes. Has anyone been here?

NORA: Here? No.

HELMER: That's odd. I saw Krogstad leaving the front door.

NORA: So? Oh yes, that's true. Krogstad was here a moment.

HELMER: Nora, I can see by your face that he's been here, begging you to put in a good word for him.

NORA: Yes.

HELMER: And it was supposed to seem like your own idea? You were to hide it from me that he'd been here. He asked you that, too, didn't he?

NORA: Yes, Torvald, but—

HELMER: Nora, Nora, and you could fall for that? Talk with that sort of person and promise him anything? And then in the bargain, tell me an untruth.

NORA: An untruth—?

HELMER: Didn't you say that no one had been here? (*Wagging his finger.*) My little songbird must never do that again. A songbird needs a clean beak to warble with. No false notes. (*Putting his arm about her waist.*) That's the way it should be, isn't it? Yes, I'm sure of it. (*Releasing her.*) And so, enough of that. (*Sitting by the stove.*) Ah, how snug and cozy it is here. (*Leafing among his papers.*)

NORA (*busy with the tree, after a short pause*): Torvald!

HELMER: Yes.

NORA: I'm so much looking forward to the Stenborgs' costume party, day after tomorrow.

HELMER: And I can't wait to see what you'll surprise me with.

NORA: Oh, that stupid business!

HELMER: What?

NORA: I can't find anything that's right. Everything seems so ridiculous, so inane.

HELMER: So my little Nora's come to *that* recognition?

NORA (*going behind his chair, her arms resting on its back*): Are you very busy, Torvald?

HELMER: Oh—

NORA: What papers are those?

HELMER: Bank matters.

NORA: Already?

HELMER: I've gotten full authority from the retiring management to make all necessary changes in personnel and procedure. I'll need Christmas week for that. I want to have everything in order by New Year's.

NORA: So that was the reason this poor Krogstad—

HELMER: Hm.

NORA (*still leaning on the chair and slowly stroking the nape of his neck*): If you weren't so very busy, I would have asked you an enormous favor, Torvald.

HELMER: Let's hear. What is it?

NORA: You know, there isn't anyone who has your good taste—and I want so much to look well at the costume party. Torvald, couldn't you take over and decide what I should be and plan my costume?

HELMER: Ah, is my stubborn little creature calling for a lifeguard?

NORA: Yes, Torvald, I can't get anywhere without your help.

HELMER: All right—I'll think it over. We'll hit on something.

NORA: Oh, how sweet of you. (*Goes to the tree again. Pause.*) Aren't the red flowers pretty—? But tell me, was it really such a crime that this Krogstad committed?

HELMER: Forgery. Do you have any idea what that means?

NORA: Couldn't he have done it out of need?

HELMER: Yes, or thoughtlessness, like so many others. I'm not so heartless that I'd condemn a man categorically for just one mistake.

NORA: No, of course not, Torvald!

HELMER: Plenty of men have redeemed themselves by openly confessing their crimes and taking their punishment.

NORA: Punishment — ?

HELMER: But now Krogstad didn't go that way. He got himself out by sharp practices, and that's the real cause of his moral breakdown.

NORA: Do you really think that would — ?

HELMER: Just imagine how a man with that sort of guilt in him has to lie and cheat and deceive on all sides, has to wear a mask even with the nearest and dearest he has, even with his own wife and children. And with the children, Nora — that's where it's most horrible.

NORA: Why?

HELMER: Because that kind of atmosphere of lies infects the whole life of a home. Every breath the children take in is filled with the germs of something degenerate.

NORA (*coming closer behind him*): Are you sure of that?

HELMER: Oh, I've seen it often enough as a lawyer. Almost everyone who goes bad early in life has a mother who's a chronic liar.

NORA: Why just — the mother?

HELMER: It's usually the mother's influence that's dominant, but the father's works in the same way, of course. Every lawyer is quite familiar with it. And still this Krogstad's been going home year in, year out, poisoning his own children with lies and pretense; that's why I call him morally lost. (*Reaching his hands out toward her.*) So my sweet little Nora must promise me never to plead his cause. Your hand on it. Come, come, what's this? Give me your hand. There, now. All settled. I can tell you it'd be impossible for me to work alongside of him. I literally feel physically revolted when I'm anywhere near such a person.

NORA (*withdraws her hand and goes to the other side of the Christmas tree*): How hot it is here! And I've got so much to do.

HELMER (*getting up and gathering his papers*): Yes, and I have to think about getting some of these read through before dinner. I'll think about your costume, too. And something to hang on the tree in gilt paper, I may even see about that. (*Putting his hand on her head.*) Oh you, my darling little songbird. (*He goes into his study and closes the door after him.*)

NORA (*softly, after a silence*): Oh, really! It isn't so. It's impossible. It must be impossible.

ANNE-MARIE (*in the doorway left*): The children are begging so hard to come in to Mama.

NORA: No, no, no, don't let them in to me! You stay with them, Anne-Marie.

ANNE-MARIE: Of course, ma'am. (*Closes the door.*)

NORA (*pale with terror*): Hurt my children — ! Poison my home? (*A moment's pause; then she tosses her head.*) That's not true. Never. Never in all the world.

ACT II

(*Same room. Beside the piano the Christmas tree now stands stripped of ornament, burned-down candle stubs on its ragged branches. Nora's street clothes lie on the sofa. Nora, alone in the room, moves restlessly about; at last she stops at the sofa and picks up her coat.*)

NORA (*dropping the coat again*): Someone's coming! (*Goes toward the door, listens.*) No — there's no one. Of course — nobody's coming today, Christmas Day — or tomorrow, either. But maybe — (*Opens the door and looks out.*) No, nothing in the mailbox. Quite empty. (*Coming forward.*) What nonsense! He won't do anything serious. Nothing terrible could happen. It's impossible. Why, I have three small children.

(*Anne-Marie, with a large carton, comes in from the room to the left.*)

ANNE-MARIE: Well, at last I found the box with the masquerade clothes.

NORA: Thanks. Put it on the table.

ANNE-MARIE (*does so*): But they're all pretty much of a mess.

NORA: Ahh! I'd love to rip them in a million pieces!

ANNE-MARIE: Oh, mercy, they can be fixed right up. Just a little patience.

NORA: Yes, I'll go get Mrs. Linde to help me.

ANNE-MARIE: Out again now? In this nasty weather? Miss Nora will catch cold — get sick.

NORA: Oh, worse things could happen — How are the children?

ANNE-MARIE: The poor mites are playing with their Christmas presents, but —

NORA: Do they ask for me much?

ANNE-MARIE: They're so used to having Mama around, you know.

NORA: Yes, but Anne-Marie, I *can't* be together with them as much as I was.

ANNE-MARIE: Well, small children get used to anything.

NORA: You think so? Do you think they'd forget their mother if she was gone for good?

ANNE-MARIE: Oh, mercy — gone for good!

NORA: Wait, tell me. Anne-Marie — I've wondered so often — how could you ever have the heart to give your child over to strangers?

ANNE-MARIE: But I had to, you know, to become little Nora's nurse.

NORA: Yes, but how could you *do* it?

ANNE-MARIE: When I could get such a good place? A girl who's poor and who's gotten in trouble is glad enough for that. Because that slippery fish, he didn't do a thing for me, you know.

NORA: But your daughter's surely forgotten you.

ANNE-MARIE: Oh, she certainly has not. She's written to me, both when she was confirmed and when she was married.

NORA (*clasping her about the neck*): You old Anne-Marie, you were a good mother for me when I was little.

ANNE-MARIE: Poor little Nora, with no other mother but me.

NORA: And if the babies didn't have one, then I know that you'd — What silly talk! (*Opening the carton.*) Go in to them. Now I'll have to — Tomorrow you can see how lovely I'll look.

ANNE-MARIE: Oh, there won't be anyone at the party as lovely as Miss Nora. (*She goes off into the room, left.*)

NORA (*begins unpacking the box, but soon throws it aside*): Oh, if I dared to go out. If only nobody would come. If only nothing would happen here while I'm out. What craziness — nobody's coming. Just don't think. This muff — needs a brushing. Beautiful gloves, beautiful gloves. Let it go. Let it go! One, two, three, four, five, six — (*With a cry.*) Oh, there they are! (*Poises to move toward the door, but remains irresolutely standing. Mrs. Linde enters from the hall, where she has removed her street clothes.*)

NORA: Oh, it's you, Kristine. There's no one else out there? How good that you've come.

MRS. LINDE: I hear you were up asking for me.

NORA: Yes, I just stopped by. There's something you really can help me with. Let's get settled on the sofa. Look, there's going to be a costume party tomorrow evening at the Stenborgs' right above us, and now Torvald wants me to go as a Neapolitan peasant girl and dance the tarantella° that I learned in Capri.

MRS. LINDE: Really, are you giving a whole performance?

NORA: Torvald says yes, I should. See, here's the dress. Torvald had it made for me down there; but now it's all so tattered that I just don't know —

MRS. LINDE: Oh, we'll fix that up in no time. It's nothing more than the trimmings — they're a bit loose here and there. Needle and thread? Good, now we have what we need.

NORA: Oh, how sweet of you!

MRS. LINDE (*sewing*): So you'll be in disguise tomorrow, Nora. You know what? I'll stop by then for a moment and have a look at you all dressed up. But listen, I've absolutely forgotten to thank you for that pleasant evening yesterday.

NORA (*getting up and walking about*): I don't think it was as pleasant as usual yesterday. You should have come to town a bit sooner, Kristine — Yes, Torvald really knows how to give a home elegance and charm.

MRS. LINDE: And you do, too, if you ask me. You're not your father's daughter for nothing. But tell me, is Dr. Rank always so down in the mouth as yesterday?

NORA: No, that was quite an exception. But he goes around critically ill all the time — tuberculosis of the spine, poor man. You know, his father was a disgusting thing who kept mistresses and so on — and that's why the son's been sickly from birth.

MRS. LINDE (*lets her sewing fall to her lap*): But my dearest Nora, how do you know about such things?

---

tarantella: A rapid whirling dance long popular in southern Italy.

NORA (*walking more jauntily*): Hmp! When you've had three children, then you've had a few visits from—from women who know something of medicine, and they tell you this and that.

MRS. LINDE (*resumes sewing; a short pause*): Does Dr. Rank come here every day?

NORA: Every blessed day. He's Torvald's best friend from childhood, and *my* good friend, too. Dr. Rank almost belongs to this house.

MRS. LINDE: But tell me—is he quite sincere? I mean, doesn't he rather enjoy flattering people?

NORA: Just the opposite. Why do you think that?

MRS. LINDE: When you introduced us yesterday, he was proclaiming that he'd often heard my name in this house; but later I noticed that your husband hadn't the slightest idea who I really was. So how could Dr. Rank—?

NORA: But it's all true, Kristine. You see, Torvald loves me beyond words, and, as he puts it, he'd like to keep me all to himself. For a long time he'd almost be jealous if I even mentioned any of my old friends back home. So of course I dropped that. But with Dr. Rank I talk a lot about such things because he likes hearing about them.

MRS. LINDE: Now listen, Nora; in many ways you're still like a child. I'm a good deal older than you, with a little more experience. I'll tell you something: You ought to put an end to all this with Dr. Rank.

NORA: What should I put an end to?

MRS. LINDE: Both parts of it, I think. Yesterday you said something about a rich admirer who'd provide you with money—

NORA: Yes, one who doesn't exist—worse luck. So?

MRS. LINDE: Is Dr. Rank well off?

NORA: Yes, he is.

MRS. LINDE: With no dependents?

NORA: No, no one. But—

MRS. LINDE: And he's over here every day?

NORA: Yes, I told you that.

MRS. LINDE: How can a man of such refinement be so grasping?

NORA: I don't follow you at all.

MRS. LINDE: Now don't try to hide it, Nora. You think I can't guess who loaned you the forty-eight hundred crowns?

NORA: Are you out of your mind? How could you think such a thing! A friend of ours, who comes here every single day. What an intolerable situation that would have been!

MRS. LINDE: Then it really wasn't him.

NORA: No, absolutely not. It never even crossed my mind for a moment— And he had nothing to lend in those days; his inheritance came later.

MRS. LINDE: Well, I think that was a stroke of luck for you, Nora dear.

NORA: No, it never would have occurred to me to ask Dr. Rank—Still, I'm quite sure that if I had asked him—

MRS. LINDE: Which you won't, of course.

NORA: No, of course not. I can't see that I'd ever need to. But I'm quite positive that if I talked to Dr. Rank—

MRS. LINDE: Behind your husband's back?

NORA: I've got to clear up this other thing; *that's* also behind his back. I've *got* to clear it all up.

MRS. LINDE: Yes, I was saying that yesterday, but—

NORA (*pacing up and down*): A man handles these problems so much better than a woman—

MRS. LINDE: One's husband does, yes.

NORA: Nonsense. (*Stopping.*) When you pay everything you owe, then you get your note back, right?

MRS. LINDE: Yes, naturally.

NORA: And can rip it into a million pieces and burn it up—that filthy scrap of paper!

MRS. LINDE (*looking hard at her, laying her sewing aside, and rising slowly*): Nora, you're hiding something from me.

NORA: You can see it in my face?

MRS. LINDE: Something's happened to you since yesterday morning. Nora, what is it?

NORA (*hurrying toward her*): Kristine! (*Listening.*) Shh! Torvald's home. Look, go in with the children a while. Torvald can't bear all this snipping and stitching. Let Anne-Marie help you.

MRS. LINDE (*gathering up some of the things*): All right, but I'm not leaving here until we've talked this out. (*She disappears into the room, left, as Torvald enters from the hall.*)

NORA: Oh, how I've been waiting for you, Torvald dear.

HELMER: Was that the dressmaker?

NORA: No, that was Kristine. She's helping me fix up my costume. You know, it's going to be quite attractive.

HELMER: Yes, wasn't that a bright idea I had?

NORA: Brilliant! But then wasn't I good as well to give in to you?

HELMER: Good—because you give in to your husband's judgment? All right, you little goose, I know you didn't mean it like that. But I won't disturb you. You'll want to have a fitting, I suppose.

NORA: And you'll be working?

HELMER: Yes. (*Indicating a bundle of papers.*) See. I've been down to the bank. (*Starts toward his study.*)

NORA: Torvald.

HELMER (*stops*): Yes.

NORA: If your little squirrel begged you, with all her heart and soul, for something—?

HELMER: What's that?

NORA: Then would you do it?

HELMER: First, naturally, I'd have to know what it was.

NORA: Your squirrel would scamper about and do tricks, if you'd only be sweet and give in.

HELMER: Out with it.

NORA: Your lark would be singing high and low in every room—

HELMER: Come on, she does that anyway.

NORA: I'd be a wood nymph and dance for you in the moonlight.

HELMER: Nora—don't tell me it's that same business from this morning?

NORA (*coming closer*): Yes, Torvald, I beg you, please!

HELMER: And you actually have the nerve to drag that up again?

NORA: Yes, yes, you've got to give in to me; you *have* to let Krogstad keep his job in the bank.

HELMER: My dear Nora, I've slated his job for Mrs. Linde.

NORA: That's awfully kind of you. But you could just fire another clerk instead of Krogstad.

HELMER: This is the most incredible stubbornness! Because you go and give an impulsive promise to speak up for him, I'm expected to—

NORA: That's not the reason, Torvald. It's for your own sake. That man does writing for the worst papers; you said it yourself. He could do you any amount of harm. I'm scared to death of him—

HELMER: Ah, I understand. It's the old memories haunting you.

NORA: What do you mean by that?

HELMER: Of course, you're thinking about your father.

NORA: Yes, all right. Just remember how those nasty gossips wrote in the papers about Papa and slandered him so cruelly. I think they'd have had him dismissed if the department hadn't sent you up to investigate, and if you hadn't been so kind and open-minded toward him.

HELMER: My dear Nora, there's a notable difference between your father and me. Your father's official career was hardly above reproach. But mine is; and I hope it'll stay that way as long as I hold my position.

NORA: Oh, who can ever tell what vicious minds can invent? We could be so snug and happy now in our quiet, carefree home—you and I and the children, Torvald! That's why I'm pleading with you so—

HELMER: And just by pleading for him you make it impossible for me to keep him on. It's already known at the bank that I'm firing Krogstad. What if it's rumored around now that the new bank manager was vetoed by his wife—

NORA: Yes, what then—?

HELMER: Oh yes—as long as our little bundle of stubbornness gets her way—! I should go and make myself ridiculous in front of the whole office—give people the idea I can be swayed by all kinds of outside pressure. Oh, you can bet I'd feel the effects of that soon enough! Besides—there's something that rules Krogstad right out at the bank as long as I'm the manager.

NORA: What's that?

HELMER: His moral failings I could maybe overlook if I had to—

NORA: Yes, Torvald, why not?

HELMER: And I hear he's quite efficient on the job. But he was a crony of mine back in my teens — one of those rash friendships that crop up again and again to embarrass you later in life. Well, I might as well say it straight out: We're on a first-name basis. And that tactless fool makes no effort at all to hide it in front of others. Quite the contrary — he thinks that entitles him to take a familiar air around me, and so every other second he comes booming out with his, "Yes, Torvald!" and "Sure thing, Torvald!" I tell you, it's been excruciating for me. He's out to make my place in the bank unbearable.

NORA: Torvald, you can't be serious about all this.

HELMER: Oh no? Why not?

NORA: Because these are such petty considerations.

HELMER: What are you saying? Petty? You think I'm petty!

NORA: No, just the opposite, Torvald dear. That's exactly why —

HELMER: Never mind. You call my motives petty; then I might as well be just that. Petty! All right! We'll put a stop to this for good. (*Goes to the hall door and calls.*) Helene!

NORA: What do you want?

HELMER (*searching among his papers*): A decision. (*The Maid comes in.*) Look here; take this letter; go out with it at once. Get hold of a messenger and have him deliver it. Quick now. It's already addressed. Wait, here's some money.

MAID: Yes, sir. (*She leaves with the letter.*)

HELMER (*straightening his papers*): There, now, little Miss Willful.

NORA (*breathlessly*): Torvald, what was that letter?

HELMER: Krogstad's notice.

NORA: Call it back, Torvald! There's still time. Oh, Torvald, call it back! Do it for my sake — for your sake, for the children's sake! Do you hear, Torvald; do it! You don't know how this can harm us.

HELMER: Too late.

NORA: Yes, too late.

HELMER: Nora, dear, I can forgive you this panic, even though basically you're insulting me. Yes, you are! Or isn't it an insult to think that *I* should be afraid of a courtroom hack's revenge? But I forgive you anyway, because this shows so beautifully how much you love me. (*Takes her in his arms.*) This is the way it should be, my darling Nora. Whatever comes, you'll see: When it really counts, I have strength and courage enough as a man to take on the whole weight myself.

NORA (*terrified*): What do you mean by that?

HELMER: The whole weight, I said.

NORA (*resolutely*): No, never in all the world.

HELMER: Good. So we'll share it, Nora, as man and wife. That's as it should be. (*Fondling her.*) Are you happy now? There, there, there — not these frightened dove's eyes. It's nothing at all but empty fantasies — Now you should run through your tarantella and practice your tambourine. I'll go to the inner office, and shut both doors, so I won't hear a thing; you can make all the noise you like. (*Turning in the doorway.*) And when Rank comes, just tell him where he can find me. (*He nods to her and goes with his papers into the study, closing the door.*)

NORA (*standing as though rooted, dazed with fright, in a whisper*): He really could do it. He will do it. He'll do it in spite of everything. No, not that, never, never! Anything but that! Escape! A way out — (*The doorbell rings.*) Dr. Rank! Anything but that! *Anything*, whatever it is! (*Her hands pass over her face, smoothing it; she pulls herself together, goes over and opens the hall door. Dr. Rank stands outside, hanging his fur coat up. During the following scene, it begins getting dark.*)

NORA: Hello, Dr. Rank. I recognized your ring. But you mustn't go in to Torvald yet; I believe he's working.

RANK: And you?

NORA: For you, I always have an hour to spare — you know that. (*He has entered, and she shuts the door after him.*)

RANK: Many thanks. I'll make use of these hours while I can.

NORA: What do you mean by that? While you can?

RANK: Does that disturb you?

NORA: Well, it's such an odd phrase. Is anything going to happen?

RANK: What's going to happen is what I've been expecting so long — but I honestly didn't think it would come so soon.

NORA (*gripping his arm*): What is it you've found out? Dr. Rank, you have to tell me!

RANK (*sitting by the stove*): It's all over with me. There's nothing to be done about it.

NORA (*breathing easier*): Is it you — then — ?

RANK: Who else? There's no point in lying to one's self. I'm the most miserable of all my patients, Mrs. Helmer. These past few days I've been auditing my internal accounts. Bankrupt! Within a month I'll probably be laid out and rotting in the churchyard.

NORA: Oh, what a horrible thing to say.

RANK: The thing itself is horrible. But the worst of it is all the other horror before it's over. There's only one final examination left; when I'm finished with that, I'll know about when my disintegration will begin. There's something I want to say. Helmer with his sensitivity has such a sharp distaste for anything ugly. I don't want him near my sickroom.

NORA: Oh, but Dr. Rank —

RANK: I won't have him in there. Under no condition. I'll lock my door to him — As soon as I'm completely sure of the worst, I'll send you my calling card marked with a black cross, and you'll know then the wreck has started to come apart.

NORA: No, today you're completely unreasonable. And I wanted you so much to be in a really good humor.

RANK: With death up my sleeve? And then to suffer this way for somebody else's sins. Is there any justice in that? And in every single family, in some way or another, this inevitable retribution of nature goes on —

NORA (*her hands pressed over her ears*): Oh, stuff! Cheer up! Please — be gay!

RANK: Yes, I'd just as soon laugh at it all. My poor, innocent spine, serving time for my father's gay army days.

NORA (*by the table, left*): He was so infatuated with asparagus tips and pâté de foie gras,° wasn't that it?

RANK: Yes — and with truffles.

NORA: Truffles, yes. And then with oysters, I suppose?

RANK: Yes, tons of oysters, naturally.

NORA: And then the port and champagne to go with it. It's so sad that all these delectable things have to strike at our bones.

RANK: Especially when they strike at the unhappy bones that never shared in the fun.

NORA: Ah, that's the saddest of all.

RANK (*looks searchingly at her*): Hm.

NORA (*after a moment*): Why did you smile?

RANK: No, it was you who laughed.

NORA: No, it was you who smiled, Dr. Rank!

RANK (*getting up*): You're even a bigger tease than I'd thought.

NORA: I'm full of wild ideas today.

RANK: That's obvious.

NORA (*putting both hands on his shoulders*): Dear, dear Dr. Rank, you'll never die for Torvald and me.

RANK: Oh, that loss you'll easily get over. Those who go away are soon forgotten.

NORA (*looks fearfully at him*): You believe that?

RANK: One makes new connections, and then —

NORA: Who makes new connections?

RANK: Both you and Torvald will when I'm gone. I'd say you're well under way already. What was that Mrs. Linde doing here last evening?

NORA: Oh, come — you can't be jealous of poor Kristine?

RANK: Oh yes, I am. She'll be my successor here in the house. When I'm down under, that woman will probably —

NORA: Shh! Not so loud. She's right in there.

RANK: Today as well. So you see.

NORA: Only to sew on my dress. Good gracious, how unreasonable you are. (*Sitting on the sofa.*) Be nice now, Dr. Rank. Tomorrow you'll see how beautifully I'll dance; and you can imagine then that I'm dancing only for you — yes, and of course for Torvald, too — that's understood. (*Takes various items out of the carton.*) Dr. Rank, sit over here and I'll show you something.

---

pâté de foie gras: Pâté of goose liver.

RANK (*sitting*): What's that?

NORA: Look here. Look.

RANK: Silk stockings.

NORA: Flesh-colored. Aren't they lovely? Now it's so dark here, but tomorrow — No, no, no, just look at the feet. Oh well, you might as well look at the rest.

RANK: Hm —

NORA: Why do you look so critical? Don't you believe they'll fit?

RANK: I've never had any chance to form an opinion on that.

NORA (*glancing at him a moment*): Shame on you. (*Hits him lightly on the ear with the stockings.*) That's for you. (*Puts them away again.*)

RANK: And what other splendors am I going to see now?

NORA: Not the least bit more, because you've been naughty. (*She hunts a little and rummages among her things.*)

RANK (*after a short silence*): When I sit here together with you like this, completely easy and open, then I don't know — I simply can't imagine — whatever would have become of me if I'd never come into this house.

NORA (*smiling*): Yes, I really think you feel completely at ease with us.

RANK (*more quietly, staring straight ahead*): And then to have to go away from it all —

NORA: Nonsense, you're not going away.

RANK (*his voice unchanged*): — and not even be able to leave some poor show of gratitude behind, scarcely a fleeting regret — no more than a vacant place that anyone can fill.

NORA: And if I asked you now for — No —

RANK: For what?

NORA: For a great proof of your friendship —

RANK: Yes, yes?

NORA: No, I mean — for an exceptionally big favor —

RANK: Would you really, for once, make me so happy?

NORA: Oh, you haven't the vaguest idea what it is.

RANK: All right, then tell me.

NORA: No, but I can't, Dr. Rank — it's all out of reason. It's advice and help, too — and a favor —

RANK: So much the better. I can't fathom what you're hinting at. Just speak out. Don't you trust me?

NORA: Of course. More than anyone else. You're my best and truest friend, I'm sure. That's why I want to talk to you. All right, then, Dr. Rank: There's something you can help me prevent. You know how deeply, how inexpressibly dearly Torvald loves me; he'd never hesitate a second to give up his life for me.

RANK (*leaning close to her*): Nora — do you think he's the only one —

NORA (*with a slight start*): Who — ?

RANK: Who'd gladly give up his life for you.

NORA (*heavily*): I see.

RANK: I swore to myself you should know this before I'm gone. I'll never find a better chance. Yes, Nora, now you know. And also you know now that you can trust me beyond anyone else.

NORA (*rising, natural and calm*): Let me by.

RANK (*making room for her, but still sitting*): Nora —

NORA (*in the hall doorway*): Helene, bring the lamp in. (*Goes over to the stove.*) Ah, dear Dr. Rank, that was really mean of you.

RANK (*getting up*): That I've loved you just as deeply as somebody else? Was *that* mean?

NORA: No, but that you came out and told me. That was quite unnecessary —

RANK: What do you mean? Have you known — ?

(*The Maid comes in with the lamp, sets it on the table, and goes out again.*)

RANK: Nora — Mrs. Helmer — I'm asking you: Have you known about it?

NORA: Oh, how can I tell what I know or don't know? Really, I don't know what to say — Why did you have to be so clumsy, Dr. Rank! Everything was so good.

RANK: Well, in any case, you now have the knowledge that my body and soul are at your command. So won't you speak out?

NORA (*looking at him*): After that?

RANK: Please, just let me know what it is.

NORA: You can't know anything now.

RANK: I have to. You mustn't punish me like this. Give me the chance to do whatever is humanly possible for you.

NORA: Now there's nothing you can do for me. Besides, actually, I don't need any help. You'll see — it's only my fantasies. That's what it is. Of course! (*Sits in the rocker, looks at him, and smiles.*) What a nice one you are, Dr. Rank. Aren't you a little bit ashamed, now that the lamp is here?

RANK: No, not exactly. But perhaps I'd better go — for good?

NORA: No, you certainly can't do that. You must come here just as you always have. You know Torvald can't do without you.

RANK: Yes, but *you*?

NORA: You know how much I enjoy it when you're here.

RANK: That's precisely what threw me off. You're a mystery to me. So many times I've felt you'd almost rather be with me than with Helmer.

NORA: Yes — you see, there are some people that one loves most and other people that one would almost prefer being with.

RANK: Yes, there's something to that.

NORA: When I was back home, of course I loved Papa most. But I always thought it was so much fun when I could sneak down to the maids' quarters, because they never tried to improve me, and it was always so amusing, the way they talked to each other.

RANK: Aha, so it's their place that I've filled.

NORA (*jumping up and going to him*): Oh, dear, sweet Dr. Rank, that's not what I meant at all. But you can understand that with Torvald it's just the same as with Papa—

(*The Maid enters from the hall.*)

MAID: Ma'am—please! (*She whispers to Nora and hands her a calling card.*)

NORA (*glancing at the card*): Ah! (*Slips it into her pocket.*)

RANK: Anything wrong?

NORA: No, no, not at all. It's only some—it's my new dress—

RANK: Really? But—there's your dress.

NORA: Oh, that. But this is another one—I ordered it—Torvald mustn't know—

RANK: Ah, now we have the big secret.

NORA: That's right. Just go in with him—he's back in the inner study. Keep him there as long as—

RANK: Don't worry. He won't get away. (*Goes into the study.*)

NORA (*to the Maid*): And he's standing waiting in the kitchen?

MAID: Yes, he came up by the back stairs.

NORA: But didn't you tell him somebody was here?

MAID: Yes, but that didn't do any good.

NORA: He won't leave?

MAID: No, he won't go till he's talked with you, ma'am.

NORA: Let him come in, then—but quietly. Helene, don't breathe a word about this. It's a surprise for my husband.

MAID: Yes, yes, I understand— (*Goes out.*)

NORA: This horror—it's going to happen. No, no, no, it can't happen, it mustn't. (*She goes and bolts Helmer's door. The Maid opens the hall door for Krogstad and shuts it behind him. He is dressed for travel in a fur coat, boots, and a fur cap.*)

NORA (*going toward him*): Talk softly. My husband's home.

KROGSTAD: Well, good for him.

NORA: What do you want?

KROGSTAD: Some information.

NORA: Hurry up, then. What is it?

KROGSTAD: You know, of course, that I got my notice.

NORA: I couldn't prevent it, Mr. Krogstad. I fought for you to the bitter end, but nothing worked.

KROGSTAD: Does your husband's love for you run so thin? He knows everything I can expose you to, and all the same he dares to—

NORA: How can you imagine he knows anything about this?

KROGSTAD: Ah, no—I can't imagine it either, now. It's not at all like my fine Torvald Helmer to have so much guts—

NORA: Mr. Krogstad, I demand respect for my husband!

KROGSTAD: Why, of course—all due respect. But since the lady's keeping it so carefully hidden, may I presume to ask if you're also a bit better informed than yesterday about what you've actually done?

NORA: More than you ever could teach me.

KROGSTAD: Yes, I *am* such an awful lawyer.

NORA: What is it you want from me?

KROGSTAD: Just a glimpse of how you are, Mrs. Helmer. I've been thinking about you all day long. A cashier, a night-court scribbler, a — well, a type like me also has a little of what they call a heart, you know.

NORA: Then show it. Think of my children.

KROGSTAD: Did you or your husband ever think of mine? But never mind. I simply wanted to tell you that you don't need to take this thing too seriously. For the present, I'm not proceeding with any action.

NORA: Oh no, really! Well — I knew that.

KROGSTAD: Everything can be settled in a friendly spirit. It doesn't have to get around town at all; it can stay just among us three.

NORA: My husband must never know anything of this.

KROGSTAD: How can you manage that? Perhaps you can pay me the balance?

NORA: No, not right now.

KROGSTAD: Or you know some way of raising the money in a day or two?

NORA: No way that I'm willing to use.

KROGSTAD: Well, it wouldn't have done you any good, anyway. If you stood in front of me with a fistful of bills, you still couldn't buy your signature back.

NORA: Then tell me what you're going to do with it.

KROGSTAD: I'll just hold onto it — keep it on file. There's no outsider who'll even get wind of it. So if you've been thinking of taking some desperate step —

NORA: I have.

KROGSTAD: Been thinking of running away from home —

NORA: I have!

KROGSTAD: Or even of something worse —

NORA: How could you guess that?

KROGSTAD: You can drop those thoughts.

NORA: How could you guess I was thinking of *that*?

KROGSTAD: Most of us think about *that* at first. I thought about it too, but I discovered I hadn't the courage —

NORA (*lifelessly*): I don't either.

KROGSTAD (*relieved*): That's true, you haven't the courage? You too?

NORA: I don't have it — I don't have it.

KROGSTAD: It would be terribly stupid, anyway. After that first storm at home blows out, why, then — I have here in my pocket a letter for your husband —

NORA: Telling everything?

KROGSTAD: As charitably as possible.

NORA (*quickly*): He mustn't ever get that letter. Tear it up. I'll find some way to get money.

KROGSTAD: Beg pardon, Mrs. Helmer, but I think I just told you —

NORA: Oh, I don't mean the money I owe you. Let me know how much you want from my husband, and I'll manage it.

KROGSTAD: I don't want any money from your husband.

NORA: What do you want, then?

KROGSTAD: I'll tell you what. I want to recoup, Mrs. Helmer; I want to get on in the world — and there's where your husband can help me. For a year and a half I've kept myself clean of anything disreputable — all that time struggling with the worst conditions; but I was satisfied, working my way up step by step. Now I've been written right off, and I'm just not in the mood to come crawling back. I tell you, I want to move on. I want to get back in the bank — in a better position. Your husband can set up a job for me —

NORA: He'll never do that!

KROGSTAD: He'll do it. I know him. He won't dare breathe a word of protest. And once I'm in there together with him, you just wait and see! Inside of a year, I'll be the manager's right-hand man. It'll be Nils Krogstad, not Torvald Helmer, who runs the bank.

NORA: You'll never see the day!

KROGSTAD: Maybe you think you can —

NORA: I have the courage now — for *that*.

KROGSTAD: Oh, you don't scare me. A smart, spoiled lady like you —

NORA: You'll see; you'll see!

KROGSTAD: Under the ice, maybe? Down in the freezing, coal-black water? There, till you float up in the spring, ugly unrecognizable, with your hair falling out —

NORA: You don't frighten me.

KROGSTAD: Nor do you frighten me. One doesn't do these things, Mrs. Helmer. Besides what good would it be? I'd still have him safe in my pocket.

NORA: Afterwards? When I'm no longer — ?

KROGSTAD: Are you forgetting that *I'll* be in control then over your final reputation? (*Nora stands speechless, staring at him.*) Good; now I've warned you. Don't do anything stupid. When Helmer's read my letter, I'll be waiting for his reply. And bear in mind that it's your husband himself who's forced me back to my old ways. I'll never forgive him for that. Good-bye, Mrs. Helmer. (*He goes out through the hall.*)

NORA (*goes to the hall door, opens it a crack, and listens*): He's gone. Didn't leave the letter. Oh no, no, that's impossible too! (*Opening the door more and more.*) What's that? He's standing outside — not going downstairs. He's thinking it over? Maybe he'll — ? (*A letter falls in the mailbox; then Krogstad's footsteps are heard, dying away down a flight of stairs. Nora gives a muffled cry and runs over toward the sofa table. A short pause.*) In the mailbox. (*Slips warily over to the hall door.*) It's lying there. Torvald, Torvald — now we're lost!

MRS. LINDE (*entering with the costume from the room, left*): There now, I can't see anything else to mend. Perhaps you'd like to try —

NORA (*in a hoarse whisper*): Kristine, come here.

MRS. LINDE (*tossing the dress on the sofa*): What's wrong? You look upset.

NORA: Come here. See that letter? There! Look—through the glass in the mailbox.

MRS. LINDE: Yes, yes, I see it.

NORA: That letter's from Krogstad—

MRS. LINDE: Nora—it's Krogstad who loaned you the money!

NORA: Yes, and now Torvald will find out everything.

MRS. LINDE: Believe me, Nora, it's best for both of you.

NORA: There's more you don't know. I forged a name.

MRS. LINDE: But for heaven's sake—?

NORA: I only want to tell you that, Kristine, so that you can be my witness.

MRS. LINDE: Witness? Why should I—?

NORA: If I should go out of my mind—it could easily happen—

MRS. LINDE: Nora!

NORA: Or anything else occurred—so I couldn't be present here—

MRS. LINDE: Nora, Nora, you aren't yourself at all!

NORA: And someone should try to take on the whole weight, all of the guilt, you follow me—

MRS. LINDE: Yes, of course, but why do you think—?

NORA: Then you're the witness that it isn't true, Kristine. I'm very much myself; my mind right now is perfectly clear; and I'm telling you: Nobody else has known about this; I alone did everything. Remember that.

MRS. LINDE: I will. But I don't understand all this.

NORA: Oh, how could you ever understand it? It's the miracle now that's going to take place.

MRS. LINDE: The miracle?

NORA: Yes, the miracle. But it's so awful, Kristine. It mustn't take place, not for anything in the world.

MRS. LINDE: I'm going right over and talk with Krogstad.

NORA: Don't go near him; he'll do you some terrible harm!

MRS. LINDE: There was a time once when he'd gladly have done anything for me.

NORA: He?

MRS. LINDE: Where does he live?

NORA: Oh, how do I know? Yes. (*Searches in her pocket.*) Here's his card. But the letter, the letter—!

HELMER (*from the study, knocking on the door*): Nora!

NORA (*with a cry of fear*): Oh! What is it? What do you want?

HELMER: Now, now, don't be so frightened. We're not coming in. You locked the door—are you trying on the dress?

NORA: Yes, I'm trying it. I'll look just beautiful, Torvald.

MRS. LINDE (*who has read the card*): He's living right around the corner.

NORA: Yes, but what's the use? We're lost. The letter's in the box.

MRS. LINDE: And your husband has the key?

NORA: Yes, always.

MRS. LINDE: Krogstad can ask for his letter back unread; he can find some excuse —

NORA: But it's just this time that Torvald usually —

MRS. LINDE: Stall him. Keep him in there. I'll be back as quick as I can. (*She hurries out through the hall entrance.*)

NORA (*goes to Helmer's door, opens it, and peers in*): Torvald!

HELMER (*from the inner study*): Well — does one dare set foot in one's own living room at last? Come on, Rank, now we'll get a look — (*In the doorway.*) But what's this?

NORA: What, Torvald dear?

HELMER: Rank had me expecting some grand masquerade.

RANK (*in the doorway*): That was my impression, but I must have been wrong.

NORA: No one can admire me in my splendor — not till tomorrow.

HELMER: But Nora dear, you look so exhausted. Have you practiced too hard?

NORA: No, I haven't practiced at all yet.

HELMER: You know, it's necessary —

NORA: Oh, it's absolutely necessary, Torvald. But I can't get anywhere without your help. I've forgotten the whole thing completely.

HELMER: Ah, we'll soon take care of that.

NORA: Yes, take care of me, Torvald, please! Promise me that? Oh, I'm so nervous. That big party — You must give up everything this evening for me. No business — don't even touch your pen. Yes? Dear Torvald, promise?

HELMER: It's a promise. Tonight I'm totally at your service — you little helpless thing. Hm — but first there's one thing I want to — (*Goes toward the hall door.*)

NORA: What are you looking for?

HELMER: Just to see if there's any mail.

NORA: No, no, don't do that, Torvald!

HELMER: Now what?

NORA: Torvald, please. There isn't any.

HELMER: Let me look, though. (*Starts out. Nora, at the piano, strikes the first notes of the tarantella. Helmer, at the door, stops.*) Aha!

NORA: I can't dance tomorrow if I don't practice with you.

HELMER (*going over to her*): Nora dear, are you really so frightened?

NORA: Yes, so terribly frightened. Let me practice right now; there's still time before dinner. Oh, sit down and play for me, Torvald. Direct me. Teach me, the way you always have.

HELMER: Gladly, if it's what you want. (*Sits at the piano.*)

NORA (*snatches the tambourine up from the box, then a long, varicolored shawl, which she throws around herself, whereupon she springs forward and cries out*): Play for me now! Now I'll dance!

(*Helmer plays and Nora dances. Rank stands behind Helmer at the piano and looks on.*)

HELMER (*as he plays*): Slower. Slow down.

NORA: Can't change it.

HELMER: Not so violent, Nora!

NORA: Has to be just like this.

HELMER (*stopping*): No, no, that won't do at all.

NORA (*laughing and swinging her tambourine*): Isn't that what I told you?

RANK: Let me play for her.

HELMER (*getting up*): Yes, go on. I can teach her more easily then.

(*Rank sits at the piano and plays, Nora dances more and more wildly. Helmer has stationed himself by the stove and repeatedly gives her directions; she seems not to hear them; her hair loosens and falls over her shoulders; she does not notice, but goes on dancing. Mrs. Linde enters.*)

MRS. LINDE (*standing dumbfounded at the door*): Ah—!

NORA (*still dancing*): See what fun, Kristine!

HELMER: But Nora darling, you dance as if your life were at stake.

NORA: And it is.

HELMER: Rank, stop! This is pure madness. Stop it, I say!

(*Rank breaks off playing, and Nora halts abruptly.*)

HELMER (*going over to her*): I never would have believed it. You've forgotten everything I taught you.

NORA (*throwing away the tambourine*): You see for yourself.

HELMER: Well, there's certainly room for instruction here.

NORA: Yes, you see how important it is. You've got to teach me to the very last minute. Promise me that, Torvald?

HELMER: You can bet on it.

NORA: You mustn't, either today or tomorrow, think about anything else but me; you mustn't open any letters — or the mailbox —

HELMER: Ah, it's still the fear of that man —

NORA: Oh yes, yes, that too.

HELMER: Nora, it's written all over you — there's already a letter from him out there.

NORA: I don't know. I guess so. But you mustn't read such things now; there mustn't be anything ugly between us before it's all over.

RANK (*quietly to Helmer*): You shouldn't deny her.

HELMER (*putting his arm around her*): The child can have her way. But tomorrow night, after you've danced —

NORA: Then you'll be free.

MAID (*in the doorway, right*): Ma'am, dinner is served.

NORA: We'll be wanting champagne, Helene.

MAID: Very good, ma'am. (*Goes out.*)

HELMER: So — a regular banquet, hm?

NORA: Yes, a banquet — champagne till daybreak! (*Calling out.*) And some macaroons, Helene. Heaps of them — just this once.

HELMER (*taking her hands*): Now, now, now — no hysterics. Be my own little lark again.

NORA: Oh, I will soon enough. But go on in — and you, Dr. Rank. Kristine, help me put up my hair.

RANK (*whispering, as they go*): There's nothing wrong — really wrong, is there?

HELMER: Oh, of course not. It's nothing more than this childish anxiety I was telling you about. (*They go out, right.*)

NORA: Well?

MRS. LINDE: Left town.

NORA: I could see by your face.

MRS. LINDE: He'll be home tomorrow evening. I wrote him a note.

NORA: You shouldn't have. Don't try to stop anything now. After all, it's a wonderful joy, this waiting here for the miracle.

MRS. LINDE: What is it you're waiting for?

NORA: Oh, you can't understand that. Go in to them; I'll be along in a moment.

(*Mrs. Linde goes into the dining room. Nora stands a short while as if composing herself; then she looks at her watch.*)

NORA: Five. Seven hours to midnight. Twenty-four hours to the midnight after, and then the tarantella's done. Seven and twenty-four? Thirty-one hours to live.

HELMER (*in the doorway, right*): What's become of the little lark?

NORA (*going toward him with open arms*): Here's your lark!

ACT III

(*Same scene. The table, with chairs around it, has been moved to the center of the room. A lamp on the table is lit. The hall door stands open. Dance music drifts down from the floor above. Mrs. Linde sits at the table, absently paging through a book, trying to read, but apparently unable to focus her thoughts. Once or twice she pauses, tensely listening for a sound at the outer entrance.*)

MRS. LINDE (*glancing at her watch*): Not yet — and there's hardly any time left. If only he's not — (*Listening again.*) Ah, there it is. (*She goes out in the hall and cautiously opens the outer door. Quiet footsteps are heard on the stairs. She whispers.*) Come in. Nobody's here.

KROGSTAD (*in the doorway*): I found a note from you at home. What's back of all this?

MRS. LINDE: I just *had* to talk to you.

KROGSTAD: Oh? And it just *had* to be here in this house?

MRS. LINDE: At my place it was impossible; my room hasn't a private entrance. Come in, we're all alone. The maid's asleep, and the Helmers are at the dance upstairs.

KROGSTAD (*entering the room*): Well, well, the Helmers are dancing tonight? Really?

MRS. LINDE: Yes, why not?

KROGSTAD: How true — why not?

MRS. LINDE: All right, Krogstad, let's talk.

KROGSTAD: Do we two have anything more to talk about?

MRS. LINDE: We have a great deal to talk about.

KROGSTAD: I wouldn't have thought so.

MRS. LINDE: No, because you've never understood me, really.

KROGSTAD: Was there anything more to understand — except what's all too common in life? A calculating woman throws over a man the moment a better catch comes by.

MRS. LINDE: You think I'm so thoroughly calculating? You think I broke it off lightly?

KROGSTAD: Didn't you?

MRS. LINDE: Nils — is that what you really thought?

KROGSTAD: If you cared, then why did you write me the way you did?

MRS. LINDE: What else could I do? If I had to break off with you, then it was my job as well to root out everything you felt for me.

KROGSTAD (*wringing his hands*): So that was it. And this — all this, simply for money!

MRS. LINDE: Don't forget I had a helpless mother and two small brothers. We couldn't wait for you, Nils; you had such a long road ahead of you then.

KROGSTAD: That may be; but you still hadn't the right to abandon me for somebody else's sake.

MRS. LINDE: Yes — I don't know. So many, many times I've asked myself if I did have that right.

KROGSTAD (*more softly*): When I lost you, it was as if all the solid ground dissolved from under my feet. Look at me; I'm a half-drowned man now, hanging onto a wreck.

MRS. LINDE: Help may be near.

KROGSTAD: It was near — but then you came and blocked it off.

MRS. LINDE: Without my knowing it, Nils. Today for the first time I learned that it's you I'm replacing at the bank.

KROGSTAD: All right — I believe you. But now that you know, will you step aside?

MRS. LINDE: No, because that wouldn't benefit you in the slightest.

KROGSTAD: Not "benefit" me, hm! I'd step aside anyway.

MRS. LINDE: I've learned to be realistic. Life and hard, bitter necessity have taught me that.

KROGSTAD: And life's taught me never to trust fine phrases.

MRS. LINDE: Then life's taught you a very sound thing. But you do have to trust in actions, don't you?

KROGSTAD: What does that mean?

MRS. LINDE: You said you were hanging on like a half-drowned man to a wreck.

KROGSTAD: I've good reason to say that.

MRS. LINDE: I'm also like a half-drowned woman on a wreck. No one to suffer with; no one to care for.

KROGSTAD: You made your choice.

MRS. LINDE: There wasn't any choice then.

KROGSTAD: So — what of it?

MRS. LINDE: Nils, if only we two shipwrecked people could reach across to each other.

KROGSTAD: What are you saying?

MRS. LINDE: Two on one wreck are at least better off than each on his own.

KROGSTAD: Kristine!

MRS. LINDE: Why do you think I came into town?

KROGSTAD: Did you really have some thought of me?

MRS. LINDE: I have to work to go on living. All my born days, as long as I can remember, I've worked, and it's been my best and my only joy. But now I'm completely alone in the world; it frightens me to be so empty and lost. To work for yourself — there's no joy in that. Nils, give me something — someone to work for.

KROGSTAD: I don't believe all this. It's just some hysterical feminine urge to go out and make a noble sacrifice.

MRS. LINDE: Have you ever found me to be hysterical?

KROGSTAD: Can you honestly mean this? Tell me — do you know everything about my past?

MRS. LINDE: Yes.

KROGSTAD: And you know what they think I'm worth around here.

MRS. LINDE: From what you were saying before, it would seem that with me you could have been another person.

KROGSTAD: I'm positive of that.

MRS. LINDE: Couldn't it happen still?

KROGSTAD: Kristine — you're saying this in all seriousness? Yes, you are! I can see it in you. And do you really have the courage, then — ?

MRS. LINDE: I need to have someone to care for, and your children need a mother. We both need each other. Nils, I have faith that you're good at heart — I'll risk everything together with you.

KROGSTAD (*gripping her hands*): Kristine, thank you, thank you — Now I know I can win back a place in their eyes. Yes — but I forgot —

MRS. LINDE (*listening*): Shh! The tarantella. Go now! Go on!

KROGSTAD: Why? What is it?

MRS. LINDE: Hear the dance up there? When that's over, they'll be coming down.

KROGSTAD: Oh, then I'll go. But — it's all pointless. Of course, you don't know the move I made against the Helmers.

MRS. LINDE: Yes, Nils, I know.

KROGSTAD: And all the same, you have the courage to — ?

MRS. LINDE: I know how far despair can drive a man like you.

KROGSTAD: Oh, if I only could take it all back.

MRS. LINDE: You easily could — your letter's still lying in the mailbox.

KROGSTAD: Are you sure of that?

MRS. LINDE: Positive. But—

KROGSTAD (*looks at her searchingly*): Is that the meaning of it, then? You'll save your friend at any price. Tell me straight out. Is that it?

MRS. LINDE: Nils—anyone who's sold herself for somebody else once isn't going to do it again.

KROGSTAD: I'll demand my letter back.

MRS. LINDE: No, no.

KROGSTAD: Yes, of course. I'll stay here till Helmer comes down; I'll tell him to give me my letter again—that it only involves my dismissal—that he shouldn't read it—

MRS. LINDE: No, Nils, don't call the letter back.

KROGSTAD: But wasn't that exactly why you wrote me to come here?

MRS. LINDE: Yes, in that first panic. But it's been a whole day and night since then, and in that time I've seen such incredible things in this house. Helmer's got to learn everything; this dreadful secret has to be aired; those two have to come to a full understanding; all these lies and evasions can't go on.

KROGSTAD: Well, then, if you want to chance it. But at least there's one thing I can do, and do right away—

MRS. LINDE (*listening*): Go now, go, quick! The dance is over. We're not safe another second.

KROGSTAD: I'll wait for you downstairs.

MRS. LINDE: Yes, please do; take me home.

KROGSTAD: I can't believe it; I've never been so happy. (*He leaves by way of the outer door; the door between the room and the hall stays open.*)

MRS. LINDE (*straightening up a bit and getting together her street clothes*): How different now! How different! Someone to work for, to live for—a home to build. Well, it is worth the try! Oh, if they'd only come! (*Listening.*) Ah, there they are. Bundle up. (*She picks up her hat and coat. Nora's and Helmer's voices can be heard outside; a key turns in the lock, and Helmer brings Nora into the hall almost by force. She is wearing the Italian costume with a large black shawl about her; he has on evening dress, with a black domino open over it.*)

NORA (*struggling in the doorway*): No, no, no, not inside! I'm going up again. I don't want to leave so soon.

HELMER: But Nora dear—

NORA: Oh, I beg you, please, Torvald. From the bottom of my heart, *please*—only an hour more!

HELMER: Not a single minute, Nora darling. You know our agreement. Come on, in we go; you'll catch cold out here. (*In spite of her resistance, he gently draws her into the room.*)

MRS. LINDE: Good evening.

NORA: Kristine!

HELMER: Why, Mrs. Linde—are you here so late?

MRS. LINDE: Yes, I'm sorry, but I did want to see Nora in costume.

NORA: Have you been sitting here, waiting for me?

MRS. LINDE: Yes. I didn't come early enough; you were all upstairs; and then I thought I really couldn't leave without seeing you.

HELMER (*removing Nora's shawl*): Yes, take a good look. She's worth looking at, I can tell you that, Mrs. Linde. Isn't she lovely?

MRS. LINDE: Yes, I should say—

HELMER: A dream of loveliness, isn't she? That's what everyone thought at the party, too. But she's horribly stubborn—this sweet little thing. What's to be done with her? Can you imagine, I almost had to use force to pry her away.

NORA: Oh, Torvald, you're going to regret you didn't indulge me, even for just a half hour more.

HELMER: There, you see. She danced her tarantella and got a tumultuous hand—which was well earned, although the performance may have been a bit too naturalistic—I mean it rather overstepped the proprieties of art. But never mind—what's important is, she made a success, an overwhelming success. You think I could let her stay on after that and spoil the effect? Oh no; I took my lovely little Capri girl—my capricious little Capri girl, I should say—took her under my arm; one quick tour of the ballroom, a curtsy to every side, and then—as they say in novels— the beautiful vision disappeared. An exit should always be effective, Mrs. Linde, but that's what I can't get Nora to grasp. Phew, it's hot in here. (*Flings the domino on a chair and opens the door to his room.*) Why's it dark in here? Oh yes, of course. Excuse me. (*He goes in and lights a couple of candles.*)

NORA (*in a sharp, breathless whisper*): So?

MRS. LINDE (*quietly*): I talked with him.

NORA: And—?

MRS. LINDE: Nora—you must tell your husband everything.

NORA (*dully*): I knew it.

MRS. LINDE: You've got nothing to fear from Krogstad, but you have to speak out.

NORA: I won't tell.

MRS. LINDE: Then the letter will.

NORA: Thanks, Kristine. I know now what's to be done. Shh!

HELMER (*reentering*): Well, then, Mrs. Linde—have you admired her?

MRS. LINDE: Yes, and now I'll say good night.

HELMER: Oh, come, so soon? Is this yours, this knitting?

MRS. LINDE: Yes, thanks. I nearly forgot it.

HELMER: Do you knit, then?

MRS. LINDE: Oh yes.

HELMER: You know what? You should embroider instead.

MRS. LINDE: Really? Why?

HELMER: Yes, because it's a lot prettier. See here, one holds the embroidery so, in the left hand, and then one guides the needle with the right—so— in an easy, sweeping curve—right?

MRS. LINDE: Yes, I guess that's —

HELMER: But, on the other hand, knitting — it can never be anything but ugly. Look, see here, the arms tucked in, the knitting needles going up and down — there's something Chinese about it. Ah, that was really a glorious champagne they served.

MRS. LINDE: Yes, good night, Nora, and don't be stubborn anymore.

HELMER: Well put, Mrs. Linde!

MRS. LINDE: Good night, Mr. Helmer.

HELMER (*accompanying her to the door*): Good night, good night. I hope you get home all right. I'd be very happy to — but you don't have far to go. Good night, good night. (*She leaves. He shuts the door after her and returns.*) There, now, at last we got her out the door. She's a deadly bore, that creature.

NORA: Aren't you pretty tired, Torvald?

HELMER: No, not a bit.

NORA: You're not sleepy?

HELMER: Not at all. On the contrary, I'm feeling quite exhilarated. But you? Yes, you really look tired and sleepy.

NORA: Yes, I'm very tired. Soon now I'll sleep.

HELMER: See! You see! I was right all along that we shouldn't stay longer.

NORA: Whatever you do is always right.

HELMER (*kissing her brow*): Now my little lark talks sense. Say, did you notice what a time Rank was having tonight?

NORA: Oh, was he? I didn't get to speak with him.

HELMER: I scarcely did either, but it's a long time since I've seen him in such high spirits. (*Gazes at her a moment, then comes nearer her.*) Hm — it's marvelous, though, to be back home again — to be completely alone with you. Oh, you bewitchingly lovely young woman!

NORA: Torvald, don't look at me like that!

HELMER: Can't I look at my richest treasure? At all that beauty that's mine, mine alone — completely and utterly.

NORA (*moving around to the other side of the table*): You mustn't talk to me that way tonight.

HELMER (*following her*): The tarantella is still in your blood. I can see — and it makes you even more enticing. Listen. The guests are beginning to go. (*Dropping his voice.*) Nora — it'll soon be quiet through this whole house.

NORA: Yes, I hope so.

HELMER: You do, don't you, my love? Do you realize — when I'm out at a party like this with you — do you know why I talk to you so little, and keep such a distance away; just send you a stolen look now and then — you know why I do it? It's because I'm imagining then that you're my secret darling, my secret young bride-to-be, and that no one suspects there's anything between us.

NORA: Yes, yes; oh, yes, I know you're always thinking of me.

HELMER: And then when we leave and I place the shawl over those fine young rounded shoulders — over that wonderful curving neck — then I pretend that you're my young bride, that we're just coming from the wedding, that for the first time I'm bringing you into my house — that for the first time I'm alone with you — completely alone with you, your trembling young beauty! All this evening I've longed for nothing but you. When I saw you turn and sway in the tarantella — my blood was pounding till I couldn't stand it — that's why I brought you down here so early —

NORA: Go away, Torvald! Leave me alone. I don't want all this.

HELMER: What do you mean? Nora, you're teasing me. You will, won't you? Aren't I your husband — ?

(A knock at the outside door.)

NORA *(startled)*: What's that?

HELMER *(going toward the hall)*: Who is it?

RANK *(outside)*: It's me. May I come in a moment?

HELMER *(with quiet irritation)*: Oh, what does he want now? *(Aloud.)* Hold on. *(Goes and opens the door.)* Oh, how nice that you didn't just pass us by!

RANK: I thought I heard your voice, and then I wanted so badly to have a look in. *(Lightly glancing about.)* Ah, me, these old familiar haunts. You have it snug and cozy in here, you two.

HELMER: You seemed to be having it pretty cozy upstairs, too.

RANK: Absolutely. Why shouldn't I? Why not take in everything in life? As much as you can, anyway, and as long as you can. The wine was superb —

HELMER: The champagne especially.

RANK: You noticed that too? It's amazing how much I could guzzle down.

NORA: Torvald also drank a lot of champagne this evening.

RANK: Oh?

NORA: Yes, and that always makes him so entertaining.

RANK: Well, why shouldn't one have a pleasant evening after a well-spent day?

HELMER: Well spent? I'm afraid I can't claim that.

RANK *(slapping him on the back)*: But I can, you see!

NORA: Dr. Rank, you must have done some scientific research today.

RANK: Quite so.

HELMER: Come now — little Nora talking about scientific research!

NORA: And can I congratulate you on the results?

RANK: Indeed you may.

NORA: Then they were good?

RANK: The best possible for both doctor and patient — certainty.

NORA *(quickly and searchingly)*: Certainty?

RANK: Complete certainty. So don't I owe myself a gay evening afterwards?

NORA: Yes, you're right, Dr. Rank.

HELMER: I'm with you — just so long as you don't have to suffer for it in the morning.

RANK: Well, one never gets something for nothing in life.

NORA: Dr. Rank — are you very fond of masquerade parties?

RANK: Yes, if there's a good array of odd disguises —

NORA: Tell me, what should we two go as at the next masquerade?

HELMER: You little featherhead — already thinking of the next!

RANK: We two? I'll tell you what: You must go as Charmed Life —

HELMER: Yes, but find a costume for that!

RANK: Your wife can appear just as she looks every day.

HELMER: That was nicely put. But don't you know what you're going to be?

RANK: Yes, Helmer, I've made up my mind.

HELMER: Well?

RANK: At the next masquerade I'm going to be invisible.

HELMER: That's a funny idea.

RANK: They say there's a hat — black, huge — have you never heard of the hat that makes you invisible? You put it on, and then no one on earth can see you.

HELMER (*suppressing a smile*): Ah, of course.

RANK: But I'm quite forgetting what I came for. Helmer, give me a cigar, one of the dark Havanas.

HELMER: With the greatest pleasure. (*Holds out his case.*)

RANK: Thanks. (*Takes one and cuts off the tip.*)

NORA (*striking a match*): Let me give you a light.

RANK: Thank you. (*She holds the match for him; he lights the cigar.*) And now good-bye.

HELMER: Good-bye, good-bye, old friend.

NORA: Sleep well, Doctor.

RANK: Thanks for that wish.

NORA: Wish me the same.

RANK: You? All right, if you like — Sleep well. And thanks for the light. (*He nods to them both and leaves.*)

HELMER (*his voice subdued*): He's been drinking heavily.

NORA (*absently*): Could be. (*Helmer takes his keys from his pocket and goes out in the hall.*) Torvald — what are you after?

HELMER: Got to empty the mailbox; it's nearly full. There won't be room for the morning papers.

NORA: Are you working tonight?

HELMER: You know I'm not. Why — what's this? Someone's been at the lock.

NORA: At the lock — ?

HELMER: Yes, I'm positive. What do you suppose — ? I can't imagine one of the maids — ? Here's a broken hairpin. Nora, it's yours —

NORA (*quickly*): Then it must be the children —

HELMER: You'd better break them of that. Hm, hm — well, opened it after all. (*Takes the contents out and calls into the kitchen.*) Helene! Helene, would you put out the lamp in the hall. (*He returns to the room, shutting the hall door, then displays the handful of mail.*) Look how it's piled up. (*Sorting through them.*) Now what's this?

NORA (*at the window*): The letter! Oh, Torvald, no!

HELMER: Two calling cards — from Rank.

NORA: From Dr. Rank?

HELMER (*examining them*): "Dr. Rank, Consulting Physician." They were on top. He must have dropped them in as he left.

NORA: Is there anything on them?

HELMER: There's a black cross over the name. See? That's a gruesome notion. He could almost be announcing his own death.

NORA: That's just what he's doing.

HELMER: What! You've heard something? Something he's told you?

NORA: Yes. That when those cards came, he'd be taking his leave of us. He'll shut himself in now and die.

HELMER: Ah, my poor friend! Of course I knew he wouldn't be here much longer. But so soon — And then to hide himself away like a wounded animal.

NORA: If it has to happen, then it's best it happens in silence — don't you think so, Torvald?

HELMER (*pacing up and down*): He's grown right into our lives. I simply can't imagine him gone. He with his suffering and loneliness — like a dark cloud setting off our sunlit happiness. Well, maybe it's best this way. For him, at least. (*Standing still.*) And maybe for us too, Nora. Now we're thrown back on each other, completely. (*Embracing her.*) Oh you, my darling wife, how can I hold you close enough? You know what, Nora — time and again I've wished you were in some terrible danger, just so I could stake my life and soul and everything, for your sake.

NORA (*tearing herself away, her voice firm and decisive*): Now you must read your mail, Torvald.

HELMER: No, no, not tonight. I want to stay with you, dearest.

NORA: With a dying friend on your mind?

HELMER: You're right. We've both had a shock. There's ugliness between us — these thoughts of death and corruption. We'll have to get free of them first. Until then — we'll stay apart.

NORA (*clinging about his neck*): Torvald — good night! Good night!

HELMER (*kissing her on the cheek*): Good night, little songbird. Sleep well, Nora. I'll be reading my mail now. (*He takes the letters into his room and shuts the door after him.*)

NORA (*with bewildered glances, groping about, seizing Helmer's domino, throwing it around her, and speaking in short, hoarse, broken whispers*): Never see him again. Never, never. (*Putting her shawl over her head.*) Never see the children either — them, too. Never, never. Oh, the freezing black water! The depths — down — Oh, I wish it were over — He has it now; he's reading it — now. Oh no, no, not yet. Torvald, good-bye, you and the children — (*She starts for the hall; as she does, Helmer throws open his door and stands with an open letter in his hand.*)

HELMER: Nora!

NORA (*screams*): Oh — !

HELMER: What is this? You know what's in this letter?

NORA: Yes, I know. Let me go! Let me out!

HELMER (*holding her back*): Where are you going?

NORA (*struggling to break loose*): You can't save me, Torvald!

HELMER (*slumping back*): True! Then it's true what he writes? How horrible! No, no, it's impossible — it can't be true.

NORA: It *is* true. I've loved you more than all this world.

HELMER: Ah, none of your slippery tricks.

NORA (*taking one step toward him*): Torvald — !

HELMER: What *is* this you've blundered into!

NORA: Just let me loose. You're not going to suffer for my sake. You're not going to take on my guilt.

HELMER: No more playacting. (*Locks the hall door.*) You stay right here and give me a reckoning. You understand what you've done? Answer! You understand?

NORA (*looking squarely at him, her face hardening*): Yes. I'm beginning to understand everything now.

HELMER (*striding about*): Oh, what an awful awakening! In all these eight years — she who was my pride and joy — a hypocrite, a liar — worse, worse — a criminal! How infinitely disgusting it all is! The shame! (*Nora says nothing and goes on looking straight at him. He stops in front of her.*) I should have suspected something of the kind. I should have known. All your father's flimsy values — Be still! All your father's flimsy values have come out in you. No religion, no morals, no sense of duty — Oh, how I'm punished for letting him off! I did it for your sake, and you repay me like this.

NORA: Yes, like this.

HELMER: Now you've wrecked all my happiness — ruined my whole future. Oh, it's awful to think of. I'm in a cheap little grafter's hands; he can do anything he wants with me, ask for anything, play with me like a puppet — and I can't breathe a word. I'll be swept down miserably into the depths on account of a featherbrained woman.

NORA: When I'm gone from this world, you'll be free.

HELMER: Oh, quit posing. Your father had a mess of those speeches too. What good would that ever do me if you were gone from this world, as you say? Not the slightest. He can still make the whole thing known; and if he does, I could be falsely suspected as your accomplice. They might even think that I was behind it — that I put you up to it. And all that I can thank you for — you that I've coddled the whole of our marriage. Can you see now what you've done to me?

NORA (*icily calm*): Yes.

HELMER: It's so incredible, I just can't grasp it. But we'll have to patch up whatever we can. Take off the shawl. I said, take it off! I've got to appease him somehow or other. The thing has to be hushed up at any cost. And as for you and me, it's got to seem like everything between us is just as it was — to the outside world, that is. You'll go right on living in this house, of course. But you can't be allowed to bring up the children; I don't dare trust you with them — Oh, to have to say this to someone I've loved so much! Well, that's done with. From now on happiness doesn't matter; all that matters is saving the bits and pieces, the appearance — (*The doorbell rings. Helmer starts.*) What's that? And so late. Maybe the worst — ? You think he'd — ? Hide, Nora! Say you're sick. (*Nora remains standing motionless. Helmer goes and opens the door.*)

MAID (*half dressed, in the hall*): A letter for Mrs. Helmer.

HELMER: I'll take it. (*Snatches the letter and shuts the door.*) Yes, it's from him. You don't get it; I'm reading it myself.

NORA: Then read it.

HELMER (*by the lamp*): I hardly dare. We may be ruined, you and I. But — I've got to know. (*Rips open the letter, skims through a few lines, glances at an enclosure, then cries out joyfully.*) Nora! (*Nora looks inquiringly at him.*) Nora! Wait — better check it again — Yes, yes, it's true. I'm saved. Nora, I'm saved!

NORA: And I?

HELMER: You too, of course. We're both saved, both of us. Look. He's sent back your note. He says he's sorry and ashamed — that a happy development in his life — oh, who cares what he says! Nora, we're saved! No one can hurt you. Oh, Nora, Nora — but first, this ugliness all has to go. Let me see — (*Takes a look at the note.*) No, I don't want to see it; I want the whole thing to fade like a dream. (*Tears the note and both letters to pieces, throws them into the stove and watches them burn.*) There — now there's nothing left — He wrote that since Christmas Eve you — Oh, they must have been three terrible days for you, Nora.

NORA: I fought a hard fight.

HELMER: And suffered pain and saw no escape but — No, we're not going to dwell on anything unpleasant. We'll just be grateful and keep on repeating: It's over now, it's over! You hear me, Nora? You don't seem to realize — it's over. What's it mean — that frozen look? Oh, poor little Nora, I understand. You can't believe I've forgiven you. But I have, Nora; I swear I have. I know that what you did, you did out of love for me.

NORA: That's true.

HELMER: You loved me the way a wife ought to love her husband. It's simply the means that you couldn't judge. But you think I love you any the less for not knowing how to handle your affairs? No, no — just lean on me; I'll guide you and teach you. I wouldn't be a man if this feminine helplessness didn't make you twice as attractive to me. You mustn't mind those sharp words I said — that was all in the first confusion of thinking my world had collapsed. I've forgiven you, Nora; I swear I've forgiven you.

NORA: My thanks for your forgiveness. (*She goes out through the door, right.*)

HELMER: No, wait — (*Peers in.*) What are you doing in there?

NORA (*inside*): Getting out of my costume.

HELMER (*by the open door*): Yes, do that. Try to calm yourself and collect your thoughts again, my frightened little songbird. You can rest easy now; I've got wide wings to shelter you with. (*Walking about close by the door.*) How snug and nice our home is, Nora. You're safe here; I'll keep you like a hunted dove I've rescued out of a hawk's claws. I'll bring peace to your poor, shuddering heart. Gradually it'll happen, Nora; you'll see. Tomorrow all this will look different to you; then everything will be as it was. I won't have to go on repeating I forgive you; you'll feel it for yourself. How can you imagine I'd ever conceivably want to disown you — or even blame you in any way? Ah, you don't know a man's heart, Nora. For a man there's something indescribably sweet and satisfying in knowing he's forgiven his wife — and forgiven her out of a full and open heart. It's as if she belongs to him in two ways now: In a sense he's given her fresh into the world again, and she's become his wife and his child as well. From now on that's what you'll be to me — you little, bewildered, helpless thing. Don't be afraid of anything, Nora; just open your heart to me, and I'll be conscience and will to you both — (*Nora enters in her regular clothes.*) What's this? Not in bed? You've changed your dress?

NORA: Yes, Torvald, I've changed my dress.

HELMER: But why now, so late?

NORA: Tonight I'm not sleeping.

HELMER: But Nora dear —

NORA (*looking at her watch*): It's still not so very late. Sit down, Torvald; we have a lot to talk over. (*She sits at one side of the table.*)

HELMER: Nora — what is this? That hard expression —

NORA: Sit down. This'll take some time. I have a lot to say.

HELMER (*sitting at the table directly opposite her*): You worry me, Nora. And I don't understand you.

NORA: No, that's exactly it. You don't understand me. And I've never understood you either — until tonight. No, don't interrupt. You can just listen to what I say. We're closing out accounts, Torvald.

HELMER: How do you mean that?

NORA (*after a short pause*): Doesn't anything strike you about our sitting here like this?

HELMER: What's that?

NORA: We've been married now eight years. Doesn't it occur to you that this is the first time we two, you and I, man and wife, have ever talked seriously together?

HELMER: What do you mean — seriously?

NORA: In eight whole years — longer even — right from our first acquaintance, we've never exchanged a serious word on any serious thing.

HELMER: You mean I should constantly go and involve you in problems you couldn't possibly help me with?

NORA: I'm not talking of problems. I'm saying that we've never sat down seriously together and tried to get to the bottom of anything.

HELMER: But dearest, what good would that ever do you?

NORA: That's the point right there: You've never understood me. I've been wronged greatly, Torvald — first by Papa, and then by you.

HELMER: What! By us — the two people who've loved you more than anyone else?

NORA (*shaking her head*): You never loved me. You've thought it fun to be in love with me, that's all.

HELMER: Nora, what a thing to say!

NORA: Yes, it's true now, Torvald. When I lived at home with Papa, he told me all his opinions, so I had the same ones too; or if they were different I hid them, since he wouldn't have cared for that. He used to call me his doll-child, and he played with me the way I played with my dolls. Then I came into your house —

HELMER: How can you speak of our marriage like that?

NORA (*unperturbed*): I mean, then I went from Papa's hands into yours. You arranged everything to your own taste, and so I got the same taste as you — or I pretended to; I can't remember. I guess a little of both, first one, then the other. Now when I look back, it seems as if I'd lived here like a beggar — just from hand to mouth. I've lived by doing tricks for you, Torvald. But that's the way you wanted it. It's a great sin what you and Papa did to me. You're to blame that nothing's become of me.

HELMER: Nora, how unfair and ungrateful you are! Haven't you been happy here?

NORA: No, never. I thought so — but I never have.

HELMER: Not — not happy!

NORA: No, only lighthearted. And you've always been so kind to me. But our home's been nothing but a playpen. I've been your doll-wife here, just as at home I was Papa's doll-child. And in turn the children have been my dolls. I thought it was fun when you played with me, just as they thought it fun when I played with them. That's been our marriage, Torvald.

HELMER: There's some truth in what you're saying — under all the raving exaggeration. But it'll all be different after this. Playtime's over; now for the schooling.

NORA: Whose schooling — mine or the children's?

HELMER: Both yours and the children's, dearest.

NORA: Oh, Torvald, you're not the man to teach me to be a good wife to you.

HELMER: And you can say that?

NORA: And I — how am I equipped to bring up children?

HELMER: Nora!

NORA: Didn't you say a moment ago that that was no job to trust me with?

HELMER: In a flare of temper! Why fasten on that?

NORA: Yes, but you were so very right. I'm not up to the job. There's another job I have to do first. I have to try to educate myself. You can't help me with that. I've got to do it alone. And that's why I'm leaving you now.

HELMER (*jumping up*): What's that?

NORA: I have to stand completely alone, if I'm ever going to discover myself and the world out there. So I can't go on living with you.

HELMER: Nora, Nora!

NORA: I want to leave right away. Kristine should put me up for the night —

HELMER: You're insane! You've no right! I forbid you!

NORA: From here on, there's no use forbidding me anything. I'll take with me whatever is mine. I don't want a thing from you, either now or later.

HELMER: What kind of madness is this!

NORA: Tomorrow I'm going home — I mean, home where I came from. It'll be easier up there to find something to do.

HELMER: Oh, you blind, incompetent child!

NORA: I must learn to be competent, Torvald.

HELMER: Abandon your home, your husband, your children! And you're not even thinking what people will say.

NORA: I can't be concerned about that. I only know how essential this is.

HELMER: Oh, it's outrageous. So you'll run out like this on your most sacred vows.

NORA: What do you think are my most sacred vows?

HELMER: And I have to tell you that! Aren't they your duties to your husband and children?

NORA: I have other duties equally sacred.

HELMER: That isn't true. What duties are they?

NORA: Duties to myself.

HELMER: Before all else, you're a wife and a mother.

NORA: I don't believe in that anymore. I believe that before all else, I'm a human being, no less than you — or anyway, I ought to try to become one. I know the majority thinks you're right, Torvald, and plenty of books agree with you, too. But I can't go on believing what the majority says, or what's written in books. I have to think over these things myself and try to understand them.

HELMER: Why can't you understand your place in your own home? On a point like that, isn't there one everlasting guide you can turn to? Where's your religion?

NORA: Oh, Torvald, I'm really not sure what religion is.

HELMER: What — ?

NORA: I only know what the minister said when I was confirmed. He told me religion was this thing and that. When I get clear and away by myself, I'll go into that problem too. I'll see if what the minister said was right, or, in any case, if it's right for me.

HELMER: A young woman your age shouldn't talk like that. If religion can't move you, I can try to rouse your conscience. You do have some moral feeling? Or, tell me — has that gone too?

NORA: It's not easy to answer that, Torvald. I simply don't know. I'm all confused about these things. I just know I see them so differently from you.

I find out for one thing, that the law's not at all what I'd thought — but I can't get it through my head that the law is fair. A woman hasn't a right to protect her dying father or save her husband's life! I can't believe that.

HELMER: You talk like a child. You don't know anything of the world you live in.

NORA: No, I don't. But now I'll begin to learn for myself. I'll try to discover who's right, the world or I.

HELMER: Nora, you're sick; you've got a fever. I almost think you're out of your head.

NORA: I've never felt more clearheaded and sure in my life.

HELMER: And — clearheaded and sure — you're leaving your husband and children?

NORA: Yes.

HELMER: Then there's only one possible reason.

NORA: What?

HELMER: You no longer love me.

NORA: No. That's exactly it.

HELMER: Nora! You can't be serious!

NORA: Oh, this is so hard, Torvald — you've been so kind to me always. But I can't help it. I don't love you anymore.

HELMER (*struggling for composure*): Are you also clearheaded and sure about that?

NORA: Yes, completely. That's why I can't go on staying here.

HELMER: Can you tell me what I did to lose your love?

NORA: Yes, I can tell you. It was this evening when the miraculous thing didn't come — then I knew you weren't the man I'd imagined.

HELMER: Be more explicit; I don't follow you.

NORA: I've waited now so patiently eight long years — for, my Lord, I know miracles don't come every day. Then this crisis broke over me, and such a certainty filled me: *Now* the miraculous event would occur. While Krogstad's letter was lying out there, I never for an instant dreamed that you could give in to his terms. I was so utterly sure you'd say to him: Go on, tell your tale to the whole wide world. And when he'd done that —

HELMER: Yes, what then? When I'd delivered my own wife into shame and disgrace — !

NORA: When he'd done that, I was so utterly sure that you'd step forward, take the blame on yourself and say: I am the guilty one.

HELMER: Nora — !

NORA: You're thinking I'd never accept such a sacrifice from you? No, of course not. But what good would my protests be against you? That was the miracle I was waiting for, in terror and hope. And to stave that off, I would have taken my life.

HELMER: I'd gladly work for you day and night, Nora — and take on pain and deprivation. But there's no one who gives up honor for love.

NORA: Millions of women have done just that.

HELMER: Oh, you think and talk like a silly child.

NORA: Perhaps. But you neither think nor talk like the man I could join my-self to. When your big fright was over — and it wasn't from any threat against me, only for what might damage you — when all the danger was past, for you it was just as if nothing had happened. I was exactly the same, your little lark, your doll, that you'd have to handle with double care now that I'd turned out so brittle and frail. (*Gets up.*) Torvald — in that instant it dawned on me that for eight years I've been living here with a stranger, and that I'd even conceived three children — oh, I can't stand the thought of it! I could tear myself to bits.

HELMER (*heavily*): I see. There's a gulf that's opened between us — that's clear. Oh, but Nora, can't we bridge it somehow?

NORA: The way I am now, I'm no wife for you.

HELMER: I have the strength to make myself over.

NORA: Maybe — if your doll gets taken away.

HELMER: But to part! To part from you! No, Nora, no — I can't imagine it.

NORA (*going out, right*): All the more reason why it has to be. (*She reenters with her coat and a small overnight bag, which she puts on a chair by the table.*)

HELMER: Nora, Nora, not now! Wait till tomorrow.

NORA: I can't spend the night in a strange man's room.

HELMER: But couldn't we live here like brother and sister —

NORA: You know very well how long that would last. (*Throws her shawl about her.*) Good-bye, Torvald. I won't look in on the children. I know they're in better hands than mine. The way I am now, I'm no use to them.

HELMER: But someday, Nora — someday — ?

NORA: How can I tell? I haven't the least idea what'll become of me.

HELMER: But you're my wife, now and wherever you go.

NORA: Listen, Torvald — I've heard that when a wife deserts her husband's house just as I'm doing, then the law frees him from all responsibility. In any case, I'm freeing you from being responsible. Don't feel yourself bound, any more than I will. There has to be absolute freedom for us both. Here, take your ring back. Give me mine.

HELMER: That too?

NORA: That too.

HELMER: There it is.

NORA: Good. Well, now it's all over. I'm putting the keys here. The maids know all about keeping up the house — better than I do. Tomorrow, after I've left town, Kristine will stop by to pack up everything that's mine from home. I'd like those things shipped up to me.

HELMER: Over! All over! Nora, won't you ever think about me?

NORA: I'm sure I'll think of you often, and about the children and the house here.

HELMER: May I write you?

NORA: No — never. You're not to do that.

HELMER: Oh, but let me send you—

NORA: Nothing. Nothing.

HELMER: Or help you if you need it.

NORA: No. I accept nothing from strangers.

HELMER: Nora—can I never be more than a stranger to you?

NORA (*picking up the overnight bag*): Ah, Torvald—it would take the greatest miracle of all—

HELMER: Tell me the greatest miracle!

NORA: You and I both would have to transform ourselves to the point that— Oh, Torvald, I've stopped believing in miracles.

HELMER: But I'll believe. Tell me! Transform ourselves to the point that—?

NORA: That our living together could be a true marriage. (*She goes out down the hall.*)

HELMER (*sinks down on a chair by the door, face buried in his hands*): Nora! Nora! (*Looking about and rising.*) Empty. She's gone. (*A sudden hope leaps in him.*) The greatest miracle—?

(*From below, the sound of a door slamming shut.*)

CD-ROM: Research Henrik Ibsen and *A Doll House* in depth with cultural documents and multimedia resources on *LiterActive*.

Arthur Miller b. 1915

Death of a Salesman   [1949]
Certain Private Conversations in Two Acts and a Requiem

CHARACTERS

WILLY LOMAN	UNCLE BEN
LINDA	HOWARD WAGNER
BIFF	JENNY
HAPPY	STANLEY
BERNARD	MISS FORSYTHE
THE WOMAN	LETTA
CHARLEY	

The action takes place in Willy Loman's house and yard and in various places he visits in the New York and Boston of today.

(*Throughout the play, in the stage directions, left and right mean stage left and stage right.*)

ACT I

(*A melody is heard, played upon a flute. It is small and fine, telling of grass and trees and the horizon. The curtain rises.*)

(*Before us is the Salesman's house. We are aware of towering, angular shapes behind it, surrounding it on all sides. Only the blue light of the sky falls upon the house and forestage; the surrounding area shows an angry glow of orange. As more light appears, we see a solid vault of apartment houses around the small, fragile-seeming home. An air of the dream clings to the place, a dream rising out of reality. The kitchen at center seems actual enough, for there is a kitchen table with three chairs, and a refrigerator. But no other fixtures are seen. At the back of the kitchen there is a draped entrance, which leads to the living room. To the right of the kitchen, on a level raised two feet, is a bedroom furnished only with a brass bedstead and a straight chair. On a shelf over the bed a silver athletic trophy stands. A window opens onto the apartment house at the side.*)

(*Behind the kitchen, on a level raised six and a half feet, is the boys' bedroom, at present barely visible. Two beds are dimly seen, and at the back of the room a dormer window. [This bedroom is above the unseen living room.] At the left a stairway curves up to it from the kitchen.*)

(*The entire setting is wholly or, in some places, partially transparent. The roofline of the house is one-dimensional; under and over it we see the apartment buildings. Before the house lies an apron, curving beyond the forestage into the orchestra. This forward area serves as the back yard as well as the locale of all Willy's imaginings and of his city scenes. Whenever the action is in the present the actors observe the imaginary wall-lines, entering the house only through its door at the left. But in the scenes of the past these boundaries are broken, and characters enter or leave a room by stepping "through" a wall onto the forestage.*)

(*From the right, Willy Loman, the Salesman, enters, carrying two large sample cases. The flute plays on. He hears but is not aware of it. He is past sixty years of age, dressed quietly. Even as he crosses the stage to the doorway of the house, his exhaustion is apparent. He unlocks the door, comes into the kitchen, and thankfully lets his burden down, feeling the soreness of his palms. A word-sigh escapes his lips — it might be "Oh, boy, oh, boy." He closes the door then carries his cases out into the living room, through the draped kitchen doorway.*)

(*Linda, his wife, has stirred in her bed at the right. She gets out and puts on a robe, listening. Most often jovial, she has developed an iron repression of her exceptions to Willy's behavior — she more than loves him, she admires him, as though his mercurial nature, his temper, his massive dreams and little cruelties, served her only as sharp reminders of the turbulent longings within him, longings which she shares but lacks the temperament to utter and follow to their end.*)

LINDA (*hearing Willy outside the bedroom, calls with some trepidation*): Willy!
WILLY: It's all right. I came back.
LINDA: Why? What happened? (*Slight pause.*) Did something happen, Willy?
WILLY: No, nothing happened.
LINDA: You didn't smash the car, did you?
WILLY (*with casual irritation*): I said nothing happened. Didn't you hear me?
LINDA: Don't you feel well?
WILLY: I'm tired to the death. (*The flute has faded away. He sits on the bed beside her, a little numb.*) I couldn't make it. I just couldn't make it, Linda.

LINDA (*very carefully, delicately*): Where were you all day? You look terrible.

WILLY: I got as far as a little above Yonkers. I stopped for a cup of coffee. Maybe it was the coffee.

LINDA: What?

WILLY (*after a pause*): I suddenly couldn't drive anymore. The car kept going off onto the shoulder, y'know?

LINDA (*helpfully*): Oh. Maybe it was the steering again. I don't think Angelo knows the Studebaker.

WILLY: No, it's me, it's me. Suddenly I realize I'm goin' sixty miles an hour and I don't remember the last five minutes. I'm — I can't seem to — keep my mind to it.

LINDA: Maybe it's your glasses. You never went for your new glasses.

WILLY: No, I see everything. I came back ten miles an hour. It took me nearly four hours from Yonkers.

LINDA (*resigned*): Well, you'll just have to take a rest, Willy, you can't continue this way.

WILLY: I just got back from Florida.

LINDA: But you didn't rest your mind. Your mind is overactive, and the mind is what counts, dear.

WILLY: I'll start out in the morning. Maybe I'll feel better in the morning. (*She is taking off his shoes.*) These goddam arch supports are killing me.

LINDA: Take an aspirin. Should I get you an aspirin? It'll soothe you.

WILLY (*with wonder*): I was driving along, you understand? And I was fine. I was even observing the scenery. You can imagine, me looking at scenery, on the road every week of my life. But it's so beautiful up there, Linda, the trees are so thick, and the sun is warm. I opened the windshield and just let the warm air bathe over me. And then all of a sudden I'm goin' off the road! I'm tellin' ya, I absolutely forgot I was driving. If I'd've gone the other way over the white line I might've killed somebody. So I went on again — and five minutes later I'm dreamin' again, and I nearly — (*He presses two fingers against his eyes.*) I have such thoughts, I have such strange thoughts.

LINDA: Willy, dear. Talk to them again. There's no reason why you can't work in New York.

WILLY: They don't need me in New York. I'm the New England man. I'm vital in New England.

LINDA: But you're sixty years old. They can't expect you to keep traveling every week.

WILLY: I'll have to send a wire to Portland. I'm supposed to see Brown and Morrison tomorrow morning at ten o'clock to show the line. Goddammit, I could sell them! (*He starts putting on his jacket.*)

LINDA (*taking the jacket from him*): Why don't you go down to the place tomorrow and tell Howard you've simply got to work in New York? You're too accommodating, dear.

WILLY: If old man Wagner was alive I'd a been in charge of New York now! That man was a prince, he was a masterful man. But that boy of his, that Howard, he don't appreciate. When I went north the first time, the Wagner Company didn't know where New England was!

LINDA: Why don't you tell those things to Howard, dear?

WILLY (*encouraged*): I will, I definitely will. Is there any cheese?

LINDA: I'll make you a sandwich.

WILLY: No, go to sleep. I'll take some milk. I'll be up right away. The boys in?

LINDA: They're sleeping. Happy took Biff on a date tonight.

WILLY (*interested*): That so?

LINDA: It was so nice to see them shaving together, one behind the other, in the bathroom. And going out together. You notice? The whole house smells of shaving lotion.

WILLY: Figure it out. Work a lifetime to pay off a house. You finally own it, and there's nobody to live in it.

LINDA: Well, dear, life is a casting off. It's always that way.

WILLY: No, no, some people — some people accomplish something. Did Biff say anything after I went this morning?

LINDA: You shouldn't have criticized him, Willy, especially after he just got off the train. You mustn't lose your temper with him.

WILLY: When the hell did I lose my temper? I simply asked him if he was making any money. Is that a criticism?

LINDA: But, dear, how could he make any money?

WILLY (*worried and angered*): There's such an undercurrent in him. He became a moody man. Did he apologize when I left this morning?

LINDA: He was crestfallen, Willy. You know how he admires you. I think if he finds himself, then you'll both be happier and not fight any more.

WILLY: How can he find himself on a farm? Is that a life? A farmhand? In the beginning, when he was young, I thought, well, a young man, it's good for him to tramp around, take a lot of different jobs. But it's more than ten years now and he has yet to make thirty-five dollars a week!

LINDA: He's finding himself, Willy.

WILLY: Not finding yourself at the age of thirty-four is a disgrace!

LINDA: Shh!

WILLY: The trouble is he's lazy, goddammit!

LINDA: Willy, please!

WILLY: Biff is a lazy bum!

LINDA: They're sleeping. Get something to eat. Go on down.

WILLY: Why did he come home? I would like to know what brought him home.

LINDA: I don't know. I think he's still lost, Willy. I think he's very lost.

WILLY: Biff Loman is lost. In the greatest country in the world a young man with such — personal attractiveness, gets lost. And such a hard worker. There's one thing about Biff — he's not lazy.

LINDA: Never.

WILLY (*with pity and resolve*): I'll see him in the morning; I'll have a nice talk with him. I'll get him a job selling. He could be big in no time. My God! Remember how they used to follow him around in high school? When he smiled at one of them their faces lit up. When he walked down the street . . . (*He loses himself in reminiscences.*)

LINDA (*trying to bring him out of it*): Willy, dear, I got a new kind of American-type cheese today. It's whipped.

WILLY: Why do you get American when I like Swiss?

LINDA: I just thought you'd like a change—

WILLY: I don't want a change! I want Swiss cheese. Why am I always being contradicted?

LINDA (*with a covering laugh*): I thought it would be a surprise.

WILLY: Why don't you open a window in here, for God's sake?

LINDA (*with infinite patience*): They're all open, dear.

WILLY: The way they boxed us in here. Bricks and windows, windows and bricks.

LINDA: We should've bought the land next door.

WILLY: The street is lined with cars. There's not a breath of fresh air in the neighborhood. The grass don't grow anymore, you can't raise a carrot in the back yard. They should've had a law against apartment houses. Remember those two beautiful elm trees out there? When I and Biff hung the swing between them?

LINDA: Yeah, like being a million miles from the city.

WILLY: They should've arrested the builder for cutting those down. They massacred the neighborhood. (*Lost.*) More and more I think of those days, Linda. This time of year it was lilac and wisteria. And then the peonies would come out, and the daffodils. What fragrance in this room!

LINDA: Well, after all, people had to move somewhere.

WILLY: No, there's more people now.

LINDA: I don't think there's more people. I think—

WILLY: There's more people! That's what's ruining this country! Population is getting out of control. The competition is maddening! Smell the stink from that apartment house! And another one on the other side . . . How can they whip cheese?

(*On Willy's last line, Biff and Happy raise themselves up in their beds, listening.*)

LINDA: Go down, try it. And be quiet.

WILLY (*turning to Linda, guiltily*): You're not worried about me, are you, sweetheart?

BIFF: What's the matter?

HAPPY: Listen!

LINDA: You've got too much on the ball to worry about.

WILLY: You're my foundation and my support, Linda.

LINDA: Just try to relax, dear. You make mountains out of molehills.

WILLY: I won't fight with him any more. If he wants to go back to Texas, let him go.

LINDA: He'll find his way.

WILLY: Sure. Certain men just don't get started till later in life. Like Thomas Edison, I think. Or B. F. Goodrich.° One of them was deaf. (*He starts for the bedroom doorway.*) I'll put my money on Biff.

LINDA: And Willy — if it's warm Sunday we'll drive in the country. And we'll open the windshield, and take lunch.

WILLY: No, the windshields don't open on the new cars.

LINDA: But you opened it today.

WILLY: Me? I didn't. (*He stops.*) Now isn't that peculiar! Isn't that a remarkable — (*He breaks off in amazement and fright as the flute is heard distantly.*)

LINDA: What, darling?

WILLY: That is the most remarkable thing.

LINDA: What, dear?

WILLY: I was thinking of the Chevvy. (*Slight pause.*) Nineteen twenty-eight . . . when I had that red Chevvy — (*Breaks off.*) That funny? I coulda sworn I was driving that Chevvy today.

LINDA: Well, that's nothing. Something must've reminded you.

WILLY: Remarkable. Ts. Remember those days? The way Biff used to simonize that car? The dealer refused to believe there was eighty thousand miles on it. (*He shakes his head.*) Heh! (*To Linda.*) Close your eyes, I'll be right up. (*He walks out of the bedroom.*)

HAPPY (*to Biff*): Jesus, maybe he smashed up the car again!

LINDA (*calling after Willy*): Be careful on the stairs, dear! The cheese is on the middle shelf! (*She turns, goes over to the bed, takes his jacket, and goes out of the bedroom.*)

(*Light has risen on the boys' room. Unseen, Willy is heard talking to himself, "Eighty thousand miles," and a little laugh. Biff gets out of bed, comes downstage a bit, and stands attentively. Biff is two years older than his brother Happy, well built, but in these days bears a worn air and seems less self-assured. He has succeeded less, and his dreams are stronger and less acceptable than Happy's. Happy is tall, powerfully made. Sexuality is like a visible color on him, or a scent that many women have discovered. He, like his brother, is lost, but in a different way, for he has never allowed himself to turn his face toward defeat and is thus more confused and hard-skinned, although seemingly more content.*)

HAPPY (*getting out of bed*): He's going to get his license taken away if he keeps that up. I'm getting nervous about him, y'know, Biff?

Edison, Goodrich: Thomas Alva Edison (1847–1931) was one of the greatest and most productive inventors of his time, especially of electronic equipment; he suffered from deafness for much of his life. Benjamin Franklin Goodrich (1841–1888) founded the B. F. Goodrich Company. Neither man was a late starter, though Edison did not thrive in conventional classroom settings.

BIFF: His eyes are going.

HAPPY: No, I've driven with him. He sees all right. He just doesn't keep his mind on it. I drove into the city with him last week. He stops at a green light and then it turns red and he goes. (*He laughs.*)

BIFF: Maybe he's color-blind.

HAPPY: Pop? Why he's got the finest eye for color in the business. You know that.

BIFF (*sitting down on his bed*): I'm going to sleep.

HAPPY: You're not still sour on Dad, are you, Biff?

BIFF: He's all right, I guess.

WILLY (*underneath them, in the living room*): Yes, sir, eighty thousand miles — eighty-two thousand!

BIFF: You smoking?

HAPPY (*holding out a pack of cigarettes*): Want one?

BIFF (*taking a cigarette*): I can never sleep when I smell it.

WILLY: What a simonizing job, heh!

HAPPY (*with deep sentiment*): Funny, Biff, y'know? Us sleeping in here again? The old beds. (*He pats his bed affectionately.*) All the talk that went across those two beds, huh? Our whole lives.

BIFF: Yeah. Lotta dreams and plans.

HAPPY (*with a deep and masculine laugh*): About five hundred women would like to know what was said in this room.

(*They share a soft laugh.*)

BIFF: Remember that big Betsy something — what the hell was her name — over on Bushwick Avenue?

HAPPY (*combing his hair*): With the collie dog!

BIFF: That's the one. I got you in there, remember?

HAPPY: Yeah, that was my first time — I think. Boy, there was a pig. (*They laugh, almost crudely.*) You taught me everything I know about women. Don't forget that.

BIFF: I bet you forgot how bashful you used to be. Especially with girls.

HAPPY: Oh, I still am, Biff.

BIFF: Oh, go on.

HAPPY: I just control it, that's all. I think I got less bashful and you got more so. What happened, Biff? Where's the old humor, the old confidence? (*He shakes Biff's knee. Biff gets up and moves restlessly about the room.*) What's the matter?

BIFF: Why does Dad mock me all the time?

HAPPY: He's not mocking you, he —

BIFF: Everything I say there's a twist of mockery on his face. I can't get near him.

HAPPY: He just wants you to make good, that's all. I wanted to talk to you about Dad for a long time, Biff. Something's — happening to him. He — talks to himself.

BIFF: I noticed that this morning. But he always mumbled.

HAPPY: But not so noticeable. It got so embarrassing I sent him to Florida. And you know something? Most of the time he's talking to you.

BIFF: What's he say about me?

HAPPY: I can't make it out.

BIFF: What's he say about me?

HAPPY: I think the fact that you're not settled, that you're still kind of up in the air . . .

BIFF: There's one or two other things depressing him, Happy.

HAPPY: What do you mean?

BIFF: Never mind. Just don't lay it all to me.

HAPPY: But I think if you just got started — I mean — is there any future for you out there?

BIFF: I tell ya, Hap, I don't know what the future is. I don't know — what I'm supposed to want.

HAPPY: What do you mean?

BIFF: Well, I spent six or seven years after high school trying to work myself up. Shipping clerk, salesman, business of one kind or another. And it's a measly manner of existence. To get on that subway on the hot mornings in summer. To devote your whole life to keeping stock, or making phone calls, or selling or buying. To suffer fifty weeks of the year for the sake of a two-week vacation, when all you really desire is to be outdoors, with your shirt off. And always to have to get ahead of the next fella. And still — that's how you build a future.

HAPPY: Well, you really enjoy it on a farm? Are you content out there?

BIFF (*with rising agitation*): Hap, I've had twenty or thirty different kinds of jobs since I left home before the war, and it always turns out the same. I just realized it lately. In Nebraska when I herded cattle, and the Dakotas, and Arizona, and now in Texas. It's why I came home now, I guess, because I realized it. This farm I work on, it's spring there now, see? And they've got about fifteen new colts. There's nothing more inspiring or — beautiful than the sight of a mare and a new colt. And it's cool there now, see? Texas is cool now, and it's spring. And whenever spring comes to where I am, I suddenly get the feeling, my God, I'm not gettin' anywhere! What the hell am I doing, playing around with horses, twenty-eight dollars a week! I'm thirty-four years old, I oughta be makin' my future. That's when I come running home. And now, I get here, and I don't know what to do with myself. (*After a pause.*) I've always made a point of not wasting my life, and every time I come back here I know that all I've done is to waste my life.

HAPPY: You're a poet, you know that, Biff? You're a — you're an idealist!

BIFF: No, I'm mixed up very bad. Maybe I oughta get married. Maybe I oughta get stuck into something. Maybe that's my trouble. I'm like a boy. I'm not married, I'm not in business, I just — I'm like a boy. Are you content, Hap? You're a success, aren't you? Are you content?

HAPPY: Hell, no!

BIFF: Why? You're making money, aren't you?

HAPPY (*moving about with energy, expressiveness*): All I can do now is wait for the merchandise manager to die. And suppose I get to be merchandise manager? He's a good friend of mine, and he just built a terrific estate on Long Island. And he lived there about two months and sold it, and now he's building another one. He can't enjoy it once it's finished. And I know that's just what I would do. I don't know what the hell I'm workin' for. Sometimes I sit in my apartment — all alone. And I think of the rent I'm paying. And it's crazy. But then, it's what I always wanted. My own apartment, a car, and plenty of women. And still, goddammit, I'm lonely.

BIFF (*with enthusiasm*): Listen, why don't you come out West with me?

HAPPY: You and I, heh?

BIFF: Sure, maybe we could buy a ranch. Raise cattle, use our muscles. Men built like we are should be working out in the open.

HAPPY (*avidly*): The Loman Brothers, heh?

BIFF (*with vast affection*): Sure, we'd be known all over the counties!

HAPPY (*enthralled*): That's what I dream about, Biff. Sometimes I want to just rip my clothes off in the middle of the store and outbox that goddam merchandise manager. I mean I can outbox, outrun and outlift anybody in that store, and I have to take orders from those common, petty sons-of-bitches till I can't stand it anymore.

BIFF: I'm tellin' you, kid, if you were with me I'd be happy out there.

HAPPY (*enthused*): See, Biff, everybody around me is so false that I'm constantly lowering my ideals . . .

BIFF: Baby, together we'd stand up for one another, we'd have someone to trust.

HAPPY: If I were around you —

BIFF: Hap, the trouble is we weren't brought up to grub for money. I don't know how to do it.

HAPPY: Neither can I!

BIFF: Then let's go!

HAPPY: The only thing is — what can you make out there?

BIFF: But look at your friend. Builds an estate and then hasn't the peace of mind to live in it.

HAPPY: Yeah, but when he walks into the store the waves part in front of him. That's fifty-two thousand dollars a year coming through the revolving door, and I got more in my pinky finger than he's got in his head.

BIFF: Yeah, but you just said —

HAPPY: I gotta show some of those pompous, self-important executives over there that Hap Loman can make the grade. I want to walk into the store the way he walks in. Then I'll go with you, Biff. We'll be together yet, I swear. But take those two we had tonight. Now weren't they gorgeous creatures?

BIFF: Yeah, yeah, most gorgeous I've had in years.

HAPPY: I get that any time I want, Biff. Whenever I feel disgusted. The only trouble is, it gets like bowling or something. I just keep knockin' them over and it doesn't mean anything. You still run around a lot?

BIFF: Naa. I'd like to find a girl — steady, somebody with substance.

HAPPY: That's what I long for.

BIFF: Go on! You'd never come home.

HAPPY: I would! Somebody with character, with resistance! Like Mom, y'know? You're gonna call me a bastard when I tell you this. That girl Charlotte I was with tonight is engaged to be married in five weeks. (*He tries on his new hat.*)

BIFF: No kiddin'!

HAPPY: Sure, the guy's in line for the vice-presidency of the store. I don't know what gets into me, maybe I just have an overdeveloped sense of competition or something, but I went and ruined her, and furthermore I can't get rid of her. And he's the third executive I've done that to. Isn't that a crummy characteristic? And to top it all, I go to their weddings! (*Indignantly, but laughing.*) Like I'm not supposed to take bribes. Manufacturers offer me a hundred-dollar bill now and then to throw an order their way. You know how honest I am, but it's like this girl, see. I hate myself for it. Because I don't want the girl, and, still, I take it and — I love it!

BIFF: Let's go to sleep.

HAPPY: I guess we didn't settle anything, heh?

BIFF: I just got one idea that I think I'm going to try.

HAPPY: What's that?

BIFF: Remember Bill Oliver?

HAPPY: Sure, Oliver is very big now. You want to work for him again?

BIFF: No, but when I quit he said something to me. He put his arm on my shoulder, and he said, "Biff, if you ever need anything, come to me."

HAPPY: I remember that. That sounds good.

BIFF: I think I'll go to see him. If I could get ten thousand or even seven or eight thousand dollars I could buy a beautiful ranch.

HAPPY: I bet he'd back you. 'Cause he thought highly of you, Biff. I mean, they all do. You're well liked, Biff. That's why I say to come back here, and we both have the apartment. And I'm tellin' you, Biff, any babe you want . . .

BIFF: No, with a ranch I could do the work I like and still be something. I just wonder though. I wonder if Oliver still thinks I stole that carton of basketballs.

HAPPY: Oh, he probably forgot that long ago. It's almost ten years. You're too sensitive. Anyway, he didn't really fire you.

BIFF: Well, I think he was going to. I think that's why I quit. I was never sure whether he knew or not. I know he thought the world of me, though. I was the only one he'd let lock up the place.

WILLY (*below*): You gonna wash the engine, Biff?
HAPPY: Shh!

(*Biff looks at Happy, who is gazing down, listening. Willy is mumbling in the parlor.*)

HAPPY: You hear that?

(*They listen. Willy laughs warmly.*)

BIFF (*growing angry*): Doesn't he know Mom can hear that?
WILLY: Don't get your sweater dirty, Biff!

(*A look of pain crosses Biff's face.*)

HAPPY: Isn't that terrible? Don't leave again, will you? You'll find a job here.
     You gotta stick around. I don't know what to do about him, it's getting
     embarrassing.
WILLY: What a simonizing job!
BIFF: Mom's hearing that!
WILLY: No kiddin', Biff, you got a date? Wonderful!
HAPPY: Go on to sleep. But talk to him in the morning, will you?
BIFF (*reluctantly getting into bed*): With her in the house. Brother!
HAPPY (*getting into bed*): I wish you'd have a good talk with him.

(*The light on their room begins to fade.*)

BIFF (*to himself in bed*): That selfish, stupid . . .
HAPPY: Sh . . . Sleep, Biff.

(*Their light is out. Well before they have finished speaking, Willy's form is dimly seen
below in the darkened kitchen. He opens the refrigerator, searches in there, and takes
out a bottle of milk. The apartment houses are fading out, and the entire house and
surroundings become covered with leaves. Music insinuates itself as the leaves appear.*)

WILLY: Just wanna be careful with those girls, Biff, that's all. Don't make any
     promises. No promises of any kind. Because a girl, y'know, they always
     believe what you tell 'em, and you're very young, Biff, you're too young
     to be talking seriously to girls.

(*Light rises on the kitchen. Willy, talking, shuts the refrigerator door and comes
downstage to the kitchen table. He pours milk into a glass. He is totally immersed in
himself, smiling faintly.*)

WILLY: Too young entirely, Biff. You want to watch your schooling first. Then
     when you're all set, there'll be plenty of girls for a boy like you. (*He smiles
     broadly at a kitchen chair.*) That so? The girls pay for you? (*He laughs.*) Boy,
     you must really be makin' a hit.

(*Willy is gradually addressing—physically—a point offstage, speaking through the
wall of the kitchen, and his voice has been rising in volume to that of a normal conversation.*)

WILLY: I been wondering why you polish the car so careful. Ha! Don't leave the hubcaps, boys. Get the chamois to the hubcaps. Happy, use newspaper on the windows, it's the easiest thing. Show him how to do it, Biff! You see, Happy? Pad it up, use it like a pad. That's it, that's it, good work. You're doin' all right, Hap. (*He pauses, then nods in approbation for a few seconds, then looks upward.*) Biff, first thing we gotta do when we get time is clip that big branch over the house. Afraid it's gonna fall in a storm and hit the roof. Tell you what. We get a rope and sling her around, and then we climb up there with a couple of saws and take her down. Soon as you finish the car, boys, I wanna see ye. I got a surprise for you, boys.

BIFF (*offstage*): Whatta ya got, Dad?

WILLY: No, you finish first. Never leave a job till you're finished — remember that. (*Looking toward the "big trees."*) Biff, up in Albany I saw a beautiful hammock. I think I'll buy it next trip, and we'll hang it right between those two elms. Wouldn't that be something? Just swingin' there under those branches. Boy, that would be . . .

(*Young Biff and Young Happy appear from the direction Willy was addressing. Happy carries rags and a pail of water. Biff, wearing a sweater with a block "S," carries a football.*)

BIFF (*pointing in the direction of the car offstage*): How's that, Pop, professional?

WILLY: Terrific. Terrific job, boys. Good work, Biff.

HAPPY: Where's the surprise, Pop?

WILLY: In the back seat of the car.

HAPPY: Boy! (*He runs off.*)

BIFF: What is it, Dad? Tell me, what'd you buy?

WILLY (*laughing, cuffs him*): Never mind, something I want you to have.

BIFF (*turns and starts off*): What is it, Hap?

HAPPY (*offstage*): It's a punching bag!

BIFF: Oh, Pop!

WILLY: It's got Gene Tunney's signature on it!

(*Happy runs onstage with a punching bag.*)

BIFF: Gee, how'd you know we wanted a punching bag?

WILLY: Well, it's the finest thing for the timing.

HAPPY (*lies down on his back and pedals with his feet*): I'm losing weight, you notice, Pop?

WILLY (*to Happy*): Jumping rope is good too.

BIFF: Did you see the new football I got?

WILLY (*examining the ball*): Where'd you get a new ball?

BIFF: The coach told me to practice my passing.

WILLY: That so? And he gave you the ball, heh?

BIFF: Well, I borrowed it from the locker room. (*He laughs confidentially.*)

WILLY (*laughing with him at the theft*): I want you to return that.

HAPPY: I told you he wouldn't like it!

BIFF (*angrily*): Well, I'm bringing it back!

WILLY (*stopping the incipient argument, to Happy*): Sure, he's gotta practice with a regulation ball, doesn't he? (*To Biff.*) Coach'll probably congratulate you on your initiative!

BIFF: Oh, he keeps congratulating my initiative all the time, Pop.

WILLY: That's because he likes you. If somebody else took that ball there'd be an uproar. So what's the report, boys, what's the report?

BIFF: Where'd you go this time, Dad? Gee we were lonesome for you.

WILLY (*pleased, puts an arm around each boy and they come down to the apron*): Lonesome, heh?

BIFF: Missed you every minute.

WILLY: Don't say? Tell you a secret, boys. Don't breathe it to a soul. Someday I'll have my own business, and I'll never have to leave home anymore.

HAPPY: Like Uncle Charley, heh?

WILLY: Bigger than Uncle Charley! Because Charley is not — liked. He's liked, but he's not — well liked.

BIFF: Where'd you go this time, Dad?

WILLY: Well, I got on the road, and I went north to Providence. Met the Mayor.

BIFF: The Mayor of Providence!

WILLY: He was sitting in the hotel lobby.

BIFF: What'd he say?

WILLY: He said, "Morning!" And I said, "You got a fine city here, Mayor." And then he had coffee with me. And then I went to Waterbury. Waterbury is a fine city. Big clock city, the famous Waterbury clock. Sold a nice bill there. And then Boston — Boston is the cradle of the Revolution. A fine city. And a couple of other towns in Mass., and on to Portland and Bangor and straight home!

BIFF: Gee, I'd love to go with you sometime, Dad.

WILLY: Soon as summer comes.

HAPPY: Promise?

WILLY: You and Hap and I, and I'll show you all the towns. America is full of beautiful towns and fine, upstanding people. And they know me, boys, they know me up and down New England. The finest people. And when I bring you fellas up, there'll be open sesame for all of us, 'cause one thing, boys: I have friends. I can park my car in any street in New England, and the cops protect it like their own. This summer, heh?

BIFF AND HAPPY (*together*): Yeah! You bet!

WILLY: We'll take our bathing suits.

HAPPY: We'll carry your bags, Pop!

WILLY: Oh, won't that be something! Me comin' into the Boston stores with you boys carryin' my bags. What a sensation!

(*Biff is prancing around, practicing passing the ball.*)

WILLY: You nervous, Biff, about the game?

BIFF: Not if you're gonna be there.

WILLY: What do they say about you in school, now that they made you captain?

HAPPY: There's a crowd of girls behind him every time the classes change.

BIFF (*taking Willy's hand*): This Saturday, Pop, this Saturday — just for you, I'm going to break through for a touchdown.

HAPPY: You're supposed to pass.

BIFF: I'm takin' one play for Pop. You watch me, Pop, and when I take off my helmet, that means I'm breakin' out. Then you watch me crash through that line!

WILLY (*kisses Biff*): Oh, wait'll I tell this in Boston!

(*Bernard enters in knickers. He is younger than Biff, earnest and loyal, a worried boy.*)

BERNARD: Biff, where are you? You're supposed to study with me today.

WILLY: Hey, looka Bernard. What're you lookin' so anemic about, Bernard?

BERNARD: He's gotta study, Uncle Willy. He's got Regents next week.

HAPPY (*tauntingly, spinning Bernard around*): Let's box, Bernard!

BERNARD: Biff! (*He gets away from Happy.*) Listen, Biff, I heard Mr. Birnbaum say that if you don't start studyin' math he's gonna flunk you, and you won't graduate. I heard him!

WILLY: You better study with him, Biff. Go ahead now.

BERNARD: I heard him!

BIFF: Oh, Pop, you didn't see my sneakers! (*He holds up a foot for Willy to look at.*)

WILLY: Hey, that's a beautiful job of printing!

BERNARD (*wiping his glasses*): Just because he printed University of Virginia on his sneakers doesn't mean they've got to graduate him, Uncle Willy!

WILLY (*angrily*): What're you talking about? With scholarships to three universities they're gonna flunk him?

BERNARD: But I heard Mr. Birnbaum say —

WILLY: Don't be a pest, Bernard! (*To his boys.*) What an anemic!

BERNARD: Okay, I'm waiting for you in my house, Biff.

(*Bernard goes off. The Lomans laugh.*)

WILLY: Bernard is not well liked, is he?

BIFF: He's liked, but he's not well liked.

HAPPY: That's right, Pop.

WILLY: That's just what I mean. Bernard can get the best marks in school, y'understand, but when he gets out in the business world, y'understand, you are going to be five times ahead of him. That's why I thank Almighty God you're both built like Adonises. Because the man who makes an appearance in the business world, the man who creates personal interest, is the man who gets ahead. Be liked and you will never want. You take me, for instance. I never have to wait in line to see a buyer. "Willy Loman is here!" That's all they have to know, and I go right through.

BIFF: Did you knock them dead, Pop?

WILLY: Knocked 'em cold in Providence, slaughtered 'em in Boston.
HAPPY (*on his back, pedaling again*): I'm losing weight, you notice, Pop?

(*Linda enters as of old, a ribbon in her hair, carrying a basket of washing.*)

LINDA (*with youthful energy*): Hello, dear!
WILLY: Sweetheart!
LINDA: How'd the Chevvy run?
WILLY: Chevrolet, Linda, is the greatest car ever built. (*To the boys.*) Since when do you let your mother carry wash up the stairs?
BIFF: Grab hold there, boy!
HAPPY: Where to, Mom?
LINDA: Hang them up on the line. And you better go down to your friends, Biff. The cellar is full of boys. They don't know what to do with themselves.
BIFF: Ah, when Pop comes home they can wait!
WILLY (*laughs appreciatively*): You better go down and tell them what to do, Biff.
BIFF: I think I'll have them sweep out the furnace room.
WILLY: Good work, Biff.
BIFF (*goes through wall-line of kitchen to doorway at back and calls down*): Fellas! Everybody sweep out the furnace room! I'll be right down!
VOICES: All right! Okay, Biff.
BIFF: George and Sam and Frank, come out back! We're hangin' up the wash! Come on, Hap, on the double! (*He and Happy carry out the basket.*)
LINDA: The way they obey him!
WILLY: Well, that's training, the training. I'm tellin' you, I was sellin' thousands and thousands, but I had to come home.
LINDA: Oh, the whole block'll be at that game. Did you sell anything?
WILLY: I did five hundred gross in Providence and seven hundred gross in Boston.
LINDA: No! Wait a minute, I've got a pencil. (*She pulls pencil and paper out of her apron pocket.*) That makes your commission . . . Two hundred — my God! Two hundred and twelve dollars!
WILLY: Well, I didn't figure it yet, but . . .
LINDA: How much did you do?
WILLY: Well, I — I did — about a hundred and eighty gross in Providence. Well, no — it came to — roughly two hundred gross on the whole trip.
LINDA (*without hesitation*): Two hundred gross. That's . . . (*She figures.*)
WILLY: The trouble was that three of the stores were half-closed for inventory in Boston. Otherwise I woulda broke records.
LINDA: Well, it makes seventy dollars and some pennies. That's very good.
WILLY: What do we owe?
LINDA: Well, on the first there's sixteen dollars on the refrigerator —
WILLY: Why sixteen?
LINDA: Well, the fan belt broke, so it was a dollar eighty.

WILLY: But it's brand new.

LINDA: Well, the man said that's the way it is. Till they work themselves in, y'know.

(*They move through the wall-line into the kitchen.*)

WILLY: I hope we didn't get stuck on that machine.

LINDA: They got the biggest ads of any of them!

WILLY: I know, it's a fine machine. What else?

LINDA: Well, there's nine-sixty for the washing machine. And for the vacuum cleaner there's three and a half due on the fifteenth. Then the roof, you got twenty-one dollars remaining.

WILLY: It don't leak, does it?

LINDA: No, they did a wonderful job. Then you owe Frank for the carburetor.

WILLY: I'm not going to pay that man! That goddam Chevrolet, they ought to prohibit the manufacture of that car!

LINDA: Well, you owe him three and a half. And odds and ends, comes to around a hundred and twenty dollars by the fifteenth.

WILLY: A hundred and twenty dollars! My God, if business don't pick up I don't know what I'm gonna do!

LINDA: Well, next week you'll do better.

WILLY: Oh, I'll knock 'em dead next week. I'll go to Hartford. I'm very well liked in Hartford. You know, the trouble is, Linda, people don't seem to take to me.

(*They move onto the forestage.*)

LINDA: Oh, don't be foolish.

WILLY: I know it when I walk in. They seem to laugh at me.

LINDA: Why? Why would they laugh at you? Don't talk that way, Willy.

(*Willy moves to the edge of the stage. Linda goes into the kitchen and starts to darn stockings.*)

WILLY: I don't know the reason for it, but they just pass me by. I'm not noticed.

LINDA: But you're doing wonderful, dear. You're making seventy to a hundred dollars a week.

WILLY: But I gotta be at it ten, twelve hours a day. Other men — I don't know — they do it easier. I don't know why — I can't stop myself — I talk too much. A man oughta come in with a few words. One thing about Charley. He's a man of few words, and they respect him.

LINDA: You don't talk too much, you're just lively.

WILLY (*smiling*): Well, I figure, what the hell, life is short, a couple of jokes. (*To himself.*) I joke too much! (*The smile goes.*)

LINDA: Why? You're —

WILLY: I'm fat. I'm very — foolish to look at, Linda. I didn't tell you, but Christmas time I happened to be calling on F. H. Stewarts, and a salesman I know, as I was going in to see the buyer I heard him say something about—walrus. And I—I cracked him right across the face. I won't take that. I simply will not take that. But they do laugh at me. I know that.

LINDA: Darling . . .

WILLY: I gotta overcome it. I know I gotta overcome it. I'm not dressing to advantage, maybe.

LINDA: Willy, darling, you're the handsomest man in the world—

WILLY: Oh, no, Linda.

LINDA: To me you are. (*Slight pause.*) The handsomest.

(*From the darkness is heard the laughter of a woman. Willy doesn't turn to it, but it continues through Linda's lines.*)

LINDA: And the boys, Willy. Few men are idolized by their children the way you are.

(*Music is heard as behind a scrim, to the left of the house, The Woman, dimly seen, is dressing.*)

WILLY (*with great feeling*): You're the best there is, Linda, you're a pal, you know that? On the road — on the road I want to grab you sometimes and just kiss the life outa you.

(*The laughter is loud now, and he moves into a brightening area at the left, where The Woman has come from behind the scrim and is standing, putting on her hat, looking into a "mirror" and laughing.*)

WILLY: 'Cause I get so lonely—especially when business is bad and there's nobody to talk to. I get the feeling that I'll never sell anything again, that I won't make a living for you, or a business, a business for the boys. (*He talks through The Woman's subsiding laughter; The Woman primps at the "mirror."*) There's so much I want to make for—

THE WOMAN: Me? You didn't make me, Willy. I picked you.

WILLY (*pleased*): You picked me?

THE WOMAN (*who is quite proper-looking, Willy's age*): I did. I've been sitting at that desk watching all the salesmen go by, day in, day out. But you've got such a sense of humor, and we do have such a good time together, don't we?

WILLY: Sure, sure. (*He takes her in his arms.*) Why do you have to go now?

THE WOMAN: It's two o'clock . . .

WILLY: No, come on in! (*He pulls her.*)

THE WOMAN: . . . my sisters'll be scandalized. When'll you be back?

WILLY: Oh, two weeks about. Will you come up again?

THE WOMAN: Sure thing. You do make me laugh. It's good for me. (*She squeezes his arm, kisses him.*) And I think you're a wonderful man.

WILLY: You picked me, heh?

THE WOMAN: Sure. Because you're so sweet. And such a kidder.

WILLY: Well, I'll see you next time I'm in Boston.

THE WOMAN: I'll put you right through to the buyers.

WILLY (*slapping her bottom*): Right. Well, bottoms up!

THE WOMAN (*slaps him gently and laughs*): You just kill me, Willy. (*He suddenly grabs her and kisses her roughly.*) You kill me. And thanks for the stockings. I love a lot of stockings. Well, good night.

WILLY: Good night. And keep your pores open!

THE WOMAN: Oh, Willy!

(*The Woman bursts out laughing, and Linda's laughter blends in. The Woman disappears into the dark. Now the area at the kitchen table brightens. Linda is sitting where she was at the kitchen table, but now is mending a pair of her silk stockings.*)

LINDA: You are, Willy. The handsomest man. You've got no reason to feel that —

WILLY (*coming out of The Woman's dimming area and going over to Linda*): I'll make it all up to you, Linda, I'll —

LINDA: There's nothing to make up, dear. You're doing fine, better than —

WILLY (*noticing her mending*): What's that?

LINDA: Just mending my stockings. They're so expensive —

WILLY (*angrily, taking them from her*): I won't have you mending stockings in this house! Now throw them out!

(*Linda puts the stockings in her pocket.*)

BERNARD (*entering on the run*): Where is he? If he doesn't study!

WILLY (*moving to the forestage, with great agitation*): You'll give him the answers!

BERNARD: I do, but I can't on a Regents! That's a state exam! They're liable to arrest me!

WILLY: Where is he? I'll whip him, I'll whip him!

LINDA: And he'd better give back that football, Willy, it's not nice.

WILLY: Biff! Where is he? Why is he taking everything?

LINDA: He's too rough with the girls, Willy. All the mothers are afraid of him!

WILLY: I'll whip him!

BERNARD: He's driving the car without a license!

(*The Woman's laugh is heard.*)

WILLY: Shut up!

LINDA: All the mothers —

WILLY: Shut up!

BERNARD (*backing quietly away and out*): Mr. Birnbaum says he's stuck up.

WILLY: Get outa here!

BERNARD: If he doesn't buckle down he'll flunk math! (*He goes off.*)

LINDA: He's right, Willy, you've gotta —

WILLY (*exploding at her*): There's nothing the matter with him! You want him to be a worm like Bernard? He's got spirit, personality . . .

(As he speaks, Linda, almost in tears, exits into the living room. Willy is alone in the kitchen, wilting and staring. The leaves are gone. It is night again, and the apartment houses look down from behind.)

WILLY: Loaded with it. Loaded! What is he stealing? He's giving it back, isn't he? Why is he stealing? What did I tell him? I never in my life told him anything but decent things.

(Happy in pajamas has come down the stairs; Willy suddenly becomes aware of Happy's presence.)

HAPPY: Let's go now, come on.

WILLY *(sitting down at the kitchen table)*: Huh! Why did she have to wax the floors herself? Everytime she waxes the floors she keels over. She knows that!

HAPPY: Shh! Take it easy. What brought you back tonight?

WILLY: I got an awful scare. Nearly hit a kid in Yonkers. God! Why didn't I go to Alaska with my brother Ben that time! Ben! That man was a genius, that man was success incarnate! What a mistake! He begged me to go.

HAPPY: Well, there's no use in —

WILLY: You guys! There was a man started with the clothes on his back and ended up with diamond mines!

HAPPY: Boy, someday I'd like to know how he did it.

WILLY: What's the mystery? The man knew what he wanted and went out and got it! Walked into a jungle, and comes out, the age of twenty-one, and he's rich! The world is an oyster, but you don't crack it open on a mattress!

HAPPY: Pop, I told you I'm gonna retire you for life.

WILLY: You'll retire me for life on seventy goddam dollars a week? And your women and your car and your apartment, and you'll retire me for life! Christ's sake, I couldn't get past Yonkers today! Where are you guys, where are you? The woods are burning! I can't drive a car!

(Charley has appeared in the doorway. He is a large man, slow of speech, laconic, immovable. In all he says, despite what he says, there is pity, and, now, trepidation. He has a robe over pajamas, slippers on his feet. He enters the kitchen.)

CHARLEY: Everything all right?

HAPPY: Yeah, Charley, everything's . . .

WILLY: What's the matter?

CHARLEY: I heard some noise. I thought something happened. Can't we do something about the walls? You sneeze in here, and in my house hats blow off.

HAPPY: Let's go to bed, Dad. Come on.

(Charley signals to Happy to go.)

WILLY: You go ahead, I'm not tired at the moment.

HAPPY *(to Willy)*: Take it easy, huh? *(He exits.)*

WILLY: What're you doin' up?

CHARLEY (*sitting down at the kitchen table opposite Willy*): Couldn't sleep good. I had a heartburn.

WILLY: Well, you don't know how to eat.

CHARLEY: I eat with my mouth.

WILLY: No, you're ignorant. You gotta know about vitamins and things like that.

CHARLEY: Come on, let's shoot. Tire you out a little.

WILLY (*hesitantly*): All right. You got cards?

CHARLEY (*taking a deck from his pocket*): Yeah, I got them. Someplace. What is it with those vitamins?

WILLY (*dealing*): They build up your bones. Chemistry.

CHARLEY: Yeah, but there's no bones in a heartburn.

WILLY: What are you talkin' about? Do you know the first thing about it?

CHARLEY: Don't get insulted.

WILLY: Don't talk about something you don't know anything about.

(*They are playing. Pause.*)

CHARLEY: What're you doin' home?

WILLY: A little trouble with the car.

CHARLEY: Oh. (*Pause.*) I'd like to take a trip to California.

WILLY: Don't say.

CHARLEY: You want a job?

WILLY: I got a job, I told you that. (*After a slight pause.*) What the hell are you offering me a job for?

CHARLEY: Don't get insulted.

WILLY: Don't insult me.

CHARLEY: I don't see no sense in it. You don't have to go on this way.

WILLY: I got a good job. (*Slight pause.*) What do you keep comin' in here for?

CHARLEY: You want me to go?

WILLY (*after a pause, withering*): I can't understand it. He's going back to Texas again. What the hell is that?

CHARLEY: Let him go.

WILLY: I got nothin' to give him, Charley, I'm clean, I'm clean.

CHARLEY: He won't starve. None a them starve. Forget about him.

WILLY: Then what have I got to remember?

CHARLEY: You take it too hard. To hell with it. When a deposit bottle is broken you don't get your nickel back.

WILLY: That's easy enough for you to say.

CHARLEY: That ain't easy for me to say.

WILLY: Did you see the ceiling I put up in the living room?

CHARLEY: Yeah, that's a piece of work. To put up a ceiling is a mystery to me. How do you do it?

WILLY: What's the difference?

CHARLEY: Well, talk about it.

WILLY: You gonna put up a ceiling?

CHARLEY: How could I put up a ceiling?

WILLY: Then what the hell are you bothering me for?

CHARLEY: You're insulted again.

WILLY: A man who can't handle tools is not a man. You're disgusting.

CHARLEY: Don't call me disgusting, Willy.

(*Uncle Ben, carrying a valise and an umbrella, enters the forestage from around the right corner of the house. He is a stolid man, in his sixties, with a mustache and an authoritative air. He is utterly certain of his destiny, and there is an aura of far places about him. He enters exactly as Willy speaks.*)

WILLY: I'm getting awfully tired, Ben.

(*Ben's music is heard. Ben looks around at everything.*)

CHARLEY: Good, keep playing; you'll sleep better. Did you call me Ben?

(*Ben looks at his watch.*)

WILLY: That's funny. For a second there you reminded me of my brother Ben.

BEN: I only have a few minutes. (*He strolls, inspecting the place. Willy and Charley continue playing.*)

CHARLEY: You never heard from him again, heh? Since that time?

WILLY: Didn't Linda tell you? Couple of weeks ago we got a letter from his wife in Africa. He died.

CHARLEY: That so.

BEN (*chuckling*): So this is Brooklyn, eh?

CHARLEY: Maybe you're in for some of his money.

WILLY: Naa, he had seven sons. There's just one opportunity I had with that man . . .

BEN: I must make a train, William. There are several properties I'm looking at in Alaska.

WILLY: Sure, sure! If I'd gone with him to Alaska that time, everything would've been totally different.

CHARLEY: Go on, you'd froze to death up there.

WILLY: What're you talking about?

BEN: Opportunity is tremendous in Alaska, William. Surprised you're not up there.

WILLY: Sure, tremendous.

CHARLEY: Heh?

WILLY: There was the only man I ever met who knew the answers.

CHARLEY: Who?

BEN: How are you all?

WILLY (*taking a pot, smiling*): Fine, fine.

CHARLEY: Pretty sharp tonight.

BEN: Is Mother living with you?

WILLY: No, she died a long time ago.

CHARLEY: Who?

BEN: That's too bad. Fine specimen of a lady, Mother.

WILLY (*to Charley*): Heh?

BEN: I'd hoped to see the old girl.

CHARLEY: Who died?

BEN: Heard anything from Father, have you?

WILLY (*unnerved*): What do you mean, who died?

CHARLEY (*taking a pot*): What're you talkin' about?

BEN (*looking at his watch*): William, it's half-past eight!

WILLY (*as though to dispel his confusion he angrily stops Charley's hand*): That's my build!

CHARLEY: I put the ace —

WILLY: If you don't know how to play the game I'm not gonna throw my money away on you!

CHARLEY (*rising*): It was my ace, for God's sake!

WILLY: I'm through, I'm through!

BEN: When did Mother die?

WILLY: Long ago. Since the beginning you never knew how to play cards.

CHARLEY (*picks up the cards and goes to the door*): All right! Next time I'll bring a deck with five aces.

WILLY: I don't play that kind of game!

CHARLEY (*turning to him*): You ought to be ashamed of yourself!

WILLY: Yeah?

CHARLEY: Yeah! (*He goes out.*)

WILLY (*slamming the door after him*): Ignoramus!

BEN (*as Willy comes toward him through the wall-line of the kitchen*): So you're William.

WILLY (*shaking Ben's hand*): Ben! I've been waiting for you so long! What's the answer? How did you do it?

BEN: Oh, there's a story in that.

(*Linda enters the forestage, as of old, carrying the wash basket.*)

LINDA: Is this Ben?

BEN (*gallantly*): How do you do, my dear.

LINDA: Where've you been all these years? Willy's always wondered why you —

WILLY (*pulling Ben away from her impatiently*): Where is Dad? Didn't you follow him? How did you get started?

BEN: Well, I don't know how much you remember.

WILLY: Well, I was just a baby, of course, only three or four years old —

BEN: Three years and eleven months.

WILLY: What a memory, Ben!

BEN: I have many enterprises, William, and I have never kept books.

WILLY: I remember I was sitting under the wagon in — was it Nebraska?

BEN: It was South Dakota, and I gave you a bunch of wild flowers.

WILLY: I remember you walking away down some open road.

BEN (*laughing*): I was going to find Father in Alaska.

WILLY: Where is he?

BEN: At that age I had a very faulty view of geography, William. I discovered after a few days that I was heading due south, so instead of Alaska, I ended up in Africa.

LINDA: Africa!

WILLY: The Gold Coast!

BEN: Principally diamond mines.

LINDA: Diamond mines!

BEN: Yes, my dear. But I've only a few minutes—

WILLY: No! Boys! Boys! (*Young Biff and Happy appear.*) Listen to this. This is your Uncle Ben, a great man! Tell my boys, Ben!

BEN: Why, boys, when I was seventeen I walked into the jungle, and when I was twenty-one I walked out. (*He laughs.*) And by God I was rich.

WILLY (*to the boys*): You see what I been talking about? The greatest things can happen!

BEN (*glancing at his watch*): I have an appointment in Ketchikan Tuesday week.

WILLY: No, Ben! Please tell about Dad. I want my boys to hear. I want them to know the kind of stock they spring from. All I remember is a man with a big beard, and I was in Mamma's lap, sitting around a fire, and some kind of high music.

BEN: His flute. He played the flute.

WILLY: Sure, the flute, that's right!

(*New music is heard, a high, rollicking tune.*)

BEN: Father was a very great and a very wild-hearted man. We would start in Boston, and he'd toss the whole family into the wagon, and then he'd drive the team right across the country; through Ohio, and Indiana, Michigan, Illinois, and all the Western states. And we'd stop in the towns and sell the flutes that he'd made on the way. Great inventor Father. With one gadget he made more in a week than a man like you could make in a lifetime.

WILLY: That's just the way I'm bringing them up, Ben—rugged, well liked, all-around.

BEN: Yeah? (*To Biff.*) Hit that, boy—hard as you can. (*He pounds his stomach.*)

BIFF: Oh, no, sir!

BEN (*taking boxing stance*): Come on, get to me! (*He laughs.*)

WILLY: Go to it, Biff! Go ahead, show him!

BIFF: Okay! (*He cocks his fists and starts in.*)

LINDA (*to Willy*): Why must he fight, dear?

BEN (*sparring with Biff*): Good boy! Good boy!

WILLY: How's that, Ben, heh?

HAPPY: Give him the left, Biff!

LINDA: Why are you fighting?

BEN: Good boy! (*Suddenly comes in, trips Biff, and stands over him, the point of his umbrella poised over Biff's eye.*)

LINDA: Look out, Biff!

BIFF: Gee!

BEN (*patting Biff's knee*): Never fight fair with a stranger, boy. You'll never get out of the jungle that way. (*Taking Linda's hand and bowing.*) It was an honor and a pleasure to meet you, Linda.

LINDA (*withdrawing her hand coldly, frightened*): Have a nice — trip.

BEN (*to Willy*): And good luck with your — what do you do?

WILLY: Selling.

BEN: Yes. Well . . . (*He raises his hand in farewell to all.*)

WILLY: No, Ben, I don't want you to think . . . (*He takes Ben's arm to show him.*) It's Brooklyn, I know, but we hunt too.

BEN: Really, now.

WILLY: Oh, sure, there's snakes and rabbits and — that's why I moved out here. Why, Biff can fell any one of these trees in no time! Boys! Go right over to where they're building the apartment house and get some sand. We're gonna rebuild the entire front stoop right now! Watch this, Ben!

BIFF: Yes, sir! On the double, Hap!

HAPPY (*as he and Biff run off*): I lost weight, Pop, you notice?

(*Charley enters in knickers, even before the boys are gone.*)

CHARLEY: Listen, if they steal any more from that building the watchman'll put the cops on them!

LINDA (*to Willy*): Don't let Biff . . .

(*Ben laughs lustily.*)

WILLY: You shoulda seen the lumber they brought home last week. At least a dozen six-by-tens worth all kinds a money.

CHARLEY: Listen, if that watchman —

WILLY: I gave them hell, understand. But I got a couple of fearless characters there.

CHARLEY: Willy, the jails are full of fearless characters.

BEN (*clapping Willy on the back, with a laugh at Charley*): And the stock exchange, friend!

WILLY (*joining in Ben's laughter*): Where are the rest of your pants?

CHARLEY: My wife bought them.

WILLY: Now all you need is a golf club and you can go upstairs and go to sleep. (*To Ben.*) Great athlete! Between him and his son Bernard they can't hammer a nail!

BERNARD (*rushing in*): The watchman's chasing Biff!

WILLY (*angrily*): Shut up! He's not stealing anything!

LINDA (*alarmed, hurrying off left*): Where is he? Biff, dear! (*She exits.*)

WILLY (*moving toward the left, away from Ben*): There's nothing wrong. What's the matter with you?

BEN: Nervy boy. Good!

WILLY (*laughing*): Oh, nerves of iron, that Biff!

CHARLEY: Don't know what it is. My New England man comes back and he's bleedin', they murdered him up there.

WILLY: It's contacts, Charley, I got important contacts!

CHARLEY (*sarcastically*): Glad to hear it, Willy. Come in later, we'll shoot a little casino. I'll take some of your Portland money. (*He laughs at Willy and exits.*)

WILLY (*turning to Ben*): Business is bad, it's murderous. But not for me, of course.

BEN: I'll stop by on my way back to Africa.

WILLY (*longingly*): Can't you stay a few days? You're just what I need, Ben, because I — I have a fine position here, but I — well, Dad left when I was such a baby and I never had a chance to talk to him and I still feel — kind of temporary about myself.

BEN: I'll be late for my train.

(*They are at opposite ends of the stage.*)

WILLY: Ben, my boys — can't we talk? They'd go into the jaws of hell for me, see, but I —

BEN: William, you're being first-rate with your boys. Outstanding, manly chaps!

WILLY (*hanging on to his words*): Oh, Ben, that's good to hear! Because sometimes I'm afraid that I'm not teaching them the right kind of — Ben, how should I teach them?

BEN (*giving great weight to each word, and with a certain vicious audacity*): William, when I walked into the jungle, I was seventeen. When I walked out I was twenty-one. And, by God, I was rich! (*He goes off into darkness around the right corner of the house.*)

WILLY: . . . was rich! That's just the spirit I want to imbue them with! To walk into a jungle! I was right! I was right! I was right!

(*Ben is gone, but Willy is still speaking to him as Linda, in nightgown and robe, enters the kitchen, glances around for Willy, then goes to the door of the house, looks out and sees him. Comes down to his left. He looks at her.*)

LINDA: Willy, dear? Willy?

WILLY: I was right!

LINDA: Did you have some cheese? (*He can't answer.*) It's very late, darling. Come to bed, heh?

WILLY (*looking straight up*): Gotta break your neck to see a star in this yard.

LINDA: You coming in?

WILLY: Whatever happened to that diamond watch fob? Remember? When Ben came from Africa that time? Didn't he give me a watch fob with a diamond in it?

LINDA: You pawned it, dear. Twelve, thirteen years ago. For Biff's radio correspondence course.

WILLY: Gee, that was a beautiful thing. I'll take a walk.

LINDA: But you're in your slippers.

WILLY (*starting to go around the house at the left*): I was right! I was! (*Half to Linda, as he goes, shaking his head.*) What a man! There was a man worth talking to. I was right!

LINDA (*calling after Willy*): But in your slippers, Willy!

(*Willy is almost gone when Biff, in his pajamas, comes down the stairs and enters the kitchen.*)

BIFF: What is he doing out there?

LINDA: Sh!

BIFF: God Almighty, Mom, how long has he been doing this?

LINDA: Don't, he'll hear you.

BIFF: What the hell is the matter with him?

LINDA: It'll pass by morning.

BIFF: Shouldn't we do anything?

LINDA: Oh, my dear, you should do a lot of things, but there's nothing to do, so go to sleep.

(*Happy comes down the stair and sits on the steps.*)

HAPPY: I never heard him so loud, Mom.

LINDA: Well, come around more often, you'll hear him. (*She sits down at the table and mends the lining of Willy's jacket.*)

BIFF: Why didn't you ever write me about this, Mom?

LINDA: How would I write to you? For over three months you had no address.

BIFF: I was on the move. But you know I thought of you all the time. You know that, don't you, pal?

LINDA: I know, dear, I know. But he likes to have a letter. Just to know that there's still a possibility for better things.

BIFF: He's not like this all the time, is he?

LINDA: It's when you come home he's always the worst.

BIFF: When I come home?

LINDA: When you write you're coming, he's all smiles and talks about the future, and—he's just wonderful. And then the closer you seem to come, the more shaky he gets, and then, by the time you get here, he's arguing, and he seems angry at you. I think it's just that maybe he can't bring himself to—to open up to you. Why are you so hateful to each other? Why is that?

BIFF (*evasively*): I'm not hateful, Mom.

LINDA: But you no sooner come in the door than you're fighting!

BIFF: I don't know why. I mean to change. I'm tryin', Mom, you understand?

LINDA: Are you home to stay now?

BIFF: I don't know. I want to look around, see what's goin'.

LINDA: Biff, you can't look around all your life, can you?

BIFF: I just can't take hold, Mom. I can't take hold of some kind of a life.

LINDA: Biff, a man is not a bird, to come and go with the springtime.

BIFF: Your hair . . . (*He touches her hair.*) Your hair got so gray.

LINDA: Oh, it's been gray since you were in high school. I just stopped dyeing it, that's all.

BIFF: Dye it again, will ye? I don't want my pal looking old. (*He smiles.*)

LINDA: You're such a boy! You think you can go away for a year and . . . You've got to get it into your head now that one day you'll knock on this door and there'll be strange people here —

BIFF: What are you talking about? You're not even sixty, Mom.

LINDA: But what about your father?

BIFF (*lamely*): Well, I meant him too.

HAPPY: He admires Pop.

LINDA: Biff, dear, if you don't have any feeling for him, then you can't have any feeling for me.

BIFF: Sure I can, Mom.

LINDA: No. You can't just come to see me, because I love him. (*With a threat, but only a threat, of tears.*) He's the dearest man in the world to me, and I won't have anyone making him feel unwanted and low and blue. You've got to make up your mind now, darling, there's no leeway any more. Either he's your father and you pay him that respect, or else you're not to come here. I know he's not easy to get along with — nobody knows that better than me — but . . .

WILLY (*from the left, with a laugh*): Hey, hey, Biffo!

BIFF (*starting to go out after Willy*): What the hell is the matter with him? (*Happy stops him.*)

LINDA: Don't — don't go near him!

BIFF: Stop making excuses for him! He always, always wiped the floor with you. Never had an ounce of respect for you.

HAPPY: He's always had respect for —

BIFF: What the hell do you know about it?

HAPPY (*surlily*): Just don't call him crazy!

BIFF: He's got no character — Charley wouldn't do this. Not in his own house — spewing out that vomit from his mind.

HAPPY: Charley never had to cope with what he's got to.

BIFF: People are worse off than Willy Loman. Believe me, I've seen them!

LINDA: Then make Charley your father, Biff. You can't do that, can you? I don't say he's a great man. Willy Loman never made a lot of money. His name was never in the paper. He's not the finest character that ever lived. But he's a human being, and a terrible thing is happening to him. So attention must be paid. He's not to be allowed to fall into his grave like an old dog. Attention, attention must be finally paid to such a person. You called him crazy —

BIFF: I didn't mean —

LINDA: No, a lot of people think he's lost his — balance. But you don't have to be very smart to know what his trouble is. The man is exhausted.

HAPPY: Sure!

LINDA: A small man can be just as exhausted as a great man. He works for a company thirty-six years this March, opens up unheard-of territories to their trademark, and now in his old age they take his salary away.

HAPPY (*indignantly*): I didn't know that, Mom.

LINDA: You never asked, my dear! Now that you get your spending money someplace else you don't trouble your mind with him.

HAPPY: But I gave you money last—

LINDA: Christmas time, fifty dollars! To fix the hot water it cost ninety-seven fifty! For five weeks he's been on straight commission, like a beginner, an unknown!

BIFF: Those ungrateful bastards!

LINDA: Are they any worse than his sons? When he brought them business, when he was young, they were glad to see him. But now his old friends, the old buyers that loved him so and always found some order to hand him in a pinch—they're all dead, retired. He used to be able to make six, seven calls a day in Boston. Now he takes his valises out of the car and puts them back and takes them out again and he's exhausted. Instead of walking he talks now. He drives seven hundred miles, and when he gets there no one knows him anymore, no one welcomes him. And what goes through a man's mind, driving seven hundred miles home without having earned a cent? Why shouldn't he talk to himself? Why? When he has to go to Charley and borrow fifty dollars a week and pretend to me that it's his pay? How long can that go on? How long? You see what I'm sitting here and waiting for? And you tell me he has no character? The man who never worked a day but for your benefit? When does he get the medal for that? Is this his reward—to turn around at the age of sixty-three and find his sons, who he loved better than his life, one a philandering bum—

HAPPY: Mom!

LINDA: That's all you are, my baby! (*To Biff.*) And you! What happened to the love you had for him? You were such pals! How you used to talk to him on the phone every night! How lonely he was till he could come home to you!

BIFF: All right, Mom. I'll live here in my room, and I'll get a job. I'll keep away from him, that's all.

LINDA: No, Biff. You can't stay here and fight all the time.

BIFF: He threw me out of this house, remember that.

LINDA: Why did he do that? I never knew why.

BIFF: Because I know he's a fake and he doesn't like anybody around who knows!

LINDA: Why a fake? In what way? What do you mean?

BIFF: Just don't lay it all at my feet. It's between me and him—that's all I have to say. I'll chip in from now on. He'll settle for half my pay check. He'll be all right. I'm going to bed. (*He starts for the stairs.*)

LINDA: He won't be all right.

BIFF (*turning on the stairs, furiously*): I hate this city and I'll stay here. Now what do you want?

LINDA: He's dying, Biff.

(*Happy turns quickly to her, shocked.*)

BIFF (*after a pause*): Why is he dying?

LINDA: He's been trying to kill himself.

BIFF (*with great horror*): How?

LINDA: I live from day to day.

BIFF: What're you talking about?

LINDA: Remember I wrote you that he smashed up the car again? In February?

BIFF: Well?

LINDA: The insurance inspector came. He said that they have evidence. That all these accidents in the last year — weren't — weren't — accidents.

HAPPY: How can they tell that? That's a lie.

LINDA: It seems there's a woman . . . (*She takes a breath as*)

BIFF (*sharply but contained*):   ⎱ What woman?
LINDA (*simultaneously*):   ⎰ . . . and this woman . . .

LINDA: What?

BIFF: Nothing. Go ahead.

LINDA: What did you say?

BIFF: Nothing. I just said what woman?

HAPPY: What about her?

LINDA: Well, it seems she was walking down the road and saw his car. She says that he wasn't driving fast at all, and that he didn't skid. She says he came to that little bridge, and then deliberately smashed into the railing, and it was only the shallowness of the water that saved him.

BIFF: Oh, no, he probably just fell asleep again.

LINDA: I don't think he fell asleep.

BIFF: Why not?

LINDA: Last month . . . (*With great difficulty.*) Oh, boys, it's so hard to say a thing like this! He's just a big stupid man to you, but I tell you there's more good in him than in many other people. (*She chokes, wipes her eyes.*) I was looking for a fuse. The lights blew out, and I went down the cellar. And behind the fuse box — it happened to fall out — was a length of rubber pipe — just short.

HAPPY: No kidding!

LINDA: There's a little attachment on the end of it. I knew right away. And sure enough, on the bottom of the water heater there's a new little nipple on the gas pipe.

HAPPY (*angrily*): That — jerk.

BIFF: Did you have it taken off?

LINDA: I'm — I'm ashamed to. How can I mention it to him? Every day I go down and take away that little rubber pipe. But, when he comes home, I put it back where it was. How can I insult him that way? I don't know what to do. I live from day to day, boys. I tell you, I know every thought in his mind. It sounds so old-fashioned and silly, but I tell you he put his whole life into you and you've turned your backs on him. (*She is bent over in the chair, weeping, her face in her hands.*) Biff, I swear to God! Biff, his life is in your hands!

HAPPY (*to Biff*): How do you like that damned fool!

BIFF (*kissing her*): All right, pal, all right. It's all settled now. I've been remiss. I know that, Mom. But now I'll stay, and I swear to you, I'll apply myself. (*Kneeling in front of her, in a fever of self-reproach.*) It's just — you see, Mom, I don't fit in business. Not that I won't try. I'll try, and I'll make good.

HAPPY: Sure you will. The trouble with you in business was you never tried to please people.

BIFF: I know, I —

HAPPY: Like when you worked for Harrison's. Bob Harrison said you were tops, and then you go and do some damn fool thing like whistling whole songs in the elevator like a comedian.

BIFF (*against Happy*): So what? I like to whistle sometimes.

HAPPY: You don't raise a guy to a responsible job who whistles in the elevator!

LINDA: Well, don't argue about it now.

HAPPY: Like when you'd go off and swim in the middle of the day instead of taking the line around.

BIFF (*his resentment rising*): Well, don't you run off? You take off sometimes, don't you? On a nice summer day?

HAPPY: Yeah, but I cover myself!

LINDA: Boys!

HAPPY: If I'm going to take a fade the boss can call any number where I'm supposed to be and they'll swear to him that I just left. I'll tell you something that I hate to say, Biff, but in the business world some of them think you're crazy.

BIFF (*angered*): Screw the business world!

HAPPY: All right, screw it! Great, but cover yourself!

LINDA: Hap, Hap!

BIFF: I don't care what they think! They've laughed at Dad for years, and you know why? Because we don't belong in this nuthouse of a city! We should be mixing cement on some open plain, or — or carpenters. A carpenter is allowed to whistle!

(*Willy walks in from the entrance of the house, at left.*)

WILLY: Even your grandfather was better than a carpenter. (*Pause. They watch him.*) You never grew up. Bernard does not whistle in the elevator, I assure you.

BIFF (*as though to laugh Willy out of it*): Yeah, but you do, Pop.

WILLY: I never in my life whistled in an elevator! And who in the business world thinks I'm crazy?

BIFF: I didn't mean it like that, Pop. Now don't make a whole thing out of it,
    will ye?

WILLY: Go back to the West! Be a carpenter, a cowboy, enjoy yourself!

LINDA: Willy, he was just saying —

WILLY: I heard what he said!

HAPPY (*trying to quiet Willy*): Hey, Pop, come on now . . .

WILLY (*continuing over Happy's line*): They laugh at me, heh? Go to Filene's, go
    to the Hub, go to Slattery's, Boston. Call out the name Willy Loman and
    see what happens! Big shot!

BIFF: All right, Pop.

WILLY: Big!

BIFF: All right!

WILLY: Why do you always insult me?

BIFF: I didn't say a word. (*To Linda.*) Did I say a word?

LINDA: He didn't say anything, Willy.

WILLY (*going to the doorway of the living room*): All right, good night, good night.

LINDA: Willy, dear, he just decided . . .

WILLY (*to Biff*): If you get tired hanging around tomorrow, paint the ceiling I
    put up in the living room.

BIFF: I'm leaving early tomorrow.

HAPPY: He's going to see Bill Oliver, Pop.

WILLY (*interestedly*): Oliver? For what?

BIFF (*with reserve, but trying, trying*): He always said he'd stake me. I'd like to
    go into business, so maybe I can take him up on it.

LINDA: Isn't that wonderful?

WILLY: Don't interrupt. What's wonderful about it? There's fifty men in the
    City of New York who'd stake him. (*To Biff.*) Sporting goods?

BIFF: I guess so. I know something about it and —

WILLY: He knows something about it! You know sporting goods better than
    Spalding, for God's sake! How much is he giving you?

BIFF: I don't know, I didn't even see him yet, but —

WILLY: Then what're you talkin' about?

BIFF (*getting angry*): Well, all I said was I'm gonna see him, that's all!

WILLY (*turning away*): Ah, you're counting your chickens again.

BIFF (*starting left for the stairs*): Oh, Jesus, I'm going to sleep!

WILLY (*calling after him*): Don't curse in this house!

BIFF (*turning*): Since when did you get so clean?

HAPPY (*trying to stop them*): Wait a . . .

WILLY: Don't use that language to me! I won't have it!

HAPPY (*grabbing Biff, shouts*): Wait a minute! I got an idea. I got a feasible
    idea. Come here, Biff, let's talk this over now, let's talk some sense here.
    When I was down in Florida last time, I thought of a great idea to sell
    sporting goods. It just came back to me. You and I, Biff — we have a line,
    the Loman Line. We train a couple of weeks, and put on a couple of ex-
    hibitions, see?

WILLY: That's an idea!

HAPPY: Wait! We form two basketball teams, see? Two water polo teams. We play each other. It's a million dollars' worth of publicity. Two brothers, see? The Loman Brothers. Displays in the Royal Palms — all the hotels. And banners over the ring and the basketball court: "Loman Brothers." Baby, we could sell sporting goods!

WILLY: That is a one-million-dollar idea!

LINDA: Marvelous!

BIFF: I'm in great shape as far as that's concerned.

HAPPY: And the beauty of it is, Biff, it wouldn't be like a business. We'd be out playin' ball again . . .

BIFF (*enthused*): Yeah, that's . . .

WILLY: Million-dollar . . .

HAPPY: And you wouldn't get fed up with it, Biff. It'd be the family again. There'd be the old honor, and comradeship, and if you wanted to go off for a swim or somethin' — well, you'd do it! Without some smart cooky gettin' up ahead of you!

WILLY: Lick the world! You guys together could absolutely lick the civilized world.

BIFF: I'll see Oliver tomorrow. Hap, if we could work that out . . .

LINDA: Maybe things are beginning to —

WILLY (*wildly enthused, to Linda*): Stop interrupting! (*To Biff.*) But don't wear sport jacket and slacks when you see Oliver.

BIFF: No, I'll —

WILLY: A business suit, and talk as little as possible, and don't crack any jokes.

BIFF: He did like me. Always liked me.

LINDA: He loved you!

WILLY (*to Linda*): Will you stop! (*To Biff.*) Walk in very serious. You are not applying for a boy's job. Money is to pass. Be quiet, fine, and serious. Everybody likes a kidder, but nobody lends him money.

HAPPY: I'll try to get some myself, Biff. I'm sure I can.

WILLY: I see great things for you kids, I think your troubles are over. But remember, start big and you'll end big. Ask for fifteen. How much you gonna ask for?

BIFF: Gee, I don't know —

WILLY: And don't say "Gee." "Gee" is a boy's word. A man walking in for fifteen thousand dollars does not say "Gee!"

BIFF: Ten, I think, would be top though.

WILLY: Don't be so modest. You always started too low. Walk in with a big laugh. Don't look worried. Start off with a couple of your good stories to lighten things up. It's not what you say, it's how you say it — because personality always wins the day.

LINDA: Oliver always thought the highest of him —

WILLY: Will you let me talk?

BIFF: Don't yell at her, Pop, will ye?

WILLY (*angrily*): I was talking, wasn't I?

BIFF: I don't like you yelling at her all the time, and I'm tellin' you, that's all.

WILLY: What're you, takin' over this house?

LINDA: Willy —

WILLY (*turning to her*): Don't take his side all the time, goddammit!

BIFF (*furiously*): Stop yelling at her!

WILLY (*suddenly pulling on his cheek, beaten down, guilt ridden*): Give my best to Bill Oliver — he may remember me. (*He exits through the living room doorway.*)

LINDA (*her voice subdued*): What'd you have to start that for? (*Biff turns away.*) You see how sweet he was as soon as you talked hopefully? (*She goes over to Biff.*) Come up and say good night to him. Don't let him go to bed that way.

HAPPY: Come on, Biff, let's buck him up.

LINDA: Please, dear. Just say good night. It takes so little to make him happy. Come. (*She goes through the living room doorway, calling upstairs from within the living room.*) Your pajamas are hanging in the bathroom, Willy!

HAPPY (*looking toward where Linda went out*): What a woman! They broke the mold when they made her. You know that, Biff?

BIFF: He's off salary. My God, working on commission!

HAPPY: Well, let's face it: he's no hot-shot selling man. Except that sometimes, you have to admit, he's a sweet personality.

BIFF (*deciding*): Lend me ten bucks, will ye? I want to buy some new ties.

HAPPY: I'll take you to a place I know. Beautiful stuff. Wear one of my striped shirts tomorrow.

BIFF: She got gray. Mom got awful old. Gee, I'm gonna go in to Oliver tomorrow and knock him for a —

HAPPY: Come on up. Tell that to Dad. Let's give him a whirl. Come on.

BIFF (*steamed up*): You know, with ten thousand bucks, boy!

HAPPY (*as they go into the living room*): That's the talk, Biff, that's the first time I've heard the old confidence out of you! (*From within the living room, fading off.*) You're gonna live with me, kid, and any babe you want just say the word . . . (*The last lines are hardly heard. They are mounting the stairs to their parents' bedroom.*)

LINDA (*entering her bedroom and addressing Willy, who is in the bathroom. She is straightening the bed for him.*): Can you do anything about the shower? It drips.

WILLY (*from the bathroom*): All of a sudden everything falls to pieces. Goddam plumbing, oughta be sued, those people. I hardly finished putting it in and the thing . . . (*His words rumble off.*)

LINDA: I'm just wondering if Oliver will remember him. You think he might?

WILLY (*coming out of the bathroom in his pajamas*): Remember him? What's the matter with you, you crazy? If he'd've stayed with Oliver he'd be on top by now! Wait'll Oliver gets a look at him. You don't know the average caliber any more. The average young man today — (*he is getting into bed*) —

is got a caliber of zero. Greatest thing in the world for him was to bum around.

(*Biff and Happy enter the bedroom. Slight pause.*)

WILLY (*stops short, looking at Biff*): Glad to hear it, boy.

HAPPY: He wanted to say good night to you, sport.

WILLY (*to Biff*): Yeah. Knock him dead, boy. What'd you want to tell me?

BIFF: Just take it easy, Pop. Good night. (*He turns to go.*)

WILLY (*unable to resist*): And if anything falls off the desk while you're talking to him — like a package or something — don't you pick it up. They have office boys for that.

LINDA: I'll make a big breakfast —

WILLY: Will you let me finish? (*To Biff.*) Tell him you were in the business in the West. Not farm work.

BIFF: All right, Dad.

LINDA: I think everything —

WILLY (*going right through her speech*): And don't undersell yourself. No less than fifteen thousand dollars.

BIFF (*unable to bear him*): Okay. Good night, Mom. (*He starts moving.*)

WILLY: Because you got a greatness in you, Biff, remember that. You got all kinds of greatness . . . (*He lies back, exhausted. Biff walks out.*)

LINDA (*calling after Biff*): Sleep well, darling!

HAPPY: I'm gonna get married, Mom. I wanted to tell you.

LINDA: Go to sleep, dear.

HAPPY (*going*): I just wanted to tell you.

WILLY: Keep up the good work. (*Happy exits.*) God . . . remember that Ebbets Field game? The championship of the city?

LINDA: Just rest. Should I sing to you?

WILLY: Yeah. Sing to me. (*Linda hums a soft lullaby.*) When that team came out — he was the tallest, remember?

LINDA: Oh, yes. And in gold.

(*Biff enters the darkened kitchen, takes a cigarette, and leaves the house. He comes downstage into a golden pool of light. He smokes, staring at the night.*)

WILLY: Like a young god. Hercules — something like that. And the sun, the sun all around him. Remember how he waved to me? Right up from the field, with the representatives of three colleges standing by? And the buyers I brought, and the cheers when he came out — Loman, Loman, Loman! God Almighty, he'll be great yet. A star like that, magnificent, can never really fade away!

(*The light on Willy is fading. The gas heater begins to glow through the kitchen wall, near the stairs, a blue flame beneath red coils.*)

LINDA (*timidly*): Willy dear, what has he got against you?

WILLY: I'm so tired. Don't talk anymore.

(*Biff slowly returns to the kitchen. He stops, stares toward the heater.*)

LINDA: Will you ask Howard to let you work in New York?
WILLY: First thing in the morning. Everything'll be all right.

(*Biff reaches behind the heater and draws out a length of rubber tubing. He is horrified and turns his head toward Willy's room, still dimly lit, from which the strains of Linda's desperate but monotonous humming rise.*)

WILLY (*staring through the window into the moonlight*): Gee, look at the moon moving between the buildings!

(*Biff wraps the tubing around his hand and quickly goes up the stairs.*)

ACT II

(*Music is heard, gay and bright. The curtain rises as the music fades away. Willy, in shirt sleeves is sitting at the kitchen table, sipping coffee, his hat in his lap. Linda is filling his cup when she can.*)

WILLY: Wonderful coffee. Meal in itself.
LINDA: Can I make you some eggs?
WILLY: No. Take a breath.
LINDA: You look so rested, dear.
WILLY: I slept like a dead one. First time in months. Imagine, sleeping till ten on a Tuesday morning. Boys left nice and early, heh?
LINDA: They were out of here by eight o'clock.
WILLY: Good work!
LINDA: It was so thrilling to see them leaving together. I can't get over the shaving lotion in this house!
WILLY (*smiling*): Mmm —
LINDA: Biff was very changed this morning. His whole attitude seemed to be hopeful. He couldn't wait to get downtown to see Oliver.
WILLY: He's heading for a change. There's no question, there simply are certain men that take longer to get — solidified. How did he dress?
LINDA: His blue suit. He's so handsome in that suit. He could be a — anything in that suit!

(*Willy gets up from the table. Linda holds his jacket for him.*)

WILLY: There's no question, no question at all. Gee, on the way home tonight I'd like to buy some seeds.
LINDA (*laughing*): That'd be wonderful. But not enough sun gets back there. Nothing'll grow any more.
WILLY: You wait, kid, before it's all over we're gonna get a little place out in the country, and I'll raise some vegetables, a couple of chickens . . .
LINDA: You'll do it yet, dear.

(*Willy walks out of his jacket. Linda follows him.*)

WILLY: And they'll get married, and come for a weekend. I'd build a little guest house. 'Cause I got so many fine tools, all I'd need would be a little lumber and some peace of mind.

LINDA (*joyfully*): I sewed the lining . . .

WILLY: I could build two guest houses, so they'd both come. Did he decide how much he's going to ask Oliver for?

LINDA (*getting him into the jacket*): He didn't mention it, but I imagine ten or fifteen thousand. You going to talk to Howard today?

WILLY: Yeah. I'll put it to him straight and simple. He'll just have to take me off the road.

LINDA: And Willy, don't forget to ask for a little advance, because we've got the insurance premium. It's the grace period now.

WILLY: That's a hundred . . . ?

LINDA: A hundred and eight, sixty-eight. Because we're a little short again.

WILLY: Why are we short?

LINDA: Well, you had the motor job on the car . . .

WILLY: That goddam Studebaker!

LINDA: And you got one more payment on the refrigerator . . .

WILLY: But it just broke again!

LINDA: Well, it's old, dear.

WILLY: I told you we should've bought a well-advertised machine. Charley bought a General Electric and it's twenty years old and it's still good, that son-of-a-bitch.

LINDA: But, Willy —

WILLY: Whoever heard of a Hastings refrigerator? Once in my life I would like to own something outright before it's broken! I'm always in a race with the junkyard! I just finished paying for the car and it's on its last legs. The refrigerator consumes belts like a goddamn maniac. They time those things. They time them so when you finally paid for them, they're used up.

LINDA (*buttoning up his jacket as he unbuttons it*): All told, about two hundred dollars would carry us, dear. But that includes the last payment on the mortgage. After this payment, Willy, the house belongs to us.

WILLY: It's twenty-five years!

LINDA: Biff was nine years old when we bought it.

WILLY: Well, that's a great thing. To weather a twenty-five year mortgage is —

LINDA: It's an accomplishment.

WILLY: All the cement, the lumber, the reconstruction I put in this house! There ain't a crack to be found in it anymore.

LINDA: Well, it served its purpose.

WILLY: What purpose? Some stranger'll come along, move in, and that's that. If only Biff would take this house, and raise a family . . . (*He starts to go.*) Good-by, I'm late.

LINDA (*suddenly remembering*): Oh, I forgot! You're supposed to meet them for dinner.

WILLY: Me?

LINDA: At Frank's Chop House on Forty-eighth near Sixth Avenue.

WILLY: Is that so! How about you?

LINDA: No, just the three of you. They're gonna blow you to a big meal!

WILLY: Don't say! Who thought of that?

LINDA: Biff came to me this morning, Willy, and he said, "Tell Dad, we want to blow him to a big meal." Be there six o'clock. You and your two boys are going to have dinner.

WILLY: Gee whiz! That's really somethin'. I'm gonna knock Howard for a loop, kid. I'll get an advance, and I'll come home with a New York job. Goddammit, now I'm gonna do it!

LINDA: Oh, that's the spirit, Willy!

WILLY: I will never get behind a wheel the rest of my life!

LINDA: It's changing, Willy, I can feel it changing!

WILLY: Beyond a question. G'by, I'm late. (*He starts to go again.*)

LINDA (*calling after him as she runs to the kitchen table for a handkerchief*): You got your glasses?

WILLY (*feels for them, then comes back in*): Yeah, yeah, got my glasses.

LINDA (*giving him the handkerchief*): And a handkerchief.

WILLY: Yeah, handkerchief.

LINDA: And your saccharine?

WILLY: Yeah, my saccharine.

LINDA: Be careful on the subway stairs.

(*She kisses him, and a silk stocking is seen hanging from her hand. Willy notices it.*)

WILLY: Will you stop mending stockings? At least while I'm in the house. It gets me nervous. I can't tell you. Please.

(*Linda hides the stocking in her hand as she follows Willy across the forestage in front of the house.*)

LINDA: Remember, Frank's Chop House.

WILLY (*passing the apron*): Maybe beets would grow out there.

LINDA (*laughing*): But you tried so many times.

WILLY: Yeah. Well, don't work hard today. (*He disappears around the right corner of the house.*)

LINDA: Be careful!

(*As Willy vanishes, Linda waves to him. Suddenly the phone rings. She runs across the stage and into the kitchen and lifts it.*)

LINDA: Hello? Oh, Biff! I'm so glad you called, I just . . . Yes, sure, I just told him. Yes, he'll be there for dinner at six o'clock, I didn't forget. Listen, I was just dying to tell you. You know that little rubber pipe I told you about? That he connected to the gas heater? I finally decided to go down the cellar this morning and take it away and destroy it. But it's gone! Imagine? He took it away himself, it isn't there! (*She listens.*) When? Oh, then you took it. Oh—nothing, it's just that I'd hoped he'd taken it away himself. Oh, I'm not worried, darling, because this morning he left in such high spirits, it was like the old days! I'm not afraid any more. Did Mr. Oliver see you? . . . Well, you wait there then. And make a nice impression on him, darling. Just don't perspire too much before you see him. And have a nice time with Dad. He may have big news too! . . . That's right, a New York job. And be sweet to him tonight, dear. Be loving to him. Because he's only a little boat looking for a harbor. (*She is trembling with sorrow and joy.*) Oh, that's wonderful, Biff, you'll save his life. Thanks, darling. Just put your arm around him when he comes into the restaurant. Give him a smile. That's the boy . . . Good-by, dear. . . . You got your comb? . . . That's fine. Good-by, Biff dear.

(*In the middle of her speech, Howard Wagner, thirty-six, wheels in a small typewriter table on which is a wire-recording machine and proceeds to plug it in. This is on the left forestage. Light slowly fades on Linda as it rises on Howard. Howard is intent on threading the machine and only glances over his shoulder as Willy appears.*)

WILLY: Pst! Pst!

HOWARD: Hello, Willy, come in.

WILLY: Like to have a little talk with you, Howard.

HOWARD: Sorry to keep you waiting. I'll be with you in a minute.

WILLY: What's that, Howard?

HOWARD: Didn't you ever see one of these? Wire recorder.

WILLY: Oh. Can we talk a minute?

HOWARD: Records things. Just got delivery yesterday. Been driving me crazy, the most terrific machine I ever saw in my life. I was up all night with it.

WILLY: What do you do with it?

HOWARD: I bought it for dictation, but you can do anything with it. Listen to this. I had it home last night. Listen to what I picked up. The first one is my daughter. Get this. (*He flicks the switch and "Roll out the Barrel" is heard being whistled.*) Listen to that kid whistle.

WILLY: That is lifelike, isn't it?

HOWARD: Seven years old. Get that tone.

WILLY: Ts, ts. Like to ask a little favor if you . . .

(*The whistling breaks off, and the voice of Howard's daughter is heard.*)

HIS DAUGHTER: Now you, Daddy.

HOWARD: She's crazy for me! (*Again the same song is whistled.*) That's me! Ha! (*He winks.*)

WILLY: You're very good!

(*The whistling breaks off again. The machine runs silent for a moment.*)

HOWARD: Sh! Get this now, this is my son.

HIS SON: "The capital of Alabama is Montgomery; the capital of Arizona is Phoenix; the capital of Arkansas is Little Rock; the capital of California is Sacramento . . ." (*and on, and on.*)

HOWARD (*holding up five fingers*): Five years old, Willy!

WILLY: He'll make an announcer some day!

HIS SON (*continuing*): "The capita . . ."

HOWARD: Get that — alphabetical order! (*The machine breaks off suddenly.*) Wait a minute. The maid kicked the plug out.

WILLY: It certainly is a —

HOWARD: Sh, for God's sake!

HIS SON: "It's nine o'clock, Bulova watch time. So I have to go to sleep."

WILLY: That really is —

HOWARD: Wait a minute! The next is my wife.

(*They wait.*)

HOWARD'S VOICE: "Go on, say something." (*Pause.*) "Well, you gonna talk?"

HIS WIFE: "I can't think of anything."

HOWARD'S VOICE: "Well, talk — it's turning."

HIS WIFE (*shyly, beaten*): "Hello." (*Silence.*) "Oh, Howard, I can't talk into this . . ."

HOWARD (*snapping the machine off*): That was my wife.

WILLY: That is a wonderful machine. Can we —

HOWARD: I tell you, Willy, I'm gonna take my camera, and my bandsaw, and all my hobbies, and out they go. This is the most fascinating relaxation I ever found.

WILLY: I think I'll get one myself.

HOWARD: Sure, they're only a hundred and a half. You can't do without it. Supposing you wanna hear Jack Benny,° see? But you can't be at home at that hour. So you tell the maid to turn the radio on when Jack Benny comes on, and this automatically goes on with the radio . . .

WILLY: And when you come home you . . .

HOWARD: You can come home twelve o'clock, one o'clock, any time you like, and you get yourself a Coke and sit yourself down, throw the switch, and there's Jack Benny's program in the middle of the night!

WILLY: I'm definitely going to get one. Because lots of times I'm on the road, and I think to myself, what I must be missing on the radio!

HOWARD: Don't you have a radio in the car?

WILLY: Well, yeah, but who ever thinks of turning it on?

HOWARD: Say, aren't you supposed to be in Boston?

WILLY: That's what I want to talk to you about, Howard. You got a minute? (*He draws a chair in from the wing.*)

HOWARD: What happened? What're you doing here?

WILLY: Well . . .

HOWARD: You didn't crack up again, did you?

Jack Benny: The comedian Jack Benny (1894–1974) starred in the variety show *The Jack Benny Program,* broadcast on radio from 1932 until 1955.

WILLY: Oh, no. No . . .

HOWARD: Geez, you had me worried there for a minute. What's the trouble?

WILLY: Well, tell you the truth, Howard. I've come to the decision that I'd rather not travel anymore.

HOWARD: Not travel! Well, what'll you do?

WILLY: Remember, Christmas time, when you had the party here? You said you'd try to think of some spot for me here in town.

HOWARD: With us?

WILLY: Well, sure.

HOWARD: Oh, yeah, yeah. I remember. Well, I couldn't think of anything for you, Willy.

WILLY: I tell ya, Howard. The kids are all grown up, y'know. I don't need much anymore. If I could take home — well, sixty-five dollars a week, I could swing it.

HOWARD: Yeah, but Willy, see I —

WILLY: I tell ya why, Howard. Speaking frankly and between the two of us, y'know — I'm just a little tired.

HOWARD: Oh, I could understand that, Willy. But you're a road man, Willy, and we do a road business. We've only got a half-dozen salesmen on the floor here.

WILLY: God knows, Howard, I never asked a favor of any man. But I was with the firm when your father used to carry you in here in his arms.

HOWARD: I know that, Willy, but —

WILLY: Your father came to me the day you were born and asked me what I thought of the name Howard, may he rest in peace.

HOWARD: I appreciate that, Willy, but there just is no spot here for you. If I had a spot I'd slam you right in, but I just don't have a single solitary spot.

(*He looks for his lighter. Willy has picked it up and gives it to him. Pause.*)

WILLY (*with increasing anger*): Howard, all I need to set my table is fifty dollars a week.

HOWARD: But where am I going to put you, kid?

WILLY: Look, it isn't a question of whether I can sell merchandise, is it?

HOWARD: No, but it's business, kid, and everybody's gotta pull his own weight.

WILLY (*desperately*): Just let me tell you a story, Howard —

HOWARD: 'Cause you gotta admit, business is business.

WILLY (*angrily*): Business is definitely business, but just listen for a minute. You don't understand this. When I was a boy — eighteen, nineteen — I was already on the road. And there was a question in my mind as to whether selling had a future for me. Because in those days I had a yearning to go to Alaska. See, there were three gold strikes in one month in Alaska, and I felt like going out. Just for the ride, you might say.

HOWARD (*barely interested*): Don't say.

WILLY: Oh, yeah, my father lived many years in Alaska. He was an adventurous man. We've got quite a little streak of self-reliance in our family. I
thought I'd go out with my older brother and try to locate him, and
maybe settle in the North with the old man. And I was almost decided
to go, when I met a salesman in the Parker House. His name was Dave
Singleman. And he was eighty-four years old, and he'd drummed merchandise in thirty-one states. And old Dave, he'd go up to his room,
y'understand, put on his green velvet slippers — I'll never forget — and
pick up his phone and call the buyers, and without ever leaving his
room, at the age of eighty-four, he made his living. And when I saw that,
I realized that selling was the greatest career a man could want. 'Cause
what could be more satisfying than to be able to go, at the age of eighty-
four, into twenty or thirty different cities, and pick up a phone, and be
remembered and loved and helped by so many different people? Do you
know? When he died — and by the way he died the death of a salesman,
in his green velvet slippers in the smoker of the New York, New Haven
and Hartford, going into Boston — when he died, hundreds of salesmen
and buyers were at his funeral. Things were sad on a lotta trains for
months after that. (*He stands up. Howard has not looked at him.*) In those
days there was personality in it, Howard. There was respect and comradeship, and gratitude in it. Today, it's all cut and dried, and there's no
chance for bringing friendship to bear — or personality. You see what I
mean? They don't know me any more.

HOWARD (*moving away, to the right*): That's just the thing, Willy.

WILLY: If I had forty dollars a week — that's all I'd need. Forty dollars, Howard.

HOWARD: Kid, I can't take blood from a stone, I —

WILLY (*desperation is on him now*): Howard, the year Al Smith was nominated,
your father came to me and —

HOWARD (*starting to go off*): I've got to see some people, kid.

WILLY (*stopping him*): I'm talking about your father! There were promises
made across this desk! You mustn't tell me you've got people to see — I
put thirty-four years into this firm, Howard, and now I can't pay my insurance! You can't eat the orange and throw the peel away — a man is
not a piece of fruit! (*After a pause.*) Now pay attention. Your father — in
1928 I had a big year. I averaged a hundred and seventy dollars a week in
commissions.

HOWARD (*impatiently*): Now, Willy, you never averaged —

WILLY (*banging his hand on the desk*): I averaged a hundred and seventy dollars
a week in the year of 1928! And your father came to me — or rather I was
in the office here — it was right over this desk — and he put his hand on
my shoulder —

HOWARD (*getting up*): You'll have to excuse me, Willy, I gotta see some
people. Pull yourself together. (*Going out.*) I'll be back in a little while.

(*On Howard's exit, the light on his chair grows very bright and strange.*)

WILLY: Pull myself together! What the hell did I say to him? My God, I was yelling at him! How could I? (*Willy breaks off, staring at the light, which occupies the chair, animating it. He approaches this chair, standing across the desk from it.*) Frank, Frank, don't you remember what you told me that time? How you put your hand on my shoulder, and Frank . . . (*He leans on the desk and as he speaks the dead man's name he accidentally switches on the recorder, and instantly*)

HOWARD'S SON: ". . . of New York is Albany. The capital of Ohio is Cincinnati, the capital of Rhode Island is . . ." (*The recitation continues.*)

WILLY (*leaping away with fright, shouting*): Ha! Howard! Howard! Howard!

HOWARD (*rushing in*): What happened?

WILLY (*pointing at the machine, which continues nasally, childishly, with the capital cities*): Shut it off! Shut it off!

HOWARD (*pulling the plug out*): Look, Willy . . .

WILLY (*pressing his hands to his eyes*): I gotta get myself some coffee. I'll get some coffee . . .

(*Willy starts to walk out. Howard stops him.*)

HOWARD (*rolling up the cord*): Willy, look . . .

WILLY: I'll go to Boston.

HOWARD: Willy, you can't go to Boston for us.

WILLY: Why can't I go?

HOWARD: I don't want you to represent us. I've been meaning to tell you for a long time now.

WILLY: Howard, are you firing me?

HOWARD: I think you need a good long rest, Willy.

WILLY: Howard —

HOWARD: And when you feel better, come back, and we'll see if we can work something out.

WILLY: But I gotta earn money, Howard. I'm in no position to —

HOWARD: Where are your sons? Why don't your sons give you a hand?

WILLY: They're working on a very big deal.

HOWARD: This is no time for false pride, Willy. You go to your sons and you tell them that you're tired. You've got two great boys, haven't you?

WILLY: Oh, no question, no question, but in the meantime . . .

HOWARD: Then that's that, heh?

WILLY: All right, I'll go to Boston tomorrow.

HOWARD: No, no.

WILLY: I can't throw myself on my sons. I'm not a cripple!

HOWARD: Look, kid, I'm busy this morning.

WILLY (*grasping Howard's arm*): Howard, you've got to let me go to Boston!

HOWARD (*hard, keeping himself under control*): I've got a line of people to see this morning. Sit down, take five minutes, and pull yourself together, and then go home, will ya? I need the office, Willy. (*He starts to go, turns, remembering the recorder, starts to push off the table holding the recorder.*) Oh, yeah. Whenever you can this week, stop by and drop off the samples. You'll feel better, Willy, and then come back and we'll talk. Pull yourself together, kid, there's people outside.

(*Howard exits, pushing the table off left. Willy stares into space, exhausted. Now the music is heard—Ben's music—first distantly, then closer, closer. As Willy speaks, Ben enters from the right. He carries valise and umbrella.*)

WILLY: Oh, Ben, how did you do it? What is the answer? Did you wind up the Alaska deal already?

BEN: Doesn't take much time if you know what you're doing. Just a short business trip. Boarding ship in an hour. Wanted to say good-by.

WILLY: Ben, I've got to talk to you.

BEN (*glancing at his watch*): Haven't the time, William.

WILLY (*crossing the apron to Ben*): Ben, nothing's working out. I don't know what to do.

BEN: Now, look here, William. I've bought timberland in Alaska and I need a man to look after things for me.

WILLY: God, timberland! Me and my boys in those grand outdoors!

BEN: You've a new continent at your doorstep, William. Get out of these cities, they're full of talk and time payments and courts of law. Screw on your fists and you can fight for a fortune up there.

WILLY: Yes, yes! Linda, Linda!

(*Linda enters as of old, with the wash.*)

LINDA: Oh, you're back?

BEN: I haven't much time.

WILLY: No, wait! Linda, he's got a proposition for me in Alaska.

LINDA: But you've got — (*To Ben.*) He's got a beautiful job here.

WILLY: But in Alaska, kid, I could —

LINDA: You're doing well enough, Willy!

BEN (*to Linda*): Enough for what, my dear?

LINDA (*frightened of Ben and angry at him*): Don't say those things to him! Enough to be happy right here, right now. (*To Willy, while Ben laughs.*) Why must everybody conquer the world? You're well liked, and the boys love you, and someday — (*To Ben*) — why, old man Wagner told him just the other day that if he keeps it up he'll be a member of the firm, didn't he, Willy?

WILLY: Sure, sure. I am building something with this firm, Ben, and if a man is building something he must be on the right track, mustn't he?

BEN: What are you building? Lay your hand on it. Where is it?

WILLY (*hesitantly*): That's true, Linda, there's nothing.

LINDA: Why? (*To Ben.*) There's a man eighty-four years old —

WILLY: That's right, Ben, that's right. When I look at that man I say, what is there to worry about?

BEN: Bah!

WILLY: It's true, Ben. All he has to do is go into any city, pick up the phone, and he's making his living and you know why?

BEN (*picking up his valise*): I've got to go.

WILLY (*holding Ben back*): Look at this boy!

(*Biff, in his high school sweater, enters carrying suitcase. Happy carries Biff's shoulder guards, gold helmet, and football pants.*)

WILLY: Without a penny to his name, three great universities are begging for him, and from there the sky's the limit, because it's not what you do, Ben. It's who you know and the smile on your face! It's contacts, Ben, contacts! The whole wealth of Alaska passes over the lunch table at the Commodore Hotel, and that's the wonder, the wonder of this country, that a man can end with diamonds here on the basis of being liked! (*He turns to Biff.*) And that's why when you get out on that field today it's important. Because thousands of people will be rooting for you and loving you. (*To Ben, who has again begun to leave.*) And Ben! when he walks into a business office his name will sound out like a bell and all the doors will open to him! I've seen it, Ben, I've seen it a thousand times! You can't feel it with your hand like timber, but it's there!

BEN: Good-by, William.

WILLY: Ben, am I right? Don't you think I'm right? I value your advice.

BEN: There's a new continent at your doorstep, William. You could walk out rich. Rich! (*He is gone.*)

WILLY: We'll do it here, Ben! You hear me? We're gonna do it here!

(*Young Bernard rushes in. The gay music of the Boys is heard.*)

BERNARD: Oh, gee, I was afraid you left already!

WILLY: Why? What time is it?

BERNARD: It's half-past one!

WILLY: Well, come on, everybody! Ebbets Field° next stop! Where's the pennants? (*He rushes through the wall-line of the kitchen and out into the living room.*)

LINDA (*to Biff*): Did you pack fresh underwear?

BIFF (*who has been limbering up*): I want to go!

BERNARD: Biff, I'm carrying your helmet, ain't I?

HAPPY: No, I'm carrying the helmet.

BERNARD: Oh, Biff, you promised me.

HAPPY: I'm carrying the helmet.

BERNARD: How am I going to get in the locker room?

LINDA: Let him carry the shoulder guards. (*She puts her coat and hat on in the kitchen.*)

Ebbets Field: Stadium in Brooklyn, opened in 1913, demolished in 1960, and the home of the Brooklyn Dodgers until 1957.

BERNARD: Can I, Biff? 'Cause I told everybody I'm going to be in the locker room.
HAPPY: In Ebbets Field it's the clubhouse.
BERNARD: I meant the clubhouse. Biff!
HAPPY: Biff!
BIFF (*grandly, after a slight pause*): Let him carry the shoulder guards.
HAPPY (*as he gives Bernard the shoulder guards*): Stay close to us now.

(*Willy rushes in with the pennants.*)

WILLY (*handing them out*): Everybody wave when Biff comes out on the field. (*Happy and Bernard run off.*) You set now, boy?

(*The music has died away.*)

BIFF: Ready to go, Pop. Every muscle is ready.
WILLY (*at the edge of the apron*): You realize what this means?
BIFF: That's right, Pop.
WILLY (*feeling Biff's muscles*): You're comin' home this afternoon captain of the All-Scholastic Championship Team of the City of New York.
BIFF: I got it, Pop. And remember, pal, when I take off my helmet, that touchdown is for you.
WILLY: Let's go! (*He is starting out, with his arm around Biff, when Charley enters, as of old, in knickers.*) I got no room for you, Charley.
CHARLEY: Room? For what?
WILLY: In the car.
CHARLEY: You goin' for a ride? I wanted to shoot some casino.
WILLY (*furiously*): Casino! (*Incredulously.*) Don't you realize what today is?
LINDA: Oh, he knows, Willy. He's just kidding you.
WILLY: That's nothing to kid about!
CHARLEY: No, Linda, what's goin' on?
LINDA: He's playing in Ebbets Field.
CHARLEY: Baseball in this weather?
WILLY: Don't talk to him. Come on, come on! (*He is pushing them out.*)
CHARLEY: Wait a minute, didn't you hear the news?
WILLY: What?
CHARLEY: Don't you listen to the radio? Ebbets Field just blew up.
WILLY: You go to hell! (*Charley laughs. Pushing them out.*) Come on, come on! We're late.
CHARLEY (*as they go*): Knock a homer, Biff, knock a homer!
WILLY (*the last to leave, turning to Charley*): I don't think that was funny, Charley. This is the greatest day of his life.
CHARLEY: Willy, when are you going to grow up?
WILLY: Yeah, heh? When this game is over, Charley, you'll be laughing out of the other side of your face. They'll be calling him another Red Grange. Twenty-five thousand a year.
CHARLEY (*kidding*): Is that so?

WILLY: Yeah, that's so.
CHARLEY: Well, then, I'm sorry, Willy. But tell me something.
WILLY: What?
CHARLEY: Who is Red Grange?
WILLY: Put up your hands. Goddam you, put up your hands!

(*Charley, chuckling, shakes his head and walks away, around the left corner of the stage. Willy follows him. The music rises to a mocking frenzy.*)

WILLY: Who the hell do you think you are, better than everybody else? You don't know everything, you big, ignorant, stupid . . . Put up your hands!

(*Light rises, on the right side of the forestage, on a small table in the reception room of Charley's office. Traffic sounds are heard. Bernard, now mature, sits whistling to himself. A pair of tennis rackets and an overnight bag are on the floor beside him.*)

WILLY (*offstage*): What are you walking away for? Don't walk away! If you're going to say something say it to my face! I know you laugh at me behind my back. You'll laugh out of the other side of your goddam face after this game. Touchdown! Touchdown! Eighty thousand people! Touchdown! Right between the goal posts.

(*Bernard is a quiet, earnest, but self-assured young man. Willy's voice is coming from right upstage now. Bernard lowers his feet off the table and listens. Jenny, his father's secretary, enters.*)

JENNY (*distressed*): Say, Bernard, will you go out in the hall?
BERNARD: What is that noise? Who is it?
JENNY: Mr. Loman. He just got off the elevator.
BERNARD (*getting up*): Who's he arguing with?
JENNY: Nobody. There's nobody with him. I can't deal with him anymore, and your father gets all upset everytime he comes. I've got a lot of typing to do, and your father's waiting to sign it. Will you see him?
WILLY (*entering*): Touchdown! Touch — (*He sees Jenny.*) Jenny, Jenny, good to see you. How're ya? Workin'? Or still honest?
JENNY: Fine. How've you been feeling?
WILLY: Not much any more, Jenny. Ha, ha! (*He is surprised to see the rackets.*)
BERNARD: Hello, Uncle Willy.
WILLY (*almost shocked*): Bernard! Well, look who's here! (*He comes quickly, guiltily, to Bernard and warmly shakes his hand.*)
BERNARD: How are you? Good to see you.
WILLY: What are you doing here?
BERNARD: Oh, just stopped by to see Pop. Get off my feet till my train leaves. I'm going to Washington in a few minutes.
WILLY: Is he in?
BERNARD: Yes, he's in his office with the accountant. Sit down.
WILLY (*sitting down*): What're you going to do in Washington?

BERNARD: Oh, just a case I've got there, Willy.

WILLY: That so? (*Indicating the rackets.*) You going to play tennis there?

BERNARD: I'm staying with a friend who's got a court.

WILLY: Don't say. His own tennis court. Must be fine people, I bet.

BERNARD: They are, very nice. Dad tells me Biff's in town.

WILLY (*with a big smile*): Yeah, Biff's in. Working on a very big deal, Bernard.

BERNARD: What's Biff doing?

WILLY: Well, he's been doing very big things in the West. But he decided to
     establish himself here. Very big. We're having dinner. Did I hear your
     wife had a boy?

BERNARD: That's right. Our second.

WILLY: Two boys! What do you know!

BERNARD: What kind of a deal has Biff got?

WILLY: Well, Bill Oliver — very big sporting-goods man — he wants Biff very
     badly. Called him in from the West. Long distance, carte blanche, spe-
     cial deliveries. Your friends have their own private tennis court?

BERNARD: You still with the old firm, Willy?

WILLY (*after a pause*): I'm — I'm overjoyed to see how you made the grade,
     Bernard, overjoyed. It's an encouraging thing to see a young man really —
     really — Looks very good for Biff — very — (*He breaks off, then.*) Bernard —
     (*He is so full of emotion, he breaks off again.*)

BERNARD: What is it, Willy?

WILLY (*small and alone*): What — what's the secret?

BERNARD: What secret?

WILLY: How — how did you? Why didn't he ever catch on?

BERNARD: I wouldn't know that, Willy.

WILLY (*confidentially, desperately*): You were his friend, his boyhood friend.
     There's something I don't understand about it. His life ended after that
     Ebbets Field game. From the age of seventeen nothing good ever hap-
     pened to him.

BERNARD: He never trained himself for anything.

WILLY: But he did, he did. After high school he took so many correspondence
     courses. Radio mechanics; television; God knows what, and never made
     the slightest mark.

BERNARD (*taking off his glasses*): Willy, do you want to talk candidly?

WILLY (*rising, faces Bernard*): I regard you as a very brilliant man, Bernard. I
     value your advice.

BERNARD: Oh, the hell with the advice, Willy. I couldn't advise you. There's
     just one thing I've always wanted to ask you. When he was supposed to
     graduate, and the math teacher flunked him —

WILLY: Oh, that son-of-a-bitch ruined his life.

BERNARD: Yeah, but, Willy, all he had to do was go to summer school and
     make up that subject.

WILLY: That's right, that's right.

BERNARD: Did you tell him not to go to summer school?

WILLY: Me? I begged him to go. I ordered him to go!

BERNARD: Then why wouldn't he go?

WILLY: Why? Why! Bernard, that question has been trailing me like a ghost for the last fifteen years. He flunked the subject, and laid down and died like a hammer hit him!

BERNARD: Take it easy, kid.

WILLY: Let me talk to you — I got nobody to talk to. Bernard, Bernard, was it my fault? Y'see? It keeps going around in my mind, maybe I did something to him. I got nothing to give him.

BERNARD: Don't take it so hard.

WILLY: Why did he lay down? What is the story there? You were his friend!

BERNARD: Willy, I remember, it was June, and our grades came out. And he'd flunked math.

WILLY: That son-of-a-bitch!

BERNARD: No, it wasn't right then. Biff just got very angry, I remember, and he was ready to enroll in summer school.

WILLY (surprised): He was?

BERNARD: He wasn't beaten by it at all. But then, Willy, he disappeared from the block for almost a month. And I got the idea that he'd gone up to New England to see you. Did he have a talk with you then?

(Willy stares in silence.)

BERNARD: Willy?

WILLY (with a strong edge of resentment in his voice): Yeah, he came to Boston. What about it?

BERNARD: Well, just that when he came back — I'll never forget this, it always mystifies me. Because I'd thought so well of Biff, even though he'd always taken advantage of me. I loved him, Willy, y'know? And he came back after that month and took his sneakers — remember those sneakers with "University of Virginia" printed on them? He was so proud of those, wore them every day. And he took them down in the cellar, and burned them up in the furnace. We had a fist fight. It lasted at least half an hour. Just the two of us, punching each other down the cellar, and crying right through it. I've often thought of how strange it was that I knew he'd given up his life. What happened in Boston, Willy?

(Willy looks at him as at an intruder.)

BERNARD: I just bring it up because you asked me.

WILLY (angrily): Nothing. What do you mean, "What happened?" What's that got to do with anything?

BERNARD: Well, don't get sore.

WILLY: What are you trying to do, blame it on me? If a boy lays down is that my fault?

BERNARD: Now, Willy, don't get —

WILLY: Well, don't — don't talk to me that way! What does that mean, "What happened?"

(*Charley enters. He is in his vest, and he carries a bottle of bourbon.*)

CHARLEY: Hey, you're going to miss that train. (*He waves the bottle.*)

BERNARD: Yeah, I'm going. (*He takes the bottle.*) Thanks, Pop. (*He picks up his rackets and bag.*) Good-by, Willy, and don't worry about it. You know, "If at first you don't succeed . . ."

WILLY: Yes, I believe in that.

BERNARD: But sometimes, Willy, it's better for a man just to walk away.

WILLY: Walk away?

BERNARD: That's right.

WILLY: But if you can't walk away?

BERNARD (*after a slight pause*): I guess that's when it's tough. (*Extending his hand.*) Good-by, Willy.

WILLY (*shaking Bernard's hand*): Good-by, boy.

CHARLEY (*an arm on Bernard's shoulder*): How do you like this kid? Gonna argue a case in front of the Supreme Court.

BERNARD (*protesting*): Pop!

WILLY (*genuinely shocked, pained, and happy*): No! The Supreme Court!

BERNARD: I gotta run. 'By, Dad!

CHARLEY: Knock 'em dead, Bernard!

(*Bernard goes off.*)

WILLY (*as Charley takes out his wallet*): The Supreme Court! And he didn't even mention it!

CHARLEY (*counting out money on the desk*): He don't have to — he's gonna do it.

WILLY: And you never told him what to do, did you? You never took any interest in him.

CHARLEY: My salvation is that I never took any interest in anything. There's some money — fifty dollars. I got an accountant inside.

WILLY: Charley, look . . . (*With difficulty.*) I got my insurance to pay. If you can manage it — I need a hundred and ten dollars.

(*Charley doesn't reply for a moment; merely stops moving.*)

WILLY: I'd draw it from my bank but Linda would know, and I . . .

CHARLEY: Sit down, Willy.

WILLY (*moving toward the chair*): I'm keeping an account of everything, remember. I'll pay every penny back. (*He sits.*)

CHARLEY: Now listen to me, Willy.

WILLY: I want you to know I appreciate . . .

CHARLEY (*sitting down on the table*): Willy, what're you doin'? What the hell is goin' on in your head?

WILLY: Why? I'm simply . . .

CHARLEY: I offered you a job. You make fifty dollars a week. And I won't send you on the road.

WILLY: I've got a job.

CHARLEY: Without pay? What kind of a job is a job without pay? (*He rises.*) Now, look, kid, enough is enough. I'm no genius but I know when I'm being insulted.

WILLY: Insulted!

CHARLEY: Why don't you want to work for me?

WILLY: What's the matter with you? I've got a job.

CHARLEY: Then what're you walkin' in here every week for?

WILLY (*getting up*): Well, if you don't want me to walk in here —

CHARLEY: I'm offering you a job.

WILLY: I don't want your goddam job!

CHARLEY: When the hell are you going to grow up?

WILLY (*furiously*): You big ignoramus, if you say that to me again I'll rap you one! I don't care how big you are! (*He's ready to fight.*)

(*Pause.*)

CHARLEY (*kindly, going to him*): How much do you need, Willy?

WILLY: Charley, I'm strapped. I'm strapped. I don't know what to do. I was just fired.

CHARLEY: Howard fired you?

WILLY: That snotnose. Imagine that? I named him. I named him Howard.

CHARLEY: Willy, when're you gonna realize that them things don't mean anything? You named him Howard, but you can't sell that. The only thing you got in this world is what you can sell. And the funny thing is that you're a salesman, and you don't know that.

WILLY: I've always tried to think otherwise, I guess. I always felt that if a man was impressive, and well liked, that nothing —

CHARLEY: Why must everybody like you? Who liked J. P. Morgan?° Was he impressive? In a Turkish bath he'd look like a butcher. But with his pockets on he was very well liked. Now listen, Willy, I know you don't like me, and nobody can say I'm in love with you, but I'll give you a job because — just for the hell of it, put it that way. Now what do you say?

WILLY: I — I just can't work for you, Charley.

CHARLEY: What're you, jealous of me?

WILLY: I can't work for you, that's all, don't ask me why.

CHARLEY (*angered, takes out more bills*): You been jealous of me all your life, you dammed fool! Here, pay your insurance. (*He puts the money in Willy's hand.*)

WILLY: I'm keeping strict accounts.

J. P. Morgan: John Pierpont Morgan (1837–1913), wealthy and ruthless American financier, railroad developer, and industrialist.

CHARLEY: I've got some work to do. Take care of yourself. And pay your insurance.

WILLY (*moving to the right*): Funny, y'know? After all the highways, and the trains, and the appointments, and the years, you end up worth more dead than alive.

CHARLEY: Willy, nobody's worth nothin' dead. (*After a slight pause.*) Did you hear what I said?

(*Willy stands still, dreaming.*)

CHARLEY: Willy!

WILLY: Apologize to Bernard for me when you see him. I didn't mean to argue with him. He's a fine boy. They're all fine boys, and they'll end up big — all of them. Someday they'll all play tennis together. Wish me luck, Charley. He saw Bill Oliver today.

CHARLEY: Good luck.

WILLY (*on the verge of tears*): Charley, you're the only friend I got. Isn't that a remarkable thing? (*He goes out.*)

CHARLEY: Jesus!

(*Charley stares after him a moment and follows. All light blacks out. Suddenly raucous music is heard, and a red glow rises behind the screen at right. Stanley, a young waiter, appears, carrying a table, followed by Happy, who is carrying two chairs.*)

STANLEY (*putting the table down*): That's all right, Mr. Loman, I can handle it myself. (*He turns and takes the chairs from Happy and places them at the table.*)

HAPPY (*glancing around*): Oh, this is better.

STANLEY: Sure, in the front there you're in the middle of all kinds of noise. Whenever you got a party, Mr. Loman, you just tell me and I'll put you back here. Y'know, there's a lotta people they don't like it private, because when they go out they like to see a lotta action around them because they're sick and tired to stay in the house by theirself. But I know you, you ain't from Hackensack. You know what I mean?

HAPPY (*sitting down*): So how's it coming, Stanley?

STANLEY: Ah, it's a dog life. I only wish during the war they'd a took me in the Army. I coulda been dead by now.

HAPPY: My brother's back, Stanley.

STANLEY: Oh, he come back, heh? From the Far West.

HAPPY: Yeah, big cattle man, my brother, so treat him right. And my father's coming too.

STANLEY: Oh, your father too!

HAPPY: You got a couple of nice lobsters?

STANLEY: Hundred percent, big.

HAPPY: I want them with the claws.

STANLEY: Don't worry, I don't give you no mice. (*Happy laughs.*) How about some wine? It'll put a head on the meal.

HAPPY: No. You remember, Stanley, that recipe I brought you from overseas? With the champagne in it?

STANLEY: Oh, yeah, sure. I still got it tacked up yet in the kitchen. But that'll have to cost a buck apiece anyways.

HAPPY: That's all right.

STANLEY: What'd you, hit a number or somethin'?

HAPPY: No, it's a little celebration. My brother is — I think he pulled off a big deal today. I think we're going into business together.

STANLEY: Great! That's the best for you. Because a family business, you know what I mean? — that's the best.

HAPPY: That's what I think.

STANLEY: 'Cause what's the difference? Somebody steals? It's in the family. Know what I mean? (*Sotto voce.*°) Like this bartender here. The boss is goin' crazy what kinda leak he's got in the cash register. You put it in but it don't come out.

HAPPY (*raising his head*): Sh!

STANLEY: What?

HAPPY: You notice I wasn't lookin' right or left, was I?

STANLEY: No.

HAPPY: And my eyes are closed.

STANLEY: So what's the — ?

HAPPY: Strudel's comin'.

STANLEY (*catching on, looks around*): Ah, no, there's no —

(*He breaks off as a furred, lavishly dressed girl enters and sits at the next table. Both follow her with their eyes.*)

STANLEY: Geez, how'd ya know?

HAPPY: I got radar or something. (*Staring directly at her profile.*) Oooooooo . . . Stanley.

STANLEY: I think that's for you, Mr. Loman.

HAPPY: Look at that mouth. Oh, God. And the binoculars.

STANLEY: Geez, you got a life, Mr. Loman.

HAPPY: Wait on her.

STANLEY (*going to the girl's table*): Would you like a menu, ma'am?

GIRL: I'm expecting someone, but I'd like a —

HAPPY: Why don't you bring her — excuse me, miss, do you mind? I sell champagne, and I'd like you to try my brand. Bring her a champagne, Stanley.

GIRL: That's awfully nice of you.

HAPPY: Don't mention it. It's all company money. (*He laughs.*)

GIRL: That's a charming product to be selling, isn't it?

HAPPY: Oh, gets to be like everything else. Selling is selling, y'know.

GIRL: I suppose.

---

s.d. *Sotto voce:* "Under [the] voice" (Italian); in a low, soft voice.

HAPPY: You don't happen to sell, do you?

GIRL: No, I don't sell.

HAPPY: Would you object to a compliment from a stranger? You ought to be on a magazine cover.

GIRL (*looking at him a little archly*): I have been.

(*Stanley comes in with a glass of champagne.*)

HAPPY: What'd I say before, Stanley? You see? She's a cover girl.

STANLEY: Oh, I could see, I could see.

HAPPY (*to the Girl*): What magazine?

GIRL: Oh, a lot of them. (*She takes the drink.*) Thank you.

HAPPY: You know what they say in France, don't you? "Champagne is the drink of the complexion" — Hya, Biff!

(*Biff has entered and sits with Happy.*)

BIFF: Hello, kid. Sorry I'm late.

HAPPY: I just got here. Uh, Miss — ?

GIRL: Forsythe.

HAPPY: Miss Forsythe, this is my brother.

BIFF: Is Dad here?

HAPPY: His name is Biff. You might've heard of him. Great football player.

GIRL: Really? What team?

HAPPY: Are you familiar with football?

GIRL: No, I'm afraid I'm not.

HAPPY: Biff is quarterback with the New York Giants.

GIRL: Well, that is nice, isn't it? (*She drinks.*)

HAPPY: Good health.

GIRL: I'm happy to meet you.

HAPPY: That's my name. Hap. It's really Harold, but at West Point they called me Happy.

GIRL (*now really impressed*): Oh, I see. How do you do? (*She turns her profile.*)

BIFF: Isn't Dad coming?

HAPPY: You want her?

BIFF: Oh, I could never make that.

HAPPY: I remember the time that idea would never come into your head. Where's the old confidence, Biff?

BIFF: I just saw Oliver —

HAPPY: Wait a minute. I've got to see that old confidence again. Do you want her? She's on call.

BIFF: Oh, no. (*He turns to look at the Girl.*)

HAPPY: I'm telling you. Watch this. (*Turning to the Girl*): Honey? (*She turns to him.*) Are you busy?

GIRL: Well, I am . . . but I could make a phone call.

HAPPY: Do that, will you, honey? And see if you can get a friend. We'll be here for a while. Biff is one of the greatest football players in the country.

GIRL (*standing up*): Well, I'm certainly happy to meet you.
HAPPY: Come back soon.
GIRL: I'll try.
HAPPY: Don't try, honey, try hard.

(*The Girl exits. Stanley follows, shaking his head in bewildered admiration.*)

HAPPY: Isn't that a shame now? A beautiful girl like that? That's why I can't get married. There's not a good woman in a thousand. New York is loaded with them, kid!
BIFF: Hap, look —
HAPPY: I told you she was on call!
BIFF (*strangely unnerved*): Cut it out, will ya? I want to say something to you.
HAPPY: Did you see Oliver?
BIFF: I saw him all right. Now look, I want to tell Dad a couple of things and I want you to help me.
HAPPY: What? Is he going to back you?
BIFF: Are you crazy? You're out of your goddam head, you know that?
HAPPY: Why? What happened?
BIFF (*breathlessly*): I did a terrible thing today, Hap. It's been the strangest day I ever went through. I'm all numb, I swear.
HAPPY: You mean he wouldn't see you?
BIFF: Well, I waited six hours for him, see? All day. Kept sending my name in. Even tried to date his secretary so she'd get me to him, but no soap.
HAPPY: Because you're not showin' the old confidence Biff. He remembered you, didn't he?
BIFF (*stopping Happy with a gesture*): Finally, about five o'clock, he comes out. Didn't remember who I was or anything. I felt like such an idiot, Hap.
HAPPY: Did you tell him my Florida idea?
BIFF: He walked away. I saw him for one minute. I got so mad I could've torn the walls down! How the hell did I ever get the idea I was a salesman there? I even believed myself that I'd been a salesman for him! And then he gave me one look and — I realized what a ridiculous lie my whole life has been! We've been talking in a dream for fifteen years. I was a shipping clerk.
HAPPY: What'd you do?
BIFF (*with great tension and wonder*): Well, he left, see. And the secretary went out. I was all alone in the waiting room. I don't know what came over me, Hap. The next thing I know I'm in his office — paneled walls, everything. I can't explain it. I — Hap, I took his fountain pen.
HAPPY: Geez, did he catch you?
BIFF: I ran out. I ran down all eleven flights. I ran and ran and ran.
HAPPY: That was an awful dumb — what'd you do that for?
BIFF (*agonized*): I don't know, I just — wanted to take something, I don't know. You gotta help me, Hap. I'm gonna tell Pop.
HAPPY: You crazy? What for?

BIFF: Hap, he's got to understand that I'm not the man somebody lends that kind of money to. He thinks I've been spiting him all these years and it's eating him up.

HAPPY: That's just it. You tell him something nice.

BIFF: I can't.

HAPPY: Say you got a lunch date with Oliver tomorrow.

BIFF: So what do I do tomorrow?

HAPPY: You leave the house tomorrow and come back at night and say Oliver is thinking it over. And he thinks it over for a couple of weeks, and gradually it fades away and nobody's the worse.

BIFF: But it'll go on forever!

HAPPY: Dad is never so happy as when he's looking forward to something!

(Willy enters.)

HAPPY: Hello, scout!

WILLY: Gee, I haven't been here in years!

(Stanley has followed Willy in and sets a chair for him. Stanley starts off but Happy stops him.)

HAPPY: Stanley!

(Stanley stands by, waiting for an order.)

BIFF *(going to Willy with guilt, as to an invalid)*: Sit down, Pop. You want a drink?

WILLY: Sure, I don't mind.

BIFF: Let's get a load on.

WILLY: You look worried.

BIFF: N-no. *(To Stanley.)* Scotch all around. Make it doubles.

STANLEY: Doubles, right. *(He goes.)*

WILLY: You had a couple already, didn't you?

BIFF: Just a couple, yeah.

WILLY: Well, what happened, boy? *(Nodding affirmatively, with a smile.)* Everything go all right?

BIFF *(takes a breath, then reaches out and grasps Willy's hand)*: Pal . . . *(He is smiling bravely, and Willy is smiling too.)* I had an experience today.

HAPPY: Terrific, Pop.

WILLY: That so? What happened?

BIFF *(high, slightly alcoholic, above the earth)*: I'm going to tell you everything from first to last. It's been a strange day. *(Silence. He looks around, composes himself as best he can, but his breath keeps breaking the rhythm of his voice.)* I had to wait quite a while for him, and —

WILLY: Oliver?

BIFF: Yeah, Oliver. All day, as a matter of cold fact. And a lot of — instances — facts, Pop, facts about my life came back to me. Who was it, Pop? Who ever said I was a salesman with Oliver?

WILLY: Well, you were.

BIFF: No, Dad, I was a shipping clerk.

WILLY: But you were practically—

BIFF (*with determination*): Dad, I don't know who said it first, but I was never a salesman for Bill Oliver.

WILLY: What're you talking about?

BIFF: Let's hold on to the facts tonight, Pop. We're not going to get anywhere bullin' around. I was a shipping clerk.

WILLY (*angrily*): All right, now listen to me—

BIFF: Why don't you let me finish?

WILLY: I'm not interested in stories about the past or any crap of that kind because the woods are burning, boys, you understand? There's a big blaze going on all around. I was fired today.

BIFF (*shocked*): How could you be?

WILLY: I was fired, and I'm looking for a little good news to tell your mother, because the woman has waited and the woman has suffered. The gist of it is that I haven't got a story left in my head, Biff. So don't give me a lecture about facts and aspects. I am not interested. Now what've you got to say to me?

(*Stanley enters with three drinks. They wait until he leaves.*)

WILLY: Did you see Oliver?

BIFF: Jesus, Dad!

WILLY: You mean you didn't go up there?

HAPPY: Sure he went up there.

BIFF: I did. I—saw him. How could they fire you?

WILLY (*on the edge of his chair*): What kind of a welcome did he give you?

BIFF: He won't even let you work on commission?

WILLY: I'm out! (*Driving.*) So tell me, he gave you a warm welcome?

HAPPY: Sure, Pop, sure!

BIFF (*driven*): Well, it was kind of—

WILLY: I was wondering if he'd remember you. (*To Happy.*) Imagine, man doesn't see him for ten, twelve years and gives him that kind of a welcome!

HAPPY: Damn right!

BIFF (*trying to return to the offensive*): Pop, look—

WILLY: You know why he remembered you, don't you? Because you impressed him in those days.

BIFF: Let's talk quietly and get this down to the facts, huh?

WILLY (*as though Biff had been interrupting*): Well, what happened? It's great news, Biff. Did he take you into his office or'd you talk in the waiting room?

BIFF: Well, he came in, see, and—

WILLY (*with a big smile*): What'd he say? Betcha he threw his arm around you.

BIFF: Well, he kinda—

WILLY: He's a fine man. (*To Happy.*) Very hard man to see, y'know.

HAPPY (*agreeing*): Oh, I know.

WILLY (*to Biff*): Is that where you had the drinks?

BIFF: Yeah, he gave me a couple of — no, no!

HAPPY (*cutting in*): He told him my Florida idea.

WILLY: Don't interrupt. (*To Biff.*) How'd he react to the Florida idea?

BIFF: Dad, will you give me a minute to explain?

WILLY: I've been waiting for you to explain since I sat down here! What happened? He took you into his office and what?

BIFF: Well — I talked. And — and he listened, see.

WILLY: Famous for the way he listens, y'know. What was his answer?

BIFF: His answer was — (*He breaks off, suddenly angry.*) Dad, you're not letting me tell you what I want to tell you!

WILLY (*accusing, angered*): You didn't see him, did you?

BIFF: I did see him!

WILLY: What'd you insult him or something? You insulted him, didn't you?

BIFF: Listen, will you let me out of it, will you just let me out of it!

HAPPY: What the hell!

WILLY: Tell me what happened!

BIFF (*to Happy*): I can't talk to him!

(*A single trumpet note jars the ear. The light of green leaves stains the house, which holds the air of night and a dream. Young Bernard enters and knocks on the door of the house.*)

YOUNG BERNARD (*frantically*): Mrs. Loman, Mrs. Loman!

HAPPY: Tell him what happened!

BIFF (*to Happy*): Shut up and leave me alone!

WILLY: No, no! You had to go and flunk math!

BIFF: What math? What're you talking about?

YOUNG BERNARD: Mrs. Loman, Mrs. Loman!

(*Linda appears in the house, as of old.*)

WILLY (*wildly*): Math, math, math!

BIFF: Take it easy, Pop!

YOUNG BERNARD: Mrs. Loman!

WILLY (*furiously*): If you hadn't flunked you'd've been set by now!

BIFF: Now, look, I'm gonna tell you what happened, and you're going to listen to me.

YOUNG BERNARD: Mrs. Loman!

BIFF: I waited six hours —

HAPPY: What the hell are you saying?

BIFF: I kept sending in my name but he wouldn't see me. So finally he . . . (*He continues unheard as light fades low on the restaurant.*)

YOUNG BERNARD: Biff flunked math!

LINDA: No!

YOUNG BERNARD: Birnbaum flunked him! They won't graduate him!

LINDA: But they have to. He's gotta go to the university. Where is he? Biff! Biff!

YOUNG BERNARD: No, he left. He went to Grand Central.

LINDA: Grand — You mean he went to Boston!

YOUNG BERNARD: Is Uncle Willy in Boston?

LINDA: Oh, maybe Willy can talk to the teacher. Oh, the poor, poor boy!

(*Light on house area snaps out.*)

BIFF (*at the table, now audible, holding up a gold fountain pen*): . . . so I'm washed up with Oliver, you understand? Are you listening to me?

WILLY (*at a loss*): Yeah, sure. If you hadn't flunked —

BIFF: Flunked what? What're you talking about?

WILLY: Don't blame everything on me! I didn't flunk math — you did! What pen?

HAPPY: That was awful dumb, Biff, a pen like that is worth —

WILLY (*seeing the pen for the first time*): You took Oliver's pen?

BIFF (*weakening*): Dad, I just explained it to you.

WILLY: You stole Bill Oliver's fountain pen!

BIFF: I didn't exactly steal it! That's just what I've been explaining to you!

HAPPY: He had it in his hand and just then Oliver walked in, so he got nervous and stuck it in his pocket!

WILLY: My God, Biff!

BIFF: I never intended to do it, Dad!

OPERATOR'S VOICE: Standish Arms, good evening!

WILLY (*shouting*): I'm not in my room!

BIFF (*frightened*): Dad, what's the matter? (*He and Happy stand up.*)

OPERATOR: Ringing Mr. Loman for you!

WILLY: I'm not there, stop it!

BIFF (*horrified, gets down on one knee before Willy*): Dad, I'll make good, I'll make good. (*Willy tries to get to his feet. Biff holds him down.*) Sit down now.

WILLY: No, you're no good, you're no good for anything.

BIFF: I am, Dad, I'll find something else, you understand? Now don't worry about anything. (*He holds up Willy's face.*) Talk to me, Dad.

OPERATOR: Mr. Loman does not answer. Shall I page him?

WILLY (*attempting to stand, as though to rush and silence the Operator*): No, no, no!

HAPPY: He'll strike something, Pop.

WILLY: No, no . . .

BIFF (*desperately, standing over Willy*): Pop, listen! Listen to me! I'm telling you something good. Oliver talked to his partner about the Florida idea. You listening? He — he talked to his partner, and he came to me . . . I'm going to be all right, you hear? Dad, listen to me, he said it was just a question of the amount!

WILLY: Then you . . . got it?

HAPPY: He's gonna be terrific, Pop!

WILLY (*trying to stand*): Then you got it, haven't you? You got it! You got it!

BIFF (*agonized, holds Willy down*): No, no. Look, Pop. I'm supposed to have lunch with them tomorrow. I'm just telling you this so you'll know that I can still make an impression, Pop. And I'll make good somewhere, but I can't go tomorrow, see?

WILLY: Why not? You simply —

BIFF: But the pen, Pop!

WILLY: You give it to him and tell him it was an oversight!

HAPPY: Sure, have lunch tomorrow!

BIFF: I can't say that —

WILLY: You were doing a crossword puzzle and accidentally used his pen!

BIFF: Listen, kid, I took those balls years ago, now I walk in with his fountain pen? That clinches it, don't you see? I can't face him like that! I'll try elsewhere.

PAGE'S VOICE: Paging Mr. Loman!

WILLY: Don't you want to be anything?

BIFF: Pop, how can I go back?

WILLY: You don't want to be anything, is that what's behind it?

BIFF (*now angry at Willy for not crediting his sympathy*): Don't take it that way! You think it was easy walking into that office after what I'd done to him? A team of horses couldn't have dragged me back to Bill Oliver!

WILLY: Then why'd you go?

BIFF: Why did I go? Why did I go! Look at you! Look at what's become of you!

(*Off left, The Woman laughs.*)

WILLY: Biff, you're going to go to that lunch tomorrow, or —

BIFF: I can't go. I've got no appointment!

HAPPY: Biff, for . . . !

WILLY: Are you spiting me?

BIFF: Don't take it that way! Goddammit!

WILLY (*strikes Biff and falters away from the table*): You rotten little louse! Are you spiting me?

THE WOMAN: Someone's at the door, Willy!

BIFF: I'm no good, can't you see what I am?

HAPPY (*separating them*): Hey, you're in a restaurant! Now cut it out, both of you! (*The girls enter.*) Hello, girls, sit down.

(*The Woman laughs, off left.*)

MISS FORSYTHE: I guess we might as well. This is Letta.

THE WOMAN: Willy, are you going to wake up?

BIFF (*ignoring Willy*): How're ya, miss, sit down. What do you drink?

MISS FORSYTHE: Letta might not be able to stay long.

LETTA: I gotta get up very early tomorrow. I got jury duty. I'm so excited! Were you fellows ever on a jury?

BIFF: No, but I been in front of them! (*The girls laugh.*) This is my father.

LETTA: Isn't he cute? Sit down with us, Pop.

HAPPY: Sit him down, Biff!

BIFF (*going to him*): Come on, slugger, drink us under the table. To hell with it! Come on, sit down, pal.

(*On Biff's last insistence, Willy is about to sit.*)

THE WOMAN (*now urgently*): Willy, are you going to answer the door!

(*The Woman's call pulls Willy back. He starts right, befuddled.*)

BIFF: Hey, where are you going?

WILLY: Open the door.

BIFF: The door?

WILLY: The washroom . . . the door . . . where's the door?

BIFF (*leading Willy to the left*): Just go straight down.

(*Willy moves left.*)

THE WOMAN: Willy, Willy, are you going to get up, get up, get up, get up?

(*Willy exits left.*)

LETTA: I think it's sweet you bring your daddy along.

MISS FORSYTHE: Oh, he isn't really your father!

BIFF (*at left, turning to her resentfully*): Miss Forsythe, you've just seen a prince walk by. A fine, troubled prince. A hard-working, unappreciated prince. A pal, you understand? A good companion. Always for his boys.

LETTA: That's so sweet.

HAPPY: Well, girls, what's the program? We're wasting time. Come on, Biff. Gather round. Where would you like to go?

BIFF: Why don't you do something for him?

HAPPY: Me!

BIFF: Don't you give a damn for him, Hap?

HAPPY: What're you talking about? I'm the one who —

BIFF: I sense it, you don't give a good goddam about him. (*He takes the rolled-up hose from his pocket and puts it on the table in front of Happy.*) Look what I found in the cellar, for Christ's sake. How can you bear to let it go on?

HAPPY: Me? Who goes away? Who runs off and —

BIFF: Yeah, but he doesn't mean anything to you. You could help him — I can't! Don't you understand what I'm talking about? He's going to kill himself, don't you know that?

HAPPY: Don't I know it! Me!

BIFF: Hap, help him! Jesus . . . help him . . . Help me, help me, I can't bear to look at his face! (*Ready to weep, he hurries out, up right.*)

HAPPY (*starting after him*): Where are you going?

MISS FORSYTHE: What's he so mad about?

HAPPY: Come on, girls, we'll catch up with him.

MISS FORSYTHE (*as Happy pushes her out*): Say, I don't like that temper of his!

HAPPY: He's just a little overstrung, he'll be all right!

WILLY (*off left, as The Woman laughs*): Don't answer! Don't answer!

LETTA: Don't you want to tell your father —

HAPPY: No, that's not my father. He's just a guy. Come on, we'll catch Biff, and, honey, we're going to paint this town! Stanley, where's the check! Hey, Stanley!

(*They exit. Stanley looks toward left.*)

STANLEY (*calling to Happy indignantly*): Mr. Loman! Mr. Loman!

(*Stanley picks up a chair and follows them off. Knocking is heard off left. The Woman enters, laughing. Willy follows her. She is in a black slip; he is buttoning his shirt. Raw, sensuous music accompanies their speech.*)

WILLY: Will you stop laughing? Will you stop?

THE WOMAN: Aren't you going to answer the door? He'll wake the whole hotel.

WILLY: I'm not expecting anybody.

THE WOMAN: Whyn't you have another drink, honey, and stop being so damn self-centered?

WILLY: I'm so lonely.

THE WOMAN: You know you ruined me, Willy? From now on, whenever you come to the office, I'll see that you go right through to the buyers. No waiting at my desk anymore, Willy. You ruined me.

WILLY: That's nice of you to say that.

THE WOMAN: Gee, you are self-centered! Why so sad? You are the saddest, self-centeredest soul I ever did see-saw. (*She laughs. He kisses her.*) Come on inside, drummer boy. It's silly to be dressing in the middle of the night. (*As knocking is heard.*) Aren't you going to answer the door?

WILLY: They're knocking on the wrong door.

THE WOMAN: But I felt the knocking. And he heard us talking in here. Maybe the hotel's on fire!

WILLY (*his terror rising*): It's a mistake.

THE WOMAN: Then tell him to go away!

WILLY: There's nobody there.

THE WOMAN: It's getting on my nerves, Willy. There's somebody standing out there and it's getting on my nerves!

WILLY (*pushing her away from him*): All right, stay in the bathroom here, and don't come out. I think there's a law in Massachusetts about it, so don't come out. It may be that new room clerk. He looked very mean. So don't come out. It's a mistake, there's no fire.

(*The knocking is heard again. He takes a few steps away from her, and she vanishes into the wing. The light follows him, and now he is facing Young Biff, who carries a suitcase. Biff steps toward him. The music is gone.*)

BIFF: Why didn't you answer?

WILLY: Biff! What are you doing in Boston?

BIFF: Why didn't you answer? I've been knocking for five minutes, I called you on the phone —

WILLY: I just heard you. I was in the bathroom and had the door shut. Did anything happen home?

BIFF: Dad — I let you down.

WILLY: What do you mean?

BIFF: Dad . . .

WILLY: Biffo, what's this about? (*Putting his arm around Biff.*) Come on, let's go downstairs and get you a malted.

BIFF: Dad, I flunked math.

WILLY: Not for the term?

BIFF: The term. I haven't got enough credits to graduate.

WILLY: You mean to say Bernard wouldn't give you the answers?

BIFF: He did, he tried, but I only got a sixty-one.

WILLY: And they wouldn't give you four points?

BIFF: Birnbaum refused absolutely. I begged him, Pop, but he won't give me those points. You gotta talk to him before they close the school. Because if he saw the kind of man you are, and you just talked to him in your way, I'm sure he'd come through for me. The class came right before practice, see, and I didn't go enough. Would you talk to him? He'd like you, Pop. You know the way you could talk.

WILLY: You're on. We'll drive right back.

BIFF: Oh, Dad, good work! I'm sure he'll change it for you!

WILLY: Go downstairs and tell the clerk I'm checkin' out. Go right down.

BIFF: Yes, sir! See, the reason he hates me, Pop — one day he was late for class so I got up at the blackboard and imitated him. I crossed my eyes and talked with a lithp.

WILLY (*laughing*): You did? The kids like it?

BIFF: They nearly died laughing!

WILLY: Yeah? What'd you do?

BIFF: The thquare root of thixty twee is . . . (*Willy bursts out laughing; Biff joins.*) And in the middle of it he walked in!

(*Willy laughs and The Woman joins in offstage.*)

WILLY (*without hesitation*): Hurry downstairs and —

BIFF: Somebody in there?

WILLY: No, that was next door.

(*The Woman laughs offstage.*)

BIFF: Somebody got in your bathroom!

WILLY: No, it's the next room, there's a party —

THE WOMAN (*enters, laughing. She lisps this.*): Can I come in? There's something in the bathtub, Willy, and it's moving!

(*Willy looks at Biff, who is staring open-mouthed and horrified at The Woman.*)

WILLY: Ah — you better go back to your room. They must be finished painting by now. They're painting her room so I let her take a shower here. Go back, go back . . . (*He pushes her.*)

THE WOMAN (*resisting*): But I've got to get dressed, Willy, I can't —

WILLY: Get out of here! Go back, go back . . . (*Suddenly striving for the ordinary.*) This is Miss Francis, Biff, she's a buyer. They're painting her room. Go back, Miss Francis, go back . . .

THE WOMAN: But my clothes, I can't go out naked in the hall!

WILLY (*pushing her offstage*): Get outa here! Go back, go back!

(*Biff slowly sits down on his suitcase as the argument continues offstage.*)

THE WOMAN: Where's my stockings? You promised me stockings, Willy!

WILLY: I have no stockings here!

THE WOMAN: You had two boxes of size nine sheers for me, and I want them!

WILLY: Here, for God's sake, will you get outa here!

THE WOMAN (*enters holding a box of stockings*): I just hope there's nobody in the hall. That's all I hope. (*To Biff.*) Are you football or baseball?

BIFF: Football.

THE WOMAN (*angry, humiliated*): That's me too. G'night. (*She snatches her clothes from Willy, and walks out.*)

WILLY (*after a pause*): Well, better get going. I want to get to the school first thing in the morning. Get my suits out of the closet. I'll get my valise. (*Biff doesn't move.*) What's the matter! (*Biff remains motionless, tears falling.*) She's a buyer. Buys for J. H. Simmons. She lives down the hall — they're painting. You don't imagine — (*He breaks off. After a pause.*) Now listen, pal, she's just a buyer. She sees merchandise in her room and they have to keep it looking just so . . . (*Pause. Assuming command.*) All right, get my suits. (*Biff doesn't move.*) Now stop crying and do as I say. I gave you an order. Biff, I gave you an order! Is that what you do when I give you an order? How dare you cry! (*Putting his arm around Biff.*) Now look, Biff, when you grow up you'll understand about these things. You mustn't — you mustn't overemphasize a thing like this. I'll see Birnbaum first thing in the morning.

BIFF: Never mind.

WILLY (*getting down beside Biff*): Never mind! He's going to give you those points. I'll see to it.

BIFF: He wouldn't listen to you.

WILLY: He certainly will listen to me. You need those points for the U. of Virginia.

BIFF: I'm not going there.

WILLY: Heh? If I can't get him to change that mark you'll make it up in summer school. You've got all summer to —

BIFF (*his weeping breaking from him*): Dad . . .

WILLY (*infected by it*): Oh, my boy . . .

BIFF: Dad . . .

WILLY: She's nothing to me, Biff. I was lonely, I was terribly lonely.

BIFF: You—you gave her Mama's stockings! (*His tears break through and he rises to go.*)

WILLY (*grabbing for Biff*): I gave you an order!

BIFF: Don't touch me, you—liar!

WILLY: Apologize for that!

BIFF: You fake! You phony little fake! You fake! (*Overcome, he turns quickly and weeping fully goes out with his suitcase. Willy is left on the floor on his knees.*)

WILLY: I gave you an order! Biff, come back here or I'll beat you! Come back here! I'll whip you!

(*Stanley comes quickly in from the right and stands in front of Willy.*)

WILLY (*shouts at Stanley*): I gave you an order . . .

STANLEY: Hey, let's pick it up, pick it up, Mr. Loman. (*He helps Willy to his feet.*) Your boys left with the chippies. They said they'll see you home.

(*A second waiter watches some distance away.*)

WILLY: But we were supposed to have dinner together.

(*Music is heard, Willy's theme.*)

STANLEY: Can you make it?

WILLY: I'll—sure, I can make it. (*Suddenly concerned about his clothes.*) Do I—I look all right?

STANLEY: Sure, you look all right. (*He flicks a speck off Willy's lapel.*)

WILLY: Here—here's a dollar.

STANLEY: Oh, your son paid me. It's all right.

WILLY (*putting it in Stanley's hand*): No, take it. You're a good boy.

STANLEY: Oh, no, you don't have to . . .

WILLY: Here—here's some more, I don't need it anymore. (*After a slight pause.*) Tell me—is there a seed store in the neighborhood?

STANLEY: Seeds? You mean like to plant?

(*As Willy turns, Stanley slips the money back into his jacket pocket.*)

WILLY: Yes. Carrots, peas . . .

STANLEY: Well, there's hardware stores on Sixth Avenue, but it may be too late now.

WILLY (*anxiously*): Oh, I'd better hurry. I've got to get some seeds. (*He starts off to the right.*) I've got to get some seeds, right away. Nothing's planted. I don't have a thing in the ground.

(*Willy hurries out as the light goes down. Stanley moves over to the right after him, watches him off. The other waiter has been staring at Willy.*)

STANLEY (*to the waiter*): Well, whatta you looking at?

(*The waiter picks up the chairs and moves off right. Stanley takes the table and follows him. The light fades on this area. There is a long pause, the sound of the flute coming over. The light gradually rises on the kitchen, which is empty. Happy appears at the door of the house, followed by Biff. Happy is carrying a large bunch of long-stemmed roses. He enters the kitchen, looks around for Linda. Not seeing her, he turns to Biff, who is just outside the house door, and makes a gesture with his hands, indicating "Not here, I guess." He looks into the living room and freezes. Inside, Linda, unseen, is seated, Willy's coat on her lap. She rises ominously and quietly and moves toward Happy, who backs up into the kitchen, afraid.)*

HAPPY: Hey, what're you doing up? (*Linda says nothing but moves toward him implacably.*) Where's Pop? (*He keeps backing to the right, and now Linda is in full view in the doorway to the living room.*) Is he sleeping?

LINDA: Where were you?

HAPPY (*trying to laugh it off*): We met two girls, Mom, very fine types. Here, we brought you some flowers. (*Offering them to her.*) Put them in your room, Ma.

(She knocks them to the floor at Biff's feet. He has now come inside and closed the door behind him. She stares at Biff, silent.)

HAPPY: Now what'd you do that for? Mom, I want you to have some flowers —

LINDA (*cutting Happy off, violently to Biff*): Don't you care whether he lives or dies?

HAPPY (*going to the stairs*): Come upstairs, Biff.

BIFF (*with a flare of disgust, to Happy*): Go away from me! (*To Linda.*) What do you mean, lives or dies? Nobody's dying around here, pal.

LINDA: Get out of my sight! Get out of here!

BIFF: I wanna see the boss.

LINDA: You're not going near him!

BIFF: Where is he? (*He moves into the living room and Linda follows.*)

LINDA (*shouting after Biff*): You invite him for dinner. He looks forward to it all day — (*Biff appears in his parents' bedroom, looks around, and exits*) — and then you desert him there. There's no stranger you'd do that to!

HAPPY: Why? He had a swell time with us. Listen, when I — (*Linda comes back into the kitchen*) — desert him I hope I don't outlive the day!

LINDA: Get out of here!

HAPPY: Now look, Mom . . .

LINDA: Did you have to go to women tonight? You and your lousy rotten whores!

(Biff reenters the kitchen.)

HAPPY: Mom, all we did was follow Biff around trying to cheer him up! (*To Biff.*) Boy, what a night you gave me!

LINDA: Get out of here, both of you, and don't come back! I don't want you tormenting him any more. Go on now, get your things together! (*To Biff.*) You can sleep in his apartment. (*She starts to pick up the flowers and stops herself.*) Pick up this stuff, I'm not your maid anymore. Pick it up, you bum, you!

(*Happy turns his back to her in refusal. Biff slowly moves over and gets down on his knees, picking up the flowers.*)

LINDA: You're a pair of animals! Not one, not another living soul would have had the cruelty to walk out on that man in a restaurant!

BIFF (*not looking at her*): Is that what he said?

LINDA: He didn't have to say anything. He was so humiliated he nearly limped when he came in.

HAPPY: But, Mom, he had a great time with us —

BIFF (*cutting him off violently*): Shut up!

(*Without another word, Happy goes upstairs.*)

LINDA: You! You didn't even go in to see if he was all right!

BIFF (*still on the floor in front of Linda, the flowers in his hand; with self-loathing*): No. Didn't. Didn't do a damned thing. How do you like that, heh? Left him babbling in a toilet.

LINDA: You louse. You . . .

BIFF: Now you hit it on the nose! (*He gets up, throws the flowers in the wastebasket.*) The scum of the earth, and you're looking at him!

LINDA: Get out of here!

BIFF: I gotta talk to the boss, Mom. Where is he?

LINDA: You're not going near him. Get out of this house!

BIFF (*with absolute assurance, determination*): No. We're gonna have an abrupt conversation, him and me.

LINDA: You're not talking to him.

(*Hammering is heard from outside the house, off right. Biff turns toward the noise.*)

LINDA (*suddenly pleading*): Will you please leave him alone?

BIFF: What's he doing out there?

LINDA: He's planting the garden!

BIFF (*quietly*): Now? Oh, my God!

(*Biff moves outside, Linda following. The light dies down on them and comes up on the center of the apron as Willy walks into it. He is carrying a flashlight, a hoe, and a handful of seed packets. He raps the top of the hoe sharply to fix it firmly, and then moves to the left, measuring off the distance with his foot. He holds the flashlight to look at the seed packets, reading off the instructions. He is in the blue of night.*)

WILLY: Carrots . . . quarter-inch apart. Rows . . . one-foot rows. (*He measures it off.*) One foot. (*He puts down a package and measures off.*) Beets. (*He puts down another package and measures again.*) Lettuce. (*He reads the package, puts it down.*) One foot — (*He breaks off as Ben appears at the right and moves slowly down to him.*) What a proposition, ts, ts. Terrific, terrific. 'Cause she's suffered, Ben, the woman has suffered. You understand me? A man can't go out the way he came in, Ben, a man has got to add up to something. You can't, you can't — (*Ben moves toward him as though to interrupt.*) You gotta consider, now. Don't answer so quick. Remember, it's a guaranteed twenty-thousand-dollar proposition. Now look, Ben, I want you to go through the ins and outs of this thing with me. I've got nobody to talk to, Ben, and the woman has suffered, you hear me?

BEN (*standing still, considering*): What's the proposition?

WILLY: It's twenty thousand dollars on the barrelhead. Guaranteed, giltedged, you understand?

BEN: You don't want to make a fool of yourself. They might not honor the policy.

WILLY: How can they dare refuse? Didn't I work like a coolie to meet every premium on the nose? And now they don't pay off? Impossible!

BEN: It's called a cowardly thing, William.

WILLY: Why? Does it take more guts to stand here the rest of my life ringing up a zero?

BEN (*yielding*): That's a point, William. (*He moves, thinking, turns.*) And twenty thousand—that is something one can feel with the hand, it is there.

WILLY (*now assured, with rising power*): Oh, Ben, that's the whole beauty of it! I see it like a diamond, shining in the dark, hard and rough, that I can pick up and touch in my hand. Not like—like an appointment! This would not be another damned-fool appointment, Ben, and it changes all the aspects. Because he thinks I'm nothing, see, and so he spites me. But the funeral—(*Straightening up.*) Ben, that funeral will be massive! They'll come from Maine, Massachusetts, Vermont, New Hampshire! All the old-timers with the strange license plates—that boy will be thunderstruck, Ben, because he never realized—I am known! Rhode Island, New York, New Jersey—I am known, Ben and he'll see it with his eyes once and for all. He'll see what I am, Ben! He's in for a shock, that boy!

BEN (*coming down to the edge of the garden*): He'll call you a coward.

WILLY (*suddenly fearful*): No, that would be terrible.

BEN: Yes. And a damned fool.

WILLY: No, no, he mustn't, I won't have that! (*He is broken and desperate.*)

BEN: He'll hate you, William.

(*The gay music of the Boys is heard.*)

WILLY: Oh, Ben, how do we get back to all the great times? Used to be so full of light, and comradeship, the sleigh-riding in winter, and the ruddiness on his cheeks. And always some kind of good news coming up, always something nice coming up ahead. And never even let me carry the valises in the house, and simonizing, simonizing that little red car! Why, why can't I give him something and not have him hate me?

BEN: Let me think about it. (*He glances at his watch.*) I still have a little time. Remarkable proposition, but you've got to be sure you're not making a fool of yourself.

(*Ben drifts off upstage and goes out of sight. Biff comes down from the left.*)

WILLY (*suddenly conscious of Biff, turns and looks up at him, then begins picking up the packages of seeds in confusion*): Where the hell is that seed? (*Indig-*

nantly.) You can't see nothing out here! They boxed in the whole goddam neighborhood!

BIFF: There are people all around here. Don't you realize that?

WILLY: I'm busy. Don't bother me.

BIFF (*taking the hoe from Willy*): I'm saying good-by to you, Pop. (*Willy looks at
him, silent, unable to move.*) I'm not coming back any more.

WILLY: You're not going to see Oliver tomorrow?

BIFF: I've got no appointment, Dad.

WILLY: He put his arm around you, and you've got no appointment?

BIFF: Pop, get this now, will you? Everytime I've left it's been a fight that sent
me out of here. Today I realized something about myself and I tried to
explain it to you and I—I think I'm just not smart enough to make any
sense out of it for you. To hell with whose fault it is or anything like
that. (*He takes Willy's arm.*) Let's just wrap it up, heh? Come on in, we'll
tell Mom. (*He gently tries to pull Willy to left.*)

WILLY (*frozen, immobile, with guilt in his voice*): No, I don't want to see her.

BIFF: Come on! (*He pulls again, and Willy tries to pull away.*)

WILLY (*highly nervous*): No, no, I don't want to see her.

BIFF (*tries to look into Willy's face, as if to find the answer there*): Why don't you
want to see her?

WILLY (*more harshly now*): Don't bother me, will you?

BIFF: What do you mean, you don't want to see her? You don't want them
calling you yellow, do you? This isn't your fault; it's me, I'm a bum. Now
come inside! (*Willy strains to get away.*) Did you hear what I said to you?

(*Willy pulls away and quickly goes by himself into the house. Biff follows.*)

LINDA (*to Willy*): Did you plant, dear?

BIFF (*at the door, to Linda*): All right, we had it out. I'm going and I'm not
writing any more.

LINDA (*going to Willy in the kitchen*): I think that's the best way, dear. 'Cause
there's no use drawing it out, you'll just never get along.

(*Willy doesn't respond.*)

BIFF: People ask where I am and what I'm doing, you don't know, and you
don't care. That way it'll be off your mind and you can start brightening
up again. All right? That clears it, doesn't it? (*Willy is silent, and Biff goes
to him.*) You gonna wish me luck, scout? (*He extends his hand.*) What do
you say?

LINDA: Shake his hand, Willy.

WILLY (*turning to her, seething with hurt*): There's no necessity to mention the
pen at all, y'know.

BIFF (*gently*): I've got no appointment, Dad.

WILLY (*erupting fiercely*): He put his arm around . . . ?

BIFF: Dad, you're never going to see what I am, so what's the use of arguing?
If I strike oil I'll send you a check. Meantime forget I'm alive.

WILLY (*to Linda*): Spite, see?

BIFF: Shake hands, Dad.

WILLY: Not my hand.

BIFF: I was hoping not to go this way.

WILLY: Well, this is the way you're going. Good-by.

(*Biff looks at him a moment, then turns sharply and goes to the stairs.*)

WILLY (*stops him with*): May you rot in hell if you leave this house!

BIFF (*turning*): Exactly what is it that you want from me?

WILLY: I want you to know, on the train, in the mountains, in the valleys, wherever you go, that you cut down your life for spite!

BIFF: No, no.

WILLY: Spite, spite, is the word of your undoing! And when you're down and out, remember what did it. When you're rotting somewhere beside the railroad tracks, remember, and don't you dare blame it on me!

BIFF: I'm not blaming it on you!

WILLY: I won't take the rap for this, you hear?

(*Happy comes down the stairs and stands on the bottom step, watching.*)

BIFF: That's just what I'm telling you!

WILLY (*sinking into a chair at a table, with full accusation*): You're trying to put a knife in me — don't think I don't know what you're doing!

BIFF: All right, phony! Then let's lay it on the line. (*He whips the rubber tube out of his pocket and puts it on the table.*)

HAPPY: You crazy . . .

LINDA: Biff! (*She moves to grab the hose, but Biff holds it down with his hand.*)

BIFF: Leave it there! Don't move it!

WILLY (*not looking at it*): What is that?

BIFF: You know goddam well what that is.

WILLY (*caged, wanting to escape*): I never saw that.

BIFF: You saw it. The mice didn't bring it into the cellar! What is this supposed to do, make a hero out of you? This supposed to make me sorry for you?

WILLY: Never heard of it.

BIFF: There'll be no pity for you, you hear it? No pity!

WILLY (*to Linda*): You hear the spite!

BIFF: No, you're going to hear the truth — what you are and what I am!

LINDA: Stop it!

WILLY: Spite!

HAPPY (*coming down toward Biff*): You cut it now!

BIFF (*to Happy*): The man don't know who we are! The man is gonna know! (*To Willy.*) We never told the truth for ten minutes in this house!

HAPPY: We always told the truth!

BIFF (*turning on him*): You big blow, are you the assistant buyer? You're one of the two assistants to the assistant, aren't you?

HAPPY: Well, I'm practically . . .

BIFF: You're practically full of it! We all are! and I'm through with it. (*To Willy.*) Now hear this, Willy, this is me.

WILLY: I know you!

BIFF: You know why I had no address for three months? I stole a suit in Kansas City and I was in jail. (*To Linda, who is sobbing.*) Stop crying. I'm through with it.

(*Linda turns away from them, her hands covering her face.*)

WILLY: I suppose that's my fault!

BIFF: I stole myself out of every good job since high school!

WILLY: And whose fault is that?

BIFF: And I never got anywhere because you blew me so full of hot air I could never stand taking orders from anybody! That's whose fault it is!

WILLY: I hear that!

LINDA: Don't, Biff!

BIFF: It's goddam time you heard that! I had to be boss big shot in two weeks, and I'm through with it!

WILLY: Then hang yourself! For spite, hang yourself!

BIFF: No! Nobody's hanging himself, Willy! I ran down eleven flights with a pen in my hand today. And suddenly I stopped, you hear me? And in the middle of that office building, do you hear this? I stopped in the middle of that building and I saw — the sky. I saw the things that I love in this world. The work and the food and time to sit and smoke. And I looked at the pen and said to myself, what the hell am I grabbing this for? Why am I trying to become what I don't want to be? What am I doing in an office, making a contemptuous begging fool of myself, when all I want is out there, waiting for me the minute I say I know who I am! Why can't I say that, Willy? (*He tries to make Willy face him, but Willy pulls away and moves to the left.*)

WILLY (*with hatred, threateningly*): The door of your life is wide open!

BIFF: Pop! I'm a dime a dozen, and so are you!

WILLY (*turning on him now in an uncontrolled outburst*): I am not a dime a dozen! I am Willy Loman, and you are Biff Loman!

(*Biff starts for Willy, but is blocked by Happy. In his fury, Biff seems on the verge of attacking his father.*)

BIFF: I am not a leader of men, Willy, and neither are you. You were never anything but a hard-working drummer who landed in the ash can like all the rest of them! I'm one dollar an hour, Willy! I tried seven states and couldn't raise it. A buck an hour! Do you gather my meaning? I'm not bringing home any prizes any more, and you're going to stop waiting for me to bring them home!

WILLY (*directly to Biff*): You vengeful, spiteful mutt!

(*Biff breaks from Happy. Willy, in fright, starts up the stairs. Biff grabs him.*)

BIFF (*at the peak of his fury*): Pop, I'm nothing! I'm nothing, Pop. Can't you understand that? There's no spite in it any more. I'm just what I am, that's all.

(*Biff's fury has spent itself and he breaks down, sobbing, holding on to Willy, who dumbly fumbles for Biff's face.*)

WILLY (*astonished*): What're you doing? What're you doing? (*To Linda.*) Why is he crying?

BIFF (*crying, broken*): Will you let me go, for Christ's sake? Will you take that phony dream and burn it before something happens? (*Struggling to contain himself he pulls away and moves to the stairs.*) I'll go in the morning. Put him — put him to bed. (*Exhausted, Biff moves up the stairs to his room.*)

WILLY (*after a long pause, astonished, elevated*): Isn't that — isn't that remarkable? Biff — he likes me!

LINDA: He loves you, Willy!

HAPPY (*deeply moved*): Always did, Pop.

WILLY: Oh, Biff! (*Staring wildly.*) He cried! Cried to me. (*He is choking with his love, and now cries out his promise.*) That boy — that boy is going to be magnificent!

(*Ben appears in the light just outside the kitchen.*)

BEN: Yes, outstanding, with twenty thousand behind him.

LINDA (*sensing the racing of his mind, fearfully, carefully*): Now come to bed, Willy. It's all settled now.

WILLY (*finding it difficult not to rush out of the house*): Yes, we'll sleep. Come on. Go to sleep, Hap.

BEN: And it does take a great kind of a man to crack the jungle.

(*In accents of dread, Ben's idyllic music starts up.*)

HAPPY (*his arm around Linda*): I'm getting married, Pop, don't forget it. I'm changing everything. I'm gonna run that department before the year is up. You'll see, Mom. (*He kisses her.*)

BEN: The jungle is dark but full of diamonds, Willy.

(*Willy turns, moves, listening to Ben.*)

LINDA: Be good. You're both good boys, just act that way, that's all.

HAPPY: 'Night, Pop. (*He goes upstairs.*)

LINDA (*to Willy*): Come, dear.

BEN (*with greater force*): One must go in to fetch a diamond out.

WILLY (*to Linda, as he moves slowly along the edge of kitchen, toward the door*): I just want to get settled down, Linda. Let me sit alone for a little.

LINDA (*almost uttering her fear*): I want you upstairs.

WILLY (*taking her in his arms*): In a few minutes, Linda. I couldn't sleep right now. Go on, you look awful tired. (*He kisses her.*)

BEN: Not like an appointment at all. A diamond is rough and hard to the touch.

WILLY: Go on now. I'll be right up.

LINDA: I think this is the only way, Willy.

WILLY: Sure, it's the best thing.

BEN: Best thing!

WILLY: The only way. Everything is gonna be — go on, kid, get to bed. You look so tired.

LINDA: Come right up.

WILLY: Two minutes.

(Linda goes into the living room, then reappears in her bedroom. Willy moves just outside the kitchen door.)

WILLY: Loves me. *(Wonderingly.)* Always loved me. Isn't that a remarkable thing? Ben, he'll worship me for it!

BEN *(with promise)*: It's dark there, but full of diamonds.

WILLY: Can you imagine that magnificence with twenty thousand dollars in his pocket?

LINDA *(calling from her room)*: Willy! Come up!

WILLY *(calling into the kitchen)*: Yes! yes. Coming! It's very smart, you realize that, don't you, sweetheart? Even Ben sees it. I gotta go, baby. 'By! 'By! *(Going over to Ben, almost dancing.)* Imagine? When the mail comes he'll be ahead of Bernard again!

BEN: A perfect proposition all around.

WILLY: Did you see how he cried to me? Oh, if I could kiss him, Ben!

BEN: Time, William, time!

WILLY: Oh, Ben, I always knew one way or another we were gonna make it, Biff and I!

BEN *(looking at his watch)*: The boat. We'll be late. *(He moves slowly off into the darkness.)*

WILLY *(elegiacally, turning to the house)*: Now when you kick off, boy, I want a seventy-yard boot, and get right down the field under the ball, and when you hit, hit low and hit hard, because it's important, boy. *(He swings around and faces the audience.)* There's all kinds of important people in the stands, and the first thing you know . . . *(Suddenly realizing he is alone.)* Ben! Ben, where do I . . . ? *(He makes a sudden movement of search.)* Ben, how do I . . . ?

LINDA *(calling)*: Willy, you coming up?

WILLY *(uttering a gasp of fear, whirling about as if to quiet her)*: Sh! *(He turns around as if to find his way; sounds, faces, voices, seem to be swarming in upon him and he flicks at them, crying, Sh! Sh! Suddenly music, faint and high, stops him. It rises in intensity, almost to an unbearable scream. He goes up and down on his toes, and rushes off around the house.)* Shhh!

LINDA: Willy?

(There is no answer. Linda waits. Biff gets up off his bed. He is still in his clothes. Happy sits up. Biff stands listening.)

LINDA *(with real fear)*: Willy, answer me! Willy!

(*There is the sound of a car starting and moving away at full speed.*)

LINDA: No!

BIFF (*rushing down the stairs*): Pop!

(*As the car speeds off, the music crashes down in a frenzy of sound, which becomes the soft pulsation of a single cello string. Biff slowly returns to his bedroom. He and Happy gravely don their jackets. Linda slowly walks out of her room. The music has developed into a dead march. The leaves of day are appearing over everything. Charley and Bernard, somberly dressed, appear and knock on the kitchen door. Biff and Happy slowly descend the stairs to the kitchen as Charley and Bernard enter. All stop a moment when Linda, in clothes of mourning, bearing a little bunch of roses, comes through the draped doorway into the kitchen. She goes to Charley and takes his arm. Now all move toward the audience, through the wall-line of the kitchen. At the limit of the apron, Linda lays down the flowers, kneels, and sits back on her heels. All stare down at the grave.*)

REQUIEM

CHARLEY: It's getting dark, Linda.

(*Linda doesn't react. She stares at the grave.*)

BIFF: How about it, Mom? Better get some rest, heh? They'll be closing the gate soon.

(*Linda makes no move. Pause.*)

HAPPY (*deeply angered*): He had no right to do that. There was no necessity for it. We would've helped him.

CHARLEY (*grunting*): Hmmm.

BIFF: Come along, Mom.

LINDA: Why didn't anybody come?

CHARLEY: It was a very nice funeral.

LINDA: But where are all the people he knew? Maybe they blame him.

CHARLEY: Naa. It's a rough world, Linda. They wouldn't blame him.

LINDA: I can't understand it. At this time especially. First time in thirty-five years we were just about free and clear. He only needed a little salary. He was even finished with the dentist.

CHARLEY: No man only needs a little salary.

LINDA: I can't understand it.

BIFF: There were a lot of nice days. When he'd come home from a trip; or on Sundays, making the stoop; finishing the cellar; putting on the new porch; when he built the extra bathroom; and put up the garage. You know something, Charley, there's more of him in that front stoop than in all the sales he ever made.

CHARLEY: Yeah. He was a happy man with a batch of cement.

LINDA: He was so wonderful with his hands.

BIFF: He had the wrong dreams. All, all, wrong.

HAPPY (*almost ready to fight Biff*): Don't say that!

BIFF: He never knew who he was.

CHARLEY (*stopping Happy's movement and reply. To Biff*): Nobody dast blame this man. You don't understand: Willy was a salesman. And for a salesman, there is no rock bottom to the life. He don't put a bolt to a nut, he don't tell you the law or give you medicine. He's a man way out there in the blue, riding on a smile and a shoeshine. And when they start not smiling back — that's an earthquake. And then you get yourself a couple of spots on your hat, and you're finished. Nobody dast blame this man. A salesman is got to dream, boy. It comes with the territory.

BIFF: Charley, the man didn't know who he was.

HAPPY (*infuriated*): Don't say that!

BIFF: Why don't you come with me, Happy?

HAPPY: I'm not licked that easily. I'm staying right in this city, and I'm gonna beat this racket! (*He looks at Biff, his chin set.*) The Loman Brothers!

BIFF: I know who I am, kid.

HAPPY: All right, boy. I'm gonna show you and everybody else that Willy Loman did not die in vain. He had a good dream. It's the only dream you can have — to come out number-one man. He fought it out here, and this is where I'm gonna win it for him.

BIFF (*with a hopeless glance at Happy, bends toward his mother*): Let's go, Mom.

LINDA: I'll be with you in a minute. Go on, Charley. (*He hesitates.*) I want to, just for a minute. I never had a chance to say good-by.

(*Charley moves away, followed by Happy. Biff remains a slight distance up and left of Linda. She sits there, summoning herself. The flute begins, not far away, playing behind her speech.*)

LINDA: Forgive me, dear. I can't cry. I don't know what it is, but I can't cry. I don't understand it. Why did you ever do that? Help me, Willy, I can't cry. It seems to me that you're just on another trip. I keep expecting you. Willy, dear, I can't cry. Why did you do it? I search and search and I search, and I can't understand it, Willy. I made the last payment on the house today. Today, dear. And there'll be nobody home. (*A sob rises in her throat.*) We're free and clear. (*Sobbing more fully, released.*) We're free. (*Biff comes slowly toward her.*) We're free . . . We're free . . .

(*Biff lifts her to her feet and moves out up right with her in his arms. Linda sobs quietly. Bernard and Charley come together and follow them, followed by Happy. Only the music of the flute is left on the darkening stage as over the house the hard towers of the apartment buildings rise into sharp focus, and the curtain falls.*)

CD-ROM: Research Arthur Miller and *Death of a Salesman* in depth with cultural documents and multimedia resources on *LiterActive*.

William Shakespeare 1564–1616

Othello the Moor of Venice   [1604]

THE NAMES OF THE ACTORS

OTHELLO, THE MOOR
BRABANTIO, [a Venetian senator,] father to Desdemona
CASSIO, an honorable lieutenant [to Othello]
IAGO, [Othello's ancient,] a villain
RODERIGO, a gulled gentleman
DUKE OF VENICE
SENATORS [of Venice]
MONTANO, governor of Cyprus
LODOVICO AND GRATIANO, [kinsmen to Brabantio,] two noble Venetians
SAILORS
CLOWNS
DESDEMONA, wife to Othello
EMILIA, wife to Iago
BIANCA, a courtesan
[MESSENGER, HERALD, OFFICERS, VENETIAN GENTLEMEN, MUSICIANS, ATTENDANTS

SCENE

Venice and Cyprus]

ACT I / Scene I

A street in Venice.

Enter Roderigo and Iago.

RODERIGO: Tush, never tell me! I take it much unkindly
   That thou, Iago, who hast had my purse
   As if the strings were thine, shouldst know of this.°
IAGO: 'Sblood,° but you'll not hear me!
   If ever I did dream of such a matter,   5
   Abhor me.
RODERIGO: Thou told'st me thou didst hold him in thy hate.
IAGO: Despise me if I do not. Three great ones of the city,
   In personal suit to make me his lieutenant,

Note: *Othello* was first published in 1622, some six years after Shakespeare's death, in a slender book called a "quarto" (made up of printer's paper folded twice, creating four leaves — eight pages — approximately 9½ by 12 inches in size). The following year the play was printed a second time, in the 1623 collected edition of Shakespeare's plays called the First Folio (with paper folded once, creating pages twice as large as a quarto). The Folio text is around 160 lines longer, but the quarto text contains some things omitted from the Folio text. The play as printed here mainly follows the Folio text, but passages from the quarto text have been inserted and enclosed in square brackets. ACT I, SCENE I. **3. this:** I.e., Desdemona's elopement. **4. 'Sblood:** By God's blood.

Off-capped to him;° and, by the faith of man,   10
I know my price; I am worth no worse a place.
But he, as loving his own pride and purposes,
Evades them with a bombast circumstance.°
Horribly stuffed with epithets of war;
[And, in conclusion,]   15
Nonsuits° my mediators; for, "Certes," says he,
"I have already chose my officer."
And what was he?
Forsooth, a great arithmetician,°
One Michael Cassio, a Florentine   20
(A fellow almost damned in a fair wife°)
That never set a squadron in the field,
Nor the division of a battle knows
More than a spinster; unless the bookish theoric,
Wherein the togèd consuls can propose   25
As masterly as he. Mere prattle without practice
Is all his soldiership. But he, sir, had th' election;
And I (of whom his eyes had seen the proof
At Rhodes, at Cyprus, and on other grounds
Christian and heathen) must be belee'd and calmed°   30
By debitor and creditor; this counter-caster,°
He, in good time, must his lieutenant be,
And I — God bless the mark! — his Moorship's ancient.°
RODERIGO: By heaven, I rather would have been his hangman.
IAGO: Why, there's no remedy; 'tis the curse of service.   35
Preferment goes by letter and affection,°
And not by old gradation, where each second
Stood heir to th' first. Now, sir, be judge yourself,
Whether I in any just term am affined°
To love the Moor.
RODERIGO: I would not follow him then.   40
IAGO: O, sir, content you;
I follow him to serve my turn upon him.
We cannot all be masters, nor all masters
Cannot be truly followed. You shall mark
Many a duteous and knee-crooking knave   45
That, doting on his own obsequious bondage,
Wears out his time, much like his master's ass,

---

10. **him:** I.e., Othello.   13. **a bombast circumstance:** Pompous circumlocutions.   16. **Non-suits:** Rejects.   19. **arithmetician:** Theoretician.   21. **almost . . . wife:** (An obscure allusion; Cassio is unmarried, but see 4.1.125–26).   30. **belee'd and calmed:** Left in the lurch.   31. **counter-caster:** Bookkeeper.   33. **ancient:** Ensign.   36. **affection:** Favoritism. 39. **affined:** Obliged.

For naught but provender; and when he's old, cashiered.°
Whip me such honest knaves! Others there are
Who, trimmed° in forms and visages of duty,   50
Keep yet their hearts attending on themselves;
And, throwing but shows of service on their lords,
Do well thrive by them, and when they have lined their coats,
Do themselves homage. These fellows have some soul;
And such a one do I profess myself. For, sir,   55
It is as sure as you are Roderigo,
Were I the Moor, I would not be Iago.
In following him, I follow but myself;
Heaven is my judge, not I for love and duty,
But seeming so, for my peculiar end;   60
For when my outward action doth demonstrate
The native act and figure of my heart°
In compliment extern,° 'tis not long after
But I will wear my heart upon my sleeve
For daws to peck at; I am not what I am.   65
RODERIGO: What a full fortune does the thick-lips° owe°
    If he can carry't thus!
IAGO: Call up her father,
    Rouse him. Make after him, poison his delight,
    Proclaim him in the streets. Incense her kinsmen,
    And though he in a fertile climate dwell,   70
    Plague him with flies; though that his joy be joy,
    Yet throw such changes of vexation on't
    As it may lose some color.
RODERIGO: Here is her father's house. I'll call aloud.
IAGO: Do, with like timorous° accent and dire yell   75
    As when, by night and negligence, the fire
    Is spied in populous cities.
RODERIGO: What, ho, Brabantio! Signior Brabantio, ho!
IAGO: Awake! What, ho, Brabantio! Thieves! thieves! thieves!
    Look to your house, your daughter, and your bags!   80
    Thieves! thieves!

Brabantio at a window.°

BRABANTIO (*above*): What is the reason of this terrible summons?
    What is the matter there?
RODERIGO: Signior, is all your family within?

---

48. **cashiered:** Turned off.   50. **trimmed:** Dressed up.   62. **The . . . heart:** What I really believe and intend.   63. **compliment extern:** Outward appearance.   66. **thick-lips:** An Elizabethan epithet for blacks, including Moors; **owe:** Own.   75. **timorous:** Terrifying.   s.d. **Brabantio at a window:** (added from quarto).

IAGO: Are your doors locked?

BRABANTIO: Why, wherefore ask you this?   85

IAGO: Zounds, sir, y' are robbed! For shame, put on your gown!
    Your heart is burst; you have lost half your soul.
    Even now, now, very now, an old black ram
    Is tupping your white ewe. Arise, arise!
    Awake the snorting° citizens with the bell.   90
    Or else the devil will make a grandsire of you.
    Arise, I say!

BRABANTIO: What, have you lost your wits?

RODERIGO: Most reverend signior, do you know my voice?

BRABANTIO: Not I. What are you?   95

RODERIGO: My name is Roderigo.

BRABANTIO: The worser welcome!
    I have charged thee not to haunt about my doors.
    In honest plainness thou hast heard me say
    My daughter is not for thee; and now, in madness,
    Being full of supper and distemp'ring draughts,   100
    Upon malicious knavery dost thou come
    To start my quiet.

RODERIGO: Sir, sir, sir—

BRABANTIO: But thou must needs be sure
    My spirit and my place have in them power   105
    To make this bitter to thee.

RODERIGO: Patience, good sir.

BRABANTIO: What tell'st thou me of robbing? This is Venice;
    My house is not a grange.°

RODERIGO: Most grave Brabantio,
    In simple and pure soul I come to you.

IAGO: Zounds, sir, you are one of those that will not serve God if the   110
    devil bid you. Because we come to do you service, and you think we
    are ruffians, you'll have your daughter covered with a Barbary horse;
    you'll have your nephews° neigh to you; you'll have coursers for
    cousins, and gennets for germans.°

BRABANTIO: What profane wretch art thou?   115

IAGO: I am one, sir, that comes to tell you your daughter and the Moor
    are now making the beast with two backs.

BRABANTIO: Thou are a villain.

IAGO: You are—a senator.

BRABANTIO: This thou shalt answer. I know thee, Roderigo.

RODERIGO: Sir, I will answer anything. But I beseech you,   120
    If 't be your pleasure and most wise consent,

---

90. snorting: Snoring.   **108. grange:** Isolated farmhouse.   **113. nephews:** I.e., grandsons.
114. gennets for germans: Spanish horses for near kinsmen.

As partly I find it is, that your fair daughter,
At this odd-even° and dull watch o' th' night,
Transported, with no worse nor better guard
But with a knave of common hire, a gondolier,   125
To the gross clasps of a lascivious Moor —
If this be known to you, and your allowance,°
We then have done you bold and saucy wrongs;
But if you know not this, my manners tell me
We have your wrong rebuke. Do not believe   130
That, from the sense° of all civility,
I thus would play and trifle with your reverence.
Your daughter, if you have not given her leave,
I say again, hath made a gross revolt,
Tying her duty, beauty, wit, and fortunes   135
In an extravagant and wheeling° stranger
Of here and everywhere. Straight satisfy yourself.
If she be in her chamber, or your house,
Let loose on me the justice of the state
For thus deluding you.
BRABANTIO: Strike on the tinder, ho!   140
Give me a taper! Call up all my people!
This accident° is not unlike my dream.
Belief of it oppresses me already.
Light, I say! light!   *Exit [above].*
IAGO: Farewell, for I must leave you.
It seems not meet, nor wholesome to my place,   145
To be produced — as, if I stay, I shall —
Against the Moor. For I do know the state,
However this may gall him with some check,°
Cannot with safety cast° him; for he's embarked
With such loud reason to the Cyprus wars,   150
Which even now stand in act,° that for their souls
Another of his fathom° they have none
To lead their business; in which regard,
Though I do hate him as I do hell-pains,
Yet, for necessity of present life,   155
I must show out a flag and sign of love,
Which is indeed but sign. That you shall surely find him,
Lead to the Sagittary° the raisèd search;
And there will I be with him. So farewell.   *Exit.*

---

123. **odd-even:** Between night and morning.   127. **allowance:** Approval.   131. **from the sense:** In violation.   136. **extravagant and wheeling:** Expatriate and roving.   142. **accident:** Occurrence.   148. **check:** Reprimand.   149. **cast:** Discharge.   151. **stand in act:** Are going on.   152. **fathom:** Capacity.   158. **Sagittary:** An inn.

Enter [below] Brabantio in his nightgown,° and Servants with torches.

BRABANTIO: It is too true an evil. Gone she is;   160
    And what's to come of my despisèd time
    Is naught but bitterness. Now, Roderigo,
    Where didst thou see her? — O unhappy girl! —
    With the Moor, say'st thou? — Who would be a father? —
    How didst thou know 'twas she! — O, she deceives me   165
    Past thought! — What said she to you? — Get moe° tapers!
    Raise all my kindred! — Are they married, think you?
RODERIGO: Truly I think they are.
BRABANTIO: O heaven! How got she out? O treason of the blood!
    Fathers, from hence trust not your daughters' minds   170
    By what you see them act. Is there not charms
    By which the property° of youth and maidhood
    May be abused? Have you not read, Roderigo,
    Of some such thing?
RODERIGO: Yes, sir, I have indeed.
BRABANTIO: Call up my brother. — O, would you had had her! —   175
    Some one way, some another. — Do you know
    Where we may apprehend her and the Moor?
RODERIGO: I think I can discover him, if you please
    To get good guard and go along with me.
BRABANTIO: I pray you lead on. At every house I'll call;   180
    I may command at most. — Get weapons, ho!
    And raise some special officers of night. —
    On, good Roderigo; I'll deserve° your pains.   *Exeunt.*

Scene II

Before the lodgings of Othello.

Enter Othello, Iago, and Attendants with torches.

IAGO: Though in the trade of war I have slain men,
    Yet do I hold it very stuff o' th' conscience
    To do no contrived murther. I lack iniquity
    Sometimes to do me service. Nine or ten times
    I had thought t' have yerked° him here under the ribs.   5
OTHELLO: 'Tis better as it is.
IAGO: Nay, but he prated,
    And spoke such scurvy and provoking terms
    Against your honor
    That with the little godliness I have

---

s.d. **nightgown:** Dressing gown. **166. moe:** More. **172. property:** Nature. **183. de-**
serve: Show gratitude for. SCENE II. **5. yerked:** Stabbed.

    I did full hard forbear him. But I pray you, sir,   10
    Are you fast° married? Be assured of this,
    That the magnifico° is much beloved,
    And hath in his effect a voice potential°
    As double° as the Duke's. He will divorce you,
    Or put upon you what restraint and grievance   15
    The law, with all his might to enforce it on,
    Will give him cable.
OTHELLO: Let him do his spite.
    My services which I have done the signiory°
    Shall out-tongue his complaints. 'Tis yet to know° —
    Which, when I know that boasting is an honor,   20
    I shall promulgate — I fetch my life and being
    From men of royal siege;° and my demerits°
    May speak unbonneted to as proud a fortune
    As this that I have reached.° For know, Iago,
    But that I love the gentle Desdemona,   25
    I would not my unhousèd° free condition
    Put into circumscription and confine
    For the sea's worth. But look what lights come yond?
IAGO: Those are the raisèd father and his friends.
    You were best go in.
OTHELLO: Not I; I must be found.   30
    My parts, my title, and my perfect soul°
    Shall manifest me rightly. Is it they?
IAGO: By Janus, I think no.

Enter Cassio, with torches, Officers.

OTHELLO: The servants of the Duke, and my lieutenant.
    The goodness of the night upon you, friends!   35
    What is the news?
CASSIO: The Duke does greet you, general;
    And he requires your haste-post-haste appearance
    Even on the instant.
OTHELLO: What's the matter, think you?
CASSIO: Something from Cyprus, as I may divine.
    It is a business of some heat. The galleys   40
    Have sent a dozen sequent° messengers
    This very night at one another's heels,

---

11. fast: Securely. **12. magnifico:** Grandee (Brabantio). **13. potential:** Powerful.
14. double: Doubly influential. **18. signiory:** Venetian government. **19. yet to know:**
Still not generally known. **22. siege:** Rank; **demerits:** Deserts. **23–24. May speak . . .
reached:** Are equal, I modestly assert, to those of Desdemona's family. **26. unhousèd:** Unrestrained. **31. perfect soul:** Stainless conscience. **41. sequent:** Consecutive.

And many of the consuls, raised and met,
Are at the Duke's already. You have been hotly called for;
When, being not at your lodging to be found,   45
The Senate hath sent about three several quests
To search you out.
OTHELLO: 'Tis well I am found by you.
I will but spend a word here in the house,
And go with you.   [*Exit*]
CASSIO: Ancient, what makes he here?
IAGO: Faith, he to-night hath boarded a land carack.°   50
If it prove lawful prize, he's made for ever.
CASSIO: I do not understand.
IAGO: He's married.
CASSIO: To who?

[*Enter Othello.*]

IAGO: Marry, to — Come, captain, will you go?
OTHELLO: Have with you.
CASSIO: Here comes another troop to seek for you.

Enter Brabantio, Roderigo, and others with lights and weapons.

IAGO: It is Brabantio. General, be advised.   55
He comes to bad intent.
OTHELLO: Holla! stand there!
RODERIGO: Signior, it is the Moor.
BRABANTIO: Down with him, thief!

[*They draw on both sides.*]

IAGO: You, Roderigo! Come, sir, I am for you.
OTHELLO: Keep up° your bright swords, for the dew will rust them.
Good signior, you shall more command with years   60
Than with your weapons.
BRABANTIO: O thou foul thief, where hast thou stowed my daughter?
Damned as thou art, thou hast enchanted her!
For I'll refer me to all things of sense,
If she in chains of magic were not bound,   65
Whether a maid so tender, fair, and happy,
So opposite to marriage that she shunned
The wealthy curlèd darlings of our nation,
Would ever have, t' incur a general mock,
Run from her guardage to the sooty bosom   70
Of such a thing as thou — to fear, not to delight.
Judge me the world if 'tis not gross in sense°

---

50. carack: Treasure ship.   **59. Keep up:** I.e., sheath.   **72. gross in sense:** Obvious.

That thou hast practiced on her with foul charms,
Abused her delicate youth with drugs or minerals
That weaken motion.° I'll have't disputed on;   75
'Tis probable, and palpable to thinking.
I therefore apprehend and do attach° thee
For an abuser of the world, a practicer
Of arts inhibited and out of warrant.
Lay hold upon him. If he do resist,   80
Subdue him at his peril.
OTHELLO: Hold your hands,
Both you of my inclining and the rest.
Were it my cue to fight, I should have known it
Without a prompter. Where will you that I go
To answer this your charge?
BRABANTIO: To prison, till fit time   85
Of law and course of direct session°
Call thee to answer.
OTHELLO: What if I do obey?
How may the Duke be therewith satisfied,
Whose messengers are here about my side
Upon some present business of the state   90
To bring me to him?
OFFICER: 'Tis true, most worthy signior.
The Duke's in council, and your noble self
I am sure is sent for.
BRABANTIO: How? The Duke in council?
In this time of the night? Bring him away.
Mine's not an idle° cause. The Duke himself,   95
Or any of my brothers of the state,
Cannot but feel this wrong as 'twere their own;
For if such actions may have passage free,
Bondslaves and pagans shall our statesmen be.   *Exeunt.*

Scene III

The Venetian Senate Chamber.

Enter Duke and Senators, set at a table, with lights and Attendants.

DUKE: There is no composition° in these news
That gives them credit.
1. SENATOR: Indeed they are disproportioned.
My letters say a hundred and seven galleys.

---

75. **motion:** Perception.   77. **attach:** Arrest.   86. **direct session:** Regular trial.   95. **idle:**
Trifling.   SCENE III.   1. **composition:** Consistency.

DUKE: And mine a hundred forty.
2. SENATOR: And mine two hundred.
    But though they jump° not on a just account —   5
    As in these cases where the aim° reports
    'Tis oft with difference — yet do they all confirm
    A Turkish fleet, and bearing up to Cyprus.
DUKE: Nay, it is possible enough to judgment.
    I do not so secure me° in the error   10
    But the main article° I do approve°
    In fearful sense.
SAILOR (*within*):   What, ho! what, ho! what, ho!
OFFICER: A messenger from the galleys.

Enter Sailor.

DUKE: Now, what's the business?
SAILOR: The Turkish preparation makes for Rhodes.
    So was I bid report here to the state   15
    By Signior Angelo.
DUKE: How say you by this change?
1. SENATOR: This cannot be
    By no assay° of reason. 'Tis a pageant
    To keep us in false gaze.° When we consider
    Th' importancy of Cyprus to the Turk,   20
    And let ourselves again but understand
    That, as it more concerns the Turk than Rhodes,
    So may he with more facile question bear° it,
    For that it stands not in such warlike brace,°
    But altogether lacks th' abilities   25
    That Rhodes is dressed in — if we make thought of this,
    We must not think the Turk is so unskillful
    To leave that latest which concerns him first,
    Neglecting an attempt of ease and gain
    To wake and wage° a danger profitless.   30
DUKE: Nay, in all confidence, he's not for Rhodes.
OFFICER: Here is more news.

Enter a Messenger.

MESSENGER: The Ottomites, reverend and gracious,
    Steering with due course toward the isle of Rhodes,
    Have there injointed them with an after fleet.   35

---

5. jump: Agree. **6. aim:** Conjecture. **10. so secure me:** Take such comfort. **11. article:** Substance; **approve:** Accept. **18. assay:** Test. **19. in false gaze:** Looking the wrong way. **23. with . . . bear:** More easily capture. **24. brace:** Posture of defense. **30. wake and wage:** Rouse and risk.

1. SENATOR: Ay, so I thought. How many, as you guess?
MESSENGER: Of thirty sail; and now they do restem°
  Their backward course, bearing with frank appearance
  Their purposes toward Cyprus, Signior Montano,
  Your trusty and most valiant servitor,   40
  With his free duty recommends you thus,
  And prays you to believe him.
DUKE: 'Tis certain then for Cyprus.
  Marcus Luccicos,° is not he in town?
1. SENATOR: He's now in Florence.   45
DUKE: Write from us to him; post, post-haste dispatch.
1. SENATOR: Here comes Brabantio and the valiant Moor.

Enter Brabantio, Othello, Cassio, Iago, Roderigo, and Officers.

DUKE: Valiant Othello, we must straight employ you
  Against the general enemy Ottoman.   [*To Brabantio.*]
  I did not see you. Welcome, gentle signior.   50
  We lacked your counsel and your help to-night.
BRABANTIO: So did I yours. Good your grace, pardon me.
  Neither my place, nor aught I heard of business,
  Hath raised me from my bed; nor doth the general care
  Take hold on me; for my particular grief   55
  Is of so floodgate° and o'erbearing nature
  That it engluts° and swallows other sorrows,
  And it is still itself.
DUKE: Why, what's the matter?
BRABANTIO: My daughter! O, my daughter!
ALL: Dead?
BRABANTIO: Ay, to me.
  She is abused, stol'n from me, and corrupted   60
  By spells and medicines bought of mountebanks;
  For nature so prepost'rously to err,
  Being not deficient,° blind, or lame of sense,
  Sans witchcraft could not.
DUKE: Whoe'er he be that in this foul proceeding   65
  Hath thus beguiled your daughter of herself,
  And you of her, the bloody book of law
  You shall yourself read in the bitter letter
  After your own sense; yea, though our proper° son
  Stood in your action.°
BRABANTIO: Humbly I thank your grace.   70
  Here is the man — this Moor, whom now, it seems,

---

37. restem: Steer again.   **44. Marcus Luccicos:** (Presumably a Venetian envoy).   **56. flood-
gate:** Torrential.   **57. engluts:** Devours.   **63. deficient:** Feeble-minded.   **69. our proper:**
My own.   **70. Stood in your action:** Were accused by you.

Your special mandate for the state affairs
Hath hither brought.

ALL: We are very sorry for't.

DUKE [*to Othello*]: What, in your own part, can you say to this?

BRABANTIO: Nothing, but this is so.   75

OTHELLO: Most potent, grave, and reverend signiors,
My very noble, and approved° good masters,
That I have ta'en away this old man's daughter,
It is most true; true I have married her.
The very head and front of my offending   80
Hath this extent, no more. Rude° am I in my speech,
And little blessed with the soft phrase of peace;
For since these arms of mine had seven years' pith°
Till now some nine moons wasted, they have used
Their dearest action in the tented field;   85
And little of this great world can I speak
More than pertains to feats of broil and battle;
And therefore little shall I grace my cause
In speaking for myself. Yet, by your gracious patience,
I will a round° unvarnished tale deliver   90
Of my whole course of love — what drugs, what charms,
What conjuration, and what mighty magic
(For such proceeding am I charged withal)
I won his daughter.

BRABANTIO: A maiden never bold;
Of spirit so still and quiet that her motion   95
Blushed° at herself; and she — in spite of nature,
Of years, of country, credit, everything —
To fall in love with what she feared to look on!
It is a judgment maimed and most imperfect
That will confess perfection so could err   100
Against all rules of nature, and must be driven
To find out practices° of cunning hell
Why this should be. I therefore vouch° again
That with some mixtures pow'rful o'er the blood,°
Or with some dram, conjured to this effect,   105
He wrought upon her.

DUKE: To vouch this is no proof,
Without more certain and more overt test
Than these thin habits° and poor likelihoods
Of modern seeming° do prefer against him.

---

77. **approved:** Tested by experience.   81. **Rude:** Unpolished.   83. **pith:** Strength.   90. **round:**
Plain.   95–96. **her motion Blushed:** Her own emotions caused her to blush.   102. **practices:** Plots.   103. **vouch:** Assert.   104. **blood:** Passions.   108. **thin habits:** Slight appearances.   109. **modern seeming:** Everyday supposition.

1. SENATOR: But, Othello, speak.   110
  Did you by indirect and forcèd° courses
  Subdue and poison this young maid's affections?
  Or came it by request, and such fair question°
  As soul to soul affordeth?
OTHELLO: I do beseech you,
  Send for the lady to the Sagittary   115
  And let her speak of me before her father.
  If you do find me foul in her report,
  The trust, the office, I do hold of you
  Not only take away, but let your sentence
  Even fall upon my life.
DUKE: Fetch Desdemona hither.   120
OTHELLO: Ancient, conduct them; you best know the place.
        Exit [Iago, with] two or three [Attendants].
  And till she come, as truly as to heaven
  I do confess the vices of my blood,
  So justly to your grave ears I'll present
  How I did thrive in this fair lady's love,   125
  And she in mine.
DUKE: Say it, Othello.
OTHELLO: Her father loved me, oft invited me;
  Still° questioned me the story of my life
  From year to year—the battles, sieges, fortunes   130
  That I have passed.
  I ran it through, even from my boyish days
  To th' very moment that he bade me tell it.
  Wherein I spoke of most disastrous chances,
  Of moving accidents by flood and field;   135
  Of hairbreadth scapes i' th' imminent deadly breach;
  Of being taken by the insolent foe
  And sold to slavery; of my redemption thence
  And portance° in my travels' history;
  Wherein of anters° vast and deserts idle,   140
  Rough quarries, rocks, and hills whose heads touch heaven,
  It was my hint° to speak—such was the process;
  And of the Cannibals that each other eat,
  The Anthropophagi,° and men whose heads
  Do grow beneath their shoulders. This to hear   145
  Would Desdemona seriously incline;
  But still the house affairs would draw her thence;

---

111. forcèd: Violent.   **113. question:** Conversation.   **129. Still:** Continually.   **139. portance:** Behavior.   **140. anters:** Caves.   **142. hint:** Occasion.   **144. Anthropophagi:** Man-eaters.

Which ever as she could with haste dispatch,
She'ld come again, and with a greedy ear
Devour up my discourse. Which I observing,   150
Took once a pliant° hour, and found good means
To draw from her a prayer of earnest heart
That I would all my pilgrimage dilate,°
Whereof by parcels° she had something heard,
But not intentively.° I did consent,   155
And often did beguile her of her tears
When I did speak of some distressful stroke
That my youth suffered. My story being done,
She gave me for my pains a world of sighs.
She swore, i' faith, 'twas strange, 'twas passing strange;   160
'Twas pitiful, 'twas wondrous pitiful.
She wished she had not heard it; yet she wished
That heaven had made her such a man. She thanked me;
And bade me, if I had a friend that loved her,
I should but teach him how to tell my story,   165
And that would woo her. Upon this hint° I spake.
She loved me for the dangers I had passed,
And I loved her that she did pity them.
This only is the witchcraft I have used.
Here comes the lady. Let her witness it.   170

Enter Desdemona, Iago, Attendants.

DUKE: I think this tale would win my daughter too.
    Good Brabantio,
    Take up this mangled matter at the best.
    Men do their broken weapons rather use
    Than their bare hands.
BRABANTIO: I pray you hear her speak.   175
    If she confess that she was half the wooer,
    Destruction on my head if my bad blame
    Light on the man! Come hither, gentle mistress.
    Do you perceive in all this noble company
    Where most you owe obedience?
DESDEMONA: My noble father,   180
    I do perceive here a divided duty.
    To you I am bound for life and education;°
    My life and education both do learn me
    How to respect you: you are the lord of duty;
    I am hitherto your daughter. But here's my husband;   185

---

151. **pliant:** Propitious. **153. dilate:** Recount in full. **154. parcels:** Portions. **155. intentively:** With full attention. **166. hint:** Opportunity. **182. education:** Upbringing.

And so much duty as my mother showed
To you, preferring you before her father,
So much I challenge° that I may profess
Due to the Moor my lord.

BRABANTIO: God be with you! I have done.   190
    Please it your grace, on to the state affairs.
    I had rather to adopt a child than get° it.
    Come hither, Moor.
    I here do give thee that with all my heart
    Which, but thou hast already, with all my heart
    I would keep from thee. For your sake,° jewel,   195
    I am glad at soul I have no other child;
    For thy escape° would teach me tyranny,
    To hang clogs on them. I have done, my lord.

DUKE: Let me speak like yourself° and lay a sentence°
    Which, as a grise° or step, may help these lovers   200
    [Into your favor.]
    When remedies are past, the griefs are ended
    By seeing the worst, which late on hopes depended.
    To mourn a mischief that is past and gone
    Is the next way to draw new mischief on.   205
    What cannot be preserved when fortune takes,
    Patience her injury a mock'ry makes.
    The robbed that smiles steals something from the thief;
    He robs himself that spends a bootless grief.

BRABANTIO: So let the Turk of Cyprus us beguile: 210
    We lose it not so long as we can smile.
    He bears the sentence well that nothing bears
    But the free comfort which from thence he hears;
    But he bears both the sentence and the sorrow
    That to pay grief must of poor patience borrow.   215
    These sentences, to sugar, or to gall,
    Being strong on both sides, are equivocal.
    But words are words. I never yet did hear
    That the bruisèd heart was piercèd through the ear.
    Beseech you, now to the affairs of state.   220

DUKE: The Turk with a most mighty preparation makes for Cyprus. Oth-
    ello, the fortitude° of the place is best known to you; and though we
    have there a substitute of most allowed° sufficiency, yet opinion,° a
    more sovereign mistress of effects, throws a more safer voice on you.

---

188. challenge: Claim the right.   **191. get:** Beget.   **195. For your sake:** Because of you.
197. escape: Escapade.   **199. like yourself:** As you should; **sentence:** Maxim.   **200. grise:**
Step.   **222. fortitude:** Fortification.   **223. allowed:** Acknowledged; **opinion:** Public opinion.

You must therefore be content to slubber° the gloss of your new for- 225
tunes with this more stubborn and boist'rous expedition.
OTHELLO: The tyrant custom, most grave senators,
Hath made the flinty and steel couch of war
My thrice-driven bed of down. I do agnize
A natural and prompt alacrity 230
I find in hardness;° and do undertake
These present wars against the Ottomites.
Most humbly, therefore, bending to your state,
I crave fit disposition for my wife,
Due reference of place, and exhibition,° 235
With such accommodation and besort°
As levels° with her breeding.
DUKE: If you please,
Be't at her father's.
BRABANTIO: I will not have it so.
OTHELLO: Nor I.
DESDEMONA: Nor I. I would not there reside, 240
To put my father in impatient thoughts
By being in his eye. Most gracious Duke,
To my unfolding lend your prosperous° ear,
And let me find a charter in your voice,
T' assist my simpleness.° 245
DUKE: What would you, Desdemona?
DESDEMONA: That I did love the Moor to live with him,
My downright violence, and storm of fortunes,
May trumpet to the world. My heart's subdued
Even to the very quality of my lord. 250
I saw Othello's visage in his mind,
And to his honors and his valiant parts
Did I my soul and fortunes consecrate.
So that, dear lords, if I be left behind,
A moth of peace, and he go to the war, 255
The rites for which I love him are bereft me,
And I a heavy interim shall support
By his dear absence. Let me go with him.
OTHELLO: Let her have your voice.
Vouch with me, heaven, I therefore beg it not 260
To please the palate of my appetite,
Not to comply with heat° — the young affects°

---

225. **slubber:** Sully.   229–31. **agnize . . . hardness:** Recognize in myself a natural and easy
response to hardship.   235. **exhibition:** Allowance of money.   236. **besort:** Suitable company.   237. **levels:** Corresponds.   243. **prosperous:** Favorable.   245. **simpleness:** Lack of
skill.   262. **heat:** Passions; **young affects:** Tendencies of youth.

In me defunct — and proper satisfaction;
But to be free and bounteous to her mind;
And heaven defend your good souls that you think   265
I will your serious and great business scant
When she is with me. No, when light-winged toys
Of feathered Cupid seel° with wanton dullness
My speculative and officed instruments,°
That° my disports corrupt and taint my business,   270
Let housewives make a skillet of my helm,
And all indign° and base adversities
Make head against my estimation!°
DUKE: Be it as you shall privately determine,
        Either for her stay or going. Th' affair cries haste,   275
        And speed must answer it.
1. SENATOR: You must away to-night.
OTHELLO: With all my heart.
DUKE: At nine i' th' morning here we'll meet again.
        Othello, leave some officer behind,
        And he shall our commission bring to you,   280
        With such things else of quality and respect
        As doth import° you.
OTHELLO: So please your grace, my ancient;
        A man he is of honesty and trust
        To his conveyance I assign my wife,
        With what else needful your good grace shall think   285
        To be sent after me.
DUKE: Let it be so.
        Good night to every one.
                [To Brabantio.]   And, noble signior,
        If virtue no delighted° beauty lack,
        Your son-in-law is far more fair than black.
1. SENATOR: Adieu, brave Moor. Use Desdemona well.   290
BRABANTIO: Look to her, Moor, if thou hast eyes to see:
        She has deceived her father, and may thee.
                        Exeunt [Duke, Senators, Officers, &c.].
OTHELLO: My life upon her faith! — Honest Iago,
        My Desdemona must I leave to thee.
        I prithee let thy wife attend on her,   295
        And bring them after in the best advantage.°
        Come, Desdemona. I have but an hour

---

268. **seel:** Blind.   269. **My . . . instruments:** My perceptive and responsible faculties.
270. **That:** So that.   272. **indign:** Unworthy.   273. **estimation:** Reputation.   282. **import:**
Concern.   288. **delighted:** Delightful.   296. **in the best advantage:** At the best opportunity.

Of love, of worldly matters and direction,
To spend with thee. We must obey the time.

Exit Moor and Desdemona.

RODERIGO: Iago,—   300

IAGO: What say'st thou, noble heart?

RODERIGO: What will I do, think'st thou?

IAGO: Why, go to bed and sleep.

RODERIGO: I will incontinently° drown myself.

IAGO: If thou dost, I shall never love thee after. Why, thou silly gentle- 305
man!

RODERIGO: It is silliness to live when to live is torment; and then have we
a prescription to die when death is our physician.

IAGO: O villainous! I have looked upon the world for four times seven
years; and since I could distinguish betwixt a benefit and an injury, I 310
never found man that knew how to love himself. Ere I would say I
would drown myself for the love of a guinea hen, I would change my
humanity with a baboon.

RODERIGO: What should I do? I confess it is my shame to be so fond, but
it is not in my virtue to amend it.   315

IAGO: Virtue? a fig! 'Tis in ourselves that we are thus or thus. Our bodies
are our gardens, to which our wills are gardeners; so that if we will
plant nettles or sow lettuce, set hyssop and weed up thyme, supply it
with one gender° of herbs or distract it with many—either to have it
sterile with idleness or manured with industry—why, the power and 320
corrigible authority° of this lies in our wills. If the balance of our
lives had not one scale of reason to poise° another of sensuality, the
blood and baseness° of our natures would conduct us to most pre-
posterous conclusions. But we have reason to cool our raging
motions,° our carnal strings, our unbitted° lusts; whereof I take this 325
that you call love to be a sect or scion.°

RODERIGO: It cannot be.

IAGO: It is merely a lust of the blood and a permission of the will. Come,
be a man! Drown thyself? Drown cats and blind puppies! I have
professed me thy friend, and I confess me knit to thy deserving with 330
cables of perdurable toughness. I could never better stead thee than
now. Put money in thy purse. Follow thou the wars; defeat thy
favor° with an usurped beard. I say, put money in thy purse. It cannot be that Desdemona should long continue her love to the
Moor—put money in thy purse—nor he his to her. It was a violent 335

---

304. incontinently: Forthwith.   **319. gender:** Species.   **321. corrigible authority:** Correc-
tive power.   **322. poise:** Counterbalance.   **323. blood and baseness:** Animal instincts.
325. motions: Appetites; **unbitted:** Uncontrolled.   **326. sect or scion:** Offshoot, cutting.
332–33. defeat thy favor: Spoil thy appearance.

commencement in her, and thou shalt see an answerable sequestra-
tion° — put but money in thy purse. These Moors are changeable in
their wills — fill thy purse with money. The food that to him now is
as luscious as locusts shall be to him shortly as bitter as coloquintida.° She must change for youth: when she is sated with his body,   340
she will find the error of her choice. [She must have change, she
must.] Therefore put money in thy purse. If thou wilt needs damn
thyself, do it a more delicate way than drowning. Make° all the
money thou canst. If sanctimony and a frail vow betwixt an erring°
barbarian and a supersubtle Venetian be not too hard for my wits   345
and all the tribe of hell, thou shalt enjoy her. Therefore make
money. A pox of drowning thyself! 'Tis clean out of the way. Seek
thou rather to be hanged in compassing thy joy than to be drowned
and go without her.

RODERIGO: Wilt thou be fast to my hopes, if I depend on the issue?   350

IAGO: Thou art sure of me. Go, make money. I have told thee often, and
I retell thee again and again, I hate the Moor. My cause is hearted;°
thine hath no less reason. Let us be conjunctive in our revenge
against him. If thou canst cuckold him, thou dost thyself a pleasure,
me a sport. There are many events in the womb of time, which will   355
be delivered. Traverse,° go, provide thy money! We will have more of
this to-morrow. Adieu.

RODERIGO: Where shall we meet i' th' morning?

IAGO: At my lodging.

RODERIGO: I'll be with thee betimes.   360

IAGO: Go to, farewell — Do you hear, Roderigo?

[RODERIGO: What say you?

IAGO: No more of drowning, do you hear?

RODERIGO: I am changed.

IAGO: Go to, farewell. Put money enough in your purse.]   365

RODERIGO: I'll sell all my land.   *Exit.*

IAGO: Thus do I ever make my fool my purse;
For I mine own gained knowledge should profane
If I would time expend with such a snipe°
But for my sport and profit. I hate the Moor;   370
And it is thought abroad that 'twixt my sheets
H'as done my office. I know not if't be true;
But I, for mere suspicion in that kind,
Will do as if for surety. He holds me well;°
The better shall my purpose work on him.   375
Cassio's a proper man. Let me see now:

336–37. sequestration: Estrangement.   339–40. coloquintida: A medicine.   343. Make:
Raise.   344. erring: Wandering.   352. My cause is hearted: My heart is in it.   356. Traverse: Forward march.   369. snipe: Fool.   374. well: In high regard.

To get his place, and to plume up° my will
In double knavery—How, how?—Let's see:—
After some time, to abuse Othello's ears
That he is too familiar with his wife.   380
He hath a person and a smooth dispose°
To be suspected—framed to make women false.
The Moor is of a free° and open nature
That thinks men honest that but seem to be so;
And will as tenderly be led by th' nose   385
As asses are.
I have't! It is engend'red! Hell and night
Must bring this monstrous birth to the world's light.   *Exit.*

ACT II / Scene I

An open place in Cyprus, near the harbor.

Enter Montano and two Gentlemen.

MONTANO: What from the cape can you discern at sea?
1. GENTLEMAN: Nothing at all: it is a high-wrought flood.
    I cannot 'twixt the heaven and the main
    Descry a sail.
MONTANO: Methinks the wind hath spoke aloud at land;   5
    A fuller blast ne'er shook our battlements.
    If it hath ruffianed so upon the sea,
    What ribs of oak, when mountains melt on them,
    Can hold the mortise?° What shall we hear of this?
2. GENTLEMAN: A segregation° of the Turkish fleet.   10
    For do but stand upon the foaming shore,
    The chidden billow seems to pelt the clouds;
    The wind-shaked surge, with high and monstrous mane,
    Seems to cast water on the burning Bear
    And quench the Guards° of th' ever-fixèd pole.°   15
    I never did like molestation° view
    On the enchafèd flood.
MONTANO: If that the Turkish fleet
    Be not ensheltered and embayed, they are drowned;
    It is impossible to bear it out.

Enter a third Gentleman.

3. GENTLEMAN: News, lads! Our wars are done.   20
    The desperate tempest hath so banged the Turks

---

377. plume up: Gratify.   **381. dispose:** Manner.   **383. free:** Frank.   ACT II, SCENE I.
9. hold the mortise: Hold their joints together.   **10. segregation:** Scattering.   **15. Guards:**
Stars near the North Star; **pole:** Polestar.   **16. molestation:** Tumult.

That their designment halts.° A noble ship of Venice
Hath seen a grievous wrack and sufferance°
On most part of their fleet.
MONTANO: How? Is this true?
3. GENTLEMAN: The ship is here put in,   25
A Veronesa;° Michael Cassio,
Lieutenant to the warlike Moor Othello,
Is come on shore; the Moor himself at sea,
And is in full commission here for Cyprus.
MONTANO: I am glad on't. 'Tis a worthy governor.   30
3. GENTLEMAN: But his same Cassio, though he speak of comfort
Touching the Turkish loss, yet he looks sadly
And prays the Moor be safe, for they were parted
With foul and violent tempest.
MONTANO: Pray heaven he be;
For I have served him, and the man commands   35
Like a full soldier. Let's to the seaside, ho!
As well to see the vessel that's come in
As to throw out our eyes for brave Othello,
Even till we make the main and th' aerial blue
An indistinct regard.°
3. GENTLEMAN: Come, let's do so;   40
For every minute is expectancy
Of more arrivance.

Enter Cassio.

CASSIO: Thanks, you the valiant of this warlike isle,
That so approve the Moor! O, let the heavens
Give him defense against the elements,   45
For I have lost him on a dangerous sea!
MONTANO: Is he well shipped?
CASSIO: His bark is stoutly timbered, and his pilot
Of very expert and approved allowance;
Therefore my hopes, not surfeited to death,°   50
Stand in bold cure.°
(*Within.*)   A sail, a sail, a sail!   *Enter a messenger.*
CASSIO: What noise?
MESSENGER: The town is empty; on the brow o' th' sea
Stand ranks of people, and they cry "A sail!"
CASSIO: My hopes do shape him for the governor.   55

A shot.

---

22. **designment halts:** Plan is crippled.   23. **sufferance:** Disaster.   26. **Veronesa:** Ship furnished by Verona.   40. **an indistinct regard:** Indistinguishable.   50. **surfeited to death:** Overindulged.   51. **in bold cure:** A good chance of fulfillment.

2. GENTLEMAN: They do discharge their shot of courtesy:
    Our friends at least.
CASSIO: I pray you, sir, go forth
    And give us truth who 'tis that is arrived.
2. GENTLEMAN: I shall.   *Exit.*
MONTANO: But, good lieutenant, is your general wived?   60
CASSIO: Most fortunately. He hath achieved a maid
    That paragons° description and wild fame;
    One that excels the quirks° of blazoning° pens,
    And in th' essential vesture of creation
    Does tire the ingener.°

Enter Second Gentleman.

                        How now? Who has put in?   65
2. GENTLEMAN: 'Tis one Iago, ancient to the general.
CASSIO: H'as had most favorable and happy speed:
    Tempests themselves, high seas, and howling winds,
    The guttered° rocks and congregated sands,
    Traitors ensteeped° to clog the guiltless keel,   70
    As having sense of beauty, do omit
    Their mortal° natures, letting go safely by
    The divine Desdemona.
MONTANO: What is she?
CASSIO: She that I spake of, our great captain's captain,
    Left in the conduct of the bold Iago,   75
    Whose footing° here anticipates our thoughts
    A se'nnight's° speed. Great Jove, Othello guard,
    And swell his sail with thine own pow'rful breath,
    That he may bless this bay with his tall ship,
    Make love's quick pants in Desdemona's arms,   80
    Give renewed fire to our extincted spirits,
    [And bring all Cyprus comfort!]

Enter Desdemona, Iago, Roderigo, and Emilia [with Attendants].

                        O, behold!
    The riches of the ship is come on shore!
    You men of Cyprus, let her have your knees.°
    Hail to thee, lady! and the grace of heaven,   85
    Before, behind thee, and on every hand,
    Enwheel thee round!

---

62. **paragons:** Surpasses.   63. **quirk:** Ingenuities; **blazoning:** Describing.   64–65. **And . . . ingener:** Merely to describe her as God made her exhaust her praiser.   69. **guttered:** Jagged.
70. **ensteeped:** Submerged.   72. **mortal:** Deadly.   76. **footing:** Landing.   77. **se'nnight's:** Week's.   84. **knees:** I.e., kneeling.

DESDEMONA: I thank you, valiant Cassio.
    What tidings can you tell me of my lord?
CASSIO: He is not yet arrived; nor know I aught
    But that he's well and will be shortly here.   90
DESDEMONA: O but I fear! How lost you company?
CASSIO: The great contention of the sea and skies
    Parted our fellowship.
        (*Within.*)   A sail, a sail! [*A shot.*]
                                              But hark. A sail!
2. GENTLEMAN: They give their greeting to the citadel;
    This likewise is a friend.
CASSIO: See for the news.   95

                                              [*Exit Gentleman.*]

    Good ancient, you are welcome.
        [*To Emilia.*]   Welcome, mistress. —
    Let it not gall your patience, good Iago,
    That I extend my manners. 'Tis my breeding
    That gives me this bold show of courtesy.
        [*Kisses Emilia.*°]
IAGO: Sir, would she give you so much of her lips   100
    As of her tongue she oft bestows on me,
    You would have enough.
DESDEMONA: Alas, she has no speech!
IAGO: In faith, too much.
    I find it still when I have list to sleep.
    Marry, before your ladyship, I grant,   105
    She puts her tongue a little in her heart
    And chides with thinking.
EMILIA: You have little cause to say so.
IAGO: Come on, come on! You are pictures out of doors,
    Bells in your parlors, wildcats in your kitchens,   110
    Saints in your injuries, devils being offended,
    Players in your housewifery,° and housewives° in your beds.
DESDEMONA: O, fie upon thee, slanderer!
IAGO: Nay, it is true, or else I am a Turk:
    You rise to play, and go to bed to work.   115
EMILIA: You shall not write my praise.
IAGO: No, let me not.
DESDEMONA: What wouldst thou write of me, if thou shouldst praise me?
IAGO: O gentle lady, do not put me to't,
    For I am nothing if not critical.

---

s.d. Kisses Emilia: (Kissing was a common Elizabethan form of social courtesy).   **112. house-
wifery:** Housekeeping; **housewives:** Hussies.

DESDEMONA: Come on, assay.° — There's one gone to the harbor?   120
IAGO: Ay, madam.
DESDEMONA: I am not merry; but I do beguile
    The thing I am by seeming otherwise. —
    Come, how wouldst thou praise me?
IAGO: I am about it; but indeed my invention   125
    Comes from my pate as birdlime° does from frieze° —
    It plucks out brains and all. But my Muse labors,
    And thus she is delivered:
    If she be fair and wise, fairness and wit —
    The one's for use, the other useth it.   130
DESDEMONA: Well praised! How if she be black° and witty?
IAGO: If she be black, and thereto have a wit,
    She'll find a white that shall her blackness fit.
DESDEMONA: Worse and worse!
EMILIA: How if fair and foolish?   135
IAGO: She never yet was foolish that was fair,
    For even her folly° helped her to an heir.
DESDEMONA: These are old fond° paradoxes to make fools laugh i' th'
    alehouse. What miserable praise hast thou for her that's foul° and
    foolish?   140
IAGO: There's none so foul, and foolish thereunto,
    But does foul pranks which fair and wise ones do.
DESDEMONA: O heavy ignorance! Thou praisest the worst best. But what
    praise couldst thou bestow on a deserving woman indeed — one that
    in the authority of her merit did justly put on the vouch° of very   145
    malice itself?
IAGO: She that was ever fair, and never proud;
    Had tongue at will, and yet was never loud;
    Never lacked gold, and yet went never gay;
    Fled from her wish, and yet said "Now I may";   150
    She that, being ang'red, her revenge being nigh,
    Bade her wrong stay, and her displeasure fly;
    She that in wisdom never was so frail
    To change the cod's head for the salmon's tail;°
    She that could think, and ne'er disclose her mind;   155
    See suitors following, and not look behind:
    She was a wight (if ever such wight were) —
DESDEMONA: To do what?
IAGO: To suckle fools and chronicle small beer.°

---

120. **assay:** Try.   126. **birdlime:** A sticky paste; **frieze:** Rough cloth.   131. **black:** Brunette.   137. **folly:** Wantonness.   138. **fond:** Foolish.   139. **foul:** Ugly.   145. **put on the vouch:** Compel the approval.   154. **To . . . tail:** I.e., to exchange the good for the poor but expensive.   159. **chronicle small beer:** Keep petty household accounts.

DESDEMONA: O most lame and impotent conclusion! Do not learn of 160
him, Emilia, though he be thy husband. How say you, Cassio? Is he
not a most profane and liberal° counsellor?

CASSIO: He speaks home,° madam. You may relish him more in the soldier than in the scholar.

IAGO [aside]: He takes her by the palm. Ay, well said, whisper! With as 165
little a web as this will I ensnare as great a fly as Cassio. Ay, smile
upon her, do! I will give thee in thine own courtship.° — You say
true; 'tis so, indeed! — If such tricks as these strip you out of your
lieutenantry, it had been better you had not kissed your three fingers
so oft — which now again you are most apt to play the sir° in. Very 170
good! well kissed! an excellent courtesy! 'Tis so, indeed. Yet again
your fingers to your lips? Would they were clyster pipes° for your
sake! (*Trumpet within.*)
The Moor! I know his trumpet.

CASSIO: 'Tis truly so.   175

DESDEMONA: Let's meet him and receive him.

CASSIO: Lo, where he comes.

Enter Othello and Attendants.

OTHELLO: O my fair warrior!

DESDEMONA: My dear Othello!

OTHELLO: It gives me wonder great as my content
To see you here before me. O my soul's joy!   180
If after every tempest come such calms,
May the winds blow till they have wakened death!
And let the laboring bark climb hills of seas
Olympus-high, and duck again as low
As hell's from heaven! If it were now to die,   185
'Twere now to be most happy;° for I fear
My soul hath her content so absolute
That not another comfort like to this
Succeeds in unknown fate.

DESDEMONA: The heavens forbid
But that our loves and comforts should increase   190
Even as our days do grow.

OTHELLO: Amen to that, sweet powers!
I cannot speak enough of this content;
It stops me here; it is too much of joy.
And this, and this, the greatest discords be

They kiss.

---

162. **profane and liberal:** Worldly and licentious.   163. **home:** Bluntly.   167. **give . . .
courtship:** Manacle you by means of your courtly manners.   170. **sir:** Courtly gentleman.
172. **clyster pipes:** Syringes.   186. **happy:** Fortunate.

That e'er our hearts shall make!

IAGO [*aside*]:   O, you are well tuned now!   195
But I'll set down° the pegs that make this music,
As honest as I am.

OTHELLO: Come, let us to the castle.
News, friends! Our wars are done; the Turks are drowned.
How does my old acquaintance of this isle? —
Honey, you shall be well desired° in Cyprus;   200
I have found great love amongst them. O my sweet,
I prattle out of fashion, and I dote
In mine own comforts. I prithee, good Iago,
Go to the bay and disembark my coffers.
Bring thou the master° to the citadel;   205
He is a good one, and his worthiness
Does challenge° much respect. — Come, Desdemona,
Once more well met at Cyprus.

       Exit Othello [with all but Iago and Roderigo].

IAGO [*to an Attendant, who goes out*]: Do thou meet me presently at the
harbor. [*To Roderigo.*] Come hither. If thou be'st valiant (as they say   210
base men being in love have then a nobility in their natures more
than is native to them), list me. The lieutenant to-night watches on
the court of guard.° First, I must tell thee this: Desdemona is directly in love with him.

RODERIGO: With him? Why, 'tis not possible.   215

IAGO: Lay thy finger thus,° and let thy soul be instructed. Mark me with
what violence she first loved the Moor, but for bragging and telling
her fantastical lies; and will she love him still for prating? Let not
thy discreet heart think it. Her eye must be fed; and what delight
shall she have to look on the devil? When the blood is made dull   220
with the act of sport, there should be, again to inflame it and to give
satiety a fresh appetite, loveliness in favor, sympathy in years, manners, and beauties; all which the Moor is defective in. Now for want
of these required conveniences,° her delicate tenderness will find itself abused, begin to heave the gorge,° disrelish and abhor the Moor. 225
Very nature will instruct her in it and compel her to some second
choice. Now, sir, this granted — as it is a most pregnant° and un-
forced position — who stands so eminent in the degree of this fortune as Cassio does? A knave very voluble; no further conscionable°
than in putting on the mere form of civil and humane° seeming for 230

---

196. **set down:** Loosen.   200. **well desired:** Warmly welcomed.   205. **master:** Ship captain.
207. **challenge:** Deserve.   213. **court of guard:** Headquarters.   216. **thus:** I.e., on your lips.
224. **conveniences:** Compatibilities.   225. **heave the gorge:** Be nauseated.   227. **pregnant:**
Evident.   229. **conscionable:** Conscientious.   230. **humane:** Polite.

the better compassing of his salt° and most hidden loose affection?
Why, none! why, none! A slipper° and subtle knave; a finder-out of
occasions; that has an eye can stamp and counterfeit advantages,
though true advantage never present itself; a devilish knave! Besides, the knave is handsome, young, and hath all those requisites in   235
him that folly and green minds look after. A pestilent complete
knave! and the woman hath found him already.

RODERIGO: I cannot believe that in her; she's full of most blessed condition.°

IAGO: Blessed fig's-end! The wine she drinks is made of grapes. If she   240
had been blessed, she would never have loved the Moor. Blessed
pudding! Didst thou not see her paddle with the palm of his hand?
Didst not mark that?

RODERIGO: Yes, that I did; but that was but courtesy.

IAGO: Lechery, by this hand! an index and obscure prologue to the his-   245
tory of lust and foul thoughts. They met so near with their lips that
their breaths embraced together. Villainous thoughts, Roderigo!
When these mutualities° so marshal the way, hard at hand comes
the master and main exercise, th' incorporate° conclusion. Pish!
But, sir, be you ruled by me: I have brought you from Venice. Watch   250
you to-night; for the command, I'll lay't upon you. Cassio knows
you not. I'll not be far from you: do you find some occasion to anger
Cassio, either by speaking too loud, or tainting° his discipline, or
from what other course you please which the time shall more favorably minister.   255

RODERIGO: Well.

IAGO: Sir, he's rash and very sudden in choler,° and haply with his trun-
cheon may strike at you. Provoke him that he may; for even out of
that will I cause these of Cyprus to mutiny; whose qualification°
shall come into no true taste° again but by the displanting of Cas-   260
sio. So shall you have a shorter journey to your desires by the means
I shall then have to prefer° them; and the impediment most profitably removed with-out the which there were no expectation of our
prosperity.

RODERIGO: I will do this if you can bring it to any opportunity.   265

IAGO: I warrant thee. Meet me by and by at the citadel; I must fetch his
necessaries ashore. Farewell.

RODERIGO: Adieu.   *Exit.*

IAGO: That Cassio loves her, I do well believe't;
That she loves him, 'tis apt° and of great credit.   270

---

231. salt: Lecherous.   232. slipper: Slippery.   238–39. condition: Character.   248. mutu-
alities: Exchanges.   249. incorporate: Carnal.   253. tainting: Discrediting.   257. sudden
in choler: Violent in anger.   259. qualification: Appeasement.   260. true taste: Satisfactory state.   262. prefer: Advance.   270. apt: Probable.

The Moor, howbeit that I endure him not,
Is of a constant, loving, noble nature,
And I dare think he'll prove to Desdemona
A most dear husband. Now I do love her too;
Not out of absolute lust, though peradventure   275
I stand accountant° for as great a sin,
But partly led to diet° my revenge,
For that I do suspect the lusty Moor
Hath leaped into my seat; the thought whereof
Doth, like a poisonous mineral, gnaw my inwards;   280
And nothing can or shall content my soul
Till I am evened with him, wife for wife;
Or failing so, yet that I put the Moor
At least into a jealousy so strong
That judgment cannot cure. Which thing to do,   285
If this poor trash of Venice, whom I trash°
For° his quick hunting, stand the putting on,°
I'll have our Michael Cassio on the hip,°
Abuse him to the Moor in the rank garb°
(For I fear Cassio with my nightcap too),   290
Make the Moor thank me, love me, and reward me
For making him egregiously an ass
And practicing upon° his peace and quiet
Even to madness. 'Tis here, but yet confused:
Knavery's plain face is never seen till used.   *Exit.* 295

Scene II

A street in Cyprus.

Enter Othello's Herald, with a proclamation.

HERALD: It is Othello's pleasure, our noble and valiant general, that,
    upon certain tidings now arrived, importing the mere perdition° of
    the Turkish fleet, every man put himself into triumph; some to
    dance, some to make bonfires, each man to what sport and revels
    his addiction leads him. For, besides these beneficial news, it is the   5
    celebration of his nuptial. So much was his pleasure should be pro-
    claimed. All offices° are open, and there is full liberty of feasting
    from the present hour of five till the bell have told eleven. Heaven
    bless the isle of Cyprus and our noble general Othello!   *Exit.*

---

276. accountant: Accountable.   277. diet: Feed.   286. I trash: I weight down (in order to
keep under control).   287. For: In order to develop; stand the putting on: Responds to my
inciting.   288. on the hip: At my mercy.   289. rank garb: Gross manner.   293. practicing
upon: Plotting against.   SCENE II.   2. mere perdition: Complete destruction.   7. offices:
Kitchens and storerooms.

Scene III

The Cyprian Castle.

Enter Othello, Desdemona, Cassio, and Attendants.

OTHELLO: Good Michael, look you to the guard to-night.
Let's teach ourselves that honorable stop,
Not to outsport discretion.
CASSIO: Iago hath direction what to do;
But not withstanding, with my personal eye   5
Will I look to't.
OTHELLO: Iago is most honest.
Michael, good night. To-morrow with your earliest
Let me have speech with you.
          [*To Desdemona.*]   Come, my dear love.
The purchase made, the fruits are to ensue;
That profit 's yet to come 'tween me and you. —   10
Good night.

                         Exit [Othello with Desdemona and Attendants].

Enter Iago.

CASSIO: Welcome, Iago. We must to the watch.
IAGO: Not this hour, lieutenant; 'tis not yet ten o' th' clock. Our general
cast° us thus early for the love of his Desdemona; who let us not
therefore blame. He hath not yet made wanton the night with her,   15
and she is sport for Jove.
CASSIO: She's a most exquisite lady.
IAGO: And, I'll warrant her, full of game.
CASSIO: Indeed, she's a most fresh and delicate creature.
IAGO: What an eye she has! Methinks it sounds a parley to provocation.   20
CASSIO: An inviting eye; and yet methinks right modest.
IAGO: And when she speaks, is it not an alarum to love?
CASSIO: She is indeed perfection.
IAGO: Well, happiness to their sheets! Come, lieutenant, I have a stoup°
of wine, and here without are a brace of Cyprus gallants that would   25
fain have a measure to the health of black Othello.
CASSIO: Not to-night, good Iago. I have very poor and unhappy brains
for drinking; I could well wish courtesy would invent some other
custom of entertainment.
IAGO: O, they are our friends. But one cup! I'll drink for you.   30
CASSIO: I have drunk but one cup to-night, and that was craftily quali-
fied° too; and behold what innovation° it makes here. I am unfor-

---

SCENE III.   **14. cast:** Dismissed.   **24. stoup:** Two-quart tankard.   **31–32. qualified:** Diluted.
32. innovation: Disturbance.

tunate in the infirmity and dare not task my weakness with any
more.

IAGO: What, man! 'Tis a night of revels: the gallants desire it.   35

CASSIO: Where are they?

IAGO: Here at the door; I pray you call them in.

CASSIO: I'll do't, but it dislikes me.   *Exit.*

IAGO: If I can fasten but one cup upon him
    With that which he hath drunk to-night already,   40
    He'll be as full of quarrel and offense
    As my young mistress' dog. Now my sick fool Roderigo,
    Whom love hath turned almost the wrong side out,
    To Desdemona hath to-night caroused
    Potations pottle-deep;° and he's to watch.   45
    Three lads of Cyprus—noble swelling spirits,
    That hold their honors in a wary distance,°
    The very elements° of this warlike isle—
    Have I to-night flustered with flowing cups,
    And they watch too. Now, 'mongst this flock of drunkards   50
    Am I to put our Cassio in some action
    That may offend the isle.

Enter Cassio, Montano, and Gentlemen [; Servants following with wine].

                But here they come.
    If consequence do but approve my dream,
    My boat sails freely, both with wind and stream.

CASSIO: 'Fore God, they have given me a rouse° already.   55

MONTANO: Good faith, a little one; not past a pint, as I am a soldier.

IAGO: Some wine, ho!
    [*Sings.*]   And let me the canakin clink, clink;
              And let me the canakin clink
                A soldier's a man;   60
                A life's but a span,
             Why then, let a soldier drink.
    Some wine, boys!

CASSIO: 'Fore God, an excellent song!

IAGO: I learned it in England, where indeed they are most potent in pot-   65
ting. Your Dane, your German, and your swag-bellied Hollander—
Drink, ho!—are nothing to your English.

CASSIO: Is your Englishman so expert in his drinking?

IAGO: Why, he drinks you with facility your Dane dead drunk; he sweats
not to overthrow your Almain; he gives your Hollander a vomit ere   70
the next pottle can be filled.

---

45. pottle-deep: Bottoms up. **47. That . . . distance:** Very sensitive about their honor.
48. very elements: True representatives. **55. rouse:** Bumper.

CASSIO: To the health of our general!
MONTANO: I am for it, lieutenant, and I'll do you justice.
IAGO: O sweet England!
    [*Sings.*]   King Stephen was a worthy peer;   75
               His breeches cost him but a crown;
           He held 'em sixpence all too dear,
               With that he called the tailor lown.°
           He was a wight of high renown,
               And thou art but of low degree.   80
           'Tis pride that pulls the country down;
               Then take thine auld cloak about thee.
    Some wine, ho!
CASSIO: 'Fore God, this is a more exquisite song than the other.
IAGO: Will you hear't again?   85
CASSIO: No, for I hold him to be unworthy of his place that does those
    things.° Well, God's above all; and there be souls must be saved, and
    there be souls must not be saved.
IAGO: It's true, good lieutenant.
CASSIO: For mine own part — no offense to the general, nor any man of   90
    quality — I hope to be saved.
IAGO: And so do I too, lieutenant.
CASSIO: Ay, but, by your leave, not before me. The lieutenant is to be
    saved before the ancient. Let's have no more of this; let's to our af-
    fairs. — God forgive us our sins! — Gentlemen, let's look to our busi-   95
    ness. Do not think, gentlemen, I am drunk. This is my ancient; this
    is my right hand, and this is my left. I am not drunk now. I can
    stand well enough, and I speak well enough.
ALL: Excellent well!
CASSIO: Why, very well then. You must not think then that I am drunk.   100
                                                      Exit.

MONTANO: To th' platform, masters. Come, let's set the watch.
IAGO: You see this fellow that is gone before.
    He's a soldier fit to stand by Caesar
    And give direction; and do but see his vice.
    'Tis to his virtue a just equinox,°   105
    The one as long as th' other. 'Tis pity of him.
    I fear the trust Othello puts him in,
    On some odd time of his infirmity,
    Will shake this island.
MONTANO: But is he often thus?
IAGO: 'Tis evermore his prologue to his sleep: 110
    He'll watch the horologe a double set°
    If drink rock not his cradle.

---

78. **lown:** Rascal.   **86–87. does . . . things:** I.e., behaves in this fashion.   **105. just equi-
nox:** Exact equivalent.   **111. watch . . . set:** Stay awake twice around the clock.

MONTANO: It were well
    The general were put in mind of it.
    Perhaps he sees it not, or his good nature
    Prizes the virtue that appears in Cassio   115
    And looks not on his evils. Is not this true?

Enter Roderigo.

IAGO [*aside to him*]: How now, Roderigo?
    I pray you after the lieutenant, go!   *Exit Roderigo.*
MONTANO: And 'tis great pity that the noble Moor
    Should hazard such a place as his own second   120
    With one of an ingraft° infirmity.
    It were an honest action to say
    So to the Moor.
IAGO: Not I, for this fair island!
    I do love Cassio well and would do much
    To cure him of this evil.   125
        (*Within.*) Help! help!
                  But hark! What noise?

Enter Cassio, driving in Roderigo.

CASSIO: Zounds, you rogue! you rascal!
MONTANO: What's the matter, lieutenant?
CASSIO: A knave to teach me my duty?
    I'll beat the knave into a twiggen° bottle.
RODERIGO: Beat me?
CASSIO: Dost thou prate, rogue? [*Strikes him.*]
MONTANO: Nay, good lieutenant!   130
                         [*Stays him.*]
    I pray you, sir, hold your hand.
CASSIO: Let me go, sir
    Or I'll knock you o'er the mazzard.°
MONTANO: Come, come, you're drunk!
CASSIO: Drunk?

They fight.

IAGO [*aside to Roderigo*]: Away, I say! Go out and cry a mutiny!
                                     Exit Roderigo.
    Nay, good lieutenant. God's will, gentlemen!   135
    Help, ho! — lieutenant — sir — Montano — sir —
    Help, masters! — Here's a goodly watch indeed!

A bell rung.

    Who's that which rings the bell? Diablo, ho!

---

121. ingraft: I.e., ingrained. **129. twiggen:** Wicker-covered. **132. mazzard:** Head.

The town will rise.° God's will, lieutenant, hold!
You'll be shamed for ever.

Enter Othello and Gentlemen with weapons.

OTHELLO: What is the matter here?   140
MONTANO: Zounds, I bleed still. I am hurt to th' death.
    He dies!
OTHELLO: Hold for your lives!
IAGO: Hold, hold! Lieutenant — sir — Montano — gentlemen!
    Have you forgot all sense of place and duty?   145
    Hold! The general speaks to you. Hold, for shame!
OTHELLO: Why, how now ho? From whence ariseth this?
    Are we turned Turks, and to ourselves do that
    Which heaven hath forbid the Ottomites?
    For Christian shame put by this barbarous brawl!   150
    He that stirs next to carve for° his own rage.
    Holds his soul light; he dies upon his motion.
    Silence that dreadful bell! It frights the isle
    From her propriety.° What is the matter, masters?
    Honest Iago, that looks dead with grieving,   155
    Speak. Who began this? On thy love, I charge thee.
IAGO: I do not know. Friends all, but now, even now,
    In quarter,° and in terms like bride and groom
    Devesting them for bed; and then, but now —
    As if some planet had unwitted men —   160
    Swords out, and tilting one at other's breast
    In opposition bloody. I cannot speak
    Any beginning to this peevish odds,°
    And would in action glorious I had lost
    Those legs that brought me to a part of it!   165
OTHELLO: How comes it, Michael, you are thus forgot?
CASSIO: I pray you pardon me; I cannot speak.
OTHELLO: Worthy Montano, you were wont to be civil;
    The gravity and stillness of your youth
    The world hath noted, and your name is great   170
    In months of wisest censure.° What's the matter
    That you unlace° your reputation thus
    And spend your rich opinion° for the name
    Of a night-brawler? Give me answer to it.
MONTANO: Worthy Othello, I am hurt to danger.   175
    Your officer, Iago, can inform you,

---

139. **rise:** Grow riotous.   151. **carve for:** Indulge.   154. **propriety:** Proper self.
158. **quarter:** Friendliness.   163. **peevish odds:** Childish quarrel.   171. **censure:** Judgment.   172. **unlace:** Undo.   173. **rich opinion:** High reputation.

While I spare speech, which something now offends° me,
Of all that I do know; nor know I aught
By me that's said or done amiss this night,
Unless self-charity be sometimes a vice,   180
And to defend ourselves it be a sin
When violence assails us.

OTHELLO: Now, by heaven,
My blood° begins my safer guides to rule,
And passion, having my best judgment collied,°
Assays° to lead the way. If I once stir   185
Or do but lift this arm, the best of you
Shall sink in my rebuke. Give me to know
How this foul rout began, who set it on;
And he that is approved in° this offense,
Though he had twinned with me, both at a birth,   190
Shall lose me. What! in a town of war,
Yet wild, the people's hearts brimful of fear,
To manage° private and domestic quarrel?
In night, and on the court and guard of safety?
'Tis monstrous. Iago, who began't?   195

MONTANO: If partially affined, or leagued in office,°
Thou dost deliver more or less than truth,
Thou art no soldier.

IAGO: Touch me not so near.
I had rather have this tongue cut from my mouth
Than it should do offense to Michael Cassio;   200
Yet I persuade myself, to speak the truth
Shall nothing wrong him. This it is, general.
Montano and myself being in speech,
There comes a fellow crying out for help,
And Cassio following him with determined sword   205
To execute° upon him. Sir, this gentleman
Steps in to Cassio and entreats his pause.
Myself the crying fellow did pursue,
Lest by his clamor — as it so fell out —
The town might fall in fright. He, swift of foot,   210
Outran my purpose; and I returned then rather
For that I heard the clink and fall of swords,
And Cassio high in oath;° which till to-night
I ne'er might say before. When I came back —

---

177. offends: Pains.   **183. blood:** Passion.   **184. collied:** Darkened.   **185. Assays:** Tries.
189. approved in: Proved guilty of.   **193. manage:** Carry on.   **196. partially . . . office:**
Prejudiced by comradeship or official relations.   **206. execute:** Work his will.   **213. high in
oath:** Cursing.

For this was brief—I found them close together   215
At blow and thrust, even as again they were
When you yourself did part them.
More of this matter cannot I report;
But men are men; the best sometimes forget.
Though Cassio did some little wrong to him,   220
As men in rage strike those that wish them best,
Yet surely Cassio I believe received
From him that fled some strange indignity,
Which patience could not pass.°
OTHELLO: I know, Iago,
Thy honesty and love doth mince this matter,   225
Making it light to Cassio. Cassio, I love thee;
But never more be officer of mine.

Enter Desdemona, attended.

Look if my gentle love be not raised up!
I'll make thee an example.
DESDEMONA: What's the matter?
OTHELLO: All's well now, sweeting; come away to bed.   230
  [*To Montano.*]
Sir, for your hurts, myself will be your surgeon.
Lead him off.

[*Montano is led off.*]

Iago, look with care about the town
And silence those whom this vile brawl distracted.°
Come, Desdemona; 'tis the soldiers' life   235
To have their balmy slumbers waked with strife.
                              Exit [*with all but Iago and Cassio*].
IAGO: What, are you hurt, lieutenant?
CASSIO: Ay, past all surgery.
IAGO: Marry, God forbid!
CASSIO: Reputation, reputation, reputation! O, I have lost my reputa- 240
  tion! I have lost the immortal part of myself, and what remains is
  bestial. My reputation, Iago, my reputation!
IAGO: As I am an honest man, I thought you had received some bodily
  wound. There is more sense in that than in reputation. Reputation
  is an idle and most false imposition; oft got without merit and lost 245
  without deserving. You have lost no reputation at all unless you repute yourself such a loser. What, man! there are ways to recover°
  the general again. You are but now cast in his mood°—a punish-

---
224. pass: Pass over, ignore.   **234. distracted:** Excited.   **247. recover:** Regain favor with.
248. in his mood: Dismissed because of his anger.

ment more in policy than in malice, even so as one would beat his
offenseless dog to affright an imperious lion. Sue to him again, and 250
he's yours.

CASSIO: I will rather sue to be despised than to deceive so good a com-
mander with so slight, so drunken, and so indiscreet an officer.
Drunk! and speak parrot!° and squabble! swagger! swear! and discourse fustian° with one's own shadow! O thou invisible spirit of 255
wine, if thou hast no name to be known by, let us call thee devil!

IAGO: What was he that you followed with your sword? What had he
done to you?

CASSIO: I know not.

IAGO: Is't possible?   260

CASSIO: I remember a mass of things, but nothing distinctly; a quarrel,
but nothing wherefore. O God, that men should put an enemy in
their mouths to steal away their brains! that we should with joy,
pleasance, revel, and applause° transform ourselves into beasts!

IAGO: Why, but you are now well enough. How came you thus recovered? 265

CASSIO: It hath pleased the devil drunkenness to give place to the devil
wrath. One unperfectness shows me another, to make me frankly
despise myself.

IAGO: Come, you are too severe a moraler. As the time, the place, and
the condition of this country stands, I could heartily wish this had 270
not so befall'n; but since it is as it is, mend it for your own good.

CASSIO: I will ask him for my place again: he shall tell me I am a drunk-
ard! Had I as many mouths as Hydra,° such an answer would stop
them all. To be now a sensible man, by and by a fool, and presently a
beast! O strange! Every inordinate cup is unblest, and the ingredi- 275
ent° is a devil.

IAGO: Come, come, good wine is a good familiar creature if it be well
used. Exclaim no more against it. And, good lieutenant, I think you
think I love you.

CASSIO: I have well approved° it, sir. I drunk!   280

IAGO: You or any man living may be drunk at some time, man. I'll tell
you what you shall do. Our general's wife is now the general. I may
say so in this respect, for that he hath devoted and given up himself
to the contemplation, mark, and denotement of her parts and
graces. Confess yourself freely to her; importune her help to put you 285
in your place again. She is of so free,° so kind, so apt, so blessed a
disposition she holds it a vice in her goodness not to do more than
she is requested. This broken joint between you and her husband
entreat her to splinter;° and my fortunes against any lay° worth

---

254. **parrot:** Meaningless phrases. 255. **fustian:** Bombastic nonsense. 264. **applause:**
Desire to please. 273. **Hydra:** Monster with many heads. 275–76. **ingredient:** Contents.
280. **approved:** Proved. 286. **free:** Bounteous. 289. **splinter:** Bind up with splints; **lay:**
Wager.

naming, this crack of your love shall grow stronger than it was   290
before.

CASSIO: You advise me well.

IAGO: I protest, in the sincerity of love and honest kindness.

CASSIO: I think it freely; and betimes in the morning will I beseech the
virtuous Desdemona to undertake for me. I am desperate of my for-   295
tunes if they check me here.

IAGO: You are in the right. Good night, lieutenant; I must to the watch.

CASSIO: Good night, honest Iago.   *Exit Cassio.*

IAGO: And what's he then that says I play the villain,
When this advice is free I give and honest,   300
Probal° to thinking, and indeed the course
To win the Moor again? For 'tis most easy
Th' inclining Desdemona to subdue°
In an honest suit; she's framed as fruitful
As the free elements. And then for her   305
To win the Moor — were't to renounce his baptism,
All seals and symbols of redeemèd sin —
His soul is so enfettered to her love
That she may make, unmake, do what she list,
Even as her appetite shall play the god   310
With his weak function. How am I then a villain
To counsel Cassio to this parallel° course,
Directly to his good? Divinity° of hell!
When devils will the blackest sins put on,°
They do suggest at first with heavenly shows,   315
As I do now. For whiles this honest fool
Plies Desdemona to repair his fortunes,
And she for him pleads strongly to the Moor,
I'll pour this pestilence into his ear,
That she repeals him° for her body's lust;   320
And by how much she strives to do him good,
She shall undo her credit with the Moor.
So will I turn her virtue into pitch,
And out of her own goodness make the net
That shall enmesh them all.

Enter Roderigo.

                                    How, now, Roderigo?   325

RODERIGO: I do follow here in the chase, not like a hound that hunts,
but one that fills up the cry.° My money is almost spent; I have been
to-night exceedingly well cudgelled; and I think the issue will be — I

---

301. Probal: Probable.   **303. subdue:** Persuade.   **312. parallel:** Corresponding.   **313. Divinity:** Theology.   **314. put on:** Incite.   **320. repeals him:** Seeks his recall.   **327. cry:** Pack.

shall have so much experience for my pains; and so, with no money
at all, and a little more wit, return again to Venice.   330

IAGO: How poor are they that have not patience!
What wound did ever heal but by degrees?
Thou know'st we work by wit, and not by witchcraft;
And wit depends on dilatory time.
Does't not go well? Cassio hath beaten thee,   335
And thou by that small hurt hast cashiered Cassio.°
Though other things grow fair against the sun,
Yet fruits that blossom first will first be ripe.
Content thyself awhile. By the mass, 'tis morning!
Pleasure and action make the hours seem short.   340
Retire thee; go where thou art billeted.
Away, I say! Thou shalt know more hereafter.
Nay, get thee gone!   *Exit Roderigo.*
                 Two things are to be done:
My wife must move for Cassio to her mistress;
I'll set her on;   345
Myself the while to draw the Moor apart
And bring him jump° when he may Cassio find
Soliciting his wife. Ay, that's the way!
Dull no device by coldness and delay.   *Exit.*

ACT III / Scene I

Before the chamber of Othello and Desdemona.

Enter Cassio, with Musicians and the Clown.

CASSIO: Masters, play here, I will content° your pains:
Something that's brief; and bid "Good morrow, general."

[*They play.*]

CLOWN: Why, masters, ha' your instruments been in Naples,° that they
speak i' th' nose thus?
MUSICIAN: How, sir, how?   5
CLOWN: Are these, I pray you, called wind instruments?
MUSICIAN: Ay, marry, are they, sir.
CLOWN: O, thereby hangs a tail.
MUSICIAN: Whereby hangs a tail, sir?
CLOWN: Marry, sir, by many a wind instrument that I know. But, mas-   10
ters, here's money for you; and the general so likes your music that
he desires you, for love's sake, to make no more noise with it.
MUSICIAN: Well, sir, we will not.

---

336. **cashiered Cassio:** Maneuvered Cassio's discharge.   347. **jump:** At the exact moment.
ACT III, SCENE I.   1. **content:** Reward.   3. **Naples:** (Notorious for its association with venereal disease).

CLOWN: If you have any music that may not be heard, to't again: but, as
    they say, to hear music the general does not greatly care.   15
MUSICIAN: We have none such, sir.
CLOWN: Then put up your pipes in your bag, for I'll away. Go, vanish into
    air, away!   *Exit Musician [with his fellows].*
CASSIO: Dost thou hear, my honest friend?
CLOWN: No, I hear not your honest friend. I hear you.   20
CASSIO: Prithee keep up thy quillets.° There's a poor piece of gold for
    thee. If the gentlewoman that attends the general's wife be stirring,
    tell her there's one Cassio entreats her a little favor of speech. Wilt
    thou do this?
CLOWN: She is stirring sir. If she will stir hither, I shall seem to notify   25
    unto her.
CASSIO: [Do, good my friend.]   *Exit Clown.*

Enter Iago.

                     In happy time,° Iago.
IAGO: You have not been abed then?
CASSIO: Why, no; the day had broke
    Before we parted. I have made bold, Iago,   30
    To send in to your wife: my suit to her
    Is that she will to virtuous Desdemona
    Procure me some access.
IAGO: I'll send her to you presently;
    And I'll devise a mean to draw the Moor
    Out of the way, that your converse and business   35
    May be more free.
CASSIO: I humbly thank you for't.   *Exit [Iago].*
                    I never knew
    A Florentine° more kind and honest.

Enter Emilia.

EMILIA: Good morrow, good lieutenant. I am sorry
    For your displeasure: but all will sure be well.   40
    The general and his wife are talking of it,
    And she speaks for you stoutly. The Moor replied
    That he you hurt is of great fame in Cyprus
    And great affinity,° and that in wholesome wisdom
    He might not but refuse you; but he protests he loves you,   45
    And needs no other suitor but his likings
    [To take the safest occasion° by the front°]
    To bring you in again.

---

21. quillets: Quips.   **27. In happy time:** Well met.   **38. Florentine:** I.e., even a Florentine
(like Cassio; Iago was a Venetian).   **44. affinity:** Family connections.   **47. occasion:** Opportunity; **front:** Forelock.

CASSIO: Yet I beseech you,
   If you think fit, or that it may be done,
   Give me advantage of some brief discourse   50
   With Desdemona alone.
EMILIA: Pray you come in.
   I will bestow you where you shall have time
   To speak your bosom° freely.
CASSIO: I am much bound to you.   *Exeunt.*

Scene II

The castle.

Enter Othello, Iago, and Gentlemen.

OTHELLO: These letters give, Iago, to the pilot
   And by him do my duties to the Senate.
   That done, I will be walking on the works;°
   Repair there to me.
IAGO: Well, my good lord, I'll do't.
OTHELLO: This fortification, gentlemen, shall we see't?   5
GENTLEMEN: We'll wait upon your lordship.   *Exeunt.*

Scene III

The castle grounds.

Enter Desdemona, Cassio, and Emilia.

DESDEMONA: Be thou assured, good Cassio, I will do
   All my abilities in thy behalf.
EMILIA: Good madam, do. I warrant it grieves my husband
   As if the cause were his.
DESDEMONA: O, that's an honest fellow. Do not doubt, Cassio,   5
   But I will have my lord and you again
   As friendly as you were.
CASSIO: Bounteous madam,
   Whatever shall become of Michael Cassio,
   He's never anything but your true servant.
DESDEMONA: I know't; I thank you. You do love my lord;   10
   You have known him long; and be you well assured
   He shall in strangeness° stand no farther off
   Than in a politic distance.°
CASSIO: Ay, but, lady,
   That policy may either last so long,
   Or feed upon such nice and waterish diet,°   15

---

53. your bosom: Your inmost thoughts.   SCENE II.   **3. works:** Fortifications.   SCENE III.
12. strangeness: Aloofness.   **13. Than ... distance:** Than wise policy requires.   **15. Or ...
diet:** Or be continued for such slight reasons.

> Or breed itself so out of circumstance,
> That, I being absent, and my place supplied,
> My general will forget my love and service.
>
> DESDEMONA: Do not doubt° that; before Emilia here
> I give thee warrant of thy place. Assure thee,   20
> If I do vow a friendship, I'll perform it
> To the last article. My lord shall never rest;
> I'll watch him tame° and talk him out of patience;
> His bed shall seem a school, his board a shrift;°
> I'll intermingle everything he does   25
> With Cassio's suit. Therefore be merry, Cassio,
> For thy solicitor shall rather die
> Than give thy cause away.

Enter Othello and Iago [at a distance].

> EMILIA: Madam, here comes my lord.
> CASSIO: Madam, I'll take my leave.   30
> DESDEMONA: Why, stay, and hear me speak.
> CASSIO: Madam, not now: I am very ill at ease,
>   Unfit for mine own purposes.
> DESDEMONA: Well, do your discretion.   *Exit Cassio.*
> IAGO: Ha! I like not that.
> OTHELLO: What dost thou say?   35
> IAGO: Nothing, my lord; or if—I know not what.
> OTHELLO: Was not that Cassio parted from my wife?
> IAGO: Cassio, my lord? No, sure, I cannot think it,
>   That he would steal away so guilty-like,
>   Seeing your coming.
> OTHELLO: I do believe 'twas he.   40
> DESDEMONA: How now, my lord?
>   I have been talking with a suitor here,
>   A man that languishes in your displeasure.
> OTHELLO: What is't you mean?
> DESDEMONA: Why, your lieutenant, Cassio. Good my lord,   45
>   If I have any grace or power to move you,
>   His present° reconciliation take;
>   For if he be not one that truly loves you,
>   That errs in ignorance, and not in cunning,
>   I have no judgment in an honest face,   50
>   I prithee call him back.
> OTHELLO: Went he hence now?
> DESDEMONA: Yes, faith; so humbled

---

19. **doubt:** Fear.   23. **watch him tame:** Keep him awake until he gives in.   24. **shrift:** Confessional.   47. **present:** Immediate.

That he hath left part of his grief with me
To suffer with him. Good love, call him back.
OTHELLO: Not now, sweet Desdemon; some other time.   55
DESDEMONA: But shall't be shortly?
OTHELLO: The sooner, sweet, for you.
DESDEMONA: Shall't be to-night at supper?
OTHELLO: No, not to-night.
DESDEMONA: To-morrow dinner then?
OTHELLO: I shall not dine at home;
    I meet the captains at the citadel.
DESDEMONA: Why then, to-morrow night, or Tuesday morn,   60
    On Tuesday noon or night, or Wednesday morn.
    I prithee name the time, but let it not
    Exceed three days. I' faith, he's penitent;
    And yet his trespass, in our common reason
    (Save that, they say, the wars must make examples   65
    Out of their best), is not almost° a fault
    T' incur a private check.° When shall he come?
    Tell me, Othello. I wonder in my soul
    What you could ask me that I should deny
    Or stand so mamm'ring on.° What? Michael Cassio,   70
    That came a-wooing with you, and so many a time,
    When I have spoke of you dispraisingly,
    Hath ta'en your part — to have so much to do
    To bring him in? By'r Lady, I could do much —
OTHELLO: Prithee no more. Let him come when he will!   75
    I will deny thee nothing.
DESDEMONA: Why, this is not a boon;
    'Tis as I should entreat you wear your gloves,
    Or feed on nourishing dishes, or keep you warm,
    Or sue to you to do a peculiar profit
    To your own person. Nay, when I have a suit   80
    Wherein I mean to touch your love indeed,
    It shall be full of poise and difficult weight,
    And fearful° to be granted.
OTHELLO: I will deny thee nothing!
    Whereon I do beseech thee grant me this,
    To leave me but a little to myself.   85
DESDEMONA: Shall I deny you? No. Farewell, my lord.
OTHELLO: Farewell, my Desdemon: I'll come to thee straight.
DESDEMONA: Emilia, come. — Be as your fancies teach you;
    Whate'er you be, I am obedient.   *Exit [with Emilia].*

---

66. **not almost:** Hardly.   67. **a private check:** Even a private reprimand.   70. **mamm'ring
on:** Hesitating about.   83. **fearful:** Dangerous.

OTHELLO: Excellent wretch!° Perdition catch my soul   90
    But I do love thee! and when I love thee not,
    Chaos is come again.
IAGO: My noble lord —
OTHELLO: What dost thou say, Iago?
IAGO: Did Michael Cassio, when you wooed my lady,
    Know of your love?   95
OTHELLO: He did, from first to last. Why dost thou ask?
IAGO: But for a satisfaction of my thought;
    No further harm.
OTHELLO: Why of thy thought, Iago?
IAGO: I did not think he had been acquainted with her.
OTHELLO: O, yes, and went between us° very oft.   100
IAGO: Indeed?
OTHELLO: Indeed? Ay, indeed! Discern'st thou aught in that?
    Is he not honest?
IAGO: Honest, my lord?
OTHELLO: Honest. Ay, honest.
IAGO: My lord, for aught I know.
OTHELLO: What dost thou think?
IAGO: Think, my lord?
OTHELLO: Think, my lord?   105
    By heaven, he echoes me,
    As if there were some monster in his thought
    Too hideous to be shown. Thou dost mean something:
    I heard thee say even now, thou lik'st not that,
    When Cassio left my wife. What didst not like?   110
    And when I told thee he was of my counsel
    In my whole course of wooing, thou cried'st "Indeed?"
    And didst contract and purse thy brow together,
    As if thou then hadst shut up in thy brain
    Some horrible conceit.° If thou dost love me,   115
    Show me thy thought
IAGO: My lord, you know I love you.
OTHELLO: I think thou dost;
    And, for I know thou'rt full of love and honesty
    And weigh'st thy words before thou giv'st them breath,
    Therefore these stops of thine fright me the more;   120
    For such things in a false disloyal knave
    Are tricks of custom; but in a man that's just
    They are close dilations, working from the heart
    That passion cannot rule.°

---

90. wretch: (A term of endearment).   100. went . . . us: (I.e., as messenger).   115. conceit:
Fancy.   123–24. close dilations . . . rule: Secret emotions which well up in spite of restraint.

IAGO: For Michael Cassio,
    I dare be sworn I think that he is honest.   125
OTHELLO: I think so too.
IAGO: Men should be what they seem;
    Or those that be not, would they might seem none!°
OTHELLO: Certain, men should be what they seem.
IAGO: Why then, I think Cassio's an honest man.
OTHELLO: Nay, yet there's more in this.   130
    I prithee speak to me as to thy thinkings,
    As thou dost ruminate, and give thy worst of thoughts
    The worst of words.
IAGO: Good my lord, pardon me:
    Though I am bound to every act of duty,
    I am not bound to that all slaves are free to.°   135
    Utter my thoughts? Why, say they are vile and false,
    As where's that palace whereinto foul things
    Sometimes intrude not? Who has a breast so pure
    But some uncleanly apprehensions
    Keep leets and law days,° and in Sessions sit   140
    With meditations lawful?
OTHELLO: Thou dost conspire against thy friend, Iago,
    If thou but think'st him wronged, and mak'st his ear
    A stranger to thy thoughts.
IAGO: I do beseech you —
    Though I perchance am vicious in my guess   145
    (As I confess it is my nature's plague
    To spy into abuses, and oft my jealousy°
    Shapes faults that are not), that your wisdom yet
    From one that so imperfectly conjects°
    Would take no notice, nor build yourself a trouble   150
    Out of his scattering and unsure observance.
    It were not for your quiet nor your good,
    Nor for my manhood, honesty, and wisdom,
    To let you know my thoughts.
OTHELLO: What dost thou mean?
IAGO: Good name in man and woman, dear my lord,   155
    Is the immediate° jewel of their souls.
    Who steals my purse steals trash; 'tis something, nothing;
    'Twas mine, 'tis his, and has been slave to thousands;
    But he that filches from me my good name

---

127. **seem none:** I.e., not pretend to be men when they are really monsters.   **135. bound . . . free to:** Bound to tell that which even slaves are allowed to keep to themselves.   **140. leets and law days:** Sittings of the courts.   **147. jealousy:** Suspicion.   **149. conjects:** Conjectures.   **156. immediate:** Nearest the heart.

Robs me of that which not enriches him   160
    And makes me poor indeed.
OTHELLO: By heaven, I'll know thy thoughts!
IAGO: You cannot, if my heart were in your hand;
    Nor shall not whilst 'tis in my custody.
OTHELLO: Ha!
IAGO: O, beware, my lord, of jealousy!   165
    It is the green-eyed monster, which doth mock°
    The meat it feeds on. That cuckold lives in bliss
    Who, certain of his fate, loves not his wronger;
    But O, what damnèd minutes tells he o'er
    Who dotes, yet doubts—suspects, yet strongly loves!   170
OTHELLO: O misery!
IAGO: Poor and content is rich, and rich enough;
    But riches fineless° is as poor as winter
    To him that ever fears he shall be poor.
    Good God, the souls of all my tribe defend   175
    From jealousy!
OTHELLO: Why, why is this?
    Think'st thou I'ld make a life of jealousy,
    To follow still the changes of the moon
    With fresh suspicions? No! To be once in doubt
    Is once to be resolved. Exchange me for a goat   180
    When I shall turn the business of my soul
    To such exsufflicate and blown° surmises,
    Matching this inference. 'Tis not to make me jealous
    To say my wife is fair, feeds well, loves company,
    Is free of speech, sings, plays, and dances;   185
    Where virtue is, these are more virtuous.
    Nor from mine own weak merits will I draw
    The smallest fear or doubt of her revolt,°
    For she had eyes, and chose me. No, Iago;
    I'll see before I doubt; when I doubt, prove;   190
    And on the proof there is no more but this—
    Away at once with love or jealousy!
IAGO: I am glad of this; for now I shall have reason
    To show the love and duty that I bear you
    With franker spirit. Therefore, as I am bound,   195
    Receive it from me. I speak not yet of proof.
    Look at your wife; observe her well with Cassio;
    Wear your eyes thus, not jealous nor secure:°

---

166. **mock:** Play with, like a cat with a mouse.   173. **fineless:** Unlimited.   182. **exsufflicate and blown:** Spat out and flyblown.   188. **revolt:** Unfaithfulness.   198. **secure:** Overconfident.

I would not have your free and noble nature,
Out of self-bounty,° be abused. Look to't.   200
I know our country disposition well:
In Venice they do let God see the pranks
They dare not show their husbands; their best conscience
Is not to leave't undone, but keep't unknown.
OTHELLO: Dost thou say so?   205
IAGO: She did deceive her father, marrying you;
   And when she seemed to shake and fear your looks,
   She loved them most.
OTHELLO: And so she did.
IAGO: Why, go to then!
   She that, so young, could give out such a seeming
   To seel° her father's eyes up close as oak° —   210
   He thought 'twas witchcraft — but I am much to blame.
   I humbly do beseech you of your pardon
   For too much loving you.
OTHELLO: I am bound to thee for ever.
IAGO: I see this hath a little dashed your spirits.
OTHELLO: Not a jot, not a jot.
IAGO: I' faith, I fear it has.   215
   I hope you will consider what is spoke
   Comes from my love. But I do see y' are moved.
   I am to pray you not to strain my speech
   To grosser issues° nor to larger reach
   Than to suspicion.   220
OTHELLO: I will not.
IAGO: Should you do so, my lord,
   My speech should fall into such vile success°
   As my thoughts aim not at. Cassio's my worthy friend —
   My lord, I see y' are moved.
OTHELLO: No, not much moved:
   I do not think but Desdemona's honest.°   225
IAGO: Long live she so! and long live you to think so!
OTHELLO: And yet, how nature erring from itself —
IAGO: Ay, there's the point! as (to be bold with you)
   Not to affect many proposèd matches
   Of her own clime, complexion, and degree,   230
   Whereto we see in all things nature tends —
   Foh! one may smell in such a will most rank,
   Foul disproportions, thought unnatural —

---

200. **self-bounty:** Natural goodness.   210. **seel:** Close; **oak:** Oak grain.   219. **To grosser issues:** To mean something more monstrous.   222. **vile success:** Evil outcome.   225. **honest:** Chaste.

But pardon me — I do not in position°
Distinctly speak of her; though I may fear   235
Her will, recoiling° to her better judgment,
May fall to match° you with her country forms,
And happily° repent.
OTHELLO: Farewell, farewell!
If more thou dost perceive, let me know more.
Set on thy wife to observe. Leave me, Iago.   240
IAGO: My lord, I take my leave.   [*Going.*]
OTHELLO: Why did I marry? This honest creature doubtless
Sees and knows more, much more, than he unfolds.
IAGO [*returns*]: My lord, I would I might entreat your honor
To scan this thing no further: leave it to time.   245
Although 'tis fit that Cassio have his place,
For sure he fills it up with great ability,
Yet, if you please to hold off a while,
You shall by that perceive him and his means.
Note if your lady strain his entertainment°   250
With any strong or vehement importunity;
Much will be seen in that. In the mean time
Let me be thought too busy° in my fears
(As worthy cause I have to fear I am)
And hold her free,° I do beseech your honor.   255
OTHELLO: Fear not my government.°
IAGO: I once more take my leave.   *Exit.*
OTHELLO: This fellow 's of exceeding honesty,
And knows all qualities,° with a learned spirit
Of° human dealings. If I do prove her haggard,°   260
Though that her jesses° were my dear heartstrings,
I'd whistle her off and let her down the wind
To prey at fortune.° Haply, for I am black
And have not those soft parts of conversation°
That chamberers° have, or for I am declined   265
Into the vale of years — yet that's not much —
She's gone. I am abused, and my relief
Must be to loathe her. O curse of marriage,
That we can call these delicate creatures ours,
And not their appetites! I had rather be a toad   270

---

234. position: Definite assertion.   **236. recoiling:** Reverting.   **237. fall to match:** Happen
to compare.   **238. happily:** Haply, perhaps.   **250. strain his entertainment:** Urge his recall.
253. busy: Meddlesome.   **255. hold her free:** Consider her guiltless.   **256. government:**
Self-control.   **259. qualities:** Natures.   **259–60. learned spirit Of:** Mind informed about.
260. haggard: A wild hawk.   **261. jesses:** Thongs for controlling a hawk.   **262–63. whistle
. . . fortune:** Turn her out and let her take care of herself.   **264. soft . . . conversation:** In-
gratiating manners.   **265. chamberers:** Courtiers.

And live upon the vapor of a dungeon
Than keep a corner in the thing I love
For others' uses. Yet 'tis the plague of great ones;°
Prerogatived° are they less than the base.
'Tis destiny unshunnable, like death.　　　　　　　　　　　　275
Even then this forkèd plague° is fated to us
When we do quicken.° Look where she comes.

Enter Desdemona and Emilia.

If she be false, O, then heaven mocks itself!
I'll not believe't.
DESDEMONA:　　　　　How now, my dear Othello?
Your dinner, and the generous° islanders　　　　　　　　280
By you invited, do attend your presence.
OTHELLO: I am to blame.
DESDEMONA:　　　　　　Why do you speak so faintly?
Are you not well?
OTHELLO: I have a pain upon my forehead, here.
DESDEMONA: Faith, that's with watching;° 'twill away again.　　　285
Let me but bind it hard, within this hour
It will be well.
OTHELLO:　　　　Your napkin° is too little;

[*He pushes the handkerchief from him, and it falls unnoticed.*]

Let it° alone. Come, I'll go in with you.
DESDEMONA: I am very sorry that you are not well.　　　　*Exit [with Othello].*
EMILIA: I am glad I have found this napkin;　　　　　　　290
This was her first remembrance from the Moor,
My wayward husband hath a hundred times
Wooed me to steal it; but she so loves the token
(For he conjured her she should ever keep it)
That she reserves it evermore about her　　　　　　　　295
To kiss and talk to. I'll have the work ta'en out°
And give't Iago.
What he will do with it heaven knows, not I;
I nothing but to please his fantasy.°

Enter Iago.

IAGO: How now? What do you here alone?　　　　　　　300
EMILIA: Do not you chide; I have a thing for you.

---

273. **great ones:** Prominent men.　274. **Prerogatived:** Privileged.　276. **forkèd plague:** I.e.,
horns of a cuckold.　277. **do quicken:** Are born.　280. **generous:** Noble.　285. **watching:**
Working late.　287. **napkin:** Handkerchief.　288. **it:** I.e., his forehead.　296. **work ta'en
out:** Pattern copied.　299. **fantasy:** Whim.

IAGO: A thing for me? It is a common thing —
EMILIA: Ha?
IAGO: To have a foolish wife.
EMILIA: O, is that all? What will you give me now   305
    For that same handkerchief?
IAGO: What handkerchief?
EMILIA: What handkerchief!
    Why, that the Moor first gave to Desdemona;
    That which so often you did bid me steal.
IAGO: Hast stol'n it from her?   310
EMILIA: No, faith; she let it drop by negligence,
    And to th' advantage,° I, being here, took't up.
    Look, here it is.
IAGO: A good wench! Give it me.
EMILIA: What will you do with't, that you have been so earnest
    To have me filch it?
IAGO: Why, what is that to you?   315

[*Snatches it.*]

EMILIA: If it be not for some purpose of import,°
    Give't me again. Poor lady, she'll run mad
    When she shall lack it.
IAGO: Be not acknown on't;° I have use for it.
    Go, leave me.   *Exit Emilia.* 320
    I will in Cassio's lodgings lose this napkin
    And let him find it. Trifles light as air
    Are to the jealous confirmations strong
    As proofs of holy writ. This may do something.
    The Moor already changes with my poison: 325
    Dangerous conceits° are in their nature poisons,
    Which at the first are scarce found to distaste,
    But with a little act upon the blood
    Burn like the mines of sulphur.

Enter Othello.

                                       I did say so.
    Look where he comes! Not poppy nor mandragora,°   330
    Nor all the drowsy syrups of the world,
    Shall ever med'cine thee to that sweet sleep
    Which thou owedst yesterday.
OTHELLO: Ha! ha! false to me?
IAGO: Why, how now, general? No more of that!

---

312. **to th' advantage:** Opportunely.   316. **import:** Importance.   319. **Be . . . on't:** Do not
acknowledge it.   326. **conceits:** Ideas.   330. **mandragora:** A narcotic.

OTHELLO: Avaunt! be gone! Thou hast set me on the rack.   335
    I swear 'tis better to be much abused
    Than but to know't a little.
IAGO: How now, my lord?
OTHELLO: What sense had I of her stol'n hours of lust?
    I saw't not, thought it not, it harmed not me;
    I slept the next night well, fed well, was free° and merry;   340
    I found not Cassio's kisses on her lips
    He that is robbed, not wanting° what is stol'n,
    Let him not know't, and he's not robbed at all.
IAGO: I am sorry to hear this.
OTHELLO: I had been happy if the general camp,   345
    Pioneers° and all, had tasted her sweet body,
    So I had nothing known. O, now for ever
    Farewell the tranquil mind! farewell content!
    Farewell the plumèd troop, and the big° wars
    That make ambition virtue! O, farewell!   350
    Farewell the neighing steed and the shrill trump,
    The spirit-stirring drum, th' ear-piercing fife,
    The royal banner, and all quality,
    Pride, pomp, and circumstance° of glorious war!
    And O you mortal engines° whose rude throats   355
    Th' immortal Jove's dread clamors counterfeit,°
    Farewell! Othello's occupation's gone!
IAGO: Is't possible, my lord?
OTHELLO: Villain, be sure thou prove my love a whore!
    Be sure of it; give me the ocular proof;   360
    Or, by the worth of mine eternal soul,
    Thou hadst been better have been born a dog
    Than answer my waked wrath!
IAGO: Is't come to this?
OTHELLO: Make me to see't; or at the least so prove it
    That the probation° bear no hinge nor loop   365
    To hang a doubt on — or woe upon thy life!
IAGO: My noble lord —
OTHELLO: If thou dost slander her and torture me,
    Never pray more; abandon all remorse;
    On horror's head horrors accumulate;   370
    Do deeds to make heaven weep, all earth amazed;
    For nothing canst thou to damnation add
    Greater than that.

---

340. **free:** Carefree. 342. **wanting:** Missing. 346. **Pioneers:** Sappers, laborers. 349. **big:** Stately. 354. **circumstance:** Pageantry. 355. **mortal engines:** Deadly artillery. 356. **counterfeit:** Imitate. 365. **probation:** Proof.

IAGO: O grace! O heaven forgive me!
  Are you a man? Have you a soul or sense? —
  God b' wi' you! take mine office. O wretched fool,   375
  That liv'st to make thine honesty a vice!
  O monstrous world! Take note, take note, O world,
  To be direct and honest is not safe.
  I thank you for this profit;° and from hence
  I'll love no friend, sith love breeds such offense.   380
OTHELLO: Nay, stay. Thou shouldst be honest.
IAGO: I should be wise; for honesty's a fool
  And loses that it works for.
OTHELLO: By the world,
  I think my wife be honest, and think she is not;
  I think that thou art just, and think thou art not.   385
  I'll have some proof. Her name, that was as fresh
  As Dian's visage, is now begrimed and black
  As mine own face. If there be cords, or knives,
  Poison, or fire, or suffocating streams,
  I'll not endure it. Would I were satisfied!°   390
IAGO: I see, sir, you are eaten up with passion:
  I do repent me that I put it to you.
  You would be satisfied?
OTHELLO: Would? Nay, I will.
IAGO: And may; but how? how satisfied, my lord?
  Would you, the supervisor,° grossly gape on?   395
  Behold her topped?
OTHELLO: Death and damnation! O!
IAGO: It were a tedious difficulty, I think,
  To bring them to that prospect. Damn them then,
  If ever mortal eyes do see them bolster°
  More than their own! What then? How then?   400
  What shall I say? Where's satisfaction?
  It is impossible you should see this,
  Were they as prime° as goats, as hot as monkeys,
  As salt° as wolves in pride,° and fools as gross
  As ignorance made drunk. But yet, I say,   405
  If imputation and strong circumstances
  Which lead directly to the door of truth
  Will give you satisfaction, you may have't.
OTHELLO: Give me a living reason she's disloyal.
IAGO: I do not like the office.   410
  But sith I am ent'red in this cause so far,

---

379. profit: Profitable lesson. **390. satisfied:** Completely informed. **395. supervisor:** Spectator. **399. bolster:** Lie together. **403. prime:** Lustful. **404. salt:** Lecherous; **pride:** Heat.

Pricked to't by foolish honesty and love,
I will go on. I lay with Cassio lately,
And being troubled with a raging tooth,
I could not sleep.   415
There are a kind of men so loose of soul
That in their sleeps will mutter their affairs.
One of this kind is Cassio.
In sleep I heard him say, "Sweet Desdemona,
Let us be wary, let us hide our loves!"   420
And then, sir, would he gripe and wring my hand,
Cry "O sweet creature!" and then kiss me hard,
As if he plucked up kisses by the roots
That grew upon my lips; then laid his leg
Over my thigh, and sighed, and kissed, and then   425
Cried "Cursèd fate that gave thee to the Moor!"
OTHELLO: O monstrous! monstrous!
IAGO: Nay, this was but his dream.
OTHELLO: But this denoted a foregone conclusion;°
'Tis a shrewd doubt,° though it be but a dream.
IAGO: And this may help to thicken other proofs   430
That do demonstrate thinly.
OTHELLO: I'll tear her all to pieces!
IAGO: Nay, but be wise. Yet we see nothing done;
She may be honest yet. Tell me but this —
Have you not sometimes seen a handkerchief
Spotted with strawberries in your wife's hand?   435
OTHELLO: I gave her such a one; 'twas my first gift.
IAGO: I know not that; but such a handkerchief —
I am sure it was your wife's — did I to-day
See Cassio wipe his beard with.
OTHELLO: If it be that —
IAGO: If it be that, or any that was hers,   440
It speaks against her with the other proofs.
OTHELLO: O, that the slave had forty thousand lives!
One is too poor, too weak for my revenge.
Now do I see 'tis true. Look here, Iago:
All my fond love thus do I blow to heaven.   445
'Tis gone.
Arise, black vengeance, from the hollow hell!
Yield up, O love, thy crown and hearted throne
To tyrannous hate! Swell, bosom, with thy fraught,°
For 'tis of aspics'° tongues!
IAGO: Yet be content.   450

428. **foregone conclusion:** Previous experience.   429. **a shrewd doubt:** Cursedly suspicious.
449. **fraught:** Burden.   450. **aspics:** Deadly poisonous snakes.

OTHELLO: O, blood, blood, blood!

IAGO: Patience, I say. Your mind perhaps may change.

OTHELLO: Never, Iago. Like to the Pontic sea,°
    Whose icy current and compulsive course
    Ne'er feels retiring ebb, but keeps due on   455
    To the Propontic and the Hellespont,
    Even so my bloody thoughts, with violent pace,
    Shall ne'er look back, ne'er ebb to humble love,
    Till that a capable° and wide revenge
    Swallow them up.
    (*He kneels.*)   Now, by yond marble heaven,   460
    In the due reverence of a sacred vow
    I here engage my words.

IAGO: Do not rise yet.
(*Iago kneels.*)
    Witness, you ever-burning lights above,
    You elements that clip° us round about,
    Witness that here Iago doth give up   465
    The execution° of his wit,° hands, heart
    To wronged Othello's service! Let him command,
    And to obey shall be in me remorse,°
    What bloody business ever.

[*They rise.*]

OTHELLO: I greet thy love,
    Not with vain thanks but with acceptance bounteous,   470
    And will upon the instant put thee to't.
    Within these three days let me hear thee say
    That Cassio's not alive.

IAGO: My friend is dead; 'tis done at your request.
    But let her live.   475

OTHELLO: Damn her, lewd minx! O, damn her! damn her!
    Come, go with me apart. I will withdraw
    To furnish me with some swift means of death
    For the fair devil. Now art thou my lieutenant.

IAGO: I am your own forever.   *Exeunt.* 480

Scene IV

The environs of the castle.

Enter Desdemona, Emilia, and Clown.

DESDEMONA: Do you know, sirrah, where Lieutenant Cassio lies?°

CLOWN: I dare not say he lies anywhere.

---

453. **Pontic sea:** Black Sea.   459. **capable:** All-embracing.   464. **clip:** Encompass.   466. **execution:** Activities; **wit:** Mind.   468. **remorse:** Pity.   SCENE IV.   1. **lies:** Lives, lodges.

DESDEMONA: Why, man?

CLOWN: He's a soldier, and for me to say a soldier lies is stabbing.

DESDEMONA: Go to. Where lodges he?   5

CLOWN: To tell you where he lodges is to tell you where I lie.

DESDEMONA: Can anything be made of this?

CLOWN: I know not where he lodges; and for me to devise a lodging, and
    say he lies here or he lies there, were to lie in mine own throat.

DESDEMONA: Can you enquire him out, and be edified by report?   10

CLOWN: I will catechize the world for him; that is, make questions, and
    by them answer.

DESDEMONA: Seek him, bid him come hither. Tell him I have moved° my
    lord on his behalf and hope all will be well.

CLOWN: To do this is within the compass of man's wit, and therefore   15
    I'll attempt the doing of it.   *Exit.*

DESDEMONA: Where should I lose that handkerchief, Emilia?

EMILIA: I know not, madam.

DESDEMONA: Believe me, I had rather have lost my purse
    Full of crusadoes;° and but my noble Moor   20
    Is true of mind, and made of no such baseness
    As jealous creatures are, it were enough
    To put him to ill thinking.

EMILIA: Is he not jealous?

DESDEMONA: Who? he? I think the sun where he was born
    Drew all such humors° from him.

Enter Othello.

EMILIA: Look where he comes.   25

DESDEMONA: I will not leave him now till Cassio
    Be called to him — How is't with you, my lord?

OTHELLO: Well, my good lady. [*Aside.*] O, hardness to dissemble! —
    How do you, Desdemona?

DESDEMONA: Well, my good lord.

OTHELLO: Give me your hand. This hand is moist, my lady.   30

DESDEMONA: It yet hath felt no age nor known no sorrow.

OTHELLO: This argues fruitfulness and liberal heart.
    Hot, hot, and moist. This hand of yours requires
    A sequester° from liberty, fasting and prayer,
    Much castigation, exercise devout;   35
    For here's a young and sweating devil here
    That commonly rebels. 'Tis a good hand,
    A frank one.

DESDEMONA: You may, indeed, say so;
    For 'twas that hand that gave away my heart.   40

---

13. moved: Made proposals to. **20. crusadoes:** Portuguese gold coins. **25. humors:** Inclinations. **34. sequester:** Removal.

OTHELLO: A liberal hand! The hearts of old gave hands;
    But our new heraldry° is hands, not hearts.
DESDEMONA: I cannot speak of this. Come now, your promise!
OTHELLO: What promise, chuck?
DESDEMONA: I have sent to bid Cassio come speak with you.   45
OTHELLO: I have a salt and sorry rheum° offends me.
    Lend me thy handkerchief.
DESDEMONA: Here, my lord.
OTHELLO: That which I gave you.
DESDEMONA: I have it not about me.
OTHELLO: Not?
DESDEMONA: No, faith, my lord.
OTHELLO: That's a fault.
    That handkerchief   50
    Did an Egyptian° to my mother give.
    She was a charmer,° and could almost read
    The thoughts of people. She told her, while she kept it,
    'Twould make her amiable° and subdue my father
    Entirely to her love; but if she lost it   55
    Or made a gift of it, my father's eye
    Should hold her loathèd, and his spirits should hunt
    After new fancies. She, dying, gave it me,
    And bid me, when my fate would have me wive;
    To give it her. I did so; and take heed on't;   60
    Make it a darling like your precious eye.
    To lose't or give't away were such perdition°
    As nothing else could match.
DESDEMONA: Is't possible?
OTHELLO: 'Tis true. There's magic in the web of it.
    A sibyl that had numb'red in the world   65
    The sun to course two hundred compasses,°
    In her prophetic fury sewed the work;
    The worms were hallowed that did breed the silk;
    And it was dyed in mummy° which the skillful
    Conserved of maidens' hearts.
DESDEMONA: I' faith? Is't true?   70
OTHELLO: Most veritable. Therefore look to't well.
DESDEMONA: Then would to God that I had never seen't!
OTHELLO: Ha! Wherefore?
DESDEMONA: Why do you speak so startingly and rash?
OTHELLO: Is't lost? Is't gone? Speak, is it out o' th' way?   75

---

42. **heraldry:** Heraldic symbolism.   46. **salt . . . rheum:** Distressing head cold.   51. **Egyptian:** Gypsy.   52. **charmer:** Sorceress.   54. **amiable:** Lovable.   62. **perdition:** Disaster.   66. **compasses:** Annual rounds.   69. **mummy:** A drug made from mummies.

DESDEMONA: Heaven bless us!
OTHELLO: Say you?
DESDEMONA: It is not lost. But what an if it were?
OTHELLO: How?
DESDEMONA: I say it is not lost.
OTHELLO: Fetch't, let me see't!   80
DESDEMONA: Why, so I can, sir; but I will not now.
   This is a trick to put° me from my suit:
   Pray you let Cassio be received again.
OTHELLO: Fetch me the handkerchief! My mind misgives.
DESDEMONA: Come, come!   85
   You'll never meet a more sufficient man.
OTHELLO: The handkerchief!
[DESDEMONA: I pray talk me of Cassio.
OTHELLO: The handkerchief!]
DESDEMONA: A man that all his time°
   Hath founded his good fortunes on your love,
   Shared dangers with you —   90
OTHELLO: The handkerchief!
DESDEMONA: I' faith, you are to blame.
OTHELLO: Zounds!   *Exit Othello.*
EMILIA: Is not this man jealous?
DESDEMONA: I ne'er saw this before.   95
   Sure there's some wonder in this handkerchief;
   I am most unhappy in the loss of it.
EMILIA: 'Tis not a year or two shows us a man.
   They are all but stomachs, and we all but food;
   They eat us hungerly, and when they are full,   100
   They belch us.

Enter Iago and Cassio.

          Look you — Cassio and my husband!
IAGO: There is no other way; 'tis she must do't.
   And lo the happiness!° Go and importune her.
DESDEMONA: How now, good Cassio? What's the news with you?
CASSIO: Madam, my former suit. I do beseech you   105
   That by your virtuous means I may again
   Exist, and be a member of his love
   Whom I with all the office of my heart
   Entirely honor. I would not be delayed.
   If my offense be of such mortal kind   110
   That neither service past, nor present sorrows,
   Nor purposed merit in futurity,

---

82. put: Divert.   88. all . . . time: During his whole career.   103. happiness: Good luck.

Can ransom me into his love again,
But to know so must be my benefit.
So shall I clothe me in a forced content,   115
And shut myself up in° some other course,
To fortune's alms.
DESDEMONA: Alas, thrice-gentle Cassio!
My advocation° is not now in tune.
My lord is not my lord; nor should I know him,
Were he in favor° as in humor altered.   120
So help me every spirit sanctified
As I have spoken for you all my best
And stood within the blank° of his displeasure
For my free speech! You must a while be patient.
What I can do I will; and more I will   125
Than for myself I dare. Let that suffice you.
IAGO: Is my lord angry?
EMILIA: He went hence but now,
And certainly in strange unquietness.
IAGO: Can he be angry? I have seen the cannon
When it hath blown his ranks into the air   130
And, like the devil, from his very arm
Puffed his own brother—and is he angry?
Something of moment then. I will go meet him.
There's matter in't indeed if he be angry.
DESDEMONA: I prithee do so.   *Exit [Iago]*.
                      Something sure of state,°   135
Either from Venice or some unhatched practice°
Made demonstrable here in Cyprus to him,
Hath puddled° his clear spirit; and in such cases
Men's natures wrangle with inferior things,
Though great ones are their object. 'Tis even so;   140
For let our finger ache, and it endues°
Our other, healthful members even to a sense
Of pain. Nay, we must think men are not gods,
Nor of them look for such observancy
As fits the bridal. Beshrew me much, Emilia,   145
I was, unhandsome warrior° as I am,
Arraigning his unkindness with my soul;°
But now I find I had suborned the witness,
And he's indicted falsely.

---

116. **shut myself up in:** Confine myself to.   118. **advocation:** Advocacy.   120. **favor:** Appearance.   123. **blank:** Bull's-eye of the target.   135. **state:** Public affairs.   136. **unhatched practice:** Budding plot.   138. **puddled:** Muddied.   141. **endues:** Brings.   146. **unhandsome warrior:** Inadequate soldier.   147. **Arraigning . . . soul:** Indicting his unkindness before the bar of my soul.

EMILIA: Pray heaven it be state matters, as you think,   150
    And no conception nor no jealous toy°
    Concerning you.
DESDEMONA: Alas the day! I never gave him cause.
EMILIA: But jealous souls will not be answered so;
    They are not ever jealous for the cause,   155
    But jealous for they're jealous. 'Tis a monster
    Begot upon itself,° born on itself.
DESDEMONA: Heaven keep that monster from Othello's mind!
EMILIA: Lady, amen.
DESDEMONA: I will go seek him. Cassio, walk here about: 160
    If I do find him fit, I'll move your suit
    And seek to effect it to my uttermost.
CASSIO: I humbly thank your ladyship.

                                Exeunt Desdemona and Emilia.
Enter Bianca.

BIANCA: Save you, friend Cassio!
CASSIO: What make you from home?
    How is't with you, my most fair Bianca?   165
    I' faith, sweet love, I was coming to your house.
BIANCA: And I was going to your lodging, Cassio.
    What, keep a week away? seven days and nights?
    Eightscore eight hours? and lovers' absent hours,
    More tedious than the dial° eightscore times?   170
    O weary reck'ning!
CASSIO: Pardon me, Bianca:
    I have this while with leaden thoughts been pressed;
    But I shall in a more continuate° time
    Strike off this score of absence. Sweet Bianca,

[Gives her Desdemona's handkerchief.]

    Take me this work out.°
BIANCA: O Cassio, whence came this?   175
    This is some token from a newer friend.
    To the felt absence now I feel a cause.
    Is't come to this? Well, well.
CASSIO: Go to, woman!
    Throw your vile guesses in the devil's teeth,
    From whence you have them. You are jealous now   180
    That this is from some mistress, some remembrance.
    No, by my faith, Bianca.

---

151. toy: Fancy.   157. Begot . . . itself: Self-engendered.   170. dial: Clock.   173. continuate: Uninterrupted.   175. Take . . . out: Copy this embroidery for me.

BIANCA: Why, whose is it?
CASSIO: I know not, sweet; I found it in my chamber.
    I like the work° well; ere it be demanded,
    As like enough it will, I'd have it copied.   185
    Take it and do't, and leave me for this time.
BIANCA: Leave you? Wherefore?
CASSIO: I do attend here on the general
    And think it no addition, nor my wish,
    To have him see me womaned.
BIANCA: Why, I pray you?   190
CASSIO: Not that I love you not.
BIANCA: But that you do not love me!
    I pray you bring me on the way a little,
    And say if I shall see you soon at night.
CASSIO: 'Tis but a little way that I can bring you,
    For I attend here; but I'll see you soon.   195
BIANCA: 'Tis very good. I must be circumstanced.°   *Exeunt.*

ACT IV / Scene I

The environs of the castle.

Enter Othello and Iago.

IAGO: Will you think so?
OTHELLO: Think so, Iago?
IAGO: What,
    To kiss in private?
OTHELLO: An unauthorized kiss.
IAGO: Or to be naked with her friend in bed
    An hour or more, not meaning any harm?
OTHELLO: Naked in bed, Iago, and not mean harm?   5
    It is hypocrisy against the devil.°
    They that mean virtuously, and yet do so,
    The devil their virtue tempts, and they tempt heaven.
IAGO: So they do nothing, 'tis a venial slip.
    But if I give my wife a handkerchief—   10
OTHELLO: What then?
IAGO: Why, then 'tis hers, my lord; and being hers,
    She may, I think, bestow't on any man.
OTHELLO: She is protectress of her honor too;
    May she give that?   15
IAGO: Her honor is an essence that's not seen;
    They have it very oft that have it not.
    But for the handkerchief—

---

184. work: Needlework.   **196. circumstanced:** Governed by circumstances.   Act IV, Scene I.
6. hypocrisy . . . devil: I.e., feigned sin instead of feigned virtue.

OTHELLO: By heaven, I would most gladly have forgot it!
        Thou said'st — O, it comes o'er my memory   20
        As doth the raven o'er the infected° house,
        Boding to all! — he had my handkerchief.
IAGO: Ay, what of that?
OTHELLO: That's not so good now.
IAGO: What
        If I had said I had seen him do you wrong?
        Or heard him say — as knaves be such abroad   25
        Who having, by their own importunate suit,
        Or voluntary dotage of some mistress,
        Convincèd or supplied° them, cannot choose
        But they must blab —
OTHELLO: Hath he said anything?
IAGO: He hath, my lord; but be you well assured,   30
        No more than he'll unswear.
OTHELLO: What hath he said?
IAGO: Faith, that he did — I know not what he did.
OTHELLO: What? what?
IAGO: Lie —
OTHELLO: With her?
IAGO: With her, on her; what you will.   35
OTHELLO: Lie with her? lie on her? — We say lie on her when they belie
        her. — Lie with her! Zounds, that's fulsome. — Handkerchief — con-
        fessions — handkerchief! — To confess, and be hanged for his labor —
        first to be hanged, and then to confess! I tremble at it. Nature would
        not invest herself in such shadowing passion without some instruc-   40
        tion.° It is not words that shakes me thus. — Pish! Noses, ears, and
        lips? Is't possible? — Confess? — Handkerchief? — O devil!

(Falls in a trance.)

IAGO: Work on,
        My med'cine, work! Thus credulous fools are caught,
        And many worthy and chaste dames even thus,   45
        All guiltless, meet reproach. — What, ho! my lord!
        My lord, I say! Othello!
        Enter Cassio.   How now, Cassio?
CASSIO: What's the matter?
IAGO: My lord is fall'n into an epilepsy.
        This is his second fit; he had one yesterday.   50
CASSIO: Rub him about the temples.
IAGO: No, forbear.

---

21. **infected:** Plague-stricken.   28. **Convincèd or supplied:** Overcome or gratified.   **39–41. Nature . . . instruction:** My natural faculties would not be so overcome by passion without
reason.

The lethargy° must have his quiet course.
If not, he foams at mouth, and by and by
Breaks out to savage madness. Look, he stirs.
Do you withdraw yourself a little while.   55
He will recover straight. When he is gone,
I would on great occasion speak with you.   [*Exit Cassio.*]
How is it, general? Have you not hurt your head?

OTHELLO: Dost thou mock me?

IAGO: I mock you? No, by heaven.
Would you would bear your fortune like a man!   60

OTHELLO: A hornèd man's° a monster and a beast.

IAGO: There's many a beast then in a populous city,
And many a civil monster.

OTHELLO: Did he confess it?

IAGO: Good sir, be a man.
Think every bearded fellow that's but yoked   65
May draw with you. There's millions now alive
That nightly lie in those unproper° beds
Which they dare swear peculiar:° your case is better.
O, 'tis the spite of hell, the fiend's arch-mock,
To lip a wanton in a secure° couch,   70
And to suppose her chaste! No, let me know;
And knowing what I am, I know what she shall be.

OTHELLO: O, thou art wise! 'Tis certain.

IAGO: Stand you awhile apart;
Confine yourself but in a patient list.°
Whilst you were here, o'erwhelmèd with your grief —   75
A passion most unsuiting such a man —
Cassio came hither. I shifted him away
And laid good 'scuse upon your ecstasy;°
Bade him anon return, and here speak with me;
The which he promised. Do but encave° yourself   80
And mark the fleers, the gibes, and notable scorns
That dwell in every region of his face;
For I will make him tell the tale anew —
Where, how, how oft, how long ago, and when
He hath, and is again to cope° your wife.   85
I say, but mark his gesture. Marry, patience!
Or I shall say y'are all in all in spleen,°
And nothing of a man.

---

52. **lethargy:** Coma.   61. **hornèd man:** Cuckold.   67. **unproper:** Not exclusively their
own.   68. **peculiar:** Exclusively their own.   70. **secure:** Free from fear of rivalry.   74. **in a
patient list:** Within the limits of self-control.   78. **ecstasy:** Trance.   80. **encave:** Conceal.
85. **cope:** Meet.   87. **all in all in spleen:** Wholly overcome by your passion.

OTHELLO: Dost thou hear, Iago?
I will be found most cunning in my patience;
But — dost thou hear? — most bloody.
IAGO: That's not amiss: 90
But yet keep time in all. Will you withdraw?

[*Othello retires.*]

Now will I question Cassio of Bianca,
A huswife° that by selling her desires
Buys herself bread and clothes. It is a creature
That dotes on Cassio, as 'tis the strumpet's plague   95
To beguile many and be beguiled by one.
He, when he hears of her, cannot refrain
From the excess of laughter. Here he comes.

Enter Cassio.

As he shall smile, Othello shall go mad;
And his unbookish° jealousy must conster°   100
Poor Cassio's smiles, gestures, and light behavior
Quite in the wrong. How do you now, lieutenant?
CASSIO: The worser that you give me the addition°
Whose want even kills me.
IAGO: Ply Desdemona well, and you are sure on't.   105
Now, if this suit lay in Bianca's power,
How quickly should you speed!
CASSIO: Alas, poor caitiff!°
OTHELLO: Look how he laughs already!
IAGO: I never knew a woman love man so.
CASSIO: Alas, poor rogue! I think, i' faith, she loves me.   110
OTHELLO: Now he denies it faintly, and laughs it out.
IAGO: Do you hear, Cassio?
OTHELLO: Now he importunes him
To tell it o'er. Go to! Well said, well said!
IAGO: She gives out that you shall marry her.
Do you intend it?   115
CASSIO: Ha, ha, ha!
OTHELLO: Do you triumph, Roman? Do you triumph?
CASSIO: I marry her? What, a customer?° Prithee bear some charity to
my wit; do not think it so unwholesome. Ha, ha, ha!
OTHELLO: So, so, so, so! They laugh that win!   120
IAGO: Faith, the cry goes that you shall marry her.
CASSIO: Prithee say true.

---

93. **huswife:** Hussy. 100. **unbookish:** Uninstructed; **conster:** Construe, interpret. 103. **addition:** Title. 107. **caitiff:** Wretch. 118. **customer:** Prostitute.

IAGO: I am a very villain else.

OTHELLO: Have you scored me?° Well.

CASSIO: This is the monkey's own giving out. She is persuaded I will   125
marry her out of her own love and flattery, not out of my promise.

OTHELLO: Iago beckons° me; now he begins the story.

CASSIO: She was here even now; she haunts me in every place. I was t'
other day talking on the sea bank with certain Venetians, and thither
comes the bauble,° and, by this hand, she falls me thus about my   130
neck—

OTHELLO: Crying "O dear Cassio!" as it were. His gesture imports it.

CASSIO: So hangs, and lolls, and weeps upon me; so shakes and pulls
me! Ha, ha, ha!

OTHELLO: Now he tells how she plucked him to my chamber. O, I see   135
that nose of yours, but not that dog I shall throw it to.

CASSIO: Well, I must leave her company.

Enter Bianca.

IAGO: Before me! Look where she comes.

CASSIO: 'Tis such another fitchew!° marry, a perfumed one. What do
you mean by this haunting of me?   140

BIANCA: Let the devil and his dam haunt you! What did you mean by
that same handkerchief you gave me even now? I was a fine fool to
take it. I must take out the whole work? A likely piece of work that
you should find it in your chamber and know not who left it there!
This is some minx's token, and I must take out the work? There!   145
Give it your hobby-horse.° Wheresoever you had it, I'll take out no
work on't.

CASSIO: How now, my sweet Bianca? How now? how now?

OTHELLO: By heaven, that should be my handkerchief!

BIANCA: An you'll come to supper to-night, you may; an you will not,   150
come when you are next prepared for.   *Exit.*

IAGO: After her, after her!

CASSIO: Faith, I must; she'll rail in the street else.

IAGO: Will you sup there?

CASSIO: Yes, I intend so.   155

IAGO: Well, I may chance to see you; for I would very fain speak with you.

CASSIO: Prithee come. Will you?

IAGO: Go to! say no more.   *Exit Cassio.*

OTHELLO [*comes forward*]: How shall I murder him, Iago?

IAGO: Did you perceive how he laughed at his vice?°   160

---

124. scored me: Settled my account (?).   **127. beckons:** Signals.   **130. bauble:** Plaything.
139. fitchew: Polecat (slang for whore).   **146. hobby-horse:** Harlot.   **160. vice:** I.e., vicious conduct.

OTHELLO: O Iago!

IAGO: And did you see the handkerchief?

OTHELLO: Was that mine?

IAGO: Your, by this hand! And to see how he prizes° the foolish woman
    your wife! She gave it him, and he hath giv'n it his whore.   165

OTHELLO: I would have him nine years a-killing—A fine woman! a fair
    woman! a sweet woman!

IAGO: Nay, you must forget that.

OTHELLO: Ay, let her rot, and perish, and be damned to-night; for she
    shall not live. No, my heart is turned to stone; I strike it, and it hurts   170
    my hand. O, the world hath not a sweeter creature! She might lie by
    an emperor's side and command him tasks.

IAGO: Nay, that's not your way.

OTHELLO: Hang her! I do but say what she is. So delicate with her needle!
    an admirable musician! O, she will sing the savageness out of a   175
    bear! Of so high and plenteous wit and invention°—

IAGO: She's the worse for all this.

OTHELLO: O, a thousand thousand times! And then, of so gentle a con-
    dition!°

IAGO: Ay, too gentle.   180

OTHELLO: Nay, that's certain. But yet the pity of it, Iago! O Iago, the pity
    of it, Iago!

IAGO: If you are so fond over her iniquity, give her patent° to offend; for
    if it touch not you, it comes near nobody.

OTHELLO: I will chop her into messes! Cuckold me!   185

IAGO: O, 'tis foul in her.

OTHELLO: With mine officer!

IAGO: That's fouler.

OTHELLO: Get me some poison, Iago, this night. I'll not expostulate with
    her, lest her body and beauty unprovide° my mind again. This night,   190
    Iago!

IAGO: Do it not with poison. Strangle her in her bed, even the bed she
    hath contaminated.

OTHELLO: Good, good! The justice of it pleases. Very good!

IAGO: And for Cassio, let me be his undertaker;° you shall hear more by   195
    midnight.

OTHELLO: Excellent good!

A trumpet.

    What trumpet is that same?

IAGO: I warrant something from Venice.

---

164. **prizes:** Values. 176. **invention:** Imagination. 178–79. **condition:** Disposition.
183. **patent:** License. 190. **unprovide:** Disarm. 195. **be his undertaker:** Undertake to
deal with him.

Enter Lodovico, Desdemona, and Attendants.

                                              'Tis Lodovico.
    This comes from the Duke; and see, your wife is with him.   200
LODOVICO: God save you, worthy general!
OTHELLO: With all my heart, sir.
LODOVICO: The Duke and senators of Venice greet you.

[Gives him a letter.]

OTHELLO: I kiss the instrument of their pleasures.

[Opens the letter and reads.]

DESDEMONA: And what's the news, good cousin Lodovico?
IAGO: I am very glad to see you, signior.   205
    Welcome to Cyprus.
LODOVICO: I thank you. How does Lieutenant Cassio?
IAGO: Lives, sir.
DESDEMONA: Cousin, there's fall'n between him and my lord
    An unkind breach; but you shall make all well.
OTHELLO: Are you sure of that?   210
DESDEMONA: My lord?
OTHELLO [*reads*]: "This fail you not to do, as you will —"
LODOVICO: He did not call; he's busy in the paper.
    Is there division 'twixt thy lord and Cassio?
DESDEMONA: A most unhappy one. I would do much   215
    T' atone° them, for the love I bear to Cassio.
OTHELLO: Fire and brimstone!
DESDEMONA: My lord?
OTHELLO: Are you wise?
DESDEMONA: What, is he angry?
LODOVICO: May be the letter moved him;
    For, as I think, they do command him home,
    Deputing Cassio in his government.   220
DESDEMONA: By my troth, I am glad on't.
OTHELLO: Indeed?
DESDEMONA: My lord?
OTHELLO: I am glad to see you mad.°
DESDEMONA: Why, sweet Othello —
OTHELLO: Devil!

[Strikes her.]

DESDEMONA: I have not deserved this.
LODOVICO: My lord, this would not be believed in Venice,   225

---

216. atone: Reconcile.   **222. mad:** I.e., waggish.

Though I should swear I saw't. 'Tis very much.
Make her amends; she weeps.
OTHELLO: O devil, devil!
If that the earth could teem° with woman's tears,
Each drop she falls would prove a crocodile.°
Out of my sight!
DESDEMONA: I will not stay to offend you.   [*Going.*] 230
LODOVICO: Truly, an obedient lady.
I do beseech your lordship call her back.
OTHELLO: Mistress!
DESDEMONA: My lord?
OTHELLO: What would you with her, sir?
LODOVICO: Who? I, my lord?   235
OTHELLO: Ay! You did wish that I would make her turn.
Sir, she can turn, and turn, and yet go on
And turn again; and she can weep, sir, weep;
And she's obedient; as you say, obedient,
Very obedient. — Proceed you in your tears. —   240
Concerning this, sir — O well-painted passion!° —
I am commanded home. — Get you away;
I'll send for you anon. — Sir, I obey the mandate
And will return to Venice. — Hence, avaunt!

                                        [*Exit Desdemona.*]
Cassio shall have my place. And, sir, to-night   245
I do entreat that we may sup together.
You are welcome, sir, to Cyprus — Goats and monkeys!

                                                        Exit.

LODOVICO: Is this the noble Moor whom our full Senate
Call all in all sufficient? Is this the nature
Whom passion could not shake? whose solid virtue   250
The shot of accident nor dart of chance
Could neither graze nor pierce?
IAGO: He is much changed.
LODOVICO: Are his wits safe? Is he not light of brain?
IAGO: He's that he is; I may not breathe my censure.
What he might be — if what he might he is not —   255
I would to heaven he were!
LODOVICO: What, strike his wife?
IAGO: Faith, that was not so well; yet would I knew
That stroke would prove the worst!
LODOVICO: Is it his use?°
Or did the letters work upon his blood

---

228. teem: Breed.   **229. crocodile:** (Crocodiles were supposed to shed hypocritical tears to
lure men to destruction).   **241. passion:** Grief.   **258. use:** Custom.

And new-create this fault?
IAGO: Alas, alas!   260
    It is not honesty in me to speak
    What I have seen and known. You shall observe him,
    And his own courses will denote him so
    That I may save my speech. Do but go after
    And mark how he continues.   265
LODOVICO: I am sorry that I am deceived in him.   *Exeunt.*

Scene II

Within the castle.

Enter Othello and Emilia.

OTHELLO: You have seen nothing then?
EMILIA: Nor ever heard, nor ever did suspect.
OTHELLO: Yes, you have seen Cassio and she together.
EMILIA: But then I saw no harm, and then I heard
    Each syllable that breath made up between them.   5
OTHELLO: What, did they never whisper?
EMILIA: Never, my lord.
OTHELLO: Nor send you out o' th' way?
EMILIA: Never.
OTHELLO: To fetch her fan, her gloves, her mask, nor nothing?
EMILIA: Never, my lord.   10
OTHELLO: That's strange.
EMILIA: I durst, my lord, to wager she is honest,
    Lay down my soul at stake. If you think other,
    Remove your thought; it doth abuse your bosom.°
    If any wretch have put this in your head,   15
    Let heaven requite it with the serpent's curse!°
    For if she be not honest, chaste, and true,
    There's no man happy; the purest of their wives
    Is foul as slander.
OTHELLO: Bid her come hither. Go.   *Exit Emilia.*
    She says enough; yet she's a simple bawd   20
    That cannot say as much. This is a subtle whore,
    A closet lock and key of villainous secrets;
    And yet she'll kneel and pray; I have seen her do't.

Enter Desdemona and Emilia.

DESDEMONA: My lord, what is your will?
OTHELLO: Pray, chuck, come hither.
DESDEMONA: What is your pleasure?

SCENE II.   **14. abuse . . . bosom:** Deceive your heart.   **16. serpent's curse:** (cf. Genesis 3:14).

OTHELLO: Let me see your eyes.   25
    Look in my face.
DESDEMONA: What horrible fancy's this?
OTHELLO [*to Emilia*]: Some of your function, mistress.
    Leave procreants° alone and shut the door;
    Cough or cry hem if anybody come.
    Your mystery, your mystery!° Nay, dispatch!   30
                             Exit Emilia.

DESDEMONA: Upon my knees, what doth your speech import?
    I understand a fury in your words,
    [But not the words.]
OTHELLO: Why, what art thou?
DESDEMONA: Your wife, my lord; your true
    And loyal wife.
OTHELLO: Come, swear it, damn thyself;   35
    Lest, being like one of heaven,° the devils themselves
    Should fear to seize thee. Therefore be double-damned —
    Swear thou art honest.°
DESDEMONA: Heaven doth truly know it.
OTHELLO: Heaven truly knows that thou art false as hell.
DESDEMONA: To whom, my lord? With whom? How am I false?   40
OTHELLO: Ah, Desdemona! away! away! away!
DESDEMONA: Alas the heavy day! Why do you weep?
    Am I the motive of these tears, my lord?
    If haply you my father do suspect
    An instrument° of this your calling back,   45
    Lay not your blame on me. If you have lost him,
    Why, I have lost him too.
OTHELLO: Had it pleased heaven
    To try me with affliction, had they rained
    All kinds of sores and shames on my bare head,
    Steeped me in poverty to the very lips,   50
    Given to captivity me and my utmost hopes,
    I should have found in some place of my soul
    A drop of patience. But, alas, to make me
    A fixèd figure for the time of scorn°
    To point his slow unmoving finger at!   55
    Yet could I bear that too; well, very well.
    But there where I have garnered up my heart,
    Where either I must live or bear no life,
    The fountain from the which my current runs

---

28. procreants: Mating couples.   **30. mystery:** Trade, occupation.   **36. being . . . heaven:** Looking like an angel.   **38. honest:** Chaste.   **45. An instrument:** To be the cause.   **54. time of scorn:** Scornful world.

Or else dries up — to be discarded thence,   60
Or keep it as a cistern for foul toads
To knot and gender in — turn thy complexion there,°
Patience, thou young and rose-lipped cherubin!
Ay, there look grim as hell!
DESDEMONA: I hope my noble lord esteems me honest.   65
OTHELLO: O, ay; as summer flies are in the shambles,°
That quicken° even with blowing. O thou weed,
Who art so lovely fair, and smell'st so sweet,
That the sense aches at thee, would thou hadst ne'er been born!
DESDEMONA: Alas, what ignorant sin have I committed?   70
OTHELLO: Was this fair paper, this most goodly book,
Made to write "whore" upon? What committed?
Committed? O thou public commoner!°
I should make very forges of my cheeks
That would to cinders burn up modesty,   75
Did I but speak thy deeds. What committed?
Heaven stops the nose at it, and the moon winks;°
The bawdy wind, that kisses all it meets,
Is hushed within the hollow mine of earth
And will not hear it. What committed?   80
Impudent strumpet!
DESDEMONA: By heaven, you do me wrong!
OTHELLO: Are not you a strumpet?
DESDEMONA: No, as I am a Christian!
If to preserve this vessel for my lord
From any other foul unlawful touch
Be not to be a strumpet, I am none.   85
OTHELLO: What, not a whore?
DESDEMONA: No, as I shall be saved!
OTHELLO: Is't possible?
DESDEMONA: O, heaven forgive us!
OTHELLO: I cry you mercy° then.
I took you for that cunning whore of Venice
That married with Othello. — [*Calling.*] You, mistress,   90
That have the office opposite to Saint Peter
And keep the gate of hell!

Enter Emilia.

                        You, you, ay, you!
We have done our course; there's money for your pains:
I pray you turn the key, and keep our counsel.   *Exit.*

---

62. turn thy complexion there: Change thy color at that point.   **66. shambles:** Slaughter-
house.   **67. quicken:** Come to life.   **73. commoner:** Harlot.   **77. winks:** Closes her eyes.
88. cry you mercy: Beg your pardon.

EMILIA: Alas, what does this gentleman conceive?   95
 How do you, madam? How do you, my good lady?
DESDEMONA: Faith, half asleep.°
EMILIA: Good madam, what's the matter with my lord?
DESDEMONA: With who?
EMILIA: Why, with my lord, madam.   100
DESDEMONA: Who is thy lord?
EMILIA: He that is yours, sweet lady.
DESDEMONA: I have none. Do not talk to me, Emilia.
 I cannot weep; nor answer have I none
 But what should go by water. Prithee to-night
 Lay on my bed my wedding sheets, remember;   105
 And call thy husband hither.
EMILIA: Here's a change indeed!   *Exit.*
DESDEMONA: 'Tis meet I should be used so, very meet.
 How have I been behaved, that he might stick
 The small'st opinion° on my least misuse?°

Enter Iago and Emilia.

IAGO: What is your pleasure, madam? How is't with you?   110
DESDEMONA: I cannot tell. Those that do teach young babes
 Do it with gentle means and easy tasks:
 He might have chid me so; for, in good faith,
 I am a child to chiding.
IAGO: What is the matter, lady?
EMILIA: Alas, Iago, my lord hath so bewhored her,   115
 Thrown such despite and heavy terms upon her
 As true hearts cannot bear.
DESDEMONA: Am I that name, Iago?
IAGO: What name, fair lady?
DESDEMONA: Such as she said my lord did say I was.
EMILIA: He called her whore. A beggar in his drink   120
 Could not have laid such terms upon his callet.°
IAGO: Why did he so?
DESDEMONA: I do not know; I am sure I am none such.
IAGO: Do not weep, do not weep. Alas the day!
EMILIA: Hath she forsook so many noble matches,   125
 Her father and her country, and her friends,
 To be called whore? Would it not make one weep?
DESDEMONA: It is my wretched fortune.
IAGO: Beshrew him for't!
 How comes this trick° upon him?

---

97. **half asleep:** I.e., stunned.   109. **small'st opinion:** Least suspicion; **least misuse:** Slightest misconduct.   121. **callet:** Whore.   129. **trick:** Freakish behavior.

DESDEMONA: Nay, heaven doth know.
EMILIA: I will be hanged if some eternal villain,   130
    Some busy and insinuating rogue,
    Some cogging, cozening° slave, to get some office,
    Have not devised this slander. I'll be hanged else.
IAGO: Fie, there is no such man! It is impossible.
DESDEMONA: If any such there be, heaven pardon him!   135
EMILIA: A halter pardon him! and hell gnaw his bones!
    Why should he call her whore? Who keeps her company?
    What place? what time? what form? what likelihood?
    The Moor 's abused by some most villainous knave,
    Some base notorious knave, some scurvy fellow.   140
    O heaven, that such companions° thou 'dst unfold,°
    And put in every honest hand a whip
    To lash the rascals naked through the world
    Even from the east to th' west!
IAGO: Speak within door.°
EMILIA: O, fie upon them! Some such squire he was   145
    That turned your wit the seamy side without
    And made you to suspect me with the Moor.
IAGO: You are a fool. Go to.
DESDEMONA: Alas, Iago,
    What shall I do to win my lord again?
    Good friend, go to him; for, by this light of heaven,   150
    I know not how I lost him. Here I kneel:
    If e'er my will did trespass 'gainst his love
    Either in discourse° of thought or actual deed,
    Or that mine eyes, mine ears, or any sense
    Delighted them in any other form,   155
    Or that I do not yet, and ever did,
    And ever will (though he do shake me off
    To beggarly divorcement) love him dearly,
    Comfort forswear° me! Unkindness may do much;
    And his unkindness may defeat° my life,   160
    But never taint my love. I cannot say "whore."
    It does abhor me now I speak the word;
    To do the act that might the addition earn
    Not the world's mass of vanity could make me.
IAGO: I pray you be content. 'Tis but his humor.   165
    The business of the state does him offense,
    [And he does chide with you.]
DESDEMONA: If 'twere no other —

---

132. **cogging, cozening:** Cheating, defrauding.   141. **companions:** Rogues; **unfold:** Expose.
144. **within door:** With restraint.   153. **discourse:** Course.   159. **Comfort forswear:** Happiness forsake.   160. **defeat:** Destroy.

IAGO: 'Tis but so, I warrant.

[*Trumpets within.*]

Hark how these instruments summon you to supper.
The messengers of Venice stay the meat: 170
Go in, and weep not. All things shall be well.

Exeunt Desdemona and Emilia.

Enter Roderigo.

How now, Roderigo?
RODERIGO: I do not find that thou deal'st justly with me.
IAGO: What in the contrary?
RODERIGO: Every day thou daff'st me with some device,° Iago, and rather,   175
    as it seems to me now, keep'st from me all conveniency° than sup-
    pliest me with the least advantage of hope. I will indeed no longer
    endure it; nor am I yet persuaded to put up in peace what already I
    have foolishly suffered.
IAGO: Will you hear me, Roderigo?   180
RODERIGO: Faith, I have heard too much; for your words and perfor-
    mances are no kin together.
IAGO: You charge me most unjustly.
RODERIGO: With naught but truth. I have wasted myself out of my
    means. The jewels you have had from me to deliver to Desdemona   185
    would half have corrupted a votarist.° You have told me she hath re-
    ceived them, and returned me expectations and comforts of sudden
    respect° and acquaintance; but I find none.
IAGO: Well, go to; very well.
RODERIGO: Very well! go to! I cannot go to, man; nor 'tis not very well.   190
    By this hand, I say 'tis very scurvy, and begin to find myself fopped°
    in it.
IAGO: Very well.
RODERIGO: I tell you 'tis not very well. I will make myself known to Des-
    demona. If she will return me my jewels, I will give over my suit and   195
    repent my unlawful solicitation; if not, assure yourself I will seek
    satisfaction of you.
IAGO: You have said now.
RODERIGO: Ay, and said nothing but what I protest intendment of doing.
IAGO: Why, now I see there's mettle in thee; and even from this instant   200
    do build on thee a better opinion than ever before. Give me thy
    hand, Roderigo. Thou has taken against me a most just exception;
    but yet I protest I have dealt most directly° in thy affair.

---

175. thou . . . device: You put me off with some trick.   **176. conveniency:** Favorable opportunities.   **186. votarist:** Nun.   **187–88. sudden respect:** Immediate notice.   **191. fopped:**
Duped.   **203. directly:** Straightforwardly.

RODERIGO: It hath not appeared.

IAGO: I grant indeed it hath not appeared, and your suspicion is not 205
without wit and judgment. But, Roderigo, if thou hast that in thee
indeed which I have greater reason to believe now than ever, I mean
purpose, courage, and valor, this night show it. If thou the next
night following enjoy not Desdemona, take me from this world with
treachery and devise engines for° my life.   210

RODERIGO: Well, what is it? Is it within reason and compass?

IAGO: Sir, there is especial commission come from Venice to depute
Cassio in Othello's place.

RODERIGO: Is that true? Why, then Othello and Desdemona return
again to Venice.   215

IAGO: O, no; he goes into Mauritania and takes away with him the fair
Desdemona, unless his abode be lingered here° by some accident;
wherein none can be so determinate° as the removing of Cassio.

RODERIGO: How do you mean removing of him?

IAGO: Why, by making him uncapable of Othello's place — knocking out 220
his brains.

RODERIGO: And that you would have me to do?

IAGO: Ay, if you dare do yourself a profit and a right. He sups to-night
with a harlotry, and thither will I go to him. He knows not yet of his
honorable fortune. If you will watch his going thence, which I will 225
fashion to fall out between twelve and one, you may take him at
your pleasure. I will be near to second your attempt, and he shall fall
between us. Come, stand not amazed at it, but go along with me. I
will show you such a necessity in his death that you shall think
yourself bound to put it on him. It is now high supper time, and the 230
night grows to waste. About it!

RODERIGO: I will hear further reason for this.

IAGO: And you shall be satisfied.   *Exeunt.*

Scene III

Within the castle.

Enter Othello, Lodovico, Desdemona, Emilia, and Attendants.

LODOVICO: I do beseech you, sir, trouble yourself no further.

OTHELLO: O, pardon me; 'twill do me good to walk.

LODOVICO: Madam, good night. I humbly thank your ladyship.

DESDEMONA: Your honor is most welcome.

OTHELLO: Will you walk, sir?

O, Desdemona —   5

DESDEMONA: My lord?

---

210. engines for: Plots against.   **217. abode . . . here:** Stay here be extended.   **218. determinate:** Effective.

OTHELLO: Get you to bed on th' instant; I will be returned forthwith.
  Dismiss your attendant there. Look't be done.
DESDEMONA: I will, my lord.

Exit [Othello, with Lodovico and Attendants].

EMILIA: How goes it now? He looks gentler than he did.   10
DESDEMONA: He says he will return incontinent.°
  He hath commanded me to go to bed,
  And bade me to dismiss you.
EMILIA: Dismiss me?
DESDEMONA: It was his bidding; therefore, good Emilia,
  Give me my nightly wearing, and adieu.   15
  We must not now displease him.
EMILIA: I would you had never seen him!
DESDEMONA: So would not I. My love doth so approve him
  That even his stubbornness,° his checks,° his frowns —
  Prithee unpin me — have grace and favor in them.   20
EMILIA: I have laid those sheets you bade me on the bed.
DESDEMONA: All's one. Good faith, how foolish are our minds!
  If I do die before thee, prithee shroud me
  In one of those same sheets.
EMILIA: Come, come! You talk.
DESDEMONA: My mother had a maid called Barbary.   25
  She was in love; and he she loved proved mad°
  And did forsake her. She had a song of "Willow";
  An old thing 'twas; but it expressed her fortune,
  And she died singing it. That song to-night
  Will not go from my mind; I have much to do   30
  But to go hang my head all at one side
  And sing it like poor Barbary. Prithee dispatch.
EMILIA: Shall I go fetch your nightgown?°
DESDEMONA: No, unpin me here.
  This Lodovico is a proper man.
EMILIA: A very handsome man.   35
DESDEMONA: He speaks well.
EMILIA: I know a lady in Venice would have walked barefoot to Palestine
  for a touch of his nether lip.
DESDEMONA (*sings*): "The poor soul sat sighing by a sycamore tree
          Sing all a green willow;   40
  Her hand on her bosom, her head on her knee,
          Sing willow, willow, willow.

SCENE III.   **11. incontinent:** At once.   **19. stubbornness:** Roughness; **checks:** Rebukes.
26. mad: Wild, faithless.   **33. nightgown:** Dressing gown.

The fresh streams ran by her and murmured her moans;
    Sing willow, willow, willow;
Her salt tears fell from her, and soft'ned the stones" —   45
Lay by these.
    "Sing willow, willow, willow" —
Prithee hie thee;° he'll come anon.
    "Sing all a green willow must be my garland.
    Let nobody blame him; his scorn I approve" —   50
Nay, that's not next. Hark! who is't that knocks?
EMILIA: It's the wind.
DESDEMONA (*sings*): "I call my love false love; but what said he then?
    Sing willow, willow, willow:
    If I court moe women, you'll couch with moe men."   55
So get thee gone; good night. Mine eyes do itch.
Doth that bode weeping?
EMILIA: 'Tis neither here nor there.
DESDEMONA: I have heard it said so. O, these men, these men!
    Dost thou in conscience think — tell me, Emilia —
    That there be women do abuse their husbands   60
    In such gross kind?
EMILIA: There be some such, no question.
DESDEMONA: Wouldst thou do such a deed for all the world?
EMILIA: Why, would not you?
DESDEMONA: No, by this heavenly light!
EMILIA: Nor I neither by this heavenly light.
    I might do't as well i' th' dark.   65
DESDEMONA: Wouldst thou do such a deed for all the world?
EMILIA: The world's a huge thing; it is a great price for a small vice.
DESDEMONA: In troth, I think thou wouldst not.
EMILIA: In troth, I think I should; and undo't when I had done it. Marry,
    I would not do such a thing for a joint-ring,° nor for measures of 70
    lawn, nor for gowns, petticoats, nor caps, nor any petty exhibition;°
    but, for all the whole world — 'Ud's pity! who would not make her
    husband a cuckold to make him a monarch? I should venture pur-
    gatory for't.
DESDEMONA: Beshrew me if I would do such a wrong   75
    For the whole world.
EMILIA: Why, the wrong is but a wrong i' th' world; and having the world
    for your labor, 'tis a wrong in your own world, and you might
    quickly make it right.
DESDEMONA: I do not think there is any such woman.   80
EMILIA: Yes, a dozen; and as many to th' vantage° as
    would store° the world they played for.

---

48. hie thee: Hurry.   **70. joint-ring:** Ring made in separable halves.   **71. exhibition:** Gift.
81. to th' vantage: Besides.   **82. store:** Populate.

But I do think it is their husbands' faults
If wives do fall. Say that they slack their duties
And pour our treasures into foreign laps;   85
Or else break out in peevish° jealousies,
Throwing restraint upon us; or say they strike us,
Or scant our former having° in despite —
Why, we have galls;° and though we have some grace,
Yet have we some revenge. Let husbands know   90
Their wives have sense like them. They see, and smell,
And have their palates both for sweet and sour,
As husbands have. What is it that they do
When they change us for others? Is it sport?
I think it is. And doth affection breed it?   95
I think it doth. Is't frailty that thus errs?
It is so too. And have not we affections,
Desires for sport, and frailty, as men have?
Then let them use us well; else let them know,
The ills we do, their ills instruct us so.   100
DESDEMONA: Good night, good night. God me such usage° send,
    Not to pick bad from bad, but by bad mend!   *Exeunt.*

ACT V / Scene I

A street in Cyprus.

Enter Iago and Roderigo.

IAGO: Here, stand behind this bulk;° straight will he come.
    Wear thy good rapier bare, and put it home.
    Quick, quick! Fear nothing; I'll be at thy elbow.
    It makes us, or it mars us — think on that,
    And fix most firm thy resolution.   5
RODERIGO: Be near at hand; I may miscarry in't.
IAGO: Here, at thy hand. Be bold, and take thy stand.

[Stands aside.]

RODERIGO: I have no great devotion to the deed,
    And yet he hath given me satisfying reasons.
    'Tis but a man gone. Forth my sword! He dies!   10
IAGO: I have rubbed this young quat° almost to the sense,°
    And he grows angry. Now whether he kill Cassio,
    Or Cassio him, or each do kill the other,
    Every way makes my gain. Live Roderigo,
    He calls me to a restitution large   15

---

86. peevish: Senseless. **88. having:** Allowance. **89. galls:** Spirits to resent. **101. usage:**
Habits. ACT V, SCENE I. **1. bulk:** Projecting shop-front. **11. quat:** Pimple; **sense:** Quick.

Of gold and jewels that I bobbed° from him
As gifts to Desdemona.
It must not be. If Cassio do remain,
He hath a daily beauty in his life
That makes me ugly; and besides, the Moor   20
May unfold me to him; there stand I in much peril.
No, he must die. Be't so! I hear him coming.

Enter Cassio.

RODERIGO: I know his gait. 'Tis he. Villain, thou diest!

[*Makes a pass at Cassio.*]

CASSIO: That thrust had been mine enemy indeed
          But that my coat° is better than thou know'st.   25
          I will make proof of thine.

[*Draws, and wounds Roderigo.*]

RODERIGO: O, I am slain!

[*Iago darts from concealment behind Cassio, wounds him in the leg, and exit.*]

CASSIO: I am maimed for ever. Help, ho! Murder! murder!

[*Falls.*]
Enter Othello.

OTHELLO: The voice of Cassio. Iago keeps his word.
RODERIGO: O, villain that I am!
OTHELLO: It is even so.
CASSIO: O, help, ho! light! a surgeon!   30
OTHELLO: 'Tis he. O brave Iago, honest and just,
          That hast such noble sense of thy friend's wrong!
          Thou teachest me. Minion,° your dear lies dead,
          And your unblest fate hies.° Strumpet, I come.
          Forth of my heart those charms, thine eyes, are blotted.   35
          Thy bed, lust-stained, shall with lust's blood be spotted.

                                                          Exit Othello.

Enter Lodovico and Gratiano.

CASSIO: What, ho? No watch? No passage?° Murder! murder!
GRATIANO: 'Tis some mischance. The cry is very direful.
CASSIO: O, help!
LODOVICO: Hark!   40
RODERIGO: O wretched villain!

---

16. bobbed: Swindled.   25. coat: Undershirt of mail.   33. Minion: Mistress.   34. hies:
Hurries on.   37. passage: Passersby.

LODOVICO: Two or three groan. It is a heavy° night.
  These may be counterfeits. Let's think't unsafe
  To come in to the cry without more help.
RODERIGO: Nobody come? Then shall I bleed to death.   45
LODOVICO: Hark!

Enter Iago, with a light.

GRATIANO: Here's one comes in his shirt, with light and weapons.
IAGO: Who's there? Whose noise is this that cries on° murder?
LODOVICO: We do not know.
IAGO: Did not you hear a cry?
CASSIO: Here, here! For heaven's sake, help me!
IAGO: What's the matter?   50
GRATIANO: This is Othello's ancient, as I take it.
LODOVICO: The same indeed, a very valiant fellow.
IAGO: What are you here that cry so grievously?
CASSIO: Iago? O, I am spoiled, undone by villains!
  Give me some help.   55
IAGO: O me, lieutenant! What villains have done this?
CASSIO: I think that one of them is hereabout
  And cannot make° away.
IAGO: O treacherous villains!

[To Lodovico and Gratiano.]

  What are you there? Come in, and give some help.
RODERIGO: O, help me here!   60
CASSIO: That's one of them.
IAGO: O murd'rous slave! O villain!

[Stabs Roderigo.]

RODERIGO: O damned Iago! O inhuman dog!
IAGO: Kill men i' th' dark? — Where be these bloody thieves? —
  How silent is this town! — Ho! murder! murder! —
  What may you be? Are you of good or evil?   65
LODOVICO: As you shall prove us, praise us.
IAGO: Signior Lodovico?
LODOVICO: He, sir.
IAGO: I cry you mercy. Here's Cassio hurt by villains.
GRATIANO: Cassio?   70
IAGO: How is't, brother?
CASSIO: My leg is cut in two.
IAGO: Marry,° heaven forbid!
  Light, gentlemen. I'll bind it with my shirt.

---

42. **heavy:** Cloudy, dark. 48. **cries on:** Raises the cry of. 58. **make:** Get. 72. **Marry:** (From "By Mary").

Enter Bianca.

BIANCA: What is the matter, ho? Who is't that cried?
IAGO: Who is't that cried?   75
BIANCA: O my dear Cassio! my sweet Cassio!
    O Cassio, Cassio, Cassio!
IAGO: O notable strumpet! — Cassio, may you suspect
    Who they should be that have thus mangled you?
CASSIO: No.   80
GRATIANO: I am sorry to find you thus. I have been to seek you.
IAGO: Lend me a garter. So. O for a chair°
    To bear him easily hence!
BIANCA: Alas, he faints! O Cassio, Cassio, Cassio!
IAGO: Gentlemen all, I do suspect this trash   85
    To be a party in this injury. —
    Patience a while, good Cassio. — Come, come!
    Lend me a light. Know we this face or no?
    Alas, my friend and my dear countryman
    Roderigo? No — Yes, sure. — O heaven, Roderigo!   90
GRATIANO: What, of Venice?
IAGO: Even he, sir. Did you know him?
GRATIANO: Know him? Ay.
IAGO: Signior Gratiano? I cry your gentle pardon.
    These bloody accidents must excuse my manners
    That so neglected you.
GRATIANO: I am glad to see you.   95
IAGO: How do you, Cassio? — O, a chair, a chair!
GRATIANO: Roderigo?
IAGO: He, he, 'tis he!

[A chair brought in.]

    O, that's well said;° the chair.
    Some good man bear him carefully from hence.   100
    I'll fetch the general's surgeon. *[To Bianca.]* For you, mistress,
    Save you your labor. — He that lies slain here, Cassio,
    Was my dear friend. What malice was between you?
CASSIO: None in the world; nor do I know the man.
IAGO *[to Bianca]*: What, look you pale? — O, bear him out o' th' air.   105

                                        [Cassio and Roderigo are borne off.]

    Stay you, good gentlemen. — Look you pale, mistress? —
    Do you perceive the gastness° of her eye? —
    Nay, if you stare, we shall hear more anon.

---

82. chair: Litter.   **99. well said:** Well done.   **107. gastness:** Terror.

Behold her well; I pray you look upon her.
Do you see, gentlemen? Nay, guiltiness will speak.   110
Though tongues were out of use.

Enter Emilia.

EMILIA: 'Las, what's the matter? What's the matter, husband?
IAGO: Cassio hath here been set on in the dark
    By Roderigo, and fellows that are scaped.
    He's almost slain, and Roderigo dead.   115
EMILIA: Alas, good gentlemen! alas, good Cassio!
IAGO: This is the fruits of whoring. Prithee, Emilia,
    Go know of Cassio where he supped to-night.

[To Bianca.]

    What, do you shake at that?
BIANCA: He supped at my house; but I therefore shake not.   120
IAGO: O, did he so? I charge you go with me.
EMILIA: Fie, fie upon thee, strumpet!
BIANCA: I am no strumpet, but of life as honest°
    As you that thus abuse me.
EMILIA: As I? Foh! fie upon thee!
IAGO: Kind gentlemen, let's go see poor Cassio dressed.   125

[To Bianca.]

    Come, mistress, you must tell 's another tale.
    Emilia, run you to the citadel
    And tell my lord and lady what hath happed.
                                                    [Exit Emilia.]
                                                Exeunt [all but Iago].
    Will you go on afore?
                    This is the night
    That either makes me or fordoes° me quite.   *[Exit.]* 130

Scene II

A bedchamber in the castle.

Desdemona [asleep] in her bed. Enter Othello with a light.

OTHELLO: It is the cause, it is the cause,° my soul.
    Let me not name it to you, you chaste stars!
    It is the cause. Yet I'll not shed her blood,
    Nor scar that whiter skin of hers than snow,
    And smooth as monumental alabaster.   5

---

123. **honest:** Chaste. 130. **fordoes:** Destroys. SCENE II. 1. **cause:** Cause of justice.

Yet she must die, else she'll betray more men.
Put out the light, and then put out the light.
If I quench thee, thou flaming minister,°
I can again thy former light restore,
Should I repent me; but once put out thy light,   10
Thou cunning'st pattern of excelling nature,
I know not where is that Promethean heat°
That can thy light relume.° When I have plucked the rose,
I cannot give it vital growth again;
It needs must wither. I'll smell thee on the tree.   15

(*He kisses her.*)

O balmy breath, that dost almost persuade
Justice to break her sword! One more, one more!
Be thus when thou art dead, and I will kill thee,
And love thee after. One more, and that's the last!
So sweet was ne'er so fatal. I must weep,   20
But they are cruel tears. This sorrow's heavenly;
It strikes where it doth love. She wakes.
DESDEMONA: Who's there? Othello?
OTHELLO: Ay, Desdemona.
DESDEMONA: Will you come to bed, my lord?
OTHELLO: Have you prayed to-night, Desdemon?
DESDEMONA: Ay, my lord.   25
OTHELLO: If you bethink yourself of any crime°
    Unreconciled as yet to heaven and grace,
    Solicit for it straight.
DESDEMONA: Alack, my lord, what may you mean by that?
OTHELLO: Well, do it, and be brief; I will walk by.   30
    I would not kill thy unpreparèd spirit.
    No, heaven forfend!° I would not kill thy soul.
DESDEMONA: Talk you of killing?
OTHELLO: Ay, I do.
DESDEMONA: Then heaven
    Have mercy on me!
OTHELLO: Amen, with all my heart!
DESDEMONA: If you say so, I hope you will not kill me.   35
OTHELLO: Hum!
DESDEMONA: And yet I fear you; for you're fatal then
    When your eyes roll so. Why I should fear I know not,
    Since guiltiness I know not; but yet I feel I fear.
OTHELLO: Think on thy sins.

---

8. minister: Servant.   **12. Promethean heat:** Divine fire.   **13. relume:** Relight.   **26. crime:**
Sin.   **32. forfend:** Forbid.

DESDEMONA: They are loves I bear to you.   40
OTHELLO: Ay, and for that thou diest.
DESDEMONA: That death 's unnatural that kills for loving.
    Alas, why gnaw you so your nether lip?
    Some bloody passion shakes your very frame.
    These are portents,° but yet I hope, I hope,   45
    They do not point on me.
OTHELLO: Peace and be still!
DESDEMONA: I will so. What's the matter?
OTHELLO: That handkerchief which I so loved and gave thee
    Thou gav'st to Cassio.
DESDEMONA: No, by my life and soul!
    Send for the man and ask him.
OTHELLO: Sweet soul, take heed,   50
    Take heed of perjury; thou art on thy deathbed.
DESDEMONA: Ay, but not yet to die.
OTHELLO: Yes, presently.°
    Therefore confess thee freely of thy sin;
    For to deny each article with oath
    Cannot remove nor choke the strong conception°   55
    That I do groan withal. Thou art to die.
DESDEMONA: Then Lord have mercy on me!
OTHELLO: I say amen.
DESDEMONA: And have you mercy too! I never did
    Offend° you in my life; never loved Cassio
    But with such general warranty of heaven   60
    As I might love. I never gave him token.
OTHELLO: By heaven, I saw my handkerchief in's hand!
    O perjured woman! thou dost stone my heart,°
    And mak'st me call what I intend to do
    A murder, which I thought a sacrifice.   65
    I saw the handkerchief.
DESDEMONA: He found it then.
    I never gave it him. Send for him hither.
    Let him confess a truth.
OTHELLO: He hath confessed.
DESDEMONA: What, my lord?
OTHELLO: That he hath used thee.
DESDEMONA: How? Unlawfully?
OTHELLO: Ay.   70
DESDEMONA: He will not say so.
OTHELLO: No, his mouth is stopped.

---

45. portents: Signs of impending violence.   **52. presently:** At once.   **55. conception:** Belief.
59. Offend: Wrong.   **63. stone my heart:** Turn my heart to stone.

Honest Iago hath ta'en order° for't.
DESDEMONA: O, my fear interprets. What, is he dead?
OTHELLO: Had all his hairs been lives, my great revenge
    Had stomach for them all.   75
DESDEMONA: Alas, he is betrayed, and I undone!
OTHELLO: Out, strumpet! Weep'st thou for him to my face?
DESDEMONA: O, banish me, my lord, but kill me not!
OTHELLO: Down, strumpet!
DESDEMONA: Kill me to-morrow; let me live to-night!   80
OTHELLO: Nay, if you strive —
DESDEMONA: But half an hour!
OTHELLO: Being done, there is no pause.
DESDEMONA: But while I say one prayer!
OTHELLO: It is too late.

(Smothers her.)

[DESDEMONA: O Lord, Lord, Lord!]

Emilia at the door.

EMILIA *(calls within)*: My lord, my lord! What, ho! my lord, my lord!   85
OTHELLO: What noise is this? Not dead? not yet quite dead?
    I that am cruel am yet merciful;
    I would not have thee linger in thy pain.
    So, so.
EMILIA *(within)*: What, ho! my lord, my lord!
OTHELLO: Who's there?   90
EMILIA *(within)*: O, good my lord, I would speak a word with you!
OTHELLO: Yes, 'tis Emilia. — By and by.° — She's dead. —
    'Tis like she comes to speak of Cassio's death.
    The noise was here. Ha! no more moving?
    Still as the grave. — Shall she come in? Were't good! —   95
    I think she stirs again. No. — What's best to do?
    If she come in, she'll sure speak to my wife.
    My wife! my wife! what wife? I have no wife.
    O, insupportable! O heavy hour!
    Methinks it should be now a huge eclipse   100
    Of sun and moon, and that th' affrighted globe
    Should yawn° at alteration.
EMILIA *(within)*:   I do beseech you
    That I may speak with you, O good my lord!
OTHELLO: I had forgot thee. O, come in, Emilia.
    Soft, by and by. — Let me the curtains draw. —   105

---

72. **ta'en order**: Taken measures. **92. By and by**: Just a moment (addressed to Emilia).
102. yawn: Open, as in an earthquake.

[*Closes the bed-curtains.*]

    Where art thou?

[*Opens the door.*]
Enter Emilia.

               What's the matter with thee now?
EMILIA: O my good lord, yonder's foul murder done!
OTHELLO: What? Now?
EMILIA: But now, my lord.
OTHELLO: It is the very error° of the moon.   110
    She comes more nearer earth than she was wont
    And makes men mad.
EMILIA: Cassio, my lord, hath killed a young Venetian
    Called Roderigo.
OTHELLO: Roderigo killed?
    And Cassio killed?
EMILIA: No, Cassio is not killed.   115
OTHELLO: Not Cassio killed? Then murder's out of tune,
    And sweet revenge grows harsh.
DESDEMONA: O, falsely, falsely murdered?
EMILIA: O, Lord! what cry is that?
OTHELLO: That? What?
EMILIA: Out and alas! that was my lady's voice.   120
    Help! help, ho! help! O lady, speak again!
    Sweet Desdemona! O sweet mistress, speak!
DESDEMONA: A guiltless death I die.
EMILIA: O, who hath done this deed?
DESDEMONA: Nobody—I myself. Farewell.   125
    Commend° me to my kind lord. O, farewell!

(*She dies.*)

OTHELLO: Why, how should she be murd'red?
EMILIA: Alas, who knows?
OTHELLO: You heard her say herself, it was not I.
EMILIA: She said so. I must needs report the truth.
OTHELLO: She's like a liar gone to burning hell!   130
    'Twas I that killed her.
EMILIA: O, the more angel she,
    And you the blacker devil!
OTHELLO: She turned to folly, and she was a whore.
EMILIA: Thou dost belie her, and thou art a devil.
OTHELLO: She was false as water.°

---

110. error: Straying off course.　**126. Commend:** Remember.　**135. water:** (Which is yielding).

EMILIA: Thou art rash as fire to say   135
  That she was false. O, she was heavenly true!
OTHELLO: Cassio did top her. Ask thy husband else.
  O, I were damned beneath all depth in hell
  But that I did proceed upon just grounds
  To this extremity. Thy husband knew it all.   140
EMILIA: My husband?
OTHELLO: Thy husband.
EMILIA: That she was false to wedlock?
OTHELLO: Ay, with Cassio. Nay, had she been true,
  If heaven would make me such another world   145
  Of one entire and perfect chrysolite,°
  I'ld not have sold her for it.
EMILIA: My husband?
OTHELLO: Ay 'twas he that told me first.
  An honest man he is, and hates the slime
  That sticks on filthy deeds.
EMILIA: My husband?   150
OTHELLO: What needs this iterance,° woman? I say thy husband.
EMILIA: O mistress, villainy hath made mocks with love!
  My husband say that she was false?
OTHELLO: He, woman.
  I say, thy husband. Dost understand the word?
  My friend, thy husband; honest, honest Iago.   155
EMILIA: If he say so, may his pernicious soul
  Rot half a grain a day! he lies to th' heart.
  She was too fond of her most filthy bargain.
OTHELLO: Ha!
EMILIA: Do thy worst.   160
  This deed of thine is no more worthy heaven
  Than thou wast worthy her.
OTHELLO: Peace, you were best.
EMILIA: Thou hast not half the power to do me harm
  As I have to be hurt.° O gull! O dolt!
  As ignorant as dirt! thou hast done a deed —   165
  I care not for thy sword; I'll make thee known,
  Though I lost twenty lives. Help! help! Ho! help!
  The Moor hath killed my mistress! Murder! murder!

Enter Montano, Gratiano, Iago, and others.

MONTANO: What is the matter? How now, general?
EMILIA: O, are you come, Iago? You have done well,   170
  That men must lay their murders on your neck.
GRATIANO: What is the matter?

---

146. **chrysolite:** (Precious topaz).   151. **iterance:** Repetition.   164. **to be hurt:** To endure hurt.

EMILIA: Disprove this villain, if thou be'st a man.
    He says thou told'st him that his wife was false.
    I know thou didst not; thou'rt not such a villain. 175
    Speak, for my heart is full.
IAGO: I told him what I thought, and told no more
    Than what he found himself was apt and true.
EMILIA: But did you ever tell him she was false?
IAGO: I did. 180
EMILIA: You told a lie, an odious damnèd lie!
    Upon my soul, a lie! a wicked lie!
    She false with Cassio? Did you say with Cassio?
IAGO: With Cassio, mistress. Go to, charm° your tongue.
EMILIA: I will not charm my tongue; I am bound to speak: 185
    My mistress here lies murdered in her bed—
ALL: O heavens forfend!
EMILIA: And your reports have set the murder on.
OTHELLO: Nay, stare not, masters. It is true indeed.
GRATIANO: 'Tis a strange truth. 190
MONTANO: O monstrous act!
EMILIA: Villainy, villainy, villainy!
    I think upon't—I think I smell't!—O villainy!
    I thought so then.—I'll kill myself for grief.—
    O villainy, villainy!
IAGO: What, are you mad? I charge you get you home. 195
EMILIA: Good gentlemen, let me have leave to speak.
    'Tis proper I obey him, but not now.
    Perchance, Iago, I will ne'er go home.
OTHELLO: O! O! O! *(Falls on the bed.)*
EMILIA: Nay, lay thee down and roar!
    For thou hast killed the sweetest innocent 200
    That e'er did lift up eye.
OTHELLO: O, she was foul!

[*Rises.*]

    I scarce did know you, uncle. There lies your niece,
    Whose breath, indeed, these hands have newly stopped.
    I know this act shows° horrible and grim.
GRATIANO: Poor Desdemon! I am glad thy father's dead. 205
    Thy match was mortal to him, and pure grief
    Shore his old thread in twain. Did he live now,
    This sight would make him do a desperate turn;°
    Yea, curse his better angel from his side,
    And fall to reprobation.° 210

---

184. **charm:** Cast a spell on. 204. **shows:** Appears. 208. **turn:** Act. 210. **reprobation:** Rejection by God, damnation.

OTHELLO: 'Tis pitiful; but yet Iago knows
       That she with Cassio hath the act of shame
       A thousand times committed. Cassio confessed it;
       And she did gratify° his amorous works
       With that recognizance° and pledge of love   215
       Which I first gave her. I saw it in his hand.
       It was a handkerchief, an antique token
       My father gave my mother.
EMILIA: O God! O heavenly God!
IAGO: Zounds, hold your peace!
EMILIA: 'Twill out, 'twill out! I peace?   220
       No, I will speak as liberal as the north,°
       Let heaven and men and devils, let them all,
       All, all, cry shame against me, yet I'll speak.
IAGO: Be wise, and get you home.
EMILIA: I will not.

[Iago draws and threatens Emilia.]

GRATIANO: Fie!
       Your sword upon a woman?   225
EMILIA: O thou dull Moor, that handkerchief thou speak'st of
       I found by fortune, and did give my husband;
       For often with a solemn earnestness —
       More than indeed belonged to such a trifle —
       He begged of me to steal't.
IAGO: Villainous whore!   230
EMILIA: She give it Cassio? No, alas, I found it,
       And I did give't my husband.
IAGO: Filth, thou liest!
EMILIA: By heaven, I do not, I do not, gentlemen.
       O murd'rous coxcomb! what should such a fool
       Do with so good a wife?
OTHELLO: Are there no stones° in heaven   235
       But what serves for the thunder? Precious villain!

The Moor runs at Iago [but is disarmed by Montano].

Iago kills his wife.

GRATIANO: The woman falls. Sure he hath killed his wife.
EMILIA: Ay, ay. O, lay me by my mistress' side.   *Exit Iago.*
GRATIANO: He's gone, but his wife's killed.
MONTANO: 'Tis a notorious° villain. Take you this weapon,   240
       Which I have here recovered from the Moor.

---

214. gratify: Reward. **215. recognizance:** Token. **221. liberal as the north:** Unchecked as the north wind blows. **235. stones:** Bolts like those used for thunderbolts. **240. notorious:** Notable.

Come, guard the door without. Let him not pass,
But kill him rather. I'll after that same villain,
For 'tis a damnèd slave.

Exit [Montano, with all but Othello and Emilia].

OTHELLO: I am not valiant neither;
But every puny whipster° gets my sword.   245
But why should honor outlive honesty?
Let it go all.
EMILIA: What did thy song bode, lady?
Hark, canst thou hear me? I will play the swan,
And die in music. [*Sings.*] "Willow, willow, willow."
Moor, she was chaste. She loved thee, cruel Moor: 250
So come my soul to bliss as I speak true.
So speaking as I think, alas, I die.

(*She dies.*)

OTHELLO: I have another weapon in this chamber;
It is a sword of Spain, the ice brook's° temper.
O, here it is. — Uncle, I must come forth.   255
GRATIANO (*within*): If thou attempt it, it will cost thee dear.
Thou hast no weapon, and perforce must suffer.
OTHELLO: Look in upon me then and speak with me,
Or, naked° as I am, I will assault thee.

[*Enter Gratiano.*]

GRATIANO: What is the matter?
OTHELLO: Behold, I have a weapon;   260
A better never did itself sustain
Upon a soldier's thigh. I have seen the day
That with this little arm and this good sword
I have made my way through more impediments
Than twenty times your stop.° But O vain boast!   265
Who can control his fate? 'Tis not so now.
Be not afraid, though you do see me weaponed.
Here is my journey's end, here is my butt,°
And very seamark° of my utmost sail:
Do you go back dismayed? 'Tis a lost° fear.   270
Man but a rush° against Othello's breast,
And he retires. Where should Othello go?
Now, how dost thou look now? O ill-starred wench!

---

245. puny whipster: Whippersnapper.   **254. ice brook:** I.e., a Spanish blade, tempered in
cold running water.   **259. naked:** Disarmed.   **265. stop:** Power to stop.   **268. butt:** Limit.
269. seamark: Beacon, destination.   **270. lost:** Wasted.   **271. Man but a rush:** Wield only
a reed.

Pale as thy smock! When we shall meet at compt,°
This look of thine will hurl my soul from heaven,   275
And fiends will snatch at it. Cold, cold, my girl?
Even like thy chastity.
O cursèd, cursèd slave! Whip me, ye devils,
From the possession of this heavenly sight!
Blow me about in winds! roast me in sulphur!   280
Wash me in steep-down gulfs of liquid fire!
Oh Desdemon! dead Desdemon! dead! Oh! Oh!

Enter Lodovico, Montano, Iago [as prisoner], and Officers; Cassio in a chair.

LODOVICO: Where is this rash and most unfortunate man?
OTHELLO: That's he that was Othello. Here I am.
LODOVICO: Where is that viper? Bring the villain forth.   285
OTHELLO: I look down towards his feet° — but that's a fable.
      If that thou be'st a devil, I cannot kill thee.

[Wounds Iago.]

LODOVICO: Wrench his sword from him.

[Othello is disarmed.]

IAGO: I bleed, sir, but not killed.
OTHELLO: I am not sorry neither. I'd have thee live;
      For in my sense, 'tis happiness to die.   290
LODOVICO: O thou Othello that wert once so good,
      Fall'n in the practice° of a damnèd slave,
      What shall be said to thee?
OTHELLO: Why, anything;
      An honorable murderer, if you will;
      For naught did I in hate, but all in honor.   295
LODOVICO: This wretch hath part confessed his villainy.
      Did you and he consent in° Cassio's death?
OTHELLO: Ay.
CASSIO: Dear general, I never gave you cause.
OTHELLO: I do believe it, and I ask your pardon.   300
      Will you, I pray, demand that demi-devil
      Why he hath thus ensnared my soul and body?
IAGO: Demand me nothing. What you know, you know.
      From this time forth I never will speak word.
LODOVICO: What, not to pray?
GRATIANO: Torments will ope your lips.   305
OTHELLO: Well, thou dost best.

---

274. **compt:** Final accounting, Last Judgment.   286. **I . . . feet:** I.e., to see if they are cloven, like the Devil's.   292. **practice:** Plot.   297. **consent in:** Agree upon.

LODOVICO: Sir, you shall understand what hath befall'n,
    Which, as I think, you know not. Here is a letter
    Found in the pocket of the slain Roderigo;
    And here another. The one of them imports   310
    The death of Cassio to be undertook
    By Roderigo.
OTHELLO: O villain!
CASSIO: Most heathenish and most gross!
LODOVICO: Now here's another discontented paper
    Found in the pocket too; and this, it seems,   315
    Roderigo meant t' have sent this damnèd villain;
    But that, belike, Iago in the nick°
    Came in and satisfied him.
OTHELLO: O thou pernicious caitiff! —
    How came you, Cassio, by that handkerchief
    That was my wife's?
CASSIO: I found it in my chamber;   320
    And he himself confessed but even now
    That there he dropped it for a special purpose
    Which wrought to his desire.
OTHELLO: O fool! fool! fool!
CASSIO: There is besides in Roderigo's letter,
    How he upbraids Iago that he made him   325
    Brave me upon the watch; whereon it came
    That I was cast;° and even but now he spake,
    After long seeming dead — Iago hurt him,
    Iago set him on.
LODOVICO: You must forsake this room and go with us.   330
    Your power and your command is taken off,
    And Cassio rules in Cyprus. For this slave,
    If there be any cunning cruelty
    That can torment him much and hold him long,
    It shall be his. You shall close prisoner rest   335
    Till that the nature of your fault be known
    To the Venetian state. Come, bring away.
OTHELLO: Soft you! a word or two before you go.
    I have done the state some service, and they know't.
    No more of that. I pray you, in your letters,   340
    When you shall these unlucky° deeds relate,
    Speak of me as I am. Nothing extenuate,
    Nor set down aught in malice. Then must you speak
    Of one that loved not wisely, but too well;
    Of one not easily jealous, but, being wrought,   345

317. nick: Nick of time.   327. cast: Dismissed.   341. unlucky: Fatal.

Perplexed° in the extreme; of one whose hand,
Like the base Judean,° threw a pearl away
Richer than all his tribe; of one whose subdued° eyes,
Albeit unusèd to the melting mood,
Drop tears as fast as the Arabian trees   350
Their med'cinable gum. Set you down this.
And say besides that in Aleppo once,
Where a malignant and a turbaned Turk
Beat a Venetian and traduced the state,
I took by th' throat the circumcisèd dog   355
And smote him — thus.

(*He stabs himself.*)

LODOVICO: O bloody period!°
GRATIANO: All that's spoke is marred.
OTHELLO: I kissed thee ere I killed thee. No way but this,
    Killing myself, to die upon a kiss.

(*He [falls upon the bed and] dies.*)

CASSIO: This did I fear, but thought he had no weapon;   360
    For he was great of heart.
LODOVICO [*to Iago*]:   O Spartan dog,
    More fell° than anguish, hunger, or the sea!
    Look on the tragic loading of this bed.
    This is thy work. The object poisons sight;
    Let it be hid.° Gratiano, keep the house,   365
    And seize upon° the fortunes of the Moor,
    For they succeed on you. To you, lord governor,
    Remains the censure° of this hellish villain,
    The time, the place, the torture. O, enforce it!
    Myself will straight aboard, and to the state   370
    This heavy act with heavy heart relate.

                                                        Exeunt.

---

346. **Perplexed:** Distracted.   347. **Judean:** Judas Iscariot (?) (quarto reads "Indian").
348. **subdued:** I.e., conquered by grief.   357. **period:** Ending.   362. **fell:** Cruel.   365. **Let
it be hid:** I.e., draw the bed curtains.   366. **seize upon:** Take legal possession of.   368. **censure:** Judicial sentence.

WEB: Research William Shakespeare in depth, including images and cultural documents, with
VirtuaLit Drama at bedfordstmartins.com/approachinglit.

Sophocles c. 496–c. 406 B.C.

Oedipus Rex°   [c. 430 B.C.]

Translated by Dudley Fitts and Robert Fitzgerald

CHARACTERS

OEDIPUS, King of Thebes, supposed son of Polybos and Merope, King and
    Queen of Corinth
IOKASTE,° wife of Oedipus and widow of the late King Laios
KREON,° brother of Iokaste, a prince of Thebes
TEIRESIAS, a blind seer who serves Apollo
PRIEST
MESSENGER, from Corinth
SHEPHERD, former servant of Laios
SECOND MESSENGER, from the palace
CHORUS OF THEBAN ELDERS
CHORAGOS, leader of the Chorus
ANTIGONE and ISMENE, young daughters of Oedipus and Iokaste. They appear
    in the Exodus but do not speak.
SUPPLIANTS, GUARDS, SERVANTS

SCENE: *Before the palace of Oedipus, King of Thebes. A central door and two lateral
doors open onto a platform which runs the length of the facade. On the platform,
right and left, are altars; and three steps lead down into the orchestra, or chorus-
ground. At the beginning of the action these steps are crowded by suppliants who have
brought branches and chaplets of olive leaves and who sit in various attitudes of despair. Oedipus enters.*

PROLOGUE°

OEDIPUS: My children, generations of the living
    In the line of Kadmos,° nursed at his ancient hearth:
    Why have you strewn yourselves before these altars
    In supplication, with your boughs and garlands?
    The breath of incense rises from the city   5
    With a sound of prayer and lamentation.

                                              Children,
    I would not have you speak through messengers,
    And therefore I have come myself to hear you —
    I, Oedipus, who bear the famous name.

Oedipus Rex: "Oedipus the King" (Latin). The name *Oedipus* derives from *oida,* "to know"
(from a root word meaning "to see"). *Oedipus* means "swollen foot" or "clubfoot."   **Iokaste:**
The Anglicized spelling is *Jocasta.*   **Kreon:** The Anglicized spelling is *Creon.*   **Prologue:** The
first part the play, providing exposition and establishing the scene.   **2. Kadmos:** The Anglicized spelling is Cadmus. According to tradition, the founder of Thebes.

(*To a Priest.*) You, there, since you are eldest in the company,   10
Speak for them all, tell me what preys upon you,
Whether you come in dread, or crave some blessing:
Tell me, and never doubt that I will help you
In every way I can; I should be heartless
Were I not moved to find you suppliant here.   15
PRIEST: Great Oedipus, O powerful king of Thebes!
You see how all the ages of our people
Cling to your altar steps: here are boys
Who can barely stand alone, and here are priests
By weight of age, as I am a priest of God,   20
And young men chosen from those yet unmarried;
As for the others, all that multitude,
They wait with olive chaplets in the squares,
At the two shrines of Pallas,° and where Apollo°
Speaks in the glowing embers.

                                  Your own eyes   25
Must tell you: Thebes is tossed on a murdering sea
And can not lift her head from the death surge.
A rust consumes the buds and fruits of the earth;
The herds are sick; children die unborn,
And labor is vain. The god of plague and pyre   30
Raids like detestable lightning through the city,
And all the house of Kadmos is laid waste,
All emptied, and all darkened: Death alone
Battens upon the misery of Thebes.

You are not one of the immortal gods, we know;   35
Yet we have come to you to make our prayer
As to the man surest in mortal ways
And wisest in the ways of God. You saved us
From the Sphinx,° that flinty singer, and the tribute
We paid to her so long; yet you were never   40
Better informed than we, nor could we teach you:
A god's touch, it seems, enabled you to help us.

Therefore, O mighty power, we turn to you:
Find us our safety, find us a remedy,

---

24. Pallas: Pallas Athena, goddess of wisdom and warfare, and guardian of cities; **Apollo:** Phoebus Apollo, god of prophesy as well as of learning and the arts.   **39. Sphinx:** In Greek mythology, the Sphinx was a winged monster with the head and breasts of a woman and the body of a lion. The Sphinx terrorized Thebes, confronting those who came near her with a riddle — "What walks on four feet in the morning, two at noon, and three in the evening?" — and killing them when they did not answer correctly. When Oedipus correctly answered "Man" (as a baby crawling on all fours, as an adult walking erect, and in old age using a cane), the Sphinx killed herself and the city was freed.

Whether by counsel of the gods or of men.   45
A king of wisdom tested in the past
Can act in a time of troubles, and act well.
Noblest of men, restore
Life to your city! Think how all men call you
Liberator for your boldness long ago;   50
Ah, when your years of kingship are remembered,
Let them not say *We rose, but later fell* —
Keep the State from going down in the storm!
Once, years ago, with happy augury,
You brought us fortune; be the same again!   55
No man questions your power to rule the land:
But rule over men, not over a dead city!
Ships are only hulls, high walls are nothing,
When no life moves in the empty passageways.

OEDIPUS: Poor children! You may be sure I know   60
All that you longed for in your coming here.
I know that you are deathly sick; and yet,
Sick as you are, not one is as sick as I.
Each of you suffers in himself alone
His anguish, not another's; but my spirit   65
Groans for the city, for myself, for you.

I was not sleeping, you are not waking me.
No, I have been in tears for a long while
And in my restless thought walked many ways.
In all my search I found one remedy,   70
And I have adopted it: I have sent Kreon,
Son of Menoikeus, brother of the queen,
To Delphi,° Apollo's place of revelation,
To learn there, if he can,
What act or pledge of mine may save the city.   75
I have counted the days, and now, this very day,
I am troubled, for he has overstayed his time.
What is he doing? He has been gone too long.
Yet whenever he comes back, I should do ill
Not to take any action the god orders.   80

PRIEST: It is a timely promise. At this instant
They tell me Kreon is here.

OEDIPUS: O Lord Apollo!
May his news be fair as his face is radiant!

PRIEST: Good news, I gather! he is crowned with bay,
The chaplet is thick with berries.

---

73. Delphi: Site of the temple that housed the most famous and most powerful oracle (priestess uttering a message from the gods) of ancient Greece.

OEDIPUS: We shall soon know;   85
 He is near enough to hear us now. (*Enter Kreon.*) O prince:
 Brother: son of Menoikeus:
 What answer do you bring us from the god?
KREON: A strong one. I can tell you, great afflictions
 Will turn out well, if they are taken well.   90
OEDIPUS: What was the oracle? These vague words
 Leave me still hanging between hope and fear.
KREON: Is it your pleasure to hear me with all these
 Gathered around us? I am prepared to speak,
 But should we not go in?
OEDIPUS: Speak to them all,   95
 It is for them I suffer, more than for myself.
KREON: Then I will tell you what I heard at Delphi.
 In plain words
 The god commands us to expel from the land of Thebes
 An old defilement we are sheltering.   100
 It is a deathly thing, beyond cure;
 We must not let it feed upon us longer.
OEDIPUS: What defilement? How shall we rid ourselves of it?
KREON: By exile or death, blood for blood. It was
 Murder that brought the plague-wind on the city.   105
OEDIPUS: Murder of whom? Surely the god has named him?
KREON: My Lord: Laios once ruled this land,
 Before you came to govern us.
OEDIPUS: I know;
 I learned of him from others; I never saw him.
KREON: He was murdered; and Apollo commands us now   110
 To take revenge upon whoever killed him.
OEDIPUS: Upon whom? Where are they? Where shall we find a clue
 To solve that crime, after so many years?
KREON: Here in this land, he said. Search reveals
 Things that escape an inattentive man.   115
OEDIPUS: Tell me: Was Laios murdered in his house,
 Or in the fields, or in some foreign country?
KREON: He said he planned to make a pilgrimage.
 He did not come home again.
OEDIPUS: And was there no one,
 No witness, no companion, to tell what happened?   120
KREON: They were all killed but one, and he got away
 So frightened that he could remember one thing only.
OEDIPUS: What was that one thing? One may be the key
 To everything, if we resolve to use it.
KREON: He said that a band of highwaymen attacked them,   125
 Outnumbered them, and overwhelmed the king.

OEDIPUS: Strange, that a highwayman should be so daring —
　Unless some faction here bribed him to do it.
KREON: We thought of that. But after Laios' death
　New troubles arose and we had no avenger.　　　　　　　　　　130
OEDIPUS: What troubles could prevent your hunting down the killers?
KREON: The riddling Sphinx's song
　Made us deaf to all mysteries but her own.
OEDIPUS: Then once more I must bring what is dark to light.
　It is most fitting that Apollo shows,　　　　　　　　　　　　135
　As you do, this compunction for the dead.
　You shall see how I stand by you, as I should,
　Avenging this country and the god as well,
　And not as though it were for some distant friend,
　But for my own sake, to be rid of evil.　　　　　　　　　　140
　Whoever killed King Laios might — who knows? —
　Lay violent hands even on me — and soon.
　I act for the murdered king in my own interest.

　Come, then, my children: leave the altar steps,
　Lift up your olive boughs!
　　　　　　　　　　　　One of you go　　　　　　　　　　145
　And summon the people of Kadmos to gather here.
　I will do all that I can; you may tell them that.　　　　(*Exit a Page.*)
　So, with the help of God,
　We shall be saved — or else indeed we are lost.
PRIEST: Let us rise, children. It was for this we came,　　　　150
　And now the king has promised it.
　Phoibos° has sent us an oracle; may he descend
　Himself to save us and drive out the plague.

(*Exeunt*° *Oedipus and Kreon into the palace by the central door. The Priest and
the Suppliants disperse right and left. After a short pause the Chorus enters the orchestra.*)

PARODOS° / Strophe° 1

CHORUS: What is God singing in his profound
　Delphi of gold and shadow?
　What oracle for Thebes, the Sunwhipped city?
　Fear unjoints me, the roots of my heart tremble.
　Now I remember, O Healer, your power, and wonder:　　　　5
　Will you send doom like a sudden cloud, or weave it

---

152. Phoibos: Apollo.　s.d. Exeunt: "They go out" or leave the stage (Latin).　**Parodos:** The
introductory section of a choral ode, sung (or chanted) by the Chorus on their entry.　**Strophe:** The first stanza of a choral ode sung by the Chorus as they move from stage right to stage
left.

Like nightfall of the past?
Speak to me, tell me, O
Child of golden Hope, immortal Voice.

Antistrophe° 1

Let me pray to Athene, the immortal daughter of Zeus,   10
And to Artemis° her sister
Who keeps her famous throne in the market ring,
And to Apollo, archer from distant heaven—
O gods, descend! Like three streams leap against
The fires of our grief, the fires of darkness;   15
Be swift to bring us rest!
As in the old time from the brilliant house
Of air you stepped to save us, come again!

Strophe 2

Now our afflictions have no end,
Now all our stricken host lies down   20
And no man fights off death with his mind;
The noble plowland bears no grain,
And groaning mothers can not bear—
See, how our lives like birds take wing,
Like sparks that fly when a fire soars,   25
To the shore of the god of evening.

Antistrophe 2

The plague burns on, it is pitiless,
Though pallid children laden with death
Lie unwept in the stony ways,
And old gray women by every path   30
Flock to the strand about the altars
There to strike their breasts and cry
Worship of Phoibos in wailing prayers:
Be kind, God's golden child!

Strophe 3

There are no swords in this attack by fire,   35
No shields, but we are ringed with cries.
Send the besieger plunging from our homes
Into the vast sea-room of the Atlantic

Antistrophe: The second stanza of a choral ode sung by the Chorus as they move back from stage left to stage right.   **11. Artemis:** Twin sister of Apollo, goddess of the moon, hunting, and female chastity.

Or into the waves that foam eastward of Thrace —
For the day ravages what the night spares —   40
Destroy our enemy, lord of the thunder!
Let him be riven by lightning from heaven!

Antistrophe 3

Phoibos Apollo, stretch the sun's bowstring,
That golden cord, until it sing for us,
Flashing arrows in heaven!
                            Artemis, Huntress,   45
Race with flaring lights upon our mountains!
O scarlet god,° O golden-banded brow,
O Theban Bacchos in a storm of Maenads,°

(Enter Oedipus, center.)

Whirl upon Death, that all the Undying hate!
Come with blinding torches, come in joy!   50

SCENE 1

OEDIPUS: Is this your prayer? It may be answered. Come,
Listen to me, act as the crisis demands,
And you shall have relief from all these evils.

Until now I was a stranger to this tale,
As I had been a stranger to the crime.   5
Could I track down the murderer without a clue?
But now, friends,
As one who became a citizen after the murder,
I make this proclamation to all Thebans:
If any man knows by whose hand Laios, son of Labdakos,   10
Met his death, I direct that man to tell me everything,
No matter what he fears for having so long withheld it.
Let it stand as promised that no further trouble
Will come to him, but he may leave the land in safety.
Moreover: If anyone knows the murderer to be foreign,   15
Let him not keep silent: he shall have his reward from me.
However, if he does conceal it; if any man
Fearing for his friend or for himself disobeys this edict,
Hear what I propose to do:

I solemnly forbid the people of this country,   20
Where power and throne are mine, ever to receive that man
Or speak to him, no matter who he is, or let him

---

47. **scarlet god:** Dionysus (Bacchus), god of wine.   48. **Maenads:** Female celebrants who accompany Dionysus.

Join in sacrifice, lustration, or in prayer.
I decree that he be driven from every house,
Being, as he is, corruption itself to us: the Delphic   25
Voice of Apollo has pronounced this revelation.
Thus I associate myself with the oracle
And take the side of the murdered king.

As for the criminal, I pray to God —
Whether it be a lurking thief, or one of a number —   30
I pray that that man's life be consumed in evil and wretchedness.
And as for me, this curse applies no less
If it should turn out that the culprit is my guest here,
Sharing my hearth.
                    You have heard the penalty.
I lay it on you now to attend to this   35
For my sake, for Apollo's, for the sick
Sterile city that heaven has abandoned.
Suppose the oracle had given you no command:
Should this defilement go uncleansed for ever?
You should have found the murderer: your king,   40
A noble king, had been destroyed!
                    Now I,
Having the power that he held before me,
Having his bed, begetting children there
Upon his wife, as he would have, had he lived —
Their son would have been my children's brother,   45
If Laios had had luck in fatherhood!
(And now his bad fortune has struck him down) —
I say I take the son's part, just as though
I were his son, to press the fight for him
And see it won! I'll find the hand that brought   50
Death to Labdakos' and Polydoros' child,
Heir of Kadmos' and Agenor's line.°
And as for those who fail me,
May the gods deny them the fruit of the earth,
Fruit of the womb, and may they rot utterly!   55
Let them be wretched as we are wretched, and worse!

For you, for loyal Thebans, and for all
Who find my actions right, I pray the favor
Of justice, and of all the immortal gods.
CHORAGOS:° Since I am under oath, my lord, I swear   60
    I did not do the murder, I can not name

51–52. Labdakos, Polydoros, Kadmos, and Agenor: Laios's father, grandfather, great-grandfather, and great-great-grandfather.   **60. Choragos:** Leader of the Chorus.

The murderer. Phoibos ordained the search;
    Why did he not say who the culprit was?
OEDIPUS: An honest question. But no man in the world
    Can make the gods do more than the gods will.   65
CHORAGOS: There is an alternative, I think —
OEDIPUS: Tell me.
    Any or all, you must not fail to tell me.
CHORAGOS: A lord clairvoyant to the lord Apollo,
    As we all know, is the skilled Teiresias.
    One might learn much about this from him, Oedipus.   70
OEDIPUS: I am not wasting time:
    Kreon spoke of this, and I have sent for him —
    Twice, in fact; it is strange that he is not here.
CHORAGOS: The other matter — that old report — seems useless.
OEDIPUS: What was that? I am interested in all reports.   75
CHORAGOS: The king was said to have been killed by highwaymen.
OEDIPUS: I know. But we have no witnesses to that.
CHORAGOS: If the killer can feel a particle of dread,
    Your curse will bring him out of hiding!
OEDIPUS: No.
    The man who dared that act will fear no curse.   80

(*Enter the blind seer Teiresias, led by a Page.*)

CHORAGOS: But there is one man who may detect the criminal.
    This is Teiresias, this is the holy prophet
    In whom, alone of all men, truth was born.
OEDIPUS: Teiresias: seer: student of mysteries,
    Of all that's taught and all that no man tells,   85
    Secrets of Heaven and secrets of the earth:
    Blind though you are, you know the city lies
    Sick with plague; and from this plague, my lord,
    We find that you alone can guard or save us.

    Possibly you did not hear the messengers?   90
    Apollo, when we sent to him,
    Sent us back word that this great pestilence
    Would lift, but only if we established clearly
    The identity of those who murdered Laios.
    They must be killed or exiled.
                            Can you use   95
    Birdflight° or any art of divination
    To purify yourself, and Thebes, and me
    From this contagion? We are in your hands.

---

96. Birdflight: Prophecy of future events based on the flight of birds.

    There is no fairer duty
    Than that of helping others in distress.   100
TEIRESIAS: How dreadful knowledge of the truth can be
    When there's no help in truth! I knew this well,
    But did not act on it; else I should not have come.
OEDIPUS: What is troubling you? Why are your eyes so cold?
TEIRESIAS: Let me go home. Bear your own fate, and I'll   105
    Bear mine. It is better so: trust what I say.
OEDIPUS: What you say is ungracious and unhelpful
    To your native country. Do not refuse to speak.
TEIRESIAS: When it comes to speech, your own is neither temperate
    Nor opportune. I wish to be more prudent.   110
OEDIPUS: In God's name, we all beg you —
TEIRESIAS: You are all ignorant.
    No; I will never tell you what I know.
    Now it is my misery; then, it would be yours.
OEDIPUS: What! You do know something, and will not tell us?
    You would betray us all and wreck the State?   115
TEIRESIAS: I do not intend to torture myself, or you.
    Why persist in asking? You will not persuade me.
OEDIPUS: What a wicked old man you are! You'd try a stone's
    Patience! Out with it! Have you no feeling at all?
TEIRESIAS: You call me unfeeling. If you could only see   120
    The nature of your own feelings . . .
OEDIPUS: Why,
    Who would not feel as I do? Who could endure
    Your arrogance toward the city?
TEIRESIAS: What does it matter?
    Whether I speak or not, it is bound to come.
OEDIPUS: Then, if "it" is bound to come, you are bound to tell me.   125
TEIRESIAS: No, I will not go on. Rage as you please.
OEDIPUS: Rage? Why not!
                And I'll tell you what I think:
    You planned it, you had it done, you all but
    Killed him with your own hands: if you had eyes,
    I'd say the crime was yours, and yours alone.   130
TEIRESIAS: So? I charge you, then,
    Abide by the proclamation you have made:
    From this day forth
    Never speak again to these men or to me;
    You yourself are the pollution of this country.   135
OEDIPUS: You dare say that! Can you possibly think you have
    Some way of going free, after such insolence?
TEIRESIAS: I have gone free. It is the truth sustains me.
OEDIPUS: Who taught you shamelessness? It was not your craft.

TEIRESIAS: You did. You made me speak. I did not want to.   140
OEDIPUS: Speak what? Let me hear it again more clearly.
TEIRESIAS: Was it not clear before? Are you tempting me?
OEDIPUS: I did not understand it. Say it again.
TEIRESIAS: I say that you are the murderer whom you seek.
OEDIPUS: Now twice you have spat out infamy. You'll pay for it!   145
TEIRESIAS: Would you care for more? Do you wish to be really angry?
OEDIPUS: Say what you will. Whatever you say is worthless.
TEIRESIAS: I say you live in hideous shame with those
    Most dear to you. You can not see the evil.
OEDIPUS: Can you go on babbling like this for ever?   150
TEIRESIAS: I can, if there is power in truth.
OEDIPUS: There is:
    But not for you, not for you,
    You sightless, witless, senseless, mad old man!
TEIRESIAS: You are the madman. There is no one here
    Who will not curse you soon, as you curse me.   155
OEDIPUS: You child of total night! I would not touch you;
    Neither would any man who sees the sun.
TEIRESIAS: True: it is not from you my fate will come.
    That lies within Apollo's competence,
    As it is his concern.
OEDIPUS: Tell me, who made   160
    These fine discoveries? Kreon? or someone else?
TEIRESIAS: Kreon is no threat. You weave your own doom.
OEDIPUS: Wealth, power, craft of statemanship!
    Kingly position, everywhere admired!
    What savage envy is stored up against these,   165
    If Kreon, whom I trusted, Kreon my friend,
    For this great office which the city once
    Put in my hands unsought — if for this power
    Kreon desires in secret to destroy me!

    He has bought this decrepit fortune-teller, this   170
    Collector of dirty pennies, this prophet fraud —
    Why, he is no more clairvoyant than I am!
                         Tell us:
    Has your mystic mummery ever approached the truth?
    When that hellcat the Sphinx was performing here,
    What help were you to these people?   175
    Her magic was not for the first man who came along:
    It demanded a real exorcist. Your birds —
    What good were they? or the gods, for the matter of that?
    But I came by,
    Oedipus, the simple man, who knows nothing —   180

I thought it out for myself, no birds helped me!
And this is the man you think you can destroy,
That you may be close to Kreon when he's king!
Well, you and your friend Kreon, it seems to me,
Will suffer most. If you were not an old man,   185
You would have paid already for your plot.
CHORAGOS: We can not see that his words or yours
    Have been spoken except in anger, Oedipus,
    And of anger we have no need. How to accomplish
    The god's will best: that is what most concerns us.   190
TEIRESIAS: You are a king. But where argument's concerned
    I am your man, as much a king as you.
    I am not your servant, but Apollo's.
    I have no need of Kreon or Kreon's name.

    Listen to me. You mock my blindness, do you?   195
    But I say that you, with both your eyes, are blind:
    You can not see the wretchedness of your life,
    Nor in whose house you live, no, nor with whom.
    Who are your father and mother? Can you tell me?
    You do not even know the blind wrongs   200
    That you have done them, on earth and in the world below.
    But the double lash of your parents' curse will whip you
    Out of this land some day, with only night
    Upon your precious eyes.
    Your cries then—where will they not be heard?   205
    What fastness of Kithairon° will not echo them?
    And that bridal-descant of yours—you'll know it then,
    The song they sang when you came here to Thebes
    And found your misguided berthing.
    All this, and more, that you can not guess at now,   210
    Will bring you to yourself among your children.

    Be angry, then. Curse Kreon. Curse my words.
    I tell you, no man that walks upon the earth
    Shall be rooted out more horribly than you.
OEDIPUS: Am I to bear this from him?—Damnation   215
    Take you! Out of this place! Out of my sight!
TEIRESIAS: I would not have come at all if you had not asked me.
OEDIPUS: Could I have told that you'd talk nonsense, that
    You'd come here to make a fool of yourself, and of me?
TEIRESIAS: A fool? Your parents thought me sane enough.   220
OEDIPUS: My parents again!—Wait: who were my parents?
TEIRESIAS: This day will give you a father, and break your heart.
OEDIPUS: Your infantile riddles! Your damned abracadabra!

---

206. Kithairon: Mountain where Oedipus was abandoned as an infant.

TEIRESIAS: You were a great man once at solving riddles.
OEDIPUS: Mock me with that if you like; you will find it true.   225
TEIRESIAS: It was true enough. It brought about your ruin.
OEDIPUS: But if it saved this town?
TEIRESIAS (*to the Page*):   Boy, give me your hand.
OEDIPUS: Yes, boy; lead him away.
                              — While you are here
        We can do nothing. Go; leave us in peace.
TEIRESIAS: I will go when I have said what I have to say.   230
        How can you hurt me? And I tell you again:
        The man you have been looking for all this time,
        The damned man, the murderer of Laios,
        That man is in Thebes. To your mind he is foreign-born,
        But it will soon be shown that he is a Theban,   235
        A revelation that will fail to please.
                              A blind man,
        Who has his eyes now; a penniless man, who is rich now;
        And he will go tapping the strange earth with his staff.
        To the children with whom he lives now he will be
        Brother and father — the very same; to her   240
        Who bore him, son and husband — the very same
        Who came to his father's bed, wet with his father's blood.
        Enough. Go think that over.
        If later you find error in what I have said,
        You may say that I have no skill in prophecy.   245

(*Exit Teiresias, led by his Page. Oedipus goes into the palace.*)

ODE° 1 / Strophe 1

CHORUS: The Delphic stone of prophecies
        Remembers ancient regicide
        And a still bloody hand.
        That killer's hour of flight has come.
        He must be stronger than riderless   5
        Coursers of untiring wind,
        For the son of Zeus° armed with his father's thunder
        Leaps in lightning after him;
        And the Furies° hold his track, the sad Furies.

Antistrophe 1

Holy Parnassos'° peak of snow   10
Flashes and blinds that secret man,

Ode: Song chanted by the Chorus.   **7. son of Zeus:** Apollo.   **9. Furies:** Three female spirits who sought out and punished evildoers.   **10. Parnassos:** Parnassus, mountain in Greece sacred to Apollo.

That all shall hunt him down:
Though he may roam the forest shade
Like a bull gone wild from pasture
To rage through glooms of stone.   15
Doom comes down on him; flight will not avail him;
For the world's heart calls him desolate,
And the immortal voices follow, for ever follow.

Strophe 2

But now a wilder thing is heard
From the old man skilled at hearing Fate in the wing-beat of a bird.   20
Bewildered as a blown bird, my soul hovers and can not find
Foothold in this debate, or any reason or rest of mind.
But no man ever brought—none can bring
Proof of strife between Thebes' royal house,
Labdakos' line,° and the son of Polybos;°   25
And never until now has any man brought word
Of Laios' dark death staining Oedipus the King.

Antistrophe 2

Divine Zeus and Apollo hold
Perfect intelligence alone of all tales ever told;
And well though this diviner works, he works in his own night;   30
No man can judge that rough unknown or trust in second sight,
For wisdom changes hands among the wise.
Shall I believe my great lord criminal
At a raging word that a blind old man let fall?
I saw him, when the carrion woman° faced him of old,   35
Prove his heroic mind. These evil words are lies.

SCENE 2

KREON: Men of Thebes:
I am told that heavy accusations
Have been brought against me by King Oedipus.

I am not the kind of man to bear this tamely.

If in these present difficulties   5
He holds me accountable for any harm to him
Through anything I have said or done—why, then,
I do not value life in this dishonor.

---

25. **Labdakos' line:** Laios's family; **Polybos:** Corinthian king who had adopted Oedipus.
35. **carrion woman:** The Sphinx.

It is not as though this rumor touched upon
Some private indiscretion. The matter is grave.   10
The fact is that I am being called disloyal
To the State, to my fellow citizens, to my friends.
CHORAGOS: He may have spoken in anger, not from his mind.
KREON: But did you not hear him say I was the one
    Who seduced the old prophet into lying?   15
CHORAGOS: The thing was said; I do not know how seriously.
KREON: But you were watching him! Were his eyes steady?
    Did he look like a man in his right mind?
CHORAGOS: I do not know.
I can not judge the behavior of great men.
But here is the king himself.

(Enter Oedipus.)

OEDIPUS: So you dared come back.   20
Why? How brazen of you to come to my house,
You murderer!
            Do you think I do not know
That you plotted to kill me, plotted to steal my throne?
Tell me, in God's name: am I coward, a fool,
That you should dream you could accomplish this?   25
A fool who could not see your slippery game?
A coward, not to fight back when I saw it?
You are the fool, Kreon, are you not? hoping
Without support or friends to get a throne?
Thrones may be won or bought: you could do neither.   30
KREON: Now listen to me. You have talked; let me talk, too.
    You can not judge unless you know the facts.
OEDIPUS: You speak well: there is one fact; but I find it hard
    To learn from the deadliest enemy I have.
KREON: That above all I must dispute with you.   35
OEDIPUS: That above all I will not hear you deny.
KREON: If you think there is anything good in being stubborn
    Against all reason, then I say you are wrong.
OEDIPUS: If you think a man can sin against his own kind
    And not be punished for it, I say you are mad.   40
KREON: I agree. But tell me: what have I done to you?
OEDIPUS: You advised me to send for that wizard, did you not?
KREON: I did. I should do it again.
OEDIPUS: Very well. Now tell me:
    How long has it been since Laios —
KREON: What of Laios?
OEDIPUS: Since he vanished in that onset by the road?   45
KREON: It was long ago, a long time.

OEDIPUS: And this prophet,
    Was he practicing here then?
KREON: He was; and with honor, as now.
OEDIPUS: Did he speak of me at that time?
KREON: He never did,
    At least, not when I was present.
OEDIPUS: But . . . the enquiry?
    I suppose you held one?
KREON: We did, but we learned nothing.   50
OEDIPUS: Why did the prophet not speak against me then?
KREON: I do not know; and I am the kind of man
    Who holds his tongue when he has no facts to go on.
OEDIPUS: There's one fact that you know, and you could tell it.
KREON: What fact is that? If I know it, you shall have it.   55
OEDIPUS: If he were not involved with you, he could not say
    That it was I who murdered Laios.
KREON: If he says that, you are the one that knows it! —
    But now it is my turn to question you.
OEDIPUS: Put your questions. I am no murderer.   60
KREON: First, then: You married my sister?
OEDIPUS: I married your sister.
KREON: And you rule the kingdom equally with her?
OEDIPUS: Everything that she wants she has from me.
KREON: And I am the third, equal to both of you?
OEDIPUS: That is why I call you a bad friend.   65
KREON: No. Reason it out, as I have done.
    Think of this first: would any sane man prefer
    Power, with all a king's anxieties,
    To that same power and the grace of sleep?
    Certainly not I.   70
    I have never longed for the king's power — only his rights.
    Would any wise man differ from me in this?
    As matters stand, I have my way in everything
    With your consent, and no responsibilities.
    If I were king, I should be a slave to policy.   75
    How could I desire a scepter more
    Than what is now mine — untroubled influence?
    No, I have not gone mad; I need no honors,
    Except those with the perquisites I have now.
    I am welcome everywhere; every man salutes me,   80
    And those who want your favor seek my ear,
    Since I know how to manage what they ask.
    Should I exchange this ease for that anxiety?
    Besides, no sober mind is treasonable.
    I hate anarchy   85

And never would deal with any man who likes it.
Test what I have said. Go to the priestess
At Delphi, ask if I quoted her correctly.
And as for this other thing: if I am found
Guilty of treason with Teiresias,   90
Then sentence me to death. You have my word
It is a sentence I should cast my vote for—
But not without evidence!
                      You do wrong
When you take good men for bad, bad men for good.
A true friend thrown aside—why, life itself   95
Is not more precious!
                    In time you will know this well:
For time, and time alone, will show the just man,
Though scoundrels are discovered in a day.
CHORAGOS: This is well said, and a prudent man would ponder it.
    Judgments too quickly formed are dangerous.   100
OEDIPUS: But is he not quick in his duplicity?
    And shall I not be quick to parry him?
    Would you have me stand still, hold my peace, and let
    This man win everything, through my inaction?
KREON: And you want—what is it, then? To banish me?   105
OEDIPUS: No, not exile. It is your death I want,
    So that all the world may see what treason means.
KREON: You will persist, then? You will not believe me?
OEDIPUS: How can I believe you?
KREON: Then you are a fool.
OEDIPUS: To save myself?
KREON: In justice, think of me.   110
OEDIPUS: You are evil incarnate.
KREON: But suppose that you are wrong?
OEDIPUS: Still I must rule.
KREON: But not if you rule badly.
OEDIPUS: O city, city!
KREON: It is my city, too!
CHORAGOS: Now, my lords, be still. I see the queen,
    Iokaste, coming from her palace chambers;   115
    And it is time she came, for the sake of you both.
    This dreadful quarrel can be resolved through her.

(*Enter Iokaste.*)

IOKASTE: Poor foolish men, what wicked din is this?
    With Thebes sick to death, is it not shameful
    That you should take some private quarrel up?   120
    (*To Oedipus.*) Come into the house.

—And you, Kreon, go now:
Let us have no more of this tumult over nothing.
KREON: Nothing? No, sister: what your husband plans for me
Is one of two great evils: exile or death.
OEDIPUS: He is right.
                              Why, woman I have caught him squarely   125
Plotting against my life.
KREON: No! Let me die
Accurst if ever I have wished you harm!
IOKASTE: Ah, believe it, Oedipus!
In the name of the gods, respect this oath of his
For my sake, for the sake of these people here!   130

Strophe 1

CHORAGOS: Open your mind to her, my lord. Be ruled by her, I beg you!
OEDIPUS: What would you have me do?
CHORAGOS: Respect Kreon's word. He has never spoken like a fool,
And now he has sworn an oath.
OEDIPUS: You know what you ask?
CHORAGOS: I do.
OEDIPUS: Speak on, then.
CHORAGOS: A friend so sworn should not be baited so,   135
In blind malice, and without final proof.
OEDIPUS: You are aware, I hope, that what you say
Means death for me, or exile at the least.

Strophe 2

CHORAGOS: No, I swear by Helios, first in heaven!
May I die friendless and accurst,   140
The worst of deaths, if ever I meant that!
It is the withering fields
That hurt my sick heart:
Must we bear all these ills,
And now your bad blood as well?   145
OEDIPUS: Then let him go. And let me die, if I must,
Or be driven by him in shame from the land of Thebes.
It is your unhappiness, and not his talk,
That touches me.
                    As for him—
Wherever he goes, hatred will follow him.   150
KREON: Ugly in yielding, as you were ugly in rage!
Natures like yours chiefly torment themselves.
OEDIPUS: Can you not go? Can you not leave me?

KREON: I can.
 You do not know me; but the city knows me,
 And in its eyes I am just, if not in yours.   (*Exit Kreon.*) 155

Antistrophe 1

CHORAGOS: Lady Iokaste, did you not ask the King to go to his chambers?
IOKASTE: First tell me what has happened.
CHORAGOS: There was suspicion without evidence; yet it rankled
 As even false charges will.
IOKASTE: On both sides?
CHORAGOS: On both.
IOKASTE: But what was said?   160
CHORAGOS: Oh let it rest, let it be done with!
 Have we not suffered enough?
OEDIPUS: You see to what your decency has brought you:
 You have made difficulties where my heart saw none.

Antistrophe 2

CHORAGOS: Oedipus, it is not once only I have told you —   165
 You must know I should count myself unwise
 To the point of madness, should I now forsake you —
            You, under whose hand,
                 In the storm of another time,
                 Our dear land sailed out free.   170
                 But now stand fast at the helm!
IOKASTE: In God's name, Oedipus, inform your wife as well:
 Why are you so set in this hard anger?
OEDIPUS: I will tell you, for none of these men deserves
 My confidence as you do. It is Kreon's work,   175
 His treachery, his plotting against me.
IOKASTE: Go on, if you can make this clear to me.
OEDIPUS: He charges me with the murder of Laios.
IOKASTE: Has he some knowledge? Or does he speak from hearsay?
OEDIPUS: He would not commit himself to such a charge,   180
 But he has brought in that damnable soothsayer
 To tell his story.
IOKASTE: Set your mind at rest.
 If it is a question of soothsayers, I tell you
 That you will find no man whose craft gives knowledge
 Of the unknowable.
                    Here is my proof: 185
 An oracle was reported to Laios once
 (I will not say from Phoibos himself, but from

His appointed ministers, at any rate)
That his doom would be death at the hands of his own son —
His son, born of his flesh and of mine!   190

Now, you remember the story: Laios was killed
By marauding strangers where three highways meet;
But his child had not been three days in this world
Before the king had pierced the baby's ankles
And left him to die on a lonely mountainside.   195

Thus, Apollo never caused that child
To kill his father, and it was not Laios' fate
To die at the hands of his son, as he had feared.
This is what prophets and prophecies are worth!
Have no dread of them.
                              It is God himself   200
Who can show us what he wills, in his own way.
OEDIPUS: How strange a shadowy memory crossed my mind,
     Just now while you were speaking; it chilled my heart.
IOKASTE: What do you mean? What memory do you speak of?
OEDIPUS: If I understand you, Laios was killed   205
     At a place where three roads meet.
IOKASTE: So it was said;
     We have no later story.
OEDIPUS: Where did it happen?
IOKASTE: Phokis, it is called: at a place where the Theban Way
     Divides into the roads toward Delphi and Daulia.
OEDIPUS: When?
IOKASTE: We had the news not long before you came   210
     And proved the right to your succession here.
OEDIPUS: Ah, what net has God been weaving for me?
IOKASTE: Oedipus! Why does this trouble you?
OEDIPUS: Do not ask me yet.
     First, tell me how Laios looked, and tell me
     How old he was.
IOKASTE: He was tall, his hair just touched   215
     With white; his form was not unlike your own.
OEDIPUS: I think that I myself may be accurst
     By my own ignorant edict.
IOKASTE: You speak strangely.
     It makes me tremble to look at you, my king.
OEDIPUS: I am not sure that the blind man can not see.   220
     But I should know better if you were to tell me —
IOKASTE: Anything — though I dread to hear you ask it.
OEDIPUS: Was the king lightly escorted, or did he ride
     With a large company, as a ruler should?

IOKASTE: There were five men with him in all: one was a herald;   225
    And a single chariot, which he was driving.
OEDIPUS: Alas, that makes it plain enough!
                                      But who —
    Who told you how it happened?
IOKASTE: A household servant,
    The only one to escape.
OEDIPUS: And is he still
    A servant of ours?
IOKASTE: No; for when he came back at last   230
    And found you enthroned in the place of the dead king,
    He came to me, touched my hand with his, and begged
    That I would send him away to the frontier district
    Where only the shepherds go —
    As far away from the city as I could send him.   235
    I granted his prayer; for although the man was a slave,
    He had earned more than this favor at my hands.
OEDIPUS: Can he be called back quickly?
IOKASTE: Easily.
    But why?
OEDIPUS: I have taken too much upon myself   240
    Without enquiry; therefore I wish to consult him.
IOKASTE: Then he shall come.
                      But am I not one also
    To whom you might confide these fears of yours?
OEDIPUS: That is your right; it will not be denied you,
    Now least of all; for I have reached a pitch   245
    Of wild foreboding. Is there anyone
    To whom I should sooner speak?

    Polybos of Corinth is my father.
    My mother is a Dorian: Merope.
    I grew up chief among the men of Corinth   250
    Until a strange thing happened —
    Not worth my passion, it may be, but strange.
    At a feast, a drunken man maundering in his cups
    Cries out that I am not my father's son!
    I contained myself that night, though I felt anger   255
    And a sinking heart. The next day I visited
    My father and mother, and questioned them. They stormed,
    Calling it all the slanderous rant of a fool;
    And this relieved me. Yet the suspicion
    Remained always aching in my mind;   260
    I knew there was talk; I could not rest;
    And finally, saying nothing to my parents,
    I went to the shrine at Delphi.

The god dismissed my question without reply;
He spoke of other things.

      Some were clear,   265
Full of wretchedness, dreadful, unbearable:
As, that I should lie with my own mother, breed
Children from whom all men would turn their eyes;
And that I should be my father's murderer.

I heard all this, and fled. And from that day   270
Corinth to me was only in the stars
Descending in that quarter of the sky,
As I wandered farther and farther on my way
To a land where I should never see the evil
Sung by the oracle. And I came to this country   275
Where, so you say, King Laios was killed.

I will tell you all that happened there, my lady.
There were three highways
Coming together at a place I passed;
And there a herald came towards me, and a chariot   280
Drawn by horses, with a man such as you describe
Seated in it. The groom leading the horses
Forced me off the road at his lord's command;
But as this charioteer lurched over towards me
I struck him in my rage. The old man saw me   285
And brought his double goad down upon my head
As I came abreast.

      He was paid back, and more!
Swinging my club in this right hand I knocked him
Out of his car, and he rolled on the ground.

            I killed him.

I killed them all.   290
Now if that stranger and Laios were — kin,
Where is a man more miserable than I?
More hated by the gods? Citizen and alien alike
Must never shelter me or speak to me —
I must be shunned by all.

       And I myself   295
Pronounced this malediction upon myself!

Think of it: I have touched you with these hands,
These hands that killed your husband. What defilement!

Am I all evil, then? It must be so,
Since I must flee from Thebes, yet never again   300

See my own countrymen, my own country,
For fear of joining my mother in marriage
And killing Polybos, my father.
                                    Ah,
If I was created so, born to this fate,
Who could deny the savagery of God?   305

O holy majesty of heavenly powers!
May I never see that day! Never!
Rather let me vanish from the race of men
Than know the abomination destined me!

CHORAGOS: We too, my lord, have felt dismay at this.   310
   But there is hope: you have yet to hear the shepherd.

OEDIPUS: Indeed, I fear no other hope is left me.

IOKASTE: What do you hope from him when he comes?

OEDIPUS: This much:
   If his account of the murder tallies with yours,
   Then I am cleared.

IOKASTE: What was it that I said   315
   Of such importance?

OEDIPUS: Why, "marauders," you said,
   Killed the king, according to this man's story.
   If he maintains that still, if there were several,
   Clearly the guilt is not mine: I was alone.
   But if he says one man, singlehanded, did it,   320
   Then the evidence all points to me.

IOKASTE: You may be sure that he said there were several;
   And can he call back that story now? He can not.
   The whole city heard it as plainly as I.
   But suppose he alters some detail of it: 325
   He can not ever show that Laios' death
   Fulfilled the oracle: for Apollo said
   My child was doomed to kill him; and my child—
   Poor baby!—it was my child that died first.

   No. From now on, where oracles are concerned,   330
   I would not waste a second thought on any.

OEDIPUS: You may be right.
                           But come: let someone go
   For the shepherd at once. This matter must be settled.

IOKASTE: I will send for him.
   I would not wish to cross you in anything,   335
   And surely not in this.—Let us go in.

                                        (*Exeunt into the palace.*)

ODE 2 / Strophe 1

CHORUS: Let me be reverent in the ways of right,
    Lowly the paths I journey on;
    Let all my words and actions keep
    The laws of the pure universe
    From highest Heaven handed down.   5
    For Heaven is their bright nurse,
    Those generations of the realms of light;
    Ah, never of mortal kind were they begot,
    Nor are they slaves of memory, lost in sleep:
    Their Father is greater than Time, and ages not.   10

Antistrophe 1

The tyrant is a child of Pride
Who drinks from his great sickening cup
Recklessness and vanity,
Until from his high crest headlong
He plummets to the dust of hope.   15
That strong man is not strong.
But let no fair ambition be denied;
May God protect the wrestler for the State
In government, in comely policy,
Who will fear God, and on his ordinance wait.   20

Strophe 2

Haughtiness and the high hand of disdain
Tempt and outrage God's holy law;
And any mortal who dares hold
No immortal Power in awe
Will be caught up in a net of pain: 25
The price for which his levity is sold.
Let each man take due earnings, then,
And keep his hands from holy things,
And from blasphemy stand apart—
Else the crackling blast of heaven   30
Blows on his head, and on his desperate heart.
Though fools will honor impious men,
In their cities no tragic poet sings.

Antistrophe 2

Shall we lose faith in Delphi's obscurities,
We who have heard the world's core   35
Discredited, and the sacred wood
Of Zeus at Elis praised no more?

The deeds and the strange prophecies
Must make a pattern yet to be understood.
Zeus, if indeed you are lord of all,   40
Throned in light over night and day,
Mirror this in your endless mind:
Our masters call the oracle
Words on the wind, and the Delphic vision blind!
Their hearts no longer know Apollo,   45
And reverence for the gods has died away.

SCENE 3

(*Enter Iokaste.*)

IOKASTE: Princes of Thebes, it has occurred to me
    To visit the altars of the gods, bearing
    These branches as a suppliant, and this incense.
    Our king is not himself: his noble soul
    Is overwrought with fantasies of dread,   5
    Else he would consider
    The new prophecies in the light of the old.
    He will listen to any voice that speaks disaster,
    And my advice goes for nothing. (*She approaches the altar, right.*)
                                            To you, then, Apollo,
    Lycean lord, since you are nearest, I turn in prayer   10
    Receive these offerings, and grant us deliverance
    From defilement. Our hearts are heavy with fear
    When we see our leader distracted, as helpless sailors
    Are terrified by the confusion of their helmsman.

(*Enter Messenger.*)

MESSENGER: Friends, no doubt you can direct me: 15
    Where shall I find the house of Oedipus,
    Or, better still, where is the king himself?
CHORAGOS: It is this very place, stranger; he is inside.
    This is his wife and mother of his children.
MESSENGER: I wish her happiness in a happy house,   20
    Blest in all the fulfillment of her marriage.
IOKASTE: I wish as much for you: your courtesy
    Deserves a like good fortune. But now, tell me:
    Why have you come? What have you to say to us?
MESSENGER: Good news, my lady, for your house and your husband.   25
IOKASTE: What news? Who sent you here?
MESSENGER: I am from Corinth.
    The news I bring ought to mean joy for you,
    Though it may be you will find some grief in it.

IOKASTE: What is it? How can it touch us in both ways?

MESSENGER: The word is that the people of the Isthmus   30
    Intend to call Oedipus to be their king.

IOKASTE: But old King Polybos — is he not reigning still?

MESSENGER: No. Death holds him in his sepulchre.

IOKASTE: What are you saying? Polybos is dead?

MESSENGER: If I am not telling the truth, may I die myself.   35

IOKASTE (*to a Maidservant*): Go in, go quickly; tell this to your master.
    O riddlers of God's will, where are you now!
    This was the man whom Oedipus, long ago,
    Feared so, fled so, in dread of destroying him —
    But it was another fate by which he died.   40

(*Enter Oedipus, center.*)

OEDIPUS: Dearest Iokaste, why have you sent for me?

IOKASTE: Listen to what this man says, and then tell me
    What has become of the solemn prophecies.

OEDIPUS: Who is this man? What is his news for me?

IOKASTE: He has come from Corinth to announce your father's death!   45

OEDIPUS: Is it true, stranger? Tell me in your own words.

MESSENGER: I can not say it more clearly: the king is dead.

OEDIPUS: Was it by treason? Or by an attack of illness?

MESSENGER: A little thing brings old men to their rest.

OEDIPUS: It was sickness, then?

MESSENGER: Yes, and his many years.   50

OEDIPUS: Ah!
    Why should a man respect the Pythian hearth,° or
    Give heed to the birds that jangle above his head?
    They prophesied that I should kill Polybos,
    Kill my own father; but he is dead and buried,   55
    And I am here — I never touched him, never,
    Unless he died of grief for my departure,
    And thus, in a sense, through me. No. Polybos
    Has packed the oracles off with him underground.
    They are empty words.

IOKASTE: Had I not told you so?   60

OEDIPUS: You had; it was my faint heart that betrayed me.

IOKASTE: From now on never think of those things again.

OEDIPUS: And yet — must I not fear my mother's bed?

IOKASTE: Why should anyone in this world be afraid
    Since Fate rules us and nothing can be foreseen?   65
    A man should live only for the present day.

---

52. Pythian hearth: Altar in the temple at Delphi, where offerings to Apollo were made by the priestess.

Have no more fear of sleeping with your mother:
How many men, in dreams, have lain with their mothers!
No reasonable man is troubled by such things.
OEDIPUS: That is true, only —   70
If only my mother were not still alive!
But she is alive. I can not help my dread.
IOKASTE: Yet this news of your father's death is wonderful.
OEDIPUS: Wonderful. But I fear the living woman.
MESSENGER: Tell me, who is this woman that you fear?   75
OEDIPUS: It is Merope, man; the wife of King Polybos.
MESSENGER: Merope? Why should you be afraid of her?
OEDIPUS: An oracle of the gods, a dreadful saying.
MESSENGER: Can you tell me about it or are you sworn to silence?
OEDIPUS: I can tell you, and I will.   80
Apollo said through his prophet that I was the man
Who should marry his own mother, shed his father's blood
With his own hands. And so, for all these years
I have kept clear of Corinth, and no harm has come —
Though it would have been sweet to see my parents again.   85
MESSENGER: And is this the fear that drove you out of Corinth?
OEDIPUS: Would you have me kill my father?
MESSENGER: As for that
You must be reassured by the news I gave you.
OEDIPUS: If you could reassure me, I would reward you.
MESSENGER: I had that in mind, I will confess: I thought   90
I could count on you when you returned to Corinth.
OEDIPUS: No: I will never go near my parents again.
MESSENGER: Ah, son, you still do not know what you are doing —
OEDIPUS: What do you mean? In the name of God tell me!
MESSENGER: — If these are your reasons for not going home.   95
OEDIPUS: I tell you, I fear the oracle may come true.
MESSENGER: And guilt may come upon you through your parents?
OEDIPUS: That is the dread that is always in my heart.
MESSENGER: Can you not see that all your fears are groundless?
OEDIPUS: Groundless? Am I not my parents' son?   100
MESSENGER: Polybos was not your father.
OEDIPUS: Not my father?
MESSENGER: No more your father than the man speaking to you.
OEDIPUS: But you are nothing to me!
MESSENGER: Neither was he.
OEDIPUS: Then why did he call me son?
MESSENGER: I will tell you:
Long ago he had you from my hands, as a gift.   105
OEDIPUS: Then how could he love me so, if I was not his?
MESSENGER: He had no children, and his heart turned to you.

OEDIPUS: What of you? Did you buy me? Did you find me by chance?

MESSENGER: I came upon you in the woody vales of Kithairon.

OEDIPUS: And what were you doing there?

MESSENGER: Tending my flocks.   110

OEDIPUS: A wandering shepherd?

MESSENGER: But your savior, son, that day.

OEDIPUS: From what did you save me?

MESSENGER: Your ankles should tell you that.

OEDIPUS: Ah, stranger, why do you speak of that childhood pain?

MESSENGER: I pulled the skewer that pinned your feet together.

OEDIPUS: I have had the mark as long as I can remember.   115

MESSENGER: That was why you were given the name you bear.°

OEDIPUS: God! Was it my father or my mother who did it?
    Tell me!

MESSENGER: I do not know. The man who gave you to me
    Can tell you better than I.

OEDIPUS: It was not you that found me, but another?   120

MESSENGER: It was another shepherd gave you to me.

OEDIPUS: Who was he? Can you tell me who he was?

MESSENGER: I think he was said to be one of Laios' people.

OEDIPUS: You mean the Laios who was king here years ago?

MESSENGER: Yes; King Laios; and the man was one of his herdsmen.   125

OEDIPUS: Is he still alive? Can I see him?

MESSENGER: These men here
    Know best about such things.

OEDIPUS: Does anyone here
    Know this shepherd that he is talking about?
    Have you seen him in the fields, or in the town?
    If you have, tell me. It is time things were made plain.   130

CHORAGOS: I think the man he means is that same shepherd
    You have already asked to see. Iokaste perhaps
    Could tell you something.

OEDIPUS: Do you know anything
    About him, Lady? Is he the man we have summoned?
    Is that the man this shepherd means?

IOKASTE: Why think of him?   135
    Forget this herdsman. Forget it all.
    This talk is a waste of time.

OEDIPUS: How can you say that,
    When the clues to my true birth are in my hands?

IOKASTE: For God's love, let us have no more questioning!
    Is your life nothing to you?   140
    My own is pain enough for me to bear.

----

116. **name you bear:** *Oedipus* means "swollen foot."

OEDIPUS: You need not worry. Suppose my mother a slave,
   And born of slaves: no baseness can touch you.
IOKASTE: Listen to me, I beg you: do not do this thing!
OEDIPUS: I will not listen; the truth must be made known.   145
IOKASTE: Everything that I say is for your own good!
OEDIPUS: My own good
   Snaps my patience, then; I want none of it.
IOKASTE: You are fatally wrong! May you never learn who you are!
OEDIPUS: Go, one of you, and bring the shepherd here.
   Let us leave this woman to brag of her royal name.   150
IOKASTE: Ah, miserable!
   That is the only word I have for you now.
   That is the only word I can ever have.   (*Exit into the palace.*)
CHORAGOS: Why has she left us, Oedipus? Why has she gone
   In such a passion of sorrow? I fear this silence: 155
   Something dreadful may come of it.
OEDIPUS: Let it come!
   However base my birth, I must know about it.
   The Queen, like a woman, is perhaps ashamed
   To think of my low origin. But I
   Am a child of Luck, I can not be dishonored.   160
   Luck is my mother; the passing months, my brothers,
   Have seen me rich and poor.
                            If this is so,
   How could I wish that I were someone else?
   How could I not be glad to know my birth?

ODE 3 / Strophe

CHORUS: If ever the coming time were known
   To my heart's pondering,
   Kithairon, now by Heaven I see the torches
   At the festival of the next full moon
   And see the dance, and hear the choir sing   5
   A grace to your gentle shade:
   Mountain where Oedipus was found,
   O mountain guard of a noble race!
   May the god° who heals us lend his aid,
   And let that glory come to pass   10
   For our king's cradling-ground.

Antistrophe

Of the nymphs that flower beyond the years,
Who bore you, royal child,

---

9. god: Apollo.

To Pan° of the hills or the timberline Apollo,
Cold in delight where the upland clears,   15
Or Hermes° for whom Kyllene's° heights are piled?
Or flushed as evening cloud,
Great Dionysos, roamer of mountains,
He — was it he who found you there,
And caught you up in his own proud   20
Arms from the sweet god-ravisher
Who laughed by the Muses'° fountains?

SCENE 4

OEDIPUS: Sirs: though I do not know the man,
    I think I see him coming, this shepherd we want:
    He is old, like our friend here, and the men
    Bringing him seem to be servants of my house.
    But you can tell, if you have ever seen him.   5

(*Enter Shepherd escorted by Servants.*)

CHORAGOS: I know him, he was Laios' man. You can trust him.
OEDIPUS: Tell me first, you from Corinth: is this the shepherd
    We were discussing?
MESSENGER: This is the very man.
OEDIPUS (*to Shepherd*): Come here. No, look at me. You must answer
    Everything I ask. — You belonged to Laios?   10
SHEPHERD: Yes: born his slave, brought up in his house.
OEDIPUS: Tell me: what kind of work did you do for him?
SHEPHERD: I was a shepherd of his, most of my life.
OEDIPUS: Where mainly did you go for pasturage?
SHEPHERD: Sometimes Kithairon, sometimes the hills near-by.   15
OEDIPUS: Do you remember ever seeing this man out there?
SHEPHERD: What would he be doing there? This man?
OEDIPUS: This man standing here. Have you ever seen him before?
SHEPHERD: No. At least, not to my recollection.
MESSENGER: And that is not strange, my lord. But I'll refresh   20
    His memory: he must remember when we two
    Spent three whole seasons together, March to September,
    On Kithairon or thereabouts. He had two flocks;
    I had one. Each autumn I'd drive mine home
    And he would go back with his to Laios' sheepfold. —   25
    Is this not true, just as I have described it?

---

14. Pan: Pastoral god of fertility and patron of shepherds; associated with the wilderness.
16. Hermes: The messenger of the gods; **Kyllene:** Rural mountain on which Hermes was born and that was raised by the gods for that purpose.   **22. Muses:** Nine sisters, patron goddesses of the arts.

SHEPHERD: True, yes; but it was all so long ago.

MESSENGER: Well, then: do you remember, back in those days,
      That you gave me a baby boy to bring up as my own?

SHEPHERD: What if I did? What are you trying to say?   30

MESSENGER: King Oedipus was once that little child.

SHEPHERD: Damn you, hold your tongue!

OEDIPUS: No more of that!
      It is your tongue needs watching, not this man's.

SHEPHERD: My king, my master, what is it I have done wrong?

OEDIPUS: You have not answered his question about the boy.   35

SHEPHERD: He does not know . . . He is only making trouble . . .

OEDIPUS: Come, speak plainly, or it will go hard with you.

SHEPHERD: In God's name, do not torture an old man!

OEDIPUS: Come here, one of you; bind his arms behind him.

SHEPHERD: Unhappy king! What more do you wish to learn?   40

OEDIPUS: Did you give this man the child he speaks of?

SHEPHERD: I did.
      And I would to God I had died that very day.

OEDIPUS: You will die now unless you speak the truth.

SHEPHERD: Yet if I speak the truth, I am worse than dead.

OEDIPUS (to Attendant): He intends to draw it out, apparently —   45

SHEPHERD: No! I have told you already that I gave him the boy.

OEDIPUS: Where did you get him? From your house? From somewhere
      else?

SHEPHERD: Not from mine, no. A man gave him to me.

OEDIPUS: Is that man here? Whose house did he belong to?

SHEPHERD: For God's love, my king, do not ask me any more!   50

OEDIPUS: You are a dead man if I have to ask you again.

SHEPHERD: Then . . . Then the child was from the palace of Laios.

OEDIPUS: A slave child? or a child of his own line?

SHEPHERD: Ah, I am on the brink of dreadful speech!

OEDIPUS: And I of dreadful hearing. Yet I must hear.   55

SHEPHERD: If you must be told, then . . .
                            They said it was Laios' child;
      But it is your wife who can tell you about that.

OEDIPUS: My wife — Did she give it to you?

SHEPHERD: My lord, she did.

OEDIPUS: Do you know why?

SHEPHERD: I was told to get rid of it.

OEDIPUS: Oh heartless mother!

SHEPHERD: But in dread of prophecies . . .   60

OEDIPUS: Tell me.

SHEPHERD: It was said that the boy would kill his own father.

OEDIPUS: Then why did you give him over to this old man?

SHEPHERD: I pitied the baby, my king,
      And I thought that this man would take him far away

To his own country.
                He saved him — but for what a fate!   65
For if you are what this man says you are,
No man living is more wretched than Oedipus.
OEDIPUS: Ah God!
    It was true!
          All the prophecies!
                  — Now,
    O Light, may I look on you for the last time!   70
    I, Oedipus,
    Oedipus, damned in his birth, in his marriage damned,
    Damned in the blood he shed with his own hand!

(He rushes into the palace.)

ODE 4 / Strophe 1

CHORUS: Alas for the seed of men.
    What measure shall I give these generations
    That breathe on the void and are void
    And exist and do not exist?
    Who bears more weight of joy   5
    Than mass of sunlight shifting in images,
    Or who shall make his thought stay on
    That down time drifts away?
    Your splendor is all fallen.
    O naked brow of wrath and tears,   10
    O change of Oedipus!
    I who saw your days call no man blest —
    Your great days like ghosts gone.

Antistrophe 1

That mind was a strong bow.
Deep, how deep you drew it then, hard archer,   15
At a dim fearful range,
And brought dear glory down!
You overcame the stranger° —
The virgin with her hooking lion claws —
And though death sang, stood like a tower   20
To make pale Thebes take heart.
Fortress against our sorrow!
True king, giver of laws,
Majestic Oedipus!

---

18. **stranger:** The Sphinx.

No prince in Thebes had ever such renown,   25
No prince won such grace of power.

Strophe 2

And now of all men ever known
Most pitiful is this man's story:
His fortunes are most changed; his state
Fallen to a low slave's   30
Ground under bitter fate.
O Oedipus, most royal one!
The great door that expelled you to the light
Gave at night — ah, gave night to your glory:
As to the father, to the fathering son.   35
All understood too late.
How could that queen whom Laios won,
The garden that he harrowed at his height,
Be silent when that act was done?

Antistrophe 2

But all eyes fail before time's eye,   40
All actions come to justice there.
Though never willed, though far down the deep past,
Your bed, your dread sirings,
Are brought to book at last.
Child by Laios doomed to die,   45
Then doomed to lose that fortunate little death,
Would God you never took breath in this air
That with my wailing lips I take to cry:
For I weep the world's outcast.
I was blind, and now I can tell why: 50
Asleep, for you had given ease of breath
To Thebes, while the false years went by.

EXODOS°

(*Enter, from the palace, Second Messenger.*)

SECOND MESSENGER: Elders of Thebes, most honored in this land,
What horrors are yours to see and hear, what weight
Of sorrow to be endured, if, true to your birth,
You venerate the line of Labdakos!
I think neither Istros nor Phasis, those great rivers,   5
Could purify this place of all the evil

Exodos: The final scene.

It shelters now, or soon must bring to light—
Evil not done unconsciously, but willed.

The greatest griefs are those we cause ourselves.
CHORAGOS: Surely, friend, we have grief enough already;   10
What new sorrow do you mean?
SECOND MESSENGER: The queen is dead.
CHORAGOS: O miserable queen! But at whose hand?
SECOND MESSENGER: Her own.
The full horror of what happened you can not know,
For you did not see it; but I, who did, will tell you
As clearly as I can how she met her death.   15

When she had left us,
In passionate silence, passing through the court,
She ran to her apartment in the house,
Her hair clutched by the fingers of both hands.
She closed the doors behind her; then, by that bed   20
Where long ago the fatal son was conceived—
That son who should bring about his father's death—
We heard her call upon Laios, dead so many years,
And heard her wail for the double fruit of her marriage,
A husband by her husband, children by her child.   25

Exactly how she died I do not know:
For Oedipus burst in moaning and would not let us
Keep vigil to the end: it was by him
As he stormed about the room that our eyes were caught.
From one to another of us he went, begging a sword,   30
Hunting the wife who was not his wife, the mother
Whose womb had carried his own children and himself.
I do not know: it was none of us aided him,
But surely one of the gods was in control!
For with a dreadful cry   35
He hurled his weight, as though wrenched out of himself,
At the twin doors: the bolts gave, and he rushed in.
And there we saw her hanging, her body swaying
From the cruel cord she had noosed about her neck.
A great sob broke from him, heartbreaking to hear,   40
As he loosed the rope and lowered her to the ground.

I would blot out from my mind what happened next!
For the king ripped from her gown the golden brooches
That were her ornament, and raised them, and plunged them down
Straight into his own eyeballs, crying, "No more,   45
No more shall you look on the misery about me,

The horrors of my own doing! Too long you have known
The faces of those whom I should never have seen,
Too long been blind to those for whom I was searching!
From this hour, go in darkness!" And as he spoke,   50
He struck at his eyes — not once, but many times;
And the blood spattered his beard,
Bursting from his ruined sockets like red hail.

So from the unhappiness of two this evil has sprung,
A curse on the man and woman alike. The old   55
Happiness of the house of Labdakos
Was happiness enough: where is it today?
It is all wailing and ruin, disgrace, death — all
The misery of mankind that has a name —
And it is wholly and for ever theirs.   60

CHORAGOS: Is he in agony still? Is there no rest for him?
SECOND MESSENGER: He is calling for someone to open the doors wide
     So that all the children of Kadmos may look upon
     His father's murderer, his mother's — no,
     I can not say it!
                    And then he will leave Thebes,   65
     Self-exiled, in order that the curse
     Which he himself pronounced may depart from the house.
     He is weak, and there is none to lead him,
     So terrible is his suffering.
                              But you will see:
     Look, the doors are opening; in a moment   70
     You will see a thing that would crush a heart of stone.

(*The central door is opened; Oedipus, blinded, is led in.*)

CHORAGOS: Dreadful indeed for men to see.
     Never have my own eyes
     Looked on a sight so full of fear.

     Oedipus!   75
     What madness came upon you, what demon
     Leaped on your life with heavier
     Punishment than a mortal man can bear?
     No: I can not even
     Look at you, poor ruined one.   80
     And I would speak, question, ponder,
     If I were able. No.
     You make me shudder.
OEDIPUS: God. God.
     Is there a sorrow greater?
     Where shall I find harbor in this world?   85

My voice is hurled far on a dark wind.
What has God done to me?
CHORAGOS: Too terrible to think of, or to see.

Strophe 1

OEDIPUS: O cloud of night,   90
Never to be turned away: night coming on,
I can not tell how: night like a shroud!
My fair winds brought me here.
                          O God. Again
The pain of the spikes where I had sight,
The flooding pain   95
Of memory, never to be gouged out.
CHORAGOS: This is not strange.
You suffer it all twice over, remorse in pain,
Pain in remorse.

Antistrophe 1

OEDIPUS: Ah dear friend   100
Are you faithful even yet, you alone?
Are you still standing near me, will you stay here,
Patient, to care for the blind?
                        The blind man!
Yet even blind I know who it is attends me,
By the voice's tone—   105
Though my new darkness hide the comforter.
CHORAGOS: Oh fearful act!
What god was it drove you to rake black
Night across your eyes?

Strophe 2

OEDIPUS: Apollo. Apollo. Dear   110
Children, the god was Apollo.
He brought my sick, sick fate upon me.
But the blinding hand was my own!
How could I bear to see
When all my sight was horror everywhere?   115
CHORAGOS: Everywhere; that is true.
OEDIPUS: And now what is left?
Images? Love? A greeting even,
Sweet to the senses? Is there anything?
Ah, no, friends: lead me away.   120
Lead me away from Thebes.
                      Lead the great wreck
And hell of Oedipus, whom the gods hate.

CHORAGOS: Your misery, you are not blind to that.
> Would God you had never found it out!

Antistrophe 2

OEDIPUS: Death take the man who unbound   125
> My feet on that hillside
> And delivered me from death to life! What life?
> If only I had died,
> This weight of monstrous doom
> Could not have dragged me and my darlings down.   130

CHORAGOS: I would have wished the same.

OEDIPUS: Oh never to have come here
> With my father's blood upon me! Never
> To have been the man they call his mother's husband!
> Oh accurst! Oh child of evil,   135
> To have entered that wretched bed —
> > the selfsame one!
> More primal than sin itself, this fell to me.

CHORAGOS: I do not know what words to offer you.
> You were better dead than alive and blind.

OEDIPUS: Do not counsel me any more. This punishment   140
> That I have laid upon myself is just.
> If I had eyes,
> I do not know how I could bear the sight
> Of my father, when I came to the house of Death,
> Or my mother: for I have sinned against them both   145
> So vilely that I could not make my peace
> By strangling my own life.
> > Or do you think my children,
> Born as they were born, would be sweet to my eyes?
> Ah never, never! Nor this town with its high walls,
> Nor the holy images of the gods.
> > For I,   150
> Thrice miserable! — Oedipus, noblest of all the line
> Of Kadmos, have condemned myself to enjoy
> These things no more, by my own malediction
> Expelling that man whom the gods declared
> To be a defilement in the house of Laios.   155
> After exposing the rankness of my own guilt,
> How could I look men frankly in the eyes?
> No, I swear it,
> If I could have stifled my hearing at its source,
> I would have done it and made all this body   160
> A tight cell of misery, blank to light and sound:
> So I should have been safe in my dark mind

Beyond external evil.
                    Ah Kithairon!
Why did you shelter me? When I was cast upon you,
Why did I not die? Then I should never   165
Have shown the world my execrable birth.

Ah Polybos! Corinth, city that I believed
The ancient seat of my ancestors: how fair
I seemed, your child! And all the while this evil
Was cancerous within me!
                    For I am sick   170
In my own being, sick in my origin.
O three roads, dark ravine, woodland and way
Where three roads met; you, drinking my father's blood,
My own blood, spilled by my own hand: can you remember
The unspeakable things I did there, and the things   175
I went on from there to do?
                    O marriage, marriage!
The act that engendered me, and again the act
Performed by the son in the same bed—
                                        Ah, the net
Of incest, mingling fathers, brothers, sons,
With brides, wives, mothers: the last evil   180
That can be known by men: no tongue can say
How evil!
                No. For the love of God, conceal me
Somewhere far from Thebes; or kill me; or hurl me
Into the sea, away from men's eyes for ever.

Come, lead me. You need not fear to touch me.   185
Of all men, I alone can bear this guilt.

(*Enter Kreon.*)

CHORAGOS: Kreon is here now. As to what you ask,
        He may decide the course to take. He only
        Is left to protect the city in your place.
OEDIPUS: Alas, how can I speak to him? What right have I   190
        To beg his courtesy whom I have deeply wronged?
KREON: I have not come to mock you, Oedipus,
        Or to reproach you, either.
        (*To Attendants.*)   —You, standing there:
        If you have lost all respect for man's dignity,
        At least respect the flame of Lord Helios:°   195

---

195. **Lord Helios:** The sun god.

Do not allow this pollution to show itself
Openly here, an affront to the earth
And Heaven's rain and the light of day. No, take him
Into the house as quickly as you can.
For it is proper   200
That only the close kindred see his grief.

OEDIPUS: I pray you in God's name, since your courtesy
Ignores my dark expectation, visiting
With mercy this man of all men most execrable:
Give me what I ask — for your good, not for mine.   205

KREON: And what is it that you turn to me begging for?

OEDIPUS: Drive me out of this country as quickly as may be
To a place where no human voice can ever greet me.

KREON: I should have done that before now — only,
God's will had not been wholly revealed to me.   210

OEDIPUS: But his command is plain: the parricide
Must be destroyed. I am that evil man.

KREON: That is the sense of it, yes; but as things are,
We had best discover clearly what is to be done.

OEDIPUS: You would learn more about a man like me?   215

KREON: You are ready now to listen to the god.

OEDIPUS: I will listen. But it is to you
That I must turn for help. I beg you, hear me.

The woman is there —
Give her whatever funeral you think proper: 220
She is your sister.
                    — But let me go, Kreon!
Let me purge my father's Thebes of the pollution
Of my living here, and go out to the wild hills,
To Kithairon, that has won such fame with me,
The tomb my mother and father appointed for me,   225
And let me die there, as they willed I should.
And yet I know
Death will not ever come to me through sickness
Or in any natural way: I have been preserved
For some unthinkable fate. But let that be.   230

As for my sons, you need not care for them.
They are men, they will find some way to live.
But my poor daughters, who have shared my table,
Who never before have been parted from their father —
Take care of them, Kreon; do this for me.   235

And will you let me touch them with my hands
A last time, and let us weep together?
Be kind, my lord,

Great prince, be kind!
                    Could I but touch them,
They would be mine again, as when I had my eyes.   240

(*Enter Antigone and Ismene, attended.*)

Ah, God!
Is it my dearest children I hear weeping?
Has Kreon pitied me and sent my daughters?
KREON: Yes, Oedipus: I knew that they were dear to you
In the old days, and know you must love them still.   245
OEDIPUS: May God bless you for this — and be a friendlier
Guardian to you than he has been to me!

Children, where are you?
Come quickly to my hands: they are your brother's —
Hands that have brought your father's once clear eyes   250
To this way of seeing —
                        Ah dearest ones,
I had neither sight nor knowledge then, your father
By the woman who was the source of his own life!
And I weep for you — having no strength to see you —,
I weep for you when I think of the bitterness   255
That men will visit upon you all your lives.
What homes, what festivals can you attend
Without being forced to depart again in tears?
And when you come to marriageable age,
Where is the man, my daughters, who would dare   260
Risk the bane that lies on all my children?
Is there any evil wanting? Your father killed
His father; sowed the womb of her who bore him;
Engendered you at the fount of his own existence!
That is what they will say of you.

                            Then, whom   265
Can you ever marry? There are no bridegrooms for you,
And your lives must wither away in sterile dreaming.

O Kreon, son of Menoikeus!
You are the only father my daughters have,
Since we, their parents, are both of us gone for ever.   270
They are your own blood: you will not let them
Fall into beggary and loneliness;
You will keep them from the miseries that are mine!
Take pity on them; see, they are only children,
Friendless except for you. Promise me this,   275
Great prince, and give me your hand in token of it.

(*Kreon clasps his right hand.*)

> Children:
> I could say much, if you could understand me,
> But as it is, I have only this prayer for you:
> Live where you can, be as happy as you can —   280
> Happier, please God, than God has made your father.

KREON: Enough. You have wept enough. Now go within.

OEDIPUS: I must, but it is hard.

KREON: Time eases all things.

OEDIPUS: You know my mind, then?

KREON: Say what you desire.

OEDIPUS: Send me from Thebes!

KREON: God grant that I may!   285

OEDIPUS: But since God hates me . . .

KREON: No, he will grant your wish.

OEDIPUS: You promise?

KREON: I can not speak beyond my knowledge.

OEDIPUS: Then lead me in.

KREON: Come now, and leave your children.   290

OEDIPUS: No! Do not take them from me!

KREON: Think no longer
> That you are in command here, but rather think
> How, when you were, you served your own destruction.

(*Exeunt into the house all but the Chorus; the Choragos chants directly to the audience.*)

CHORAGOS: Men of Thebes: look upon Oedipus.

> This is the king who solved the famous riddle   295
> And towered up, most powerful of men.
> No mortal eyes but looked on him with envy,
> Yet in the end ruin swept over him.

> Let every man in mankind's frailty
> Consider his last day; and let none   300
> Presume on his good fortune until he find
> Life, at his death, a memory without pain.

WEB: Research Sophocles in depth, including images and cultural documents, with VirtuaLit Drama at bedfordstmartins.com/approachinglit.

August Wilson   b. 1945

Fences   [1986]

When the sins of our fathers visit us
We do not have to play host.
We can banish them with forgiveness
As God, in His Largeness and Laws.
                        — *August Wilson*

CHARACTERS

TROY MAXSON
JIM BONO, Troy's friend
ROSE, Troy's wife
LYONS, Troy's oldest son by previous marriage
GABRIEL, Troy's brother
CORY, Troy and Rose's son
RAYNELL, Troy's daughter

SETTING

The setting is the yard which fronts the only entrance to the Maxson household, an ancient two-story brick house set back off a small alley in a big-city neighborhood. The entrance to the house is gained by two or three steps leading to a wooden porch badly in need of paint.

A relatively recent addition to the house and running its full width, the porch lacks congruence. It is a sturdy porch with a flat roof. One or two chairs of dubious value sit at one end where the kitchen window opens onto the porch. An old-fashioned icebox stands silent guard at the opposite end.

The yard is a small dirt yard, partially fenced, except for the last scene, with a wooden sawhorse, a pile of lumber, and other fence-building equipment set off to the side. Opposite is a tree from which hangs a ball made of rags. A baseball bat leans against the tree. Two oil drums serve as garbage receptacles and sit near the house at right to complete the setting.

ACT ONE / Scene One

It is 1957. Troy and Bono enter the yard, engaged in conversation. Troy is fifty-three years old, a large man with thick, heavy hands; it is this largeness that he strives to fill out and make an accommodation with. Together with his blackness, his largeness informs his sensibilities and the choices he has made in his life.

Of the two men, Bono is obviously the follower. His commitment to their friendship of thirty-odd years is rooted in his admiration of Troy's honesty, capacity for hard work, and his strength, which Bono seeks to emulate.

It is Friday night, payday, and the one night of the week the two men engage in a ritual of talk and drink. Troy is usually the most talkative and at times he can be crude and almost vulgar, though he is capable of rising to profound heights of expres-

sion. *The men carry lunch buckets and wear or carry burlap aprons and are dressed in clothes suitable to their jobs as garbage collectors.*

BONO: Troy, you ought to stop that lying!

TROY: I ain't lying! The nigger had a watermelon this big.

(He indicates with his hands.)

Talking about . . . "What watermelon, Mr. Rand?" I liked to fell out! "What watermelon, Mr. Rand?" . . . And it sitting there big as life.

BONO: What did Mr. Rand say?

TROY: Ain't said nothing. Figure if the nigger too dumb to know he carrying a watermelon, he wasn't gonna get much sense out of him. Trying to hide that great big old watermelon under his coat. Afraid to let the white man see him carry it home.

BONO: I'm like you . . . I ain't got no time for them kind of people.

TROY: Now what he look like getting mad cause he see the man from the union talking to Mr. Rand?

BONO: He come to me talking about . . . "Maxson gonna get us fired." I told him to get away from me with that. He walked away from me calling you a troublemaker. What Mr. Rand say?

TROY: Ain't said nothing. He told me to go down the Commissioner's office next Friday. They called me down there to see them.

BONO: Well, as long as you got your complaint filed, they can't fire you. That's what one of them white fellows tell me.

TROY: I ain't worried about them firing me. They gonna fire me cause I asked a question? That's all I did. I went to Mr. Rand and asked him, "Why? Why you got the white mens driving and the colored lifting?" Told him, "what's the matter, don't I count? You think only white fellows got sense enough to drive a truck. That ain't no paper job! Hell, anybody can drive a truck. How come you got all whites driving and the colored lifting?" He told me "take it to the union." Well, hell, that's what I done! Now they wanna come up with this pack of lies.

BONO: I told Brownie if the man come and ask him any questions . . . just tell the truth! It ain't nothing but something they done trumped up on you cause you filed a complaint on them.

TROY: Brownie don't understand nothing. All I want them to do is change the job description. Give everybody a chance to drive the truck. Brownie can't see that. He ain't got that much sense.

BONO: How you figure he be making out with that gal be up at Taylors' all the time . . . that Alberta gal?

TROY: Same as you and me. Getting just as much as we is. Which is to say nothing.

BONO: It is, huh? I figure you doing a little better than me . . . and I ain't saying what I'm doing.

TROY: Aw, nigger, look here . . . I know you. If you had got anywhere near
    that gal, twenty minutes later you be looking to tell somebody. And the
    first one you gonna tell . . . that you gonna want to brag to . . . is gonna
    be me.
BONO: I ain't saying that. I see where you be eyeing her.
TROY: I eye all the women. I don't miss nothing. Don't never let nobody tell
    you Troy Maxson don't eye the women.
BONO: You been doing more than eyeing her. You done bought her a drink
    or two.
TROY: Hell yeah, I bought her a drink! What that mean? I bought you one,
    too. What that mean cause I buy her a drink? I'm just being polite.
BONO: It's alright to buy her one drink. That's what you call being polite.
    But when you wanna be buying two or three . . . that's what you call
    eyeing her.
TROY: Look here, as long as you known me . . . you ever known me to chase
    after women?
BONO: Hell yeah! Long as I done known you. You forgetting I knew you when.
TROY: Naw, I'm talking about since I been married to Rose?
BONO: Oh, not since you been married to Rose. Now, that's the truth, there.
    I can say that.
TROY: Alright then! Case closed.
BONO: I see you be walking up around Alberta's house. You supposed to be
    at Taylors' and you be walking up around there.
TROY: What you watching where I'm walking for? I ain't watching after you.
BONO: I seen you walking around there more than once.
TROY: Hell, you liable to see me walking anywhere! That don't mean nothing
    cause you see me walking around there.
BONO: Where she come from anyway? She just kinda showed up one day.
TROY: Tallahassee. You can look at her and tell she one of them Florida gals.
    They got some big healthy women down there. Grow them right up out
    the ground. Got a little bit of Indian in her. Most of them niggers down
    in Florida got some Indian in them.
BONO: I don't know about that Indian part. But she damn sure big and
    healthy. Woman wear some big stockings. Got them great big old legs
    and hips as wide as the Mississippi River.
TROY: Legs don't mean nothing. You don't do nothing but push them out of
    the way. But them hips cushion the ride!
BONO: Troy, you ain't got no sense.
TROY: It's the truth! Like you riding on Goodyears!

(*Rose enters from the house. She is ten years younger than Troy, her devotion to him
stems from her recognition of the possibilities of her life without him: a succession of
abusive men and their babies, a life of partying and running the streets, the Church,
or aloneness with its attendant pain and frustration. She recognizes Troy's spirit as a
fine and illuminating one and she either ignores or forgives his faults, only some of*

which she recognizes. Though she doesn't drink, her presence is an integral part of the Friday night rituals. She alternates between the porch and the kitchen, where supper preparations are under way.)

ROSE: What you all out here getting into?

TROY: What you worried about what we getting into for? This is men talk, woman.

ROSE: What I care what you all talking about? Bono, you gonna stay for supper?

BONO: No, I thank you, Rose. But Lucille say she cooking up a pot of pigfeet.

TROY: Pigfeet! Hell, I'm going home with you! Might even stay the night if you got some pigfeet. You got something in there to top them pigfeet, Rose?

ROSE: I'm cooking up some chicken. I got some chicken and collard greens.

TROY: Well, go on back in the house and let me and Bono finish what we was talking about. This is men talk. I got some talk for you later. You know what kind of talk I mean. You go on and powder it up.

ROSE: Troy Maxson, don't you start that now!

TROY (*puts his arm around her*): Aw, woman . . . come here. Look here, Bono . . . when I met this woman . . . I got out that place, say, "Hitch up my pony, saddle up my mare . . . there's a woman out there for me somewhere. I looked here. Looked there. Saw Rose and latched on to her." I latched on to her and told her — I'm gonna tell you the truth — I told her, "Baby, I don't wanna marry, I just wanna be your man." Rose told me . . . tell him what you told me, Rose.

ROSE: I told him if he wasn't the marrying kind, then move out the way so the marrying kind could find me.

TROY: That's what she told me. "Nigger, you in my way. You blocking the view! Move out the way so I can find me a husband." I thought it over two or three days. Come back —

ROSE: Ain't no two or three days nothing. You was back the same night.

TROY: Come back, told her . . . "Okay, baby . . . but I'm gonna buy me a banty rooster and put him out there in the backyard . . . and when he see a stranger come, he'll flap his wings and crow . . ." Look here, Bono, I could watch the front door by myself . . . it was that back door I was worried about.

ROSE: Troy, you ought not talk like that. Troy ain't doing nothing but telling a lie.

TROY: Only thing is . . . when we first got married . . . forget the rooster . . . we ain't had no yard!

BONO: I hear you tell it. Me and Lucille was staying down there on Logan Street. Had two rooms with the outhouse in the back. I ain't mind the outhouse none. But when that goddamn wind blow through there in the winter . . . that's what I'm talking about! To this day I wonder why in the hell I ever stayed down there for six long years. But see, I didn't know I could do no better. I thought only white folks had inside toilets and things.

ROSE: There's a lot of people don't know they can do no better than they
doing now. That's just something you got to learn. A lot of folks still
shop at Bella's.

TROY: Ain't nothing wrong with shopping at Bella's. She got fresh food.

ROSE: I ain't said nothing about if she got fresh food. I'm talking about what
she charge. She charge ten cents more than the A&P.°

TROY: The A&P ain't never done nothing for me. I spends my money where
I'm treated right. I go down to Bella, say, "I need a loaf of bread, I'll pay
you Friday." She give it to me. What sense that make when I got money
to go and spend it somewhere else and ignore the person who done right
by me? That ain't in the Bible.

ROSE: We ain't talking about what's in the Bible. What sense it make to shop
there when she overcharge?

TROY: You shop where you want to. I'll do my shopping where the people
been good to me.

ROSE: Well, I don't think it's right for her to overcharge. That's all I was saying.

BONO: Look here . . . I got to get on. Lucille going be raising all kind of hell.

TROY: Where you going, nigger? We ain't finished this pint. Come here, finish this pint.

BONO: Well, hell, I am . . . if you ever turn the bottle loose.

TROY (*hands him the bottle*): The only thing I say about the A&P is I'm glad
Cory got that job down there. Help him take care of his school clothes
and things. Gabe done moved out and things getting tight around here.
He got that job. . . . He can start to look out for himself.

ROSE: Cory done went and got recruited by a college football team.

TROY: I told that boy about that football stuff. The white man ain't gonna let
him get nowhere with that football. I told him when he first come to me
with it. Now you come telling me he done went and got more tied up in
it. He ought to go and get recruited in how to fix cars or something
where he can make a living.

ROSE: He ain't talking about making no living playing football. It's just
something the boys in school do. They gonna send a recruiter by to talk
to you. He'll tell you he ain't talking about making no living playing
football. It's a honor to be recruited.

TROY: It ain't gonna get him nowhere. Bono'll tell you that.

BONO: If he be like you in the sports . . . he's gonna be alright. Ain't but two
men ever played baseball as good as you. That's Babe Ruth and Josh Gibson.° Them's the only two men ever hit more home runs than you.

A&P: Chain of grocery stores operated by the Great Atlantic and Pacific Tea Company.   **Babe Ruth and Josh Gibson:** George Herman Ruth (1895–1948) was a pitcher and then outfielder for the Boston Red Sox (1914–1919), New York Yankees (1920–1934), and Boston Braves (1935). His sixty home runs in the 1927 season set a major league record that stood until 1961. Joshua Gibson (1911–1947), the greatest power hitter in the Negro Leagues and often referred to as the black Babe Ruth, was credited with having hit eighty-four home runs in a single sea-son. In 1972 he was elected to the Baseball Hall of Fame, the second Negro League player (after Satchel Paige) to be so honored.

TROY: What it ever get me? Ain't got a pot to piss in or a window to throw it out of.

ROSE: Times have changed since you was playing baseball, Troy. That was before the war. Times have changed a lot since then.

TROY: How in hell they done changed?

ROSE: They got lots of colored boys playing ball now. Baseball and football.

BONO: You right about that, Rose. Times have changed, Troy. You just come along too early.

TROY: There ought not never have been no time called too early! Now you take that fellow . . . what's that fellow they had playing right field for the Yankees back then? You know who I'm talking about, Bono. Used to play right field for the Yankees.

ROSE: Selkirk?°

TROY: Selkirk! That's it! Man batting .269, understand? .269. What kind of sense that make? I was hitting .432 with thirty-seven home runs! Man batting .269 and playing right field for the Yankees! I saw Josh Gibson's daughter yesterday. She walking around with raggedy shoes on her feet. Now I bet you Selkirk's daughter ain't walking around with raggedy shoes on her feet! I bet you that!

ROSE: They got a lot of colored baseball players now. Jackie Robinson° was the first. Folks had to wait for Jackie Robinson.

TROY: I done seen a hundred niggers play baseball better than Jackie Robinson. Hell, I know some teams Jackie Robinson couldn't even make! What you talking about Jackie Robinson. Jackie Robinson wasn't nobody. I'm talking about if you could play ball then they ought to have let you play. Don't care what color you were. Come telling me I come along too early. If you could play . . . then they ought to have let you play.

(Troy takes a long drink from the bottle.)

ROSE: You gonna drink yourself to death. You don't need to be drinking like that.

TROY: Death ain't nothing. I done seen him. Done wrassled with him. You can't tell me nothing about death. Death ain't nothing but a fastball on the outside corner. And you know what I'll do to that! Lookee here, Bono . . . am I lying? You get one of them fastballs, about waist high, over the outside corner of the plate where you can get the meat of the bat on it . . . and good god! You can kiss it goodbye. Now, am I lying?

BONO: Naw, you telling the truth there. I seen you do it.

TROY: If I'm lying . . . that 450 feet worth of lying!

(Pause.)

Selkirk: George Selkirk (1934–1987), successor to Babe Ruth in right field for the Yankees. In nine seasons (1934–1942) he had a cumulative batting average of .290 with 108 home runs. In 1940 his average was .269 with 19 home runs.   **Jackie Robinson:** Jack Roosevelt Robinson (1919–1972), first and second baseman for the Brooklyn Dodgers from 1947 to 1956, was the first African American to play in the major leagues.

That's all death is to me. A fastball on the outside corner.

ROSE: I don't know why you want to get on talking about death.

TROY: Ain't nothing wrong with talking about death. That's part of life. Everybody gonna die. You gonna die, I'm gonna die. Bono's gonna die. Hell, we all gonna die.

ROSE: But you ain't got to talk about it. I don't like to talk about it.

TROY: You the one brought it up. Me and Bono was talking about baseball . . . you tell me I'm gonna drink myself to death. Ain't that right, Bono? You know I don't drink this but one night out of the week. That's Friday night. I'm gonna drink just enough to where I can handle it. Then I cuts it loose. I leave it alone. So don't you worry about me drinking myself to death. 'Cause I ain't worried about Death. I done seen him. I done wrestled with him.

Look here, Bono . . . I looked up one day and Death was marching straight at me. Like Soldiers on Parade! The Army of Death was marching straight at me. The middle of July, 1941. It got real cold just like it be winter. It seem like Death himself reached out and touched me on the shoulder. He touch me just like I touch you. I got cold as ice and Death standing there grinning at me.

ROSE: Troy, why don't you hush that talk.

TROY: I say . . . What you want, Mr. Death? You be wanting me? You done brought your army to be getting me? I looked him dead in the eye. I wasn't fearing nothing. I was ready to tangle. Just like I'm ready to tangle now. The Bible say be ever vigilant. That's why I don't get but so drunk. I got to keep watch.

ROSE: Troy was right down there in Mercy Hospital. You remember he had pneumonia? Laying there with a fever talking plumb out of his head.

TROY: Death standing there staring at me . . . carrying that sickle in his hand. Finally he say, "You want bound over for another year?" See, just like that . . . "You want bound over for another year?" I told him, "Bound over hell! Let's settle this now!"

It seem like he kinda fell back when I said that, and all the cold went out of me. I reached down and grabbed that sickle and threw it just as far as I could throw it . . . and me and him commenced to wrestling.

We wrestled for three days and three nights. I can't say where I found the strength from. Every time it seemed like he was gonna get the best of me, I'd reach way down deep inside myself and find the strength to do him one better.

ROSE: Every time Troy tell that story he find different ways to tell it. Different things to make up about it.

TROY: I ain't making up nothing. I'm telling you the facts of what happened. I wrestled with Death for three days and three nights and I'm standing here to tell you about it.

(*Pause.*)

Alright. At the end of the third night we done weakened each other to where we can't hardly move. Death stood up, throwed on his robe . . .

had him a white robe with a hood on it. He threw on that robe and went off to look for his sickle. Say, "I'll be back." Just like that. "I'll be back." I told him, say, "Yeah, but . . . you gonna have to find me!" I wasn't no fool. I wan't going looking for him. Death ain't nothing to play with. And I know he's gonna get me. I know I got to join his army . . . his camp followers. But as long as I keep my strength and see him coming . . . as long as I keep up my vigilance . . . he's gonna have to fight to get me. I ain't going easy.

BONO: Well, look here, since you got to keep up your vigilance . . . let me have the bottle.

TROY: Aw hell, I shouldn't have told you that part. I should have left out that part.

ROSE: Troy be talking that stuff and half the time don't even know what he be talking about.

TROY: Bono know me better than that.

BONO: That's right. I know you. I know you got some Uncle Remus in your blood. You got more stories than the devil got sinners.

TROY: Aw hell, I done seen him too! Done talked with the devil.

ROSE: Troy, don't nobody wanna be hearing all that stuff.

(*Lyons enters the yard from the street. Thirty-four years old, Troy's son by a previous marriage, he sports a neatly trimmed goatee, sport coat, white shirt, tieless and buttoned at the collar. Though he fancies himself a musician, he is more caught up in the rituals and "idea" of being a musician than in the actual practice of the music. He has come to borrow money from Troy, and while he knows he will be successful, he is uncertain as to what extent his lifestyle will be held up to scrutiny and ridicule.*)

LYONS: Hey, Pop.

TROY: What you come "Hey, Popping" me for?

LYONS: How you doing, Rose?

(*He kisses her.*)

Mr. Bono. How you doing?

BONO: Hey, Lyons . . . how you been?

TROY: He must have been doing alright. I ain't seen him around here last week.

ROSE: Troy, leave your boy alone. He come by to see you and you wanna start all that nonsense.

TROY: I ain't bothering Lyons.

(*Offers him the bottle.*)

Here . . . get you a drink. We got an understanding. I know why he come by to see me and he know I know.

LYONS: Come on, Pop . . . I just stopped by to say hi . . . see how you was doing.

TROY: You ain't stopped by yesterday.

ROSE: You gonna stay for supper, Lyons? I got some chicken cooking in the oven.

LYONS: No, Rose . . . thanks. I was just in the neighborhood and thought I'd
    stop by for a minute.

TROY: You was in the neighborhood alright, nigger. You telling the truth
    there. You was in the neighborhood cause it's my payday.

LYONS: Well, hell, since you mentioned it . . . let me have ten dollars.

TROY: I'll be damned! I'll die and go to hell and play blackjack with the devil
    before I give you ten dollars.

BONO: That's what I wanna know about . . . that devil you done seen.

LYONS: What . . . Pop done seen the devil? You too much, Pops.

TROY: Yeah, I done seen him. Talked to him too!

ROSE: You ain't seen no devil. I done told you that man ain't had nothing to
    do with the devil. Anything you can't understand, you want to call it the
    devil.

TROY: Look here, Bono . . . I went down to see Hertzberger about some fur-
    niture. Got three rooms for two-ninety-eight. That what it say on the
    radio. "Three rooms . . . two-ninety-eight." Even made up a little song
    about it. Go down there . . . man tell me I can't get no credit. I'm work-
    ing every day and can't get no credit. What to do? I got an empty house
    with some raggedy furniture in it. Cory ain't got no bed. He's sleeping
    on a pile of rags on the floor. Working every day and can't get no credit.
    Come back here—Rose'll tell you—madder than hell. Sit down . . . try
    to figure what I'm gonna do. Come a knock on the door. Ain't been liv-
    ing here but three days. Who know I'm here? Open the door . . . devil
    standing there bigger than life. White fellow . . . got on good clothes
    and everything. Standing there with a clipboard in his hand. I ain't had
    to say nothing. First words come out of his mouth was . . . "I under-
    stand you need some furniture and can't get no credit." I liked to fell
    over. He say, "I'll give you all the credit you want, but you got to pay the
    interest on it." I told him, "Give me three rooms worth and charge
    whatever you want." Next day a truck pulled up here and two men un-
    loaded them three rooms. Man what drove the truck give me a book. Say
    send ten dollars, first of every month to the address in the book and
    everything will be alright. Say if I miss a payment the devil was coming
    back and it'll be hell to pay. That was fifteen years ago. To this day . . .
    the first of the month I send my ten dollars, Rose'll tell you.

ROSE: Troy lying.

TROY: I ain't never seen that man since. Now you tell me who else that could
    have been but the devil? I ain't sold my soul or nothing like that, you
    understand. Naw, I wouldn't have truck with the devil about nothing
    like that. I got my furniture and pays my ten dollars the first of the
    month just like clockwork.

BONO: How long you say you been paying this ten dollars a month?

TROY: Fifteen years!

BONO: Hell, ain't you finished paying for it yet? How much the man done
    charged you?

TROY: Aw hell, I done paid for it. I done paid for it ten times over! The fact is I'm scared to stop paying it.

ROSE: Troy lying. We got that furniture from Mr. Glickman. He ain't paying no ten dollars a month to nobody.

TROY: Aw hell, woman. Bono know I ain't that big a fool.

LYONS: I was just getting ready to say . . . I know where there's a bridge for sale.

TROY: Look here, I'll tell you this . . . it don't matter to me if he was the devil. It don't matter if the devil give credit. Somebody has got to give it.

ROSE: It ought to matter. You going around talking about having truck with the devil . . . God's the one you gonna have to answer to. He's the one gonna be at the Judgment.

LYONS: Yeah, well, look here, Pop . . . let me have that ten dollars. I'll give it back to you. Bonnie got a job working at the hospital.

TROY: What I tell you, Bono? The only time I see this nigger is when he wants something. That's the only time I see him.

LYONS: Come on, Pop, Mr. Bono don't want to hear all that. Let me have the ten dollars. I told you Bonnie working.

TROY: What that mean to me? "Bonnie working." I don't care if she working. Go ask her for the ten dollars if she working. Talking about "Bonnie working." Why ain't you working?

LYONS: Aw, Pop, you know I can't find no decent job. Where am I gonna get a job at? You know I can't get no job.

TROY: I told you I know some people down there. I can get you on the rubbish if you want to work. I told you that the last time you came by here asking me for something.

LYONS: Naw, Pop . . . thanks. That ain't for me. I don't wanna be carrying nobody's rubbish. I don't wanna be punching nobody's time clock.

TROY: What's the matter, you too good to carry people's rubbish? Where you think that ten dollars you talking about come from? I'm just supposed to haul people's rubbish and give my money to you cause you too lazy to work. You too lazy to work and wanna know why you ain't got what I got.

ROSE: What hospital Bonnie working at? Mercy?

LYONS: She's down at Passavant working in the laundry.

TROY: I ain't got nothing as it is. I give you that ten dollars and I got to eat beans the rest of the week. Naw . . . you ain't getting no ten dollars here.

LYONS: You ain't got to be eating no beans. I don't know why you wanna say that.

TROY: I ain't got no extra money. Gabe done moved over to Miss Pearl's paying her the rent and things done got tight around here. I can't afford to be giving you every payday.

LYONS: I ain't asked you to give me nothing. I asked you to loan me ten dollars. I know you got ten dollars.

TROY: Yeah, I got it. You know why I got it? Cause I don't throw my money away out there in the streets. You living the fast life . . . wanna be a musician . . . running around in them clubs and things . . . then, you learn to take care of yourself. You ain't gonna find me going and asking nobody for nothing. I done spent too many years without.

LYONS: You and me is two different people, Pop.

TROY: I done learned my mistake and learned to do what's right by it. You still trying to get something for nothing. Life don't owe you nothing. You owe it to yourself. Ask Bono. He'll tell you I'm right.

LYONS: You got your way of dealing with the world . . . I got mine. The only thing that matters to me is the music.

TROY: Yeah, I can see that! It don't matter how you gonna eat . . . where your next dollar is coming from. You telling the truth there.

LYONS: I know I got to eat. But I got to live too. I need something that gonna help me to get out of the bed in the morning. Make me feel like I belong in the world. I don't bother nobody. I just stay with the music cause that's the only way I can find to live in the world. Otherwise there ain't no telling what I might do. Now I don't come criticizing you and how you live. I just come by to ask you for ten dollars. I don't wanna hear all that about how I live.

TROY: Boy, your mamma did a hell of a job raising you.

LYONS: You can't change me, Pop. I'm thirty-four years old. If you wanted to change me, you should have been there when I was growing up. I come by to see you . . . ask for ten dollars and you want to talk about how I was raised. You don't know nothing about how I was raised.

ROSE: Let the boy have ten dollars, Troy.

TROY (*to Lyons*): What the hell you looking at me for? I ain't got no ten dollars. You know what I do with my money.

(*To Rose.*)

Give him ten dollars if you want him to have it.

ROSE: I will. Just as soon as you turn it loose.

TROY (*handing Rose the money*): There it is. Seventy-six dollars and forty-two cents. You see this, Bono? Now, I ain't gonna get but six of that back.

ROSE: You ought to stop telling that lie. Here, Lyons.

(*She hands him the money.*)

LYONS: Thanks, Rose. Look . . . I got to run . . . I'll see you later.

TROY: Wait a minute. You gonna say, "thanks, Rose" and ain't gonna look to see where she got that ten dollars from? See how they do me, Bono?

LYONS: I know she got it from you, Pop. Thanks. I'll give it back to you.

TROY: There he go telling another lie. Time I see that ten dollars . . . he'll be owing me thirty more.

LYONS: See you, Mr. Bono.

BONO: Take care, Lyons!

LYONS: Thanks, Pop. I'll see you again.

(Lyons exits the yard.)

TROY: I don't know why he don't go and get him a decent job and take care of that woman he got.

BONO: He'll be alright, Troy. The boy is still young.

TROY: The *boy* is thirty-four years old.

ROSE: Let's not get off into all that.

BONO: Look here . . . I got to be going. I got to be getting on. Lucille gonna be waiting.

TROY *(puts his arm around Rose)*: See this woman, Bono? I love this woman. I love this woman so much it hurts. I love her so much . . . I done run out of ways of loving her. So I got to go back to basics. Don't you come by my house Monday morning talking about time to go to work . . . 'cause I'm still gonna be stroking!

ROSE: Troy! Stop it now!

BONO: I ain't paying him no mind, Rose. That ain't nothing but gin-talk. Go on, Troy. I'll see you Monday.

TROY: Don't you come by my house, nigger! I done told you what I'm gonna be doing.

(The lights go down to black.)

Scene Two

The lights come up on Rose hanging up clothes. She hums and sings softly to herself. It is the following morning.

ROSE *(sings)*: Jesus, be a fence all around me every day
Jesus, I want you to protect me as I travel on my way.
Jesus, be a fence all around me every day.

(Troy enters from the house.)

ROSE *(continued)*: Jesus, I want you to protect me
As I travel on my way.

(To Troy)

'Morning. You ready for breakfast? I can fix it soon as I finish hanging up these clothes.

TROY: I got the coffee on. That'll be alright. I'll just drink some of that this morning.

ROSE: That 651 hit yesterday. That's the second time this month. Miss Pearl hit for a dollar . . . seem like those that need the least always get lucky. Poor folks can't get nothing.

TROY: Them numbers don't know nobody. I don't know why you fool with them. You and Lyons both.

ROSE: It's something to do.

TROY: You ain't doing nothing but throwing your money away.

ROSE: Troy, you know I don't play foolishly. I just play a nickel here and a nickel there.

TROY: That's two nickels you done thrown away.

ROSE: Now I hit sometimes . . . that makes up for it. It always comes in handy when I do hit. I don't hear you complaining then.

TROY: I ain't complaining now. I just say it's foolish. Trying to guess out of six hundred ways which way the number gonna come. If I had all the money niggers, these Negroes, throw away on numbers for one week — just one week — I'd be a rich man.

ROSE: Well, you wishing and calling it foolish ain't gonna stop folks from playing numbers. That's one thing for sure. Besides . . . some good things come from playing numbers. Look where Pope done bought him that restaurant off of numbers.

TROY: I can't stand niggers like that. Man ain't had two dimes to rub together. He walking around with his shoes all run over bumming money for cigarettes. Alright. Got lucky there and hit the numbers . . .

ROSE: Troy, I know all about it.

TROY: Had good sense, I'll say that for him. He ain't throwed his money away. I seen niggers hit the numbers and go through two thousand dollars in four days. Man bought him that restaurant down there . . . fixed it up real nice . . . and then didn't want nobody to come in it! A Negro go in there and can't get no kind of service. I seen a white fellow come in there and order a bowl of stew. Pope picked all the meat out the pot for him. Man ain't had nothing but a bowl of meat! Negro come behind him and ain't got nothing but the potatoes and carrots. Talking about what numbers do for people, you picked a wrong example. Ain't done nothing but make a worser fool out of him than he was before.

ROSE: Troy, you ought to stop worrying about what happened at work yesterday.

TROY: I ain't worried. Just told me to be down there at the Commissioner's office on Friday. Everybody think they gonna fire me. I ain't worried about them firing me. You ain't got to worry about that.

(Pause.)

Where's Cory? Cory in the house? *(Calls.)* Cory?

ROSE: He gone out.

TROY: Out, huh? He gone out 'cause he know I want him to help me with this fence. I know how he is. That boy scared of work.

(Gabriel enters. He comes halfway down the alley and, hearing Troy's voice, stops.)

TROY *(continues)*: He ain't done a lick of work in his life.

ROSE: He had to go to football practice. Coach wanted them to get in a little extra practice before the season start.

TROY: I got his practice . . . running out of here before he get his chores done.

ROSE: Troy, what is wrong with you this morning? Don't nothing set right with you. Go on back in there and go to bed . . . get up on the other side.

TROY: Why something got to be wrong with me? I ain't said nothing wrong with me.

ROSE: You got something to say about everything. First it's the numbers . . . then it's the way the man runs his restaurant . . . then you done got on Cory. What's it gonna be next? Take a look up there and see if the weather suits you . . . or is it gonna be how you gonna put up the fence with the clothes hanging in the yard.

TROY: You hit the nail on the head then.

ROSE: I know you like I know the back of my hand. Go on in there and get you some coffee . . . see if that straighten you up. 'Cause you ain't right this morning.

(Troy starts into the house and sees Gabriel. Gabriel starts singing. Troy's brother, he is seven years younger than Troy. Injured in World War II, he has a metal plate in his head. He carries an old trumpet tied around his waist and believes with every fiber of his being that he is the Archangel Gabriel. He carries a chipped basket with an assortment of discarded fruits and vegetables he has picked up in the strip district and which he attempts to sell.)

GABRIEL *(singing)*: Yes, ma'am, I got plums
You ask me how I sell them
Oh ten cents apiece
Three for a quarter
Come and buy now
'Cause I'm here today
And tomorrow I'll be gone

(Gabriel enters.)

Hey, Rose!

ROSE: How you doing, Gabe?

GABRIEL: There's Troy . . . Hey, Troy!

TROY: Hey, Gabe.

(Exit into kitchen.)

ROSE *(to Gabriel)*: What you got there?

GABRIEL: You know what I got, Rose. I got fruits and vegetables.

ROSE *(looking in basket)*: Where's all these plums you talking about?

GABRIEL: I ain't got no plums today, Rose. I was just singing that. Have some tomorrow. Put me in a big order for plums. Have enough plums tomorrow for St. Peter and everybody.

(Troy re-enters from kitchen, crosses to steps.)
(To Rose.)

Troy's mad at me.

TROY: I ain't mad at you. What I got to be mad at you about? You ain't done nothing to me.

GABRIEL: I just moved over to Miss Pearl's to keep out from in your way. I ain't mean no harm by it.

TROY: Who said anything about that? I ain't said anything about that.

GABRIEL: You ain't mad at me, is you?

TROY: Naw . . . I ain't mad at you, Gabe. If I was mad at you I'd tell you about it.

GABRIEL: Got me two rooms. In the basement. Got my own door too. Wanna see my key?

(He holds up a key.)

That's my own key! Ain't nobody else got a key like that. That's my key! My two rooms!

TROY: Well, that's good, Gabe. You got your own key . . . that's good.

ROSE: You hungry, Gabe? I was just fixing to cook Troy his breakfast.

GABRIEL: I'll take some biscuits. You got some biscuits? Did you know when I was in heaven . . . every morning me and St. Peter would sit down by the gate and eat some big fat biscuits? Oh, yeah! We had us a good time. We'd sit there and eat us them biscuits and then St. Peter would go off to sleep and tell me to wake him up when it's time to open the gates for the judgment.

ROSE: Well, come on . . . I'll make up a batch of biscuits.

(Rose exits into the house.)

GABRIEL: Troy . . . St. Peter got your name in the book. I seen it. It say . . . Troy Maxson. I say . . . I know him! He got the same name like what I got. That's my brother!

TROY: How many times you gonna tell me that, Gabe?

GABRIEL: Ain't got my name in the book. Don't have to have my name. I done died and went to heaven. He got your name though. One morning St. Peter was looking at his book . . . marking it up for the judgment . . . and he let me see your name. Got it in there under M. Got Rose's name . . . I ain't seen it like I seen yours . . . but I know it's in there. He got a great big book. Got everybody's name what was ever been born. That's what he told me. But I seen your name. Seen it with my own eyes.

TROY: Go on in the house there. Rose going to fix you something to eat.

GABRIEL: Oh, I ain't hungry. I done had breakfast with Aunt Jemimah. She come by and cooked me up a whole mess of flapjacks. Remember how we used to eat them flapjacks?

TROY: Go on in the house and get you something to eat now.

GABRIEL: I got to sell my plums. I done sold some tomatoes. Got me two quarters. Wanna see?

(He shows Troy his quarters.)

I'm gonna save them and buy me a new horn so St. Peter can hear me when it's time to open the gates.

(*Gabriel stops suddenly. Listens.*)

Hear that? That's the hellhounds. I got to chase them out of here. Go on get out of here! Get out!

(*Gabriel exits singing.*)

Better get ready for the judgment
Better get ready for the judgment
My Lord is coming down

(*Rose enters from the house.*)

TROY: He gone off somewhere.

GABRIEL (*offstage*): Better get ready for the judgment
Better get ready for the judgment morning
Better get ready for the judgment
My God is coming down

ROSE: He ain't eating right. Miss Pearl say she can't get him to eat nothing.

TROY: What you want me to do about it, Rose? I done did everything I can for the man. I can't make him get well. Man got half his head blown away . . . what you expect?

ROSE: Seem like something ought to be done to help him.

TROY: Man don't bother nobody. He just mixed up from that metal plate he got in his head. Ain't no sense for him to go back into the hospital.

ROSE: Least he be eating right. They can help him take care of himself.

TROY: Don't nobody wanna be locked up, Rose. What you wanna lock him up for? Man go over there and fight the war . . . messin' around with them Japs, get half his head blown off . . . and they give him a lousy three thousand dollars. And I had to swoop down on that.

ROSE: Is you fixing to go into that again?

TROY: That's the only way I got a roof over my head . . . cause of that metal plate.

ROSE: Ain't no sense you blaming yourself for nothing. Gabe wasn't in no condition to manage that money. You done what was right by him. Can't nobody say you ain't done what was right by him. Look how long you took care of him . . . till he wanted to have his own place and moved over there with Miss Pearl.

TROY: That ain't what I'm saying, woman! I'm just stating the facts. If my brother didn't have that metal plate in his head . . . I wouldn't have a pot to piss in or a window to throw it out of. And I'm fifty-three years old. Now see if you can understand that!

(*Troy gets up from the porch and starts to exit the yard.*)

ROSE: Where you going off to? You been running out of here every Saturday for weeks. I thought you was gonna work on this fence?

TROY: I'm gonna walk down to Taylors'. Listen to the ball game. I'll be back in a bit. I'll work on it when I get back.

(*He exits the yard. The lights go to black.*)

Scene Three

The lights come up on the yard. It is four hours later. Rose is taking down the clothes from the line. Cory enters carrying his football equipment.

ROSE: Your daddy like to had a fit with you running out of here this morning without doing your chores.

CORY: I told you I had to go to practice.

ROSE: He say you were supposed to help him with this fence.

CORY: He been saying that the last four or five Saturdays, and then he don't never do nothing, but go down to Taylors. Did you tell him about the recruiter?

ROSE: Yeah, I told him.

CORY: What he say?

ROSE: He ain't said nothing too much. You get in there and get started on your chores before he gets back. Go on and scrub down them steps before he gets back here hollering and carrying on.

CORY: I'm hungry. What you got to eat, Mama?

ROSE: Go on and get started on your chores. I got some meat loaf in there. Go on and make you a sandwich . . . and don't leave no mess in there.

(*Cory exits into the house. Rose continues to take down the clothes. Troy enters the yard and sneaks up and grabs her from behind.*)

Troy! Go on, now. You liked to scared me to death. What was the score of the game? Lucille had me on the phone and I couldn't keep up with it.

TROY: What I care about the game? Come here, woman. (*He tries to kiss her.*)

ROSE: I thought you went down Taylors' to listen to the game. Go on, Troy! You supposed to be putting up this fence.

TROY (*attempting to kiss her again*): I'll put it up when I finish with what is at hand.

ROSE: Go on, Troy. I ain't studying you.

TROY (*chasing after her*): I'm studying you . . . fixing to do my homework!

ROSE: Troy, you better leave me alone.

TROY: Where's Cory? That boy brought his butt home yet?

ROSE: He's in the house doing his chores.

TROY (*calling*): Cory! Get your butt out here, boy!

(*Rose exits into the house with the laundry. Troy goes over to the pile of wood, picks up a board, and starts sawing. Cory enters from the house.*)

TROY: You just now coming in here from leaving this morning?

CORY: Yeah, I had to go to football practice.

TROY: Yeah, what?

CORY: Yessir.

TROY: I ain't but two seconds off you noway. The garbage sitting in there overflowing . . . you ain't done none of your chores . . . and you come in here talking about "Yeah."

CORY: I was just getting ready to do my chores now, Pop . . .

TROY: Your first chore is to help me with this fence on Saturday. Everything else come after that. Now get that saw and cut them boards.

(*Cory takes the saw and begins cutting the boards. Troy continues working. There is a long pause.*)

CORY: Hey, Pop . . . why don't you buy a TV?

TROY: What I want with a TV? What I want one of them for?

CORY: Everybody got one. Earl, Ba Bra . . . Jesse!

TROY: I ain't asked you who had one. I say what I want with one?

CORY: So you can watch it. They got lots of things on TV. Baseball games and everything. We could watch the World Series.

TROY: Yeah . . . and how much this TV cost?

CORY: I don't know. They got them on sale for around two hundred dollars.

TROY: Two hundred dollars, huh?

CORY: That ain't that much, Pop.

TROY: Naw, it's just two hundred dollars. See that roof you got over your head at night? Let me tell you something about that roof. It's been over ten years since that roof was last tarred. See now . . . the snow come this winter and sit up there on that roof like it is . . . and it's gonna seep inside. It's just gonna be a little bit . . . ain't gonna hardly notice it. Then the next thing you know, it's gonna be leaking all over the house. Then the wood rot from all that water and you gonna need a whole new roof. Now, how much you think it cost to get that roof tarred?

CORY: I don't know.

TROY: Two hundred and sixty-four dollars . . . cash money. While you thinking about a TV, I got to be thinking about the roof . . . and whatever else go wrong here. Now if you had two hundred dollars, what would you do . . . fix the roof or buy a TV?

CORY: I'd buy a TV. Then when the roof started to leak . . . when it needed fixing . . . I'd fix it.

TROY: Where you gonna get the money from? You done spent it for a TV. You gonna sit up and watch the water run all over your brand new TV.

CORY: Aw, Pop. You got money. I know you do.

TROY: Where I got it at, huh?

CORY: You got it in the bank.

TROY: You wanna see my bankbook? You wanna see that seventy-three dollars and twenty-two cents I got sitting up in there.

CORY: You ain't got to pay for it all at one time. You can put a down payment on it and carry it on home with you.

TROY: Not me. I ain't gonna owe nobody nothing if I can help it. Miss a payment and they come and snatch it right out your house. Then what you got? Now, soon as I get two hundred dollars clear, then I'll buy a TV. Right now, as soon as I get two hundred and sixty-four dollars, I'm gonna have this roof tarred.

CORY: Aw . . . Pop!

TROY: You go on and get you two hundred dollars and buy one if ya want it. I got better things to do with my money.

CORY: I can't get no two hundred dollars. I ain't never seen two hundred dollars.

TROY: I'll tell you what . . . you get you a hundred dollars and I'll put the other hundred with it.

CORY: Alright, I'm gonna show you.

TROY: You gonna show me how you can cut them boards right now.

(Cory begins to cut the boards. There is a long pause.)

CORY: The Pirates won today. That makes five in a row.

TROY: I ain't thinking about the Pirates. Got an all-white team. Got that boy . . . that Puerto Rican boy . . . Clemente.° Don't even half-play him. That boy could be something if they give him a chance. Play him one day and sit him on the bench the next.

CORY: He gets a lot of chances to play.

TROY: I'm talking about playing regular. Playing every day so you can get your timing. That's what I'm talking about.

CORY: They got some white guys on the team that don't play every day. You can't play everybody at the same time.

TROY: If they got a white fellow sitting on the bench . . . you can bet your last dollar he can't play! The colored guy got to be twice as good before he get on the team. That's why I don't want you to get all tied up in them sports. Man on the team and what it get him? They got colored on the team and don't use them. Same as not having them. All them teams the same.

CORY: The Braves got Hank Aaron and Wes Covington.° Hank Aaron hit two home runs today. That makes forty-three.

TROY: Hank Aaron ain't nobody. That's what you supposed to do. That's how you supposed to play the game. Ain't nothing to it. It's just a matter of

---

Clemente: Roberto Clemente (1934–1972), right fielder for the Pittsburgh Pirates from 1955 to 1971, was the first player of Latin American descent to be elected into the Baseball Hall of Fame. In 1956 he played in 147 games and had a .311 batting average; in 1957 he played in 111 games and his average dropped to .253.   **Hank Aaron and Wes Covington:** Henry Louis Aaron (b. 1934), African American outfielder, hit 44 home runs for the Milwaukee Braves in 1957 and went on to break Babe Ruth's career home run record. John Wesley Covington (b. 1932), African American outfielder, hit 21 homers for the Milwaukee Braves in 1957.

timing . . . getting the right follow-through. Hell, I can hit forty-three home runs right now!

CORY: Not off no major-league pitching, you couldn't.

TROY: We had better pitching in the Negro leagues. I hit seven home runs off of Satchel Paige.° You can't get no better than that!

CORY: Sandy Koufax.° He's leading the league in strike-outs.

TROY: I ain't thinking of no Sandy Koufax.

CORY: You got Warren Spahn and Lew Burdette.° I bet you couldn't hit no home runs off of Warren Spahn.

TROY: I'm through with it now. You go on and cut them boards.

(*Pause.*)

Your mama tell me you done got recruited by a college football team? Is that right?

CORY: Yeah. Coach Zellman say the recruiter gonna be coming by to talk to you. Get you to sign the permission papers.

TROY: I thought you supposed to be working down there at the A&P. Ain't you suppose to be working down there after school?

CORY: Mr. Stawicki say he gonna hold my job for me until after the football season. Say starting next week I can work weekends.

TROY: I thought we had an understanding about this football stuff? You suppose to keep up with your chores and hold that job down at the A&P. Ain't been around here all day on a Saturday. Ain't none of your chores done . . . and now you telling me you done quit your job.

CORY: I'm gonna to be working weekends.

TROY: You damn right you are! And ain't no need for nobody coming around here to talk to me about signing nothing.

CORY: Hey, Pop . . . you can't do that. He's coming all the way from North Carolina.

TROY: I don't care where he coming from. The white man ain't gonna let you get nowhere with that football noway. You go on and get your book-learning so you can work yourself up in that A&P or learn how to fix cars or build houses or something, get you a trade. That way you have

---

Satchel Paige: Leroy "Satchel" Paige (1906–1982), star pitcher in the Negro Leagues from 1926 to 1947, played in the major leagues for the Cleveland Indians (1948–1949), the St. Louis Browns (1951–1953), and the Kansas City Athletics (1965). He was the first African American elected to the Baseball Hall of Fame.   **Sandy Koufax:** Sanford Koufax (b. 1935), pitcher for the Brooklyn and Los Angeles Dodgers from 1955 to 1966. He recorded 122 strikeouts in 1957. Jack Sanford ended up leading the league that year with 188 strikeouts for the Philadelphia Phillies.   **Warren Spahn and Lew Burdette:** Warren Edward Spahn (1921–2003) is the winningest left-handed pitcher in major league history with 363 victories, all but seven of those wins coming with the Boston-Milwaukee Braves, 1942–1964. He had a 21-11 record in 1957 when he won the Cy Young Award and won the fourth game of the 1958 World Series. Selva Lewis Burdette (b. 1926), pitcher for six major league teams from 1950 to 1967, had a 17-9 record for Milwaukee in 1957, won three games in the 1957 World Series, and was named that series' Most Valuable Player.

something can't nobody take away from you. You go on and learn how to put your hands to some good use. Besides hauling people's garbage.

CORY: I get good grades, Pop. That's why the recruiter wants to talk with you. You got to keep up your grades to get recruited. This way I'll be going to college. I'll get a chance . . .

TROY: First you gonna get your butt down there to the A&P and get your job back.

CORY: Mr. Stawicki done already hired somebody else 'cause I told him I was playing football.

TROY: You a bigger fool than I thought . . . to let somebody take away your job so you can play some football. Where you gonna get your money to take out your girlfriend and whatnot? What kind of foolishness is that to let somebody take away your job?

CORY: I'm still gonna be working weekends.

TROY: Naw . . . naw. You getting your butt out of here and finding you another job.

CORY: Come on, Pop! I got to practice. I can't work after school and play football too. The team needs me. That's what Coach Zellman say . . .

TROY: I don't care what nobody else say. I'm the boss . . . you understand? I'm the boss around here. I do the only saying what counts.

CORY: Come on, Pop!

TROY: I asked you . . . did you understand?

CORY: Yeah . . .

TROY: What?!

CORY: Yessir.

TROY: You go on down there to that A&P and see if you can get your job back. If you can't do both . . . then you quit the football team. You've got to take the crookeds with the straights.

CORY: Yessir.

(Pause.)

Can I ask you a question?

TROY: What the hell you wanna ask me? Mr. Stawicki the one you got the questions for.

CORY: How come you ain't never liked me?

TROY: Liked you? Who the hell say I got to like you? What law is there say I got to like you? Wanna stand up in my face and ask a damn fool-ass question like that. Talking about liking somebody. Come here, boy, when I talk to you.

(Cory comes over to where Troy is working. He stands slouched over and Troy shoves him on his shoulder.)

Straighten up, goddammit! I asked you a question . . . what law is there say I got to like you?

CORY: None.

TROY: Well, alright then! Don't you eat every day?

(*Pause.*)

Answer me when I talk to you! Don't you eat every day?
CORY: Yeah.
TROY: Nigger, as long as you in my house, you put that sir on the end of it
   when you talk to me!
CORY: Yes . . . sir.
TROY: You eat every day.
CORY: Yessir!
TROY: Got a roof over your head.
CORY: Yessir!
TROY: Got clothes on your back.
CORY: Yessir.
TROY: Why you think that is?
CORY: Cause of you.
TROY: Aw, hell I know it's 'cause of me . . . but why do you think that is?
CORY (*hesitant*): Cause you like me.
TROY: Like you? I go out of here every morning . . . bust my butt . . . putting
   up with them crackers every day . . . cause I like you? You about the
   biggest fool I ever saw.

(*Pause.*)

It's my job. It's my responsibility! You understand that? A man got to
take care of his family. You live in my house . . . sleep you behind on my
bedclothes . . . fill you belly up with my food . . . cause you my son. You
my flesh and blood. Not 'cause I like you! Cause it's my duty to take care
of you. I owe a responsibility to you! Let's get this straight right here . . .
before it go along any further . . . I ain't got to like you. Mr. Rand don't
give me my money come payday cause he likes me. He gives me cause he
owe me. I done give you everything I had to give you. I gave you your life!
Me and your mama worked that out between us. And liking your black
ass wasn't part of the bargain. Don't you try and go through life worrying about if somebody like you or not. You best be making sure they
doing right by you. You understand what I'm saying, boy?
CORY: Yessir.
TROY: Then get the hell out of my face, and get on down to that A&P.

(*Rose has been standing behind the screen door for much of the scene. She enters as
Cory exits.*)

ROSE: Why don't you let the boy go ahead and play football, Troy? Ain't no
   harm in that. He's just trying to be like you with the sports.
TROY: I don't want him to be like me! I want him to move as far away from
   my life as he can get. You the only decent thing that ever happened to
   me. I wish him that. But I don't wish him a thing else from my life. I decided seventeen years ago that boy wasn't getting involved in no sports.
   Not after what they did to me in the sports.

ROSE: Troy, why don't you admit you was too old to play in the major leagues? For once . . . why don't you admit that?

TROY: What do you mean too old? Don't come telling me I was too old. I just wasn't the right color. Hell, I'm fifty-three years old and can do better than Selkirk's .269 right now!

ROSE: How's was you gonna play ball when you were over forty? Sometimes I can't get no sense out of you.

TROY: I got good sense, woman. I got sense enough not to let my boy get hurt over playing no sports. You been mothering that boy too much. Worried about if people like him.

ROSE: Everything that boy do . . . he do for you. He wants you to say "Good job, son." That's all.

TROY: Rose, I ain't got time for that. He's alive. He's healthy. He's got to make his own way. I made mine. Ain't nobody gonna hold his hand when he get out there in that world.

ROSE: Times have changed from when you was young, Troy. People change. The world's changing around you and you can't even see it.

TROY (*slow, methodical*): Woman . . . I do the best I can do. I come in here every Friday. I carry a sack of potatoes and a bucket of lard. You all line up at the door with your hands out. I give you the lint from my pockets. I give you my sweat and my blood. I ain't got no tears. I done spent them. We go upstairs in that room at night . . . and I fall down on you and try to blast a hole into forever. I get up Monday morning . . . find my lunch on the table. I go out. Make my way. Find my strength to carry me through to the next Friday.

(*Pause.*)

That's all I got, Rose. That's all I got to give. I can't give nothing else.

(*Troy exits into the house. The lights go down to black.*)

Scene Four

It is Friday. Two weeks later. Cory starts out of the house with his football equipment. The phone rings.

CORY (*calling*): I got it!

(*He answers the phone and stands in the screen door talking.*)

Hello? Hey, Jesse. Naw . . . I was just getting ready to leave now.

ROSE (*calling*): Cory!

CORY: I told you, man, them spikes is all tore up. You can use them if you want, but they ain't no good. Earl got some spikes.

ROSE (*calling*): Cory!

CORY (*calling to Rose*): Mam? I'm talking to Jesse.

(*Into phone.*)

When she say that? (*Pause.*) Aw, you lying, man. I'm gonna tell her you
said that.
ROSE (*calling*): Cory, don't you go nowhere!
CORY: I got to go to the game, Ma!

(*Into the phone.*)

Yeah, hey, look, I'll talk to you later. Yeah, I'll meet you over Earl's house.
Later. Bye, Ma.

(*Cory exits the house and starts out the yard.*)

ROSE: Cory, where you going off to? You got that stuff all pulled out and
thrown all over your room.
CORY (*in the yard*): I was looking for my spikes. Jesse wanted to borrow my
spikes.
ROSE: Get up there and get that cleaned up before your daddy get back in
here.
CORY: I got to go to the game! I'll clean it up *when I get back.*

(*Cory exits.*)

ROSE: That's all he need to do is see that room all messed up.

(*Rose exits into the house. Troy and Bono enter the yard. Troy is dressed in clothes
other than his work clothes.*)

BONO: He told him the same thing he told you. Take it to the union.
TROY: Brownie ain't got that much sense. Man wasn't thinking about nothing. He wait until I confront them on it . . . then he wanna come crying
seniority.

(*Calls.*)

Hey, Rose!
BONO: I wish I could have seen Mr. Rand's face when he told you.
TROY: He couldn't get it out of his mouth! Liked to bit his tongue! When
they called me down there to the Commissioner's office . . . he thought
they was gonna fire me. Like everybody else.
BONO: I didn't think they was gonna fire you. I thought they was gonna put
you on the warning paper.
TROY: Hey, Rose!

(*To Bono.*)

Yeah, Mr. Rand like to bit his tongue.

(*Troy breaks the seal on the bottle, takes a drink, and hands it to Bono.*)

BONO: I see you run right down to Taylors' and told that Alberta gal.
TROY (*calling*): Hey Rose! (*To Bono.*) I told everybody. Hey, Rose! I went down
there to cash my check.

ROSE (*entering from the house*): Hush all that hollering, man! I know you out here. What they say down there at the Commissioner's office?

TROY: You supposed to come when I call you, woman. Bono'll tell you that.

(*To Bono.*)

Don't Lucille come when you call her?

ROSE: Man, hush your mouth. I ain't no dog . . . talk about "come when you call me."

TROY (*puts his arm around Rose*): You hear this, Bono? I had me an old dog used to get uppity like that. You say, "C'mere, Blue!" . . . and he just lay there and look at you. End up getting a stick and chasing him away trying to make him come.

ROSE: I ain't studying you and your dog. I remember you used to sing that old song.

TROY (*he sings*): Hear it ring! Hear it ring!
I had a dog his name was Blue.

ROSE: Don't nobody wanna hear you sing that old song.

TROY (*sings*): You know Blue was mighty true.

ROSE: Used to have Cory running around here singing that song.

BONO: Hell, I remember that song myself.

TROY (*sings*): You know Blue was a good old dog.
Blue treed a possum in a hollow log.

That was my daddy's song. My daddy made up that song.

ROSE: I don't care who made it up. Don't nobody wanna hear you sing it.

TROY (*makes a song like calling a dog*): Come here, woman.

ROSE: You come in here carrying on, I reckon they ain't fired you. What they say down there at the Commissioner's office?

TROY: Look here, Rose . . . Mr. Rand called me into his office today when I got back from talking to them people down there . . . it come from up top . . . he called me in and told me they was making me a driver.

ROSE: Troy, you kidding!

TROY: No I ain't. Ask Bono.

ROSE: Well, that's great, Troy. Now you don't have to hassle them people no more.

(*Lyons enters from the street.*)

TROY: Aw hell, I wasn't looking to see you today. I thought you was in jail. Got it all over the front page of the *Courier* about them raiding Sefus's place . . . where you be hanging out with all them thugs.

LYONS: Hey, Pop . . . that ain't got nothing to do with me. I don't go down there gambling. I go down there to sit in with the band. I ain't got nothing to do with the gambling part. They got some good music down there.

TROY: They got some rogues . . . is what they got.

LYONS: How you been, Mr. Bono? Hi, Rose.

BONO: I see where you playing down at the Crawford Grill tonight.

ROSE: How come you ain't brought Bonnie like I told you. You should have brought Bonnie with you, she ain't been over in a month of Sundays.

LYONS: I was just in the neighborhood . . . thought I'd stop by.

TROY: Here he come . . .

BONO: Your daddy got a promotion on the rubbish. He's gonna be the first colored driver. Ain't got to do nothing but sit up there and read the paper like them white fellows.

LYONS: Hey, Pop . . . if you knew how to read you'd be alright.

BONO: Naw . . . naw . . . you mean if the nigger knew how to *drive* he'd be all right. Been fighting with them people about driving and ain't even got a license. Mr. Rand know you ain't got no driver's license?

TROY: Driving ain't nothing. All you do is point the truck where you want it to go. Driving ain't nothing.

BONO: Do Mr. Rand know you ain't got no driver's license? That's what I'm talking about. I ain't asked if driving was easy. I asked if Mr. Rand know you ain't got no driver's license.

TROY: He ain't got to know. The man ain't got to know my business. Time he find out, I have two or three driver's licenses.

LYONS (*going into his pocket*): Say, look here, Pop . . .

TROY: I knew it was coming. Didn't I tell you, Bono? I know what kind of "Look here, Pop" that was. The nigger fixing to ask me for some money. It's Friday night. It's my payday. All them rogues down there on the avenue . . . the ones that ain't in jail . . . and Lyons is hopping in his shoes to get down there with them.

LYONS: See, Pop . . . if you give somebody else a chance to talk sometime, you'd see that I was fixing to pay you back your ten dollars like I told you. Here . . . I told you I'd pay you when Bonnie got paid.

TROY: Naw . . . you go ahead and keep that ten dollars. Put it in the bank. The next time you feel like you wanna come by here and ask me for something . . . you go on down there and get that.

LYONS: Here's your ten dollars, Pop. I told you I don't want you to give me nothing. I just wanted to borrow ten dollars.

TROY: Naw . . . you go on and keep that for the next time you want to ask me.

LYONS: Come on, Pop . . . here go your ten dollars.

ROSE: Why don't you go on and let the boy pay you back, Troy?

LYONS: Here you go, Rose. If you don't take it I'm gonna have to hear about it for the next six months. (*He hands her the money.*)

ROSE: You can hand yours over here too, Troy.

TROY: You see this, Bono. You see how they do me.

BONO: Yeah, Lucille do me the same way.

(*Gabriel is heard singing onstage. He enters.*)

GABRIEL: Better get ready for the Judgment! Better get ready for . . . Hey! . . . Hey! . . . There's Troy's boy!

LYONS: How you doing, Uncle Gabe?

GABRIEL: Lyons . . . The King of the Jungle! Rose . . . hey, Rose. Got a flower for you.

(*He takes a rose from his pocket.*)

Picked it myself. That's the same rose like you is!

ROSE: That's right nice of you, Gabe.

LYONS: What you been doing, Uncle Gabe?

GABRIEL: Oh, I been chasing hellhounds and waiting on the time to tell St. Peter to open the gates.

LYONS: You been chasing hellhounds, huh? Well . . . you doing the right thing, Uncle Gabe. Somebody got to chase them.

GABRIEL: Oh, yeah . . . I know it. The devil's strong. The devil ain't no pushover. Hellhounds snipping at everybody's heels. But I got my trumpet waiting on the judgment time.

LYONS: Waiting on the Battle of Armageddon, huh?

GABRIEL: Ain't gonna be too much of a battle when God get to waving that Judgment sword. But the people's gonna have a hell of a time trying to get into heaven if them gates ain't open.

LYONS (*putting his arm around Gabriel*): You hear this, Pop. Uncle Gabe, you alright!

GABRIEL (*laughing with Lyons*): Lyons! King of the Jungle.

ROSE: You gonna stay for supper, Gabe? Want me to fix you a plate?

GABRIEL: I'll take a sandwich, Rose. Don't want no plate. Just wanna eat with my hands. I'll take a sandwich.

ROSE: How about you, Lyons? You staying? Got some short ribs cooking.

LYONS: Naw, I won't eat nothing till after we finished playing.

(*Pause.*)

You ought to come down and listen to me play, Pop.

TROY: I don't like that Chinese music. All that noise.

ROSE: Go on in the house and wash up, Gabe . . . I'll fix you a sandwich.

GABRIEL (*to Lyons, as he exits*): Troy's mad at me.

LYONS: What you mad at Uncle Gabe for, Pop.

ROSE: He thinks Troy's mad at him cause he moved over to Miss Pearl's.

TROY: I ain't mad at the man. He can live where he want to live at.

LYONS: What he move over there for? Miss Pearl don't like nobody.

ROSE: She don't mind him none. She treats him real nice. She just don't allow all that singing.

TROY: She don't mind that rent he be paying . . . that's what she don't mind.

ROSE: Troy, I ain't going through that with you no more. He's over there cause he want to have his own place. He can come and go as he please.

TROY: Hell, he could come and go as he please here. I wasn't stopping him. I ain't put no rules on him.

ROSE: It ain't the same thing, Troy. And you know it.

(Gabriel comes to the door.)

Now, that's the last I wanna hear about that. I don't wanna hear nothing else about Gabe and Miss Pearl. And next week . . .

GABRIEL: I'm ready for my sandwich, Rose.

ROSE: And next week . . . when that recruiter come from that school . . . I want you to sign that paper and go on and let Cory play football. Then that'll be the last I have to hear about that.

TROY *(to Rose as she exits into the house)*: I ain't thinking about Cory nothing.

LYONS: What . . . Cory got recruited? What school he going to?

TROY: That boy walking around here smelling his piss . . . thinking he's grown. Thinking he's gonna do what he want, irrespective of what I say. Look here, Bono . . . I left the Commissioner's office and went down to the A&P . . . that boy ain't working down there. He lying to me. Telling me he got his job back . . . telling me he working weekends . . . telling me he working after school . . . Mr. Stawicki tell me he ain't working down there at all!

LYONS: Cory just growing up. He's just busting at the seams trying to fill out your shoes.

TROY: I don't care what he's doing. When he get to the point where he wanna disobey me . . . then it's time for him to move on. Bono'll tell you that. I bet he ain't never disobeyed his daddy without paying the consequences.

BONO: I ain't never had a chance. My daddy came on through . . . but I ain't never knew him to see him . . . or what he had on his mind or where he went. Just moving on through. Searching out the New Land. That's what the old folks used to call it. See a fellow moving around from place to place . . . woman to woman . . . called it searching out the New Land. I can't say if he ever found it. I come along, didn't want no kids. Didn't know if I was gonna be in one place long enough to fix on them right as their daddy. I figured I was going searching too. As it turned out I been hooked up with Lucille near about as long as your daddy been with Rose. Going on sixteen years.

TROY: Sometimes I wish I hadn't known my daddy. He ain't cared nothing about no kids. A kid to him wasn't nothing. All he wanted was for you to learn how to walk so he could start you to working. When it come time for eating . . . he ate first. If there was anything left over, that's what you got. Man would sit down and eat two chickens and give you the wing.

LYONS: You ought to stop that, Pop. Everybody feed their kids. No matter how hard times is . . . everybody care about their kids. Make sure they have something to eat.

TROY: The only thing my daddy cared about was getting them bales of cotton in to Mr. Lubin. That's the only thing that mattered to him. Sometimes I used to wonder why he was living. Wonder why the devil hadn't come and got him. "Get them bales of cotton in to Mr. Lubin" and find out he owe him money . . .

LYONS: He should have just went on and left when he saw he couldn't get nowhere. That's what I would have done.

TROY: How he gonna leave with eleven kids? And where he gonna go? He ain't knew how to do nothing but farm. No, he was trapped and I think he knew it. But I'll say this for him . . . he felt a responsibility toward us. Maybe he ain't treated us the way I felt he should have . . . but without that responsibility he could have walked off and left us . . . made his own way.

BONO: A lot of them did. Back in those days what you talking about . . . they walk out their front door and just take on down one road or another and keep on walking.

LYONS: There you go! That's what I'm talking about.

BONO: Just keep on walking till you come to something else. Ain't you never heard of nobody having the walking blues? Well, that's what you call it when you just take off like that.

TROY: My daddy ain't had them walking blues! What you talking about? He stayed right there with his family. But he was just as evil as he could be. My mama couldn't stand him. Couldn't stand that evilness. She run off when I was about eight. She sneaked off one night after he had gone to sleep. Told me she was coming back for me. I ain't never seen her no more. All his women run off and left him. He wasn't good for nobody.

When my turn come to head out, I was fourteen and got to sniffing around Joe Canewell's daughter. Had us an old mule we called Greyboy. My daddy sent me out to do some plowing and I tied up Greyboy and went to fooling around with Joe Canewell's daughter. We done found us a nice little spot, got real cozy with each other. She about thirteen and we done figured we was grown anyway . . . so we down there enjoying ourselves . . . ain't thinking about nothing. We didn't know Greyboy had got loose and wandered back to the house and my daddy was looking for me. We down there by the creek enjoying ourselves when my daddy come up on us. Surprised us. He had them leather straps off the mule and commenced to whupping me like there was no tomorrow. I jumped up, mad and embarrassed. I was scared of my daddy. When he commenced to whupping on me . . . quite naturally I run to get out of the way.

(*Pause.*)

Now I thought he was mad cause I ain't done my work. But I see where he was chasing me off so he could have the gal for himself. When I see what the matter of it was, I lost all fear of my daddy. Right there is where I become a man . . . at fourteen years of age.

(*Pause.*)

Now it was my turn to run him off. I picked up them same reins that he had used on me. I picked up them reins and commenced to whupping on him. The gal jumped up and run off . . . and when my daddy turned to face me, I could see why the devil had never come to get him . . . cause he was the devil himself. I don't know what happened. When I woke up, I was laying right there by the creek, and Blue . . . this old dog we had . . . was licking my face. I thought I was blind. I couldn't see nothing. Both my eyes were swollen shut. I layed there and cried. I didn't know what I was gonna do. The only thing I knew was the time had come for me to leave my daddy's house. And right there the world suddenly got big. And it was a long time before I could cut it down to where I could handle it.

Part of that cutting down was when I got to the place where I could feel him kicking in my blood and knew that the only thing that sepa- rated us was the matter of a few years.

(*Gabriel enters from the house with a sandwich.*)

LYONS: What you got there, Uncle Gabe?

GABRIEL: Got me a ham sandwich. Rose gave me a ham sandwich.

TROY: I don't know what happened to him. I done lost touch with everybody except Gabriel. But I hope he's dead. I hope he found some peace.

LYONS: That's a heavy story, Pop. I didn't know you left home when you was fourteen.

TROY: And didn't know nothing. The only part of the world I knew was the forty-two acres of Mr. Lubin's land. That's all I knew about life.

LYONS: Fourteen's kinda young to be out on your own. (*Phone rings.*) I don't even think I was ready to be out on my own at fourteen. I don't know what I would have done.

TROY: I got up from the creek and walked on down to Mobile. I was through with farming. Figured I could do better in the city. So I walked the two hundred miles to Mobile.

LYONS: Wait a minute . . . you ain't walked no two hundred miles, Pop. Ain't nobody gonna walk no two hundred miles. You talking about some walking there.

BONO: That's the only way you got anywhere back in them days.

LYONS: Shhh. Damn if I wouldn't have hitched a ride with somebody!

TROY: Who you gonna hitch it with? They ain't had no cars and things like they got now. We talking about 1918.

ROSE (*entering*): What you all out here getting into?

TROY (*to Rose*): I'm telling Lyons how good he got it. He don't know nothing about this I'm talking.

ROSE: Lyons, that was Bonnie on the phone. She say you supposed to pick her up.

LYONS: Yeah, okay, Rose.

TROY: I walked on down to Mobile and hitched up with some of them fel- lows that was heading this way. Got up here and found out . . . not only couldn't you get a job . . . you couldn't find no place to live. I thought I was in freedom. Shhh. Colored folks living down there on the river-banks in whatever kind of shelter they could find for themselves. Right down there under the Brady Street Bridge. Living in shacks made of sticks and tarpaper. Messed around there and went from bad to worse. Started stealing. First it was food. Then I figured, hell, if I steal money I can buy me some food. Buy me some shoes too! One thing led to another. Met your mama. I was young and anxious to be a man. Met your mama and had you. What I do that for? Now I got to worry about feeding you and her. Got to steal three times as much. Went out one day looking for somebody to rob . . . that's what I was, a robber. I'll tell you the truth. I'm ashamed of it today. But it's the truth. Went to rob this fellow . . . pulled out my knife . . . and he pulled out a gun. Shot me in the chest. I felt just like somebody had taken a hot branding iron and laid it on me. When he shot me I jumped at him with my knife. They told me I killed him and they put me in the penitentiary and locked me up for fifteen years. That's where I met Bono. That's where I learned how to play baseball. Got out that place and your mama had taken you and went on to make life without me. Fifteen years was a long time for her to wait. But that fifteen years cured me of that robbing stuff. Rose'll tell you. She asked me when I met her if I had gotten all that foolishness out of my system. And I told her, "Baby, it's you and baseball all what count with me." You hear me, Bono? I meant it too. She say, "Which one comes first?" I told her, "Baby, ain't no doubt it's baseball . . . but you stick and get old with me and we'll both outlive this baseball." Am I right, Rose? And it's true.

ROSE: Man, hush your mouth. You ain't said no such thing. Talking about, "Baby, you know you'll always be number one with me." That's what you was talking.

TROY: You hear that, Bono. That's why I love her.

BONO: Rose'll keep you straight. You get off the track, she'll straighten you up.

ROSE: Lyons, you better get on up and get Bonnie. She waiting on you.

LYONS (gets up to go): Hey, Pop, why don't you come on down to the Grill and hear me play?

TROY: I ain't going down there. I'm too old to be sitting around in them clubs.

BONO: You got to be good to play down at the Grill.

LYONS: Come on, Pop . . .

TROY: I got to get up in the morning.

LYONS: You ain't got to stay long.

TROY: Naw, I'm gonna get my supper and go on to bed.

LYONS: Well, I got to go. I'll see you again.

TROY: Don't you come around my house on my payday.

ROSE: Pick up the phone and let somebody know you coming. And bring Bonnie with you. You know I'm always glad to see her.

LYONS: Yeah, I'll do that, Rose. You take care now. See you, Pop. See you, Mr.
   Bono. See you, Uncle Gabe.
GABRIEL: Lyons! King of the Jungle!

(*Lyons exits.*)

TROY: Is supper ready, woman? Me and you got some business to take care
   of. I'm gonna tear it up too.
ROSE: Troy, I done told you now!
TROY (*puts his arm around Bono*): Aw hell, woman . . . this is Bono. Bono like
   family. I done known this nigger since . . . how long I done know you?
BONO: It's been a long time.
TROY: I done known this nigger since Skippy was a pup. Me and him done
   been through some times.
BONO: You sure right about that.
TROY: Hell, I done know him longer than I known you. And we still standing
   shoulder to shoulder. Hey, look here, Bono . . . a man can't ask for no
   more than that.

(*Drinks to him.*)

   I love you, nigger.
BONO: Hell, I love you too . . . but I got to get home see my woman. You got
   yours in hand. I got to go get mine.

(*Bono starts to exit as Cory enters the yard, dressed in his football uniform. He gives
Troy a hard, uncompromising look.*)

CORY: What you do that for, Pop?

(*He throws his helmet down in the direction of Troy.*)

ROSE: What's the matter? Cory . . . what's the matter?
CORY: Papa done went up to the school and told Coach Zellman I can't play
   football no more. Wouldn't even let me play the game. Told him to tell
   the recruiter not to come.
ROSE: Troy . . .
TROY: What you Troying me for. Yeah, I did it. And the boy know why I did it.
CORY: Why you wanna do that to me? That was the one chance I had.
ROSE: Ain't nothing wrong with Cory playing football, Troy.
TROY: The boy lied to me. I told the nigger if he wanna play football . . . to
   keep up his chores and hold down that job at the A&P. That was the
   conditions. Stopped down there to see Mr. Stawicki . . .
CORY: I can't work after school during the football season, Pop! I tried to tell
   you that Mr. Stawicki's holding my job for me. You don't never want to
   listen to nobody. And then you wanna go and do this to me!
TROY: I ain't done nothing to you. You done it to yourself.
CORY: Just cause you didn't have a chance! You just scared I'm gonna be better than you, that's all.

TROY: Come here.

ROSE: Troy . . .

(*Cory reluctantly crosses over to Troy.*)

TROY: Alright! See. You done made a mistake.

CORY: I didn't even do nothing!

TROY: I'm gonna tell you what your mistake was. See . . . you swung at the ball and didn't hit it. That's strike one. See, you in the batter's box now. You swung and you missed. That's strike one. Don't you strike out!

(*Lights fade to black.*)

ACT TWO / Scene One

The following morning. Cory is at the tree hitting the ball with the bat. He tries to mimic Troy, but his swing is awkward, less sure. Rose enters from the house.

ROSE: Cory, I want you to help me with this cupboard.

CORY: I ain't quitting the team. I don't care what Poppa say.

ROSE: I'll talk to him when he gets back. He had to go see about your Uncle Gabe. The police done arrested him. Say he was disturbing the peace. He'll be back directly. Come on in here and help me clean out the top of this cupboard.

(*Cory exits into the house. Rose sees Troy and Bono coming down the alley.*)

Troy . . . what they say down there?

TROY: Ain't said nothing. I give them fifty dollars and they let him go. I'll talk to you about it. Where's Cory?

ROSE: He's in there helping me clean out these cupboards.

TROY: Tell him to get his butt out here.

(*Troy and Bono go over to the pile of wood. Bono picks up the saw and begins sawing.*)

TROY (*to Bono*): All they want is the money. That makes six or seven times I done went down there and got him. See me coming they stick out their hands.

BONO: Yeah. I know what you mean. That's all they care about . . . that money. They don't care about what's right.

(*Pause.*)

Nigger, why you got to go and get some hard wood? You ain't doing nothing but building a little old fence. Get you some soft pine wood. That's all you need.

TROY: I know what I'm doing. This is outside wood. You put pine wood inside the house. Pine wood is inside wood. This here is outside wood. Now you tell me where the fence is gonna be?

BONO: You don't need this wood. You can put it up with pine wood and it'll stand as long as you gonna be here looking at it.

TROY: How you know how long I'm gonna be here, nigger? Hell, I might just live forever. Live longer than old man Horsely.

BONO: That's what Magee used to say.

TROY: Magee's a damn fool. Now you tell me who you ever heard of gonna pull their own teeth with a pair of rusty pliers.

BONO: The old folks . . . my granddaddy used to pull his teeth with pliers. They ain't had no dentists for the colored folks back then.

TROY: Get clean pliers! You understand? Clean pliers! Sterilize them! Besides we ain't living back then. All Magee had to do was walk over to Doc Goldblum's.

BONO: I see where you and that Tallahassee gal . . . that Alberta . . . I see where you all done got tight.

TROY: What you mean "got tight"?

BONO: I see where you be laughing and joking with her all the time.

TROY: I laughs and jokes with all of them, Bono. You know me.

BONO: That ain't the kind of laughing and joking I'm talking about.

(*Cory enters from the house.*)

CORY: How you doing, Mr. Bono?

TROY: Cory? Get that saw from Bono and cut some wood. He talking about the wood's too hard to cut. Stand back there, Jim, and let that young boy show you how it's done.

BONO: He's sure welcome to it.

(*Cory takes the saw and begins to cut the wood.*)

Whew-e-e! Look at that. Big old strong boy. Look like Joe Louis.° Hell, must be getting old the way I'm watching that boy whip through that wood.

CORY: I don't see why Mama want a fence around the yard noways.

TROY: Damn if I know either. What the hell she keeping out with it? She ain't got nothing nobody want.

BONO: Some people build fences to keep people out . . . and other people build fences to keep people in. Rose wants to hold on to you all. She loves you.

TROY: Hell, nigger, I don't need nobody to tell me my wife loves me. Cory . . . go on in the house and see if you can find that other saw.

CORY: Where's it at?

TROY: I said find it! Look for it till you find it!

(*Cory exits into the house.*)

What's that supposed to mean? Wanna keep us in?

Joe Louis: Joseph Louis Barrow (1914–1981), African American boxer, was known as the "Brown Bomber" and held the world heavyweight title from 1937 to 1949, longer than any other man in history.

BONO: Troy . . . I done known you seem like damn near my whole life. You
and Rose both. I done know both of you all for a long time. I remember
when you met Rose. When you was hitting them baseball out the park.
A lot of them old gals was after you then. You had the pick of the litter.
When you picked Rose, I was happy for you. That was the first time I
knew you had any sense. I said . . . My man Troy knows what he's
doing . . . I'm gonna follow this nigger . . . he might take me somewhere. I been following you too. I done learned a whole heap of things
about life watching you. I done learned how to tell where the shit lies.
How to tell it from the alfalfa. You done learned me a lot of things. You
showed me how to not make the same mistakes . . . to take life as it
comes along and keep putting one foot in front of the other.

(*Pause.*)

Rose a good woman, Troy.

TROY: Hell, nigger, I know she a good woman. I been married to her for
eighteen years. What you got on your mind, Bono?

BONO: I just say she a good woman. Just like I say anything. I ain't got to
have nothing on my mind.

TROY: You just gonna say she a good woman and leave it hanging out there
like that? Why you telling me she a good woman?

BONO: She loves you, Troy. Rose loves you.

TROY: You saying I don't measure up. That's what you trying to say. I don't
measure up cause I'm seeing this other gal. I know what you trying
to say.

BONO: I know what Rose means to you, Troy. I'm just trying to say I don't
want to see you mess up.

TROY: Yeah, I appreciate that, Bono. If you was messing around on Lucille I'd
be telling you the same thing.

BONO: Well, that's all I got to say. I just say that because I love you both.

TROY: Hell, you know me . . . I wasn't out there looking for nothing. You
can't find a better woman than Rose. I know that. But seems like this
woman just stuck onto me where I can't shake her loose. I done wrestled
with it, tried to throw her off me . . . but she just stuck on tighter. Now
she's stuck on for good.

BONO: You's in control . . . that's what you tell me all the time. You responsible for what you do.

TROY: I ain't ducking the responsibility of it. As long as it sets right in my
heart . . . then I'm okay. Cause that's all I listen to. It'll tell me right
from wrong every time. And I ain't talking about doing Rose no bad
turn. I love Rose. She done carried me a long ways and I love and respect
her for that.

BONO: I know you do. That's why I don't want to see you hurt her. But what
you gonna do when she find out? What you got then? If you try and
juggle both of them . . . sooner or later you gonna drop one of them.
That's common sense.

TROY: Yeah, I hear what you saying, Bono. I been trying to figure a way to work it out.

BONO: Work it out right, Troy. I don't want to be getting all up between you and Rose's business . . . but work it so it come out right.

TROY: Aw hell, I get all up between you and Lucille's business. When you gonna get that woman that refrigerator she been wanting? Don't tell me you ain't got no money now. I know who your banker is. Mellon don't need that money bad as Lucille want that refrigerator. I'll tell you that.

BONO: Tell you what I'll do . . . when you finish building this fence for Rose . . . I'll buy Lucille that refrigerator.

TROY: You done stuck your foot in your mouth now!

(Troy grabs up a board and begins to saw. Bono starts to walk out the yard.)

    Hey, nigger . . . where you going?

BONO: I'm going home. I know you don't expect me to help you now. I'm protecting my money. I wanna see you put that fence up by yourself. That's what I want to see. You'll be here another six months without me.

TROY: Nigger, you ain't right.

BONO: When it comes to my money . . . I'm right as fireworks on the Fourth of July.

TROY: Alright, we gonna see now. You better get out your bankbook.

(Bono exits, and Troy continues to work. Rose enters from the house.)

ROSE: What they say down there? What's happening with Gabe?

TROY: I went down there and got him out. Cost me fifty dollars. Say he was disturbing the peace. Judge set up a hearing for him in three weeks. Say to show cause why he shouldn't be recommitted.

ROSE: What was he doing that cause them to arrest him?

TROY: Some kids was teasing him and he run them off home. Say he was howling and carrying on. Some folks seen him and called the police. That's all it was.

ROSE: Well, what's you say? What'd you tell the judge?

TROY: Told him I'd look after him. It didn't make no sense to recommit the man. He stuck out his big greasy palm and told me to give him fifty dollars and take him on home.

ROSE: Where's he at now? Where'd he go off to?

TROY: He's gone about his business. He don't need nobody to hold his hand.

ROSE: Well, I don't know. Seem like that would be the best place for him if they did put him into the hospital. I know what you're gonna say. But that's what I think would be best.

TROY: The man done had his life ruined fighting for what? And they wanna take and lock him up. Let him be free. He don't bother nobody.

ROSE: Well, everybody got their own way of looking at it I guess. Come on and get your lunch. I got a bowl of lima beans and some cornbread in the oven. Come and get something to eat. Ain't no sense you fretting over Gabe.

(*Rose turns to go into the house.*)

TROY: Rose . . . got something to tell you.

ROSE: Well, come on . . . wait till I get this food on the table.

TROY: Rose!

(*She stops and turns around.*)

I don't know how to say this.

(*Pause.*)

I can't explain it none. It just sort of grows on you till it gets out of hand. It starts out like a little bush . . . and the next thing you know it's a whole forest.

ROSE: Troy . . . what is you talking about?

TROY: I'm talking, woman, let me talk. I'm trying to find a way to tell you . . . I'm gonna be a daddy. I'm gonna be somebody's daddy.

ROSE: Troy . . . you're not telling me this? You're gonna be . . . what?

TROY: Rose . . . now . . . see . . .

ROSE: You telling me you gonna be somebody's daddy? You telling your *wife* this?

(*Gabriel enters from the street. He carries a rose in his hand.*)

GABRIEL: Hey, Troy! Hey, Rose!

ROSE: I have to wait eighteen years to hear something like this.

GABRIEL: Hey, Rose . . . I got a flower for you.

(*He hands it to her.*)

That's a rose. Same rose like you is.

ROSE: Thanks, Gabe.

GABRIEL: Troy, you ain't mad at me is you? Them bad mens come and put me away. You ain't mad at me is you?

TROY: Naw, Gabe, I ain't mad at you.

ROSE: Eighteen years and you wanna come with this.

GABRIEL (*takes a quarter out of his pocket*): See what I got? Got a brand new quarter.

TROY: Rose . . . it's just . . .

ROSE: Ain't nothing you can say, Troy. Ain't no way of explaining that.

GABRIEL: Fellow that give me this quarter had a whole mess of them. I'm gonna keep this quarter till it stop shining.

ROSE: Gabe, go on in the house there. I got some watermelon in the frigidaire. Go on and get you a piece.

GABRIEL: Say, Rose . . . you know I was chasing hellhounds and them bad mens come and get me and take me away. Troy helped me. He come down there and told them they better let me go before he beat them up. Yeah, he did!

ROSE: You go on and get you a piece of watermelon, Gabe. Them bad mens is gone now.

GABRIEL: Okay, Rose . . . gonna get me some watermelon. The kind with the stripes on it.

(*Gabriel exits into the house.*)

ROSE: Why, Troy? Why? After all these years to come dragging this in to me now. It don't make no sense at your age. I could have expected this ten or fifteen years ago, but not now.

TROY: Age ain't got nothing to do with it, Rose.

ROSE: I done tried to be everything a wife should be. Everything a wife could be. Been married eighteen years and I got to live to see the day you tell me you been seeing another woman and done fathered a child by her. And you know I ain't never wanted no half nothing in my family. My whole family is half. Everybody got different fathers and mothers . . . my two sisters and my brother. Can't hardly tell who's who. Can't never sit down and talk about Papa and Mama. It's your papa and your mama and my papa and my mama . . .

TROY: Rose . . . stop it now.

ROSE: I ain't never wanted that for none of my children. And now you wanna drag your behind in here and tell me something like this.

TROY: You ought to know. It's time for you to know.

ROSE: Well, I don't want to know, goddamn it!

TROY: I can't just make it go away. It's done now. I can't wish the circumstance of the thing away.

ROSE: And you don't want to either. Maybe you want to wish me and my boy away. Maybe that's what you want? Well, you can't wish us away. I've got eighteen years of my life invested in you. You ought to have stayed upstairs in my bed where you belong.

TROY: Rose . . . now listen to me . . . we can get a handle on this thing. We can talk this out . . . come to an understanding.

ROSE: All of a sudden it's "we." Where was "we" at when you was down there rolling around with some god-forsaken woman? "We" should have come to an understanding before you started making a damn fool of yourself. You're a day late and a dollar short when it comes to an understanding with me.

TROY: It's just . . . She gives me a different idea . . . a different understanding about myself. I can step out of this house and get away from the pressures and problems . . . be a different man. I ain't got to wonder how I'm gonna pay the bills or get the roof fixed. I can just be a part of myself that I ain't never been.

ROSE: What I want to know . . . is do you plan to continue seeing her. That's all you can say to me.

TROY: I can sit up in her house and laugh. Do you understand what I'm saying. I can laugh out loud . . . and it feels good. It reaches all the way down to the bottom of my shoes.

(*Pause.*)

Rose, I can't give that up.

ROSE: Maybe you ought to go on and stay down there with her . . . if she a better woman than me.

TROY: It ain't about nobody being a better woman or nothing. Rose, you ain't the blame. A man couldn't ask for no woman to be a better wife than you've been. I'm responsible for it. I done locked myself into a pattern trying to take care of you all that I forgot about myself.

ROSE: What the hell was I there for? That was my job, not somebody else's.

TROY: Rose, I done tried all my life to live decent . . . to live a clean . . . hard . . . useful life. I tried to be a good husband to you. In every way I knew how. Maybe I come into the world backwards, I don't know. But . . . you born with two strikes on you before you come to the plate. You got to guard it closely . . . always looking for the curve ball on the inside corner. You can't afford to let none get past you. You can't afford a call strike. If you going down . . . you going down swinging. Everything lined up against you. What you gonna do. I fooled them, Rose. I bunted. When I found you and Cory and a halfway decent job . . . I was safe. Couldn't nothing touch me. I wasn't gonna strike out no more. I wasn't going back to the penitentiary. I wasn't gonna lay in the streets with a bottle of wine. I was safe. I had me a family. A job. I wasn't gonna get that last strike. I was on first looking for one of them boys to knock me in. To get me home.

ROSE: You should have stayed in my bed, Troy.

TROY: Then when I saw that gal . . . she firmed up my backbone. And I got to thinking that if I tried . . . I just might be able to steal second. Do you understand after eighteen years I wanted to steal second.

ROSE: You should have held me tight. You should have grabbed me and held on.

TROY: I stood on first base for eighteen years and I thought . . . well, goddamn it . . . go on for it!

ROSE: We're not talking about baseball! We're talking about you going off to lay in bed with another woman . . . and then bring it home to me. That's what we're talking about. We ain't talking about no baseball.

TROY: Rose, you're not listening to me. I'm trying the best I can to explain it to you. It's not easy for me to admit that I been standing in the same place for eighteen years.

ROSE: I been standing with you! I been right here with you, Troy. I got a life too. I gave eighteen years of my life to stand in the same spot with you. Don't you think I ever wanted other things? Don't you think I had dreams and hopes? What about my life? What about me? Don't you think it ever crossed my mind to want to know other men? That I wanted to lay up somewhere and forget about my responsibilities? That I wanted someone to make me laugh so I could feel good? You not the only one who's got wants and needs. But I held on to you, Troy. I took all my feelings, my wants and needs, my dreams . . . and I buried them inside you. I planted a seed and watched and prayed over it. I planted myself inside you and waited to bloom. And it didn't take me no eighteen years to find out the soil was hard and rocky and it wasn't never gonna bloom.

But I held on to you, Troy. I held you tighter. You was my husband. I owed you everything I had. Every part of me I could find to give you. And upstairs in that room . . . with the darkness falling in on me . . . I gave everything I had to try and erase the doubt that you wasn't the finest man in the world. And wherever you was going . . . I wanted to be there with you. Cause you was my husband. Cause that's the only way I was gonna survive as your wife. You always talking about what you give . . . and what you don't have to give. But you take too. You take . . . and don't even know nobody's giving!

(Rose turns to exit into the house; Troy grabs her arm.)

TROY: You say I take and don't give!

ROSE: Troy! You're hurting me!

TROY: You say I take and don't give.

ROSE: Troy . . . you're hurting my arm! Let go!

TROY: I done give you everything I got. Don't you tell that lie on me.

ROSE: Troy!

TROY: Don't you tell that lie on me!

(Cory enters from the house.)

CORY: Mama!

ROSE: Troy. You're hurting me.

TROY: Don't you tell me about no taking and giving.

(Cory comes up behind Troy and grabs him. Troy, surprised, is thrown off balance just as Cory throws a glancing blow that catches him on the chest and knocks him down. Troy is stunned, as is Cory.)

ROSE: Troy. Troy. No!

(Troy gets to his feet and starts at Cory.)

Troy . . . no. Please! Troy!

(Rose pulls on Troy to hold him back. Troy stops himself.)

TROY *(to Cory):* Alright. That's strike two. You stay away from around me, boy. Don't you strike out. You living with a full count. Don't you strike out.

(Troy exits out the yard as the lights go down.)

Scene Two

It is six months later, early afternoon. Troy enters from the house and starts to exit the yard. Rose enters from the house.

ROSE: Troy, I want to talk to you.

TROY: All of a sudden, after all this time, you want to talk to me, huh? You ain't wanted to talk to me for months. You ain't wanted to talk to me last night. You ain't wanted no part of me then. What you wanna talk to me about now?

ROSE: Tomorrow's Friday.

TROY: I know what day tomorrow is. You think I don't know tomorrow's Friday? My whole life I ain't done nothing but look to see Friday coming and you got to tell me it's Friday.

ROSE: I want to know if you're coming home.

TROY: I always come home, Rose. You know that. There ain't never been a night I ain't come home.

ROSE: That ain't what I mean . . . and you know it. I want to know if you're coming straight home after work.

TROY: I figure I'd cash my check . . . hang out at Taylors' with the boys . . . maybe play a game of checkers . . .

ROSE: Troy, I can't live like this. I won't live like this. You livin' on borrowed time with me. It's been going on six months now you ain't been coming home.

TROY: I be here every night. Every night of the year. That's 365 days.

ROSE: I want you to come home tomorrow after work.

TROY: Rose . . . I don't mess up my pay. You know that now. I take my pay and I give it to you. I don't have no money but what you give me back. I just want to have a little time to myself . . . a little time to enjoy life.

ROSE: What about me? When's my time to enjoy life?

TROY: I don't know what to tell you, Rose. I'm doing the best I can.

ROSE: You ain't been home from work but time enough to change your clothes and run out . . . and you wanna call that the best you can do?

TROY: I'm going over to the hospital to see Alberta. She went into the hospital this afternoon. Look like she might have the baby early. I won't be gone long.

ROSE: Well, you ought to know. They went over to Miss Pearl's and got Gabe today. She said you told them to go ahead and lock him up.

TROY: I ain't said no such thing. Whoever told you that is telling a lie. Pearl ain't doing nothing but telling a big fat lie.

ROSE: She ain't had to tell me. I read it on the papers.

TROY: I ain't told them nothing of the kind.

ROSE: I saw it right there on the papers.

TROY: What it say, huh?

ROSE: It said you told them to take him.

TROY: Then they screwed that up, just the way they screw up everything. I ain't worried about what they got on the paper.

ROSE: Say the government send part of his check to the hospital and the other part to you.

TROY: I ain't got nothing to do with that if that's the way it works. I ain't made up the rules about how it work.

ROSE: You did Gabe just like you did Cory. You wouldn't sign the paper for Cory . . . but you signed for Gabe. You signed that paper.

(*The telephone is heard ringing inside the house.*)

TROY: I told you I ain't signed nothing, woman! The only thing I signed was the release form. Hell, I can't read, I don't know what they had on that paper! I ain't signed nothing about sending Gabe away.

ROSE: I said send him to the hospital . . . you said let him be free . . . now you done went down there and signed him to the hospital for half his money. You went back on yourself, Troy. You gonna have to answer for that.

TROY: See now . . . you been over there talking to Miss Pearl. She done got mad cause she ain't getting Gabe's rent money. That's all it is. She's liable to say anything.

ROSE: Troy, I seen where you signed the paper.

TROY: You ain't seen nothing I signed. What she doing got papers on my brother anyway? Miss Pearl telling a big fat lie. And I'm gonna tell her about it too! You ain't seen nothing I signed. Say . . . you ain't seen nothing I signed.

(*Rose exits into the house to answer the telephone. Presently she returns.*)

ROSE: Troy . . . that was the hospital. Alberta had the baby.

TROY: What she have? What is it?

ROSE: It's a girl.

TROY: I better get on down to the hospital to see her.

ROSE: Troy . . .

TROY: Rose . . . I got to go see her now. That's only right . . . what's the matter . . . the baby's all right, ain't it?

ROSE: Alberta died having the baby.

TROY: Died . . . you say she's dead? Alberta's dead?

ROSE: They said they done all they could. They couldn't do nothing for her.

TROY: The baby? How's the baby?

ROSE: They say it's healthy. I wonder who's gonna bury her.

TROY: She had family, Rose. She wasn't living in the world by herself.

ROSE: I know she wasn't living in the world by herself.

TROY: Next thing you gonna want to know if she had any insurance.

ROSE: Troy, you ain't got to talk like that.

TROY: That's the first thing that jumped out your mouth. "Who's gonna bury her?" Like I'm fixing to take on that task for myself.

ROSE: I am your wife. Don't push me away.

TROY: I ain't pushing nobody away. Just give me some space. That's all. Just give me some room to breathe.

(*Rose exits into the house. Troy walks about the yard.*)

TROY (*with a quiet rage that threatens to consume him*): Alright . . . Mr. Death. See now . . . I'm gonna tell you what I'm gonna do. I'm gonna take and build me a fence around this yard. See? I'm gonna build me a fence around what belongs to me. And then I want you to stay on the other side. See? You stay over there until you're ready for me. Then you come on. Bring your army. Bring your sickle. Bring your wrestling clothes. I ain't gonna fall down on my vigilance this time. You ain't gonna sneak up on me no more. When you ready for me . . . when the top of your list say Troy Maxson . . . that's when you come around here. You come up and knock on the front door. Ain't nobody else got nothing to do with this. This is between you and me. Man to man. You stay on the other side of that fence until you ready for me. Then you come up and knock on the front door. Anytime you want. I'll be ready for you.

(*The lights go down to black.*)

Scene Three

The lights come up on the porch. It is late evening three days later. Rose sits listening to the ball game waiting for Troy. The final out of the game is made and Rose switches off the radio. Troy enters the yard carrying an infant wrapped in blankets. He stands back from the house and calls.

(*Rose enters and stands on the porch. There is a long, awkward silence, the weight of which grows heavier with each passing second.*)

TROY: Rose . . . I'm standing here with my daughter in my arms. She ain't but a wee bittie little old thing. She don't know nothing about grownups' business. She innocent . . . and she ain't got no mama.
ROSE: What you telling me for, Troy?

(*She turns and exits into the house.*)

TROY: Well . . . I guess we'll just sit out here on the porch.

(*He sits down on the porch. There is an awkward indelicateness about the way he handles the baby. His largeness engulfs and seems to swallow it. He speaks loud enough for Rose to hear.*)

A man's got to do what's right for him. I ain't sorry for nothing I done. It felt right in my heart.

(*To the baby.*)

What you smiling at? Your daddy's a big man. Got these great big old hands. But sometimes he's scared. And right now your daddy's scared cause we sitting out here and ain't got no home. Oh, I been homeless before. I ain't had no little baby with me. But I been homeless. You just be out on the road by your lonesome and you see one of them trains coming and you just kinda go like this . . .

(*He sings as a lullaby.*)

Please, Mr. Engineer let a man ride the line
Please, Mr. Engineer let a man ride the line
I ain't got no ticket please let me ride the blinds

(*Rose enters from the house. Troy, hearing her steps behind him, stands and faces her.*)

She's my daughter, Rose. My own flesh and blood. I can't deny her no more than I can deny them boys.

(*Pause.*)

You and them boys is my family. You and them and this child is all I got in the world. So I guess what I'm saying is . . . I'd appreciate it if you'd help me take care of her.

ROSE: Okay, Troy . . . you're right. I'll take care of your baby for you . . . cause . . . like you say . . . she's innocent . . . and you can't visit the sins of the father upon the child. A motherless child has got a hard time.

(*She takes the baby from him.*)

From right now . . . this child got a mother. But you a womanless man.

(*Rose turns and exits into the house with the baby. Lights go down to black.*)

Scene Four

It is two months later. Lyons enters from the street. He knocks on the door and calls.

LYONS: Hey, Rose! (*Pause.*) Rose!

ROSE (*from inside the house*): Stop that yelling. You gonna wake up Raynell. I just got her to sleep.

LYONS: I just stopped by to pay Papa this twenty dollars I owe him. Where's Papa at?

ROSE: He should be here in a minute. I'm getting ready to go down to the church. Sit down and wait on him.

LYONS: I got to go pick up Bonnie over her mother's house.

ROSE: Well, sit it down there on the table. He'll get it.

LYONS (*enters the house and sets the money on the table*): Tell Papa I said thanks. I'll see you again.

ROSE: Alright, Lyons. We'll see you.

(*Lyons starts to exit as Cory enters.*)

CORY: Hey, Lyons.

LYONS: What's happening, Cory? Say man, I'm sorry I missed your graduation. You know I had a gig and couldn't get away. Otherwise, I would have been there, man. So what you doing?

CORY: I'm trying to find a job.

LYONS: Yeah I know how that go, man. It's rough out here. Jobs are scarce.

CORY: Yeah, I know.

LYONS: Look here, I got to run. Talk to Papa . . . he know some people. He'll
be able to help get you a job. Talk to him . . . see what he say.

CORY: Yeah . . . alright, Lyons.

LYONS: You take care. I'll talk to you soon. We'll find some time to talk.

(Lyons exits the yard. Cory wanders over to the tree, picks up the bat, and assumes a batting stance. He studies an imaginary pitcher and swings. Dissatisfied with the result, he tries again. Troy enters. They eye each other for a beat. Cory puts the bat down and exits the yard. Troy starts into the house as Rose exits with Raynell. She is carrying a cake.)

TROY: I'm coming in and everybody's going out.

ROSE: I'm taking this cake down to the church for the bakesale. Lyons was by
to see you. He stopped by to pay you your twenty dollars. It's laying in
there on the table.

TROY *(going into his pocket)*: Well . . . here go this money.

ROSE: Put it in there on the table, Troy. I'll get it.

TROY: What time you coming back?

ROSE: Ain't no use in you studying me. It don't matter what time I come
back.

TROY: I just asked you a question, woman. What's the matter . . . can't I ask
you a question?

ROSE: Troy, I don't want to go into it. Your dinner's in there on the stove. All
you got to do is heat it up. And don't you be eating the rest of them
cakes in there. I'm coming back for them. We having a bakesale at the
church tomorrow.

(Rose exits the yard. Troy sits down on the steps, takes a pint bottle from his pocket, opens it, and drinks. He begins to sing.)

TROY: Hear it ring! Hear it ring!
Had an old dog his name was Blue
You know Blue was mighty true
You know Blue was a good old dog
Blue trees a possum in a hollow log
You know from that he was a good old dog

(Bono enters the yard.)

BONO: Hey, Troy.

TROY: Hey, what's happening, Bono?

BONO: I just thought I'd stop by to see you.

TROY: What you stop by and see me for? You ain't stopped by in a month of
Sundays. Hell, I must owe you money or something.

BONO: Since you got your promotion I can't keep up with you. Used to see
you every day. Now I don't even know what route you working.

TROY: They keep switching me around. Got me out in Greentree now . . .
hauling white folks' garbage.

BONO: Greentree, huh? You lucky, at least you ain't got to be lifting them barrels. Damn if they ain't getting heavier. I'm gonna put in my two years and call it quits.

TROY: I'm thinking about retiring myself.

BONO: You got it easy. You can *drive* for another five years.

TROY: It ain't the same, Bono. It ain't like working the back of the truck. Ain't got nobody to talk to . . . feel like you working by yourself. Naw, I'm thinking about retiring. How's Lucille?

BONO: She alright. Her arthritis get to acting up on her sometime. Saw Rose on my way in. She going down to the church, huh?

TROY: Yeah, she took up going down there. All them preachers looking for somebody to fatten their pockets.

(*Pause.*)

   Got some gin here.

BONO: Naw, thanks. I just stopped by to say hello.

TROY: Hell, nigger . . . you can take a drink. I ain't never known you to say no to a drink. You ain't got to work tomorrow.

BONO: I just stopped by. I'm fixing to go over to Skinner's. We got us a domino game going over his house every Friday.

TROY: Nigger, you can't play no dominoes. I used to whup you four games out of five.

BONO: Well, that learned me. I'm getting better.

TROY: Yeah? Well, that's alright.

BONO: Look here . . . I got to be getting on. Stop by sometime, huh?

TROY: Yeah, I'll do that, Bono. Lucille told Rose you bought her a new refrigerator.

BONO: Yeah, Rose told Lucille you had finally built your fence . . . so I figured we'd call it even.

TROY: I knew you would.

BONO: Yeah . . . okay. I'll be talking to you.

TROY: Yeah, take care, Bono. Good to see you. I'm gonna stop over.

BONO: Yeah. Okay, Troy.

(*Bono exits. Troy drinks from the bottle.*)

TROY: Old Blue died and I dig his grave
       Let him down with a golden chain
       Every night when I hear old Blue bark
       I know Blue treed a possum in Noah's Ark.
       Hear it ring! Hear it ring!

(*Cory enters the yard. They eye each other for a beat. Troy is sitting in the middle of the steps. Cory walks over.*)

CORY: I got to get by.

TROY: Say what? What's you say?

CORY: You in my way. I got to get by.

TROY: You got to get by where? This is my house. Bought and paid for. In full. Took me fifteen years. And if you wanna go in my house and I'm sitting on the steps . . . you say excuse me. Like your mama taught you.

CORY: Come on, Pop . . . I got to get by.

(*Cory starts to maneuver his way past Troy. Troy grabs his leg and shoves him back.*)

TROY: You just gonna walk over top of me?

CORY: I live here too!

TROY (*advancing toward him*): You just gonna walk over top of me in my own house?

CORY: I ain't scared of you.

TROY: I ain't asked if you was scared of me. I asked you if you was fixing to walk over top of me in my own house? That's the question. You ain't gonna say excuse me? You just gonna walk over top of me?

CORY: If you wanna put it like that.

TROY: How else am I gonna put it?

CORY: I was walking by you to go into the house cause you sitting on the steps drunk, singing to yourself. You can put it like that.

TROY: Without saying excuse me???

(*Cory doesn't respond.*)

I asked you a question. Without saying excuse me???

CORY: I ain't got to say excuse me to you. You don't count around here no more.

TROY: Oh, I see . . . I don't count around here no more. You ain't got to say excuse me to your daddy. All of a sudden you done got so grown that your daddy don't count around here no more . . . Around here in his own house and yard that he done paid for with the sweat of his brow. You done got so grown to where you gonna take over. You gonna take over my house. Is that right? You gonna wear my pants. You gonna go in there and stretch out on my bed. You ain't got to say excuse me cause I don't count around here no more. Is that right?

CORY: That's right. You always talking this dumb stuff. Now, why don't you just get out my way.

TROY: I guess you got someplace to sleep and something to put in your belly. You got that, huh? You got that? That's what you need. You got that, huh?

CORY: You don't know what I got. You ain't got to worry about what I got.

TROY: You right! You one hundred percent right! I done spent the last seventeen years worrying about what you got. Now it's your turn, see? I'll tell you what to do. You grown . . . we done established that. You a man. Now, let's see you act like one. Turn your behind around and walk out this yard. And when you get out there in the alley . . . you can forget about this house. See? Cause this is my house. You go on and be a man

and get your own house. You can forget about this. Cause this is mine.
You go on and get yours cause I'm through with doing for you.

CORY: You talking about what you did for me . . . what'd you ever give me?

TROY: Them feet and bones! That pumping heart, nigger! I give you more
than anybody else is ever gonna give you.

CORY: You ain't never gave me nothing! You ain't never done nothing but
hold me back. Afraid I was gonna be better than you. All you ever did
was try and make me scared of you. I used to tremble every time you
called my name. Every time I heard your footsteps in the house. Wondering all the time . . . what's Papa gonna say if I do this? . . . What's he
gonna say if I do that? . . . What's Papa gonna say if I turn on the radio?
And Mama, too . . . she tries . . . but she's scared of you.

TROY: You leave your mama out of this. She ain't got nothing to do with this.

CORY: I don't know how she stand you . . . after what you did to her.

TROY: I told you to leave your mama out of this!

(He advances toward Cory.)

CORY: What you gonna do . . . give me a whupping? You can't whup me no
more. You're too old. You just an old man.

TROY *(shoves him on his shoulder)*: Nigger! That's what you are. You just another nigger on the street to me!

CORY: You crazy! You know that?

TROY: Go on now! You got the devil in you. Get on away from me!

CORY: You just a crazy old man . . . talking about I got the devil in me.

TROY: Yeah, I'm crazy! If you don't get on the other side of that yard . . . I'm
gonna show you how crazy I am! Go on . . . get the hell out of my yard.

CORY: It ain't your yard. You took Uncle Gabe's money he got from the army
to buy this house and then you put him out.

TROY *(advances on Cory)*: Get your black ass out of my yard!

(Troy's advance backs Cory up against the tree. Cory grabs up the bat.)

CORY: I ain't going nowhere! Come on . . . put me out! I ain't scared of you.

TROY: That's my bat!

CORY: Come on!

TROY: Put my bat down!

CORY: Come on, put me out.

(Cory swings at Troy, who backs across the yard.)

What's the matter? You so bad . . . put me out!

(Troy advances toward Cory.)

CORY *(backing up)*: Come on! Come on!

TROY: You're gonna have to use it! You wanna draw that bat back on me . . .
you're gonna have to use it.

CORY: Come on! . . . Come on!

(*Cory swings the bat at Troy a second time. He misses. Troy continues to advance toward him.*)

TROY: You're gonna have to kill me! You wanna draw that bat back on me. You're gonna have to kill me.

(*Cory, backed up against the tree, can go no farther. Troy taunts him. He sticks out his head and offers him a target.*)

Come on! Come on!

(*Cory is unable to swing the bat. Troy grabs it.*)

TROY: Then I'll show you.

(*Cory and Troy struggle over the bat. The struggle is fierce and fully engaged. Troy ultimately is the stronger and takes the bat from Cory and stands over him ready to swing. He stops himself.*)

Go on and get away from around my house.

(*Cory, stung by his defeat, picks himself up, walks slowly out of the yard and up the alley.*)

CORY: Tell Mama I'll be back for my things.
TROY: They'll be on the other side of that fence.

(*Cory exits.*)

TROY: I can't taste nothing. Helluljah! I can't taste nothing no more. (*Troy assumes a batting posture and begins to taunt Death, the fastball on the outside corner.*) Come on! It's between you and me now! Come on! Anytime you want! Come on! I be ready for you . . . but I ain't gonna be easy.

(*The lights go down on the scene.*)

Scene Five

The time is 1965. The lights come up in the yard. It is the morning of Troy's funeral. A funeral plaque with a light hangs beside the door. There is a small garden plot off to the side. There is noise and activity in the house as Rose, Gabriel, and Bono have gathered. The door opens and Raynell, seven years old, enters dressed in a flannel nightgown. She crosses to the garden and pokes around with a stick. Rose calls from the house.

ROSE: Raynell!
RAYNELL: Mam?
ROSE: What you doing out there?
RAYNELL: Nothing.

(*Rose comes to the door.*)

ROSE: Girl, get in here and get dressed. What you doing?
RAYNELL: Seeing if my garden growed.

ROSE: I told you it ain't gonna grow overnight. You got to wait.

RAYNELL: It don't look like it never gonna grow. Dag!

ROSE: I told you a watched pot never boils. Get in here and get dressed.

RAYNELL: This ain't even no pot, Mama.

ROSE: You just have to give it a chance. It'll grow. Now you come on and do what I told you. We got to be getting ready. This ain't no morning to be playing around. You hear me?

RAYNELL: Yes, mam.

(*Rose exits into the house. Raynell continues to poke at her garden with a stick. Cory enters. He is dressed in a Marine corporal's uniform, and carries a duffel bag. His posture is that of a military man, and his speech has a clipped sternness.*)

CORY (*to Raynell*): Hi.

(*Pause.*)

I bet your name is Raynell.

RAYNELL: Uh huh.

CORY: Is your mama home?

(*Raynell runs up on the porch and calls through the screendoor.*)

RAYNELL: Mama . . . there's some man out here. Mama?

(*Rose comes to the door.*)

ROSE: Cory? Lord have mercy! Look here, you all!

(*Rose and Cory embrace in a tearful reunion as Bono and Lyons enter from the house dressed in funeral clothes.*)

BONO: Aw, looka here . . .

ROSE: Done got all grown up!

CORY: Don't cry, Mama. What you crying about?

ROSE: I'm just so glad you made it.

CORY: Hey Lyons. How you doing, Mr. Bono.

(*Lyons goes to embrace Cory.*)

LYONS: Look at you, man. Look at you. Don't he look good, Rose. Got them Corporal stripes.

ROSE: What took you so long.

CORY: You know how the Marines are, Mama. They got to get all their paperwork straight before they let you do anything.

ROSE: Well, I'm sure glad you made it. They let Lyons come. Your Uncle Gabe's still in the hospital. They don't know if they gonna let him out or not. I just talked to them a little while ago.

LYONS: A Corporal in the United States Marines.

BONO: Your daddy knew you had it in you. He used to tell me all the time.

LYONS: Don't he look good, Mr. Bono?

BONO: Yeah, he remind me of Troy when I first met him.

(*Pause.*)

> Say, Rose, Lucille's down at the church with the choir. I'm gonna go down and get the pallbearers lined up. I'll be back to get you all.

ROSE: Thanks, Jim.

CORY: See you, Mr. Bono.

LYONS (*with his arm around Raynell*): Cory . . . look at Raynell. Ain't she precious? She gonna break a whole lot of hearts.

ROSE: Raynell, come and say hello to your brother. This is your brother, Cory. You remember Cory.

RAYNELL: No, Mam.

CORY: She don't remember me, Mama.

ROSE: Well, we talk about you. She heard us talk about you. (*To Raynell.*) This is your brother, Cory. Come on and say hello.

RAYNELL: Hi.

CORY: Hi. So you're Raynell. Mama told me a lot about you.

ROSE: You all come on into the house and let me fix you some breakfast. Keep up your strength.

CORY: I ain't hungry, Mama.

LYONS: You can fix me something, Rose. I'll be in there in a minute.

ROSE: Cory, you sure you don't want nothing? I know they ain't feeding you right.

CORY: No, Mama . . . thanks. I don't feel like eating. I'll get something later.

ROSE: Raynell . . . get on upstairs and get that dress on like I told you.

(*Rose and Raynell exit into the house.*)

LYONS: So . . . I hear you thinking about getting married.

CORY: Yeah, I done found the right one, Lyons. It's about time.

LYONS: Me and Bonnie been split up about four years now. About the time Papa retired. I guess she just got tired of all them changes I was putting her through.

(*Pause.*)

> I always knew you was gonna make something out yourself. Your head was always in the right direction. So . . . you gonna stay in . . . make it a career . . . put in your twenty years?

CORY: I don't know. I got six already, I think that's enough.

LYONS: Stick with Uncle Sam and retire early. Ain't nothing out here. I guess Rose told you what happened with me. They got me down the workhouse. I thought I was being slick cashing other people's checks.

CORY: How much time you doing?

LYONS: They give me three years. I got that beat now. I ain't got but nine more months. It ain't so bad. You learn to deal with it like anything else. You got to take the crookeds with the straights. That's what Papa used to say. He used to say that when he struck out. I seen him strike out three times in a row . . . and the next time up he hit the ball over the grandstand. Right out there in Homestead Field. He wasn't satisfied hitting in the seats . . . he want to hit it over everything! After the game he had two hundred people standing around waiting to shake his hand. You got to take the crookeds with the straights. Yeah, Papa was something else.

CORY: You still playing?

LYONS: Cory . . . you know I'm gonna do that. There's some fellows down there we got us a band . . . we gonna try and stay together when we get out . . . but yeah, I'm still playing. It still helps me to get out of bed in the morning. As long as it do that I'm gonna be right there playing and trying to make some sense out of it.

ROSE (*calling*): Lyons, I got these eggs in the pan.

LYONS: Let me go on and get these eggs, man. Get ready to go bury Papa.

(*Pause.*)

How you doing? You doing alright?

(*Cory nods. Lyons touches him on the shoulder and they share a moment of silent grief. Lyons exits into the house. Cory wanders about the yard. Raynell enters.*)

RAYNELL: Hi.

CORY: Hi.

RAYNELL: Did you used to sleep in my room?

CORY: Yeah . . . that used to be my room.

RAYNELL: That's what Papa call it. "Cory's room." It got your football in the closet.

(*Rose comes to the door.*)

ROSE: Raynell, get in there and get them good shoes on.

RAYNELL: Mama, can't I wear these? Them other one hurt my feet.

ROSE: Well, they just gonna have to hurt your feet for a while. You ain't said they hurt your feet when you went down to the store and got them.

RAYNELL: They didn't hurt then. My feet done got bigger.

ROSE: Don't you give me no backtalk now. You get in there and get them shoes on.

(*Raynell exits into the house.*)

Ain't too much changed. He still got that piece of rag tied to that tree. He was out here swinging that bat. I was just ready to go back in the house. He swung that bat and then he just fell over. Seem like he swung it and stood there with this grin on his face . . . and then he just fell over. They carried him on down to the hospital, but I knew there wasn't no need . . . why don't you come on in the house?

CORY: Mama . . . I got something to tell you. I don't know how to tell you this . . . but I've got to tell you . . . I'm not going to Papa's funeral.

ROSE: Boy, hush your mouth. That's your daddy you talking about. I don't want hear that kind of talk this morning. I done raised you to come to this? You standing there all healthy and grown talking about you ain't going to your daddy's funeral?

CORY: Mama . . . listen . . .

ROSE: I don't want to hear it, Cory. You just get that thought out of your head.

CORY: I can't drag Papa with me everywhere I go. I've got to say no to him. One time in my life I've got to say no.

ROSE: Don't nobody have to listen to nothing like that. I know you and your daddy ain't seen eye to eye, but I ain't got to listen to that kind of talk this morning. Whatever was between you and your daddy . . . the time has come to put it aside. Just take it and set it over there on the shelf and forget about it. Disrespecting your daddy ain't gonna make you a man, Cory. You got to find a way to come to that on your own. Not going to your daddy's funeral ain't gonna make you a man.

CORY: The whole time I was growing up . . . living in his house . . . Papa was like a shadow that followed you everywhere. It weighed on you and sunk into your flesh. It would wrap around you and lay there until you couldn't tell which one was you anymore. That shadow digging in your flesh. Trying to crawl in. Trying to live through you. Everywhere I looked, Troy Maxson was staring back at me . . . hiding under the bed . . . in the closet. I'm just saying I've got to find a way to get rid of that shadow, Mama.

ROSE: You just like him. You got him in you good.

CORY: Don't tell me that, Mama.

ROSE: You Troy Maxson all over again.

CORY: I don't want to be Troy Maxson. I want to be me.

ROSE: You can't be nobody but who you are, Cory. That shadow wasn't nothing but you growing into yourself. You either got to grow into it or cut it down to fit you. But that's all you got to make life with. That's all you got to measure yourself against that world out there. Your daddy wanted you to be everything he wasn't . . . and at the same time he tried to make you into everything he was. I don't know if he was right or wrong . . . but I do know he meant to do more good than he meant to do harm. He wasn't always right. Sometimes when he touched he bruised. And sometimes when he took me in his arms he cut.

  When I first met your daddy I thought . . . Here is a man I can lay down with and make a baby. That's the first thing I thought when I seen him. I was thirty years old and had done seen my share of men. But when he walked up to me and said, "I can dance a waltz that'll make you dizzy," I thought, Rose Lee, here is a man that you can open yourself up to and be filled to bursting. Here is a man that can fill all them empty spaces you been tipping around the edges of. One of them empty spaces was being somebody's mother.

I married your daddy and settled down to cooking his supper and keeping clean sheets on the bed. When your daddy walked through the house he was so big he filled it up. That was my first mistake. Not to make him leave some room for me. For my part in the matter. But at that time I wanted that. I wanted a house that I could sing in. And that's what your daddy gave me. I didn't know to keep up his strength I had to give up little pieces of mine. I did that. I took on his life as mine and mixed up the pieces so that you couldn't hardly tell which was which anymore. It was my choice. It was my life and I didn't have to live it like that. But that's what life offered me in the way of being a woman and I took it. I grabbed hold of it with both hands.

By the time Raynell came into the house, me and your daddy had done lost touch with one another. I didn't want to make my blessing off of nobody's misfortune . . . but I took on to Raynell like she was all them babies I had wanted and never had.

(*The phone rings.*)

Like I'd been blessed to relive a part of my life. And if the Lord see fit to keep up my strength . . . I'm gonna do her just like your daddy did you . . . I'm gonna give her the best of what's in me.

RAYNELL (*entering, still with her old shoes*): Mama . . . Reverend Tollivier on the phone.

(*Rose exits into the house.*)

RAYNELL: Hi.

CORY: Hi.

RAYNELL: You in the Army or the Marines?

CORY: Marines.

RAYNELL: Papa said it was the Army. Did you know Blue?

CORY: Blue? Who's Blue?

RAYNELL: Papa's dog what he sing about all the time.

CORY (*singing*): Hear it ring! Hear it ring!
   I had a dog his name was Blue
   You know Blue was mighty true
   You know Blue was a good old dog
   Blue treed a possum in a hollow log
   You know from that he was a good old dog.
   Hear it ring! Hear it ring!

(*Raynell joins in singing.*)

CORY and RAYNELL: Blue treed a possum out on a limb
   Blue looked at me and I looked at him
   Grabbed that possum and put him in a sack
   Blue stayed there till I came back

Old Blue's feets was big and round
Never allowed a possum to touch the ground.

Old Blue died and I dug his grave
I dug his grave with a silver spade
Let him down with a golden chain
And every night I call his name
Go on Blue, you good dog you
Go on Blue, you good dog you

RAYNELL: Blue laid down and died like a man
Blue laid down and died . . .

BOTH: Blue laid down and died like a man
Now he's treeing possums in the Promised Land
I'm gonna tell you this to let you know
Blue's gone where the good dogs go
When I hear old Blue bark
When I hear old Blue bark
Blue treed a possum in Noah's Ark
Blue treed a possum in Noah's Ark.

(*Rose comes to the screen door.*)

ROSE: Cory, we gonna be ready to go in a minute.

CORY (*to Raynell*): You go on in the house and change them shoes like Mama
    told you so we can go to Papa's funeral.

RAYNELL: Okay, I'll be back.

(*Raynell exits into the house. Cory gets up and crosses over to the tree. Rose stands in
the screen door watching him. Gabriel enters from the alley.*)

GABRIEL (*calling*): Hey, Rose!

ROSE: Gabe?

GABRIEL: I'm here, Rose. Hey Rose, I'm here!

(*Rose enters from the house.*)

ROSE: Lord . . . Look here, Lyons!

LYONS: See, I told you, Rose . . . I told you they'd let him come.

CORY: How you doing, Uncle Gabe?

LYONS: How you doing, Uncle Gabe?

GABRIEL: Hey, Rose. It's time. It's time to tell St. Peter to open the gates. Troy,
    you ready? You ready, Troy. I'm gonna tell St. Peter to open the gates.
    You get ready now.

(*Gabriel, with great fanfare, braces himself to blow. The trumpet is without a
mouthpiece. He puts the end of it into his mouth and blows with great force, like a
man who has been waiting some twenty-odd years for this single moment. No sound
comes out of the trumpet. He braces himself and blows again with the same result. A
third time he blows. There is a weight of impossible description that falls away and*)

leaves him bare and exposed to a frightful realization. It is a trauma that a sane and normal mind would be unable to withstand. He begins to dance. A slow, strange dance, eerie and life-giving. A dance of atavistic signature and ritual. Lyons attempts to embrace him. Gabriel pushes Lyons away. He begins to howl in what is an attempt at song, or perhaps a song turning back into itself in an attempt at speech. He finishes his dance and the gates of heaven stand open as wide as God's closet.)

That's the way that go!

(*BLACKOUT.*)

PART 5

Approaching
WRITERS
IN DEPTH

Overleaf: Langston Hughes (left) smiles in a photograph taken by Jack Delano in 1942. Judith Ortiz Cofer (right) is seen here on the campus of the University of Georgia where she teaches English and creative writing. Sherman Alexie (bottom) gives a reading from his book Ten Little Indians *in 2003.* Judith Oriz Cofer photo reprinted by permission of Judith Ortiz Cofer. Sherman Alexie photo © 2003 Rob Casey.

To me jazz is a montage of a dream deferred. A great big dream — yet to come — and always *yet* — to become ultimately and finally true.

Langston Hughes

Langston Hughes: Dreams Deferred

James Langston Hughes was born February 1, 1902, in Joplin, Missouri. His parents divorced when he was a small child, his father moving to Mexico. Aside from short periods with his mother, until he was twelve he lived mostly with his grandmother in Lawrence, Kansas. Lonely and unhappy there, he immersed himself in "the wonderful world of books." After his grandmother's death, he spent a year with an aunt, then moved to Lincoln, Illinois, to live with his mother and her husband. He began writing poetry when he was elected Class Poet, because — he speculated later — his grade-school classmates knew poems need to have rhythm and even at that age had absorbed the stereotype that all African Americans sing, dance, and have a sense of rhythm.

Soon after Hughes graduated from the eighth grade, the family moved to Cleveland, Ohio, where he attended Central High School. Heavily influenced by Paul Laurence Dunbar, Carl Sandberg, and Walt Whitman, he continued to create poems: on love, the steel mills, the slums, and girls who came up from the South. He began sending his poems to magazines, but in reply received only rejection slips.

Following graduation, he spent a year in Mexico with his father, teaching English to Spanish-speaking students. Then, in 1920, his ability began to be recognized when "The Negro Speaks of Rivers" (p. 1267), which would become one of his most famous poems, was published in *The Crisis*. In September 1921, he went to New York to attend Columbia University, just as the New Negro Movement, later known as the Harlem Renaissance, was beginning. The Harlem Renaissance was a flowering of creative activity in the arts and radical social thinking that lasted from 1920 until about 1930. It was initiated by the large numbers of African Americans who had moved from the South to northern industrial cities before and during World War I. Their hope for new opportunities gave them a sense of liberty and empowerment, of racial consciousness and pride in all things black. Harlem's artistic and intellectual vibrancy in the visual arts, music, dance, theater, and literature — poetry, fiction, drama, and essay — deeply inspired Hughes. Although he left Columbia after a year and traveled to Africa and Europe, working as a seaman, Hughes maintained his connection to Harlem, and he is recognized as one of the central figures of the Harlem Renaissance (in 1940 he wrote an autobiographical account of the movement, *The Big Sea*).

When he was still living with his grandmother, Hughes attended a blues concert in Kansas City. He was immediately struck by its power and deeply impressed by its mixture of heartache and hope, the way "the music seemed to cry, but the words somehow laughed" (Arnold Rampersad, as quoted in Yusef Komunyakaa's essay on p. 1276). About the time he arrived in New York, jazz, in part an outgrowth from the blues, was moving north and taking hold in Harlem — and in Hughes. As a result, his poetry came under the influence of both jazz and the blues, especially the rhythms linked back to spirituals and work songs of the slavery era. Hughes describes his poetry as putting jazz into words. These qualities are evident in his poem "The Weary Blues" (p. 1266), which won first prize in a literary contest organized by *Opportunity* magazine, a prize that brought him valuable attention.

In 1926, Hughes enrolled at historically black Lincoln University in Pennsylvania, from which he graduated in 1929. His first book of poetry, *The Weary Blues*, was published in 1926 by Alfred A. Knopf. *Fine Clothes to the Jew*, which some call his most accomplished book of poetry, followed in 1927. In 1930, his first novel, *Not Without Laughter*, won the Harmon gold medal for literature. His first collection of short stories, *The Ways of White Folks*, appeared in 1934, but he was occupied primarily during the 1930s in writing for the theater.

In 1943, he created Jesse B. Semple, or Simple, arguably his most memorable character. In weekly columns for the *Chicago Defender*, Hughes described humorous episodes involving this ordinary Harlemite, out of whose simplicity came pearls of wisdom. They were collected in *Simple Speaks His Mind* (1950), *Simple Takes a Wife* (1952), and *Simple Stakes a Claim* (1957). He also wrote lyrics for the musical theater, including *Street Scene* (1947), with music by Kurt Weill.

Hughes died of prostate cancer in May 1967, in New York. Recognized as one of the most important figures in the development of African American literature, as well as of literature generally, he was often referred to as Poet Laureate of the Negro Race. In his memory, his Harlem residence at 20 East 127th Street was given landmark status by the New York City Preservation Commission, and East 127th Street was renamed Langston Hughes Place.

Hughes was a flexible and versatile author, skilled in many genres — lyric poems, political verse, songs, children's literature, fiction, drama, essays, and autobiography. One can't appreciate his abilities and accomplishments as a writer without recognizing the breadth of his work and the high quality

An early drawing of Langston Hughes (drawn in 1927, the year Fine Clothes to the Jew *was published) by the renowned Harlem Renaissance portraitist Winold Reiss.*

he achieved in so many different forms. Reading this chapter is a beginning, but no more than that, toward seeing Hughes fully as an artist. We include in this book examples from a number of genres. One of his most famous poems, "Harlem," is in Chapter 13 (p. 546). Before looking at the material in the rest of this chapter, read "Harlem" again because it has such a central place in Hughes's work (notice how several works in this chapter echo wordings in it) and is so influential in other writers' works, most notably Lorraine Hansberry's well-known play *A Raisin in the Sun* (1959), which uses the poem as its epigraph and the poem's third line as its title.

This chapter contains a short story, "One Friday Morning"; an essay, "Jazz as Communication"; five poems; lyrics for a song from the opera *Troubled Island;* a chapter from his autobiographical book *The Big Sea;* and a one-act play, *Soul Gone Home.* As you read them, watch for Hughes's ways of working with the literary elements of fiction, poetry, and drama covered earlier in this book. Think critically as you read the works to see the distinctions of style and achievement in the wide variety of genres that Hughes worked in, including poems, song lyrics, stories, memoir, and drama.

The chapter concludes with three essays that discuss some important aspects of Hughes's work and can give you some different or deeper ways of understanding it. The first analyzes the use of symbolism to explore racial

Langston Hughes with two actors rehearsing a scene from one of his plays in Chicago, Illinois, 1942.

themes in *Soul Gone Home*. The second discusses the way Hughes's attraction to the blues influences the style of his poetry. The third examines how central the themes of heritage and strength are to Hughes's poems and how Hughes created his poems' brilliant imagery. Read the works by Hughes at least once, preferably twice, before you go on to the essays written about them. The essays should expand the insights and interpretations you reach on your own, not take the place of your own analyses or influence your thoughts before they have a chance to fill out on their own. For specific suggestions of ways to use such essays as you reflect on Hughes, see "Approaching the Readings" at the end of the chapter (p. 1282).

Most writers have topics, themes, styles, techniques, and images that keep coming up in their works that get treated differently depending on the literary elements specific to the genre the author is working in. A striking image, for example, might be handled differently depending on if the author is working on a poem or a play or a story. One of the pleasures of reading widely in an author and reading across genres is to notice such recurring motifs and make connections between works and between genres. Watch for repeated elements as you read the works in this chapter. You might focus, for example, on the theme of freedom and dreams. "Harlem" asks, "What happens to a dream deferred?" In the story "One Friday Morning," Nancy Lee believes she lives in a free country and pursues the American dream, only to have her dream deferred because of racist restrictions on freedom. She continues to believe in the ideal of freedom and could well have sung the lyrics

Hughes wrote for *Troubled Island,* "I dream a world where all / Will know sweet freedom's way." "Good Morning" repeats the "dream deferred" question, and "Dream Variations" echoes the sentiments of "I Dream a World." And the son in *Soul Gone Home* is denied his dreams in part by his mother's neglect and in part by the effects of the racial and economic systems.

As you read, give attention to the influence of the blues. Hughes says in "I've Known Rivers" that his best poems were written when he felt the worst; notice how much the blues aesthetic influences many of the poems in this chapter, as well as *Soul Gone Home.* Notice also the influence of jazz on his rhythmic structures and tones, particularly the prose of "Jazz as Communication" and poems such as "The Weary Blues," "The Negro Speaks of Rivers," "Good Morning," and "Freedom's Plow." And watch in various works and in the critical essays for the impact on Hughes of Harlem as both place and symbol. These are just examples of the kinds of things you might look for as you read the works included here. Any of these themes would reward further research and could be expanded into topics for research papers, which are covered in Chapter 26.

> Research Langston Hughes in depth with cultural documents and multimedia resources on *LiterActive.*

One Friday Morning   [1952]

The thrilling news did not come directly to Nancy Lee, but it came in little indirections that finally added themselves up to one tremendous fact: she had won the prize! But being a calm and quiet young lady, she did not say anything, although the whole high school buzzed with rumors, guesses, reportedly authentic announcements on the part of students who had no right to be making announcements at all — since no student really knew yet who had won this year's art scholarship.

But Nancy Lee's drawing was so good, her lines so sure, her colors so bright and harmonious, that certainly no other student in the senior art class at George Washington High was thought to have very much of a chance. Yet you never could tell. Last year nobody had expected Joe Williams to win the Artist Club scholarship with that funny modernistic water color he had done of the high-level bridge. In fact, it was hard to make out there was a bridge until you had looked at the picture a long time. Still, Joe Williams got the prize, was feted by the community's leading painters, club women, and society folks at a big banquet at the Park-Rose Hotel, and was now an award student at the Art School — the city's only art school.

Nancy Lee Johnson was a colored girl, a few years out of the South. But seldom did her high-school classmates think of her as colored. She was smart, pretty and brown, and fitted in well with the life of the school. She stood high in scholarship, played a swell game of basketball, had taken part in the senior musical in a soft, velvety voice, and had never seemed to intrude or stand out except in pleasant ways, so it was seldom even mentioned — her color.

Nancy Lee sometimes forgot she was colored herself. She liked her classmates and her school. Particularly she liked her art teacher, Miss Dietrich, the tall red-haired woman who taught her law and order in doing things; and the beauty of working step by step until a job is done; a picture finished; a design created; or a block print carved out of nothing but an idea and a smooth square of linoleum, inked, proofs made, and finally put down on paper — clean, sharp, beautiful, individual, unlike any other in the world, thus making the paper have a meaning nobody else could give it except Nancy Lee. That was the wonderful thing about true creation. You made something nobody else on earth could make — but you.

Miss Dietrich was the kind of teacher who brought out the best in her students — but their own best, not anybody else's copied best. For anybody else's best, great though it might be, even Michelangelo's, wasn't enough to please Miss Dietrich dealing with the creative impulses of young men and women living in an American city in the Middle West, and being American.

Nancy Lee was proud of being American, a Negro American with blood out of Africa a long time ago, too many generations back to count. But her parents had taught her the beauties of Africa, its strength, its song, its mighty rivers, its early smelting of iron, its building of the pyramids, and its ancient and important civilizations. And Miss Dietrich had discovered for her the sharp and humorous lines of African sculpture, Benin, Congo, Makonde. Nancy Lee's father was a mail carrier, her mother a social worker in a city settlement house. Both parents had been to Negro colleges in the South. And her mother had gotten a further degree in social work from a Northern university. Her parents were, like most Americans, simple ordinary people who had worked hard and steadily for their education. Now they were trying to make it easier for Nancy Lee to achieve learning than it had been for them. They would be very happy when they heard of the award to their daughter — yet Nancy did not tell them. To surprise them would be better. Besides, there had been a promise.

Casually, one day, Miss Dietrich asked Nancy Lee what color frame she thought would be best on her picture. That had been the first inkling.

"Blue," Nancy Lee said. Although the picture had been entered in the Artist Club contest a month ago, Nancy Lee did not hesitate in her choice of a color for the possible frame since she could still see her picture clearly in her mind's eye — for that picture waiting for the blue frame had come out of her soul, her own life, and had bloomed into miraculous being with Miss Dietrich's help. It was, she knew, the best water color she had painted in her four years as a high-school art student, and she was glad she had made something Miss Dietrich liked well enough to permit her to enter in the contest before she graduated.

It was not a modernistic picture in the sense that you had to look at it a long time to understand what it meant. It was just a simple scene in the city park on a spring day with the trees still leaflessly lacy against the sky, the new grass fresh and green, a flag on a tall pole in the center, children playing, and an old Negro woman sitting on a bench with her head turned. A lot for one picture, to be sure, but it was not there in heavy and final detail like a calendar. Its charm was that everything was light and airy, happy like spring, with a lot of blue sky, paper-white clouds, and air showing through. You could tell that the old Negro woman was looking at the flag, and that the flag was proud in the spring breeze, and that the breeze helped to make the children's dresses billow as they played.

Miss Dietrich had taught Nancy Lee how to paint spring, people, and a breeze on what was only a plain white piece of paper from the supply closet. But Miss Dietrich had not said make it like any other spring-people-breeze ever seen before. She let it remain Nancy Lee's own. That is how the old Negro woman happened to be there looking at the flag—for in her mind the flag, the spring, and the woman formed a kind of triangle holding a dream Nancy Lee wanted to express. White stars on a blue field, spring, children, ever-growing life, and an old woman. Would the judges at the Artist Club like it?

One wet, rainy April afternoon Miss O'Shay, the girls' vice-principal, sent for Nancy Lee to stop by her office as school closed. Pupils without umbrellas or raincoats were clustered in doorways hoping to make it home between showers. Outside the skies were gray. Nancy Lee's thoughts were suddenly gray, too.

She did not think she had done anything wrong, yet that tight little knot came in her throat just the same as she approached Miss O'Shay's door. Perhaps she had banged her locker too often and too hard. Perhaps the note in French she had written to Sallie halfway across the study hall just for fun had never gotten to Sallie but into Miss O'Shay's hands instead. Or maybe she was failing in some subject and wouldn't be allowed to graduate. Chemistry! A pang went through the pit of her stomach.

She knocked on Miss O'Shay's door. That familiarly solid and competent voice said, "Come in."

Miss O'Shay had a way of making you feel welcome, even if you came to be expelled.

"Sit down, Nancy Lee Johnson," said Miss O'Shay. "I have something to tell you." Nancy Lee sat down. "But I must ask you to promise not to tell anyone yet."

"I won't, Miss O'Shay," Nancy Lee said, wondering what on earth the principal had to say to her.

"You are about to graduate," Miss O'Shay said. "And we shall miss you. You have been an excellent student, Nancy, and you will not be without honors on the senior list, as I am sure you know."

At that point there was a light knock on the door. Miss O'Shay called out, "Come in," and Miss Dietrich entered. "May I be a part of this, too?" she asked, tall and smiling.

"Of course," Miss O'Shay said. "I was just telling Nancy Lee what we thought of her. But I hadn't gotten around to giving her the news. Perhaps, Miss Dietrich, you'd like to tell her yourself."

Miss Dietrich was always direct. "Nancy Lee," she said, "your picture has won the Artist Club scholarship."

The slender brown girl's eyes widened, her heart jumped, then her throat tightened again. She tried to smile, but instead tears came to her eyes.

"Dear Nancy Lee," Miss O'Shay said, "we are so happy for you." The elderly white woman took her hand and shook it warmly while Miss Dietrich beamed with pride.

Nancy Lee must have danced all the way home. She never remembered quite how she got there through the rain. She hoped she had been dignified. But certainly she hadn't stopped to tell anybody her secret on the way. Raindrops, smiles, and tears mingled on her brown cheeks. She hoped her mother hadn't yet gotten home and that the house was empty. She wanted to have time to calm down and look natural before she had to see anyone. She didn't want to be bursting with excitement — having a secret to contain.

Miss O'Shay's calling her to the office had been in the nature of a preparation and a warning. The kind, elderly vice-principal said she did not believe in catching young ladies unawares, even with honors, so she wished her to know about the coming award. In making acceptance speeches she wanted her to be calm, prepared, not nervous, overcome, and frightened. So Nancy Lee was asked to think what she would say when the scholarship was conferred upon her a few days hence, both at the Friday morning high-school assembly hour when the announcement would be made, and at the evening banquet of the Artist Club. Nancy Lee promised the vice-principal to think calmly about what she would say.

Miss Dietrich had then asked for some facts about her parents, her background, and her life, since such material would probably be desired for the papers. Nancy Lee had told her how, six years before, they had come up from the Deep South, her father having been successful in achieving a transfer from the one post office to another, a thing he had long sought in order to give Nancy Lee a chance to go to school in the North. Now, they lived in a modest Negro neighborhood, went to see the best plays when they came to town, and had been saving to send Nancy Lee to art school, in case she were permitted to enter. But the scholarship would help a great deal, for they were not rich people.

"Now Mother can have a new coat next winter," Nancy Lee thought, "because my tuition will all be covered for the first year. And once in art school, there are other scholarships I can win."

Dreams began to dance through her head, plans and ambitions, beauties she would create for herself, her parents, and the Negro people — for

Nancy Lee possessed a deep and reverent race pride. She could see the old woman in her picture (really her grandmother in the South) lifting her head to the bright stars on the flag in the distance. A Negro in America! Often hurt, discriminated against, sometimes lynched — but always there were the stars on the blue body of the flag. Was there any other flag in the world that had so many stars? Nancy Lee thought deeply but she could remember none in all the encyclopedias or geographies she had ever looked into.

"Hitch your wagon to a star," Nancy Lee thought, dancing home in the rain. "Who were our flag-makers?"

Friday morning came, the morning when the world would know — her high-school world, the newspaper world, her mother and dad. Dad could not be there at the assembly to hear the announcement, nor see her prize picture displayed on the stage, nor listen to Nancy Lee's little speech of acceptance, but Mother would be able to come, although Mother was much puzzled as to why Nancy Lee was so insistent she be at school on that particular Friday morning.

When something is happening, something new and fine, something that will change your very life, it is hard to go to sleep at night for thinking about it, and hard to keep your heart from pounding, or a strange little knot of joy from gathering in your throat. Nancy Lee had taken her bath, brushed her hair until it glowed, and had gone to bed thinking about the next day, the big day when, before three thousand students, she would be the one student honored, her painting the one painting to be acclaimed as the best of the year from all the art classes of the city. Her short speech of gratitude was ready. She went over it in her mind, not word for word (because she didn't want it to sound as if she had learned it by heart) but she let the thoughts flow simply and sincerely through her consciousness many times.

When the president of the Artist Club presented her with the medal and scroll of the scholarship award, she would say:

"Judges and members of the Artist Club. I want to thank you for this award that means so much to me personally and through me to my people, the colored people of this city who, sometimes, are discouraged and bewildered, thinking that color and poverty are against them. I accept this award with gratitude and pride, not for myself alone, but for my race that believes in American opportunity and American fairness — and the bright stars in our flag. I thank Miss Dietrich and the teachers who made it possible for me to have the knowledge and training that lie behind this honor you have conferred upon my painting. When I came here from the South a few years ago, I was not sure how you would receive me. You received me well. You have given me a chance and helped me along the road I wanted to follow. I suppose the judges know that every week here at assembly the students of this school pledge allegiance to the flag. I shall try to be worthy of that pledge, and of the help and friendship and understanding of my fellow citizens of whatever race or creed, and of our American dream of 'Liberty and justice for all!'"

That would be her response before the students in the morning. How proud and happy the Negro pupils would be, perhaps almost as proud as they were of the one colored star on the football team. Her mother would probably cry with happiness. Thus Nancy Lee went to sleep dreaming of a wonderful tomorrow.

The bright sunlight of an April morning woke her. There was breakfast with her parents — their half-amused and puzzled faces across the table, wondering what could be this secret that made her eyes so bright. The swift walk to school; the clock in the tower almost nine; hundreds of pupils streaming into the long, rambling old building that was the city's largest high school; the sudden quiet of the homeroom after the bell rang; then the teacher opening her record book to call the roll. But just before she began, she looked across the room until her eyes located Nancy Lee.

"Nancy," she said, "Miss O'Shay would like to see you in her office, please."

Nancy Lee rose and went out while the names were being called and the word *present* added its period to each name. Perhaps, Nancy Lee thought, the reporters from the papers had already come. Maybe they wanted to take her picture before assembly, which wasn't until ten o'clock. (Last year they had had the photograph of the winner of the award in the morning papers as soon as the announcement had been made.)

Nancy Lee knocked at Miss O'Shay's door.

"Come in."

The vice-principal stood at her desk. There was no one else in the room. It was very quiet.

"Sit down, Nancy Lee," she said. Miss O'Shay did not smile.

There was a long pause. The seconds went by slowly. "I do not know how to tell you what I have to say," the elderly woman began, her eyes on the papers on her desk. "I am indignant and ashamed for myself and for this city." Then she lifted her eyes and looked at Nancy Lee in the neat blue dress sitting there before her. "You are not to receive the scholarship this morning."

Outside in the hall the electric bells announcing the first period rang, loud and interminably long. Miss O'Shay remained silent. To the brown girl there in the chair, the room grew suddenly smaller, smaller, smaller, and there was no air. She could not speak.

Miss O'Shay said, "When the committee learned that you were colored, they changed their plans."

Still Nancy Lee said nothing, for there was no air to give breath to her lungs.

"Here is the letter from the committee, Nancy Lee." Miss O'Shay picked it up and read the final paragraph to her.

" 'It seems to us wiser to arbitrarily rotate the award among the various high schools of the city from now on. And especially in this case since the student chosen happens to be colored, a circumstance which unfortunately, had we known, might have prevented this embarrassment. But there have never been any Negro students in the local art school, and the presence of one there might create difficulties for all concerned. We have high regard for the quality of Nancy Lee Johnson's talent, but we do not feel it would be fair to honor it with the Artist Club award.'" Miss O'Shay paused. She put the letter down.

"Nancy Lee, I am very sorry to have to give you this message."

"But my speech," Nancy Lee said, "was about. . . ." The words stuck in her throat. ". . . about America. . . ."

Miss O'Shay had risen, she turned her back and stood looking out the window at the spring tulips in the school yard.

"I thought, since the award would be made at assembly right after our oath of allegiance," the words tumbled almost hysterically from Nancy Lee's throat now, "I would put part of the flag salute in my speech. You know, Miss O'Shay, that part about 'liberty and justice for all.'"

"I know," said Miss O'Shay slowly facing the room again. "But America is only what we who believe in it, make it. I am Irish. You may not know, Nancy Lee, but years ago we were called the dirty Irish, and mobs rioted against us in the big cities, and we were invited to go back where we came from. But we didn't go. And we didn't give up, because we believed in the American dream, and in our power to make that dream come true. Difficulties, yes. Mountains to climb, yes. Discouragements to face, yes. Democracy to make, yes. That is it, Nancy Lee! We still have in this world of ours democracy to *make*. You and I, Nancy Lee. But the premise and the base are here, the lines of the Declaration of Independence and the words of Lincoln are here, and the stars in our flag. Those who deny you this scholarship do not know the meaning of those stars, but it's up to us to make them know. As a teacher in the public schools of this city, I myself will go before the school board and ask them to remove from our system the offer of any prizes or awards denied to any student because of race or color."

Suddenly Miss O'Shay stopped speaking. Her clear, clear blue eyes looked into those of the girl before her. The woman's eyes were full of strength and courage. "Lift up your head, Nancy Lee, and smile at me."

Miss O'Shay stood against the open window with the green lawn and the tulips beyond, the sunlight tangled in her gray hair, her voice an electric flow of strength to the hurt spirit of Nancy Lee. The Abolitionists who believed in freedom when there was slavery must have been like that. The first white teachers who went into the Deep South to teach the freed slaves must have been like that. All those who stand against ignorance, narrowness, hate, and mud on stars must be like that.

Nancy Lee lifted her head and smiled. The bell for assembly rang. She went through the long hall filled with students toward the auditorium.

"There will be other awards," Nancy Lee thought. "There're schools in other cities. This won't keep me down. But when I'm a woman, I'll fight to see that these things don't happen to other girls as this has happened to me. And men and women like Miss O'Shay will help me."

She took her seat among the seniors. The doors of the auditorium closed. As the principal came onto the platform, the students rose and turned their eyes to the flag on the stage.

One hand went to the heart, the other outstretched toward the flag. Three thousand voices spoke. Among them was the voice of a dark girl whose cheeks were suddenly wet with tears, ". . . one nation indivisible, with liberty and justice for all."

"That is the land we must make," she thought.

I Dream a World   [1945]

I dream a world where man
No other man will scorn,
Where love will bless the earth
And peace its paths adorn.
I dream a world where all   5
Will know sweet freedom's way,
Where greed no longer saps the soul
Nor avarice blights our day.
A world I dream where black or white,
Whatever race you be,   10
Will share the bounties of the earth
And every man is free,
Where wretchedness will hang its head
And joy, like a pearl,
Attends the needs of all mankind —   15
Of such I dream, my world!

Good Morning   [1951]

Good morning, daddy!
I was born here, he said,
watched Harlem grow
until colored folks spread
from river to river   5
across the middle of Manhattan
out of Penn Station
dark tenth of a nation,
planes from Puerto Rico,

and holds of boats, chico,   10
up from Cuba Haiti Jamaica,
in busses marked NEW YORK
from Georgia Florida Louisiana
to Harlem Brooklyn the Bronx
but most of all to Harlem   15
dusky sash across Manhattan
I've seen them come dark
    wondering
    wide-eyed
    dreaming   20
out of Penn Station —
but the trains are late.
The gates open —
    Yet there're bars
    at each gate.   25

        What happens
        to a dream deferred?

    Daddy, ain't you heard?

Dream Variations   [1926]

To fling my arms wide
In some place of the sun,
To whirl and to dance
Till the white day is done.
Then rest at cool evening   5
Beneath a tall tree
While night comes on gently,
    Dark like me —
That is my dream!

To fling my arms wide   10
In the face of the sun,
Dance! Whirl! Whirl!
Till the quick day is done.
Rest at pale evening . . .
A tall, slim tree . . .   15
Night coming tenderly
    Black like me.

Freedom's Plow

[1943; rev. 1959]

When a man starts out with nothing,
When a man starts out with his hands
Empty, but clean,
When a man starts out to build a world,
He starts first with himself   5
And the faith that is in his heart—
The strength there,
The will there to build.

First in the heart is the dream.
Then the mind starts seeking a way.   10
His eyes look out on the world,
On the great wooded world,
On the rich soil of the world,
On the rivers of the world.

The eyes see there materials for building,   15
See the difficulties, too, and the obstacles.
The hand seeks tools to cut the wood,
To till the soil, and harness the power of the waters.
Then the hand seeks other hands to help,
A community of hands to help—   20
Thus the dream becomes not one man's dream alone,
But a community dream.
Not my dream alone, but *our* dream.
Not my world alone,
But *your world and my world*,   25
Belonging to all the hands who build.

A long time ago, but not too long ago,
Ships came from across the sea
Bringing Pilgrims and prayer-makers,
Adventurers and booty seekers,   30
Free men and indentured servants,
Slave men and slave masters, all new—
To a new world, America!

With billowing sails the galleons came
Bringing men and dreams, women and dreams.   35
In little bands together,
Heart reaching out to heart,
Hand reaching out to hand,
They began to build our land.
Some were free hands   40

Seeking a greater freedom,
Some were indentured hands
Hoping to find their freedom,
Some were slave hands
Guarding in their hearts the seed of freedom.   45
But the word was there always:
   FREEDOM.

Down into the earth went the plow
In the free hands and the slave hands,
In indentured hands and adventurous hands,   50
Turning the rich soil went the plow in many hands
That planted and harvested the food that fed
And the cotton that clothed America.
Clang against the trees went the ax in many hands
That hewed and shaped the rooftops of America.   55
Splash into the rivers and the seas went the boat-hulls
That moved and transported America.
Crack went the whips that drove the horses
Across the plains of America.
Free hands and slave hands,   60
Indentured hands, adventurous hands,
White hands and black hands
Held the plow handles,
Ax handles, hammer handles,
Launched the boats and whipped the horses   65
That fed and housed and moved America.
Thus together through labor,
All these hands made America.
Labor! Out of labor came the villages
And the towns that grew to cities.   70
Labor! Out of labor came the rowboats
And the sailboats and the steamboats,
Came the wagons, stage coaches,
Out of labor came the factories,
Came the foundries, came the railroads,   75
Came the marts and markets, shops and stores,
Came the mighty products moulded, manufactured,
Sold in shops, piled in warehouses,
Shipped the wide world over:
Out of labor — white hands and black hands —   80
Came the dream, the strength, the will,
And the way to build America.
Now it is Me here, and You there.
Now it's Manhattan, Chicago,
Seattle, New Orleans,   85

Boston and El Paso—
Now it is the U.S.A.

A long time ago, but not too long ago, a man said:

    ALL MEN ARE CREATED EQUAL . . .
    ENDOWED BY THEIR CREATOR   90
    WITH CERTAIN INALIENABLE RIGHTS . . .
    AMONG THESE LIFE, LIBERTY
    AND THE PURSUIT OF HAPPINESS.

His name was Jefferson. There were slaves then,
But in their hearts the slaves believed him, too,   95
And silently took for granted
That what he said was also meant for them.
It was a long time ago,
But not so long ago at that, Lincoln said:

    NO MAN IS GOOD ENOUGH   100
    TO GOVERN ANOTHER MAN
    WITHOUT THAT OTHER'S CONSENT.

There were slaves then, too,
But in their hearts the slaves knew
What he said must be meant for every human being—   105
Else it had no meaning for anyone.
Then a man said:

    BETTER TO DIE FREE,
    THAN TO LIVE SLAVES.

He was a colored man who had been a slave   110
But had run away to freedom.
And the slaves knew
What Frederick Douglass said was true.
With John Brown at Harpers Ferry, Negroes died.
John Brown was hung.   115
Before the Civil War, days were dark,
And nobody knew for sure
When freedom would triumph.
"Or if it would," thought some.
But others knew it had to triumph.   120
In those dark days of slavery,
Guarding in their hearts the seed of freedom,
The slaves made up a song:

    KEEP YOUR HAND ON THE PLOW!
        HOLD ON!   125

    *   *   *

That song meant just what it said: *Hold on!*
Freedom will come!

    KEEP YOUR HAND ON THE PLOW!
      HOLD ON!

Out of war, it came, bloody and terrible!   130
But it came!
Some there were, as always,
Who doubted that the war would end right,
That the slaves would be free,
Or that the union would stand.   135
But now we know how it all came out.
Out of the darkest days for a people and a nation,
We know now how it came out.
There was light when the battle clouds rolled away.
There was a great wooded land,   140
And men united as a nation.

America is a dream.
The poet says it was promises.
The people say it *is* promises — that will come true.
The people do not always say things out loud,   145
Nor write them down on paper.
The people often hold
Great thoughts in their deepest hearts
And sometimes only blunderingly express them,
Haltingly and stumbling say them,   150
And faultily put them into practice.
The people do not always understand each other.
But there is, somewhere there,
Always the *trying* to understand,
And the *trying* to say,   155
"You are a man. Together we are building our land."

America!
Land created in common,
Dream nourished in common,
Keep your hand on the plow! Hold on!   160
If the house is not yet finished,
Don't be discouraged, builder!
If the fight is not yet won,
Don't be weary, soldier!
The plan and the pattern is here,   165
Woven from the beginning
Into the warp and woof of America:

    *   *   *

ALL MEN ARE CREATED EQUAL.

NO MAN IS GOOD ENOUGH
TO GOVERN ANOTHER MAN WITHOUT   170
THAT OTHER'S CONSENT.

BETTER DIE FREE,
THAN LIVE SLAVES.

Who said those things? Americans!
Who owns those words? America!   175
Who is America? You, me!
We are America!
To the enemy who would conquer us from without,
We say, NO!
To the enemy who would divide   180
and conquer us from within,
We say, NO!

   FREEDOM!
     BROTHERHOOD!
      DEMOCRACY!   185

To all the enemies of these great words:
We say, NO!

A long time ago,
An enslaved people heading toward freedom
Made up a song: 190
   Keep Your Hand On The Plow! Hold On!
That plow plowed a new furrow
Across the field of history.
Into that furrow the freedom seed was dropped.
From that seed a tree grew, is growing, will ever grow. 195
That tree is for everybody,
For all America, for all the world.
May its branches spread and its shelter grow
Until all races and all peoples know its shade.

   KEEP YOUR HAND ON THE PLOW!   200
   HOLD ON!

Jazz as Communication   [1958]

You can start anywhere—Jazz as Communication—since it's a circle, and you yourself are the dot in the middle. You, me. For example, I'll start with the Blues. I'm not a Southerner. I never worked on a levee. I hardly ever saw a cotton field except from the highway. But women behave the same on

Park Avenue as they do on a levee: when you've got hold of one part of them the other part escapes you. That's the Blues!

Life is as hard on Broadway as it is in Blues-originating-land. The Brill Building Blues is just as hungry as the Mississippi Levee Blues. One communicates to the other, brother! Somebody is going to rise up and tell me that nothing that comes out of Tin Pan Alley is jazz. I disagree. Commercial, yes. But so was Storyville,° so was Basin Street.° What do you think Tony Jackson and Jelly Roll Morton and King Oliver and Louis Armstrong° were playing for? Peanuts? No, money, even in Dixieland. They were communicating for money. For fun, too — because they had fun. But the money helped the fun along.

Now; To skip a half century, somebody is going to rise up and tell me Rock and Roll isn't jazz. First, two or three years ago, there were all these songs about too young to know — *but.* . . . The songs are right. You're never too young to know how bad it is to love and not have love come back to you. That's as basic as the Blues. And that's what Rock and Roll is — teenage *Heartbreak Hotel*° — the old songs reduced to the lowest common denominator. The music goes way back to Blind Lemon and Leadbelly — Georgia Tom merging into the Gospel Songs — Ma Rainey,° and the most primitive of the Blues. It borrows their gut-bucket heartache. It goes back to the jubilees and stepped-up Spirituals — Sister Tharpe° — and borrows their I'm-gonna-be-happy-anyhow-in-spite-of-this-world kind of hope. It goes back further and borrows the steady beat of the drums of Congo Square — that going-on beat — and the Marching Bands' loud and blatant *yes!!* Rock and roll puts them all together and makes a music so basic it's like the meat cleaver the butcher uses — before the cook uses the knife — before you use the sterling silver at the table on the meat that by then has been rolled up into a commercial filet mignon.

A few more years and Rock and Roll will no doubt be washed back half forgotten into the sea of jazz. Jazz is a great big sea. It washes up all kinds of fish and shells and spume and waves with a steady old beat, or off-beat. And Louis must be getting old if he thinks J. J. and Kai° — and even Elvis — didn't

---

Storyville: A district of legalized prostitution in New Orleans from 1897 through 1917 and an area where jazz flourished (the earliest forms of jazz music are often termed "Storyville Jazz"). **Basin Street:** A street in New Orleans long associated with jazz clubs. **Tony Jackson . . . Louis Armstrong:** Antony Jackson (1876–1921), American ragtime pianist, blues singer, and composer; Ferdinand Joseph "Jelly Roll" Morton (1890–1941), American jazz pianist and composer; Joseph "King" Oliver (1885–1938), innovative New Orleans cornet player; Louis "Satchmo" Armstrong (1901–1971), American jazz trumpet virtuoso, singer, and bandleader. **Heartbreak Hotel:** Rock'n'roll song recorded by Elvis Presley in 1956. **Blind Lemon . . . Ma Rainey:** Clarence "Blind Lemon" Jefferson (1897–1929), American guitarist and blues singer; Huddie "Leadbelly" Ledbetter (1885–1949), American blues singer and guitarist; Thomas "Georgia Tom" Dorsey (1899–1993), American blues singer, gospel songwriter, and pianist; Gertrude "Ma" Rainey (1886–1939), American singer known as the "Mother of the Blues." **Sister Tharpe:** Sister Rosetta Tharpe (1915–1973), American jazz singer. **J. J. and Kai:** James Louis "J. J." Johnson (1924–2001), American jazz trombonist and composer; Kai Winding (1922–1983), Danish American trombonist best known for the two-trombone combo Jay and Kai that he formed with Johnson in 1954.

come out of the same sea he came out of, too. Some water has chlorine in it and some doesn't. There're all kinds of water. There's salt water and Saratoga water and Vichy water, Quinine water and Pluto water — and Newport rain. And it's all water. Throw it all in the sea, and the sea'll keep on rolling along toward shore and crashing and booming back into itself again. The sun pulls the moon. The moon pulls the sea. They also pull jazz and me. Beyond Kai to Count to Lonnie to Texas Red, beyond June to Sarah to Billie to Bessie° to Ma Rainey. And the Most is the It — the all of it.

Jazz seeps into words — spelled out words. Nelson Algren is influenced by jazz. Ralph Ellison is, too. Sartre, too. Jacques Prévert.° Most of the best writers today are. Look at the end of the *Ballad of the Sad Café.*° Me as the public, *my* dot in the middle — it was fifty years ago, the first time I heard the Blues on Independence Avenue in Kansas City. Then State Street in Chicago. Then Harlem in the twenties with J. P. and J. C. Johnson and Fats and Willie the Lion and Nappy° playing piano — with the Blues running all up and down the keyboard through the ragtime and the jazz. House rent party cards. I wrote *The Weary Blues:*

Droning a drowsy syncopated tune . . . . . . etc. . . . .

Shuffle Along was running then — the Sissle and Blake tunes.° A little later *Runnin' Wild* and the Charleston and Fletcher and Duke and Cab.° Jimmie Lunceford, Chick Webb, and Ella. Tiny Parham° in Chicago. And at the

---

Count . . . Bessie: William "Count" Basie (1904–1984), American pianist and big band leader; Alfonzo "Lonnie" Johnson (1889–1970), American guitarist and jazz singer; William M. "Texas Red" Garland (1923–1984), American jazz pianist; Sarah Vaughn (1924–1990), American jazz singer and pianist; Billie Holiday (Eleanora Fagan Gough, 1915–1959), American jazz singer; Bessie Smith (1895–1937), American blues singer. **Nelson Algren . . . Jacques Prévert:** Nelson Algren (1909–1981), American fiction writer and poet; Ralph Ellison (1914–1994), American novelist, jazz musician, and music critic; Jean-Paul Sartre (1905–1980), French existentialist philosopher, playwright, novelist, and literary critic; Jacques Prévert (1900–1977), French poet. **Ballad of the Sad Café:** Short 1953 novel by Carson McCullers (1917–1967). **J. P. . . . Nappy:** James Price "J. P." Johnson (1891–1955), American ragtime and jazz pianist and composer; J. C. Johnson (1896–1981), jazz pianist and songwriter; Thomas Wright "Fats" Waller (1904–1943), American pianist, jazz pianist, organist, and composer; Willie "The Lion" Smith (1897–1973), American ragtime and jazz pianist and composer; Hilton Napoleon "Nappy" Lamare (1907–1988), American guitarist, singer, and composer. **Shuffle Along . . . Sissle and Blake tunes:** *Shuffle Along,* an all-black musical comedy with lyrics by Noble Sissle (1889–1975) and music by Eubie Blake (1883–1983), opened in Harlem and in 1921 became the first African American Broadway musical. **Runnin' Wild . . . Cab:** *Runnin' Wild,* an African American musical by J. P. Johnson (see earlier note), opened in 1923. Its hit number, "Charleston," became one of the best-known and most widely recorded songs of the 1920s. Fletcher Henderson (1897–1952), American pianist, arranger, and band leader. Edward K. "Duke" Ellington (1899–1974), American composer, bandleader, and pianist. Cabell "Cab" Calloway (1907–1994), American singer and bandleader. **Jimmie Lunceford . . . Tiny Parham:** Jimmie Lunceford (1904–1942), American saxophonist and bandleader; William Henry "Chick" Webb (1909–1939), American drummer and bandleader; Ella Fitzgerald (1917–1996), American jazz singer; Hartzell Strathdene "Tiny" Parham (1900–1943), Canadian American pianist, organist, and bandleader.

end of the Depression times, what I heard at Minton's.° A young music —
coming out of young people. Billy — the male and female of them — both the
Eckstein and the Holiday — and Dizzy and Tad and the Monk.° Some of it
came out in poems of mine in *Montage of a Dream Deferred* later. Jazz again
putting itself into words . . .

But I wasn't the only one putting jazz into words. Better poets of the
heart of jazz beat me to it. W. C. Handy a long time before. Benton Overstreet. Mule Bradford. Then Buddy DeSylva on the pop level. Ira Gershwin.
By and by Dorothy Baker° in the novel — to name only the most obvious —
the ones with labels. I mean the ones you can spell out easy with a-b-c's —
the word mongers — outside the music. But always the ones of the music
were the best — Charlie Christian, for example, Bix, Louis, Joe Sullivan,°
Count.

Now, to wind it all up, with you in the middle — jazz is only what you
yourself get out of it. Louis's famous quote — or misquote probably — "Lady,
if you have to ask what it is, you'll never know." Well, I wouldn't be so
positive. The lady just might know — without being able to let loose the cry —
to follow through — to light up before the fuse blows out. To me jazz is a
montage of a dream deferred. A great big dream — yet to come — and always
yet — to become ultimately and finally true. Maybe in the next seminar — for
Saturday — Nat Hentoff and Billy Strayhorn and Tony Scott° and the others
on that panel will tell us about it — when they take up "The Future of Jazz."
The Bird was looking for that future like mad. The Newborns, Chico, Dave,
Gulda, Milt, Charlie Mingus.° That future is what you call pregnant. Poten-

---

Minton's: Minton's Playhouse, a Harlem nightclub that opened in 1940 on 118th Street in the
Hotel Cecil, was famous for after-hours experimental jam sessions in the 1940s and is known
as the "Birthplace of Bebop."   **Eckstein . . . Monk:** William Clarence "Billy" Eckstein
(1914–1993), American jazz singer and bandleader; Billie Holiday (see earlier note); John Birks
"Dizzy" Gillespie (1917–1993), American trumpeter and bandleader; Tadley Ewing "Tadd"
Dameron (1917–1965), American jazz pianist, arranger, composer, and bandleader; Thelonius
Monk (1917–1982), American jazz pianist and composer.   **W. C. Handy . . . Dorothy Baker:**
William Christopher Handy (1873–1958), American composer and arranger known as the
"Father of the Blues"; W. Benton Overstreet, American songwriter; Perry "Mule" Bradford
(1893–1970), American blues pianist, songwriter, and singer; Buddy DeSylva (1895–1950),
American songwriter; Ira Gershwin (1896–1983), American songwriter; Dorothy Baker
(1907–1968), jazz writer and author of *Young Man with a Horn,* a novel based on the life of Bix
Beiderbecke.   **Charlie Christian . . . Joe Sullivan:** Charlie Christian (1916–1942), American
jazz guitarist; Leon "Bix" Beiderbecke (1903–1931), American jazz cornetist and pianist; Louis
Armstrong (see earlier note); Joe Sullivan (1906–1971), American jazz pianist and composer.
Nat Hentoff . . . Tony Scott: Nathan Irving "Nat" Hentoff (b. 1925), American novelist and
jazz historian; Billy Strayhorn (1915–1967), American jazz pianist, composer, and arranger;
Tony Scott (b. 1921), American jazz clarinetist.   **Bird . . . Charlie Mingus:** Charlie "Bird"
Parker (1920–1955), American jazz saxophonist and composer; Phineas Newborn Jr. (1931–
1989), American jazz pianist; (Edwin) Calvin Newborn (b. 1933), American jazz guitarist;
Foreststorn "Chico" Hamilton (b. 1921), American jazz drummer; Dave Brubeck (b. 1920),
American jazz pianist and composer; Friedrich Gulda (1930–2000), Austrian classical and jazz
pianist and composer; Milt Jackson (1923–1999), American jazz vibraphonist; Charles Mingus
(1922–1979), American bass player, pianist, composer, and bandleader.

tial papas and mamas of tomorrow's jazz are all known. But THE papa and THE mama — maybe both — are anonymous. But the child will communicate. Jazz is a heartbeat — its heartbeat is yours. You will tell me about its perspectives when you get ready.

The Weary Blues   [1926]

Droning a drowsy syncopated tune,
Rocking back and forth to a mellow croon,
   I heard a Negro play.
Down on Lenox Avenue the other night
By the pale dull pallor of an old gas light   5
   He did a lazy sway . . .
   He did a lazy sway . . .
To the tune o' those Weary Blues.
With his ebony hands on each ivory key
He made that poor piano moan with melody.   10
   O Blues!
Swaying to and fro on his rickety stool
He played that sad raggy tune like a musical fool.
   Sweet Blues!
Coming from a black man's soul.   15
   O Blues!
In a deep song voice with a melancholy tone
I heard that Negro sing, that old piano moan —
   "Ain't got nobody in all this world,
   Ain't got nobody but ma self.   20
   I's gwine to quit ma frownin'
   And put ma troubles on the shelf."
Thump, thump, thump, went his foot on the floor.
He played a few chords then he sang some more —
   "I got the Weary Blues   25
   And I can't be satisfied.
   Got the Weary Blues
   And can't be satisfied —
   I ain't happy no mo'
   And I wish that I had died."   30
And far into the night he crooned that tune.
The stars went out and so did the moon.
The singer stopped playing and went to bed
While the Weary Blues echoed through his head.
He slept like a rock or a man that's dead.   35

The Negro Speaks of Rivers   [1926]

I've known rivers:
I've known rivers ancient as the world and older than the flow of
    human blood in human veins.

My soul has grown deep like the rivers.

I bathed in the Euphrates when dawns were young.
I built my hut near the Congo and it lulled me to sleep.   5
I looked upon the Nile and raised the pyramids above it.
I heard the singing of the Mississippi when Abe Lincoln went down
    to New Orleans, and I've seen its muddy bosom turn all golden
    in the sunset.

I've known rivers:
Ancient, dusky rivers.

My soul has grown deep like the rivers.   10

I've Known Rivers   [1940]

That November the First World War ended. In Cleveland, everybody
poured into the streets to celebrate the Armistice. Negroes, too, although
Negroes were increasingly beginning to wonder where, for them, was that
democracy they had fought to preserve. In Cleveland, a liberal city, the color
line began to be drawn tighter and tighter. Theaters and restaurants in the
downtown area began to refuse to accommodate colored people. Landlords
doubled and tripled the rents at the approach of a dark tenant. And when
the white soldiers came back from the war, Negroes were often discharged
from their jobs and white men hired in their places.

The end of the war! But many of the students at Central kept talking,
not about the end of the war, but about Russia, where Lenin had taken
power in the name of the workers, who made everything, and who would
now own everything they made. "No more pogroms," the Jews said, "no
more race hatred, no more landlords." John Reed's *Ten Days That Shook the
World* shook Central High School, too.

The daily papers pictured the Bolsheviki as the greatest devils on earth,
but I didn't see how they could be that bad if they had done away with race
hatred and landlords—two evils that I knew well at first hand.

My father raised my allowance that year, so I was able to help my
mother with the expenses of our household. It was a pleasant year for me,
for I was a senior. I was elected Class Poet and Editor of our Year Book. As an
officer in the drill corps, I wore a khaki uniform and leather puttees, and
gave orders. I went calling on a little brownskin girl, who was as old as I

was — seventeen — but only in junior high school, because she had just come up from the poor schools of the South. I met her at a dance at the Longwood Gym. She had big eyes and skin like rich chocolate. Sometimes she wore a red dress that was very becoming to her, so I wrote a poem about her that declared:

> When Susanna Jones wears red
> Her face is like an ancient cameo
> Turned brown by the ages.
>
> Come with a blast of trumpets,
>   Jesus!
>
> When Susanna Jones wears red
> A queen from some time-dead Egyptian night
> Walks once again.
>
> Blow trumpets, Jesus!
>
> And the beauty of Susanna Jones in red
> Burns in my heart a love-fire sharp like pain.
>
> Sweet silver trumpets,
>   Jesus!

I had a whole notebook full of poems by now, and another one full of verses and jingles. I always tried to keep verses and poems apart, although I saw no harm in writing verses if you felt like it, and poetry if you could.

June came. And graduation. Like most graduations, it made you feel both sorry and glad: sorry to be leaving and glad to be going. Some students were planning to enter college, but not many, because there was no money for college in most of Central's families.

My father had written me to come to Mexico again to discuss with him my future plans. He hinted that he would send me to college if I intended to go, and he thought I had better go.

I didn't want to return to Mexico, but I had a feeling I'd never get any further education if I didn't, since my mother wanted me to go to work and be, as she put it, "of some use to her." She demanded to know how I would look going off to college and she there working like a dog!

I said I thought I could be of more help to her once I got an education than I could if I went to work fresh out of high school, because nobody could do much on the salary of a porter or a bus boy. And such jobs offered no advancement for a Negro.

But about my going to join my father, my mother acted much as she had done the year before. I guess it is the old story of divorced parents who don't like each other, and take their grievances out on the offspring. I got the feeling then that I'd like to get away from home altogether, both homes, and that maybe if I went to Mexico one more time, I could go to college somewhere in some new place, and be on my own.

So I went back to Toluca.

My mother let me go to the station alone, and I felt pretty bad when I got on the train. I felt bad for the next three or four years, to tell the truth, and those were the years when I wrote most of my poetry. (For my best poems were all written when I felt the worst. When I was happy, I didn't write anything.)

The one of my poems that has perhaps been most often reprinted in anthologies was written on the train during this trip to Mexico when I was feeling very bad. It's called "The Negro Speaks of Rivers" and was written just outside St. Louis, as the train rolled toward Texas.

It came about in this way. All day on the train I had been thinking about my father and his strange dislike of his own people. I didn't understand it, because I was a Negro, and I liked Negroes very much. One of the happiest jobs I had ever had was during my freshman year in high school, when I worked behind the soda fountain for a Mrs. Kitzmiller, who ran a refreshment parlor on Central Avenue in the heart of the colored neighborhood. People just up from the South used to come in for ice cream and sodas and watermelon. And I never tired of hearing them talk, listening to the thunderclaps of their laughter, to their troubles, to their discussions of the war and the men who had gone to Europe from the Jim Crow South, their complaints over the high rent and the long overtime hours that brought what seemed like big checks, until the weekly bills were paid. They seemed to me like the gayest and the bravest people possible — these Negroes from the Southern ghettos — facing tremendous odds, working and laughing and trying to get somewhere in the world.

I had been in to dinner early that afternoon on the train. Now it was just sunset, and we crossed the Mississippi, slowly, over a long bridge. I looked out the window of the Pullman at the great muddy river flowing down toward the heart of the South, and I began to think what that river, the old Mississippi, had meant to Negroes in the past — how to be sold down the river was the worst fate that could overtake a slave in times of bondage. Then I remembered reading how Abraham Lincoln had made a trip down the Mississippi on a raft to New Orleans, and how he had seen slavery at its worst, and had decided within himself that it should be removed from American life. Then I began to think about other rivers in our past — the Congo, and the Niger, and the Nile in Africa — and the thought came to me: "I've known rivers," and I put it down on the back of an envelope I had in my pocket, and within the space of ten or fifteen minutes, as the train gathered speed in the dusk, I had written this poem, which I called "The Negro Speaks of Rivers":

I've known rivers:
I've known rivers ancient as the world and older than the flow of human
    blood in human veins.

My soul has grown deep like the rivers.

*   *   *

I bathed in the Euphrates when dawns were young.
I built my hut near the Congo and it lulled me to sleep.
I looked upon the Nile and raised the pyramids above it.
I heard the singing of the Mississippi when Abe Lincoln went down to New
  Orleans, and I've seen its muddy bosom turn all golden in the sunset.

I've known rivers:
Ancient, dusky rivers.

My soul has grown deep like the rivers.

No doubt I changed a few words the next day, or maybe crossed out a line or two. But there are seldom many changes in my poems, once they're down. Generally, the first two or three lines come to me from something I'm thinking about, or looking at, or doing, and the rest of the poem (if there is to be a poem) flows from those first few lines, usually right away. If there is a chance to put the poem down then, I write it down. If not, I try to remember it until I get to a pencil and paper; for poems are like rainbows: they escape you quickly.

Soul Gone Home   [1936]
A One-Act Play

CHARACTERS

THE MOTHER
THE SON
TWO MEN

Night.

A tenement room, bare, ugly, dirty. An unshaded electric-light bulb. In the middle of the room a cot on which the body of a Negro youth is lying. His hands are folded across his chest. There are pennies on his eyes. He is a soul gone home.

As the curtain rises, his Mother, a large, middle-aged woman in a red sweater, kneels weeping beside the cot, loudly simulating grief.

MOTHER: Oh, Gawd! Oh, Lawd! Why did you take my son from me? Oh, Gawd, why did you do it? He was all I had! Oh, Lawd, what am I gonna do? (*Looking at the dead boy and stroking his head*) Oh, son! Oh, Ronnie! Oh, my boy, speak to me! Ronnie, say something to me! Son, why don't you talk to your mother? Can't you see she's bowed down in sorrow? Son, speak to me, just a word! Come back from the spirit-world and speak to me! Ronnie, come back from the dead and speak to your mother!

SON (*Lying there dead as a doornail. Speaking loudly*): I wish I wasn't dead, so I *could* speak to you. You been a hell of a mama!

MOTHER (*Falling back from the cot in astonishment, but still on her knees*): Ronnie! Ronnie! What's that you say? What you sayin' to your mother? (*Wild-eyed*) Is you done opened your mouth and spoke to me?

SON: I said you a hell of a mama!

MOTHER (*Rising suddenly and backing away, screaming loudly*): Awo-ooo-o! Ronnie, that ain't you talkin'!

SON: Yes, it is me talkin', too! I say you been a no-good mama.

MOTHER: What for you talkin' to me like that, Ronnie? You ain't never said nothin' like that to me before.

SON: I know it, but I'm dead now—and I can say what I want to say. (*Stirring*) You done called on me to talk, ain't you? Lemme take these pennies off my eyes so I can see. (*He takes the coins off his eyes, throws them across the room, and sits up in bed. He is a very dark boy in a torn white shirt. He looks hard at his mother*) Mama, you know you ain't done me right.

MOTHER: What you mean, I ain't done you right? (*She is rooted in horror*) What you mean, huh?

SON: You know what I mean.

MOTHER: No, I don't neither. (*Trembling violently*) What you mean comin' back to haunt your poor old mother? Ronnie, what does you mean?

SON (*Leaning forward*): I'll tell you just what I mean! You been a bad mother to me.

MOTHER: Shame! Shame! Shame, talkin' to your mama that away. Damn it! Shame! I'll slap your face. (*She starts toward him, but he rolls his big white eyes at her, and she backs away*) Me, what borned you! Me, what suffered the pains o' death to bring you into this world! Me, what raised you up, what washed your dirty didies. (*Sorrowfully*) And now I'm left here mighty nigh prostrate 'cause you gone from me! Ronnie, what you mean talkin' to *me* like that—what brought you into this world?

SON: You never did feed me good, that's what I mean! Who wants to come into the world hongry, and go out the same way?

MOTHER: What you mean hongry? When I had money, ain't I fed you?

SON (*Sullenly*): Most of the time you ain't had no money.

MOTHER: 'Twarn't my fault then.

SON: 'Twarn't *my* fault neither.

MOTHER (*Defensively*): You always was so weak and sickly, you couldn't earn nothin' sellin' papers.

SON: I know it.

MOTHER: You never was no use to me.

SON: So you just lemme grow up in the street, and I ain't had no manners nor morals, neither.

MOTHER: Manners and morals? Ronnie, where'd you learn all them big words?

SON: I learnt 'em just now in the spirit-world.

MOTHER (*Coming nearer*): But you ain't been dead no more'n an hour.

SON: That's long enough to learn a lot.

MOTHER: Well, what else did you find out?

SON: I found out you was a hell of a mama puttin' me out in the cold to sell papers soon as I could even walk.

MOTHER: What? You little liar!

SON: If I'm lyin', I'm dyin'! And lettin' me grow up all bowlegged and stunted from undernourishment.

MOTHER: Under-nurse-mint?

SON: Undernourishment. You heard what the doctor said last week?

MOTHER: Naw, what'd he say?

SON: He said I was dyin' o' undernourishment, that's what he said. He said I had TB 'cause I didn't have enough to eat never when I were a child. And he said I couldn't get well, nohow eating nothin' but beans ever since I been sick. Said I needed milk and eggs. And you said you ain't got no money for milk and eggs, which I know you ain't. (*Gently*) We never had no money, mama, not even since you took up hustlin' on the streets.

MOTHER: Son, money ain't everything.

SON: Naw, but when you got TB you have to have milk and eggs.

MOTHER (*Advancing sentimentally*): Anyhow, I love you, Ronnie!

SON (*Rudely*): Sure you love me — but here I am dead.

MOTHER (*Angrily*): Well, damn your hide, you ain't even decent dead. If you was, you wouldn't be sittin' there jawin' at your mother when she's sheddin' every tear she's got for you tonight.

SON: First time you ever did cry for me, far as I know.

MOTHER: Tain't! You's a liar! I cried when I borned you — you was such a big child — ten pounds.

SON: Then *I* did the cryin' after that, I reckon.

MOTHER (*Proudly*): Sure, I could of let you die, but I didn't. Naw, I kept you with me — off and on. And I lost the chance to marry many a good man, too — if it weren't for you. No man wants to take care o' nobody else's child. (*Self-pityingly*) You been a burden to me, Randolph.

SON (*Angrily*): What did you have me for then, in the first place?

MOTHER: How could I help havin' you, you little bastard? Your father ruint me — and you's the result. And I been worried with you for sixteen years. (*Disgustedly*) Now, just when you get big enough to work and do me some good, you have to go and die.

SON: I sure am dead!

MOTHER: But you ain't decent dead! Here you come back to haunt your poor old mama, and spoil her cryin' spell, and spoil the mournin'. (*There is the noise of an ambulance gong outside. The Mother goes to the window and looks down into the street. Turns to Son*) Ronnie, lay down quick! Here comes the city's ambulance to take you to the undertaker's. Don't let them white men see you dead, sitting up here quarrelin' with your mother. Lay down and fold your hands back like I had 'em.

SON (*Passing his hand across his head*): All right, but gimme that comb yonder and my stocking cap. I don't want to go out of here with my hair standin' straight up in front, even if I is dead. (*The Mother hands him a* comb and his stocking cap. *The Son combs his hair and puts the cap on. Noise of men coming up the stairs)*

MOTHER: Hurry up, Ronnie, they'll be here in no time.

SON: Aw, they got another flight to come yet. Don't rush me, ma!

MOTHER: Yes, but I got to put these pennies back on your eyes, boy! *(She searches in a corner for the coins as her Son lies down and folds his hands, stiff in death. She finds the coins and puts them nervously on his eyes, watching the door meanwhile. A knock)* Come in.

(Enter two Men in the white coats of city health employees)

MAN: Somebody sent for us to get the body of Ronnie Bailey? Third floor, apartment five.

MOTHER: Yes, sir, here he is! *(Weeping loudly)* He's my boy! Oh, Lawd, he's done left me! Oh, Lawdy, he's done gone home! His soul's gone home! Oh, what am I gonna do? Mister! Mister! Mister, the Lawd's done took him home! *(As the Men unfold the stretchers, she continues to weep hysterically. They place the boy's thin body on the stretchers and cover it with a rubber cloth. Each man takes his end of the stretchers. Silently, they walk out the door as the Mother wails)* Oh, my son! Oh, my boy! Come back, come back, come back! Ronnie, come back! *(One loud scream as the door closes)* Awo-ooo-o!

(As the footsteps of the men die down on the stairs, the Mother becomes suddenly quiet. She goes to a broken mirror and begins to rouge and powder her face. In the street the ambulance gong sounds fainter and fainter in the distance. The Mother takes down an old fur coat from a nail and puts it on. Before she leaves, she smooths back the quilts on the cot from which the dead boy has been removed. She looks into the mirror again, and once more whitens her face with powder. She dons a red hat. From a handbag she takes a cigarette, lights it, and walks slowly out the door. At the door she switches off the light. The hallway is dimly illuminated. She turns before closing the door, looks back into the room, and speaks)

MOTHER: Tomorrow, Ronnie, I'll buy you some flowers — if I can pick up a dollar tonight. You was a hell of a no-good son, I swear!

CURTAIN

Philip C. Kolin and Maureen Curley

Hughes's *Soul Gone Home* [2003]

Langston Hughes's one-act play *Soul Gone Home*, first published in 1936, mirrors some of his longer, more ambitious works. In the tradition of a haunting or ghost play, *Soul Gone Home* is the story of a sixteen-year old black boy, Randolph Bailey, who comes back from the dead after only one hour in the "spirit-world" (Hughes 39) to chastise his mourning mother, a prostitute, for having "been a bad mother to me" (Hughes 40). This short play blends Hughes's wry comedy with the deep tragedy of his social criticism. Unfortunately, *Soul* has received very little attention, and when it has been noticed, the play has been interpreted in simple biographical terms. Arnold Rampersad, for example, claims that Hughes penned *Soul Gone Home* as a diatribe against his mother "who kept him broke" and "Instead of leaving her . . . vented his anger in [this] macabre little play" (1.319). But *Soul Gone Home* goes beyond the limits of Hughes's family circle.

The title of the play is expansively ambiguous, partaking of the spiritual and the satiric. Young Ronnie (Randolph) is indeed a soul on his journey to his heavenly home, but he comes back to his earthly home — "a tenement room, bare, ugly, dirty" (Hughes 39) — to interrogate his mother and to add to her tears. Their painful encounter calls to mind other mother-son relationships — Hamlet and Gertrude, Nora and her drowned son in John Millington Synge's *Riders to the Sea,* and Hughes's own *Mulatto* and *Mother to Son* — but includes some tragicomic fantasy. Ronnie blames his mother's not giving him enough to eat — he came into the world hungry and leaves the same way — and his mother, in a wonderfully self-accusatory pun, renders Ronnie's charge that he was "stunted from undernourishment" as "under-nurse-mint" (Hughes 41). Though she was dry of the milk of motherly kindness, the fact that Ronnie came into this world a ten-pound strapling suggests that his mother hardly starved herself. She in turn accuses him of not being a help to her; he could not even sell newspapers because he was so sickly. "Now, just when you get big enough to work and do me some good, you have to go and die" (Hughes 41). She also blames Ronnie for her not having a husband — "No man wants to take care o' nobody else's child" (Hughes 41). Ella Forbes rationalizes that the mother's "ability to truly love has been crushed out of [her]" by poverty (169), an interpretation that may be too kind, for Ronnie's mother gives as good as she gets. She lashes out at Ronnie, calling him a "bastard," cursing him — "damn your hide," and fuming that "you ain't even decent dead" (Hughes 41). Ronnie does not escape his mother's nagging instruction, even after death. She worries about what the ambulance attendants will think when they come for Ronnie's corpse. "Don't let them white men see you dead, sitting up here quarrelin' with your mother. Lay down and fold your hands back like I had 'em" (Hughes 41).

Soul Gone Home powerfully expresses Hughes's repeated theme about racial identity in a world dominated by whites. The symbolism in this short play — in its stage directions, costumes, and verbal imagery — underscores the racial tensions that Ronnie, his mother, and Hughes himself felt. White imagery haunts both reader and characters. The white world is most clearly represented by the two white-coated attendants who carry Ronnie away and for whom he had to dress. To prepare for the ride, his mother hands him a comb and his "stocking cap" (Hughes 42). As the play begins, Ronnie is described as a "dark boy in a torn white shirt" (Hughes 39), a perfect image of the divided, split world in which a black boy has to live and to die. Even in death, the black man is not allowed to wear a sign of whiteness undefiled; Ronnie's tattered shroud cannot be wholly white. Ironically, Ronnie "rolls his big white eyes at her" (Hughes 40) as if a white world had freakishly drawn the color out of them.

When Ronnie starts talking to his mother, he removes the coins that she had put on his eyes and "throws them across the room, and sits up" (Hughes 39). Putting coins on the eyes of the dead, a tradition rooted in antiquity, is supposed to symbolize payment to Charon, the ferryman over the river Styx. But in Hughes's symbolism, the coins symbolize that Ronnie's mother wanted him to see the world in terms of money and to see how useful it (and he) would be to her in such a capitalist world. She wants his eyes to be blinded by money. At the end of the play, she "searches in a corner for the coins . . . and puts them nervously on his eyes" (Hughes 42), again to make the right impression on the men in white coats. As a starving child, Ronnie needed "milk and eggs" (41—further icons of a wealthy, unobtainable white world) to help him recover from TB.

Hughes's most disarming commentary on a cruel white world occurs at the end of *Soul Gone Home*. After Ronnie's corpse has been removed, his mother puts "rouge and powder [on] her face" (Hughes 42) and then again "whitens her face with powder" (Hughes 42). She makes herself white — what might today be labeled colonial mimicry — to attract the johns who she hopes will pay her a dollar for flowers for Ronnie — and to compete/earn more in a capitalist world. Her rouge, symbolic of her sexual energy, is useful only for the commodification of sex in her world. (Three decades later, Adrienne Kennedy would show the grotesque consequences of black women who put on white faces to exist in a white world.) Victimized by a white economy and her own (and her son's) miserable trade in it, Ronnie's mother and Ronnie are split apart like Ronnie's burial shroud even after death. The last line of the play, spoken by the mother, "You was a hell of a no-good son" (42), is rank with Hughes's indictments of a society where children must go begging even to death.

Works Cited

Forbes, Ella. "Hughes as Dramatist." *Langston Hughes: The Man, His Art, and His Continuing Influence.* Ed. James C. Trotman. New York: Garland, 1995. 167–69.

Hughes, Langston. *Soul Gone Home.* In *Five Plays by Langston Hughes.* Ed. Webster Smalley. Bloomington: Indiana UP, 1963. 37–42.

Rampersad, Arnold. *The Life of Langston Hughes.* 2 vols. New York: Oxford UP, 1986–88.

Yusef Komunyakaa

Langston Hughes + Poetry = The Blues [2002]

And far into the night he crooned that tune.
The stars went out and so did the moon.
The singer stopped playing and went to bed
While the Weary Blues echoed through his head.
— *Langston Hughes*, The Weary Blues

When we analyze and weigh the most innovative voices of the Harlem Renaissance, Langston Hughes — alongside Zora Neale Hurston, Jean Toomer, and Helene Johnson — remains at the axis. Where Countee Cullen and Claude McKay embraced the archaism of the Keatsian ode and the Elizabethan sonnet,[1] respectively, Hughes grafted on to his modernist vision traditional blues as well as the Chicago Renaissance (Vachel Lindsay and Carl Sandburg).[2] So, as the other voices grew silent during the Great Depression of 1929 — with modernism[3] and imagism[4] having taken a firm hold and reshaped the tongue and heart of American poetry — the 1930s found a prolific Hughes. From the outset an American-ness had been at the center of Hughes's work, which is one of the reasons he has endured. Even his benchmark poem "The Negro Speaks of Rivers" plumbs the "muddy bosom" of the Mississippi after its narrator praises the Euphrates and the Congo (i.e., after taking readers on a tour through African heritage, the poem focuses on racial tensions in America).

Like Walt Whitman, the pulse and throb of Hughes's vision is driven by an acute sense of beauty and tragedy in America's history. Arnold Rampersad says in *The Life of Langston Hughes* that "On a visit to Kansas City he became aware of yet another aspect of black culture on which he would draw later as an artist and an individual. At an open air theatre on Independence Avenue, from an orchestra of blind musicians, Hughes first heard the blues. The music seemed to cry, but the words somehow laughed." Where Whitman had embraced the aria of the Italian opera (horizontal music), Hughes's divining rod quivered over the bedrock of the blues (vertical music).[5] The short lines of the blues poems create a syncopated insistence and urgency. Art has to have tension. And it is the simultaneous laughter and crying that create the tension in Hughes's blues poetry.[6] Hughes writes in "Homesick Blues": "Homesick blues is / A terrible thing to have. / To keep from cryin' / I opens ma mouth an' laughs."

In "Midwinter Blues" we find the same tension:

Don't know's I'd mind his goin'
But he left me when the coal was low.
Don't know's I'd mind his goin'
But he left when the coal was low.
Now, if a man loves a woman
That ain't no time to go.

Hughes also incorporates a jagged lyricism and modulation into his poetry by using short lines — a modern feeling that depends on a vertical movement that sidesteps contemplation but invites action/motion. There is confrontation in the blues. Stephen Henderson states in *Understanding the New Black Poetry:* "In oral tradition, the dogged determination of the work songs, the tough-minded power of the blues, the inventive energy of jazz, and the transcendent vision of God in the spirituals and the sermons, all energize the idea of Freedom, of Liberation, which is itself liberated from the temporal, the societal, and the political."

Hughes seems to have set out to take poetry off the page and toss it up into the air we breathe; he desired to bring poetry into our daily lives. In essence, he wanted his blues chants to parallel the improvisation in the lives of African Americans:

> To fling my arms wide
> In the face of the sun,
> Dance! Whirl! Whirl!
> Till the quick day is done.
> Rest at pale evening . . .
> A tall, slim tree . . .
> Night coming tenderly
>   Black like me.

Hughes speaks here about daring joy to enter black life. The poem, "Dream Variations," is more than the speaker day-dreaming about bringing images of nature into Harlem (the first black metropolis of the modern world): this is celebration and revolution in the same breath. Hughes addresses the future, forging through imagery and metaphor, the possibility of a new black culture in literature, music, and the arts.

To date, Amiri Baraka is one of the first names that light on the tongue if one were to ask, Who is the rightful heir to the Langston Hughes legacy? This is mainly due to his long allegiance to jazz and the blues through essays and poetry. But some would argue that his most successful poems are informed by his Black Mountain School[7] connection (the poems in *The Dead Lecturer* are touched by a blues feeling). He says in his "Blues, Poetry, and the New Music" essay that "I begin with blues because it is the basic national voice of the African American people. It is the fundamental verse form (speech, dance, verse/song) and musical form of the African American slave going through successive transformations."[8] Undoubtedly, Baraka owes much to Hughes, as do many other voices — black and white. But some would say, What about Sherley Anne Williams? Just mentioning her name is enough to almost bring Hughes to life; her tribute to Bessie Smith underlines what Hughes was striving for in the blues idiom:

> She was looking in
> my mouth and I knowed

no matter what words
come to my mind the
song'd be her'n jes as
well as it be mine.

Sherley Anne Williams receives my vote. But one of the most recent voices associated with Hughes is Willie Perdomo. Claude Brown's blurb on the cover of Perdomo's book of verse, *Where a Nickel Costs a Dime* (the title is a Hughes line), proclaims the following: "Langston Hughes has been reincarnated and lives in Spanish Harlem." True, some of the same anger is there; true, most of Perdomo's lines are short, with a similar jagged rhythm that is often linked to the blues; true, the urban subject matter might force the reader or listener to think of Hughes's simplicity with that which is simple. Yet Hughes's poetry is rather complex because it filters through the lenses of insinuation and satire. The laughter fuses with the crying, and the synthesis is affirmation. This is what Albert Murray seems to address in *The Blue Devils of Nada* [(New York: Pantheon Books, 1996), 208–9]:

> As for the blues statement, regardless of what it reflects, what it *expresses* is a sense of life that is affirmative. The blues lyrics reflect that which they confront, of course, which includes the absurd, the unfortunate, and the catastrophic; but they also reflect the person making the confrontation, his self-control, his sense of structure and style; and they express, among other things, his sense of humor as well as his sense of ambiguity and his sense of possibility. Thus, the very existence of the blues tradition is irrefutable evidence that those who evolved it respond to the vicissitudes of the human condition not with hysterics and desperation but through the wisdom of poetry informed by pragmatic insight.

Notes

1. Cullen modeled his poetry on the verse of the nineteenth-century British poet John Keats; McKay's models were the seventeenth-century Elizabethan poets, including William Shakespeare.
2. According to Hughes's biographer, Faith Berry, Hughes's high school English teacher (at Central High in Cleveland), "introduced her class to the Chicago school of poets: Vachel Lindsay, Edgar Lee Masters, and—the poet Hughes admired most, and eventually his greatest influence in the matter of form—Carl Sandburg."
3. Modernist poets like T. S. Eliot, Wallace Stevens, and Ezra Pound broke away from poetic traditions of the nineteenth century, such as rhyme and "flowery" language, the kind of poetry Cullen and Claude McKay continued to write.
4. Imagism was a post–World War I literary movement that rebelled against nineteenth-century Romanticism and promoted the use of free verse and precise, concentrated imagery. The early poems of William Carlos Williams and the poetry of H. D. exemplify this tradition.

5. The lines of Whitman's verse are very long, giving his poetry a horizontal feel. Hughes's lines are short, so the reader's eyes move quickly down the page, giving the poetry a sense of verticalness.

6. In a review of W. C. Handy's *Blues: An Anthology* Langston Hughes says the blues grew out of "the racial hurt and the racial ecstasy," out of "trouble with incongruous overtones of laughter [and] joy with strange undertones of pain."

7. The Black Mountain School refers to an artists' colony in North Carolina with which Baraka was associated during the 1950s.

8. Hughes said much the same thing about jazz.

Onwuchekwa Jemie
Langston Hughes: An Introduction to the Poetry [1976]

Amiri Baraka (LeRoi Jones) once defined the black writer's function as follows:

> The Black Artist's role in America is to aid in the destruction of America as he knows it. His role is to report and reflect so precisely the nature of the society, and of himself in that society, that other men will be moved by the exactness of his rendering and, if they are black men, grow strong through this moving, having seen their own strength, and weakness; and if they are white men, tremble, curse, and go mad, because they will be drenched with the filth of their evil.[1]

The statement is at once descriptive and prescriptive, not unlike Aristotle's *Poetics,* which is both a description of the practice of leading Greek playwrights of his day and a recommendation or prescription to future playwrights. Except for the anticipated effect of the work of art on the audience (and such effect is always a theoretical ideal and difficult to measure), Baraka's statement accurately describes the main tradition of Afro-American writing from the slave narratives and abolitionist fiction to the novels of Wright, Himes, and Ellison, the essays of Du Bois, Baldwin, and Cleaver, and the poetry and drama of the Black Consciousness era of the 1960s and 70s. Certainly, it describes Hughes's lifelong artistic theory and practice. We have already seen, in the blues and jazz poems, how precisely Hughes reports and reflects the nature of American society and the black man's life in it. His other poems, those not modeled on black musical forms, are informed by the same vision.

Hughes's "report" includes a picture of America as a cage, a zoo, a circus, a gory monster cannibal, and a syphilitic whore, and the black man as deracinated, alienated, exiled, groping for reconnection with his African past. Africa is "time lost," surviving only in fragments and in dim racial memories felt, like the music that is its chief surrogate, in the blood and bones, in received culture not fully understood.[2] Hughes was more fortunate than most of his contemporaries in that he had actually visited the coastal areas of West Africa, a region rich in history for Afro-Americans. But the contact was brief — too brief to save his early evocations of Africa wholly from the romanticism which characterized, for instance, Countee Cullen's "Heritage" or Claude McKay's "In Bondage," "Outcast," and "Africa."

In any case, what is crucial is not so much Hughes's image of Africa as his image of America. In his early poems, Africa is for him a distant ideal, foil and backdrop for his portrait of the present reality that is America. America to him is a cold, joyless wilderness, Africa a carefree tropical paradise,[3] a land where it would be customary, for instance, to "work maybe a little today, rest a little tomorrow. Play awhile. Sing awhile. O, let's dance."[4] Uprooted from a natural environment of palms and forests and silver moons, blacks in America suffocate in a prison of skyscrapers and industrial smog.[5] And as lions, tigers, and elephants, nature's majestic creatures created to live free, are trapped and harnessed for entertainment and profit, so have the non-white peoples of the world been converted from human beings into natural resources in the Western "circus of civilization."[6] . . .

"The Negro Speaks of Rivers" is perhaps the most profound of these poems of heritage and strength. Composed when Hughes was a mere 17 years old, and dedicated to W. E. B. Du Bois, it is a sonorous evocation of transcendent essences so ancient as to appear timeless, predating human existence, longer than human memory. The rivers are part of God's body, and participate in his immortality. They are the earthly analogues of eternity: deep, continuous, mysterious. They are named in the order of their association with black history. The black man has drunk of their life-giving essences, and thereby borrowed their immortality. He and the rivers have become one. The magical transformation of the Mississippi from mud to gold by the sun's radiance is mirrored in the transformation of slaves into free men by Lincoln's Proclamation (and, in Hughes's poems, the transformation of shabby cabarets into gorgeous palaces, dancing girls into queens and priestesses by the spell of black music).

As the rivers deepen with time, so does the black man's soul; as their waters ceaselessly flow, so will the black soul endure. The black man has seen the rise and fall of civilizations from the earliest times, seen the beauty and death-changes of the world over the thousands of years, and will survive even this America. . . . In a time and place where black life is held cheap and the days of black men appear to be numbered, the poem is a majestic reminder of the strength and fullness of history, of the source of that life which transcends even ceaseless labor and burning crosses. . . .

The deferred dream was overwhelming, yet not even its great weight could crush the purely lyric impulse totally. The world of beauty and lyricism may have been distant from Hughes's daily life and the concerns of his art, as he claims in "My Adventures as a Social Poet," but, all the same, he made frequent and pleasurable excursions into that world. Especially in his early years he maintains a respectable balance between social and lyric poems. Of his first five books, only *Fine Clothes to the Jew* and *The Negro Mother* are entirely social and/or modeled on black folk forms. Lyric poetry with no immediate social or political content occupies most of *Dear Lovely Death* (1931) and roughly a half of *The Weary Blues* (1926) and of *The Dream Keeper* (1932) (although two-thirds of the latter were reprints). But after that it was three or four lyric poems per volume, except for *Fields of Wonder* (1947), which was almost entirely lyric.

The most prominent feature of Hughes's lyric verse is its brilliance of imagery. Hughes makes frequent use of poetic conceits as we find them in Shakespeare, the Metaphysical Poets, and Emily Dickinson, and of the brief and bright flashes that characterize Japanese haiku and the early 20th-century Imagists. The lyric poem is the particular vehicle of the dream as romantic fantasy and wish fulfillment ("love, roses, and moonlight"). . . .

"When Sue Wears Red" is perhaps the most powerful of Hughes's love poems:

> When Susanna Jones wears red
> Her face is like an ancient cameo
> Turned brown by the ages.
>
> Come with a blast of trumpets,
>   Jesus!
>
> When Susanna Jones wears red
> A queen from some time-dead Egyptian night
> Walks once again.
>
> Blow trumpets, Jesus!
>
> And the beauty of Susanna Jones in red
> Burns in my heart a love-fire sharp like pain.
>
> Sweet silver trumpets,
>   Jesus!

Like "The Negro Speaks of Rivers," which it rivals in brilliance, this too is an early poem, written while Hughes was in high school, a poetically mature 17. And just as that poem fuses into one timeless flow the soul-deep rivers of the black experience through the ages, so does this reincarnate in one woman the feminine beauty and majesty of the ages. The poem derives its power from its vision of eternity and from the holler and shout of religious enthusiasm ("Come with a blast of trumpets, Jesus!"). In addition, it has its literary antecedents in Dunbar's "The Colored Band" and "When Malindy Sings":[7] Malindy, whose voice in "Come to Jesus" sets sinners' hearts atremble and compels their feet Christ-ward; Malindy, whose "Swing Low, Sweet Chariot" echoes "from de valley to de hill / . . . Th'oo de bresh of angels' wings, / Sof' an' sweet." In both poets the vision is of transfiguration through art/magic: through Sue's red dress, a type of magic mantle, which resurrects in her the queens of other ages; through the Colored Band's syncopated rhythms in response to which "de hea't goes into bus'ness fu' to he'p erlong de eah"; and through the mesmeric power of Malindy's downhome voice.

Notes

1. LeRoi Jones (Amiri Baraka), "State/Meant," *Home: Social Essays* (New York: Apollo, 1966), 251.
2. "Afro-American Fragment," *Dear Lovely Death,* n.p.
3. See "Dream Variation" and "Our Land," *Weary Blues,* 43, 99.
4. "The Negro Artist and the Racial Mountain."
5. "Afraid," "Poem: For the Portrait of an African Boy," *Weary Blues,* 101, 102.
6. "Lament for Dark Peoples," ibid., 100.
8. Dunbar, *Complete Poems,* 82, 178.

APPROACHING THE READINGS

1. The intensity of much effective writing comes from tensions within a work. Choose any work in this chapter, pick out artistic and thematic tensions in it, and discuss how they contribute to its intensity and effectiveness.

2. Yusef Komunyakaa points out the way the mixture of heartache and hope in the blues influenced Hughes's work. Consider the extent to which various works with the "dream deferred" theme can be illuminated by viewing them in terms of a tension between heartache and hope.

3. According to Onwuchekwa Jemie, a prominent feature of Hughes's poetry is "its brilliance of imagery" (p. 1281). Consider the relevance of that statement to such lyric poems as "When Sue Wears Red" (p. 1281) and "The Weary Blues" (p. 1266), and to more political poems such as "Dream Variations" (p. 1257), "The Negro Speaks of Rivers" (p. 1267), "Good Morning" (p. 1256), and "Freedom's Plow" (p. 1258).

4. Philip Kolin and Maureen Curley say in their article that *Soul Gone Home* "powerfully expresses Hughes's repeated theme about racial identity in a world dominated by whites" (p. 1274). Trace that theme in other works included in this chapter.

5. Yusef Komunyakaa asserts that "from the outset an American-ness had been at the center of Hughes's work, which is one of the reasons he has endured" (p. 1276), and Amiri Baraka is quoted by Onwuchekwa Jemie as saying that "the Black Artist's role in America is to aid in the destruction of

America as he knows it" (p. 1279). Consider ways the two statements coincide and ways they differ, and ways both are illustrated in the story, various poems, and the play included in this chapter.

RESPONDING THROUGH WRITING

Journal Entries

1. In "Jazz as Communication" Hughes says, "jazz is a montage of a dream deferred" (p. 1265). Write a journal entry explaining what the line means and how it contributes to Hughes's exploration of the dream deferred theme.

Research Langston Hughes in depth with cultural documents and multimedia resources on *LiterActive.*

2. Write a journal entry discussing the picture, or views, of America that emerge from Hughes's story "One Friday Morning" (p. 1249).

3. Select one poem by Hughes from this chapter. Focus on the imagery in it. In your journal, list examples of particularly striking or powerful images and discuss how they help make the poem "work" effectively.

Literary Analysis Papers

4. Write a thematic paper on dreams deferred and on their effect in Hughes's poems and stories.

5. Write an analytic paper on irony as an important recurring technique in Hughes's works.

6. Write a paper analyzing the use and effect of sound techniques (alliteration, assonance, consonance, repetition, catalogs, rhythm) in "Freedom's Plow" (p. 1258).

Making Connections

7. Read the excerpts from Walt Whitman's *Song of Myself* (p. 748) and write an analytic/research paper on parallels between it and Hughes's "Freedom's Plow" (p. 1258) or on the influence of Whitman on Hughes's work.

8. Write a research paper on the influence of the blues and jazz on the poetic style of Langston Hughes.

Cultural Criticism Papers

9. Write a research paper on the Harlem Renaissance and the place and importance of Hughes in it.

10. Find collections of visual art works done during the Harlem Renaissance, or about it, and write a paper that compares their vision to that of Hughes.

RESPONDING THROUGH THE ARTS

1. Create a CD "soundtrack" for Hughes's works using blues and jazz works from both his time and later. Write liner notes for it explaining your choices and what works you associate with each piece.

2. Choreograph a dance piece for "Freedom's Plow" (p. 1258) or for two or three of Hughes's shorter poems.

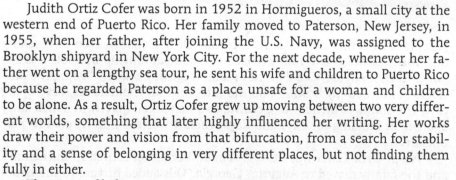

M̲ost of the stories in my work date back to the times when I would sit around at my grandmother's house and listen to the women telling their stories.

Judith Ortiz Cofer

Judith Ortiz Cofer: Thinking Back Through Her Mothers

Judith Ortiz Cofer was born in 1952 in Hormigueros, a small city at the western end of Puerto Rico. Her family moved to Paterson, New Jersey, in 1955, when her father, after joining the U.S. Navy, was assigned to the Brooklyn shipyard in New York City. For the next decade, whenever her father went on a lengthy sea tour, he sent his wife and children to Puerto Rico because he regarded Paterson as a place unsafe for a woman and children to be alone. As a result, Ortiz Cofer grew up moving between two very different worlds, something that later highly influenced her writing. Her works draw their power and vision from that bifurcation, from a search for stability and a sense of belonging in very different places, but not finding them fully in either.

The sense of bifurcation was accentuated by the differences between her father and mother. Her father, quiet and intellectual, sought always to escape Puerto Rico and the limitations he felt it imposed on him. He joined the navy, moved to New Jersey, made it a goal to move outside the barrio, the Puerto Rican neighborhood, and made sure his children mastered English and received good educations. His wife, on the other hand, loved Puerto Rico and longed for it whenever she was on the mainland. She never learned English because she thought of her life in New Jersey as an "exile" and a temporary stay. She made every attempt to surround herself with a Puerto Rican environment: She bought groceries at Puerto Rican shops, served only Puerto Rican foods, listened to Puerto Rican music.

Ortiz Cofer and her brother tried to deal with a new language and culture on the mainland, but at the same time, they were torn between their

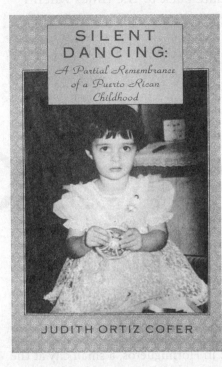

SILENT
DANCING:
*A Partial Remembrance
of a Puerto Rican
Childhood*

JUDITH ORTIZ COFER

*Judith Ortiz Cofer's well-received collection
of essays and poems,* Silent Dancing, *was
published in 1990 with an image of Ortiz
Cofer as a young girl on the cover.*

Reprinted with permission from the publisher of
*Silent Dancing: A Partial Remembrance of a Puerto
Rican Childhood* (Houston: Arte Público Press–
University of Houston, 1990).

parents' conflicting outlooks. As a result, Ortiz Cofer, instead of reaching out, turned inward and found solace and companionship in books. As she put it in the chapter "Casa" in her memoir *Silent Dancing,* "Being the outsiders . . . turned my brother and me into cultural chameleons, developing early the ability to blend into a crowd, to sit and read quietly in a fifth story apartment building for days and days when it was too bitterly cold to play outside."

When Ortiz Cofer was in high school, her father retired from the navy and the family moved to Augusta, Georgia. This added further to the issues that result from having a diverse cultural background. The South was so overwhelmingly different from New Jersey that in *The Latin Deli* Ortiz Cofer compares it to "moving from one planet to another." She was the only Puerto Rican in a high school of almost two thousand students. Her academic life was very successful, but her social life was all but nonexistent. Upon graduation, she received a scholarship from Augusta College, from which she graduated in 1971.

Soon after graduation, she married and had a daughter. She then completed a graduate degree and began teaching English. But, she says, something was missing from her life: She realized that she needed to write. The problem was finding time; so she began getting up at 5:00 to give herself two hours for writing, a ritual she refined and continues today as she describes in *The Latin Deli*: "I get up at five and put on a pot of coffee. Then I sit in my rocking chair and read what I did the previous day until the coffee is ready. I take fifteen minutes to drink two cups of coffee . . . [and] when I'm ready, I write." This decision, she goes on, "to get up early and to work every day, forced me to come to terms with the discipline of art. I wrote my poems in this manner for nearly ten years before my first book was published. When I decided to give my storytelling impulse full rein and write a novel, I divided my two hours: the first hour for poetry, the second for fiction: two pages minimum per day."

Her first book of poetry, *Reaching for the Mainland,* was published in 1987, followed by *Terms of Survival* in 1989. *The Latin Deli: Prose and Poetry* (1993) received the Anisfield Wolf Book Award, and *The Year of Our Revolution: New and Selected Stories and Poems* (1998) received the Paterson Book Prize given by the Poetry Center at Passaic County Community College. In addition to poetry and stories, she has published a novel, *The Line of the Sun* (1989); a memoir, *Silent Dancing: A Partial Remembrance of a Puerto Rican Childhood* (1990); and a book about writing, *Woman in Front of the Sun: On Becoming a Writer* (2000). Her most recent book is a novel, *The Meaning of Consuelo* (2003). Her young adult book *An Island Like You: Stories of the Barrio* (1996) was awarded The American Library Association Reforma Pura Belpre Medal and the Fanfare Best Book of the Year award. She is the Franklin Professor of English and Creative Writing at the University of Georgia, and lives with her husband on the family farm near Louisville, Georgia.

As that paragraph indicates, Ortiz Cofer writes successfully in a wide variety of genres, even combining them in the same collection. She started with and remains centered in poetry ("Poetry is my obsession"), and has moved from it to short stories, adolescent fiction, a novel, creative nonfiction, and memoir. She looks on the different genres as closely related, in craft as well as themes and imagery: "Poetry fine tunes my writing. When I go from working on my poetry to working on a novel, the demands of language are already established." In her prose, she seeks the same economy, concentration, and intensity of style that she seeks in her poetry. For Ortiz Cofer, prose and poetry are less different than they are for many writers. She works in each genre not because she feels they are all that distinctive in effect but to explore each form and to challenge her writing by the demands of each. To achieve a deeper understanding and appreciation of Ortiz Cofer as a writer, one needs to read her work in all the genres she writes in, and to read widely, not just a single poem or story.

That is one purpose of this chapter. We include in it and in earlier chapters examples from several different genres. Before going on to the rest of the material in this chapter, reread Ortiz Cofer's story "Not for Sale" in Chapter 6 (p. 134) and her poem "Cold as Heaven" in Chapter 13 (p. 558). The rest of this chapter contains several more of her poems; another story, "Abuela Invents the Zero," from *An Island Like You;* a chapter from *Silent Dancing;* an essay, "And Are You a Latina Writer?" written in the form of an

A recent portrait of Judith Ortiz Cofer.
Reprinted by permission of UGA Photographic
Services.

interview; and an actual interview, "Speaking in Puerto Rican," on being a writer and an ethnic writer. As you read them, be alert for the literary elements that are covered in the earlier sections of this book on fiction and poetry. Think critically as you read the various works to notice the influence of poetry on her prose and to see how her exploration of genres has a variety of effects. Think about the result if she had written a prose piece as poetry and a poem as a work of prose.

The chapter concludes with excerpts from three critical essays intended to help you understand and engage more fully with some of the complexity of Ortiz Cofer's themes and approaches. In "And Are You a Latina Writer?" Ortiz Cofer says that when she began writing her mission was to use her art to build bridges between the two cultures in which she grew up. To Ortiz Cofer, being a Puerto Rican American writer means "to claim my heritage." The essays reprinted here illuminate different ways of both building bridges and claiming a heritage. Teresa Derrickson's essay focuses on the effect on Puerto Rican Americans of the lack of a concrete, physical border between their previous home and their new home. Viviana Rangil examines the effect of Ortiz Cofer's mixing of languages — writing in English but blending in Spanish words and phrases. And Juan Bruce-Novoa looks closely at some specific poems in which Ortiz Cofer creates a sense of place and identity through her work as a writer. Before you read the pieces about Ortiz Cofer, however, get to know the works by her well — read them at least once, preferably twice. Discussions of an author can enable you to notice things you didn't see before and to gain a fuller, deeper understanding of what you read. But it's important that you formulate insights and interpretations through your own reading of the works first, so your thinking won't be unduly influenced by what others think about them. For examples of how such essays can be applied to the works by Ortiz Cofer, refer to "Approaching the Readings" at the end of this chapter (p. 1316).

Like most writers, particular themes, techniques, and images appear repeatedly in Ortiz Cofer's work. One of the rewards of reading a writer in depth, especially one who is comfortable working in multiple genres, is to trace such recurring motifs and make connections between works and between genres. As you read this chapter, watch for such repeated elements. Notice, for example, the way the importance of place and its accompanying images is a continuing motif in many of Ortiz Cofer's works. We seek to identify people, perhaps categorize them, by asking "Where are you from?" That is a complicated question for Ortiz Cofer. How should she answer: Puerto Rico? New Jersey? Georgia? Works such as "The Birthplace," "The Latin Deli," "Abuela Invents the Zero," "Not for Sale," and "Silent Dancing" explore her sense of having two homes — the island of Puerto Rico and the mainland United States — and yet being an outsider in both.

Another such recurring theme is the importance of story. In "Speaking in Puerto Rican," Ortiz Cofer says, "Most of the stories in my work date back to the times when I would sit around at my grandmother's house and listen to the women telling their stories" (p. 1307). In that light, consider the way story is emphasized and treated in "Not for Sale," "The Changeling," "Silent Dancing," and "And Are You a Latina Writer?" Still another theme is the importance of mother and grandmother in Ortiz Cofer's life as evidenced in such works as "And Are You a Latina Writer?" and "Speaking in Puerto Rican." These are only a few examples of the kinds of themes that recur throughout Ortiz Cofer's work and of the type of work that you can do when you read and explore one writer in depth. Tracing the evolution of theme or style or a series of images through Ortiz Cofer's poems, stories, and memoirs would make a good topic for a research paper, the subject of Chapter 26.

Research Judith Ortiz Cofer with LitLinks at bedfordstmartins.com/approachinglit.

The Birthplace [1987]

There is no danger now
that these featureless hills
will hold me.
That church
sitting on the highest one   5
like a great hen

spreading her marble wings
over the penitent houses
does not beckon to me.
This dusty road under my feet   10
is like any other road
I have traveled,
it leads only
to other roads.
Towns everywhere are the same   15
when shadows thicken.
Yet, each window
casting a square of light,
that grassy plain under a weighted sky
turning to plum,   20
tell me
that as surely as my dreams are mine,
I must be home.

On the Island I Have Seen   [1987]

Men cutting cane under a sun relentless
as an overseer with a quota,
measuring their days
with each swing of their machetes,
mixing their sweat with the sugar   5
destined to sweeten half a continent's coffee.

Old men playing dominoes in the plazas
cooled by the flutter of palms,
divining from the ivory pieces
that clack like their bones, the future   10
of the children who pass by on their way to school,
ducklings following the bobbing beak
of the starched nun who leads them in silence.

Women in black dresses keeping all the holy days,
asking the priest in dark confessionals   15
what to do about the anger in their sons' eyes.
Sometimes their prayers are answered
and the young men take their places
atop the stacked wedding cakes.
The ones who are lost to God and mothers   20
may take to the fields, the dry fields,
where a man learns the danger of words,
where even a curse can start a fire.

The Latin Deli: An Ars Poetica   [1993]

Presiding over a formica counter,
plastic Mother and Child magnetized
to the top of an ancient register,
the heady mix of smells from the open bins
of dried codfish, the green plantains   5
hanging in stalks like votive offerings,
she is the Patroness of Exiles,
a woman of no-age who was never pretty,
who spends her days selling canned memories
while listening to Puerto Ricans complain   10
that it would be cheaper to fly to San Juan
than to buy a pound of Bustelo coffee here,
and to Cubans perfecting their speech
of a "glorious return" to Havana — where no one
has been allowed to die and nothing to change until then;   15
to Mexicans who pass through, talking lyrically
of *dólares* to be made in El Norte —
                        all wanting the comfort
of spoken Spanish, to gaze upon the family portrait
of her plain wide face, her ample bosom   20
resting on her plump arms, her look of maternal interest
as they speak to her and each other
of their dreams and their disillusions —
how she smiles understanding,
when they walk down the narrow aisles of her store   25
reading the labels of packages aloud, as if
they were the names of lost lovers: *Suspiros,*
Merengues, the stale candy of everyone's childhood.

                        She spends her days
slicing *jamón y queso*° and wrapping it in wax paper   30
tied with string: plain ham and cheese
that would cost less at the A&P, but it would not satisfy
the hunger of the fragile old man lost in the folds
of his winter coat, who brings her lists of items
that he reads to her like poetry, or the others,   35
whose needs she must divine, conjuring up products
from places that now exist only in their hearts —
closed ports she must trade with.

---

30. *jamón y queso*: Ham and cheese.

The Changeling   [1993]

As a young girl
vying for my father's attention,
I invented a game that made him look up
from his reading and shake his head
as if both baffled and amused.   5

In my brother's closet, I'd change
into his dungarees — the rough material
molding me into boy shape; hide
my long hair under an army helmet
he'd been given by Father, and emerge   10
transformed into the legendary Che
of grown-up talk.

Strutting around the room,
I'd tell of life in the mountains,
of carnage and rivers of blood,   15
and of manly feasts with rum and music
to celebrate victories *para la libertad.*°   *for freedom*
He would listen with a smile
to my tales of battles and brotherhood
until Mother called us to dinner.   20

She was not amused
by my transformations, sternly forbidding me
from sitting down with them as a man.
She'd order me back to the dark cubicle
that smelled of adventure, to shed   25
my costume, to braid my hair furiously
with blind hands, and to return invisible,
as myself,
to the real world of her kitchen.

Abuela Invents the Zero   [1995]

"You made me feel like a zero, like a nothing," she says in Spanish, *un cero, nada.* She is trembling, an angry little old woman lost in a heavy winter coat that belongs to my mother. And I end up being sent to my room, like I was a child, to think about my grandmother's idea of math.

It all began with Abuela coming up from the Island for a visit — her first time in the United States. My mother and father paid her way here so that she wouldn't die without seeing snow, though if you asked me, and nobody has, the dirty slush in this city is not worth the price of a ticket. But I guess she deserves some kind of award for having had ten kids and survived to tell about it. My mother is the youngest of the bunch. Right up to the time when we're supposed to pick up the old lady at the airport, my mother is telling me stories about how hard times were for la familia on la isla, and how *la abuela* worked night and day to support them after their father died of a heart attack. I'd die of a heart attack too if I had a troop like that to support. Anyway, I had seen her only three or four times in my entire life, whenever we would go for somebody's funeral. I was born here and I have lived in this building all my life. But when Mami says, "Connie, please be nice to Abuela. She doesn't have too many years left. Do you promise me, Constancia?" — when she uses my full name, I know she means business. So I say, "Sure." Why wouldn't I be nice? I'm not a monster, after all.

So we go to Kennedy to get la abuela and she is the last to come out of the airplane, on the arm of the cabin attendant, all wrapped up in a black shawl. He hands her over to my parents like she was a package sent airmail. It is January, two feet of snow on the ground, and she's wearing a shawl over a thin black dress. That's just the start.

Once home, she refuses to let my mother buy her a coat because it's a waste of money for the two weeks she'll be in *el Polo Norte,* as she calls New Jersey, the North Pole. So since she's only four feet eleven inches tall, she walks around in my mother's big black coat looking ridiculous. I try to walk far behind them in public so that no one will think we're together. I plan to stay very busy the whole time she's with us so that I won't be asked to take her anywhere, but my plan is ruined when my mother comes down with the flu and Abuela absolutely *has* to attend Sunday mass or her soul will be eternally damned. She's more Catholic than the Pope. My father decides that he should stay home with my mother and that I should escort la abuela to church. He tells me this on Saturday night as I'm getting ready to go out to the mall with my friends.

"No way," I say.

I go for the car keys on the kitchen table: he usually leaves them there for me on Friday and Saturday nights. He beats me to them.

"No way," he says, pocketing them and grinning at me.

Needless to say, we come to a compromise very quickly. I do have a responsibility to Sandra and Anita, who don't drive yet. There is a Harley-Davidson fashion show at Brookline Square that we *cannot* miss.

"The mass in Spanish is at ten sharp tomorrow morning, entiendes?" My father is dangling the car keys in front of my nose and pulling them back when I try to reach for them. He's really enjoying himself.

"I understand. Ten o'clock. I'm out of here." I pry his fingers off the key ring. He knows that I'm late, so he makes it just a little difficult. Then he laughs. I run out of our apartment before he changes his mind. I have no idea what I'm getting myself into.

Sunday morning I have to walk two blocks on dirty snow to retrieve the car. I warm it up for Abuela as instructed by my parents, and drive it to the front of our building. My father walks her by the hand in baby steps on the slippery snow. The sight of her little head with a bun on top of it sticking out of that huge coat makes me want to run back into my room and get under the covers. I just hope that nobody I know sees us together. I'm dreaming, of course. The mass is packed with people from our block. It's a holy day of obligation and everyone I ever met is there.

I have to help her climb the steps, and she stops to take a deep breath after each one, then I lead her down the aisle so that everybody can see me with my bizarre grandmother. If I were a good Catholic, I'm sure I'd get some purgatory time taken off for my sacrifice. She is walking as slow as Captain Cousteau exploring the bottom of the sea, looking around, taking her sweet time. Finally she chooses a pew, but she wants to sit in the *other* end. It's like she had a spot picked out for some unknown reason, and although it's the most inconvenient seat in the house, that's where she has to sit. So we squeeze by all the people already sitting there, saying, "Excuse me, please, *con permiso,* pardon me," getting annoyed looks the whole way. By the time we settle in, I'm drenched in sweat. I keep my head down like I'm praying so as not to see or be seen. She is praying loud, in Spanish, and singing hymns at the top of her creaky voice.

I ignore her when she gets up with a hundred other people to go take communion. I'm actually praying hard now—that this will all be over soon. But the next time I look up, I see a black coat dragging around and around the church, stopping here and there so a little gray head can peek out like a periscope on a submarine. There are giggles in the church, and even the priest has frozen in the middle of a blessing, his hands above his head like he is about to lead the congregation in a set of jumping jacks.

I realize to my horror that my grandmother is lost. She can't find her way back to the pew. I am so embarrassed that even though the woman next to me is shooting daggers at me with her eyes, I just can't move to go get her. I put my hands over my face like I'm praying, but it's really to hide my burning cheeks. I would like for her to disappear. I just know that on Monday my friends, and my enemies, in the barrio will have a lot of senile-grandmother jokes to tell in front of me. I am frozen to my seat. So the same woman who wants me dead on the spot does it for me. She makes a big deal out of getting up and hurrying to get Abuela.

The rest of the mass is a blur. All I know is that my grandmother kneels the whole time with her hands over *her* face. She doesn't speak to me on the way home, and she doesn't let me help her walk, even though she almost falls a couple of times.

When we get to the apartment, my parents are at the kitchen table, where my mother is trying to eat some soup. They can see right away that something is wrong. Then Abuela points her finger at me like a judge passing a sentence on a criminal. She says in Spanish, "You made me feel like a zero, like a nothing." Then she goes to her room.

I try to explain what happened. "I don't understand why she's so upset. She just got lost and wandered around for a while," I tell them. But it sounds lame, even to my own ears. My mother gives me a look that makes me cringe and goes in to Abuela's room to get her version of the story. She comes out with tears in her eyes.

"Your grandmother says to tell you that of all the hurtful things you can do to a person, the worst is to make them feel as if they are worth nothing."

I can feel myself shrinking right there in front of her. But I can't bring myself to tell my mother that I think I understand how I made Abuela feel. I might be sent into the old lady's room to apologize, and it's not easy to admit you've been a jerk — at least, not right away with everybody watching. So I just sit there not saying anything.

My mother looks at me for a long time, like she feels sorry for me. Then she says, "You should know, Constancia, that if it wasn't for this old woman whose existence you don't seem to value, you and I would not be here."

That's when *I'm* sent to *my* room to consider a number I hadn't thought much about — until today.

Silent Dancing   [1990]

We have a home movie of this party. Several times my mother and I have watched it together, and I have asked questions about the silent revellers coming in and out of focus. It is grainy and of short duration but a great visual aid to my first memory of life in Paterson at that time. And it is in color — the only complete scene in color I can recall from those years.

We lived in Puerto Rico until my brother was born in 1954. Soon after, because of economic pressures on our growing family, my father joined the United States Navy. He was assigned to duty on a ship in Brooklyn Yard, New York City — a place of cement and steel that was to be his home base in the States until his retirement more than twenty years later.

He left the Island first, tracking down his uncle who lived with his family across the Hudson River, in Paterson, New Jersey. There he found a tiny apartment in a huge apartment building that had once housed Jewish families and was just being transformed into a tenement by Puerto Ricans overflowing from New York City. In 1955 he sent for us. My mother was only twenty years old, I was not quite three, and my brother was a toddler when we arrived at *El Building,* as the place had been christened by its new residents.

My memories of life in Paterson during those first few years are in shades of gray. Maybe I was too young to absorb vivid colors and details, or to discriminate between the slate blue of the winter sky and the darker hues of the snow-bearing clouds, but the single color washes over the whole period. The building we lived in was gray, the streets were gray with slush the first few months of my life there, the coat my father had bought for me was dark in color and too big. It sat heavily on my thin frame.

I do remember the way the heater pipes banged and rattled, startling all of us out of sleep until we got so used to the sound that we automatically either shut it out or raised our voices above the racket. The hiss from the valve punctuated my sleep, which has always been fitful, like a nonhuman presence in the room — the dragon sleeping at the entrance of my childhood. But the pipes were a connection to all the other lives being lived around us. Having come from a house made for a single family back in Puerto Rico — my mother's extended-family home — it was curious to know that strangers lived under our floor and above our heads, and that the heater pipe went through everyone's apartments. (My first spanking in Paterson came as a result of playing tunes on the pipes in my room to see if there would be an answer.) My mother was as new to this concept of beehive life as I was, but had been given strict orders by my father to keep the doors locked, the noise down, ourselves to ourselves.

It seems that Father had learned some painful lessons about prejudice while searching for an apartment in Paterson. Not until years later did I hear how much resistance he had encountered with landlords who were panicking at the influx of Latinos into a neighborhood that had been Jewish for a couple of generations. But it was the American phenomenon of ethnic turnover that was changing the urban core of Paterson, and the human flood could not be held back with an accusing finger.

"You Cuban?" the man had asked my father, pointing a finger at his name tag on the Navy uniform — even though my father had the fair skin and light brown hair of his northern Spanish family background and our name is as common in Puerto Rico as Johnson is in the U.S.

"No," my father had answered looking past the finger into his adversary's angry eyes "I'm Puerto Rican."

"Same shit." And the door closed. My father could have passed as European, but we couldn't. My brother and I both have our mother's black hair and olive skin, and so we lived in El Building and visited our great-uncle and his fair children on the next block. It was their private joke that they were the German branch of the family. Not many years later that area too would be mainly Puerto Rican. It was as if the heart of the city map were being gradually colored in brown — *café-con-leche* brown. Our color.

The movie opens with a sweep of the living room. It is "typical" immigrant Puerto Rican decor for the time: the sofa and chairs are square and hard-looking, upholstered in bright colors (blue and yellow in this instance, and covered in the transparent plastic) that furniture salesmen then were adept at making women buy. The linoleum on the floor is light blue, and if it was subjected to the spike heels as it was in most places, there were dime-sized indentations all over it that cannot be seen in this movie. The room is full of people dressed in mainly two colors: dark suits for the men, red dresses for the women. I have asked my mother why most of the women are in red that night, and she shrugs, "I don't remember. Just a coincidence." She doesn't have my obsession for assigning symbolism to everything.

The three women in red sitting on the couch are my mother, my eighteen-year-old cousin, and her brother's girlfriend. The "novia" is just up from the

Island, which is apparent in her body language. She sits up formally, and her dress is carefully pulled over her knees. She is a pretty girl but her posture makes her look insecure, lost in her full skirted red dress which she has carefully tucked around her to make room for my gorgeous cousin, her future sister-in-law. My cousin has grown up in Paterson and is in her last year of high school. She doesn't have a trace of what Puerto Ricans call "la mancha" (literally, the stain: the mark of the new immigrant — something about the posture, the voice, or the humble demeanor making it obvious to everyone that that person has just arrived on the mainland; has not yet acquired the polished look of the city dweller). My cousin is wearing a tight red-sequined cocktail dress. Her brown hair has been lightened with peroxide around the bangs, and she is holding a cig-arette very expertly between her fingers, bringing it up to her mouth in a sensu-ous arc of her arm to her as she talks animatedly with my mother, who has come to sit between the two women, both only a few years younger than herself. My mother is somewhere halfway between the poles they represent in our culture.

It became my father's obsession to get out of the barrio, and thus we were never permitted to form bonds with the place or with the people who lived there. Yet the building was a comfort to my mother, who never got over yearning for *la isla*. She felt surrounded by her language: the walls were thin, and voices speaking and arguing in Spanish could be heard all day. *Salsas* blasted out of radios turned on early in the morning and left on for com-pany. Women seemed to cook rice and beans perpetually — the strong aroma of red kidney beans boiling permeated the hallways.

Though Father preferred that we do our grocery shopping at the super-market when he came home on weekend leaves, my mother insisted that she could cook only with products whose labels she could read, and so, during the week, I accompanied her and my little brother to *La Bodega* — a hole-in-the-wall grocery store across the street from El Building. There we squeezed down three narrow aisles jammed with various products. Goya and Libby's — those were the trademarks trusted by her Mamá, and so my mother bought cans of Goya beans, soups and condiments. She bought little cans of Libby's fruit juices for us. And she bought Colgate toothpaste and Palmolive soap. (The final *e* is pronounced in both those products in Spanish, and for many years I believed that they were manufactured on the Island. I remember my surprise at first hearing a commercial on television for the toothpaste in which Colgate rhymed with "ate.")

We would linger at La Bodega, for it was there that mother breathed best, taking in the familiar aromas of the foods she knew from Mamá's kitchen, and it was also there that she got to speak to the other women of El Building without violating outright Father's dictates against fraternizing with our neighbors.

But he did his best to make our "assimilation" painless. I can still see him carrying a Christmas tree up several flights of stairs to our apartment, leaving a trail of aromatic pine. He carried it formally, as if it were a flag in a parade. We were the only ones in El Building that I knew of who got presents on both Christmas Day and on *Día de Reyes*, the day when the Three Kings brought gifts to Christ and to Hispanic children.

Our greatest luxury in El Building was having our own television set. It must have been a result of Father's guilt feelings over the isolation he had imposed on us, but we were one of the first families in the barrio to have one. My brother quickly became an avid watcher of Captain Kangaroo and Jungle Jim. I loved all the family series, and by the time I started first grade in school, I could have drawn a map of Middle America as exemplified by the lives of characters in "Father Knows Best," "The Donna Reed Show," "Leave It to Beaver," "My Three Sons," and (my favorite) "Bachelor Father," where John Forsythe treated his adopted teenage daughter like a princess because he was rich and had a Chinese houseboy to do everything for him. Compared to our neighbors in El Building, we were rich. My father's Navy check provided us with financial security and a standard of life that the factory workers envied. The only thing his money could not buy us was a place to live away from the barrio — his greatest wish and Mother's greatest fear.

In the home movie the men are shown next, sitting around a card table set up in one corner of the living room, playing dominoes. The clack of the ivory pieces is a familiar sound. I heard it in many houses on the Island and in many apartments in Paterson. In "Leave It To Beaver," the Cleavers played bridge in every other episode; in my childhood, the men started every social occasion with a hotly debated round of dominoes: the women would sit around and watch, but they never participated in the games.

Here and there you can see a small child. Children were always brought to parties and, whenever they got sleepy, put to bed in the host's bedrooms. Babysitting was a concept unrecognized by the Puerto Rican women I knew: a responsible mother did not leave her children with any stranger. And in a culture where children are not considered intrusive, there is no need to leave the children at home. We went where our mother went.

Of my pre-school years I have only impressions: the sharp bite of the wind in December as we walked with our parents towards the brightly lit stores downtown, how I felt like a stuffed doll in my heavy coat, boots and mittens; how good it was to walk into the five-and-dime and sit at the counter drinking hot chocolate.

On Saturdays our whole family would walk downtown to shop at the big department stores on Broadway. Mother bought all our clothes at Penny's and Sears, and she liked to buy her dresses at the women's specialty shops like Lerner's and Diana's. At some point we would go into Woolworth's and sit at the soda fountain to eat.

We never ran into other Latinos at these stores or eating out, and it became clear to me only years later that the women from El Building shopped mainly at other places — stores owned either by other Puerto Ricans, or by Jewish merchants who had philosophically accepted our presence in the city and decided to make us their good customers, if not neighbors and friends. These establishments were located not downtown, but in the blocks around our street, and they were referred to generically as *La Tienda, El Bazar, La Bodega, La Botánica*. Everyone knew what was meant. These were the stores where your face did not turn a clerk to stone, where your money was as green as anyone else's.

On New Year's Eve we were dressed up like child models in the Sears catalogue — my brother in a miniature man's suit and bow tie, and I in black patent leather shoes and a frilly dress with several layers of crinolines underneath. My mother wore a bright red dress that night, I remember, and spike heels; her long black hair hung to her waist. Father, who usually wore his Navy uniform during his short visits home, had put on a dark civilian suit for the occasion: we had been invited to his uncle's house for a big celebration. Everyone was excited because my mother's brother, Hernán — a bachelor who could indulge himself in such luxuries — had bought a movie camera which he would be trying out that night.

Even the home movie cannot fill in the sensory details such a gathering left imprinted in a child's brain. The thick sweetness of women's perfume mixing with the ever-present smells of food cooking in the kitchen: meat and plantain *pasteles*, the ubiquitous rice dish made special with pigeon peas — *gandules* — and seasoned with the precious *sofrito* sent up from the island by somebody's mother or smuggled in by a recent traveler. *Sofrito* was one of the items that women hoarded, since it was hardly ever in stock at La Bodega. It was the flavor of Puerto Rico.

The men drank Palo Viejo rum and some of the younger ones got weepy. The first time I saw a grown man cry was at a New Year's Eve party. He had been reminded of his mother by the smells in the kitchen. But what I remember most were the boiled *pasteles* — the plantain or yucca rectangles stuffed with corned beef or other meats, olives, and many other savory ingredients, all wrapped in banana leaves. Everyone had to fish one out with a fork. There was always a "trick" pastel — one without stuffing — and whoever got that one was the "New Year's Fool."

There was also the music. Long-playing albums were treated like precious china in these homes. Mexican recordings were popular, but the songs that brought tears to my mother's eyes were sung by the melancholic Daniel Santos, whose life as a drug addict was the stuff of legend. Felipe Rodríguez was a particular favorite of couples. He sang about faithless women and broken-hearted men. There is a snatch of a lyric that has stuck in my mind like a needle on a worn groove: "De piedra ha de ser mi cama, de piedra la cabecera . . . la mujer que a mi me quiera . . . ha de quererme de veras. Ay, Ay, corazón, ¿por qué no amas . . . ?" I must have heard it a thousand times since the idea of a bed made of stone, and its connection to love, first troubled me with its disturbing images.

The five-minute home movie ends with people dancing in a circle. The creative filmmaker must have asked them to do that so that they could file past him. It is both comical and sad to watch silent dancing. Since there is no justification for the absurd movements that music provides for some of us, people appear frantic, their faces embarrassingly intense. It's as if you were watching sex. Yet for years, I've had dreams in the form of this home movie. In a recurring scene, familiar faces push themselves forward into my mind's eye, plastering their features into distorted close-ups. And I'm asking them: "Who is she? Who is the woman I don't recognize? Is she an aunt? Somebody's wife? Tell me who she is. Tell me who these people are."

"No, see the beauty mark on her cheek as big as a hill on the lunar land-scape of her face — well, that runs in the family. The women on your father's side of the family wrinkle early; it's the price they pay for that fair skin. The young girl with the green stain on her wedding dress is *La Novia* — just up from the island. See, she lowers her eyes as she approaches the camera like she's supposed to. Decent girls never look you directly in the face. *Humilde,* humble, a girl should express humility in all her actions. She will make a good wife for your cousin. He should consider himself lucky to have met her only weeks after she arrived here. If he marries her quickly, she will make him a good Puerto Rican-style wife; but if he waits too long, she will be cor-rupted by the city, just like your cousin there."

"She means me. I do what I want. This is not some primitive island I live on. Do they expect me to wear a black *mantilla* on my head and go to mass every day? Not me. I'm an American woman and I will do as I please. I can type faster than anyone in my senior class at Central High, and I'm going to be a secretary to a lawyer when I graduate. I can pass for an American girl anywhere — I've tried it — at least for Italian, anyway. I never speak Spanish in public. I hate these parties, but I wanted the dress. I look better than any of these *humildes* here. My life is going to be different. I have an American boyfriend. He is older and has a car. My parents don't know it, but I sneak out of the house late at night sometimes to be with him. If I marry him, even my name will be American. I hate rice and beans. It's what makes these women fat."

"Your *prima* is pregnant by that man she's been sneaking around with. Would I lie to you? I'm your great-uncle's common-law wife — the one he abandoned on the island to marry your cousin's mother. I was not invited to this party, but I came anyway. I came to tell you that story about your cousin that you've always wanted to hear. Remember that comment your mother made to a neighbor that has always haunted you? The only thing you heard was your cousin's name and then you saw your mother pick up your doll from the couch and say: 'It was as big as this doll when they flushed it down the toilet.' This image has bothered you for years, hasn't it? You had night-mares about babies being flushed down the toilet, and you wondered why anyone would do such a horrible thing. You didn't dare ask your mother about it. She would only tell you that you had not heard her right and yell at you for listening to adult conversations. But later, when you were old enough to know about abortions, you suspected. I am here to tell you that you were right. Your cousin was growing an *Americanito* in her belly when this movie was made. Soon after she put something long and pointy into her pretty self, thinking maybe she could get rid of the problem before breakfast and still make it to her first class at the high school. Well, *Niña,* her screams could be heard downtown. Your aunt, her Mamá, who had been a midwife on the Island, managed to pull the little thing out. Yes, they probably flushed it down the toilet, what else could they do with it—give it a Christian burial in a little white casket with blue bows and ribbons? Nobody wanted that baby—least of all the father, a teacher at her school with a house in West Paterson that he was filling with real children, and a wife who was a natural blond.

"Girl, the scandal sent your uncle back to the bottle. And guess where your cousin ended up? Irony of ironies. She was sent to a village in Puerto Rico to live with a relative on her mother's side: a place so far away from civilization that you have to ride a mule to reach it. A real change in scenery. She found a man there. Women like that cannot live without male company. But believe me, the men in Puerto Rico know how to put a saddle on a woman like her. *La Gringa,* they call her. Ha, ha. ha. *La Gringa* is what she always wanted to be . . ."

The old woman's mouth becomes a cavernous black hole I fall into. And as I fall, I can feel the reverberations of her laughter. I hear the echoes of her last mocking words: *La Gringa, La Gringa!* And the conga line keeps moving silently past me. There is no music in my dream for the dancers.

When Odysseus visits Hades asking to see the spirit of his mother, he makes an offering of sacrificial blood, but since all of the souls crave an audience with the living, he has to listen to many of them before he can ask questions. I, too, have to hear the dead and the forgotten speak in my dream. Those who are still part of my life remain silent, going around and around in their dance. The others keep pressing their faces forward to say things about the past.

My father's uncle is last in line. He is dying of alcoholism, shrunken and shriveled like a monkey, his face is a mass of wrinkles and broken arteries. As he comes closer I realize that in his features I can see my whole family. If you were to stretch that rubbery flesh, you could find my father's face, and deep within *that* face—mine. I don't want to look into those eyes ringed in purple. In a few years he will retreat into silence, and take a long, long time to die. *Move back, Tío,* I tell him. *I don't want to hear what you have to say. Give the dancers room to move, soon it will be midnight. Who is the New Year's Fool this time?*

And Are You a Latina Writer? [2000]

Back in 1978, having just finished graduate school and feeling somewhat inhibited by having read and dissected the major works of great, dead men of letters, I thought I'd be glad if someday someone referred to me simply as a "writer." Now I find myself not just a writer, but bearing the added responsibility of being a *Latina* writer. What is a Latina writer, and how did I become one? My case as a developing Latina writer is somewhat different from others in that, except for the years during my childhood when my family lived in Puerto Rico and in a Puerto Rican neighborhood in Paterson, New Jersey, I have lived in relative geographical isolation from the Latino communities of the United States.

I stress the word *geographical* because, in my mind, I have never abandoned the island of my birth, or perhaps that obsession called "the Island" has never left me. It is the subject of much of my writing. However, I am not a scholar in the field of Latino literature, but rather a writer of books written in English whose main subjects and settings often reflect the author's emigrant background and issues pertaining to her ethnicity. I would like to reiterate some of the questions that have been put to me by persons trying to determine whether I am a Puerto Rican writer:

Why don't you write in Spanish? Isn't writing in English a selling out to the mainstream culture on your part?

My choice of languages is not a political statement: English is my literary language, the language I learned in the schools of the country where my parents brought me to live as a child. Spanish is my familial language, the tongue I speak with my blood relatives, that I dream in, that lies between the lines of my English sentences. The Puerto Rican American writer, Nicholasa Mohr, summed it up best when she stated in an essay about her work, "Because I am a daughter of the Puerto Rican Diaspora, English is the language that gives life to my work, the characters I create, and that stimulates me as a writer."[1]

Isn't the barrio what you write about? Don't you need a sense of place and community for your art? What are you doing in Georgia?

These are the questions I am often asked by people who cannot imagine what a *puertorriqueña* is doing in the Deep South. Once I heard that a Puerto Rican writer had asked where I lived; on hearing the answer, she had said, "No wonder she's mad." At first, offended, I took that "mad" to mean "crazy," but I decided that a benevolent interpretation would be better: What my colleague had obviously meant was that my isolation from others like her, like myself by extension, had not prevented me from being a part of what Las Vasquez has referred to as the phenomenon of the Latina as "the angry storyteller." I choose to believe that my fellow writer, my *compañera* in art, meant that living in the piney woods has not dissipated the passion of my art. Because my literary universe exists within me, and although admitting the need for "community" where the free exchange of

---

[1]"Puerto Rican Writers in the U.S., Puerto Rican Writers in Puerto Rico: A Separation Beyond Language," in *Breaking Boundaries: Latina Writing and Critical Readings,* edited by Asunsion Horno-Delgado, Eliana Ortega, Nina M. Scott, and Nancy Saporta Sternback (Amherst: University of Massachusetts Press, 1989), 12.

ideas can be stimulating, I write in isolation and anywhere that I can find a room of my own.

In the isolation of my art I find a significant relation to the separateness that is an inherent component of my psyche as the child of emigrants. In his Nobel lecture, Octavio Paz spoke of "this consciousness of being separate [as a] constant feature of our [Latino] spiritual history." He also proposed that our divided souls may be the genesis for our most powerful artistic expression: "[Our isolation creates] an anguished awareness that invites self-examination, at other times it appears as a challenge, a spur to action, to go forth and encounter others and the outside world." His conclusion is that, although he speaks as a Mexican writer, out of his particular experiences and worldview, aloneness is the condition of humankind, and as artists our goal is to build the bridges "to overcome the separation and reunite us with the world and our fellow beings."

In the 1960s, growing up in two confusing and increasingly fragmented cultures, I absorbed literature, both the spoken *cuentos* I heard the women in my family tell and the books I buried my head in as if I were a creature who consumed paper and ink for sustenance. As a young college student I first majored in sociology, hoping to find a way to change the world. With the Vietnam War on my TV screen daily and the other ongoing attacks on my political naïveté, it was not long before the spell of innocence was broken. For the spiritual sustenance I craved I returned to my first love, literature. Although the world was tearing itself asunder, each author I read put it back together for me, giving order to chaos, however fleetingly. While I was visiting the realm of its creator, the poem, the story, or the novel made sense of things for me. I decided that words were my medium; language could be tamed. I could make it perform for me, if I could only hold back the madness outside with my pen. In other words, I had to believe that my work was important to my being. My mission as an emerging writer became to use my art as a bridge, so that I would not be like my parents, who precariously straddled cultures, always fearing the fall, anxious as to which side they really belonged to; I would be crossing the bridge of my design and construction, at will, not abandoning either side, but traveling back and forth without fear and confusion as to where I belonged—I belong to both.

This is what it means to me to be a Puerto Rican American writer: to claim my heritage—to drink from the life-giving waters of my own backyard well, to eat the mango fruit of knowledge of good and evil that grows in Borinquen, the tropical island of my grandmother's tales, as well as to acknowledge the troubled, real country of Puerto Rico I can travel back to any time I desire—and also to claim the language of my education, English, the culture and literature of the country I was brought to as a child. I claim both. I plant my little writer's flag on both shores. There are exclusivists who would have me choose sides: I do not find such a choice necessary, any more than Isaac Bashevis Singer gave up being Jewish when he wrote his universal tales, any more than Alice Walker denies her African American roots and Deep South

beginnings to write her American novels. It is neither necessary nor beneficial to me as a writer and an individual to give up anything that makes me a
whole person.

Where does your work belong in the American literature canon?

I am glad to have to consider this question at all. I feel that I risk hubris
in addressing it. I believe that the work of Latina writers, myself included,
belongs, if it is judged worthy enough, alongside the work of other American
writers whose work reflects the concerns of people experiencing our time.
There common ground is found, at the level of our obsessions. In an important essay that defines Latina writing, the editors of *Breaking Boundaries:
Latina Writings and Critical Readings* have stated, "the Latina writer will
often prioritize the lives of women who have, like themselves, carved an existence within a woman's space. More specifically, their recognition and celebration of what we call 'a matriarchal heritage' can be expressed in remarks
such as Ana Castillo's: 'We all have our *abuelita* (little grandmother)
poems.' It is not infrequent in Latina discourse to pay tribute to a long line
of female ancestors" (12).

I had no idea when I wrote the following early poem about my grandmother that I was falling into the category of Latina writer. The only major
woman writer I had heard "speak" directly to me from the canon I was following in graduate school was Virginia Woolf, and it would be many years
later that I would read her "A Room of One's Own" in which she stated: "A
Woman Writing thinks back through her mothers."

Claims

Last time I saw her, Grandmother
had grown seamed as a Bedouin tent.
She had claimed the right
to sleep alone, to own
her nights, to never bear
the weight of sex again, nor to accept
its gift of comfort, for the luxury
of stretching her bones.
She'd carried eight children,
three had sunk in her belly, *náufragos*,
she'd called them, shipwrecked babies
drowned in her black waters.
*Children are made in the night and
steal your days
for the rest of your life, amen.* She said this
to each of her daughters in turn.
Once she had made a pact with man and nature
and kept it. Now like the sea
she is claiming back her territory.

Since then I have thought back through my mothers through dozens of poems, essays, short stories, and a novel. And not just my mothers through biology, but also my literary mothers who include a wealthy Victorian called Woolf; several African American matriarchs such as Mother Morrison and Sisters Walker and Dove; my southern muses, greatest among them Flannery O'Connor; the cousins from South and Central America, Allende and Esquivel; my closest contemporary Puerto Rican kin-through-art from my own Island and the U.S.; and the work of my contemporary Latina writers whose example inspires and encourages me. My mothers are all strong women, but they are not all *puertorriqueñas*.

Finally, I am not lost in America. I am not searching for an identity. I know who I am and what I am. And although community is nice for a writer to have — a group to discuss work in progress with, a cafe to socialize with others who share her interests — I do not believe those things are necessary to the production of a work. In my case, specifically, I don't feel a need to have others authenticate my work as "Puerto Rican" literature.

Although I often seek the counsel of my scholarly colleagues who are experts in the field of Puerto Rican literature and culture — which I'm not, and I freely and gratefully accept their assistance and expertise — I do my best work in a room alone. I am not confused about my cultural identity. I know what I am because my *puertorricanness* was not awarded to me: it is part of me; it cannot be legislated out. It can be said and it can be written that one is or is not a Puerto Rican writer, but one's essence cannot be either given or taken away. Whether I write in Spanish or English, I am who I am: a writer who is a Puerto Rican woman, whether I live in New York City or on a farm in Georgia.

Because I am vigilant about keeping my work free from the constraints of external interference, the push for political and other agendas, I have an even greater need to get back to what Octavio Paz described as "that time I wrote without wondering why I was doing it."

In my books I follow memories, *cuentos*, events, and characters that I see as my guides back to what Virginia Woolf calls "moments of being" in my life, both in Puerto Rico and in the United States. It is a process of discovery. My books are neither Puerto Rican emigrant history nor sociological case studies; at least, I didn't write them as such. I tell stories that recount the suffering and joy of the Puerto Rican emigrants of my experience, mainly women; I re-envision the scenes of my youth and transform them through my imagination, attempting to synthesize the collective yearnings of these souls into a collage that means Puerto Rican to me, that gives shape to my individual vision. If these *cuentos* I create out of my memory and imbue with my perceptions add up to a universal message, then I consider myself fortunate to have accomplished much more than I allow myself to hope for when I sit down in front of that blank sheet of paper that calls to my restless spirit like a believer's candle. No longer the idealistic young poet hoping to find big answers to big questions, I am content now to be the solitary traveler, the *caminante:* my main hope — to find a pattern in the trees, the path less traveled by in the woods. I know to whom these woods belong: if I'm lucky I will find her *casa* in the clearing, always just ahead of me — my little-old-lady muse, my *abuela,* sitting in her rocking chair waiting to tell me another *cuento;* through her storytelling, she teaches me the way back home.

Rafael Ocasio

Speaking in Puerto Rican:
An Interview with Judith Ortiz Cofer   [1990]

Rafael Ocasio: *Maybe you should start by talking about your poetry. You are a poet by trade and that was your first literary work.*

Judith Ortiz Cofer: Poetry is my obsession. I think that poetry has taught me the craft of writing. I have known for a long time that I needed to express myself creatively. For a while I wanted to be a sociologist and save the world. Eventually, I even looked into the visual arts but found out very rapidly that I had no talent in that area. It dawned on me that the one thing I had consistently been doing was writing and that I loved studying literature, particularly poetry.

RO: *When did you start publishing your poetry?*

JOC: Only after I finished graduate school did I really attempt to write poems that I wanted to show other people. I was frankly surprised when they were taken for publication, because one of the first poems that was published was called "Latin Women Pray." It's an ironic little poem about being a Puerto Rican and praying to an Anglo god with a Jewish heritage, and all you can hope is that He's bilingual. It was a political statement as well as a sarcastic poem. It was published in *The New Mexico Humanities Review* and an editorial member wrote a note and said, "Please send us more, we don't get this kind of stuff." . . .

RO: *How would you describe your poetry?*

JOC: The more I wrote poetry, the more I learned about it, the more I understood that I was passionately committed to the art form. Writing a poem is a discipline; most people think that you just sit down and you let the Muse strike you on the head and out comes a poem. My poems go through 15, 20, 25 drafts. In fact, I'm working on one now about going back to see my mother ten years after my father had died and finding out that she had a lover. It was a traumatic experience for me. I must have 30 drafts of

This interview was conducted in November 1990 at Lanier Plaza Hotel, Atlanta, Georgia, by Rafael Ocasio. The written transcript was edited by Rita Ganey.

that. It's a delicate subject, and I love my mother so much that if she ever reads it, I want her to understand that it's done with affection. Poetry fine tunes my writing. When I go from working on my poetry to working on a novel, the demands of language are already established. I don't want to write 20 pages a day and find 18 of them are disposable. When I sit down to write a page of prose, it is as economical, as concentrated, and as strong as a poem.

RO: *Does poetry writing have a personal commitment for you?*

JOC: Yes. Because I've lived physically isolated from the Puerto Rican community, my poetry has kept me connected emotionally. Even though I live in rural Georgia, my husband is North American, and my daughter was born here, I feel connected to the island and to my heritage. Every time I sit down to write a poem about my grandmother, I have to call her back. In a sense it's like being a medium. You sit down at a table and call back the spirits of your ancestors. When the novel [*The Line of the Sun* (1989)] was published my mother said, "Everybody is amazed that you write as if you've been here all your life." In a sense I have been connected through my imagination. It's like having a child who is away. You don't stop loving them. My poetry is my emotional and intellectual connection to my heritage. . . .

RO: *It is obvious that women, specifically your grandmother, are influences in your work.*

JOC: A lot of my stories have to do with the fact that my grandmother, who is slightly suspicious of books, is a woman connected to her work, her children, her family, and has not had the opportunity or the time to be educated. She loves storytelling, though. If she can teach something by telling a story, she'll do it. My book of essays, *Silent Dancing,* is dedicated to that very strong narrative impulse. Most of the stories in my work date back to the times when I would sit around at my grandmother's house and listen to the women telling their stories.

RO: *How did you make the transition from poetry to prose writing?*

JOC: I don't feel that I've made a transition. I've added a genre. I've never stopped writing poetry. What the public mainly sees between books is my poems. The poem is an immediate source for telling a story. I found a few years ago that I got an immense amount of satisfaction from telling a story. I knew that there were certain characters I wanted to create and let them act. I chose my black sheep Angel Guzmán, who is a real person and who was a real black sheep of my family. In my childhood, I had heard only stories that my mother thought a small child should hear about Guzmán. I let my imagination run wild. The novel developed out of my strong sense that I could tell a story and that the natural form for it should be a novel. . . .

RO: *Let's talk more specifically about your novel. The Spanish tone which permeates your English prose resembles the* criollismo [*mixed languages*] *techniques as it presents universal values through original Latin American motifs. Would you comment on that particular style or do you feel that there is a special affinity with American and Spanish American, including Puerto Rican writers?*

JOC: I intended to make the language relate to the theme. I was writing about rural Puerto Ricans, leading their lives in connections to each other and the land. I felt that idiomatic American English would defeat that purpose, because Spanish is lyrical. These people were thinking and speaking in Spanish, but I was writing my novel in English. I wrote as if it were being translated at the moment of writing. It preserved the flavor of the Spanish, because Spanish is syntactically different from English. It is also more poetic in its expression. My poems that deal with Puerto Rico are syntactically different than my poems that deal with my life in the United States. The tone is a direct result of the different syntactical construction I used in order to make it seem credible and feasible that these people were actually Spanish speakers and thinkers, not Americans impersonating Puerto Ricans. . . .

RO: *What do you think will be the reaction of the Puerto Rican scholar and reader to your novel? What will be the reaction of the American scholar and reader?*

JOC: Interestingly enough, I've gotten mainly the reaction of the American readers to my novel. . . . I was at a conference in Paris where different writers were being discussed. A publisher said, "We don't know where to put Judith Cofer." Judith Cofer is writing in standard English, and she lives in Georgia. Until recently, I was somewhere in limbo. I'm not a mainstream North American writer, but I publish in mainstream North American journals. I'm not an island writer. All I know is that I'm a writer, period, writing about the one thing that defines me as a human being — my biculturalism.

Teresa Derrickson

"Cold/Hot, English/Spanish": The Puerto Rican American Divide in Judith Ortiz Cofer's *Silent Dancing*   [2003]

On more than one occasion Puerto Rican American writer Judith Ortiz Cofer has been questioned about her use of standard American English to express the bicultural experiences of the immigrant Puerto Ricans featured in her poetry and prose fiction. The suggestion that her linguistic selection renders suspect her ethnic identity as well as the authenticity of her literary accounts is never far from the surface of such inquiries. Ortiz Cofer's response, however, has been consistently unapologetic. In a recent interview conducted by Rafael Ocasio, she speaks forcefully about the "varied and ever changing" character of the Puerto Rican experience ("Infinite Variety" 735), asserting, "I want my work to be recognized as coming out of the Puerto Rican tradition, even though it sounds different" (734). . . .

Ortiz Cofer's response is significant not only because it rejects facile definitions of cultural identity, definitions based almost exclusively on linguistic proficiency, but more importantly, because it challenges writers and scholars to adopt a more nuanced approach in their investigation of Latin peoples. . . . *Silent Dancing* breaks new ground in Latino/a literature by speaking specifically about the bicultural experience of Puerto Rican Americans, and by demonstrating the way in which this experience is fundamentally distinct from that found in Chicano/a literature.

. . . The cultural reality encountered by the characters in *Silent Dancing* is neither random nor monolithically shared, but one that is shaped instead by the unique physical reality that divides these characters from their homeland. Unlike the U.S. Texas-Mexican border . . . , the Puerto Rican American border is not a land formation, and hence it has an entirely different psychic impact on those who traverse it. This notion is one of the most compelling insights of Ortiz Cofer's work. . . .

Unlike the concrete land border that divides Mexico and America, the U.S.-Puerto Rican border is a seeming gap, a stretch of water whose shifting consistency and apparent intangibility masquerades in the human psyche as a gulf of space, a void not easily traversed. It is thus, for all practical purposes, an imaginary division, and hence one that operates in a fundamentally different way from its land-based corollary. Ortiz Cofer's work never refers to this defining space as it charts the family's journeys to and from the American mainland, and yet this fact does not negate the importance of such a boundary as a formidable influence on the family's bicultural experience. The Ortiz Cofers' "gypsy lifestyle" as cultural commuters (52), combined with the "carefully constructed facsimile of a Puerto Rican home" painstakingly maintained by the speaker's mother in their cramped New Jersey apartment (125), do indeed create a situation in which, for them, "two . . . cultures edge each other," a situation in which life is shaped by geography.

Ortiz Cofer confirms her status as an inhabitant of such a political landscape by observing of her daily routine to and from her American school, "Every day I crossed the border of two countries" (125). An earlier passage reflects a similar assessment of the reality in which she lives: "I had spent my early childhood in the U.S. where I lived in a bubble created by my Puerto Rican parents" (52). Both statements communicate important insights about how the Puerto Rican American border functions in the consciousness of the Ortiz Cofer family. As the speaker of the text indicates, the formal water border dividing the island from the mainland has become unimportant, reconstituting itself in the form of a surrogate boundary which, in its new location outside the Ortiz Cofer family apartment, has the isolating effect of turning the speaker's American home into its own self-sustaining "bubble," into its own diminutive "country."

The defining nature of this displaced border is not the fact that it exists apart from its official counterpart in the Atlantic, but the fact that its confines are so narrowly prescribed (limited, as they are, to the periphery of a neighborhood, a parking lot, or a small apartment) that they allow for no actual borderland to speak of, no mediating "land" or space in which a person is allowed to transition from one cultural sphere to another. The pronounced cultural "purity" that such a tenuous border preserves is indicated in a number of passages in which Ortiz Cofer expresses genuine bewilderment at the acute contrast between one cultural environment and another. Such is her reaction in the following description of her mother's obsessive efforts to refashion her American apartment into a Puerto Rican homeland: "My mother . . . kept herself 'pure' for her eventual return to the island by . . . her ability to create an environment in our home that was a comfort to her, but a shock to my senses, and I suppose, to my younger brother's, both of us having to enter and exit this twilight zone of sights and smells that meant *casa*° to her" (127).

The key phrase of this passage is the term "twilight zone," a word that expresses the extent to which the speaker's home atmosphere is disparate, distinct, and altogether alien from the surrounding dominant environment. Ortiz Cofer's use of the words "enter" and "exit" assume a weighty importance as well, underscoring the abrupt contours that mark the distinction between the end of one culture — in this case just outside the Ortiz Cofer dwelling — and the beginning of another — just inside the front door. That such a boundary is indeed as rigidly defined as implied by these words is conveyed by the "shock" the speaker continues to experience upon entering a domain that by all rights ought to be completely familiar to her. . . .

The Puerto Rican American border as defined in Ortiz Cofer's book, . . . occurring as it does at a much more intimate and individualized locale, is significantly more abrupt and more acutely defined than land-based borders of an institutional nature. The effect of this reality . . . is to disallow the occurrence of a middle ground, to preclude the possibility of a singular space where cultures might intersect and combine. Instead, the fundamental aspect of the displaced Puerto Rican American border and its "real" counterpart works aggressively to protect the "purity" of both sides. There is no melding, no crossover, and no diffusion.

Such a fact is communicated in one of the most controlling motifs of the work: the text's pervasive trope of dichotomy. This figure is made most apparent in the strikingly antithetical nature of Ortiz Cofer's mother and father, two individuals who separately embody the extremes of the disparate cultures they straddle: Ortiz Cofer's mother personifying Latin culture and her father personifying American culture. . . . While Ortiz Cofer's mother pines for her homeland, reproducing her own island *casa* in the middle of her American living room, Ortiz Cofer's father is plagued with opposite obsessions, drilling his children on their English pronunciation and scheming to escape the barrio which he perceives as holding them back. Their status as two people who are paradoxically "separate but joined" offers a powerful characterization of the borderland dynamic at play in this work. Ortiz Cofer

casa: Home.

is mindful of this dynamic as she literally maps it out for her reader in a line that reads, "Cold/hot, English/Spanish; that was our life" (129). The juxtapositioning of the antithetical terms of each set (e.g., "cold/hot" and "English/Spanish") mimics the territorial juxtapositioning of the American and Puerto Rican cultures that figure so prominently in Ortiz Cofer's childhood. Her two worlds, like the printed words in this crude sentence diagram, share a common edge but remain distinct, divided as they are by a tangible line that sets them apart.

Unlike, therefore, the contiguous land-based borders of other territories whose pronounced boundaries arrange for a middle space of cultural negotiation, Puerto Rico and America have no such common ground and hence make none of the same accommodations. Instead, the two environments, occupying separate but adjacent spheres, remain for all practical purposes culturally intact, rarely spilling across the careful line that defines them so resolutely.

Works Cited

Ocasio, Rafael. "The Infinite Variety of the Puerto Rican Reality: An Interview with Judith Ortiz Cofer." *Callaloo* 17.3 (1994): 730–42.

Ortiz Cofer, Judith. *Silent Dancing: A Partial Remembrance of a Puerto Rican Childhood.* Houston: Arte Publico Press, 1990.

Viviana Rangil

Pro-Claiming a Space: The Poetry of Sandra Cisneros and Judith Ortiz Cofer   [2000]

Latina writing, that is, literature written by Latinas, is . . . marked by its double outsider status. . . . [In it] we see a search for identity that is a way of asserting the particularity of Latinas' existences in the United States, existences marked by inequalities stemming from the often ignored categories of race, class, and gender. Latinas experience these inequalities differently than men and respond to them differently. . . .

Latinas' experiences are defined by the condition of in-betweenness and straddling in which they claim their space. Living with a leg on each side of both cultures is part of a daily existence and is manifested in a variety of cultural practices. Literature is perhaps one of the most transparent means through which Latinas' in-betweenness is manifested, and Judith Ortiz Cofer and Sandra Cisneros provide us with powerful and salient examples. . . .

Both Cisneros and Ortiz Cofer acknowledge their bilingualism/interlinguism as an integral part of their identities, one of the main roads in which their itineraries, as opposed to frontiers or boundaries, between and inside two cultures get inscribed. Ortiz Cofer uses Spanish to define a particular set of characteristics that she cannot articulate in English, as in the case of her description of the goods one can get at the *Latin Deli:*

> when they walk down the narrow aisles of her store
> reading the labels of packages aloud, as if
> they were the names of lost lovers: *Suspiros,*
> *Merengues,* the stale candy of everyone's childhood . . .
> slicing *jamón y queso*° and wrapping it in wax paper.
> (Ortiz Cofer 3)

Spanish is a medium, a conduit that enables these writers to experience and comprehend more fully, but it is also a burden since, in a way, it has to compete with English, the everyday language of the outside world. This playful and painful duality represents separation and assimilation at the same time.

The ability to create and produce in one language with the imprint of both languages is . . . the mark of a transnational subject that constantly acknowledges the interrelations between the historical and the social, the diachronic and synchronic axes of identity. At times, Ortiz Cofer's voice can be vociferous, as in the case of the poem entitled "Changeling" where the poet, as a child, dresses up as Che and tells of feasts "to celebrate victories *para la libertad*"° (Ortiz Cofer 38). This fleeting freedom disappears when her mother orders her to put on girl's clothes and "to return invisible, as myself, to the real world of her kitchen." . . .

English and Spanish are not juxtaposed, they are incorporated into each other, giving us the impression that Ortiz Cofer, like the eponymous character of "Paciencia," "weaves an endless pattern of intersecting lines" (90). . . . When referring to her poem "The Latin Deli," Ortiz Cofer says, "I don't put in Spanish words as decoration. They are used to transmit a special kind of reality, to communicate to my English-speaking reader, to say, 'Yes, this is a different reality, but you can understand it by paying close attention'" (Kallet 69). Rather than being a materialization of a "patois," or her own "third world" (Deleuze 18), this language reflects a reality inscribed within the borders of the United States, enriched by the collapse of the language borders and barriers and the incorporation of intersecting cultural lines.

It is evident that for a large proportion of U.S. society the daily language is double, and that existing in only one of them is unsustainable and impossible. By using both languages, Latinas create a new space, a new territory where they reaffirm and reinscribe their Hispanic cultural and historic traditions within the U.S. cultural milieu, and therefore they propose a culture that is different from the traditional. . . .

For Cisneros as well as Ortiz Cofer, writing not only allows them to reappropriate their cultural heritage but also provides the space for a re-vision

---

jamón y queso: Ham and cheese.   *para la libertad:* For freedom.

of that heritage in light of a new and pressing specific historical circumstance: being Latinas living in the United States. Writing inside a culture that marginalizes them as individuals and being outsiders in their own cultures as well, these poets try to restore balance, to debunk the traditional patriarchal mythology. They address the importance of the written word and the variety of obstacles they have had to overcome in order to generate spaces for new forms of expression. . . .

The writing process is not only a self-affirming, identity-creating quest but also a way of disrupting learned and expected roles. Writing is a way of redefining the boundaries that seem to enclose Latinas. It opens up a space for a new reality in which women can "fill in the omissions" [of history] (Horno-Delgado 13), expand and thrive between the gaps, and expose the contradictions of history, society, and culture. Writing, then, becomes a practice for asserting a positionality: that of being a Latina in the United States. For Ortiz Cofer and Cisneros the United States is home. There is no sense of exile or displacement but rather a need to reconfigure the boundaries of a space that has been arbitrarily marked. If territory is a space of containment and belonging circumscribed by political geography, the poetry of Sandra Cisneros and Judith Ortiz Cofer becomes the cultural proof that *pertenencia*° is much more than what can be contained by a map.

Works Cited

Deleuze, Gilles. *Kafka: Toward a Minor Literature.* Minneapolis: U of Minnesota P, 1986.

Horno-Delgado, Asunción, Eliana Ortega, and Nancy Saporta Sternbach, eds. *Breaking Boundaries: Latina Writing and Critical Readings.* Amherst: U of Massachusetts P, 1989.

Kallet, Marilyn. "The Art of Not Forgetting: An Interview with Judith Ortiz Cofer." *Prairie Schooner* 68.4 (1994): 68–75.

Ortiz Cofer, Judith. *The Latin Deli.* New York: Norton, 1995.

---

pertenencia: Belonging.

Juan Bruce-Novoa

Judith Ortiz Cofer's Rituals of Movement   [1991]

[Since Judith Ortiz Cofer is] a product of U.S. schools, complet[ed] a Masters degree in English, and [was] awarded a graduate fellowship from the English-Speaking Union of America to study at Oxford University, it should come as no surprise that [she] writes predominantly in English. It is the language of her literary training. Yet, by choice she foregrounds her Puerto Rican identity in her texts. Only her chapbook *Among the Ancestors*[1] avoids linkage to her Latino heritage, exploring instead the rural environment of Georgia, her home state since 1968. In the rest of her works she openly seeks to create and document herself as a writer of Puerto Rican lineage. It is this project of self-identification and ethnogenesis within her poetry that interests us here.[2]

The goal of establishing a Puerto Rican identity leads Ortiz Cofer inevitably to confront the question of the island's role in her personal ontology. Her answer may seem simple and predictable: the island is encoded as her place of origin and, thus, synonymous with her source of existence. Yet, it is one thing for a person to say, as we in the United States are called on to say so many times, "I am from . . . ," and another for an artist to create the sense of spatial and cultural origin for the persona of her or his production. In the latter case we have arrived at one of the basic questions of ethnic literature. . . .

Ortiz Cofer desires and chooses to place her origin in the island. Puerto Rico is "The Birthplace" of her persona, as the subtitle to the initial section of *Reaching for the Mainland,* her first full-length collection, announces in 1987. The first poem, an account of her birth, begins: "They say / when I arrived."[3] This conscious, even self-conscious, act of recreating one's beginning is highly significant in its implications. Not only does she place herself in the space of Puerto Rico, she evokes as her foundation ritual the act of speaking, specifically the oral tradition garnered from Puerto Rican relatives. Thus, the author transforms herself here into both the object and subject of the island's traditional system of genealogical accounting. . . . Her aim seems clear: she is Puerto Rican. Yet questions arise which she and we must eventually consider: in what language do "they say"? What does it mean for the poet to translate the tradition into English, further compounding the transmutation by passing the foundation act from the spoken to the written word? To respond, however, we ourselves must investigate the origins and evolution of Ortiz Cofer's foundation story.

Her first two chapbooks already had revealed a similar, yet slightly different orientation. While they display the author's intention of identifying with Puerto Rico, unlike the later *Reaching* they specifically place her not on the Island, but rather in the camp of the Latinos who reside within the mainland U.S. context. The title itself of *Latin Women Pray,*[4] her first publication, contextualized all subsequent work within the distinguishing difference of a Latino ethnicity, as distinct from what might be construed as a separate Puerto Rican "nationality" — albeit problematic to utilize such a term when referring to a territory of the United States. "Latino" is a U.S. ethnic marker which loses its signifying context when removed to Latin America. In other words, it connotes a U.S. mainland space of residence, thus serving to distinguish between an island and a mainland context. . . .

Significantly, in their function as generative foundation works, these first publications establish a point of origin in the dynamic tension between two cultural spaces. The author's response is not a simple return to the Island itself, but an exploration of the experience of finding oneself in the mainland U.S. space while simultaneously knowing that one is the Latino Other, and specifically the migrant Puerto Rican. The Latin women who pray do so not in a monoculture ruled by Spanish, as Puerto Rico might ideally be considered when seen as part of Latin America, but in a situation that can only be characterized as intercultural, where a blending of traditions is imposed: "They pray in Spanish to an Anglo God / With a Jewish Heritage. / And this Great White Father / . . . Looks down upon his brown daughters."[5] Trapped in this environment, which in the Puerto Rican context is called either Yankee colonialism on the island or just the reality on the mainland, Ortiz Cofer's characters do not petition for a return to a monolingual state — the linguistic equivalent of an independent national space — but that God "be bilingual," yet another implicit mainland marker. A bilingual God would, in effect, signal an interlingual cosmos. . . .

Existence for the Ortiz Cofer poetic persona [begins]. . . , then, not as an experience of foreign nationality, but as an ethnic one already on the mainland. It starts in the situation of finding herself in a foreign and hostile exterior environment, characterized by the extreme cold of New Jersey winters, within which security and identity were derived from a small inner circle of personal relationships: "in a sealed room. / . . . we learned / early to extract warmth and color from ourselves / . . . we'd shout each other's names across the room, / our existence for the moment confirmed."[6] When the exterior, material reality refuses to reflect one's existence, then interior reality must be brought forth to manifest it. This is the situation of threat which necessitates response, and Ortiz Cofer offers us an image of children practicing inchoate cultural production. They respond by voicing the word which coincides with their self, their identity: their names. They have entered into the process of creating the ethnic identity, ethnogenesis. . . .

Yet, we should not stray from the above image too soon, for it harbors still more significant detail. The act of calling to each other produces warmth, a nurturing characteristic, while at the same time creating a spatial dimension — an interior area between brother and sister, marked off from the outside world. Within that space created by their bodies and hollowed out and filled with signifying sounds by their voices, they identify each other and, thus, know who and where they really are. In turn, this allows them to characterize the outside reality as other, as foreign, but more importantly, it locates it on a self-created map of identity on which the children are protagonists of the center. . . . And it is unavoidable to read the words *warmth and color* beyond their universal symbolism of life and nurturing to their specific allusion to the Puerto Rican climate and environment. In truth, the two sets of signifieds are fused in Ortiz Cofer's code: the memory of Puerto Rico is the nurturing source of her life which allows her to survive the hostile daily existence on the mainland. . . .

These poetic works guide readers eventually to the acceptance by the author of the impossibility of returning to her birthplace island and being a

Puerto Rican. Her "reaching for the mainland" is a placement of herself where she knows she cannot fully be, or at least not remain permanently, revealing its true, ironic message: through her writing Ortiz Cofer reaches not for the mainland, which is, after all, her normal habitat, but for the island which is the distant object of her desire. Once grasped or recreated, however, the island turns out to be a place, a reality, which she can only experience as a yearning to return to her mainland existence. . . .

It is clear from these poems that Judith Ortiz Cofer fully realizes that her existence can never be reduced to a single geographic area, and even less to one or the other side of the political opposition of island versus mainland. No simple choice is open to her. Hence, she makes virtue out of necessity, opting for the state of movement as her defining characteristic, and her writing as her real home, simultaneously her origin, place of residence, and guest house for fellow travelers called readers.

Notes

1. No location, no publisher, 1981.
2. For a definition of ethnogenesis, see Werner Sollors, *Beyond Ethnicity, Consent and Descent in American Culture* (New York: Oxford University Press, 1986): 56–59. In an article entitled "Rituals in Ortiz Cofer's *The Line of the Sun*," to appear in the collected papers of Fetes et Celebrations des Grupes Ethniques en Amerique de Nord, University of Paris VII, I study the author's novel.
3. J. Ortiz Cofer, *Reaching for the Mainland*, in *Triple Crown* (Tempe: Bilingual Press, 1987): 69.
4. Fort Lauderdale: The Florida Arts Gazette Press, 1980.
5. Ortiz Cofer, *Latin Women Pray*, 5.
6. Ortiz Cofer, *The Native Dancer*, 6.

APPROACHING THE READINGS

1. In "Speaking in Puerto Rican" (p. 1306), Ortiz Cofer says poetry taught her the craft of writing. Her poems go through multiple drafts to make the language economical, concentrated, and intense. Look for those qualities in one of her poems — and in one of her stories, since she says she aims for the same qualities in her prose.

2. Ortiz Cofer says her work was strongly influenced by the storytelling of her grandmother and other Puerto Rican women telling their stories. Consider the theme of storytelling in "Silent Dancing" (p. 1295) and "Not for Sale" (p. 134).

3. Viviana Rangil (p. 1311) describes the "double outsider" status faced by writers like Cisneros and Ortiz Cofer: the need to find a racial and a gender "space" and identity — both as a Latina and as a woman. Watch for ways that theme is evident in Ortiz Cofer's personal writings and explored in her poems and stories.

4. Teresa Derrickson (p. 1308) points out the difference in effect between having a concrete land border, like that between the United States and Mexico, and an imaginary border, like that between the mainland United States and Puerto Rico. The latter becomes a moveable border, surrounding the barrio in Paterson, New Jersey, or even the apartment in which the Ortiz family lives. People can go back and forth across that border — they live simultaneously in two cultures, rather than moving from one and settling in the other. Watch for and be ready to discuss ways and places this cultural simultaneity appears in Ortiz Cofer's poems and stories.

5. Juan Bruce-Novoa (p. 1313) examines the issue of identity for someone born in Puerto Rico but living on the mainland. Look for and be ready to discuss ways identity is explored for the young narrators of "Not for Sale" (p. 134) and "Abuela Invents the Zero" (p. 1292).

RESPONDING THROUGH WRITING

Journal Entries

1. In "And Are You a Latina Writer?" Ortiz Cofer refers to Mexican writer Octavio Paz's Nobel Prize lecture in which he says aloneness is the condition of humankind and artists build bridges "'to overcome the separation and reunite us with the world and our fellow beings'" (p. 1303). Write a journal entry on ways literature achieves that goal for you, using Ortiz Cofer or another author to illustrate.

www

Research Judith Ortiz Cofer with LitLinks at bedfordstmartins.com/approachinglit.

2. Viviana Rangil, in "Pro-Claiming a Space," says that "for a large proportion of U.S. society the daily language is double, and that existing in only one of them is unsustainable and impossible" (p. 1312). Collect examples of such doubleness of language from everyday life — signs in ethnic neighborhoods, labels in stores, radio and TV broadcasting — and write a journal entry assessing and commenting on what Rangil says in the rest of that paragraph.

3. Write a journal entry in which you discuss at least two places you realize you are from. They may not be simply physical places. And they may be in the same environment. Many of us feel as if we are from many places even if we have seldom left our neighborhoods.

Literary Analysis Papers

4. Write an analytic paper on the role of the home movie in "Silent Dancing" (p. 1295).

5. Write an analytic paper on figures of speech and theme in "The Birthplace" (p. 1289), perhaps relating the poem to ideas and images in "Silent Dancing" (p. 1295) and "And Are You a Latina Writer?" (p. 1301).

6. Write a thematic paper on what Ortiz Cofer says in "And Are You a Latina Writer?" (p. 1301) and "Speaking in Puerto Rican" (p. 1306) about "thinking back through mothers" and the importance of mothers and grandmothers, and their stories, in her poems and stories.

Making Connections

7. The subtitle of Ortiz Cofer's poem "The Latin Deli" (p. 1291) is "An Ars Poetica." *Ars Poetica* is the title of a poem by the Roman poet Horace (65 B.C.E.–8 B.C.E.). The "Art of Poetry" is his theory of literature, spelling out the qualities that should be evident in literary works and in writers of them. Write a paper relating "The Latin Deli" to what Ortiz Cofer says about writing in other works included in this chapter and explain in what senses this poem can be seen as her "art of poetry."

8. Learn more about the experiences of other writers of Puerto Rican origins or heritage, such as Julia de Burgos, Jesus Colon, Victor Hernández Cruz, and Sandra Maria Esteves, to name just a few, and write a paper discussing how Ortiz Cofer's response to her cultural background is similar to and different from theirs.

Cultural Criticism Papers

9. Write a research paper on the *abuela,* or grandmother, in Ortiz Cofer's writing. Read what she said about the importance of her grandmother in "And Are You a Latina Writer?" (p. 1301) and "Speaking in Puerto Rican" (p. 1306), and look for similar comments elsewhere in personal writings and other published interviews. Bring what you find to bear on poems and stories that feature her grandmother—ones in this book, such as "Cold as Heaven" (p. 558) and "Abuela Invents the Zero" (p. 1292)—and ones you find in other books by her.

10. Watch the much-acclaimed film of the early 1960s, *West Side Story,* and compare that film's depiction of Puerto Rican-American culture with that depicted by Ortiz Cofer.

RESPONDING THROUGH THE ARTS

1. Create a PowerPoint presentation or Web page illuminating cultural allusions in "Silent Dancing." You might include, for example, maps, music clips, visual images of food (with click-on recipes), clothing, and links to Internet sites about TV shows. Use your creativity for what else could be added.

2. Make a collection of pieces by Latin musicians whom you feel are most appropriate for evoking themes and reactions similar to those of the work of Ortiz Cofer, and explain your choices.

A s I have been working with film, I've come to realize sitting in a movie theater is the contemporary equivalent of sitting around the fire listening to a storyteller.
Sherman Alexie

Sherman Alexie: Listening for Stories

CHAPTER **24**

Sherman Alexie was born in 1966 in Wellpinit, a tiny town on the 150,000-acre Spokane Indian Reservation in eastern Washington, about fifty miles northeast of Spokane. His father is Coeur d'Alene Indian and his mother is Spokane Indian. When he was six months old, he was diagnosed with hydrocephalus, an abnormal buildup of fluid creating too much pressure on the brain, and underwent surgery. It was expected that he would not survive or, if he survived, that he would be left mentally retarded. But he did survive, without retardation, though he suffered seizures and uncontrollable bed-wetting well into childhood.

Alexie learned to read by age three, and his love of reading as he grew up created barriers between him and his peers: He describes himself as a geek during his school years. His parents decided to have him attend high school in nearby Reardan, where he could receive a better education than he could on the reservation. He was the only Native American in the school. Throughout his time there, he was an excellent student and a star basketball player. He attended Gonzaga University in Spokane for two years, then Washington State University in Pullman, from which he graduated in 1991. He started out as a premed student, but a human anatomy class on the one hand and a poetry workshop on the other changed his direction. He discovered he loved writing, and was good at it, and didn't love human anatomy. Writing soon became the center of his life.

His early efforts as a poet were supported by a Washington State Arts Commission Poetry Fellowship in 1991 and a National Endowment for the Arts Poetry Fellowship in 1992. He wrote prolifically and found success immediately, publishing two poetry collections — *The Business of Fancydancing* (1992) and *I Would Steal Horses* (1993). His first collection of short stories, *The Lone Ranger and Tonto Fistfight in Heaven* (1993), was equally successful,

A still from Sherman Alexie's movie Smoke Signals, *with Adam Beach (left) as Victor
Joseph and Evan Adams as Thomas Builds-the-Fire.*
© Miramax Films. Jill Sabella/Everett Collection. Reprinted by permission.

receiving a PEN/Hemingway Award and the Great Lakes Colleges Associa-
tion Award for best first book of fiction, and a Lila Wallace-Reader's Digest
Writers' Award. His first novel, *Reservation Blues* (1995), won the Before
Columbus Foundation's American Book Award and the Murray Morgan
Prize, and he was named one of Granta's Best of Young American Novelists.
His second novel, *Indian Killer* (1996), was selected as one of *People*'s Best
of Pages and a *New York Times* Notable Book. In June 1999, Alexie was fea-
tured in *The New Yorker*'s Summer Fiction Edition, "20 Writers for the 21st
Century."

In 1997 he began work on a screenplay based on "This Is What It Means
to Say Phoenix, Arizona," a short story from *The Lone Ranger and Tonto
Fistfight in Heaven*. Written in collaboration with Chris Eyre, a Cheyenne/
Arapaho Indian who also directed, the film was produced by Shadow Catcher
Entertainment as *Smoke Signals*. Released at the Sundance Film Festival in
January 1998, it won two awards, the Audience Award and the Filmmakers
Trophy, and was subsequently distributed by Miramax Films. *Smoke Signals*
was the first Indian-produced, Indian-directed, Indian-written feature film
ever distributed in the United States. It received a Christopher Award, pre-
sented to the creators of artistic works "which affirm the highest values of
the human spirit." Alexie was also nominated for the Independent Feature
Project/West 1999 Independent Spirit Award for Best First Screenplay.

Cover of the Jim Boyd (music) and Sherman Alexie (words) collaboration Reservation Blues.

Reprinted by permission of Jim Boyd.

Alexie wrote another screenplay, *The Business of Fancydancing,* which he directed and produced in 2002 as a low-budget, independent film production filmed on digital video, thus freeing him from the artistic constraints imposed by commercial filmmakers. His most recent books are two collections of short stories, *The Toughest Indian in the World* (2000) and *Ten Little Indians* (2003), and a collection of poetry, *One Stick Song* (2000).

Alexie does occasional reading and stand-up performances with musician Jim Boyd, a Colville Indian. They recorded an album, *Reservation Blues,* made up of songs from Alexie's novel by that name. Alexie made his debut as a stand-up comedian at the Foolproof Northwest Comedy Festival in Seattle in April 1999 and was the featured performer at the Vancouver International Comedy Festival's opening night gala in July 1999. Alexie continues making public appearances as an author and writing in several genres from his home in Seattle, where he lives with his wife and two sons.

Alexie's talent is displayed in many genres — poetry, stories, novels, screenplays. As he indicates in the *Sidewalk* interview later in this chapter, in each format he seeks to make an impact on both Native American readers and those outside the Native culture. To understand and appreciate Alexie fully as a writer, one needs to read widely in his work in two or three genres and to see his films.

That is one purpose of this chapter. In it and in an earlier chapter, we include examples from several different genres. His personal essay "Superman and Me," on the importance of reading and writing in his life, appears in Chapter 1 (p. 4). It would be useful to go back to it after reading the material in this chapter. You will probably find a more complex and rewarding meaning in it after having done so. The pages that follow include several poems, the short story "This Is What It Means to Say Phoenix, Arizona," excerpts from the *Smoke Signals* screenplay, an interview with Alexie mainly about *Smoke Signals,* and an interview about being an ethnic writer. As you read them, be alert for the literary elements of fiction, poetry, and drama covered in the earlier sections of this book. Think critically as you read the various works and try to discern why Alexie may have chosen one form over another to fulfill his purposes. The chapter concludes with excerpts from two critical essays intended to help you participate in the ongoing conversation about Alexie's achievements. One of the essays is on Alexie as a storyteller, drawing on and moving beyond traditional Native American techniques and styles. The other discusses his uses of humor, especially how the Trickster figures in his works. Do not read them until after you have read the works by Alexie at least once, preferably twice. What you read should add to and expand the insights and interpretations you reach through your own reading and reflection, not substitute for your own active reading of and critical thinking about Alexie's works. The "Approaching the Readings" section at the end of the chapter (p. 1357) suggests some ways the pieces about Alexie can be incorporated into your reading and thinking.

One of the rewards of exploring a writer in depth, particularly one who works in multiple genres, is to read for the way themes, styles, and images reoccur and are used differently depending on the genre the writer is working in. As you read this chapter, watch for such repeated elements. Notice, for example, the way the image of a jumping salmon appears as part of a traditional Coyote tale in a poem ("That Place Where the Ghosts of Salmon Jump"), then as a magical vision triggered by a simile in a story ("This Is What It Means to Say Phoenix, Arizona"), and then as a crucial symbol at the conclusion of *Smoke Signals.* Similarly, compare the use of basketball imagery in "Father and Farther" (a typical Alexie poem, mixing sections of rhythmic prose and verse), in *Smoke Signals,* and in the *Sidewalk* interview, especially the way the sport serves as a symbol, or synecdoche, for something larger than itself.

Consider also the importance of story and the oral storytelling tradition: the way it weaves through "The Summer of Black Widows," "That Place Where Ghosts of Salmon Jump," and the character of Thomas Builds-the-Fire in "This Is What It Means to Say Phoenix, Arizona" and *Smoke Signals.* Susan Berry Brill de Ramírez's essay shows how Alexie uses oral storytelling traditions, adapting them to convey an authentic voice, to write about "the way we live" rather than a romanticized stereotype of Indian life. Consider as well the theme of the relationships of fathers (or father figures) and sons as it appears in "Father and Farther," "This Is What It Means to Say Phoenix, Arizona," and *Smoke Signals.* And notice what Alexie says, in the interviews and articles discussing his work, about being a Native American writer; then

www

Research Sherman Alexie with LitLinks at bedfordstmartins.com/approachinglit.

think back through the works and pick out ways the works exemplify the things he says he aims to achieve. These are just a few examples to give you some idea of how rewarding it can be to read a writer in depth, and the kinds of work you can do with this kind of material. Any of these topics can be expanded into a research paper, the subject of Chapter 26.

The Business of Fancydancing   [1992]

After driving all night, trying to reach
Arlee in time for the fancydance
finals, a case of empty
beer bottles shaking our foundations, we
stop at a liquor store, count out money,   5
and would believe in the promise

of any man with a twenty, a promise
thin and wrinkled in his hand, reaching into the window of our car. Money
is an Indian Boy who can fancydance   10
from powwow to powwow. We
got our boy, Vernon WildShoe, to fill our empty

wallets and stomachs, to fill our empty
cooler. Vernon is like some promise
to pay the light bill, a credit card we   15
Indians get to use. When he reach-
es his hands up, feathers held high, in a dance
that makes old women speak English, the money

for first place belongs to us, all in cash, money
we tuck in our shoes, leaving our wallets empty   20
in case we pass out. At the modern dance,
where Indians dance white, a twenty is a promise
that can last all night long, a promise reaching into back pockets of unfamiliar Levis. We

get Vernon there in time for the finals and we   25
watch him like he was dancing on money,
which he is, watch the young girls reaching for him like he was Elvis in braids and an empty
tipi, like Vernon could make a promise
with every step he took, like a fancydance   30

could change their lives. We watch him dance
and he never talks. It's all a business we
understand. Every drum beat is a promise

note written in the dust, measured exactly. Money
is a tool, putty to fill all the empty   35
spaces, a ladder so we can reach

for more. A promise is just like money.
Something we can hold, in twenties, a dream we reach.
It's business, a fancydance to fill where it's empty.

The Summer of Black Widows   [1996]

The spiders appeared suddenly
after that summer rainstorm.

Some people still insist the spiders fell with the rain
while other believe the spiders grew from the damp soil like weeds
    with eight thin roots.

The elders knew the spiders   5
carried stories in their stomachs.

We tucked our pants into our boots when we walked through fields
    of fallow stories.
An Indian girl opened the closet door and a story fell into her hair.
We lived in the shadow of a story trapped in the ceiling lamp.
The husk of a story museumed on the windowsill.   10
Before sleep, we shook our blankets and stories fell to the floor.
A story floated in a glass of water left on the kitchen table.
We opened doors slowly and listened for stories.
The stories rose on hind legs and offered their red bellies to the most
    beautiful Indians.
Stories in our cereal boxes.   15
Stories in our firewood.
Stories in the pockets of our coats.
We captured stories and offered them to the ants, who carried the
    stories back to their queen.
A dozen stories per acre.
We poisoned the stories and gathered their remains with broom
    and pan.   20

The spiders disappeared suddenly
after that summer lightning storm.

Some people still insist the spiders were burned to ash
while others believe the spiders climbed the lightning bolts and
    became a new constellation.

*   *   *

The elders knew the spiders   25
had left behind bundles of stories.

Up in the corners of our old houses
we still find those small, white bundles
and nothing, neither fire
nor water, neither rock nor wind,   30
can bring them down.

That Place Where Ghosts of Salmon Jump   [1996]

Coyote was alone and angry because he could not find love.
Coyote was alone and angry because he demanded a wife

from the Spokane, the Coeur d'Alene, the Palouse, all those tribes
camped on the edge of the Spokane River, and received only laughter.

So Coyote rose up with his powerful and senseless magic   5
and smashed a paw across the water, which broke the river bottom

in two, which created rain that lasted for forty days and nights,
which created Spokane Falls, that place where salmon travelled

more suddenly than Coyote imagined, that place where salmon
        swam
larger than any white man dreamed. Coyote, I know you broke   10

the river because of love, and pretended it was all done by your
        design.
Coyote, you're a liar and I don't trust you. I never have

but I do trust all the stories the grandmothers told me.
They said the Falls were built because of your unrequited love

and I can understand that rage, Coyote. We can all understand   15
but look at the Falls now and tell me what you see. Look

at the Falls now, if you can see beyond all of the concrete
the white man has built here. Look at all of this

and tell me that concrete ever equals love. Coyote,
these white men sometimes forget to love their own mothers   20

so how could they love this river which gave birth
to a thousand lifetimes of salmon? How could they love

these Falls, which have fallen farther, which sit dry
and quiet as a graveyard now? These Falls are that place

*   *   *

where ghosts of salmon jump, where ghosts of women mourn   25
their children who will never find their way back home,

where I stand now and search for any kind of love,
where I sing softly, under my breath, alone and angry.

Father and Farther   [1996]

> Such waltzing was not easy.
> —*Theodore Roethke*

1.

In McNeil Island Prison for bad checks, my father worked to pay back his debts. One morning, a few weeks before his scheduled release date, he climbed the power tower for some routine line repair and touched a live wire. Unconscious and burned, he fell five feet before his safety line snapped taut.

2.

My father knows how to jitterbug.
How many Indians can say that?

3.

He attended Catholic school on purpose. There, the nuns taught him how to play piano. He refuses to play now, and offers no explanations for his refusal. There is a photograph of my father and his sister sitting side by side at a piano. She is wearing a silk dress. He is wearing a coat and tie. Did she know how to play the piano? I assume she could. She attended the same Catholic school as my father. She died in 1980. My father stood beside her coffin and did not sing.

4.

Late night, Yakama Indian Reservation, my father drunk, telling stories. We had traveled there to play in an all-Indian basketball tournament. My father was the coach. I was the shooting guard. We had a bad team and were eliminated quickly. We camped in a cheap hotel. Four players to a room, though my father and I were alone for some reason. "Listen," my father said, "I was a paratrooper in the war." "Which war?" I asked. "All of them," he said.

5.

My father drinks cough syrup
because he believes it heals everything.

My father drinks cough syrup
because he watched RFK's last news conference.

My father drinks cough syrup
because he has a tickle in the back of his throat.

My father drinks cough syrup
because he has survived twenty-three car wrecks.

My father drinks cough syrup
because he wants to stop the influenza virus at the door.

My father drinks cough syrup
because he once saw Lana Turner in a parade.

My father drinks cough syrup
because he is afraid of medicine.

6.

Of course, by now, you realize this is a poem about my father. It could also be a series of exaggerations and outright lies. I might be talking about another man who wears my father's mask. Behind that mask, he could be anybody.

7.

Summer evening, 1976. Our father is thirsty. He knows his children are thirsty. He rummages through our house in search of loose change. He finds a handful of coins. He walks to the Spokane Tribal Jail which, for some unknown reason, has the only soda pop machine on the reservation. My father has enough change for six Pepsis. It is quiet. We can hear mosquitoes slamming against the screen door. The jail is only a few hundred feet from our house. If we listen closely, we can hear our father dropping change into the machine. We can hear the sodas drop into the dispenser. My father gathers the cans. He carries them back to us.

8.

Basketball is
a series of prayers.

Shoot the ball
and tell me

*   *   *

you believe
otherwise.

My father
shoots the ball.

As it spins away
my father prays.

9.

My father often climbed into a van with our crazy cousins and left us for
days to drink. When he came back, still drunk, he always popped "Deer
Hunter" into the VCR. He never made it past the wedding scene. I kept
watching it after he'd passed out. Halfway through the movie, John Savage
and Robert De Niro play a sick game of Russian Roulette while their Viet-
cong captors make wagers on the probable survivor. De Niro asks for more
bullets. Two bullets, three. He knows the odds. He holds the gun to his head.
He has a plan.

10.

As he dribbles
past you, into the
paint, then stops, pivots
and gives the big man
a head fake, you must
remember that my
father can shoot with either
the right or left hand.

11.

During the World's Fair in 1974, my father and I rode over Spokane
Falls in a blue gondola. No. It was more like a chair. Our legs and feet floated
free. I looked down into the water. My father held his left arm around me.
He must have been afraid of gravity. Then my left shoe came loose because
the laces were not tight enough. My shoe would have slipped from my foot if
I hadn't pressed my other shoe against it. My father told me to hang on. He
was smiling as I struggled to keep my shoe. I had written my name across the
top of it. I looked down into the water. My father was laughing. The chair
was blue. It was 1974. The entire world was walking the streets below us. My
mother was dancing for tourists in the Native American exhibit. My siblings
were sleeping in the station wagon. Gravity. The water. My shoe. I looked at
my father. He held me tightly. He told me to hold on.

This Is What It Means to Say Phoenix, Arizona   [1993]

Just after Victor lost his job at the BIA, he also found out that his father had died of a heart attack in Phoenix, Arizona. Victor hadn't seen his father in a few years, only talked to him on the telephone once or twice, but there still was a genetic pain, which was soon to be pain as real and immediate as a broken bone.

Victor didn't have any money. Who does have money on a reservation, except the cigarette and fireworks salespeople? His father had a savings account waiting to be claimed, but Victor needed to find a way to get to Phoenix. Victor's mother was just as poor as he was, and the rest of his family didn't have any use at all for him. So Victor called the Tribal Council.

"Listen," Victor said. "My father just died. I need some money to get to Phoenix to make arrangements."

"Now, Victor," the council said. "You know we're having a difficult time financially."

"But I thought the council had special funds set aside for stuff like this."

"Now, Victor, we do have some money available for the proper return of tribal members' bodies. But I don't think we have enough to bring your father all the way back from Phoenix."

"Well," Victor said. "It ain't going to cost all that much. He had to be cremated. Things were kind of ugly. He died of a heart attack in his trailer and nobody found him for a week. It was really hot, too. You get the picture."

"Now, Victor, we're sorry for your loss and the circumstances. But we can really only afford to give you one hundred dollars."

"That's not even enough for a plane ticket."

"Well, you might consider driving down to Phoenix."

"I don't have a car. Besides, I was going to drive my father's pickup back up here."

"Now, Victor," the council said. "We're sure there is somebody who could drive you to Phoenix. Or is there somebody who could lend you the rest of the money?"

"You know there ain't nobody around with that kind of money."

"Well, we're sorry, Victor, but that's the best we can do."

Victor accepted the Tribal Council's offer. What else could he do? So he signed the proper papers, picked up his check, and walked over to the Trading Post to cash it.

While Victor stood in line, he watched Thomas Builds-the-Fire standing near the magazine rack, talking to himself. Like he always did. Thomas was a storyteller that nobody wanted to listen to. That's like being a dentist in a town where everybody has false teeth.

Victor and Thomas Builds-the-Fire were the same age, had grown up and played in the dirt together. Ever since Victor could remember, it was Thomas who always had something to say.

Once, when they were seven years old, when Victor's father still lived with the family, Thomas closed his eyes and told Victor this story: "Your father's heart is weak. He is afraid of his own family. He is afraid of you. Late at night he sits in the dark. Watches the television until there's nothing but that white noise. Sometimes he feels like he wants to buy a motorcycle and ride away. He wants to run and hide. He doesn't want to be found."

Thomas Builds-the-Fire had known that Victor's father was going to leave, knew it before anyone. Now Victor stood in the Trading Post with a one-hundred-dollar check in his hand, wondering if Thomas knew that Victor's father was dead, if he knew what was going to happen next.

Just then Thomas looked at Victor, smiled, and walked over to him.

"Victor, I'm sorry about your father," Thomas said.

"How did you know about it?" Victor asked.

"I heard it on the wind. I heard it from the birds. I felt it in the sunlight. Also, your mother was just in here crying."

"Oh," Victor said and looked around the Trading Post. All the other Indians stared, surprised that Victor was even talking to Thomas. Nobody talked to Thomas anymore because he told the same damn stories over and over again. Victor was embarrassed, but he thought that Thomas might be able to help him. Victor felt a sudden need for tradition.

"I can lend you the money you need," Thomas said suddenly. "But you have to take me with you."

"I can't take your money," Victor said. "I mean, I haven't hardly talked to you in years. We're not really friends anymore. "

"I didn't say we were friends. I said you had to take me with you."

"Let me think about it."

Victor went home with his one hundred dollars and sat at the kitchen table. He held his head in his hands and thought about Thomas Builds-the-Fire, remembered little details, tears and scars, the bicycle they shared for a summer, so many stories.

Thomas Builds-the-Fire sat on the bicycle, waited in Victor's yard. He was ten years old and skinny. His hair was dirty because it was the Fourth of July.

"Victor," Thomas yelled. "Hurry up. We're going to miss the fireworks."

After a few minutes, Victor ran out of his house, jumped the porch railing, and landed gracefully on the sidewalk.

"And the judges award him a 9.95, the highest score of the summer," Thomas said, clapped, laughed.

"That was perfect, cousin," Victor said. "And it's my turn to ride the bike."

Thomas gave up the bike and they headed for the fairgrounds. It was nearly dark and the fireworks were about to start.

"You know," Thomas said. "It's strange how us Indians celebrate the Fourth of July. It ain't like it was *our* independence everybody was fighting for."

"You think about things too much," Victor said. "It's just supposed to be fun. Maybe Junior will be there."

"Which Junior? Everybody on this reservation is named Junior."

And they both laughed.

The fireworks were small, hardly more than a few bottle rockets and a fountain. But it was enough for two Indian boys. Years later, they would need much more.

Afterwards, sitting in the dark, fighting off mosquitoes, Victor turned to Thomas Builds-the-Fire.

"Hey," Victor said. "Tell me a story."

Thomas closed his eyes and told this story: "There were these two Indian boys who wanted to be warriors. But it was too late to be warriors in the old way. All the horses were gone. So the two Indian boys stole a car and drove to the city. They parked the stolen car in front of the police station and then hitchhiked back home to the reservation. When they got back, all their friends cheered and their parents' eyes shone with pride. *You were very brave,* everybody said to the two Indian boys. *Very brave.*"

"Ya-hey," Victor said. "That's a good one. I wish I could be a warrior."

"Me too," Thomas said.

They went home together in the dark, Thomas on the bike now, Victor on foot. They walked through shadows and light from streetlamps.

"We've come a long ways," Thomas said. "We have outdoor lighting."

"All I need is the stars," Victor said. "And besides, you still think about things too much."

They separated then, each headed for home, both laughing all the way.

Victor sat at his kitchen table. He counted his one hundred dollars again and again. He knew he needed more to make it to Phoenix and back. He knew he needed Thomas Builds-the-Fire. So he put his money in his wallet and opened the front door to find Thomas on the porch.

"Ya-hey, Victor," Thomas said. "I knew you'd call me."

Thomas walked into the living room and sat down on Victor's favorite chair.

"I've got some money saved up," Thomas said. "It's enough to get us down there, but you have to get us back."

"I've got this hundred dollars," Victor said. "And my dad had a savings account I'm going to claim."

"How much in your dad's account?"

"Enough. A few hundred."

"Sounds good. When we leaving?"

When they were fifteen and had long since stopped being friends, Victor and Thomas got into a fistfight. That is, Victor was really drunk and beat Thomas up for no reason at all. All the other Indian boys stood around and watched it happen. Junior was there and so were Lester, Seymour, and a lot of others. The beating might have gone on until Thomas was dead if Norma Many Horses hadn't come along and stopped it.

"Hey, you boys," Norma yelled and jumped out of her car. "Leave him alone."

If it had been someone else, even another man, the Indian boys would've just ignored the warnings. But Norma was a warrior. She was powerful. She could have picked up any two of the boys and smashed their skulls together. But worse than that, she would have dragged them all over to some tipi and made them listen to some elder tell a dusty old story.

The Indian boys scattered, and Norma walked over to Thomas and picked him up.

"Hey, little man, are you okay?" she asked.

Thomas gave her a thumbs up.

"Why they always picking on you?"

Thomas shook his head, closed his eyes, but no stories came to him, no words or music. He just wanted to go home, to lie in his bed and let his dreams tell his stories for him.

Thomas Builds-the-Fire and Victor sat next to each other in the airplane, coach section. A tiny white woman had the window seat. She was busy twisting her body into pretzels. She was flexible.

"I have to ask," Thomas said, and Victor closed his eyes in embarrassment.

"Don't," Victor said.

"Excuse me, miss," Thomas asked. "Are you a gymnast or something?"

"There's no something about it," she said. "I was first alternate on the 1980 Olympic team."

"Really?" Thomas asked.

"Really."

"I mean, you used to be a world-class athlete?" Thomas asked.

"My husband still thinks I am."

Thomas Builds-the-Fire smiled. She was a mental gymnast, too. She pulled her leg straight up against her body so that she could've kissed her kneecap.

"I wish I could do that," Thomas said.

Victor was ready to jump out of the plane. Thomas, that crazy Indian storyteller with ratty old braids and broken teeth, was flirting with a beautiful Olympic gymnast. Nobody back home on the reservation would ever believe it.

"Well," the gymnast said. "It's easy. Try it."

Thomas grabbed at his leg and tried to pull it up into the same position as the gymnast. He couldn't even come close, which made Victor and the gymnast laugh.

"Hey," she asked. "You two are Indian, right?"

"Full-blood," Victor said.

"Not me," Thomas said. "I'm half magician on my mother's side and half clown on my father's."

They all laughed.

"What are your names?" she asked.

"Victor and Thomas."

"Mine is Cathy. Pleased to meet you all."

The three of them talked for the duration of the flight. Cathy the gymnast complained about the government, how they screwed the 1980 Olympic team by boycotting.

"Sounds like you all got a lot in common with Indians," Thomas said.

Nobody laughed.

After the plane landed in Phoenix and they had all found their way to the terminal, Cathy the gymnast smiled and waved good-bye.

"She was really nice," Thomas said.

"Yeah, but everybody talks to everybody on airplanes," Victor said. "It's too bad we can't always be that way."

"You always used to tell me I think too much," Thomas said. "Now it sounds like you do."

"Maybe I caught it from you."

"Yeah."

Thomas and Victor rode in a taxi to the trailer where Victor's father died.

"Listen," Victor said as they stopped in front of the trailer. "I never told you I was sorry for beating you up that time."

"Oh, it was nothing. We were just kids and you were drunk."

"Yeah, but I'm still sorry."

"That's all right."

Victor paid for the taxi and the two of them stood in the hot Phoenix summer. They could smell the trailer.

"This ain't going to be nice," Victor said. "You don't have to go in."

"You're going to need help."

Victor walked to the front door and opened it. The stink rolled out and made them both gag. Victor's father had lain in that trailer for a week in hundred-degree temperatures before anyone found him. And the only reason anyone found him was because of the smell. They needed dental records to identify him. That's exactly what the coroner said. They needed dental records.

"Oh, man," Victor said. "I don't know if I can do this."

"Well, then don't."

"But there might be something valuable in there."

"I thought his money was in the bank."

"It is. I was talking about pictures and letters and stuff like that."

"Oh," Thomas said as he held his breath and followed Victor into the trailer.

*   *   *

When Victor was twelve, he stepped into an underground wasp nest. His foot was caught in the hole, and no matter how hard he struggled, Victor couldn't pull free. He might have died there, stung a thousand times, if Thomas Builds-the-Fire had not come by.

"Run," Thomas yelled and pulled Victor's foot from the hole. They ran then, hard as they ever had, faster than Billy Mills, faster than Jim Thorpe, faster than the wasps could fly.

Victor and Thomas ran until they couldn't breathe, ran until it was cold and dark outside, ran until they were lost and it took hours to find their way home. All the way back, Victor counted his stings.

"Seven," Victor said. "My lucky number."

Victor didn't find much to keep in the trailer. Only a photo album and a stereo. Everything else had that smell stuck in it or was useless anyway.

"I guess this is all," Victor said. "It ain't much."

"Better than nothing," Thomas said.

"Yeah, and I do have the pickup."

"Yeah," Thomas said. "It's in good shape."

"Dad was good about that stuff."

"Yeah, I remember your dad."

"Really?" Victor asked. "What do you remember?"

Thomas Builds-the-Fire closed his eyes and told this story: "I remember when I had this dream that told me to go to Spokane, to stand by the Falls in the middle of the city and wait for a sign. I knew I had to go there but I didn't have a car. Didn't have a license. I was only thirteen. So I walked all the way, took me all day, and I finally made it to the Falls. I stood there for an hour waiting. Then your dad came walking up. *What the hell are you doing here?* he asked me. I said, *Waiting for a vision.* Then your father said, *All you're going to get here is mugged.* So he drove me over to Denny's, bought me dinner, and then drove me home to the reservation. For a long time I was mad because I thought my dreams had lied to me. But they didn't. Your dad was my vision. *Take care of each other* is what my dreams were saying. *Take care of each other.*"

Victor was quiet for a long time. He searched his mind for memories of his father, found the good ones, found a few bad ones, added it all up, and smiled.

"My father never told me about finding you in Spokane," Victor said.

"He said he wouldn't tell anybody. Didn't want me to get in trouble. But he said I had to watch out for you as part of the deal."

"Really?"

"Really. Your father said you would need the help. He was right."

"That's why you came down here with me, isn't it?" Victor asked.

"I came because of your father."

Victor and Thomas climbed into the pickup, drove over to the bank, and claimed the three hundred dollars in the savings account.

* * *

Thomas Builds-the-Fire could fly.

Once, he jumped off the roof of the tribal school and flapped his arms like a crazy eagle. And he flew. For a second, he hovered, suspended above all the other Indian boys who were too smart or too scared to jump.

"He's flying," Junior yelled, and Seymour was busy looking for the trick wires or mirrors. But it was real. As real as the dirt when Thomas lost altitude and crashed to the ground.

He broke his arm in two places.

"He broke his wing," Victor chanted, and the other Indian boys joined in, made it a tribal song.

"He broke his wing, he broke his wing, he broke his wing," all the Indian boys chanted as they ran off, flapping their wings, wishing they could fly, too. They hated Thomas for his courage, his brief moment as a bird. Everybody has dreams about flying. Thomas flew.

One of his dreams came true for just a second, just enough to make it real.

Victor's father, his ashes, fit in one wooden box with enough left over to fill a cardboard box.

"He always was a big man," Thomas said.

Victor carried part of his father and Thomas carried the rest out to the pickup. They set him down carefully behind the seats, put a cowboy hat on the wooden box and a Dodgers cap on the cardboard box. That's the way it was supposed to be.

"Ready to head back home," Victor asked.

"It's going to be a long drive."

"Yeah, take a couple days, maybe."

"We can take turns," Thomas said.

"Okay," Victor said, but they didn't take turns. Victor drove for sixteen hours straight north, made it halfway up Nevada toward home before he finally pulled over.

"Hey, Thomas," Victor said. "You got to drive for a while."

"Okay."

Thomas Builds-the-Fire slid behind the wheel and started off down the road. All through Nevada, Thomas and Victor had been amazed at the lack of animal life, at the absence of water, of movement.

"Where is everything?" Victor had asked more than once.

Now when Thomas was finally driving they saw the first animal, maybe the only animal in Nevada. It was a long-eared jackrabbit.

"Look," Victor yelled. "It's alive."

Thomas and Victor were busy congratulating themselves on their discovery when the jackrabbit darted out into the road and under the wheels of the pickup.

"Stop the goddamn car," Victor yelled, and Thomas did stop, backed the pickup off the dead jackrabbit.

"Oh, man, he's dead," Victor said as he looked at the squashed animal.

"Really dead."

"The only thing alive in this whole state and we just killed it."

"I don't know," Thomas said. "I think it was suicide."

Victor looked around the desert, sniffed the air, felt the emptiness and loneliness, and nodded his head.

"Yeah," Victor said. "It had to be suicide."

"I can't believe this," Thomas said. "You drive for a thousand miles and there ain't even any bugs smashed on the windshield. I drive for ten seconds and kill the only living thing in Nevada."

"Yeah," Victor said. "Maybe I should drive."

"Maybe you should."

Thomas Builds-the-Fire walked through the corridors of the tribal school by himself. Nobody wanted to be anywhere near him because of all those stories. Story after story.

Thomas closed his eyes and this story came to him: "We are all given one thing by which our lives are measured, one determination. Mine are the stories which can change or not change the world. It doesn't matter which as long as I continue to tell the stories. My father, he died on Okinawa in World War II, died fighting for this country, which had tried to kill him for years. My mother, she died giving birth to me, died while I was still inside her. She pushed me out into the world with her last breath. I have no brothers or sisters. I have only my stories which came to me before I even had the words to speak. I learned a thousand stories before I took my first thousand steps. They are all I have. It's all I can do."

Thomas Builds-the-Fire told his stories to all those who would stop and listen. He kept telling them long after people had stopped listening.

Victor and Thomas made it back to the reservation just as the sun was rising. It was the beginning of a new day on earth, but the same old shit on the reservation.

"Good morning," Thomas said.

"Good morning."

The tribe was waking up, ready for work, eating breakfast, reading the newspaper, just like everybody else does. Willene LeBret was out in her garden wearing a bathrobe. She waved when Thomas and Victor drove by.

"Crazy Indians made it," she said to herself and went back to her roses.

Victor stopped the pickup in front of Thomas Builds-the-Fire's HUD house. They both yawned, stretched a little, shook dust from their bodies.

"I'm tired," Victor said.

"Of everything," Thomas added.

They both searched for words to end the journey. Victor needed to thank Thomas for his help, for the money, and make the promise to pay it all back.

"Don't worry about the money," Thomas said. "It don't make any difference anyhow."

"Probably not, enit?"

"Nope."

Victor knew that Thomas would remain the crazy storyteller who talked to dogs and cars, who listened to the wind and pine trees. Victor knew that he couldn't really be friends with Thomas, even after all that had happened. It was cruel but it was real. As real as the ashes, as Victor's father, sitting behind the seats.

"I know how it is," Thomas said. "I know you ain't going to treat me any better than you did before. I know your friends would give you too much shit about it."

Victor was ashamed of himself. Whatever happened to the tribal ties, the sense of community? The only real thing he shared with anybody was a bottle and broken dreams. He owed Thomas something, anything.

"Listen," Victor said and handed Thomas the cardboard box which contained half of his father. "I want you to have this."

Thomas took the ashes and smiled, closed his eyes, and told this story: "I'm going to travel to Spokane Falls one last time and toss these ashes into the water. And your father will rise like a salmon, leap over the bridge, over me, and find his way home. It will be beautiful. His teeth will shine like silver, like a rainbow. He will rise, Victor, he will rise."

Victor smiled.

"I was planning on doing the same thing with my half," Victor said. "But I didn't imagine my father looking anything like a salmon. I thought it'd be like cleaning the attic or something. Like letting things go after they've stopped having any use."

"Nothing stops, cousin," Thomas said. "Nothing stops."

Thomas Builds-the Fire got out of the pickup and walked up his driveway. Victor started the pickup and began the drive home.

"Wait," Thomas yelled suddenly from his porch. "I just got to ask one favor."

Victor stopped the pickup, leaned out the window, and shouted back. "What do you want?"

"Just one time when I'm telling a story somewhere, why don't you stop and listen?" Thomas asked.

"Just once?"

"Just once."

Victor waved his arms to let Thomas know that the deal was good. It was a fair trade, and that was all Victor had ever wanted from his whole life. So Victor drove his father's pickup toward home while Thomas went into his house, closed the door behind him, and heard a new story come to him in the silence afterwards.

From Smoke Signals   [1998]

SCENE 8
Exterior baseball diamond (1988) — day.

Angle on Young Thomas Builds-the-Fire, twelve years old, standing on the left side of the frame and Young Victor Joseph, twelve years old, standing on the right side of the frame with a burning barrel sitting between them.

Young Thomas is wearing a thirdhand sport coat with blue jeans and T-shirt.

He also wears very traditionally braided hair and thick glasses.

He is very much an Indian nerd.

Young Victor is wearing a red T-shirt and blue jeans.

He is a very handsome and confident boy.

YOUNG THOMAS: Hey, Victor, what do you know about fire?

YOUNG VICTOR: Thomas, I don't know what you're talking about.

YOUNG THOMAS: No, really, Victor. I mean, did you know that things burn in colors? I mean, sodium burns yellow and carbon burns orange. Just like that. You can tell what's in a fire by the color of the flames. *(beat)* Hey, Victor, I heard your dad is living in Phoenix, Arizona, now.

YOUNG VICTOR: Yeah, Thomas, what about it?

YOUNG THOMAS: Man, he's lived everywhere since he left you, huh?

Victor ignores Thomas.

YOUNG THOMAS *(cont'd)*: I mean, he lived in Neah Bay, and then in Eureka, and then in Riverside, and then in Tijuana, and now in Phoenix, Arizona. *(beat)* Man, Phoenix is like a million miles away from here, enit?

YOUNG VICTOR: Is that so, Thomas? *(beat)* You know, I was wondering. What color do you think your mom and dad were when they burned up?

Young Thomas is hurt by this. He is silent for a moment.

YOUNG THOMAS: You know, your dad ain't coming back.

YOUNG VICTOR: Yes, he is.

YOUNG THOMAS: No, he's gone. When Indians go away, they don't come back. Last of the Mohicans, last of the Sioux, last of the Navajo, last of the Winnebago, last of the Coeur d'Alene people . . .

YOUNG VICTOR *(interrupting Thomas)*: Shut up, Thomas. Or I'll beat you up again.

Long beat.

YOUNG THOMAS: What does it mean?

YOUNG VICTOR: What does what mean?

YOUNG THOMAS: What does Phoenix, Arizona, mean?

Cut to: opening credits roll

SCENE 13

Ext. basketball court — Coeur d'Alene reservation — day.

Angle on Victor Joseph and his basketball buddies, Junior and Boo, as they sit on the court.

In the background we see Thomas is still sitting with his radio, chair, and little plastic table.

JUNIOR POLATKIN: Hey, Victor, who do you think is the best basketball player ever?

VICTOR: That's easy. Geronimo.

JUNIOR POLATKIN: Geronimo? He couldn't play basketball, man. He was Apache, man. Those suckers are about three feet tall.

VICTOR: It's Geronimo, man. He was lean, mean, and bloody. Would have dunked on your flat Indian ass and then cut it off.

JUNIOR POLATKIN: Yeah, sometimes it's a good day to die. Sometimes, it's a good day to play basketball.

BOO: What about Sitting Bull?

VICTOR: A veteran player. Would have used those old-man moves. Stepping on your foot so you can't jump. Holding your shirt when you tried to run by him. Poke you in the belly when you take a shot.

JUNIOR POLATKIN: Yeah, he played in the Six-Feet-and-Under, Forty-Years-and-Older, Indian Spiritual Leader Basketball League.

VICTOR: Kind of a slow league, though, enit? All those old guys running up and down the court with their drums and medicine bundles and singing and shit. (*pounding his leg in rhythm and singing a makeshift powwow song*) Oh, I took the ball to the hoop and what did I see? Oh, I took the ball to the hoop and what did I see? General George Armstrong Custer was a-guarding me! Way, ya, hi, ye! Way, ya, hi, ye! (*Junior and Boo join in*) Oh, I took the ball to the hoop and what did I see? Oh, I took the ball to the hoop and what did I see. General George Armstrong Custer was a-guarding me! Way, ya, hi, ye! Way, ya, hi, ye!

JUNIOR POLATKIN: What about Chief Joseph? He had to be good.

VICTOR: He retired young, man. He will play basketball no more forever.

BOO: What about Pocahontas? Was she a cheerleader or what?

VICTOR: Shit, old Pokey was a point guard. Strapped on a rawhide athletic bra to cover up those big ol' Technicolor Disney boobs and kicked some white boys' asses.

JUNIOR POLATKIN: What about Thomas?

VICTOR: What about him?

Angle on Thomas sitting alone in his chair.

SCENE 14
Ext. Suzy Song's trailer house — Phoenix, Arizona — day.

Angle on Suzy Song as she sits alone on her porch.
She is still wearing her business suit, though she holds her jacket in her arms.
She holds it up to her face and breathes in the terrible smell of Arnold's death.
Disgusted, she throws the jacket to the ground.
She stares into the distance.

SCENE 15
Ext. outdoor basketball court — day.

Angle on Victor, Junior, and Boo leaving the outdoor basketball court.
Victor is dribbling the basketball.
Thomas is still sitting on his chair beside the court.
He stands and watches Victor and his pals walk away.

THOMAS: Hey, Victor!

Victor ignores Thomas.
He continues to dribble the basketball.

JUNIOR POLATKIN: Hey, Victor, how come you don't hello Thomas when you know him so easy.

Victor ignores Junior.
Junior and Boo laugh together as if sharing some secret joke.

JUNIOR POLATKIN (*to Victor*): Jeez, look at you, leaving your *se-sen-sah*° behind.
VICTOR: He's not my brother!

Junior and Boo laugh harder.
They are having a good time at Victor's expense.
The three continue to walk away from Thomas.

THOMAS: Hey, Victor!

Victor continues to ignore Thomas.
Victor dribbles the basketball.
He fakes left, right, dribbles past an imaginary defender.
Angle on Thomas standing all alone.

---

se-sen-sah: Little brother.

SCENE 16

Interior Suzy's mobile-home living room — day.

Angle on Suzy Song sitting on her couch.

She is now wearing a T-shirt and blue jeans.

The room is simple and neat.

A recliner, couch, coffee table, television.

There are many books of all kinds stacked in piles everywhere.

She must be quite a reader.

She picks up a beaded wallet, completely beaded with an eagle design, Arnold's wallet.

Suzy opens it and pulls out a photograph.

Insert shot of the photograph of Arnold, Arlene, and Baby Victor.

A happy family photograph.

Suzy looks at the back side of the photograph.

There is nothing.

Angle on Suzy as she picks up the phone and dials a phone number.

SCENE 17

Int. Josephs' house — day.

Angle on Arlene Joseph.

We hear the phone ringing.

She picks it up and holds the phone to her ear.

We see the shock, then grief on her face as Suzy gives her the news.

Angle on Victor as he comes through the front door.

Arlene turns to face him.

They share a long look.

Victor is standing very still.

SCENE 18

Int. Coeur d'Alene Indian Trading Post — day.

Angle on Victor as he stands very still in line at the checkout counter, looking down at a forty-dollar check from his mom.

He looks up to see the Cashier, a large Indian woman.

VICTOR: Can you cash this? It's from my mom.

The Cashier takes the check, throws it in her register, gives Victor forty dollars.

He looks at the money, knowing it isn't very much.

THOMAS: Hey, Victor.

Victor turns to face Thomas Builds-the-Fire.

THOMAS: I'm sorry about your father.
VICTOR: How'd you hear about it?
THOMAS: I heard it on the wind. I heard it from the birds. I felt it in the sunlight. And your mother was just in here crying.

Victor is suddenly very uncomfortable.

VICTOR: Listen, Thomas. I got to go. I've got things to take care of.

Victor turns to leave again, but Thomas grabs his arm.

THOMAS: Victor, your mom said she only had forty bucks. That ain't enough money to get you to Phoenix. (*beat*) I can help, you know?
VICTOR: Help what?
THOMAS: I can help you get to Phoenix. I have some money. (*pleading, Thomas holds up a glass jar, his piggy bank, filled with paper money and coins*) I can help.
VICTOR: Listen, Thomas, I can't take your money. Why don't you go buy a car or something. Go find a woman. Anything. But leave me alone, okay?
THOMAS: I can get you to Phoenix.
VICTOR: Okay, so you can get me to Phoenix. But what do you get out of the deal?
THOMAS: You have to take me with you.
VICTOR (*laughing, dismissive*): Sure, Thomas, whatever.

Thomas watches as the adult Victor walks out the trading post door, which is covered with red handbills advertising The Last Goodbye Powwow . . .

MATCH CUT TO:

SCENE 19
Ext. Coeur d'Alene Indian Trading Post (July 4, 1988) — day.

. . . and then we see the Young Victor walk out of the trading post into the parking lot.

A few beat-up cars are there, as are a few Indians standing around, laughing and talking.

Young Victor is wearing a red T-shirt and blue jeans.

From behind him, out of the trading post door, the Young Thomas comes racing out.

He is wearing his typical three-piece suit.

He is also holding a burning sparkler firework.

YOUNG THOMAS: Hey, Victor, happy Fourth of July! Look at this. Ain't it cool?

Victor walks over to Thomas.

Together, they both stare at the sparkler.

Thomas is grinning like crazy.

His happiness is infectious.

Victor has to smile too.

YOUNG THOMAS (*cont'd*): Hey, Victor, you want to hold it?
YOUNG VICTOR: Nah, Thomas, it's yours. You hang on to it.

Angle on Young Victor as he is suddenly picked up from behind.

He is scared at first but then we see it is Arnold Joseph who has picked up his son.

ARNOLD JOSEPH: Hey, little Thomas, you better get home. Your grandma is looking for you.

Young Thomas smiles and runs away.

Arnold Joseph carries Young Victor over his shoulder to his pickup and deposits him inside.

Young Victor is giggling like crazy.

Arnold gets inside the pickup.

SCENE 20
Int. pickup (July 4, 1988) — day.

Arnold and Young Victor sit in the pickup.

Arnold reaches into a cooler sitting on the seat between them and pulls out a beer.

He opens it, takes a big drink, hands it to Young Victor.

Young Victor is holding it tightly.

He looks up at his father and smiles.

Arnold smiles at his son.

He shows empty hands and then magically pulls a coin from behind Young Victor's ear.

Arnold starts the car and pulls out of the trading post parking lot, heading for home.

As he drives, he talks.

Arnold is not drunk.

He is just beginning to catch a buzz.

As he talks, Young Victor listens with rapt attention.

ARNOLD JOSEPH: Happy Independence Day, Victor. You feeling independent? I'm feeling independent. I'm feeling extra magical today, Victor. Like I could make anything disappear. Houdini with braids, you know? Wave my hand and poof! The white people are gone, sent back to where they belong. Poof! Paris, London, Moscow. Poof! Berlin, Rome, Athens. Poof! Poof! Poof! Wave my hand and the reservation is gone. The trading post and the post office, the tribal school and the pine trees, the dogs and cats, the drunks and the Catholics, and the drunk Catholics. Poof! And all the little Indian boys named Victor.

Arnold looks at his son with a big smile, musses his hair.

ARNOLD JOSEPH: I'm magic. I'm magic. I just wave my hand and make it disappear, send it somewhere else. I can make you disappear. Where do you want to go, Victor? You want to go to Disneyland? The moon? The North Pole? I'm so good, I can make myself disappear. Poof! And I'm gone.

Arnold focuses on the road, dreaming of places he'd go.
He pulls the truck up in front of their house.
Young Victor looks up at him.

ARNOLD JOSEPH: Here, give me that beer.

Young Victor holds the beer out to his father.
But the beer slips from Young Victor's hand and falls to the seat.
Beer spills.
Angrily, Arnold slaps his son across the face.

ARNOLD JOSEPH: Look what you did!

Young Victor is crying.
Arnold cleans up the mess, drinks the rest of the beer from the bottle.
He grabs a new beer.

ARNOLD JOSEPH: Ah, quit your crying. I didn't hit you that hard. (*beat*) Now, go see your mom. Tell her I'll be right in.

Angle on Young Victor, still crying, as he climbs out of the pickup.
Arnold's POV [point of view] on Young Victor as he runs toward the Josephs' house.
Angle on Arnold as he takes a big drink of beer. He looks out the window.
Angle on Young Victor as he runs onto the porch, opens the front door, and walks inside . . .

MATCH CUT TO:

SCENE 21
Int. Josephs' house (present day) — night.

. . . and we see the Adult Victor walk into the house.
He walks through the living room into kitchen.
Arlene Joseph is making fry bread.
She looks up when Victor walks into the room.

ARLENE JOSEPH: Did you cash the check?
VICTOR: Yeah.
ARLENE JOSEPH: That's all the money I got.
VICTOR: I know.
ARLENE JOSEPH: Is it enough?
VICTOR: No.

Arlene drops a piece of fry bread to the floor.
She smiles and rubs her hands.

ARLENE JOSEPH: Damn arthritis.
VICTOR: Hurting bad today, enit?

Arlene shrugs her shoulders.
Victor walks over to his mother, takes her hands in his, and gently rubs them.

SCENE 22
Int. Builds-the-Fires' House — night.

Angle on Grandma and Thomas standing in their kitchen.
Defying gender expectations, Thomas is making the fry bread.
He kneads the dough and drops it into hot oil.

GRANDMA: Do you think Victor is going to take your money?

Angle on Thomas as he shrugs his shoulders.

GRANDMA: I don't trust him, you know. He's mean to you.
THOMAS: He wasn't always mean.

Angle on the fry bread sizzling in the pan.

SCENE 23
Int. Josephs' house — night.

Angle on fry bread sizzling in a different pan.
Wide angle on Arlene and Victor standing in their kitchen.
Arlene pulls a piece of hot fry bread from the grease and drops it into a basket.
Victor leans against the refrigerator, drinking a Coke.

VICTOR: Thomas says he'll give me the money. But he wants to go with me.

Victor reaches over and grabs a piece of fry bread from the basket.
It's hot, so he bounces it from hand to hand to cool it off.
He takes a bite, swallows some Coke to wash it down.
He looks at his mother.
She looks up at him.

ARLENE JOSEPH: You know, people always tell me I make the best fry bread in
    the world. Maybe it's true. But I don't make it by myself, you know? I got
    the recipe from your grandmother, who got it from her grandmother.
    And I listen to people when they eat my bread, too. Sometimes, they
    might say, "Arlene, there's too much flour," or "Arlene, you should

knead the dough a little more." I listen to them. And I watch that Julia Child all the time. (*beat*) She's a pretty good cook, too. But she's got lots of help.

VICTOR: So, do you think I should go with Thomas?

ARLENE JOSEPH: That's your decision. (*beat*) But if you go, I want you to promise me you'll come back.

VICTOR: Come on, Mom.

ARLENE JOSEPH: Promise me.

VICTOR: Jeez, Mom. You want me to sign something?

ARLENE JOSEPH: No way. You know how Indians feel about signing papers.

Angle on Arlene as she picks a piece of fry bread from the pan.

Close angle on that piece of fry bread being dropped onto a plate.

SCENE 24
Int. Builds-the-Fires' house — night.

Close angle on a different piece of fry bread dropping onto a different plate.

Wide angle on Grandma and Thomas sitting at the kitchen table, silently eating dinner.

Both look up as they hear a knock on the door.

They look at each other and smile.

We hear Victor's voice over this.

VICTOR (*V.O.*): Okay, Thomas, I need the money and you can come with me. But I have a few rules. First of all, you can't wear that stupid suit.

SCENE 25
Ext. reservation road — morning.

Wide angle on Thomas, still wearing his suit, and Victor.

Both are carrying small backpacks.

Victor has clothes and toiletries inside his pack.

Thomas probably has just about everything, but he is definitely carrying his glass jar piggy bank inside the pack.

Thomas also has a big army surplus canteen hanging from his belt.

They are walking on opposite sides of the road, heading north off the reservation.

We hear Victor shouting across the road at Thomas.

They are hitchhiking away from the reservation toward the city of Spokane.

VICTOR: . . . and secondly, I don't want you telling me a million of your damn stories. And third, we're going right down there and coming right back.

Close angle on Thomas, who doesn't say anything.

He just smiles.

We begin to hear loud rock music.

SCENE 26

Ext. KREZ Radio station—morning.

As we continue to hear loud rock music we see a close angle on a flimsy antenna on top of an even flimsier house. . . .

SCENE 88

Int. Arnold's trailer—night.

Angle on the front door as somebody (Victor) rattles the doorknob.

It turns one way, then another, then is furiously rattled.

A sudden thump against the door as Victor throws his shoulder to it, and the door opens.

We see Victor stumble into the living room.

The smell of his father's death is horrible.

Victor covers his mouth and nose, sick to his stomach, wanting to leave immediately, but knowing that he must search the house.

The camera follows Victor as he walks from room to room, in search of some trace of himself.

We began to hear a very familiar sad song, "The Ballad of Arlene and Arnold."

That same sad song keeps playing throughout the scene.

Victor walks into the kitchen and opens the refrigerator and checks the contents.

He pulls out a Tupperware container filled with something.

He shakes it a little and then returns it to the fridge, leaving the door open.

He opens all of the cupboard doors, looks inside, and then leaves the cupboard doors open.

In fact, during this search, throughout the entire trailer, Victor opens every drawer, jar, container, cabinet, and door he can find, and leaves them open after he inspects their contents.

He also rubs his hands along all of the maps hanging on the walls of the trailer.

In the living room, he picks up books and magazines and drops them to the floor.

In the bathroom, he opens up jars of cologne and shaving cream.

Finally, he comes to the bedroom.

He looks at the bed.

That bed is where his father died.

A red shirt and blue jeans are draped over a chair at a desk near the bed.

Victor sits at the desk.

He looks through the drawers, but finds nothing.

He looks over the top of the desk and finds nothing.

Victor grabs his father's shirt, holds it to his nose, and inhales deeply.

Through all the smell of Arnold's death, Victor is still trying to smell part of his life, too.

Victor digs through the pockets of his father's blue jeans and finds his father's wallet, completely beaded with an eagle design, the same beaded one that Suzy had held earlier in the film when she was calling Arlene Joseph to tell them of Arnold's death.

Victor looks through his father's wallet, and finds no money, but in a compartment behind his father's driver's license, Victor finds the same photograph that Suzy held earlier in the film.

Insert shot of the photograph of Arlene Joseph, Arnold Joseph, and the Baby Victor.

Victor looks at the back of the photograph.

It had been blank when Suzy first held it.

Now, a single word written there: HOME.

Angle on Victor as he stares down at the photograph.

He cannot begin to understand the complex swirl of emotions inside himself.

But he knows he is in mourning for his dead father.

He knows his father kept some small memento of their life together.

Victor has found evidence of himself in his father's house.

Victor is ready to break.

He digs through his father's blue jeans and finds a pocketknife in the other pocket.

Victor stares at the blade for a while, contemplating his options.

Slowly and methodically, Victor begins to cut his long, black, beautiful hair, and drops the strands onto the bed where his father died.

The hair falls like rain onto the sheets.

SCENE 89
Ext. Suzy's trailer — night.

Angle on the moon shining brightly.

The yellow pickup is parked in front of Suzy's trailer.

SCENE 90
Ext. yellow pickup — morning.

Angle on Suzy, Thomas, and Victor standing near the yellow pickup. . . .

SCENE 151
Ext. Spokane Falls (Thomas's story) — dawn.

As we see the following, we hear Thomas's voice over this.

Angle on Victor standing on the bridge over the Falls.

He holds his father's ash can in his hands.

He opens the can and a strong wind blows up.

It blows the ash up and out of the can, back into Victor's face.

His mouth is open wide and he is screaming a silent scream.

Instead of his voice, we hear the singing voices of Ulali [a First Nations female a capella trio]. We hear them until end.

THOMAS (V.O.): How do we forgive our fathers? Maybe in a dream. He's in your power. You twist his arm. But you're not sure it was he that stole your money. You feel calmer and you decide to let him go free.

Moving shot of the ash as it blows into Victor's mouth, past his head, falls behind him, off the bridge, and down toward the water.

Just before the ash reaches the water, a salmon rises from the water through the ash and splashes back into the river . . .

THOMAS (V.O.): Or he's the one, as in a dream of mine, I must pull from the water, but I never knew it or wouldn't have done it, until I saw the street-theater play so close up I was moved to actions I'd never before taken.

Moving shot begins to flow up the river, slowly at first, then following the course of the river, quickly through the city of Spokane, to the outskirts, then to more remote areas, then coming to a fork in the river, one fork a stream that feeds the river . . .

THOMAS (V.O.): Do we forgive our fathers for leaving us too often or forever when we were little? Maybe for scaring us with unexpected rage or making us nervous because there never seemed to be any rage there at all?

Moving shot then following that stream upstream for a while, as it grows smaller and smaller, then another fork, one fork which is a small creek, following that creek, which grows smaller and smaller.

As we follow the creek, more and more Indians start appearing beside the creek . . .

THOMAS (V.O.): Do we forgive our fathers for marrying or not marrying our mothers? For divorcing or not divorcing our mothers? And shall we forgive them for their excesses of warmth or coldness?

Moving shot very quickly up the creek now as we see a group of people standing ahead at the very source of the river.

Moving shot toward them quickly, then slowing, and stopping on them . . .

THOMAS (V.O.): Shall we forgive them for pushing or leaning? For shutting doors? For speaking only through layers of cloth, or never speaking, or never being silent?

Angle on the Young Victor and the Young Thomas standing together.

Behind them, Arlene Joseph, Grandma Builds-the-Fire, Suzy Song, the Adult Victor, and the Adult Thomas.

THOMAS (*V.O., cont'd*):   Do we forgive our fathers in our age or in theirs? Or in their deaths? Saying it to them or not saying it? If we forgive our fathers, what is left?

Closer angle on the Young Thomas and the Young Victor as they suddenly take each other's hands . . .

Wider angle on the group, creek in the foreground, as Arnold Joseph rises suddenly from the water, his back to us.

He walks toward the shore.

Jeannette Johnston

Sidewalk Interview with Sherman Alexie   [1999]

Sherman Alexie was the geek of his Indian reservation: the misfit kid who marched to a different drummer.

But the 31-year-old writer has since turned that skewed perspective into one of the most unique and creative voices in American literature. Absent from the award-winning poet and novelist's writings are the hackneyed portrayals of Indians as loincloth-clad, befeathered warriors or disillusioned drunks. They've been replaced by funny and flawed contemporary people who bear little resemblance to the caricatures we've come to expect.

Fueled by his literary success and the impact his writings have had on perceptions of Indians, Alexie is now shifting his art to the big screen. His first feature film, *Smoke Signals,* which follows the stoic Victor and his nerdy sidekick Thomas on their road trip to recover Victor's estranged father's ashes, is one of the most notable films of the season. And as the first film ever produced, directed, and written by Native Americans, it's also a cinematic milestone.

We caught up with Alexie at the Nantucket Film Festival, where *Smoke Signals* was screening to a rapt audience. Here's what he had to tell us about himself, his career, and the impact of his ground-breaking debut film.

Sidewalk: *Thomas Builds-the-Fire seems so at odds with the kinds of stereotypical Indian film roles we've come to expect. He's a garrulous geek, and annoys the hell out of everyone. Why create such a surprising character?*

Alexie: Because Thomas explodes the myth and stereotype about the huge, stoic, warrior Indian. He's the exact opposite of what people have come to expect — the idea of an Indian geek just doesn't happen. He's something of a trickster figure, sort of a coyote figure, and he's mythological in that sense. He's always subverting conventions, not only Indian conventions about Indians but white conventions about Indians.

The funny thing is that while he's over the top in many ways, he's a recognizable cultural character for Indians, because there's two or three of those guys on every reservation. I was the one on mine. He's very much like me, or like I was. I've since learned to hide my geekiness. Well, a little bit.

Sidewalk: *When you were a boy, did you dream of writing poetry and making films?*

Alexie: I never dreamed of either thing. Growing up on a reservation, nobody tells you you can do this. I never read a book written by an Indian until I was 21 years old and in college. So the idea of creating art in that way was completely outside my realm of possibility, beyond anything I ever imagined. I was going to be a pediatrician, but I kept fainting in human anatomy class.

Sidewalk: *Practicing medicine on the reservation is one way to give back to your people. Is making movies another?*

Alexie: In a different sort of way. The thing is, being a good artist and being a good member of a tribe are often mutually exclusive. Being an artist is all about being iconoclastic and rebellious and questioning the status quo at all times. But being a good member of a tribe is about filling and accepting your role. So I'm often at odds with members of my tribe simply because of what I do as an artist. That's been the case forever.

Sidewalk: *What kind of reception did you get during the filming?*

Alexie: It was a huge event on the Coeur d'Alene reservation. Although our actors may not be all that well-known in the outside world, Adam Beach is Elvis on the reservation. No matter what time we were filming, there would be big crowds watching. On the night we did the fire, it was freezing and rainy and horrible, and there were 40 people watching the filming. Our assistant directors had to keep shushing everybody because they were so excited.

Sidewalk: *Writing is a silent and lonely project. Making a film involves collaboration. Was the adjustment difficult?*

Alexie: In writing books, I am the Fidel Castro of my world. I determine everything. In the filmmaking project, I'm more like the senator from Wyoming. So getting used to that took some doing. Making this film was like being on a basketball team. There are certainly stars and people who take the last shot of the game, but also people who pass the ball — everybody's a part of the team. Once I started thinking of it that way, then it got to be fun.

Sidewalk: *Why is this the first major film ever to be written, directed, and produced by Indians?*

Alexie: First of all, I don't think movie producers in general think there's an economic audience for these kind of films. There are only a million and a half Indians in the country, so the built-in audience isn't as large as it is for a Chicano or a black filmmaker. So they didn't think they'd make their money back, which is already wrong — without even selling a ticket [to *Smoke Signals*] we've already made all the money back twofold.

Secondly, most Indian filmmakers who've been making Indian feature films have been so didactic and political that the art suffers. This film doesn't work that way. It's highly political, highly politically aware, but we do it in ways that are very artful and funny and interesting. This film is subtle enough and clever enough to get its political messages across without hammering people over the head with it.

People have never clamored to get Indian directors or writers to work on their projects. But with this movie, things are changing. Already I've seen eight different Trail of Tears screenplays. I need to get a T-shirt that says "no loincloth movies."

Sidewalk: *What kind of impact do you think this film is going to have on Indians?*

Alexie: I've already seen that impact. At a special screening at Sundance for the Indian community in Utah, there was a 70-year-old Indian man sitting next to me. He chuckled through the whole movie. Just rubbing his belly kind of chuckling. He was so delighted. And that was so wonderful to see him so happy with something I'd helped create. Another time, an Indian woman walked up to me, and she'd had serious issues with her father. And she said, "Now I know how to talk to him."

Sidewalk: *Why do Indian stereotypes continue to persist?*

Alexie: It's part of the national consciousness. If people start dealing with Indian culture and Indian peoples truthfully in this country, we're going to have to start dealing with the genocide that happened here. In order to start dealing truthfully with our cultures, they have to start dealing truthfully with that great sin, the original sin of this country, and that's not going to happen.

Just look at the sports teams. You couldn't have a team called the Washington Kikes or the Washington Micks. But yet you can have the Washington Redskins and this Indian with a big nose and big lips running around. How would you feel if it was the Washington Rabbis and you had a guy with braids running around throwing bagels? Or the Washington Jesuits with some guy handing out communion wafers? It wouldn't happen. So, it's an insult. It's proof of the ways in which we get ignored.

Tomson Highway

Interview with Sherman Alexie   [1997]

Tomson Highway: *When did you start writing?*

Sherman Alexie: I started writing because I kept fainting in human anatomy class and needed a career change. The only class that fit where the human anatomy class had been was a poetry writing workshop. I always liked poetry. I'd never heard of, or nobody'd ever showed me, a book written by a First Nations person, ever. I got into the class, and my professor, Alex Kwo, gave me an anthology of contemporary Native American poetry called *Songs from This Earth on Turtle's Back*. I opened it up and — oh my gosh — I saw my life in poems and stories for the very first time.

T.H.: *Who were some of the writers in the book?*

S.A.: Linda Hogan, Simon Ortiz, Joy Harjo, James Welch, Adrian Lewis. There were poems about reservation life: fry bread, bannock, 49's, fried baloney, government food, and terrible housing. But there was also joy and happiness.

There's a line by a Paiute poet named Adrian Lewis that says, "Oh, Uncle Adrian, I'm in the reservation of my mind." I thought, "Oh my God, somebody understands me!" At that moment I realized, "I can do this!" That's when I started writing — in 1989.

T.H.: *The poetry that you would have studied in American Studies, for instance, the poetry of Wallace Stevens or e. e. cummings or Emily Dickinson never influenced you at all?*

S.A.: Of course it did. I loved that stuff. I still love it. Walt Whitman and Emily Dickinson are two of my favorites. Wallace Stevens leaves me kind of dry, but the other poets, they're still a primary influence. I always tell people my literary influences are Stephen King, John Steinbeck, my mother, my grandfather, and the Brady Bunch.

T.H.: *Then you moved on to short stories.*

S.A.: I'd written a couple of them in college. After my first book of poems, *The Business of Fancydancing,* was published by Hanging Loose Press in Brooklyn, New York, I got a great *New York Times* book review. The review called me "one of the major lyric voices of our time." I was a 25-year-old Spokane Indian guy working as a secretary at a high school exchange program in Spokane, Washington, when my poetry editor faxed that review to me. I pulled it out of the fax machine beside my desk and read, "one of the major lyric voices of our time." I thought, "Great! Where do I go from here!?" After that, the agents started calling *me*.

T.H.: *Where did that book of poetry come from?*

S.A.: It was my first semester poetry manuscript. Part of the assignment was to submit to literary magazines. The one I liked in the Washington State library was *Hanging Loose* magazine. I liked that it started the same year I was born. The magazine, the press, and I are the same age. Over the next year and a half they kept taking poems of mine to publish. Then they asked if I had a manuscript. I said, "Yes!" and sent it in.

It was a *thousand* copies. I figured I'd sell a hundred and fifty to my family. My mom would buy a hundred herself and that would be about it. But, it took off. I never expected it. Sometimes I think it would have been nicer if it had not been as big, because my career has been a rocket ride. There's a lot of pressure.

Susan Berry Brill de Ramírez
Fancy Dancer: A Profile of Sherman Alexie   [1999]

Alexie contrasts his most recent collection of poetry, *The Summer of Black Widows,* with his earlier volume, *The Business of Fancydancing.* . . . The earlier collection of stories and poems was very popular in Indian country, presenting direct and often raw depictions of reservation life. Its realities are stark and troubling, guaranteed to disturb any preconceived notions readers might have about Indian America. And the poems and stories are told with engaging strategies of oral storytelling traditions, including the humor and epigrammatic statements that sum up centuries of struggle. As Alexie writes in the title poem, "A promise is just like money. / Something we can hold . . . / It's business, a fancydance to fill where it's empty." The pieces in this book are orally driven and very accessible.

In contrast, Alexie's recent book of poetry has been received more positively by the literary community than in Indian country. He explains that these poems are more literary and less accessible to the broader audience he wants to reach. The title poem, "The Summer of Black Widows," is a tightly crafted work in which Alexie uses repetition, meter, and alliteration to convey a story about the power of stories to survive and endure regardless of the extent to which people and cultures attempt to silence them or twist them into lies. These are stories created by the woven webs of black widow spiders. Alexie's choice of naming these story weavers "black widows" underscores the fact that the stories, like their creators, are venomous and dangerous. And even though some might try to destroy ("poison") or contain ("capture") the stories, there is no power in this world ("nothing, neither fire / nor water, neither rock nor wind") that "can bring them down" — not literally from the rafters where they are safely out of our reach, nor metaphorically from their protected positions as harbingers of truth.

Alexie warns us that we fear the truths in those stories, so we try to capture them and poison them. Like the "bundles of stories / . . . Up in the corners of our old houses," stories that previously fell like rain now must be protected from our reach so that we will not destroy them. Perhaps this poem, in some ways, serves as a metaphor for Alexie's own writing as he grapples with the process of telling his stories and truths in ways that compromise neither them, him, or his readers. Either way, the poem, aimed at a literary audience, serves as a warning to his readers to respect both the presences and absences of stories. . . .

When asked why he made the switch from poetry to prose, from short stories to novels, and from writing to film, Alexie immediately responds with two answers: sales and access. Novels and films pay the bills better than poetry, and with the broader sales he can get his work out to more people, particularly Indian youth. . . . "As I have been working with the film," Alexie says, "I've come to realize sitting in a movie theater is the contemporary equivalent of sitting around the fire listening to a storyteller. . . . And because of this, Indian peoples, all peoples, will respond more powerfully to movies than to books." . . .

Another of Alexie's concerns is that Indian literatures are erroneously assumed by non-Indian readers to represent social and historical realities in ways that other literatures do not. When readers' expectations take an anthropological turn, writers are put in the extremely awkward position of being expected to represent their tribes, communities, and Native America. "Most of us [Indian writers] are outcasts," Alexie says. "We don't really fit in within the Indian community, so we write to try to fit in and sound Indian. So it's ironic that we become the spokespeople for Indian country, that we are supposed to be representative of our tribes." . . .

What does Alexie want to see within the ranks of Indian writers? "I want us to write books about the way we live." He wants Indian writers to write from their own lived experiences, not from some nostalgic and romanticized notion of what it means to be Indian. "When I see words like *the Creator, Father Sky, Mother Earth, Four Leggeds,* I almost feel like we're colonizing ourselves. These words, this is how we're supposed to talk — what it means to be Indian according to white America. But it's not who we really are; it's not what it means to be Navajo or Spokane or Coeur d'Alene."

Joseph L. Coulombe

The Approximate Size of His Favorite Humor: Sherman Alexie's Comic Connections and Disconnections in *The Lone Ranger and Tonto Fistfight in Heaven*   [2002]

In this essay I will argue that Alexie's humor is central to a constructive social and moral purpose evident throughout his fiction but particularly in his collection of short stories, *The Lone Ranger and Tonto Fistfight in Heaven.* He uses humor — or his characters use humor — to reveal injustice, protect self-esteem, heal wounds, and create bonds. The function of humor changes from scene to scene, shifting to serve these myriad goals. In *Indi'n Humor* Kenneth Lincoln explains the many different roles of humor within Indian communities. He describes "the contrary powers of Indian humor" as "[t]he powers to heal and to hurt, to bond and to exorcize, to renew and to purge" (5). Like the legendary Trickster figure, humor in Indian communities embodies shifting meanings and serves conflicting ends. However, rather than a sign of his "hip" irreverence for all things Indian, Alexie's sophisticated use of humor unsettles conventional ways of thinking and compels re-evaluation and growth, which ultimately allows Indian characters to connect to their heritage in novel ways and forces non-Indian readers to reconsider simplistic generalizations.

In his best work to date, *The Lone Ranger and Tonto Fistfight in Heaven,* humor allows his characters to display strengths and hide weaknesses, to expose prejudices and avoid realities, and to create bonds and construct barricades. These "contrary powers" often coexist simultaneously, requiring the characters and readers to position and then reposition themselves within shifting personal and cultural contexts. Alexie's cross-cultural humor alternately engages readers — creating positive connections between individuals of diverse backgrounds — and disrupts communities (both Indian and white), erecting barriers that make constructive communication difficult. Here lies its principal challenge for readers. Alexie's shifting treatment of humor serves as a means of connection as well as an instrument of separation. However, it is precisely this complexity and plasticity that allow him to negotiate successfully the differences between Indian communities and mainstream American society, while simultaneously instigating crucial dialogue about social and moral issues especially important to Indian communities. . . .

I contend that Alexie's brand of humor, more than others perhaps, is "that trickster at the heart of the Native American imagination." As such, it embodies the potential for facilitating mutual understanding and respect between diverse peoples. By exploding expectations and compelling dialogue, humor teaches self-knowledge and social awareness, much like Trickster. Alexie's use of humor encourages readers to think anew by creating a space of shared inquiry and reciprocal empathy. . . . Alexie's humor . . . provides an emotional and intellectual meeting ground for his readers to reconsider reductive stereotypes and expectations. . . . Alexie challenges readers of diverse backgrounds to join together to re-evaluate past and present ideologies. Humor generates a freely occupied space in which readers can begin sorting through the myriad connections and disconnections that face us all today. Stephen Evans, in an evaluation of Alexie's refashioning of stereotypes (particularly that of the "drunken Indian"), correctly notes how satire compels "the collaborative making of meaning between Alexie and his readers" (54). Readers are not passive receptacles; they engage, question, resist, learn, and grow during the reading process. They join Alexie . . . to hash out interpretations of the past, responses to the present, and prospects for the future. This delicate alliance between author and audience — facilitated in large part by humor — promises to be more effective than purely logical, historical, or traditional efforts to promote understanding. With its shifting layers and elaborate surprises, Alexie's humor disrupts readers' complacency and necessitates analysis, clarification, and, ultimately, identification.

Works Cited

Alexie, Sherman. *The Lone Ranger and Tonto Fistfight in Heaven*. New York: Harper Perennial, 1993.

Evans, Stephen F. "'Open Containers': Sherman Alexie's Drunken Indians." *American Indian Quarterly* 25.1 (Winter 2001): 46–72.

Lincoln, Kenneth. *Indi'n Humor: Bicultural Play in Native America*. New York: Oxford UP, 1993.

APPROACHING THE READINGS

1. In "Superman and Me" (p. 4) and the interviews with *Sidewalk* (p. 1350) and Tomson Highway (p. 1352), Alexie talks about what it means to be a Native American writer. Pick out the key points he makes and be ready to discuss the ways the works in this chapter illustrate them.

2. In his *Sidewalk* interview, Alexie says that *Smoke Signals* is "highly political, highly politically aware, but we do it in ways that are very artful and funny and interesting" (p. 1352). Explain what he means by that. Find illustrations of that in *Smoke Signals* and look for examples of the same qualities in his poetry and stories as well.

3. In his interview with Tomson Highway (p. 1352), Alexie says that he was influenced by the poetry of Walt Whitman. Whitman was also an important influence on Langston Hughes (Chapter 22). Read the selections from *Song of Myself* in this book (pp. 748–52) and consider what it is about Whitman, in style or theme, that appeals to Alexie and to Hughes.

4. Susan Berry Brill de Ramírez, discussing "The Summer of Black Widows," writes that in it Alexie asserts that "we fear the truths in . . . stories, so we try to capture them and poison them" (p. 1354). What kinds of truths that we fear and try to avoid are conveyed in the Alexie poems and story in this chapter? Or, applying the point more broadly, what kinds of truths that we fear and try to avoid are conveyed by any of the stories, poems, and plays in this book, or by literature generally?

5. Joseph Coulombe says in his critical essay that Alexie "uses humor — or his characters use humor — to reveal injustice, protect self-esteem, heal wounds, and create bonds" (p. 1355). Discuss what Coulombe's statement means and find examples in Alexie's works that support it.

RESPONDING THROUGH WRITING

Journal Entries

1. The epigraph to "Father and Farther" (p. 1326) is a line from Theodore Roethke's poem "My Papa's Waltz" (p. 492). Reread that poem and write a journal entry on what makes the epigraph appropriate for Alexie's poem.

2. In your journal, make a list of the ways stories are imaged in "The Summer of Black Widows" (p. 1324) — different ways they are referred to or different metaphors used for them. Discuss briefly the cumulative effect of depicting story in this variety of ways.

WWW

Research Sherman Alexie with LitLinks at bedfordstmartins.com/ approachinglit.

3. Write a journal entry on how the things you've read in this chapter, by and about Sherman Alexie, make the line "I read to save my life" (in "Superman and Me," p. 4) take on more implications and significance.

Literary Analysis Papers

4. Write a critical paper on ways the screenplay for *Smoke Signals* (p. 1338) uses and adapts the structure and the style of "This Is What It Means to Say Phoenix, Arizona" (p. 1329).

5. Write a paper on the theme of fathers (or father figures) and sons in Alexie's poems and stories.

6. Write an analytical paper on types of humor, and the uses and effects of humor, in "This Is What It Means to Say Phoenix, Arizona" (p. 1329).

Making Connections

7. Write an analytical paper on how actions, characters, and details in "This Is What It Means to Say Phoenix, Arizona" (p. 1329) were changed as the story was turned into the screenplay *Smoke Signals* (p. 1338) and/or how aspects of the screenplay were changed in the course of shooting and editing the film.

8. Write a paper connecting "The Business of Fancydancing" (p. 1323) to the sestina tradition. A sestina — like a chant or litany — relies on repetitions in which words or phrases take on a magical quality as they appear and reappear, but change in meaning and impact as the context changes. Do some research on the characteristics of the form and its history and discuss why that form seems appropriate for this poem and may appeal to a Native American writer.

Cultural Criticism Papers

9. Write a paper in which you compare the depiction of Native Americans in three or four films (some before 1960, some later) with their depiction in Alexie's poems, stories, and films.

10. Write a research paper on the archetypal Trickster figure in Native American mythology and literature, focusing particularly on how it is adapted in selected works by Alexie.

RESPONDING THROUGH THE ARTS

1. Make a collage of images that capture aspects of the poems, stories, and screenplay included in this chapter and aspects of Alexie's life. Be sure to include a fancydancer.

2. Using the excerpts from *Smoke Signals* (p. 1338) as a model, try converting "That Place Where Ghosts of Salmon Jump" (p. 1325) into a screenplay, conveying its action and meaning through dialogue, scene, and directions to actors and camera operators.

Approaching
LITERARY
RESEARCH

Overleaf: Toni Morrison giving a reading for her book Love *(2003) at Barnes and Noble in New York, 2003. Morrison's 1983 short story "Recitatif" is the subject of Kristina Martinez's student research paper, "The Structure of Story in Toni Morrison's 'Recitatif'" in Chapter 26. (See page 1447 for a short biography of Morrison.)*

Photo © Nancy Kaszerman/ZUMA/Corbis.

A good critic is one who narrates the adventures of his mind among masterpieces.

Anatole France

Reading Critical Essays

CHAPTER 25

When you see a movie you really like, you may not only want to see it again but also to find out more about it — what other films an actor has appeared in (and perhaps some details about her or his life), some background on the director and information on the screenwriter, what changes were made from the work on which it was based (if adapted from another source), and what well-informed film critics said about it. As you look for information about these topics in newspapers, in magazines, or on the Internet, you are engaging in research. You can do the same for literary works. Even if you learn a lot about a work by reading it several times, reflecting on it and taking notes about it, listening to what is said about it in class, and discussing it with your classmates, for rich, complex works there is always more to learn, beyond the classroom.

Learning more in this case can be interesting and even exciting as it brings you deeper into the great ongoing conversation about literature that we've referred to several times in this book. That conversation starts with people talking about works they like and sharing their enthusiasms, dislikes, and questions. It continues as they move that exchange to paper (or computer screens). It extends further through the efforts of literary scholars who publish their critical insights about a particular work or era or theme. Obviously, you can participate in early stages of that conversation. But it's important for you, as a student of literature, to enter the later stages as well by reading, reflecting upon, and responding to the critical writings of literary scholars, thus incorporating them into your own literary experience. This chapter offers suggestions on how to read and assess critical essays about literary works, something that can be an important step toward an even more interesting and provocative involvement in the wider world of literary study.

WHAT ARE CRITICAL ESSAYS?

The word *critical* in its literary use (and in its use for the arts in general) does not mean "inclined to find fault or judge severely," as in "My uncle is such a critical person—always ripping somebody apart." Rather, it means exercising skillful and well-informed judgment as to the techniques, ideas, or merits in, for example, a work of literature or a play, a concert, a dance performance, or an art exhibit. Literary critics are scholars who have learned a great deal about literature, usually through work toward academic degrees but sometimes through extensive reading on their own. When they prepare to write a critical essay on a work, they read the work many times; they read everything else the author has written; and they read critical essays and books written about the work and author by other critics. Through previous study they probably already have learned a good deal about the time and places in which the author lived, and about writers and works that may have influenced the author, but they may do additional study as preparation for a particular essay. For us to read what such expert authorities write about a work can yield insights—which we otherwise might miss—and a fuller understanding of the work itself, its context, and how it came into being.

WHY READ CRITICAL ESSAYS?

Reading critical essays helps in a number of ways. However, you will find them most useful if you read them at the right point. We recommend strongly that you not begin reading critical essays about a story, poem, or play until you have read the work itself several times and formulated your own thoughts about it. If you start reading criticism before you know the text well and have articulated your ideas about it, the ideas in the essays may overwhelm your own thoughts and lead you merely to accept or adapt what you read. If you've already formed ideas, you'll be better able to evaluate what you read, to disagree with the critic as well as agree, and to accept refinements on your own insights.

Once you know a work well and have begun shaping your ideas about it, here are five good reasons for reading critical studies of the work:

1. To see how your own ideas are like and unlike those of other readers
2. To have your attention drawn to parts or aspects of the work whose significance you haven't recognized and to begin to imagine new ways of reading a text—new interpretations of or perspectives on it
3. To learn where the literary conversation about an author or a work stands and what scholars regard as strengths and weaknesses in what other critics have written
4. To discover new ways of constructing a literary argument, refuting earlier positions, offering counterarguments, and using explanation, elaboration, and evidence effectively

5. To gain a better understanding of the background or culture or literary tradition of a work by reading the results of a scholar's primary research (because you don't have time to do research on everything yourself, you often learn through reading the results of other people's research)

Each of these reasons has a practical benefit when you are working on a paper. Reading critical essays can give you a more informed and balanced stance as you explore a work. You can be more confident about your ability to find support for a position you want to uphold, and for entering the on-going discussion as you write your paper. If need be, you may be able to re-fine your tentative thesis into a more effective argumentative thesis by connecting with places where critics disagree with each other, or where one modifies what another has said — the way Susan Farrell challenges prevailing views about "Everyday Use" in the sample essay later in this chapter.

ACTIVE READING: Critical Essays

In Chapters 2, 8, 15, and 21, we describe a number of conventions you should follow in writing a literary paper — being sure you state a thesis in the in-troduction, start each paragraph with a topic sentence, and so on. There is a strategic reason for following those conventions: They enable your reader to grasp your paper easily and establish confidence in you as a writer worth attend-ing to. The importance of what we say in those chapters may become more evi-dent as you read critical essays and find yourself using those conventions as a way of tracing the steps in the argument and understanding what is being said. Here are some guidelines for reading critical essays. (For reading critical books, begin by looking at the table of contents, noticing the overall outline of the book, and reading the preface to find out the aims, approach, and outlook of the book; then apply the guidelines to each chapter.)

- *Pick out the thesis and identify the central idea the paper will explore.* The the-sis is likely found near the end of the introductory paragraph or section. Look also for references to previous studies and notice how this essay differs from or disagrees with them. Use such references to identify what is new about the central idea and about the essay.

- *Look for the topic sentence in each paragraph.* The first sentence usually states the central idea to be discussed in the paragraph. (The second sen-tence may do this instead if the first is mainly a transitional sentence.)

- *Watch for the way the ideas are advanced and supported.* Outline the steps in the argument (the thesis sentence and topic sentences may provide an outline). Consider the reasoning used in laying out ideas and connecting points to each other. Consider the nature and adequacy of the evidence provided in support of the reasoning.

- *Identify and take into account the theoretical approach being taken in the essay.* The appendix on theoretical approaches to literature (p. 1479) summarizes a number of ways scholars approach literature, such as doing literary analysis, literary interpretation, historical background research, or analysis from a Marxist, psychoanalytic, or feminist perspective. Knowing where a critical work is coming from — what its assumptions and intentions are — helps you to follow its arguments and to do justice to its ideas.

- *Look at the footnotes and/or works cited list to see if there are other studies you might want to read yourself.*

SAMPLE ESSAY

Try out those strategies in reading the following essay. If you did not read Alice Walker's story "Everyday Use" in Chapter 5 (p. 101) or if you do not remember it well, read it before going on to the essay. For the convenience of readers, we have changed the page numbers for quotations of "Everyday Use" originally given in the essay to the pages on which they are found in this book.

Notice as you read the essay that the first paragraph situates the study in the ongoing discussion of "Everyday Use." It sketches out the position held by other critics, summarizing and quoting from a few representative analyses of the story and listing many other studies in a footnote. Then it states the thesis to be explored in this paper, one that clearly is argumentative because it asserts a position almost directly opposite to the one most critics hold. The rest of the essay elaborates on that argument and explains why the author adheres to it. As you read, it is important to differentiate between sentences that *advance* the argument and sentences that *support* and *illustrate* the argument. To make that easier, we have put the former in boldface and added some marginal notes.

Susan Farrell

Fight vs. Flight: A Re-evaluation of Dee in Alice Walker's "Everyday Use"   [1998]

Method: summary of views held by other critics.

Most readers of Alice Walker's short story "Everyday Use," published in her 1973 collection, *In Love and Trouble,* agree that the point of the story is to show, as Nancy Tuten argues, a mother's "awakening to one daughter's superficiality and to the other's deepseated understanding of heritage" (125).[1] These readers praise the "simplicity" of Maggie and her mother, along with their allegiance to their specific family identity and folk heritage as well as their refusal to change at the whim of an outside world that doesn't really have much to do with them. Such a reading condemns the older, more worldly sister, Dee, as "shallow," "condescending," and "manipulative," as overly concerned with style, fashion, and aesthetics, and thus as lacking a "true" understanding of her heritage. **In this essay, conversely, I will argue that this popular view is far too simple a reading of the story. While Dee is certainly insensitive and selfish to a certain degree, she nevertheless offers a view of heritage and a strategy for contemporary African Americans to cope with an oppressive society that is, in some ways, more valid than that offered by Mama and Maggie.**

Thesis.

We must remember from the beginning that the story is told by Mama; the perceptions are filtered through her mind and her views of her two daughters are not to be accepted uncritically. Several readers have pointed out that Mama's view of Maggie is not quite accurate — that Maggie is not as passive or as "hangdog" as she appears.[2] **Might Mama's view of her older daughter, Dee, not be especially accurate as well? Dee obviously holds a central place in Mama's world.** The story opens with the line: "I will wait for her in the yard that Maggie and I made so clean and wavy yesterday afternoon" (101). As Houston Baker and Charlotte Pierce-Baker point out, "The mood at the story's beginning is one of ritualistic waiting," of preparation "for the arrival of a goddess" (715). Thus, Dee seems to attain almost mythic stature in Mama's imagination as she and Maggie wait for the as-yet unnamed "her" to appear. Such an opening may lead readers to suspect that Mama has a rather troubled relationship with her older daughter. Dee inspires in Mama a type of awe and fear more suitable to the advent of a goddess than the love one might expect a mother to feel for a returning daughter.

Method: building on earlier critics.

Central idea for Section I.

Mama, in fact, **displaces what seem to be her own fears onto Maggie** when she speculates that Maggie will be cowed by Dee's arrival. Mama conjectures that

> Maggie will be nervous until after her sister goes: she will stand hopelessly in corners, homely and ashamed of the burn scars down her arms and legs, eyeing her sister with a mixture of envy and awe. She thinks her sister has held life always in the palm of one hand, that "no" is a word the world never learned to say to her. (101)

But Mama here emphasizes the perceptual nature of this observation — she says that Maggie *thinks* these things, encouraging readers to wonder whether or not this first perception of Dee is true. We also find out in the next section, when Mama relates her Johnny Carson television fantasy, that she herself is the one that will be "nervous"

Method: close reading of text.

*Evidence: sum-
mary and quo-
tation.*

until after Dee goes, that she is ashamed of her own appearance and very much seeks her daughter's approval. Mama confesses that, in "real life," she is "a large, big-boned woman with rough, man-working hands" (102). However, in her television fantasy, as Mama tells us,

> all this does not show. . . . I am the way my daughter would want me to be: a hundred pounds lighter, my skin like an un-cooked barley pancake. My hair glistens in the hot bright lights. Johnny Carson has much to do to keep up with my quick and witty tongue. (102)

It is important to remember, though, that **this Johnny Carson daydream is Mama's fantasy of a mother-child reunion, *not* Dee's.** In fact, Mama even acknowledges that this particular scenario might not be to Dee's taste — she imagines Dee pinning an orchid on her even though Dee had previously told Mama she thinks orchids are "tacky flowers" (101). Thus, although Tuten equates Dee's values with those of "the white Johnny Carson society" (126), it seems to me that we have to question whether Mama's vision of her light-skinned, slender, witty self is actually Dee's wish or only Mama's perception of what she imagines Dee would like her to be.

Elsewhere, as well, we see that **Mama is often wrong about her expectations of Dee and her readings of Dee's emotions.** She writes that she "used to think" Dee hated Maggie as much as she hated the previous house that burned down (102). Mama implies, though, that she has since changed her mind about this. Further, as Mama and Maggie continue to wait for Dee's arrival, Mama "de-liberately" turns her back on the house, expecting Dee to hate this house as much as Mama believes she hated the earlier one: "No doubt when Dee sees it she will want to tear it down" (103). When Dee does arrive, however, she has a camera with her and "never takes a shot without making sure the house is included" (104). Of course,

*Method: con-
trast with other
critics.*

most readers see this as evidence of Dee's fickle changing with what-ever fad happens to be current. Once it becomes fashionable to have rural, poverty-stricken roots, Dee wants a record of her own humble beginnings. This might very well be true. Yet **I would argue that we have only Mama's word for Dee's earlier haughtiness, and this could have been exaggerated,** much as Mama hints that her earlier suspicion of Dee's hatred for Maggie was inaccurate. The more sub-tle point here is that **Mama's expectations of Dee tell us more about Mama herself than they do about Dee.** Again, Mama seems to view Dee with a mixture of awe, envy, and fear. Although she re-sents Dee because she expects Dee will want "to tear the house down," Mama still takes her cue from her older daughter, herself turning her back on the house, perhaps in an effort to appease this daughter, who looms so large in Mama's imagination.

In contrast to her own fearfulness, **Mama, with grudging admi-ration, remembers Dee as a fearless girl.** While Mama imagines herself unable to look white people in the eye, talking to them only "with one foot raised in flight," Dee "would always look anyone in the eye. Hesitation was no part of her nature" (102). Mama remem-bers Dee as self-centered and demanding, yes, but she also remem-bers this daughter as **a determined fighter.** Dee is concerned with style, but she'll do whatever is necessary to improve her circum-stances. For instance, when Dee wants a new dress, she "makes over" an old green suit someone had given her mother. Rather than passively accept her lot, as Mama seems trained to do, Dee "was de-termined to stare down any disaster in her efforts" (103). **Mama's fearful nature is also apparent in her reaction to knowledge.** Words for Mama are associated with "lies" and "other folks' habits" (102). She remembers feeling "trapped and ignorant" as Dee reads to her and Maggie "without pity" (102). This is partly because Mama never had an education herself. When her school was closed down in 1927, after she had completed only the second grade, Mama, like the other African Americans in her community, didn't fight: "colored asked fewer questions than they do now," she tells us (103). Again, Mama is trained in acquiescence while Dee refuses to meekly accept the status quo.

Central idea for Section II.

Method: accu-mulation of details.

Most critics see Dee's education and her insistence on reading to Mama and Maggie as further evidence of her separation from and lack of understanding for her family identity and heritage. Tuten, for instance, argues that, in this story, "Walker stresses not only the importance of language but also the destructive effects of its mis-use. . . . Rather than providing a medium for newfound awareness and for community, . . . verbal skill equips Dee to oppress and manip-ulate others and to isolate herself" (125). Similarly, Donna Winchell writes that "Dee tries to force on" Maggie and her mother "knowl-edge they probably do not need." She continues,

Method: con-trast with other critics.

> Mrs. Johnson can take an objective look at who and what she is and find not disillusionment but an easy satisfaction. Simple pleasures — a dip of snuff, a cooling breeze across a clean swept yard, church songs, the soothing movements of milk cows — are enough. (82)

But are these "simple pleasures" really enough for Mama in the story? When she imagines her future she seems vaguely unhappy and apprehensive about it: "[Maggie] will marry John Thomas (who has mossy teeth in an earnest face) and then I'll be free to sit here and I guess just sing church songs to myself. Although I never was a good singer. Never could carry a tune" (103). Not quite sure what she will do with herself when Maggie marries, Mama can only imagine

Method: show-ing other critics may be mis-taken.

herself alone, engaging in an activity which she feels she is not even very good at. Although she perhaps goes about it in the wrong way— Mama says that Dee "pressed us to her with the serious way she read," only to "shove us away at just the moment, like dimwits, we seemed about to understand" (102)—Dee at least tries to change what she foresees as Mama's fairly dismal future, a vision of her future Mama herself seems to reinforce rather than dispute. **Thus, I'd suggest the possibility that Dee's attempt to educate Mama and Maggie may be read much more positively than other critics have suggested.** Again, we must remember that Mama's perspective is the only one we see throughout the story. Told from Dee's point of view, we might expect a very different rendering of this incident. Rather than simply abandon her mother and sister in their ignorance and poverty, in their acquiescence to an oppressive system, Dee tries her best to extend her own education to them, which is surely not such a bad thing.

When Dee does finally arrive, **both Maggie and her mother react again with fear of the unknown, of something strange and different.** But as Dee approaches, Mama notices that the brightly colored African dress that Dee wears "throw[s] back the light of the sun" (104). Mama feels her "whole face warming from the heat waves it throws out" (104). She also admires the way that the "dress is loose and flows," and, despite her initial reaction, even decides that she likes it as Dee moves closer to her. In her admiration of the dress, **Mama illustrates Walker's point that everything new is not to be feared, that change can be positive, not only negative.** Maggie, however, remains fearful, even in the face of the friendliness of Dee's companion, who grins and greets Mrs. Johnson and Maggie warmly: "Asalamalakim, my mother and sister!" (104). When he tries to hug Maggie, though, she falls back against a chair and trembles. And later, when he tries to teach Maggie a new handshake, her hand remains limp and she quickly withdraws it from his.

Central idea for Section III.

Shortly after this, Dee announces that she is no longer Dee but "Wangero Leewanika Kemanjo." She has newly adopted an African name since, as she explains: "I couldn't bear it any longer, being named after the people who oppress me" (104). Many readers point to Dee's proclamation of her new name as the turning point in the story, the point at which Dee pushes her mother too far. They point out that Dee is rejecting her family heritage and identity in this scene. **Yet it seems to me that Dee and Mama are *both* right here.** Mama's recounting of the family history of the name is surely accurate, but what the critics fail to point out is that Dee's assertion that the name comes from "the people who oppress" her is also accurate. While most readers see Mama and Maggie as having a "true" sense

Method: contrast with other critics.

of heritage as opposed to Dee's false or shallow understanding of the past, both Mama and Dee are blind to particular aspects of heritage. Dee has much to learn about honoring her particular and individual family history, but Mama has much to learn about the history of African Americans in general, and about fighting oppression. Although each is stubborn, both Dee and Mama do make a concession to the other here. Dee tells Mama that she needn't use the new name if she doesn't want to, while Mama shows her willingness to learn and to use the name.

Mama's secret admiration for Dee's fighting spirit leaks out again when she explicitly connects the "beef-cattle peoples down the road" to Dee and her boyfriend, "Hakim-a-barber." We see that the neighbors down the road, like Dee's boyfriend, are most likely black Muslims: they also say "Asalamalakim" when they meet, and Hakim explains that he accepts "some of their doctrines," although farming is not his style. Like Dee, these neighbors are also fighters. When "white folks" poison some of their cattle, they "stayed up all night with rifles in their hands" (105). Tellingly, Mama, who can't look white people in the eye and who never asked questions when her school closed down, is intrigued by this younger generation's refusal to acquiesce. She "walked a mile and a half" down the road "just to see the sight" of blacks armed for resistance (105). **Mixed with her resentment against her older daughter's worldliness and self-centered attitude, Mama also grudgingly respects and even envies the willingness to fight evinced both by Dee and the black Muslim neighbors.**

Method: new way of reading the text.

Maggie's forbearance in the story contrasts with Dee's boldness. When Dee haughtily insists that Maggie would ruin Grandma's quilts by using them every day, and that hanging the quilts would be the only way to preserve them, Maggie, "like somebody used to never winning anything, or having anything reserved for her," meekly replies: "She can have them, Mama, . . . I can 'member Grandma Dee without the quilts" (107). Mama, though, does not react so meekly. She sees Maggie standing with her scarred hands hidden in her skirt and says: "When I looked at her like that something hit me in the top of my head and ran down to the soles of my feet. Just like when I'm in church and the spirit of God touches me and I get happy and shout" (107). This powerful feeling causes Mama to do something she "never had done before": she "snatched the quilts out of Miss Wangero's hands and dumped them into Maggie's lap" (107). **Ironically, in acting against Dee's wishes here, Mama is truly behaving more like Dee, with her refusal to back down, her willingness to stand up for herself, than she is like the patient and long-suffering Maggie.** So perhaps, along with the younger, changing generation coming of age in the early 1970s that she is associated with, Dee, despite her outward obnoxiousness, has taught Mama something about fighting back. Or perhaps Dee has inherited more of her stubbornness and self-determination from her Mama than previously suspected. But, in any case, it seems too easy and neat a reading to simply praise Mama and Maggie for understanding their heritage while dismissing Dee as shallow and self-serving, when Mama's final courageous act ties her more closely to this older daughter than to the younger one she is trying to protect.

Central idea for Section IV.

Walker raised similar problems concerning the willingness to fight for a cause versus the desire to remain passive in her novel *Meridian*, published in 1976, three years after *In Love and Trouble.*

Method: parallel situation in another work by Walker.

In this novel, Walker's main character, Meridian Hill, is at first passive and dreamy. She drifts into an early marriage and pregnancy, since these things seem to be expected of her, but she doesn't truly find direction in her life until she becomes involved with the early Civil Rights movement. As a movement worker, though, Meridian is tempted toward becoming a martyr for her cause. When asked if she would "kill for the revolution," Meridian remains unable to answer. Although readers see the complexities of Meridian's ambivalence here, other activists call her a coward and a masochist for her lack of commitment. In her forbearance and initial willingness to sacrifice her own needs if necessary, Meridian shares much in common with Maggie of "Everyday Use." Meridian's college roommate, Anne-Marion Coles, on the other hand, is similar to Dee. Aggressive and determined to change her life, Anne-Marion, unlike Meridian, easily asserts her willingness to kill if necessary. But, also like Dee in the way she treats Mama and Maggie, Anne-Marion is self-centered and at times unthinkingly cruel to the weaker, more fragile Meridian.

Summary to bring out similarities between the two works.

While Meridian is certainly a more sympathetic character than Anne-Marion throughout the novel, just as Maggie and Mama are more appealing than Dee in many ways, by the end Walker shows us that Meridian has something to learn from Anne-Marion and her other militant colleagues in the movement. . . .

Readers of these two works may at first be seduced into affirming the passive acquiescence of characters such as Mama, Maggie, and Meridian because they are, in many ways, more palatable, more likeable, than such aggressive fighters as Dee and Anne-Marion. These determined, fierce women, however, have much to teach the more forbearing, self-sacrificing characters in both works. Yet, at the same time, we see that a spirit of rebellion, without a corresponding spirituality and respect for such traditional black institutions as the church or the folk arts of "Everyday Use," can be empty as well. Though defiant and aggressive, both Dee and Anne-Marion are selfish and capricious in their social activism. Finally, then, in "Everyday Use,"

Walker shows that Mama's moment of triumph is achieved be- *Completion of*
cause she is able to attain a balance between the two types of her *thesis idea.*
heritage represented by her very different daughters—at the end
Mama combines Maggie's respect for tradition with Dee's pride and
refusal to back down, the combination Walker seems to feel is necessary if true social change is to come about.

Notes

Informative endnotes.

1. See especially, along with Tuten's *Explicator* article, Houston
Baker and Charlotte Pierce-Baker's "Patches: Quilts and Community
in Alice Walker's 'Everyday Use,'" Margaret D. Bauer's "Alice Walker: *Note listing re-*
Another Southern Writer Criticizing Codes Not Put to 'Everyday *lated critical*
Use,'" and Donna Haisty Winchell's Twayne Series book on Alice *studies.*
Walker (80–84).

2. Tuten, for instance, argues that the "action of the story . . . *Note providing*
in no way supports Mama's reading of her younger daughter," that *further support-*
Maggie "conveys disgust with her sister rather than envy and awe" as *ing evidence.*
Mama believes (127). Similarly, Baker and Pierce-Baker point out that,
"in her epiphanic moment of recognition," Mama must perceive "the
fire-scarred Maggie—the stay-at-home victim of southern scarifica-
tions—in a revised light," that she must reassess "what she wrongly
interprets as Maggie's hang-dog resignation before Dee" (717).

Works Cited

Baker, Houston, and Charlotte Pierce-Baker. "Patches: Quilts and
    Community in Alice Walker's 'Everyday Use.'" *The Southern Re-
    view* 21 (1985): 706–20.
Bauer, Margaret D. "Alice Walker: Another Southern Writer Criticiz-
    ing Codes Not Put to 'Everyday Use.'" *Studies in Short Fiction* 29
    (1992): 143–51.
Tuten, Nancy. "Alice Walker's 'Everyday Use.'" *The Explicator* 51.2
    (Winter 1993): 125–28.
Walker, Alice. "Everyday Use." *In Love and Trouble.* New York: Har-
    court, 1973. 47–59.
——. *Meridian.* New York: Harcourt, 1976.
Winchell, Donna Haisty. *Alice Walker.* New York: Twayne, 1992.

Most scholars, when they read such an essay, pick out the central idea in
each paragraph and jot down an outline of the main steps in the argument. Here
is an example of the sort of outline a reader might sketch out:

Thesis: Dee offers a view of heritage and way of coping with society more valid than those of Mama and Maggie
  I. Mama's view of Dee may not be reliable
      A. She displaces her fears of Dee onto Maggie
      B. The Johnny Carson daydream is Mama's fantasy, not Dee's
      C. Mama is often wrong about Dee
  II. Contrast between Dee's fearlessness and Mama's fearfulness
      A. Dee as a determined fighter
      B. Mama's fear of knowledge
      C. Mama's fear of the future
 III. Mama's attitude change as she interacts with Dee
      A. Mama seems more open to new things than Maggie
      B. Both Mama and Dee need to gain a more adequate under-
         standing of heritage
      C. Mama admires Dee's fighting spirit
      D. Mama behaves like Dee (not like Maggie) by fighting back
         against Dee's demands
 IV. The same pattern (passivity vs. fighting back) is evident in *Meridian*
Restatement of thesis: Mama triumphs as she achieves a balance between the approaches and attitudes of Dee and Maggie.

Such an outline enables you to view the argument as a whole—what the individual points are and how they relate to each other. That's valuable in understanding the essay and in assessing the strength of what it says.

It's also important to notice the kinds of evidence an author uses to support her or his argument. In Farrell's essay, most of the evidence comes through close reading of the text, with supporting details and quotations from it. But the author also uses the authoritative opinions of other scholars in support of her own positions when she regards them as sound, and she argues against them when she believes their interpretations are not accurate or adequate. And the author uses as a further kind of supporting evidence a parallel situation in another work by Walker, the novel *Meridian*. (We include only the first paragraph of that section, to show how the author introduces the comparison, and omit the following three paragraphs because they discuss a work that is not included in this book and will be unfamiliar to many of you.)

REREADING: Critical Essays

An important step in the reading process of critical essays is evaluation: After all, the essay is trying to persuade you, so it is crucial that you not simply accept automatically what has been written, that you have the skills necessary to decide how good the points and arguments in the essay are. Making that decision usually requires rereading all, or the key parts of, the essay. To evaluate the essay well, start by comparing the critic's ideas with your own ideas. This is why it is important that you know the work itself well and that you formulate your own interpretation of it before reading any critical essay. Here are some suggestions for evaluating critical essays.

- *Compare the critic's interpretation with your own interpretation.* The first step in evaluation is to formulate your own judgment as clearly and substantially as you can. Then compare the critic's interpretations to your own — how convincing do they seem to you? Does the critic use the text accurately and fairly and draw sensible conclusions about details in it? Does the critic take everything into account or pass over details that don't support her or his conclusions? Do the steps in the critic's argument proceed logically, and is the case presented sound and convincing?

- *Compare what one critic says with what other critics say.* Perhaps comparison is the best method of evaluation. To assess fully what one critic says, read the interpretations of several or many other critics. By comparing what one says with what another says, you will begin to get a sense of what ideas need to be explored in a work, what sections or details need to be taken into consideration, what approaches prove to be most productive and illuminating. In some cases, you will find some critics agreeing with or replying to or refuting the interpretations of others (as you do in the sample essay above). What the critics say about each other will be very helpful in testing and shaping your own conclusions about a critical essay — though, of course, you will need to be evaluating the soundness of each as you make your comparisons.

W hen you're writing, you're trying to find out something that you don't know.

James Baldwin

CHAPTER **26** **Writing a Literary Research Paper**

In the introduction to Chapter 25, we talk about how you go about learning more about a movie you like. Learning more, we said there, involves doing research into the subject, and the chapter provides guidance in reading critical essays dealing with an author or literary work. But the chapter didn't tell you how to go about finding such essays. That's the subject of this chapter: the research process. It focuses on undertaking research into a literary topic, but you will see how many of the principles carry over to research into movies or other projects you may want or be asked to work on. Literary research involves finding materials, comprehending what they have to say, evaluating how sound they are, and (if the research results in writing a paper) including them in your discussion — that is, using what they say to clarify and support the points you want to make or to present points you want to refute.

> Find additional advice for finding, evaluating, and working with sources, including interactive exercises, with the Research and Documentation Guide on *LiterActive*.

TOPICS

In nature and form, a research paper is basically the same as the papers discussed in Chapters 8, 15, and 21. The specific differences are that research papers tend to be longer and that they include the results of research — those concerning details in the work, the background of the work, and what scholars and literary critics have written about the work or its author. What Chapters 8, 15, and 21 say about finding topics also applies to research papers: Research papers can be written about what goes on inside a work, the literary context surrounding a work, or the social, cultural, political, and ideological context that extends beyond the boundaries of the work. You can do the same kinds of things in these papers, but with a larger scope, in more depth, and often with more complex and extensive results.

Finding a topic starts with preliminary reading. Almost all literary research topics deal with specific texts — novels, stories, poems, or plays. Some projects concern a specific text or two and focus on them closely (for example, the importance of quilts to culture in "Everyday Use"). Others may explore literary movements (for example, the significance of the Harlem Renaissance on later twentieth-century poetry) and use literary works as one source of information and evidence. In either case, however, literary works are central, and reading in them must be your first step. Read the key text or texts several times. Get to know them well. Jot down possible ideas and questions that could become topics or that you will want to explore when you begin your research.

As with the essays discussed in Chapters 8, 15, and 21, the most important part of a research paper is what *you* say in it, the development of *your* approach and ideas and interpretations. A research paper is not a report: A report gives an account of something. Its nature is objective — the writer does not interject opinions or interpretations. Research papers in high school sometimes take the form of a report, on diabetes in children, for example: The student searches for information on the subject from various sources and pieces together an informative account of the extent of the problem, what kind of treatment is involved, why the disease is a growing concern, and what can be done to improve the situation. Often such a paper turns out to be a long string of quotations and paraphrases, with transition sentences connecting and holding them together.

That is not what we mean by a literary research paper. Like other literary essays, a research paper is unified around an argumentative thesis, a central idea that takes a position others could disagree with. The only difference from the papers discussed earlier is that, as you shape and develop and support your ideas, an additional resource is available: In addition to evidence from the text itself, you can draw on factual information found in other sources and on the ideas of authorities in the field, scholars who have commented on the texts or authors you are working with.

The thesis argued in the paper should be original to you. As you carry out your research, however, you may find that someone else has already explored the topic you were planning to focus on, perhaps even argued for the same thesis you had tentatively decided on. That should not be a problem. For a student paper, originality isn't saying something that never has been said before. Reconstructing the argument on your own should supply a freshness to the ongoing conversation. You can do this by bringing your own arguments and evidence to support your thesis, ones different from those used before, even if someone else has argued for the same point. It can also be done by taking a theoretical or critical approach different from the one used before (for example, if you use a feminist approach to examine a topic someone else discussed from a psychoanalytical perspective, you will frame different arguments and draw evidence from different passages, thus giving it a fresh slant). Or it can be done by combining ideas from different fields. Students are in an ideal situation for doing this: Try using concepts from your philosophy, sociology, psychology, or political science courses to illuminate works you study in your literature course.

TYPES OF RESEARCH AND SOURCES

Literary research falls into several different types, types that yield different kinds of information with different uses, and draw upon different kinds of sources. It is important to recognize these types, especially since a project often involves more than one type. First we sketch out types of research and then we turn to types of sources.

Primary Research

The most basic kind of research involves the reading of literary works and of any kind of texts (written, graphic, or oral) contemporary with those works. Such texts are referred to as *primary sources* — that is, literary works themselves; comments the author's contemporaries made about those works; letters, diaries, journals, or memoirs by the author or by contemporaries; contemporary newspapers, magazines, and books; contemporary (or earlier) works of art; books the author read (for example, literary works, works about current economics or politics, books of philosophy or theology). Literary scholars use research in primary sources to gain knowledge of the literary works themselves; to acquire firsthand information about an author's life, times, or culture; to locate sources an author drew upon; and to understand literary or artistic influences and traditions that affected an author or helped shape a work. They apply what they find to write critical books and essays or to write contextual books and essays — biographies; literary histories; economic, political, or social histories; cultural studies; and so forth.

You too are doing primary research for a paper when you go beyond the assigned work and read further in the author's works or in works by a contemporary author in order to understand the work's literary context. And you can engage in primary research by going back to personal letters, diaries, or journals from that time or to contemporary newspapers or magazines or works of art. You might find it not only interesting to read diaries of women in the nineteenth century, for example, but also helpful for understanding the context and implications of Kate Chopin's "The Story of an Hour" (p. 167). Primary research may not be required in a Writing and Literature course or an Introduction to Literature course, but a student doing a senior research project in literature probably would be expected to include some primary research as a way of practicing what literary scholars regularly do in their published works.

Secondary Research

A second kind of research involves reading in what other scholars have written about primary texts and about the life or literary, social, or cultural context of an author or work. Such works are called *secondary sources* — that is, not firsthand works written *by* an author or by her or his contemporaries, but secondhand ones written *about* an author or about her or his works or the era. Secondary sources include biographies of an author; history books discussing the author's times; studies of society, culture, and ideas of the time; and critical books or essays about a work or group of works. When literary scholars undertake a project, they do both primary and secondary research. They read as many works as possible by the author and by other scholars who have written about the author or the work involved. In this way, scholars build on what has been done previously. They may explore an area that earlier scholars had overlooked; apply previous insights or approaches to a new work; expand on implications that earlier scholars, or even contemporaries, didn't seem to grasp fully; or disagree with and modify or reverse what an earlier scholar wrote.

If you are assigned a research paper for this course, you probably will be expected to do secondary research — at least in critical books and essays — on a more limited basis than a professional scholar would. Even if you don't read everything about a work, reading several critical essays adds significantly to your understanding and appreciation of it. However, as we say in Chapter 25, do not begin reading critical books and essays until you know your primary works well and begin recording ideas for possible topics and tentative theses for them (see p. 1364).

Tertiary Research

A third (tertiary) level of research involves finding pertinent information about the meaning of words, the meaning of background details in a work, the source of allusions, and the biographical and historical context in which the work was written. This sort of investigation is not limited to research projects but is an integral part of ordinary active reading. It is usually carried out through use of *tertiary sources* — works such as dictionaries, encyclopedias, almanacs, and Internet personal pages whose purpose is to provide convenient access to ordinary, widely available information, not the interpretive understandings scholars convey in secondary sources. Thus, in preparing to write a research paper on Alice Walker's "Everyday Use," one might look in an encyclopedia to learn more about quilting or go to *Annina's Alice Walker Page* (luminarium.org/contemporary/alicew) to find some biographical information about Walker. Tertiary sources often do not specify who wrote the item you are reading because it does not contain anything unique to that person. The writer was probably drawing upon previous tertiary sources, not engaging in primary research.

In a research project, tertiary sources are valuable for finding or verifying factual details or perhaps for gaining an initial overview of an author or historical period. But a research paper should not be based on tertiary sources. In fact, if they are used only to find or verify details available widely or for background reading, they don't even need to be included in your bibliography (only if you quote from them — which generally shouldn't be necessary — or if they provide information that is important to the paper and not commonly known).

Warning! A word of caution about one other kind of tertiary resource. Various types of "study guides" are available, online and in print, for many literary authors and works. They typically offer plot summaries, analyses of characters and themes, and commentaries about key passages. We recommend you don't use these — they're an unnecessary substitute for doing careful attentive reading on your own. If you do use them, do so with great caution. They are seldom done by established literary scholars, and their treatment of works is usually superficial. Some even contain errors of fact. They tend to present themes as separate from one another and as absolutes (these are *the* themes in *Othello*), thus reducing the actual complexity and richness of the work and misleading the reader into thinking the work is not nearly as challenging as it actually is. If you decide to read one as preparation for a paper, its use must be acknowledged in the bibliography, even if you do not cite it in the paper. But these are not sources that will enhance the quality of your paper.

FINDING SOURCES AND CREATING A WORKING BIBLIOGRAPHY

The development of the Internet, with the many resources available on it, can make it tempting to do all one's research by computer. A wealth of information is available in convenient form on the Internet, but much of it is of the tertiary variety; so Internet sources by themselves are not adequate. A good college-level literature research paper needs to include work in your college or university library — most other libraries will not have the scholarly books and journals you will need, and the Internet does not provide an adequate substitute for them. We begin with a discussion of library searches and then move on to Internet searches.

Library Searches — Books

Each library search is unique and requires its own use of imagination and common sense — and, in many cases, help from a librarian. However, there are some steps nearly all library searches include. They almost always begin with the card catalog or online catalog, checking for books about the author you are researching. In card catalogs, books about an author are usually found after the books by the author. For online catalogs, do a *subject* search for your author or topic. For prominent authors, you are likely to find both biographical works and critical studies. Biographies can be useful to establish the context of a work, and some include critical commentary on the author's works as well. From the titles you find, select ones that seem likely to be helpful, then go to the stacks to investigate them. Use a book's preface, table of contents, and index or skim through its chapters to determine if they contain enough of value to justify checking them out and reading further in them. The titles that seem useful form the beginning of your working bibliography. Most scholarly books conclude with a bibliography; it may lead you to pertinent books and articles and is worth looking through carefully.

In addition to works about your author that turn up in a subject search, some works available in the literature area of the reference section of the library can provide good background and bibliographical information about many authors. Here is a list of the most important of these:

> *Contemporary Literary Criticism.* 106 volumes to date. Detroit: Gale, 1973–. Contains biographical sketches and excerpts of reviews and criticism for contemporary authors.
>
> *Dictionary of Literary Biography.* 289 volumes to date. Detroit: Gale, 1978–. An ongoing series that provides useful biographical and critical introductions to U.S., British, and world authors.
>
> Elliot, Emory, et al. *Columbia Literary History of the United States.* New York: Columbia University Press, 1988. An overview of literary movements and individual writers in the United States.
>
> *The Oxford History of English Literature.* 13 volumes. Oxford: Oxford University Press, 1945–. Overviews of literary movements and individual writers in England and Great Britain.
>
> Preminger, Alex, and T. V. F. Brogan, eds. *The New Princeton Encyclopedia of Poetry and Poetics.* Princeton: Princeton University Press, 1993. The most authoritative guide to concepts, terminology, and movements related to poetry.

These may be a good place to start your research. They should never be the place you stop, and you should never use them as the main sources in a paper.

Library Searches — Articles

Many of the most valuable studies of particular works appear as articles in literary journals or in books of collected essays. Scholarly journals are sometimes called "periodicals" because, like magazines, they are published at regular intervals (rather than once, like a book) — in most cases quarterly, instead of weekly or monthly like a magazine. Literary journals (edited by and intended for literary scholars) are more likely to provide the kind of criticism you'll need than are general magazines (written for broader readership and thus less complex to read but also less scholarly in approach and emphasis). Articles in scholarly journals are usually longer than magazine articles, are written by literary scholars whose academic affiliation or other credentials are indicated, and often use footnotes or endnotes and include a bibliography. You may find personal information such as interviews with an author in a general magazine, but usually not sophisticated critical studies of the kind you need in a college research paper.

Scholarly articles are sometimes published in books of collected essays focused on an author or topic. The contents may be articles previously published in journals and gathered into a book by an editor to make them more easily accessible to readers. Or the book may be made up of essays written specially for the collection and published for the first time in it. The collection as a whole can be found through a book search (indicated when "edited by" appears in front of what would otherwise be the author's name: for example, "*Critical Essays on Alice Walker,* edited by Ikenna Dieke"). Individual essays are indexed with journal articles and are found through the searches for scholarly articles described below.

The best method of locating articles is to use periodical indexes. You may be familiar with the *Readers' Guide to Periodical Literature,* which indexes articles published in over 275 periodicals, grouped by subject categories. It is widely used for general research and in high schools, but it is less useful for college research because it covers mostly popular magazines. However, resources similar to it are available for scholarly journals. One is the *Humanities Index,* available in print and online (look for it on your library's list of available electronic resources or ask a librarian). Other, more general article indexes also include scholarly materials. The Gale Group (InfoTrac) *Expanded Academic ASAP* database and the OCLC (FirstSearch) *Periodical Abstracts* database are two well-known examples. Ask a librarian for the name of the particular database of this type to which your library subscribes.

The standard resource for finding articles about authors and literary topics is the *MLA Bibliography of Books and Articles in the Modern Languages and Literature.* It is available online and on CD-ROM as well as in printed volumes. The printed volumes are divided into sections by nationality and era (English literature 1500–1599, for example, or Scottish literature 1700–1799), with special topics listed first and then authors listed alphabetically. It is much easier to search electronic versions, which pull up pertinent items from all the years covered, than the annual printed volumes, each of which contains items from only one year. Experiment with limiting your searches: A subject or keyword search for Toni Morrison in the *MLA Bibliography* yields around 1,300 hits; adding a subject or keyword search for "Recitatif" reduces the number to 7. Do a variety of searches, using different terms related to your topic. If you have difficulty with searches, ask your instructor or a librarian for assistance.

As with books, you need to sort through the results and decide which ones seem promising enough to find and read. If you're using a *MLA Bibliography* online search engine, a line of descriptors describes the content areas of the book or article and can help you decide if an article is worth reading. Some databases provide an abstract (a brief summary of what the paper is about) that can be even more helpful. Increasingly, databases are able to provide a link to the full text of articles. With this feature, you can immediately retrieve the entire article and read it on your screen or print a hard copy. You may be tempted to limit your research to items that have the full text online because they are so convenient to use, but it's a temptation that should be resisted. Sources without a link to the full text may be a better fit with your topic. If you are not sure how to find the article for which you have found information, take the information to a librarian, who will help you find the article. If your library does not subscribe to the journal, it may be possible to get a copy of the article (or of a book your library doesn't own) through interlibrary loan. This may take a week or two, which is a good reason to start your bibliography search early. Waiting until a day or two before a paper is due is a very bad idea.

In addition to indexes for finding articles, book-length bibliographies are available for many well-known authors, listing scholarly and critical studies on the author published during a given span of years, in some cases with a brief description or evaluation of the work. Look for such a volume as you do your search of the library catalog. If you are searching on Alice Walker, for example, you might find this book:

> Banks, Erma Banks, and Keith Byerman. *Alice Walker: An Annotated Bibliography 1968–1986.* New York: Garland, 1989.

It includes a list of primary works by Walker through 1986 as well as reviews and criticism of her works, with a brief description of many items. It is a very convenient way to locate studies of Walker through 1986. For studies since then, you would go to one of the indexes described above. Bibliographies are also available for periods and movements, as, for example:

> Glikin, Ronda. *Black American Women in Literature: A Bibliography, 1976 through 1987.* Jefferson: McFarland, 1989.
> Jordan, Casper LeRoy. *A Bibliographical Guide to African-American Women Writers.* Westport: Greenwood, 1993.
> Zimmerman, Marc. *U.S. Latino Literature: An Essay and Annotated Bibliography.* Chicago: MARCH/Abrazo, 1992.

To find such volumes, search the library catalog for "African American authors" or "Hispanic American authors" and look for a subheading on "Bibliography."

Searching Electronic Sources

Although the full-text articles available through the electronic indexes described above are on the Web, they originated as print sources and should be considered as such. Likewise, search engines such as AltaVista, Google, or Yahoo! locate items that originally appeared in a newspaper or magazine and subsequently were posted on the Internet; even though you encounter them online, they are print sources. Internet sources are Web sites and documents posted on the Internet that have not appeared in print and, in many cases, were never intended to appear in print. A great deal of material is available on the Web that is of interest and value to students of literature. Much of it falls into the category of tertiary sources (enjoyable but non-scholarly), but some is of scholarly significance and can fill areas not covered by books and journals. Home pages can be found for many authors, created by fans of the authors (some by academics, some by general readers), or, for contemporary writers, by the author her- or himself. Such home pages usually provide a biography and bibliography, sometimes some critical essays, and sometimes — for modern authors — an audio recording. They can be a good starting point for learning about an author.

In addition, myriad other types of pages exist: reprintings of poems or stories by an author, brief commentaries on literary works, study guides to an author or work, student papers, odd bits of information (of the "The day I met Julia Alvarez" type), collections of photos related to the author, places where books can be purchased, and so forth. One can waste a good deal of time clicking on potentially interesting sites, only to be disappointed by what comes up. One way to avoid some of the clutter is to do a more specialized search than just typing "Alice Walker" into the Google window and being confronted by over a million hits. Most search engines have a directory under which you can click on "Arts," then "Literature," then on a time period or genre category or on "Authors," and then on the first letter of the author's last name to get a shorter list of hits with the less useful ones eliminated. The path Arts/Literature/Authors/W/Walker on Google yields five selected sites and six articles and interviews. In the end, however, for college-level literary research, the most useful material is found in print sources (in library or online) rather than in Internet sources.

In addition to Internet resources, CD-ROMs are available on many authors, works, or movements. These often contain a wide variety of materials. As you read a text, for example, the CD-ROM may provide definitions, maps, pictures, critical essays or excerpts, biographical information, and materials related to historical and cultural background, all at the click of the mouse. Good CD-ROMs are enjoyable and educational to use, but — like all other electronic and printed materials — their quality varies greatly. Check reviews or ask your instructor about the quality of one you might use. And, as for Internet sources, using CD-ROMs does not take the place of library research.

EVALUATING SOURCES

A very important principle of research, in any field, is that "all sources are not equal." And a corollary to this is, "research that uses stronger sources is regarded more highly than research that uses weaker sources." An initial step in assessing a student paper or a book of literary criticism is to look at its bibliography. A bibliography that lists mostly popular magazines, or Internet sources, or books and articles from the 1960s won't be as strong as a bibliography listing scholarly articles and books written during the past ten to fifteen years. From the beginning of your research project, *be selective* about the sources you decide to consider further.

As you consider which potential sources to include in your working bibliography, *evaluate each one carefully.* In reading books, articles, and Internet material, first grasp clearly what is being said. Only then can you decide how valid and valuable the point being made is. Books and essays are not "good" just because they're in print or posted on the Web: Don't use just any source you happen to find. Evaluating the worth of a source is crucial. The quality of your sources affects (or even determines) the quality of your paper. To help you evaluate sources, here are five questions to ask.

1. *Who is the author and what are her or his qualifications?* Some people are better informed — are authorities in a field — and better qualified to comment on a work or an author than others are. The qualifications of an author are easier to determine for published criticism than for material on the Web. You can check if the author has an academic affiliation: Someone on the faculty at a reputable college or university is more likely to be regarded as an authority than someone who just decides to set up a Web site about a favorite writer. You can check where the author was educated and when. You can also check if the author has published extensively about the subject. Those who have published a great deal on a subject are more likely to qualify as authorities. It often is harder to ascertain the qualifications of the authors of pieces you find on the Web: Experts post pieces on the Web, but so do people with eccentric notions that they can't get journals to publish. Books and journals tell you the qualifications of their authors; Web sites often don't. Sometimes they don't even name the author (anonymous sites should be avoided). If an author is identified, you might search for the name in a search engine and see if that reveals more about the person and her or his credentials.

2. *Where was the work published?* The fact that something appears in print or on the Internet does not mean it is of value. Articles submitted to scholarly journals and books submitted to well-established presses are carefully screened by experts; only works that the experts regard as accurate and important are accepted for publication. The fact that an article appears in a highly regarded journal or that a book is published by a highly reputable

press in most cases can give you confidence in its quality. That does not mean that everything published by respected journals or presses is excellent or that nothing published by less well-known journals or presses is worthwhile. You still have to assess each item on its own merits. But paying attention to the publisher is still the wisest way to start. For material on the Internet, check who hosts the site. The URL can be of help — items posted by academic institutions (.edu), nonprofit organizations (.org), and the government (.gov) are more promising than items coming out of commercial sites (.com) and other sites with products for sale. In some cases, the host organization is identified at the bottom of the initial page. Try to find out more about who it is and what it has at stake.

3. *Is the source or its author cited by other scholars?* One way to help evaluate a scholarly work is to determine what other scholars think about it. For books, look for a review (*Book Review Digest,* online or in print form in your library, is a good place to start). Some specialized journals offer reviews of articles in its field. Scholars in their books and articles often evaluate what other scholars have written about a subject; what they say needs to be evaluated carefully for fairness and accuracy, but it's useful input. Another measure of acceptance by other scholars is how frequently a scholar's work is favorably cited by other scholars (that is, referred to in a footnote or included in a bibliography); if other scholars rely on a source, you can be fairly sure that its author is respected in the field.

4. *What is the date of the publication?* In some fields (especially the sciences), research more than a decade or two old may well be outdated. That tends to be less true in the humanities, but it is still true to some extent. Recent scholarship builds on earlier work, adding to earlier studies and correcting their mistakes, and it draws upon current ideas and theoretical approaches. It's acceptable to have some older studies in your bibliography, but in most cases your sources should include the most recent, up-to-date studies available. Caution is needed in using Internet sites. Often someone starts a site and keeps it up-to-date for a while but later neglects it so that its information is no longer current. Some sites give "last updated on" information. For sites that do not, the latest date mentioned in the material may indicate the last time the site was updated.

5. *How relevant is it to your topic and argument?* Avoid the temptation to add items to your bibliography or to slip quotations from them into your paper just because they are written by a leading expert or published by a major press. A source helps your paper only if what it deals with fits your topic or relates to your argument, and is something you actually can use. Readers are not impressed when your bibliography lists books by several widely known experts but all the citations in your text are to nonscholarly Web sites.

TAKING NOTES

When doing a research paper, take notes in an organized way. For a short paper, you might get by with using your memory and marking up a copy of the primary text; but in a research paper, if it's done well, too much is going on for that. In the old days, scholars took notes on 3 x 5 or 4 x 6 cards (or, earlier, on slips of paper), using one set for bibliographical information and another for summary notes and quotations, cross-referenced to the corresponding bibliography card. This produced excellent results for centuries and is still a good system (you may have been asked to use it for a high school research paper). But it is much less widely used today because of advances in electronic equipment.

Many scholars now type their notes directly into notebook computers. Many libraries are equipped to enable researchers to plug in computers at reading tables and in study carrels. Notes in a computer are easier to use because they can be searched quickly and can be copied and pasted directly into a paper. You might experiment with this form of note taking if you have never tried it before. You'll need to decide how to organize the notes into files: One large file into which you put everything? (It may become long, bulky, and cumbersome to use.) Separate files for each source? Separate files for different topics? You'll need to find a system that is searchable and enables you to find and retrieve material easily. It might be a good idea, when you've collected quite a bit of material but are far from finished, to go back over what you have, refresh your memory of it, rearrange it by grouping items together that relate to the same subtopic, and note gaps you still need to fill.

Copiers have changed the need for taking notes and the way many people take notes. For materials available in general areas of a library, many people photocopy pages of books or whole articles from journals, instead of writing or typing passages they might want to use in a paper. (In rare book and special collection areas, photocopying usually is available only by special arrangement.) Copyright protection allows photocopying of articles and selected pages from a book when used for personal research, but forbids photocopying an entire book, or even most of one. Photocopies are convenient to use because you can underline important phrases or sentences and jot notes in the margins (which you should never do directly in a library book). And they have the benefit of accuracy: One must take great care in writing out or typing passages, and then double-check them for accuracy. With photocopied pages, that's not necessary until parts are actually quoted in your paper.

No matter what system you use, some principles are the same:

- *Check for completeness.* Be sure to put down the author's name and all the data needed to complete the bibliography entry: title, place of publication, publisher, date of publication, and page numbers for a book; for a magazine article, its title, title of the magazine, date of the issue, first and last page numbers, and the number for each page you use; for a journal article, its title, title of the journal, volume number, year, first and last page numbers, and the number for each page you use; for an Internet source, its URL or the pathway used for reaching it. You certainly don't want to discover — usually the night before a paper is due! — that you forgot to include a date or page number and must to go back to the library (hoping it's still open) to find it.

- *Check for accuracy.* Make sure the bibliographical data you put down is accurate. After you write or type a quotation, check that every word and punctuation mark in it is accurate before you move on. If you omit a phrase or sentence, be sure you've indicated that with ellipsis marks (see p. 44). Remember that if you put quotation marks around a passage, you are guaranteeing that it's reproduced exactly the way the way it appears in the original source.

- *Check for clarity.* If you're writing or typing notes, indicate clearly what is quoted and what is summary. It's a good idea to write "quote" or "summary" in the margin to make sure you won't mistake the one for the other, something that can lead to unfortunate results. Also, add a label indicating what point in your paper the notes apply to. That will make it much easier for you to find and organize your notes when you get ready to use them.

You will save time later if, as you take notes, you begin preparing the actual Works Cited page for your paper, instead of leaving it to the end, when you're weary and perhaps pressed for time. It is most convenient to create a separate Works Cited file in your computer as you compile your list. But it's important, at some point, to paste the list into your paper at the end, so the pages will be paginated consecutively with the body of the paper and so the list won't get lost. We've had students remember to keep the computer file containing their paper but delete their separate Works Cited file, forgetting that they haven't copied the Works Cited list to the paper itself.

DEVELOPING YOUR PAPER AND THESIS

The steps suggested in Chapters 8, 15, and 21 for developing an essay apply equally for a research paper. After deciding on a topic, you need to narrow it to manageable size for the length assigned; you need to focus it on a central point, a tentative, argumentative thesis; you need to discuss the thesis in a draft of the paper, amplifying the ideas, supplying details and illustrations that support the points you make, and explaining how the ideas and examples support each other in a convincing way; and you need to revise and proofread the draft. Review the detailed discussion of these steps in Chapter 8 and follow them as you work on your research project. In discussing short papers, we mentioned that some people organize them in their heads, without a written outline. Research papers are more complex, so an outline is usually important, even for those who ordinarily don't make outlines. The introduction to a research paper also is more challenging than the introduction to a short paper. In addition to attracting the reader's attention, it should indicate where the literary conversation about your author or work stands and how your paper fits into it.

INCORPORATING SOURCES

The unique aspect in developing a research paper is that additional materials for clarifying ideas and supporting arguments are available from the primary and secondary research you've carried out. Such materials can be incorporated into your paper in four ways (we illustrate with examples from Susan Farrell's essay in Chapter 25, on pp. 1366–73).

1. *Citation.* In some cases you may want to mention a source as related to your argument without giving details about it. You can do so by making a passing reference to it ("citing" it), without saying more about it. Citations often are used to supply additional examples, supporting one that has been described fully. That is the case in Farrell's first endnote:

> 1. See [also] . . . Houston Baker and Charlotte Pierce-Baker's "Patches: Quilts and Community in Alice Walker's 'Everyday Use,'" Margaret D. Bauer's "Alice Walker: Another Southern Writer Criticizing Codes Not Put to 'Everyday Use,'" and Donna Haisty Winchell's Twayne Series book on Alice Walker (80–84).

In this case, three sources are cited as additional examples of Nancy Tuten's position that a central theme in "Everyday Use" is "a mother's 'awakening to one daughter's superficiality and to the other's deepseated understanding of heritage' ([Tuten] 125)."

2. *Summary.* In most cases, you will bring sources into your paper through a summary of some information, a key idea, or an overall argument you found valuable in them. The summary should be a brief restatement of the author's point into your own words. What you incorporate does not have to summarize the whole book, chapter, or article but may summarize one section or simply one paragraph. Summary is used commonly as a way to bring primary texts usefully into a paper. Farrell does that repeatedly as she builds her case, as for example,

> When he [Asalamalakim] tries to hug Maggie, though, she falls back against a chair and trembles. And later, when he tries to teach Maggie a new handshake, her hand remains limp and she quickly withdraws it from his.

Likewise, Farrell summarizes the plot of *Meridian* for the benefit of those readers who are not familiar with it.

Secondary sources can be handled through summary as well. In her first paragraph, Farrell includes a composite summary of the way many critics, represented by those cited in endnote 1, back up their contention that the point of the story is Mama's awakening to Dee and Maggie's values:

> These readers praise the "simplicity" of Maggie and her mother, along with their allegiance to their specific family identity and folk heritage as well as their refusal to change at the whim of an outside world that doesn't really have much to do with them.

These sources could have been identified separately, with Farrell discussing each in detail and illustrating them with quotations. However, since they represent the position she is contesting, setting them out in a condensed version gives them adequate attention.

   3. *Paraphrase.* A paraphrase, like a summary, is a restatement of an author's point in your own words, but at greater length — usually approximately equal in length to the original passage. Paraphrase is more commonly used for secondary sources than for primary ones; since paraphrasing wouldn't save space, most critics would tend to give readers the actual words of the text instead of a rephrased version. For secondary sources, paraphrase should be used instead of summary when it is important to supply your reader with more detail: if, for example, you want to call specific attention to each step in an argument, perhaps because you want to dispute an argument step by step. Quoting the passage, in such a case, might not work as well because a paraphrase allows you to enumerate each step even if the author didn't do so. Paraphrase can also be used not for what other critics have actually said but to articulate what they would say, as for example:

> Of course, most readers see this as evidence of Dee's fickle changing with whatever fad happens to be current. Once it becomes fashionable to have rural, poverty-stricken roots, Dee wants a record of her own humble beginnings.

This is not a quotation or a summary, but Farrell putting in her own words what she believes other critics would argue.

   4. *Quotation.* Every literary paper should include some quotations of the primary text or texts being discussed. A paper without any quotations can come across as superficial, even too general. Handling quotations from stories, poems, and plays has been discussed in Chapters 8, 15, and 21, respectively (pp. 209, 590, and 922). In a research paper, like any literary paper, the danger is quoting too extensively, turning your paper into simply a "collage of quotations." Combining quoted extracts with summary is a skill worth learning. Farrell does it well:

For instance, when Dee wants a new dress, she "makes over" an old green
suit someone had given her mother. Rather than passively accept her lot, as
Mama seems trained to do, Dee "was determined to stare down any disaster
in her efforts" (103).

Quoting only a few words is effective because we tend to pay attention to
those words, on the assumption that the critic must think these words are
particularly significant if she or he chose them for quotation.

Research papers don't need to include quotations from secondary
sources, but they usually do. Writers encounter passages written so effectively that they don't want to paraphrase them. The danger, again, is not un-
derusing quotations but using too many, and using ones that are too long.
Quotations must not carry the argument of a paper but must support and illustrate the argument you are presenting in your own words. In that regard,
it's important not to begin paragraphs with quotations: A sentence in your
own words should always precede a quotation to introduce it and set it up
properly. Although it may be tempting to quote sources at length because
their points are stated so well, keep quotations brief. Using ellipsis marks is
an effective way to shorten quotations and to focus on relevant portions
(see p. 44). Papers that quote too often, and at too great a length, can be
disconcerting and not enjoyable to read: The prose style keeps changing,
one's orientation toward the material keeps shifting, and arguments are not
articulated in as unified and coherent a manner. For secondary sources as
for primary sources, the best approach is to combine quotations with summary and to blend the quoted extracts into your prose style as gracefully as
possible. Farrell's article does this well:

> Thus, although Tuten equates Dee's values with those of "the white Johnny
> Carson society" (126), it seems to me that we have to question whether
> Mama's vision of her light-skinned, slender, witty self is actually Dee's
> wish or only Mama's perception of what she imagines Dee would like her
> to be. . . .
>   . . . Similarly, Donna Winchell writes that "Dee tries to force on" Mag-
> gie and her mother "knowledge they probably do not need." She continues,
>
>> Mrs. Johnson can take an objective look at who and what she is and find
>> not disillusionment but an easy satisfaction. Simple pleasures—a dip of
>> snuff, a cooling breeze across a clean swept yard, church songs, the sooth-
>> ing movements of milk cows—are enough. (82)
>
> But are these "simple pleasures" really enough for Mama in the story?

Only twice does Farrell quote a secondary passage at length, both times because she wanted to build an argument not just on the critic's overall point
but on the particular words and details the critic uses. Her essay provides an
excellent model for judicious, graceful handling of quotations from both the
primary text and from secondary sources.

AVOIDING PLAGIARISM

Plagiarism is the presentation of the work of others as if it were one's own. It's dishonest. You commit plagiarism if you present, without proper acknowledgment, all or part of another person's work as if it were your own. This is a serious offense. It's stealing another person's effort and ideas. It violates the expectations of trust and honesty expected in an academic community. In addition, plagiarism undercuts the basic purposes of higher education by short-circuiting the processes of inquiry, reflection, and communication that lead to learning.

Some more specific examples of plagiarism clarify that broad description:

- Buying a paper from a commercial source and submitting it as your own, or taking a paper from a classmate, friend, fraternity or sorority file, or anyone else and submitting it as if you wrote it, or using parts of such a paper even if you change the introduction or alter some of the wording
- Cutting and pasting material from the Internet into your paper without indicating where it came from
- Using the exact words of another writer in a paper without indicating that they are quoted and providing proper citations for them
- Paraphrasing or summarizing the words of another writer without providing citations that indicate they are rewordings
- Taking important ideas from sources and including them in your paper as if you thought them up, even if the wording is not the same as in the original
- Letting someone else (a friend, classmate, parent, etc.) write parts of your paper for you or correct or edit a paper so extensively that it no longer accurately reflects your work
- Submitting a drawing, painting, musical composition, computer program, or any other kind of material created originally by someone else and claiming or implying that you created it yourself

One final example of plagiarism often surprises students: Turning in the same paper more than once in different courses is plagiarism, even though all the material is yours. Instructors expect papers to be work done specifically for and during that course — it's not fair if the other students are taking the time to write a new paper and you just reuse one you wrote in high school or in an earlier college course. In some cases, you may want to do a research project that involves two courses you are taking at the same time — literature and psychology, for example. In that case, talk to both instructors. They will probably encourage you because making connections between disciplines is a valuable way of learning. But they may require you to do separate papers for each course or allow you to submit the same paper for both courses but require it to be longer than those done by other students.

Some of the examples above are deliberate cheating. Everyone knows it is unacceptable to buy a paper and turn it in as your own work. Those who do it deserve the severe penalties most instructors and institutions impose. In some cases, however, students stumble into inadvertent plagiarism by not knowing the rules for citation. They may believe, for example, that only direct quotations need to be acknowledged; therefore, they assume that if they totally rephrase a passage and avoid using any words from the original, they don't need to cite a source for it. Not so. You need to give credit to the person who came up with the idea, or who did the work of tracing a historical allusion or detail, or who thought out the interpretation of a story or poem, even though your phrasing of the material is different. And you are responsible for knowing what plagiarism is and how to avoid it: Ignorance is not an adequate excuse.

Here are a few guidelines for avoiding plagiarism:

- Put quotation marks around any groups of words taken directly from a source (phrases or whole sentences).
- Document every direct quotation (except phrases that are so common that most people would recognize the source without being told — "Four score and seven years ago," for example).
- Document any idea or information that you attained through your research, except for information that is widely available from many different sources (even if you looked up the place and date of Alice Walker's birth, you don't need to give a source because that information is readily available in many places).

Keep in mind that you are taking part in a long-honored tradition: the extension of the ongoing conversation about a literary work of art. Respecting the work of others by acknowledging their contributions is a matter of personal integrity and a standard by which you are welcomed into the community of both established and beginning scholars.

DOCUMENTING SOURCES: MLA STYLE

The method of citing sources for papers on literature preferred by most teachers is the MLA style, described in detail in the *MLA Handbook for Writers of Research Papers,* 6th ed., by Joseph Gibaldi (New York: Modern Language Association of America, 2003). It is a simple, convenient, two-step system that uses abbreviated parenthetical citations in the text and a bibliography of works cited to supply information for locating the sources. Footnotes or endnotes can be used to supply information and

www
Find additional advice for documenting sources with Diana Hacker's *Research and Documentation Online* at bedfordstmartins.com/approachinglit.

comments that do not fit into the text of the paper or that cannot be handled adequately through parenthetical citation (see the informational notes in Farrell's paper, p. 1373). But including notes is not essential.[1]

In-Text Citations

The MLA system begins with brief in-text citations. After a quotation or a sentence using facts or opinions drawn from a specific source (wherever a footnote would have been used in earlier documentation systems), one inserts a parenthesis with, ordinarily, the last name of the author and the page or pages on which the information is found.

> The point of the story is to show, in one critic's words, a mother's "awakening to one daughter's superficiality and to the other's deepseated understanding of heritage" (Tuten 125).

This is the most basic form of in-text citation. Notice three formatting conventions followed in it:

1. There is no comma after the author's name and no "page" or "p." preceding the number.
2. The quotation marks come before the parenthesis. The in-text citation identifies the source of the quotation but is not part of the quotation.
3. The punctuation mark closing the sentence follows the parenthetical citation, so that the citation is included in the sentence, not left floating unattached between sentences. (An exception is in the case of block quotations, where the period precedes the parenthetical citation.)

You'll also need to know about a few variations on that basic form:

- If the author is named in the text leading up to the quotation (and this is good practice; notice that Farrell always does so), the name is not repeated in parentheses:

> As Houston Baker and Charlotte Pierce-Baker point out, "The mood at the story's beginning is one of ritualistic waiting," of preparation "for the arrival of a goddess" (715).

---

[1]Other forms are preferred in other fields of study: APA style (American Psychological Association) is used in the social sciences; CBE style (Council of Biology Editors) in the sciences; and the *Chicago* style (Chicago Manual of Style) is generally used for history. Each focuses on the kind of information considered more useful in that discipline and on the format regarded as more convenient to use.

- If more than one work by the same author is used in the paper, the first word of the title must be included to indicate which work is being referred to.
- If you want to quote in your paper something you found quoted by someone else in an essay or book, the best procedure is to find the original source (that's one of the values of having bibliographical information provided in a work), quote from it directly, and cite it as the source. In case your library does not have the original work or it's checked out, a less desirable but accepted procedure is to copy the quote from the secondary source and use the abbreviation "qtd. in" to indicate that you are doing so.

Thus, an essay on "Everyday Use" by Houston A. Baker Jr. and Charlotte Pierce-Baker quotes the following sentence by Frederick Douglass: "I have thus far seen no book of importance written by a Negro woman and I know of no one among us who can appropriately be called famous." Baker and Pierce-Baker didn't identify the location of that statement, so if you want to quote part of it, you'll need to do something like this:

> Frederick Douglass's admission that "I have thus far seen no book of importance written by a Negro woman" provides evidence of how little impression the efforts of early African American writers made (qtd. in Baker and Pierce-Baker 713).

- If you want to cite two or more sources at once, to indicate that they say much the same thing about a point you are making, you can list them parenthetically in either of two ways:

> Among the most valuable criticism of "Everyday Use," some of the most interesting has involved a variety of viewpoints regarding Dee (see especially Baker and Pierce-Baker 715–18, Bauer 150–51, Tuten 125–28, and Farrell 181–84).
>
> Helpful discussions of Dee can be found in Baker and Pierce-Baker (715–18), Bauer (150–51), Tuten (125–28), and Farrell (181–84).

Information Notes

MLA style permits but does not require the use of informational notes either to include additional information that seems important but would disrupt the flow of the paper or to refer readers to relevant sources not discussed in the paper. Information notes may be footnotes or endnotes. Footnotes appear at the foot of the page; endnotes are placed on a separate page at the end of the paper, just before the Works Cited page. In either case, the notes are numbered consecutively throughout the paper, using raised arabic numerals (superscript).

PREPARING A WORKS CITED PAGE

WWW
Find additional advice for preparing a Works Cited page with Diana Hacker's *Research and Documentation Online* at bedfordstmartins .com/approachinglit.

The other key part of the MLA system is the bibliography. The *MLA Handbook* recommends that it be a list of Works Cited — that is, containing only works referred to within the paper. In some cases, for a student paper, a Bibliography of Works Consulted might be preferred over Works Cited to indicate the range of research, if noncited works are an important part of the context of the paper. Check with your teacher if you think that might apply to your paper.

Works Cited Page

First, here are five guidelines for preparing your Works Cited page:

1. Begin on a new page. Continue the page numbers begun in the earlier parts of the paper.
2. Center the heading "Works Cited" at the top of the page. Use capitals and lowercase letters, not bolded or italicized.
3. Arrange your list alphabetically, by the last name of the author or, for anonymous works, by the first significant word in the title (ignoring an initial *A, An,* or *The*). If two authors have the same last name, alphabetize by their first names.
4. Make the first line of each entry flush with the left margin, with subsequent lines, if any, indented one-half inch (using a hanging indent).
5. Double-space the entire list, without extra spaces between entries.

For an example of a properly formatted Works Cited page, see page 1413.

Citing Books

We include in this chapter guidelines for listing the kinds of resources that occur most commonly in literary study. If you encounter types or details not covered here, consult the *MLA Handbook* or the Bedford/St. Martin's Web site at dianahacker.com/resdoc/humanities/list.html.

For books, the asterisked items are always included; others are included as required:

*Name of the author or editor, last name first, as it appears on the title page, followed by a period. If this entry ends with an initial, only one period is needed. Only the first author's name, the one used for alphabetizing, is reversed; other names in the entry are given in the regular order.

*Title of the book, underlined or italicized, followed by a period. If the book has a subtitle, include it as well, preceded by a colon (unless the main title ends in a question mark, exclamation point, or dash).

Name of the editor (for a book that has an editor in addition to an author), **translator**, or **compiler**, preceded by the abbreviation "Ed." (even if there are two editors), "Trans.," or "Comp." and followed by a period.

Edition used, if other than the first, followed by a period.

Volume used, if a multivolume work, followed by a period.

Series name, if the book is part of a series, followed by a period.

*Place of publication, followed by a colon. If more than one city is listed on the title page, give only the first one. Identify lesser-known international cities with a country abbreviation ("Amsterdam:" but "Apeldoorn, Neth.:"; also, use "Cambridge, MA:" to distinguish it from the one in England).

*Name of the publisher, shortened, followed by a comma.

*Year of publication, followed by a period. If the date of publication is not given on the title page, look for it on the following page (the copyright page). If no date of publication is given there, use the copyright date (if more than one copyright date is listed, use the last one). Sometimes the copyright page includes the dates of successive printings of the book: These are not of interest; the date you use should be that of the first printing, its original appearance.

Here are examples of the most common kinds of entries.

A Book by One Author

Walker, Alice. *In Search of Our Mothers' Gardens: Womanist Prose.* San Diego: Harcourt, 1983.

A Book by Two Authors

To cite a book by more than one author, list the authors' names in the order they appear on the title page; invert only the first author's name, followed by a comma and the other name or names in normal order.

Pratt, L. H., and Darnell Pratt. *Alice Malsenior Walker: An Annotated Bibliography.* New York: Greenwood, 1988.

For more than three authors, you may give just the first author, followed by "et al." (abbreviation for the Latin *et alii* or *et aliae,* "and others").

An Edited Collection

To cite a book with chapters by different authors, use the same form as for a book attributed in its entirety to one or more authors, with "ed." or "eds." added after the name(s) of the editor(s), preceded by a comma.

> Gates, Henry Louis, Jr., and K. A. Appiah, eds. *Alice Walker: Critical Perspectives: Past and Present.* New York: Amistad, 1993.

To cite a specific chapter from such a collection, see below, "Citing a Scholarly Essay Published for the First Time in a Collection of Essays" or "Citing a Previously Published Article Reprinted in a Collection."

A Book in a Series

If the book you are using is part of a series as indicated by the title page or the preceding page, include the series name (not underlined or in quotation marks) and the series number after the title, followed by a period.

> Montelaro, Janet J. *Producing a Womanist Text: The Maternal as Signifier in Alice Walker's "The Color Purple."* ELS Monograph Series 70. Victoria, BC: English Literary Series, U of Victoria, 1996.

The title of a book-length work included in a book title can be enclosed in quotation marks (or, alternatively, set in contrasting roman type: *Producing a Womanist Text: The Maternal as Signifier in Alice Walker's* The Color Purple.)

Two or More Books by the Same Author

To cite two or more books by the same author, give the name only in the first entry. For the others, substitute three hyphens followed by a period. If the person edited or translated one or more of the books, place a comma after the three hyphens, then the appropriate abbreviation (that is, "ed." or "trans."), then the title. The titles should be in alphabetical order.

> Walker, Alice. *By the Light of My Father's Smile: A Novel.* New York: Random, 1998.
> ---. *The Color Purple: A Novel.* New York: Harcourt, 1982.
> ---. *Meridian.* New York: Harcourt, 1976.

A Republished Book

To cite a book that has been republished—for example, a paperback reprint of a book—give the original date of publication, followed by a period and then the publication information for the book you are using. The date of original publication can usually be found on the copyright page of the reprint; if it's not there, you may need to check library catalogs or biographical introductions to the author to find it.

> Walker, Alice. *The Color Purple*. 1982. New York: Pocket, 1985.

An Edition

To cite a work prepared for publication by someone other than the author—by an editor—provide the information you would provide for a republished book, with the name of the editor inserted before the publication information. The date of original publication is included for a republication, in edited form, of a previously published book.

> Dunbar, Paul Laurence. *Collected Poetry*. Ed. Joanne M. Bruxton. Charlottes-
> ville: UP of Virginia, 1993.

Note that although the title page reads *The Collected Poetry of Paul Laurence Dunbar,* repetition can be avoided to make it fit conventional citation form. The following example is not a reprint but the first printing of a collected edition of stories originally published in several books.

> Hughes, Langston. *The Return of Simple*. Ed. Akiba Sullivan Harper. New York:
> Hill, 1994.

A Multivolume Work

To cite two or more volumes of a multivolume work, give the total number of volumes in the set before the publication information, using an arabic numeral followed by the abbreviation "vols." Parenthetical references in the text will require volume number plus page numbers ("2: 145–47"). For a work in which volumes were published separately, in different years, give the first and last dates at the end of the citation.

> Rampersad, Arnold. *The Life of Langston Hughes*. 2 vols. New York: Oxford UP,
> 1986-88.

When you use only one volume of a multivolume work, give its volume number in the bibliographic entry and include publication information for only that volume. In this case, only the page numbers are needed in parenthetical references in the text.

> Rampersad, Arnold. *The Life of Langston Hughes*. Vol. 2. New York: Oxford UP,
> 1988.

Citing a Work in a Collection of Stories or Poems

To cite a work from a collection of stories or poems by a single author, insert the title of the story or poem, in quotation marks, between the name of the author and the title of the book, and conclude the entry with the pages on which it appears.

> Walker, Alice. "Everyday Use." *In Love and Trouble: Stories of Black Women.*
>   New York: Harcourt, 1973. 47-59.

Citations for additional works from the same collection can be abbreviated:

> ---. "The Flowers." *In Love and Trouble* 119-20.

Citing a Work in an Anthology

When citing a work published in an anthology, insert the title of the work (in quotation marks for a story, poem, or essay; underlined or italicized for a play or screenplay) and the year of original publication (unless this is its first publication) after the author's name; conclude the entry with the page numbers on which the work appears.

> Walker, Alice. "Everyday Use." 1973. *Approaching Literature in the 21st Century: Fiction. Poetry. Drama.* Ed. Peter Schakel and Jack Ridl. Boston: Bedford, 2004. 101-7.

If several works from the same anthology are cited in the paper, unnecessary repetition can be avoided by creating a main entry for the anthology and cross-referencing individual works to it.

> Ríos, Alberto. "Nani." 1982. Schakel and Ridl 713.
> Schakel, Peter, and Jack Ridl, eds. *Approaching Literature in the 21st Century: Fiction. Poetry. Drama.* Boston: Bedford, 2004.
> Walker, Alice. "Everyday Use." 1973. Schakel and Ridl 101-7.

Citing a Scholarly Essay Published for the First Time in a Collection of Essays

> Parker-Smith, Bettye J. "Alice Walker's Women: In Search of Some Peace of Mind." *Black Women Writers (1950-1980): A Critical Evaluation.* Ed. Mari Evans. Garden City: Anchor, 1984. 478-93.

If two or more works from the same volume are cited in the paper, create a main entry for the volume and cross-reference individual works to it, as above.

Citing an Entry from an Encyclopedia

The citation for an encyclopedia article or dictionary entry follows the pattern for an essay in a collection, except the editor's name should not be included and, if it's well-known, publication information can be omitted. If the article is signed, start with the author (sometimes articles in reference books are signed with initials identified elsewhere in the book); if it is anonymous, start with the title of the entry. If entries are arranged alphabetically in the encyclopedia or dictionary, volume and page numbers may be omitted.

"Clabber." *The Oxford English Dictionary*. 2nd ed. 1989.

"Quilting." *The New Encyclopedia Britannica: Micropedia*. 15th ed. 2002.

Citing an Entry in a Multivolume Reference Work

Christian, Barbara T. "Alice Walker." *Dictionary of Literary Biography*. Vol. 33: *Afro-American Fiction Writers after 1955*. Ed. Thadious M. Davis and Trudier Harris. Detroit: Gale, 1984. 258-71.

Citing Articles Published in Scholarly Journals

Scholarly journals usually publish several issues a year (often quarterly). Each year is designated as a volume, and pages are usually numbered continuously throughout the volume. Works Cited entries for an article in a scholarly journal should include the following:

* **Name of the author**, last name first, as it appears in the article, followed by a period.
* **Title of the article**, enclosed in quotation marks, followed by a period (inside the quotation mark).
* **Title of the journal**, underlined or italicized, no punctuation following it.
* **Volume number of the journal**, using arabic numerals even if a roman numeral is used in the journal, no punctuation following.
* **Year of publication**, in parentheses, followed by a colon.
* **Page numbers** (first and last), followed by a period.

Bauer, Margaret D. "Alice Walker: Another Southern Writer Criticizing Codes Not Put to 'Everyday Use.'" *Studies in Short Fiction* 29 (1992): 143-51.

Some journals paginate each issue separately. In that case, you must also include the issue number (volume, period, issue with no spaces between: "29.2").

Citing Articles Published in Magazines

Magazines usually appear more frequently than scholarly journals (often weekly, biweekly, monthly, or bimonthly) and paginate each issue separately. Magazines have volume numbers, but they are not important for locating an issue and are left out. Works Cited entries for a magazine article should include the following:

*   ***Name of the author**, last name first, as it appears in the magazine, followed by a period.
*   ***Title of the article**, enclosed in quotation marks, followed by a period (inside the quotation mark).
*   ***Title of the journal**, underlined or italicized, no punctuation following it.
*   ***Date of publication**, followed by a colon. Day, month (abbreviated), and year (in that order) are given for weekly or biweekly magazines; only month or months and year are given for magazines published monthly or bimonthly.
*   ***Page numbers** (first and last of the whole article, not just the ones you used), followed by a period. If pagination is not consecutive (for example, begins on page 4, then jumps to page 8), write only the first page number and a plus sign, with no intervening space.

Reed, J. R. "Post Feminism Playing for Keeps." *Time* 10 Jan. 1983: 60-61.

Watkins, Mel. "Sexism, Racism and Black Women Writers." *New York Times Book Review* 15 June 1986: 4+.

Citing Articles Published in Newspapers

The format for citing an article in a newspaper is exactly the same as for a weekly magazine, unless the newspaper is published in varied editions (late edition, suburban edition) — in that case, the edition is included after the date, separated by a comma. If a newspaper is divided into sections, include the section letter or section number with the page number. If the article is on more than one page and not consecutive, give the first page number followed by a plus sign, with no space between them.

Ross, Michelle. "Georgia Writer Alice Walker Didn't Know They Had Pulitzer Prize for Fiction." *Atlanta Journal* 19 Apr. 1983: A3.

Sague, Maria. "Alice Walker: A Writer with a Cause." *Sun* [Baltimore] 5 July 1987: A7-8.

Citing a Review

In citing a review, include the title and author of the work being reviewed after the review title and before the periodical title.

Giovanni, Nikki. "So Black and Blue." Rev. of *In Love and Trouble,* by Alice
Walker. *Book World* 18 Nov. 1973: 1.

Citing a Previously Published Article Reprinted in a Collection

To cite a previously published scholarly article reprinted in a collection, give the complete data for the earlier publication and then add "Rpt. in" ("Reprinted in"), the title of the collection, and its publication data.

Baker, Houston A., and Charlotte Pierce-Baker. "Patches: Quilts and Community
in Alice Walker's 'Everyday Use.'" *The Southern Review* 21 (1985): 706-20.
Rpt. in *Alice Walker: Critical Perspectives: Past and Present*. Ed. Henry
Louis Gates, Jr., and K. A. Appiah. New York: Amistad, 1993. 309-16.

Citing Print Sources Accessed Electronically

Many libraries subscribe to services such as JSTOR, InfoTrac, and Lexis-Nexis to make journal articles available online. If you use such a service to obtain the text of a printed work, you should provide as much of the usual information for the source's original publication as possible, then the title of the database used (underlined or italicized) if known, along with the name of the service subscribed to, the name of the library or library system through which it was accessed, and the date on which it was accessed. If you know the URL of the service's home page, include it at the end in angle brackets.

Farrell, Susan. "Fight vs. Flight: A Re-evaluation of Dee in Alice Walker's 'Everyday Use.'" *Studies in Short Fiction* 35 (1998): 179-86. *FirstSearch*. OCLC.
Hope College Library. 3 Nov. 2003 <http://www.firstsearch.oclc.org>.

Citing Electronic Sources

Whenever possible, give the same kinds of information for an online source as for a printed source (such as author, title, "publication" information, and date). When the source does not provide all of that information, give as much information as you can. Two dates should be included, whenever possible: the date when the document was posted or updated and the date you accessed the document. Online addresses are enclosed in angle brackets (turn off the function on your word processor that converts Web addresses into hyperlinks).

A CD-ROM

To cite a CD-ROM, treat it like a book, with "CD-ROM" and a period between its title and the publication information.

"Alice Walker." *DISCovering Authors.* CD-ROM. Detroit: Gale, 1999.

A Professional or Personal Web Page

To cite a Web page, include as much of the following as possible: author of the site or document; its title, in quotation marks, for separate documents within the site; the name of the site, underlined or italicized; the date the site or document was created or most recently updated; the sponsoring organization or institution; the date you accessed it; and the online address. If the site does not have a heading title, give an identifying phrase (not underlined or in quotation marks).

Jokinen, Anniina. *Anniina's Alice Walker Page.* 21 Mar. 2002. 3 Nov. 2003
    <http://www.luminarium.org/contemporary/alicew/>.

An Online Scholarly Project or Database

"Alice Walker." *Online Poetry Classroom.* Academy of American Poets. 2003.
    3 Nov. 2003 <http://www.onlinepoetryclassroom.org>.
Mabry, Donald J. *The Historical Text Archive.* Founded 1990 at Mississippi State
    University. 2003. 3 Nov. 2003 <http://www.historicaltextarchive.com>.

An Online Journal

Rhodes-Pitts, Sharifa. "Everyday Use: The Quilters of Gee's Bend." *Africana:*
    Gateway to the Black World. Microsoft Corp. 25 Nov. 2002. 3 Nov. 2003
    <http://www.Africana.com/articles/daily/ar20021125gees.asp>.

An Online Magazine

"LitChat: Alice Walker." *Salon.com* 11 Aug. 2000. 3 Nov. 2003 <http://
    archive.salon.com/09/departments/litchat1.htm>.

Citing Interviews

To cite an interview, give first the name of the person being interviewed. If the interview has been published, give the title (if it has one) in quotation marks or just "Interview," without quotation marks or italics, and then give the name of the interviewer and publication information.

Walker, Alice. "Authors and Editors." Interview with Barbara Bannon. *Publish-*
    ers Weekly 31 Aug. 1970: 195-97.

To cite an interview conducted personally by the author of a paper, include the name of the person interviewed, the kind of interview ("Personal interview," "Telephone interview," "E-mail interview"), and the date or dates.

Ridl, Jack. Personal interview. 7 Sept. 2003.

Schakel, Peter. E-mail interview. 13-15 Oct. 2003.

Citing a Personal Letter or E-mail

To cite a letter that you received, give the name of the sender, the type of communication, and its date.

Ridl, Jack. Letter to the author. 21 Oct. 2003.

Schakel, Peter. E-mail to the author. 28 Oct. 2003.

A STUDENT WRITER AT WORK: KRISTINA MARTINEZ ON THE RESEARCH PROCESS

Students in an Introduction to Literature class were asked to use secondary sources in writing a paper on technique and meaning in a work from the "Collection of Stories" section of this book (see Chapter 8). One of our students, Kristina Martinez, decided to do her paper on Toni Morrison's "Recitatif." We are going to follow her through the writing process in completing that assignment, using her own words as she retraces her steps.

On Finding a Topic

"There were a lot of interesting ideas in the story — racial ambiguity, social status, mother-daughter relationships, among others — and I considered several of these as a topic. But what I found tied all of these ideas together, and interested me most, was the way in which the story was told. Before I began writing the paper I knew I might have trouble with keeping the paper focused and staying with the idea of how the story is told. I hadn't read a story before that plays with readers so much, and manages to address a number of issues."

On Researching the Topic

"The first thing I did, after reading 'Recitatif' three times, was to use the online catalog to look for books on Toni Morrison. I found several, including an encyclopedia on her (*The Toni Morrison Encyclopedia*, ed. Elizabeth Ann

Beaulieu [Westport: Greenwood, 2003]). I browsed in them and photocopied sections on 'Recitatif' that looked potentially useful. Then I searched databases to find articles about the story, and again found several. I photocopied ones that looked good if we had them in the library, and printed others where full texts were available online. Then, in the notes and bibliographies of the books and articles I had collected, I looked at what those authors used as sources, found ones that seemed interesting, and made copies. I then put everything in a three-ring notebook and began reading closely. I expected the paper to focus especially on Twyla, Roberta, their mothers, and Maggie, as well as on the structure of the story. So I marked in the margins places that referred to any of those. To make it easier to return to these places, I put tabs by them, using sticky notes, a different color for each topic. (When I was writing the paper and used a passage, I removed the tab so I would not go back to the passage again.)"

On Developing and Supporting a Thesis

"I started by working on a thesis, and, after a couple of false starts, decided to focus on the way differences in stories told in 'Recitatif' leave readers feeling ambiguous about race and about Maggie. My working thesis statement was, 'Elements of story are thick throughout this piece. Morrison uses character, point of view, and time to hold readers' attention and leaves them questioning not only race but what really has happened to Maggie.' It was modified slightly in the final version, but most of it is still there.

"One of my sources was helpful in setting up the rest of the paper — it showed that Morrison used oral storytelling techniques in writing 'Recitatif.' That led me to wonder about Twyla and Roberta as oral storytellers. Both of them told stories about the same events. I tried to think about both as telling stories in order to lead their listeners (readers) or to mislead them.

"With that as a starting point, I wrote a detailed outline of the rest of the paper. Briefly:

- Narrator — Twyla as primary one; Roberta as secondary
- Race — concealing which is white and which is black
- Stories about Maggie and her race
  - Both girls identify with Maggie
  - First story about Maggie: Difference in what they remember
  - Second story about Maggie: Did they kick her? Was she black?
  - Third story about Maggie: Why they *wanted* to kick her
- Conclusion

Next, I wrote the first point in longhand, then typed and printed it, reread it, and revised it. I went on to do the same for the other points. I wrote by hand because it was easier to put my ideas from head to hand and hand to paper, plus the weather was great and I wrote outside.

"I wrote out what I wanted to say about each point, using summaries and details from the story to support it. Then I went back through my notebook, looking for places where critics could be used to clarify or back up what I was saying. I inserted summaries or quotations where they seemed to fit well."

On Revising and Proofreading

"Despite my thorough outline, I ended up writing paragraphs that turned out not to be central to my focus on storytelling. One thing I did in revision was to cut paragraphs — often keeping a sentence I could move to another paragraph and deleting the rest. I also needed to reduce quotations — there were too many, at first, and some were too long. I cut a lot. Another revision was to improve the way I led into quotations.

"I had started my Works Cited list earlier, as I photocopied materials. While revising, I used that list as I went through the paper and put a check mark by each item that I actually used in the paper. I checked each for accuracy, and deleted the ones I didn't use. Then I checked quotations, and corrected a few minor slips. Last, I proofread the whole paper, for spelling, grammar, and sentence style."

SAMPLE RESEARCH PAPER

What follows is Kristina's final revision. For the convenience of readers, we have changed the page numbers for quotations from "Recitatif" originally given in the essay to the page on which they are found in this book.

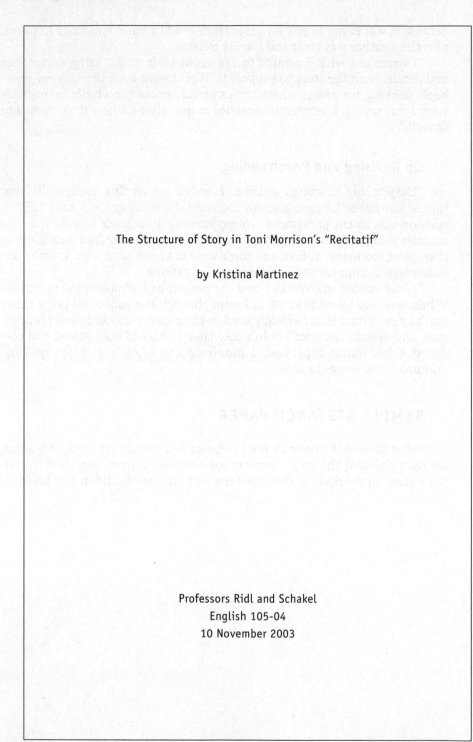

The Structure of Story in Toni Morrison's "Recitatif"

by Kristina Martinez

Professors Ridl and Schakel
English 105-04
10 November 2003

1

What do stories do? Some are told to entertain, some to inform or instruct, some to mislead. And sometimes the way a story is structured creates ambiguities that make it difficult to tell which of these it is doing. That is the case with Toni Morrison's story "Recitatif." The structure of Twyla's story, and that of Roberta's stories within it, hold a reader's attention and leave a reader questioning not only race but what happened to Maggie.

The structure relates to the kind of story this is. Robert Stepto points out that many African-American authors "choose to see them-selves as storytellers instead of storywriters" (qtd. in Goldstein-Shirley 101) because they distrust readers, and want people to *listen* to what they have to say. "Recitatif" falls into that category: "Although the text is written," David Goldstein-Shirley notes, "its structure mimics oral storytelling" (101). He goes on to spell out the effect of that form: "The distinctively 'oral' quality of 'Recitatif' also contributes to the story's strategy of recruiting the reader in its mission to decon-struct racism" (101).

The story, in fact, has two storytellers. Twyla is the overall story-teller. The story begins with her: "My mother danced all night and Roberta's was sick" ("Recitatif" 300). Twyla is a limited narrator, an outsider in her own story, lacking the understanding of things that Roberta possesses from the start ("I liked the way she understood things so fast"--"Recitatif" 301). As a result, Elizabeth Abel believes, Twyla "feels vulnerable to Roberta's judgment" (473). Twyla's story provides a frame, within which we also hear stories told by Roberta, which often conflict with Twyla's, thus creating tension between the two and forcing the reader to sort out differences and attempt to find the truth.

One of the things readers must grapple with is race. Twyla and Roberta are of different races: "we looked like salt and pepper standing there," Twyla says ("Recitatif" 301). But which is white and which is black is never stated. The reader's desire to know is paralleled later in the story by the girls' attempts to determine the race of the servant Maggie (Bennett 212). Morrison creates a racial ambiguity that, Lisa Cade Wieland argues, grows out of linguistic ambiguity: "'Recitatif'

Thesis sentence states central idea.

Use of indirect secondary source (quoted in another source) to set up argument.

Clear topic sen-tences are used throughout the paper.

Secondary source quoted to advance ar-gument, with signal phrase naming author.

Primary text quoted to back up assertion.

Secondary source quoted to expand point.

2

becomes an experiment in language, as Morrison considers whether a story can be written without the linguistic short cuts habitually employed in American literature to categorize and to stereotype its characters" (280). Race is important to our identities, Anthony Appiah concludes (499), and in that respect it is a central issue in the story. Yet the reader is not allowed to fall back on familiar language and comfortable stereotypes in understanding that issue.

Secondary source summarized.

These discrepancies and ambiguities come to bear especially on their stories about Maggie. Both girls identified to some extent with Maggie. Maggie is, as one critic states, "the lowest person in the hierarchy" (Holmes). Similarly, Twyla and Roberta were looked down upon by other children at the orphanage because "we weren't real orphans with beautiful dead parents in the sky" ("Recitatif" 301). As Maggie is mute, so the two girls while at St. Bonny's have no voice. This does not, however, lead them to bond with Maggie. On the contrary, they attempt to separate and distance themselves from her emotionally because, Jan Furman says, she makes them feel inadequate and helpless. The result was that, "Without realizing it, however, in hating Maggie, they hated themselves and each other" (Furman 110). That hatred leads them to remember Maggie differently, and thus the stories they tell are different.

Transition to Part 2.

No page number for Web source.

Shortened citation of primary text: no need to repeat "Morrison."

Paraphrase and quotation of secondary source to advance argument.

The first story about Maggie occurs when, years after St. Bonny's, they cross paths at the Food Emporium. They have lunch and as they reminisce about the orphanage, Twyla says,

Extended block quotation sets up further discussion of Maggie.

> "I don't remember a hell of a lot from those days, but Lord, St. Bonny's is as clear as daylight. Remember Maggie? The day she fell down and those gar girls laughed at her?"
>
> Roberta looked up from her salad and stared at me.
> "Maggie didn't fall," she said.
> "Yes, she did. You remember."
> "No, Twyla. They knocked her down. Those girls pushed her down and tore her clothes. In the orchard."
> "I don't--that's not what happened."
> "Sure it is. In the orchard." ("Recitatif" 309)

3

The discrepancies bother Twyla ("Roberta had messed up my past somehow with that business about Maggie. I wouldn't forget a thing like that. Would I?"--"Recitatif" 310) and create ambiguity for the reader. Which story is correct, Roberta's or Twyla's (or neither)? Are they remembering details about Maggie differently because one of them is the same race as Maggie and the other not? If so, which one is the same?

Series of questions to be explored in rest of paper.

Conflicting stories about Maggie appear again the next time they meet, later that year, outside a school at which Roberta is picketing against busing children to achieve racial balance. They have a bitter exchange about forced integration, in which Roberta blurts out to Twyla, "You're the same little state kid who kicked a poor old black lady when she was down on the ground. You kicked a black lady and you have the nerve to call me a bigot" ("Recitatif" 312). Twyla tells a different story: "Maggie wasn't black" ("Recitatif" 312), and she hadn't kicked Maggie: "I know I didn't do that, I couldn't do that" ("Recitatif" 313). On further thought, she remains convinced about the kicking, but not about the race: "When I thought about it I actually couldn't be certain" ("Recitatif" 313). The reader is left to figure out why Roberta said this to Twyla, how much of it is true, and how racial difference affects their different memories.

Summary of primary text.

Quotation of primary text to highlight crux in story.

Maggie stories emerge also in the last meeting with Roberta that Twyla tells about. The last time they meet in the story is at least a year later when Twyla stops at a downtown diner for coffee after shopping for a Christmas tree and Roberta sits with her for a few minutes. Roberta now backs away from her previous story: she acknowledges that Twyla didn't kick Maggie--neither of them did, only the gar girls did. The exchange brings out a parallel between Roberta and Twyla: each had wanted to kick Maggie because each identified Maggie with her mother as well as with herself. For Twyla, "Maggie was my dancing mother. Deaf, I thought, and dumb. Nobody inside. Nobody who would hear you if you cried in the night. Nobody who could tell you anything important that you could use" ("Recitatif" 313). Roberta thought Maggie was crazy, like her mother, and had "been brought up in an institution like my mother was and like I thought I would be too"

Primary text summarized at length to provide context.

Quotations of primary text to bring out key points.

4

(Recitatif" 314). Neither girl could accept her own mother, just as neither could accept Maggie: the reminders of the pain their mothers inflicted were too much to bear.

The structure of story creates ambiguity in racial codes, and does not attempt to resolve it. It is too complex to fit the conventional language and stereotypes. Each girl constructed a racial identity for Maggie out of her own cultural and racial context, and we as readers are tempted to do the same (Abel 471–72). What this story does is to show how literature can bring readers into a work, "the ways writers . . . tell other stories, fight secret wars, limn out all sorts of debates blanketed in their text" (Morrison, *Playing* 4). Readers are given the language, which takes them through the story and finally leads them to the point of realizing that this story will not provide answers to their questions, and that acceptance of ambiguity itself answers the need to have answers.

Secondary source summarized.

Title included in citation because two works by Morrison appear in Works Cited.

5

Works Cited

Abel, Elizabeth. "Black Writing, White Reading: Race and the Politics of Feminist Interpretation." *Critical Inquiry* 19 (1993): 470-98.

Appiah, Anthony. "'But Would That Still Be Me?' Notes on Gender, 'Race,' Ethnicity, as Sources of 'Identity.'" *Journal of Philosophy* 87 (1990): 493-99. *JSTOR*. Hope College Library. 3 Nov. 2003 <http://www.jstor.org/search>.

Bennett, Juda. "Toni Morrison and the Burden of the Passing Narrative." *African American Review* 35(2001): 205-17. *InfoTrac.* Gale. Hope College Library. 3 Nov. 2003 <http://www.0-web7.infotrac.galegroup.com>.

Furman, Jan. *Toni Morrison's Fiction*. Columbia: U of South Carolina P, 1996.

Goldstein-Shirley, David. "Race/[Gender]." *Women on the Edge: Ethnicity and Gender in Short Stories by American Women*. Ed. Corrine H. Dale and J. H. S. Paine. New York: Garland, 1999: 97-110.

Holmes, Martha Stoddard. "Literature Annotations: Morrison, Toni: 'Recitatif.'" *Literature, Arts, and Medicine Database*. 6 Nov. 2003 <http://www.endeavor.med.nyu.edu/lit-med/lit-med-db/webdocs/webdescrips/morrison11854-des-.html>.

Morrison, Toni. *Playing in the Dark: Whiteness and the Literary Imagination*. Cambridge, MA: Harvard UP, 1992.

---. "Recitatif." *Confirmation: An Anthology of African American Women*. Ed. Amiri Baraka (LeRoi Jones) and Amina Baraka. New York: Quill, 1983. 243-61.

Wieland, Lisa Cade. "Recitatif." *The Toni Morrison Encyclopedia*. Ed. Elizabeth Ann Beaulieu. Westport: Greenwood, 2003. 287-89.

Biographical Sketches

This section offers brief biographical sketches of the 235 known authors of the works included in this book. For fuller biographical information, the most convenient print sources are the *Dictionary of Literary Biography* (Detroit: Gale, 1978–), currently at 289 volumes, and *Contemporary Authors,* also published by Gale (original series, 195 volumes; new revised series, currently 103 volumes).

Biographical information for many authors is also found on the Internet. The Academy of American Poets Web site (poets.org/poets/index.cfm) is valuable and convenient for information about poets; we are indebted to it for many of our entries. *Voices from the Gaps: Women Writers of Color* (voices.cla.umn.edu/newsite/index.htm) also is very helpful. Sites for many individual authors are available as well, personal home pages for some contemporary poets and sites maintained by scholars or fans of writers old and new. To emphasize how authors work with each other and are influenced by other poets, when the names of poets represented in this anthology appear within a biographical entry, they are in small capital letters, as a reminder that those biographical notes will shed further light on the author at hand.

The companion Web site for this book, bedfordstmartins.com/approachinglit, provides access to LitLinks, which offers brief biographies of all of the writers in this book, with links to important related sites. Marginal icons throughout the book reference the companion Web site and *LiterActive,* a CD-ROM with multimedia resources, biographies, and critical and cultural documents. After each biographical entry, we've included cross-references to these two resources. Both are good places to start when researching individual authors.

CHINUA ACHEBE (b. 1930) was born in Ogidi, in eastern Nigeria. His father was a teacher in a missionary school and instilled in him strong Christian teachings as well as the values of their traditional Igbo culture. Achebe studied English, history, and theology at the University of Ibadan and graduated with a B.A. in 1953. A year later he joined the Nigerian Broadcasting Company in Lagos. He served as director of external services in charge of the Voice of Nigeria in the early 1960s and helped raise money later in the decade to alleviate suffering caused by the Biafran War. He began writing stories as an undergraduate to provide an alternative to the stories told about Africa by European writers. His acclaimed first novel, *Things Fall Apart* (1958), has been translated into some fifty languages. He has published over twenty books in various genres; has edited *Okike,* the leading journal of Nigerian new writing, since 1971; founded and edits a bilingual magazine, *Uwa ndi Igbo,* that encourages Igbo studies; and is the director of Heinemann Educational Books in Nigeria, which publishes the works of African writers.

WEB: Further research this author with LitLinks at bedfordstmartins.com/approachinglit.

AI (b. 1947), who has described herself as one-half Japanese, one-eighth Choctaw, one-half black, and one-sixteenth Irish, was born

Florence Anthony in Albany, Texas, and grew up in Tucson, Arizona. She legally changed her name to "Ai," which means "love" in Japanese. She received a B.A. in Japanese from the University of Arizona and an M.F.A. from the University of California at Irvine. She is the author of half a dozen books of poetry, among them *Vice* (1999), which won the National Book Award for Poetry. She has taught at Wayne State University, George Mason University, and the University of Kentucky, and she currently teaches at Oklahoma State University and lives in Stillwater, Oklahoma.

WEB: Further research this author with LitLinks at bedfordstmartins.com/approachinglit.

ANNA AKHMATOVA (1889–1966) was born Anna Gorenko in Bolshoy Fontan, near Odessa, Ukraine. She began writing poetry at eleven but had to adopt a pseudonym to allay her father's fears that her becoming a "decadent poetess" would dishonor the family. She attended law school in Kiev before moving to St. Petersburg to study literature. Her first collection of poetry, *Evening,* appeared in 1912 and was well received. Because she was suspected of anti-Bolshevik sentiments, her poetry was banned in Russia from 1925 until 1940 and again after World War II. During the ban she devoted herself to literary criticism and translations. In the late 1930s, her long poem *Requiem* was dedicated to the memory of Stalin's victims. In 1940, a collection of previously published poems, *From Six Books,* was published but withdrawn a few months later. After Stalin's death Akhmatova slowly gained recognition as one of the greatest Russian poets of the twentieth century, respected internationally for the quality of her literary work and for her integrity and resoluteness in the face of political oppression.

WEB: Further research this author with LitLinks at bedfordstmartins.com/approachinglit.

SHERMAN ALEXIE (b. 1966) — See page 1319.

AGHA SHAHID ALI (1949–2001) was born in New Delhi and grew up Muslim in Kashmir. He was educated at the University of Kashmir, Srinagar, and at the University of Delhi. He earned a Ph.D. from Pennsylvania State University in 1984 and an M.F.A. from the University of Arizona in 1985. He was a poet

(author of eight books of poetry), critic (author of *T. S. Eliot as Editor* [1986]), translator (*The Rebel's Silhouette: Selected Poems* by Faiz Ahmed Faiz, 1992), and editor (*Ravishing Disunities: Real Ghazals in English,* 2000). He held teaching positions at the University of Delhi and at several colleges and universities in the United States. "I Dream It Is Afternoon When I Return to Delhi" (p. 597) shows Ali's use of Western formal cultural principles in work that focuses on his own cultural background.

WEB: Further research this author with LitLinks at bedfordstmartins.com/approachinglit.

ISABEL ALLENDE (b. 1942) was born in Lima, Peru. After the divorce of her mother and father (a Chilean diplomat), she lived with her maternal grandparents in Santiago, Chile, then in Bolivia, the Middle East, and Europe with her mother and stepfather, also a diplomat. She worked for the United Nations Food and Agricultural Organization in Santiago and then embarked on a promising career as a journalist for *Paula* magazine and on television and in movie newsreels. That career ended with the overthrow and assassination in 1973 of her uncle, Salvador Allende, president of Chile, when she, her husband, and her children had to flee to Venezuela for safety. While in exile, she began to write her first novel, *The House of the Spirits* (1982), which traces personal and political conflicts in several generations of an imaginary family in a Latin American country and is based on memories of her own family and the political upheaval in Chile. She has since published several novels and a collection of short stories. Her work is known for focusing on the experience (especially the struggles) of women and for its use of the "magic realism" often found in Latin American literature.

WEB: Further research this author with LitLinks at bedfordstmartins.com/approachinglit.

JULIA ALVAREZ (b. 1950) was born in New York City, lived in the Dominican Republic until she was ten, and returned to New York when her father had to flee because he was involved in a plot to overthrow the dictator, Rafael Trujillo. Thus she needed to adjust to a new culture and a new language. Since childhood she says she loved stories — hearing them and telling them — so it was natural for her to decide she wanted to be a writer. She graduated from Middlebury College in Vermont and earned an M.A. in creative writing from Syracuse University. Since 1998 she has been writer-in-residence at Middlebury. Alvarez has published many short stories, several books for young readers, three volumes of poetry, and a book of essays about herself and her writing life, *Something to Declare* (1998).

WEB: Further research this author with LitLinks at bedfordstmartins.com/approachinglit.

YEHUDA AMICHAI (1924–2000) was born in Wurzburg, Germany, and emigrated with his family to Palestine in 1936. He later became a naturalized Israeli citizen. Although German was his native language, Amichai read Hebrew fluently by the time he moved to Palestine. He served in the Jewish Brigade of the British Army in World War II and fought with the Israeli defense forces in the 1948 Arab-Israeli war. Following the war, he attended Hebrew University to study biblical texts and Hebrew literature, and then taught in secondary schools. He published eleven volumes of poetry in Hebrew, two novels, and a book of short stories. His work has been translated into thirty-seven languages. He is regarded as one of the leading twentieth-century Hebrew poets, his contribution extending beyond his own literary achievements to his influence on the development of modern Israeli poetry.

WEB: Further research this author with LitLinks at bedfordstmartins.com/approachinglit.

SUSAN ATEFAT-PECKHAM (1970–2004) was a first-generation American born to Iranian parents. She spent most of her life in France, Switzerland, and the United States. She received her undergraduate degree at Baylor University where she planned on a career as a physician. However, part way through her college years, she discovered poetry and was encouraged to write by her future husband. She earned her Ph.D. in English and creative writing from the University of Nebraska and was a member of the M.F.A. faculty at Georgia College and State University. She died in a car accident while on a Fulbright Fellowship in Jordan. Atefat-Peckham was also a noted writer of creative nonfiction, having been cited in *Best American Essays;* an accomplished pianist; and an excellent painter, something that influenced the vibrancy and color-filled quality of her poems. Her poems lead the reader into the usually hidden lives of Iranian women living in the dual worlds of tradition and the contemporary.

WEB: Further research this author with LitLinks at bedfordstmartins.com/approachinglit.

W.[YSTAN] H.[UGH] AUDEN (1907–1973) was born in York, England. He went to private school and then to Oxford University, where he began to write poetry. He supported himself by teaching and publishing, and wrote books based on his travels to Iceland, Spain, and China. He also wrote (with Chester Kallman) several librettos, including one for Igor Stravinsky's *The Rake's Progress* (1951). He lived in the United States from 1939 until his death and became a U.S. citizen in 1946. His work combines lively intelligence, quick wit, and immense craftsmanship, and often focuses on social concerns.

WEB: Further research this author with LitLinks at bedfordstmartins.com/approachinglit.

JOSEPH AWAD (b. 1929) was born in Shenandoah, Pennsylvania, and grew up in Washington, D.C., where he earned his B.A. in English literature from Georgetown University and edited the college literary magazine. He took night courses in drawing and painting at the Corcoran School of Art and toyed with the idea of a career in art, but decided instead to do graduate studies in English at George Washington University. A job in public relations turned into a career, as he joined the Reynolds Metals Company public relations department and ultimately became vice president. He has published several collections of poetry, including *Leaning to Hear the Music* (1997). His poetry has won many awards, among them the Edgar Allan Poe Prize of the Poetry Society of Virginia, The Lyric's Nathan Haskell Dole Prize, and the Donn Goodwin Poetry Award. He lives with his wife in Richmond, Virginia, and served as poet laureate for Virginia from 1998 to 2000.

WEB: Further research this author with LitLinks at bedfordstmartins.com/approachinglit.

JIMMY SANTIAGO BACA (b. 1952) was born in Sante Fe, New Mexico, of Chicano and Apache heritage. Abandoned by his parents at the age of two, he lived with one of his grandparents for several years before being placed in an orphanage. He lived on the streets as a youth and was imprisoned for six years for drug possession. In prison, he taught himself to read and write, and began to compose poetry. A fellow inmate convinced him to submit some of his poems for publication. He has since published seven books of poetry, a memoir, a collection of stories and essays, a play, and a screenplay. He lives outside Albuquerque in a one-hundred-year-old adobe house.

WEB: Further research this author with LitLinks at bedfordstmartins.com/approachinglit.

JAMES BALDWIN (1924–1987) was born in Harlem to an unmarried domestic worker. When Baldwin was three, his mother married a factory worker and storefront preacher who was a hard, cruel man. At age fourteen, Baldwin began preaching at the small Fireside Pentecostal Church in Harlem, and the cadences of black preaching continued to influence his writing style later in his life. His first story appeared in a church newspaper when he was about twelve. He left home at seventeen and lived in Greenwich Village, where he met RICHARD WRIGHT, who encouraged him to continue his writing and helped him win a Eugene Saxton Fellowship. Strained relations with his stepfather, problems over sexual identity, the suicide of a friend, and racial oppression in the United States led Baldwin to move to France when he was nineteen, though he returned to the United States frequently to lecture and teach, and from 1957 on spent half of each year in New York City. His first novel, the partially autobiographical *Go Tell It on the Mountain,* was published in 1953. His second novel, *Giovanni's Room* (1956), dealt with a white American expatriate who must come to terms with his homosexuality, and *Another Country* (1962) explored racial and gay sexual tensions among New York intellectuals. He published several more novels, plays, and essay collections, including *Nobody Knows My Name* (1961) and *The Fire Next Time* (1963).

WEB: Further research this author with LitLinks at bedfordstmartins.com/approachinglit.

CD-ROM: Research this author in depth with cultural documents and multimedia resources on *LiterActive.*

TONI CADE BAMBARA (1939–1995) was born in New York City and grew up in Harlem and Bedford-Stuyvesant. She began writing stories when she was a child and continued writing and taking writing courses in high school and at Queens College, where she majored in Theater Arts and English. Bambara completed her master's degree in American literature while serving as program director at Colony Settlement House in Brooklyn; she then began teaching at City College of New York. She first became known for editing a groundbreaking collection of African American women's writing, *The Black Woman: An Anthology* (1970). She went on to publish four collections of stories, two novels, many screenplays, and a book for children. In addition to being an important figure among the group of African American writers who emerged in the 1960s, Bambara was an activist in the civil rights and women's movements.

WEB: Further research this author with LitLinks at bedfordstmartins.com/approachinglit.

REZA BARAHENI (b. 1935) was born in Tabriz, Iran. He earned his doctorate in literature from the University of Istanbul and in 1963 was appointed as Professor of English at Tehran University. The author of over fifty books of fiction and poetry, he has been described as "Iran's finest living poet." His best-known works in English are *The Crowned Cannibals* (1977) and *God's Shadow: Prison Poems* (1976), the latter a collection of poems based on a period of 102 days spent in solitary confinement in Iran in 1973, during the time of the Shah. Baraheni's work is also well known in France. Three of his novels — *Les saisons en enfer du jeune Ayyaz, Shéhérazade et son romancier,* and *Elias in New York* — have been published in France by Fayard, and two plays — *Enfer* and *Qeskes* — have been performed there, most of them reviewed in *Le Monde, Liberation,* and other French newspapers and periodicals. He was imprisoned in the fall of 1981 and the winter of 1982 by the

Islamic Republic of Iran, expelled from the University of Tehran, and deprived of the right to work. He escaped Iran in the fall of 1996 after an attempt on his life and presently makes his home in Canada, where he is a Professor of Comparative Literature at the University of Toronto's Centre for Comparative Literature. He was president of PEN Canada (2001–2003) and is the winner of numerous literary and human rights awards.

WEB: Further research this author with LitLinks at bedfordstmartins.com/approachinglit.

AMIRI BARAKA (b. 1934) was born Everett LeRoi Jones in Newark, New Jersey. He attended Rutgers University and then transferred to Howard where in 1954 he earned his B.A. in English. In 1958, after three years in the Air Force, he founded Totem Press, which first published the works of ALLEN GINSBERG and Jack Kerouac. His first collection, *Preface to a Twenty Volume Suicide Note* (1961), had a big impact, and he followed that work with a series of dynamic plays, most noteworthy being *Dutchman* (1964). After the assassination of Malcolm X, Jones's distrust of white society increased, and he turned his back on his former life and moved to Harlem where he founded the Black Arts Repertory Theater/School. In 1968, he became a Muslim, changing his name to Imamu (meaning "Spiritual Leader") Amiri Baraka. In 1974, following an adoption of a Marxist-Leninist stance, he dropped "Imamu." He has written jazz operas, plays, works of fiction and nonfiction, and several volumes of poetry. His poetry is charged with political content, usually challenging the dominant administrations and ideologies of the time and attacking the oppression of African Americans on all levels. Baraka has taught at Columbia University, the New School for Social Research, and Yale University, and has served as poet laureate of New Jersey.

WEB: Further research this author with LitLinks at bedfordstmartins.com/approachinglit.

JIM BARNES (b. 1933), born in Oklahoma of Choctaw and Welsh heritage, worked for ten years as a lumberjack. He studied at Southeastern Oklahoma State University and received his Ph.D. from the University of

Arkansas. Author of several books of poetry, he often uses formalist techniques to comment on the difficulties faced by Native Americans. Currently professor of comparative literature at Northeast Missouri State University, he is the founder and editor of the *Chariton Review*.

WEB: Further research this author with LitLinks at bedfordstmartins.com/approachinglit.

GERALD BARRAX (b. 1933) was born in Atalla, Alabama. He received his B.A. in English from Duquesne University and his M.A. from the University of Pittsburgh. He has published six volumes of poetry including *Leaning Against the Sun* (1992), which was nominated for both a Pulitzer Prize and the National Book Award, and *From a Person Sitting in Darkness: New and Selected Poems* (1998). Barrax acknowledges the great influence of music, all music — jazz and blues music, opera, pop, classical — on his work. He has said they are "necessary." Barrax lives in Raleigh, North Carolina, where he is Professor of English at North Carolina State University.

WEB: Further research this author with LitLinks at bedfordstmartins.com/approachinglit.

ELIZABETH BISHOP (1911–1979), born in Worcester, Massachusetts, was raised in Nova Scotia by her grandparents after her father died and her mother was committed to an asylum. She attended Vassar College, intending to study medicine, but was encouraged by MARIANNE MOORE to be a poet. From 1935 to 1937 she traveled in France, Spain, northern Africa, Ireland, and Italy and then settled in Key West, Florida, for four years, after which she lived in Rio de Janeiro for almost twenty years. She wrote slowly and carefully and produced a small body of poetry (totaling only around one hundred poems), technically sophisticated, formally varied, witty and thoughtful, revealing in precise, true-to-life images her impressions of the physical world. She served as Consultant in Poetry at the Library of Congress from 1949 to 1950. (The first appointment of a Consultant in Poetry at the Library of Congress was made in 1937. The title was changed to Poet Laureate Consultant in Poetry in 1986.

Appointments are made for one year, beginning in September, and sometimes have been renewed for a second year.)

WEB: Further research this author with LitLinks at bedfordstmartins.com/approachinglit.

CD-ROM: Research this author in depth with cultural documents and multimedia resources on *LiterActive.*

WILLIAM BLAKE (1757–1827) was born and lived in London. His only formal schooling was in art—he studied for a year at the Royal Academy and was apprenticed to an engraver. He worked as a professional engraver, doing commissions and illustrations, assisted by his wife, Catherine Boucher. Blake started writing poetry at the age of eleven and later engraved and hand-printed his own poems, in very small batches, with his own hand-colored illustrations. His early work showed a strong social conscience, and his later work turned increasingly mythic and prophetic.

WEB: Further research this author with LitLinks at bedfordstmartins.com/approachinglit.

CD-ROM: Research this author in depth with cultural documents and multimedia resources on *LiterActive.*

PETER BLUE CLOUD (b. 1935), born in Quebec, is a Turtle Mohawk and former ironworker. In addition to editing such publications as the *Alcatraz Newsletter, Akwesasne Notes,* and *Coyote's Journal,* he has published several volumes of poetry, including *White Corn Sister* (1979) and *Clans of Many Nations: Selected Poems, 1969–1994* (1995). His visionary poems often draw on native storytelling traditions, native dance structures, and native chant and drumming. One can experience in his poems the influence of these as well as the impact of industrial values on native ways of life.

WEB: Further research this author with LitLinks at bedfordstmartins.com/approachinglit.

EAVAN BOLAND (b. 1944) was born in Dublin and was educated there and in London and New York. She has taught at Trinity College and University College, Bowdoin College, and the University of Iowa. She currently is a professor of English at Stanford University. She is the author of eight volumes of poetry and a

collection of essays, coeditor of *The Making of a Poem: A Norton Anthology of Poetic Forms* (2000), and a regular reviewer for the *Irish Times.*

WEB: Further research this author with LitLinks at bedfordstmartins.com/approachinglit.

JORGE LUIS BORGES (1899–1986)—See page 762.

ANNE BRADSTREET (c. 1612–1672), born in Northampton, England, was educated by tutors, reading chiefly in religious writings and the Bible. In 1628 she married Simon Bradstreet, a brilliant young Puritan educated at Cambridge. They were among the earliest settlers of the Massachusetts Bay Colony, in 1630, and her father and husband were leading figures in its governance. She wrote regularly in both prose and verse throughout her busy and difficult years in Massachusetts.

WEB: Further research this author with LitLinks at bedfordstmartins.com/approachinglit.

GWENDOLYN BROOKS (1917–2000), born in Topeka, Kansas, was raised in Chicago and wrote her first poems at age seven. She began studying poetry at the Southside Community Art Center. Her second collection of poems, *Annie Allen* (1949), earned the first Pulitzer Prize given to an African American poet. She served as Consultant in Poetry at the Library of Congress from 1985 to 1986 and worked in community programs and poetry workshops in Chicago to encourage young African American writers.

WEB: Further research this author with LitLinks at bedfordstmartins.com/approachinglit.

CD-ROM: Research this author in depth with cultural documents and multimedia resources on *LiterActive.*

STERLING A. BROWN (1901–1989) was born in Washington, D.C., and educated at Dunbar High School, Williams College, and Harvard University. He taught for more than fifty years at Howard University. Like many other black poets of the period, he expressed his concerns about race in America. His first book of poems, *Southern Road* (1932), was well received by critics, and Brown became part of the artistic tradition of the Harlem

Renaissance. Brown was deeply interested in African American music and dialect. He became one of the great innovators in developing poetry related to jazz. His work is known for its frank, unsentimental portraits of black people and their experiences and its successful incorporation of African American folklore and contemporary idiom.

WEB: Further research this author with LitLinks at bedfordstmartins.com/approachinglit.

ELIZABETH BARRETT BROWNING (1806–1861) was born in Durham, England, and studied with her brother's tutor. Her first book of poetry was published when she was thirteen, and she soon became the most famous female poet to that point in English history. A riding accident at the age of sixteen left her a semi-invalid in the house of her possessive father, who had forbidden any of his eleven children to get married. She and Robert Browning were forced to elope (she was thirty-nine at the time); they lived in Florence, Italy, where she died fifteen years later. Her best-known book of poems was *Sonnets from the Portugese,* a sequence of forty-four sonnets recording the growth of her love for Robert.

WEB: Further research this author with LitLinks at bedfordstmartins.com/approachinglit.

ROBERT BROWNING (1812–1889) was the son of a bank clerk in Camberwell, then a suburb of London. As an aspiring poet in 1844, he admired Elizabeth Barrett's poetry and began a correspondence with her that led to one of the world's most famous romances. Their courtship lasted until 1846 when they were secretly wed and ran off to Italy, where they lived until Elizabeth's death in 1861. The years in Florence were among the happiest for both of them. To her he dedicated *Men and Women,* which contains his best poetry. Although she was the more popular poet during her lifetime, his reputation grew upon his return to London after her death, assisted somewhat by public sympathy for him. The late 1860s were the peak of his career: He and ALFRED, LORD TENNYSON were mentioned together as the foremost poets of the age. His fame and influence continued to grow through the remainder of his life until his death in 1889.

WEB: Further research this author with LitLinks at bedfordstmartins.com/approachinglit.

CD-ROM: Research this author in depth with cultural documents and multimedia resources on *LiterActive.*

DENNIS BRUTUS (b. 1924) was born in Zimbabwe of South African parents. He attended the University of Witwaterstand and taught for fourteen years in South African high schools, but was banned from teaching (and his university law studies) because of his leadership in the campaign to exclude South Africa from the Olympic Games as long as the country practiced apartheid in sports. He was arrested and sentenced to eighteen months of hard labor. His *Letters to Martha* (1968) are poems about his experiences as a prisoner on Robben Island. After leaving South Africa in 1966 with a Rhodesian passport, Brutus made his home in England. In 1983, after engaging in a protracted legal struggle and appearing on ABC's *Nightline* with Ted Koppel, he won the right to stay in the United States as a political refugee. Currently living in the United States, he is author of several books of poetry and a professor of African Studies and African Literature at the University of Pittsburgh.

WEB: Further research this author with LitLinks at bedfordstmartins.com/approachinglit.

CHARLES BUKOWSKI (1920–1994), born in Andernach, Germany, came to the United States at age three and grew up in poverty in Los Angeles, drifted extensively, and for much of his life made his home in San Pedro, working for many years in the U.S. Postal Service. He was familiar with the people of the streets, skid row residents, hustlers, and a transient lifestyle. He began writing in childhood and published his first story at age twenty-four and his first poetry when he was thirty-five. He published many books of poetry, in addition to novels and short stories reminiscent of ERNEST HEMINGWAY. He is very popular in Europe. His style, which exhibits a strong sense of immediacy and a refusal to embrace standard formal structures, was influenced by the Beat movement.

WEB: Further research this author with LitLinks at bedfordstmartins.com/approachinglit.

JULIA DE BURGOS (1917–1953), the best known female poet in Puerto Rico and one of the best of Latino America, was born in Carolina, Puerto Rico. She graduated from the University of Puerto Rico as a teacher. She also studied and worked as a journalist in Havana, Cuba. Later she moved to New York where she lived for most of the rest of her life. Her first book of poems was published when she was nineteen. She published several books of poetry and received many literary honors before and after her death.

WEB: Further research this author with LitLinks at bedfordstmartins.com/approachinglit.

RAYMOND CARVER (1938–1988) was born and grew up in Oregon. He decided he wanted to become a writer because he liked stories about hunting and fishing. He began to learn the craft of fiction in a creative writing course taught by novelist John Gardner at Chico State College in California. He earned his B.A. from Humboldt State College in California and attended the University of Iowa Writers' Workshop. Because Carver had married young and had a wife and children and little money, earning a living had to take precedence over writing and so his writing career progressed slowly. He kept at it, however, and eventually published a dozen collections of stories and books of poetry before his death from lung cancer at age fifty. He revised many of the stories in his first book, *Will You Please Be Quiet, Please?* (1976), as he moved into his much acclaimed and imitated hard-edged and minimalist style evident in the collection *What We Talk about When We Talk about Love* (1981).

WEB: Further research this author with LitLinks at bedfordstmartins.com/approachinglit.

CD-ROM: Research this author in depth with cultural documents and multimedia resources on *LiterActive.*

SANDRA CASTILLO (b. 1962) spent the first eight years of her life in Havana, Cuba, where she was born. During the Johnson administration's "Freedom Flights," she and her family were among the last Cubans to leave the island. She received her B.A. and M.A. degrees from Florida State University. She has published two collections of poetry, *Red Letters* (1991) and *My Father Sings, to My Embar-*

rassment (2002). Her work has appeared in numerous anthologies including *A Century of Cuban Writers in Florida* (1996) and *Cool Salsa: Bilingual Poems on Growing Up Latino in the United States* (1994). One can see in her poems the constant tension of dual identity. As she writes in her poem "Exile," "As we go door to door along East 4th Avenue / a street we are not supposed to be on / . . . thinking we are who we want to be."

WEB: Further research this author with LitLinks at bedfordstmartins.com/approachinglit.

ROSEMARY CATACALOS (b. 1944), of Mexican and Greek descent, grew up in San Antonio, Texas. She is the author of two books of poetry: a hand-sewn, fine-letterpress chapbook, *As Long As It Takes* (1984), and a full-length collection, *Again for the First Time* (1984), which won the 1985 Texas Institute of Letters poetry prize. From fall 1989 to spring 1991 she was a Wallace Stegner Creative Writing Fellow in Poetry at Stanford University, where she received the Patricia Smith Poetry Prize.

WEB: Further research this author with LitLinks at bedfordstmartins.com/approachinglit.

LORNA DEE CERVANTES (b. 1954) was born in San Francisco and grew up in San Jose. There she studied at San Jose City College and San Jose State University. She has been a member of the Chicana Theatre Group, worked at the Centro Cultural de la Gente, and founded Mango Publications, a small press that prints Chicano and diverse books as well as a literary journal. She is coeditor of *Red Dirt,* a cross-cultural poetry journal. Cervantes, who considers herself "a Chicana writer, a feminist writer, a political writer," lives in Colorado and is a professor at the University of Colorado at Boulder.

WEB: Further research this author with LitLinks at bedfordstmartins.com/approachinglit.

LAN SAMANTHA CHANG (b. 1965) was born and raised in Appleton, Wisconsin, where her parents settled after they left China when the Communists took over in 1949. Chang's parents were proud of their Chinese background and taught their daughters to be proud of it as well. Chang is a graduate of Yale University, where she majored in East Asian Studies, and of the University of Iowa Writers' Workshop. Her collection *Hunger: A Novella and Stories* (1999) won the Banta Award from the Wisconsin Library Association, the Bay Area Book Reviewers' Award for Fiction, and the California Book Award's Silver Medal. She received a Wallace Stegner Fellowship at Stanford University, where she was a Jones Lecturer in Fiction from 1995 to 1998. She has been a visiting faculty member at the University of Iowa Writers' Workshop and is currently Briggs-Copeland Lecturer in Fiction at Harvard University. Chang's work often shows the conscious and unconscious collisions and fusions of traditions within cultures and the incongruous effects that result.

WEB: Further research this author with LitLinks at bedfordstmartins.com/approachinglit.

ALICE CHILDRESS (1920–1994) was born in Charleston, South Carolina, but went to live with her maternal grandmother in Harlem at age nine after her parents separated. Upon completing her education in the public schools of New York, she began a career in the theater as actor, director, and playwright. Her plays include *Florence* (1949; see p. 795), *Mojo: A Black Love Story* (1970), *Wedding Band: A Love/Hate Story in Black and White* (1972), and *Moms: A Praise Play for a Black Comedienne* (1987). Childress also wrote fiction, including a novel for young adults, *A Hero Ain't Nothin' but a Sandwich* (1973), for which she also wrote the screenplay for the 1978 film. She has received numerous awards and honors for her writings, among them the first Paul Robeson Award for Outstanding Contributions to the Performing Arts. Her work is known for the frankness with which it deals with racial issues, the strength and insight of its characterizations, and the honesty and compassion with which its explores such controversial subjects as miscegenation and teenage drug addiction — qualities that caused some of her works to be banned at times in certain locations.

WEB: Further research this author with LitLinks at bedfordstmartins.com/approachinglit.

MARILYN CHIN (b. 1955) is a first-generation Chinese American, born in Hong Kong and raised in Portland, Oregon. In addition to publishing several books of poetry, she has co-edited *Dissident Song: A Contemporary Asian*

American Anthology (1991) and cotranslated *The Selected Poems of Ai Qing* (1985). An activist who sees herself pitted against the dominant culture in which she lives, she writes poetry that reflects the difficulty of bridging two cultures and conveys a sense of exile and loss. She teaches at San Diego State University.

WEB: Further research this author with LitLinks at bedfordstmartins.com/approachinglit.

KATE CHOPIN (1851–1904) was born Katherine O'Flaherty in St. Louis. Her father, an Irish immigrant and a very successful businessman, died when she was four. Her mother was of a prominent French Creole family. Chopin received an excellent education at the Academy of the Sacred Heart and from her mother and grandmother and on graduation was known as a brilliant storyteller, a youthful cynic, and an accomplished pianist. At age nineteen she married Oscar Chopin and had six children. They lived in the Creole community of Natchitoches Parish, Louisiana, until his death in 1882, when she moved back to St. Louis. After her mother died a year later, friends encouraged her to write as a way to deal with her grief and anger, and in doing so she turned to Creole country for her subjects and themes. She became both a nationally acclaimed and popular author. Her masterpiece, *The Awakening* (1899), a lyrical study of a young woman whose deep personal discontents lead to adultery and suicide, was praised for its craft but criticized for its content and created a scandal. Chopin, always sensitive to her critics and declining in health, wrote little after it.

WEB: Further research this author with LitLinks at bedfordstmartins.com/approachinglit.

CD-ROM: Research this author in depth with cultural documents and multimedia resources on *LiterActive*.

SANDRA CISNEROS (b. 1954) was born in Chicago to a Mexican father and Chicana mother. She grew up in ghetto neighborhoods of Chicago, moving frequently and thus never feeling settled. She spoke English at school and Spanish at home and on many trips to Mexico to visit her grandmother. She wrote poetry in high school and was editor of the school literary magazine, and went on to earn a B.A. from Loyola University and an M.F.A. from the University of Iowa Writers' Workshop. She discovered her literary voice in a graduate seminar, when she experimented with writing about growing up as a poor Latina in Chicago. She has published four books of poetry, two books of stories, and a bilingual children's book. Cisneros has taught at various colleges and universities, including the University of California, University of Michigan, and the University of New Mexico. She now lives in San Antonio, Texas.

WEB: Further research this author with LitLinks at bedfordstmartins.com/approachinglit.

CD-ROM: Research this author in depth with cultural documents and multimedia resources on *LiterActive.*

LUCILLE CLIFTON (b. 1936) was born in Depew, New York, and studied at Howard University. In addition to many books of poetry, she has published a memoir and more than sixteen books for children. She has taught at several colleges and worked in the Office of Education in Washington, D.C. She has served as poet laureate for the State of Maryland and is currently Distinguished Professor of Humanities at St. Mary's College of Maryland. Her poems typically reflect her ethnic pride, womanist principles, and race and gender consciousness.

WEB: Further research this author with LitLinks at bedfordstmartins.com/approachinglit.

SAMUEL TAYLOR COLERIDGE (1772–1834) was born in Devonshire and sent to school in London after his father's death. He went to Jesus College, Cambridge, in 1791, and dropped out twice without a degree. In 1798 Coleridge and WILLIAM WORDSWORTH published *Lyrical Ballads,* which initiated the Romantic movement in English poetry and established both of their reputations. After 1802 Coleridge became addicted to opium, used as a treatment for physical discomfort and seizures. He and his wife were separated, his friendship with Wordsworth broke up, and his poetic output stopped. From 1816 to his death he lived under constant medical supervision but still managed to publish a journal and write several plays, pieces of criticism, and philosophical and religious treatises.

WEB: Further research this author with LitLinks at bedfordstmartins.com/approachinglit.

BILLY COLLINS (b. 1941), born and raised in New York City, is the author of several collections of poems. Perhaps no poet since ROBERT FROST has managed to combine high critical acclaim with such broad popular appeal. The typical Collins poem opens on a clear and hospitable note but soon takes an unexpected turn; poems that begin in irony may end in a moment of lyric surprise. Collins sees his poetry as "a form of travel writing" and considers humor "a door into the serious." Collins, the author of numerous books of poetry, most recently *Nine Horses* (2003), is Distinguished Professor of Literature at Lehman College of the City University of New York and a writer-in-residence at Sarah Lawrence College. He served as Poet Laureate Consultant in Poetry at the Library of Congress from 2001 to 2003.

WEB: Further research this author with LitLinks at bedfordstmartins.com/approachinglit.

JAYNE CORTEZ (b. 1936) was born in Arizona, grew up in the Watts section of Los Angeles, and now lives in New York City. A poet and performance artist, she has published several collections of poetry and made a number of recordings, often performing her poetry with her jazz group the Firespitters. Her poems have been translated into twenty-eight languages. In 1964 she founded the Watts Repertory Company, and in 1972 she formed her own publishing company, Bola Press.

WEB: Further research this author with LitLinks at bedfordstmartins.com/approachinglit.

VICTOR HERNÁNDEZ CRUZ (b. 1949) was born in Aguas Buenas, Puerto Rico, and moved to New York City with his family at the age of five. His first book of poetry was published when he was seventeen. A year later he moved to California's Bay Area and published his second book. In 1971 Cruz visited Puerto Rico and reconnected with his ancestral heritage; eighteen years later, he returned to Puerto Rico to live. He now divides his time between Puerto Rico and New York. Much of his work explores the relation between the English language and his native Spanish, playing with grammatical and syntactical conventions within both languages to create his own bilingual idiom.

WEB: Further research this author with LitLinks at bedfordstmartins.com/approachinglit.

COUNTEE CULLEN (1903–1946) was born in either Louisville, Kentucky, Baltimore, Maryland, or (as he himself claimed) New York City. He was adopted by the Reverend Frederick A. Cullen and his wife and grew up, as he put it, "in the conservative atmosphere of a Methodist parsonage." He studied at New York University and Harvard University. A forerunner of the Harlem Renaissance movement, he was in the 1920s the most popular black literary figure in America. From the 1930s until his death, he wrote less and worked as a junior high French teacher. For many years after his death, his reputation was eclipsed by that of other Harlem Renaissance writers, particularly LANGSTON HUGHES and ZORA NEALE HURSTON; recently, however, there has been a resurgence of interest in his life and work.

WEB: Further research this author with LitLinks at bedfordstmartins.com/approachinglit.

E. E. CUMMINGS (1894–1962) was born in Cambridge, Massachusetts, where his father was a Unitarian minister and a sociology lecturer at Harvard University. He graduated from Harvard and then served as an ambulance driver during World War I. *The Enormous Room* (1922) is an account of his confinement in a French prison camp during the war. After the war, he lived in rural Connecticut and Greenwich Village, with frequent visits to Paris. In his work, cummings experimented radically with form, punctuation, spelling, and syntax, abandoning traditional techniques and structures to create a new, highly idiosyncratic means of poetic expression. At the time of his death, he was the second most widely read poet in the United States, after ROBERT FROST.

WEB: Further research this author with LitLinks at bedfordstmartins.com/approachinglit.

CD-ROM: Research this author in depth with cultural documents and multimedia resources on *LiterActive*.

BEI DAO (b. 1949), pseudonym for Zhao Zhenkai, was born in Beijing, China. During the Cultural Revolution, Bei joined the Red Guard movement, expecting a spirit of cooperation between the Chinese Communist Party and the country's intelligentsia, but he soon became disillusioned. He was sent to the countryside, where he became a construction worker. By 1974, he had finished the first draft of his novella *Waves* and began working on poems. Some of his most famous poems were directly inspired by the April Fifth Democracy Movement of 1976, in which thousands peacefully demonstrated in Beijing's Tiananmen Square. Bei Dao's poems were warmly welcomed by young educated readers as underground poems before 1976 and as unofficial poems in 1978–1980, but they provoked strong official disapproval in the 1970s and early 1980s. He was forced into exile following the Tiananmen Square Massacre in 1989, and since then readers in mainland China have had very limited access to his work. He has published several books of poetry and is the editor-in-chief of an underground literary magazine, *Jintian (Today)*, an important outlet for contemporary Chinese writing. He is currently the Mackey Poet in Residence at Beloit College in Wisconsin, where he held the Lois Wilson Mackey '45 Distinguished Professorship of Creative Writing in 2000–2001.

WEB: Further research this author with LitLinks at bedfordstmartins.com/approachinglit.

KEKI N. DARUWALLA (b. 1937) was born in Lahore, now in Pakistan, and educated in Ludhiana, India; he has a master's degree in English literature. He served an illustrious career in the Indian Police Service, rising to become a Special Assistant to the Prime Minister on International Affairs. He subsequently was in the Cabinet Secretariat until his retirement. He is the author of a dozen books of poems and short stories and the editor of *Two Decades of Indian Poetry* (1980). His collection of poems, *The Keeper of the Dead* (1982), received the Sahitya Akademi Award (Indian Academy of Letters) in 1984. He currently lives in Delhi.

WEB: Further research this author with LitLinks at bedfordstmartins.com/approachinglit.

KAMALA DAS (b. 1934) was born in Kerala, India. Her mother, Nalapat Balamani Amma, is a well-known Malayali poet. Das was privately educated until the age of fifteen when she was married to K. Madhava Das, who was considerably older. Her first child was born a year later. She was able to write only after the day's work was done and her family had gone to sleep; she would then clear the kitchen table and type until morning — a schedule that took its toll on her health. She has become one of India's foremost poets. In addition to her poetry, she has written an autobiography, *My Story,* published in 1975, and a successful syndicated column.

WEB: Further research this author with LitLinks at bedfordstmartins.com/approachinglit.

TOI DERRICOTTE (b. 1941) was born and raised in Detroit, where she earned a B.A. in special education from Wayne State University. She is the author of several collections of poetry as well as a memoir, *The Black Notebooks* (1997). With poet CORNELIUS EADY, she cofounded Cave Canem, which offers workshops and retreats for African American poets. Among many honors she has received is the Distinguished Pioneering of the Arts Award from the United Black Artists. Derricotte teaches creative writing at the University of Pittsburgh.

WEB: Further research this author with LitLinks at bedfordstmartins.com/approachinglit.

EMILY DICKINSON (1830–1886) was born in Amherst, Massachusetts, and lived there her entire life, rarely leaving. She briefly attended a women's seminary but became homesick and left before a year was out. Dickinson never married and became reclusive later in life, forgoing even the village routines and revelries she enjoyed. She published very few of the more than seventeen hundred poems she wrote; most were written for herself or for inclusion in her many letters. Not until 1955 was there a complete edition of her poems that attempted to present them as originally written.

WEB: Further research this author with LitLinks at bedfordstmartins.com/approachinglit.

CD-ROM: Research this author in depth with cultural documents and multimedia resources on *LiterActive.*

ANA DOINA (b. 1955) was born in Bucharest, Romania, when the country was under Communist rule. After she graduated from the University of Bucharest with an M.A. in philosophy and history, she taught high school and adult education. Due to increasing political pressures and social restrictions, she and her husband left Romania in 1983. She is now a U.S. citizen and lives in New Jersey with her husband and two children. In Romania, some of her poems were published in the national literary magazines *Romania Literara, Muguri,* and *Sapatmina.* In the United States, her poems have appeared in small press publications including *The Rift, El Locofoco, Icarus,* and *Timber Creek Review.*

WEB: Further research this author with LitLinks at bedfordstmartins.com/approachinglit.

JOHN DONNE (1572–1631) was born in London to a prosperous Catholic family (he was related to Sir Thomas More and the playwright John Heywood). Donne studied at Oxford University for several years but did not take a degree. He fought with SIR WALTER RALEGH in two naval strikes against Spain. In 1601 Donne's promising political career was permanently derailed by his precipitous marriage to Anne More without her father's consent. He was briefly imprisoned, lost a very promising position with Sir Thomas Egerton, and spent years seeking further political employment before finally being convinced by King James in 1615 to take holy orders as priest of the Church of England. His life was described by Isaac Walton later in the century as being divided into two parts. In Phase I he was "Jack Donne" of Lincoln's Inn: When young, Donne employed a sophisticated urban wit in his earlier poetry, like that of "A Valediction: Forbidding Mourning" (p. 638). In Phase II he was John Donne, dean of St. Paul's: After Donne took his vows in 1615, his poetry became markedly less amorous and more religious in tone. His *Holy Sonnets* (of which "Batter my heart, three-personed God" is one) are as dense and complex as his earlier work, with his talent now directed toward exploration of his relationship with God.

WEB: Further research this author with LitLinks at bedfordstmartins.com/approachinglit.

MARK DOTY (b. 1953) is the author of six collections of poetry and two memoirs —

Heaven's Coast (1996), about the loss of his partner, Wally Roberts, and *Firebird* (1999), a gay coming-of-age story and a chronicle of a gradual process of finding in art a place of personal belonging. He has taught at Brandeis University, Sarah Lawrence College, Vermont College, and the University of Iowa Writers' Workshop. He now lives in Provincetown, Massachusetts, and Houston, Texas, where he teaches at the University of Houston.

WEB: Further research this author with LitLinks at bedfordstmartins.com/approachinglit.

RITA DOVE (b. 1952) was born in Akron, Ohio. Her father was the first research chemist to break the race barrier in the tire industry. She graduated from Miami University in Oxford, Ohio, with a degree in English; after a year at Tübingen University in Germany on a Fulbright fellowship, she joined the University of Iowa Writers' Workshop, where she earned her M.F.A. in 1977. She has taught at Tuskegee Institute and Arizona State University and now is on the faculty of the University of Virginia. She was appointed Poet Laureate Consultant in Poetry at the Library of Congress in 1993, making her the youngest person to receive the highest official honor in American letters. She was awarded the Pulitzer Prize in 1987 for *Thomas and Beulah* (1986), a book-length sequence loosely based on the lives of her grandparents. "The Satisfaction Coal Company" (p. 641) is from that book ("he" is Thomas; "they" are Thomas and Beulah); the poem reflects Dove's concern for those living workaday lives and is her celebration of their worth and dignity.

WEB: Further research this author with LitLinks at bedfordstmartins.com/approachinglit.

PAUL LAURENCE DUNBAR (1872–1906) was the first African American to gain national eminence as a poet. Born and raised in Dayton, Ohio, he was the son of ex-slaves. He was an outstanding student: the only African American in his class, he was both class president and class poet. Although he lived to be only thirty-three years old, Dunbar was prolific, writing short stories, novels, librettos, plays, songs, and essays as well as the poetry for which he became well known. He was popular with both black and white readers of his day. His style encompasses two distinct voices—the standard English of the classical poet and the evocative dialect of the turn-of-the-century black community in America.

WEB: Further research this author with LitLinks at bedfordstmartins.com/approachinglit.

CORNELIUS EADY (b. 1954) was born and raised in Rochester, New York, and attended Monroe Community College and Empire State College. He began writing as a teenager. His poems are his biography, their subjects ranging from blues musicians to the witnessing of his father's death. He has published six volumes of poetry. With poet TOI DERRICOTTE, he cofounded Cave Canem, which offers workshops and retreats for African American poets, and with composer Diedre Murray he has collaborated on two highly acclaimed music dramas. Formerly the director of the Poetry Center at the State University of New York, Stony Brook, he is currently Distinguished Writer-in-Residence at the City College of New York.

WEB: Further research this author with LitLinks at bedfordstmartins.com/approachinglit.

T.[HOMAS] S.[TEARNS] ELIOT (1888–1965) was born and raised in St. Louis. He went to prep school in Massachusetts and then to Harvard University, where he earned an M.A. in philosophy in 1910 and started his doctoral dissertation. He studied at the Sorbonne, Paris, and then at Marburg, Germany, in 1914. The war forced him to Oxford, where he married and abandoned philosophy for poetry. After teaching and working in a bank, he became an editor at Faber and Faber and editor of the journal *Criterion,* and was the dominant force in English poetry for several decades. He became a British citizen and a member of the Church of England in 1927. He won the Nobel Prize for Literature in 1948. He also wrote plays, essays, and a series of poems on cats that became the basis of a musical by Andrew Lloyd Weber.

WEB: Further research this author with LitLinks at bedfordstmartins.com/approachinglit.

CD-ROM: Research this author in depth with cultural documents and multimedia resources on *LiterActive.*

RALPH ELLISON (1914–1994) was born in Oklahoma City, where his mother worked as a servant after the death of her husband when

Ellison was three. She brought home discarded books and phonograph records from houses where she worked, and from them Ellison developed an interest in literature and music. He studied music at Tuskegee Institute in Alabama and then went to New York, where he met LANGSTON HUGHES and RICHARD WRIGHT, who encouraged him in his writing. Ellison's literary reputation rests on one novel, *Invisible Man* (1952), which received the National Book Award for fiction and was listed in a Book Week poll in 1965 as the most distinguished American novel of the preceding twenty years. It deals with a young black man moving from the South to the North and learning about how racial prejudice leads to discrimination on the one hand and to being unnoticed and inconsequential on the other. "Battle Royal" (p. 237) is the first chapter of that novel. Ellison also published a scattering of short stories (collected posthumously in *Flying Home and Other Stories* [1986]) and two books of essays. A second novel was incomplete when he died (excerpts from the manuscript were published as *Juneteenth* in 1999).

WEB: Further research this author with LitLinks at bedfordstmartins.com/approachinglit.

CD-ROM: Research this author in depth with cultural documents and multimedia resources on *LiterActive.*

ANITA ENDREZZE (b. 1952), of Yaqui and European ancestry, was born in Long Beach, California, and earned her M.A. from Eastern Washington University. She is a poet, writer, and painter (in watercolor and acrylics) who also works in fiber and creates handmade books. She is a member of Atlatl, a Native American arts service organization. In addition to her poetry, she has published a children's novel in Danish, *The Mountain and the Guardian Spirit* (1986), as well as other novels, short stories, and nonfiction. Currently, she lives in Spokane, Washington, where she is a storyteller, teacher, and writer.

WEB: Further research this author with LitLinks at bedfordstmartins.com/approachinglit.

LOUISE ERDRICH (b. 1954) was born in Minnesota to a French-Ojibwe mother and a German-born father. She grew up near the Turtle Mountain Reservation in North Dakota and is a member of the Turtle Mountain Band of Chippewa. Her grandfather was tribal chief of the reservation. She was among the first women admitted to Dartmouth College, where she began writing; she also studied at Johns Hopkins University. Erdrich is best known for her novels and nonfiction.

WEB: Further research this author with LitLinks at bedfordstmartins.com/approachinglit.

CD-ROM: Research this author in depth with cultural documents and multimedia resources on *LiterActive.*

MARTÍN ESPADA (b. 1957) was born in Brooklyn and has an eclectic résumé: radio journalist in Nicaragua, welfare rights paralegal, advocate for mental patients, night desk clerk in a transient hotel, attendant in a primate nursery, groundskeeper at a minor league ballpark, bindery worker in a printing plant, bouncer in a bar, and practicing lawyer in Chelsea, Massachusetts. Author of six books of poetry, including his latest collection of poetry, *Alabanza: New and Selected Poems 1982-2002* (2003), he is regarded as one of the leading poets of Puerto Rican heritage in the United States. He lives with his wife and son in Amherst, Massachusetts, where he is an Associate Professor of English at the University of Massachusetts-Amherst.

WEB: Further research this author with LitLinks at bedfordstmartins.com/approachinglit.

SANDRA MARÍA ESTEVES (b. 1948) is a "Puerto Rican-Dominican-Boriqueña-Quisquevana-Taino-African American" born and raised in the Bronx. A founder and leading light of one of the twentieth century's most important literary/performance developments, the Nuyorican poetry movement, she was one of the first Puerto Rican-Dominican women to publish a volume of poetry in the United States. She has published six books of poetry, including *Yerba Buena,* which was selected as Best Small Press Collection for 1981 by the Library Journal. Among her awards and fellowships are the Louis Reyes Rivera Lifetime Achievement Award and the Edgar Allan Poe Literary Award. She lives in New York.

WEB: Further research this author with LitLinks at bedfordstmartins.com/approachinglit.

FAIZ AHMED FAIZ (1911–1984) was born in Sialkot in the Punjab, then a part of India under British rule. His father was a prominent lawyer who was interested in literature. Faiz was educated at mission schools in Sialkot in the English language, but he also learned Urdu, Persian, and Arabic. He worked as a teacher in Amritsar and Lahore. When the Islamic republic of Pakistan was established in 1947, Faiz moved to Pakistan with his family. In 1951 he and a number of army officers were accused of planning a coup d'etat. He spent four years in prison under a sentence of death until his release in 1955. He went into exile and wrote poems in Urdu using the diction, and often the meters, of an elaborate classical poetic tradition to address contemporary concerns, including his political condition. His work was widely read in Pakistan and in India from the time of its first publication. He returned to Pakistan in 1982 and died in Lahore two years later. His reputation spread abroad during his lifetime, and in recent years translations by the late AGHA SHAHID ALI and others have generated a following for Faiz in the English-speaking world.

WEB: Further research this author with LitLinks at bedfordstmartins.com/approachinglit.

WILLIAM FAULKNER (1897–1962) was born into an old southern family in New Albany, Mississippi. When he was five, his family moved to Oxford, a small city in northern Mississippi that was his home for most of the rest of his life. He attended the University of Mississippi for three semesters, having been admitted as a war veteran although he had not finished high school, and published poems and short stories in the campus newspaper. He continued writing while working at odd jobs for several years in New York and New Orleans and published his first novel, *Soldier's Pay,* in 1926. Success as a novelist came when he began writing about the northern Mississippi area he knew best, creating the mythical Yoknapatawpha County. His discovery that this "little postage stamp of native soil was worth writing about" enabled him to write a series of acclaimed experimental novels, including *The Sound and the Fury* (1920), *As I Lay Dying* (1930), *Light in August* (1932), and *Absalom, Absalom!*

(1936), in which he traces the disintegration of the South through several generations. Until the publication of the anthology *The Portable Faulkner* brought him wide recognition in 1946, he supported himself by publishing short stories (nearly a hundred) in magazines and by writing screenplays in Hollywood. In 1949 he received the Nobel Prize for Literature and delivered one of the most influential acceptance speeches ever given at a Nobel ceremony (available online at nobel.se/literature/laureates/1949/faulkner-speech.html).

WEB: Further research this author with LitLinks at bedfordstmartins.com/approachinglit.

CD-ROM: Research this author in depth with cultural documents and multimedia resources on *LiterActive.*

CAROLYN FORCHÉ (b. 1950) was born in Detroit, attended Michigan State University, and earned an M.F.A. from Bowling Green State University. She achieved immediate success as a writer, winning a Yale Younger Poets Prize in 1976. Her work underwent a remarkable shift following a year spent on a Guggenheim fellowship in El Salvador, where she worked with human rights activist Archbishop Oscar Humberto Romero and with Amnesty International. The shock of witnessing countless atrocities in Central America led her to begin writing what she calls "poetry of witness." The volume *The Country Between Us* (1981) stirred immediate controversy because of its overtly political topics and themes. "The Colonel" (p. 650), a prose poem in which the speaker conveys a horrific story with chilling flatness, is probably the most disturbing and memorable poem in the book. Over the years her quest to understand the individual's struggle with social upheaval and political turmoil has taken her from El Salvador to the occupied West Bank, Lebanon, and South Africa. She is currently a faculty member at George Mason University in Virginia.

WEB: Further research this author with LitLinks at bedfordstmartins.com/approachinglit.

ROBERT FROST (1874–1963) was born in San Francisco and lived there until he was eleven. When his father died, the family moved to

Massachusetts, where Robert did well in school, especially in the classics, but he dropped out of both Dartmouth College and Harvard University. He went unrecognized as a poet until 1913, when he was first published in England, where he had moved with his wife and four children. Upon returning to the United States, he quickly achieved success with more publications and became the most celebrated poet in mid-twentieth-century America. He held a teaching position at Amherst College and received many honorary degrees as well as an invitation to recite a poem at John F. Kennedy's inauguration. Although his work is principally associated with the life and landscape of New England, and though he is a poet of traditional verse forms and metrics, he is also a quintessentially modern poet in his adherence to language as it is actually spoken, in the psychological complexity of his portraits, and in the degree to which his work is infused with layers of ambiguity and irony.

WEB: Further research this author with LitLinks at bedfordstmartins.com/approachinglit.

CD-ROM: Research this author in depth with cultural documents and multimedia resources on *LiterActive*.

RICHARD GARCIA (b. 1941) was born in San Francisco, a first-generation American (his mother was from Mexico, his father from Puerto Rico). While still in high school, he had a poem published by City Lights in a Beat anthology. After publishing his first collection in 1972, however, he did not write poetry again for twelve years, until an unsolicited letter of encouragement from OCTAVIO PAZ inspired him to resume. Since then, his work has appeared widely in literary magazines as well as two later books, *The Flying Garcias* (1993) and *Rancho Notorious* (2001). He is also the author of a bilingual children's book, *My Aunt Otilia's Spirits* (1987). Garcia has lived in Colorado, Mexico, and Israel, and now makes his home in Los Angeles, where he is poet-in-residence at Childrens Hospital.

WEB: Further research this author with LitLinks at bedfordstmartins.com/approachinglit.

GABRIEL GARCÍA MÁRQUEZ (b. 1928) was born in the small town of Aracataca, situated in a tropical region of northern Colombia between the mountains and the Caribbean Sea, and he grew up there with his maternal grandparents. He studied law and then journalism at the National University of Colombia in Bogota and at the University of Cartagena. In 1954 he was sent to Rome on an assignment for his newspaper. Since then he has mostly lived abroad, in Paris, New York, Barcelona, and Mexico. He published his first book of short stories in 1955. His most famous work, the novel *One Hundred Years of Solitude,* was published in 1967. His fiction is characterized by magic realism, which, as he put it, "expands the categories of the real so as to encompass myth, magic and other extraordinary phenomena in Nature or experience" excluded by European realistic fiction. Besides his large output of fiction he has written screenplays, a memoir, and has continued to work as a journalist. In 1982 he received the Nobel Prize for Literature. His most recent book is *Living to Tell the Truth* (2002), the first volume of a projected three-part memoir.

WEB: Further research this author with LitLinks at bedfordstmartins.com/approachinglit.

DAGOBERTO GILB (b. 1950) was born and grew up in Los Angeles, raised by a Chicana mother who divorced his German father soon after Dagoberto was born. He attended the University of California, where he majored in philosophy and religion, after which he moved to El Paso and spent sixteen years making a living as a construction worker, twelve of them as a journeyman, high-rise carpenter. During this time he began writing stories, several of which were published in a variety of journals. His collection of stories *The Magic of Blood* (1993) won the 1994 PEN/Hemingway Award, and his novel *The Last Known Residence of Mickey Acuña* (1994) was named a Notable Book of the Year by the *New York Times Book Review*. His most recent books are a collection of stories, *Woodcuts of Women* (2001), and a collection of essays, *Gritos: Essays* (2003). He currently lives in Austin where he teaches creative writing at Southwest Texas State University, San Marcos.

WEB: Further research this author with LitLinks at bedfordstmartins.com/approachinglit.

CHRISTOPHER GILBERT (b. 1949) is trained in clinical and cognitive psychology and has practiced psychotherapy, and he has been a psychologist with the Worcester Youth Guidance Center, the Cambridge Family, and the Children's Service in the Boston area. This work, his concern for the impact of depravation on young people, and the influence of jazz and the blues, all contribute to the explorations in his poetry. His first book, *Across the Mutual Landscape,* was selected for the 1983 Walt Whitman Award from the Academy of American Poets.

WEB: Further research this author with LitLinks at bedfordstmartins.com/approachinglit.

ALLEN GINSBERG (1926–1997) was born in Newark, New Jersey, and graduated from Columbia University, after several suspensions, in 1948. Several years later, Ginsberg left for San Francisco to join other poets of the Beat movement. His poem "Howl," the most famous poem of the movement, was published in 1956 by Lawrence Ferlinghetti's City Lights Books; the publicity of the ensuing censorship trial brought the Beats to national attention. Ginsberg was cofounder with Anne Waldman of the Jack Kerouac School of Disembodied Poetics at the Naropa Institute in Boulder, Colorado. In his later years, he became a distinguished professor at Brooklyn College.

WEB: Further research this author with LitLinks at bedfordstmartins.com/approachinglit.

NIKKI GIOVANNI (b. 1943) was born in Knoxville, Tennessee, and returned there after spending her childhood years in Cincinnati. After receiving her B.A. from Fisk University, she organized the Black Arts Festival in Cincinnati and then entered graduate school at the University of Pennsylvania. She has received wide popular acclaim as a writer — having published numerous collections of poetry, including several for children — and as a lecturer on literature and racial and social causes. She is currently Professor of English and Gloria D. Smith Professor of Black Studies at Virginia Polytechnic Institute and State University.

WEB: Further research this author with LitLinks at bedfordstmartins.com/approachinglit.

DIANE GLANCY (b. 1941) was born in Kansas City, Missouri, to a Cherokee father and English-German mother. She graduated from the University of Missouri in 1964, married Duane Glancy, and moved to Tulsa, Oklahoma. She completed her M.A. at Central State University in Edmond, Oklahoma, in 1983 and received her M.F.A. from the University of Iowa Writers' Workshop in 1988. She is now Professor of English at Macalester College in Minneapolis. Glancy, who writes in many genres, is author of numerous plays and many books of fiction and collections of poetry. Much of her work is based upon Native American life and how traditional values and ways of life interact and are juxtaposed with those of modern America, often with harsh, even demeaning results in the midst of a character's holding fiercely to dignity.

WEB: Further research this author with LitLinks at bedfordstmartins.com/approachinglit.

SUSAN GLASPELL (1882–1948) was born and raised in Davenport, Iowa. She worked as a journalist before enrolling at Drake University in Des Moines; after graduating in 1899, she worked for two years as a reporter for the Des Moines *Daily News* and then returned to Davenport to write. Her short stories began to be accepted by magazines such as *Harper's* and *The American*. Her first novel, *The Glory of the Conquered,* was published in 1909. She married George Cram Cook, a novelist and utopian socialist, in 1916; they moved to New York and, at Cook's urging, she began to write plays. They founded the Provincetown Players in Provincetown, Massachusetts, in the summer of 1916 and moved the theater to New York that fall, where it served as a venue for producing innovative plays by American playwrights. Glaspell wrote *Trifles* (p. 822) for the Players' first season. Glaspell and Cook lived in Greece from 1922 until Cook's death in 1924, after which she settled in Provincetown for the rest of her life and continued writing. She published over fifty short stories, nine novels, eleven plays, and one biography. She was awarded a Pulitzer Prize for Drama for *Alison's House* (1931), based on the life of poet EMILY DICKINSON.

WEB: Further research this author with LitLinks at bedfordstmartins.com/approachinglit.

CD-ROM: Research this author in depth with cultural documents and multimedia resources on *LiterActive.*

Louise Glück (b. 1943) was born in New York City and educated at Sarah Lawrence College and Columbia University. She has published numerous collections of poetry, including *The Triumph of Achilles* (1985), which received the National Book Critics Circle Award and the Poetry Society of America's Melville Kane Award; *Ararat* (1990), which received the Rebekah Johnson Bobbitt National Prize for Poetry; and *The Wild Iris* (1992), which received the Pulitzer Prize and the Poetry Society of America's William Carlos Williams Award. She has also published *Proofs and Theories: Essays on Poetry* (1994). Glück was made U.S. Poet Laureate Consultant in Poetry at the Library of Congress for the year 2003–2004. She teaches at Williams College and lives in Cambridge, Massachusetts.

WEB: Further research this author with LitLinks at bedfordstmartins.com/approachinglit.

Patricia Goedicke (b. 1931) was born in Boston and grew up in Hanover, New Hampshire. She received her B.A. from Middlebury College and her M.A. in creative writing in 1956 from Ohio University. She taught at Kalamazoo College, Ohio University, and Hunter College. She lived for twelve years in San Miguel de Allende, Mexico, returning to the United States to teach first at Sarah Lawrence and then the University of Montana, where in 1991 she received the Outstanding Scholar Award. She has published twelve collections of poetry and her work has appeared in dozens of anthologies. Her poetry often combines an austerity and precision of language with a deeply felt concern for the ways environmental, political, and social issues affect the daily lives and the psyches of those who have little or no control over them.

WEB: Further research this author with LitLinks at bedfordstmartins.com/approachinglit.

Ray González (b. 1952) received his M.F.A. in creative writing from Southwest Texas State University. He has published five books of poetry, including *The Heat of Arrivals* (which won the 1997 Josephine Miles Book Award) and *Cabato Sentora* (1999). He is also the author of *Memory Fever: A Journey Beyond El Paso del Norte* (1993), a book of essays dealing with growing up in the Southwest, and is the editor of twelve anthologies. He served as poetry editor for *The Bloomsbury Review* for eighteen years. In 1989 he was awarded the Colorado Governor's Award for Excellence in the Arts. He has taught at the University of Illinois, Chicago, and now teaches at the University of Minnesota.

WEB: Further research this author with LitLinks at bedfordstmartins.com/approachinglit.

Patricia Grace (b. 1937), born in Wellington, New Zealand, is of Ngati, Raukawa, Ngati Toa, and Te Ati Awa descent, and she is connected to the Ngati Porou tribe by marriage. Grace was educated at St. Anne's School, St. Mary's College, and Wellington Teachers' Training College. She has taught in primary and secondary schools in the King Country, Northland, and Porirua. Her first collection of stories, *Waiariki*—the first published by a Maori woman writer—appeared in 1975. Her novel *Potiki* (1986) won the New Zealand Book Award for Fiction, and her novel *Dogside Story* won the 2001 Kiriyama Pacific Rim Book Prize. She has published six collections of stories, five novels, and many books for children. Though her works deal with loss, isolation, and sadness, they are tempered with joy and hope; in them, childlike innocence and insight are mixed with adult awareness.

WEB: Further research this author with LitLinks at bedfordstmartins.com/approachinglit.

Thomas Gray (1716–1771) was born in London and educated at Eton College and Cambridge University, where he studied literature and history. In November 1741 his father died, and Gray moved with his mother and aunt to the village of Stoke Poges in Buckinghamshire, where he wrote his first important English poems, the "Ode on the Spring," "Ode on a Distant Prospect of Eton College," and "Hymn to Adversity," and began his masterpiece, "Elegy Written in a Country Churchyard" (p. 660), called the most famous and diversified of all graveyard poems. These poems solidified his reputation as one of the most important English poets of the eighteenth century. In 1757 he was named poet laureate but refused the position. In 1762 he applied for the Regius Professorship of Modern History at Cambridge but was rejected; however, he was given the position in 1768 when the successful candidate was killed. A painfully shy and private person, he never delivered any lectures as a professor.

WEB: Further research this author with LitLinks at bedfordstmartins.com/approachinglit.

ANGELINA WELD GRIMKÉ (1880–1958) was born in Boston to a mixed racial background: her mother was from a prominent white family; her father was the son of a white man and a black slave. Grimké's father was able to earn a law degree from Harvard University (and become executive director of the NAACP) through the support of two white aunts in South Carolina who acknowledged their ties to their brother's mixed-race children. Her parents named her after her great aunt Angelina Grimké Weld, a famous white abolitionist and women's rights advocate. When Grimké was three years old, her mother left her father, taking her daughter with her. After four years she returned Angelina to her father and the child never saw her mother again. Grimké attended one of the finest schools in Massachusetts, the Carleton Academy in Ashburnham, graduated from the Boston Normal School with a degree in physical education, taught until 1907, and then moved to Washington, D.C., and taught English until she retired in 1926. While in Washington, she wrote poetry, fiction, reviews, and biographical sketches. Her best-known work, the only one published as a book, was the play *Rachel* (1916).

WEB: Further research this author with LitLinks at bedfordstmartins.com/approachinglit.

KIMIKO HAHN (b. 1955) was born in Mt. Kisco, New York, to two artists; her mother is from Hawaii and her father is from Wisconsin. Hahn majored in English and East Asian studies at the University of Iowa and received an M.A. in Japanese literature from Columbia University. She is the author of numerous books of poems, including *The Unbearable Heart* (1996), which received an American Book Award. In 1995 she wrote ten portraits of women for a two-hour HBO special entitled *Ain't Nuthin' but a She-Thing*. She has taught at Parsons School of Design, the Poetry Project at St. Mark's Church, and Yale University. She lives in New York and is an associate professor in the English Department at Queens College/CUNY.

WEB: Further research this author with LitLinks at bedfordstmartins.com/approachinglit.

JOY HARJO (b. 1951) was born in Tulsa, Oklahoma. Her mother was of Cherokee-French descent and her father was Creek. She moved to the Southwest and began writing poetry in her early twenties. She then earned her B.A. at the University of New Mexico and her M.F.A. from the University of Iowa Writers' Workshop. Harjo has published several volumes of poetry, including *In Mad Love and War* (1990), which received an American Book Award and the Delmore Schwartz Memorial Award; *A Map to the Next World: Poems* (2000); and *How We Became Human: New and Selected Poems* (2002). She also performs her poetry and plays saxophone with her band, Poetic Justice. She is professor of English at the University of New Mexico, Albuquerque. Of "She Had Some Horses" (p. 537) Harjo has said, "This is the poem I'm asked most about and the one I have the least to say about. I don't know where it came from."

WEB: Further research this author with LitLinks at bedfordstmartins.com/approachinglit.

MICHAEL S. HARPER (b. 1938) was born in Brooklyn and grew up surrounded by jazz. When his family moved to Los Angeles, he worked at all kinds of jobs, from the post office to professional football. He studied at the City College of Los Angeles, California State University, Los Angeles, and the University of Iowa Writers' Workshop. He has written more than ten books of poetry, including *Dear John, Dear Coltrane* (1970), which was nominated for the National Book Award, and edited or coedited several collections of African American poetry. He is University Professor and professor of English at Brown University, where he has taught since 1970. He lives in Barrington, Rhode Island.

WEB: Further research this author with LitLinks at bedfordstmartins.com/approachinglit.

NATHANIEL HAWTHORNE (1804–1864) was born in Salem, Massachusetts, into a family that had been prominent in the area since colonial times. His father died when Nathaniel was four. Later, relatives recognized his literary talent and financed his education at Bowdoin College. After graduation, he lived at home writing short "tales" and a novel *Fanshawe,* which he self-published in 1828 and later dismissed as immature. He wrote prolifically in the 1830s, producing a number of successful short stories including "Young Goodman Brown" (p. 252). He published two collections of stories that were well received — *Twice-Told Tales* (1837; expanded edition 1842) and *Mosses from an Old Manse* (1846) — but had difficulty supporting himself by his writings. In 1845 he was appointed surveyor of the Boston Custom House by President James Polk but was dismissed from this post when Zachary Taylor became president. He then worked intensely on his most famous novel, *The Scarlet Letter,* published in 1850. In addition to five novels and romances, Hawthorne published nearly 120 stories and sketches and several books for children, and left behind numerous notebooks with sketches from his travels and ideas for additional stories and novels. He was one of the first American writers to explore the hidden motivations of his characters, and often used allegorical approaches to explore the complexities of moral choices and his characters' struggles with sin and guilt.

WEB: Further research this author with LitLinks at bedfordstmartins.com/approachinglit.

CD-ROM: Research this author in depth with cultural documents and multimedia resources on *LiterActive.*

ROBERT HAYDEN (1913–1980) was raised in a poor neighborhood in Detroit and had an emotionally tumultuous childhood. Because of impaired vision, he was unable to participate in sports and spent his time reading instead. He graduated from high school in 1932 and attended Detroit City College (later Wayne State University). His first book of poems, *Heart-Shape in the Dust,* was published in 1940. After working for newspapers and on other projects, he studied under W. H. AUDEN in the graduate creative writing program at the University of Michigan. He taught at Fisk University and at the University of Michigan. His poetry gained international recognition in the 1960s, and he was awarded the grand prize for poetry at the First World Festival of Negro Arts in Dakar, Senegal, in 1966 for his book *Ballad of Remembrance.* In 1976 he became the first black American to be appointed as Consultant in Poetry at the Library of Congress.

WEB: Further research this author with LitLinks at bedfordstmartins.com/approachinglit.

SAMUEL HAZO (b. 1928), of Lebanese and Syrian heritage, is a highly influential Arab American writer of verse, educator, and advocate on behalf of poetry. He is the author of numerous collections of poetry, fiction, and essays. He is founder, director, and president of the International Poetry Forum in Pittsburgh and the McAnulty Distinguished Professor of English Emeritus at Duquesne University. He is the recipient of the 1986 Hazlett Memorial Award for Excellence in the Arts. In 1993 he was chosen to be the first state poet of the Commonwealth of Pennsylvania, a position he still holds.

WEB: Further research this author with LitLinks at bedfordstmartins.com/approachinglit.

BESSIE HEAD (1937–1986) was born in Pietermaritzburg, South Africa, to a wealthy white woman who had a relationship with a black man who worked in the stable on her family's estate. She was adopted by a Colored (mixed-race) family and educated at a mission school. She earned a teaching certificate and taught for a few years in an elementary school near Cape Town. She left teaching to become a journalist and wrote for *Drum* magazine. She married a journalist, Harold Head, in 1960. After their divorce in 1964, she left South Africa to escape apartheid and lived a precarious existence as a refugee in Serowe, Botswana. Typing at night by candlelight, after working all day, she published her first novel, *When Rain Clouds Gather,* in 1969. She went on to write four other novels (the best known is *A Question of Power* [1973], in which she documents her own mental breakdown) and a collection of short stories, *The Collector of Treasures and Other Botswana Tales* (1977).

WEB: Further research this author with LitLinks at bedfordstmartins.com/approachinglit.

SEAMUS HEANEY (b. 1939) grew up on a small farm near Castledawson, County Derry, Northern Ireland. He was educated at St. Columb's College, a Catholic boarding school situated in the city of Derry, forty miles from home, and then at Queen's University, Belfast. As a young English teacher in Belfast in the early 1960s, he joined a poetry workshop and began writing verse. Subsequently he became a major force in contemporary Irish literature. The author of many volumes of poetry and essays as well as at least one play, he is well known for his best-selling verse translation of *Beowulf* (2000). He held the chair of professor of poetry at Oxford University from 1989 to 1994. Heaney has been a resident of Dublin since 1976, but since 1981 he has spent part of each year teaching at Harvard University. He was awarded the Nobel Prize for Literature in 1995.

WEB: Further research this author with LitLinks at bedfordstmartins.com/approachinglit.

ERNEST HEMINGWAY (1899–1961) was born in Oak Park, a conservative, upper-middle-class suburb of Chicago, but spent his summers at Walloon Lake in northern Michigan, where he learned to love the outdoors and fishing and hunting. He decided to become a journalist instead of going to college and worked as a reporter for the *Kansas City Star,* where he was taught to write with short sentences, short paragraphs, active verbs, compression, clarity, and immediacy, qualities apparent in his fiction writing. He tried to enlist for service in World War I but was turned down because of poor eyesight. Instead, he volunteered as a Red Cross ambulance driver. Shortly after arriving in Italy, he was seriously wounded, with over two hundred pieces of shrapnel in his legs. After the war he lived in Paris, worked as a newspaper correspondent for the *Toronto Daily Star,* and mingled with prominent writers and artists. Between 1925 and 1929 he published four major works of fiction, including two novels — *The Sun Also Rises* (1926) and *A Farewell to Arms* (1929) — and went from being unknown to being one of the most important writers of his generation. He moved first to Key West, Florida, where he grew to love big-game fishing, and later to Havana, Cuba. He continued writing, continued his interests in fishing and big-game hunting, and served as a war correspondent during the Spanish Civil War and the Chinese-Japanese war, thus fostering further the macho persona he built throughout his life. His last major novels were *For Whom the Bell Tolls* (1940) and *The Old Man and the Sea* (1953), which was awarded the Pulitzer Prize for Fiction. He was awarded the Nobel Prize for Literature in 1954. Seven years later, in poor health and afflicted with severe depression, he committed suicide, as his father had some three decades earlier.

WEB: Further research this author with LitLinks at bedfordstmartins.com/approachinglit.

GEORGE HERBERT (1593–1633) was the fifth son in an ancient and wealthy Welsh family. He studied at Cambridge University, graduating with honors, and was elected public orator of the university. He served in Parliament for two years but fell out of political favor and become rector of Bemerton near Salisbury. Herbert was a model Anglican priest and an inspiring preacher. All of his poetry, religious in nature, was published posthumously in 1633. "The Pulley" (p. 668) is a fine example of metaphysical poetry (see the Glossary of Literary Terms, p. 1511).

WEB: Further research this author with LitLinks at bedfordstmartins.com/approachinglit.

DAVID HERNANDEZ (b. 1971) was born in Burbank, California. His first passion was drawing. His love of art continued through college at California State University, Long Beach, and it was here that his infatuation with poetry began and that he earned a B.A. in creative writing. He works full-time as a Web designer but still carves out time to write. He has published two chapbooks, *Man Climbs Out of Manhole* (2000) and *Donating the Heart* (2001) — which won the National Looking Glass Chapbook Competition — and a full-length collection of poems, *A House Waiting for Music* (2003). His drawings have appeared in literary magazines, including *Other Voices, Gargoyle,* and *Indiana Review.* He is married to writer Lisa Glatt. Their collection of collaborative poems, *A Merciful Bed,* was published in 2001.

WEB: Further research this author with LitLinks at bedfordstmartins.com/approachinglit.

ROBERT HERRICK (1591–1674), the son of a well-to-do London goldsmith, was apprenticed to his uncle (also a goldsmith), studied at Cambridge University, and then lived for nine years in London, where he hobnobbed with a group of poets that included BEN JONSON. Under familial pressure to do something more worthwhile, Herrick became an Anglican priest. He was given the parish of Dean Prior, Devonshire—a rural place that he at first hated—and there he quietly wrote poems about imagined mistresses and pagan rites as well as deft but devout religious poems. When he returned to London in 1648, having been ejected from his pulpit by the Puritan revolution, he published his poetry in a volume with two titles, *Hesperides* for the secular poems, *Noble Numbers* for those with sacred subjects. Probably his most famous poem is "To the Virgins, to Make Much of Time" (p. 669), a short lyric on the traditional *carpe diem* theme (see the Glossary of Literary Terms, p. 1504).

WEB: Further research this author with LitLinks at bedfordstmartins.com/approachinglit.

NAZIM HIKMET (1902–1963) was born in Salonica, Ottoman Empire (now Thessaloniki). He began writing poems when he was fourteen. He studied briefly at the French-language Galatasary Lycée in Istanbul and attended the Naval War School, but dropped out because of ill health. He studied sociology and economics at the University of Moscow (1921–1928) and joined the Turkish Communist Party in the 1920s. He was imprisoned for returning to Turkey in 1928 without a visa but pardoned in 1935 in a general amnesty. In 1938 the author was given a twenty-eight year sentence for anti-Nazi and anti-Franco activities and spent the following twelve years in different prisons. He was released in 1950 because of international protests and escaped in a small boat from his home country in fear of an attempt on his life. He lived first in the Soviet Union and in 1950 shared with PABLO NERUDA the Soviet Union's International Peace Prize. He became a Polish citizen and from 1951 lived his remaining days in Sofia, Warsaw, and finally in Moscow. A prolific writer in poetry, drama, and fiction, he was one of the most important figures writing in twentieth-century Turkish.

WEB: Further research this author with LitLinks at bedfordstmartins.com/approachinglit.

GEOFFREY HILL (b. 1932) is a major presence in contemporary British poetry. Born in Bromsgrove, Worcestershire, he attended the local grammar school there before going on to study English language and literature at Keble College, Oxford. He taught at Leeds University from 1954 until 1980, when he moved to Emmanuel College, Cambridge. In 1988 he became University Professor and a professor of literature and religion at Boston University.

WEB: Further research this author with LitLinks at bedfordstmartins.com/approachinglit.

LINDA HOGAN (b. 1947), a poet, novelist, essayist, playwright, and activist widely considered to be one of the most influential and provocative Native American figures in the contemporary American literary landscape, was born in Denver. Because her father, who was from the Chicksaw Nation, was in the army and was transferred frequently during Hogan's childhood, she lived in various locations while she was growing up, but she considers Oklahoma to be her true home. In her late twenties, while working with orthopedically handicapped children, she began writing during her lunch hours, though she had no previous experience as a writer and little experience reading literature. She pursued her writing by commuting to the University of Colorado, Colorado Springs, for her undergraduate degree and earning an M.A. in English and creative writing at the University of Colorado, Boulder, in 1978. She has published more than a dozen books—poetry, novels, and nonfiction—and received numerous awards for her work. She teaches creative writing at the University of Colorado.

WEB: Further research this author with LitLinks at bedfordstmartins.com/approachinglit.

MIROSLAV HOLUB (1923–1998) was born in Plzen, in Western Bohemia, and after World War II studied science and medicine at Charles University in Prague, becoming a pathologist and later a noted research scientist in immunology and author of more than 150 academic papers. He started writing poetry after World War II, publishing in newspapers and magazines, and became one of the leading Eastern European poets of the post-war period. He was part of an effort by Czech artists and intellectuals to liberalize the Communist system from within, by free cultural acts, a movement that culminated in the Prague Spring of 1968, which was ended by the Warsaw Pact invasion in August 1968. He was dismissed from his post at the Microbiological Institute in 1970 and was not allowed to travel abroad or to appear in public. He could not publish until the ban was lifted in 1982, and his books were removed from the libraries. Abroad, however, his literary and scientific work became very well known. Much of his writing was translated into more than thirty languages.

WEB: Further research this author with LitLinks at bedfordstmartins.com/approachinglit.

GARRETT KAORU HONGO (b. 1951) was born in Volcano, Hawaii, grew up on Oahu and in Los Angeles, and did graduate work in Japanese language and literature at the University of Michigan. Hongo has published several books of poetry, including *The River of Heaven* (1988), which was the Lamont Poetry Selection of the Academy of American Poets and a finalist for the Pulitzer Prize. He has also written *Volcano: A Memoir of Hawai'i* (1995) and edited collections of Asian American verse. He currently teaches at the University of Oregon, Eugene, where he directed the creative writing program from 1989 to 1993. His work often uses rich textures and sensuous details to comment on conditions endured by Japanese Americans during World War II and thereafter.

WEB: Further research this author with LitLinks at bedfordstmartins.com/approachinglit.

GERARD MANLEY HOPKINS (1844–1889) was born in London, the eldest of eight children. His father was a ship insurer who also wrote a book of poetry. Hopkins studied at Balliol College, Oxford, and, after converting to Catholicism, taught in a school in Birmingham. In 1868 he became a Jesuit and burned all of his early poetry, considering it "secular" and worthless. He then worked as a priest and teacher in working-class London, Glasgow, and Merseyside, and later as professor of classics at University College, Dublin. Hop-

kins went on to write many poems on spiritual themes, but he published little during his lifetime; his poems were not known until they were published by his friend Robert Bridges in 1918. They convey a spiritual sensuality, celebrating the wonder of nature both in their language and their rhythms.

WEB: Further research this author with LitLinks at bedfordstmartins.com/approachinglit.

A. E. HOUSMAN (1859–1936) was born in Fockbury, Worcestershire. A promising student at Oxford University, he failed his final exams because of emotional turmoil caused by his suppressed homosexual love for a fellow student and spent the next ten years feverishly studying and writing scholarly articles while working as a clerk at the patent office. Housman was rewarded with the chair of Latin at University College, London, and later at Cambridge. His poetry, like his scholarship, was meticulous, impersonal in tone, and limited in output: two slender volumes— *A Shropshire Lad* (1896) and *Last Poems* (1922)—during his lifetime, and a small book of *More Poems* (1936) after his death. His poems often take up the theme of doomed youths acting out their brief lives in the context of the human histories implicit in agricultural communities and activities, especially the English countryside and traditions he loved.

WEB: Further research this author with LitLinks at bedfordstmartins.com/approachinglit.

LANGSTON HUGHES (1902–1967)—See page 1245.

ZORA NEALE HURSTON (1891–1960) was born to a family of sharecroppers in Notasula, Alabama, but grew up in Eatonville, Florida, a town founded by African Americans. After her mother's death in 1904, Hurston lived with various relatives. She never finished grade school. At sixteen she joined a traveling theater group and later did domestic work for a white household. The woman for whom she worked arranged for her to attend high school at Morgan Academy (now known as Morgan State University) in Baltimore. In her twenties, she attended Howard University, where she published her first stories in student publications and later in newspapers and magazines. In 1925 she moved to New York City and became active in the Harlem Renaissance. She collaborated with LANGSTON HUGHES in a folk comedy, *Mule Bone* (1931). Her first book, *The Eatonville Anthology* (1927), gained her national attention. At Barnard College she took courses in anthropology and studied traditional folklore in Alabama and native culture in the Caribbean. During the 1930s and early 1940s she completed graduate work at Columbia University and published four novels and an autobiography. Hurston published more books than any other African American woman writer of her time — novels, collections of stories, non-fiction, an autobiography — but she earned very little from her writing and spent her final years in near poverty. In the mid-1970s her work was rediscovered, and she is now recognized as an important American author.

WEB: Further research this author with LitLinks at bedfordstmartins.com/approachinglit.

DAVID HENRY HWANG (b. 1957) was born in Los Angeles to parents who immigrated to the United States from China; his father was a banker, his mother a professor of music. Hwang attended Stanford University intending to study law, but he became interested in drama and changed his major to English. A year before he graduated in 1979, he wrote his first play, *FOB* [Fresh Off the Boat], which won the 1981 Obie Award as the best new play of the season for Joseph Papp's off-Broadway production in New York. Hwang attended the Yale School of Drama from 1980 to 1981. *The Dance and the Railroad* and *Family Devotions* were produced off-Broadway in 1981. Both, like *FOB*, deal with the problems of immigrants, the tension between trying to assimilate and trying to avoid assimilation in a new culture. Other plays followed in the 1980s, but his big breakthrough came with the 1988 Broadway hit, *M. Butterfly*, which won the Outer Critics Circle Award for best Broadway play, the Drama Desk Award for best new play, the John Gassner Award for best American play, and the Tony Award for best play of the year and established him as one of the leading young American playwrights.

WEB: Further research this author with LitLinks at bedfordstmartins.com/approachinglit.

HENRIK IBSEN (1828–1906) was born in Skien, a tiny coastal town in southeast Norway. Although his father was successful and wealthy at the time of Ibsen's birth, his business failed soon after, and Ibsen grew up in poverty, familiar with the economic hardships he later depicted often in his plays. He worked for six years as apprentice to a druggist in the seaport town of Grimstad to help support his family, and he intended to study medicine but failed the university entrance examinations. By his early twenties, he was deeply involved in a small local theater in Bergen. In 1857 he was appointed artistic director for the new National Theatre and held that post until it went bankrupt in 1862. He received a travel grant from the government and moved with his wife and son to Rome, living for the next twenty-seven years in various European cities. In 1875 he began to experiment with realistic plays exploring social issues related to middle-class life. He is best known for a series of "problem plays" that shocked but also fascinated audiences, among them *A Doll House* (1879; see p. 926) and *Hedda Gabler* (1890). In 1891 he returned to Norway for the rest of his life and continued to write until suffering a stroke in 1900. He received worldwide recognition on his seventieth birthday as the greatest dramatist of the nineteenth century.

WEB: Further research this author with LitLinks at bedfordstmartins.com/approachinglit.

CD-ROM: Research this author in depth with cultural documents and multimedia resources on *LiterActive*.

LAWSON FUSAO INADA (b. 1938) was born in Fresno, California, and attended Fresno State University. He has edited two important Asian American literary anthologies and published several collections of poetry. His collection *Before the War* (1971) was the first volume of poetry by an Asian American to be published by a major publishing house. Early in his life, Inada was an aspiring jazz bassist. Later, he became interested in poetry, but the influence of jazz is evident in his work. One can sense in his rhythms the beats of his bass.

WEB: Further research this author with LitLinks at bedfordstmartins.com/approachinglit.

DAVID IVES (b. 1950) was born in Chicago and attended Northwestern University. After graduating, he moved to New York and worked as an editor for *Foreign Affairs,* in addition to writing plays and short stories. He enrolled in the Yale Drama School in 1981 and earned his M.F.A. degree. Many of his plays, often described as "wacky one-act comedies," have been staged at the Manhattan Punch Line's Festival of One-Act Comedies. His full-length comedy *Don Juan in Chicago* (1994) received the Outer Critics Circle's John Gassner Playwriting Award. He was named winner of the 1994 George and Elisabeth Martin Playwriting Award from Young Playwrights Inc. He has published many plays and collections of short plays as well as a children's story, *Monsieur Eck* (2001).

WEB: Further research this author with LitLinks at bedfordstmartins.com/approachinglit.

GISH JEN (b. 1956) grew up in Scarsdale, New York, the American-born daughter of Chinese immigrant parents. After she graduated from Harvard University with a major in English, her parents expected her to go on to an M.B.A., and she dutifully enrolled in Stanford University's business school but recognized she was not well-suited for a career in business. She earned an M.F.A. in fiction from the University of Iowa Writers' Workshop and became a highly successful writer. Her first novel, *Typical American* (1991) was a *New York Times* notable book of the year and a finalist for the National Book Critics' Circle Award. Its sequel, *Mona in the Promised Land* (1996), also was a *New York Times* notable book and was named one of the ten best books of the year by the *Los Angeles Times.* Jen's works typically combine an adolescent's search for self-identity with the larger search for cultural identity, exploring themes of immigration, assimilation, tensions between ethnic communities, and the importance and complexity of the American dream.

WEB: Further research this author with LitLinks at bedfordstmartins.com/approachinglit.

CALEEN SINNETTE JENNINGS (b. 1950) received a B.A. degree from Bennington College with a major in theater and an M.F.A. in theater from New York University's Tisch School of the Arts. As she worked as an actress, her husband suggested that she try writing plays. *Casting Othello* won the 1996 Washington Summer Theater Festival Award for Outstanding New Play and was produced with its companion piece, *Playing Juliet,* by the Source Theatre Company and the Folger Library Theatre in January 1998. Jennings won Washington's Theater Lobby Award and The Source Theatre's H.D. Lewis Award and Literary Merit Award for her plays. *Sunday Dinner* was published in 1993, and her collection of plays for young performers, *A Lunch Line: Contemporary Scenes for Contemporary Teens,* was published in 1989. Jennings is also a performer and a member of the acting faculty for the Teaching Shakespeare Institute at the Folger Shakespeare Library. She is professor of theatre and director of the Theatre and Music Theatre Program at the American University in Washington, D.C., where she teaches acting and play writing courses, as well as academic courses in theater.

WEB: Further research this author with LitLinks at bedfordstmartins.com/approachinglit.

GEORGIA DOUGLAS JOHNSON (1880–1966) was born in Atlanta and attended Atlanta University. She went on to study music at the Oberlin Conservatory (Ohio) and the Cleveland College of Music. Her ambition was to be a composer, but to earn a living she taught high school in Alabama and Washington, D.C., and later worked for the federal government. She was prolific as a poet, fiction writer, playwright, songwriter, and journalist; in addition to writing a syndicated newspaper column from 1926 to 1932, she wrote twenty-eight plays, thirty-one short stories, and over two hundred poems. She was the most widely published of all the women poets of the Harlem Renaissance period. Beyond her importance as a writer, she played an influential role in Washington circles by providing a "salon" in her home as a meeting place for artists and writers.

WEB: Further research this author with LitLinks at bedfordstmartins.com/approachinglit.

HELENE JOHNSON (1907–1995) was born and raised in Boston. She attended Boston University and Columbia University. Her work began attracting attention when James Weldon Johnson and ROBERT FROST selected three of her poems for prizes in a 1926 competition. Although she was regarded in the early 1930s as one of the most gifted poets of the Harlem Renaissance, she had a limited poetic output: thirty-four poems in a range of forms and voices, published in small magazines. The last of her poems published during her lifetime was "Let Me Sing My Song," which appeared in *Challenge,* a journal founded by her cousin, the novelist Dorothy West, to revive the spirit of the Harlem Renaissance. She married in 1933 and from then on directed most of her energy and attention to motherhood and earning a living as a correspondent for *Consumer's Union.*

WEB: Further research this author with LitLinks at bedfordstmartins.com/approachinglit.

BEN JONSON (1572–1637) was born in London, the stepson of a bricklayer (father died before he was born). He attended Westminster School and then joined the army. Jonson later worked as an actor and was the author of comedies such as *Everyman in His Humor* (in which Shakespeare acted the lead), *Volpone,* and *The Alchemist.* He wrote clear, elegant, "classical" poetry, contrasting with the intricate, subtle, "metaphysical" poetry of his contemporaries JOHN DONNE and GEORGE HERBERT. He was named poet laureate and was the idol of a generation of English writers, who dubbed themselves the Sons of Ben.

WEB: Further research this author with LitLinks at bedfordstmartins.com/approachinglit.

[A.] VAN JORDAN (b. 1965) was born and raised in Akron, Ohio. He is a graduate of the M.F.A. Program for Writers at Warren Wilson College, where he taught in the undergraduate Writing Program and served as the 1999–2000 and 2000–2001 Joan Beebe Graduate Teaching Fellow. In 1995 he was awarded a D.C. Commission on the Arts and Humanities Literary Award. He was also a semifinalist for the 1999 "Discovery"/The Nation Award. His first collection of poems, *Rise,* was published in 2001. He currently teaches in the M.F.A. program at the University of North Carolina, Greensboro.

WEB: Further research this author with LitLinks at bedfordstmartins.com/approachinglit.

ALLISON JOSEPH (b. 1967) was born in London to Caribbean parents and grew up in Toronto and the Bronx. She earned her B.A. from Kenyon College and her M.F.A. from Indiana University. She is the author of four collections of poetry, *What Keeps Us Here* (winner of Ampersand Press's 1992 Women Poets Series Competition and the John C. Zacharis First Book Award), *Soul Train* (1997), *In Every Seam* (1999), and *Imitation of Life* (2002). Her poems are often attuned to the experiences of women and minorities. She formerly taught at the University of Arkansas and currently is an associate professor at Southern Illinois University, Carbondale, where she is editor of *The Crab Orchard Review.*

WEB: Further research this author with LitLinks at bedfordstmartins.com/approachinglit.

JAMES JOYCE (1882–1941) was born in Rathgar, a suburb of Dublin. His father, descended from an old, wealthy Cork family, drank his family into poverty. However, Joyce received an excellent classical education at a Jesuit school and University College, Dublin, where he studied modern languages and began writing. He became alienated from the Catholic religion and from Ireland, and in 1902 he left Dublin for Paris; he returned in 1903 to be with his mother, who was dying of cancer. From 1905 he lived on the continent, in Trieste, Zurich, and from 1920 to 1939 as part of the vibrant colony of expatriate authors in Paris. Although he was not able to live in Ireland, all of his writings concern Ireland and his memories of it. His first book was a collection of poems, *Chamber Music,* published in 1907. His major collection of stories, *Dubliners,* appeared in 1914, followed in 1916 by the autobiographical novel that established his reputation as a major writer, *A Portrait of the Artist as a Young Man.* The novel regarded generally as his masterpiece, *Ulysses,* was published 1922 in Paris. (*Ulysses* was not published in the United States until 1933 and not in England until 1937, because legal difficulties prohibited uncensored publication in those countries prior to that.) His final novel, *Finnegans Wake,* appeared in 1939. To escape the German occupation of

France, he returned that year to Zurich, where he had lived while writing *Ulysses*, and died there slightly more than a year later.

WEB: Further research this author with LitLinks at bedfordstmartins.com/approachinglit.

CD-ROM: Research this author in depth with cultural documents and multimedia resources on *LiterActive*.

JOHN KEATS (1795–1821) was born in London. His father, a worker at a livery stable who married his employer's daughter and inherited the business, was killed by a fall from a horse when Keats was eight. When his mother died of tuberculosis six years later, Keats and his siblings were entrusted to the care of a guardian, a practical-minded man who took Keats out of school at fifteen and apprenticed him to a doctor. As soon as he qualified for medical practice in 1815, he abandoned medicine for poetry, which he had begun writing two years earlier. In 1818, the year he contracted tuberculosis, he also fell madly in love with a pretty, vivacious young woman named Fanny Brawne, whom he could not marry because of his poverty, illness, and devotion to poetry. In the midst of such stress and emotional turmoil, his masterpieces poured out between January and September 1819: the great odes, a number of sonnets, and several longer lyric poems. In February 1820, his health failed rapidly; he went to Italy in the autumn, in hopes that the warmer climate would improve his health, and died there on February 23, 1821. His poems are rich with sensuous, lyrical beauty and emotional resonance, reflecting his delight in life as well as his awareness of life's brevity and difficulty.

WEB: Further research this author with LitLinks at bedfordstmartins.com/approachinglit.

CD-ROM: Research this author in depth with cultural documents and multimedia resources on *LiterActive*.

JAMAICA KINCAID (b. 1949) was born Elaine Potter Richardson in St. Johns, Antigua, on the West Indies and completed her British-style secondary education there. She lived with her stepfather, a carpenter, and her mother until 1965 when she was sent to Westchester, New York, to work as an au pair. After working for three years and taking night classes at a community college, she attended Franconia College in New Hampshire for a year. Because her family disapproved of her writing, she changed her name to Jamaica Kincaid when she began publishing stories in magazines. Her work drew the attention of William Shawn, editor of the *New Yorker*, who hired her as a staff writer in 1976. For the next nine years, she wrote columns for the "Talk of the Town" section. In 1978, she first published a story in the *New Yorker;* it later became part of her first book, a collection entitled *At the Bottom of the River* (1984), which won the Morton Dauwen Zabel Award of the American Academy and Institute of Arts and Letters. She has also published four novels; a nonfiction book about Antigua, *A Small Place* (1988); and a memoir, *My Brother* (1997). Kincaid lives in Bennington, Vermont, with her husband, composer Allen Shawn (son of the former *New Yorker* editor), and their two children and teaches creative writing at Bennington College.

WEB: Further research this author with LitLinks at bedfordstmartins.com/approachinglit.

CD-ROM: Research this author in depth with cultural documents and multimedia resources on *LiterActive*.

GALWAY KINNELL (b. 1927) was born in Providence, Rhode Island, and attended Princeton University and the University of Rochester. He served in the U.S. Navy and then visited Paris on a Fulbright fellowship. Returning to the United States, he worked for the Congress on Racial Equality and then traveled widely in the Middle East and Europe. He has taught in France, Australia, and Iran as well as at numerous colleges and universities in the United States. He has published many books of poetry, including *Selected Poems* (1980), for which he received both the Pulitzer Prize and the National Book Award. He has also published translations of works by Yves Bonnefoy, Yvanne Goll, François Villon, and Rainer Maria Rilke. He divides his time between Vermont and New York City, where he is the Erich Maria Remarque Professor of Creative Writing at New York University.

WEB: Further research this author with LitLinks at bedfordstmartins.com/approachinglit.

ETHERIDGE KNIGHT (1931–1991) was born in Corinth, Mississippi. He dropped out of school at age sixteen and served in the U.S. Army in Korea from 1947 to 1951, returning with a shrapnel wound that caused him to fall deeper into a drug addiction that had begun during his service. In 1960 he was arrested for robbery, convicted, and sentenced to eight years in an Indiana state prison. During this time he began writing poetry. His first book, *Poems from Prison* (1968), was published one year before his release. The book was a success, and Knight joined other poets in what came to be called the Black Arts movement, the aesthetic and spiritual sister of the Black Power concept. He went on to write several more books of poetry and to receive many prestigious honors and awards. In 1990 he earned a B.A. in American poetry and criminal justice from Martin Center University in Indianapolis.

WEB: Further research this author with LitLinks at bedfordstmartins.com/approachinglit.

YUSEF KOMUNYAKAA (b. 1947) was born and grew up in Bogalusa, Louisiana. He earned degrees at the University of Colorado, Colorado State University, and the University of California, Irvine. His numerous books of poems include *Neon Vernacular: New and Selected Poems, 1977–1989* (1994), for which he received the Pulitzer Prize and the Kingsley Tufts Poetry Award, and *Thieves of Paradise* (1998), which was a finalist for the National Book Critics Circle Award. Other publications include *Blues Notes: Essays, Interviews & Commentaries* (2000), *The Jazz Poetry Anthology* (coedited with J. A. Sascha Feinstein, 1991), and *The Insomnia of Fire* by Nguyen Quang Thieu (cotranslated with Martha Collins, 1995). He now lives in New York City and is a professor in the Council of Humanities and the creative writing program at Princeton University.

WEB: Further research this author with LitLinks at bedfordstmartins.com/approachinglit.

MAXINE KUMIN (b. 1925) was born in Philadelphia and received her B.A. and M.A. at Radcliffe College. She has published several books of poetry, including *Up Country: Poems of New England* (1972), for which she received the Pulitzer Prize. She is also the au-

thor of a memoir, *Inside the Halo and Beyond: The Anatomy of a Recovery* (2000); four novels; a collection of short stories; more than twenty children's books; and four books of essays. She has taught at the University of Massachusetts, Columbia University, Brandeis University, and Princeton University. She has served as Consultant in Poetry to the Library of Congress and as poet laureate of New Hampshire, where she lives.

WEB: Further research this author with LitLinks at bedfordstmartins.com/approachinglit.

JHUMPA LAHIRI (b. 1967) was born in London but grew up in Rhode Island. As a child she wrote stories in her school notebooks. She received her B.A. from Barnard College and, rejected by creative writing programs, continued to write stories while working at an office job. She was then accepted to the graduate program at Boston University and earned an M.A. in English, an M.A. in creative writing, and a Ph.D. in Renaissance studies. The daughter of parents born in India who frequently took her there as a child, she has been influenced by the culture of India and the United States. Her first collection of short fiction, *Interpreter of Maladies* (1999), won the Pulitzer Prize for Fiction in 2000, in addition to the PEN/Hemingway Award, the *New Yorker* Debut of the Year award, and an American Academy of Arts and Letters Addison Metcalf Award. Her first novel, *The Namesake,* was published in 2003. She has taught creative writing at Boston University and the Rhode Island School of Design and currently lives in New York City.

WEB: Further research this author with LitLinks at bedfordstmartins.com/approachinglit.

LI-YOUNG LEE (b. 1957) was born in Jakarta, Indonesia, to Chinese parents. His father, who had been personal physician to Mao Tse-tung, relocated his family to Indonesia, where he helped found Gamaliel University. In 1959 the Lee family fled the country to escape anti-Chinese sentiment, and they settled in the United States in 1964. Lee studied at the University of Pittsburgh, the University of Arizona, and the Brockport campus of the State University of New York. He has taught at several universities, including Northwestern University and the University of Iowa. He is the author of three collections of poetry: *Rose* (1986), which won the Delmore Schwartz Memorial Poetry Award; *The City in Which I Love You* (1991), which was the 1990 Lamont Poetry Selection; and *Book of My Nights* (2001). He has also written a memoir, *The Winged Seed: A Remembrance* (1995), which received an American Book Award from the Before Columbus Foundation. In his poems, one often senses a profound sense of exile, the influence of his father's presence, and a rich spiritual sensuality.

WEB: Further research this author with LitLinks at bedfordstmartins.com/approachinglit.

JOHN LEGUIZAMO (b. 1964) was born in Bogotá, Colombia. His family immigrated to the United States when he was four, and he grew up in New York City. In 1983 he began studying acting at Sylvia Leigh's Showcase Theater, which he picked randomly out of the Yellow Pages. After graduating from high school, he attended New York University to major in drama but left school after a year to join the comedy group Off Center Theater. He also attended the Strasberg Theater Institute and the H. B. Studio. He has performed as a stand-up comedian and in many roles on television and in movies, as well as in an off-Broadway staging of his play *Mambo Mouth*. He is author of several successful screenplays and one-actor plays — *Mambo Mouth: A Savage Comedy* (1991; see p. 874), which won an Obie Award and an Outer Critics Circle Award, *Spic-o-Rama* (1992), and *Sexaholix . . . A Love Story: Monologue* (2002) — and coauthor with David Katz of *Freak: A Semi-Demi-Quasi-Pseudo Autobiography* (1997).

WEB: Further research this author with LitLinks at bedfordstmartins.com/approachinglit.

CD-ROM: Research this author in depth with cultural documents and multimedia resources on *LiterActive*.

PHILIP LEVINE (b. 1928) was born in Detroit and received his degrees from Wayne State University and the University of Iowa. He is the author of many books of poetry, including *The Simple Truth* (1994), which won the Pulitzer Prize. He has also published a collection of essays, edited *The Essential Keats* (1987), and coedited and translated books of poetry by Spanish poet Gloria Fuertes and Mexican poet Jamie Sabines. He lives in New York City and Fresno, California, and teaches at New York University.

WEB: Further research this author with LitLinks at bedfordstmartins.com/approachinglit.

TIMOTHY LIU (b. 1965) was born in San Jose, California, to parents who had immigrated from the Chinese mainland. He studied at Brigham Young University, the University of Houston, and the University of Massachusetts, Amherst. He is author of several books of poetry (including *Vox Angelica*, which won the 1992 Norma Farber First Book Award from the Poetry Society of America) and editor of *Word of Mouth: An Anthology of Gay American Poetry* (2000). He is an assistant professor at William Paterson University and lives in Hoboken, New Jersey.

WEB: Further research this author with LitLinks at bedfordstmartins.com/approachinglit.

AUDRE LORDE (1934–1992) was born in New York City of West Indian parents. She grew up in Manhattan and attended Roman Catholic schools. While she was still in high school, her first poem appeared in *Seventeen* magazine. She earned her B.A. from Hunter College and her M.A. in library science from Columbia University. In 1968 she left her job as head librarian at the University of New York to become a lecturer and creative writer. She accepted a poet-in-residence position at Tougaloo College in Mississippi, where she discovered a love of teaching, published her first volume of poetry, *The First Cities* (1968), and met her long-term partner, Frances Clayton. Many other volumes of poetry followed, several of which won major awards. She also published four volumes of prose, among them *The Cancer Journals* (1980), which chronicled her struggles with cancer, and *A Burst of Light* (1988), which won a National Book Award. In the 1980s, Lorde and writer Barbara Smith founded Kitchen Table: Women of Color Press. She was also a founding member of Sisters in Support of Sisters in South Africa, an organization that worked to raise awareness about women under apartheid. She was the poet laureate of New York from 1991 to 1992.

WEB: Further research this author with LitLinks at bedfordstmartins.com/approachinglit.

RICHARD LOVELACE (1618–1692) was born into a prominent family in Kent, England, and went to Oxford University, where his dashing appearance and wit made him a social and literary favorite. He fought in the English civil war on the Royalist side and was imprisoned and exiled. Later he fought in France against the Spanish and was again imprisoned on his return to England. After his release he spent ten years in poverty and isolation before his death. He was a leader of the "Cavalier poets," followers of King Charles I who were soldiers and courtiers but also wrote well-crafted, light-hearted lyric poetry. "To Lucasta, Going to the Wars" (p. 683) is an excellent example of the type.

WEB: Further research this author with LitLinks at bedfordstmartins.com/approachinglit.

ROBERT LOWELL (1917–1978) was born in Boston into a prominent New England family. He attended Harvard University and then Kenyon College, where he studied under John Crowe Ransom. At Louisiana State University, he studied with Robert Penn Warren and Cleanth Brooks as well as Allen Tate. He was always politically active — a conscientious objector during World War II and a Vietnam protestor — and suffered from manic depression. Lowell's reputation was established early: His second book, *Lord Weary's Castle*, was awarded the Pulitzer Prize for Poetry in 1947. In the mid-1950s he began to write more directly from personal experience and loosened his adherence to traditional meter and form. The result was a watershed collection of the "confessional" school, *Life Studies* (1959), which changed the landscape of modern poetry, much as T. S. ELIOT's *The Waste Land* had done three decades before. He died suddenly from a heart attack at age 60.

WEB: Further research this author with LitLinks at bedfordstmartins.com/approachinglit.

HEATHER MCHUGH (b. 1948) was born to Canadian parents in San Diego and grew up in Virginia. She is a graduate of Radcliffe College and the University of Denver. McHugh has published numerous books of poetry, a book of prose, and four books of translations. She teaches as a core faculty member in the M.F.A. Program for Writers at Warren Wilson College and as Milliman Writer-in-Residence at the University of Washington, Seattle. She has been a visiting professor at the University of Iowa Writers' Workshop and has held chairs at the University of California, Berkeley, the University of Alabama, and the University of Cincinnati.

WEB: Further research this author with LitLinks at bedfordstmartins.com/approachinglit.

CLAUDE MCKAY (1890–1948), the son of poor farmworkers, was born in Sunny Ville, Jamaica. He was educated by his older brother, who possessed a library of English novels, poetry, and scientific texts. At age twenty, McKay published a book of verse in dialect called *Songs of Jamaica,* recording his impressions of black life in Jamaica. In 1912, he traveled to the United States to attend Tuskegee Institute. He soon left to study agriculture at Kansas State University. In 1914 he moved to Harlem and became an influential member of the Harlem Renaissance. After committing to communism and traveling to Moscow in 1922, he lived for some time in Europe and Morocco, writing fiction. McKay later repudiated communism, converted to Roman Catholicism, and returned to the United States. He published several books of poetry as well as an autobiography, *A Long Way from Home* (1937). He wrote a number of sonnets protesting the injustices of black life in the United States, "America" (p. 686) among them. They are of interest for the way they use the most Anglo of forms to contain and intensify what the poem's language is saying.

WEB: Further research this author with LitLinks at bedfordstmartins.com/approachinglit.

NAGUIB MAHFOUZ (b. 1911) was born in Gamaliya, Cairo. In his childhood his mother often took him to museums, and Egyptian history later became a major theme in many of his books. He graduated from Cairo University in 1934. After spending a year working on an M.A., he decided to become a professional writer. He worked as a journalist, wrote articles and short stories, and then began writing novels. His first published book was a translation of James Baikie's work on ancient Egypt. His first collection of stories appeared in 1938. From 1939 until 1954 he was a civil servant at the Ministry of Islamic

Affairs, and then worked as director of the Foundation for Support of the Cinema, the State Cinema Organization. He has written some forty novels and short story collections, screenplays, and several stage plays. In his work, Mahfouz describes the development of his country in the twentieth century, combining intellectual and cultural influences from East and West. In 1988 he won the Nobel Prize for Literature, for "works rich in nuance—now clearsightedly realistic, now evocatively ambiguous—[which form] an Arabian narrative art that applies to all mankind."

WEB: Further research this author with LitLinks at bedfordstmartins.com/approachinglit.

CLARENCE MAJOR (b. 1936) was born in Atlanta. He received his B.A. from the State University of New York and his Ph.D. from the Union of Experimenting Colleges and Universities. Major is the author of nine volumes of poetry including *Configurations: New and Selected Poems 1958–1998* (1999), more than eight novels, and a collection of literary and cultural criticism, *Necessary Distance: Essays and Criticism* (2001). He has edited collections of twentieth-century African American poetry and fiction and compiled *Black Slang: A Dictionary of Afro-American Talk* (1971). He has read and lectured in major cities throughout the United States, Europe, and North and West Africa. He is a professor of English at the University of California, Davis. Many of his poems, while centered on a narrator from the United States, are international in scope, drawing on images and rhythms especially from the history of oppressed peoples in Europe and West and North Africa.

WEB: Further research this author with LitLinks at bedfordstmartins.com/approachinglit.

CHRISTOPHER MARLOWE (1564–1593) was born in Canterbury, England, the same year as WILLIAM SHAKESPEARE. The son of a shoemaker, he needed the help of scholarships to attend King's School, Canterbury, and Corpus Christi College, Cambridge. He was involved in secret political missions for the government. He was one of the most brilliant writers of his generation, in narrative poetry, lyric poetry, and drama (his best-known play

is *Doctor Faustus*). He died after being knifed in a bar fight, reportedly over his bill, at the age of twenty-nine. "The Passionate Shepherd to His Love" (p. 687) is among the most famous of Elizabethan poems.

WEB: Further research this author with LitLinks at bedfordstmartins.com/approachinglit.

ANDREW MARVELL (1621–1678) was born in Hull, Yorkshire, and educated at Trinity College, Cambridge. After traveling in Europe, he worked as a tutor and in a government office (as assistant to JOHN MILTON) and later became a member of Parliament for Hull. Marvell was known in his lifetime as a writer of rough satires in verse and prose. His "serious" poetry, like "To His Coy Mistress" (p. 688), was not published until after his death. It is a famous exploration of the *carpe diem* theme (see the Glossary of Literary Terms, p. 1504).

WEB: Further research this author with LitLinks at bedfordstmartins.com/approachinglit.

CD-ROM: Research this author in depth with cultural documents and multimedia resources on *LiterActive*.

ORLANDO RICARDO MENES (b. 1958) was born in Lima, Peru, to Cuban parents, but has lived most of his life in Miami, Florida. He holds a B.A. and M.A. in English from the University of Florida and a Ph.D. from the University of Illinois at Chicago. His first collection of poetry, *Borderlands with Angels,* was winner of the 1994 Bacchae Press Chapbook Competition. His second collection, *Rumba Atop the Stones,* was published in 2001. He has also edited the volume *Renaming Ecstasy: Latino Writings on the Sacred* (2004). For years photography was one of his passions, and in 1992 he had an exhibition of photographs at Books and Books in Miami Beach. He teaches in the Creative Writing Program at the University of Notre Dame.

WEB: Further research this author with LitLinks at bedfordstmartins.com/approachinglit.

ARTHUR MILLER (b. 1915) was born in New York City to middle-class Jewish parents. His mother was a teacher and his father a successful clothing manufacturer whose business collapsed during the Depression. The family had to move from Manhattan to a small frame house in Brooklyn, similar to that of the Loman family in *Death of a Salesman* (p. 980). After high school he worked for two years in a warehouse to save money for college. He went to the University of Michigan to study journalism, but soon began to write and win prizes for plays. After graduation, he wrote plays for radio and worked for the Federal Theater Project. His first successful play was *All My Sons* (1947), which won a Drama Critics Circle Award. *Death of a Salesman* (1949) was the hit of the 1948–1949 Broadway season, running for 742 performances and winning the Pulitzer Prize, the Drama Critics Circle Award, the Donaldson Award, and a Tony Award for best play. The script of the play became a best seller and the only play ever to be a Book-of-the-Month selection. Miller has continued to write plays, among the most successful being *The Crucible* (1953), *A View from the Bridge* (1955), and *After the Fall* (1964). He also has published a memoir, *Timebends: A Life* (1987); a novel; a collection of short stories; and many essays on the theater and the craft of playwriting.

WEB: Further research this author with LitLinks at bedfordstmartins.com/approachinglit.

CD-ROM: Research this author in depth with cultural documents and multimedia resources on *LiterActive.*

CZESLAW MILOSZ (b. 1911) was born in Seteiniai, Lithuania, son of Aleksander Milosz, a civil engineer, and Weronika, née Kunat. His family later moved to Wilno, Lithuania. In 1930, a year after he graduated from high school, his first poems were published in a university magazine. In 1931 he cofounded the Polish avant-garde literary group Zagary; his first collection of verse appeared in 1933. He received his Master of Law degree in 1934 and then worked for Radio Wilno and Polish Radio. He spent most of World War II in Nazi-occupied Warsaw working for underground presses. After the war, he came to the United States as a diplomat, working at the Polish consulate first in New York and then in Washington. In 1950 he was transferred to Paris, and the following year requested and received political asylum. He spent the next decade in Paris as a freelance writer. In 1960 he moved to the United States to become a

lecturer at the University of California, Berkeley, where he is now professor of Slavic languages and literature. He is the author of many books of poetry (almost all of his poems are written in his native Polish). He has also translated his own works and the works of other Polish writers into English. In 1980, Milosz was awarded the Nobel Prize for Literature.

WEB: Further research this author with LitLinks at bedfordstmartins.com/approachinglit.

JOHN MILTON (1608–1674), son of a well-off London businessman, was educated at St. Paul's School and at home with private tutors. After graduating with an M.A. from Christ's College, Cambridge, he spent the next six years reading at home. Milton had written verse since his university days, but he broke off to write prose tracts in favor of Oliver Cromwell, in whose government he later headed a department. The strain of long hours of reading and writing for the revolutionary cause aggravated a genetic weakness and resulted in his total blindness around 1651. He wrote his most famous works, *Paradise Lost* (1667), *Paradise Regained* (1671), and *Samson Agonistes* (1671), by dictating them to his daughter and other amanuenses.

WEB: Further research this author with LitLinks at bedfordstmartins.com/approachinglit.

GARY MIRANDA (b. 1938) was born in Bremerton, Washington, and grew up in the Pacific Northwest. He is the author of three collections of poetry, *Listeners at the Breathing Place* (1978), *Grace Period* (1983), and *Turning Sixty* (2001) and has published a translation of Rainer Maria Rilke's *Duino Elegies* (1981). He lives in Portland, Oregon, and works at the Kaiser Permanente Center for Health Research.

WEB: Further research this author with LitLinks at bedfordstmartins.com/approachinglit.

JANICE MIRIKITANI (b. 1942) was born in California, a sansei or third-generation Japanese American. As an infant, she was interned with her family in Rohwer, Arkansas, during World War II. She has published four volumes of poetry and edited several anthologies of poetry, prose, and essays, among them *Ayumi: Japanese American Anthology* (1980) and *Watch Out, We're Talking: Speaking Out about Incest and Abuse* (1993). She is the recipient of many awards and honors, including the American Book Lifetime Achievement Award for Literature, the Woman Warrior in Arts and Culture Award from the Pacific Asian-American Bay Area Women's Coalition, and the first Woman of Words Award from the Women's Foundation. Executive Director of Glide Church and President of the Glide Foundation, she has lived in San Francisco since 1963 and was poet laureate of San Francisco for 2000–2002.

WEB: Further research this author with LitLinks at bedfordstmartins.com/approachinglit.

MISHIMA YUKIO (1925–1970) was born Kimitake Hiraoka into a samurai family (when he became a writer, he changed his name to Mishima Yukio so his anti-literary father wouldn't know). During World War II Mishima was excused from military service, but he served in a factory. This plagued Mishima throughout his life — he had survived shamefully when so many others had been killed. After graduating from the University of Tokyo in 1947, he worked briefly in the finance ministry before devoting himself entirely to writing. He completed his first novel the year he entered university and went on to write twenty-three novels, more than forty plays, over ninety short stories, several poetry and travel volumes, and hundreds of essays. He was nominated for the Nobel Prize for Literature three times. He considered his tetralogy *The Sea of Fertility* his masterpiece and frequently said he would die when it was completed, and, in fact, delivered the final pages of the last volume, *The Decay of the Angel*, to his publisher on the day of his death. In 1968 he founded the Shield Society, a private army of some one hundred youths dedicated to a revival of Bushido, the samurai knightly code of honor. In 1970 he seized control of military headquarters in Tokyo, trying to rouse the nation to prewar nationalist heroic ideals. After this failed, Mishima committed *seppuku* (ritual disembowelment) with his sword. Many critics consider him the most important Japanese novelist of the twentieth century.

WEB: Further research this author with LitLinks at bedfordstmartins.com/approachinglit.

MARIANNE MOORE (1887–1972) was born near St. Louis and grew up in Carlisle, Pennsylvania. After studying at Bryn Mawr College and Carlisle Commercial College, she taught at a government Indian school in Carlisle. She moved to Brooklyn, where she became an assistant at the New York Public Library. She loved baseball and spent a good deal of time watching her beloved Brooklyn Dodgers. She began to write Imagist poetry and to contribute to the *Dial,* a prestigious literary magazine. She served as acting editor of the *Dial* from 1925 to 1929 and later as editor for four years. Moore was widely recognized for her work, receiving among other honors the Bollingen Prize for Poetry, the National Book Award, and the Pulitzer Prize.

WEB: Further research this author with LitLinks at bedfordstmartins.com/approachinglit.

ROBERT MORGAN (b. 1944) is a native of the North Carolina mountains. He was raised on land settled by his Welsh ancestors. He is an accomplished poet, novelist, and short story writer. His four historical novels, two collections of short fiction, and nine volumes of poetry reveal an indelible sense of place for those familiar with, or strangers to, the Blue Ridge Mountains and address themes that matter to all people in all places: birth and death, love and loss, joy and sorrow, the necessity for remembrance, and the inevitability of forgetting. He was educated at the University of North Carolina, Chapel Hill, and earned an M.F.A. from the University of North Carolina, Greensboro. In 1971 Morgan began teaching at Cornell University, where, since 1992, he has been the Kappa Alpha Professor of English.

WEB: Further research this author with LitLinks at bedfordstmartins.com/approachinglit.

TONI MORRISON (b. 1931) was born Chloe Anthony Wofford in Lorain, Ohio. She spent her childhood in the Midwest, reading widely in such classic authors as Leo Tolstoy, Feodor Dostoyevski, Gustave Flaubert, and Jane Austen on the one hand, and absorbing folktales and literary culture of the black community from her father on the other. She received her B.A. from Howard University (where she began using a shortened form of her middle name because "Chloe" was difficult for others to pronounce) and her M.A. from Cornell University. She taught at Texas Southern University and Howard University and then worked as an editor for Random House. In 1958 while teaching at Howard, she married Harold Morrison, a Jamaican architect, and she began writing fiction. Her first novel, *The Bluest Eye,* was published in 1970, followed by *Sula* in 1973. Her next novel, *Song of Solomon* (1977), brought her international recognition. It was the first novel by a black writer to be a main selection of the Book-of-the-Month Club since Richard Wright's *Native Son* in 1949. In 1984 she was appointed to an Albert Schweitzer chair at the University of New York at Albany. Her fifth novel, *Beloved* (1987), was awarded the 1987 Pulitzer Prize for Fiction. In 1987, Toni Morrison was named the Robert F. Goheen Professor in the Council of Humanities at Princeton University, the first black woman writer to hold a named chair at an Ivy League University. Later novels are *Jazz* (1992), *Paradise* (1998), and *Love* (2003). In 1993, she became the eighth woman and the first black woman to receive the Nobel Prize for Literature.

WEB: Further research this author with LitLinks at bedfordstmartins.com/approachinglit.

THYLIAS MOSS (b. 1954) was born in Cleveland. She attended Syracuse University and received her B.A. from Oberlin College and M.F.A. from the University of New Hampshire. She is the author of numerous books of poetry; a memoir, *Tale of a Sky-Blue Dress* (1998); two children's books; and two plays, *Talking to Myself* (1984) and *The Dolls in the Basement* (1984). She lives in Ann Arbor, where she is a professor of English at the University of Michigan.

WEB: Further research this author with LitLinks at bedfordstmartins.com/approachinglit.

JULIE MOULDS (RYBICKI) (b. 1962) received her B.A. from Hope College and her M.F.A. from Western Michigan University. Her poetry has been published in many literary magazines and was collected in her book *The Woman with a Cubed Head* (1998). She is author of the libretto of an operetta based on the Russian witch Babba Yaga, which was given its first performance in 1996. Moulds

has taught children's literature and worked in children's bookstores. She has lived for many years with a recurring form of cancer. Her work often combines the magical with a harsh realism. She is presently working on a sonnet sequence based on the limericks of Edward Lear, her hero.

WEB: Further research this author with LitLinks at bedfordstmartins.com/approachinglit.

BHARATI MUKHERJEE (b. 1940) was born in Calcutta, India, into a wealthy traditional family. In 1947, her father was given a job in England, and he brought his family to London, where they lived until 1951 and where Mukherjee perfected her English language skills. Her parents gave their children excellent educational opportunities, Mukherjee earning a B.A. from the University of Calcutta and an M.A. from Baroda University. Having written stories since she was five, she knew she wanted to be a writer and entered the prestigious University of Iowa Writers' Workshop, intending to earn an M.F.A. and return to India and marry a bridegroom of her father's choosing after receiving her degree. However, while in Iowa City, she met a Canadian student from Harvard University, Clark Blaise, and married him after a two-week courtship. After receiving her M.F.A., she went on to earn her Ph.D. in English and comparative literature from the University of Iowa in 1969. She and her husband lived in Canada for ten difficult years, where she experienced discrimination and treatment as a member of a "visible minority." During those years she taught at McGill University and published her first two novels. In 1980, Mukherjee and her family moved to the United States, where she taught at a number of colleges and universities and published several more novels, two collections of stories, and two books with her husband about experiences in India. She is currently a Distinguished Professor of English at the University of California, Berkeley.

WEB: Further research this author with LitLinks at bedfordstmartins.com/approachinglit.

DAVID MURA (b. 1952), a third-generation Japanese American, was born in Great Lakes, Illinois, and graduated from Grinnell College in Iowa; he did graduate work at the University of Minnesota and Vermont College. Mura is a poet, creative nonfiction writer, critic, playwright, and performance artist. He is author of numerous books of poetry — including *After We Lost Our Way* (1989), which was selected as a National Poetry Series winner — and two memoirs: *Turning Japanese: Memoirs of a Sansei* (1991), which was a *New York Times* Notable Book of the Year; and *Where the Body Meets Memory: An Odyssey of Race, Sexuality & Identity* (1996). Mura is the artistic director of the Asian-American Renaissance, an arts organization in Minnesota.

WEB: Further research this author with LitLinks at bedfordstmartins.com/approachinglit.

TASLIMA NASRIN (b. 1962) was born to a Muslim family in Mymensingh, East Pakistan. Because the area became independent in 1971, her city of birth is now in Bangladesh. She started writing when she was fifteen. After earning her medical degree in 1984, she worked in public hospitals for eight years. Because of the success of her second book of poetry in 1989, editors of progressive daily and weekly newspapers suggested that she write regular columns, which she used to write about women's oppression. Her strong language and uncompromising attitude against male domination stirred many people, eliciting both admiration and hatred. Islamic fundamentalists launched a campaign against her in 1990, staging street demonstrations and processions, and she was publicly assaulted several times. In 1993, a fundamentalist organization, Soldiers of Islam, issued a fatwa against her (set a price on her head) and she went into hiding. After two more fatwas were issued, many humanist organizations outside Bangladesh came to her support. In 1994 she was granted bail but forced to leave the country. She has since been living in exile in Europe. She has written twenty-four books — novels and collections of poetry, essays, and short stories. Her applications to the Bangladesh government to be allowed to return have been denied repeatedly.

WEB: Further research this author with LitLinks at bedfordstmartins.com/approachinglit.

PABLO NERUDA (1904–1973), whose real name is Neftalí Ricardo Reyes Basoalto, was born in the town of Parral in central Chile.

He began to contribute articles to the daily *La Mañana* in 1917, including his first poem "Mis ojos." In 1920, he became a contributor to the literary journal *Selva Austral* using a pen name to avoid conflict with his family, who disapproved of his literary ambitions. He chose the name "Pablo Neruda" in memory of the Czechoslovak poet Jan Neruda (1834–1891) and used it for over twenty years before adopting it legally in 1946. Neruda studied French and pedagogy at the University of Chile in Santiago. At age twenty-three he was appointed to the first of a series of diplomatic posts in various East Asian and European Countries. In 1939, while serving as Consul General in Mexico, he transformed his *Canto General de Chile* into an epic poem about the whole South American continent, its nature, its people, and its historical destiny. This work, entitled *Canto General,* was published the same year in Mexico and underground in Chile. In 1943, Neruda returned to Chile, and in 1945 he was elected senator of the Republic. Due to his protests against President González Videla's repressive policy against striking miners in 1947, he had to live underground in his own country for two years. He managed to leave in 1949; then after living in different European countries, he returned home in 1952. When Salvador Allende was elected president, he appointed Neruda as Chile's ambassador to France (1970–1972). Neruda died of leukemia in Santiago in 1973. A prolific writer, he published more than forty volumes of poetry, translations, and verse drama and is the most widely read of the Spanish American poets. He was awarded the Nobel Prize for Literature in 1971.

WEB: Further research this author with LitLinks at bedfordstmartins.com/approachinglit.

DUANE NIATUM (b. 1938) was born in Seattle near his ancestral lands on the Washington coast. He is a Native American of mixed descent and a member of the Klallum tribe. He grew up moving among Washington, Oregon, California, and Alaska. At age seventeen, he enlisted in the navy, spending two years in Japan, after which he earned his B.A. in English at the University of Washington and his M.A. from Johns Hopkins University. He is author of several collections of poetry —

including *Songs for the Harvester of Dreams* (1982), which won the National Book Award from the Before Columbus Foundation — and editor of two important collections, *Carriers of the Dream Wheel: Contemporary Native American Poetry* (1975) and *Harper's Anthology of Twentieth-Century Native American Poetry* (1988). His poems often reveal a stunningly keen ability to observe both the human-made and the natural world, and his structures are often sharply focused sequences of such observations.

WEB: Further research this author with LitLinks at bedfordstmartins.com/approachinglit.

NAOMI SHIHAB NYE (b. 1952) was born in St. Louis of a Palestinian father and an American mother and grew up in both the United States and Jerusalem. She received her B.A. from Trinity University in San Antonio, Texas, where she still resides with her family. The author of many books of poems, she has also written short stories and books for children and has edited anthologies, several of which focus on the lives of children and represent work from around the world. She is also a singer-songwriter and on several occasions has traveled to the Middle East and Asia for the U.S. Information Agency, promoting international goodwill through the arts. Nye's work often attests to a universal sense of exile, from place, home, love, and one's self, and the way the human spirit confronts them.

WEB: Further research this author with LitLinks at bedfordstmartins.com/approachinglit.

JOYCE CAROL OATES (b. 1938) was born in Lockport, New York. She began storytelling in early childhood, composing picture stories even before she could write. Only after earning a B.A. from Syracuse University and an M.A. from the University of Wisconsin did she focus on writing as a career. Her first book was a collection of stories, *By the North Gate* (1963). Since then she has gone on to become one of the most versatile, prolific, and important American writers of her time, publishing over eighty books — novels, story collections, poetry, plays, children's books, and literary criticism. She has twice been nominated for the Nobel Prize for Literature. Oates is the Roger S. Berlind Distinguished Professor of Humanities at Princeton University.

WEB: Further research this author with LitLinks at bedfordstmartins.com/approachinglit.

TIM O'BRIEN (b. 1946) was born in Austin, Minnesota, and grew up in Worthington, Minnesota. He attended Macalester College in Minneapolis and, on graduation, was drafted for military service in Vietnam. O'Brien served from 1969 to 1970 as an infantry foot soldier in the Americal division, which was involved in the My Lai massacre in 1968, an event that figures prominently in O'Brien's novel *In the Lake of the Woods* (1994). While in Vietnam he rose to the rank of sergeant and received the Purple Heart. After Vietnam he entered graduate school at Harvard University but left to become a newspaper reporter, a career he pursued until publication of his first book, *If I Die in a Combat Zone, Box Me Up and Ship Me Home* (1973). He has gone on to write several other novels, including *Going after Cacciato* (1978), which won the National Book Award. His collection of stories *The Things They Carried* (1990) was a finalist for the National Book Critics Circle Award and for the Pulitzer Prize, and winner of the Heartland Award from the *Chicago Tribune* and of the French prize for the best foreign book of the year; it was chosen by the *New York Times Book Review* as one of the nine best books of the year in all categories. He teaches in the creative writing program at Texas State University–San Marcos.

WEB: Further research this author with LitLinks at bedfordstmartins.com/approachinglit.

CD-ROM: Research this author in depth with cultural documents and multimedia resources on *LiterActive*.

FLANNERY O'CONNOR (1925–1964) was born in Savannah, Georgia. She earned her B.A. from Georgia State College for Women in Milledgeville, Georgia, and an M.F.A. from the University of Iowa Writers' Workshop. When she was twenty-five, she was found to have disseminated lupus, an incurable disease from which her father died when she was thirteen. She returned to Milledgeville for treatments that slowed the progress of the disease. Living with her mother on the family dairy farm, she wrote in the mornings and rested, read, and carried on correspondence in the afternoons, and she traveled to give occasional lectures as health permitted. She wrote only two novels, *Wise Blood* (1952) and *The Violent Bear It Away* (1960); her literary output also includes two collections of stories, *A Good Man Is Hard to Find* (1955) and *Everything That Rises Must Converge* (1965); a collection of her lectures and essays, *Mystery and Manners* (published posthumously in 1969); and a volume of correspondence (published in 1979 as *The Habit of Being*). Despite her career being cut short, O'Connor is widely recognized as a major Southern writer. Her short stories are generally considered to be her finest work; they are carefully crafted, often focusing on grotesque characters redeemed by grace, have a crisp humor, and reflect the influence of her Catholic faith. *Complete Stories,* a collection of the thirty-one stories she wrote, won the National Book Award for fiction in 1972.

WEB: Further research this author with LitLinks at bedfordstmartins.com/approachinglit.

CD-ROM: Research this author in depth with cultural documents and multimedia resources on *LiterActive.*

DWIGHT OKITA (b. 1958) was born in Chicago and continues to live there. He began writing poems in first grade and published his first poem in the first-grade *Luella Log.* He earned a creative writing degree at University of Illinois, Chicago. His first book of poems, *Crossing with the Light,* was published in 1992. He describes himself as "Japanese American, gay, and Buddhist (Soka Gakkai International)" and says that all things are reflected in his work.

WEB: Further research this author with LitLinks at bedfordstmartins.com/approachinglit.

MARY OLIVER (b. 1935) was born in Cleveland and educated at Ohio State University and Vassar College. She is the author of ten volumes of poetry, including *American Primitive* (1983), for which she won the Pulitzer Prize, and three books of prose. She holds the Catharine Osgood Foster Chair for Distinguished Teaching at Bennington College, and lives in Provincetown, Massachusetts, and Bennington, Vermont. Oliver is one of the most respected among poets concerned for the natural world.

WEB: Further research this author with LitLinks at bedfordstmartins.com/approachinglit.

TILLIE OLSEN was born in 1912 or 1913 either near Mead, Nebraska, or in Omaha, Nebraska. Her parents were Jewish immigrants who fled from the Russian Czarist repression after the revolution of 1905. In the 1920s, her father became a leader in the Nebraska Socialist Party. After the eleventh grade she had to leave school to help support her family during the Depression. She joined the Young Communist League and throughout her life was active politically, especially in causes rooted to her attachment to poor and oppressed workers. Early in 1932, she wrote four chapters of her first novel, *Yonnondio.* Part of one chapter was published as "The Iron Throat" in the *Partisan Review* in 1934 and was acclaimed critically. She wrote very little for the next two decades, during which she married, had a child, and had to care for it alone, much as described in her story "I Stand Here Ironing" (p. 353). She then had three more children with Jack Olsen, a YCL comrade whom she moved in with in 1936 and married in 1944. When her youngest child entered school in 1953, she was able to take creative writing classes at San Francisco State College and Stanford University. "Tell Me a Riddle" won the O. Henry Award for Best Short Story of the Year (1961). It and three other stories were published in *Tell Me a Riddle* (1961), selected by *Time* magazine for its "best-ten-books" list in 1962. Olsen went on to complete *Yonnondio* (1974) and a nonfiction work, *Silences* (1978). She has played an important role in reclaiming the works of neglected women authors. Despite her limited literary output, she has received wide recognition for the quality of her fiction and for the importance of her contributions to the feminist movement.

WEB: Further research this author with LitLinks at bedfordstmartins.com/approachinglit.

MICHAEL ONDAATJE (b. 1943) was born in Colombo, Sri Lanka. He moved at age eleven to England and to Canada in 1962, where he earned a B.A. at the University of Toronto and an M.A. at Queens University. He has written more than a dozen collections of poetry, twice winning the Governor General's award, a memoir, several films, and four novels, the best known of which is *The English Patient* (1992), which shared the Booker Prize and was later made into an Academy Award–winning film. Ondaatje has also edited several anthologies, among them collections of Canadian short stories by Canadian writers, and he and his wife, novelist Linda Spalding, edit the literary magazine *Brick*. He began his teaching career at the University of Western Ontario, London, and since 1971 has been a member of the Department of English at Glendon College, York University, in Toronto.

WEB: Further research this author with LitLinks at bedfordstmartins.com/approachinglit.

SIMON J. ORTIZ (b. 1941) was born and raised in the Acoma Pueblo Community in Albuquerque. He received his early education from the Bureau of Indian Affairs school on the Acoma reservation, later attending the University of New Mexico and completing his M.F.A. at the University of Iowa, where he was a part of the International Writing Program. Unlike most Native American contemporary writers, Ortiz is a full-blooded Native American, and his first language is Keresan. By learning English, he found a way to communicate with those outside his immediate culture. His poetry explores the significance of individual origins and journeys, which he sees as forming a vital link in the continuity of life. His many writing accomplishments include poems, short stories, essays, and children's books. Ortiz has taught Native American literature and creative writing at San Diego State University, Navajo Community College, Marin College, the Institute for the Arts of the American Indian, and the University of New Mexico. He is currently a faculty member at the University of Toronto.

WEB: Further research this author with LitLinks at bedfordstmartins.com/approachinglit.

JUDITH ORTIZ COFER (b. 1952) — See page 1285.

WILFRED OWEN (1893–1918) was born in Oswestry, Shropshire, and went to school at Birkenhead Institute and Shrewsbury Technical School. He studied at London University but was forced to withdraw for financial reasons. After that he went to Dunsden, Oxfordshire, as a vicar's assistant. At Dunsden, Owen grew disaffected with the church and left to teach in France. He enlisted in 1915 and six months later was hospitalized in Edinburgh, where he met Siegfried Sassoon, whose war poems had just been published.

Owen was sent back to the front and was killed one week before the armistice. He is the most widely recognized of the "war poets," a group of World War I writers who brought the realism of war into poetry.

WEB: Further research this author with LitLinks at bedfordstmartins.com/approachinglit.

CD-ROM: Research this author in depth with cultural documents and multimedia resources on LiterActive.

RICARDO PAU-LLOSA (b. 1954) was born in Havana, Cuba, and emigrated to the United States with his family at the age of six. He is the author of five books of poems, including *Cuba* (1993), *Vereda Tropical* (1998), and *The Mastery Impulse* (2002). He is also known as a writer of short fiction. An internationally renowned art critic, he has written extensively on the visual arts, specializing in twentieth-century Latin American painting and sculpture. He lives in Coral Gables, Florida.

WEB: Further research this author with LitLinks at bedfordstmartins.com/approachinglit.

OCTAVIO PAZ (1914–1998) was born in Mexico City. His grandfather was a novelist and his father worked as a secretary to Emilio Zapata. When Zapata was driven into retreat and assassinated, the family lived in exile in the United States for a short time. After they returned to Mexico, Paz studied law and literature at the National University but his ambition had always been to be a poet. Encouraged by PABLO NERUDA, he began to write. After his first collection, *Luna Silvestre* (1933), he went on to publish over forty books. An essayist, diplomat, and cultural historian as well as a poet, he was Mexico's foremost writer of the twentieth century. His most famous prose work, *El laberinto de la soledad* (*The Labyrinth of Solitude*), which explores the Mexican psyche, was published in 1961. In 1990, he won the Nobel Prize for Literature, the first for a writer from Mexico.

WEB: Further research this author with LitLinks at bedfordstmartins.com/approachinglit.

GUSTAVO PÉREZ FIRMAT (b. 1949) was born in Cuba and raised in Miami and attended Miami-Dade Community College and the University of Miami. He earned his Ph.D. in comparative literature from the University of

Michigan and taught at Duke University from 1978 to 1999. He was named Duke University Scholar/Teacher of the Year in 1995. Currently the David Feinson Professor of Humanities at Columbia University, he is the author of several books of literary and cultural criticism, four collections of poetry, a novel, and a memoir. His study of Cuban American culture, *Life on the Hyphen,* was awarded the Eugene M. Kayden University Press National Book Award for 1994. He divides his time between New York City and Chapel Hill, North Carolina, where he lives with his wife and two children.

WEB: Further research this author with LitLinks at bedfordstmartins.com/approachinglit.

MARGE PIERCY (b. 1936) was born in working-class Detroit and studied at the University of Michigan and Northwestern University. She has published fourteen books of poetry, fifteen novels, and a collection of essays on poetry, *Parti-Colored Blocks for a Quilt* (1982). Much of her work deals with both subtle and blatant forms of oppression of women.

WEB: Further research this author with LitLinks at bedfordstmartins.com/approachinglit.

WANG PING (b. 1957) received her B.A. from Beijing University and came to the United States in 1985. She earned a Ph.D. at New York University. Ping writes not only poetry but also short stories, novels, essays, and nonfiction, and she has served as an anthology editor and translator. Her work often reveals how speaking two different languages can create very different experiences of the world.

WEB: Further research this author with LitLinks at bedfordstmartins.com/approachinglit.

ROBERT PINSKY (b. 1940) was born in Long Branch, New Jersey. He is the author of six books of poetry, including *The Figured Wheel: New and Collected Poems 1966-1996* (1996), which won the 1997 Lenore Marshall Poetry Prize and was a Pulitzer Prize nominee. He has also published four books of criticism, two books of translation, and a computer novel, *Mindwheel* (1984). In 1999 he co-edited with Maggie Dietz *Americans' Favorite Poems: The Favorite Poem Project Anthology.* He is currently poetry editor of the weekly Internet magazine *Slate.* He teaches in the grad-

uate writing program at Boston University, and in 1997 he was named Poet Laureate Consultant in Poetry at the Library of Congress. He lives in Newton Corner, Massachusetts.

WEB: Further research this author with LitLinks at bedfordstmartins.com/approachinglit.

SYLVIA PLATH (1932-1963) grew up in a middle-class family in Boston and showed early promise as a writer, having stories and poems published in magazines such as *Seventeen* while she was in high school. As a student at Smith College, she was selected for an internship at *Mademoiselle* magazine and spent a month working in New York in the summer of 1953. Upon her return home, she suffered a serious breakdown and attempted suicide, was institutionalized, and then returned to Smith College for her senior year in 1954. She received a Fulbright fellowship to study at Cambridge University in England, where she met poet Ted Hughes. They were married in 1956. They lived in the United States as well as England, and Plath studied under ROBERT LOWELL at Boston University. Her marriage to Hughes broke up in 1962, and from her letters and poems it appears that she was approaching another breakdown. On February 11, 1963, she committed suicide. Four books of poetry appeared during her lifetime, and her *Selected Poems* was published in 1985. The powerful, psychologically intense poetry for which she is best known (including "Daddy," p. 705) was written after 1960, influenced by the "confessional" style of Lowell.

WEB: Further research this author with LitLinks at bedfordstmartins.com/approachinglit.

CD-ROM: Research this author in depth with cultural documents and multimedia resources on *LiterActive.*

EDGAR ALLAN POE (1809-1849) was born in Boston. His parents were touring actors; both died before he was three years old, and he was taken into the home of John Allan, a prosperous merchant in Richmond, Virginia, and baptized Edgar Allan Poe. His childhood was uneventful, although he studied in England for five years (1815-1820). In 1826 he entered the University of Virginia but, because of gambling debts, stayed for only a year. He began to write and published a book of poems in 1827. He joined the army and gained an appointment to West Point, but was dismissed after six months for disobedience of orders. He turned to fiction writing and journalism to support himself. He began publishing stories and was appointed editor of the *Southern Literary Messenger* in Richmond, but his job was terminated after two years because of his drinking. He achieved success as an artist and editor in New York City (1837), then in Philadelphia (1838–1844), and again in New York (1844–1849), but failed to satisfy his employers and to secure a livelihood, and thus lived in or close to poverty his entire life. He is famous for his horror tales and is credited with inventing the detective story, as well as for writing poetry with a prominent use of rhythms, alliteration, and assonance that gives it a strongly musical quality.

WEB: Further research this author with LitLinks at bedfordstmartins.com/approachinglit.

CD-ROM: Research this author in depth with cultural documents and multimedia resources on *LiterActive*.

KATHERINE ANNE PORTER (1890–1980), a descendant of Daniel Boone, was born in Indian Creek, Texas. When she was two, her mother died; she was raised by her grandmother and attended convent schools. At sixteen, she ran away to get married, but left her husband a few years later to be an actress. She worked briefly as a reporter in Chicago and Denver. Between 1918 and 1921, she became involved in revolutionary politics and worked as a journalist and teacher in Mexico, the setting for several of her stories. She traveled in the late 1920s to Europe, settling in Paris during the early 1930s, and began publishing stories in magazines. Her first book, *Flowering Judas and Other Stories* (1930), won high praise. It was followed by *Noon Wine* (1937), *Pale Horse, Pale Rider: Three Short Novels* (1939), and numerous other books of essays, stories, and nonfiction. Her only novel, *Ship of Fools* (1962), on which she worked for twenty years, was published when she was seventy-two. Her *Collected Stories* (1965) won the Pulitzer Prize for Fiction and the National Book Award.

WEB: Further research this author with LitLinks at bedfordstmartins.com/approachinglit.

NAHID RACHLIN (b. 1946) was born in Iran. She is author of three novels, *Foreigner* (1978), *Married to a Stranger* (1983), and *The Heart's Desire* (1995), and a collection of short stories, *Veils* (1993). She currently lives in New York City and teaches creative writing at the New School for Social Research.

WEB: Further research this author with LitLinks at bedfordstmartins.com/approachinglit.

SIR WALTER RALEGH (1552–1618) was born in Hayes Barton, Devonshire, England. He was an undergraduate at Oxford University and read law at the Middle Temple in London, but he apparently did not complete either course of studies. He was a "Renaissance man," proficient in many fields: soldier, courtier, adventurer, colonist, student of science, historian, and poet. Ralegh was a royal favorite and, according to popular legend, once placed his cloak in the mud for Queen Elizabeth I. He undertook three expeditions to America and introduced potatoes and tobacco to Britain. In 1603, after the death of the Queen, he was arrested by James I, accused (unjustly) of treason for opposing James's succession to the throne. Ralegh's death sentence was commuted to life imprisonment in the Tower of London, where he focused on historical writing — including his *History of the World* — and scientific study. He was released in 1616 to search for gold in the Orinoco, but his expedition failed and he violated the terms of the mission by destroying a Spanish town. At the request of Spain, his death sentence was reinstated, and he was beheaded at Whitehall in 1618.

WEB: Further research this author with LitLinks at bedfordstmartins.com/approachinglit.

A. K. RAMANUJAN (1929–1993) was an internationally renowned poet and scholar as well as a professor of linguistics, anthropology, the history of religions, folklore, and literary studies. He was one of India's most published authors with an international recognition for expertise as a writer and translator. He wrote in English and Kannada and translated works from Tamil and Kannada into English and from English into Kannada. At the time of his death, he was the William H. Colvin Professor in South Asian Languages and Civilizations at the University of Chicago.

WEB: Further research this author with LitLinks at bedfordstmartins.com/approachinglit.

DUDLEY RANDALL (1914–2002) was born in Washington, D.C., but lived most of his life in Detroit. His first published poem appeared in the *Detroit Free Press* when he was thirteen. He worked for Ford Motor Company and then for the U.S. Postal Service and served in the South Pacific during World War II. He graduated from Wayne State University in 1949 and then from the library school at the University of Michigan. In 1965 Randall established the Broadside Press, one of the most important publishers of modern black poetry. "Ballad of Birmingham" (p. 708), written in response to the 1963 bombing of a church in which four African American girls were killed, has been set to music and recorded. It became an "anthem" for many in the civil rights movement.

WEB: Further research this author with LitLinks at bedfordstmartins.com/approachinglit.

DAHLIA RAVIKOVITCH (b. 1936) was born in Ramat Gan, a Tel Aviv suburb, in Israel, and after her father's death was sent to live in a kibbutz. She studied at the Hebrew University of Jerusalem and later worked as a journalist and high school teacher. Her first poems appeared in 1954. The author of several volumes of poetry, she has also published a collection of short stories and a number of children's books. Her language, rich inner life, and sensitivity have won her an enthusiastic readership in Israel and abroad as one of the most skilled and versatile Israeli poets. She has also contributed to the construction of a feminist consciousness in Israeli poetry. She has translated children's literature, including *Mary Poppins* and *Cinderella,* as well as the poetry of WILLIAM B. YEATS and T. S. ELIOT. She has received several literary awards, including the Bialik Prize and the 1990 Israel Prize.

WEB: Further research this author with LitLinks at bedfordstmartins.com/approachinglit.

ISHMAEL REED (b. 1938) was born in Chattanooga, Tennessee, and raised in Buffalo, New York, where he later attended the State University of New York, Buffalo. Reed has published nine novels, five collections of poetry, two plays, and four collections of essays. In 1971, Reed cofounded Yardbird Publishing Company. With Al Young he founded the influential magazine *Quilt.* Reed has read and lectured throughout the world. He has been a professor at the University of California, Berkeley, for more than twenty years. Reed's work is edgy, tough, outspoken, confrontational, funny, poignant, and told with a voice that is a central and dynamic presence.

WEB: Further research this author with LitLinks at bedfordstmartins.com/approachinglit.

ADRIENNE RICH (b. 1929) was born in Baltimore, the elder daughter of a forceful Jewish intellectual who encouraged and critiqued her writing. While she was at Radcliffe College in 1951, W. H. AUDEN selected her book *A Change of World* for the Yale Younger Poets Award. She became involved in radical politics, especially in the opposition to the Vietnam War, and taught inner-city minority youth. In the 1970s Rich became a feminist, freeing herself from her old models and becoming an influential figure in contemporary American literature. She is the author of nearly twenty volumes of poetry, including *Diving into the Wreck* (1973) and *Dark Fields of the Republic* (1995), and several books of nonfiction prose. In 1999 Rich received the Lifetime Achievement Award from the Lannan Foundation. Since 1984 she has lived in California.

WEB: Further research this author with LitLinks at bedfordstmartins.com/approachinglit.

ALBERTO RÍOS (b. 1952) was born to a Guatemalan father and an English mother in Nogales, Arizona, on the Mexican border. He earned a B.A. in English and one in psychology and an M.F.A. at the University of Arizona. In addition to seven books of poetry, he has published two collections of short stories. His work often fuses realism, surrealism, and magical realism, as exemplified by "Nani" (p. 713). Since 1994 he has been Regents Professor of English at Arizona State University, where he has taught since 1982. He lives in Chandler, Arizona.

WEB: Further research this author with LitLinks at bedfordstmartins.com/approachinglit.

EDWIN ARLINGTON ROBINSON (1869–1935) was born in Head Tide, Maine, and grew up in the equally provincial Maine town of Gardiner, the setting for much of his poetry. He was forced to leave Harvard University after two years because of his family's financial difficulties. He published his first two books of poetry in 1896 and 1897 ("Richard Cory" [p. 552] appeared in the latter). For the next quarter-century Robinson chose to live in poverty and write his poetry, supporting himself through temporary jobs and charity from friends. President Theodore Roosevelt, at the urging of his son Kermit, used his influence to get Robinson a sinecure in the New York Custom House in 1905, giving him time to write. He published numerous books of mediocre poetry in the next decade. The tide turned for him with *The Man against the Sky* (1916); the numerous volumes that followed received high praise and sold well. He was awarded three Pulitzer Prizes: for *Collected Poems* (1921), *The Man Who Died Twice* (1924), and *Tristram* (1927). Robinson was the first major American poet of the twentieth century, unique in that he devoted his life to poetry and willingly paid the price in poverty and obscurity.

WEB: Further research this author with LitLinks at bedfordstmartins.com/approachinglit.

LUIS RODRIGUEZ (b. 1954) was born in El Paso, Texas, but grew up in Watts and East Los Angeles. By eleven, he was already involved in gangs, and by the time he was eighteen he had lost twenty-five friends to gang fights and killings. He now works with gangs as a peacemaker. From this life came his best-selling memoir *Always Running: La Vida Loca, Gang Days in L.A.* (1993), winner of the Carl Sandburg Award from the Friends of the Chicago Library Association. Rodriguez now lives in Chicago where he is also a journalist and critic, his work appearing in a wide variety of national magazines. He is the founding director of Tia Chucha Press, publisher of writers of socially conscious works. Rodriguez has published numerous books in memoir, fiction, nonfiction, children's literature, and poetry. His work shows great understanding and reveals his experiences at the heart of violent urban conflict in a strong and compassionate voice.

WEB: Further research this author with LitLinks at bedfordstmartins.com/approachinglit.

THEODORE ROETHKE (1908–1963) was the son of a commercial greenhouse operator in Saginaw, Michigan. As a child, he spent much time in the greenhouse, and the impressions of nature he formed there later influenced the subjects and imagery of his verse. Roethke graduated from the University of Michigan and studied at Harvard University. Although he published only eight books of poetry, they were held in high regard by critics, some of whom considered him among the best poets of his generation. *The Waking* was awarded the Pulitzer Prize in 1954; *Words for the Wind* (1958) received the Bollingen Prize and the National Book Award. He taught at many colleges and universities and gained a reputation as an exceptional teacher of poetry writing, though his career was interrupted several times by serious mental breakdowns.

WEB: Further research this author with LitLinks at bedfordstmartins.com/approachinglit.

CD-ROM: Research this author in depth with cultural documents and multimedia resources on *LiterActive.*

WENDY ROSE (b. 1948) was born Bronwen Elizabeth Edwards in Oakland, California, of Hopi and Mewok ancestry. As a teenager, she dropped out of high school and became connected with the bohemian scene in San Francisco. Her experiences in the city and the struggle in finding her identity within her mixed lineage would be major influences on her poetry. Rose attended Costa College and the University of California, Berkeley, and completed a Ph.D. in anthropology. The author of a dozen volumes of poetry, she has taught American Indian studies at University of California, Berkeley, and California State University, Fresno, as well as being coordinator of American Indian studies at Fresno City College. Rose's poems often combine the world of the contemporary native culture with an elegiac voice, a quiet sense of reverence and loss.

WEB: Further research this author with LitLinks at bedfordstmartins.com/approachinglit.

SALMAN RUSHDIE (b. 1947) was born in Bombay, India, to a middle-class Muslim family. His paternal grandfather was an Urdu poet and his father a Cambridge-educated businessman. At fourteen Rushdie was sent to Rugby School in England. In 1964 his parents moved to Karachi, Pakistan, reluctantly joining the Muslim exodus from India. After graduating in 1968 from King's College, Cambridge, where he read history, he worked for a time in television in Pakistan, then as a freelance advertising copywriter in London from 1971 to 1981. His first novel, *Grimus* (1975), a work of fantastical science fiction drawing on pre-Islamic Persian mythology, anticipates the magic realism that informs much of his work. His second novel, *Midnight's Children* (1981), brought him international recognition; it won the prestigious Booker Prize for fiction and in 1993 was judged to have been the "Booker of Bookers," the best novel to have won the Booker Prize for fiction in the award's twenty-five year history. His fourth novel, *The Satanic Verses* (1988), which won the Whitbread Award, proved highly controversial. Many Muslims regarded the character modeled on the Prophet Muhammad as blasphemous, and the former Iranian spiritual leader Ayatollah Khomeini called on all zealous Muslims to execute the writer and the publishers of the book. Since then, Rushdie has lived in hiding, first in London and now in New York, but has continued to write and publish.

WEB: Further research this author with LitLinks at bedfordstmartins.com/approachinglit.

BENJAMIN ALIRE SÁENZ (b. 1954) is the author of three books of poetry, *Calendar of Dust* (1991), *Dark and Perfect Angels* (1996), and *Elegies in Blue* (2002); two novels, *Carry Me Like Water* (1995) and *House of Forgetting* (1998); and a collection of stories, *Flowers for the Broken* (1992). He also writes books for children. He is assistant professor of English at the University of Texas, El Paso.

WEB: Further research this author with LitLinks at bedfordstmartins.com/approachinglit.

SONIA SANCHEZ (b. 1934) was born Wilsonia Driver in Birmingham, Alabama. In 1943 she moved to Harlem with her sister to live with their father and his third wife. She earned a B.A. in political science from Hunter College in 1955 and studied poetry writing with Louise Bogan at New York University. In the 1960s she became actively involved in the social movements of the times, and she has continued to be a voice for social change. She has published more than a dozen books of poetry, many plays, and several books for children and has edited two anthologies of literature. She began teaching in the San Francisco area in 1965 and was a pioneer in developing black studies courses at what is now San Francisco State University, from 1968 to 1969. She was the first Presidential Fellow at Temple University, where she began teaching in 1977, and held the Laura Carnell Chair in English there until her retirement in 1999. She lives in Philadelphia.

WEB: Further research this author with LitLinks at bedfordstmartins.com/approachinglit.

MILCHA SANCHEZ-SCOTT (b. 1955) was born in Bali, the daughter of a Colombian father and a mother with Chinese, Indonesian, and Dutch ancestry. She grew up on a family ranch in San Marta, Colombia, but attended a convent boarding school near London, where she learned English. In 1969 her family moved to California, where Sanchez-Scott attended high school and the University of San Diego, majoring in philosophy. She worked at a series of jobs, including one as an actress in a Los Angeles Theatre Works' project at the women's prison in Chino. Encouraged to write a play based on her experiences working with immigrant families, she wrote *Latina*, which premiered in 1980. *Dog Lady* and *The Cuban Swimmer* (winner of a Le Compte de Nouy Foundation Award; see p. 890) were first produced in 1984. Sanchez-Scott went to New York to participate in the theater workshop of playwright Irene Fornés, where she wrote perhaps her best-known work to-date, *Roosters* (1988), which was made into a film in 1994 for which she wrote the screenplay. Her work often reflects the Latin American tradition of magic realism, known especially in the fiction of JORGE LUIS BORGES and GABRIEL GARCÍA MÁRQUEZ. She currently lives in southern California.

WEB: Further research this author with LitLinks at bedfordstmartins.com/approachinglit.

CHERYL SAVAGEAU (b. 1950) was born in central Massachusetts and grew up in an island neighborhood on Lake Quinsigamond. She is of mixed French Canadian and Abenaki heritage. She graduated from Clark University in 1978, where she began writing "by accident": she signed up for a poetry class through Continuing Education to finish her degree, and it turned out to be a writing class. She is the author of two books of poetry, *Home Country* (1992) and *Dirt Road Home* (1995). Her children's book, *Muskrat Will Be Swimming,* was named a 1996 Notable Book for Children by the Smithsonian. She worked for several years as a poet and storyteller in the schools through the Massachusetts Artist in Residence program and was a member of Wordcraft Circle of Native Writers and Storytellers, working as a mentor to apprentice native writers. She currently teaches in the Native American Studies Department at the University of New Mexico in Albuquerque.

WEB: Further research this author with LitLinks at bedfordstmartins.com/approachinglit.

VIJAY SESHADRI (b. 1954) was born in Bangalore, India, and came to the United States at the age of five. He grew up in Columbus, Ohio, and has lived in many parts of the country, including the Northwest, where he spent five years working in the fishing industry, and the Upper West Side in New York City. He earned his B.A. degree from Oberlin College and his M.F.A. from Columbia University. His poems, essays, and reviews have appeared in many literary magazines and journals. He has published two collections of poetry, the more recent of which — *The Long Meadow* (2004) — won the James Laughlin Award. He currently teaches poetry and nonfiction writing at Sarah Lawrence College and lives in Brooklyn with his wife and son.

WEB: Further research this author with LitLinks at bedfordstmartins.com/approachinglit.

WILLIAM SHAKESPEARE (1564–1616) was born in Stratford-upon-Avon, England, where his father was a glovemaker and bailiff, and presumably went to grammar school there. He married Anne Hathaway in 1582, and sometime before 1592 he left for London to work as a playwright and actor. Shakespeare joined the Lord Chamberlain's Men (later the King's

Men), an acting company for which he wrote thirty-five plays, before retiring to Stratford around 1612. In addition to being a skillful dramatist, he was perhaps the finest lyric poet of his day, as exemplified by songs scattered through his plays, two early nondramatic poems (*Venus and Adonis* and *The Rape of Lucrece*), and the sonnet sequence expected of all noteworthy writers in the Elizabethan age. Shakespeare's sonnets were probably written in the 1590s, though not published until 1609.

WEB: Further research this author with LitLinks at bedfordstmartins.com/approachinglit.

CD-ROM: Research this author in depth with cultural documents and multimedia resources on *LiterActive.*

PERCY BYSSHE SHELLEY (1792–1822) was born into a wealthy aristocratic family in Sussex County, England. He was educated at Eton, then went on to Oxford University, but was expelled after six months for writing a defense of atheism, the first price he would pay for his nonconformity and radical (for his time) commitment to social justice. The following year he eloped with Harriet Westbrook, daughter of a tavern keeper, despite his belief that marriage was a tyrannical and degrading social institution (she was sixteen, he eighteen). He became a disciple of the radical social philosopher William Godwin, fell in love with Godwin's daughter, Mary Wollstonecraft Godwin (later the author of *Frankenstein*), and went to live with her in France. Two years later, after Harriet committed suicide, Shelley and Godwin married and moved to Italy, where they shifted about restlessly and Shelley was generally short on money and in poor health. Under such trying circumstances, he wrote his greatest works. He died at age thirty, when the boat he was in was overturned by a sudden storm.

WEB: Further research this author with LitLinks at bedfordstmartins.com/approachinglit.

MASAOKA SHIKI (1867–1902) was born in Matsuyama as the son of a low-ranking samurai, who died when Masaoka was five. His mother, Yae, was a teacher. Masaoka studied classic Japanese literature at the Imperial University and began to write poetry in 1885. After withdrawing from the university in 1892, he was a haiku editor for the newspaper *Nippon*. While covering the Chinese-Japanese War as a war correspondent in 1894–1895, he contracted tuberculosis and remained an invalid for much of his life, devoting his time to the writing of haiku and waka (or tanka). In 1892 he started his reform of the haiku, which at that time was considered incapable of expressing the complexities of modern life. Masaoka advocated a realistic, descriptive style, which he regarded as the original spirit of Japanese verse, and his poetic treatises greatly influenced the Japanese literary world in defining modern Japanese modes of expression. His sickroom, when he was bound to bed, became a meeting place for his friends and followers, who gathered there to discuss literature. He died in Tokyo a few weeks before his thirty-fifth birthday.

WEB: Further research this author with LitLinks at bedfordstmartins.com/approachinglit.

KAZUKO SHIRAISHI (b. 1931) was born in Vancouver, Canada, and emigrated to Japan before the beginning of World War II. He has lived in Tokyo since then. His first collection of poems, translated as *The City Where Eggs Rained* (1951), was followed by thirty additional collections of poems and stories. His love of jazz is apparent in much of his work. "Dedicated to the Late John Coltrane" (p. 724), like all of the author's poems, was written in Japanese. The translation included here is by Ikuko Atsumi, John Solt, Carol Tinker, Yasuyo Morita, and Kenneth Rexroth.

WEB: Further research this author with LitLinks at bedfordstmartins.com/approachinglit.

LESLIE MARMON SILKO (b. 1948) was born in Albuquerque of mixed Pueblo, Mexican, and white ancestry and grew up on the Laguna Pueblo Reservation in New Mexico. She earned her B.A. with honors from the University of New Mexico. In a long and productive writing career (she was already writing stories in elementary school), she has published poetry, novels, short stories, essays, letters, and film scripts. She taught creative writing first at the University of New Mexico and later at the University of Arizona. She has been named a Living Cultural Treasure by the New Mexico Humanities Council and has received

the Native Writers' Circle of the Americas Lifetime Achievement Award. Her work is a graphic telling of the life of native peoples, maintaining its rich spiritual heritage while exposing the terrible consequences of European domination. Silko lives today on a ranch in the mountains a few miles northwest of Tucson.

WEB: Further research this author with LitLinks at bedfordstmartins.com/approachinglit.

CHARLES SIMIC (b. 1938) was born in Belgrade, Yugoslavia. In 1953 he, his mother, and his brother joined his father in Chicago, where he lived until 1958. His first poems were published in 1959, when he was twenty-one. In 1961 he was drafted into the U.S. Army, and in 1966 he earned his B.A. from New York University. His first book of poems, *What the Grass Says*, was published in 1967. Since then he has published more than sixty books of poetry, translations, and essays, including *The World Doesn't End: Prose Poems* (1990), for which he received the Pulitzer Prize for Poetry. Since 1973 he has lived in New Hampshire, where he is a professor of English at the University of New Hampshire.

WEB: Further research this author with LitLinks at bedfordstmartins.com/approachinglit.

CATHY SONG (b. 1955) was born in Hawaii and lived in the small town of Wahiawa on Oahu. She left Hawaii for the East Coast, studying at Wellesley College and then at Boston University. Her first book, *Picture Bride*, was chosen by Richard Hugo for the Yale Series of Younger Poets in 1982. Since then she has published three other books of poetry. She lives in Honolulu and teaches at the University of Hawaii, Manoa.

WEB: Further research this author with LitLinks at bedfordstmartins.com/approachinglit.

SOPHOCLES (496–406 B.C.E.), born the son of a wealthy merchant in Athens, enjoyed the advantages of the thriving Greek empire. He studied all of the arts. By the age of sixteen, he was known for his beauty and grace and was chosen to lead a choir of boys at a celebration of the victory of Salamis. He served as a statesman, general, treasurer, and priest as well as, with Aeschylus and Euripides, one of the three major authors of Greek tragedy. He was an accomplished actor and performed in many of his own plays. Fragments indicate that he wrote over 120 plays, of which only 7 are extant. His plays introduced several innovations to Greek theater, particularly adding a third actor, which allowed for more dialogue and greater complexity of action and reduced the role of the chorus. He also changed the form of drama. Aeschylus had used three tragedies to tell a single story; Sophocles made each play a complete and independent work, which required greater compression of action and resulted in greater dramatic intensity.

WEB: Further research this author with LitLinks at bedfordstmartins.com/approachinglit.

CD-ROM: Research this author in depth with cultural documents and multimedia resources on *LiterActive.*

GARY SOTO (b. 1952) grew up in Fresno, California. He earned his B.A. from California State University, Fresno, and his M.F.A. from the University of California, Irvine. He worked his way through college at jobs such as picking grapes and chopping beets. Much of his poetry comes out of and reflects his working background, that of migrant workers and tenant farmers in the fields of southern California, and provides glimpses into the lives of families in the barrio. Soto's language comes from earthy, gritty, raw everyday American speech. His first book, *The Elements of San Joaquin,* won the 1976 United States Award from the International Poetry Forum. He has published ten collections of poetry, two novels, four essay collections, and numerous young adult and children's books and has edited three anthologies. He lives in Berkeley, California.

WEB: Further research this author with LitLinks at bedfordstmartins.com/approachinglit.

CD-ROM: Research this author in depth with cultural documents and multimedia resources on *LiterActive.*

WOLE SOYINKA (b. 1934), one of contemporary Africa's greatest writers, was born Akinwande Oluwole Soyinka at Abeokuta, near Ibadan in western Nigeria, of Yoruba heritage. He studied at University College, Ibadan, then at Leeds University in England,

where he earned his doctorate. He worked for several years in London theaters where he wrote his first two mature plays, staged successfully in London and Ibadan. He returned to Nigeria and produced a new play, *A Dance of the Forests* (1964), to celebrate that nation's independence. It envisioned a "New Africa" that would escape its colonial past by grafting the technical advances of the present onto the stock of its own ancient traditions, but the play was greeted with hostility. During the civil war in Nigeria, Soyinka appealed in an article for a cease-fire. For this he was arrested in 1967, accused of conspiring with the Biafra rebels, and held in solitary confinement as a political prisoner for two years. Following his release in 1969, after an intense international campaign, Soyinka went into voluntary exile and has lived outside of Nigeria most of the time since then. Africa's most distinguished playwright, he has written many plays, both for the theater and for radio production, as well as poetry, prose fiction, and several autobiographical works. He became, in 1986, the first black African to be awarded the Nobel Prize for Literature.

WEB: Further research this author with LitLinks at bedfordstmartins.com/approachinglit.

EDMUND SPENSER (1552–1599), a contemporary of WILLIAM SHAKESPEARE, was the greatest English nondramatic poet of his time. Best known for his romantic and national epic *The Faerie Queene,* Spenser wrote poems of a number of other types as well and was important as an innovator in metrics and forms (as in his development of the special form of sonnet and unique stanza form that bear his name—see the Glossary of Literary Terms, p. 1517). The sonnet included in this anthology, beginning "One day I wrote her name upon the strand" (p. 735), is number 75 in *Amoretti,* a sequence of sonnets about a courtship addressed to a woman named Elizabeth, probably Elizabeth Boyle, who became his second wife.

WEB: Further research this author with LitLinks at bedfordstmartins.com/approachinglit.

WILLIAM STAFFORD (1914–1995) was born in Hutchinson, Kansas, and studied at the University of Kansas and then at the University of Iowa Writers' Workshop. In between, he was a conscientious objector during World War II and worked in labor camps. In 1948 Stafford moved to Oregon, where he taught at Lewis and Clark College until he retired in 1980. His first major collection of poems, *Traveling through the Dark* (1962), was published when Stafford was forty-eight. It won the National Book Award in 1963. He went on to publish more than sixty-five volumes of poetry and prose and came to be known as a very influential teacher of poetry. From 1970 to 1971 he was Consultant in Poetry at the Library of Congress.

WEB: Further research this author with LitLinks at bedfordstmartins.com/approachinglit.

WALLACE STEVENS (1879–1955) was born in Reading, Pennsylvania, and attended Harvard University for three years. He tried journalism and then attended New York University Law School, after which he worked as a legal consultant. He spent most of his life working as an executive for the Hartford Accident and Indemnity Company, spending his evenings writing some of the most imaginative and influential poetry of his time. Although now considered one of the major American poets of the century, he did not receive widespread recognition until the publication of his *Collected Poems* just a year before his death.

WEB: Further research this author with LitLinks at bedfordstmartins.com/approachinglit.

VIRGIL SUÁREZ (b. 1962) was born in Havana, Cuba. Eight years later he left with his parents for Spain, where they lived until they came to the United States in 1974. He received his B.A. from California State University, Long Beach, and his M.F.A. from Louisiana State University. He is the author of five novels and five collections of poetry, a collection of short fiction, and a memoir titled *Spared Angola: Memories from a Cuban-American Childhood* (1997). He is editor or coeditor of several important anthologies, including *Iguana Dreams: New Latino Fiction* (1993), the first anthology of Cuban American writers, and *Paper Dance: 55 Latino Poets* (2000), a collection of contemporary Latino poetry. His work has been included in hundreds of magazines, journals, and anthologies. Presently he is a professor of creative writing at Florida State University.

WEB: Further research this author with LitLinks at bedfordstmartins.com/approachinglit.

SEKOU SUNDIATA (b. 1948) was born and raised in Harlem. His work is deeply influenced by the music, poetry, and oral traditions of African American culture. A self-proclaimed radical in the 1970s, for the past several decades he has used poetry to comment on the life and times of our culture. His work, which encompasses print, performance, music, and theater, has received praise for its fusion of soul, jazz, and hip-hop grooves with political insight, humor, and rhythmic speech. He regularly records and performs on tour with artists such as Craig Harris and Vernon Reid.

WEB: Further research this author with LitLinks at bedfordstmartins.com/approachinglit.

JONATHAN SWIFT (1667–1745) was born in Ireland of English parents and educated at Kilkenny College and Trinity College, Dublin. He worked in England for a decade as a private secretary and for four years as a political writer, but spent the rest of his life in Ireland as Dean of St. Patrick's Cathedral in Dublin. Although he is best known for his satires in prose (such as *Gulliver's Travels* and "A Modest Proposal"), Swift's original ambition was to be a poet, and he wrote occasional verse throughout his life.

WEB: Further research this author with LitLinks at bedfordstmartins.com/approachinglit.

WISLAWA SZYMBORSKA (b. 1923), born in Bnin (now a part of Kórnik) in western Poland, has lived since 1931 in Krakow, where she studied Polish literature and sociology at Jagiellonian University. From 1953 to 1981 she worked as poetry editor and columnist for the Kraków literary weekly *Zycie Literackie*, for which she wrote a series of essays, "Lektury nadobowiazkowe," from which four collections have been published as books. She has published sixteen books of poetry and her poems have been translated and published in book form. She was awarded the Nobel Prize for Literature in 1996, for "poetry that with ironic precision allows the historical and biological context to come to light in fragments of human reality."

WEB: Further research this author with LitLinks at bedfordstmartins.com/approachinglit.

MARY TALL MOUNTAIN (1918–1994) was born Mary Demonski in the interior of Alaska in Nilato. Her mother was a Koyukon-Athabaskan and her father a Scotch-Irish signal corpsman. Her mother died when she was six, and she was the first child from her village to be adopted by an Anglo-American couple. Tall Mountain's poetry was fully influenced by her spiritual connections to her birthplace, her family, and her native culture. She began every day by talking with her late grandmother, mother, and two aunts. She claimed both a Christian faith and "the ritual of the Indian. We have only one God — and we know that — but we follow two paths. Why not? Why not worship Him twice. Him or Her." The Mary Tall Mountain Circle in San Francisco produces and distributes her work and her support for Native American and Tenderloin writers.

WEB: Further research this author with LitLinks at bedfordstmartins.com/approachinglit.

AMY TAN (b. 1952) was born in Oakland, California. Her father had been educated as an engineer in Beijing; her mother left China in 1949, just before the Communist revolution. After her father's death, Tan and her mother lived in Switzerland, where Tan attended high school. She received her B.A. and M.A. in English and linguistics from San Jose State University, took a job as a language development consultant to the Alameda County Association for Retarded Citizens, and later directed a training project for developmentally disabled children. She became a highly successful freelance business writer specializing in corporate communications for such companies as AT&T, IBM, and Pacific Bell, but she found the work unsatisfying and began writing fiction. A visit to China with her mother in 1987, and meeting relatives there, gave her the realization, as she put it, that "I belonged to my family and my family belonged to China." Inspired by LOUISE ERDRICH's Love Medicine (1986), she began to write stories about her own minority culture. A literary agent read one of them and secured her an advance that allowed her to write full time, resulting in her very successful first book, The Joy Luck Club (1989). She has gone on to write three more novels, two children's books, and a collection of essays, The Opposite of Fate: A Book of Musings (2003). She is also the lead singer for the Rock Bottom Remainders, a rock band made up of fellow writers who make select appearances at charities and benefits that support free-speech issues.

WEB: Further research this author with LitLinks at bedfordstmartins.com/approachinglit.

CD-ROM: Research this author in depth with cultural documents and multimedia resources on LiterActive.

ALFRED, LORD TENNYSON (1809–1892) was born in Somersby, Lincolnshire, and grew up there in the tense atmosphere of his unhappy father's rectory. He went to Trinity College, Cambridge, but was forced to leave because of family and financial problems, so he returned home to study and practice the craft of poetry. His early volumes, published in 1830 and 1832, received bad reviews, but his In Memoriam (1850), an elegy on his close friend Arthur Hallam, who died of a brain seizure, won acclaim. He was unquestionably the most popular poet of his time (the "poet of the people") and arguably the greatest of the Victorian poets. He succeeded WILLIAM WORDSWORTH as poet laureate, a position he held from 1850 until his death.

WEB: Further research this author with LitLinks at bedfordstmartins.com/approachinglit.

DYLAN THOMAS (1914–1953) was born in Swansea, Wales, and after grammar school became a journalist. He worked as a writer for the rest of his life. His first book of poetry, Eighteen Poems, appeared in 1934 and was followed by Twenty-five Poems (1936), Deaths and Entrances (1946), and Collected Poems (1952). His poems are often rich in textured rhythms and images. He also wrote prose, chiefly short stories collectively appearing as Portrait of the Artist as a Young Dog (1940), and a number of film scripts and radio plays. His most famous work, Under Milk Wood, written as a play for voices, was first performed in New York on May 14, 1953. Thomas's radio broadcasts and his lecture tours and poetry readings in the United States brought him fame and popularity. Alcoholism contributed to his early death in 1953.

WEB: Further research this author with LitLinks at bedfordstmartins.com/approachinglit.

CD-ROM: Research this author in depth with cultural documents and multimedia resources on *LiterActive.*

JEAN TOOMER (1894–1967) was born in Washington, D.C., of mixed French, Dutch, Welsh, Negro, German, Jewish, and Indian blood. Although he passed for white during certain periods of his life, he was raised in a predominantly black community and attended black high schools. He began college at the University of Wisconsin but transferred to the College of the City of New York. He spent several years publishing poems and stories in small magazines. In 1921 he took a teaching job in Georgia and remained there four months; the experience inspired *Cane* (1923), a book of prose poetry describing the Georgian people and landscape that became a central work of the Harlem Renaissance. He later experimented in communal living and both studied and tried to promulgate the ideas of the Russian mystic George Gurdjieff and later of Quakerism. From 1950 on he published no literary works and began withdrawing from public life.

WEB: Further research this author with LitLinks at bedfordstmartins.com/approachinglit.

QUINCY TROUPE (b. 1943) was born in New York City and grew up in St. Louis, Missouri. He is the author of fourteen books, including seven volumes of poetry, the latest of which, *Transcircularities: New and Selected Poems* (2002), received the Milt Kessler Award for 2003 and was a finalist for the Paterson Poetry Prize. He is recipient of two American Book Awards, for his collection of poetry *Snake-Back Solos* (1980) and his nonfiction book *Miles the Autobiography* (1989). In 1991 he received the prestigious Peabody Award for writing and coproducing the seven-part Miles Davis Radio Project aired on National Public Radio in 1990. Troupe has taught at UCLA, Ohio University, the College of Staten Island (CUNY), Columbia University (in the Graduate Writing Program), and the University of California, San Diego. He is now professor emeritus of Creative Writing and American and Caribbean Literature at UCSD. He is the founding editorial director for *Code* magazine and former artistic director of "Arts on the Cutting Edge," a reading and performance se-

ries at the Museum of Contemporary Art, San Diego. He was the first official poet laureate of the state of California, appointed to the post in 2002 by Governor Gray Davis.

WEB: Further research this author with LitLinks at bedfordstmartins.com/approachinglit.

JOHN UPDIKE (b. 1932) was born in Reading, Pennsylvania, but grew up in the small nearby city of Shillington. He earned his B.A. at Harvard University where he contributed to and later edited the *Harvard Lampoon.* He spent 1954–1955 at the Ruskin School of Drawing and Fine Arts in Oxford, England, then worked at the *New Yorker* until 1957 when he left to become a full-time writer. In 1959 he published his first book of stories, *The Same Door,* and his first novel, *The Poorhouse Fair,* and he moved from New York City to Massachusetts, where he has lived most of the time since. A prolific writer, Updike has published over fifty books — novels, collections of poems, short stories, essays, criticism, and a memoir. He has received numerous awards, including the National Medal of Art and the National Medal for the Humanities. Two of his novels, *Rabbit Is Rich* (1981) and *Rabbit at Rest* (1990), have won Pulitzer Prizes.

WEB: Further research this author with LitLinks at bedfordstmartins.com/approachinglit.

CD-ROM: Research this author in depth with cultural documents and multimedia resources on *LiterActive.*

LUIS VALDEZ (b. 1940) was born and raised in Delano, California, the son of farmworkers. He graduated from San Diego State University in 1964 with a major in drama and joined the San Francisco Mime Troupe, an important experimental theater company. In 1965 he formed El Teatro Campesino ("The Farmworkers' Theater"), which became an important Chicago theater company, performing in the Southwest and touring in other parts of the United States and in Europe. El Teatro Campesino produced one-act plays in two unique forms — *actos* (satirical plays showing the oppression of fieldworkers) and *mitos* (poetic, lyrical plays on Chicano life) — often without stage, script, or props. Valdez has written, cowritten, and directed many plays depicting the Hispanic experience. His *Zoot Suit* (1978), based on the "zoot suit riots" in Los Angeles, was the first play by a Chicano to be produced on Broadway; in 1982 it was adapted into a film that was directed by Valdez. He also directed the movie *La Bamba* in 1987.

WEB: Further research this author with LitLinks at bedfordstmartins.com/approachinglit.

HELENA MARÍA VIRAMONTES (b. 1954) was born and raised in East Los Angeles. She began writing poetry and fiction at Immaculate Heart College, from which she earned her B.A. in 1975 (one of five Chicanas in her class). In the next few years, several of her stories won prizes. She entered the M.F.A. program at the University of California, Irvine, in 1981, and completed her degree in 1994, after many years of successful writing. She has published two collections of short stories and two novels, and she is coeditor, with Maria Herrera-Sobek, of two anthologies, *Chicana Creativity and Criticism: Charting New Frontiers in American Literature* (1988) and *Chicana (W)rites: On Word and Film* (1995). Her stories are known for their vivid depictions of Chicano culture and especially of the struggles and sufferings of Chicana women. She is an associate professor of English at Cornell University.

WEB: Further research this author with LitLinks at bedfordstmartins.com/approachinglit.

GERALD VIZENOR (b. 1934) was born in Minnesota. He attended New York University for one year and then transferred to the University of Minnesota, where he earned his B.A. in 1960. He has done graduate studies at the University of Minnesota and Harvard University. He has taught at several colleges and universities in the Midwest and California. Vizenor currently is professor of Native American studies at the University of California, Berkeley. A member of the Chippewa tribe, he has been a major figure in both the literature and scholarship of Native Americans. In addition to publishing numerous books of poetry and fiction, he is the author of *Earthdrivers: Narratives on Tribal Descent* (1981) and *The People Named the Chippewa: Narrative Histories* (1985). His novel *Griever: An American Monkey King in China* won the Fiction Collective Prize for 1986. He also published a collection of original haiku, *Matsushima: Pine Island* (1984). Vizenor's work

reflects his studied relationship to the natural world as he opens himself to the influences of both his Chippewa heritage and his study of Japanese culture and haiku.

WEB: Further research this author with LitLinks at bedfordstmartins.com/approachinglit.

DEREK WALCOTT (b. 1930), born on the eastern Caribbean island of St. Lucia, moves between the African heritage of his family and the English cultural heritage of his reading and education. Both of his parents were educators who immersed themselves in the arts. His early training was in painting, which, like his poetry, was influenced by his Methodist religious training. He attended St. Mary's College and the University of the West Indies in Jamaica. His first book, *25 Poems* (1948), appeared when he was eighteen, and he has published prolifically since then: nearly twenty books of poetry, more than twenty-five plays, and a book of nonfiction. His work, which explores both the isolation of the artist and regional identity, is known for blending Caribbean, English, and African traditions. He was awarded the Nobel Prize for Literature in 1992, the academy citing him for "a poetic oeuvre of great luminosity, sustained by a historical vision, the outcome of a multicultural achievement." He teaches creative writing at Boston University every fall and lives the rest of the year in St. Lucia.

WEB: Further research this author with LitLinks at bedfordstmartins.com/approachinglit.

ALICE WALKER (b. 1944) was born in Eatonton, Georgia. Her parents were sharecropper farmers. When she was eight, she lost sight in one eye when one of her older brothers accidentally shot her with a BB gun. She was valedictorian of her high school class. Encouraged by her teachers and her mother to go on to college, she attended Spelman College in Atlanta, a school for black women, for two years, and graduated from Sarah Lawrence College. From the mid-1960s to the mid-1970s, she lived in Tougaloo, Mississippi. She was active in the civil rights movement of the 1960s and remains an involved activist today. Her first book was a collection of poetry, *Once* (1968). She is a prolific writer, having gone on to publish numerous books of poetry, novels, short story collections, and books of essays. Her best known novel, *The Color Purple* (1982), won the American Book Award and the Pulitzer Prize for Fiction and was made into a motion picture directed by Steven Spielberg.

WEB: Further research this author with LitLinks at bedfordstmartins.com/approachinglit.

JAMES WELCH (1940–2003) was born in Browning, Montana. His father was a member of the Blackfoot tribe, his mother of the Gros Ventre tribe. He attended schools on the Blackfoot and Fort Belknap reservations and earned a degree from the University of Montana, where he studied under Richard Hugo. Welch published many books of poetry, fiction, and nonfiction. His hard, spare poems often evoke the bleakest side of contemporary Native American life. He received a Lifetime Achievement Award for Literature from the Native Writers' Circle in 1997.

WEB: Further research this author with LitLinks at bedfordstmartins.com/approachinglit.

ROBERTA HILL WHITEMAN (b. 1947), a member of the Oneida tribe, grew up around Oneida and Green Bay, Wisconsin. She earned a B.A. from the University of Wisconsin and an M.F.A. from the University of Montana. Her poems have appeared in many magazines and anthologies. Her three collections of poetry — *Star Quilt* (1984), *Your Fierce Resistance* (1993), and *Philadelphia Flowers* (1996) — have been illustrated by her husband, Ernest Whiteman, an Arapaho artist.

WEB: Further research this author with LitLinks at bedfordstmartins.com/approachinglit.

WALT WHITMAN (1819–1892) was born in rural Long Island, the son of a farmer and carpenter. He attended grammar school in Brooklyn and took his first job as a printer's devil for the *Long Island Patriot*. Attending the opera, dabbling in politics, participating in street life, and gaining experience as student, printer, reporter, writer, carpenter, farmer, seashore observer, and teacher provided the bedrock for his future poetic vision of an ideal society based on the realization of self. Although Whitman liked to portray himself as uncultured, he read widely in the King James Bible, SHAKESPEARE, Homer, Dante, Aeschylus, and SOPHOCLES. He worked for many years in the newspaper business and began writing poetry only in 1847. In 1855, at his own ex-

pense, Whitman published the first edition of *Leaves of Grass*, a thin volume of twelve long untitled poems. Written in a highly original and innovative free verse, influenced significantly by music and with a wide-ranging subject matter, the work seemed strange to most of the poet's contemporaries, but they did recognize its value: Ralph Waldo Emerson wrote to him, less than three weeks after Whitman sent him a copy, "I greet you at the beginning of a great career." He spent much of the remainder of his life revising and expanding this book. *Leaves of Grass* today is considered a masterpiece of world literature, marking the beginning of modern American poetry, and Whitman is widely regarded as America's national poet.

WEB: Further research this author with LitLinks at bedfordstmartins.com/approachinglit.

CD-ROM: Research this author in depth with cultural documents and multimedia resources on *LiterActive*.

RICHARD WILBUR (b. 1921) was born in New York City and grew up in rural New Jersey. He attended Amherst College and began writing poetry during World War II while fighting in Italy and France. Afterward, he studied at Harvard University and then taught there and at Wellesley College, Wesleyan University, and Smith College. He has published many books of poetry, including *Things of This World* (1956), for which he received the Pulitzer Prize for Poetry and the National Book Award, and *New and Collected Poems* (1988), which also won a Pulitzer Prize. He has always been respected as a master of formal constraints, comparing them to the genie in the bottle: The restraints stimulate the imagination to achieve results unlikely to be reached without them. He has also published numerous translations of French plays, two books for children, a collection of prose pieces, and editions of WILLIAM SHAKESPEARE and EDGAR ALLAN POE. In 1987 he was appointed Poet Laureate Consultant in Poetry at the Library of Congress. He now lives in Cummington, Massachusetts.

WEB: Further research this author with LitLinks at bedfordstmartins.com/approachinglit.

WILLIAM CARLOS WILLIAMS (1883–1963) was born in Rutherford, New Jersey; his father was an English emigrant and his mother was of mixed Basque descent from Puerto Rico. He decided to be both a writer and a doctor while in high school in New York City. He graduated from the medical school at the University of Pennsylvania, where he was a friend of Ezra Pound and Hilda Doolittle. After an internship in New York, writing poems between seeing patients, Williams practiced general medicine in Rutherford (he was ALLEN GINSBERG's pediatrician). His first book of poems was published in 1909, and he subsequently published poems, novels, short stories, plays, criticism, and essays. Initially one of the principal poets of the Imagist movement, Williams sought later to invent an entirely fresh — and distinctly American — poetic, whose subject matter was centered on the everyday circumstances of life and the lives of common people. Williams, like WALLACE STEVENS, became one of the major poets of the twentieth century and exerted great influence on poets of his own and later generations.

WEB: Further research this author with LitLinks at bedfordstmartins.com/approachinglit.

AUGUST WILSON (b. 1945) was born Frederick August Kittel in Pittsburgh, son of German immigrant Frederick August (a baker) and Daisy (a cleaning woman; maiden name, Wilson) Kittel, and grew up in the Hill district, a black neighborhood. When his mother married David Bedford, the family moved to the largely white community of Hazelwood, Pennsylvania, where Wilson dropped out of high school because of racial harassment. He educated himself and prepared to be a writer by reading his way through the section of black authors in the local library, discovering such writers as RICHARD WRIGHT, LANGSTON HUGHES, and RALPH ELLISON. He proceeded to read voraciously in fiction, poetry, and drama by both white and black authors and then began writing poetry and fiction himself. But he found himself drawn to the theater because drama offered a better way to politicize the community and raise consciousness. He moved to Minnesota and became involved with the Playwrights Center of Minneapolis; from there Wilson began to write realistic plays depicting African American life as he experienced it in Pittsburgh. His best known plays are *Ma Rainey's Black Bottom* (1984), *Fences*

(1985), *Joe Turner's Come and Gone* (1986) — all of which won the prestigious New York Drama Critics Circle Award — and *The Piano Lesson* (1989), which, like *Fences* (p. 1186), won the Pulitzer Prize for Drama. These works form part of a planned cycle of ten plays about the experience of African Americans in the United States, one for each decade of the twentieth century, to inform later generations about the hardships and indignities experienced by earlier generations. He is probably the most widely produced and highly regarded black dramatist of the twentieth century.

WEB: Further research this author with LitLinks at bedfordstmartins.com/approachinglit.

NELLIE WONG (b. 1934) was born and raised in Oakland, California's Chinatown. Since she began writing in the 1970s, she has spoken out against the oppression of all people — in particular, workers, women, minorities, and immigrants — and has worked steadily with community-based and international organizations to achieve racial justice. She is known as both a poet and a feminist human rights activist. She is the author of three poetry volumes and coeditor of an anthology of political essays, *Voices of Color* (1999). She has taught creative writing at several colleges in the San Francisco Bay area. Until her retirement, she worked as senior analyst in the Office of Affirmative Action/Equal Opportunity at the University of San Francisco. She lives in San Francisco and continues to speak at conferences nationwide on issues of race, gender, class, literature, labor, and community organizing.

WEB: Further research this author with LitLinks at bedfordstmartins.com/approachinglit.

WILLIAM WORDSWORTH (1770–1850) was born and raised in the Lake District of England. Both of his parents died by the time he was thirteen. He studied at Cambridge University, toured Europe on foot, and lived in France for a year during the first part of the French Revolution. He returned to England, leaving behind a lover, Annette Vallon, and their daughter, Caroline, from whom he was soon cut off by war between England and France. He met SAMUEL TAYLOR COLERIDGE, and in 1798 they together published *Lyrical Bal-*

lads, the first great work of the English Romantic movement. He changed poetry forever by his decision to use common language in his poetry instead of artificial poetic diction (see the Glossary of Literary Terms, p. 1514). In 1799 he and his sister Dorothy moved to Grasmere, in the Lake District, where he married Mary Hutchinson, a childhood friend. His greatest works were produced between 1797 and 1808. He continued to write for the next forty years but never regained the heights of his early verse. In 1843 he was named poet laureate, a position he held until his death in 1850.

WEB: Further research this author with LitLinks at bedfordstmartins.com/approachinglit.

JAMES WRIGHT (1927–1980) grew up in Martin's Ferry, Ohio. He attended Kenyon College, where his study under John Crowe Ransom sent his early poetry in a formalist direction. After spending a year in Austria on a Fulbright fellowship, he returned to the United States and earned an M.A. and Ph.D. at the University of Washington, studying under THEODORE ROETHKE and Stanley Kunitz. He went on to teach at the University of Minnesota, Macalester College, and Hunter College. His working-class background and the poverty that he saw during the Depression stirred a sympathy for the poor and "outsiders" of various sorts, which shaped the tone and content of his poetry. He published numerous books of poetry; his *Collected Poems* received the Pulitzer Prize for Poetry in 1972.

WEB: Further research this author with LitLinks at bedfordstmartins.com/approachinglit.

RICHARD WRIGHT (1908–1960) was born on a plantation near Natchez, Mississippi. His father, Nathaniel, was an illiterate sharecropper and his mother, Ella Wilson, was a schoolteacher. When Wright was five, his father left the family, and his mother was forced to take domestic jobs away from the house. Wright and his brother spent a period at an orphanage. Wright attended several schools, graduating from the Smith Robertson Junior High School in Jackson as the class valedictorian in June 1925. His first story, "The Voodoo of Hell's Half Acre," was published in the *Southern Register* in 1924. He worked and read as much as possible in

Memphis for two years and then moved to Chicago where he worked as a post office clerk, joined the Communist Party, and wrote for leftist publications such as the *New Masses,* the *Daily Worker,* and *New Challenge.* He moved to New York in 1937. In 1938 his first collection of stories, *Uncle Tom's Children,* won first prize in a contest for writers in the Federal Writers' Project during the Depression. His first novel, *Native Son* (1940), was the first best-selling novel by a black American writer and the first Book-of-the-Month Club selection by an African American writer. It sold 215,000 copies in its first three weeks of publication and made him the most respected and wealthiest black writer in America. His autobiography, *Black Boy,* was published in 1945, and it too was a bestseller and Book-of-the-Month Club selection. The following year, he moved to Paris and spent the rest of his life in exile, alienated by the racism he encountered as a black man married to a white woman. He traveled a great deal and continued to write, mostly nonfiction works about his travels and political and sociological topics.

WEB: Further research this author with LitLinks at bedfordstmartins.com/approachinglit.

SIR THOMAS WYATT THE ELDER (1503–1542) was born in Kent, England, and educated at St. John's College, Cambridge. He spent most of his life as a courtier and diplomat, serving King Henry VIII as ambassador to Spain and as a member of several missions to Italy and France. These travels introduced Wyatt to Italian writers of the High Renaissance, whose work he translated, thus introducing the sonnet form into English. He was arrested twice and charged with treason, sent to the Tower of London, and acquitted in 1541. Aristocratic poets at the time rarely published their poems themselves; works circulated in manuscript and in published collections ("miscellanies") gathered by printers. The most important of these is a volume published by Richard Tottel in 1557 entitled *Songs and Sonnets* but more commonly known as *Tottel's Miscellany,* which includes ninety-seven of Wyatt's sonnets and delightful lyrics.

WEB: Further research this author with LitLinks at bedfordstmartins.com/approachinglit.

XU GANG (b. 1945) was born in Shanghai, China. He was drafted into the army in 1962 and began writing poetry in support of the Cultural Revolution. However, he gradually became disillusioned with its violent practices and disruptive results while studying at Beijing University, from which he graduated in 1974. He has authored several collections of poems.

WEB: Further research this author with LitLinks at bedfordstmartins.com/approachinglit.

JOHN YAU (b. 1950) was born in Lynn, Massachusetts, a year after his parents emigrated from China. He received a B.A. from Bard College and an M.F.A. from Brooklyn College, where he studied with John Ashbery. He has published several books of poetry and two books of criticism, edited an anthology of fiction, organized a retrospective of Ed Moses's paintings and drawings, and written a long essay on Robert Creeley's poetry and poetics. Yau lives in Manhattan and teaches at the Maryland Institute College of Art.

WEB: Further research this author with LitLinks at bedfordstmartins.com/approachinglit.

WILLIAM BUTLER YEATS (1865–1939) was born in Sandymount, Dublin, to an Anglo-Irish family. On leaving high school in 1883 he decided to be an artist, like his father, and attended art school, but soon gave it up to concentrate on poetry. His first poems were published in 1885 in the *Dublin University Review*. Religious by temperament but unable to accept orthodox Christianity, Yeats throughout his life explored esoteric philosophies in search of a tradition that would substitute for a lost religion. He became a member of the Theosophical Society and the Order of the Golden Dawn, two groups interested in Eastern occultism, and later developed a private system of symbols and mystical ideas. Through the influence of Lady Gregory, a writer and promoter of literature, he became interested in Irish nationalist art, helping to found the Irish National Theatre and the famous Abbey Theatre. He was actively involved in Irish politics, especially after the Easter Rising of 1916. He continued to write and to revise earlier poems, leaving behind, at his death, a body of verse that, in its variety and power, placed him among the greatest twentieth-century poets of the English language. He was awarded the Nobel Prize for Literature in 1923.

WEB: Further research this author with LitLinks at bedfordstmartins.com/approachinglit.

CD-ROM: Research this author in depth with cultural documents and multimedia resources on *LiterActive*.

AL YOUNG (b. 1939) was born at Ocean Springs, Mississippi, and lived for a decade in the South before moving to Detroit. He attended the University of Michigan and the University of California, Berkeley. He has been a professional guitarist and singer, a disk jockey, a medical photographer, and a warehouseman and has written six books of poetry, five novels, several memoirs, essays, and film scripts. He has edited a number of books, including *Yardbird Lives!* (1978) and *African American Literature: A Brief Introduction and Anthology* (1995). In the 1970s and 1980s, Young cofounded the journals *Yardbird Reader* and *Quilt* with poet-novelist ISHMAEL REED. He lives in Palo Alto, California.

WEB: Further research this author with LitLinks at bedfordstmartins.com/approachinglit.

RAY A. YOUNG BEAR (b. 1950) was born and grew up in the Mesquakie Tribal Settlement near Tama, Iowa. His poetry has been influenced by his maternal grandmother, Ada Kapayou Old Bear, and his wife, Stella L. Young Bear. He attended Claremont College in California as well as Grinnell College, the University of Iowa, Iowa State University, and Northern Iowa University. He has been a visiting faculty member at Eastern Washington University and the University of Iowa. Young Bear and his wife cofounded the Woodland Song and Dance Troupe of Arts Midwest in 1983. Young Bear's group has performed traditional Mesquakie music in this country and the Netherlands. A writer of poetry, fiction, and nonfiction, he has contributed to contemporary Native American poetry and to the study of it for nearly three decades.

WEB: Further research this author with LitLinks at bedfordstmartins.com/approachinglit.

Appendix on Scansion

This appendix returns to the use of meter in poetry, extending the discussion begun in Chapter 14. We said there that meter forms an important component of rhythm for poems using it, ones having a regular beat created by a repeating pattern of stressed and unstressed syllables. In Chapter 14, we indicated the beat in metrical lines by using capital letters for stressed syllables (i AM bic ME ter GOES like THIS) to show that you can hear meter by listening for the stressed (louder) syllables, those that get more emphasis than the unstressed syllables. That's the important thing for readers beginning to read poetry attentively: hearing a steady beat when it's present and being able to distinguish poetry that has such a beat from poetry that does not. As you read more poetry, however, you may want to deal with meter in a more sophisticated way. This appendix introduces the traditional system of scansion and shows how metrical analysis contributes to a fuller understanding and appreciation of a poem written in meter.

Here is a brief review of some basic concepts and terminology introduced in Chapter 14. Go back to pages 564–72 to review them if you need to.

FOOT   A two- or three-syllable metrical unit made up (usually) of one stressed and one or two unstressed syllables. The most important metrical feet are these:

Iamb: unstressed, stressed: da DA (for example, "awake")

Trochee: stressed, unstressed: DA da ("wakeful")

Anapest: unstressed, unstressed, stressed: da da DA ("in a dream")

Dactyl: stressed, unstressed, unstressed: DA da da ("sleepily")

Spondee: stressed, stressed: DA DA ("dream house")

LINE LENGTH   Line lengths are measured by the number of feet in the line and are labeled with names derived from Greek roots:

Trimeter: a line with three metrical feet

Tetrameter: a line with four metrical feet

Pentameter: a line with five metrical feet

Hexameter: a line with six metrical feet

These are the commonest line lengths; more rare are monometer (one foot) and heptameter (seven).

The meter in a poem is highlighted and clarified through a process called **scansion**. To scan a poem involves marking its stressed syllables — whether the stress is heavy or light — with an accent mark (´) and marking its unstressed syllables with a curved line (˘). You use a vertical line to indicate the way the lines divide up into feet. (You need not try to distinguish stronger from weaker stresses — only syllables that receive at least *some* stress from those that receive *none*.)

    Ĭám | bĭc mé | tĕr góes | lĭke thís.[1]

You then describe (or label) the type of foot used most often in the line and the line length — in this case, iambic tetrameter.

The ideal way to scan a poem is to listen for where you stress syllables. But read with a natural emphasis, not a singsong regularity. Where *you* stress syllables is important: Scansion is not a mechanical process; it involves your interpretation. Scansion reflects the way a poem actually is read and so will differ slightly from one reader to another. Practice hearing the stresses as a recurring background beat, somewhat like the bass guitar or drums. But do not emphasize the beat; instead, concentrate on the words as you feel the beat underneath them.

You can use logic to do a rough but generally adequate scansion. First, start with multisyllabic words, using a dictionary if necessary to put ´ on the accented syllables and ˘ on the unaccented ones. Then put stress marks on important shorter words (most nouns and verbs, for example). Rhyming syllables almost always are stressed. Helping words (such as *a, an, to*) are rarely stressed and can safely be given ˘ marks. Just examining a poem thoughtfully will show where at least three-fourths of the stressed or unstressed syllables fall. The remainder can be sounded or figured out: For example, in ˘˘ ? ˘˘, the ? will almost surely be stressed; five unstressed syllables in a row would be very unusual. After such an analysis, read the poem aloud to test how well the stress patterns you identified match what you hear.

Notice in the following stanza how the metrical substitutions control emphasis and make the sound natural, not artificially "poetic." Lines 1, 3, 5,

---

[1] In dividing lines into feet, begin by looking for the way that yields the greatest number of identical groupings of twos or threes since most feet in a poem will be the same; then figure out the exceptions.

Notice that dividing lines into feet may involve breaking up words. Feet work primarily with syllables, not words. However, in a line like "Evening traffic homeward burns" (from Yvor Winters's "Before Disaster"), which could be scanned as either iambic or trochaic, trochaic seems preferable because it keeps the words together ("Évenĭng | tráffĭc | hómewărd | búrns" rather than "Eve | nĭng tráf | fĭc home | wărd búrns").

and 6 are in regular iambic feet and have the important role of establishing the prevailing "beat," but line 2 begins with a spondee ("Lóng fiélds"), and lines 7 and 8 lack the opening, unstressed syllable; unlike the opening six lines, they begin with a stressed syllable and have only seven syllables, instead of eight.

Alfred, Lord Tennyson   1809–1892

From "The Lady of Shalott"   [1832]

On éi | thĕr síde | thĕ rí | vĕr líe
Lóng fiĕlds | ŏf bár | lĕy and² | ŏf rýe,
Thăt clóthe | thĕ wóld | ănd méet | thĕ ský;
Ănd thró' | thĕ fiéld | thĕ róad | rŭns bý
   Tŏ má | nў-tów | er'd Ca | mĕlót;   5
Ănd úp | ănd dówn | thĕ péo | plĕ gó,
Gáz | ĭng whére | thĕ líl | iĕs blów
Roúnd | ăn ís | lănd thére | bĕlów,
   Thĕ ís | lănd ŏf | Shálótt.

For practice, try scanning the following lines. Mark the stressed syllables with ´ and unstressed syllables with ˘, and use | to divide lines into feet. Try first to do it by hearing the beat; if that doesn't work, figure it out logically, following the steps we suggest above. To compare your result with the way we scanned it, see page 1478.

Samuel Taylor Coleridge   1772–1834

Metrical Feet   [1806]
Lesson for a Boy

Trochee trips from long to short.
From long to long in solemn sort
Slow Spondee stalks; strong foot! yet ill able
Ever to come up with Dactyl trisyllable.
Iambics march from short to long; —
With a leap and a bound the swift Anapests throng.   5

---

²A reserved accent [`] often is used for a very lightly stressed syllable, such as the slight stress a normally unstressed word (like *and*) receives when its position in a line calls for it.

To illustrate further, we will consider what scansion might add to our understanding, enjoyment, and appreciation of the following poem. Read it twice, once silently, once aloud, and listen for the beat.

Emily Dickinson   1830–1886

I like to see it lap the Miles   [c. *1862*; 1891]

I like to see it lap the Miles –
And lick the Valleys up –
And stop to feed itself at Tanks –
And then – prodigious step

Around a Pile of Mountains –   5
And supercilious peer
In Shanties – by the sides of Roads –
And then a Quarry pare

To fit its Ribs
And crawl between   10
Complaining all the while
In horrid – hooting stanza –
Then chase itself down Hill –

And neigh like Boanerges[3] –
Then – punctual as a Star   15
Stop – docile and omnipotent
At its own stable door –

This poem resembles a riddle — it forces the reader to supply the implied antecedent to the pronoun *it*. The answer would have been obvious to most readers in Emily Dickinson's day, and perhaps it was to you as you read it too; but cultural changes (especially the replacement of rail systems with freeways) make the riddle less obvious for many readers today. Because trains are not as much a part of our visual imagery as they were during the last century, we may be tempted to read "neigh" and "stable" as literal, rather than as parts of an extended implied metaphor. Scanning the poem can help us clarify why meter is an important aspect of this imaginative depiction of a train. Try scanning it yourself first and then compare your reading with ours.

---

[3]*Boanerges* ("sons of thunder") is the name Jesus gave to the brothers James and John, his disciples (see Mark 3:17).

The poem starts with a stanza of regular iambic feet, alternating lines of tetrameter and trimeter.

Ĭ líke | tŏ sée | ĭt láp | thĕ Míles –
Ănd líck | thĕ Vál | lĕys úp –
Ănd stóp | tŏ feéd | ĭtsélf | ăt Tánks –

Not only is the meter regular, but the rhythm is steady as well; the short, simple words can be read at an even pace, with no internal punctuation interrupting or slowing them down; the dashes at the ends of lines 1 and 2 (Dickinson had her own, unusual ideas about punctuation) give just enough pause for a breath to keep the pace in the following line. Meter and rhythm together echo the repetitive, predictable, clickity-clack sound that train wheels make as they pass over the cracks between the rails.

In line 4 the meter remains regular — "Ănd thén – | prŏdí | giŏus stép" — but the rhythm slows down because the dash creates a pause and because the multisyllabic word "prodigious" takes longer to say than the short monosyllabic words "stop to feed." Stanzas 1 and 2 have no end punctuation; in fact, the entire poem is made up of one sentence. We usually pause briefly at the end of a line even when there is no punctuation, and we pause a bit longer at the end of a stanza that lacks end punctuation. That too slows the rhythm — just as, we find in the next line, the speed of the train decreases as it curls around mountains. (We may even sense the effect of having our eyes "step around" the end of the first stanza into the beginning of the second, in imitation of the train.)

Scansion can alert us to another way of slowing the rhythm, in line 5. The pattern established in the first stanza leads us to expect that first and third lines will have eight syllables, four iambic feet. When you read line 5, your ear should hear a difference, something unexpected. Here's an example of the tension between "expected" meter and "heard" meter. Scanning the line ("Ăroúnd | ă Píle | ŏf Moún | taĭns –") reveals that the difference is that it has only seven syllables and lacks the final stressed syllable the other lines have. We tend to linger a bit on the end of that line, slowing the rhythmic pace, partly because of the dash but partly out of respect for the syllable that our ear expects to hear.

The next three lines reestablish the expected pattern of iambic trimeter, tetrameter, trimeter, at a steady pace but slower than lines 1 to 3, slower largely because the combinations of sounds cannot be said rapidly: "Ănd sŭ | pĕrcíl | iŏus péer / Ĭn Shán | tiĕs – bý | thĕ sídes | ŏf Róads – / Ănd thén | ă Quár | rў páre."

Just as we become reaccustomed to the expected pattern, we are jolted out of it again. Stanza 3 has five lines instead of the usual four and it begins with two lines of only four syllables — two iambic feet — instead of the expected eight syllables, four feet:

To fít | its Ríbs
Aňd cráwl | bětwéen
Cǒmpláin | iňg áll | thě whíle
Ǐn hór | rǐd – hǒot | iňg stán | zǎ –

Scanning the lines helps us notice that the unexpected line still fits the "pattern": lines 9 and 10 are just an expected tetrameter line divided into two. With a playfulness typical of her, almost as a poetic joke, Dickinson has the stanza become visually narrower as the train peels along the edge of a quarry, fitting its metal "ribs" into the tight space. Line 9 is made tight by the sound of the "fit its" in the middle. As the train slows down for the narrow curves, the poem's rhythm does too, because of the pauses at the ends of the short lines 9 and 10, the long, slow *craaawwll* sound in the middle of line 10, and the length of words and the sound combinations of "Complaining" and "horrid–hooting."

The poem, like the train, hesitates at the end of line 12, which like line 5 lacks the final stressed syllable, then speeds up in regular meter as the train thunders downhill —

Thěn cháse | ǐtsélf | dǒwn Híll –
Aňd neígh | lǐke Bó | aňér | gěs –

— only to pause sharply at the missing eighth syllable in line 14.

Scansion clarifies a final playful, but metrically effective, touch. After line 15 slows down, "Thén – púnc | tuǎl ás | ǎ Stár," because of the spondee, the dash, and the extra syllable (though some readers may slur "púnc | tuǎl" into two syllables and keep the meter regular), line 16 again does the unexpected. Thus far, most lines have begun with an unstressed syllable and an iambic foot, and our ears begin to expect that. This line jolts our ear, pulls us up short, by a metrical substitution — a spondee instead of an iamb: "Stóp – dóc | iǐe aňd | oǐmńi | potéńt / Ǎt íts | oǐwn stá | bǐle dóor." The substitution puts strong emphasis on "Stop," and that, together with the dash following it, interrupts the rhythm — stops us — as the train, now quiet though still powerful, stops at the end of its journey.

In this case it seems that Dickinson may have deliberately decided how meter would fit the shape and effects of the poem. However, poets who use meter do not always count syllables and decide consciously that it is time to make a substitution or to leave off a final stressed syllable. Their ears are attuned to meters, so they hear whether a line "sounds appropriate" or "right" or whether they need to make further changes. Looking back, they may be able to figure out (perhaps by scanning the line) what made it sound better, what made it "work." Scanning — and attention to meter generally — can be retrospective, part of the process of figuring out why what was done proved effective, or it can be part of the creative process.

Let's try this now on a more complex passage, a famous speech from Shakespeare's tragedy *Macbeth* (5.5.19–28). It occurs when Macbeth nears the end of his life. His evil deeds have been found out, his opponents are closing in on his castle, and he is told that his wife has just committed suicide. Full of grief and despair, Macbeth utters a bleak assessment of human existence. Read the passage and then scan it yourself before looking at the way we did it:

> Tomorrow, and tomorrow, and tomorrow
> Creeps in this petty pace from day to day
> To the last syllable of recorded time,
> And all our yesterdays have lighted fools
> The way to dusty death. Out, out, brief candle!   5
> Life's but a walking shadow, a poor player
> That struts and frets his hour upon the stage
> And then is heard no more. It is a tale
> Told by an idiot, full of sound and fury,
> Signifying nothing.   10

Here is the way we scan the lines, but it is important to realize that this is not *the one correct* way to scan it. Differences in pronunciation and interpretation can lead to entirely acceptable differences in scansion of a poem. (Acceptable differences do not include mispronunciations. You may need to look up pronunciations, as well as definitions, of unfamiliar words to be fair both to the sound and to the meaning of a poem.)

> Tŏmór | rŏw, ănd| tŏmór| rŏw, ănd| tŏmórrŏw
> Créeps ĭn| thĭs pét| tў páce| frŏm dáy| tŏ dáy
> Tŏ thĕ lást| sýllă| blĕ ŏf| rĕcórd| ĕd tíme,
> Ănd áll| ŏŭr yés| tĕrdáys| hăve líght| ĕd fóols
> Thĕ wáy| tŏ dúst| ў déath.| Oŭt, oút,| brĭef cán| dĭe!   5
> Life's bŭt| ă wálk| ĭng shád| ŏw, ă póor| pláyĕr
> Thăt strúts| ănd fréts| hĭs hóur| ŭpón| thĕ stáge
> Ănd thén| ĭs héard| nŏ móre.| Ĭt ĭs| ă tále
> Tóld bў ăn| ídĭŏt,| fúll ŏf| soúnd ănd| fúrў,
> Sígnĭ| fўĭng| nóthĭng.   10

The passage, like much of the poetry in Shakespeare's plays, is written in **blank verse** (unrhymed iambic pentameter). The first line is regular, except for the extra unstressed syllable on the final iamb. That syllable, together with the two caesuras and the time it takes to say each "tomorrow," lengthens the line and slows it down, so that rhythmically it creeps, the way Macbeth says life does. Stressing "and" twice adds to the sense of circularity and monotony Macbeth finds in life.

The second line begins with one of the most common metric substitutions, an initial trochee instead of an iamb, which puts extra emphasis on the key word "creeps." That the rest of the line is regular echoes the steady, plodding pace by which life proceeds, and it sets up the irregular, unexpected anapest and trochee of the first half of line 3 — to think of the very end, the final millisecond, of history ("recorded time") is jolting, and the meter jolts us as well. After two irregular lines the expected, regular iambics return for the rest of line 3, all of line 4, and half of line 5, again suiting the steady, plodding pace by which Macbeth says people follow one another through life toward death, the past like a lantern lighting the way as people foolishly imitate what those before them have done.

The rest of line 5 is irregular: two spondees and an extra unstressed syllable: "Oút, oút, | bríef cándle!" Although life may seem to plod, it is short; and Macbeth expresses the wish that his would end. The double stresses of the spondees, emphasized by the caesuras that make one linger, give strength to the words "Out, out," and another spondee with an extra syllable and a definite end stop make us dwell on "brief candle!" The rhythm, which had been slow but steady, becomes broken and forceful here and in the following line. Line 6 also is irregular and unusual — a trochee, two iambs, an anapest, and a trochee. This is an unusual metrical combination, difficult to enunciate, just as its thought (that there is no reality, that life is empty and meaningless) is difficult for most people to accept. That slow, contorted line rhythmically leads into a line and a half that are metrically regular, reestablishing the expected meter. The mostly monosyllabic words, full of stops and fricatives, seem almost drumlike, booming their assertions about the brevity and unreality of people's stage-play lives: "That STRUTS and FRETS his HOUR upON the STAGE / And THEN is HEARD no MORE."

After the full-stop caesura, the iambs continue for two feet but the drum disappears with the lightly stressed "is." But these quieter, softer lines ("Ĭt ĭs | ă tále / Tóld bў ăn | ídĭŏt, | fúll ŏf | soúnd ănd | fúry, / Sígnĭ | fyĭng | nóthĭng") are perhaps even more intense than those before them since they describe life as having no more shape and significance than the babblings of an insane person. The meter in lines 9 and 10 — two dactyls and six trochees — is madly unusual and amazingly effective. Emphasis on "tale | Told" is heightened by stressing both and linking them by alliteration. The two dactyls, "Told by an idiot," can only be read slowly, with difficulty, which places unmissable emphasis on "idiot." The dactyls and the six trochees following illustrate the anticlimactic potential of "falling meter," as with each foot we seem to sink lower than the one before.

The length of the ninth line, with its two extra syllables, makes an idiot's tale seem not only chaotic but also almost endless. The unifying sounds of the last six feet (alliteration linking "full" and "fury" and also "sound" and "signifying") makes them forceful; the rhythm, steady in line 9, becomes less steady in line 10 (the stress on "fy" is so light that one may hear "sígnĭfyĭng") and almost fades away (to "nothing").

When you are watching *Macbeth,* you probably do not think about the fact that much of it is poetry and can be discussed for its figures, sounds, meter, and rhythm like the short poems we examine throughout this book. Even though you are not thinking about or realizing the presence of the poetry, however, it contributes in an important way to the intensity and emotional power of the play.

For additional practice, scan the following lines and label the prevailing metrical foot and line length.

> Woman much missed, how you call to me, call to me,
> Saying that now you are not as you were
> When you had changed from the one who was all to me,
> But as at first, when our day was fair.
> —Thomas Hardy

> That time of year thou mayst in me behold
> When yellow leaves, or none, or few, do hang
> Upon those boughs which shake against the cold,
> Bare ruined choirs, where late the sweet birds sang.
> —William Shakespeare

> "Good speed!" cried the watch, as the gate-bolts undrew;
> "Speed!" echoed the wall to us galloping through;
> Behind shut the postern, the lights sank to rest,
> And into the midnight we galloped abreast.
> —Robert Browning

> Piping down the valleys wild,
> Piping songs of pleasant glee,
> On a cloud I saw a child,
> And he laughing said to me:
> —William Blake

To compare your results with ours, see page 1478.

Trŏchee | trĭps frŏm | lŏng tŏ | shŏrt.   *trochaic tetrameter*
Frŏm lŏng | tŏ lŏng | ĭn sŏl | ĕmn sŏrt.   *iambic tetrameter*
Slŏw Spŏn | dĕe stalks; | strŏng foŏt! |yĕt   *spondaic tetrameter plus*
    ĭll ăble   *two weak syllables*
Ĕvĕr tŏ | cŏme ŭp wĭth | Dăctŷl tri | syllăblĕ.   *dactylic tetrameter*
Ĭam | bĭcs march | frŏm shŏrt | tŏ lŏng;—   *iambic tetrameter*
Wĭth ă leăp | ănd ă bound | thĕ swĭft Ăn | *anapestic tetrameter*
    ăpĕsts throng.

   —Samuel Taylor Coleridge, "Metrical Feet"

Wŏmăn mŭch | mĭssed, hŏw yŏu | cáll tŏ mĕ, | cáll tŏ mĕ,
Sáyĭng thăt | nŏw yŏu ăre | nŏt ăs yŏu | wĕre   *dactylic*
Whĕn yŏu hăd | chănged frŏm thĕ | ŏne whŏ wăs | ăll tŏ mĕ,   *tetrameter*
Bŭt ăs ăt | fĭrst, whĕn oŭr | dăy wăs | făir.

   —Thomas Hardy

Thăt tĭme | ŏf yeăr | thŏu măyst | ĭn mĕ | bĕhóld
Whĕn yĕl | lŏw leăves, | ŏr nóne, | ŏr fĕw, | dŏ hăng   *iambic*
Ŭpón | thŏse boŭghs | whĭch shăke | ăgaĭnst | thĕ cŏld,   *pentameter*
Băre rú | ĭned choĭrs, | whĕre lăte | thĕ swĕet | bĭrds săng.

   —William Shakespeare

"Goŏd spĕed!" | crĭed thĕ watch, | ăs thĕ găte | -bŏlts ŭndrĕw;
"Spĕed!" ĕch | oĕd thĕ wăll | tŏ ŭs găl | lŏpĭng thróugh;   *anapestic*
Bĕhĭnd | shŭt thĕ pŏs | tĕrn, thĕ lĭghts | sănk tŏ rĕst,   *tetrameter*
Ănd ĭn | tŏ thĕ mĭd | nĭght wĕ găl | lŏpĕd ăbreăst.

   —Robert Browning

Pípĭng | dŏwn thĕ | vălleўs | wĭld,
Pípĭng | sŏngs ŏf | pleăsănt | glĕe,   *trochaic*
Ŏn ă | cloŭd Ĭ | săw ă | chĭld,   *tetrameter*
Ănd hĕ | laŭghĭng | saĭd tŏ | mĕ:
    —William Blake

Approaching Critical Theory

This book is about approaching literature. It's valuable to realize that you always approach something from somewhere. We have tried to connect reading literature to your everyday life: You come to this course with prior interests and experiences, and the way you approach what you read, even your ability to relate to it at all, depends on where you're "coming from."

In addition to this personal way to approach a work, there is another sense of approaching literature from somewhere. All readers approach their reading from a critical or theoretical perspective, even though they may not be aware of it. There are many such perspectives — some practical, others more abstract and philosophical. This appendix, though it cannot cover all of them, does indicate the range of past and present approaches used by readers.

Having an awareness of critical and theoretical perspectives helps as you read literary works themselves — helps you sharpen and refine your own approaches to reading, helps you become a more flexible reader, helps you vary your approaches for different works and in different situations. And being familiar with critical theories is beneficial as you read scholarly books and essays about literature. As we said in Chapter 25 (p. 1366), knowing where a critical work is coming from, what its assumptions and intentions are, can help in following its arguments and in understanding why two readers of the same text can arrive at quite different readings. (Note, however, that scholars usually do not limit themselves to only one approach; they often combine approaches, or elements from different approaches, to fit a particular work or problem.)

The following survey of approaches is arranged in roughly chronological order to provide a brief history of literary criticism and to indicate how some theories developed out of, or as a reaction to, other theories — though theories have often overlapped, or run simultaneously, with others. Reader-response theories, for example, arose as a reaction to the neglect of the reading process in earlier twentieth-century critical theories. Keep in mind that literary theories also come from somewhere; knowing how they relate to prior theories and to the prevailing philosophical outlook of their time helps you to better understand them.

READING FOR PERSONAL IMPROVEMENT

Until the late 1800s, literature in English was not studied but was read for pleasure and edification. Part of the enjoyment of literature for readers then was picking out — and copying or memorizing — lines or passages that said something profound or meaningful about life. And some readers then, as now, sought out books that were informative or inspirational, through which they could find personal growth. Sir Philip Sidney, asserting the value of literature in his *Defense of Poesy* (1595), one of the earliest theoretical works in English, built his case on a moral foundation: "The ending end of all earthly leaning [is] virtuous action." Sidney's case continued to be widely influential until at least the mid-twentieth century.

Such growth had potential for benefits to society in addition to individuals, as poet and critic Matthew Arnold theorized in the mid-1800s. Arnold was deeply distressed by what he called the "barbarianism" (lack of interest in ideas) of the upper classes in England; by the "philistinism" (lack of intelligence and taste) of the middle classes; and by the lack of interest among the lower classes in anything save "beer, gin, and fun." He attempted to improve society by challenging it to a commitment to "high culture" (his term again), "knowledge of the best that has been thought and said in the world."

Culture, in this view, provides a norm, or standard, for people to aspire to, and it has a unifying effect if they can be induced to strive toward the same values in aesthetics and morality. Arnold put so much emphasis on culture, especially literature, because he believed it could fill the role religion had filled, of offering society a source of moral values and an instrument for social unity and stability. For Arnold, education was the method for spreading this perspective. Through literature — especially the classics — the middle classes would be able to share some of the advantages the upper classes had always had available to them through their access to education.

Arnold's approach to literature was widely influential for over a century and continues to shape thinking today, though with some concerns about its tendency toward elitism. For decades educators in the United States used literature as an avenue for assimilating people into mainstream "American culture," with the aim of helping them rise to the middle class. This Arnoldian version of cultural criticism also critiqued literature to assess what was worthy of attention and would contribute most to cultural development and to the unifying, socializing effect a common culture helps achieve. Out of this social aim arose a "canon," or list, of "the best" works and authors, those "approved" as the most valuable and worthwhile. This canon later became a hotly contested issue, to which we will return shortly.

PHILOLOGICAL STUDIES

English literature became a subject of academic study in the late 1800s. Until then, literature students studied the Greek and Roman classics, using an approach called *philology,* or the scientific study of language and literature. Philological scholarship included language study, preparation of scholarly editions with accurate texts, and examination of literary backgrounds, sources, and influences. If you can, take a look at J. R. R. Tolkien and E. V. Gordon's edition of the medieval romance *Sir Gawain and the Green Knight* (1925). It provides an excellent example of philological scholarship, with its historical introduction, authoritative text, extensive footnotes, and thorough glossary.

When the study of English literature began, the initial emphasis was on literature from its beginnings (written in Old English) through the Middle Ages (Middle English). It was approached philologically — much the same as the way Latin and Greek were studied. Although it may seem surprising now, the assumption was that students didn't need much help with literature from Shakespeare on: Those works were considered part of their reading for pleasure, not part of the academic program.

BIOGRAPHICAL CRITICISM

By the 1930s, academic study of English literature had begun to include later authors, though still not contemporary literature, the attention focusing particularly on the historical backgrounds of works and on the lives of authors. Scholars used literary works as a source of information about authors (not always being careful to keep a first-person narrator or speaker separate from the author) and used details from an author's life to gain a better understanding of a work (not always being careful to remember that a writer can make things up).

Biographical criticism today involves research into the details of an author's life to shed light on the author's works, an important and basic form of literary study. Publishers have recognized its value by publishing biographical encyclopedias for literary figures and by including biographical sketches of the authors in anthologies such as this textbook (see p. 1415). Knowledge about an author can enable us in many cases to notice details or ideas in a work we might otherwise miss.

Chapters 22, 23, and 24 illustrate what a biographical approach offers. They provide detailed biographical sketches of Langston Hughes, Judith Ortiz Cofer, and Sherman Alexie, supplemented by excerpts from memoirs or interviews. The chapters provide initial materials for biographical studies, and some applications to particular works where that seems profitable. You could use those chapters as the starting point for a biographical paper, or you could decide to research and write about another author. Research into the lives of authors has been greatly facilitated by the Internet and by publication of literary biographies (for some titles, see the introduction to the biographical sketches in this book, on p. 1415).

If you decide to attempt biographical criticism, however, be sure it actually *is* criticism and not just a report on the author's life. The paper must involve analysis, and it must use biographical data to illuminate meaning and build its interpretations on what is in the text, not on extraneous material from outside the text.

HISTORICAL CRITICISM

As biographical knowledge enhances your understanding of a work, so does awareness of the social, political, cultural, and intellectual context in which it was conceived and written. Literary historians research such backgrounds and bring what they find to bear on a work, explaining details used in the work and clarifying the meaning of the work as its original readers would have understood it. They research sources the author drew on and influences that shaped the form and content of the work. They connect the work to others written at the time, to describe the literary environment that surrounds it, and compare it to works written earlier, to understand how it relates to the traditional handling of similar forms and ideas.

To see how historical criticism is used, look again at the discussion of "Hills Like White Elephants" in Chapter 6 (p. 125). There we describe the historical context and social milieu in which Hemingway wrote and in which the story was set. We show how awareness of events and attitudes of the time clarifies details in plot, characterization, and setting and proves helpful in understanding the story. You can try using such an approach for a paper assignment, if you'd like — probably a research paper. Learning about history almost invariably involves doing research into the era you're interested in. You use a historical approach for almost any time other than what you know firsthand. As with biographical criticism, be sure what you write is actually criticism, not just a report on the time period. The paper must involve analysis and must use historical data to illuminate meaning and build its interpretations on what is in the text, not on extraneous material from outside the text.

MARXISM AND LITERATURE

Marxist thought emerged in the United States in the 1920s and 1930s, partly as a reverberation from the Russian revolution in 1918 and the spread of Marxist philosophy across Europe. Later many people in the United States turned to Marxism as a reaction to the Great Depression and widespread unemployment and poverty that followed the fall of the stock market in

1929, with all the capitalist symbolism that carried. Many authors and literary critics embraced Marxism, as did many other artists and academics. At this point, Marxist authors wrote stories, novels, and plays advocating Marxist principles, and critics wrote books and essays endorsing works consistent with a Marxist outlook, by authors who accepted Marxism and even ones who did not. We will return to Marxist theory later in this survey and treat it more fully as it reemerges in a more sophisticated and highly influential form in the 1970s.

PSYCHOLOGICAL CRITICISM

Biographical criticism — or a good deal of it, at least — began to turn in a psychological direction during the 1940s and 1950s. This was a result of the growing interest in the parent of psychoanalysis, Sigmund Freud, who sought a scientific understanding of the mind and mental illness. His methods and conclusions were revolutionary and controversial, and have been and continue to be both applied and challenged on many grounds. The field of psychoanalysis has now moved far beyond Freud — so far, in fact, that he is given slight attention in psychology courses today. However, his work had a great impact on twentieth-century literature and twentieth-century literary criticism.

A brief summary of Freud's thought is needed before we can consider its effect on literature. Crucial to its early phase is Freud's realization of a dynamic tension between the conscious and the unconscious in mental activity. This was a radical shift. Pre-Freudian belief held that one could *know* and *control* oneself. The idea that there are parts of the self knowable only through analysis is almost universally accepted now, but it was strikingly new when Freud advanced it. He described three areas of consciousness, each of which can contain causes for human behavior. First is the *conscious* level, the things we are aware of. Second is the *preconscious* level, feelings and sensations we are not presently aware of but that can be brought to the surface if we reflect on them. Third is the *unconscious* level, the realm of things we are not aware of, though they influence us greatly.

In his second phase, Freud replaced the conscious and unconscious with the very different and now familiar concepts of the id, ego, and superego. The *id,* a reservoir of biological impulses and drives, demands instant gratification of its needs and desires — for food, relieving ourselves, sexual gratification. But instant satisfaction is not always possible, and when satisfaction must be postponed, tensions build up that cause inner conflict. We are often unaware that such tensions and conflicts exert an influence on our lives and actions. The *ego* (rational, controlled, partially conscious) is concerned first with pleasure, through the elimination of inner tensions and conflicts, but also with self-preservation, which requires that urges and needs be dealt with in a practical, realistic way. The id, for example, tells us we need to eat, and the ego *wants* to concur, but the ego, balancing the id's desire with the restraint imposed by the *superego* (the rules and taboos internalized through parental and societal influences), tells us to wait until lunchtime.

In a third phase of his work, Freud focused on the development of the ego in children. Freud held that part of the normal emotional development of a child includes an unconscious wish to replace the parent of the child's sex in the affection of the parent of the opposite sex: A little boy wants to eliminate his father and marry his mother (Oedipus complex), and a little girl to eliminate her mother and marry her father (Electra complex). Although many aspects of his approach to the stages of the early childhood development have been challenged or discredited, evidences of them are found in literary criticism, to clarify what lies behind a character's attitudes or actions, and in literary works, as authors influenced by Freudian theories apply them as they develop characters and plots.

Another controversial Freudian theory important for literary study is that of *repression*. This theory holds that memories (that is, bundles of psychic energy) of situations with painful or threatening or guilt-laden associations are unconsciously pushed out of consciousness and sealed off so we will not have to deal with them consciously. When such matters are repressed, the pent-up energy has an effect on the personality—a repressed memory of childhood abuse, for example, may interfere with a person's adult relationships. It may take something of great force to break through the barrier, but only when it has been broken through is the person freed from the pain and its effects.

Psychological criticism is most commonly used to analyze characters in a work. The psychological critic attempts to clarify a character's actions, motivations, and attitudes by bringing modern psychoanalytical insights to bear on them. The critic does with characters what a psychoanalyst does with a patient: probes beneath the surface, exploring what unconscious conflicts and tensions, or repressed memories, may underlie the character's behavior.

This approach isn't used profitably with every story, poem, or play. For example, we might be intrigued with what makes Jake tick in "Love in L.A." (p. 55). He seems to be a compulsive liar, unable to hold a job, wary of close relationships, unwilling to follow rules and regulations. Why? Could such behavior be the result of psychological problems? Perhaps so, but we don't know enough about Jake to be able to develop such an analysis. Doing so would require that the story provide details about events in his childhood and his relation to his parents; we would need to be able to tell if his attitudes or actions result from memories that are now unconscious or from experiences he has repressed. We can't know these things, however, because we aren't given enough information to work with.

It would seem much more possible to do a psychoanalytical analysis of the title character in "Young Goodman Brown" (p. 252). His is a longer story than Jake's, and we are told more about his background and behavior.

There seems adequate material in the story to show in a convincing way that many of his actions and attitudes come not from his conscious thought but from unconscious and repressed guilt, fears, and conflicts.

This is the direction you probably will want to use if you decide to write a paper taking a psychological approach. Your approach does not need to be Freudian — other psychological theories also can be used to amplify literature. But to work responsibly, you will need to know a good deal about whichever one you use. If you haven't taken at least one psychology course, trying this approach might not be advisable.

MYTHOLOGICAL CRITICISM

What Freud attempted for the individual consciousness, another group of theorists in the late 1940s began to do for cultures, or the human race as a whole. Theorists who came to be known as *mythological critics* (or *archetypal critics*) focused their attention on the myths that underlie many literary works. *Myth* here must be understood not in its popular sense of a "fictitious story, or unscientific account, theory, belief," but in its literary sense of an anonymous story arising from a culture's oral traditions that involves gods or heroic figures and explores matters beyond and above everyday life, concerning origins, endings, aspirations, purpose, and meaning. Myths often appear in the earliest and seemingly simplest stories told in a culture — folktales, fairy tales, or religious writings, for example.

Myths usually build on literary archetypes — symbols, character types, and plot lines that have been used again and again in a culture until they come to carry a wide, nearly universal significance and thus move most readers at a very deep emotional level. Throughout the centuries, writer after writer has drawn on motifs such as the quest, the journey into experience, and the Cinderella pattern in developing the plot of a story. Such writers use a typical or recurring symbol, character type, or plot motif that, in the words of archetypal theorist Northrop Frye, "connects one poem with another and thereby helps to unify and integrate our literary experience."[1]

Among the most used and most important of such archetypal images is the seasonal cycle of spring, summer, autumn, and winter; the daily cycle of dawn, zenith, sunset, and night; and the life cycle of youth, adulthood, old age, and death. Throughout history poets have seen analogies among these natural cycles. Each time we speak of the "sunset" and "golden" years of life in referring to old age or describe death as being "sleep," we are, consciously or unconsciously, invoking those archetypes.

Beyond the meaning of the individual cycles is the significance of the patterns as a whole. "In the solar cycle of the day," Frye explains, "the seasonal cycle of the year, and the organic cycle of human life, there is a single

---

[1] *Anatomy of Criticism, Four Essays* (Princeton: Princeton UP, 1957) 99.

pattern of significance"; elsewhere he calls that pattern the "story of the loss and regaining of identity," which is "the framework of all literature," the single story or "monomyth" underlying it all.[2] Other theorists hold that the "single story" focuses on the earth mother[3] or on the hero.[4] All of the theories, however, share a belief in the close relationship between literature and life. "Putting works of literature in such a context gives them an immense reverberating dimension of significance . . . , in which every literary work catches the echoes of all other works of its type in literature, and so ripples out into the rest of literature and thence into life."[5]

For an example of an essay that makes use of archetypal images and motifs, though not entirely mythological in approach, see Philip C. Kolin and Maureen Curley's "Hughes's *Soul Gone Home*" (p. 1273), as it draws connections between Langston Hughes's plays and other works with mythical overtones. William Shakespeare's sonnet "That time of year thou mayst in me behold" (p. 521) explicitly draws on the archetypes we just discussed, as the speaker uses images of winter and sunset to describe old age and approaching death.

NEW CRITICISM (FORMALISM)

The literary approach most influential in the twentieth century, and still important today, is called New Criticism, or Formalism (from its concentration on the *formal* elements of a work). It originated in the 1930s and for over forty years it dominated the study of literature. New Criticism was in part a reaction against an approach that makes biography or history primary and treats the literary text as secondary, either regarding it merely as a source of information or as material to the interpretation of which biographical and historical knowledge provides all the clues we need. New Criticism insists on the primacy of the text, appreciated as worthwhile for its own sake, for its aesthetic beauty, for its way of considering and helping understand the human condition generally. New Criticism takes texts themselves very seriously, looks at them closely as self-contained works of art, and affirms that literature has its own epistemology, or theory of knowledge.

New Criticism borrowed from France a method of teaching literature called *explication de texte*. The word *explicate* comes from Latin roots meaning "to unfold, to give an account of" and means to explain in detail. A key method of New Criticism is to explain the interconnections and ambiguities

---

[2]*Fables of Identity: Studies in Poetic Mythology* (New York: Harcourt, 1963) 15; *The Educated Imagination* (Bloomington: Indiana UP, 1964) 55.

[3]Robert Graves, *The White Goddess: A Historical Grammar of Poetic Myth* (London: Faber, 1948).

[4]Joseph Campbell, *The Hero with a Thousand Faces,* Bollingen Series XVII (Princeton: Princeton UP, 1949).

[5]Frye, *Fables of Identity* 37.

(multiple meanings) within a work, or within an important passage from a work, through a detailed, close analysis of its language — the meanings, relationships, and complexities of its words, images, figures, and symbols. In all this, what the author *intended* to do is not relevant — what matters is what the work *actually* says and does. New Critics, therefore, read works repeatedly. The first reading is less important than the later ones because one does not yet know where the work is headed and cannot see how early parts tie in with things further along.

As one rereads, again and again, one begins to see connections and to grasp the way large and small features relate to each other. Central to New Criticism are unity and universality. In the words of Cleanth Brooks, one of the developers of the approach, "The primary concern of criticism is with the problem of unity — the kind of whole which the literary work forms or fails to form, and the relation of the various parts to each other in building up this whole."[6] The unity sought is unity of meaning; but meaning, for New Critics, cannot be separated from form. Thus, a New Critic focuses on the speaker (or persona), conflicts and tensions, the arrangement of parts and details, and the relationships between them. A New Critic pays particular attention to metaphors as ways of unifying dissimilar things and to irony and paradox as ways apparent contradictions can be resolved (and thus unified).

New Criticism tends to look especially for issues of significance to all people, in all times — issues of life and relationship, worth and purpose, love, aging, death, faith, and doubt. The foundation of New Critical theory is its claim that literature has its own kind of knowledge — experiential knowledge conveyed imaginatively — and that this knowledge is superior to the abstract, impersonal knowledge of science. An overreliance on scientific approaches, New Critics believe, has led to fragmentation and "dissociation" within society and even within individuals. In the face of such disintegration, New Criticism emphasizes wholeness and unity. Literature offers a hope of wholeness, of a "unified sensibility" combining intellect and feeling, of redemption from the disintegration — the division, specialization, and alienation — that science has sometimes inflicted on the modern world.

Today New Criticism is viewed more as a critical method than as a way of knowing. Anyone who engages in detailed close reading of a text is a descendent of New Criticism, even if she or he doesn't look for universal meanings or think in terms of being a New Critic. The method we have used in this book borrows from New Criticism in the way it teaches close attention to details in literary works, though we are more concerned with readers and the reading process than New Criticism itself is.

Two of the student papers in this book offer good examples of New Critical readings. Alicia Abood's paper on "Love in L.A." (p. 213) is New Critical in the way it looks closely at the way the sounds of words, the use of similes, and the handling of verbs combine to characterize the way love happens in

---

[6]"The Formalist Critics," *Kenyon Review* 13 (1951): 72.

L.A., as a brief, hurried moment in a self-centered life. And Dan Carter's paper does an explication of "Love Poem" (p. 592), showing how the adaptation of the sonnet form, the poem's images, and the way the author uses sound unite to create a poem that expresses its sincere love through angles and slants instead of the direct approach more traditional for sonnets.

READER-RESPONSE CRITICISM

Reader-response criticism contrasts sharply with New Criticism by focusing primarily on the reader instead of the text, and on individual effect instead of universal meaning. The roots of reader-response criticism go back to the 1930s and were laid down as a reaction against historical and biographical approaches, which gave little consideration to the role of the reader. Louise Rosenblatt began developing a reader-response theory just about the time New Criticism was emerging. New Criticism caught on and became widely accepted, while for several decades Rosenblatt's work was mostly neglected. Interest in the reader reemerged in the 1960s as a reaction against New Criticism's text-centered neglect of the reader. Reader-response criticism has become increasingly popular and influential, especially as a classroom approach.

Reader-response criticism, as we say in Chapter 1, is based on the assumption that reading is a transaction between an author, a reader, and a text in a cultural context. Reader-response criticism studies the steps through which the reader, by interacting with a text, completes the work in her or his mind. It does not just *describe* the response a work elicits from a reader ("here's what the work makes me feel") but examines the *activity* involved in reading — *how* the work produces the effects and feelings it does as a reader interacts with it. Reader-response criticism focuses on the sequential apprehension of a work — on the experience of grasping each line or each paragraph without knowing what comes later and on the process of putting the pieces together. Rereading is just as important for reader-response criticism as for New Criticism, but unlike New Criticism the first reading also is regarded as crucially significant.

Most reader-response theories have a more subjective view of a text than New Criticism, thinking of a text more as a musical score that is meant to be "performed," brought to life by a reader, than as a permanent artistic object. The degrees of subjectivity vary. Some versions see the reader's interaction with the text as controlled to some extent by formal structures included in the text. For these, the text is a stable and "objective" entity that sets limits on the reader. A work cannot mean just anything the reader says it does: The reader must pay close attention to the text to notice and follow the cues it supplies and must be able to provide evidence from within the text to support the way she or he interprets it.

Other, more subjective reader-response approaches deemphasize the words on the page and place more emphasis on a text created in the reader's mind. This raises the question of whether there are any limits on the reader. Does a text then mean anything the reader says it does? Perhaps not. One way to consider that limits do exist, without giving up subjectivity of the text, is to recognize that reading occurs within "interpretive communities." In their broadest sense, interpretive communities are groups of readers who share a common situation, similar assumptions about how literary works are actualized, or an agreement about how literary conventions are used in approaching a text. The community provides a context within which individual experiencing of a work can be assessed. A class, for example, is an interpretive community. So are the readers of a professional journal and a group of scholars who specialize in a given area of literature.

The role of such a group is not to arrive at a single "best" reading or to judge which among several readings is the "right" one or is "better" than others. Rather, by its endorsements and discouragements, each interpretive community indicates which readings go too far for that community, which ones it regards as *unacceptable*. This too will vary. What is unacceptable to one group of readers may not be to another. It is the collective judgments of interpretive communities, in this view, not texts or readers, that create stability. Even within the same community readings will vary because texts are not objective and different readers enact them in individual ways. Constraints do exist, however. A text can "mean" many things, but not just anything. The constraints, however, are not *in* the text but grow out of the strategies, assumptions, and conventions of the community.

For an example of a paper using a reader-response approach, see Kristina Martinez's student paper on "Recitatif" (p. 1408). It looks closely at large-scale strategies in the work rather than on smaller details the way New Critical papers do. It focuses on discrepancies and ambiguities in the text and the way readers must sort out differences and attempt to figure out the way things really were. It brings up questions readers are forced to work through: "Which story is correct, Roberta's or Twyla's (or neither)? Are they remembering details about Maggie differently because one of them is the same race as Maggie and the other not? If so, which one is the same?" It points out how readers—like Twyla and Roberta in the story—may wrongly attempt to construct meaning out of their own contexts as a way to resolve the ambiguities, instead of acknowledging "that this story will not provide answers to their questions, and that acceptance of ambiguity itself answers the need to have answers."

MARXIST CRITICISM

Although acceptance of Marxism has waned over the past decade and a half, Karl Marx's social and economic theories had a major impact across the world through much of the twentieth century. That was true for literature as well: While Marxist ideas influenced authors and literary critics from the 1920s on, they emerged more prominently in the 1960s. They remain an important strand in literary study, one with which students of literature should be conversant. A brief introduction to the basic tenets of Marx's thought is helpful in understanding the foundations of and procedures used in Marxist criticism.

Marx's main interest was in economic power and the ways in which it is disguised and manipulated. His analysis of society starts with the exploitation of workers by owners and capitalists, which creates class conflict between the bourgeoisie (the middle and upper classes — the owners and capitalists) and the proletariat (the workers, those who must sell their labor to the owners and capitalists). The subjugation of the workers, Marx held, is maintained by *ideology,* that is, the beliefs, values, and ways of thinking through which human beings perceive what they believe to be reality and carry out their roles in society. The ideology of an era (Marx called it the "superstructure") is determined by the contemporary socioeconomic system (the "base") and reflects the beliefs, values, and interests of the dominant class in it. Ideology includes everything that shapes the individual's mental picture of life experience — not what life really is, but the way it is perceived. This ideology may seem to people at the time just the natural, inevitable way of seeing and explaining things. But Marxists claim that it seems that way only because ideology quietly, subtly works to legitimize and maintain the position, power, and economic interests of the ruling class and, for the working classes, to cover up the reality of their exploitation. Ideology helps preserve the status quo by making what is artificial and oppressive seem natural and inevitable. According to Marxists, such ideology must be exposed and overcome if people are to gain relief from their oppressors.

Early Marxist criticism concentrated on exposing the presence of bourgeois attitudes, values, and orientation in literary works. Later Marxist criticism became more sophisticated in analyzing the ideology underlying literature and societies: bringing out the beliefs, values, and ways of thinking through which people perceive what they believe to be reality and on which they carry out their roles in society. In the latter part of the twentieth century, Fredric Jameson used insights from psychoanalysis to reenergize Marxist criticism. The function of ideology, Jameson held, is to "repress" revolutionary ideas or tendencies, to push them into the "political unconscious."[7] As ideology works itself into a text, things must be omitted: "In order to say anything, there are other things *which must not be said.*"[8] As a result, gaps and contradictions occur and generally go unnoticed. Like psychoanalysts, Marxist critics focus on the text's "unconscious," on what is unspoken and repressed, and bring it into "consciousness."

To expose the ideology in literary works, the main approach of Marxist criticism is to read "against the grain." The metaphor comes from carpentry:

---

[7]*The Political Unconscious: Narrative as a Socially Symbolic Act* (Ithaca: Cornell UP, 1981).
[8]Pierre Machery, qtd. in Raman Selden, *A Reader's Guide to Contemporary Literary Theory* (Lexington: UP of Kentucky, 1985) 41.

It is easiest to plane a board by pushing "with the grain"; the plane moves easily, can glide over irregularities and inconsistencies in the wood, and produces smooth, pleasing results. Pushing "against the grain" is harder and usually causes rough edges. To apply the metaphor to reading, it is easiest and most natural to read a work "with the grain" — that is, to accept and follow the conventions and signals that correspond with the ideology behind it. Reading with the grain allows a reader to glide over problems and leads to smooth, reassuring results, compatible with what the dominant culture values and approves. It is harder to read "against the grain," to resist the conventions of the dominant culture's ideology, to challenge and question them instead of accepting and following them. The role of a Marxist approach to literature is to bring what is hidden into the open, to expose underlying ideology, and to make readers see its effect.

Marxist criticism is committed criticism: It aims not only to illuminate readers but also to arouse them to involvement and action; it seeks to impact the lives and values of readers and effect changes in society. As with psychological criticism, you should not attempt writing a paper from a Marxist perspective unless you have read and understood a good deal from Marx's works and from works studying his positions. Attempting to do so without being well informed is likely to lead to superficial and even erroneous results. And it seems fair to point out that if you write a Marxist critique without sharing Marx's beliefs about class conflict and the need for rising up against the injustices of the capitalist system, though it might fulfill an academic assignment, your work will not be authentic Marxist criticism, which requires passionate commitment to a set of ideas designed to initiate significant societal change.

The value of a Marxist approach is illustrated by using it to consider "The Homes of England," a poem written around 1825 by Felicia Hemans (1793–1835). The poem celebrates a variety of English homes, starting with the magnificent country houses of the rich: "The stately Homes of England, / How beautiful they stand! / Amidst their tall ancestral trees, / O'er all the pleasant land." Following stanzas go on to discuss "merry" and "blessed" homes in idyllic terms, moving down to "The Cottage Homes of England! / By thousands on her plains, / They are smiling o'er the silvery brooks / And round the hamlet fanes [churches]." A Marxist critic would expose the underlying ideology and point out what goes unsaid, and unseen, in the poem. Hemans, though not wealthy herself, saw her country through the lens of patriotic, upper-class landowners and capitalists. England was a land of "free, fair Homes" where all citizens lived with the "glad spirit" of children and loved their "country and its God."

But that is not how all of England was. It is how the upper classes perceived it. Hemans's setting is rural England; she makes no mention of the wretched homes in city slums where exploited factory workers and their families lived. The lower classes are invisible to the upper classes, who profit from them but are oblivious to their lives and welfare. Rural areas had their poor as well, living not in romantic cottages but in huts and hovels. These homes, too, don't appear in the poem (the poem does refer to "hut and hall," but the very phrase seems to equate them, as equally pleasant, happy dwellings). A Marxist critic would bring out how acceptance of this ideology — this sense that all are free, happy, and content — is a way to keep the lower classes from realizing the inequity of their situation and from wanting to rebel against it.

FEMINIST CRITICISM AND EXPANSION OF THE CANON

Prior to 1970, especially during the period in which New Criticism was in vogue, literary standards and agendas were dominated by white, male academics. A large majority of college and university teachers and scholars were male; all of the founders of New Criticism were male; most of the writers studied and approved of by New Criticism were male. Cleanth Brooks and Robert Penn Warren's landmark New Critical textbook *Understanding Poetry* (1938) included poems by 89 men and 5 women (11 poems are anonymous). Of poems included, 220 were by men, 8 by women (one an example of a "bad" poem). In the original edition of a very influential formalist textbook on poetry, Laurence Perrine's *Sound and Sense* (1956), 107 male, but only 10 female, poets were represented (169 poems by men, 18 by women).

The tendency of male critics to favor works by men was reinforced by the theoretical position of New Criticism. New Criticism looked in literature for universal themes — themes it assumed would apply equally to women and men of all classes, cultures, and times. The shapers of New Criticism, however, did not seem aware of the extent to which their own backgrounds and presuppositions — their ideologies — defined those "universal" issues: The issues were ones raised by well-educated, upper-class, conservative men. Just as their method of reading sought to unify and integrate aspects of literary works, so the themes they found in the works involved social unity and integration. Issues of importance to marginal groups — women, people of color, lower classes — did not fit the mold and were overlooked (only one poem by an ethnic American author — Countee Cullen's "Incident" — appears in the original *Sound and Sense,* and two are included in *Understanding Poetry,* both by William Carlos Williams).

Against this background arose a feminist protest movement, which initiated a radical rethinking of the canon. Pivotal in its development was Kate Millett's *Sexual Politics* (1970), which began to raise the consciousness of women to the fact that, generally speaking, all avenues of power in Western culture were under male control. That was true of the production and study of literature. White males set the criteria for what was good literature and decided whose books would be published and whose works would be anthologized. They, therefore, had the power to determine who would be read, who would receive attention, who would achieve fame.

Feminist criticism reacted against this power initially by asking what happens to a work written by a male when it is read from a consciously feminine perspective instead of an assumed male perspective. The first act of a feminist reader, according to critic Judith Fetterley, is to become a "resisting reader" rather than an assenting reader[9] — that is, to question and challenge the assumptions of a work about roles, power, and values. A resisting reader exposes the masculine biases (the patriarchal ideology) in a work. This requires paying attention not only to what is said, but also to what is not said. Even works in which no women are present may convey an attitude toward women: What does their absence say? How does the fact that no women are present shape and color the situation? Are there details that (perhaps unintentionally or unconsciously) demean women or treat subjects in a way that is potentially insulting to women?

From a reappraisal of works by men, feminist criticism moved on to the study of literature written by women — what Elaine Showalter has termed *gynocriticism*. This involves, on the one hand, the reexamination of woman authors who have long been accepted in the canon, and on the other hand, even more significantly, the discovery or rediscovery of many neglected or forgotten women writers, past and present. The result has been to open up the literary canon to include works by women that earlier criticism had excluded.

One criticism of early varieties of feminist criticism is that much of it treats *woman* as a universal category without recognizing differences among women — differences of race, economic and social class, and national origin — that contribute to their identity. Contemporary feminists such as Gayatri Spivak say that while all women are female, they are something else as well (such as working class or upper class, heterosexual or lesbian, African American or living in a postcolonial nation), and the "something else" is important to consider. Such an approach has led feminists to feel affinities with all those who are considered "the Other" or are marginalized on the basis of race, ethnicity, class, sexual orientation, or social background.

Thus feminist critics took the lead in raising for ethnic minorities the same questions and concerns raised about women — particularly for African Americans at first, and then for Latinos, Native Americans, and other ethnic minorities: How are they treated in works by white authors? Are they stereotyped in insensitive and demeaning ways? Are there details that (perhaps unintentionally or unconsciously) demean minorities or treat subjects in a way that is potentially insulting to the minority group? Are ethnic characters rendered invisible? Are they not included at all? If so, what does their absence say? Ethnic critics began to point out the dearth of writers of color in anthologies and literature courses, to call attention to ethnic authors who had been accepted in the canon or were on its fringes, and to discover or rediscover many neglected or forgotten writers of color, past and

---

[9]*The Resisting Reader: A Feminist Approach to American Fiction* (Bloomington: Indiana UP, 1978).

present. As the canon expanded to include woman writers, so it expanded to include ethnic authors. This textbook's table of contents is evidence of the result.

Feminist criticism, like Marxist criticism, does not focus on a *method* (the way New Criticism and reader-response criticism do). Instead, it is an orientation, a set of principles that can be fused with a variety of critical approaches. Thus there can be feminist-reader-response criticism, feminist-deconstructive criticism, and so on. Feminist criticism, in addition to indicating some things to *do* with a work of literature, points out issues to be aware of in a work. It is a committed criticism that aims to heighten awareness, to effect changes in attitudes and behavior, to correct injustices, and to improve society and individual situations.

Susan Farrell's essay "Fight vs. Flight: A Re-evaluation of Dee in Alice Walker's 'Everyday Use'" (p. 1366) illustrates how awareness of theoretical approaches can help in understanding the premises on which a scholarly essay is based. Nowhere does the essay say that it is taking a feminist approach to the story, but that is its effect. The essay undertakes a reassessment of Dee, a character with modern feminist inclinations — she went to college to prepare herself for a career, she is fearless and a fighter, she stands up for herself and refuses to back down from what she believes in. Most critics see the story as putting Dee down because she fails to recognize the difference between her own attitude toward her heritage (embracing it as fashionable, though separate from her experience) and that of her mother and sister, who continue to live in that heritage, with its values permeating their daily experiences. Farrell's essay, however, defends Dee, showing that she offers — through her feminist ways — a strategy for contemporary African Americans to cope with an oppressive society, one, Farrell argues, Dee's mother admires, envies, and eventually emulates.

GENDER STUDIES

The protest movement that began as feminist criticism has moved on in large part to the more inclusive area of gender studies. Gender studies focus on the idea that gender is socially constructed on attitudes toward masculinity and femininity that are rooted in deeply but uncritically held beliefs of a society. Most varieties of gender studies assume a difference between the terms *sex* and *gender*. *Sex* refers to the physical characteristics of women and men biologically; *gender* refers to traits designated as "feminine" and "masculine." One is born biologically female or male, but one *acquires* a "gender" (society's conceptions of "woman" and "man"). In Simone de Beauvoir's words, "One is not born a woman, one becomes one."[10]

---

[10]*The Second Sex* (1949), trans. H. M. Parshley (New York: Vintage, 1974) 301.

Gender studies show that such distinctions in the West traditionally have been shaped through the use of binary oppositions:

masculine / feminine

father / mother

son / daughter

brother / sister

active / passive

reason / emotion

intelligent / sensitive

Through the centuries, the items on the left side of these pairings generally have been favored (or *privileged*) over those on the right side. Gender criticism exposes the pairings as false oppositions, contending that all these traits can be a part of one's identity. Gender criticism covers *all* "the critical ramifications of sexual oppression,"[11] including gay, lesbian, and queer studies. Just as early feminist critics brought attention to the way women traditionally have been forced to approach literature from a masculine perspective, so gay, lesbian, and queer studies have called attention to the way texts traditionally are read from a heterosexual viewpoint. Many readers assume that a relationship described in a work is heterosexual even when that is not indicated directly. It is not a valid assumption. Lesbian and gay critics have produced revisionist rereadings — often provocative and illuminating — of many texts that previously were read as straight.

DECONSTRUCTION

One of the best known contemporary literary theories, deconstruction, is also one of the most controversial and difficult. You may have heard of deconstruction, and maybe even used the verb *deconstruct* without realizing its use in literary studies.

Deconstruction challenges the logical principles on which the thinking of the Western world since Socrates has been based. Fundamental to Western logic, for example, is the law of noncontradiction (that is, "A" is not the same as "not A") and the use of binary oppositions that have become deeply embedded in our thought: We try to understand things by considering them in pairs that differentiate them. Remember some of the binaries in the section on gender studies:

---

[11]Jonathan Culler, *On Deconstruction: Theory and Criticism after Structuralism* (Ithaca: Cornell UP, 1982) 56.

masculine / feminine
active / passive
reason / emotion
intelligent / sensitive

Here's another list similar to that one:

conscious / unconscious
being / nonbeing
reality / image
right / wrong
thing / sign
speech / writing

Western thinking, from the Greeks on, has privileged the left side of this list over the right side. Such privileging reflects the classical, or Hellenic (Greek), influence on Western philosophy, with its love of reason, logic, order, clarity, coherence, and unity. A key aspect of deconstruction is to challenge that impulse to divide and stratify. Things are not always separate and opposed. They can be different without being opposed; they can also be interdependent and interactive.

Deconstruction — like Marxist and feminist criticism — is not a critical *method* the way New Criticism is. Rather, it is a philosophical approach, a way of thinking, a critique of the assumptions that underlie such systems as New Criticism, which emphasize order, coherence, and unity. Deconstructionists posit that a text has no stable reference, and they therefore question assumptions about the ability of language to represent reality. Language is not fixed and limited: It always conveys meanings different from or beyond what we intend. Deconstruction focuses on gaps and ambiguities that expose a text's instability and indeterminacy, the "crack" in the seeming unity or coherence of its argument. "Meaning" is not present in the work but is filled in by the reader in the act of reading. According to deconstruction, meaning is totally contextual. A literary work does not *reflect* reality; rather, works *create* their own reality. One cannot go outside a text — to the author's intentions or to references to the outside world — to determine its significa-tion. The text is "self-referential": Only as we look closely at a work and con-sider its full range of interplay and implication can its signification emerge.

A deconstructive reading, therefore, looks very closely at language, per-haps even more attentively than New Criticism does. It treats language "playfully," showing how the multiple meanings in words (the doubleness of language) contribute to the instability of texts. It picks out key binary op-positions, identifying which term in those oppositions is being privileged (given preference) and showing how such privileging imposes an interpretive template on the subject being examined. It watches for inconsistencies in the apparent unity and stability of a work, as exposed by gaps (comparing what is privileged and what is passed over, or "marginalized").

The values of a deconstructive reading are illustrated through analyzing James Baldwin's "Sonny's Blues" (p. 138). The story is grounded in a binary opposition, between words and music. The narrator is strongly oriented toward words. The story opens with him reading about Sonny in a newspaper (that, ironically, is their only means of communication at that point). The story shows the narrator reading, or attempting to read, not just words but people and situations. Keith E. Byerman has said of the narrator that "the story, in part, is about his misreadings" or his "inability to read properly."[12] As Byerman explains, the narrator is constantly turning nonverbal experiences into words. For example, when the narrator listens in the nightclub, he declares that both the terribleness and triumph of music is that "it has no words"; yet, immediately afterward, he begins reading language into the music, describing it as a conversation: "The dry, low, black man *said* something awful on the drums, Creole *answered,* and the drums *talked back.* Then the horn insisted, sweet and high, slightly detached perhaps, and Creole listened, *commenting* now and then" (p. 161).

Byerman suggests that Baldwin uses the verbalizing of the nonverbal early in the story as a way to undercut the narrator and to show his need for deeper understanding. However, something more complex than that is going on near the end. Byerman does note the lack of preparation for the narrator's sophisticated analysis of music in the final scene. The narrator throughout has expressed his antipathy to music and an inability to comprehend its appeal. Yet suddenly he expresses profound understandings of how music affects a listener. A deconstructionist would recognize that what we are hearing, actually, is the author's voice breaking through the narrator's voice, conveying the meaning he finds in music. That, in turn, undermines the author's own undercutting of the narrator: The author himself cannot resist verbalizing the meaning of music. Or he cannot avoid it because the final section of the story rests on a binary opposition it attempts to deconstruct: Words and music are similar as well as different. Music, like objects and like words, must be "interpreted" — there is no escape from "reading." But the reading that music invites is open and indirect. Baldwin, however, gives a direct and closed reading in an attempt to convey openness and indirection. The story, thus, has a level of complexity, through its contradictions, which Byerman's New Critical reading does not pick up but which a deconstructive approach can bring out.

---

[12]"Words and Music: Narrative Ambiguity in 'Sonny's Blues,'" *Studies in Short Fiction* 19 (1982): 367.

CULTURAL CRITICISM

From the 1980s on, much of literary study has been focused on culture, but in a way quite different from the promotion of "high culture" advocated by Matthew Arnold in the previous century. As we said in Chapter 8 (p. 206), cultural criticism explores the relationship between an author and her or his work and the cultural context in which they exist. An author, writing at a specific time in a specific place, inevitably is influenced by contemporary events and attitudes, whether she or he accepts and reflects prevailing attitudes or ignores, rejects, or challenges them.

The work of anthropologists has changed the primary meaning of *culture* from a single, static, universal, elitist "high culture" to a set of dynamic, interactive, always-changing *cultures*. Contemporary cultural criticism (sometimes referred to as cultural studies) is inclusive ethnically, with a strong multicultural emphasis. It emphasizes that cultural achievements of worth are produced by people from a variety of social, economic, and ethnic backgrounds, past as well as present, and that criticism should enable us to appreciate this diversity of accomplishment. And it is inclusive regarding subject matter — it does not limit itself to the literature of "high culture" but also draws on popular culture as a valuable indicator of cultural values. It studies comic books as well as novels, hit movies as well as theater, MTV as well as public television, pop songs as well as jazz, graffiti as well as gallery art. The emphasis in cultural studies is on how people *relate to* all levels of art, rather than on their aesthetic standards and on getting them to recognize and work with "the best" literature, music, or art.

Cultural criticism focuses on what a work conveys about social attitudes and social relations, focusing especially on the impact of such things as social background, sex, class, ethnicity, power, and privilege. Cultural critics concentrate on the way a work embodies a cultural context, how the events, ideas, or attitudes in a work were influenced by the economic conditions, political situation, or social conventions existing when it was written; but they also explore the way a work exists as *a part of* a culture and how it can influence, and perhaps change, the economic conditions, political situation, or social conventions of its time or later times.

Thus the theory tends to work with interdisciplinary approaches. Cultural criticism often views works in relation to other works (literary works, especially ones outside the traditional canon, but also journals, memoirs, and diaries of ordinary people, church records, medical reports, architectural drawings, and so on); to social and economic conditions that affected them; to the way they were shaped by those who held power (including editors, publishers, and reviewers, for example); and to the way they reinforced conditions of power, intentionally or not.

For an example of a paper engaging in cultural criticism, see Teresa Derrickson's essay " 'Cold/Hot, English/Spanish': The Puerto Rican American Divide in Judith Ortiz Cofer's *Silent Dancing*" (p. 1308). It explores the way

Ortiz Cofer fashions a bicultural personal identity out of a divided back-ground, living between two cultures—the island (Puerto Rico) and the mainland, Spanish-speaking and English-speaking. Derrickson shows how, rather than rejecting either culture, Ortiz Cofer finds a way to move com-fortably back and forth between them. Caleb Sheng's student paper "Iden-tity and Independence in Alice Childress's *Florence*" (p. 924) draws on cultural criticism in a different way. It is a thematic paper that focuses on a cultural issue, racial assimilation. It analyzes the way Marge and Mrs. Carter represent different but equally imprisoning sides of the same problem, Mrs. Carter the tragic ignorance of mainstream society and Marge the unfortu-nate constrictions of a minority mentality.

NEW HISTORICISM

An influential variety of cultural studies, New Historicism, grew out of a sense that New Criticism and deconstruction, through their neglect of the social and cultural milieu in which a work had been written, were leaving out something important and valuable. New Historicists would say that by focusing almost wholly on what occurs within a text, New Crit-ics and deconstructionists cut themselves off from the ways historical con-text can clarify and illuminate a work. They lose referentiality. Despite many differences, the varieties of historicist critics have in common a belief in referentiality—that works of literature are influenced by, and influence, reality.

New Historicism starts from a theory of history different from that which underlies "old historicism," with its emphasis on facts and events, its selective focus on the kinds of events that get recorded in official docu-ments, and its explanations of causes and effects and of development to-ward an end. New Historicists assume that it is virtually impossible to reconstruct the past. We have only stories about the past, not objective facts and events existing independently; the stories are constructed by historians, reflecting the historians' assumptions and purposes and the choices they in-evitably make about what to include, what to emphasize, what to omit. French philosophical historian Michael Foucault emphasized that all histo-rians are "situated." It is difficult for historians to recognize their own cul-tural practices and assumptions, and even more difficult to get outside them and enter those of another age.

The work of New Historicists is influenced by deconstruction and reader-response criticism, with their emphasis on subjectivity, and by cul-tural studies generally, with its attention to the myriad forces that shape events and motivations. New Historicists do not concentrate on economic and political forces or on the better-documented activities of the rich and famous, as the old historicism did. Like other types of cultural studies, New Historicism is open to other disciplines in its attempts to elucidate how art is shaped by, and shapes, social, historical, and economic conditions, and how art is affected by politics and has political effects itself.

Consider, for example, John Keats's 1819 poem "Ode on a Grecian Urn" (p. 676). The poem was a central text in Cleanth Brooks's famous book of New Critical essays, *The Well Wrought Urn*.[13] In his close examination of the poem, Brooks suggests that it is proper for the personified urn to ignore names, dates, and special circumstances, and to concentrate instead on universal truths. Brooks ignores historical context and influences to take a few details and order them so that we better appreciate the beauty of the poem and its own impact as myth.

New Historicists, in contrast, would hold that it is important to situate the poem in its historical context and to ask, in this case, how economic and political conditions of early nineteenth-century England shaped Keats's image of ancient Greece. New Historicists tend to start their analysis by discussing a particular object or event, and then connect that object or event to the poem so that readers come to see "the event as a social text and the literary text as a social event."[14] Brook Thomas, for example, asks where Keats would have seen such an urn. The answer — in a museum — leads into a discussion of the rise of the art museum in eighteenth- and nineteenth-century Europe, as cultural artifacts from the past were placed in museums to be contemplated as art, isolated from their social setting. "In Keats's poem an urn that once had a practical social function now sparks aesthetic contemplation about the nature of truth, beauty, and the past." Thomas then says that reflecting on how the urn assumes a purely aesthetic function in a society that was becoming increasingly practical helps clarify "how our modern notion of art has been defined in response to the social order."[15]

To the New Historicist, even the urn's position in a museum raises political issues. The presence of a Grecian urn in an English museum can lead to reflections on the political implications of a cultural heritage. Englishmen in the nineteenth century, although they sympathized with the struggle for liberation in Greece, nevertheless took cultural treasures out of the country and put them on display in London. Thomas concludes that Keats's poem is "a social text, one that in telling us about the society that produced it also tells us about the society we inhabit today"[16] and should lead to reflection not just on present attitudes toward museums in the United States, but also on the implications of the way Keats's English poem has become a museum-type artifact in U.S. culture today.

---

[13]*The Well Wrought Urn: Studies in the Structure of Poetry* (New York: Reynal, 1947) ch. 8.

[14]Brook Thomas, "The New Literary Historicism," *A Companion to American Thought*, ed. Richard Wightman Fox and James T. Kloppenberg (New York: Blackwell, 1995) 490.

[15]"The Historical Necessity for — and Difficulties with — New Historical Analysis in Introductory Literature Courses," *College English* 49 (1987): 518.

[16]"The Historical Necessity" 519.

POSTCOLONIAL CRITICISM

Postcolonial theory deals with cultural expression and behavior relating to the formerly or currently colonized parts of the world. Postcolonial criticism involves the analysis of literature by native writers who are living in colonized countries or who emigrated from such countries. We limit the discussion here to literature written in English in parts of the world that were colonized by Great Britain or the United States: primarily, then, Australia, New Zealand, and parts of the Caribbean, South America, Africa, and Asia. Postcolonial criticism focuses particularly on how colonized peoples attempt to assert their identity and to claim their heritage separate from, or other than, the colonizing culture. It also involves analysis of works written about colonized countries by writers from the colonizing countries, particularly as such writers misrepresent the cultures they describe, imposing on them their own cultural values and sense of cultural superiority.

Postcolonial criticism deals with all aspects of the struggle that occurs when one culture is subjugated by another, with what happens when one culture, because of the political power behind it, is able to dominate the other and to establish the impression of being superior to the other. It deals with the creation of Otherness, especially through the use of dialectical thinking to create pairs such as us/them, same/other, white/colored, rational/irrational, ordered/chaotic. Postcolonial criticism also addresses the way colonized peoples lose their past, are removed from history, and are forced to give up many of their cultural beliefs and practices. It confronts the way colonized peoples must forsake their language and cooperate with the conquerors if they want to get ahead economically. It reveals how the colonized peoples must cope with the memories and continuing legacy of being an occupied nation.

For a discussion of some postcolonial issues, see the way Judith Ortiz Cofer's "And Are You a Latina Writer?" (p. 1301) and Teresa Derrickson's essay "'Cold/Hot, English/Spanish': The Puerto Rican American Divide in Judith Ortiz Cofer's *Silent Dancing*" (p. 1308) approach the fact that Ortiz Cofer writes in English, the language of the colonizer, and the way she is forced to deal with a dominant culture and to find a sense of personal identity in it. And two stories by writers from former colonies — Chinua Achebe's "Dead Men's Path" (p. 405) and Patricia Grace's "Butterflies" (p. 420) — explore the kind of situations and issues faced in postcolonial cultures.

Glossary of Literary Terms

Abstract language   Language that names general or intangible concepts, such as *love, truth,* and *beauty*. See also CONCRETE LANGUAGE.

Accent   The emphasis, or stress, given a syllable in articulation. Metrical accent is the placement of stress as determined by the metrical and rhythmic pattern of a poetic line. See also STRESS.

Act   One of the major divisions of a dramatic work. See also SCENE.

Alexandrine   A poetic line with six iambic feet. Also called a *hexameter*.

Allegory   A literary form or approach in which objects, persons, and actions make coherent sense on a literal level, but also are equated in a sustained and obvious way with (usually) abstract meanings that lie outside the story. A classic example in prose is John Bunyan's *The Pilgrim's Progress;* in narrative poetry, Edmund Spenser's *The Faerie Queene;* in drama, the medieval English play *Everyman.*

Alliteration   The repetition of identical initial consonant sounds in the stressed syllables of words relatively near to each other. See also CONSONANCE.

Allusion   Echoes or brief references to a literary or artistic work or a historical figure, event, or object, as, for example, the references to Lazarus and Hamlet in T. S. Eliot's "The Love Song of J. Alfred Prufrock" (see p. 645). It is usually a way of placing one's poem within, or alongside, a whole other context that is thus evoked in a very economical fashion.

Ambiguity   (1) In expository prose, an undesirable doubtfulness or uncertainty of meaning or intention, resulting from imprecision in use of words or construction of sentences. (2) In poetry, the desirable condition of admitting more than one possible meaning, resulting from the capacity of language to function on levels other than the literal. Related terms sometimes employed are *ambivalence* and *polysemy*. See also PUN.

Anapest   A metrical foot consisting of three syllables, with two unaccented syllables followed by an accented one (*da da DA*—"in a dream"). In anapestic meter, anapests are the predominant foot in a line or poem.

Antagonist   The character who opposes the protagonist in a narrative or dramatic work. See also PROTAGONIST.

Antihero   A protagonist in a narrative or dramatic work who lacks the attributes of a traditional hero.

Antistrophe   (1) The second stanza in a three-stanza segment of a choral ode in Greek drama. It is preceded by (and identical in form to) the strophe, which is sung while the chorus moves from stage right to stage left. During the antistrophe, the chorus moves back to stage right before singing the epode. (2) The second stanza in a three-stanza segment of an ode (thus, stanzas two, five, eight, and so on). See also CHORUS; EPODE; ODE; STROPHE.

Antithesis   A figure of speech in which contrasting words, sentences, or ideas are expressed in balanced, parallel grammatical structures; for example, "She had some horses she loved. / She had some horses she hated" (Joy Harjo, "She Had Some Horses," p. 537).

Apostrophe   A figure of speech in which an absent person is addressed as though present or an abstract quality or a nonhuman entity is addressed. In the latter case, it is a particular type of PERSONIFICATION.

Approximate rhyme   See SLANT RHYME.

Archetype   An image, symbol, character type, or plot line that occurs frequently enough in literature, religion, myths, folktales, and fairy tales to be recognizable as an element of universal literary experience and thus to evoke a deep emotional response.

Aside   A convention in drama in which a character utters thoughts intended for the audience to hear that supposedly cannot be heard by the other characters onstage.

Assonance   The repetition of identical or similar vowel sounds in words relatively near to each other whose consonant sounds differ. See also SLANT RHYME.

Atmosphere   The feeling, or emotional aura, created in a reader or audience by a literary work, especially as such feeling is evoked by the setting or landscape.

Ballad   A poem that tells a story and is meant to be recited or sung; originally a folk art, transmitted orally from person to person and generation to generation. Many of the popular ballads were not written down and published until the eighteenth century, though their origins may have been centuries earlier. See "Sir Patrick Spens" (p. 598) for an example of a Scottish popular ballad.

Ballad stanza   A quatrain in iambic meter rhyming *abcb* with (usually) four feet in the first and third lines, three in the second and fourth.

Biographical criticism   See page 1481.

Blank verse   Lines of unrhymed iambic pentameter.

Cacophony   A harsh or unpleasant combination of sounds, as, for example, "But when loud surges lash the sounding shore, / The hoarse, rough verse should like the torrent roar" (Alexander Pope, "An Essay on Criticism," ll. 368–69). See also EUPHONY.

Caesura   A pause or break within a line of verse, usually signaled by a mark of punctuation.

Canon   In the Christian tradition, the books accepted by the church as divinely in-spired and approved for inclusion in the Bible. In literary studies, it means (1) the list of works generally accepted as the authentic work of a particular author (e.g., the Shakespearean canon), or (2) literary works that are given special status by the liter-ary establishment within a society as works most worthy of study and emulation.

Carpe diem   "Seize the day," a Latin phrase from an ode by Horace. It is the label for a theme common in literature, especially sixteenth- and seventeenth-century English love poetry, that life is short and fleeting and that therefore one must make the most of present pleasures. See, for example, Robert Herrick's "To the Virgins, to Make Much of Time" (p. 669) and Andrew Marvell's "To His Coy Mistress" (p. 688).

Catastrophe   The concluding section of a play, particularly of a tragedy, describing the fall or death of the protagonist that results from the climax. The term *dénoue-ment* is more commonly used for comedy. See also DÉNOUEMENT.

Catharsis   Term used by Aristotle in the *Poetics* to describe the outcome of viewing a tragedy. The term has usually been translated as "purgation" or "purification," though what Aristotle meant by it is widely disputed. A tragedy, it seems to say, en-genders pity and fear in its audience, then releases and quiets those emotions, a process that has a healthy effect, psychologically and physically: The audience goes away feeling not dejected but relieved.

Center of consciousness technique   A third-person limited point of view in which a narrator relates a story through what is thought, felt, seen, and experienced by one of the characters, showing only what that character is conscious of.

Character   (1) A figure, human or personified, in a literary work; characters may be animals or some other beings. (2) A literary genre that offers a brief sketch of a personality type or an example of a virtue or vice, such as a country bumpkin or a braggart soldier.

Characterization   The process or use of techniques by which an author describes and develops the characters in a literary work.

Chaucerian stanza   A seven-line iambic stanza rhyming *ababbcc,* sometimes hav-ing an alexandrine (hexameter) closing line. See, for example, Sir Thomas Wyatt, "They flee from me" (p. 756).

Chorus   In its literary sense, the group of performers in Greek theater whose danc-ing and singing provided exposition and comment on the action of a play. In later theater, a single character identified as "chorus" who has a function similar to that of the Greek chorus.

Climax   The moment of greatest tension or emotional intensity in a plot.

Closed form   A poetic organization that evinces any repetition of meter, rhyme, or stanza. See also OPEN FORM.

Closet drama   A play that is intended to be read rather than performed.

Colloquial language   The diction, syntax, and idioms characteristic of informal speech.

Comedy   In medieval times, a literary work that has a happy ending and is written in a style less exalted than that of tragedy (e.g., Dante's *Divine Comedy*). More broadly, a humorous and entertaining work, particularly such a work in drama. See also TRAGEDY.

Comic relief   A humorous scene, passage, or character in an otherwise serious play; sometimes described as providing an audience with a momentary relief from the emotional intensity of a tragedy but at the same time heightening the seriousness of the work.

Complication   One of the traditional elements of plot, describing the protagonist's entanglements resulting from plot conflicts.

Concrete language   Language that names material things. See also ABSTRACT LANGUAGE.

Concrete poem   A poem arranged in a shape suggestive of the poem's subject matter.

Conflict   A confrontation or struggle between opposing characters or forces in a literary work, which gives rise to and is a focal point for the action of the plot.

Connotation   The shared or communal range of associations and emotional implications a word may carry in addition to its dictionary definitions. See also DENOTATION.

Consonance   The repetition of consonant sounds in the same or nearby lines. See also SLANT RHYME.

Convention   A rule, method, practice, or characteristic established by usage; a customary feature.

Couplet   A unit consisting of two consecutive lines of poetry with the same end rhyme. See also HEROIC COUPLET.

Crisis   The turning point in a plot, the moment at which a situation changes decisively for better or for worse. See also CLIMAX.

Cultural criticism   See page 1498.

Dactyl   A metrical foot consisting of three syllables, an accented one followed by two unaccented ones (*DA da da*—"sleepily"). In dactylic meter, dactyls are the predominant foot of a line or poem.

Deconstruction   See page 1495.

Denotation   The basic meaning of a word; a word's dictionary definition. See also CONNOTATION.

Dénouement   From the French for "unknotting," the untangling of events at the end of a play that resolves the conflicts (or leaves them satisfyingly unresolved), clarifies what is needed for understanding the outcome, and ties up the loose ends. It can be used in tragedy, but is generally used in comedy. See also CATASTROPHE.

Deus ex machina   From the Latin for "god out of the machine," refers to the mechanical device by which the actor playing a god was lowered to the stage in Greek drama to rescue characters from a seemingly impossible situation. It now denotes the use of any unexpected or artificial means to resolve an irresolvable conflict.

Dialect   One of several varieties of a language, differing in vocabulary, grammar, and/or pronunciation, and identified with a certain region, community, or social, ethnic, or occupational group. Often one dialect comes to be considered the "standard."

Dialogue   A conversation between two or more characters in a literary work.

Diction   Choice of words; the kind of words, phrases, and figurative language that make up a work of literature. See also POETIC DICTION.

Dimeter   A line of verse consisting of two metrical feet.

Downstage   The part of the stage closest to the audience.

Double rhyme   A rhyme in which the accented, rhyming syllable is followed by one or more identical, unstressed syllables: *thrilling* and *killing, marry* and *tarry*. An older label, *feminine rhyme,* is generally no longer used. See also SINGLE RHYME.

Drama   (1) A literary composition that tells a story, usually involving human conflict, by means of dialogue and action rather than narration. (2) In modern and contemporary theater, any play that is not a comedy or a musical. (3) The dramas of a particular writer or culture, considered as a whole (e.g., Shakespearean drama, medieval drama). See also CLOSET DRAMA; PLAY.

Dramatic irony   A situation in which a reader or audience knows more than the speakers or characters, either about future events or about the discrepancy between a meaning intended by a speaker or character and that recognized by a reader or audience. See also IRONY; SITUATIONAL IRONY; VERBAL IRONY.

Dramatic monologue   A poem consisting of speech by one speaker, overheard in a dramatic moment and usually addressing a character or characters who do not speak. The speaker's words reveal what is going on in the scene and expose significant depths of the speaker's temperament, attitudes, and values. See also SOLILOQUY.

Dramatis personae   The characters in a play, or a list of such characters.

Dynamic character   Characters shown as changing and growing because of what happens to them. See also STATIC CHARACTER.

Elegy   In Greek and Roman literature, a serious, meditative poem written in elegiac meter (alternating hexameter and pentameter lines); since the 1600s, a sustained and formal poem lamenting the death of a particular person, usually ending with a consolation, or setting forth meditations on death or another solemn theme. See, for example, Thomas Gray's "Elegy Written in a Country Churchyard" (p. 660). The adjective *elegiac* is also used to describe a general tone of sadness or a worldview that emphasizes suffering and loss. It is most often applied to Anglo-Saxon poems such as *Beowulf* or *The Seafarer* but also can be used for modern poems, as, for example, A. E. Housman's poems in *A Shropshire Lad.*

End rhyme   Rhyme at the ends of lines in a poem. See also INTERNAL RHYME.

End-stopped line   A line in which a grammatical pause (punctuation mark) and the completion of the meaning coincide at the end. See also RUN-ON LINE.

English sonnet   A sonnet consisting of three quatrains (four-line units, typically rhyming *abab cdcd efef*) and a couplet (two rhyming lines). Usually the subject is introduced in the first quatrain, expanded in the second, and expanded still further in the third; the couplet adds a logical, pithy conclusion or gives a surprising twist. Also called the *Shakespearean sonnet*. See also ITALIAN SONNET.

Enjambment   See RUN-ON LINE.

Epic   A long narrative poem that celebrates the achievements of great heroes and heroines, often determining the fate of a tribe or nation, in formal language and an elevated style. Examples include Homer's *Iliad* and *Odyssey*, Virgil's *Aeneid*, and John Milton's *Paradise Lost*.

Epic simile   An extended or elaborate simile in which the image used to describe the subject is developed in considerable detail.

Epigram   Originally, an inscription on a building, tomb, or gravestone; in modern usage, a short poem, usually polished and witty with a surprising twist at the end. (Its other dictionary definition, "any terse, witty, pointed statement," is a characteristic of some dramatic writing, for example, the comedies of Oscar Wilde.)

Epigraph   In literature, a quotation at the beginning of a poem, story, chapter, play, or book. See, for example, the epigraph from Dante at the beginning of T. S. Eliot's "The Love Song of J. Alfred Prufrock" (p. 645).

Epilogue   Final remarks by an actor after the main action of a play has ended, usually summing up or commenting on the play, or asking for critics and the audience to receive it favorably. In novels, an epilogue may be added to reveal what happened to the characters in future years, after the plot proper concluded.

Epiphany   An appearance or manifestation, especially of a divine being; in literature, since James Joyce adapted the term to secular use, a sudden sense of radiance and revelation one may feel while perceiving a commonplace object; a moment or event in which the essential nature of a person, a situation, or an object is suddenly perceived. The term is more common in the criticism of fiction, narrative poetry, and drama than in lyric poetry.

Epode   (1) The third stanza in a three-stanza segment of an ode in Greek drama, sung while the chorus is standing still. (2) The third stanza in a three-stanza segment of an ode. See also ANTISTROPHE; CHORUS; ODE; STROPHE.

Essay   A relatively brief discussion, usually in prose, of a limited, nonfictional topic or idea.

Euphony   Sounds that strike the ear as smooth, musical, and agreeable, as, for example, "Soft is the strain when Zephyr gently blows, / And the smooth stream in smoother numbers flows" (Alexander Pope, "An Essay on Criticism," ll. 366–67). See also CACOPHONY.

Exact rhyme   Rhyme in which the vowel sound and all sounds following it are the same: *spite* and *night* or *ache* and *fake*.

Exaggeration   See HYPERBOLE.

Explication   A method entailing close analysis of a text, opening it up line by line, clarifying how diction, images, figurative language, symbols, sounds, rhythm, form, and allusions contribute toward shaping the work's meaning and effect.

Exposition A nondramatized explanation, often a speech by a character or the narrator, that describes things that occurred before the initial action of a narrative or drama, filling in background information the audience needs to make sense of the story.

Extended metaphor A metaphoric comparison that is sustained and expanded over a number of lines.

Falling action The action following the climax of a traditionally structured play as the tension lessens and the play moves toward the catastrophe or dénouement. See also RISING ACTION.

Falling meter A foot (usually trochee or dactyl) in which the first syllable is stressed, followed by unstressed syllables that give a sense of stepping down. See also RISING METER.

Farce A dramatic work intended to excite laughter that depends less on plot and character than on improbable situations, gross incongruities, coarse wit, and horseplay.

Feminine rhyme See DOUBLE RHYME.

Feminist criticism See page 1492.

Fiction From the Latin verb "to make." (1) Narrated stories in prose — usually short stories, novellas, or novels — that are drawn from the imagination or are an imaginative reworking of actual experiences. Incidents and details in a work of fiction can originate in fact, history, or everyday life, but the characters and events as a whole are primarily invented, or altered, in the author's imagination. (2) The made-up situation underlying any literary work; the feigned or imagined situation underlying it. See also NOVEL; NOVELLA; SHORT STORY.

Figurative language See FIGURE OF SPEECH.

Figure of speech Uses of language that depart from customary construction, order, or significance in order to achieve a special effect or meaning. They occur in two forms: (1) trope (from a word for "turn"), or "figure of thought," in which a word or phrase is turned or twisted to make it mean something different from its usual significance; and (2) "rhetorical figure," which creates a surprising effect by using words in unexpected ways without altering what the words mean. See also METAPHOR; METONYMY; PERSONIFICATION; SIMILE; SYNECDOCHE.

First-person narrator The I who tells a story from a first-person point of view, either as an outside observer or as someone directly or indirectly involved in the action of the story.

Fixed form In poetry, definite, repeating patterns of line, rhyme scheme, or stanza.

Flashback A literary device that interrupts a narrative to present earlier material, often something that occurred before the opening of the work, through a character's memories or dreams or through juxtaposition of earlier and later events.

Flat character A character represented through only one or two main features or aspects that can often be summed up in a sentence or two. See also ROUND CHARACTER.

Foil   A character used as a contrast with another character, thus highlighting the latter's distinctive attributes or character traits.

Foot   The basic unit in metrical verse, comprised of (usually) one stressed and one or more unstressed syllables. See also ANAPEST; DACTYL; IAMB; SPONDEE; TROCHEE.

Foreshadowing   Words, gestures, or other actions that hint at future events or outcomes in a literary work.

Form   (1) Genre or literary type (e.g., the lyric form); (2) patterns of meter, lines, and rhymes (stanzaic form); or, (3) the organization of the parts of a literary work in relation to its total effect (e.g., "The form [structure] of this poem is very effective"). See also STRUCTURE.

Formalist criticism   See page 1486.

Found poem   A passage from a nonpoetic source such as a newspaper, magazine, advertisement, textbook, or elsewhere in everyday life that contains some element of poetry: meter (sometimes), effective rhythm, phrasings that can be divided into lines, imaginative uses of language and sound, and so on.

Fourth wall   The theatrical convention, dating from the nineteenth century and realistic drama, whereby an audience seems to be looking through an invisible fourth wall into the room of an actual house created by the other three walls of a box set.

Free verse   See OPEN FORM.

Gay and lesbian criticism   See page 1495.

Gender criticism   See page 1494.

Genre   A recurring type of literature; a literary form as defined by rules or conventions followed in it (e.g., tragedy, comedy, epic, lyric, pastoral, novel, short story, essay).

Gothic story   Fiction in which magic, mystery, and effects creating a sense of horror, or an atmosphere of brooding and unknown terror, play a major role.

Haiku   A lyric form, originating in Japan, of seventeen syllables in three lines, the first and third having five syllables and the second seven, presenting an image of a natural object or scene that expresses a distinct emotion or spiritual insight.

Hamartia   An error in judgment, a mistake, a frailty that, according to Aristotle's *Poetics,* results in a tragic hero's change in fortune from prosperity to adversity. *Hamartia* is sometimes mistakenly equated with tragic flaw. It does not, however, refer to a character flaw but rather to a central or defining aspect of the character. Watching for an error or misstep (*hamartia*) is more advisable to looking for a defect in character (tragic flaw). See also TRAGIC FLAW.

Heptameter   A poetic line with seven metrical feet.

Hero, heroine   The protagonist, or central character, in a literary work.

Heroic couplet   Couplet in iambic pentameter with a full stop, usually, at the end. Also called *closed couplet.*

Hexameter   See ALEXANDRINE.

Historical criticism   See page 1482.

Hubris (hybris)   Greek for "insolence"; excessive pride that can lead to the downfall of the protagonist in a tragedy.

Hyperbole   Exaggeration; a figure of speech in which something is stated more strongly than is logically warranted. See also UNDERSTATEMENT.

Iamb   A metrical foot consisting of two syllables, an unaccented one followed by an accented one (*da DA*—"awake"). In iambic meter, iambs are the predominant foot in a line or poem.

Image   (1) A word or group of words that refers to a sensory experience or to an object that can be known by one or more of the senses. *Imagery* signifies all such language in a poem or other literary work collectively and can include any of the senses (visual imagery, auditory imagery, tactile imagery, kinetic imagery, imagery of smell or taste). (2) A metaphor or other comparison. *Imagery* in this sense refers to the characteristic that several images in a poem have in common, for example, the sports imagery in Patricia Goedicke's "My Brother's Anger" (p. 559).

Imagery   See IMAGE.

Implied metaphor   Metaphor in which the *to be* verb is omitted and one aspect of the comparison is implied rather than stated directly, as, for example, "these dragonflies / filled with little men" in Julia Alvarez's "How I Learned to Sweep" (p. 560).

In medias res   Latin for "into the middle things"; used to describe the technique of starting a narrative at an engaging point well into the story and filling in the background events later as needed.

Interior monologue   The representation of unspoken mental activity—thoughts, impressions, and memories—as if directly overheard by the reader, without being selected and organized by a narrator, either in an associative, disjointed, nonlogical, nongrammatical way (stream of consciousness) or in a logical, grammatical flow of thoughts and memories moving through a person's mind, as if being spoken to an external listener. It is sometimes set off typographically, for example, by using italics rather than quotation marks.

Internal rhyme   Rhyme that occurs between words within a line, between words within lines near each other, or between a word within a line and one at the end of the same or a nearby line.

Irony   A feeling, tone, mood, or attitude arising from the awareness that what is (reality) is opposite from, and usually worse than, what seems (appearance). Irony is not the same as mere coincidence. Irony has different forms: What a person *says* may be ironic (see VERBAL IRONY); a discrepancy between what a character knows or means and what a reader or audience knows can be ironic (see DRAMATIC IRONY); a general situation can be ironic (see SITUATIONAL IRONY).

Italian sonnet   A sonnet composed of an octave (an eight-line unit), rhyming *abbaabba,* and a sestet (a six-line unit), often rhyming *cdecde* or *cdcdcd,* although variations are frequent. The octave usually develops an idea or question or problem; then the poem pauses, or "turns," and the sestet completes the idea, answers the question, or resolves the difficulty. Sometimes called a *Petrarchan sonnet.* See also ENGLISH SONNET.

Juxtaposition   Placement of things side by side or close together for comparison or contrast or to create something new from the union, without necessarily making them grammatically parallel.

Limited omniscient point of view   Use of a narrator who is omniscient in some areas or to some extent, but is not completely all-knowing.

Line   A sequence of words printed as a separate entity on a page; the basic structural unit in poetry (except prose poems).

Literal   In accordance with the primary or strict meaning of a word or words; not figurative or metaphorical.

Litotes   See UNDERSTATEMENT.

Lyric   Originally, a poem sung to the accompaniment of a lyre; now a poem, usually short, expressing the personal emotion and ideas of a single speaker.

Marxist criticism   See page 1489.

Masculine rhyme   See SINGLE RHYME.

Melodrama   Originally, a drama with musical accompaniment that enhanced its emotional impact; it became in the nineteenth century a type of play relying on broadly drawn heroes and villains, suspenseful plots, improbable escapes, the triumph of good over evil, and an excessive appeal to the emotions of the audience.

Metaphor   A figure of speech in which two things usually thought to be dissimilar are treated as if they were alike and have characteristics in common, as, for example, "My brother's anger is a helmet" in Patricia Goedicke's "My Brother's Anger" (p. 559). See also IMPLIED METAPHOR.

Metaphysical poetry   The work of a number of seventeenth-century English poets characterized by philosophical subtlety and intellectual rigor; subtle, often outrageous logic; imitation of actual speech, sometimes resulting in "rough" meter and style; and far-fetched analogies. Sometimes applied to modern verse sharing some of these characteristics.

Meter   A steady beat, or measured pulse, created by a repeating pattern of accents, syllables, or both.

Metonymy   A figure of speech in which the name of one thing is substituted for that of something closely associated with it, as in commonly used phrases such as "The *White House* announced today . . ." See also SYNECDOCHE.

Metrics   The study of the patterns of rhythm in poetry.

Monometer   A poetic line with one metrical foot.

Morality play   A form of drama that originated in the Middle Ages and presents a dramatized allegory in which abstractions (such as Mercy, Conscience, Perseverance, and Shame) are personified and engage in a struggle for a human soul.

Motif   A recurring element — image, idea, feature, action, or theme — that is elaborated or developed throughout a work.

Motivation   The combination of personality traits and circumstances that impel a character to act in a particular way.

Mystery play   A medieval play based on biblical history; a scriptural play.

Myth   Anonymous stories arising from a culture's oral traditions that involve gods or heroic figures, explore matters beyond everyday life, and concern origins, endings, aspirations, purpose, and meaning.

Mythological criticism   See page 1485.

Naïve narrator   A narrator too young or too inexperienced to understand fully the implications of what she or he is talking about. See also NARRATOR; RELIABLE NARRATOR; UNRELIABLE NARRATOR.

Narrative   A narrated story, in prose or verse; an account of events involving characters and what they do and say, told by a storyteller (narrator).

Narrator   The storyteller through whom an author relates a narrative. See also FIRST-PERSON NARRATOR; NAÏVE NARRATOR; POINT OF VIEW; RELIABLE NARRATOR; UNRELIABLE NARRATOR.

Naturalism   A literary movement of the late nineteenth and early twentieth centuries that applies the principles of scientific determinism to literature and views humans as animals in a natural world who respond to environmental forces — physical or socioeconomic — and internal stresses and drives, none of which they can control or understand.

Near rhyme   See SLANT RHYME.

New Comedy   Greek comedy of the fourth and third centuries B.C.E. that depicts the obstacles faced by young lovers and the unpredictable changes of fortune they encounter, and pokes fun at the foibles and attitudes of the lovers as well as those around them.

New Criticism   See page 1486.

New Historicism   See page 1499.

Novel   Although the term can refer to any extended fictional narrative in prose, it is generally used for narratives that emphasize complexity of character and development of a unifying theme. See also FICTION; NOVELLA; SHORT STORY.

Novella   A fictional prose narrative longer than a short story but shorter than a novel; commonly fifty to one hundred pages in length. See also FICTION; NOVEL; SHORT STORY.

Objective point of view   A narrative approach in which a narrator describes events only from the outside, without looking into the mind of any of the characters or explaining why any of the characters do what they do.

Octameter   A poetic line with eight metrical feet.

Octave   The first, eight-line segment of an Italian sonnet.

Ode   (1) In Greek drama, a speech delivered by the chorus. (2) A long lyric poem, serious (often intellectual) in tone, elevated and dignified in style, dealing with a single theme. The ode is generally more complicated in form than other lyric poems. Some odes retain a formal division into strophe, antistrophe, and epode, which reflects the ode's origins in Greek drama. See also ANTISTROPHE; CHORUS; EPODE; STROPHE.

Off rhyme   See SLANT RHYME.

Old comedy   Comedy, such as that of Aristophanes in the fifth century B.C.E., employing raucous (sometimes coarse) humor, elements of satire and farce, and often a critique of contemporary persons or political and social norms.

Omniscient point of view   The point of view in a work of fiction in which the narrator is capable of knowing everything about a story's events and characters, including their inner feelings.

One-act play   A short play that is complete in one act.

Onomatopoeia   The use of words whose sounds supposedly resemble the sounds they denote, such as *hiss* or *buzz,* or a group of words whose sounds help to convey what is being described.

Open form   A poetic form free of any predetermined metrical and stanzaic patterns. See also CLOSED FORM.

Orchestra   From the Greek word for "dance." In Greek theater, the area in front of the skene where the chorus performed its songs and dances. Later, a pit for musicians in front of the stage; still later, the group of musicians working there.

Ottava rima   An eight-line stanza in iambic pentameter rhyming *ababababcc.*

Overstatement   See HYPERBOLE.

Oxymoron   A figure of speech combining in one phrase (usually adjective-noun) two seemingly contradictory elements, such as "loving hate" or "feather of lead, bright smoke, cold fire, sick health" (Shakespeare, *Romeo and Juliet* 1.1.176–80). Oxymoron is a type of PARADOX.

Paradox   A figure of speech in which a statement initially seeming self-contradictory or absurd turns out, seen in another light, to make good sense. See also OXYMORON.

Parallelism   (1) A verbal arrangement in which elements of equal weight within phrases, sentences, or paragraphs are expressed in a similar grammatical order and structure. (2) A principle of poetic structure in which consecutive lines in open form are related by a line's repeating, expanding on, or contrasting with the idea of the lines or lines before it, as in the biblical psalms or the poems of Walt Whitman (see p. 748).

Parody   In modern usage, a humorous or satirical imitation of a serious piece of literature or writing. In the sixteenth and seventeenth centuries, poets such as George Herbert practiced "sacred parody" by adapting secular lyrics to devotional themes.

Partial rhyme   See SLANT RHYME.

Pastoral   (1) As an adjective, that which deals with a rural setting and affirms a rustic way of life. (2) As a noun, a literary type associated with shepherds and country living.

Pause   See CAESURA.

Pentameter   A poetic line with five metrical feet.

Persona   Literally, the mask through which actors spoke in Greek plays. In some critical approaches of recent decades, the "character" projected by the author, the *I* of a narrative poem or novel, or the speaker whose voice is heard in a lyric poem. In this view, the poem is an artificial construct distanced from the poet's autobiographical self. See also VOICE.

Personification   A figure of speech in which something nonhuman (an abstraction or a natural object) is treated as if it had human (not just living) characteristics or actions. See also APOSTROPHE.

Petrarchan sonnet   See ITALIAN SONNET.

Play   A drama intended for performance before a theatrical audience. See also CLOSET DRAMA.

Plot   (1) The selection and arrangement of events in a narrative to present them most effectively to the reader and bring out their causal connections. (2) The action that takes place within a play, considered by Aristotle in the *Poetics* to be the most important of the six elements of drama. See also SUBPLOT.

Poem   A term whose meaning exceeds all attempts at definition. Here is a slightly modified version of an attempt at definition by William Harmon and C. Hugh Holman in *A Handbook to Literature* (1996): A poem is a literary composition, written or oral, typically characterized by imagination, emotion, sense impressions, and concrete language that invites attention to its own physical features, such as sound or appearance on the page.

Poetic diction   In general, a specialized language used in or considered appropriate to poetry. In the late seventeenth and the eighteenth centuries, a refined use of language that excluded "common" speech from poetry as indecorous and substituted elevated circumlocutions or archaic synonyms, or such forms as *ope* and *e'er*.

Point of view   The vantage point from which an author presents a story, combining person (first, second, or third, named or anonymous) and perspective (objective, omniscient, limited). See also CENTER OF CONSCIOUSNESS; STREAM OF CONSCIOUSNESS.

Problem play   A serious work that dramatizes a real-life, usually contemporary, social, political, or ethical problem. Although in a broad sense it covers all drama dealing with problems of human life, it is used more narrowly for the "drama of ideas" that emerged in the late nineteenth century in the work, for example, of Norwegian playwright Henrik Ibsen (see p. 926).

Prologue   (1) The opening section of a Greek tragedy. (2) Words spoken before the beginning of a play, usually a monologue by one of the actors providing background information.

Property (prop)   A movable object used on stage, especially one handled by an actor while performing.

Proscenium   The part of the stage in a modern theater between the orchestra and the curtain. The proscenium arch is the arch over the front of the stage from which the curtain hangs and which separates the stage from the audience.

Prose poem   A poem printed as prose, with lines wrapping at the right margin rather than being divided through predetermined line breaks.

Prosody   The principles of versification, especially of meter, rhythm, rhyme, and stanza forms.

Protagonist   The most important or leading character in a literary work. See also ANTAGONIST.

Psychological criticism   See page 1483.

Pun   A "play on words" based on similarity in sound between two words having very different meanings, as when "Dear heart" in Sir Thomas Wyatt's "They flee from me" (p. 756) means both "heart" and "hart" (deer). Also called *paronomasia*. Often used to produce AMBIGUITY in sense 2.

Quatrain   A stanza of four lines or other four-line unit within a larger form, such as a sonnet.

Reader-response criticism   See page 1488.

Realism   (1) An approach to literature that attempts to depict accurately the everyday life of a time and place. (2) A literary movement that developed in the latter half of the nineteenth century characterized by an objective presentation of material and realistic depiction of setting, characters, and details.

Recognition   A significant realization or discovery by a character, usually the protagonist, that moves the plot forward by changing the circumstances of a play.

Refrain   One or more identical or deliberately similar lines repeated throughout a poem, sometimes with meaningful variation, such as the final line of a stanza or as a block of lines between stanzas or sections.

Reliable narrator   A narrator who tells her or his story accurately and honestly. See also NAÏVE NARRATOR; NARRATOR; UNRELIABLE NARRATOR.

Resolution   The culmination of a fictional plot that resolves the conflicts or leaves them satisfyingly unresolved.

Rhyme   The repetition of the accented vowel sound of a word and all succeeding consonant sounds. See also EXACT RHYME; SLANT RHYME.

Rhyme royal   An alternative term for Chaucerian stanza because it was used by King James I of Scotland in his poem *The Kingis Quair* ("The King's Book"), written about 1424.

Rhyme scheme   The pattern of end rhymes in a poem or stanza; the recurring sequence is usually described by assigning a letter to each word sound, the same word sounds having the same letter (e.g., *abbaabba*).

Rhythm   The patterned "movement" of language created by the choice of words and their arrangement, usually described through such metaphors as fast or slow, smooth or halting, graceful or rough, deliberate or frenzied, syncopated or disjointed. Rhythm in poetry is affected, in addition to meter, by such factors as line length; line endings; pauses (or lack of them) within lines; spaces within, at the beginning or end of, or between lines; word choice; and combinations of sounds.

Rising action   The part of a plot leading up to the climax and marked by increasingly tense and complicated conflict. See also FALLING ACTION.

Rising meter   A foot (usually an iamb or an anapest) in which the final, stressed syllable is preceded by one or two unstressed syllables, thus giving a sense of stepping up. See also FALLING METER.

Romance   (1) In medieval narrative poetry or prose, a tale involving knights and kings, adventures, ladies in distress, courtly love, and chivalric ideals. (2) In modern fiction, a work characterized by remote and exotic settings, exciting and heroic action, passionate love, and mysterious or supernatural experiences. (3) In drama, a play neither wholly comic nor wholly tragic, often containing elements of the supernatural.

Round character   A complex, fully developed character either shown as changing and growing because of what happens to her or him or described in such rich detail that we have a clear sense of how she or he would, or will, change even though we don't see it happening. See also FLAT CHARACTER.

Run-on line   A line whose sense and grammatical structure continue to the next. The technique is called *enjambment*. See also END-STOPPED LINE.

Sarcasm   A harsh and cutting form of verbal irony, often involving apparent praise that is obviously not meant seriously.

Satire   A work, or manner within a work, that combines a critical attitude with humor and wit with the intent of improving human institutions or humanity.

Scansion   The division of metrical verse into feet in order to determine and label the meter of a poem. See also FOOT; METER; page 1469.

Scene   (1) A subdivision of an ACT in drama, or — in modern drama — a section of a play that is not divided into acts. (2) See SETTING. (3) A variant spelling of *skene*.

Script   The written text of a play, which includes the stage directions, dramatic monologues, and the dialogue between characters.

Sentimentality   A term used to describe a work seeking to elicit an emotional response in a reader or spectator that exceeds what the situation warrants.

Sestet   The last six lines of an Italian sonnet.

Sestina   A lyric poem consisting of 6 six-line stanzas and a three-line concluding stanza (or "envoy"). The six end-words of the first stanza must be used as the end-words of the other five stanzas, in a specified pattern (the first line ends with the end-word from the last line of the previous stanza, the second line with that of the first line of the previous stanza, the third line with that of the previous fifth line, the fourth line with that of the previous second line, the fifth line with that of the previous fourth line, the sixth line with that of the previous third line). The three lines of the envoy must use the end-words of lines 5, 3, and 1 from the first stanza, in that order, and must include the other three end-words within the lines.

Set   The physical equipment of a stage, including backdrops, furniture, properties, and lighting.

Setting   The overall context — where, when, in what circumstances — in which the action in a fictional or dramatic work takes place.

Shakespearean sonnet   See ENGLISH SONNET.

Shaped poem   See CONCRETE POEM.

Short story   A brief prose work of narrative fiction characterized by a carefully crafted plot and style, complexity in characterization and point of view, and unity of effect. See also FICTION; NOVEL; NOVELLA.

Simile   Expression of a direct similarity, using such words as *like, as,* or *than,* between two things usually regarded as dissimilar (e.g., "His face was as white as a sheet."). It is important to distinguish *simile* from *comparison,* where the two things joined by *like* or *as* are not dissimilar.

Single rhyme   A rhyme in which the stressed, rhyming syllable is the final syllable in the rhyme: *west* and *stressed, away* and *today.* Formerly called *masculine rhyme.* See also DOUBLE RHYME.

Situational irony   A kind of irony in which a result turns out very different from, and usually more sinister than, what a character expected or hoped for. Unlike dramatic irony, in situational irony the reader does not necessarily know more than the characters and may be as surprised by what happens as the characters are. See also DRAMATIC IRONY; IRONY; VERBAL IRONY.

Slant rhyme   A form of rhyme in which words contain similar sounds but do not rhyme perfectly (usually involving assonance or — more frequently — consonance). See also ASSONANCE; CONSONANCE.

Soliloquy   A monologue delivered by a character in a play while alone on stage or otherwise out of hearing of the other characters, often revealing the character's inner thoughts or feelings. Sometimes applied to a poem imitating this feature. See also DRAMATIC MONOLOGUE.

Sonnet   A fourteen-line poem usually written in iambic pentameter. Originally lyrical love poems, sonnets came to be used also for meditations on religious themes, death, and nature, and are now open to all subjects. Some sonnets have varied from the traditional form — using hexameter lines, fewer or more than fourteen lines, or an appended coda. Sometimes sonnets are grouped in a "sonnet sequence," with implied narrative progression in the situations imagined as underlying the successive utterances. See also ENGLISH SONNET; ITALIAN SONNET; SPENSERIAN SONNET.

Speaker   The imagined voice in a nonnarrative poem of someone uttering the words of the poem, either that of the poet quite directly or of a character expressing views or feelings the poet may or may not share.

Spenserian sonnet   A variation of the English sonnet that employs the structure of three quatrains plus a couplet, but joins the quatrains by linking rhymes: *abab bcbc cdcd ee.*

Spenserian stanza   A stanza of nine iambic lines, the first eight pentameter and the ninth hexameter, rhyming *ababbcbcc.*

Spondee   A metrical foot made up of two stressed syllables (*DA DA*—"dream house"), with no unstressed syllables. Spondees cannot be the predominant foot in a poem; they are usually substituted for iambs or trochees as a way of increasing emphasis.

Stage directions   Written instructions in the script of a play, typically placed in parentheses and set in italics, telling actors how to move on the stage or how to deliver a particular word or speech.

Stage left, stage right   Areas of the stage seen from the point of view of an actor facing the audience. Stage left, therefore, is on the audience's right-hand side, and vice versa.

Stanza   A grouping of poetic lines into a section, either according to form — each section having the same number of lines and the same prosody — or according to thought, creating irregular units comparable to paragraphs in prose. Irregular stanzas are sometimes called STROPHES.

Static character   A character in a narrative or dramatic work who is not shown as changing. See also DYNAMIC CHARACTER.

Stichomythia   A form of repartee in dialogue originating in ancient Greek drama — brief, alternating lines that reply sharply to each other in wordings that echo and vary what the preceding character expressed.

Stock character   A traditional character defined by a single, stereotypical characteristic, such as innocent young woman, a rakish young man, or a clever servant.

Story   Any account of a related series of events in sequential order, usually chronological order (the order in which they happened).

Stream-of-consciousness technique   An attempt to convey the unstructured, even at times chaotic, flow of random sense perceptions, mental pictures, memories, sounds, thoughts, and feelings — prerational mental activity, before the mind orders it into a coherent form or shape — through an associative rather than logical style, usually without ordinary punctuation or complete sentences.

Stress   In metrics, the greater emphasis given to some words and syllables relative to that received by adjacent words and syllables. See also ACCENT.

Strophe   (1) The first part in a three-stanza segment of a choral ODE in Greek drama, sung while the chorus moves from stage right to stage left. (2) The first stanza in a three-stanza segment of an ode. (3) See STANZA. See also ANTISTROPHE; CHORUS; EPODE; ODE.

Structure   (1) The planned framework — the general plan or outline — of a literary work. (2) Narrower patterns within the overall framework. See also FORM.

Style   In writing, the distinctive, individual manner in which a writer uses words, constructs sentences, incorporates nonliteral expressions, and handles rhythm, timing, and tone; also, the manner characteristic of a group of writers (as in "period style").

Subplot   A subordinate or minor story in a dramatic or narrative work, often related thematically or structurally to the main plot. See also PLOT.

Substitution   The use of a different kind of foot in place of the one normally demanded by the predominant meter of a poem, as a way of calling attention to an idea, emphasizing the dominant foot by variation from it, speeding up or slowing down the pace, or signaling a switch in meaning.

Suspense   A sense of uncertainty and concern about how things in a literary work will turn out, when disaster will fall or rescue will occur, who did what, or what the effects on the characters or events will be.

Symbol   Something that represents both itself and something else. A literary symbol is a prominent or repeated image or action that is present in the poem, story, or play and is seen, touched, smelled, heard, tasted, or experienced imaginatively but also conveys a cluster of abstract meanings beyond itself.

Synecdoche   A special kind of metonymy in which a part of a thing is substituted for the whole of which it is a part, as in the commonly used phrases "give me a hand," "lend me your ears," or "many mouths to feed."

Syntax   The arrangement of words in a sentence to show their relationship to one another.

Tercet   A stanza of three lines, each usually ending with the same rhyme. See also TERZA RIMA; TRIPLET.

Terza rima   A poetic form consisting of three-line stanzas (TERCETS) with inter-linked rhymes, *aba bcb cdc ded efe,* etc., made famous by Dante's use of it in *The Divine Comedy.* Terza rima is used — with a concluding couplet — in Percy Bysshe Shelley's "Ode to the West Wind" (p. 721).

Tetrameter   A poetic line with four metrical feet.

Text   Traditionally, a piece of writing. In recent reader-response criticism, *text* has come to mean the words with which the reader interacts; in this view, a literary work is not an object, not a shape on the page or a spoken performance, but what is completed in the reader's mind.

Theme   The central idea embodied or explored in a literary work, what it all adds up to; the general concept, explicit or implied, which the work incorporates and makes persuasive to the reader.

Third-person narrator   The type of narration with a storyteller who is not identified; uses the pronouns *he, she, it,* or *they* — but not *I* — in speaking of herself or himself; asserts no connection between the narrator and the characters in the story; and tells the story with some objectivity and distance.

Title   The name attached to a work of literature. Usually a title, when assigned by the author, is an integral part of a work and needs to be considered in interpreting it. In some cases, a title for a poem has been added as a means of identifying it and is not integral to its interpretation. Sometimes a poem is untitled and the first line is used as a convenient way of referring to the poem (e.g., in Emily Dickinson's poems), but it should not be thought of as a title and does not follow the capitalization rules for titles.

Tone   The attitude, or "stance," toward the subject and toward the reader or audience implied in a literary work; the "tone of voice" it seems to project.

Tragedy   A story recounting a causally related series of serious and important events that culminate in an unhappy ending for the protagonist. See also COMEDY.

Tragic flaw   The theory, attributed to Aristotle's *Poetics,* that the downfall of the hero in a tragedy is caused by a defect, or flaw, in her or his character. See also *HAMARTIA.*

Tragicomedy   A play whose plot could be appropriate to tragedy until the final act, when it turns out unexpectedly to have the happy ending of a comedy. The tone and style of tragicomedy are serious and the outcome could well be disaster or death; but somehow the disaster is averted, and at the end order and harmony prevail. See also COMEDY; TRAGEDY.

Trimeter   A poetic line with three metrical feet.

Triplet   A group of three consecutive lines with the same rhyme, often used for variation in a long sequence of couplets. See also TERCET.

Trochee   A metrical foot consisting of two syllables, an accented one followed by an unaccented one (*DA da*—"wakeful"). In trochaic meter, trochees are the predominant foot in a line or poem.

Type   (1) See GENRE. (2) A character who represents a class or kind of person, either atypical and individualized, or stereotypical (see STOCK CHARACTER). (3) A variety of symbol, especially as used in religion for something that is to come, such as "a type of Christ."

Understatement   A figure of speech expressing something in an unexpectedly restrained way, which often has the effect of increasing rather than reducing emphasis. See also HYPERBOLE.

Unity   A sense of wholeness and cohesion in a literary work, as all of its parts work together according to some organizing principle to achieve common effect.

Unreliable narrator   A narrator who may be in error in her or his reporting or understanding of things, or who distorts things, deliberately or unintentionally. See also NAÏVE NARRATOR; NARRATOR; RELIABLE NARRATOR.

Upstage   The part of the stage farthest from the audience.

Verbal irony   A figure of speech in which what is said is nearly the opposite of what is meant. See also DRAMATIC IRONY; IRONY; SARCASM; SITUATIONAL IRONY.

Verisimilitude   The semblance of truth; the use of abundant detail to create the appearance of reality in a literary work.

Verse   (1) A unit of poetry, the same thing as a stanza or line. (2) A rhythmic composition, often in meter and rhyme, irrespective of merit (the term *poetry* is often reserved for verse of high merit).

Viewpoint   See POINT OF VIEW.

Villanelle   A nineteen-line lyric poem divided into five tercets and a final four-line stanza, rhyming *aba aba aba aba aba abaa*. Line 1 is repeated to form lines 6, 12, and 18; line 3 is repeated to form lines 9, 15, and 19. See, for example, Dylan Thomas's "Do not go gentle into that good night" (p. 741) and John Yau's "Chinese Villanelle" (p. 757).

Voice   The supposed authorial presence in poems that do not obviously employ persona as a distancing device.

Dagoberto Gilb, "Love in L.A." from *The Magic of Blood*. Reprinted by permission of the University of New Mexico Press.

Christopher Gilbert, "Horizontal Cosmology" from *Across the Mutual Landscape*. Copyright © by Christopher Gilbert. Reprinted by permission of the author.

Allen Ginsberg, "A Supermarket in California" from *Collected Poems 1947-1980*. Copyright © 1955 by Allen Ginsberg. Reprinted by permission of HarperCollins Publishers Inc.

Nikki Giovanni, "Nikka-Rosa" from *Black Feeling, Black Talk, Black Judgement*. Copyright © 1968, 1970 by Nikki Giovanni. Reprinted by permission of HarperCollins Publishers Inc.

Diane Glancy, "Aunt Parnetta's Electric Blisters" from *Trigger Dance*. Copyright © 1990 by Diane Glancy. Used by permission of the publisher, Fiction Collective Two. "Battery" from *The Stones for a Pillow*. Reprinted in *Like Thunder*, University of Iowa Press, 2002. Reprinted by permission of the author.

Susan Glaspell, *Trifles*. Copyright © 1916 by Susan Glaspell. Reprinted with permission of the Estate of Susan Glaspell.

Louise Glück, "Parable of Flight" from *Meadowlands*. Copyright © 1996 by Louise Glück. Reprinted by permission of HarperCollins Publishers Inc.

Patricia Goedicke, "My Brother's Anger" from *Paul Bunyan's Bearskin* (Minneapolis: Milkweed Editions, 1992). Copyright © 1992 by Patricia Goedicke. Reprinted with permission from Milkweed Editions.

Ray González, "Praise the Tortilla, Praise the Menudo, Praise the Chorizo" from *The Heat of Arrivals*, BOA Editions, 1996. Copyright © 1996 by Ray González. Used by permission of the author.

Patricia Grace, "Butterflies" from *Selected Stories*. Copyright © Patricia Grace and Penguin Books (NZ). Reproduced by permission of Penguin Books (NZ).

Angelina Weld Grimké, "A Winter Twilight" from the Angela Weld Grimké papers. Reprinted by permission of the Moorland-Spingarn Research Center, Howard University.

Kimiko Hahn, "When You Leave" from *Air Pocket*. Copyright © 1989 by Kimiko Hahn. Reprinted by permission of Hanging Loose Press.

Joy Harjo, "She Had Some Horses" from *She Had Some Horses*. Copyright © 1983, 1987 by Thunder's Mouth Press. Appears by permission of the publisher, Thunder's Mouth Press, a division of Avalon Publishing Group.

Michael S. Harper, "Nightmare Begins Responsibility" from *Songlines in Michaeltree: New and Collected Poems*. Copyright © 2000 by Michael S. Harper. Used with permission of the poet and the University of Illinois Press.

Robert Hayden, "Those Winter Sundays." Copyright © 1966 by Robert Hayden. From *Angle of Ascent: New and Selected Poems*. Used by permission of Liveright Publishing Corporation.

Samuel Hazo, "For Fawzi in Jerusalem" from *Blood Rights*. Copyright © 1968 by Samuel Hazo. Reprinted by permission of the author.

Bessie Head, "The Collector of Treasures" from *The Collector of Treasures*, Heinemann, 1977. Copyright © 1977 by The Estate of Bessie Head. Reprinted by permission of Johnson & Alcock Ltd.

Seamus Heaney, "Digging" from *Opened Ground: Selected Poems 1966-1998*. Copyright © 1998 by Seamus Heaney. Reprinted by permission of Farrar, Straus and Giroux, LLC, and Faber & Faber, Ltd.

Ernest Hemingway, "Hills Like White Elephants" from *Men Without Women*. Copyright 1927 by Charles Scribner's Sons and renewed 1955 by Ernest Hemingway. Reprinted with permission of Scribner, an imprint of Simon & Schuster Adult Publishing Group.

David Hernandez, "The Butterfly Effect" from *A House Waiting for Music*, Tupelo Press, Dorset, Vermont, 2003. Reprinted by permission of Tupelo Press.

Tomson Highway, excerpts from "Spokane Words: Tomson Highway Raps with Sherman Alexie" from *Aboriginal Voices* 4.1, Jan/Feb/Mar 1997. Reprinted by permission of Tomson Highway.

Nazim Hikmet, "Letters from a Man in Solitary" from *Poems of Nazim*, translated by Randy Blasing and Mutlu Konuk. Translation copyright © 1994, 2002 by Randy Blasing and Mutlu Konuk. Reprinted by permission of Persea Books, Inc. (New York).

Geoffrey Hill, "In Memory of Jane Fraser" from *Collected Poems, 1952-1992*. Copyright © 1994 by Geoffrey Hill. Reprinted by permission of Houghton Mifflin Company. All rights reserved. In Canada, from *Geoffrey Hill: Collected Poems* (Penguin Books 1985, first published in *For the Unfallen*, 1959). Copyright © 1959, 1985 by Geoffrey Hill. Reprinted by permission of Penguin Books Ltd.

Linda Hogan, "The History of Red" from *The Book of Medicines*. Copyright © 1993 by Linda Hogan. Reprinted with the permission of Coffee House Press, Minneapolis, Minnesota, USA, coffeehousepress.org.

Miroslav Holub, "Elementary School Field Trip to the Dinosaur Exhibit" from *Intensive Care: Selected and New Poems*, translated by David Young et al., FIELD Translation Series 22, Oberlin College Press, 1996. Reprinted by permission of Oberlin College Press.

Garrett Kaoru Hongo, "Yellow Light" from *Yellow Light*. Copyright © 1982 by Garrett Kaoru Hongo. Reprinted by permission of Wesleyan University Press.

Langston Hughes, "Dream Variations," "Freedom's Plow," "Good Morning," "Harlem," "I Dream a World," "The Negro Speaks of Rivers," "The Weary Blues," and "When Sue Wears Red" from *The Collected Poems of Langston Hughes*. Copyright © 1994 by The Estate of Langston Hughes. Used by permission of Alfred A. Knopf, a division of Random House, Inc. "I've Known Rivers" from *The Big Sea*. Copyright © 1940 by

Langston Hughes and renewed 1968 by Arna Bontemps and George Houston Bass. Reprinted by permission of Hill & Wang, a division of Farrar, Straus and Giroux, LLC. "Jazz as Communication" from *The Langston Hughes Reader*. Copyright © 1958 by Langston Hughes. Reprinted by permission of Harold Ober Associates Incorporated. "One Friday Morning" from *Short Stories*. Copyright © 1996 by Ramona Bass and Arnold Rampersad. Reprinted by permission of Hill & Wang, a division of Farrar, Straus and Giroux, LLC. *Soul Gone Home* from *Five Plays*, edited by Webster Smalley. Copyright © 1937 by Langston Hughes. Reprinted by permission of Harold Ober Associates Incorporated. Caution: Professionals and amateurs are hereby warned that *Soul Gone Home* is subject to a royalty. It is fully protected under the copyright laws of the United States of America, and of all countries covered by the International Copyright Union (including the Dominion of Canada, and the rest of the British Commonwealth), and of all countries covered by the Pan-American Copyright Convention and the Universal Copyright Convention, and of all countries with which the United States has reciprocal copyright relations. All rights, including professional, amateur, motion picture, recitation, lecturing, public reading, radio broadcasting, television, and the rights of translation into foreign languages, are strictly reserved. All inquiries about performing and other rights should be addressed to the author's representatives, Harold Ober Associates, 425 Madison Ave., New York, NY 10017.

David Henry Hwang, "As the Crow Flies" from *Between Worlds: Contemporary Asian-American Plays*, edited by Misha Berson. Copyright © David Henry Hwang. Reprinted by permission of the author.

Henrik Ibsen, "A Doll House" from *The Complete Major Prose Plays of Henrik Ibsen*, translated by Rolf Fjelde. Translation copyright © 1965, 1970, 1978 by Rolf Fjelde. Used by permission of Dutton Signet, a division of Penguin Group (USA) Inc.

Lawson Fusao Inada, "Plucking Out a Rhythm" from *Before the War*. Copyright © 1970 by Lawson Fusao Inada. Reprinted by permission of HarperCollins Publishers Inc.

David Ives, "Sure Thing" from *All in the Timing*. Copyright © 1989, 1990, 1992 by David Ives. Used by permission of Vintage Books, a division of Random House, Inc.

Onwuchekwa Jemie, "Or Does It Explode?" from *Langston Hughes: An Introduction to the Poetry*. Reprinted by permission of the author.

Gish Jen, "Who's Irish?" from *Who's Irish?* Copyright © 1999 by Gish Jen. Reprinted by permission of the author.

Caleen Sinnette Jennings, "Classyass" from *Humana Festival 2002: The Complete Plays*, edited by Tanya Palmer and Amy Wegener. Premiered in Actors Theatre of Louisville's 26th Annual Humana Festival of New American Plays, March 3–April 7, 2002. Copyright © 2002 by Caleen Sinnette Jennings. All rights reserved. Reprinted by permission of the author. All inquiries concerning performance rights, including amateur rights, should be addressed to: Caleen Sinnette Jennings, American University, 4400 Massachusetts Avenue, NW, Washington, D.C. 20016.

Georgia Douglas Johnson, "Wishes." First published in *The Crisis*, April 1927. Bedford/St. Martin's wishes to thank the Crisis Publishing Co., Inc., the publisher of the magazine of the National Association for the Advancement of Colored People, for the use of this material.

Jeannette Johnston, "Smashing Stereotypes with Sherman Alexie" from *boston.sidewalk*, July 1, 1998. Reprinted by permission of the author.

A. Van Jordan, "The Journey of Henry 'Box' Brown" from *Rise*. Copyright © by A. Van Jordan. Reprinted by permission of Tia Chucha Press and The Guild Complex.

Allison Joseph, "On Being Told I Don't Speak Like a Black Person." Copyright © 1999 by Allison Joseph. First appeared in *Many Mountains Moving*. Reprinted in *Imitation of Life*, Carnegie Mellon University Press, 2003. Reprinted by permission of the author.

James Joyce, "Eveline" from *Dubliners*. Copyright © 1916 by B. W. Heubsch. Definitive text copyright © 1967 by the Estate of James Joyce. Used by permission of Viking Penguin, a division of Penguin Group (USA) Inc.

Jamaica Kincaid, "Girl" from *At the Bottom of the River*. Copyright © 1983 by Jamaica Kincaid. Reprinted by permission of Farrar, Straus and Giroux, LLC.

Galway Kinnell, "Saint Francis and the Sow" from *Mortal Acts, Mortal Words*. Copyright © 1980 by Galway Kinnell. Reprinted by permission of Houghton Mifflin Co. All rights reserved.

Etheridge Knight, "Hard Rock Returns to Prison from the Hospital for the Criminal Insane" from *The Essential Etheridge Knight*. Copyright © 1986. Reprinted by permission of the University of Pittsburgh Press.

Philip C. Kolin and Maureen Curley, "Hughes's *Soul Gone Home*" from *The Explicator* 61.3, Spring 2003. Copyright © 2003. Reprinted with permission of the Helen Dwight Reid Educational Foundation. Published by Heldref Publications, 1319 Eighteenth St., NW, Washington, DC 20036-1802.

Yusef Komunyakaa, "Facing It" from *Neon Vernacular*. Copyright © 1993 by Yusef Komunyakaa. Reprinted by permission of Wesleyan University Press. "Langston Hughes + Poetry = The Blues." First appeared in *Nexus*, 1996. Reprinted in *Blue Notes: Essays, Interviews, and Commentaries*, edited by Radiclani Clytus. Copyright © 1996, 2000 by Yusef Komunyakaa. Reprinted by permission of the author.

Maxine Kumin, "The Sound of Night" from *Halfway*. Copyright © 1961 by Maxine W. Kumin. Reprinted by permission of the author.

Jhumpa Lahiri, "Interpreter of Maladies" from *The Interpreter of Maladies*. Copyright © 1999 by Jhumpa Lahiri. Reprinted by permission of Houghton Mifflin Company. All rights reserved.

Li-Young Lee, "Eating Alone" and "Visions and Interpretations" from *Rose*. Copyright © 1986 by Li-Young Lee. Reprinted with the permission of BOA Editions, Ltd.

John Leguizamo, "Pepe" from *Mambo Mouth: A Savage Comedy*. Copyright © 1993 by John Leguizamo. Reprinted by permission of the author.

Philip Levine, "What Work Is" from *What Work Is*. Copyright © 1992 by Philip Levine. Used by permission of Alfred A. Knopf, a division of Random House, Inc.

Timothy Liu, "Thoreau" from *Burnt Offerings*. Copyright © 1995 by Timothy Liu. Reprinted with the permission of Copper Canyon Press, P.O. Box 271, Port Townsend, WA 98368-0271.

Audre Lorde, "Hanging Fire." Copyright © 1978 by Audre Lorde. From *Collected Poems*. Used by permission of W. W. Norton & Company, Inc.

Robert Lowell, "Skunk Hour" from *Collected Poems*. Copyright © 2003 by Harriet Lowell and Sheridan Lowell. Reprinted by permission of Farrar, Straus and Giroux, LLC.

Heather McHugh, "What He Thought" from *Hinge & Sign: Poems 1968-1993*. Copyright © 1994 by Heather McHugh. Reprinted by permission of Wesleyan University Press.

Claude McKay, "America" and "If we must die." Reprinted courtesy of the Literary Representative for the Works of Claude McKay, Schomburg Center for Research in Black Culture, The New York Public Library, Astor, Lenox and Tilden Foundations.

Naguib Mahfouz, "Half a Day." Translated by Denys Johnson-Davies. Copyright © 1991 by the American University in Cairo Press. From *The Time and the Place and Other Stories*. Used by permission of Doubleday, a division of Random House, Inc.

Clarence Major, "Young Woman" from *Configurations: New and Selected Poems 1958-1998*. Copyright © 1998 by Clarence Major. Reprinted with the permission of Copper Canyon Press, P.O. Box 271, Port Townsend, WA 98368-0271.

Orlando Ricardo Menes, "Letter to Mirta Yáñez." Reprinted by permission of the author.

Arthur Miller, *Death of a Salesman*. Copyright © 1949 and renewed © 1977 by Arthur Miller. Used by permission of Viking Penguin, a division of Penguin Group (USA) Inc.

Czeslaw Milosz, "It Was Winter" from *The Collected Poems, 1931-1987*. Copyright © 1988 by Czeslaw Milosz Royalties, Inc. Reprinted by permission of HarperCollins Publishers Inc.

Gary Miranda, "Love Poem" from *Grace Period*. Copyright © 1983 by Princeton University Press. Reprinted by permission of Princeton University Press.

Janice Mirikitani, "For a Daughter Who Leaves" from *Love Works*. Copyright © 1993 by Janice Mirikitani. Reprinted by permission of City Lights Books.

Mishima Yukio, "Swaddling Clothes," translated by Ivan Morris, from *Death in Midsummer*. Copyright © 1966 by New Directions Publishing Corp. Reprinted by permission of New Directions Publishing Corp.

Robert Morgan, "Mountain Bride" from *Groundwork*. Copyright © 1979. Reprinted by permission of Gnomon Press.

Toni Morrison, "Recitatif." Copyright © 1983 by Toni Morrison. Reprinted by permission of International Creative Management, Inc.

Thylias Moss, "Tornados" from *Rainbow Remnants in Rock Bottom Ghetto Sky*. Copyright © 1993 by Thylias Moss. Reprinted by permission of Persea Books, Inc., New York.

Julie Moulds, "Wedding Iva" from *The Woman with a Cubed Head*. Copyright © 1998 by Julie Moulds. Reprinted by permission of the publisher, New Issues Poetry & Prose, Kalamazoo, Michigan.

Bharati Mukherjee, "Orbiting" from *The Middleman and Other Stories*. Copyright © 1988 by Bharati Mukherjee. Used by permission of Grove/Atlantic, Inc., and Penguin Group (Canada).

David Mura, "Grandfather-in-Law" from *After We Lost Our Way*. Copyright © 1989 by David Mura. Reprinted by permission of the author.

Taslima Nasrin, "Things Cheaply Had," translated by Carolyne Wright with Mohammad Nurul Huda and the author, from *The New Yorker*, October 9, 1995. Copyright © 1995 by Carolyne Wright. Reprinted by permission of Carolyne Wright.

Pablo Neruda, "The Dead Woman" from *The Captain's Verses*. Copyright © 1972 by Pablo Neruda and Donald D. Walsh. Reprinted by permission of New Directions Publishing Corp.

Duane Niatum, "First Spring" from *Songs for the Harvester of Dreams* and *Drawings of the Song Animals*. Copyright © Duane Niatum. Reprinted by permission of the author.

Naomi Shihab Nye, "The Small Vases from Hebron" from *Fuel*. Copyright © 1998 by Naomi Shihab Nye. Reprinted with the permission of BOA Editions, Ltd.

Joyce Carol Oates, "Where Are You Going, Where Have You Been?" Copyright © 1970 by The Ontario Review. Reprinted by permission of John Hawkins & Associates, Inc.

Tim O'Brien, "The Things They Carried" from *The Things They Carried*. Copyright © 1990 by Tim O'Brien. Reprinted by permission of Houghton Mifflin Company. All rights reserved.

Rafael Ocasio, "Speaking in Puerto Rican: An Interview with Judith Ortiz Cofer," edited by Rita Ganey, from *The Bilingual Review*, 17.2 (May–August 1992). Reprinted by permission of Bilingual Press/Editorial Bilingüe, Arizona State University, Tempe, Arizona.

Flannery O'Connor, "A Good Man Is Hard to Find" from *A Good Man Is Hard to Find and Other Stories*. Copyright 1953 by Flannery O'Connor and renewed 1981 by Regina O'Connor. Reprinted by permission of Harcourt, Inc.

Luis Valdez, *Los Vendidos* is reprinted with permission from the publisher of *Luis Valdez—Early Works: Actos, Bernabé, and Pensamiento Serpentino* (Houston: Arte Público Press–University of Houston, 1971).

Helena María Viramontes, "The Moths" is reprinted with permission from the publisher of *The Moths and Other Stories* (Houston: Arte Público Press–University of Houston, 1985).

Gerald Vizenor, "Shaman Breaks" from *Harper's Anthology of 20th Century Native American Literature.* Reprinted by pemission of the author.

Derek Walcott, "Sea Grapes" from *Collected Poems 1948-1984.* Copyright © 1986 by Derek Walcott. Reprinted by permission of Farrar, Straus and Giroux, LLC.

Alice Walker, "Everyday Use" and "The Flowers" from *In Love and Trouble: Stories of Black Women.* Copyright © 1973 by Alice Walker. Reprinted by permission of Harcourt, Inc.

James Welch, "Christmas Comes to Moccasin Flat" from *Riding the Earthboy 40.* Copyright © 1971 by James Welch. Reprinted by permission of the Elaine Markson Literary Agency, Inc.

Roberta Hill Whiteman, "The White Land" from *Star Quilt,* Holy Cow! Press, 1984. Reprinted by permission of Holy Cow! Press.

Richard Wilbur, "Love Calls Us to the Things of This World" from *Things of This World.* Copyright © 1956 and renewed 1984 by Richard Wilbur. Reprinted by permission of Harcourt, Inc.

William Carlos Williams, "Spring and All, Section 1" and "The Red Wheelbarrow" from *Collected Poems: 1909-1939, Volume 1.* Copyright © 1938 by New Directions Publishing Corp. Reprinted by permission of New Directions Publishing Corp.

August Wilson, *Fences.* Copyright © 1986 by August Wilson. Used by permission of Dutton Signet, a division of Penguin Group (USA) Inc.

Nellie Wong, "Grandmother's Song" from *Dreams in Harrison Railroad Park.* Copyright © 1977 by Nellie Wong. Reprinted by permission of the author.

James Wright, "A Blessing" from *The Branch Will Not Break.* Copyright © 1961 by James Wright. Reprinted by permission of Wesleyan University Press.

Richard Wright, "The Man Who Was Almost a Man" from *Eight Men.* Copyright 1940, © 1961 by Richard Wright and renewed © 1989 by Ellen Wright. Introduction by Paul Gilmore. Reprinted by permission of HarperCollins Publishers Inc.

Xu Gang, "Red Azalea on the Cliff" from *The Red Azalea: Chinese Poetry Since the Cultural Revolution,* edited by Edward Morin and translated by Fang Dai, Dennis Ding, and Edward Morin. Reprinted by permission of the University of Hawai'i Press.

John Yau, "Chinese Villanelle" from *Radiant Silhouette: New and Selected Work, 1974-1988* (Black Sparrow Press, Santa Rosa, CA, 1988). Copyright © 1989 by John Yau. Reprinted by permission of the author.

William Butler Yeats, "The Lake Isle of Innisfree" and "The Second Coming." Copyright © 1924 by The Macmillan Company and renewed © 1952 by Bertha Georgie Yeats. From *The Collected Poems of W. B. Yeats, Volume 1: The Poems, Revised,* edited by Richard J. Finneran. Reprinted with the permission of Scribner, an imprint of Simon & Schuster Adult Publishing Group.

Al Young, "A Dance for Ma Rainey." Copyright © 1969, 1992 by Al Young. Reprinted with permission of the author.

Ray A. Young Bear, "From the Spotted Night" from *The Invisible Musician.* Copyright © 1990 by Ray A. Young Bear. Reprinted by permission of Holy Cow! Press.

Index of Authors and Titles